Gleim Publications, Inc. offers five university-level study systems:

Auditing & Systems Exam Questions and Explanations with Test Prep CD-Rom
Business Law/Legal Studies Exam Questions and Explanations with Test Prep CD-Rom
Federal Tax Exam Questions and Explanations with Test Prep CD-Rom
Financial Accounting Exam Questions and Explanations with Test Prep CD-Rom
Cost/Managerial Accounting Exam Questions and Explanations with Test Prep CD-Rom

The following is a list of Gleim examination review systems:

CIA Review: Part I, Internal Audit Role in Governance, Risk, and Control
CIA Review: Part II, Conducting the Internal Audit Engagement
CIA Review: Part III, Business Analysis and Information Technology
CIA Review: Part IV, Business Management Skills

CMA Review: Part 1, Business Analysis
CMA Review: Part 2, Management Accounting and Reporting
CMA Review: Part 3, Strategic Management
CMA Review: Part 4, Business Applications

CPA Review: Financial
CPA Review: Auditing
CPA Review: Business
CPA Review: Regulation

EA Review: Part 1, Individuals
EA Review: Part 2, Businesses
EA Review: Part 3, Representation, Practice, and Procedures

An order form is provided at the back of this book, or contact us at www.gleim.com or (800) 874-5346.

Groundwood Paper and Highlighters — All Gleim books are printed on high-quality groundwood paper. We recommend you use a non-bleed-through (dry) highlighter (e.g., the Avery *Glidestick*™ – ask for it at your local office supply store) when highlighting items within these books.

Visit our Internet site (www.gleim.com) for the latest updates and information on all of our products.

REVIEWERS AND CONTRIBUTORS

Garrett W. Gleim, B.S., CPA (not in public practice), is a graduate of The Wharton School at the University of Pennsylvania. Mr. Gleim coordinated the production staff, reviewed the manuscript, and provided production assistance throughout the project.

Grady M. Irwin, J.D., is a graduate of the University of Florida College of Law, and he has taught in the University of Florida College of Business. Mr. Irwin provided substantial editorial assistance throughout the project.

D. Scott Lawton, B.S., is a graduate of Brigham Young University-Idaho and Utah Valley State College. He has been employed by the Utah State Tax Commission.

John F. Rebstock, B.S.A., is a graduate of the Fisher School of Accounting at the University of Florida. He has passed the CPA and CIA exams. Mr. Rebstock reviewed portions of the manuscript.

Stewart B. White, B.M., *Cum Laude*, University of Richmond, B.S., Virginia Commonwealth University, has passed the CPA and CISA exams and has worked in the fields of retail management, financial audit, IT audit, COBOL programming, and data warehouse management.

A PERSONAL THANKS

This manual would not have been possible without the extraordinary effort and dedication of Kyle Cadwallader, Julie Cutlip, Mumbi Ngugi, Eileen Nickl, and Teresa Soard, who typed the entire manuscript and all revisions, and drafted and laid out the diagrams and illustrations in this book.

The authors also appreciate the production and editorial assistance of Jacob Brunny, Katie Burns, Daniel Fisher, Katie Goodrich, James Harvin, Jean Marzullo, Shane Rapp, Joanne Strong, and Martha Willis.

The authors also appreciate the critical reading assistance of Ellen Buhl, Alysa Carmichael, Will Clamons, Matt Milner, Selden Ross, and Jeremy Wright.

Finally, we appreciate the encouragement, support, and tolerance of our families throughout this project.

2009 EDITION
CPA REVIEW
Financial

by

Irvin N. Gleim, Ph.D., CPA, CIA, CMA, CFM

with the assistance of
Grady M. Irwin, J.D.

The AICPA title of this section is *Financial Accounting and Reporting*, and the AICPA acronym is FAR.

ABOUT THE AUTHOR

Irvin N. Gleim is Professor Emeritus in the Fisher School of Accounting at the University of Florida and is a member of the American Accounting Association, Academy of Legal Studies in Business, American Institute of Certified Public Accountants, Association of Government Accountants, Florida Institute of Certified Public Accountants, The Institute of Internal Auditors, and the Institute of Management Accountants. He has had articles published in the *Journal of Accountancy*, *The Accounting Review*, and *The American Business Law Journal* and is author/coauthor of numerous accounting books, aviation books, and CPE courses.

Gleim Publications, Inc.
P.O. Box 12848
University Station
Gainesville, Florida 32604
(800) 87-GLEIM or (800) 874-5346
(352) 375-0772
FAX: (352) 375-6940
Internet: www.gleim.com
Email: admin@gleim.com

This is the first printing of the 2009 edition of *CPA Review: Financial*. Please email update@gleim.com with **CPA FIN 2009-1** included in the subject or text. You will receive our current update as a reply. Updates are available until the next edition is published.

EXAMPLE:

To: update@gleim.com
From: *your email address*
Subject: CPA FIN 2009-1

ISSN: 1547-8025

ISBN: 978-1-58194-709-0   *CPA Review: Auditing*
ISBN: 978-1-58194-710-6   *CPA Review: Business*
ISBN: 978-1-58194-711-3   *CPA Review: Financial*
ISBN: 978-1-58194-712-0   *CPA Review: Regulation*
ISBN: 978-1-58194-708-3   *CPA Review: A System for Success*

ACKNOWLEDGMENTS

Material from *Uniform Certified Public Accountant Examination Questions and Unofficial Answers*, Copyright © 1974-2008 by the American Institute of Certified Public Accountants, Inc. is reprinted and/or adapted with permission. Visit the AICPA web page at www.aicpa.org for more information.

The author is indebted to the Institute of Certified Management Accountants for permission to use problem materials from past CMA examinations. Questions and unofficial answers from the Certified Management Accountant Examinations, copyright by the Institute of Certified Management Accountants, are reprinted and/or adapted with permission.

The author is grateful for permission to reproduce Certified Internal Auditor Examination Questions, Copyright © 1991-1995 by The Institute of Internal Auditors, Inc.

This publication was printed and bound by Corley Printing Company, St. Louis, MO, a registered ISO-9002 company. More information about Corley Printing Company is available at www.corleyprinting.com or by calling (314) 739-3777.

This publication is designed to provide accurate and authoritative information with regard to the subject matter covered. It is sold with the understanding that the publisher is not engaged in rendering legal, accounting, or other professional service.

If legal advice or other expert assistance is required, the services of a competent professional person should be sought.

(From a declaration of principles jointly adopted by a Committee of the American Bar Association and a Committee of Publishers.)

TABLE OF CONTENTS

PREFACE FOR CPA CANDIDATES

The purpose of this Gleim *CPA Review* study book is to help YOU prepare to pass the Financial Accounting and Reporting (referred to throughout the rest of this text as Financial) section of the CPA examination. Our overriding consideration is to provide an inexpensive, effective, and easy-to-use study program. This book

1. Explains how to optimize your grade by focusing on the Financial section of the CPA exam.

2. Defines the subject matter tested on the Financial section of the CPA exam.

3. Outlines all of the subject matter tested on the Financial section in 20 easy-to-use-and-complete study units.

4. Presents multiple-choice questions from recent CPA examinations to prepare you for financial questions in future CPA exams. Our answer explanations are presented to the immediate right of each question for your convenience. Two bookmarks are provided at the back of this book. Use a bookmark to cover our answer explanations as you study the questions.

5. Presents one simulation in each study unit to acquaint you with simulation formats. Answer the simulation test questions in your book. The answers and grading instructions follow each simulation.

The outline format, the spacing, and the question and answer formats in this book are designed to facilitate readability, learning, understanding, and success on the CPA exam. Our most successful candidates use the Gleim CPA Complete System,* which includes books, *Test Prep* CD-Rom, audio CDs, *Gleim Online*, Test Prep for Pocket PC, and a Personal Counselor; or a group study CPA review program. (Check our website for live courses we recommend.) This review book and all Gleim *CPA Review* materials are compatible with other CPA review materials and courses that follow the AICPA Content Specification Outlines.

To maximize the efficiency and effectiveness of your CPA review program, begin by **studying** (not merely reading) *CPA Review: A System for Success*. It has been carefully organized and written to provide important information to assist you in passing the CPA examination.

Thank you for your interest in the Gleim *CPA Review* materials. We deeply appreciate the thousands of letters and suggestions received from CIA, CMA, EA, and CPA candidates for the past 4 decades. Please send your suggestions, comments, and corrections concerning this review book. The last page has been designed to help you note corrections and suggestions during your study process. Please tear it out and mail it to us with your comments immediately after you take the CPA exam. We will respond to each letter on an individual basis.

Good Luck on the Exam,

Irvin N. Gleim

December 2008

OPTIMIZING YOUR FINANCIAL SCORE

This introduction is a summary of Gleim's *CPA Review: A System for Success*, an 80-page booklet containing a detailed discussion of the steps to exam success. *CPA Review: A System for Success* is a necessity for all CPA candidates. It should be studied at least twice: at the start of a candidate's study program and again 1 or 2 weeks before taking the CPA exam. It is a separate booklet, so you do not have to carry it with you when you use this book, *CPA Review: Financial*.

Financial is scheduled for 4 hours.

AICPA title:	Financial Accounting and Reporting
AICPA acronym:	FAR
Gleim title:	Financial
Question format:	90 multiple-choice questions in three testlets of 30 questions each
	Two Simulations
Areas covered:	I. (20%) Concepts and Standards for Financial Statements
	II. (30%) Typical Items: Recognition, Measurement, Valuation, and Presentation in Financial Statements in Conformity with GAAP
	III. (30%) Specific Types of Transactions and Events: Recognition, Measurement, Valuation, and Presentation in Financial Statements in Conformity with GAAP
	IV. (10%) Accounting and Reporting for Governmental Entities
	V. (10%) Accounting and Reporting for Nongovernmental Not-for-Profit Organizations

OVERVIEW OF FINANCIAL

The Financial section of the CPA exam tests knowledge of generally accepted accounting principles (GAAP) in the United States of America for business enterprises, not-for-profit organizations, and governmental entities, and the skills needed to apply that knowledge. Content covered in this section includes financial accounting concepts and standards, and their application. To demonstrate such knowledge and skills, candidates will be required to

- Obtain and document information for use in financial statement presentations
- Evaluate, analyze, and process entity information for reporting in financial statements
- Communicate entity information and conclusions
- Analyze information and identify data relevant to financial accounting and reporting
- Identify financial accounting and reporting methods and select those that are suitable
- Perform calculations
- Formulate conclusions
- Present results in writing in a financial statement format or other appropriate format

AICPA CONTENT SPECIFICATION OUTLINES (CSOs)

The AICPA has indicated that the content specification outlines have several purposes, including:

1. *Ensure consistent coverage of subject matter from one examination to the next.*

2. *Provide guidance to those who are responsible for preparing the examination in order to ensure a balanced examination.*

3. *Assist candidates in preparing for the examination by indicating subjects that may be covered by the examination.*

4. *Alert accounting educators about the subject matter considered necessary to prepare for the examination.*

The next two pages contain the AICPA Financial CSOs and corresponding Gleim study units.

AICPA CONTENT SPECIFICATION OUTLINE

Financial Accounting and Reporting

I. **Concepts and standards for financial statements (20%)**
   A. Financial accounting concepts
      1. Process by which standards are set and roles of standard-setting bodies
      2. Conceptual basis for accounting standards
   B. Financial accounting standards for presentation and disclosure in general-purpose financial statements
      1. Consolidated and combined financial statements
      2. Balance sheet
      3. Statement(s) of income, comprehensive income, and changes in equity accounts
      4. Statement of cash flows
      5. Accounting policies and other notes to financial statements
   C. Other presentations and financial data (financial statements prepared in conformity with comprehensive bases of accounting other than GAAP)
   D. Financial statement analysis

II. **Typical items: recognition, measurement, valuation, and presentation in financial statements in conformity with GAAP (30%)**
   A. Cash, cash equivalents, and marketable securities
   B. Receivables
   C. Inventories
   D. Property, plant, and equipment
   E. Investments
   F. Intangibles and other assets
   G. Payables and accruals
   H. Deferred revenues
   I. Notes and bonds payable
   J. Other liabilities
   K. Equity accounts
   L. Revenues, cost, and expense accounts

III. **Specific types of transactions and events: recognition, measurement, valuation, and presentation in financial statements in conformity with GAAP (30%)**
   A. Accounting changes and corrections of errors
   B. Business combinations
   C. Contingent liabilities and commitments
   D. Discontinued operations
   E. Earnings per share
   F. Employee benefits, including stock options
   G. Extraordinary items
   H. Financial instruments, including derivatives
   I. Foreign currency transactions and translation
   J. Income taxes
   K. Interest costs
   L. Interim financial reporting
   M. Leases
   N. Non-monetary transactions
   O. Related parties
   P. Research and development costs
   Q. Segment reporting
   R. Subsequent events

GLEIM STUDY UNITS

FINANCIAL STATEMENTS
1. Concepts and Standards
2. Financial Statements
3. Income Statement Items
4. Financial Statement Disclosure

ACCOUNTING TOPICS
5. Cash and Investments
6. Receivables
7. Inventories
8. Property, Plant, Equipment, and Depletable Resources
9. Intangible Assets and Other Capitalization Issues
10. Payables and Taxes

11. Employee Benefits
12. Noncurrent Liabilities
13. Leases and Contingencies
14. Equity
15. Business Combinations
16. Derivatives, Hedging, and Other Topics

AICPA CONTENT SPECIFICATION OUTLINE   **GLEIM STUDY UNITS**

Financial Accounting and Reporting

IV. **Accounting and reporting for governmental entities (10%)**

	GOVERNMENTAL ACCOUNTING

A. Governmental accounting concepts

1. Measurement focus and basis of accounting
2. Fund accounting concepts and application
3. Budgetary process

17. Governmental Accounting I

18. Governmental Accounting II

B. Format and content of governmental financial statements

1. Government-wide financial statements
2. Governmental funds financial statements
3. Conversion from fund to government-wide financial statements
4. Proprietary fund financial statements
5. Fiduciary fund financial statements
6. Notes to financial statements
7. Required supplementary information, including management's discussion and analysis
8. Comprehensive annual financial report (CAFR)

C. Financial reporting entity, including blended and discrete component units

D. Typical items and specific types of transactions and events: recognition, measurement, valuation, and presentation in governmental entity financial statements in conformity with GAAP

1. Net assets
2. Capital assets and infrastructures
3. Transfers
4. Other financing sources and uses
5. Fund balance
6. Non-exchange revenues
7. Expenditures
8. Special items
9. Encumbrances

E. Accounting and financial reporting for governmental not-for-profit organizations

V. **Accounting and reporting for nongovernmental not-for-profit organizations (10%)**

	NOT-FOR-PROFIT ORGANIZATIONS

A. Objectives, elements and formats of financial statements

1. Statement of financial position
2. Statement of activities
3. Statement of cash flows
4. Statement of functional expenses

19. Not-for-Profit Concepts

20. Not-for-Profit Accounting and Reporting

B. Typical items and specific types of transactions and events: recognition, measurement, valuation, and presentation in the financial statements of not-for-profit organizations in conformity with GAAP

1. Revenues and contributions
2. Restrictions on resources
3. Expenses, including depreciation and functional expenses
4. Investments

A SYSTEM FOR SUCCESS

To ensure your success on the Financial section of the CPA examination, you should focus on the following steps:

1. **Understand the exam, including coverage, content, format, administration, and grading.**

    a. The better you understand the examination process from beginning to end, the better you will be able to perform.

    b. Study Gleim's *CPA Review: A System for Success*. Please be sure you have a copy of this useful booklet. (*CPA Review: A System for Success* is also available online at www.gleim.com/accounting/systemforsuccess/cpa/.)

2. **Learn and understand the subject matter tested.** The AICPA's CSOs for the Financial section, along with the questions that have appeared in recent CPA examinations and the suggestions from recent CPA candidates,* are the basis for the study outlines that are presented in each of the 20 study units that make up this book. You will also learn and understand the Financial material tested on the CPA exam by answering numerous multiple-choice questions from recent CPA exams. Multiple-choice questions with the answer explanations to the immediate right of each question are a major component of each study unit.

3. **Practice answering recent exam questions to perfect your question-answering techniques.** Answering recent exam questions helps you understand the standards to which you will be held. This motivates you to learn and understand while studying (rather than reading) the outlines in each of the 20 study units.

    a. Question-answering techniques are suggested for multiple-choice and simulation questions in Study Units 4 and 5 of *CPA Review: A System for Success*.

    b. Our *CPA Test Prep* CD-Rom and Test Prep for Pocket PC contain thousands of additional multiple-choice questions that are not offered in our books. Additionally, the CD-Rom has many useful features, including documentation of your performance and the ability to simulate the CBT (computer-based testing) exam environment.

    c. Our *CPA Gleim Online* is a powerful Internet-based program that allows CPA candidates to learn in an interactive environment and provides feedback to candidates to encourage learning. It includes multiple-choice questions and simulation (constructive response) questions in Prometric's format. Each *CPA Gleim Online* candidate has access to a Personal Counselor, who helps organize study plans that work with busy schedules.

4. **Plan exam execution.** Anticipate the exam environment and prepare yourself with a plan: When to arrive? How to dress? What exam supplies to bring? How many questions and what format? Order of answering questions? How much time to spend on each question? See Study Unit 7 in *CPA Review: A System for Success*.

    a. Expect the unexpected and adjust! Remember, your sole objective when taking an examination is to maximize your score. CPA exam grading is curved, and you must outperform your peers.

5. **Be in control.** Develop confidence and ensure success with a controlled preparation program followed by confident execution during the examination.

---

*Please complete the form on pages 809 and 810 IMMEDIATELY after you take the CPA exam so we can adapt to changes in the exam. Our approach has been approved by the AICPA.

HOW TO STUDY A STUDY UNIT USING GLEIM'S COMPLETE SYSTEM

To ensure that you are using your time effectively, we recommend that you follow the steps listed below when using all of the materials together (books, CD-Rom/Test Prep for Pocket PC, audios, and Gleim Online):

1. (25-30 minutes) In the Gleim Online course, complete Multiple-Choice Quiz #1 in 20-25 minutes (excluding the review session). It is expected that your scores will be lower on the first quiz than on subsequent quizzes.

    a. Immediately following the quiz, you will be prompted to review the questions you marked and/or answered incorrectly. For each question, analyze and understand why you marked it or answered it incorrectly. This step is an essential learning activity.

2. (15-30 minutes) Use the online audiovisual presentation for an overview of the study unit. The Gleim *CPA Review Audios* can be substituted for audiovisual presentations and can be used while driving to work, exercising, etc.

3. (30-45 minutes) Complete the 30-question True/False quiz. It is interactive and most effective if used prior to studying the Knowledge Transfer Outline.

4. (60 minutes) Study the Knowledge Transfer Outline, specifically the troublesome areas identified from the multiple-choice questions in the Gleim Online course. The Knowledge Transfer Outline can be studied either online or from the books.

5. (25-30 minutes) Complete Multiple-Choice Quiz #2 in the Gleim Online course.

    a. Immediately following the quiz, you will be prompted to review the questions you marked and/or answered incorrectly. For each question, analyze and understand why you marked it or answered it incorrectly. This step is an essential learning activity.

6. (60 minutes) Complete at least two 20-question quizzes while in Test Mode from the *CPA Test Prep* CD-Rom or Test Prep for Pocket PC.

7. (50 minutes, plus 10 minutes for review) Complete a simulation in the Gleim Online course. (This only applies to AUD, FAR, and REG since there are no simulations in BEC.)

When following these steps, you will complete all 20 study units in about 70-80 hours. Then spend about 10-20 hours using the *CPA Test Prep* CD-Rom or Test Prep for Pocket PC to create customized tests for the problem areas that you identified. To review the entire section before the exam, use the *CPA Test Prep* CD-Rom or Test Prep for Pocket PC to create 20-question quizzes that draw questions from all 20 study units. Continue taking 20-question quizzes until you approach your desired proficiency level, e.g., 75%+.

CPA GLEIM ONLINE

Gleim's *CPA Gleim Online* is a versatile, interactive, self-study review program delivered via the Internet. With *CPA Gleim Online*, Gleim guarantees that you will pass the CPA exam on your first sitting. It is divided into four courses (one for each section of the CPA exam).

Each course is broken down into 20 individual, manageable study units. Completion time per study unit will vary from 3-5 hours. Each study unit in the course contains an audiovisual presentation, 30 true/false study questions, 10-20 pages of Knowledge Transfer Outlines, and two 20-question multiple-choice quizzes. Simulation questions are also included with each study unit in AUD, FAR, and REG.

Gleim's *CPA Gleim Online* provides you with a Personal Counselor, a real person who will provide support to ensure your competitive edge. *CPA Gleim Online* is a great way to get confidence as you prepare with Gleim. This confidence will continue during and after the exam.

GLEIM BOOKS AND TEST PREP CD-ROM

Twenty-question tests in the *CPA Test Prep* CD-Rom or Test Prep for Pocket PC will help you to focus on your weaker areas. Make it a game: How much can you improve?

Our *CPA Test Prep* forces you to commit to your answer choice before looking at answer explanations; thus, you are preparing under true exam conditions. For each study unit, it also keeps track of your time and performance history, both of which are available in either a table or graphical format.

Simplify the exam preparation process by following our suggested steps listed below. DO NOT omit the step in which you diagnose the reasons for answering questions incorrectly; i.e., learn from your mistakes while studying so you avoid making similar mistakes on the CPA exam.

1. In test mode, answer a 20-question diagnostic quiz from each study unit before studying any other information.

2. Study the Knowledge Transfer Outline for the corresponding study unit in your Gleim book.

   a. Place special emphasis on the weaker areas that you identified with the initial diagnostic quiz in Step 1.

3. Take two or three 20-question quizzes in test mode after you have studied the Knowledge Transfer Outline.

4. Immediately following the quiz, you will be prompted to review the questions you marked and/or answered incorrectly. For each question, analyze and understand why you marked it or answered it incorrectly. This step is an essential learning activity.

5. Continue this process until you approach a predetermined proficiency level, e.g., 75%+.

6. Modify this process to suit your individual learning process.

   a. Learning from questions you answer incorrectly is very important. Each question you answer incorrectly is an **opportunity** to avoid missing actual test questions on your CPA exam. Thus, you should carefully study the answer explanations provided until you understand why the original answer you chose is wrong, as well as why the correct answer indicated is correct. This learning technique is clearly the difference between passing and failing for many CPA candidates.

   b. Also, you **must** determine why you answered questions incorrectly and learn how to avoid the same error in the future. Reasons for missing questions include:

      1) Misreading the requirement (stem)
      2) Not understanding what is required
      3) Making a math error
      4) Applying the wrong rule or concept
      5) Being distracted by one or more of the answers
      6) Incorrectly eliminating answers from consideration
      7) Not having any knowledge of the topic tested
      8) Employing bad intuition (WHY?) when guessing

   c. It is also important to verify that you answered correctly for the right reasons. Otherwise, if the material is tested on the CPA exam in a different manner, you may not answer it correctly.

   d. It is imperative that you complete your predetermined number of study units per week so you can review your progress and realize how attainable a comprehensive CPA review program is when using Gleim's Complete System. Remember to meet or beat your schedule to give yourself confidence.

GLEIM AUDIO REVIEWS

Gleim *CPA Review* audios provide a 20- to 40-minute overview of the outline for each study unit in the *CPA Review* book. The purpose is to get candidates "started" so they can relate to the questions they will answer before reading the study outlines in each study unit.

The audios are short and to the point, as is the entire **Gleim System for Success**. We are working to get you through the CPA exam with minimum time, cost, and frustration. You can listen to an informative discussion about the CPA exam and hear a sample of an audio review (The Equity Method) on our website at www.gleim.com/accounting/demos.

MULTIPLE-CHOICE QUESTION-ANSWERING TECHNIQUE

Expect three testlets of 30 multiple-choice questions each on the Financial section. See Study Unit 4 in *CPA Review: A System for Success* for additional discussion of how to maximize your score on multiple-choice questions.

1. **Budget your time.** We make this point with emphasis. Just as you would fill up your gas tank prior to reaching empty, so too would you finish your exam before time expires.

    a. Here is our suggested time allocation for Financial

	Minutes	Start Time	
Testlet 1 (MC)	45	4 hours	0 minutes
Testlet 2 (MC)	45	3 hours	15 minutes
Testlet 3 (MC)	45	2 hours	30 minutes
Testlet 4 (Simulation)	40	1 hour	45 minutes
Testlet 5 (Simulation)	40	1 hour	5 minutes
***Extra time	25	0 hours	25 minutes

    b. Before beginning your first testlet of multiple-choice questions, prepare a Gleim Time Management Sheet as recommended in Study Unit 7 of *CPA Review: A System for Success*.

    c. As you work through the individual items, monitor your time. In FAR, we suggest 45 minutes for each testlet of 30 questions. If you answer five items in 7 minutes, you are fine, but if you spend 10 minutes on five items, you need to speed up.

    ***Remember to allocate your budgeted "extra time," as needed, to each testlet. Your goal is to answer all of the items and achieve the maximum score possible.

2. **Answer the questions in consecutive order.**

    a. Do **not** agonize over any one item. Stay within your time budget.

    b. Mark any questions you are unsure of and return to them later as time allows.

        1) Once you have selected either the Continue or Quit option, you will no longer be able to review/change any answers in the testlet completed.

    c. Never leave a multiple-choice question unanswered. Make your best guess in the time allowed. Remember that your score is based on the number of correct responses. You will not be penalized for guessing incorrectly.

3. **For each multiple-choice question:**

    a. **Ignore the answer choices.** Do not allow the answer choices to affect your reading of the item stem (the part of the question that precedes the answer choices).

       1) If four answer choices are presented, three of them are incorrect. These choices are called **distractors** for good reason. Often, distractors are written to appear correct at first glance.

       2) In computational items, distractors are often the result of making common mistakes. Make sure to take your time and, if time permits, double-check your computations.

    b. **Read the question** carefully to determine the precise requirement.

       1) Focusing on what is required enables you to ignore extraneous information and to proceed directly to determining the correct answer.

          a) Be especially careful to note when the requirement is an **exception**; e.g., "Which of the following is **not** a required disclosure?"

       2) By adhering to these steps, you know what is required and which are the relevant facts.

    c. **Determine the correct answer** before reading the answer choices.

       1) However, some multiple-choice items are structured so that the answer cannot be determined from the question alone.

    d. **Read the answer choices carefully.**

       1) Even if answer (A) appears to be the correct choice, do **not** skip the remaining answer choices. Answer (B), (C), or (D) may be even better.

       2) Treat each answer choice as a true/false question as you analyze it.

    e. **Click on the best answer.**

       1) If you are uncertain, guess intelligently. Improve on your 25% chance of getting the correct answer with blind guessing.

       2) For many multiple-choice questions, two answer choices can be eliminated with minimal effort. This can reduce the risk of random guessing and increase your chances of success.

4. After you have answered all the items in a testlet and <u>before</u> you select either the Continue or Quit option, go back to the questions you marked and reconsider your answer choices.

5. **If you don't know the answer,**

    a. Again, guess; but make it an educated guess, which means select the best possible answer. First, rule out answers that you think are incorrect. Second, speculate on what the AICPA is looking for and/or the rationale behind the question. Third, select the best answer or guess between equally appealing answers. Your first guess is usually the most intuitive. If you cannot make an educated guess, read the stem and each answer and pick the best or most intuitive answer. It's just a guess!

    b. Make sure you accomplish this step within your predetermined time budget per testlet.

SIMULATION QUESTIONS

In Financial, testlets 4 and 5 are simulation questions. The following information and toolbar icons are located at the top of each screen.

1. **Time Remaining:** This information box displays how long you have remaining in the entire exam. Regularly note the amount of time remaining in order to stay on schedule for completion. Time for breaks and all testlets are included; i.e., the clock does not stop.

2. **Copy:** This icon provides the same function of copying text that a standard word processing program does. It copies selected text so you can move text from one document to another.

3. **Paste:** This icon provides the same function of pasting text that a standard word processing program does. It pastes/inserts previously copied text into the selected document.

4. **Calculator:** The calculator provided is a basic tool for simple computations. It is designed much like many common calculators used in software programs.

5. **Sheet:** This is a spreadsheet much like those used in many applications, e.g., Excel, and is provided as a tool available for more complex calculations. There is no information contained in the cells when the spreadsheet is opened. You may enter and execute formulas as well as enter text and numbers.

6. **Help:** This icon, when selected, provides a quick review of certain functions and tool buttons. It will also provide directions and general information and will not include information related specifically to the test content.

7. **Unsplit:** This icon, when selected, will unsplit the screen between the relevant information tab and the current in-use work tab.

8. **Split Horiz:** This icon, when selected, will split the screen horizontally between the relevant information tab and the current in-use work tab, thereby enabling you to work between screens to obtain critical information easily. However, you will not be able to view the same tab in both windows.

9. **Split Vert:** This icon, when selected, will split the screen vertically between the relevant information tab and the current in-use work tab, thereby enabling you to work between screens to obtain critical information easily. However, you will not be able to view the same tab in both windows.

10. **Done:** There are three options when you choose this icon.

   - You may choose Review to return to the beginning of the testlet to review your answers.
   - You may choose Continue to close the current testlet and go on to the next testlet. Once you have chosen Continue, you may not return to that testlet. After choosing Continue, you may choose Break in order to leave the room for a break. The clock will not stop if you choose to take a break.
   - Finally, you may choose Quit, which means either that you have completed the exam or that you chose not to complete it. If you chose not to complete it, there are security measures in place to determine that you are intentionally not completing the exam.

SIMULATION TABS

| Directions | Resources | ⑪ Treatments | ⑪ Inventory Costs | ⑪ Journal Entries | ⑪ Form 1065a | ⑪ Communication | ⑪ Research / Authoritative Literature |

There are three types of simulation tabs: informational tabs, work tabs, and the Research/ Authoritative Literature tab. Visit all tabs in each simulation to ensure your best performance.

The first two tabs are the informational tabs called Directions and Resources.* The Resources tab is informational in that it contains resources and tools for use with the spreadsheet tool. Other resources and tools may be provided within the tab and will vary depending upon the situation. These tools and resources could be tax rates, present value tables, formulas, spreadsheet operators, and spreadsheet functions. After reading the Directions tab, you should review the Resources tab.

A variety of work tabs require test-takers to respond to given information and are distinguished by a pencil icon that changes color when you enter a response. Note that the icon color change indicates only that a response has been made, NOT that the response is complete.

1. Forms Completion Tabs - This tab will contain a task that requires completion of accounting or tax forms. These tasks could include the completion of certain sections of tax return forms for personal or corporate taxes, or they could include the completion of other forms of a regulatory nature.

2. Multiple Choice/Multiple Select - This tab will contain questions and tasks that will be answered through the multiple-choice/multiple-selection method. Many of these will be drop-down boxes containing the possible answers or possibly a choice of formulas to properly complete an equation. Drop-down boxes are also referred to as "pop-up" boxes. You may need to double click the cell to produce the drop-down box.

3. Communication Tabs - This tab will contain a task that requires you to prepare a written communication or to edit an existing document, such as preparing a memo to a client or editing an audit engagement letter. The purpose is to assess your ability to logically organize ideas and communicate information effectively. Specific directions as to the type of communication will be provided.

    In written communication, the grader will not evaluate the accuracy of your answer. Rather, the grader is required to assess the strength of your writing ability. While content is not graded in the traditional sense, incorrect and inconsistently formatted answers negatively impact the grader's evaluation. Your communication grade is worth one-third of your grade for each simulation.

4. Spreadsheet Response Tabs - This tab will contain a task that requires completion of specific functions within a spreadsheet. This could include the completion of an equity section of a balance sheet, a completion of an indirect cash flow statement, or a calculation of inventory amounts.

5. Resources - The Resources tab contains resources and tools for use with the spreadsheet tool. Other resources and tools may be provided within the tab and will vary depending upon the simulation. These tools and resources could be present value tables, formulas relevant to the specific simulation, spreadsheet operators, or spreadsheet functions. You should always view the Resources tab before answering any work tabs.

* According to the AICPA, some simulations also will contain a Situation tab, as seen in the image on the next page. These tabs are available only when the information needed to answer a question does not fit on the applicable work tab.

6. Research/Authoritative Literature Tab – There are three simple steps to completing the Research/ Authoritative Literature tab. These directions are easily accessible within the tab itself by clicking on the "View Directions" tab in the top left corner.

    Step 1: Read the question, which is at the top of the screen beneath the "Step 1 – Research Question" heading.

    Step 2: Search the authoritative literature using the search function under "Step 2 – Search" heading. When you press "Search All," the middle column will display a list of all the literature that contains the search term(s). Click on the link of the document you want from the search results, and the contents of that document will be displayed in the middle column. The column on the right will automatically update itself to display all possible answers for the document. Alternatively, you can forgo a search and double click on the literature titles in the column on the left to display its contents and possible answer choices.*

    Step 3: Select your answer from the given choices under the "Step 3 – Answer" heading by clicking on the radio button to the left of the choices. Your answer will be confirmed at the top of the column.

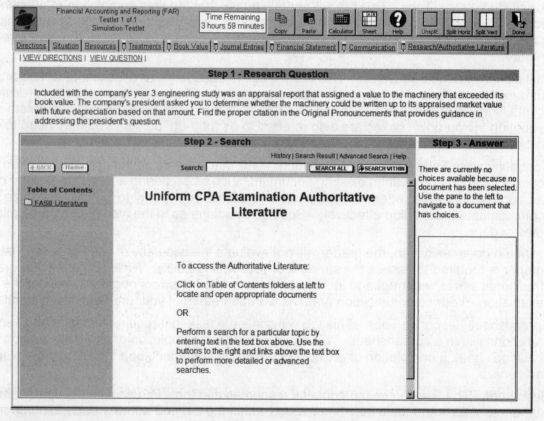

*Be aware that you may need to scroll vertically and/or horizontally to reveal the search results in their entirety. Many candidates have experienced anxiety when links associated with search results have not immediately appeared in the document pane. To be more in control during your test, practice with Gleim's full-length practice exams at www.gleim.com/practicecpaexam/.

Grading of Written Communication

AICPA graders are trained to look for the following seven attributes: thesis sentence, main ideas, support ideas, punctuation, sentence structure, conciseness, and clarity.

Assign a self-grade of 0, 1, 2, 3, 4, or 5 to your communication response. Use zero for no response or if you did not address the issue required. 3 is an average score; 4 is good; 5 is excellent; 2 is below average; 1 is poor. Divide this number by 5, then multiply the result by 1/3, which is the weighting assigned to the simulation by the AICPA. Example: If 5 points are possible and your self-grade is 3 (which is average), your communication score is 0.20 [(3 ÷ 5) × 1/3].

Other work tabs will be graded similarly:

$$\frac{\text{\# Correct Responses}}{\text{\# Gradable Items}} \times \text{\% Weight Assigned to Each Work Tab by the AICPA}$$

Please use Gleim's **CPA Simulation Wizard** to practice simulations under exam conditions to prepare you for your CPA exam. Go to www.gleim.com/accounting/cpa/simwizard.

SIMULATION QUESTION-ANSWERING TECHNIQUE

Do NOT be intimidated by simulations. Do your best so you outperform 55% of CPA candidates. Practice answering simulation questions at www.gleim.com/CPA. We have an online *CPA Simulation Wizard* with a practice simulation question for each study unit. Alternatively, we have **CPA Gleim Online**, which has audiovisuals, outlines, multiple-choice and true/false questions, and simulations.

We suggest the following simulation question-answering technique:

1. Write down the time remaining (hours/minutes) on your Gleim Time Management Sheet.

2. Read the information tabs for understanding so you can use the information as you complete the work tab requirements.

3. Answer the work tabs in order from left to right. Attempt to complete each tab before moving on to the next tab. If you become frustrated, have difficulty, etc., move on to the next tab.

4. After you have completed your first pass from left to right through the tabs, return to the first work tab at the left to review and complete your answers. Move from work tab to work tab systematically, reviewing and completing each tab. Be in control.

5. TIME: Stay within your time allocation in testlet 4 because you want the same amount of budgeted time for testlet 5. If you have stayed within your time allocation for testlets 1, 2, and 3, you will have extra minutes to add to the time allocated to testlets 4 and 5.

The start time in hours/minutes and time allocation in minutes follows:

Testlet	Format	Start Times and Time Allocation			
		REG	AUD	FAR	BEC
1	Multiple Choice	3/0 - 35	4/30 - 50	4/0 - 45	2/30 - 45
2	Multiple Choice	2/25 - 35	3/40 - 50	3/15 - 45	1/45 - 45
3	Multiple Choice	1/50 - 35	2/50 - 50	2/30 - 45	1/0 - 45
4	Simulation	1/15 - 35	2/0 - 50	1/45 - 40	NA
5	Simulation	0/40 - 35	1/10 - 50	1/5 - 40	NA
Extra Time		0/5	0/20	0/25	0/15

Simulation Recap: The following five types of work tabs appear in simulation questions. Each question format is easy and straightforward after you have practiced several under exam conditions. For guaranteed success, use *CPA Gleim Online* to learn and understand all subject matter tested as well as to practice your question-answering techniques and exam-taking skills.

1. Forms Completion
2. Multiple Choice/Multiple Select
3. Spreadsheet Response
    a. Numeric and Monetary Inputs
    b. Drop-down Selections
    c. Formula Answers
4. Communication
5. Research/Authoritative Literature

Be positive. You will have studied harder and practiced more wisely than most candidates, and you will prevail. Do your best: No one can ask for more!

ARB, APB, AND FASB PRONOUNCEMENT CROSS REFERENCE

The following listing relates FASB Statements and certain other nongovernmental accounting pronouncements to the study unit(s) where they are discussed (the subject matter may be covered without specific reference to the pronouncement). Pronouncements that do not appear in the listing have been superseded.

Accounting pronouncements may be tested 6 months after their effective date. When early application is permitted, pronouncements may be tested 6 months after the issuance date, but the old rules also are subject to testing until superseded. If no effective date is stated, the pronouncement is already in effect.

Appendix A, which begins on page 755, contains brief summaries of many of these pronouncements. If a pronouncement is extensively outlined in the main text, no summary is given. AICPA Statements of Position (SOPs) generally focus on narrow issues and are not summarized in the appendix.

Appendix A also includes summaries of GASB Statements and Interpretations. These summaries are more detailed than those for FASB Statements, most of which are outlined in the main body of the text. Because the area of governmental accounting and reporting represents only about 10% of the examination (two study units), GASB pronouncements not having broad application (i.e., the great majority) are covered only in Appendix A. Accordingly, GASB Statements and Interpretations are not included in the following cross reference.

Pronounce-ment	Gleim Study Unit(s)	Accounting Research Bulletins
ARB 43		
2A	2	Comparative Financial Statements
3A	2, 10	Current Assets and Current Liabilities
4	7	Inventory Pricing
7A	14	Quasi-Reorganization or Corporate Readjustment
7B	14	Stock Dividends and Stock Splits
9	8, A	Depreciation
10A	A	Real and Personal Property Taxes
13B	A	Compensation Involved in Stock Option and Stock Purchase Plans
ARB 45	3	Long-Term Construction Contracts
ARB 46	14	Discontinuance of Dating Earned Surplus
ARB 51	15, A	Consolidated Financial Statements

		Accounting Principles Board Opinions
APB Opinion 4	A	Accounting for the "Investment Credit"
APB Opinion 6	6, 8, 14, A	Status of Accounting Research Bulletins
APB Opinion 9	2, 3, 14	Reporting the Results of Operations
APB Opinion 10	3, A	Omnibus Opinion-1966
APB Opinion 12	2, A	Omnibus Opinion-1967
APB Opinion 14	12	Accounting for Convertible Debt and Debt Issued with Stock Purchase Warrants
APB Opinion 18	5, 9	The Equity Method of Accounting for Investments in Common Stock
APB Opinion 21	6, 12	Interest on Receivables and Payables
APB Opinion 22	4	Disclosure of Accounting Policies
APB Opinion 23	A	Accounting for Income Taxes-Special Areas
APB Opinion 26	12	Early Extinguishment of Debt
APB Opinion 28	4	Interim Financial Reporting
APB Opinion 29	8, 14	Accounting for Nonmonetary Transactions
APB Opinion 30	3	Reporting the Results of Operations – Reporting the Effects of Disposal of a Segment of a Business, and Extraordinary, Unusual, and Infrequently Occurring Events and Transactions (Guidance on disposal of a segment deleted by SFAS 144.)

Pronounce-ment	Gleim Study Unit(s)	Statements of Financial Accounting Standards
SFAS 2	9	Accounting for Research and Development Costs
SFAS 5	13	Accounting for Contingencies
SFAS 6	2, 12	Classification of Short-Term Obligations Expected to Be Refinanced
SFAS 7	9	Accounting and Reporting by Development Stage Enterprises
SFAS 13	13	Accounting for Leases
SFAS 15	12	Accounting by Debtors and Creditors for Troubled Debt Restructurings
SFAS 16	3, 4	Prior Period Adjustments
SFAS 19	A	Financial Accounting and Reporting by Oil and Gas Producing Companies
SFAS 22	A	Changes in the Provisions of Lease Agreements Resulting from Refundings of Tax-Exempt Debt
SFAS 23	A	Inception of the Lease
SFAS 25	A	Suspension of Certain Accounting Requirements for Oil and Gas Producing Companies
SFAS 27	A	Classification of Renewals or Extensions of Existing Sales-Type or Direct Financing Leases
SFAS 28	13	Accounting for Sales with Leasebacks
SFAS 29	13, A	Determining Contingent Rentals
SFAS 34	8	Capitalization of Interest Cost
SFAS 35	A	Accounting and Reporting by Defined Benefit Pension Plans
SFAS 37	A	Balance Sheet Classification of Deferred Income Taxes
SFAS 42	A	Determining Materiality for Capitalization of Interest Cost
SFAS 43	11	Accounting for Compensated Absences
SFAS 45	9	Accounting for Franchise Fee Revenue
SFAS 47	4	Disclosure of Long-Term Obligations
SFAS 48	6	Revenue Recognition When Right of Return Exists
SFAS 49	7	Accounting for Product Financing Arrangements
SFAS 50	A	Financial Reporting in the Record and Music Industry
SFAS 51	A	Financial Reporting by Cable Television Companies
SFAS 52	16	Foreign Currency Translation
SFAS 57	4	Related Party Disclosures
SFAS 58	8, A	Capitalization of Interest Cost in Financial Statements That Include Investments Accounted for by the Equity Method
SFAS 60	A	Accounting and Reporting by Insurance Enterprises
SFAS 61	A	Accounting for Title Plant
SFAS 62	A	Capitalization of Interest Cost in Situations Involving Certain Tax-Exempt Borrowings and Certain Gifts and Grants
SFAS 63	A	Financial Reporting by Broadcasters
SFAS 65	A	Accounting for Certain Mortgage Banking Activities
SFAS 66	A	Accounting for Sales of Real Estate
SFAS 67	A	Accounting for Costs and Initial Rental Operations of Real Estate Projects
SFAS 68	9	Research and Development Arrangements
SFAS 69	A	Disclosures about Oil and Gas Producing Activities
SFAS 71	A	Accounting for the Effects of Certain Types of Regulation
SFAS 72	A	Accounting for Certain Acquisitions of Banking or Thrift Institutions
SFAS 78	10, 12	Classification of Obligations That Are Callable by the Creditor
SFAS 84	12	Induced Conversions of Convertible Debt
SFAS 86	9	Accounting for the Costs of Computer Software to Be Sold, Leased, or Otherwise Marketed
SFAS 87	11	Employers' Accounting for Pensions
SFAS 88	11, A	Employers' Accounting for Settlements and Curtailments of Defined Benefit Pension Plans and for Termination Benefits
SFAS 89	16	Financial Reporting and Changing Prices
SFAS 90	A	Regulated Enterprises – Accounting for Abandonments and Disallowances of Plant Costs
SFAS 91	A	Accounting for Nonrefundable Fees and Costs Associated With Originating or Acquiring Loans and Initial Direct Costs of Leases
SFAS 92	A	Regulated Enterprises – Accounting for Phase-in Plans
SFAS 93	20	Recognition of Depreciation by Not-for-Profit Organizations
SFAS 94	15	Consolidation of All Majority-Owned Subsidiaries
SFAS 95	2, 19	Statement of Cash Flows
SFAS 97	A	Accounting and Reporting by Insurance Enterprises for Certain Long-Duration Contracts and for Realized Gains and Losses from the Sale of Investments
SFAS 98	13	Accounting for Leases: Sales-Leaseback Transactions Involving Real Estate; Sales-Type Leases of Real Estate; Definition of the Lease Term; Initial Direct Costs of Direct Financing Leases

Pronounce-ment	Gleim Study Unit(s)	Statements of Financial Accounting Standards - Cont.
SFAS 101	A	Regulated Enterprises – Accounting for the Discontinuation of Application of FASB Statement No. 71
SFAS 102	A	Statement of Cash Flows – Exemption of Certain Enterprises and Classification of Cash Flows from Certain Securities Acquired for Resale
SFAS 104	A	Statement of Cash Flows – Net Reporting of Certain Cash Receipts and Cash Payments and Classification of Cash Flows from Hedging Transactions
SFAS 106	11	Employers' Accounting for Postretirement Benefits Other Than Pensions
SFAS 107	4	Disclosures about Fair Value of Financial Instruments
SFAS 109	10	Accounting for Income Taxes
SFAS 110	A	Reporting by Defined Benefit Pension Plans of Investment Contracts
SFAS 111	A	Rescission of FASB Statement No. 32 and Technical Corrections
SFAS 112	11	Employers' Accounting for Postemployment Benefits
SFAS 113	A	Accounting and Reporting for Reissuance of Short-Duration and Long-Duration Contracts
SFAS 114	12	Accounting by Creditors for Impairment of a Loan
SFAS 115	2, 5	Accounting for Certain Investments in Debt and Equity Securities
SFAS 116	8, 14, 19, 20	Accounting for Contributions Received and Contributions Made
SFAS 117	19	Financial Statements of Not-for-Profit Organizations
SFAS 118	12	Accounting by Creditors for Impairment of a Loan – Income Recognition and Disclosures
SFAS 120	A	Accounting and Reporting by Mutual Life Insurance Enterprises and by Insurance Enterprises for Certain Long-Duration Participating Contracts
SFAS 123(R)	11	Share-Based Payment (revised 2004)
SFAS 124	19, 20	Accounting for Certain Investments Held by Not-for-Profit Organizations
SFAS 126	16	Exemption from Certain Required Disclosures about Financial Instruments for Certain Nonpublic Entities
SFAS 128	3	Earnings per Share
SFAS 129	3	Disclosure of Information about Capital Structure
SFAS 130	2	Reporting Comprehensive Income
SFAS 131	4, A	Disclosures about Segments of an Enterprise and Related Information
SFAS 132(R)	11	Employers' Disclosures about Pensions and Other Postretirement Benefits (revised 2003)
SFAS 133	5, 7, 16, 20, A	Accounting for Derivative Instruments and Hedging Activities
SFAS 134	A	Accounting for Mortgage-Backed Securities Retained after the Securitization of Mortgage Loans Held for Sale by a Mortgage Banking Enterprise
SFAS 135	A	Rescission of FASB Statement No. 75 and Technical Corrections
SFAS 136	19	Transfers of Assets to a Not-for-Profit Organization or Charitable Trust That Raises or Holds Contributions for Others
SFAS 137	A	Accounting for Derivative Instruments and Hedging Activities – Deferral of the Effective Date of FASB Statement No. 133
SFAS 138	A	Accounting for Certain Derivative Instruments and Certain Hedging Activities (an amendment of SFAS 133)
SFAS 139	A	Rescission of FASB Statement No. 53
SFAS 140	5, 6, 12	Accounting for Transfers and Servicing of Financial Assets and Extinguishment of Liabilities (a replacement of SFAS 125)
SFAS 141(R)	9, 15	Business Combinations (revised 2007) (effective December 2008, testable July 2009)
SFAS 142	5, 9, 15	Goodwill and Other Intangible Assets
SFAS 143	12, 20	Asset Retirement Obligations
SFAS 144	3, 8, 14, 20, A	Accounting for the Impairment or Disposal of Long-Lived Assets
SFAS 145	A	Rescission of FASB Statements 4, 44, and 64; Amendment of FASB Statement No. 13; and Technical Corrections
SFAS 146	12	Accounting for Costs Associated with Exit or Disposal Activities
SFAS 147	A	Acquisitions of Certain Financial Institutions
SFAS 149	A	Amendment of Statement 133 on Derivative Instruments and Hedging Activities
SFAS 150	A	Accounting for Certain Financial Instruments with Characteristics of Both Liabilities and Equity
SFAS 151	7	Inventory Costs
SFAS 152	A	Accounting for Real Estate Time-Sharing Transactions
SFAS 153	8	Exchanges of Nonmonetary Assets
SFAS 154	3, 4, 7	Accounting Changes and Error Corrections
SFAS 155	A	Accounting for Certain Hybrid Instruments
SFAS 156	A	Accounting for Servicing of Financial Assets
SFAS 157	1, 4, 5	Fair Value Measurements
SFAS 158	11	Employers' Accounting for Defined Benefit Pension and Other Postretirement Plans
SFAS 159	2, 5	The Fair Value Option for Financial Assets and Financial Liabilities

Pronounce-ment	Gleim Study Unit(s)	Statements of Financial Accounting Standards - Cont.
SFAS 160	15	Noncontrolling Interests in Consolidated Financial Statements (effective December 2008, testable July 2009)
SFAS 161	4, 16	Disclosures about Derivative Instruments and Hedging Activities
SFAS 162	1	The Hierarchy of Generally Accepted Accounting Principles (effective November 2008, testable July 2009)
SFAS 163	A	Accounting for Financial Guarantee Insurance Contracts (effective December 2008, testable July 2009)

FASB Interpretations

No. 1	3	Accounting Changes Related to the Cost of Inventory
No. 14	13	Reasonable Estimation of the Amount of Loss
No. 18	4	Accounting for Income Taxes in Interim Periods
No. 19	13	Lessee Guarantee of the Residual Value of Leased Property
No. 24	13	Leases Involving only Part of a Building
No. 30	8	Accounting for Involuntary Conversions of Nonmonetary Assets to Monetary Assets
No. 33	8	Applying SFAS 34 to Oil and Gas Producing Operations Accounted for by the Full Cost Method
No. 35	5	Criteria for Applying the Equity Method of Accounting for Investments in Common Stock
No. 37	16	Accounting for Translation Adjustments upon Sale of Part of an Investment in a Foreign Entity
No. 43	A	Real Estate Sales
No. 45	10, 13	Guarantor's Accounting and Disclosure Requirements for Guarantees, Including Indirect Guarantees of Indebtedness to Others
No. 46	15	Consolidation of Variable Interest Entities (Revised December 2003)
No. 47	12	Accounting for Conditional Asset Retirement Obligations
No. 48	10	Accounting for Uncertainty in Income Taxes

Statements of Financial Accounting Concepts

SFAC 1	1	Objectives of Financial Reporting by Business Enterprises
SFAC 2	1	Qualitative Characteristics of Accounting Information
SFAC 4	19	Objectives of Financial Reporting by Nonbusiness Organizations
SFAC 5	1	Recognition and Measurement in Financial Statements of Business Enterprises
SFAC 6	1, 19	Elements of Financial Statements
SFAC 7	1	Using Cash Flow Information and Present Value in Accounting Measurements

Selected Statements of Position

81-1	3	Accounting for Performance of Construction-Type and Certain Production-Type Contracts
82-1	2	Accounting and Financial Reporting for Personal Financial Statements
93-6	11	Employers' Accounting for Employee Stock Option Plans
93-7	9	Advertising Costs
94-6	4	Disclosure of Certain Significant Risks and Uncertainties
97-2	9	Software Revenue Recognition
98-1	9	Accounting for the Costs of Computer Software Developed or Obtained for Internal Use
98-2	20	Accounting for the Costs of Activities of Not-for-Profit Organizations and State and Local Governmental Entities That Include Fund Raising
98-5	9	Reporting on the Costs of Start-Up Activities

GLEIM FINANCIAL STUDY UNIT LISTING

		Number of Outline Pages	Number of Questions MC	First Page No.
1.	Concepts and Standards	24	44	19
2.	Financial Statements	22	39	63
3.	Income Statement Items	20	42	103
4.	Financial Statement Disclosure	16	28	145
5.	Cash and Investments	18	31	177
6.	Receivables	16	28	213
7.	Inventories	24	29	247
8.	Property, Plant, Equipment, and Depletable Resources	23	36	287
9.	Intangible Assets and Other Capitalization Issues	20	25	331
10.	Payables and Taxes	16	35	367
11.	Employee Benefits	16	26	403
12.	Noncurrent Liabilities	15	39	435
13.	Leases and Contingencies	13	20	471
14.	Equity	28	37	499
15.	Business Combinations	15	31	545
16.	Derivatives, Hedging, and Other Topics	21	28	579
17.	Governmental Accounting I	25	36	615
18.	Governmental Accounting II	20	47	657
19.	Not-for-Profit Concepts	11	30	701
20.	Not-for-Profit Accounting and Reporting	14	15	727

Also see the Financial Review Checklist presented on pages 793 and 794 and the AICPA's Content Specification Outlines on pages 3 and 4.

USER INQUIRIES (TECHNICAL ASSISTANCE) AND CUSTOMER SERVICE PROCEDURES

Technical questions about our materials should be sent to us via <u>mail</u>, <u>email</u>, or <u>fax</u>. The appropriate author, consultant, or staff member will give your correspondence thorough consideration and a prompt response.

Questions concerning orders, prices, shipments, or payments will be handled via telephone, mail, email, Internet, or fax by our competent and courteous customer service staff.

For Test Prep CD-Rom technical support, you may use our automated technical support service at www.gleim.com/support, email us at support@gleim.com, or call us at (800) 874-5346.

CONTROL: HOW TO BE IN

Remember, you must be in control to be successful during exam preparation and execution. Perhaps more importantly, control can also contribute greatly to your personal and other professional goals. Control is the process whereby you

1. Develop expectations, standards, budgets, and plans
2. Undertake activity, production, study, and learning
3. Measure the activity, production, output, and knowledge
4. Compare actual activity with what was expected or budgeted
5. Modify the activity to better achieve the expected or desired outcome
6. Revise expectations and standards in light of actual experience
7. Continue the process

Exercising control will ultimately develop the confidence you need to outperform 55% of CPA candidates and PASS the CPA exam! Obtain our *CPA Review: A System for Success* booklet for a more detailed discussion of control and other exam tactics.

STUDY UNIT ONE
CONCEPTS AND STANDARDS

(24 pages of outline)

The first topic is the **conceptual framework** underlying financial accounting and reporting. It currently consists of six **Statements of Financial Accounting Concepts (SFACs)**. The **Financial Accounting Standards Board (FASB)** is the nongovernmental organization that formulated this basis for the development, interpretation, and application of accounting standards. It also has issued **Statement of Financial Accounting Standards (SFAS) 157**, *Fair Value Measurements*, to provide a framework for the many applications of fair value accounting.

The second topic is the process of **standard setting** for financial accounting and reporting in the United States. The FASB has been recognized by the Securities and Exchange Commission (SEC) as the primary source of **generally accepted accounting principles (GAAP)**. The specific rules in the highest category of GAAP consist of the FASB's own Statements on Financial Accounting Standards (SFASs), Interpretations of SFASs, and certain currently effective pronouncements by its predecessor bodies.

The third topic is the time value of money, a concept that underlies many accounting applications.

NOTE: Throughout this book, the sources of official pronouncements often are cited to document the information provided and to facilitate further study. However, learning their formal titles or numbers is not necessary. Rather, candidates need to understand their content and how to apply it. This understanding is the focus of the study outlines and answer explanations.

1.1 INTRODUCTION TO THE CONCEPTUAL FRAMEWORK

SFACs

1. The following are the **currently effective SFACs**:

    a. **SFAC 1**, *Objectives of Financial Reporting by Business Enterprises*

    b. **SFAC 2**, *Qualitative Characteristics of Accounting Information*

    c. **SFAC 4**, *Objectives of Financial Reporting by Nonbusiness Organizations* (see Study Unit 19)

    d. **SFAC 5**, *Recognition and Measurement in Financial Statements of Business Enterprises*

    e. **SFAC 6**, *Elements of Financial Statements*

    f. **SFAC 7**, *Using Cash Flow Information and Present Value in Accounting Measurements*

2. The conceptual framework is a coherent set of **interrelated objectives and fundamental concepts** serving as a basis for accounting and reporting standards.

    a. **Objectives** state the purposes of financial reporting.

    b. **Fundamental concepts** are the basis of financial accounting. They provide guidance for

        1) Selecting the transactions, events, and circumstances to be accounted for;
        2) Recognizing and measuring the items selected; and
        3) Summarizing and communicating the resulting information.

    c. SFACs do not directly establish accounting and reporting requirements. Instead, they underlie the development, interpretation, and application of a consistent set of standards that will establish accounting and reporting requirements.

Assumptions

3. Certain **assumptions** underlie the environment in which the reporting entity operates. These assumptions are **not** found in official pronouncements. They have developed over time and are generally recognized by the accounting profession.

    a. **Economic-entity assumption.** The reporting entity is separately identified for the purpose of economic and financial accountability. Thus, the economic affairs of owners and managers are kept separate from those of the reporting entity.

        1) The legal entity and the economic entity are not necessarily the same. For example, consolidated reporting is permitted, if not required, even though the parent and its subsidiaries are legally distinct entities.

    b. **Going-concern (business continuity) assumption.** Unless stated otherwise, every business is assumed to be a going concern that will continue operating indefinitely. As a result, liquidation values are not important. It is assumed that the entity is not going to be liquidated in the near future.

    c. **Monetary-unit (unit-of-money) assumption.** Accounting records are kept in terms of money. Using money as the unit of measure is the best way of providing economic information to users of financial statements.

        1) The changing **purchasing power** of the monetary unit is assumed not to be significant.

    d. **Periodicity (time period) assumption.** Even though the most accurate way to measure an entity's results of operations is to wait until it liquidates, this method is not followed. Instead, financial statements are prepared periodically throughout the life of a business to ensure the timeliness of information.

        1) The periodicity assumption necessitates the use of **estimates** in the preparation of financial statements. It sacrifices some reliability of information for increased relevance.

Principles

4. Certain **principles** provide guidelines for recording financial information. The **revenue recognition** and **matching principles** have been formally incorporated into the conceptual framework as recognition and measurement concepts (see Subunit 5). Two additional principles are described below and on the next page.

    a. **Historical cost principle.** Transactions are recorded initially at cost because that is the most objective determination of fair value. It is a reliable measure.

        1) However, the trend is toward more extensive reporting of fair value information (see Subunits 1.6 and 1.7).

b. **Full-disclosure principle.** Financial statement users should be able to assume that financial information that could influence users' judgment is reported in the financial statements. As a result, notes typically provide information that is not shown on the face of the financial statements. Another source is supplementary information.

   1) **Notes** present information to explain financial statement amounts, for example, by describing the accounting policies used.

   2) **Supplementary information**, such as management's discussion and analysis or the effects of changing prices, provides information additional to that in the statements and notes. It may include relevant information that does not meet all recognition criteria.

   3) Full disclosure is not a substitute for reporting in accordance with GAAP.

Constraints

5. Certain **constraints (doctrines)** limit the process of recognition in the financial statements.

   a. The **cost-benefit** and **materiality constraints** are incorporated into the hierarchy of accounting qualities (see Subunit 1.3). Two additional doctrines are described below.

   b. **Industry practices constraint.** Occasionally, GAAP are not followed in an industry because adherence to them would generate misleading or unnecessary information.

      1) For example, banks and insurers typically measured marketable equity securities at fair value even before the issuance of SFAS 115, *Accounting for Certain Investments in Debt and Equity Securities*. Fair value and liquidity are most important to these industries.

   c. **Conservatism constraint.** Conservatism is "a prudent reaction to uncertainty to try to ensure that uncertainties and risks inherent in business situations are adequately considered" (SFAC 2).

      1) The conservatism doctrine originally directed accountants, when faced with two or more acceptable choices, to report the lowest amount for an asset or income.

         a) However, conservatism does not permit deliberate understatement of net assets and net income.

      2) Thus, if estimates of future amounts to be paid or received differ but are **equally likely**, conservatism requires using the **least optimistic estimate**.

         a) However, if the estimates are **not equally likely**, conservatism does not necessarily require use of the estimate that results in understatement rather than the **estimate that is the most likely**.

      3) The application of the lower-of-cost-or-market rule to inventories is an example of the conservatism constraint.

Stop and review! You have completed the outline for this subunit. Study multiple-choice questions 1 through 6 beginning on page 43.

1.2 OBJECTIVES OF FINANCIAL REPORTING (SFAC 1)

Scope of Financial Reporting

1. Objectives extend to all forms of **general purpose external financial reporting** by business entities. They are a response to the needs of external users who lack the authority to require the reporting of the information they need.

   a. **Financial statements**, including the notes and parenthetical disclosures, are crucial to financial reporting. They communicate accounting information to external parties. However, the scope of **financial reporting** is much broader. It also embraces "other information provided by the accounting system."

      1) Examples are disclosures required by authoritative pronouncements as supplementary information, annual reports, prospectuses, other filings with the SEC, news releases, and letters to shareholders. But some of this information is not subject to an external audit to enhance its reliability.

Environmental Context of Objectives

2. "Financial reporting is not an end in itself but is intended to provide information that is **useful in making business and economic decisions** – for making reasoned choices among alternative uses of scarce resources in the conduct of business and economic activities."

   a. Financial reporting is useful to people who make decisions about business entities or investments in or loans to business entities.

Characteristics and Limitations of Information

3. Certain inherent **characteristics and limitations** of financial reporting are listed below:

   a. The information **must be quantifiable** in units of money.
   b. The information pertains to **individual business entities**, not industries or an economy as a whole or individual consumers.
   c. The information often results from **approximate, rather than exact**, measures.
   d. The information largely reflects transactions and events that have **already happened**.
   e. Financial reporting is **but one source** of information.
   f. The benefits of information should be expected to **at least equal the cost** involved.

Objectives

4. **General Considerations**

   a. Although focused on investment and credit decisions, the objectives are intended to apply to information that is **useful to anyone** interested in the related entity's ability to meet its obligations or reward its investors.

   b. Financial reporting should **facilitate business and economic decisions** but not determine what those decisions should be.

5. **Information Useful in Investment and Credit Decisions**

   a. Financial reporting should provide information that is useful to current and potential investors and creditors and other users in making rational investment, credit, and other similar decisions.

   b. The information should be comprehensible to those who have a reasonable understanding of business and economic activities and who are willing to study the information with reasonable diligence.

6. **Information Useful in Assessing Cash Flow Prospects**

   a. Financial reporting should provide information to help current and potential investors and creditors and other users **assess the amounts, timing, and uncertainty of prospective cash receipts**. These may be from dividends or interest and the proceeds from the sale, redemption, or maturity of securities or loans.

   b. Financial reporting also should provide information to help investors, creditors, and others assess the amounts, timing, and uncertainty of **prospective net cash inflows** to the related entity.

   c. Investing, lending, and similar activities are undertaken to obtain not merely a return of cash expended but also a **return proportionate to the risk**. Thus, information should be useful in assessing risk.

7. **Information about Entity Resources, Claims to Those Resources, and Changes in Them**

   a. Financial reporting furnishes information that helps to identify the financial strengths and weaknesses of an entity, to assess its liquidity and solvency, and to evaluate its performance during a period.

      1) Financial reporting does not directly measure its fair value.

   b. According to SFAC 1, "The primary focus of financial reporting is information about an entity's **performance** provided by measure to earnings and its components."

      1) Although such information concerns the past, investors and creditors commonly use it to evaluate an entity's prospects. Information about past performance is most valuable when the **going-concern assumption** is appropriate, that is, when an entity is expected to continue in operation for an indefinite time.

      2) Measures of earnings and its components are of special interest to those concerned with an entity's cash flow potential. However, cash-basis financial statements for a short period, such as a year, are less valuable for this purpose than **accrual-basis statements**.

   c. Although the primary focus is on earnings, information about **cash flows** is useful for (1) understanding operations, (2) evaluating financing activities, (3) assessing liquidity and solvency, and (4) interpreting earnings information.

   d. Financial reporting should provide information about **management's stewardship** of resources, including their efficient and profitable use.

      1) However, it does not separate **management performance** from **entity performance**. The latter is affected by many factors other than management's activities. Thus, financial reporting does not directly provide information about management performance.

   e. Financial reporting should include **management's explanations and interpretations** of assumptions or methods underlying estimates and judgments.

Stop and review! You have completed the outline for this subunit. Study multiple-choice questions 7 through 9 on page 44.

1.3 QUALITATIVE CHARACTERISTICS OF ACCOUNTING INFORMATION (SFAC 2)

1. The qualities or characteristics of accounting information required by accounting standards make such information useful for decision making.

2. SFAC 2 applies to **business entities** and **not-for-profit organizations**.

   a. Without usefulness, no benefits are provided.

   b. The following chart (©, Financial Accounting Standards Board) depicts the hierarchy of accounting qualities:

A HIERARCHY OF ACCOUNTING QUALITIES

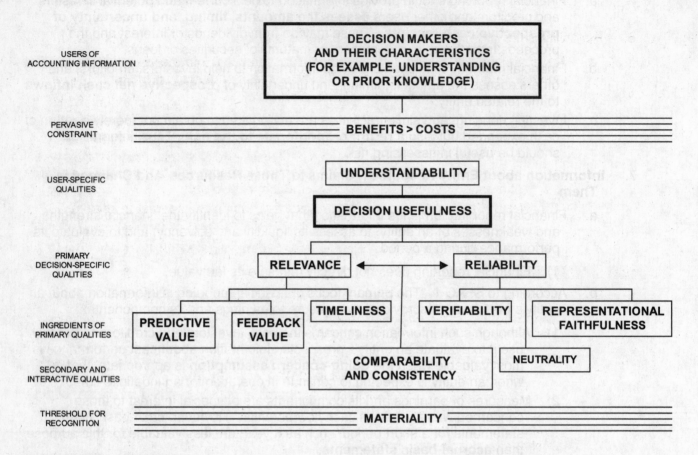

USERS OF ACCOUNTING INFORMATION	**DECISION MAKERS AND THEIR CHARACTERISTICS (FOR EXAMPLE, UNDERSTANDING OR PRIOR KNOWLEDGE)**
PERVASIVE CONSTRAINT	**BENEFITS > COSTS**
USER-SPECIFIC QUALITIES	**UNDERSTANDABILITY** / **DECISION USEFULNESS**
PRIMARY DECISION-SPECIFIC QUALITIES	**RELEVANCE** ⟷ **RELIABILITY**
INGREDIENTS OF PRIMARY QUALITIES	**PREDICTIVE VALUE** / **FEEDBACK VALUE** / **TIMELINESS** / **VERIFIABILITY** / **REPRESENTATIONAL FAITHFULNESS**
SECONDARY AND INTERACTIVE QUALITIES	**COMPARABILITY AND CONSISTENCY** / **NEUTRALITY**
THRESHOLD FOR RECOGNITION	**MATERIALITY**

User-Specific Qualities

3. **Understandability** and **decision usefulness** are **user-specific qualities**.

   a. **Decision makers.** Decision making has a central role in financial reporting. Decision makers must ultimately determine what information is **useful**.

   b. Information becomes more beneficial as it is understood by a greater number of users.

   c. **Understandability** (a user-specific quality) depends on both the characteristics of users (such as prior training and knowledge) and those of the information (reliability, relevance, etc.).

Decision-Specific Qualities

4. Relevance is the **first primary decision-specific quality**.

   a. **Relevance** is a primary decision-specific quality. It is "the capacity of information to make a difference in a decision by helping users to form predictions about the outcomes of past, present, and future events or to confirm or correct prior expectations."

   b. The following are the two **principal ingredients** of relevance:

      1) **Feedback value** is "the quality of information that enables users to confirm or correct prior expectations."

      2) **Predictive value** is "the quality of information that helps users to increase the likelihood of correctly forecasting the outcome of past or current events."

    c.   A third ingredient of relevance is timeliness. It is an **ancillary aspect** of relevance.

        1)   **Timeliness** means "having information available to a decision maker before it loses its capacity to influence decisions."

5.   Reliability is the **other primary decision-specific quality**.

    a.   **Reliability** is "the quality of information that assures that information is reasonably free from error and bias and faithfully represents what it purports to represent."

    b.   The following are the three **ingredients** of reliability:

        1)   **Representational faithfulness** is "correspondence or agreement between a measure or description and the phenomenon that it purports to represent."

        2)   **Verifiability** is "the ability through consensus among measurers to ensure that information represents what it purports to represent or that the chosen method of measurement has been used without error or bias."

        3)   **Neutrality** is "absence in reported information of bias intended to attain a predetermined result or to induce a particular mode of behavior."

            a)   Neutrality interacts with the other ingredients of reliability.

Secondary and Interactive Qualities

6.   Comparability and consistency are the **secondary and interactive qualities**.

    a.   **Comparability** is "the quality of information that enables users to identify similarities in and differences between two sets of economic phenomena."

        1)   Comparability interacts with the primary decision-specific qualities to enhance the usefulness of accounting information.

        2)   Comparability is not a quality of information in the same sense as relevance and reliability. Rather, it is a quality of the relationship among items of information.

    b.   Comparability includes **consistency**, which is "conformity from period to period with unchanging policies and procedures."

        1)   Consistency restricts entities from changing accounting methods, unless they can demonstrate that the newly adopted method is preferable to the old method.

Threshold for Recognition

7.   **Materiality** is the threshold for recognition.

    a.   Materiality is "the magnitude of an omission or misstatement of accounting information that, in the light of surrounding circumstances, makes it probable that the judgment of a reasonable person relying on the information would have been changed or influenced by the omission or misstatement."

        1)   The importance of materiality is emphasized by the exemption of immaterial items from the application of GAAP.

        2)   Judgments about materiality are primarily quantitative but are affected by qualitative concerns about the nature of particular items and the circumstances in which the judgments are made.

            a)   Because the unique circumstances affecting materiality judgments differ substantially, general standards of materiality ordinarily have not been issued.

Pervasive Constraint

8. **Costs and benefits** is the **pervasive constraint**.

    a. Like other goods, financial information will not often be sought unless its benefits exceed its costs. However, these costs and benefits cannot be objectively quantified.

Stop and review! You have completed the outline for this subunit. Study multiple-choice questions 10 through 13 beginning on page 45.

1.4 ELEMENTS OF FINANCIAL STATEMENTS (SFAC 6)

1. SFAC 6 applies to **business entities and not-for-profit entities**. The elements defined in SFAC 6 relate to measuring the performance and status of an entity based on information provided by accrual accounting.

Elements Reflecting Resources and Claims to Them in a Moment of Time

2. **Assets** are "probable future economic benefits obtained or controlled by a particular entity as a result of past transactions or events."

    a. Valuation allowances, such as premiums on notes receivable, "are part of the related assets and are neither assets in their own right nor liabilities."

3. **Liabilities** are "probable future sacrifices of economic benefits arising from present obligations of a particular entity to transfer assets or provide services to other entities in the future as a result of past transactions or events."

    a. Valuation allowances, such as discounts on bonds payable, "are part of the related liability and are neither liabilities in their own right nor assets."

4. **Equity or net assets** is "the residual interest in the assets of an entity that remains after deducting its liabilities."

Elements Describing Transactions and Other Events and Circumstances during Intervals of Time (The first three apply only to business entities.)

5. **Investments by owners** are "increases in equity of a particular business entity resulting from transfers to it from other entities of something valuable to obtain or increase ownership interests (or equity) in it."

    a. While assets are the most commonly transferred item, services also can be exchanged for equity interests.

6. **Distributions to owners** are "decreases in equity of a particular business enterprise resulting from transferring assets, rendering services, or incurring liabilities by the enterprise to owners."

    a. A distribution to owners decreases equity (the ownership interest).

7. **Comprehensive income** is "the change in equity of a business entity during a period from transactions and other events and circumstances from nonowner sources. It includes all changes in equity during a period except those resulting from investments by owners and distributions to owners."

    a. Comprehensive income encompasses net income and other comprehensive income (OCI). OCI excludes investments by and distributions to owners. It includes amounts recognized initially in equity, not earnings. See Subunit 2.2.

    b.   Comprehensive income and traditional financial statements are based on **financial capital maintenance**.

        1)   A **return** on financial capital is an excess of the monetary amount of ending net assets over the beginning amount (excluding owner transactions).

        2)   A **return** on **physical capital** is an excess of ending **productive capacity** (or the resources to achieve that capacity) over the beginning capacity (excluding owner transactions).

        3)   The physical capital approach differs because

           a)   Many **assets** are measured at **current cost**.

           b)   Effects of price changes are adjustments of equity, not the return on capital.

8.   **Revenues** are "inflows or other enhancements of assets of an entity or settlements of its liabilities (or a combination of both) from delivering or producing goods, rendering services, or other activities that constitute the entity's ongoing major or central operations."

9.   **Expenses** are "outflows or other using up of assets or incurrences of liabilities (or a combination of both) from delivering or producing goods, rendering services, or carrying out other activities that constitute the entity's ongoing major or central operations."

10.   **Gains** are increases in equity from peripheral or incidental transactions of an entity and from all other transactions and other events and circumstances affecting the entity except those that result from revenues or investments by owners."

11.   **Losses** are decreases in equity "from peripheral or incidental transactions of an entity and from all other transactions and other events and circumstances affecting the entity except those that result from expenses or distributions to owners."

12.   The elements are distributed as follows among the **financial statements** issued by business entities:

    a.   **Statement of Financial Position (Balance Sheet)**

        1)   Assets
        2)   Liabilities
        3)   Equity
        4)   Investments by owners

    b.   **Statement of Income**

        1)   Revenues
        2)   Gains
        3)   Expenses
        4)   Losses

    c.   **Statement of Changes in Equity**

        1)   Investments by and distributions to owners

        2)   Comprehensive income (but also may appear in a separate statement or be combined with the income statement)

13. The following table summarizes all transactions and other events and circumstances affecting a business entity during a period

Changes in assets and liabilities not accompanied by changes in equity	Changes in assets and liabilities accompanied by changes in equity		Changes within equity that do not affect assets or liabilities
• Exchanges of assets for assets • Exchanges of liabilities for liabilities • Acquisitions of assets by incurring liabilities • Settlements of liabilities by transferring assets	**Comprehensive income**	**Changes in equity from transfers between an entity and its owners**	
	• Revenues • Gains • Expenses • Losses	• Investments by owners • Distributions to owners	

Accrual Accounting

14. **Accrual accounting** applies to an item that meets (a) the definition of an element of financial statements and (b) the criteria for recognition and measurement. It records the financial effects of transactions and other events and circumstances when they occur rather than when their direct cash consequences occur.

 a. Accordingly, accrual accounting also considers (1) noncash exchanges of goods or services, (2) credit transactions, (3) nonreciprocal transfers, (4) price changes, (5) changes in fair values, (6) changes in form of assets or liabilities, etc.

 b. Accrual accounting embraces both accruals and deferrals.

   1) **Accruals** anticipate future cash flows. They recognize assets or liabilities and the related liabilities, assets, revenues, expenses, gains, or losses. Sales or purchases on account, interest, and taxes are common accruals.

   2) **Deferrals** reflect past cash flows. They recognize liabilities (for receipts) and assets (for payments), with deferral of the related revenues, expenses, gains, and losses. The deferral ends when the obligation is satisfied or the future economic benefit is used up. Prepaid insurance is a typical deferral.

 c. **Allocation** "is the accounting process of assigning or distributing an amount according to a plan or formula." **Amortization** is a form of allocation. It is "the accounting process of reducing an amount by periodic payments or write-downs." More specifically, it is an allocation process for deferrals. It involves reducing a liability (asset) recorded as a result of a cash receipt (payment) by recognizing revenues (expenses).

   1) Examples of allocation are the apportionment of a lump-sum purchase price among the assets acquired or the assignment of manufacturing costs to products.

   2) Examples of amortization are depreciation and depletion expenses and the recognition of earned subscriptions revenue.

 d. Concepts of realization and recognition also are crucial to accrual accounting. **Recognition** "is the process of formally recording or incorporating an item in the financial statements of an entity." **Realization** is "the process of converting noncash resources and rights into money."

   1) These concepts are covered in the next subunit.

Stop and review! You have completed the outline for this subunit. Study multiple-choice questions 14 through 20 beginning on page 46.

1.5 RECOGNITION AND MEASUREMENT CONCEPTS (SFAC 5)

1. **SFAC 5** "sets forth fundamental recognition criteria and guidance on what information should be formally incorporated into financial statements and when."

Financial Statements

2. Financial statements are the primary means of communicating financial information to external parties.

   a. A financial statement is "a formal tabulation of names and amounts of money derived from accounting records that displays either the financial position of an entity at a moment in time or one or more kinds of changes in financial position of the entity during a period of time."

   b. Additional information is provided by financial statement notes, supplementary information, and other types of disclosures.

      1) Information typically disclosed in **notes** is essential to understanding the financial statements. It is an integral part of basic financial statements.

   c. According to the conceptual framework, a **full set of financial statements** is similar to but not identical with those required by GAAP. They disclose

      1) Financial position
      2) Earnings
      3) Comprehensive income
      4) Cash flows
      5) Owner transactions (investments and distributions)

   d. The **statement of financial position (balance sheet)** provides information about assets, liabilities, and equity (the resource and financing structures of an entity) and their relationships at a moment in time.

      1) Following the guidance in SFAC 5 does not result in a measure of the fair value of a business entity.

   e. **Statements of earnings and comprehensive income** together show the nonowner changes in equity during a period.

      1) **Earnings** emphasizes what an entity receives or expects to receive (revenues) and what it sacrifices (expenses) in its ongoing major or central operations. But, in accordance with an **all-inclusive concept**, it also includes results of incidental or peripheral activities and the effects of certain environmental events (gains and losses).

      2) **Comprehensive income** is a broad measure of all recognized changes that affect equity, other than transactions with owners.

   f. A **statement of cash flows** should report, either directly or indirectly, the major sources of cash receipts and cash payments during a period.

      1) This statement provides information about operating, investing, and financing (both debt and equity) cash flows. The purpose is to aid the assessment of liquidity, financial flexibility, profitability, and risk.

         a) A cash flow statement also provides information about the differences between earnings or comprehensive income and cash flows.

g. A **statement of transactions with owners (investments by and distributions to owners)** summarizes all the changes in equity during the period not affecting comprehensive income.

　　1) The relevant transactions are those that change ownership interests. Examples are (a) declarations of cash dividends; (b) treasury stock purchases; (c) distributions in kind; and (d) increases in ownership interests through payments to the entity of cash, goods, or services, or through satisfaction of liabilities.

　　2) In current practice, **statements of retained earnings and changes in equity**, which may be combined with other statements, convey such information.

Recognition

3. **Recognition criteria** determine whether and when items should be incorporated into the financial statements, either initially or as changes in existing items.

a. Four **fundamental recognition criteria** apply to all recognition issues. However, each is subject to the pervasive cost-benefit constraint and the materiality threshold.

　　1) The item must meet the **definition** of an element of financial statements.

　　2) It must have a relevant attribute **measurable** with sufficient reliability.

　　3) The information about it must be capable of making a difference in user decisions **(relevance)**.

　　4) The information must be representationally faithful, verifiable, and neutral **(reliability)**.

Revenue Recognition

4. According to the **revenue recognition principle**, revenues and gains should be recognized when (a) realized or realizable and (b) earned.

a. Revenues and gains are **realized** when goods or services have been exchanged for cash or claims to cash.

b. Revenues and gains are **realizable** when goods or services have been exchanged for assets that are readily convertible into cash or claims to cash.

c. Revenues are **earned** when the earning process has been substantially completed, and the entity is entitled to the resulting benefits or revenues.

　　1) **Gains** ordinarily do not involve an earning process. Thus, the significant criterion for recognition of gains is being **realized or realizable**.

d. The two conditions usually are met when goods are delivered or services are rendered, that is, at the time of sale, which is customarily the **time of delivery**.

5. The following are **exceptions** to the basic revenue recognition rules:

a. Revenues from long-term contracts may be recognized using the **percentage-of-completion method**.

　　1) This method allows for revenue to be recognized **before delivery** at various stages of the contract, although the entire job is not complete.

b. **Completion of production** or a **change in prices** is an appropriate basis for recognition **before delivery** if products or other assets are readily realizable, e.g., precious metals and some agricultural products.

c. Recognition of revenues or gains or losses is appropriate in **nonmonetary exchanges**. Gains or losses also may result from **nonreciprocal transactions** (e.g., contributions received or given). However, fair values must be reasonably determinable.

d. If the collectibility of assets is relatively uncertain, revenues and gains may be recognized **after delivery** as cash is received using the **installment sales method** or the **cost recovery method**.

e.   Revenues from, for example, interest and rent may be recognized based on the **passage of time**.

Expense Recognition

6.   As a reflection of the profession's conservatism, **expenses and losses** have historically been subject to less strict recognition criteria than revenues and gains.

a.   Expenses and losses are not subject to the realization criterion.

b.   Rather, expenses and losses are recognized when (1) a **consumption of economic benefits** occurs during the entity's primary activities, or (2) an **impairment** of the ability of existing assets to provide future benefits has occurred.

1)   An expense or loss also may be recognized when a **liability** has been incurred or increased without the receipt of corresponding benefits. A probable and reasonably estimable contingent loss is an example.

c.   Long-lived assets, such as equipment, buildings, and intangible assets, are **depreciated or amortized** over their useful lives. Natural resources are **depleted**, usually on a units-of-production basis.

7.   The **pervasive expense recognition principles** are associating cause and effect, systematic and rational allocation, and immediate recognition.

a.   SFAC 6 defines matching, a term that has been given a variety of meanings in accounting literature, as essentially synonymous with **associating cause and effect**.

1)   **Matching** "is simultaneous or combined recognition of the revenues and expenses that result directly and jointly from the same transactions or other events." Such a direct relationship is found when revenue for sales of goods is recognized in the same period as the cost of goods sold.

b.   **Systematic and rational allocation** procedures do not directly relate costs and revenues but are applied when a causal relationship is "generally, but not specifically, identified."

1)   This expense recognition principle is appropriate when

a)   An asset provides benefits over several periods (its estimated useful life),

b)   The asset is used up as a result of events affecting the entity, and

c)   The expense resulting from such wastage is indirectly (not directly and traceably) related to specific revenues and particular periods.

2)   The most common example is depreciation.

c.   **Immediate recognition** is the applicable principle when costs cannot be directly or feasibly related to specific revenues, and their benefits are used up in the period in which they are incurred. Utilities expense is a common example.

Measurement Attributes

8.   Different attributes of assets and liabilities are used in current practice.

a.   **Historical cost** is the acquisition price of an asset. It is ordinarily adjusted subsequently for amortization (which includes depreciation) or other allocations. It is the relevant attribute for plant assets and most inventories.

b.   **Historical proceeds** is the cash or equivalent that is actually received when an obligation was created and may be subsequently amortized. It is the relevant attribute for liabilities incurred to provide goods or services to customers.

1)   An example is a magazine subscription.

c.   **Current (replacement) cost** is the amount of cash that would have to be paid for a current acquisition of the same or an equivalent asset.

1)   Inventory measured at the lower of cost or market may reflect current cost.

     d. **Current market value (exit value)** is the cash or equivalent realizable by selling an asset in an orderly liquidation (not in a forced sale). It is used to measure some marketable securities, e.g., those held by investment entities or assets expected to be sold at below their carrying amount.

        1) Certain liabilities, such as those incurred by writers of options who do not own the underlying assets, also are measured at current market value.

        2) More commonly, current market value is used when the lower-of-cost-or-market rule is applied to inventories and marketable securities.

     e. **Net realizable value** is the cash or equivalent expected to be received for an asset in the due course of business, minus the costs of completion and sale. It is used to measure short-term receivables and some inventories, for example, damaged inventories.

        1) Net realizable value is distinct from liquidation value, the appropriate measure of assets and liabilities when the going-concern assumption no longer holds.

     f. **Net settlement value** is the cash or equivalent that the entity expects to pay to satisfy an obligation in the due course of business. It is used to measure such items as trade payables and warranty obligations.

        1) Net settlement value ignores present value considerations. The amounts that will be realized in a liquidation are usually less than those that would have been received in the due course of business.

     g. **Present value** is in theory the most relevant method of measurement because it incorporates time value of money concepts.

        1) Determination of the present value of an asset or liability requires discounting at an appropriate interest rate the related future cash flows expected to occur in the due course of business.

        2) In practice, it is currently used only for long-term receivables and payables (but see Subunit 6).

  9. **Nominal units of money** are expected to continue as the measurement scale in current practice.

     a. The use of monetary units unadjusted for changes in purchasing power is not ideal. However, it has the virtue of simplicity and does not result in excessive distortion if inflation or deflation is relatively low.

Stop and review! You have completed the outline for this subunit. Study multiple-choice questions 21 through 26 beginning on page 48.

1.6 CASH FLOW INFORMATION AND PRESENT VALUE (SFAC 7)

Introduction

  1. Accounting measurements ordinarily use an **observable amount** determined by market forces. Absent such an amount, **estimated cash flows** often serve as a measure of an asset or a liability. Thus, SFAC 7 establishes a framework that uses cash flows for

     a. Measurements at initial recognition,
     b. Fresh-start measurements, and
     c. Applications of the interest method of allocation.

  2. SFAC 7 also states principles for the use of present value, especially when the amounts of future cash flows or their timing are uncertain, and describes the objective of present value.

3. **Definitions**

    a. An **estimated cash flow** is a future amount, whether paid or received.

    b. A **fresh-start measurement** occurs in a period subsequent to initial recognition. It results in a carrying amount not based on prior amounts or accounting treatments.

        1) An example is the reporting of trading securities at fair value at each balance sheet date.

    c. An **interest method of allocation** uses present value in the absence of a fresh-start measurement to calculate the periodic change in the carrying amount of an asset or liability.

    d. **Present value** is a current measure of an estimated cash flow after discounting.

Present Value Measurement

4. The **objective** is to estimate fair value by distinguishing the economic differences between sets of future cash flows that may vary in amount, timing, and uncertainty.

    a. For example, a series of $1,000 payments due at the end of each of the next 5 years has the same undiscounted amount as a single $5,000 payment due in 5 years.

5. For **initial recognition and fresh-start purposes**, present value is based on an observable attribute.

    a. Absent observed transaction prices, present value should encompass the elements of a **market price** if one existed (fair value). Thus, the **only objective** of present value for initial recognition and fresh-start purposes is **to estimate fair value**.

6. **Present value** should **reflect uncertainty** so that **variations in risks** are incorporated.

Elements of a PV Measurement
a. Estimates of future cash flows
b. Expected variability of their amount and timing
c. The time value of money based on the risk-free interest rate
d. The price of uncertainty inherent in an asset or liability
e. Other factors, such as lack of liquidity or market imperfections

7. The **traditional approach** to calculating present value uses one set of estimated cash flows and one interest rate. Uncertainty is reflected solely in the choice of an interest rate.

    a. This approach is expected to continue to be used in many cases, for example, when contractual cash flows are involved.

8. The **expected cash flow (ECF)** approach is applicable in more complex circumstances, such as when no market or no comparable item exists for an asset or liability.

    a. The ECF results from multiplying each possible estimated amount by its **probability** and adding the products.

    b. The ECF approach emphasizes **explicit assumptions** about the possible estimated cash flows and their probabilities.

    c. By allowing for a range of possibilities, the ECF approach permits the use of expected present value when the timing of cash flows is uncertain.

        1) **Expected present value** is the sum of present values of estimated cash flows discounted using the same interest rate and weighted according to their probabilities.

Liabilities

9. The purpose of a present value measurement of the **fair value of a liability** is to estimate the assets required currently to (a) settle it or (b) transfer it to an entity of comparable credit standing.

    a. Measurement of certain liabilities, for example, bonds payable, involves the same process as that used for assets. The measure of such a liability is the price at which another entity is willing to hold it as an asset.

        1) Some liabilities, however, are not typically held as salable assets by another entity, for example, liabilities for warranties or environmental cleanup.

            a) In this case, the estimate of the liability would be the estimate of the price a third person would have to be paid to assume the liability.

    b. **Credit standing** is always incorporated into initial and fresh-start measurements of liabilities.

Interest Methods

10. Present value is a feature of these methods.

    a. A typical example is amortization of the **discount or premium** on bonds.

        1) Unlike a fresh-start measurement, an accounting allocation does not attempt to reflect all factors that cause change in an asset or liability.

    b. Because no allocation method, whether or not interest-based, is preferable in every situation, the FASB will choose whether to require an interest method of allocation on a project-by-project basis.

        1) An interest method is most likely to be used when

            a) The transaction is a borrowing and a lending.
            b) Similar assets or liabilities are allocated using an interest method.
            c) The asset or liability has closely related estimated cash flows.
            d) The initial measurement was at present value.

11. **Changes in estimated cash flows** may result in a fresh-start measurement or in a change in the plan of amortization.

    a. If remeasurement is not done, a change in the scheme may be effected by

        1) **Prospectively** determining a new effective rate given the carrying amount and the remaining cash flows.

        2) **Retrospectively** determining a new effective rate given the original carrying amount, actual cash flows, and the newly estimated cash flows and using it to adjust the current carrying amount.

        3) Using a **catch-up** approach to adjust the carrying amount to the present value of the remaining cash flows discounted at the original rate (the FASB's preferred method).

12. The following table summarizes the conceptual framework underlying financial accounting:

Objectives
SFAC 1
Provide information
• That is useful in investment and credit decisions
• That is useful in assessing cash-flow prospects
• About entity resources, claims to those resources, and changes in them

Qualitative Characteristics	Elements of Financial Statements
SFAC 2	**SFAC 6**
Pervasive constraint:	Assets
Benefits > Costs	Liabilities
User-specific qualities:	Equity (Net assets)
Understandability	Investments by owners
Decision usefulness	Distributions to owners
Primary decision-specific qualities:	Comprehensive income
Relevance	Revenues
Feedback value	Expenses
Predictive value	Gains
Timeliness	Losses
Reliability	
Verifiability	
Neutrality	
Representational faithfulness	
Secondary and interactive qualities:	
Comparability	
Consistency	
Threshold for recognition:	
Materiality	

Recognition and Measurement		
SFAC 5		
Assumptions	**Principles**	**Constraints**
Economic entity	Historical cost	Cost-benefit
Going concern	Revenue recognition	Materiality
Monetary unit	Matching	Industry practice
Periodicity	Full disclosure	Conservatism

Stop and review! You have completed the outline for this subunit. Study multiple-choice questions 27 through 30 beginning on page 50.

1.7 FAIR VALUE MEASUREMENTS (SFAS 157)

Overview

1. SFAS 157 establishes a **framework for fair value measurements (FVMs)** required by other pronouncements. But it does not determine when FVMs are required. Accordingly, SFAS 157

   a. Defines **fair value**,
   b. Discusses **valuation techniques**,
   c. Establishes a **fair value hierarchy** of inputs to valuation techniques, and
   d. Requires expanded **disclosures** about FVMs.

2. SFAS 157 **does not affect practicability exceptions** to FVMs stated in other pronouncements. For example, it does not eliminate the exemption from the requirement to measure financial instruments at fair value if it is not feasible to do so.

Definitions

3. "**Fair value** is the price that would be received to sell an asset or paid to transfer a liability in an **orderly transaction between market participants** at the measurement date."

    a. The FVM is for a particular asset or liability that may **stand alone** (e.g., a financial instrument) or constitute **a group** (e.g., a business). The definition also applies to instruments measured at fair value that are classified as **equity**.

        1) The price is an **exit price** paid or received in a hypothetical transaction considered from the perspective of a market participant.

        2) The FVM considers **attributes** specific to the asset or liability, e.g., restrictions on sale or use, condition, and location.

        3) The **unit of account** is what is measured.

            a) For example, a **component of an entity** may be classified as held for sale and remeasured at **fair value minus cost to sell**. Thus, the component is the unit of account.

    b. **Market participants** are not related parties. They are **independent** of the reporting entity.

        1) They also are knowledgeable in the sense that they have a reasonable understanding based on all available information, including that obtainable from customary due diligence efforts.

        2) Moreover, they are willing and able (but not compelled) to engage in transactions involving the asset or liability.

        3) The FVM is market-based, not entity-specific. Thus, it is based on pricing **assumptions of hypothetical market participants**.

    c. An **orderly transaction** is not forced, and time is assumed to be sufficient to allow for **customary marketing activities**.

    d. The transaction is assumed to occur in the **principal market** for the asset or liability. In the absence of such a market, it is assumed to occur in the **most advantageous market**.

        1) Given a principal market, the FVM is the price in that market without adjustment for **transaction costs**.

            a) However, if **location** is an attribute of the asset or liability, the price includes **transportation costs**.

    e. **Assets.** The FVM is based on the **highest and best use (HBU) by market participants**.

        1) The HBU is **in-use** if the value-maximizing use is in combination with other assets in a group. An example is machinery in a factory.

        2) The HBU is **in-exchange** if the value-maximizing use is as a stand-alone asset. An example is a financial asset.

    f. **Liabilities.** The FVM assumes transfer, not settlement. Thus, the liability to the counterparty is unaffected. Accordingly, **nonperformance risk** is unaffected. It is included in the FVM.

Valuation Techniques

4. These should be consistently applied, appropriate in the circumstances, and based on sufficient data. Given a range, the FVM is the point most representative of fair value. All or any of the following should be used:

    a. The **market approach** is based on information, such as multiples of prices, from market transactions involving **identical** or **comparable items**.

  b. The **income approach** is based on current market expectations, e.g., about earnings or cash flows. It converts those amounts to a discounted current amount. Examples are present value methods and option-pricing models.

  c. The **cost approach** is based on **current replacement cost**. It is the cost to a market participant to buy or build an asset of **comparable utility** adjusted for obsolescence.

5. **Inputs to valuation techniques** are the pricing assumptions of market participants.

  a. **Observable inputs** are based on market data obtained from independent sources.

  b. **Unobservable inputs** are based on the entity's own assumptions about the assumptions of market participants that reflect the best available information. Their use should be minimized.

The Fair Value Hierarchy

6. The fair value hierarchy establishes **priorities among inputs to valuation techniques**.

  a. **Level 1 inputs** are the **most reliable**. They are unadjusted quoted prices in active markets for identical assets or liabilities that the entity can access at the measurement date.

   1) If the entity has a position in a single financial instrument that is traded in an active market, the position is measured within Level 1. The FVM equals the quantity held times the instrument's quoted price.

  b. **Level 2 inputs** are **observable**. But they exclude quoted prices included within Level 1.

   1) Examples are quoted prices for similar items in active markets, quoted prices in markets that are not active, and observable inputs that are not quoted prices.

  c. **Level 3 inputs** are the **least reliable**. They are **unobservable** inputs that are used in the absence of observable inputs. They should be based on the best available information in the circumstances.

   1) The entity need not exhaust every effort to gain information about the assumptions of market participants.

Disclosures

7. Certain **quantitative disclosures** in tabular format are required.

  a. One set of disclosures concerns assets and liabilities measured at fair value **on a recurring basis** (e.g., trading securities). A second set concerns those measured **on a nonrecurring basis** (e.g., impaired assets).

  b. The tables below and on the next page ($ in 000s) are examples of disclosures concerning assets measured at fair value **on a recurring basis**. Information is presented **separately for each major category**.

   1)

Description	12/31/Yr 1	Quoted Prices in Active Markets for Identical Assets (Level 1)	Significant Other Observable Inputs (Level 2)	Significant Unobservable Inputs (Level 3)
		Fair Value Measurements at Reporting Date Using		
Trading securities	$115	$105	$10	
Available-for-sale securities	75	75		
Derivatives	60	25	15	$20
Venture capital investments	10			10
Total	$260	$205	$25	$30

   a) A **similar table** must be disclosed for **liabilities**.

2) A **reconciliation** of the beginning and ending balances is required for any assets or liabilities measured at fair value on a recurring basis that use **significant unobservable inputs** (that is, Level 3) during the period.

| | Fair Value Measurement Using Significant Unobservable Inputs (Level 3) | | |
	Derivatives	Venture Capital Investments	Total
Beginning balance	$14	$11	$25
Total gains or losses (realized/unrealized)			
Included in earnings (or changes in net assets)	11	(3)	8
Included in other comprehensive income	4		4
Purchases, issuances, and settlements	(7)	2	(5)
Transfers in and/or out of Level 3	(2)	0	(2)
Ending balance	$20	$10	$30
The amount of total gains or losses for the period included in earnings (or changes in net assets) attributable to the change in unrealized gains or losses relating to assets still held at the reporting date	$ 7	$ 2	$ 9

© 2006, Financial Accounting Standards Board

    a) A **similar table** must be disclosed for **liabilities**.

c. For each major category of assets and liabilities measured at fair value **on a nonrecurring basis** during the period, quantitative disclosures also must be made in tabular format:

| | | Fair Value Measurement Using | | | |
Description	Year Ended 12/31/Yr 1	Quoted Prices In Active Markets for Identical Assets (Level 1)	Significant Other Observable Inputs (Level 2)	Significant Unobservable Inputs (Level 3)	Total Gains (Losses)
Long-lived assets held and used	$75		$75		$(25)
Goodwill	30			$30	(35)
Long-lived assets held for sale	26		26		(15)
					$(75)

© 2006, Financial Accounting Standards Board

    1) A **similar table** must be reported for **liabilities**.

Stop and review! You have completed the outline for this subunit. Study multiple-choice questions 31 through 35 beginning on page 51.

1.8 STANDARDS

Generally Accepted Accounting Principles (GAAP)

1. According to the AICPA, **generally accepted accounting principles (GAAP)** are the "conventions, rules, and procedures necessary to define accepted accounting practice at a particular time."

    a. They include both the **broad guidelines** and the **detailed practices** and procedures promulgated by the profession that provide uniform standards to measure financial presentations.

b.   The **hierarchies for U.S. GAAP** are presented in Statement on Auditing Standards 69 (as amended). It is codified in AICPA Professional Standards as section **AU 411**, *The Meaning of "Present Fairly in Conformity with Generally Accepted Accounting Principles" in the Independent Auditor's Report.*

Accounting Standard Setters

2.   The FASB is the body designated by the AICPA Council to establish principles for nongovernmental entities. The pronouncements in Category (a) (officially established accounting principles) are principles as contemplated in Conduct Rule 203.

3.   FASB conducts a **due process** procedure before it passes new pronouncements.

    a.   After a group of accounting experts has defined specific problems and a range of solutions for an agenda item, the FASB's staff conducts research and analysis and drafts a discussion memorandum.

    b.   The FASB then holds a public hearing, usually 60 days after the discussion memorandum is released. The next step is publication of an exposure draft.

    c.   After consideration of public comments on the exposure draft, and possibly amendments, a new statement is issued after a majority vote by the members of FASB.

4.   **Other accounting literature** may be considered in the absence of a source of established accounting principles. Other accounting literature includes FASB Concepts Statements (ordinarily, the most influential source in this category); AICPA Issues Papers; International Financial Reporting Standards; GASB Statements, Interpretations, and Technical Bulletins; Federal Accounting Standards Advisory Board (FASAB) Statements, Interpretations, and Technical Bulletins; pronouncements of other professional associations or regulatory agencies; AICPA Technical Practice Aids; and accounting textbooks, handbooks, and articles.

GAAP Hierarchy

5.   AU 411 presents GAAP hierarchies for nongovernmental entities, state and local governments, and federal governmental entities. The following is the hierarchy of **established accounting principles** for nongovernmental entities:

Category (a) Officially established (Most authoritative)	FASB Statements and Interpretations	APB Opinions	CAP Accounting Research Bulletins
Category (b)	FASB Technical Bulletins	AICPA Industry Audit and Accounting Guides	AICPA Statements of Position
Category (c)	FASB Emerging Issues Task Force Consensus Positions	AICPA Accounting Standards Executive Committee (AcSec) Practice Bulletins	
Category (d)	AICPA Accounting Interpretations	FASB Implementation Guides ("Qs and As")	Common Industry Practice

    a.   The FASB must clear the AICPA pronouncements in Categories (b) and (c).

    b.   **Mandatory SEC pronouncements** applying only to SEC registrants also have the highest priority.

6.   The FASB issues formal interpretations of its own statements.

    a.   Unlike the AICPA's Accounting Interpretations, **FASB Interpretations** are developed and voted upon by the FASB itself and have the same status as SFASs.

    b.   **ARBs** issued by the CAP and **APB Opinions** continue to be authoritative until they are amended or superseded by FASB pronouncements.

7. **Conduct Rule 203** of the AICPA's Code of Professional Conduct provides that a member shall not express assurances about conformity with GAAP if the financial statements contain a **material departure** from a principle issued by bodies designated by the AICPA Council to establish such principles.

    a. However, in unusual circumstances, a **departure may be permissible** if literal application of a principle would be misleading.

8. SFAS 162, *The Hierarchy of Generally Accepted Accounting Principles*, became effective in November 2008. Thus, it will be testable no later than July 2009.

    a. SFAS 162 moves the **nongovernmental GAAP hierarchy** into the "accounting literature established by the FASB."

        1) Accordingly, the **PCAOB** has deleted the entire GAAP hierarchy (governmental as well as nongovernmental) from its Interim Auditing Standards. These standards apply only to audits of public companies.

Sarbanes-Oxley Act of 2002

9. This act authorizes the **Securities and Exchange Commission (SEC)** to recognize as generally accepted for purposes of the securities laws any **accounting principles** issued by an appropriate entity.

    a. Such an **accounting standard setter** must have the following characteristics:

        1) It is organized as a private entity.
        2) The majority of the members of its governing body are not associated with a registered public accounting firm during their period of service and were not associated with such a firm during the prior 2 years.
        3) **Funding** of the entity is similar to that of the **Public Company Accounting Oversight Board (PCAOB)** created by the act. The source of funding is an **annual accounting support fee** assessed against public companies.
        4) Its procedures provide for prompt consideration by **majority vote** of changes in accounting principles in response to emerging accounting issues and changing business practices.

            a) For example, the FASB's five members decide questions by a simple majority.

        5) The entity considers the need to keep standards current.
        6) The entity considers the desirability of the **convergence** of U.S. and international accounting standards.

    b. The SEC will continue to recognize the **FASB** as the accounting standard setter for filings of issuers (public companies) under the securities laws.

Other Comprehensive Bases of Accounting (OCBOA)

10. The applicable pronouncement is **AU 623**, *Special Reports*.

    a. A comprehensive basis of accounting other than GAAP may be

        1) A basis used to comply with the requirements of a regulator
        2) A basis used for tax purposes
        3) The cash basis and modifications of the cash basis having substantial support
        4) A definite set of criteria having substantial support that is applied to all material items, for example, the price-level basis

    b. Statements prepared using an OCBOA should include a summary of significant accounting policies, including discussion of the basis used and how it differs from GAAP.

Stop and review! You have completed the outline for this subunit. Study multiple-choice questions 36 through 41 beginning on page 52.

1.9 TIME VALUE OF MONEY

1.   Time value of money concepts pervade financial accounting. For example, they affect the accounting for noncurrent receivables and payables (bonds and notes), leases, and certain employee benefits.

2.   A quantity of money to be received or paid in the future is worth less than the same amount now. The difference is measured in terms of interest calculated using the appropriate **discount rate**. Interest is the payment received by holders of money from the current consumer to forgo current consumption.

3.   Standard tables have been developed to facilitate the calculation of present and future values. Each entry in one of these tables represents the factor by which any monetary amount can be modified to obtain its present or future value.

Amounts

4.   The **present value (PV) of an amount** is the value today of some future payment.

   a.   It equals the future payment times the present value of 1 (a factor found in a standard table) for the given number of periods and interest rate.

	EXAMPLE		
	Present Value		
No. of Periods	6%	8%	10%
1	0.943	0.926	0.909
2	0.890	0.857	0.826
3	0.840	0.794	0.751
4	0.792	0.735	0.683
5	0.747	0.681	0.621

The present value of $1,000, to be received in 3 years and discounted at 8%, is $794 ($1,000 × 0.794).

5.   The **future value (FV) of an amount** is the amount available at a specified time in the future based on a single investment (deposit) today. The FV is the amount to be computed if one knows the present value and the appropriate discount rate.

   a.   It equals the current payment times the future value of 1 (a factor found in a standard table) for the given number of periods and interest rate.

	EXAMPLE		
	Future Value		
No. of Periods	6%	8%	10%
1	1.0600	1.0800	1.1000
2	1.1236	1.1664	1.2100
3	1.1910	1.2597	1.3310
4	1.2625	1.3605	1.4641
5	1.3382	1.4693	1.6105

The future value of $1,000 invested today for 4 years at 10% interest will be $1,464 ($1,000 × 1.464).

Annuities

6. An **annuity** is usually a series of equal payments at equal intervals of time, e.g., $1,000 at the end of every year for 10 years.

    a. An **ordinary annuity (annuity in arrears)** is a series of payments occurring at the end of each period. In an **annuity due (annuity in advance)**, the payments are made (received) at the beginning of each period.

        1) **Present value.** The first payment of an ordinary annuity is discounted. The first payment of an annuity due is not discounted.

        2) **Future value.** Interest is not earned for the first period of an ordinary annuity. Interest is earned on the first payment of an annuity due.

    b. The **PV of an annuity**. A typical present value table is for an ordinary annuity, but the factor for an annuity due can be easily derived. Select the factor for an ordinary annuity for one less period (n − 1) and add 1.000 to it to include the initial payment (which is not discounted).

        ### EXAMPLE

No. of Periods	Present Value		
	6%	8%	10%
1	0.943	0.926	0.909
2	1.833	1.783	1.736
3	2.673	2.577	2.487
4	3.465	3.312	3.170
5	4.212	3.993	3.791

        To calculate the present value of an **ordinary annuity** of four payments of $1,000 each discounted at 10%, multiply $1,000 by the appropriate factor ($1,000 × 3.170 = $3,170).

        Using the same table, the present value of an **annuity due** of four payments of $1,000 each also may be calculated. This value equals $1,000 times the factor for one less period (4 − 1 = 3), increased by 1.0. Thus, the present value of the annuity due for four periods at 10% is $3,487 [$1,000 × (2.487 + 1.0)].

        The present value of the annuity due ($3,487) is greater than the present value of the ordinary annuity ($3,170) because the payments occur 1 year sooner.

    c. The **FV of an annuity** is the value that a series of equal payments will have at a certain moment in the future if interest is earned at a given rate.

        ### EXAMPLE

No. of Periods	Future Value		
	6%	8%	10%
1	1.0000	1.0000	1.0000
2	2.0600	2.0800	2.1000
3	3.1836	3.2464	3.3100
4	4.3746	4.5061	4.6410
5	5.6371	5.8667	6.1051

        To calculate the FV of a 3-year **ordinary annuity** with payments of $1,000 each at 6% interest, multiply $1,000 by the appropriate factor ($1,000 × 3.184 = $3,184).

        The FV of an **annuity due** also may be determined from the same table. Multiply the $1,000 payment by the factor for one additional period (3 + 1 = 4) decreased by 1.0 (4.375 − 1.0 = 3.375) to arrive at a FV of $3,375 ($1,000 × 3.375).

        The future value of the annuity due ($3,375) is greater than the future value of an ordinary annuity ($3,184). The deposits are made earlier.

Stop and review! You have completed the outline for this subunit. Study multiple-choice questions 42 through 44 beginning on page 54.

QUESTIONS

1.1 Introduction to the Conceptual Framework

1. What are the Statements of Financial Accounting Concepts intended to establish?

A. Generally accepted accounting principles in financial reporting by business enterprises.

B. The meaning of "present fairly in accordance with generally accepted accounting principles."

C. The objectives and concepts for use in developing standards of financial accounting and reporting.

D. The hierarchy of sources of generally accepted accounting principles.

Answer (C) is correct. *(CPA, adapted)*
REQUIRED: The purpose of the SFACs.
DISCUSSION: SFACs do not establish accounting and reporting requirements. They are classified as other accounting literature, not established accounting principles, in the GAAP hierarchy [SAS 69 (AU 411)]. SFACs describe the objectives, qualitative characteristics, and other fundamental concepts that guide the FASB in developing sound accounting principles.
Answer (A) is incorrect because SFACs are intended to guide the development of accounting standards by the FASB. Answer (B) is incorrect because SAS 69 (AU 411) clarifies the meaning of "present fairly in accordance with generally accepted accounting principles." Answer (D) is incorrect because the hierarchy of sources of GAAP is presented in SAS 69 (AU 411).

2. A Midwestern public utility reports noncurrent assets as the first item on its statement of financial position. This practice is an example of the

A. Going-concern assumption.

B. Conservatism.

C. Economic-entity assumption.

D. Industry practice constraint.

Answer (D) is correct. *(CMA, adapted)*
REQUIRED: The reason a public utility reports noncurrent assets as the first item on the balance sheet.
DISCUSSION: Assets are normally listed in the order of their importance, with current assets typically being the most important. For a public utility, the physical plant is the most important asset. Thus, public utilities often report their noncurrent assets as the first item on the balance sheet. This departure from the customary presentation in accordance with GAAP is justified by the peculiarities of the industry.
Answer (A) is incorrect because the assumed continuity of the business is the basis for reporting financial statement items at other than liquidation value. Answer (B) is incorrect because conservatism is a prudent reaction to uncertainty. For example, if different estimates are available and none is more likely than another, the least optimistic should be used. However, conservatism is not a bias toward understatement. Answer (C) is incorrect because the affairs of an economic entity are distinct from those of its owners.

3. Reporting inventory at the lower of cost or market is a departure from the accounting principle of

A. Historical cost.

B. Consistency.

C. Conservatism.

D. Full disclosure.

Answer (A) is correct. *(CPA, adapted)*
REQUIRED: The principle from which reporting inventory at the lower of cost or market is a departure.
DISCUSSION: Historical cost is the amount of cash, or its equivalent, paid to acquire an asset. Thus, the LCM rule departs from the historical cost principle when the utility of the inventory is judged no longer to be as great as its cost.
Answer (B) is incorrect because LCM does not violate the consistency principle as long as it is consistently applied. Answer (C) is incorrect because LCM yields a conservative inventory valuation. Answer (D) is incorrect because, as long as the basis of stating inventories is disclosed, LCM does not violate the full disclosure principle.

4. The accounting measurement that is not consistent with the going concern concept is

A. Historical cost.

B. Realization.

C. The transaction approach.

D. Liquidation value.

Answer (D) is correct. *(CMA, adapted)*
REQUIRED: The accounting measurement inconsistent with the going concern concept.
DISCUSSION: Financial accounting principles assume that a business entity is a going concern in the absence of evidence to the contrary. The concept justifies the use of depreciation and amortization schedules, and the recording of assets and liabilities using attributes other than liquidation value.
Answer (A) is incorrect because historical cost is part of the basic structure of accrual accounting. Answer (B) is incorrect because realization is part of the basic structure of accrual accounting. Answer (C) is incorrect because the transaction approach is part of the basic structure of accrual accounting.

5. A newly acquired plant asset is to be depreciated over its useful life. The rationale for this process is the

A. Economic-entity assumption.

B. Monetary-unit assumption.

C. Materiality assumption.

D. Going-concern assumption.

Answer (D) is correct. *(CIA, adapted)*
REQUIRED: The rationale for depreciating a plant asset.
DISCUSSION: A basic feature of financial accounting is that the business entity is assumed to be a going concern in the absence of evidence to the contrary. The going-concern concept is based on the empirical observation that many enterprises have an indefinite life. The reporting entity is assumed to have a life long enough to fulfill its objectives and commitments and therefore to depreciate wasting assets over their useful lives.
Answer (A) is incorrect because the economic-entity assumption provides that economic activity can be identified with a particular unit of accountability. Answer (B) is incorrect because the monetary-unit assumption provides that all transactions and events can be measured in terms of a common denominator, for instance, the dollar. Answer (C) is incorrect because the materiality assumption simply implies that items of insignificant value can be expensed rather than capitalized and depreciated or amortized.

6. What is the underlying concept governing the generally accepted accounting principles pertaining to recording gain contingencies?

A. Conservatism.

B. Relevance.

C. Consistency.

D. Reliability.

Answer (A) is correct. *(CPA, adapted)*
REQUIRED: The underlying concept governing the GAAP relating to gain contingencies.
DISCUSSION: Conservatism is "a prudent reaction to uncertainty to try to ensure that uncertainty and risks inherent in business situations are adequately considered" (SFAC 2). Thus, a loss but not a gain contingency is recorded in the financial statements. If the probability of realization of a gain is high, the contingency is disclosed in the notes.
Answer (B) is incorrect because relevance relates to the capacity of information to affect a decision. Answer (C) is incorrect because consistency requires the application of the same methods to similar accounting events from period to period. Answer (D) is incorrect because reliable information is reasonably free from error and bias and faithfully represents what it purports to represent.

1.2 Objectives of Financial Reporting (SFAC 1)

7. Which of the following statements reflects the basic purposes of financial reporting for business enterprises?

A. The primary focus of financial reporting is information about an enterprise's resources.

B. The best indication of an enterprise's ability to generate favorable cash flows is information based on previous cash receipts and payments.

C. Financial accounting is expressly designed to measure directly the value of a business enterprise.

D. Investment and credit decisions often are based, at least in part, on evaluations of the past performance of an enterprise.

Answer (D) is correct. *(Publisher, adapted)*
REQUIRED: The basic purpose of financial reporting.
DISCUSSION: SFAC 1 states that, although investment and credit decisions reflect investors' and creditors' expectations about future enterprise performance, those expectations are commonly based, at least in part, on evaluations of past enterprise performance.
Answer (A) is incorrect because the primary focus of financial reporting is information about earnings and its components (not resources). Answer (B) is incorrect because the best indication of an enterprise's present and continuing ability to generate favorable cash flows is information about enterprise earnings based on accrual (not cash basis) accounting. Answer (C) is incorrect because financial accounting is not designed to measure the value of a business enterprise directly, but the information provided may be helpful to those who wish to estimate its value.

8. According to the FASB's conceptual framework, the objectives of financial reporting for business enterprises are based on

A. Generally accepted accounting principles.

B. Reporting on management's stewardship.

C. The need for conservatism.

D. The needs of the users of the information.

Answer (D) is correct. *(CPA, adapted)*
REQUIRED: The objectives of financial reporting for business enterprises.
DISCUSSION: SFAC 1 states that one objective of financial reporting is to provide information that is useful to present and potential investors, creditors, and other users in making rational investment, credit, and similar decisions.
Answer (A) is incorrect because GAAP governs how to account for items in the financial statements. Answer (B) is incorrect because financial reporting provides information that is helpful in evaluating management's stewardship but does not directly provide information about that performance. Answer (C) is incorrect because conservatism is a qualitative characteristic.

9. During a period when an enterprise is under the direction of a particular management, its financial statements will directly provide information about

A. Both enterprise performance and management performance.

B. Management performance but not directly provide information about enterprise performance.

C. Enterprise performance but not directly provide information about management performance.

D. Neither enterprise performance nor management performance.

Answer (C) is correct. *(CPA, adapted)*
REQUIRED: The information directly provided by financial statements.
DISCUSSION: Financial reporting provides information about an enterprise's performance during a period when it was under the direction of a particular management but does not directly provide information about that management's performance. Financial reporting does not try to separate the impact of a particular management's performance from the effects of prior management actions, general economic conditions, the supply and demand for an enterprise's inputs and outputs, price changes, and other events.

1.3 Qualitative Characteristics of Accounting Information (SFAC 2)

10. According to the FASB's conceptual framework, predictive value is an ingredient of

	Relevance	Reliability
A.	No	No
B.	Yes	Yes
C.	No	Yes
D.	Yes	No

Answer (D) is correct. *(CPA, adapted)*
REQUIRED: The primary quality of which predictive value is an ingredient.
DISCUSSION: The primary quality of relevance is the capacity of information to make a difference in a decision. It is composed of (1) predictive value, (2) feedback value, and (3) timeliness. Predictive value is the quality of information that helps users increase the likelihood of correctly forecasting the outcome of past and present events. The ingredients of reliability are verifiability, neutrality, and representational faithfulness.

11. According to the FASB conceptual framework, what does the concept of reliability in financial reporting include?

A. Effectiveness.

B. Certainty.

C. Precision.

D. Neutrality.

Answer (D) is correct. *(CPA, adapted)*
REQUIRED: The item included in the concept of reliability.
DISCUSSION: Reliability and relevance are the primary decision-specific qualitative characteristics of accounting information. Reliable information is "reasonably free from error and bias and faithfully represents what it purports to represent." Reliability includes the ingredients of representational faithfulness and verifiability and the secondary and interactive quality of neutrality. Neutrality is "absence in reported information of bias intended to attain a predetermined result or to induce a particular mode of behavior" (SFAC 2).
Answer (A) is incorrect because accounting information is effective if it is relevant. Reliable information is not necessarily relevant. Answer (B) is incorrect because certainty and precision are not implied by reliability. The financial statements are a model of the reporting entity. This model may be representationally faithful for its intended purposes without corresponding precisely to the real-world original. Thus, uncertainty that does not reach the materiality threshold does not impair reliability. Answer (C) is incorrect because information may be reliable within materiality limits but lack precision.

12. According to the FASB's conceptual framework, the usefulness of providing information in financial statements is subject to the constraint of

- A. Consistency.
- B. Cost-benefit.
- C. Reliability.
- D. Representational faithfulness.

Answer (B) is correct. *(CPA, adapted)*
REQUIRED: The constraint on financial reporting.
DISCUSSION: The cost-benefit principle is a pervasive constraint. Financial information will not be sought unless its benefits exceed the costs of reporting.
Answer (A) is incorrect because consistency is a quality of useful information, not constraints. Answer (C) is incorrect because reliability is a quality of useful information, not constraints. Answer (D) is incorrect because representational faithfulness is a quality of useful information, not constraints.

13. According to the FASB's conceptual framework, which of the following situations violates the concept of reliability?

- A. Data on segments having the same expected risks and growth rates are reported to analysts estimating future profits.
- B. Financial statements are issued 9 months late.
- C. Management reports to shareholders regularly refer to new projects undertaken, but the financial statements never report project results.
- D. Financial statements include property with a carrying amount increased to management's estimate of market value.

Answer (D) is correct. *(CPA, adapted)*
REQUIRED: The violation of the concept of reliability.
DISCUSSION: The ingredients of reliability are verifiability, neutrality, and representational faithfulness. Verifiability is the "ability through consensus among measurers to ensure that information represents what it purports to represent or that the chosen method of measurement has been used without error or bias." Management's estimate of market value may not be verifiable because it may not reflect a consensus and may be biased or in error.
Answer (A) is incorrect because the reliability of any given information is logically unrelated to the identity of the users. Answer (B) is incorrect because late issuance is a matter of timeliness, which is an ingredient of relevance, not reliability. Answer (C) is incorrect because failure to report results is a matter of relevance, in particular, timeliness.

1.4 Elements of Financial Statements (SFAC 6)

14. According to the FASB's conceptual framework, which of the following is an essential characteristic of an asset?

- A. The claims to an asset's benefits are legally enforceable.
- B. An asset is tangible.
- C. An asset is obtained at a cost.
- D. An asset provides future benefits.

Answer (D) is correct. *(CPA, adapted)*
REQUIRED: The essential characteristic of an asset.
DISCUSSION: One of the three essential characteristics of an asset is that the transaction or event giving rise to the entity's right to or control of its assets has already occurred, i.e., it is not expected to occur in the future. A second essential characteristic of an asset is that an entity can obtain the benefits of and control others' access to the asset. The third essential characteristic is that an asset must embody a probable future benefit that involves a capacity to contribute to future net cash inflows (SFAC 6).
Answer (A) is incorrect because claims to an asset's benefits may not be legally enforceable. Goodwill is an example.
Answer (B) is incorrect because some assets are intangible.
Answer (C) is incorrect because assets may be obtained through donations or investments by owners.

15. According to the FASB's conceptual framework, asset valuation accounts are

- A. Assets.
- B. Neither assets nor liabilities.
- C. Part of equity.
- D. Liabilities.

Answer (B) is correct. *(CPA, adapted)*
REQUIRED: The conceptual framework's definition of asset valuation accounts.
DISCUSSION: Asset valuation accounts are separate items sometimes found in financial statements that reduce or increase the carrying amount of an asset. The conceptual framework considers asset valuation accounts to be part of the related asset account. They are not considered to be assets or liabilities in their own right (SFAC 6).
Answer (A) is incorrect because asset valuation accounts are not assets. Answer (C) is incorrect because an asset valuation account is part of the related asset account. Answer (D) is incorrect because asset valuation accounts are not liabilities.

16. Under SFAC 6, *Elements of Financial Statements*, interrelated elements of financial statements that are directly related to measuring the performance and status of a business enterprise include

	Distributions to Owners	Notes to Financial Statements
A.	Yes	Yes
B.	Yes	No
C.	No	Yes
D.	No	No

Answer (B) is correct. *(CPA, adapted)*
REQUIRED: The interrelated elements directly related to measuring performance and status.
DISCUSSION: The elements of financial statements directly related to measuring the performance and status of business enterprises and not-for-profit organizations are assets, liabilities, equity of a business or net assets of a not-for-profit organization, revenues, expenses, gains, and losses. The elements of investments by owners, distributions to owners, and comprehensive income relate only to business enterprises. Information disclosed in notes or parenthetically on the face of financial statements amplifies or explains information recognized in the financial statements.

17. The FASB's conceptual framework explains both financial and physical capital maintenance concepts. Which capital maintenance concept is applied to currently reported net income, and which is applied to comprehensive income?

	Currently Reported Net Income	Comprehensive Income
A.	Financial capital	Physical capital
B.	Physical capital	Physical capital
C.	Financial capital	Financial capital
D.	Physical capital	Financial capital

Answer (C) is correct. *(CPA, adapted)*
REQUIRED: The capital maintenance concepts applicable to currently reported net income and comprehensive income.
DISCUSSION: The financial capital maintenance concept is the traditional basis of financial statements as well as the full set of financial statements, including comprehensive income, discussed in the conceptual framework. Under this concept, a return on investment (defined in terms of financial capital) results only if the financial amount of net assets at the end of the period exceeds the amount at the beginning after excluding the effects of transactions with owners. Under a physical capital concept, a return on investment (in terms of physical capital) results only if the physical productive capacity (or the resources needed to achieve that capacity) at the end of the period exceeds the capacity at the beginning after excluding the effects of transactions with owners. The latter concept requires many assets to be measured at current (replacement) cost.

18. According to the FASB's conceptual framework, an entity's revenue may result from a(n)

A. Decrease in an asset from primary operations.

B. Increase in an asset from incidental transactions.

C. Increase in a liability from incidental transactions.

D. Decrease in a liability from primary operations.

Answer (D) is correct. *(CPA, adapted)*
REQUIRED: The possible source of revenue.
DISCUSSION: According to SFAC 6, revenues are inflows or other enhancements of assets or settlements of liabilities from activities that constitute the entity's ongoing major or central operations. Thus, a revenue may result from a decrease in a liability from primary operations, for example, by delivering goods that were paid for in advance.
Answer (A) is incorrect because a decrease in an asset from primary operations results in an expense. Answer (B) is incorrect because an increase in an asset from incidental transactions results in a gain. Answer (C) is incorrect because an increase in a liability from incidental transactions results in a loss.

19. The FASB's conceptual framework classifies gains and losses based on whether they are related to an entity's major ongoing or central operations. These gains or losses may be classified as

	Nonoperating	Operating
A.	Yes	No
B.	Yes	Yes
C.	No	Yes
D.	No	No

Answer (B) is correct. *(CPA, adapted)*
REQUIRED: The classification of gains and losses.
DISCUSSION: SFAC 6 states that gains and losses result from "peripheral or incidental transactions and from other events and circumstances stemming from the environment that may be largely beyond the control of individual entities and their management." These gains and losses may be described or classified as either operating or nonoperating, depending on their relation to an entity's major ongoing or central operations.

20. According to the FASB's conceptual framework, comprehensive income includes which of the following?

	Gross Margin	Operating Income
A.	No	Yes
B.	No	No
C.	Yes	No
D.	Yes	Yes

Answer (D) is correct. *(CPA, adapted)*
REQUIRED: The items included in comprehensive income.
DISCUSSION: SFAC 6 defines comprehensive income of a business enterprise as "the change in equity of a business enterprise during a period from transactions and other events and circumstances from nonowner sources. It includes all changes in equity during a period except those resulting from investments by owners and distributions to owners." Accordingly, comprehensive income is a broad concept that embraces not only revenues, expenses, gains, and losses, but also cumulative accounting adjustments and other nonowner changes in equity. Such intermediate components as gross margin, income from continuing operations before taxes, income from continuing operations, and operating income are therefore included.

1.5 Recognition and Measurement Concepts (SFAC 5)

21. What is the purpose of information presented in notes to the financial statements?

A. To provide disclosures required by generally accepted accounting principles.

B. To correct improper presentation in the financial statements.

C. To provide recognition of amounts not included in the totals of the financial statements.

D. To present management's responses to auditor comments.

Answer (A) is correct. *(CPA, adapted)*
REQUIRED: The purpose of information presented in notes to the financial statements.
DISCUSSION: Notes are an integral part of the basic financial statements. Notes provide information essential to understanding the financial statements, including disclosures required by GAAP (SFAC 5).
Answer (B) is incorrect because notes may not be used to rectify an improper presentation. Answer (C) is incorrect because disclosure in notes is not a substitute for recognition in financial statements for items that meet recognition criteria. Answer (D) is incorrect because management's responses to auditor comments are not an appropriate subject of financial reporting.

22. According to SFAC 5, *Recognition and Measurement in Financial Statements of Business Enterprises*, the appropriate attribute for measuring plant assets is

A. Historical cost.

B. Current cost.

C. Net realizable value.

D. Present value of future cash flows.

Answer (A) is correct. *(Publisher, adapted)*
REQUIRED: The appropriate attribute for measuring plant assets.
DISCUSSION: According to SFAC 5, plant assets should be valued at historical cost. "Property, plant, and equipment and most inventories are reported at their historical cost, which is the amount of cash, or its equivalent, paid to acquire an asset, commonly adjusted after acquisition for amortization or other allocations."
Answer (B) is incorrect because current cost is used to measure certain inventories. Answer (C) is incorrect because net realizable value is most often used to measure short-term receivables and some inventories. Answer (D) is incorrect because present value is most often used for long-term receivables and payables.

23. According to the FASB's conceptual framework, which of the following attributes should not be used to measure inventory?

A. Historical cost.

B. Replacement cost.

C. Net realizable value.

D. Present value of future cash flows.

Answer (D) is correct. *(CPA, adapted)*
REQUIRED: The attribute not used to measure inventory.
DISCUSSION: The present value of future cash flows is not an acceptable measure of inventory. Present value is typically used for long-term receivables and payables.

24. On December 31, Year 1, Brooks Co. decided to end operations and dispose of its assets within 3 months. At December 31, Year 1, the net realizable value of the equipment was below historical cost. What is the appropriate measurement basis for equipment included in Brooks' December 31, Year 1, balance sheet?

A. Historical cost.

B. Current reproduction cost.

C. Liquidation value.

D. Current replacement cost.

Answer (C) is correct. *(CPA, adapted)*
REQUIRED: The attribute used to measure equipment after a decision to end operations.
DISCUSSION: Financial accounting principles assume that a business entity is a going concern in the absence of evidence to the contrary. This concept justifies the use of depreciation and amortization schedules and the recording of assets and liabilities at attributes other than liquidation value. However, the going concern assumption is no longer applicable when the entity's existence will be terminated in 3 months. Accordingly, historical cost is no longer appropriate as a measurement attribute, and assets should be restated at liquidation value.
Answer (A) is incorrect because historical cost is of little usefulness when the entity is about to discontinue operations. Answer (B) is incorrect because current reproduction cost reflects the cost of reproducing equipment or inventories and is inconsistent with a liquidation basis of measurement. Answer (D) is incorrect because current replacement cost reflects the cost of replacing equipment and is inconsistent with a liquidation basis of measurement.

25. According to the FASB's conceptual framework, which of the following statements conforms to the realization concept?

A. Equipment depreciation was assigned to a production department and then to product unit costs.

B. Depreciated equipment was sold in exchange for a note receivable.

C. Cash was collected on accounts receivable.

D. Assigning costs to products is realization.

Answer (B) is correct. *(CPA, adapted)*
REQUIRED: The statement that conforms to the realization concept.
DISCUSSION: The term "realization" is used most precisely in accounting and financial reporting with regard to sales of assets for cash or claims to cash. According to SFACs 5 and 6, the terms "realized" and "unrealized" identify revenues or gains and losses on assets sold and unsold, respectively. Thus, the sale of depreciated equipment results in realization.
Answer (A) is incorrect because assigning costs based on depreciation is allocation, not realization. Answer (C) is incorrect because realization occurred when the accounts receivable (claims to cash) were recognized. Answer (D) is incorrect because assigning costs to products is allocation, not realization.

26. According to the FASB's conceptual framework, the process of reporting an item in the financial statements of an entity is

A. Allocation.

B. Matching.

C. Realization.

D. Recognition.

Answer (D) is correct. *(CPA, adapted)*
REQUIRED: The process of reporting an item in an entity's financial statements.
DISCUSSION: Recognition is the process of formally recording or incorporating an item in the financial statements as an asset, liability, revenue, expense, gain, or loss.
Answer (A) is incorrect because allocation is the process of assigning or distributing an amount according to a plan or formula. Answer (B) is incorrect because matching is the simultaneous recognition of the revenues and expenses that result directly and jointly from the same transactions or events. Answer (C) is incorrect because realization is the identification of revenues or gains or losses on assets sold.

1.6 Cash Flow Information and Present Value (SFAC 7)

27. According to SFAC 7, *Using Cash Flow Information and Present Value in Accounting Measurements*, the objective of present value when used to determine an accounting measurement for initial recognition purposes is to

A. Capture the value of an asset or liability in the context of a given entity.

B. Estimate fair value.

C. Calculate the effective-settlement amount of assets.

D. Estimate value in use.

Answer (B) is correct. *(Publisher, adapted)*
REQUIRED: The objective of present value in an initial recognition measurement.
DISCUSSION: SFAC 7 states that the only objective of present value in an initial recognition or fresh-start measurement is to estimate fair value. In other words, "present value should attempt to capture the elements that taken together would comprise a market price if one existed, that is, fair value." A present value measurement includes five elements: estimates of cash flows, expectations about their variability, the time value of money, the price of uncertainty inherent in an asset or liability, and other factors (e.g., illiquidity or market imperfections). Fair value encompasses all these elements using the estimates and expectations of participants in the market.
Answer (A) is incorrect because entity-specific measurements are based on the entity's assumptions. Answer (C) is incorrect because an effective-settlement measurement (the current assets needed to be invested today at a given interest rate to generate future cash inflows to match future cash outflows for a liability) excludes the price components related to uncertainty and the entity's credit standing. Parties that hold an entity's liabilities consider its credit standing when determining the prices they will pay. Answer (D) is incorrect because value-in-use measurements are based on the entity's assumptions.

28. Which of the following is(are) a necessary element(s) of present value measurement?

A. Estimates of future cash flows.

B. The price of uncertainty inherent in an asset or liability.

C. Liquidity or market imperfections.

D. All of the answers are correct.

Answer (D) is correct. *(Publisher, adapted)*
REQUIRED: The necessary elements of present value measurement.
DISCUSSION: A measurement based on present value should reflect uncertainty so that variations in risks are incorporated. Accordingly, the following are the necessary elements of a present value measurement:

1. Estimates of future cash flows,
2. Expected variability of their amount and timing,
3. The time value of money (risk-free interest rate),
4. The price of uncertainty inherent in an asset or liability, and
5. Other factors, such as liquidity or market imperfections.

29. According to SFAC 7, *Using Cash Flow Information and Present Value in Accounting Measurements*, the objective of present value is to estimate fair value when used to determine accounting measurements for

	Initial-Recognition Purposes	Fresh-Start Purposes
A.	No	No
B.	Yes	Yes
C.	Yes	No
D.	No	Yes

Answer (B) is correct. *(Publisher, adapted)*
REQUIRED: The purposes for using present value measurement to estimate fair value.
DISCUSSION: SFAC 7 states that the objective of present value in initial-recognition or fresh-start measurements is to estimate fair value. "Present value should attempt to capture the elements that taken together would comprise a market price if one existed, that is, fair value." A present value measurement includes five elements: estimates of cash flows, expectations about their variability, the time value of money (the risk-free interest rate), the price of uncertainty inherent in an asset or liability, and other factors (e.g., illiquidity or market imperfections). Fair value encompasses all these elements using the estimates and expectations of participants in the market.

30. An interest method of allocation is most likely relevant when

I. The transaction giving rise to the asset or liability is viewed as a borrowing and a lending

II. Similar assets or liabilities are allocated using an interest method

III. The initial measurement was at present value

IV. The asset or liability has closely related estimated cash flows

    A. I only.

    B. I and II only.

    C. I, II, and III only.

    D. I, II, III, and IV.

Answer (D) is correct. *(Publisher, adapted)*
REQUIRED: The conditions when an interest method of allocation is most likely relevant.
DISCUSSION: Because no allocation method is preferable in every situation, the FASB will choose whether to require an interest method of allocation on a project-by-project basis. However, an interest method of allocation is most likely relevant when (1) the transaction giving rise to the asset or liability is viewed as a borrowing and a lending, (2) similar assets or liabilities are allocated using an interest method, (3) the initial measurement was at present value, or (4) the asset or liability has closely related estimated cash flows.

1.7 Fair Value Measurements (SFAS 157)

31. According to SFAS 157, *Fair Value Measurements*, fair value is

    A. An entry price.

    B. An exit price.

    C. Based on an actual transaction.

    D. An entity-specific measurement.

Answer (B) is correct. *(Publisher, adapted)*
REQUIRED: The nature of fair value.
DISCUSSION: "Fair value is the price that would be received to sell an asset or paid to transfer a liability in an orderly transaction between market participants at the measurement date" (SFAS 157). Thus, fair value is an exit price.
Answer (A) is incorrect because an entry price is what is paid or received in an orderly exchange to acquire an asset or assume a liability, respectively. Answer (C) is incorrect because fair value is an exit price paid or received in a hypothetical transaction considered from the perspective of a market participant. Answer (D) is incorrect because fair value is market-based. It is based on pricing assumptions of market participants.

32. For the purpose of a fair value measurement (FVM) of an asset or liability, a transaction is assumed to occur in the

    A. Principal market if one exists.

    B. Most advantageous market.

    C. Market in which the result is optimized.

    D. Principal market or most advantageous market at the election of the reporting entity.

Answer (A) is correct. *(Publisher, adapted)*
REQUIRED: The market in which a transaction is assumed to occur.
DISCUSSION: For FVM purposes, a transaction is assumed to occur in the principal market for an asset or liability if one exists. The principal market has the greatest volume or level of activity. If no such market exists, the transaction is assumed to occur in the most advantageous market.

33. Fair value measurements (FVMs) of assets and liabilities are based on transactions between market participants at the measurement date. Market participants

    A. Must be specifically identified.

    B. May be related parties if they are knowledgeable about the asset or liability.

    C. Include parties who are forced to engage in the transactions if they are independent of the entity.

    D. Are willing and able to engage in transactions involving the asset or liability.

Answer (D) is correct. *(Publisher, adapted)*
REQUIRED: The characteristic of market participants.
DISCUSSION: Market participants are not related parties. They are independent of the reporting entity. They also are knowledgeable and willing and able (but not compelled) to engage in transactions involving the asset or liability.
Answer (A) is incorrect because market participants need not be specifically identified. Instead, the entity must identify their general characteristics, with consideration of factors specific to (1) the asset or liability, (2) the market, and (3) parties with whom the entity would deal. Answer (B) is incorrect because market participants must be independent of the entity. Answer (C) is incorrect because market participants do not include parties who engage in forced or liquidation sales or are otherwise compelled to act.

34. The fair value measurement (FVM) of an asset

    A. Assumes transfer, not a settlement.

    B. Is based on the expected use by the reporting entity.

    C. Reflects the highest and best use by market participants.

    D. Includes the entity's own credit risk.

Answer (C) is correct. *(Publisher, adapted)*
    REQUIRED: The true statement about the FVM of an asset.
    DISCUSSION: The FVM is based on the highest and best use (HBU) by market participants. This use maximizes the value of the asset. The HBU is in-use if the value-maximizing use is in combination with other assets in a group. An example is machinery. The HBU is in-exchange if the value-maximizing use is as a standalone asset. An example is a financial asset.
    Answer (A) is incorrect because the FVM of a liability, not an asset, assumes transfer without settlement. Answer (B) is incorrect because the FVM assumes use by market participants. Answer (D) is incorrect because the FVM of a liability includes nonperformance risk. An element of nonperformance risk is the entity's own credit risk (credit standing).

35. Valuation techniques for fair value measurement (FVM) must use

    A. The market approach or income approach but not the cost approach.

    B. The pricing assumptions of market participants.

    C. Only observable inputs.

    D. Current replacement cost to approximate fair value.

Answer (B) is correct. *(Publisher, adapted)*
    REQUIRED: The element used in valuation techniques for FVM.
    DISCUSSION: Inputs to valuation techniques are the pricing assumptions of market participants. The assumptions include those about the risk of a given technique or its inputs.
    Answer (A) is incorrect because the entity may use all or any of the following: (1) the market approach (based on information, such as prices, from market transactions involving identical or comparable items), (2) the income approach (based on current market expectations about future amounts, such as earnings or cash flows converted to a discounted current amount), and (3) the cost approach (based on current replacement cost, which is the cost to a market participant to buy or build an asset of comparable utility adjusted for obsolescence). Answer (C) is incorrect because unobservable inputs are based on the entity's own assumptions about the assumptions of market participants that reflect the best available information in the circumstances. They should be minimized but are allowable in proper circumstances. Answer (D) is incorrect because the market and income approaches also may be used.

1.8 Standards

36. Arpco, Inc., a for-profit provider of healthcare services, recently purchased two smaller companies and is researching accounting issues arising from the two business combinations. Which of the following accounting pronouncements are the most authoritative?

    A. AICPA Statements of Position.

    B. AICPA Industry and Audit Guides.

    C. FASB Statements of Financial Accounting Concepts.

    D. FASB Statements of Financial Accounting Standards.

Answer (D) is correct. *(CPA, adapted)*
    REQUIRED: The most authoritative pronouncements.
    DISCUSSION: In the GAAP hierarchy, the highest of the four categories of established accounting principles, Category (a), consists of pronouncements issued by a body designated by the AICPA to establish principles covered by Conduct Rule 203 of the *Code of Professional Conduct*. This category (officially established accounting principles) includes FASB Statements (SFASs) and Interpretations, APB Opinions, and ARBs.
    Answer (A) is incorrect because, if they are cleared by the FASB, AICPA SOPs are in Category (b) of established accounting principles. Answer (B) is incorrect because, if they are cleared by the FASB, AICPA Industry and Audit Guides are in Category (b) of established accounting principles. Answer (C) is incorrect because SFACs are considered other accounting literature.

37. Which of the following official pronouncements ranks the highest in the accounting hierarchy?

A. APB Opinions.

B. Consensus positions of the EITF.

C. AICPA Audit and Accounting Guides.

D. AICPA Statements of Position.

Answer (A) is correct. *(Publisher, adapted)*
REQUIRED: The highest ranking pronouncement in the hierarchy of accounting principles (GAAP).
DISCUSSION: The highest level pronouncements, as defined in Statement on Auditing Standards No. 69 (as amended), are the Statements of the FASB, the Opinions of the former Accounting Principles Board (APB), and the Statements issued by the former Committee on Accounting Procedure (CAP).
Answer (B) is incorrect because positions of the Emerging Issues Task Force are level (c) GAAP. Answer (C) is incorrect because AICPA Industry Audit and Accounting Guides are level (b) GAAP. Answer (D) is incorrect because AICPA Statements of Position are level (b) GAAP.

38. Which of the following statements is false with respect to the FASB?

A. The FASB is composed of seven voting members.

B. At least four members of the FASB must be CPAs.

C. A vote by a majority of the FASB members decides the Board's agenda.

D. Official pronouncements require an affirmative vote by a super majority (five) of the Board's members.

Answer (D) is correct. *(Publisher, adapted)*
REQUIRED: The false statement with respect to the FASB.
DISCUSSION: A majority vote is required to decide on the agenda of the Board, and official pronouncements of the FASB also require only an affirmative vote by four of the members. After the accounting scandals of 2002, the FASB eliminated its super majority requirement.

39. Which of the following is not a comprehensive basis of accounting other than generally accepted accounting principles?

A. Cash receipts and disbursements basis of accounting.

B. Basis of accounting used by an entity to file its income tax returns.

C. Basis of accounting used by an entity to comply with the financial reporting requirements of a government regulatory agency.

D. Basis of accounting used by an entity to comply with the financial reporting requirements of a lending institution.

Answer (D) is correct. *(CPA, adapted)*
REQUIRED: The item not a comprehensive basis of accounting other than GAAP.
DISCUSSION: The applicable pronouncement is AU 623 (SAS 62), *Special Reports.* A comprehensive basis of accounting other than GAAP may be (1) a basis that the reporting entity uses to comply with the requirements or financial reporting provisions of a regulatory agency; (2) a basis used for tax purposes; (3) the cash basis, and modifications of the cash basis having substantial support, such as recording depreciation on fixed assets or accruing income taxes; or (4) a definite set of criteria having substantial support that is applied to all material items, for example, the price-level basis. However, a basis of accounting used by an entity to comply with the financial reporting requirements of a lending institutions does not qualify as governmentally mandated or as having substantial support.

40. The SEC has affirmed that it will recognize which of the following entities as an accounting standard setter for filings under the securities laws?

A. The GASB.

B. The AICPA.

C. The FASB.

D. The IASB.

Answer (C) is correct. *(Publisher, adapted)*
REQUIRED: The entity that is recognized by the SEC as the accounting standard setter for filings under the securities laws.
DISCUSSION: The Sarbanes-Oxley Act of 2002 authorizes the SEC to recognize as generally accepted for purposes of the securities laws any accounting principles promulgated by an appropriate entity. The SEC has affirmed that it will continue to recognize the FASB as an accounting standard setter for filings by issuers (public companies) under the securities laws.

41. According to the Sarbanes-Oxley Act of 2002, which of the following is a characteristic that an accounting standard setter must possess?

A. Be organized as a public entity.

B. The majority of its governing body must have been associated with a registered public accounting firm within 2 years before their period of service.

C. Its procedures provide for prompt consideration by a super-majority vote of changes in accounting principles.

D. The entity works toward convergence of U.S. and international accounting standards.

Answer (D) is correct.   *(Publisher, adapted)*
REQUIRED: The characteristic of an accounting standard setter according to the Sarbanes-Oxley Act.
DISCUSSION: The Sarbanes-Oxley Act of 2002 authorizes the SEC to recognize as generally accepted for purposes of the securities laws any accounting principles promulgated by an appropriate entity. Such an entity must possess certain characteristics required by the act. One characteristic is that the entity must consider the desirability of the convergence of U.S. and international accounting standards.
Answer (A) is incorrect because the standard setter must be a private entity. Answer (B) is incorrect because the majority must not be associated with a registered public accounting firm during their service. Moreover, the majority must not have been associated with such a firm within the prior 2 years. Answer (C) is incorrect because decisions of the standard setter must be by simple majority.

1.9 Time Value of Money

42. On December 30, Chang Co. sold a machine to Door Co. in exchange for a noninterest-bearing note requiring ten annual payments of $10,000. Door made the first payment on December 30. The market interest rate for similar notes at date of issuance was 8%. Information on present value factors is as follows:

Number of Periods	Present Value of $1 at 8%	Present Value of Ordinary Annuity of $1 at 8%
9	0.50	6.25
10	0.46	6.71

In its December 31 balance sheet, what amount should Chang report as note receivable?

A. $45,000

B. $46,000

C. $62,500

D. $67,100

Answer (C) is correct.   *(CPA, adapted)*
REQUIRED: The carrying amount of a noninterest-bearing note receivable at the date of issuance.
DISCUSSION: The purchase agreement calls for a $10,000 initial payment and equal payments of $10,000 to be received at the end of each of the next 9 years. The amount reported for the receivable should consist of the present value of the nine future payments. The present value factor to be used is the present value of an ordinary annuity for nine periods at 8%, or 6.25. The note receivable should be recorded at $62,500 ($10,000 × 6.25).
Answer (A) is incorrect because $45,000 results from multiplying $90,000 ($10,000 payments × 9 years) by 0.50. Answer (B) is incorrect because $46,000 results from multiplying the $100,000 total by 0.46. Answer (D) is incorrect because $67,100 results from using the present value of an ordinary annuity of $1 at 8% for 10 years instead of 9 years.

43. A pension fund is projecting the amount necessary today to fund a retiree's pension benefits. The retiree's first annual pension check will be in 10 years. Payments are expected to last for a total of 20 annual payments. Which of the following best describes the computation of the amount needed today to fund the retiree's annuity?

A. Present value of $1 for 10 periods, times the present value of an ordinary annuity of 20 payments, times the annual annuity payment.

B. Present value of $1 for nine periods, times the present value of an ordinary annuity of 20 payments, times the annual annuity payment.

C. Future value of $1 for 10 periods, times the present value of an ordinary annuity of 20 payments, times the annual annuity payment.

D. Future value of $1 for nine periods, times the present value of an ordinary annuity of 20 payments, times the annual annuity payment.

Answer (B) is correct. *(CIA, adapted)*
REQUIRED: The formula to compute the amount needed today to fund a pension that will begin in the future.
DISCUSSION: Multiplying the annual annuity pension payment times the present value of an ordinary annuity of 20 payments factor results in a present value determination 1 year prior to the start of the payments, or 9 years hence. Multiplying the present value of ordinary annuity pension payments by a present value of $1 factor for 9 years results in the amount needed today to fund the retiree's annuity.

44. Based on 8% interest compounded annually from day of deposit to day of withdrawal, what is the present value today of $4,000 to be received 6 years from today?

Periods	Present Value of $1 Discounted at 8% per Period
1	.926
2	.857
3	.794
4	.735
5	.681

A. $4,000 × 0.926 × 6.

B. $4,000 × 0.794 × 2.

C. $4,000 × 0.681 × 0.926.

D. Cannot be determined from the information given.

Answer (C) is correct. *(CPA, adapted)*
REQUIRED: The present value today of an amount to be received at a given future date.
DISCUSSION: To calculate the present value of an amount to be received 6 years from today when present value factors for only five periods are available, multiply $4,000 by the present value of $1 factor for five periods. This discounts the $4,000 back 5 years. This new product should then be discounted back one additional year, i.e., multiplied by the present value factor for one period.

Use Gleim's ***CPA Test Prep*** CD-Rom/Pocket PC for interactive testing with over 4,000 additional questions!

1.10 PRACTICE SIMULATION

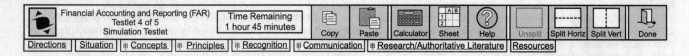

| Financial Accounting and Reporting (FAR) Testlet 4 of 5 Simulation Testlet | Time Remaining 1 hour 45 minutes | Copy | Paste | Calculator | Sheet | Help | Unsplit | Split Horiz | Split Vert | Done |

Directions | Situation | ⫼ Concepts | ⫼ Principles | ⫼ Recognition | ⫼ Communication | ⫼ Research/Authoritative Literature | Resources

---

1. Directions

In the following simulation, you will be asked to complete various tasks. You may use the content in the **Information Tabs** to complete the tasks in the **Work Tabs**.

Information Tabs:

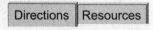

Directions | Resources

FIG 1

- Go through each of the **Information Tabs** to familiarize yourself with the simulation content
- The **Resources** tab will contain information, including formulas and definitions, that may help you to complete the tasks
- Your simulation may have more **Information Tabs** than those shown in Fig. 1

Work Tabs:

⫼ SysTrust | ⫼ Engagement Letter | ⫼ Authoritative Sources | ⫼ Communication

FIG. 2

- **Work Tabs**, to the right of **Information Tabs**, contain the tasks for you to complete
- **Work Tabs** contain directions for completing each task - be sure to read these directions carefully
- The tab names in Fig. 2 are for illustration only - yours may differ
- Once you complete any part of a task, the pencil for that tab will be shaded (see **Communication** in Fig. 2)
- The shaded pencil does **NOT** indicate that you have completed the entire task
- You must complete all of the tasks in the **Work Tabs** to receive full credit

Research/Authoritative Literature Tab:

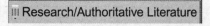

⫼ Research/Authoritative Literature

FIG. 3

- This tab contains both the Research task and the Authoritative Literature
- Detailed instructions for completing the Research task, and for using the Authoritative Literature, appear on this tab
- You may use the Authoritative Literature as a resource for completing other tasks

NOTE: If you believe you have encountered a software malfunction, report it to the test center staff immediately.

2. Situation

As a new CPA at a local accounting firm, you are charged with explaining to a staff bookkeeper some of the finer points of accounting concepts and standards. You have some old test materials that you would like to show the bookkeeper; however, no answers are available. You must review the materials located in the following tabs and complete the required information.

3. Concepts

This set of questions has a matching format. Select the best match for each numbered item from the terms in the drop-down list and write its letter in the column provided. Each choice may be used once, more than once, or not at all. Accordingly, each accounting concept should be matched with the term it defines.

Concepts	*Answer*
1. Probable future economic benefits	
2. Residual interest in assets	
3. Enhancements of assets or settlements of liabilities from an entity's major or central operations	
4. The accounting process of reducing an amount by periodic payments or write-downs	
5. Formal recording of an item	
6. The change in equity during a period from transactions and other events and circumstances from nonowner sources	
7. Probable future sacrifices of economic benefits	
8. Use of assets or incurrence of liabilities by an entity's major or central operations	
9. Recording the financial effects of transactions when they occur rather than when direct cash effects are felt in the future	
10. Assigning an amount according to a plan or formula	
11. Increases in equity from incidental transactions of an entity, except from investments by owners	
12. An accounting process concerned with cash prepayments received or paid	
13. Conversion of noncash resources into money	
14. Decreases in equity resulting from transfers by the enterprise to owners	
15. Increases in equity resulting from transfers to the enterprise for the purpose of increasing an ownership interest	

Select Term
A) Liabilities
B) Revenues
C) Gains
D) Realization
E) Assets
F) Losses
G) Accrual
H) Financial statement
I)   Recognition
J) Deferrals
K) Amortization
L) Earnings
M) Allocation
N) Comprehensive income
O) Dividends
P) Capital contributions
Q) Equity
R) Expenses

4. Established Accounting Principles

This set of questions has a matching format. Select the best match for each numbered item from the terms in the drop-down list and write its letter in the column provided. Each choice may be used once, more than once, or not at all. Accordingly, each source of established accounting principles should be matched with its appropriate category in the GAAP hierarchy for nongovernmental entities.

Source	Answer
1. FASB Statements and Interpretations	
2. AICPA Accounting Interpretations	
3. Qs and As published by the FASB staff cleared by the FASB	
4. AcSEC Practice Bulletins	
5. FASB Emerging Issues Task Force Positions	
6. APB Opinions	
7. CAP Accounting Research Bulletins	
8. FASB Technical Bulletins	
9. AICPA Statements of Position cleared by the FASB	
10. AICPA Audit and Accounting Guides cleared by the FASB	
11. Widely used accounting practices	

Category
A) Category (a)
B) Category (b)
C) Category (c)
D) Category (d)

5. Recognition

This set of questions has a matching format. Select the best match for each numbered item from the terms in the drop-down list and write its letter in the column provided. Each choice may be used once, more than once, or not at all. The concept of recognition requires that an item have a relevant attribute capable of being quantified in monetary units with reasonable reliability. Different measurement attributes of assets and liabilities are used in current practice. Accordingly, each recognition concept should be matched with the related attribute.

Recognition Concept	Answer
1. The relevant attribute for plant assets and most inventories.	
2. The relevant attribute for liabilities incurred to provide goods or services to customers.	
3. The relevant attribute defined as the cash or equivalent that would be paid for a current acquisition of the same or an equivalent asset.	
4. The relevant attribute used to measure assets expected to be sold at below their carrying amount.	
5. The relevant attribute used to measure short-term receivables.	
6. The relevant attribute used to measure such items as trade payables and warranty obligations.	
7. The relevant attribute that incorporates time value of money concepts.	

Attributes
A) Current market value
B) Net realizable value
C) Historical cost
D) Historical proceeds
E) Replacement cost
F) Present value
G) Net settlement value

6. Communication

Prepare a memorandum to the bookkeeper explaining the recognition criteria that relate specifically to revenues and gains. This explanation should address how the criteria are applied. Do not describe the four fundamental recognition criteria.

REMINDER: Your response will be graded for both technical content and writing skills. Technical content will be evaluated for information that is helpful to the intended reader and clearly relevant to the issue. Writing skills will be evaluated for development, organization, and the appropriate expression of ideas in professional correspondence. Use a standard business memo or letter format with a clear beginning, middle, and end. Do not convey information in the form of a table, bullet point list, or other abbreviated presentation.

To: Staff Member
From: CPA
Reference: Revenue and gain recognition criteria

7. Research/Authoritative Literature

See page 12 in the Introduction of this book for a detailed explanation of the AICPA's new Research/Authoritative Literature work tab as well as a screenshot of how the tab will actually look on your exam.

Research and cite the appropriate paragraph from the FASB Current Text or Original Pronouncements that describes the importance of relevance and reliability in the hierarchy of accounting qualities.

Unofficial Answers

3. Concepts (15 Gradable Items)

1. <u>E) Assets</u> are "probable future economic benefits obtained or controlled by a particular entity as a result of past transactions or events."

2. <u>Q) Equity</u> is the "residual interest in the assets of an entity that remains after deducting its liabilities." In a business enterprise, the equity is the ownership interest.

3. <u>B) Revenues</u> are "inflows or other enhancements of assets of an entity or settlements of its liabilities (or a combination of both) from delivering or producing goods, rendering services, or other activities that constitute the entity's ongoing major or central operations."

4. <u>K) Amortization</u> is a form of allocation. It is "the accounting process of reducing an amount by periodic payments or write-downs." This process entails reducing a liability (asset) recorded as a result of a cash receipt (payment) by recognizing revenues (expenses).

5. <u>I) Recognition</u> "is the process of formally recording or incorporating an item in the financial statements of an entity." The SFACs do not use recognition and realization as synonyms.

6. <u>N) Comprehensive income</u> is the "change in equity of a business enterprise during a period from transactions and other events and circumstances from nonowner sources. It includes all changes in equity during a period except those resulting from investments by owners and distributions to owners."

7. <u>A) Liabilities</u> are "probable future sacrifices of economic benefits arising from present obligations of a particular entity to transfer assets or provide services to other entities in the future as a result of past transactions or events."

8. <u>R) Expenses</u> are "outflows or other using up of assets or incurrences of liabilities (or a combination of both) from delivering or producing goods, rendering services, or carrying out other activities that constitute the entity's ongoing major or central operations."

9. <u>G) Accrual</u> "is the accounting process of recognizing assets or liabilities and the related liabilities, assets, revenues, expenses, gains, or losses for amounts expected to be received or paid, usually in cash, in the future."

10. <u>M) Allocation</u> is "the accounting process of assigning or distributing an amount according to a plan or formula." Allocation is broader than amortization. Product costing is an example of an allocation. Depreciation is a common example of amortization.

11. <u>C) Gains</u> are "increases in equity (net assets) from peripheral or incidental transactions of an entity and from all other transactions and other events and circumstances affecting the entity except those that result from revenues or investments by owners."

12. <u>J) Deferral</u> "is the accounting process of recognizing a liability resulting from a current cash receipt (or the equivalent) or an asset resulting from a current cash payment (or the equivalent) with deferred recognition of revenues, expenses, gains, or losses."

13. <u>D) Realization</u> is "the process of converting noncash resources and rights into money." The term is most precisely used to refer to sales of assets for cash or claims to cash.

14. <u>O) Dividends</u> (distributions to owners) are "decreases in equity of a particular business enterprise resulting from transferring assets, rendering services, or incurring liabilities by the enterprise to owners. Distributions to owners decrease ownership interest (or equity) in an enterprise." They are sometimes called dividends; distributions of earnings, profits, or income; or capital distributions.

15. <u>P) Capital contributions</u> (investments by owners) "are increases in equity of a particular business enterprise resulting from transfers to it from other entities of something valuable to obtain or increase ownership interests (or equity) in it."

4. Established Accounting Principles (11 Gradable Items)

1. <u>A) Category (a)</u> includes the primary sources of nongovernmental GAAP: FASB Statements and Interpretations, APB Opinions, and CAP Accounting Research Bulletins

2. <u>D) Category (d)</u> consists of AICPA Accounting Interpretations, FASB Staff Implementation Guides ("Qs and As"), and practices widely recognized and prevalent generally or in the industry.

3. <u>D) Category (d)</u> consists of AICPA Accounting Interpretations, FASB Staff Implementation Guides ("Qs and As"), and practices widely recognized and prevalent generally or in the industry.

4. <u>C) Category (c)</u> includes consensus positions of the FASB Emerging Issues Task Force and, if cleared by the FASB, AcSEC Practice Bulletins.

5. <u>C) Category (c)</u> includes consensus positions of the FASB Emerging Issues Task Force and, if cleared by the FASB, AcSEC Practice Bulletins.

6. <u>A) Category (a)</u> includes the primary sources of nongovernmental GAAP: FASB Statements and Interpretations, APB Opinions, and CAP Accounting Research Bulletins.

7. <u>A) Category (a)</u> includes the primary sources of nongovernmental GAAP: FASB Statements and Interpretations, APB Opinions, and CAP Accounting Research Bulletins.

8. <u>B) Category (b)</u> consists of FASB Technical Bulletins and, if cleared by the FASB, AICPA Audit and Accounting Guides and AICPA Statements of Position.

9. <u>B) Category (b)</u> consists of FASB Technical Bulletins and, if cleared by the FASB, AICPA Audit and Accounting Guides and AICPA Statements of Position.

10. <u>B) Category (b)</u> consists of FASB Technical Bulletins and, if cleared by the FASB, AICPA Audit and Accounting Guides and AICPA Statements of Position.

11. <u>D) Category (d)</u> consists of AICPA Accounting Interpretations, FASB Staff Implementation Guides ("Qs and As"), and practices widely recognized and prevalent generally or in the industry.

5. Recognition (7 Gradable Items)

1. <u>C) Historical cost</u> is the relevant attribute for plant assets and most inventories. It is the cash or equivalent actually paid for an asset and is ordinarily adjusted subsequently for amortization (which includes depreciation) or other allocations.

2. <u>D) Historical proceeds</u> is the relevant attribute for liabilities incurred to provide goods or services to customers. It is the cash or equivalent actually received when the obligation was created and may be subsequently amortized.

3. <u>E) Replacement cost</u> (current cost) is used to measure certain inventories, e.g., inventories valued at LCM. It is the cash or equivalent that would be paid for a current acquisition of the same or an equivalent asset.

4. <u>A) Current market value</u> is used to measure some marketable securities, e.g., those held by investment companies, or assets expected to be sold at below their carrying amount.

5. <u>B) Net realizable value</u> is used to measure short-term receivables and some inventories. It is the cash or equivalent expected to be received for an asset in the due course of business, minus the costs of completion and sale.

6. <u>G) Net settlement value</u> is used to measure such items as trade payables and warranty obligations. It is the cash or its equivalent that the entity expects to pay to satisfy an obligation in the due course of business.

7. <u>F) Present value</u> is, in theory, the most relevant method of measurement because it incorporates time value of money concepts. In practice, it is currently used only for long-term receivables and payables.

6. Communication (5 Gradable Items; for grading instructions, please refer to page 12.)

Revenues and gains are usually measured by the exchange prices of the items involved and, assuming the four fundamental criteria have been met, these measurements will be incorporated into the financial statements if two additional criteria are satisfied. Revenues and gains should be realized or realizable. Realizable means that assets are readily convertible to known amounts of cash or claims to cash. Such assets are fungible and can be traded in an active market that can absorb the quantity held without affecting the quoted prices. Revenues also should be earned. Revenues are earned when an earning process has been substantially completed and the entity is entitled to the resulting benefits. The earning process consists of the entity's ongoing major or central activities, such as delivering or producing goods. Gains ordinarily flow from events that do not involve an earning process, and the first criterion is therefore more significant than the second for determining when to recognize gains.

The two criteria are usually met when goods are delivered or services are rendered, that is, at the time of sale (customarily the time of delivery). If the sale or the receipt of cash precedes production and delivery, revenues may be recognized as production and delivery occur. Magazine subscriptions are an example. Revenues from long-term contracts may be recognized using the percentage-of-completion method. Revenues from, for example, interest and rent may be recognized based on the passage of time. Completion of production or a change in prices is the basis for recognition if products or other assets are readily realizable, e.g., precious metals and some agricultural products. Recognition of revenues or gains or losses is appropriate in nonmonetary exchanges. Revenues and gains or losses also may arise from nonreciprocal transactions involving nonmonetary assets, for example, contributions received. However, fair values must be reasonably determinable. If collectibility of assets received is relatively uncertain, revenues and gains may be recognized only as cash is received, such as under the installment and cash recovery methods.

7. Research/Authoritative Literature (1 Gradable Item)

Answer: SFAC 2, Par. 33

SFAC 2 -- *Qualitative Characteristics of Accounting Information*

33. The primary qualities are that accounting information shall be relevant and reliable. If either of those qualities is completely missing, the information will not be useful. Relevance and reliability can be further analyzed into a number of components. To be relevant, information must be timely, and it must have predictive value or feedback value or both. To be reliable, information must have representational faithfulness, and it must be verifiable and neutral.

Scoring Schedule:

	Correct Responses		Gradable Items		Weights		
Tab 3	_____	÷	15	×	20%	=	_____
Tab 4	_____	÷	11	×	20%	=	_____
Tab 5	_____	÷	7	×	15%	=	_____
Tab 6	_____	÷	5	×	30%	=	_____
Tab 7	_____	÷	1	×	15%	=	_____
							(Your Score)

Use Gleim's *CPA Gleim Online* to practice more simulations in a realistic environment.

STUDY UNIT TWO
FINANCIAL STATEMENTS

(22 pages of outline)

This study unit covers the **basic financial statements**: the statements of financial position, income, retained earnings (changes in equity), comprehensive income, and cash flows. However, specific names and formats for these statements are **not** specified under GAAP. Instead, the formats of these statements have evolved to fulfill the requirements of GAAP.

The accompanying **notes** are considered an integral part of the financial statements. The notes and statements together are a vehicle for achieving the objectives of financial reporting. Supplementary information (e.g., on changing prices) and various other means of financial reporting (such as management's discussion and analysis) also are useful for attaining those objectives.

Financial statements **complement** each other. They describe different aspects of the same transactions, and more than one statement will be necessary to provide information for a specific economic decision. Moreover, the **elements** of one statement **articulate** (interrelate) with those of other statements.

2.1 BALANCE SHEET

Definition

1. The balance sheet (statement of financial position) "provides information about an entity's assets, liabilities, and equity and their relationships to each other at a moment in time." It helps users to assess "the entity's liquidity, financial flexibility, profitability, and risk" (SFAC 5).

2. **Elements.** The balance sheet is a detailed presentation of the basic accounting equation:

Assets = Liabilities + Equity

3. **Classifications.** Some variation of the following classifications is used by most entities:

Assets	Liabilities
Current assets	Current liabilities
Cash	Accounts payable
Accounts and notes receivable	Current notes payable
Inventory	Noncurrent liabilities
Prepaid expenses	Bonds payable
Certain investments	Noncurrent notes payable
Noncurrent assets	
Certain investments and funds	Equity
Property, plant, and equipment (PPE)	Contributed capital
Intangible assets	Retained earnings
Other noncurrent assets	Accumulated other comprehensive income
	Noncontrolling interest

The Resource Structure

4.   **Current assets** consist of "cash and other assets or resources commonly identified as reasonably expected to be realized in cash or sold or consumed during the normal operating cycle of the business" (ARB 43, Ch. 3A, *Working Capital – Current Assets and Current Liabilities*).

    a.   The **operating cycle** is the average time between the acquisition of resources and the final receipt of cash from their sale as the culmination of revenue generating activities. If the cycle is less than a year, 1 year is the period used for segregating current from noncurrent assets.

    b.   Current assets include (1) cash and cash equivalents; (2) receivables; (3) inventories; (4) certain individual trading, available-for-sale, and held-to-maturity securities; and (5) prepaid expenses.

5.   **Noncurrent assets** are those not qualifying as current.

    a.   **Investments and funds** include a variety of nonoperating items intended to be held beyond the longer of 1 year or the operating cycle. The following assets are typically included:

        1)   (a) Advances or investments in securities made to control or influence another entity and (b) other noncurrent securities

            a)   Certain individual trading, available-for-sale, and held-to-maturity securities may be noncurrent

        2)   Funds restricted as to withdrawal or use for other than current operations, for example, to (a) retire long-term debt, (b) satisfy pension obligations, or (c) pay for the acquisition or construction of noncurrent assets

        3)   Cash surrender value of life insurance policies

        4)   Capital assets not used in current operations, such as (a) idle facilities or (b) land held for a future plant site

    b.   **Property, plant, and equipment (PPE)** are tangible operating items recorded at cost and reported net of any accumulated depreciation. They include

        1)   Land and natural resources subject to depletion, e.g., oil and gas

        2)   (a) Buildings, (b) equipment, (c) furniture, (d) fixtures, (e) leasehold improvements, (f) land improvements, (g) assets held under capital leases, (h) noncurrent assets under construction, and (i) other depreciable assets

    c.   **Intangible assets** are nonfinancial assets without physical substance. Examples are patents and goodwill.

    d.   **Other noncurrent assets** include noncurrent assets not readily classifiable elsewhere. Examples are

        1)   Bond issue costs

        2)   Machinery rearrangement costs (also classifiable as PPE)

        3)   Long-term prepayments

        4)   Deferred tax assets arising from interperiod tax allocation

        5)   Long-term receivables from unusual transactions, e.g., loans to officers or employees and sales of capital assets [NOTE: The Sarbanes-Oxley Act generally prohibits an issuer (defined under federal securities law) from extending personal credit to directors or officers.]

    e.   The category **deferred charges** (long-term prepayments) appears on some balance sheets.

        1)   Many of these items, for example, bond issue costs and rearrangement costs, which involve long-term prepayments, are frequently classified as other assets.

The Financing Structure

6. **Current liabilities** are "obligations whose liquidation is reasonably expected to require the use of existing resources properly classifiable as current assets, or the creation of other current liabilities" (ARB 43, Ch. 3A).

   a. This classification includes the following:

      1) **Payables** for items entering into the operating cycle, e.g., for materials and supplies used in producing goods or services for sale.

      2) Payables arising from operations **directly related to the operating cycle**, such as accrued wages, salaries, rentals, royalties, and taxes.

      3) **Collections in advance** of delivering goods or performing services, e.g., ticket sales revenue.

      4) Other obligations expected to be liquidated in the **ordinary course of business** during the longer of the next year or the operating cycle.

         a) These include

            i) Short-term notes given to acquire capital assets
            ii) Payments required under sinking-fund provisions
            iii) Payments on the current portion of serial bonds
            iv) Agency obligations incurred by the collection of assets on behalf of third parties.

      5) Amounts expected to be required within a relatively short time to pay known obligations even though

         a) Outlays can only be estimated, e.g., accrual of bonus payments, or

         b) Specific payees have not been designated, for example, in the case of warranties for repair of products sold.

      6) Obligations that, by their terms, are **due on demand** within the longer of 1 year or the operating cycle. Liquidation need not be expected.

      7) **Long-term obligations callable** at the balance sheet date because of a violation of the debt agreement or that will become callable if the violation is not cured within a specified period.

   b. Current liabilities **do not include**

      1) Short-term obligations if an entity (a) **intends to refinance** them on a **long-term basis** and (b) demonstrates an ability to consummate such refinancing (SFAS 6, *Classification of Short-term Obligations Expected to be Refinanced*).

      2) Dividends not yet declared.

      3) Debts to be paid from funds accumulated in **noncurrent asset accounts**. Thus, a liability for bonds payable in the next period will not be classified as current if payment is to be from a noncurrent fund.

   c. The difference between current assets and current liabilities is **working capital**.

7. **Noncurrent liabilities** are those not qualifying as current. The noncurrent portions of the following items are shown in this section of the balance sheet:

   a. Long-term notes and bonds
   b. Liabilities under capital leases
   c. Most postretirement benefit obligations
   d. Deferred tax liabilities arising from interperiod tax allocation
   e. Obligations under product or service warranty agreements
   f. Advances for long-term commitments to provide goods or services
   g. Advances from affiliated entities
   h. Deferred revenue

8.   **Equity** (or **net assets** for a not-for-profit organization) is the residual after total liabilities are subtracted from total assets. Any recognized transaction that does not have equal and offsetting effects on total assets and total liabilities changes equity.

    a.   Equity consists of

        1)   Capital contributed by owners

        2)   Retained earnings (income reinvested)

        3)   Accumulated other comprehensive income (all comprehensive income items not included in net income)

        4)   The noncontrolling interest in a consolidated entity.

    b.   **Treasury stock** recorded at **cost** is a reduction of total equity and listed as an asset. Treasury stock recorded at **par** is a direct reduction of the pertinent contributed capital balance, e.g., common stock or preferred stock.

Fair Value Option (FVO)

9.   Assets and liabilities measured using the FVO are reported in a way that **separates their fair values** from the carrying amounts of similar items measured using another attribute, such as net realizable value, amortized cost, or present value (SFAS 159, *The Fair Value Option for Financial Assets and Financial Liabilities*).

    a.   The main FVO outline is in Study Unit 5.

Stop and review! You have completed the outline for this subunit. Study multiple-choice questions 1 through 5 beginning on page 84.

2.2 STATEMENTS OF INCOME, RETAINED EARNINGS, AND COMPREHENSIVE INCOME

Definition

1.   The results of operations are reported in the income statement (statement of earnings) on the **accrual basis** using an approach oriented to historical transactions.

    a.   The traditional income statement reports **revenues** from, and **expenses** of, the entity's major activities and **gains** and **losses** from other activities. The sum of these **income statement elements** is net income (loss) for an interval of time.

Revenues – Expenses + Gains – Losses = Net Income or Loss

        1)   Income statement elements are reported in temporary **(nominal)** accounts that are periodically closed to permanent **(real)** accounts. The accountant need not close each transaction directly to equity.

        2)   **Income or loss** is closed to **retained earnings** at the end of the period.

        3)   Recognized amounts not included in continuing operations are reported in separate sections for **discontinued operations** and **extraordinary items** (if any).

            a)   The term "continuing operations" is used only when a discontinued operation is reported.

Transactions Included in Income

2. Under the **all-inclusive approach**, all transactions **affecting the net change in equity during the period** are included with certain exceptions (APB Opinion 9, *Reporting the Results of Operations*.

    a. The **transactions not included** in net income are (1) transactions with owners, (2) prior-period adjustments, (3) items reported initially in other comprehensive income, (4) transfers to and from appropriated retained earnings, (5) adjustments made in a quasi-reorganization, and (6) effects on prior periods of accounting changes.

    b. The net income reported in this way over the life of the entity reflects the **sum of the periodic net incomes**, including the **nonrecurring items** that are an appropriate part of the earnings history.

        1) An additional advantage of the all-inclusive approach is that it reduces variation caused by differences in judgment.

        2) The utility of the statement as a predictor of future income is not impaired if **full disclosure** of unusual, irregular, or nonrecurring items is made, and an appropriate format is used.

Income Statement Format

3. Three formats are commonly used for presentation of recurring items of revenue, expense, gain, or loss.

    a. The **single-step income statement** provides one grouping for revenue and gain items and one for expense and loss items. The single step is the one subtraction necessary to arrive at net income.

EXAMPLE

Bonilla Company
Income Statement
For Year Ended December 31, Year 1

Revenues and gains:		
Net sales	$XXX	
Other revenues	XXX	
Gains	XXX	
Total revenues and gains		$ XXX
Expenses and losses:		
Costs of goods sold	$XXX	
Selling and administrative expenses	XXX	
Interest expense	XXX	
Losses	XXX	
Income tax expense	XXX	
Total expenses and losses		(XXX)
Net income		$ XXX
Earnings per common share (simple capital structure)		$ Y.YY

---

b. The **multiple-step income statement** matches operating revenues and expenses in a section separate from nonoperating items. It enhances disclosure by presenting subtotals.

EXAMPLE

Willis Company
Income Statement
For Year Ended December 31, Year 1

Revenues:			
Gross sales			$ XXX
Minus: Sales discounts		$(XXX)	
Sales returns and allowances		(XXX)	(XXX)
Net sales			$ XXX
Cost of goods sold:			
Beginning inventory		$ XXX	
Purchases	$XXX		
Minus: Purchase returns and discounts	(XXX)		
Net purchases	$XXX		
Transportation-in	XXX	XXX	
Goods available for sale		$ XXX	
Minus: Ending inventory		(XXX)	
Cost of goods sold			(XXX)
Gross profit			$ XXX
Operating expenses:			
Selling expenses:			
Sales salaries and commissions	$XXX		
Freight-out	XXX		
Travel	XXX		
Advertising	XXX		
Office supplies	XXX	XXX	
Administrative expenses:			
Executive salaries	XXX		
Professional salaries	XXX		
Wages of office staff	XXX		
Depreciation	XXX		
Office supplies	XXX	XXX	
Total operating expenses			(XXX)
Income from operations			$ XXX
Other revenues and gains:			
Dividend revenue		$ XXX	XXX
Other expenses and losses:			
Interest expense		$ XXX	
Loss on disposal of equipment		XXX	(XXX)
Income before taxes *			$ XXX
Income taxes			(XXX)
Net income *			$ XXX
Earnings per common share (simple capital structure)			$ Y.YY

* If a discontinued operation is reported, these line items are "Income from continuing operations before taxes" and "Income from continuing operations," respectively.

c. The **condensed income statement** includes only the section totals of the multiple-step format.

EXAMPLE

Marzullo Company
Income Statement
For Year Ended December 31, Year 1

Net sales		$ XXX
Cost of goods sold		(XXX)
Gross profit		$ XXX
Selling expenses	$XXX	
Administrative expenses	XXX	(XXX)
Income from operations		$ XXX
Other revenues and gains		XXX
Other expenses and losses		(XXX)
Income before taxes *		$ XXX
Income taxes		(XXX)
Net income *		$ XXX
Earnings per common share		$ Y.YY
(Simple capital structure)		

* If a discontinued operation is reported, these line items are "Income from continuing operations before taxes" and "Income from continuing operations," respectively.

Other Income Statement Sections

4. **Cost of goods sold** equals purchases for a retailer or cost of goods manufactured (CGM) for a manufacturer, adjusted for the change in finished goods (FG) in inventory:

>   Beginning (FG) inventory
> \+ Purchases (CGM)
>   Goods available for sale
> – Ending (FG) inventory
>   Cost of goods sold

a. **Cost of goods manufactured** equals the period's manufacturing costs adjusted for the change in work-in-process. It also may be stated as cost of goods sold adjusted for the change in finished goods inventory.

>   Beginning work in process
> \+ Sum of periodic manufacturing costs
> – Ending work-in-process
>   Cost of goods manufactured

>   Ending FG inventory
> \+ Cost of goods sold
> – Beginning FG inventory
>   Cost of goods manufactured

5. **Operating Expenses**

a. **Selling expenses** are those incurred in selling or marketing.

1) Examples include (a) sales representatives' salaries, commissions, and traveling expenses; (b) sales department rent, salaries, and depreciation; and (c) communications (e.g., Internet) costs. Shipping costs also are often classified as selling costs.

b. **Administrative (general) expenses** are incurred for the direction of the entity as a whole and are not related wholly to a specific function, e.g., selling or manufacturing.

1) They include (a) accounting, legal, and other fees for professional services; (b) officers' salaries; (c) insurance; (d) wages of office staff; (e) miscellaneous supplies; and (f) office occupancy costs.

6. **Interest expense** is recognized based on the passage of time. In the case of bonds, notes, and capital leases, the **effective interest method** is used.

7. When an entity reports a **discontinued operation or an extraordinary item**, it must be presented in a separate section after income from continuing operations.

    a. **Intraperiod tax allocation** is required. Thus, income tax expense or benefit is allocated to (1) continuing operations, (2) discontinued operations, (3) extraordinary items, (4) other comprehensive income, and (5) items debited or credited directly to other components of equity (SFAS 109, *Accounting for Income Taxes*).

    b. The following items are reported separately in the **discontinued operations** section:

        1) Income or loss from operations of the component unit (including any gain or loss on disposal)

        2) Income tax expense or benefit

    c. **Extraordinary items** arise from material transactions that are **both unusual in nature and infrequent in occurrence** in the environment in which the entity operates. If an item meets one but not both criteria, it should be presented separately as a component of income from continuing operations.

    d. Appropriate **earnings per share** amounts must be disclosed, either on the face of the statement or in the accompanying notes.

EXAMPLE
(complex capital structure)

Income from continuing operations before income from discontinued operation and loss on extraordinary item		$XXX
Discontinued operations:		
Income from discontinued component unit (net of loss on disposal of $XX)	$XXX	
Income tax expense	(XXX)	XXX
Income before extraordinary item		XXX
Extraordinary item:		
Loss from volcanic eruption (net of applicable income tax benefit of $XXX)		(XXX)
Net income		$XXX

	Basic	Diluted
Basic and diluted EPS:		
Income from continuing operations before income from discontinued operation and loss on extraordinary item	$Y.YY	$Y.YY
Income from discontinued component unit, net of tax	Y.YY	Y.YY
Income before extraordinary item	$Y.YY	$Y.YY
Extraordinary loss, net of tax	(Y.YY)	(Y.YY)
Net income	$Y.YY	$Y.YY

---

    e. Also see Study Unit 3.

Statement of Retained Earnings

8. The statement of retained earnings is a **basic financial statement**. The income statement and the statement of retained earnings (presented separately or combined) broadly reflect the results of operations.

   a. Most entities report changes in retained earnings in a **statement of equity (changes in equity)** or a separate statement.

      1) Disclosures of **changes in equity** and in the number of shares of equity securities are necessary whenever financial position and results of operations are presented. These disclosures may occur in the basic statements, in the notes, or in separate statements (APB Opinion 12, *Omnibus Opinion -- 1967*).

   b. The **statement of retained earnings** displays

      1) Beginning retained earnings, plus or minus any prior-period adjustments (net of tax);
      2) Net income (loss);
      3) Dividends paid or declared;
      4) Certain other rare items, e.g., quasi-reorganizations; and
      5) Ending retained earnings.

   > **EXAMPLE**
   >
   > Statement of Retained Earnings
   > For Year Ended December 31, Year 1
   >
   > | | |
   > |---|---|
   > | Beginning retained earnings (originally reported) | $XXX |
   > | Overstatement of depreciation expense in prior period | XXX |
   > | Beginning retained earnings (restated) | $XXX |
   > | Net income | XXX |
   > | Cash dividends paid | (XXX) |
   > | Ending retained earnings | $XXX |

   c. Retained earnings is sometimes **appropriated** (restricted) to a special account to disclose that earnings retained in the business (not paid out in dividends) are being used for special purposes. See Study Unit 14.

   d. **Quasi-reorganizations** are undertaken by entities with **negative retained earnings**. In many states, such entities are **not permitted to pay dividends**. Accordingly, a now-profitable entity may not be able to pay dividends because of accumulated losses. See Study Unit 14.

Comprehensive Income

9. Comprehensive income includes all changes in equity of a business entity during a period except those resulting from investments by owners and distributions to owners (SFAC 6, *Elements of Financial Statements*).

   a. GAAP require certain items of comprehensive income to bypass net income. Requiring these items to be included in net income would be misleading. They typically represent valuation adjustments, not independent economic events.

   b. Comprehensive income has **two major categories**: net income and other comprehensive income (OCI) (SFAS 130, *Reporting Comprehensive Income*).

10. **Other comprehensive income (OCI)** includes all items of comprehensive income not included in net income. An entity need not report comprehensive income if it has no items of OCI. Under existing accounting standards, OCI includes

   a. Unrealized gains and losses on **available-for-sale securities** (except those that are hedged items in a fair value hedge).

      1) But OCI does **not** include unrealized gains or losses on trading securities, held-to-maturity securities, or securities for which the fair value option (measurement at fair value, with unrealized gains or losses included in earnings) has been elected.

   b. Gains and losses on **derivatives** designated, qualifying, and effective as **cash flow hedges**.

   c. Certain amounts associated with recognition of the **funded status of postretirement benefit plans** (e.g., defined benefit pension plans and defined other postretirement benefit plans). These amounts are included in OCI, net of tax, to the extent they are not included in income.

      1) Gains (losses)
      2) Prior service cost (credit)
      3) Transition asset or obligation

   d. **Foreign Currency Items**

      1) **Translation adjustments**
      2) Gains and losses on a hedge of a **net investment in a foreign operation**
      3) Gains and losses on derivatives designated, qualifying, and effective as hedging instruments in **foreign currency cash flow hedges**

Reporting and Display

11. The components of comprehensive income are reported in the financial statements when they are recognized. **Total comprehensive income** is displayed where the components of OCI are shown.

12. Comprehensive income and its components must be displayed in a financial statement given **the same prominence** as other statements.

   a. **No specific format** is specified. However, SFAS 130 encourages an entity to display the components of OCI and comprehensive income **below net income**.

   b. Regardless of the format, **net income** must be presented as a component of comprehensive income in the statement.

   c. The following are **possible formats** for reporting comprehensive income:

      1) **Separate statement of comprehensive income**

> ### EXAMPLE
>
> Statement of Comprehensive Income
> For Year Ended December 31, Year 1
>
> | | | |
> |---|---:|---:|
> | Net income | | $XXX |
> | OCI (net of tax): | | |
> | Foreign currency translation adjustment | $XXX | |
> | Unrealized holding loss | (XXX) | XXX |
> | Comprehensive income | | $XXX |

      2) **One statement of income and comprehensive income**

         a) The OCI section is displayed **beneath net income**. The total for OCI is added to (subtracted from) net income to arrive at comprehensive income. This format has the disadvantage of drawing attention away from net income.

3) **Part of the statement of changes in equity**

EXAMPLE

Statement of Changes in Equity
For Year Ended December 31, Year 1

Retained earnings at 1/1	$XXX	
Net income	XXX	$XXX
Dividends on common stock	(XXX)	
Balance at 12/31	$XXX	
Accumulated OCI at 1/1 (All items net of tax)	$XXX	
Unrealized gains on securities		
(Net of reclassified amounts)		$XXX
Foreign currency translation adjustment		XXX
OCI	XXX	$XXX
Comprehensive income		$XXX
Balance at 12/31	$XXX	
Common stock at 1/1	$XXX	
Shares issued	XXX	
Balance at 12/31	$XXX	
Additional paid-in capital at 1/1	$XXX	
Common stock issued	XXX	
Balance at 12/31	$XXX	
Total equity	$XXX	

---

d.   Each component of OCI is displayed **net of tax**, or one amount is shown for the aggregate tax effect on OCI. In either case, the tax effect on each component must be disclosed.

e.   **EPS** information about comprehensive income need not be disclosed.

Other Considerations

13.   The components of OCI are recorded initially in a temporary **(nominal)** account. The **total OCI** for a period is transferred to a component of equity (a permanent or **real** account) separate from retained earnings and additional paid-in capital. The component should have a descriptive title, e.g., **accumulated OCI**.

a.   The accumulated balance for each classification in that component must be disclosed in the balance sheet, a statement of changes in equity, or the notes.

14.   **Reclassification adjustments** are made for each component of OCI.

a.   Their purpose is to avoid double counting when an item included in net income also was included in OCI for the same or a prior period.

1)   For example, if a gain or loss on available-for-sale securities is realized in the current period, the prior recognition of an unrealized holding gain or loss must be eliminated from accumulated OCI.

b.   A total for comprehensive income is reported in **interim-period condensed statements**.

c.   The terms "comprehensive income" and "other comprehensive income" need not be used.

Stop and review! You have completed the outline for this subunit. Study multiple-choice questions 6 through 10 beginning on page 86.

2.3 STATEMENT OF CASH FLOWS

Definition

1. The **primary purpose** of a statement of cash flows is to provide information about the cash receipts and payments of an entity during a period. A secondary purpose is to provide information about significant **operating, investing, and financing activities**.

    a. The statement presents cash-basis amounts in a format that reconciles the cash balance at the beginning of the period with the balance at the end of the period.

    b. A statement of cash flows is **required** as part of a full set of financial statements of most business and not-for-profit entities (SFAS 95, *Statement of Cash Flows*).

        1) If an entity reports financial position and results of operations, it must present a statement of cash flows for any period for which results of operations are presented.

        2) **Cash flow per share** is **not** reported.

2. If an entity invests its cash in cash equivalents, it should use the descriptive term "cash and cash equivalents." Otherwise, the term "cash" is acceptable. Terms such as "funds" or "quick assets" may not be used.

    a. **Cash equivalents** are readily convertible to known amounts of cash and are **so near maturity** that they present insignificant risk of changes in value because of changes in interest rates.

    b. Usually, only investments with **original maturities of 3 months or less** qualify. Thus, a 3-year Treasury note meets the definition if purchased 3 months from maturity. However, if the note was purchased 3 years ago, it does not meet the definition when its remaining maturity is 3 months.

        1) Other examples of cash equivalents are Treasury bills, commercial paper, and money market funds.

    c. Not all qualifying investments must be classified as cash equivalents. An entity should **consistently apply a policy** for classifying cash equivalents.

        1) For example, an entity with operations that primarily involve investing in short-term, highly liquid investments may choose not to treat them as cash equivalents. Any change in policy is a **change in accounting principle** that requires retrospective application.

Classification of Cash Flows

3. **Operating activities** are all transactions and other events that are not financing or investing activities. In general, operating activities involve the production and delivery of goods and the provision of services. Their effects are normally reported in the income statement.

    a. **Cash inflows from operating activities** include receipts from collection or sale of accounts and notes resulting from sales to customers. They also include cash receipts in the form of **interest and dividends**, that is, **returns** on loans, other debt instruments of other entities, and equity securities.

    b. **Cash outflows from operating activities** include cash payments to buy materials for manufacture of goods for resale, including principle payments on accounts and notes payable to suppliers. They also include cash payments to

        1) Other suppliers and employees for other goods and services
        2) Governments for taxes, fees, and penalties
        3) Creditors for **interest**

    c. Other operating cash flows result from items **acquired for resale**:

        1) Certain securities and other assets carried at market value in a trading account (e.g., by banks, brokers, and dealers in securities), or
        2) Loans carried at lower of cost or market.

    d.   Cash flows from purchases, sales, and maturities of **trading securities** (securities bought and held primarily for sale in the near term) are classified based on the **nature and purpose** for which the securities were acquired.

    e.   **Operating cash outflows** are **assumed** to include the cash that would have been paid for income taxes if **excess tax benefits** from **share-based payment** arrangements had not been available.

          1)   The same amount also is reported as a **financing cash inflow**. The reason is that two transactions are deemed to exist:

               a)   Incurrence of compensation cost (operating)

               b)   Exercise of share options resulting in excess tax benefits (financing)

4.   **Investing activities** include (a) making and collecting loans; (b) acquiring and disposing of debt or equity instruments; and (c) acquiring and disposing of property, plant, and equipment and other productive assets (but not materials in inventory) held for or used in the production of goods or services.

    a.   Investing activities **exclude** transactions in (1) cash equivalents and (2) certain loans or other debt or equity instruments acquired for resale.

    b.   Cash flows from purchases, sales, and maturities of **available-for-sale and held-to-maturity securities** are from investing activities. They are reported gross for each classification of security in the cash flows statement.

5.   **Financing activities** include (a) issuance of stock, (b) payment of dividends, (c) treasury stock transactions, (d) incurrence of debt, (e) repayment or other settlement of debt obligations, and (f) the exercise of share options resulting in excess tax benefits.

    a.   They also include receiving restricted resources that, by donor stipulation, must be used for long-term purposes.

Foreign Currency Cash Flows

6.   The statement of cash flows also must include a translation of any foreign currency cash flows from transactions that occur during the reported period.

    a.   A **weighted-average exchange rate** may be used if the result is substantially the same as would be obtained by using the rates in effect when the flows occurred.

    b.   The effect of exchange rate fluctuations must be separately reported as part of the **reconciliation** of the change in cash and cash equivalents.

Noncash Investing and Financing Activities

7.   Information about all **investing and financing activities** that affect recognized assets or liabilities but not **cash flows** must be disclosed outside the body of the statement. Examples include (a) converting debt to equity, (b) obtaining assets by assuming liabilities or entering into a capital lease, (c) obtaining a building or investment asset by receiving a gift, and (d) exchanging a noncash asset or liability for another.

Stop and review! You have completed the outline for this subunit. Study multiple-choice questions 11 through 16 beginning on page 88.

2.4 DIRECT AND INDIRECT METHODS OF PRESENTING OPERATING CASH FLOWS

1.   The FASB **encourages use of the direct method**. However, it states that "if the direct method is used, a **reconciliation** of net income and net cash flow from operating activities is required to be provided in a separate schedule." Because the reconciliation is based on the indirect method, the **indirect method** is used most often in practice. The same net operating cash flow is reported under both methods.

2.   The **direct method** converts the accrual-basis amounts in the income statement to the cash basis. An entity using this method must, at a minimum, report the following:

   a.   Cash collected from customers
   b.   Interest and dividends received (unless donor-restricted for long-term purposes)
   c.   Other operating cash receipts, if any
   d.   Cash paid to employees and other suppliers of goods or services
   e.   Interest paid
   f.   Income taxes paid and the separately reported amount that would have been paid if excess tax benefits from share-based payment arrangements had not been available
   g.   Other operating cash payments, if any

3.   The **indirect method** reconciles net income of a business or the change in net assets of a not-for-profit entity to net operating cash flow. It removes the effects of

   a.   All **deferrals** of past operating cash receipts and payments. Examples are changes in (1) inventory, (2) deferred income, (3) prepaid expenses, and (4) amortization of premium on bonds.
   b.   All **accruals** of estimated future operating cash receipts and payments. Examples are changes in receivables and payables and amortization of discount on bonds.
   c.   Items whose cash effects are **investing or financing cash flows**. Examples include (1) bad debt expense and (2) depreciation. Others are gains or losses on (1) sales of property, plant, and equipment; (2) discontinued operations; and (3) debt extinguishment.

4.   Indirect vs. direct method.

EXAMPLE

Dice Corp's balance sheet accounts as of December 31, Year 6 and Year 5, are presented below. Information relating to Year 6 activities is to the left.

Information Relating to Year 6 Activities

- Net income for Year 6 was $690,000.
- Cash dividends of $240,000 were declared and paid in Year 6.
- Equipment costing $400,000 and having a carrying amount of $150,000 was sold on January 1, Year 6, for $150,000 in cash.
- A long-term investment was sold in Year 6 for $135,000 in cash.
- 10,000 shares of common stock were issued in Year 6 for $22 a share.
- Short-term investments consist of Treasury bills maturing on 6/30/Year 7. They are not cash equivalents because their maturities are not 3 months or less and they are not classified as trading securities.
- The provision for Year 6 income taxes was $210,000.
- The accounts receivable balances at the beginning and end of Year 6 were net of allowances for bad debts of $50,000 and $60,000, respectively. Dice wrote off $40,000 of bad debts during Year 6. The only transactions affecting accounts receivable and the allowance were credit sales, collections, write-offs, and recognition of bad debt expense.
- During Year 6, Dice constructed a plant asset. The accumulated expenditures during the year included $11,000 of capitalized interest.
- Dice accounts for its interest in Thrice Corp. under the equity method. Its equity in Thrice's Year 6 earnings was $25,000. At the end of Year 6, Dice received a $10,000 cash dividend from Thrice.

	December 31	
Assets	Year 6	Year 5
Cash	$ 195,000	$ 100,000
Short-term investments	300,000	0
Accounts receivable (net)	480,000	510,000
Inventory	680,000	600,000
Prepaid expenses	15,000	20,000
Long-term investments	215,000	300,000
Plant assets	1,700,000	1,000,000
Accumulated depreciation	(450,000)	(450,000)
Goodwill	90,000	100,000
Total assets	$3,225,000	$2,180,000
Liabilities and Equity		
Accounts payable	$ 825,000	$ 720,000
Interest payable	15,000	10,000
Income tax payable	20,000	30,000
Short-term debt	325,000	0
Deferred taxes	250,000	300,000
Common stock, $10 par	800,000	700,000
Additional paid-in capital	370,000	250,000
Retained earnings	620,000	170,000
Total liabilities and equity	$3,225,000	$2,180,000

Example explanations continue on the following six pages.

Indirect Presentation

5.   The following computations are required to determine **net cash provided by operations** ($905,000 as shown in the reconciliation on page 78).

    a.   **Depreciation.** Equipment costing $400,000 and having a carrying amount of $150,000 was sold on January 1, Year 6, for $150,000 in cash. Thus, the debit to accumulated depreciation must have been $250,000 ($400,000 – $150,000). In Year 6, Dice must have recognized $250,000 of depreciation [$450,000 accumulated depreciation at 12/31/Year 6 – ($450,000 accumulated depreciation at 12/31/Year 5 – $250,000 accumulated depreciation on equipment sold]. The depreciation should be added to net income because it is included in the determination of net income but had no cash effect.

Accumulated Depreciation			
1/1/Year 6	$250,000	$450,000	12/31/Year 5
(Equipment sale)		250,000	Exp. Year 6
		$450,000	12/31/Year 6

    b.   **Goodwill.** The $10,000 ($100,000 at 12/31/Year 5 – $90,000 at 12/31/Year 6) loss on impairment of goodwill should be added to net income because it is included in the determination of net income but had no cash effect.

    c.   **Inventory and accounts payable.** The adjustment from cost of goods sold (an accrual accounting amount used to calculate net income) to cash paid to suppliers requires two steps: (1) from **cost of goods sold to purchases** and (2) from **purchases to cash paid to suppliers**. The $80,000 ($680,000 – $600,000) increase in inventory is subtracted from net income. It indicates that purchases were $80,000 greater than cost of goods sold. The $105,000 ($825,000 – $720,000) increase in accounts payable is added to net income. It indicates that cash paid to suppliers was $105,000 less than purchases. Thus, the net effect of the changes in inventory and accounts payable is that cash paid to suppliers was $25,000 less than the accrual basis cost of goods sold.

    d.   **Accounts receivable.** The net accounts receivable balance declined by $30,000 ($510,000 – $480,000), implying that cash collections exceeded sales. Given that sales, collections, write-offs, and recognition of bad debt expense were the only relevant transactions, $30,000 should be added to net income. Use of the change in net accounts receivable as a reconciliation adjustment is a short-cut method. It yields the same net adjustment to net income as separately including the effects of the change in gross accounts receivable [($510,000 + $50,000 bad debt allowance) – ($480,000 + $60,000 bad debt allowance) = an addition of $20,000], bad debt expense (a noncash item resulting in an addition of $50,000), and bad debt write-offs (a subtraction of $40,000 to reflect that write-offs did not result in collections).

Gross Accounts Receivable					Allowance for Bad Debts			
12/31/Year 5	$560,000	$40,000	Writeoffs		Writeoffs	$40,000	$50,000	12/31/Year 5.
($510,000 + $50,000)							50,000	Year 6 expense
	20,000						$60,000	12/31/Year 6
12/31/Year 6	$540,000							
($480,000 + $60,000)								

    e.   **Prepaid expenses.** The $5,000 decrease in prepaid expenses signifies that noncash expenses were recognized and should be added back to net income.

    f.   **Dividends received.** Earnings of an affiliate accounted for under the equity method are debited to the investment account and credited to net income. A cash dividend from the affiliate is debited to cash and credited to the investment account. Thus, an adjustment of $15,000 ($25,000 earnings – $10,000 cash dividend) for undistributed earnings is necessary.

g.   **Long-term investments.** A $100,000 ($300,000 + $25,000 equity in affiliate's earnings – $10,000 cash dividend – $215,000) decrease in the long-term investments balance occurred when investments were sold for $135,000. The resulting $35,000 gain was included in net income. The cash effect is classified as a cash flow from an investing activity under SFAS 95. (SFAS 115, which distinguishes among trading, available-for-sale, and held-to-maturity securities, does not apply because the investment in Thrice Corp. is accounted for under the equity method.) Thus, the $35,000 should be subtracted from net income to remove it from the determination of cash flows from operating activities.

h.   **Interest payable** increased by $5,000, a noncash expense and a reconciling addition to net income. The interest capitalized is ignored for reconciliation purposes because it is not reported as interest expense in the income statement or as interest paid in the statement of cash flows or in related disclosures. The $11,000 of capitalized interest is included in the capitalized cost of the plant asset constructed for Dice's use.

i.   **Income tax payable** decreased by $10,000, giving rise to a reconciling reduction of net income because tax expense was less than cash paid for taxes.

j.   **Deferred taxes** decreased by $50,000. This reconciling deduction from net income resulted when temporary differences reversed and cash payments for taxes exceeded tax expense.

Reconciliation of Net Income to Net Operating Cash Flow		
Net income for Year 6	$690,000	
Depreciation	250,000	a.
Loss on impairment	10,000	b.
Inventory	(80,000)	c.
Accounts payable	105,000	c.
Accounts receivable (net)	30,000	d.
Prepaid expenses	5,000	e.
Undistributed earnings of an affiliate	(15,000)	f.
Gain on sale of investments	(35,000)	g.
Interest payable	5,000	h.
Income tax payable	(10,000)	i.
Deferred taxes	(50,000)	j.
Net operating cash flow	$905,000	

6.   **Net Investing Cash Flow**

a.   The $300,000 increase in short-term investments indicates that a purchase occurred.

b.   The balance sheet further indicates that plant assets increased by $700,000 ($1,700,000 – $1,000,000). Moreover, plant assets (equipment) costing $400,000 were sold. The cost of constructing the plant asset thus equaled the $700,000 increase plus the $400,000 cost of the equipment sold, or $1,100,000.

c.   The cash flows from investing activities include the cash effects of the sale of equipment and the long-term investments, the purchases of short-term investments (given that they are not trading securities), and the construction of a plant asset. The equipment was sold for $150,000 and the long-term investments for $135,000. Thus, the net cash used in investing activities was $1,115,000.

Purchases:		
Short-term investments	$ (300,000)	a.
Plant assets	(1,100,000)	b.
Sales:		
Equipment	150,000	c.
Long-term investments	135,000	c.
Net investing cash flow	$(1,115,000)	

7. **Net Financing Cash Flow**

   a. Dice Corp.'s Year 6 financing activities included the issuance of short-term debt ($325,000 – $0 = $325,000), the issuance of common stock and the recording of additional paid-in capital [($800,000 – $700,000) + ($370,000 – $250,000) = $220,000], and the payment of cash dividends ($240,000). The net cash provided by these financing activities was $305,000.

Short-term debt	$325,000	a.
Common stock	220,000	a.
Cash dividends	(240,000)	a.
Net financing cash flow	$305,000	

8. **Net change in cash.** According to Dice Corp.'s balance sheets, the net change in cash was an increase of $95,000 ($195,000 – $100,000).

   a. This amount reconciles with the net cash provided by (used in) operating, investing, and financing activities ($905,000 – $1,115,000 + $305,000 = $95,000).

9. **Noncash financing and investing activities.** Dice Corp. had no such transactions in Year 6 to be reported in supplemental disclosures.

10. **Supplemental cash flow disclosures.** If Dice Corp. uses the indirect method to present its statement of cash flows, the interest paid (excluding amounts capitalized) and income taxes paid must be reported in related disclosures.

    a. Calculation of interest paid requires the income statement data for Dice Corp. See the following page.

    b. Income taxes paid were $270,000 ($210,000 provision for income taxes + $50,000 decrease in deferred taxes + $10,000 decrease in taxes payable).

Dice Corp.
Statement of Cash Flows -- Indirect Method
for the Year Ended December 31, Year 6
Increase (Decrease) in Cash and Cash Equivalents

Operating cash flows:		Investing cash flows:		
Net income for Year 6	$ 690,000	Proceeds from sale of		
Depreciation	250,000	equipment	$ 150,000	
Loss on impairment	10,000	Proceeds from sale of		
Inventory	(80,000)	long-term investments	135,000	
Accounts payable	105,000	Payments for short-term		
Accounts receivable (net)	30,000	investments	(300,000)	
Prepaid expenses	5,000	Payments for plant assets	(1,100,000)	
Undistributed earnings		Net cash used in		
of an affiliate	(15,000)	investing activities		$(1,115,000)
Gain on sale of investments	(35,000)			
Interest payable	5,000	Financing cash flows:		
Income tax payable	(10,000)	Proceeds from short-term		
Deferred taxes	(50,000)	debt	$ 325,000	
		Proceeds from issuing		
Net cash provided by		common stock	220,000	
operating activities	$ 905,000	Dividends paid	(240,000)	
		Net cash provided by		
		financing activities		305,000
		Net increase		$ 95,000
		Beginning balance		100,000
		Ending balance		$ 195,000

Direct Presentation

11. In SFAS 95, the FASB presents a method for directly deriving information about the major classes of gross operating cash receipts and payments at the minimum specified level of detail. The direct method adjusts **nominal accounts** (revenues and expenses) for changes in related **real accounts** (assets and liabilities).

12. **Collections from customers** may be determined by adjusting sales for the changes in customer receivables. This calculation requires information similar to that used in an indirect presentation to reconcile net income to net operating cash flow: total operating receivables (which are usually separate from those for interest and dividends), bad debt write-offs, and any other noncash entries in customer accounts.

13. **Cash paid to employees and other suppliers** of goods and services may be determined by adjusting cost of goods sold and expenses (excluding interest, income tax, and depreciation) for the changes in inventory, prepaid expenses, and operating payables. This calculation is also similar to the process used in reconciling net income to net operating cash flow. It requires that operating payables and expenses be separated from interest and income tax payable.

14. **Additional information.** The indirect presentation analysis on the previous page and the additional facts from Dice Corp.'s income statement for the year ended December 31, Year 6, given below, are necessary to derive the amounts of the major classes of gross operating cash inflows and outflows required in a direct presentation.

Income Statement

Sales	$7,810,000
Cost of sales	(5,500,000)
Depreciation and impairment loss	(260,000)
Selling, general, administrative expenses	(1,100,000)
Interest expense	(140,000)
Equity in earnings of affiliate	25,000
Gain on sale of investments	35,000
Interest income	30,000
Income before income taxes	$ 900,000
Income tax expense	(210,000)
Net income	$ 690,000

15. **Cash collected from customers** is derived as follows:

Sales			$7,810,000
Change in balance of receivables:			
Gross receivables (12/31/Year 5)	$560,000	a.	
Write-offs	(40,000)	b.	
Gross receivables (12/31/Year 6)	(540,000)	a.	
Increase in gross receivables			(20,000) c.
Cash received from customers			$7,790,000

a. The beginning and ending balances ($510,000 and $480,000, respectively) of accounts receivable were net of $50,000 and $60,000 bad debt allowances, respectively. Hence, the beginning gross receivables balance was $560,000 and the ending balance was $540,000. If the direct presentation is used, the change in gross receivables, write-offs, and bad debt expense must be shown separately. The shortcut or net method is inappropriate because bad debt expense is not included in the determination of sales. It is included in selling, general, and administrative expenses and must be deducted in the derivation of cash paid to employees and suppliers as calculated on the next page.

b. Subtracting write-offs eliminates noncash credits to accounts receivable.

c. An increase in receivables signifies cash collected was less than sales.

16. **Cash paid to employees and suppliers** is derived as follows:

Cost of sales		$5,500,000
Selling, general, administrative expenses	$1,100,000	
Noncash expense (bad debts)	(50,000) a.	
Net cash expenses		1,050,000
Inventory (12/31/Year 5)	$ (600,000) b.	
Inventory (12/31/Year 6)	680,000 b.	
Net inventory increase from operations		80,000
Accounts payable (12/31/Year 5)	$ 720,000 c.	
Accounts payable (12/31/Year 6)	(825,000) c.	
Net increase in accounts payable		(105,000)
Prepaid expenses (12/31/Year 5)	$ (20,000) d.	
Prepaid expenses (12/31/Year 6)	15,000 d.	
Net decrease in prepaid expenses		(5,000)
Cash paid to employees and suppliers		$6,520,000

a. Bad debt expense is a noncash item included in selling, general, and administrative expenses and should be deducted from them. Given that the bad debt allowance increased by $10,000 ($60,000 – $50,000) despite $40,000 of write-offs, bad debt expense must have been $50,000.

b. An increase in inventory means that purchases exceeded cost of sales.

c. An increase in accounts payable indicates that purchases exceeded cash paid to suppliers. This amount is a deduction.

d. A decrease in prepaid expenses signifies recognition of a noncash expense related to a prior-period cash payment. Accordingly, this amount is a deduction.

17. Operating Activities Section Prepared Using the Direct Method

Dice Corp.
Statement of Cash Flows -- Direct Method
for the Year Ended December 31, Year 6
Increase (Decrease) in Cash and Cash Equivalents

Operating cash flows:
Cash collected from customers	$7,790,000	a.
Cash paid to employees and suppliers	(6,520,000)	b.
Dividend from affiliate	10,000	c.
Interest received	30,000	d.
Interest paid	(135,000)	e.
Income taxes paid	(270,000)	f.
Net cash provided by operating activities	$ 905,000	g.

Investing cash flows:
Proceeds from sale of equipment	$ 150,000	
Proceeds from sale of long-term investments	135,000	
Payments for short-term investments	(300,000)	
Payments for plant assets	(1,100,000)	
Net cash used in investing activities	(1,115,000)	h.

Financing cash flows:
Proceeds from short-term debt	$ 325,000	
Proceeds from issuing common stock	220,000	
Dividends paid	(240,000)	
Net cash provided by financing activities	305,000	h.
Net increase	$ 95,000	i.
Beginning balance	100,000	i.
Ending balance	$ 195,000	i.

The difference between the direct and indirect method is the determination of operating cash flows. Compare the direct method format presented above with the indirect method format on page 79. The only difference is in how the $905,000 of cash provided by operations is calculated.

a. This amount was derived in 15. on page 80.

b. This amount was derived in 16. on the previous page.

c. The dividend received, not the amount of equity-based earnings recognized in net income, is included.

d. Interest income was $30,000. Given no interest receivable, cash interest collected must also have been $30,000.

e. Interest capitalized is not considered in determining interest paid because it is included in payments for plant assets, not in interest expense ($140,000) reported in the income statement. Given that interest payable increased by $5,000, interest paid must have been $135,000. No supplemental disclosure of interest paid or of income taxes paid is necessary because the amounts are reported directly in this format.

f. Income taxes paid equaled tax expense ($210,000), plus the decrease in deferred taxes ($50,000), plus the decrease in taxes payable ($10,000), or $270,000.

g. This amount is the same regardless of the statement format used.

h. These sections are the same regardless of the method of presentation.

i. The statement of cash flows (direct or indirect method) reconciles the beginning and ending balances of cash (including cash equivalents).

18. Dice Corp. had no noncash investing and financing transactions to report in supplemental disclosures.

19. The reconciliation of net income to net operating cash flow (the operating section of the indirect method format) must be provided in a separate schedule if Dice Corp. uses the direct method.

Stop and review! You have completed the outline for this subunit. Study multiple-choice questions 17 through 32 beginning on page 89.

2.5 OTHER FINANCIAL STATEMENT PRESENTATIONS

Other Comprehensive Bases of Accounting

1. Financial statements based on a reporting system other than GAAP are said to be prepared using an **other comprehensive basis of accounting (OCBOA)**.

    a. Examples of OCBOAs are

    1) A basis used for tax purposes

    2) A basis used to comply with the requirements of a regulator

    3) The cash basis and modifications of the cash basis having substantial support

    4) A definite set of criteria having substantial support that is applied to all material items, for example, the price-level basis

    b. Statements prepared using an OCBOA should include a summary of significant accounting policies, including discussion of the basis used and how it differs from GAAP.

    c. Guidance on auditing statements prepared using an OCBOA is given by the AICPA in AU 623, *Special Reports*.

Personal Financial Statements

2. Personal financial statements of individuals or families are prepared to plan their financial affairs in general or for a specific purpose, e.g., tax or retirement planning.

    a. Assets should be presented at their estimated current values.

    1) The **estimated current value** is "the amount at which the item could be exchanged between a buyer and seller, each of whom is well informed and willing, and neither of whom is compelled to buy or sell" (AICPA SOP 82-1, *Accounting and Financial Reporting for Personal Financial Statements*).

    b. Liabilities, including payables, are presented at their estimated current amounts at the date of the statement.

    1) The **estimated current amount** is the discounted amount of cash to be paid. The interest rate is the rate implicit in the transaction in which the debt was incurred. But if the amount at which the debt can currently be discharged is lower, that amount should be used.

    c. A **statement of financial condition** must be prepared. It presents assets, liabilities, estimated income taxes, and net worth (total assets – total liabilities – estimated income tax) at a given date.

    1) Estimated income taxes are calculated as if the assets had been realized or the liabilities liquidated. Estimated income taxes are based on the differences between assets and liabilities and their tax bases.

    a) **Taxes payable**, including estimated taxes, are reported between liabilities and net worth.

    2) A **statement of changes in net worth** and comparative financial statements may be presented.

    3) Assets and liabilities and changes in them are recognized on the accrual basis.

d.   Estimated current values (amounts) may be based on recent transactions involving similar assets (liabilities) in similar circumstances. Absent such transactions, other valuation bases, such as discounted cash flow or appraisal value, may be used if they are consistently applied.

e.   **Noncancelable commitments to pay future sums** are presented at their discounted amounts as liabilities if they are for fixed or determinable amounts, are not contingent, and do not require the future performance of service by another.

1)   **Nonforfeitable rights to receive future sums** are presented as assets at their discounted amounts if they meet the same criteria.

f.   The assets and liabilities of an investment in a **limited business activity** not conducted in a separate business entity (such as an investment in real estate and a related mortgage) are separately presented.

g.   A **business interest** that is a large part of an individual's total assets is presented separately as a single amount equal to the estimated current value of the business interest.

Stop and review! You have completed the outline for this subunit. Study multiple-choice questions 33 through 39 beginning on page 94.

QUESTIONS

2.1 Balance Sheet

1. In analyzing a company's financial statements, which financial statement will a potential investor primarily use to assess the company's liquidity and financial flexibility?

A.   Balance sheet.

B.   Income statement.

C.   Statement of retained earnings.

D.   Statement of cash flows.

Answer (A) is correct. *(CPA, adapted)*
REQUIRED: The statement used to assess liquidity and financial flexibility.
DISCUSSION: The balance sheet includes "information that is often used in assessing an entity's liquidity and financial flexibility," but it provides an incomplete picture "unless it is used in conjunction with at least a cash flow statement." Liquidity reflects nearness to cash. Financial flexibility is the ability to take action to alter cash flows so that the entity can respond to unexpected events (SFAC 5).
Answer (B) is incorrect because the income statement is primarily concerned with profitability. Answer (C) is incorrect because the statement of retained earnings shows changes in equity for the year. Answer (D) is incorrect because the statement of cash flows provides an incomplete basis for assessing future cash flows. It cannot show interperiod relationships.

2. Zinc Co.'s adjusted trial balance at December 31, Year 6, includes the following account balances:

Common stock, $3 par	$600,000
Additional paid-in capital	800,000
Treasury stock, at cost	50,000
Net unrealized holding loss on available-for-sale securities	20,000
Retained earnings: appropriated for uninsured earthquake losses	150,000
Retained earnings: unappropriated	200,000

What amount should Zinc report as total equity in its December 31, Year 6, balance sheet?

A. $1,680,000

B. $1,720,000

C. $1,780,000

D. $1,820,000

Answer (A) is correct. *(CPA, adapted)*
REQUIRED: The total equity.
DISCUSSION: Total credits to equity equal $1,750,000 ($600,000 common stock at par + $800,000 additional paid-in capital + $350,000 retained earnings). The treasury stock recorded at cost is subtracted from (debited to) total equity, and the unrealized holding loss on available-for-sale securities is debited to other comprehensive income, a component of equity. Because total debits equal $70,000 ($50,000 cost of treasury stock + $20,000 unrealized loss on available-for-sale securities), total equity equals $1,680,000 ($1,750,000 – $70,000).
Answer (B) is incorrect because $1,720,000 treats the unrealized loss as a credit. Answer (C) is incorrect because $1,780,000 treats the treasury stock as a credit. Answer (D) is incorrect because $1,820,000 treats the treasury stock and the unrealized loss as credits.

Questions 3 and 4 are based on the following information.

The following trial balance of Trey Co. at December 31, Year 6, has been adjusted except for income tax expense.

	Dr.	Cr.
Cash	$ 550,000	
Accounts receivable, net	1,650,000	
Prepaid taxes	300,000	
Accounts payable		$ 120,000
Common stock		500,000
Additional paid-in capital		680,000
Retained earnings		630,000
Foreign currency translation adjustment	430,000	
Revenues		3,600,000
Expenses	2,600,000	
	$5,530,000	$5,530,000

Additional Information

- During Year 6, estimated tax payments of $300,000 were charged to prepaid taxes. Trey has not yet recorded income tax expense. There were no differences between financial statement and income tax income, and Trey's tax rate is 30%.

- Included in accounts receivable is $500,000 due from a customer. Special terms granted to this customer require payment in equal semiannual installments of $125,000 every April 1 and October 1.

3. In Trey's December 31, Year 6, balance sheet, what amount should be reported as total current assets?

A. $1,950,000

B. $2,200,000

C. $2,250,000

D. $2,500,000

Answer (A) is correct. *(CPA, adapted)*
REQUIRED: The total current assets.
DISCUSSION: Trey's current assets include cash, accounts receivable, and prepaid taxes. However, income tax expense is $300,000 [30% × ($3,600,000 revenues – $2,600,000 expenses)]. After recording income tax expense, prepaid taxes equal $0. Moreover, $250,000 of the receivables is due in Year 8 and is therefore noncurrent. Thus, total current assets equal $1,950,000 [$550,000 cash + ($1,650,000 – $250,000 noncurrent A/R)].
Answer (B) is incorrect because $2,200,000 includes the noncurrent accounts receivable. Answer (C) is incorrect because $2,250,000 includes $300,000 of prepaid taxes. Answer (D) is incorrect because $2,500,000 includes $300,000 of prepaid taxes and the noncurrent accounts receivable.

4. In Trey's December 31, Year 6, balance sheet, what amount should be reported as total retained earnings?

A. $1,029,000

B. $1,200,000

C. $1,330,000

D. $1,630,000

Answer (C) is correct. *(CPA, adapted)*
REQUIRED: The total retained earnings.
DISCUSSION: Retained earnings equal $1,330,000 {$630,000 beginning retained earnings + [($3,600,000 revenues – $2,600,000 expenses) × (1.0 – .3 tax rate)]}.
Answer (A) is incorrect because $1,029,000 results from subtracting the $430,000 foreign currency translation adjustment from retained earnings and subtracting $171,000 of taxes [($1,000,000 – $430,000) × 30%]. Answer (B) is incorrect because $1,200,000 results from subtracting the $430,000 foreign currency translation adjustment and from not subtracting the $300,000 in taxes. Answer (D) is incorrect because $1,630,000 results from not subtracting the $300,000 in taxes.

5. Brite Corp. had the following liabilities at December 31, Year 6:

Accounts payable	$ 55,000
Unsecured notes, 8%, due 7/1/Year 7	400,000
Accrued expenses	35,000
Contingent liability	450,000
Deferred income tax liability	25,000
Senior bonds, 7%, due 3/31/Year 7	1,000,000

The contingent liability is an accrual for possible losses on a $1 million lawsuit filed against Brite. Brite's legal counsel expects the suit to be settled in Year 8 and has estimated that Brite will be liable for damages in the range of $450,000 to $750,000. The deferred income tax liability is not related to an asset for financial reporting and is expected to reverse in Year 8. What amount should Brite report in its December 31, Year 6, balance sheet for current liabilities?

- A. $515,000
- B. $940,000
- C. $1,490,000
- D. $1,515,000

Answer (C) is correct. *(CPA, adapted)*
   REQUIRED: The amount reported for current liabilities.
   DISCUSSION: SFAS 78 includes the following as current liabilities: (1) obligations that, by their terms, are or will be due on demand within 1 year (or the operating cycle if longer), and (2) obligations that are or will be callable by the creditor within 1 year because of a violation of a debt covenant. Thus, the current liabilities are calculated as

Accounts payable	$ 55,000
Unsecured notes, 8%, due 7/1/Year 7	400,000
Accrued expenses	35,000
Senior bonds, 7%, due 3/31/Year 7	1,000,000
	$1,490,000

   Answer (A) is incorrect because $515,000 excludes the senior bonds due within 1 year and includes the deferred income tax liability that will not reverse within 1 year. Whether a deferred tax asset or liability is current depends on the classification of the related asset or liability. If it is not related to an asset or liability, the expected reversal date of the temporary difference determines the classification. Answer (B) is incorrect because $940,000 includes the contingent liability not expected to be settled until Year 8 and excludes the senior bonds. Answer (D) is incorrect because $1,515,000 includes the deferred income tax liability not expected to reverse until Year 8.

2.2 Statements of Income, Retained Earnings, and Comprehensive Income

6. The changes in account balances of the Vel Corporation during Year 6 are presented below:

	Increase
Assets	$356,000
Liabilities	108,000
Capital stock	240,000
Additional paid-in capital	24,000

Vel has no items of other comprehensive income (OCI), and the only charge to retained earnings was for a dividend payment of $52,000. Thus, the net income for Year 6 is

- A. $16,000
- B. $36,000
- C. $52,000
- D. $68,000

Answer (B) is correct. *(CPA, adapted)*
   REQUIRED: The net income for the year given the increase in assets, liabilities, and paid-in capital.
   DISCUSSION: Assets equal the sum of liabilities and equity (contributed capital, retained earnings, and accumulated OCI). To calculate net income, the dividend payment ($52,000) should be added to the increase in assets ($356,000). The excess of this sum ($408,000) over the increase in liabilities ($108,000) gives the total increase in equity ($300,000). Given no items of OCI, the excess of this amount over the combined increases in the capital accounts ($264,000) equals the increase in retained earnings ($36,000) arising from net income.
   Answer (A) is incorrect because $16,000 is the excess of the sum of the increases in the capital accounts other than retained earnings over the increase in net assets. Answer (C) is incorrect because $52,000 is the dividend. Answer (D) is incorrect because $68,000 equals the sum of the dividend and the excess of the sum of the increases in the capital accounts other than retained earnings over the increase in net assets.

7. The effect of a material transaction that is infrequent in occurrence but not unusual in nature should be presented separately as a component of income from continuing operations when the transaction results in a

	Gain	Loss
A.	Yes	Yes
B.	Yes	No
C.	No	No
D.	No	Yes

Answer (A) is correct. *(CPA, adapted)*
   REQUIRED: The circumstances in which an infrequent but not unusual transaction is shown as a separate component of income from continuing operations.
   DISCUSSION: To be classified as an extraordinary item, a transaction must be both unusual in nature and infrequent in occurrence within the environment in which the business operates. If an item meets one but not both of these criteria, it should be presented separately as a component of income from continuing operations (but not net of tax). Whether it is a gain or a loss does not affect this presentation.

8. In Baer Food Co.'s Year 3 single-step income statement, the section titled *Revenues* consisted of the following:

Net sales revenue	$187,000
Discontinued operations:	
Income from operations of	
component unit (including gain	
on disposal of $21,600)	18,000
Income tax	(6,000)
Interest revenue	10,200
Gain on sale of equipment	4,700
Total revenues	$213,900

In the revenues section of the Year 3 income statement, Baer Food should have reported total revenues of

A. $213,900

B. $209,200

C. $203,700

D. $201,900

Answer (D) is correct. *(CPA, adapted)*
REQUIRED: The total revenues.
DISCUSSION: This single-step income statement classifies the items included in income from continuing operations as either revenues or expenses. Discontinued operations is a classification in the income statement separate from continuing operations. Hence, total revenues (including interest and the gain) were $201,900 ($213,900 – $12,000 after-tax results from discontinued operations).
Answer (A) is incorrect because $213,900 equals reported total revenues. Answer (B) is incorrect because $209,200 excludes the gain. Answer (C) is incorrect because $203,700 excludes the interest.

9. The correction of an error in the financial statements of a prior period should be reported, net of applicable income taxes, in the current

A. Retained earnings statement after net income but before dividends.

B. Retained earnings statement as an adjustment of the opening balance.

C. Income statement after income from continuing operations and before extraordinary items.

D. Income statement after income from continuing operations and after extraordinary items.

Answer (B) is correct. *(CPA, adapted)*
REQUIRED: The proper recording of a prior period adjustment (correction of an error).
DISCUSSION: APB Opinion 9, *Reporting the Results of Operations*, as amended by SFAS 16, *Prior Period Adjustments*, requires that prior-period adjustments of single period statements be reflected net of applicable income taxes as changes in the opening balance in the statement of retained earnings of the current period. In comparative financial statements, all prior periods affected by the prior-period adjustment should be restated to reflect the adjustment.

10. Which of the following describes how comprehensive income should be reported?

A. Must be reported in a separate statement, as part of a complete set of financial statements.

B. Should not be reported in the financial statements but should only be disclosed in the notes.

C. May be reported in a separate statement, in a combined statement of income and comprehensive income, or within a statement of equity.

D. May be reported in a combined statement of income and comprehensive income or disclosed within a statement of equity; separate statements of comprehensive income are not permitted.

Answer (C) is correct. *(Publisher, adapted)*
REQUIRED: The reporting of comprehensive income.
DISCUSSION: Comprehensive income and its components must be displayed in a financial statement given the same prominence as other statements. No specific format is required, but SFAS 130 encourages an entity to display the components of other comprehensive income and comprehensive income below net income. Regardless of the format, net income must be presented as a component of comprehensive income in the statement. Among the possible formats for reporting comprehensive income are a (1) separate statement of comprehensive income, (2) combined statement of income and comprehensive income, or (3) statement of changes in equity.
Answer (A) is incorrect because no specific format is required as long as (1) comprehensive income and its components are displayed in a statement given the same prominence as other statements that constitute a full set and (2) net income is presented as a classification within comprehensive income. Answer (B) is incorrect because comprehensive income and its components must be displayed in a financial statement. Answer (D) is incorrect because an entity may report a separate statement of comprehensive income that includes a classification for net income and is displayed with the same prominence as the other statements.

2.3 Statement of Cash Flows

11. Which of the following should be disclosed as supplemental information in the statement of cash flows?

	Cash Flow per Share	Conversion of Debt to Equity
A.	Yes	Yes
B.	Yes	No
C.	No	Yes
D.	No	No

Answer (D) is correct. *(CPA, adapted)*
REQUIRED: The information that should be disclosed as supplemental information in the statement of cash flows.
DISCUSSION: SFAS 95 states, "Financial statements shall not report an amount of cash flow per share." Reporting a per-share amount might improperly imply that cash flow is an alternative to net income as a performance measure. Moreover, noncash transactions are excluded from the statement of cash flows. Conversion of debt to equity is a noncash financing activity. If material, it should be disclosed as a narrative or summarized in a separate schedule. It should not be included in the body of the statement of cash flows.

12. The primary purpose of a statement of cash flows is to provide relevant information about

A. Differences between net income and associated cash receipts and disbursements.

B. An entity's ability to generate future positive net cash flows.

C. The cash receipts and cash disbursements of an entity during a period.

D. An entity's ability to meet cash operating needs.

Answer (C) is correct. *(CPA, adapted)*
REQUIRED: The primary purpose of a statement of cash flows.
DISCUSSION: The primary purpose is to provide information about the cash receipts and cash payments of a business entity during a period. This information helps investors, creditors, and other users to assess the entity's ability to generate net cash inflows, meet its obligations, pay dividends, and secure external financing. It also helps assess reasons for the differences between net income and net cash flow and the effects of cash and noncash financing and investing activities (SFAS 95).

13. In a statement of cash flows, interest payments to lenders and other creditors should be classified as cash outflows for

A. Operating activities.

B. Borrowing activities.

C. Lending activities.

D. Financing activities.

Answer (A) is correct. *(CPA, adapted)*
REQUIRED: The classification of interest payments to lenders and other creditors.
DISCUSSION: Cash receipts from sales of goods and services, from interest on loans, and from dividends on equity securities are from operating activities. Cash payments to (1) suppliers for inventory; (2) employees for services; (3) other suppliers for other goods and services; (4) governments for taxes, duties, fines, and fees; (5) and lenders for interest are also from operating activities.
Answer (B) is incorrect because borrowing is not among the three categories of cash flows. Answer (C) is incorrect because lending is not among the three categories of cash flows. Answer (D) is incorrect because financing activities include (1) issuance of stock, (2) payment of distributions to owners, (3) treasury stock transactions, (4) issuance of debt, (5) repayment or other settlement of debt obligations, and (6) receipt of resources donor-restricted for long-term purposes.

14. The following information is available from Sand Corp.'s accounting records for the year ended December 31, Year 6:

Cash received from customers	$870,000
Rent received	10,000
Cash paid to suppliers and employees	510,000
Taxes paid	110,000
Cash dividends paid	30,000

Net cash flow provided by operations for Year 6 was

A. $220,000

B. $230,000

C. $250,000

D. $260,000

Answer (D) is correct. *(CPA, adapted)*
REQUIRED: The net cash flow provided by operations.
DISCUSSION: Payment of dividends is a financing activity. All other transactions listed are cash flows from operating activities. Accordingly, the net cash flow provided by operations is $260,000 ($870,000 + $10,000 − $510,000 − $110,000).
Answer (A) is incorrect because $220,000 includes the $30,000 dividend payment as an operating, not a financing, cash outflow and omits the rent received. Answer (B) is incorrect because $230,000 includes the $30,000 dividend payment as an operating, not a financing, cash outflow. Answer (C) is incorrect because $250,000 omits the rent received.

Questions 15 and 16 are based on the following information. Kollar Corp.'s transactions for the year ended December 31, Year 6, included the following:

- Purchased real estate for $550,000 cash borrowed from a bank
- Sold available-for-sale securities for $500,000
- Paid dividends of $600,000
- Issued 500 shares of common stock for $250,000

- Purchased machinery and equipment for $125,000 cash
- Paid $450,000 toward a bank loan
- Reduced accounts receivable by $100,000
- Increased accounts payable by $200,000

---

15. Kollar's net cash used in investing activities for Year 6 was

A. $675,000

B. $375,000

C. $175,000

D. $50,000

Answer (C) is correct. *(CPA, adapted)*
REQUIRED: The net cash used in investing activities.
DISCUSSION: The purchases of real estate and of machinery and equipment were uses of cash in investing activities. The sale of available-for-sale securities provided cash from an investing activity. Consequently, the net cash used in investing activities was $175,000 ($550,000 – $500,000 + $125,000). The reduction in accounts receivable and the increase in accounts payable were operating activities.

Answer (A) is incorrect because $675,000 omits the sale of securities. Answer (B) is incorrect because $375,000 results from either (1) improperly including the increase in accounts payable, a noncash transaction, as a use of cash in an investing activity ($550,000 cash borrowed – $500,000 sale of securities + $125,000 purchase of machinery + $200,000 increase in accounts payable) or (2) improperly calculating the net cash used in investing activities as the difference between the $500,000 sale of securities and the $125,000 purchase of machinery. Answer (D) is incorrect because $50,000 does not include the purchase of machinery and equipment.

16. Kollar's net cash used in financing activities for Year 6 was

A. $50,000

B. $250,000

C. $450,000

D. $500,000

Answer (B) is correct. *(CPA, adapted)*
REQUIRED: The net cash used in financing activities.
DISCUSSION: The dividend payment and the payment of the bank loan were uses of cash in financing activities. The borrowing from the bank and the issuance of stock provided cash from financing activities. Thus, the net cash used in financing activities was $250,000 ($600,000 – $550,000 – $250,000 + $450,000).

Answer (A) is incorrect because $50,000 omits the issuance of stock and the repayment of the bank loan. Answer (C) is incorrect because $450,000 results from including the increase in accounts payable, a noncash transaction, as a use of cash in a financing activity. Answer (D) is incorrect because $500,000 excludes the issuance of stock.

2.4 Direct and Indirect Methods of Presenting Operating Cash Flows

17. Which of the following is not disclosed on the statement of cash flows when prepared under the direct method, either on the face of the statement or in a separate schedule?

A. The major classes of gross cash receipts and gross cash payments.

B. The amount of income taxes paid.

C. A reconciliation of net income to net cash flow from operations.

D. A reconciliation of ending retained earnings to net cash flow from operations.

Answer (D) is correct. *(CPA, adapted)*
REQUIRED: The item not disclosed on the statement of cash flows.
DISCUSSION: A reconciliation of ending retained earnings to net cash flow from operations is not disclosed on the statement of cash flows, regardless of whether a direct or an indirect presentation is made. A reconciliation of net income to net cash flow from operations is reported in a separate schedule if the direct method is used. This reconciliation may be reported within the statement or provided in a separate schedule if the indirect method is used.

18. In its Year 6 income statement, Kilm Co. reported cost of goods sold (CGS) of $450,000. Changes occurred in several balance sheet accounts as follows:

Inventory	$160,000 decrease
Accounts payable -- suppliers	40,000 decrease

What amount should Kilm report as cash paid to suppliers in its Year 6 cash flow statement, prepared under the direct method?

A. $250,000

B. $330,000

C. $570,000

D. $650,000

Answer (B) is correct. *(CPA, adapted)*
REQUIRED: The cash paid to suppliers given CGS and the changes in inventory and accounts payable.
DISCUSSION: CGS is included in the determination of net income. Cash paid to suppliers, however, is the amount included in determining net cash flows from operating activities. To determine cash paid to suppliers, a two-step adjustment to CGS is necessary. The first step adjusts for the difference between CGS and purchases. The second step adjusts for the difference between purchases and the amounts disbursed to suppliers. The decrease in inventory is therefore subtracted from CGS to arrive at purchases. The decrease in accounts payable is then added to purchases to determine cash paid to suppliers. Accordingly, cash paid to suppliers equals $330,000 ($450,000 CGS – $160,000 + $40,000).
Answer (A) is incorrect because $250,000 results from subtracting the accounts payable decrease. Answer (C) is incorrect because $570,000 results from adding the inventory decrease and subtracting the accounts payable decrease. Answer (D) is incorrect because $650,000 results from adding the inventory decrease.

19. In its cash flow statement for the current year, Elliot Co. reported cash paid for interest of $70,000. Elliot did not capitalize any interest during the current year. Changes occurred in several balance sheet accounts as follows:

Accrued interest payable	$17,000 decrease
Prepaid interest	23,000 decrease

In its income statement for the current year, what amount should Elliot report as interest expense?

A. $30,000

B. $64,000

C. $76,000

D. $110,000

Answer (C) is correct. *(Publisher, adapted)*
REQUIRED: The interest expense given cash paid for interest and changes in interest payable and prepaid interest.
DISCUSSION: To reconcile cash paid for interest ($70,000) to interest expense, the decrease in interest payable (a prior-period expense and a current-period cash outflow) is subtracted. The decrease in prepaid interest (a prior-period cash outflow and a current-period expense) is added. Current interest expense is $76,000 ($70,000 – $17,000 + $23,000).
Answer (A) is incorrect because a decrease in prepaid interest must be added to cash paid to arrive at interest expense. Answer (B) is incorrect because a decrease in interest payable must be subtracted and a decrease in prepaid interest must be added to arrive at interest expense. Answer (D) is incorrect because a decrease in accrued interest payable must be subtracted, not added, to arrive at interest expense.

Questions 20 through 23 are based on the following information. Flax Corp. uses the direct method to prepare its statement of cash flows. Flax's trial balances at December 31, Year 6 and Year 5, are as follows:

	December 31		Credits	Year 6	Year 5
	Year 6	Year 5	Allowance for uncollectible accounts	$ 1,300	$ 1,100
Debits			Accumulated depreciation	16,500	15,000
Cash	$ 35,000	$ 32,000	Trade accounts payable	25,000	17,500
Accounts receivable	33,000	30,000	Income taxes payable	21,000	27,100
Inventory	31,000	47,000	Deferred income taxes	5,300	4,600
Property, plant, & equipment	100,000	95,000	8% callable bonds payable	45,000	20,000
Unamortized bond discount	4,500	5,000	Common stock	50,000	40,000
Cost of goods sold	250,000	380,000	Additional paid-in capital	9,100	7,500
Selling expenses	141,500	172,000	Retained earnings	44,700	64,600
General and administrative			Sales	538,800	778,700
expenses	137,000	151,300		$756,700	$976,100
Interest expense	4,300	2,600			
Income tax expense	20,400	61,200			
	$756,700	$976,100			

- Flax purchased $5,000 in equipment during Year 6.

- Flax allocated one-third of its depreciation expense to selling expenses and the remainder to general and administrative expenses, which include the provision for uncollectible accounts.

20. What amount should Flax report in its statement of cash flows for the year ended December 31, Year 6, for cash collected from customers?

A. $541,800

B. $541,600

C. $536,000

D. $535,800

Answer (D) is correct. *(CPA, adapted)*
REQUIRED: The cash collected from customers.
DISCUSSION: Collections from customers equal sales minus the increase in gross accounts receivable, or $535,800 ($538,800 – $33,000 + $30,000).
Answer (A) is incorrect because $541,800 results from adding the increase in receivables. Answer (B) is incorrect because $541,600 results from adding the increase in receivables and subtracting the increase in the allowance for uncollectible accounts, that is, from adding net accounts receivable. Answer (C) is incorrect because $536,000 results from subtracting net accounts receivable, a procedure that is appropriate when reconciling net income to net operating cash flow, not sales to cash collected from customers.

21. What amount should Flax report in its statement of cash flows for the year ended December 31, Year 6, for cash paid for interest?

A. $4,800

B. $4,300

C. $3,800

D. $1,700

Answer (C) is correct. *(CPA, adapted)*
REQUIRED: The cash paid for interest.
DISCUSSION: Interest expense is $4,300. This amount includes $500 of discount amortization, a noncash item. Hence, the cash paid for interest was $3,800 ($4,300 – $500).
Answer (A) is incorrect because $4,800 results from adding the amortized discount. Answer (B) is incorrect because $4,300 is the total interest expense. Answer (D) is incorrect because $1,700 is the increase in interest expense.

22. What amount should Flax report in its statement of cash flows for the year ended December 31, Year 6, for cash paid for income taxes?

A. $25,800

B. $20,400

C. $19,700

D. $15,000

Answer (A) is correct. *(CPA, adapted)*
REQUIRED: The cash paid for income taxes.
DISCUSSION: To reconcile income tax expense to cash paid for income taxes, a two-step adjustment is needed. The first step is to add the decrease in income taxes payable. The second step is to subtract the increase in deferred income taxes. Hence, cash paid for income taxes equals $25,800 [$20,400 + ($27,100 – $21,000) – ($5,300 – $4,600)].
Answer (B) is incorrect because $20,400 is income tax expense. Answer (C) is incorrect because $19,700 equals income tax expense minus the increase in deferred income taxes. Answer (D) is incorrect because $15,000 results from subtracting the decrease in income taxes payable and adding the increase in deferred taxes payable.

23. What amount should Flax report in its statement of cash flows for the year ended December 31, Year 6, for cash paid for selling expenses?

A. $142,000

B. $141,500

C. $141,000

D. $140,000

Answer (C) is correct. *(CPA, adapted)*
REQUIRED: The cash paid for selling expenses.
DISCUSSION: The cash paid for selling expenses equals selling expenses minus the depreciation allocated to selling expenses, or $141,000 {$141,500 Year 6 expense – [($16,500 – $15,000) Year 6 depreciation × 33 1/3% allocated to selling]}.
Answer (A) is incorrect because $142,000 results from adding the depreciation allocated to selling expenses. Answer (B) is incorrect because $141,500 equals the selling expenses for Year 6. Answer (D) is incorrect because $140,000 results from subtracting all of the year's depreciation expense from selling expenses.

24. The statement of cash flows may be presented in either a direct or an indirect (reconciliation) format. In which of these formats would cash collected from customers be presented as a gross amount?

	Direct	Indirect
A.	No	No
B.	No	Yes
C.	Yes	Yes
D.	Yes	No

Answer (D) is correct. *(R. O'Keefe)*
REQUIRED: The format in which cash collected from customers would be presented as a gross amount.
DISCUSSION: The statement of cash flows may report cash flows from operating activities in either an indirect (reconciliation) or a direct format. The direct format reports the major classes of operating cash receipts and cash payments as gross amounts. The indirect presentation reconciles net income to the same amount of net cash flow from operations that would be determined in accordance with the direct method. To arrive at net operating cash flow, the indirect method adjusts net income by removing the effects of (1) all deferrals of past operating cash receipts and payments, (2) all accruals of expected future operating cash receipts and payments, (3) all financing and investing activities, and (4) all noncash operating transactions.

25. With respect to the content and form of the statement of cash flows,

A. The pronouncements covering the cash flow statement encourage the use of the indirect method.

B. The indirect method adjusts ending retained earnings to reconcile it to net cash flows from operations.

C. The direct method of reporting cash flows from operating activities includes disclosing the major classes of gross cash receipts and gross cash payments.

D. The reconciliation of the net income to net operating cash flow need not be presented when using the direct method.

Answer (C) is correct. *(CMA, adapted)*
REQUIRED: The true statement about the content and form of the statement of cash flows.
DISCUSSION: SFAS 95 encourages use of the direct method of reporting major classes of operating cash receipts and payments, but the indirect method may be used. The minimum disclosures of operating cash flows under the direct method are (1) cash collected from customers, (2) interest and dividends received (unless donor-restricted to long-term purposes), (3) other operating cash receipts, (4) cash paid to employees and other suppliers of goods or services, (5) interest paid, (6) income taxes paid (and the amount that would have been paid if excess tax benefits from share-based payment arrangements had not been available), and (7) other operating cash payments.
Answer (A) is incorrect because SFAS 95 encourages use of the direct method. Answer (B) is incorrect because the indirect method reconciles net income with the net cash flow from operations. Answer (D) is incorrect because the reconciliation is required regardless of the method used.

Questions 26 through 28 are based on the following information. Royce Company had the following transactions during the fiscal year ended December 31, Year 2:

- Accounts receivable decreased from $115,000 on December 31, Year 1, to $100,000 on December 31, Year 2.

- Royce's board of directors declared dividends on December 31, Year 2, of $.05 per share on the 2.8 million shares outstanding, payable to shareholders of record on January 31, Year 3. The company did not declare or pay dividends for fiscal Year 1.

- Sold a truck with a net carrying amount of $7,000 for $5,000 cash, reporting a loss of $2,000.

- Paid interest to bondholders of $780,000.

- The cash balance was $106,000 on December 31, Year 1, and $284,000 on December 31, Year 2.

---

26. Royce Company uses the direct method to prepare its statement of cash flows at December 31, Year 2. The interest paid to bondholders is reported in the

A. Financing section, as a use or outflow of cash.

B. Operating section, as a use or outflow of cash.

C. Investing section, as a use or outflow of cash.

D. Debt section, as a use or outflow of cash.

Answer (B) is correct. *(CMA, adapted)*
REQUIRED: The proper reporting of interest paid.
DISCUSSION: Payment of interest on debt is considered an operating activity, although repayment of debt principal is a financing activity.
Answer (A) is incorrect because interest paid on bonds is an operating cash flow. Answer (C) is incorrect because investing activities include the lending of money and the acquisition, sale, or other disposal of securities that are not cash equivalents and the acquisition, sale, or other disposal of long-lived productive assets. Answer (D) is incorrect because SFAS 95 does not provide for a debt section.

---

27. Royce Company uses the indirect method to prepare its Year 2 statement of cash flows. It reports a(n)

A. Source or inflow of funds of $5,000 from the sale of the truck in the financing section.

B. Use or outflow of funds of $140,000 in the financing section, representing dividends.

C. Deduction of $15,000 in the operating section, representing the decrease in year-end accounts receivable.

D. Addition of $2,000 in the operating section for the $2,000 loss on the sale of the truck.

Answer (D) is correct. *(CMA, adapted)*
REQUIRED: The correct presentation of an item on a statement of cash flows prepared under the indirect method.
DISCUSSION: The indirect method determines net operating cash flow by adjusting net income. Under the indirect method, the $5,000 cash inflow from the sale of the truck is shown in the investing section. A $2,000 loss was recognized and properly deducted to determine net income. This loss, however, did not require the use of cash and should be added to net income in the operating section.
Answer (A) is incorrect because, under SFAS 95, the $5,000 inflow is shown in the investing section. Answer (B) is incorrect because no outflow of cash dividends occurred in Year 2. Answer (C) is incorrect because the decrease in receivables should be added to net income.

28. The total of cash provided (used) by operating activities plus cash provided (used) by investing activities plus cash provided (used) by financing activities is

- A. Cash provided of $284,000.
- B. Cash provided of $178,000.
- C. Cash used of $582,000.
- D. Equal to net income reported for fiscal year ended December 31, Year 2.

Answer (B) is correct. *(CMA, adapted)*
   REQUIRED: The net total of cash provided and used.
   DISCUSSION: The total of cash provided (used) by the three activities (operating, investing, and financing) should equal the increase or decrease in cash for the year. During Year 2, the cash balance increased from $106,000 to $284,000. Thus, the sources of cash must have exceeded the uses by $178,000.
   Answer (A) is incorrect because $284,000 is the ending cash balance, not the change in the cash balance; it ignores the beginning balance. Answer (C) is incorrect because the cash balance increased during the year. Answer (D) is incorrect because net income must be adjusted for noncash expenses and other accruals and deferrals.

29. The following data were extracted from the financial statements of a company for the year ended December 31:

Net income	$70,000
Depreciation expense	14,000
Amortization of intangible assets	1,000
Decrease in accounts receivable	2,000
Increase in inventories	9,000
Increase in accounts payable	4,000
Increase in plant assets	47,000
Increase in contributed capital	31,000
Decrease in short-term notes payable	55,000

There were no disposals of plant assets during the year. Based on the above, a statement of cash flows will report a net increase in cash of

- A. $11,000
- B. $17,000
- C. $54,000
- D. $69,000

Answer (A) is correct. *(CIA, adapted)*
   REQUIRED: The net increase in cash as reported on the statement of cash flows.
   DISCUSSION: Depreciation and amortization are noncash expenses and are added to net income. A decrease in receivables indicates that cash collections exceed sales on an accrual basis, so it is added to net income. To account for the difference between cost of goods sold (a reduction of income) and cash paid to suppliers, a two-step adjustment of net income is necessary. The difference between cost of goods sold and purchases is the change in inventory. The difference between purchases and the amount paid to suppliers is the change in accounts payable. Accordingly, the conversion of cost of goods sold to cash paid to suppliers requires deducting the inventory increase and adding the accounts payable increase. An increase in plant assets indicates an acquisition of plant assets, causing a decrease in cash, so it is deducted. An increase in contributed capital represents a cash inflow and is added to net income. A decrease in short-term notes payable is deducted from net income because it reflects a cash outflow. Thus, cash increased by $11,000 ($70,000 NI + $14,000 + $1,000 + $2,000 − $9,000 + $4,000 − $47,000 + $31,000 − $55,000).
   Answer (B) is incorrect because $17,000 results from subtracting the amortization and the decrease in receivables and adding the increase in inventories. Answer (C) is incorrect because $54,000 results from adjusting net income for the increase in plant assets and the increase in contributed capital only. Answer (D) is incorrect because $69,000 results from not making the adjustments for receivables, inventories, notes payable, and accounts payable.

30. Depreciation expense is added to net income under the indirect method of preparing a statement of cash flows in order to

- A. Report all assets at gross carrying amount.
- B. Ensure depreciation has been properly reported.
- C. Reverse noncash charges deducted from net income.
- D. Calculate net carrying amount.

Answer (C) is correct. *(CMA, adapted)*
   REQUIRED: The reason depreciation expense is added to net income under the indirect method.
   DISCUSSION: The indirect method begins with net income and then removes the effects of (1) deferrals of past operating cash receipts and payments, (2) accruals of estimated future operating cash receipts and payments, and (3) net income items not affecting operating cash flows (e.g., depreciation).
   Answer (A) is incorrect because assets other than cash are not shown on the statement of cash flows. Answer (B) is incorrect because depreciation is recorded on the income statement. On the statement of cash flows, depreciation is added back to net income because it was previously deducted on the income statement. Answer (D) is incorrect because net carrying amount of assets is shown on the balance sheet, not the statement of cash flows.

31. The net income for Cypress, Inc. was $3,000,000 for the year ended December 31. Additional information is as follows:

Depreciation on fixed assets	$1,500,000
Gain from cash sale of land	200,000
Increase in accounts payable	300,000
Dividends paid on preferred stock	400,000

The net cash provided by operating activities in the statement of cash flows for the year ended December 31 is

   A. $4,200,000

   B. $4,500,000

   C. $4,600,000

   D. $4,800,000

Answer (C) is correct. *(CMA, adapted)*
   REQUIRED: The net cash provided by operations.
   DISCUSSION: Net operating cash flow may be determined by adjusting net income. Depreciation is an expense not directly affecting cash flows that should be added back to net income. The increase in accounts payable is added to net income because it indicates that an expense has been recorded but not paid. The gain on the sale of land is an inflow from an investing, not an operating, activity and should be subtracted from net income. The dividends paid on preferred stock are cash outflows from financing, not operating, activities and do not require an adjustment. Thus, net cash flow from operations is $4,600,000 ($3,000,000 + $1,500,000 – $200,000 + $300,000).
   Answer (A) is incorrect because $4,200,000 equals net cash provided by operating activities minus the $400,000 financing activity. Answer (B) is incorrect because $4,500,000 equals net income, plus depreciation. Answer (D) is incorrect because $4,800,000 equals net income, plus depreciation, plus the increase in accounts payable.

32. Which is the most appropriate financial statement to use to determine if a company obtained financing during a year by issuing debt or equity securities?

   A. Balance sheet.

   B. Statement of cash flows.

   C. Statement of changes in equity.

   D. Income statement.

Answer (B) is correct. *(Publisher, adapted)*
   REQUIRED: The financial statement that shows financing operations.
   DISCUSSION: SFAS 95 requires a statement of cash flows as part of a full set of financial statements of all business and not-for-profit entities. The primary purpose of a statement of cash flows is to provide information about the cash receipts and payments of an entity during a period. A secondary purpose is to provide information about operating, investing, and financing activities. The financing activities section of a cash flow statement would clearly show if the company has cash inflows from the sale of debt or equity securities.
   Answer (A) is incorrect because a company may pay off certain bonds and reissue new bonds and the bond balances on the balance sheet would look identical or similar. Answer (C) is incorrect because the issuance of bonds would not be shown on a statement of changes in equity. Answer (D) is incorrect because the issuance of debt or equity securities will not affect any income item on the income statement.

2.5 Other Financial Statement Presentations

33. Personal financial statements usually consist of

   A. A statement of net worth and a statement of changes in net worth.

   B. A statement of net worth, an income statement, and a statement of changes in net worth.

   C. A statement of financial condition and a statement of changes in net worth.

   D. A statement of financial condition, a statement of changes in net worth, and a statement of cash flows.

Answer (C) is correct. *(CPA, adapted)*
   REQUIRED: The basic financial statements that should be included in personal financial statements.
   DISCUSSION: SOP 82-1 requires that personal financial statements include at least a statement of financial condition. SOP 82-1 further recommends, but does not require, a statement of changes in net worth and comparative financial statements. A personal statement of cash flows is neither required nor recommended.
   Answer (A) is incorrect because SOP 82-1 requires a statement of financial condition and recommends a statement of changes in net worth. Answer (B) is incorrect because SOP 82-1 requires a statement of financial condition and recommends a statement of changes in net worth. Answer (D) is incorrect because SOP 82-1 requires a statement of financial condition and recommends a statement of changes in net worth.

34. Green, a calendar-year taxpayer, is preparing a personal statement of financial condition as of April 30, Year 4. Green's Year 3 income tax liability was paid in full on April 15, Year 4. Green's tax on income earned between January and April Year 4 is estimated at $20,000. In addition, $40,000 is estimated for income tax on the differences between the estimated current values and current amounts of Green's assets and liabilities and their tax bases at April 30, Year 4. No withholdings or payments have been made towards the Year 4 income tax liability. In Green's April 30, Year 4, statement of financial condition, what amount should be reported, between liabilities and net worth, as estimated income taxes?

A. $0

B. $20,000

C. $40,000

D. $60,000

Answer (D) is correct. *(CPA, adapted)*
REQUIRED: The reported amount of estimated income taxes.
DISCUSSION: No amount should be reported for Year 3 taxes because the Year 3 liability was paid in full. Thus, Green will report estimated income taxes for amounts earned through April Year 4 and for the differences between the estimated current values of assets and the estimated current amounts of liabilities and their tax bases, a sum of $60,000 ($20,000 + $40,000).
Answer (A) is incorrect because Green must report estimated income taxes. Answer (B) is incorrect because $20,000 excludes estimated income taxes for the differences between the estimated current values of assets and the estimated current amounts of liabilities and their tax bases. Answer (C) is incorrect because $40,000 excludes the estimated income taxes on Year 4 income earned to date.

35. Mrs. Taft owns a $150,000 insurance policy on her husband's life. The cash value of the policy is $125,000, and a $50,000 loan is secured by the policy. In the Tafts' personal statement of financial condition at December 31, what amount should be shown as an investment in life insurance?

A. $150,000

B. $125,000

C. $100,000

D. $75,000

Answer (D) is correct. *(CPA, adapted)*
REQUIRED: The amount at which an investment in life insurance should be presented in a personal statement of financial condition.
DISCUSSION: SOP 82-1 requires that assets be presented at their estimated current values in a personal statement of financial condition. SOP 82-1 further specifies that investments in life insurance be reported at their cash values minus the amount of any outstanding loans. Thus, the amount that should be reported in Mrs. Taft's personal financial statement is $75,000 ($125,000 cash value – $50,000 loan).
Answer (A) is incorrect because $150,000 is the amount of the policy. Answer (B) is incorrect because $125,000 is the cash value. Answer (C) is incorrect because $100,000 is the amount of the policy minus the loan.

36. On December 31, Year 4, Shane is a fully vested participant in a company-sponsored pension plan. According to the plan's administrator, Shane has at that date the nonforfeitable right to receive a lump sum of $100,000 on December 28, Year 5. The discounted amount of $100,000 is $90,000 at December 31, Year 4. The right is not contingent on Shane's life expectancy and requires no future performance on Shane's part. In Shane's December 31, Year 4, personal statement of financial condition, the vested interest in the pension plan should be reported at

A. $0

B. $90,000

C. $95,000

D. $100,000

Answer (B) is correct. *(CPA, adapted)*
REQUIRED: The amount at which the vested interest in a pension plan should be reported in a personal statement of financial condition.
DISCUSSION: SOP 82-1 requires that noncancelable rights to receive future sums be presented at their estimated current value as assets in personal financial statements if they (1) are for fixed or determinable amounts; (2) are not contingent on the holder's life expectancy or the occurrence of a particular event, such as disability or death; and (3) do not require the future performance of service by the holder. The fully vested rights in the company-sponsored pension plan therefore should be reported at their current value, which is equal to the $90,000 discounted amount.
Answer (A) is incorrect because the current value of the right should be reported. Answer (C) is incorrect because $95,000 is a nonsense amount. Answer (D) is incorrect because $100,000 is the undiscounted amount.

37. Quinn is preparing a personal statement of financial condition as of April 30. Included in Quinn's assets are the following:

- 50% of the voting stock of Ink Corp. A shareholders' agreement restricts the sale of the stock and, under certain circumstances, requires Ink to repurchase the stock. Quinn's tax basis for the stock is $430,000, and at April 30, the buyout value is $675,000.

- Jewelry with a fair value aggregating $70,000 based on an independent appraisal on April 30 for insurance purposes. This jewelry was acquired by purchase and gift over a 10-year period and has a total tax basis of $40,000.

What is the total amount at which the Ink stock and jewelry should be reported in Quinn's April 30 personal statement of financial condition?

- A. $470,000
- B. $500,000
- C. $715,000
- D. $745,000

Answer (D) is correct. *(CPA, adapted)*
REQUIRED: The amount at which stock and jewelry should be reported in a personal statement of financial condition.
DISCUSSION: SOP 82-1 requires that all assets be reported at estimated current value. An interest in a closely held business is an asset and should be shown at its estimated current value. The buyout value is a better representation of the current value of the Ink stock than the tax basis. The appraisal value is the appropriate basis for reporting the jewelry. Thus, the stock and jewelry should be reported at $745,000 ($675,000 + $70,000).
Answer (A) is incorrect because $470,000 reports both assets at their tax basis. Answer (B) is incorrect because $500,000 includes the stock at its tax basis. Answer (C) is incorrect because $715,000 includes the jewelry's tax basis rather than its fair value.

38. On December 31, Year 5, Mr. and Mrs. Blake owned a parcel of land held as an investment. The land was purchased for $95,000 in Year 1, and was encumbered by a mortgage with a principal balance of $60,000 at December 31, Year 5. On this date, the fair value of the land was $150,000. In the Blakes' December 31, Year 5, personal statement of financial condition, at what amount should the land investment and mortgage payable be reported?

	Land Investment	Mortgage Payable
A.	$150,000	$60,000
B.	$95,000	$60,000
C.	$90,000	$0
D.	$35,000	$0

Answer (A) is correct. *(CPA, adapted)*
REQUIRED: The amounts at which the land investment and mortgage payable should be reported.
DISCUSSION: For an investment in a limited business activity not conducted in a separate business entity (such as an investment in real estate and a related mortgage), SOP 82-1 requires that the assets and liabilities not be presented as a net amount. Instead, they should be presented as separate assets at their estimated current values and separate liabilities at their estimated current amounts. This presentation is particularly important if a large portion of the liabilities may be satisfied with funds from sources unrelated to the investments. Thus, the land should be reported at its $150,000 fair value and the mortgage principal at $60,000 (the amount at which the debt could currently be discharged).
Answer (B) is incorrect because $95,000 was the cost of the land. Answer (C) is incorrect because the asset and liability should be presented separately and not as a net amount. Answer (D) is incorrect because $35,000 equals the cost minus the mortgage balance.

39. A business interest that constitutes a large part of an individual's total assets should be presented in a personal statement of financial condition as

- A. A separate listing of the individual assets and liabilities at cost.
- B. Separate line items of both total assets and total liabilities at cost.
- C. A single amount equal to the proprietorship equity.
- D. A single amount equal to the estimated current value of the business interest.

Answer (D) is correct. *(CPA, adapted)*
REQUIRED: The amount at which a business interest constituting a large part of an individual's total assets should be presented in a personal financial statement.
DISCUSSION: SOP 82-1 requires that a business interest constituting a large part of an individual's total assets be presented in a personal statement of financial condition as a single amount equal to the estimated current value of the business interest. This investment should be disclosed separately from other investments if the entity is marketable as a going concern.
Answer (A) is incorrect because the business interest should be reported as a net amount. Answer (B) is incorrect because the business interest should be reported as a net amount. Answer (C) is incorrect because the business interest should be reported at its estimated current value.

Use Gleim's ***CPA Test Prep*** CD-Rom/Pocket PC for interactive testing with over 4,000 additional questions!

2.6 PRACTICE SIMULATION

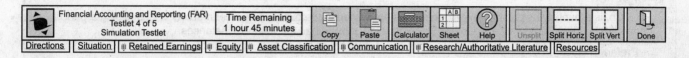

Financial Accounting and Reporting (FAR)
Testlet 4 of 5
Simulation Testlet
Time Remaining
1 hour 45 minutes
Copy
Paste
Calculator
Sheet
Help
Unsplit
Split Horiz
Split Vert
Done
Directions
Situation
Retained Earnings
Equity
Asset Classification
Communication
Research/Authoritative Literature
Resources

1. Directions

In the following simulation, you will be asked to complete various tasks. You may use the content in the **Information Tabs** to complete the tasks in the **Work Tabs**.

Information Tabs:

Directions
Resources

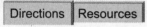

FIG 1

- Go through each of the **Information Tabs** to familiarize yourself with the simulation content
- The **Resources** tab will contain information, including formulas and definitions, that may help you to complete the tasks
- Your simulation may have more **Information Tabs** than those shown in Fig. 1

Work Tabs:

SysTrust
Engagement Letter
Authoritative Sources
Communication

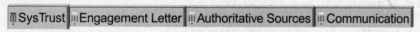

FIG. 2

- **Work Tabs**, to the right of **Information Tabs**, contain the tasks for you to complete
- **Work Tabs** contain directions for completing each task - be sure to read these directions carefully
- The tab names in Fig. 2 are for illustration only - yours may differ
- Once you complete any part of a task, the pencil for that tab will be shaded (see **Communication** in Fig. 2)
- The shaded pencil does **NOT** indicate that you have completed the entire task
- You must complete all of the tasks in the **Work Tabs** to receive full credit

Research/Authoritative Literature Tab:

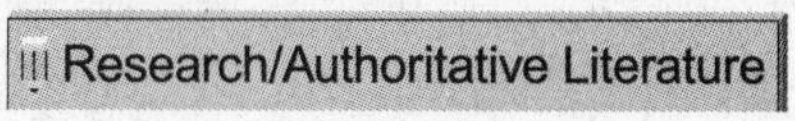

Research/Authoritative Literature

FIG. 3

- This tab contains both the Research task and the Authoritative Literature
- Detailed instructions for completing the Research task, and for using the Authoritative Literature, appear on this tab
- You may use the Authoritative Literature as a resource for completing other tasks

NOTE: If you believe you have encountered a software malfunction, report it to the test center staff immediately.

2. Situation

Min Co. is a publicly held company whose shares are traded in the over-the-counter market. It issues single-period statements only. The equity accounts at December 31, Year 5, had the following balances:

Preferred stock, $100 par value, 6% noncumulative; 5,000 shares authorized; 2,000 issued and outstanding	$ 200,000
Common stock, $1 par value, 150,000 shares authorized; 100,000 issued and outstanding	100,000
Additional paid-in capital	800,000
Retained earnings	1,586,000
Accumulated other comprehensive income	312,000
Total equity	$2,998,000

Transactions during Year 6 and other information relating to the equity accounts were as follows:

- February 1, Year 6--Issued 13,000 shares of common stock to Ram Co. in exchange for land. On the date issued, the stock had a market price of $11 per share. The land had a carrying amount on Ram's books of $135,000 and an assessed value for property tax purposes of $90,000.

- March 1, Year 6--Purchased 5,000 shares of its own common stock to be held as treasury stock for $14 per share. Min uses the cost method to account for treasury stock. Transactions in treasury stock are legal in Min's state of incorporation.

- May 10, Year 6--Declared a property dividend of marketable securities to be distributed to common shareholders. The securities had a carrying amount of $600,000. Fair values on relevant dates were

Date of declaration (May 10, Year 6)	$ 720,000
Date of record (May 25, Year 6)	758,000
Date of distribution (June 1, Year 6)	736,000

- September 17, Year 6--Purchased 150,000 shares of Max Co. stock classified as available for sale for $12 per share.

- October 1, Year 6--Reissued 2,000 shares of treasury stock for $16 per share.

- November 4, Year 6--Declared a cash dividend of $1.50 per share to all common shareholders of record on November 15, Year 6. The dividend was paid on November 25, Year 6.

- December 20, Year 6--Declared the required annual cash dividend on preferred stock for Year 6. The dividend was paid on January 5, Year 7.

- January 16, Year 7--After issuance of the financial statements for Year 6, Min became aware that no amortization had been recorded for Year 6 for a patent purchased on July 1, Year 6. The patent was properly capitalized at $320,000 and had an estimated useful life of 8 years when purchased. Min's income tax rate is 30%.

- Adjusted net income for Year 6 was $838,000.

- Max Co. stock traded at $14 per share on December 31, Year 6.

3. Retained Earnings

This type of question has a spreadsheet response format that requires you to fill in the correct amounts in the shaded cells provided. For the following listed retained earnings items, calculate the amounts requested using the information listed on the situation tab. These items will be reported on Min's statement of changes in equity or in a separate statement of retained earnings.

Retained Earnings Item	Amount Charged To Retained Earnings
1. Prior-period adjustment	
2. Preferred dividends	
3. Common dividends--cash	
4. Common dividends--property	

4. Equity

This type of question has a spreadsheet response format that requires you to fill in the correct amounts in the shaded cells provided. For the following listed equity items, calculate the amounts requested using the information listed on the situation tab. These items will be reported on Min's statement of changes in equity at December 31, Year 6.

Equity Item	Amount To Be Included in Equity
1. Number of common shares issued	
2. Dollar amount of common stock issued	
3. Additional paid-in capital, including treasury stock transactions	
4. Treasury stock	

5. Asset Classification

This set of questions has a matching format. Select the best match for each numbered item from the terms in the drop-down list and write its letter in the column provided. Each choice may be used once, more than once, or not at all. Accordingly, each asset should be matched with its appropriate balance sheet classification.

Asset	Answers
1. Cash surrender value of life insurance policies	
2. Land	
3. Leasehold improvements	
4. Debt sinking fund	
5. Loans to officers	
6. Capital lease	
7. Bond issue costs	
8. Inventory	
9. Trading securities	
10. Purchased goodwill	
11. Trademarks	

Classification
A) Plant, property, and equipment
B) Investments and funds
C) Other non-current assets
D) Current assets
E) Intangible assets

6. Communication

In a memorandum to a client, describe the purposes of the statement of cash flows, including the reporting of operating, financing, and investing activities.

REMINDER: Your response will be graded for both technical content and writing skills. Technical content will be evaluated for information that is helpful to the intended reader and clearly relevant to the issue. Writing skills will be evaluated for development, organization, and the appropriate expression of ideas in professional correspondence. Use a standard business memo or letter format with a clear beginning, middle, and end. Do not convey information in the form of a table, bullet point list, or other abbreviated presentation.

To: Client
From: CPA
Subject: Statement of Cash Flows

7. Research/Authoritative Literature

See page 12 in the Introduction of this book for a detailed explanation of the AICPA's new Research/Authoritative Literature work tab as well as a screenshot of how the tab will actually look on your exam.

Research and cite the specific paragraph in SFAC 5 that describes the kind of information the balance sheet provides.

Unofficial Answers

3. Retained Earnings (4 Gradable Items)

1. <u>$14,000</u>. The prior-period adjustment to beginning retained earnings for the Year 7 fiscal year is to correct the failure to record 6 months of patent amortization for Year 6. The patent was capitalized at $320,000 and had an expected useful life of 8 years. Thus, Year 6 amortization was $20,000 [($320,000 ÷ 8) × (6 ÷ 12)], and the prior-period adjustment to beginning retained earnings (net of tax) is $14,000 [$20,000 × (1 − .30)].

2. <u>$12,000</u>. The preferred stock is 6% noncumulative. The dividend is $12,000 ($200,000 × .06). When a dividend is declared, retained earnings is debited.

3. <u>$165,000</u>. At the beginning of the year, 100,000 shares of common stock were outstanding. Given that 13,000 shares were issued in February, 5,000 shares were purchased as treasury stock in March, and 2,000 shares were reissued in October, 110,000 shares were outstanding at November 4 (100,000 + 13,000 − 5,000 + 2,000). The dividend is $165,000 (110,000 shares × $1.50).

4. $720,000. Most nonreciprocal transfers of nonmonetary assets to owners are recorded at the fair value of the assets transferred. Thus, on the declaration date, the property should be restated at fair value. Any gain or loss should be recognized. The entries for Min on the date of declaration are

Investment in securities	$120,000	
Gain on appreciation of securities		$120,000
Retained earnings	$720,000	
Property dividends payable		$720,000

4. Equity (4 Gradable Items)

1. 113,000 shares. Given that 100,000 shares of common stock were issued and outstanding at the beginning of the year and that 13,000 shares were issued in February, 113,000 shares had been issued as of year-end. Of these 110,000 were outstanding (113,000 shares issued – 5,000 shares repurchased + 2,000 shares reissued).

2. $113,000. The number of shares issued is 113,000 (100,000 beginning shares issued + 13,000 issued in February). The stock has a par value of $1. Thus, the dollar amount of common stock issued is $113,000.

3. $934,000. Beginning additional paid-in capital was $800,000. When 13,000 shares were issued for land, the most clearly evident basis for measuring the transaction was the fair value of the stock ($11 per share). Hence, additional paid-in capital would have been credited for $130,000 [$143,000 – (13,000 shares × $1 par)]. When 2,000 shares of treasury stock purchased at $14 per share were reissued for $16 per share, additional paid-in capital was credited for $4,000 [2,000 shares × ($16 – $14)]. Thus, additional paid-in capital is $934,000 ($800,000 + $130,000 + $4,000).

4. $42,000. When 5,000 shares were reacquired, treasury stock was debited for $70,000 (5,000 shares × $14). When 2,000 shares of treasury stock were reissued at $16, treasury stock was credited for $28,000 (2,000 shares × $14), and additional paid-in capital was credited for $4,000 (2,000 shares × $2). The balance in the treasury stock account is therefore $42,000 ($70,000 – $28,000).

5. Asset Classification (11 Gradable Items)

1. Investments and funds. These noncurrent assets include a variety of nonoperating items intended to be held beyond the longer of 1 year or the operating cycle, e.g., cash surrender value.

2. Property, plant, and equipment. These noncurrent assets are tangible operating items recorded at cost and reported net of any accumulated depreciation. An example is land, a nondepreciable asset.

3. Property, plant, and equipment. These noncurrent assets are tangible operating items recorded at cost and reported net of any accumulated depreciation, e.g., leasehold improvements.

4. Investments and funds. These noncurrent assets include a variety of nonoperating items intended to be held beyond the longer of 1 year or the operating cycle, e.g., funds restricted to retirement of long-term debt.

5. Other non-current assets. These items include long-term prepaid expenses, called deferred charges, and any other noncurrent assets not readily classifiable elsewhere. They include such long-term receivables arising from unusual transactions as loans to officers. (NOTE: The Sarbanes-Oxley Act of 2002 generally prohibits an issuer from extending personal credit to directors or officers.)

6. Property, plant, and equipment. These noncurrent assets are tangible operating items recorded at cost and reported net of any accumulated depreciation. An example is a leased asset held under a capital lease.

7. Other non-current assets. These items include long-term prepaid expenses, called deferred charges, and any other noncurrent assets not readily classifiable elsewhere. Bond issue costs are a type of deferred charge.

8. Current assets. These assets consist of "cash and other assets or resources commonly identified as reasonably expected to be realized in cash or sold or consumed during the normal operating cycle of the business" (ARB 43, Ch. 3A). Current assets include inventory.

9. Current assets. These assets consist of "cash and other assets or resources commonly identified as reasonably expected to be realized in cash or sold or consumed during the normal operating cycle of the business" (ARB 43, Ch. 3A). Current assets include certain individual trading, available-for-sale, and held-to-maturity securities.

10. Intangible assets. These assets are nonfinancial assets without physical substance. Goodwill is an intangible asset that is recorded only in a business combination when the cost of the acquired entity exceeds the net of the amounts assigned to the assets acquired and liabilities assumed.

11. Intangible assets. These assets are nonfinancial assets without physical substance. An example is a trademark.

6. Communication (5 Gradable Items; for grading instructions, please refer to page 12.)

To: Client
From: CPA
Subject: Statement of Cash Flows

The primary purpose of a statement of cash flows is to provide relevant information about the cash receipts and payments of an entity during a period. A secondary purpose is to provide information about investing and financing activities. If used with information in the other financial statements, the statement of cash flows should help investors, creditors, donors, and others to assess the entity's ability to generate positive future net cash flows, meet its obligations, and pay dividends. Cash flow information also helps users to assess (1) the entity's needs for external financing, (2) the reasons for differences between income and associated cash receipts and payments, and (3) the cash and noncash aspects of investing and financing activities.

Information about noncash investing and financing activities that affect recognized assets or liabilities but do not directly affect cash flow for the period must be disclosed. These transactions are excluded from the body of the statement to avoid undue complexity and detraction from the objective of providing information about cash flows. Examples include converting debt to equity, obtaining assets by assuming liabilities or entering into a capital lease, obtaining a building or investment asset by receiving a gift, and exchanging a noncash asset or liability for another.

A statement of cash flows reports the cash effects of operating activities, investing activities, and financing activities during the period. Operating activities include all transactions and other events not classified as investing and financing activities. In general, the cash effects of transactions and other events that enter into the determination of income are to be classified as operating activities. Cash flows from operating activities include cash receipts from interest on loans and dividends on equity securities. They also include cash payments to employees and suppliers; to governments for taxes, duties, and fees; and to lenders for interest. Moreover, operating cash outflows are assumed to include the cash that would have been paid for income taxes if excess tax benefits from share-based payment arrangements had not been available. The same amount also is reported as a financing cash inflow. Investing activities include making and collecting loans and acquiring and disposing of (1) debt or equity instruments and (2) property, plant, and equipment and other productive assets, that is, assets held for or used in the production of goods or services (other than the materials held in inventory). Financing activities include the issuance of stock, the payment of dividends, treasury stock transactions, the issuance of debt, and the repayment or other settlement of debt obligations. It also includes receiving restricted resources that by donor stipulation must be used for long-term purposes.

7. Research/Authoritative Literature (1 Gradable Item)

Answer: SFAC 5, Par. 26

SFAC 5 -- *Recognition and Measurement in Financial Statements of Business Enterprises.*

26. A statement of financial position provides information about an entity's assets, liabilities, and equity and their relationships to each other at a moment in time. The statement delineates the entity's resource structure . . . major classes and amounts of assets . . . and its financing structure . . . major classes and amounts of liabilities and equity.

Scoring Schedule:

	Correct Responses		Gradable Items		Weights		
Tab 3	_____	÷	4	×	15%	=	_____
Tab 4	_____	÷	4	×	20%	=	_____
Tab 5	_____	÷	11	×	20%	=	_____
Tab 6	_____	÷	5	×	30%	=	_____
Tab 7	_____	÷	1	×	15%	=	_____
							(Your Score)

Use Gleim's **CPA Gleim Online** to practice more simulations in a realistic environment.

STUDY UNIT THREE
INCOME STATEMENT ITEMS

(20 pages of outline)

The first four subunits of this study unit concern the proper presentation of certain items on the income statement. The remaining subunits address various revenue recognition issues.

3.1 DISCONTINUED OPERATIONS

1. The operating results of a **discontinued operation** are reported separately in the income statement (or statement of activities of a not-for-profit organization) if

   a. A component of the entity has been **disposed of** or is classified as **held for sale**,

   b. Its **operations and cash flows** are or will be eliminated from the entity's operations, and

   c. The entity will have **no significant continuing involvement** after disposal (SFAS 144).

2. A **component** of an entity has operations and cash flows that are clearly distinguishable for operating and financial reporting purposes. A component may be a(n)

   a. Reportable segment,
   b. Operating segment,
   c. Reporting unit,
   d. Subsidiary, or
   e. Asset group (a **disposal group** if it is to be disposed of).

3. If a long-lived asset (or disposal group) is **not a component**, then it is not a discontinued operation. In this case, a gain or loss on its sale is included in **income from continuing operations before income taxes**.

Income Statement Presentation

4. The operating results of a component that has been disposed of or is classified as held for sale are reported in a section labeled **discontinued operations**. This section is presented after continuing operations but before extraordinary items.

   a. When a component is **classified as held for sale**, it is measured at the lower of its carrying amount or **fair value minus cost to sell**. Its operating results are reported in discontinued operations in the period(s) **when they occur**.

      1) **Operating results** include any loss for a writedown to fair value minus cost to sell. They also include a gain arising from an increase in fair value minus cost to sell (limited to losses previously recognized).

      2) Operating results do **not recognize depreciation or amortization**.

b.   The results of discontinued operations are reported **minus (plus) income tax (benefit)**. The following format may be used by a business:

EXAMPLE

Each of ING Company's divisions is a component of the entity. The X Division's results are declining. Consequently, ING decided on July 15, Year 1, to commit to a plan to sell X. The sale was completed on December 1, Year 1. The operations and cash flows of X were eliminated from the ongoing operations of ING. Moreover, the entity will have no continuing post-sale involvement in X's operations. The following is ING's single-step income statement after the disposal:

ING Company
INCOME STATEMENT
For the Year Ended 12/31/Yr 1

Revenue:		
Net sales	$1,500,000	
Other revenue	40,000	
Total revenue		$1,540,000
Expenses:		
Cost of goods sold	$ 750,000	
Selling expense	75,000	
Administrative expense	90,000	
Interest expense	70,000	
Total expenses		(985,000)
Income from continuing operations before income taxes		$ 555,000
Income taxes		(206,000)
Income from continuing operations		$ 349,000
Discontinued operations (see Note Z)		
Loss from operations of component unit -- X Division		
(including gain on disposal of $200,000)	$ (340,000)	
Income tax benefit	56,000	
Loss on discontinued operations		(284,000)
Net income		$ 65,000

---

1)   The **gain or loss on disposal** must be disclosed on the face of the income statement or in the notes.

2)   **Basic and diluted EPS** amounts for a discontinued operation are presented on the face of the income statement or in the notes (SFAS 128).

3)   The caption "Income from continuing operations" should be revised to "Income from continuing operations before extraordinary item" if an extraordinary item is reported. The EPS presentation also may require revision.

Adjustments

5.   **Amounts reported in discontinued operations** of a prior period may require adjustment in the current period. If the adjustment is **directly related** to a **prior-period disposal** of a component, it is reported **currently and separately** in discontinued operations. Its nature and amount are disclosed. Adjustments may include the following:

a.   **Contingencies** arising under the terms of the disposal transaction may be resolved, for example, by purchase price adjustments.

b.   Contingencies directly related to the **pre-disposal operations** of the component may be resolved. Examples are the seller's environmental and warranty obligations.

   c.   **Employee benefit plan obligations** for pensions and other postemployment benefits may be settled. Reporting in discontinued operations is required if the settlement is **directly related** to the disposal.

Stop and review! You have completed the outline for this subunit. Study multiple-choice questions 1 through 4 beginning on page 123.

3.2 EXTRAORDINARY ITEMS

1.   A material transaction or event that is **unusual in nature** and **infrequent in occurrence** in the environment in which the entity operates is an extraordinary item (APB Opinion 30, *Reporting the Results of Operations*).

   a.   A transaction or event is **unusual** if it has a high degree of abnormality and is of a type clearly unrelated to, or only incidentally related to, the ordinary and typical activities of the entity.

> ### EXAMPLE
> A warehouse fire is clearly unrelated to an enterprise's ordinary and typical activities.

   b.   A transaction or event is **infrequent** if it is not reasonably expected to recur in the foreseeable future.

> ### EXAMPLE
> An earthquake in Florida (but not in California) is not reasonably expected to recur.

   c.   Sometimes a pronouncement will specifically classify an item as extraordinary even if these criteria are not met.

Income Statement Presentation

2.   Extraordinary items should be reported individually in a separate section in the income statement, **net of tax**, after results of discontinued operations. Note: disclosure of individual items included in the section also is acceptable.

   a.   **Basic and diluted EPS** amounts for extraordinary items are presented on the face of the income statement or in the notes (SFAS 128).

3.   If a material transaction or event is **unusual or infrequent but not both**, it is not an extraordinary item. Thus, it is reported, **not net of tax**, as a separate component of income from continuing operations. No EPS disclosure is made on the income statement.

Items Not Extraordinary

4.   Certain items are **not considered extraordinary**.

   a.   APB Opinion 30 gives the following examples:

      1)   Write-downs of receivables, inventories, intangible assets, etc.

      2)   Gains and losses from exchange or translation of foreign currencies, including those resulting from major devaluations and revaluations

      3)   Gains and losses on disposal of a component of an entity

      4)   Other gains and losses from sale or abandonment of property, plant, and equipment used in the business

      5)   Effects of a strike, including those against competitors and major suppliers

      6)   Adjustments of accruals on long-term contracts

b.   However, an extraordinary event or transaction may occur that includes a gain or loss listed just above. In this rare case, gains or losses, such as those in 4.a.1) and 4.a.4) [but not 4.a.3)], may be classified as extraordinary.

    1)   The gains or losses that qualify are those directly resulting from a(n)

        a)   **Major casualty** (e.g., flood),
        b)   **Expropriation**, or
        c)   **Prohibition under a new law or regulation**.

c.   Any portion of the losses described in 4.b. that would have resulted from measurement of assets on a **going-concern basis** (e.g., writing down assets to fair value) is not included in the extraordinary items.

Adjustments of Estimates

5.   **Adjustments of estimates** included in extraordinary items previously reported are separately presented and disclosed in the current statements. They are classified in the same way as the original items.

Stop and review! You have completed the outline for this subunit. Study multiple-choice questions 5 through 9 beginning on page 124.

3.3 ACCOUNTING CHANGES AND ERROR CORRECTIONS

1.   If financial information is to have the qualities of **comparability** and **consistency**, entities must not make voluntary changes in accounting principles unless they can be justified as **preferable** (an improvement in financial reporting).

a.   Thus, the **general presumption** is that a principle once adopted is applied **consistently** in preparing financial statements.

2.   SFAS 154, *Accounting Changes and Error Corrections*, defines the following types of **accounting changes:**

a.   A change in accounting principle
b.   A change in accounting estimate
c.   A change in reporting entity

Change in Accounting Principle

3.   A change in accounting principle occurs when an entity (a) adopts a generally accepted principle different from the one previously used, (b) changes the **method** of applying a generally accepted principle, or (c) changes to a generally accepted principle when the principle previously used is no longer generally accepted.

a.   A change in principle does not include the initial adoption of a principle because of an **event or transaction occurring for the first time** or that previously had an immaterial effect. It also does not include adoption or modification of a principle to account for an event or transaction that clearly **differs in substance** from a previously occurring event or transaction.

4.   **Retrospective application** is required for all direct effects and the related income tax effects of a change in principle. Exceptions are made when it is impracticable to determine the cumulative effect or the period-specific effects of the change. **Direct effects** are the changes in assets or liabilities necessary to make the change in principle. An example is an adjustment of an inventory balance to implement a change in the method of measurement. (However, a new pronouncement may prescribe a different transition method.)

a. Retrospective application should not include **indirect effects**. They are changes in current or future cash flows from a change in principle applied retrospectively.

    1) An example of an indirect effect is a required profit-sharing payment based on a reported amount that was directly affected (e.g., revenue).

    2) Indirect effects actually incurred and recognized are reported in the period when the change in principle is made.

b. Retrospective application requires that carrying amounts of (1) assets, (2) liabilities, and (3) retained earnings at the beginning of the first period reported be adjusted for the **cumulative effect** of the new principle on all periods not reported. All periods reported must be individually adjusted for the **period-specific effects** of applying the new principle.

    1) It may be **impracticable** to determine the **cumulative effect** of applying a new principle to any prior period (for example, when the change is from FIFO to LIFO). In that case, the new principle is applied as if the change had been made prospectively at the earliest date practicable.

    2) It may be practicable to determine the cumulative effect of applying the new principle to all prior periods. However, determining the **period-specific effects** on all prior periods presented may be **impracticable**. In these circumstances, cumulative-effect adjustments should be made to the beginning balances for the first period to which the new principle can be applied.

    3) Retrospective application is **impracticable** when

        a) The entity cannot apply the new principle after all **reasonable efforts**;

        b) Assumptions about **management's intent** in a prior period are required that cannot be independently substantiated; or

        c) **Significant estimates** are required, and it is not possible to obtain objective evidence (1) about circumstances existing when amounts would have been recognized, measured, or disclosed and (2) that would have been available when the prior statements were issued.

Change in Accounting Estimate

5. A **change in accounting estimate** results from new information and a reassessment of the future benefits and obligations represented by assets and liabilities. The effects of a change in estimate should be accounted for only in the period of change and any future periods affected.

    a. A **change in estimate inseparable from (effected by) a change in principle** is accounted for as a change in estimate. An example is a change in a method of **depreciation, amortization, or depletion** of long-lived, nonfinancial assets.

Change in Reporting Entity

6. A **change in reporting entity** is retrospectively applied to interim and annual statements. It results when (a) consolidated or combined statements are presented in place of statements of individual entities, (b) consolidated statements include subsidiaries different from those previously included, or (c) combined statements include entities different from those previously included.

    a. A change in reporting entity does not result from a business combination or consolidation of a **variable interest entity**.

Error Correction

7.   An **accounting error** results from (a) a mathematical mistake, (b) a mistake in the application of GAAP, or (c) an oversight or misuse of facts existing when the statements were prepared. A change to a generally accepted accounting principle from one that is not is an error correction, **not an accounting change**.

   a.   An accounting error related to a prior period is reported as a **prior period adjustment** by restating the prior-period statements. **Restatement** requires the same adjustments as retrospective application of a new principle.

8.   Items of profit or loss related to **corrections of errors** in prior-period statements are prior-period adjustments.

   a.   They are debited or credited (net of tax) to **retained earnings** and reported as adjustments in the statement of changes in equity or in the statement of retained earnings. They are not included in net income. Prior-period adjustments reported in **single-period statements** are adjustments of the opening balance of retained earnings (SFAS 16, *Prior Period Adjustments*).

   b.   If **comparative statements** are presented, corresponding adjustments should be made to net income (and its components) and retained earnings (and other affected balances) for all periods reported (APB Opinion 9, *Reporting the Results of Operations*).

9.   **Error analysis.** A correcting journal entry combines the reversal of the error with the correct entry. Thus, it requires a determination of the journal entry originally recorded, event or transaction that occurred, and correct journal entry.

EXAMPLE

If the purchase of a fixed asset on account had been debited to purchases:

Incorrect Entry	Correct Entry	Correcting Entry
Purchases	Fixed asset	Fixed asset
Payables	Payables	Purchases

If cash had been incorrectly credited:

Incorrect Entry	Correct Entry	Correcting Entry
Purchases	Fixed asset	Fixed Asset
Cash	Payables	Cash
		Purchases
		Payables

---

   a.   Error analysis addresses (1) whether an error affects prior-period statements, (2) the timing of error detection, (3) whether comparative statements are presented, and (4) whether the error is counterbalancing.

   1)   An error affecting **prior-period statements** may or may not affect net income. For example, misclassifying an item as a gain rather than a revenue does not affect income and is readily correctable. No prior-period adjustment to retained earnings is required.

2)   An error that affects prior-period net income is **counterbalancing** if it self-corrects over two periods. For example, understating ending inventory for one period (and the beginning inventory of the next period) understates **(U)** the net income and retained earnings of the first period but overstates **(O)** the net income and retained earnings of the next period by the same amount (assuming no tax changes). However, despite the self-correction, the financial statements remain misstated. They are restated if **presented comparatively** in a later period.

EXAMPLE			
Year 1		**Year 2**	
Beginning inventory		Beginning inventory	U
+ Purchases		+ Purchases	
– Ending inventory	(U)	– Ending inventory	
= Cost of goods sold	(O)	= Cost of goods sold	(U)
Net income	(U)	Net income	(O)
Retained earnings	(U)	Retained earnings	(O)

a)   An example of a **noncounterbalancing** error is a misstatement of depreciation. Such an error does not self-correct over two periods. Thus, a prior-period adjustment will be necessary.

b)   In principle, a counterbalancing error requires no correcting entry if detection occurs two or more periods afterward (assuming no tax changes). Earlier detection necessitates a correcting entry.

Stop and review! You have completed the outline for this subunit. Study multiple-choice questions 10 through 17 beginning on page 126.

3.4 EARNINGS PER SHARE (EPS)

1.   **Earnings per share (EPS)** is the amount of current-period earnings that can be associated with a **single share** of a corporation's **common stock**. The guidance regarding calculation and presentation of EPS must be followed by public entities and by other entities that choose to report EPS (SFAS 128, *Earnings per Share*).

a.   EPS is calculated **only for common stock** because common shareholders are the residual owners of a corporation.

1)   Because preferred shareholders have a superior claim to the entity's earnings, amounts associated with **preferred stock** must be **removed** during the calculation of EPS.

Simple Capital Structure

2.   An entity with a simple capital structure must report one category of EPS: **basic earnings per share (BEPS)**.

$$BEPS = \frac{Income\ available\ to\ common\ shareholders\ (IACS)}{Weighted\text{-}average\ number\ of\ common\ shares\ outstanding}$$

a.   "Entities with simple capital structures, that is, those with **only common stock outstanding**, shall present basic per-share amounts for **income from continuing operations** and for **net income** on the face of the income statement" (SFAS 128).

   b.   Thus, IACS must be calculated twice.

EXAMPLE

At year-end, an entity had only 10,000,000 shares of $1 par value common stock in its capital structure. The entity issued no new shares during the year. Its income from continuing operations and net income for the year were $1,278,000 and $1,141,000 respectively.

BEPS calculations:

Income from continuing operations:	$1,278,000 ÷ 10,000,000 = $0.128
Net income:	$1,141,000 ÷ 10,000,000 = $0.114

---

3.   All other entities must report diluted earnings per share (DEPS) as well as BEPS.

   a.   The DEPS calculation includes the effects of **dilutive potential common stock (PCS)**.

       1)   PCS is a security or other contract that may entitle the holder to obtain common stock. Examples include

           a)   **Convertible securities** (preferred stock or debt)
           b)   **Options, warrants, and their equivalents**

               i)   Equivalents include nonvested stock granted to employees, stock purchase contracts, and partially paid stock subscriptions.

           c)   **Contingently issuable common stock**

               i)   The conditions for contingent issuance (passage of time or a specified market price, level of earnings, etc.) may be satisfied by year-end. The shares are then deemed to have been issued at the beginning of the period or date of the contingent stock agreement.

               ii) However, the conditions may not have been met at year-end. In this case, the shares included in the DEPS denominator equal those that would have been issued if the end of the year were the end of the contingency interval.

EXAMPLE

The contingency may involve earnings. The contingently issuable shares equal those issuable (if any) based on the current period's earnings if the result is dilutive.

---

       2)   PCS is **dilutive** if its inclusion in the calculation of EPS results in a **reduction** of EPS (or an increase in loss per share).

Basic Earnings per Share (BEPS)

4.   **Calculation of the BEPS Numerator**

   a.   **Income available to common shareholders (IACS)** is the BEPS numerator.

       1)   Neither BEPS amount (income from continuing operations and net income) is calculated directly from the amount reported for that line item on the GAAP-based income statement. The reason is that EPS is based on the amount available to holders of common stock.

2) Preferred dividends **declared or accumulated in the current period** affect the calculation of the BEPS numerator.

    a) Undistributed accumulated preferred dividends for prior years do not affect the calculation. They are included in BEPS of prior years.

3) The following calculation is performed for net income and income from continuing operations (or other number):

           Income statement amount
Minus: Dividends on preferred stock for the current period
           (cumulative or declared noncumulative)
Equals: Income available to common shareholders

EXAMPLE

An entity has two classes of preferred stock. It declared a 4% dividend on its $100,000 of noncumulative preferred stock. The entity did not declare a dividend on its $200,000 of 6% cumulative preferred stock. Undistributed dividends for the past four years have accumulated on this stock. The following is an excerpt from the entity's condensed income statement for the year:

Income from continuing operations before income taxes	**$1,666,667**
Income taxes	(666,667)
Income from continuing operations	**$1,000,000**
Discontinued operations:	
Income from operations of component unit -- Pipeline	
Division (including gain on disposal of $2,897) $15,283	
Income tax expense (5,283)	10,000
Income before extraordinary item	**$1,010,000**
Loss from volcano damage, net of applicable income	
taxes of $52,221	(140,000)
Net income	**$ 870,000**

The numerators for income from continuing operations and for net income are calculated as follows:

	Income from continuing operations	Net income
Income statement amounts	**$1,000,000**	**$870,000**
Declared or accumulated preferred dividends:		
Dividends declared on noncumulative preferred stock in the current period	(4,000)	(4,000)
Dividends accumulated on cumulative preferred stock in the current period	(12,000)	(12,000)
Income available to common shareholders	**$ 984,000**	**$854,000**

b. Given an extraordinary item but no discontinued operation, BEPS is reported for **income before extraordinary items**, not income from continuing operations.

5.   **Calculation of the BEPS Denominator**

   a.   The **weighted-average number of common shares outstanding** is determined by relating the portion of the reporting period that the shares were outstanding to the total time in the period.

      1)   Weighting is necessary because some shares may have been issued or reacquired during the period.

EXAMPLE

In the previous example, assume the following common stock transactions during the year just ended:

Date	Stock Transactions	Shares Outstanding	Times: Portion of Year	Equals: Weighted Average
Jan 1	Beginning balance	240,000	2 ÷ 12	40,000
Mar 1	Issued 60,000 shares	300,000	5 ÷ 12	125,000
Aug 1	Repurchased 20,000 shares	280,000	3 ÷ 12	70,000
Nov 1	Issued 80,000 shares	360,000	2 ÷ 12	60,000
	Total			295,000

The **BEPS** amounts for income from continuing operations and net income are **$3.336** ($984,000 ÷ 295,000) and **$2.895** ($854,000 ÷ 295,000), respectively.

---

   b.   **Stock dividends and stock splits** require an adjustment to the weighted-average of common shares outstanding.

      1)   EPS amounts for all periods presented are **adjusted retroactively** to reflect the change in capital structure **as if it had occurred at the beginning** of the first period presented.

      2)   Adjustments are made for such changes **even if they occur after the end of the current period** but before issuance of the statements.

EXAMPLE

In the previous example, assume declaration of a 50% common stock dividend and a 2-for-1 common stock split during the year:

Date	Stock Transactions	Shares Outstanding	Times: Restate for Stock Div.	Times: Restate for Stock Split	Times: Portion of Year	Equals: Weighted Average
Jan 1	Beginning balance	240,000	1.5	2	2 ÷ 12	120,000
Mar 1	Issued 60,000 shares	300,000	1.5	2	5 ÷ 12	375,000
Jun 1	Distributed 50% stock dividend	450,000				
Aug 1	Repurchased 20,000 shares	430,000		2	3 ÷ 12	215,000
Oct 1	Distributed 2-for-1 stock split	860,000				
Nov 1	Issued 80,000 shares	940,000			2 ÷ 12	156,667
	Total					866,667

The **BEPS** amounts for income from continuing operations and net income are **$1.135** ($984,000 ÷ 866,667) and **$0.985** ($854,000 ÷ 866,667), respectively.

Diluted Earnings per Share (DEPS)

6. **Calculation of DEPS**

   a. DEPS measures performance after considering the effect on the numerator and denominator of **dilutive** PCS. DEPS is calculated as follows:

      1) **The BEPS denominator is increased** to include the weighted-average number of additional shares of common stock that would have been outstanding if dilutive PCS had been issued.

      2) **Amounts are added back to the BEPS numerator** for any dividends on convertible preferred stock and the after-tax interest (after amortization of discount or premium) related to any convertible debt.

         a) The numerator also is adjusted for **other changes in income or loss**, such as profit-sharing expenses, that would result from the assumed issuance of PCS.

         $$DEPS = \frac{BEPS\ numerator + Effect\ of\ dilutive\ PCS}{BEPS\ denominator + Effect\ of\ dilutive\ PCS}$$

      3) Amounts are based on the **most advantageous conversion rate or exercise price** from the perspective of the holder.

         a) Previously reported DEPS is **not** retroactively adjusted for subsequent conversions or changes in the market price of the common stock.

         b) The calculation of DEPS does not assume the conversion, exercise, or contingent issuance of **antidilutive** securities, i.e., securities that increase EPS or decrease loss per share.

         c) Dilutive securities issued during a period and dilutive convertible securities for which (1) conversion options lapse, (2) preferred stock is redeemed, or (3) debt is extinguished are included in the DEPS denominator for the **period they were outstanding**.

            i) Moreover, dilutive convertible securities that were actually converted are included for the **period before conversion**. Common shares actually issued are included for the **period after conversion**.

   b. Three methods are used to determine the **dilutive effect** of PCS: (a) the if-converted method for convertible securities, (b) the treasury stock method for call options and warrants, and (c) the reverse treasury stock method for put options.

The If-Converted Method

7. The if-converted method calculates DEPS assuming the conversion of all dilutive **convertible securities** at the beginning of the period (or time of issue, if later).

   a. The conversion of **antidilutive** securities (those whose conversion would **increase EPS** or decrease loss per share) is **not** assumed. Thus, convertible PCS is antidilutive if the current dividend or after-tax interest per common share issuable exceeds BEPS.

8. **Dilution.** In determining whether PCS is dilutive, each issue or series of issues is considered **separately and in sequence** from the most dilutive to the least dilutive.

   a. The issue with the **lowest earnings per incremental share** is included in DEPS before issues with higher earnings per incremental share.

   b. If the issue with the lowest earnings per incremental share is found to be dilutive with respect to BEPS, it is included in a **trial calculation** of DEPS.

   c. If the issue with the next lowest earnings per incremental share is dilutive with respect to the first trial calculation of DEPS, it is included in a new DEPS calculation that adjusts the numerator and denominator from the prior calculation.

   d. This process continues until all issues of PCS have been tested.

9.   If a **discontinued operation** or **extraordinary item** is reported, the same number of shares used to adjust the denominator for **income from continuing operations** (or income before extraordinary items) is used to adjust the DEPS denominator for all other reported earnings amounts.

   a.   This rule applies even if the effect on the other amounts is antidilutive.

10. If a **loss from continuing operations** or a loss from continuing operations available to common shareholders is reported, PCS is **not** included in the calculation of DEPS for any reported earnings amount. Its effect on the continuing operations calculation is **antidilutive**.

EXAMPLE

In the continuing example, assume that the noncumulative preferred stock is convertible into 20,000 shares of common stock. Also assume that, on the first day of the year, the entity issued $2,400,000 of 8% debt, convertible into 20,000 shares of common stock. Its tax rate is 40%.

The entity has two issues of PCS: the 4% noncumulative preferred stock and the 8% convertible debt. The earnings per incremental share of the stock is $.067 [($100,000 × .04) ÷ 60,000 PCS as adjusted for the stock dividend and stock split]. The earnings per incremental share of the debt is $1.92 {[($2,400,000 × .08) × (1.0 − .4)] ÷ 60,000 PCS}.

Because the $.067 incremental effect of the convertible preferred is lower, it is more dilutive. Thus, it is compared with the $1.135 BEPS amount for income from continuing operations. Because $.067 is lower than $1.135, the convertible preferred is dilutive and is included in the trial calculation of DEPS. The result is $1.066 [($984,000 + $4,000) ÷ (866,667 shares + 60,000 PCS)].

However, the $1.92 incremental effect of the convertible debt is higher than the $1.066 trial calculation. The convertible debt is therefore antidilutive. It is excluded from the DEPS calculation.

No test for dilution is performed for net income.

The Treasury Stock Method

11. The second method used to determine the dilutive effect of PCS is the **treasury stock method**. It is used to determine the dilutive effect of outstanding **call options and warrants**. They are **dilutive** if the **average market price** for the period **exceeds the exercise price**.

   a.   The options and warrants are assumed to be exercised at the beginning of the period (or time of issuance, if later). The **assumed proceeds** equal the weighted-average number of shares issuable upon exercise times the option or warrant price.

      1)   The options or warrants may relate to **unrecognized compensation cost for future services**. In this case, the assumed proceeds also include (a) such cost and (b) the amount of any **excess tax benefit** (tax deduction in excess of compensation expense recognized for financial reporting).

         a)   The excess benefit results from an increase in the fair value of the optioned shares between the measurement date and the date at which the tax deduction is calculated.

b. The proceeds are assumed to be used to purchase common stock at the **average market price** during the period.

c. To arrive at the **DEPS denominator**, the BEPS denominator is assumed to be increased by the excess, if any, of the shares issued over the number purchased.

EXAMPLE

Troupe Company had 100,000 shares of common stock issued and outstanding at January 1. On July 1, Troupe issued a 10% stock dividend. Unexercised call options to purchase 20,000 shares of Troupe's common stock (adjusted for the stock dividend) at $20 per share were outstanding at the beginning and end of the year. The average market price of the stock (not affected by the stock dividend) was $25 per share. Net income for the year ended December 31 was $550,000. What is DEPS for the year?

A stock dividend occurring before issuance of the financial statements requires a retroactive adjustment at the beginning of the first period presented. Hence, the 110,000 shares outstanding after the stock dividend are deemed to have been outstanding during the entire year.

The options are not antidilutive because the exercise price was less than the average market price. Accordingly, exercise of the options is assumed to have occurred at the beginning of the year at the exercise price of $20. Under the treasury stock method, the assumed proceeds of $400,000 (20,000 shares × $20) are used to repurchase 16,000 shares ($400,000 ÷ $25) at the average market price. Thus, DEPS equals $4.82 {$550,000 ÷ [110,000 shares + (20,000 assumed issued − 16,000 assumed repurchased)]}.

Reverse Treasury Stock Method

12. The third method used to determine the dilutive effect of PCS is the **reverse treasury stock method**. It is used when the entity has entered into contracts to repurchase its own stock, for example, when it has **written put options** held by other parties. When the contracts are **in the money** (the exercise price exceeds the average market price), the potential dilutive effect on EPS is calculated by

a. Assuming the issuance at the beginning of the period of sufficient shares to raise the proceeds needed to satisfy the contracts,

b. Assuming those proceeds are used to repurchase shares, and

c. Including the excess of shares assumed to be issued over those assumed to be repurchased in the calculation of the DEPS denominator.

13. Options held by the entity on its own stock, whether they are puts or calls, are not included in the DEPS denominator because their effect is antidilutive.

Income Statement Presentation

14. An entity with a **simple capital structure** must report BEPS for income from continuing operations and net income on the **face of the income statement**. It does not report DEPS.

a. **Any other entity** must present BEPS and DEPS for income from continuing operations and net income with equal prominence on the **face of the income statement**.

b. An entity that reports a **discontinued operation**, an **extraordinary item**, or both must report BEPS and DEPS for the item(s) on the **face of the income statement or in the notes**.

15. EPS disclosures are **made for all periods** for which an income statement or earnings summary is presented.

   a. For each period for which an income statement is presented, the following are **disclosed**:

      1) A reconciliation by individual security of the numerators and denominators of BEPS and DEPS for income from continuing operations, including income and share effects

      2) The effect of preferred dividends on the BEPS numerator

      3) PCS not included in DEPS because it would have had an antidilutive effect in the periods reported

16. If DEPS data are **reported for at least one period**, they are **reported for all periods** shown, even if they are equal to BEPS amounts.

17. **Subsequent events** occur after the end of a reporting period but before the statements are issued. For the latest period for which an income statement is presented, an entity must disclose subsequent events that would have had a material effect on common shares or PCS outstanding if the transaction had occurred prior to the balance sheet date.

18. An entity must explain within its financial statements the **rights of outstanding securities**. It also must disclose the number of shares issued upon conversion, exercise, or satisfaction of conditions during the last fiscal year and any subsequent interim period presented (SFAS 129, *Disclosure of Information about Capital Structure*).

   a. The equity section should disclose in the aggregate the **preferences** given in involuntary liquidation to senior stock that are considerably greater than par or stated value. The entity also must disclose the aggregate or per-share amounts at which preferred stock is callable and the aggregate and per-share amounts of preferred dividends in arrears.

   b. Other necessary disclosures are the **redemption requirements** for the next 5 years for capital stock redeemable at fixed or determinable prices and dates.

Stop and review! You have completed the outline for this subunit. Study multiple-choice questions 18 through 26 beginning on page 129.

3.5 LONG-TERM CONSTRUCTION CONTRACTS

The Completed-Contract Method

1. The **completed-contract** method is used to account for a long-term contracted-for project when the percentage-of-completion method is inappropriate. It **defers all contract costs** until the project is completed. It then matches the costs of completion with revenue. Revenue and gross profit are recognized only upon completion.

   a. All costs are deferred in a **construction-in-progress** (inventory) account that is closed to cost of sales when the project is completed.

The Percentage-of-Completion Method

2. The **percentage-of-completion method** is presumed to be preferable. It is used to recognize revenue on long-term contracts when the

   a. Extent of progress toward completion, contract revenue, and contract costs are reasonably estimable;

   b. Enforceable rights regarding goods or services to be provided, the consideration to be exchanged, and the terms of settlement are clearly specified; and

   c. Obligations of the parties are expected to be fulfilled (AICPA SOP 81-1, *Accounting for Performance of Construction-Type and Certain Production-Type Contracts*).

3. Recognition of **revenue or gross profit** is based upon three factors:

a. Estimated total revenue or gross profit

b. Percentage completed based on the **progress toward completion** (the relationship of costs incurred to estimated total costs is the recommended but not the only basis for determining such progress)

$$\% \ completed = \frac{Costs \ incurred \ to \ date}{Estimated \ total \ costs}$$

c. Revenue or gross profit recognized to date

1) The **estimated total gross profit** equals the contract price (total revenue) minus the total estimated costs. The percentage completed times the total expected revenue or gross profit equals the total revenue or gross profit to be **recognized to date**. The revenue or gross profit recognized in prior periods is then subtracted from the total to date to determine the amount to be **recognized in the current period**.

Contract price	$ XX
Minus: cost incurred to date	(XX)
Minus: estimated cost to complete	(XX)
Estimated total gross profit	$ XX
Times: % completed	XX
Gross profit recognized to date	$ XX
Minus: gross profit recognized in prior periods	(XX)
Gross profit recognized in current period	$ XX

4. When estimated revenue and costs are revised, a **change in accounting estimate** is recognized. Recognition of the change is in (a) the period of change if only that period is affected or (b) the period of change and future periods if both are affected.

5. Under both the percentage-of-completion and completed-contract methods, the **full estimated loss** on any project is recognized as soon as it becomes apparent.

EXAMPLE

A contractor agrees to build a bridge that will take 3 years to complete. The contract price is $2 million and expected total costs are $1.2 million.

	Year 1	Year 2	Year 3
Costs incurred during each year	$300,000	$600,000	$550,000
Costs expected in future	900,000	600,000	0

By the end of Year 1, 25% ($300,000 ÷ $1,200,000) of expected costs has been incurred. Thus, the contractor will recognize 25% of the revenue or gross profit that will be earned on the project. The **total gross profit is expected to be** $800,000 ($2,000,000 – $1,200,000), so $200,000 ($800,000 × 25%) of gross profit should be recognized in Year 1.

At the end of Year 2, total costs incurred are $900,000 ($300,000 + $600,000). Given that $600,000 is expected to be incurred in the future, the **total expected cost** is $1,500,000 ($900,000 + $600,000), and the estimate of gross profit is $500,000 ($2,000,000 contract price – $1,500,000 costs). If the project is 60% complete ($900,000 ÷ $1,500,000), $300,000 of **cumulative gross profit** should be recognized for Years 1 and 2 ($500,000 × 60%). Because $200,000 was recognized in Year 1, $100,000 should be recognized in Year 2.

At the end of the third year, total costs are $1,450,000. Thus, the **total gross profit** is known to be $550,000. Because a total of $300,000 was recognized in Years 1 and 2, $250,000 should be recognized in Year 3.

Comparative Journal Entries

6.   Journal entries, assuming payment is made at the end of the contract:

	%-of-Completion		Completed-Contract	
Year 1: Construction in progress	$300,000		$300,000	
Cash or accounts payable		$300,000		$300,000
			--	
Construction in progress	$200,000			
Construction gross profit		$200,000		--
Year 2: Construction in progress	$600,000		$600,000	
Cash or accounts payable		$600,000		$600,000
			--	
Construction in progress	$100,000			
Construction gross profit		$100,000		--
Year 3: Construction in progress	$550,000		$550,000	
Cash or accounts payable		$550,000		$550,000
Cash	$2,000,000		$2,000,000	
Construction in progress		$1,750,000		$1,450,000
Construction gross profit		250,000		550,000

a.   Ordinarily, **progress billings** are made and payments are received during the term of the contract. The entries are

Accounts receivable	$XXX	
Progress billings		$XXX
Cash	$XXX	
Accounts receivable		$XXX

1)   Neither billing nor the receipt of cash affects gross profit. Moreover, billing, receipt of payment, and incurrence of cost have the same effects under both accounting methods.

b.   The difference between construction in progress (costs and recognized gross profit) and progress billings to date is reported as a **current asset** if construction in progress exceeds total billings and as a **current liability** if billings exceed construction in progress. The **closing entry** is

Progress billings	$XXX	
Construction in progress		$XXX

c.   A variation on the foregoing entries is to credit periodic revenue for the gross amount. This practice requires a **debit to a nominal account** (a cost of revenue earned account similar to cost of goods sold) that equals the costs incurred in the current period. For example, in Year 1, the second entry would be

Construction in progress (gross profit)	$200,000	
Construction expenses (a nominal account)	300,000	
Gross revenue		$500,000

Stop and review! You have completed the outline for this subunit. Study multiple-choice questions 27 through 30 beginning on page 132.

3.6 REVENUE RECOGNITION AFTER DELIVERY

The Installment Method

1. The installment method is not acceptable **except** when receivables are collectible over an extended period, and "there is no reasonable basis for estimating the degree of collectibility" (APB Opinion 10, *Omnibus Opinion – 1966*).

    a. The installment method recognizes a partial profit on a sale as each installment is collected.

       1) This approach differs from the ordinary procedure, that is, recognition of revenue when a transaction is complete. Thus, when collection problems (bad debts) can be **reasonably estimated**, the full profit is usually recognized at the point of sale.

    b. The amount recognized each period under the installment method is the **realized gross profit**. This amount equals the **gross profit percentage** (gross profit ÷ selling price) on installment sales for the period times the cash collected. In addition, **interest income** must be accounted for separately from the gross profit on the sale.

$$Gross\ profit\ percentage = \frac{Gross\ profit}{Installment\ sales}$$

	Year 1	Year 2	Year 3
Installment sales	$ XX	$ XX	$ XX
Minus: cost of installment sales	(XX)	(XX)	(XX)
Gross profit	$ XX	$ XX	$ XX

c. If the goods sold are **repossessed** due to nonpayment, their net realizable value, remaining deferred gross profit, and any loss are debited. The remaining receivable is credited.

EXAMPLE

Assume that a TV costing $600 is the only item sold on the installment basis in Year 1. Also assume that it was sold for a price of $1,000 on November 1, Year 1. A down payment of $100 was received, and the remainder is due in nine monthly payments of $100 each. The entry for the sale is

Cash	$100	
Installment receivable (Year 1)	900	
Inventory		$600
Deferred gross profit (Year 1)		400

In December when the first installment is received, the entry is

Cash	$100	
Installment receivable (Year 1)		$100

At December 31, the **deferred gross profit** must be adjusted to report the portion that has been earned. Given that 20% ($200 ÷ $1,000) of the total price has been received, 20% of the gross profit has been earned. The entry is

Deferred gross profit (Year 1)	$80	
Realized gross profit		$80

Net income should include only the $80 realized gross profit for the period. The balance sheet should report a receivable of $800 minus the deferred gross profit of $320. Thus, the net receivable is $480.

Balance sheet presentation

Installment receivable	$ 800
Minus: deferred gross profit	(320)
Net installment receivable	$480

In Year 2, the remaining $800 is received, and the $320 balance of deferred gross profit is recognized. If only $400 were received in Year 2 (if payments were extended), the December, Year 2, statements would report a $400 installment receivable and $160 of deferred gross profit.

Assume the TV had to be **repossessed** because no payments after the down payment were made by the buyer. The realized gross profit at December 31 would be only $40 [$400 × ($100 ÷ $1,000)]. Moreover, the used TV would be recorded at its net realizable value minus a resale profit. Assume that fair value at the time of repossession was $500 and that repair costs and sales commissions will equal $100.

Inventory of used merchandise	$400	
Deferred gross profit	360	
Loss on repossession	140	
Installment receivable		$900

The **loss on repossession** is the difference between the $400 NRV ($500 fair value – $100 repair and sales costs) and the $540 carrying amount [$900 remaining receivable – ($400 deferred gross profit – $40 realized gross profit)] of the receivable.

Cost Recovery Method

2. The **cost-recovery method** may be used only in the same circumstances as the installment method. However, no profit is recognized until collections exceed the cost of the item sold. Subsequent receipts are treated entirely as revenues.

> ### EXAMPLE
>
> In Year 1, Creditor made a $100,000 sale. The cost of the item sold was $70,000, and Year 1 collections equaled $50,000. In Year 2, collections equaled $25,000, and $10,000 of the receivable was determined to be uncollectible. The net receivable (receivable – deferred profit) was $0 at the end of Year 2. The following entries are based on the cost-recovery method:
>
> | | | | |
> |---|---|---|---|
> | Year 1: | Receivable | $100,000 | |
> | | Inventory | | $70,000 |
> | | Deferred gross profit | | 30,000 |
> | | | | |
> | | Cash | $50,000 | |
> | | Receivable | | $50,000 |
> | | | | |
> | Year 2: | Cash | $25,000 | |
> | | Deferred gross profit | 5,000 | |
> | | Receivable | | $25,000 |
> | | Realized gross profit | | 5,000 |
> | | | | |
> | | Deferred gross profit | $10,000 | |
> | | Receivable | | $10,000 |

Deposit Method

3. This method is used when cash is received, but the criteria for a sale have not been met. Thus, the seller continues to account for the property in the same way as an owner. No revenue or profit is recognized because it has not been earned, e.g., by transferring the property. The entry is

Cash	$XXX	
Deposit liability		$XXX

Stop and review! You have completed the outline for this subunit. Study multiple-choice questions 31 through 37 beginning on page 134.

3.7 CONSIGNMENT ACCOUNTING

Consignment Sales

1. A **consignment sale** is an arrangement between the owner of goods and a sales agent. Consigned goods are not sold but rather transferred to an agent for possible sale. The consignor records **sales** only when the goods are sold to third parties by the consignee.

   a. Goods on consignment are included in **inventory**. Costs of transporting the goods to the consignee are inventoriable costs, not selling expenses.

   b. The consignee never records the consigned goods as an asset.

2. The **consignee** does not recognize the initial acquisition.

   a. **Sales** are recorded with a debit to cash (or accounts receivable) and credits to commission income and accounts payable to the consignor.

   b. Any **expenses** incurred by the consignee on behalf of the consignor (such as freight-in or service costs) are reductions of the payable to the consignor.

   c. Payments to the consignor result in a debit to the payable and a credit to cash.

3. The **consignor** records the initial shipment by a debit to **consigned goods out** (a separate inventory account) and a credit to inventory at cost.

    a. Receipts and expenses incurred by the consignee are recorded by debits to cash, commission expense, consigned goods out, and cost of goods sold. Credits are to sales and consigned goods out.

Comparative Journal Entries

EXAMPLE

The consignor ships 100 units, costing $50 each, to the consignee:

CONSIGNOR			CONSIGNEE
Consigned goods out	$5,000		Only a memorandum entry
Inventory		$5,000	

The consignee pays $120 for freight-in:

CONSIGNOR			CONSIGNEE		
No entry at this time			Payable to consignor	$120	
			Cash		$120

The consignee sells 80 units at $80 each. The consignee is to receive a 20% commission on all sales:

CONSIGNOR		CONSIGNEE		
No entry at this time		Cash	$6,400	
		Payable to consignor		$5,120
		Commission income		$1,280

The consignee sends a monthly statement to the consignor with the balance owed. The cost of shipping goods to the consignee, including the $120 payment by the consignee, is debited as a cost of consigned inventory:

CONSIGNOR			CONSIGNEE		
Cash	$5,000		Payable to consignor	$5,000	
Commission expense	1,280		Cash		$5,000
Consigned goods out	120				
Cost of goods sold	4,096				
Sales		$6,400			
Consigned goods out		4,096			

The consignee may use **consignment in** rather than payable to consignor. Consignment is in a receivable/payable account.

4. **Consigned goods out** is used in a perpetual or periodic inventory system when consignments are recorded in separate accounts.

    a. If the consignor uses a **perpetual system**, the credit on shipment is to inventory.

    b. If a **periodic** system is used, the credit is to **consignment shipments**, a contra cost of goods sold account. Its balance is then closed at the end of the period when the inventory adjustments are made.

Stop and review! You have completed the outline for this subunit. Study multiple-choice questions 38 through 41 beginning on page 136.

QUESTIONS

3.1 Discontinued Operations

1. For the purpose of reporting discontinued operations, a component of an entity is best defined as

A. An operating segment or one level below an operating segment.

B. A set of operations and cash flows clearly distinguishable from the rest of the entity for operational and financial reporting purposes.

C. A separate major line of business or class of customer.

D. A significant disposal group.

Answer (B) is correct. *(Publisher, adapted)*
REQUIRED: The nature of a component of an entity.
DISCUSSION: According to SFAS 144, a component of an entity is a set of operations and cash flows clearly distinguishable from the rest of the entity for operational and financial reporting purposes. It may be, but is not limited to, a reportable segment or an operating segment (SFAS 131), a reporting unit (SFAS 142), a subsidiary, or an asset group [a long-lived asset(s) to be held and used included with other assets and liabilities not covered by SFAS 144, provided that the group is the unit of accounting for the long-lived asset(s)].
Answer (A) is incorrect because the term "component of an entity" was broadly defined to improve the usefulness of information by requiring more frequent reporting of discontinued operations. Thus, a component of an entity is not restricted to a reporting unit, that is, an operating segment (SFAS 131) or one level below an operating segment (SFAS 142). Answer (C) is incorrect because, under the pronouncement superseded by SFAS 144, reporting of a discontinued operation was limited to a separate major line of business or class of customer. Answer (D) is incorrect because the criteria for the reporting of discontinued operations do not emphasize either the significance of a component or any quantitative threshold.

2. On January 1, Year 4, Dart, Inc. entered into an agreement to sell the assets and product line of its Jay Division, which met the criteria for classification as an operating segment. The sale was consummated on December 31, Year 4, and resulted in a gain on disposal of $400,000. The division's operations resulted in losses before income tax of $225,000 in Year 4 and $125,000 in Year 3. Dart's income tax rate is 30% for both years, and the criteria for reporting a discontinued operation have been met. In a comparative statement of income for Year 4 and Year 3, under the caption discontinued operations, Dart should report a gain (loss) of

	Year 4	Year 3
A.	$122,500	$(87,500)
B.	$122,500	$0
C.	$(157,500)	$(87,500)
D.	$(157,500)	$0

Answer (A) is correct. *(CPA, adapted)*
REQUIRED: The amounts reported for discontinued operations in comparative statements.
DISCUSSION: When a component (e.g., an operating segment) has been disposed of or is classified as held for sale, and the criteria for reporting a discontinued operation have been met, the income statements for current and prior periods must report its operating results in discontinued operations. The gain from operations of the component for Year 4 equals the $225,000 operating loss for Year 4, plus the $400,000 gain on disposal. The pretax gain is therefore $175,000 ($400,000 – $225,000). The after-tax amount is $122,500 [$175,000 × (1 – .30)]. Because Year 3 was prior to the time that the component was classified as held for sale, the $125,000 of operating losses would have been reported under income from continuing operations in the Year 3 income statement as originally issued. This loss is now attributable to discontinued operations, and the Year 3 financial statements presented for comparative purposes must be reclassified. In the reclassified Year 3 income statement, the $125,000 pretax loss should be shown as an $87,500 [$125,000 × (1 – .30)] loss from discontinued operations.
Answer (B) is incorrect because the comparative statement of income for Year 4 and Year 3 should report a loss on discontinued operations for Year 3. Answer (C) is incorrect because an after-tax loss of $157,500 for Year 4 does not consider the gain on disposal. Answer (D) is incorrect because the comparative statement of income for Year 4 and Year 3 should report a loss on discontinued operations for Year 3, and an after-tax loss of $157,500 for Year 4 does not consider the gain on disposal.

3. On April 30, Deer Corp. committed to a plan to sell a component of the entity. As a result, the component's operations and cash flows will be eliminated from the entity's operations, and the entity will have no significant continuing post-disposal involvement in the component's operations. For the period January 1 through April 30, the component had revenues of $500,000 and expenses of $800,000. The assets of the component were sold on October 15 at a loss for which no tax benefit is available. In its income statement for the year ended December 31, how should Deer report the component's operations from January 1 to April 30?

A. $500,000 and $800,000 should be included with revenues and expenses, respectively, as part of continuing operations.

B. $300,000 should be reported as part of the loss on disposal of a component.

C. $300,000 should be reported as an extraordinary loss.

D. $300,000 should be included in the determination of income or loss from operations of a discontinued component.

Answer (D) is correct. *(CPA, adapted)*
REQUIRED: The proper reporting of a loss related to operations of a discontinued component.
DISCUSSION: The results of operations of a component that has been disposed of or is classified as held for sale, together with any loss on a writedown to fair value minus cost to sell (or a gain from recoupment thereof), minus applicable income taxes (benefit), should be reported separately as a component of income (discontinued operations) before extraordinary items. These results should be reported in the period(s) when they occur (SFAS 144). Thus, the operating results of the component from January 1 through October 15 and the loss on disposal are included in the determination of income or loss from operations of the discontinued component.
Answer (A) is incorrect because discontinued operations should not be reported as part of continuing operations. Answer (B) is incorrect because discontinued operations should be presented in two categories: income or loss from operations of the discontinued component and the applicable income taxes (benefit). The loss on disposal is included in the determination of income or loss from the discontinued component. Answer (C) is incorrect because income or loss from discontinued operations should be reported separately as a component of income before extraordinary items.

4. During January of Year 6, Doe Corp. agreed to sell the assets and product line of its Hart division. The sale was completed on January 15, Year 7, and resulted in a gain on disposal of $900,000. Hart's operating losses were $600,000 for Year 6 and $50,000 for the period January 1 through January 15, Year 7. Disregarding income taxes and assuming that the criteria for reporting a discontinued operation are met, what amount of net gain (loss) should be reported in Doe's comparative Year 7 and Year 6 income statements?

	Year 7	Year 6
A.	$0	$250,000
B.	$250,000	$0
C.	$850,000	$(600,000)
D.	$900,000	$(650,000)

Answer (C) is correct. *(CPA, adapted)*
REQUIRED: The amounts reported in comparative statements for discontinued operations.
DISCUSSION: The results of operations of a component classified as held for sale are reported separately in the income statement under discontinued operations in the periods when they occur. Thus, in its Year 6 income statement, Doe should recognize a $600,000 loss. For Year 7, a gain of $850,000 should be recognized ($900,000 – $50,000).
Answer (A) is incorrect because $250,000 is the net gain for Year 6 and Year 7. However, the results for Year 7 may not be anticipated. Answer (B) is incorrect because the results for Year 6 should not be deferred. Answer (D) is incorrect because the operating loss for January Year 7 should be recognized in Year 7.

3.2 Extraordinary Items

5. A transaction that is unusual in nature and infrequent in occurrence should be reported separately as a component of income

A. Before cumulative effect of a change in accounting principle and after discontinued operations of a component unit.

B. After cumulative effect of a change in accounting principle and before net income.

C. Before cumulative effect of a change in accounting principle and discontinued operations of a component unit.

D. After discontinued operations and before net income.

Answer (D) is correct. *(CPA, adapted)*
REQUIRED: The position in the income statement of a transaction that is unusual in nature and infrequent in occurrence.
DISCUSSION: A material transaction or event that is unusual and infrequent in the environment in which the entity operates is an extraordinary item. The following is the order of items to be reported in separate captions of the income statement: income from continuing operations, discontinued operations, extraordinary items, and net income. No caption is reported for the cumulative effect of a change in accounting principle. This accounting change is applied retrospectively.

6. A material loss should be presented separately as a component of income from continuing operations when it is

   A. An extraordinary item.

   B. The cumulative effect of a change in accounting principle.

   C. Unusual in nature and infrequent in occurrence.

   D. Not unusual in nature but infrequent in occurrence.

Answer (D) is correct. *(CPA, adapted)*
   REQUIRED: The material loss presented separately as a component of income from continuing operations.
   DISCUSSION: To be classified as an extraordinary item, a material transaction or event must be both unusual in nature and infrequent in occurrence within the environment in which the entity operates. If an item meets one but not both of these criteria, it should be presented separately (not net of tax) as a component of income from continuing operations.
   Answer (A) is incorrect because an extraordinary item is presented after discontinued operations. Answer (B) is incorrect because the cumulative effect of a change in accounting principle is not reported separately in the income statement. Answer (C) is incorrect because, if the item were both unusual in nature and infrequent in occurrence, it would be an extraordinary item.

7. Strand, Inc. incurred the following infrequent losses during the year just ended:

- A $90,000 write-down of equipment leased to others
- A $50,000 adjustment of accruals on long-term contracts
- A $75,000 write-off of obsolete inventory

In its income statement for the year, what amount should Strand report as total infrequent losses that are not considered extraordinary?

   A. $215,000

   B. $165,000

   C. $140,000

   D. $125,000

Answer (A) is correct. *(CPA, adapted)*
   REQUIRED: The amount to be reported as total infrequent losses not considered extraordinary.
   DISCUSSION: To be classified as an extraordinary item, a material transaction or event must be both unusual in nature and infrequent in occurrence in the environment in which the entity operates. APB Opinion 30 specifies six items that are not normally considered extraordinary. These items include the write-down of equipment, the adjustment of accruals on long-term contracts, and the write-off of obsolete inventory. Thus, Strand should report $215,000 ($90,000 + $50,000 + $75,000) of total infrequent losses as a component of income from continuing operations (not net of tax).
   Answer (B) is incorrect because $165,000 improperly excludes the adjustment of accruals. Answer (C) is incorrect because $140,000 improperly excludes the write-off of inventory. Answer (D) is incorrect because $125,000 improperly excludes the write-down of equipment.

8. During the year just ended, Teller Co. incurred losses arising from its guilty plea in its first antitrust action and from a substantial increase in production costs caused when a major supplier's workers went on strike. Which of these losses should be reported as an extraordinary item?

	Antitrust Action	Production Costs
A.	No	No
B.	No	Yes
C.	Yes	No
D.	Yes	Yes

Answer (C) is correct. *(CPA, adapted)*
   REQUIRED: The loss(es), if any, reported as an extraordinary item.
   DISCUSSION: APB Opinion 30 specifically states that the effects of a strike are not extraordinary. However, a loss from the company's first antitrust action is clearly infrequent and most likely unusual, that is, abnormal and of a type unrelated to the typical activities of the entity in the environment in which it operates.

9. An extraordinary item should be reported separately on the income statement as a component of income

	Net of Income Taxes	Before Discontinued Operations of a Component of an Entity
A.	Yes	Yes
B.	Yes	No
C.	No	No
D.	No	Yes

Answer (B) is correct. *(CPA, adapted)*
   REQUIRED: The presentation of an extraordinary item.
   DISCUSSION: Extraordinary items should be shown separately in the income statement, net of tax, after results of discontinued operations.

3.3 Accounting Changes and Error Corrections

10. When the Sonia Co. began business, it included such indirect costs of manufacturing as janitorial expenses, depreciation of machinery, and insurance on the factory as inventory costs. At the beginning of the current year, the company began expensing all insurance costs when they are incurred. The company must justify and disclose the reason for the change. The most appropriate reason is that the new principle

A. Constitutes an improvement in financial reporting.

B. Has been and continues to be the treatment used for tax purposes.

C. Is easier to apply because no assumptions about allocation must be made.

D. Is one used by the company for insurance costs other than those on factory-related activities.

Answer (A) is correct. *(Publisher, adapted)*
REQUIRED: The most appropriate reason for making a change in accounting principle.
DISCUSSION: The presumption is that, once adopted, an accounting principle should not be changed in accounting for events and transactions of a similar type. This presumption in favor of continuity may be overcome if the enterprise justifies the use of an alternative acceptable principle. The new principle should be preferable because it constitutes an improvement in financial reporting. If the GAAP hierarchy is followed, preferability automatically is established if a pronouncement of the FASB (or other designated standard setter) (1) requires use of a new principle, (2) expresses a preference for a principle not being used, (3) interprets an existing principle, or (4) rejects a specific principle. FASB Interpretation No. 1, *Accounting Changes Related to the Cost of Inventory*, states that preferability should be determined on the basis of whether the new principle constitutes an improvement in financial reporting. Other bases are not sufficient justification.

Questions 11 through 13 are based on the following information. Loire Co. has used the FIFO method since it began operations in Year 3. Loire changed to the weighted-average method for inventory measurement at the beginning of Year 6. This change was justified. In its Year 6 financial statements, Loire included comparative statements for Year 5 and Year 4. The following shows year-end inventory balances under the FIFO and weighted-average methods:

Year	FIFO	Weighted-Average
3	$ 90,000	$108,000
4	156,000	142,000
5	166,000	150,000

11. What adjustment, before taxes, should Loire make retrospectively to the balance reported for retained earnings at the beginning of Year 4?

A. $18,000 increase.

B. $18,000 decrease.

C. $4,000 increase.

D. $0.

Answer (A) is correct. *(Publisher, adapted)*
REQUIRED: The pretax retrospective adjustment to retained earnings at the beginning of the first period reported.
DISCUSSION: Retrospective application requires that the carrying amounts of assets, liabilities, and retained earnings at the beginning of the first period reported be adjusted for the cumulative effect of the new principle on periods prior to the first period reported. The pretax cumulative-effect adjustment to retained earnings at the beginning of Year 4 equals the $18,000 increase ($108,000 – $90,000) in inventory. If the weighted-average method had been applied in Year 3, cost of goods sold would have been $18,000 lower. Pretax net income and ending retained earnings for Year 3 (beginning retained earnings for Year 4) would have been $18,000 greater.
Answer (B) is incorrect because beginning retained earnings for Year 4 is increased. Answer (C) is incorrect because $4,000 is equal to the difference at the end of Year 3 minus the difference at the end of Year 4. Answer (D) is incorrect because a cumulative-effect adjustment should be recorded.

12. What amount should Loire report as inventory in its financial statements for the year ended December 31, Year 4, presented for comparative purposes?

A. $90,000

B. $108,000

C. $142,000

D. $156,000

Answer (C) is correct. *(Publisher, adapted)*
REQUIRED: The amount to be reported as inventory at December 31, Year 4.
DISCUSSION: Retrospective application requires that all periods reported be individually adjusted for the period-specific effects of applying the new principle. Thus, the ending inventory for Year 4 following the retrospective adjustment should be reported as the weighted-average amount of $142,000.
Answer (A) is incorrect because $90,000 is the FIFO amount at December 31, Year 3. Answer (B) is incorrect because $108,000 is the weighted-average amount at December 31, Year 3. Answer (D) is incorrect because $156,000 is the FIFO amount at December 31, Year 4.

13. By what amount should Loire's cost of sales be retrospectively adjusted for the year ended December 31, Year 5?

A. $0.

B. $2,000 increase.

C. $14,000 increase.

D. $16,000 increase.

Answer (B) is correct. *(Publisher, adapted)*
REQUIRED: The retrospective adjustment to cost of sales for the year ended December 31, Year 5.
DISCUSSION: Retrospective application requires that all periods reported be individually adjusted for the period-specific effects of applying the new principle. Cost of sales equals beginning inventory, plus purchases, minus ending inventory. Purchases are the same under FIFO and weighted average. Thus, the retrospective adjustment to cost of sales equals the change in beginning inventory resulting from the change from FIFO to weighted average minus the change in ending inventory. This adjustment equals an increase in cost of sales of $2,000 [($156,000 – $142,000) – ($166,000 – $150,000)].
Answer (A) is incorrect because period-specific adjustments are required. Answer (C) is incorrect because $14,000 is the difference between FIFO and weighted-average inventory amounts at the end of Year 4. Answer (D) is incorrect because $16,000 is the difference between FIFO and weighted-average inventory amounts at the end of Year 5.

14. How should the effect of a change in accounting estimate be accounted for?

A. By retrospectively applying the change to amounts reported in financial statements of prior periods.

B. By reporting pro forma amounts for prior periods.

C. As a prior-period adjustment to beginning retained earnings.

D. By prospectively applying the change to current and future periods.

Answer (D) is correct. *(CPA, adapted)*
REQUIRED: The accounting for the effect of a change in accounting estimate.
DISCUSSION: The effect of a change in accounting estimate is accounted for in the period of change, if the change affects that period only, or in the period of change and future periods, if the change affects both. For a change in accounting estimate, the entity may not (1) restate or retrospectively adjust prior-period statements or (2) report pro forma amounts for prior periods.

15. In early January of Year 6, Off-Line Co. changed its method of accounting for demo costs from writing off the costs over 2 years to expensing the costs immediately. Off-Line made the change in recognition that an increasing number of demos placed with potential customers did not result in sales. Off-Line had deferred demo costs of $500,000 at December 31, Year 5, of which $300,000 were to be written off in Year 6 and the remainder in Year 7. Off-Line's income tax rate is 30%. In its Year 6 statement of retained earnings, what amount should Off-Line report as a retrospective adjustment of its January 1, Year 6, retained earnings?

  A. $0

  B. $210,000

  C. $300,000

  D. $500,000

Answer (A) is correct. *(CPA, adapted)*
  REQUIRED: The retrospective adjustment of retained earnings at the beginning of the year in which an entity changed from capitalizing a cost to expensing it as incurred.
  DISCUSSION: In general, the retrospective application method is used to account for a change in accounting principle. However, a change in accounting estimate inseparable from (effected by) a change in principle should be accounted for as a change in estimate. A change in estimate results from new information, such as the decreasing sales resulting from the demo placements. The effects of a change in estimate should be accounted for prospectively. Thus, the effects should be recognized in the period of change and any future periods affected. Accordingly, the write-off of the $500,000 in deferred demo costs should be reported in the Year 6 income statement. Retained earnings at the beginning of the year should not be retrospectively adjusted.
  Answer (B) is incorrect because $210,000 is the after-tax effect of expensing $300,000 of the deferred costs in Year 6. Answer (C) is incorrect because $300,000 is the amount that had been scheduled to be expensed in Year 6. Answer (D) is incorrect because $500,000 is the pretax write-off to be recorded in the Year 6 income statement.

16. In which of the following situations should a company report a prior-period adjustment?

  A. A change in the estimated useful lives of fixed assets purchased in prior years.

  B. The correction of a mathematical error in the calculation of prior years' depreciation.

  C. A switch from the straight-line to double-declining-balance method of depreciation.

  D. The scrapping of an asset prior to the end of its expected useful life.

Answer (B) is correct. *(CPA, adapted)*
  REQUIRED: The basis for a prior-period adjustment.
  DISCUSSION: Items of profit or loss related to corrections of errors in prior-period statements are accounted for as prior-period adjustments. Errors include mathematical mistakes, mistakes in applying accounting principles, and oversight or misuse of facts existing when the statements were prepared. A prior-period adjustment requires restatement of the prior-period statements presented (SFAS 16 and SFAS 154).
  Answer (A) is incorrect because a change in the estimated useful lives of fixed assets is a change in estimate. It is accounted for prospectively. Answer (C) is incorrect because a switch from the straight-line to double-declining-balance method of depreciation is a change in estimate inseparable from a change in accounting principle. It is accounted for prospectively. Answer (D) is incorrect because the scrapping of an asset prior to the end of its expected useful life is accounted for prospectively. The gain or loss is recognized in earnings in the period of disposal.

17. Troop Co. frequently borrows from the bank to maintain sufficient operating cash. The following loans were at a 12% interest rate, with interest payable at maturity. Troop repaid each loan on its scheduled maturity date.

Date of Loan	Amount	Maturity Date	Term of Loan
11/1/Yr 3	$10,000	10/31/Yr 4	1 year
2/1/Yr 4	30,000	7/31/Yr 4	6 months
5/1/Yr 4	16,000	1/31/Yr 5	9 months

Troop records interest expense when the loans are repaid. Accordingly, interest expense of $3,000 was recorded in Year 4. If no correction is made, by what amount would Year 4 interest expense be understated?

  A. $1,080

  B. $1,240

  C. $1,280

  D. $1,440

Answer (A) is correct. *(CPA, adapted)*
  REQUIRED: The understatement of interest expense in Year 4 if no correction is made.
  DISCUSSION: Interest expense for the 1-year loan that should be recognized in Year 4 is $1,000 [$10,000 × 12% × (10 ÷ 12 months)]. Interest expense for the 6-month loan that should be recognized in Year 4 is $1,800 [$30,000 × 12% × (6 ÷ 6 months) × (6 ÷ 12 months)]. Interest expense for the 9-month loan that should be recognized in Year 4 is $1,280 [$16,000 × 12% × (8 ÷ 9 months) × (9 ÷ 12 months)]. Accordingly, if $3,000 of interest is recorded, the understatement of interest expense is $1,080 [($1,000 + $1,800 + $1,280) – $3,000].
  Answer (B) is incorrect because $1,240 assumes that a full year's interest should be recognized in Year 4 on the 9-month loan. Answer (C) is incorrect because $1,280 assumes that a full year's interest should be recognized in Year 4 on the 1-year loan. Answer (D) is incorrect because $1,440 equals the total interest on the loans minus $3,000.

3.4 Earnings per Share (EPS)

18. In computing the weighted-average number of shares outstanding during the year, which of the following midyear events must be treated as if it had occurred at the beginning of the year?

A. Declaration and distribution of a stock dividend.

B. Purchase of treasury stock.

C. Sale of additional common stock.

D. Sale of convertible preferred stock.

Answer (A) is correct. *(CPA, adapted)*

REQUIRED: The item that is treated as if it had occurred at the beginning of the year.

DISCUSSION: The weighted-average number of common shares outstanding is determined by relating the portion of the reporting period that the shares were outstanding to the total time in the period. Weighting is necessary because some shares may have been issued or reacquired during the period. However, a stock dividend increases the shares outstanding (the number of parts into which ownership is divided) with no effect on the company's net assets and therefore future earnings. Accordingly, unlike sales or purchases of shares, that is, transactions affecting net assets and future earnings, stock dividends must be accounted for retroactively for the sake of comparability. SFAS 128 therefore requires that the increase in shares resulting from a stock dividend be given retroactive recognition in the EPS computations for all periods presented. Nonretroactive treatment of stock dividends would create a dilution in EPS of the current period compared with prior periods that would give the false impression of a decline in profitability.

Answer (B) is incorrect because purchase of treasury stock is accounted for currently but not retroactively in the EPS computations. Answer (C) is incorrect because sale of additional common stock is accounted for currently but not retroactively in the EPS computations. Answer (D) is incorrect because sale of convertible preferred stock is accounted for currently but not retroactively in the EPS computations.

19. During the current year, Comma Co. had outstanding: 25,000 shares of common stock; 8,000 shares of $20 par, 10% cumulative preferred stock; and 3,000 bonds that are $1,000 par and 9% convertible. The bonds were originally issued at par, and each bond was convertible into 30 shares of common stock. During the year, net income was $200,000, no dividends were declared, and the tax rate was 30%. What amount was Comma's basic earnings per share for the current year?

A. $6.78

B. $7.36

C. $7.07

D. $8.00

Answer (B) is correct. *(CPA, adapted)*

REQUIRED: The basic earnings per share.

DISCUSSION: Basic earnings per share (BEPS) is calculated by first determining the income available to common shareholders. Declared dividends and accumulated dividends on preferred stock are removed from net income for the period. The undeclared but cumulative dividends on preferred stock equal $16,000 (8,000 shares × $20 par × 10%). Thus, given no dividends declared, the income available to common shareholders is $184,000 ($200,000 – $16,000). This amount is divided by the weighted average shares outstanding. All 25,000 of the common shares were outstanding during the entire period. Accordingly, BEPS equals $7.36 ($184,000 ÷ 25,000 shares).

Answer (A) is incorrect because $6.78 is diluted EPS [(BEPS numerator + $189,000 after-tax bond interest saved by a hypothetical bond conversion) ÷ (BEPS denominator + 30,000 common shares assumed to have been issued at the beginning of the period after the conversion of the bonds)]. Answer (C) is incorrect because $7.07 is the DEPS amount if the preferred stock is not cumulative. Answer (D) is incorrect because $8.00 ignores the undeclared cumulative preferred dividends.

Questions 20 through 26 are based on the following information.

Pubco is a public company that uses a calendar year and has a complex capital structure. In the computation of its basic and diluted earnings per share (BEPS and DEPS, respectively) in accordance with SFAS 128, *Earnings per Share*, Pubco uses income before extraordinary items as the control number. Pubco reported no discontinued operations, but it had an extraordinary loss (net of tax) of $1.2 million in the first quarter when its income before the extraordinary item was $1 million.

The average market price of Pubco's common stock for the first quarter was $25, the shares outstanding at the beginning of the period equaled 300,000, and 12,000 shares were issued on March 1.

At the beginning of the quarter, Pubco had outstanding $2 million of 5% convertible bonds, with each $1,000 bond convertible into 10 shares of common stock. No bonds were converted.

At the beginning of the quarter, Pubco also had outstanding 120,000 shares of preferred stock paying a quarterly dividend of $.10 per share and convertible to common stock on a one-to-one basis. Holders of 60,000 shares of preferred stock exercised their conversion privilege on February 1.

Throughout the first quarter, warrants to buy 50,000 shares of Pubco's common stock for $28 per share were outstanding but unexercised.

Pubco's tax rate was 30%.

20. The weighted-average number of shares used to calculate Pubco's BEPS amounts for the first quarter is

A. 444,000

B. 372,000

C. 344,000

D. 300,000

Answer (C) is correct. *(Publisher, adapted)*
REQUIRED: The weighted-average number of shares used to calculate BEPS amounts for the first quarter.
DISCUSSION: The number of shares outstanding at January 1 was 300,000, 12,000 shares were issued on March 1, and 60,000 shares of preferred stock were converted to 60,000 shares of common stock on February 1. Thus, the weighted-average number of shares used to calculate BEPS amounts for the first quarter is 344,000 {300,000 + [12,000 × (1 ÷ 3)] + [60,000 × (2 ÷ 3)]}.
Answer (A) is incorrect because 444,000 is the adjusted weighted-average number of shares used in the DEPS calculation. Answer (B) is incorrect because 372,000 is the total outstanding at March 31. Answer (D) is incorrect because 300,000 equals the shares outstanding at January 1.

21. The control number for determining whether Pubco's potential common shares are dilutive or antidilutive for the first quarter is

A. $1,000,000

B. $994,000

C. $(206,000)

D. $(1,200,000)

Answer (B) is correct. *(Publisher, adapted)*
REQUIRED: The control number for determining whether potential common shares are dilutive or antidilutive.
DISCUSSION: If a company reports discontinued operations or extraordinary items, it uses income from continuing operations (in Pubco's case, income before extraordinary item), adjusted for preferred dividends, as the control number for determining whether potential common shares are dilutive or antidilutive. Hence, the number of potential common shares used in calculating DEPS for income from continuing operations is also used in calculating the other DEPS amounts even if the effect is antidilutive with respect to the corresponding BEPS amounts. However, if the entity has a loss from continuing operations available to common shareholders, no potential common shares are included in the calculation of any DEPS amount (SFAS 128). The control number for Pubco is $994,000 {$1,000,000 income before extraordinary item – [$.10 per share dividend × (120,000 preferred shares – 60,000 preferred shares converted)]}.
Answer (A) is incorrect because $1,000,000 is unadjusted income from continuing operations. Answer (C) is incorrect because $(206,000) is the net loss available to common shareholders after subtracting the extraordinary loss. Answer (D) is incorrect because $(1,200,000) is the extraordinary loss.

22. The BEPS amount for Pubco's net income or loss available to common shareholders for the first quarter after the extraordinary item is

A. $2.89

B. $(0.46)

C. $(0.60)

D. $(3.49)

Answer (C) is correct. *(Publisher, adapted)*
REQUIRED: The BEPS amount for the net income or loss available to common shareholders after the extraordinary item.
DISCUSSION: The weighted-average number of shares used in the BEPS denominator is 344,000 {300,000 + [12,000 × (1 ÷ 3)] + [60,000 × (2 ÷ 3)]}. The numerator equals income before extraordinary item, minus preferred dividends, minus the extraordinary loss. Thus, it equals the control number minus the extraordinary loss, or $(206,000) [$994,000 – $1,200,000]. The BEPS amount for the net income or loss available to common shareholders after the extraordinary item is $(0.60) [$(206,000) ÷ 344,000 shares].
Answer (A) is incorrect because $2.89 is the BEPS amount for income available to common shareholders before the extraordinary item. Answer (B) is incorrect because $(0.46) uses the denominator of the DEPS calculation. Answer (D) is incorrect because $(3.49) is the BEPS amount for the extraordinary loss.

23. The weighted-average number of shares used to calculate Pubco's DEPS amounts for the first quarter is

A. 444,000

B. 438,000

C. 372,000

D. 344,000

Answer (A) is correct. *(Publisher, adapted)*
REQUIRED: The weighted-average number of shares used to calculate DEPS amounts for the first quarter.
DISCUSSION: The denominator of DEPS equals the weighted-average number of shares used in the BEPS calculation (344,000) plus dilutive potential common shares (assuming the control number is not a loss). The incremental shares from assumed conversion of warrants is zero because they are antidilutive. The $25 market price is less than the $28 exercise price. The assumed conversion of all the preferred shares at the beginning of the quarter results in 80,000 incremental shares {[120,000 shares × (3 ÷ 3)] – [60,000 shares × (2 ÷ 3)]}. The assumed conversion of all the bonds at the beginning of the quarter results in 20,000 incremental shares [10 common shares per bond × ($2,000,000 ÷ $1,000 per bond)]. Consequently, the weighted-average number of shares used to calculate DEPS amounts for the first quarter is 444,000 (344,000 + 0 + 80,000 + 20,000).
Answer (B) is incorrect because 438,000 assumes the hypothetical exercise of all the warrants at the beginning of the period at a price of $28 and the repurchase of shares using the proceeds at a price of $25. Answer (C) is incorrect because 372,000 is the total outstanding at March 31. Answer (D) is incorrect because 344,000 is the denominator of the BEPS fraction.

24. The effect of assumed conversions on the numerator of the DEPS fraction for Pubco's first quarter is

A. $31,000

B. $25,000

C. $23,500

D. $17,500

Answer (C) is correct. *(Publisher, adapted)*
REQUIRED: The effect of assumed conversions on the numerator of the DEPS fraction.
DISCUSSION: If all of the convertible preferred shares are assumed to be converted on January 1, $6,000 of dividends [(120,000 – 60,000) × $.10 preferred shares] will not be paid. Furthermore, if the bonds are assumed to be converted on January 1, interest of $17,500 {[$2,000,000 ÷ 4 × 5%] × (1.0 – .3 tax rate)} will not be paid. Accordingly, the effect of assumed conversions on the numerator of the DEPS fraction is an addition of $23,500 ($6,000 + $17,500) to the income available to common shareholders.
Answer (A) is incorrect because $31,000 disregards the tax shield provided by bond interest. Answer (B) is incorrect because $25,000 equals one quarter's bond interest payment. Answer (D) is incorrect because $17,500 is the effect of the assumed conversion of the bonds alone.

25. Refer to the information on the preceding page(s). The difference between BEPS and DEPS for the extraordinary item in Pubco's first quarter is

A. $2.89

B. $2.10

C. $.79

D. $.60

Answer (C) is correct. *(Publisher, adapted)*
REQUIRED: The difference between BEPS and DEPS for the extraordinary item.
DISCUSSION: The BEPS amount for the extraordinary loss is $(3.49) [$(1,200,000) ÷ 344,000]. The DEPS amount for the extraordinary item is $(2.70) [$(1,200,000) ÷ 444,000 shares].
Answer (A) is incorrect because $2.89 is the difference between DEPS and BEPS for the extraordinary loss. Answer (B) is incorrect because $2.10 is the difference between DEPS for the extraordinary loss and BEPS for the net loss available to common shareholders after the extraordinary loss. Answer (D) is incorrect because $.60 is the BEPS for the net loss available to common shareholders after the extraordinary loss.

26. Refer to the information on the preceding page(s). The DEPS amount for Pubco's net income or loss available to common shareholders after the extraordinary item for the first quarter is

A. $2.29

B. $(0.41)

C. $(0.53)

D. $(2.70)

Answer (B) is correct. *(Publisher, adapted)*
REQUIRED: The DEPS amount for the net income or loss available to common shareholders.
DISCUSSION: The numerator equals the income available to common shareholders (the control number), plus the effect of the assumed conversions, minus the extraordinary loss. The denominator equals the weighted-average of shares outstanding plus the dilutive potential common shares. Hence, the DEPS amount for the net income or loss available to common shareholders after the extraordinary item is $(.41) [($994,000 + $23,500 − $1,200,000) ÷ 444,000].
Answer (A) is incorrect because $2.29 is the DEPS amount for income before the extraordinary item. Answer (C) is incorrect because $(0.53) is based on the BEPS denominator. Answer (D) is incorrect because $(2.70) is the DEPS for the extraordinary item.

3.5 Long-Term Construction Contracts

27. The calculation of the income recognized in the third year of a five-year construction contract accounted for using the percentage-of-completion method includes the ratio of

A. Costs incurred in year 3 to total billings.

B. Costs incurred in year 3 to total estimated costs.

C. Total costs incurred to date to total billings.

D. Total costs incurred to date to total estimated costs.

Answer (D) is correct. *(CPA, adapted)*
REQUIRED: The ratio used in calculating income under the percentage-of-completion method.
DISCUSSION: The percentage-of-completion method recognizes gross profit or revenue based on the ratio of costs to date and estimated total costs. (This relationship is the recommended but not the only basis for determining progress.) The total anticipated gross profit or revenue is multiplied by this ratio. The product is then reduced by previously recognized gross profit or revenue.
Answer (A) is incorrect because the estimate of progress may be based on various methods, e.g., units delivered, units of work performed, efforts expended, or cost incurred. However, billings do not necessarily measure progress. Also, the elements of the ratio should be measured on the same basis, but billings are not measured in terms of costs. Moreover, the gross profit or revenue recognized to date should be based on a cumulative calculation that reflects changes in estimates. Answer (B) is incorrect because the ratio of costs in one year to total costs does not estimate progress. Answer (C) is incorrect because billings do not necessarily measure progress, and the elements of the ratio should be measured on the same basis.

28. Haft Construction Co. has consistently used the percentage-of-completion method. On January 10, Year 3, Haft began work on a $3 million construction contract. At the inception date, the estimated cost of construction was $2,250,000. The following data relate to the progress of the contract:

Gross profit recognized at 12/31/Yr 3	$ 300,000
Costs incurred 1/10/Yr 3 through	
12/31/Yr 4	1,800,000
Estimated cost to complete at 12/31/Yr 4	600,000

In its income statement for the year ended December 31, Year 4, what amount of gross profit should Haft report?

- A. $450,000
- B. $300,000
- C. $262,500
- D. $150,000

Answer (D) is correct. *(CPA, adapted)*
REQUIRED: The amount of gross profit reported using the percentage-of-completion method.
DISCUSSION: The percentage-of-completion method provides for the recognition of gross profit based on the relationship between the costs incurred to date and estimated total costs for the completion of the contract. The total anticipated gross profit is multiplied by the ratio of the costs incurred to date to the total estimated costs, and the product is reduced by previously recognized gross profit. The percentage-of-completion at 12/31/Yr 4 is 75% [$1,800,000 ÷ ($1,800,000 + $600,000)]. The total anticipated gross profit is $600,000 ($3,000,000 contract price – $2,400,000 expected total costs). Consequently, a gross profit of $150,000 [($600,000 total gross profit × 75%) – $300,000 previously recognized gross profit] is recognized for Year 4.
Answer (A) is incorrect because the current year's profit equals the cumulative income minus the previously recognized gross profit. Answer (B) is incorrect because $300,000 is the previously recognized gross profit. Answer (C) is incorrect because $262,500 assumes the total estimated gross profit is $750,000 ($3,000,000 price – $2,250,000 originally estimated total cost).

29. A company appropriately uses the completed-contract method to account for a long-term construction contract. Revenue is recognized when progress billings are

	Recorded	Collected
A.	No	Yes
B.	Yes	Yes
C.	Yes	No
D.	No	No

Answer (D) is correct. *(CPA, adapted)*
REQUIRED: The effect of progress billings on the recognition of revenue.
DISCUSSION: GAAP require that revenue be recognized when it is realized or realizable and earned. Under the completed-contract method, revenue recognition is appropriate only at the completion of the contract. Neither the recording nor the collection of progress billings affects this recognition.

30. Pell Co.'s construction jobs (described below) commenced during the year just ended.

	Project 1	Project 2
Contract price	$420,000	$300,000
Costs incurred during the year	240,000	280,000
Estimated costs to complete	120,000	40,000
Billed to customers during the year	150,000	270,000
Received from customers during the year	90,000	250,000

If Pell appropriately used the completed-contract method, what amount of gross profit (loss) should Pell report in its income statement for the year?

- A. $(20,000)
- B. $0
- C. $340,000
- D. $420,000

Answer (A) is correct. *(CPA, adapted)*
REQUIRED: The gross profit (loss) reported under the completed-contract method.
DISCUSSION: Under the completed-contract method, gross profit is deemed to meet the revenue recognition criteria (realized or realizable and earned) when the contract is completed. Neither project will be completed by the end of the year. Hence, no gross profit is recognized for Project 1 even though estimated data predict a gross profit of $60,000 ($420,000 contract price – $240,000 costs incurred – $120,000 additional estimated costs). However, when the current estimate of total contract costs indicates a loss, an immediate provision for the entire loss should be made regardless of the method of accounting used. Thus, a $20,000 loss ($300,000 contract price – $280,000 costs incurred – $40,000 additional estimated costs) will be reported for Project 2.

3.6 Revenue Recognition after Delivery

31. For financial statement purposes, the installment method of accounting may be used if the

A. Collection period extends over more than 12 months.

B. Installments are due in different years.

C. Ultimate amount collectible is indeterminate.

D. Percentage-of-completion method is inappropriate.

Answer (C) is correct. *(CPA, adapted)*
REQUIRED: The use of the installment method.
DISCUSSION: APB Opinion 10, *Omnibus Opinion-1966*, reaffirms that profits from sales in the ordinary course of business should usually be recognized at the time of sale unless collection of the sales price is not reasonably assured. When receivables are collected over an extended period and, because of the terms of the transaction or other conditions, no reasonable basis exists for estimating the degree of collectibility, the installment method or the cost-recovery method of accounting may be used.
Answer (A) is incorrect because, regardless of the length of the collection period, sales in the ordinary course of business should usually be recognized at the time of sale unless collectibility is not reasonably assured. Answer (B) is incorrect because, even if installments are due in different years, sales should be recognized at the time of sale unless collectibility is not reasonably assured. Answer (D) is incorrect because the installment method is not an alternative to the percentage-of-completion method, which is ordinarily used to account for long-term construction contracts.

32. It is proper to recognize revenue prior to the sale of merchandise when

I. The revenue will be reported as an installment sale.

II. The revenue will be reported under the cost-recovery method.

A. I only.

B. II only.

C. Both I and II.

D. Neither I nor II.

Answer (D) is correct. *(CPA, adapted)*
REQUIRED: The condition(s) under which it is proper to recognize revenue prior to the sale of merchandise.
DISCUSSION: The installment method recognizes income on a sale as the related receivable is collected. Under the cost-recovery method, profit is recognized only after collections exceed the cost of the item sold.

33. Dolce Co., which began operations on January 1, Year 8, appropriately uses the installment method of accounting to record revenues. The following information is available for the years ended December 31, Year 8 and Year 9:

	Year 8	Year 9
Sales	$1,000,000	$2,000,000
Gross profit realized on sales made in:		
Year 8	150,000	90,000
Year 9	--	200,000
Gross profit percentages	30%	40%

What amount of installment accounts receivable should Dolce report in its December 31, Year 9, balance sheet?

A. $1,100,000

B. $1,300,000

C. $1,700,000

D. $1,900,000

Answer (C) is correct. *(CPA, adapted)*
REQUIRED: The amount of installment accounts receivable.
DISCUSSION: Gross profit realized equals the gross profit percentage times cash collected. Hence, cash collected on Year 8 sales was $800,000 [($150,000 + $90,000) ÷ 30%], and cash collected on Year 9 sales was $500,000 ($200,000 ÷ 40%). The remaining balance of installment receivables is therefore $1,700,000 ($1,000,000 + $2,000,000 − $800,000 − $500,000).
Answer (A) is incorrect because $1,100,000 equals the total gross profit (both realized and unrealized) for Year 8 and Year 9. Answer (B) is incorrect because $1,300,000 is the total cash collected. Answer (D) is incorrect because $1,900,000 equals total sales minus total gross profit for Year 8 and Year 9.

34. Given no reasonable basis for estimating the degree of collectibility, Astor Co. uses the installment method of revenue recognition for the following sales:

	Year 6	Year 5
Sales	$900,000	$600,000
Collections from:		
Year 5 sales	100,000	200,000
Year 6 sales	300,000	--
Accounts written off:		
Year 5 sales	150,000	50,000
Year 6 sales	50,000	--
Gross profit percentage	40%	30%

What amount should Astor report as deferred gross profit in its December 31, Year 6, balance sheet for the Year 5 and Year 6 sales?

A. $150,000

B. $210,000

C. $220,000

D. $250,000

Answer (D) is correct. *(CPA, adapted)*
REQUIRED: The deferred gross profit.
DISCUSSION: The remaining balance of Year 5 installment receivables is $100,000 [$600,000 sales – ($200,000 + $100,000) collections – ($50,000 + $150,000) write-offs]. The remaining balance of Year 6 installment receivables is $550,000 ($900,000 sales – $300,000 collections – $50,000 write-offs). Hence, total deferred gross profit reported at year-end is $250,000 [($100,000 × 30%) + ($550,000 × 40%)].
Answer (A) is incorrect because $150,000 is the profit included in the determination of net income as a result of Year 6 collections. Answer (B) is incorrect because $210,000 is the total gross profit included in the determination of net income to date. Answer (C) is incorrect because $220,000 is the year-end deferred gross profit on Year 6 sales.

35. Bear Co., which began operations on January 2, appropriately uses the installment sales method of accounting. The following information is available for the year:

Installment sales	$1,400,000
Realized gross profit on installment sales	240,000
Gross profit percentage on sales	40%

For the year ended December 31, what amounts should Bear report as accounts receivable and deferred gross profit?

	Accounts Receivable	Deferred Gross Profit
A.	$600,000	$320,000
B.	$600,000	$360,000
C.	$800,000	$320,000
D.	$800,000	$560,000

Answer (C) is correct. *(CPA, adapted)*
REQUIRED: The accounts receivable balance and deferred gross profit under the installment sales method.
DISCUSSION: The installment method recognizes income on a sale as the related receivable is collected. The amount recognized each period is the gross profit percentage (gross profit ÷ selling price) on the sale multiplied by the cash collected. Given realized gross profit on installment sales of $240,000 and a gross profit percentage on sales of 40%, cash collections must have been $600,000 ($240,000 ÷ 40%). The accounts receivable at year-end is the difference between total installment sales and cash collected; therefore, accounts receivable must be $800,000 ($1,400,000 – $600,000) on December 31. Deferred gross profit on the year-end accounts receivable is $320,000 ($800,000 × 40%).
Answer (A) is incorrect because $600,000 equals cash collections for the year. Answer (B) is incorrect because $600,000 equals cash collections for the year, and $360,000 is the difference between cash collections and realized gross profit. Answer (D) is incorrect because $560,000 is the total of realized and unrealized gross profit.

36. On December 31, Year 3, Mill Co. sold construction equipment to Drew, Inc. for $1.8 million. The equipment had a carrying amount of $1.2 million. Drew paid $300,000 cash on December 31, Year 3, and signed a $1.5 million note bearing interest at 10%, payable in five annual installments of $300,000. Mill appropriately accounts for the sale under the installment method. On December 31, Year 4, Drew paid $300,000 principal and $150,000 interest. For the year ended December 31, Year 4, what total amount of revenue should Mill recognize from the construction equipment sale and financing?

A. $250,000

B. $150,000

C. $120,000

D. $100,000

Answer (A) is correct. *(CPA, adapted)*
REQUIRED: The total amount of income to be recognized from an equipment sale and resulting financing.
DISCUSSION: Under the installment method, interest income must be accounted for separately from the gross profit to be recognized. The gross profit margin on the sale is equal to 33 1/3%. This rate is determined by dividing the $600,000 gross profit ($1,800,000 selling price – $1,200,000 cost) by the $1,800,000 selling price. Based on collection of $300,000 of principal on December 31, Year 4, Mill should recognize $100,000 ($300,000 × 33 1/3% gross profit margin) of realized gross profit from the construction equipment sale. In addition, Mill should recognize $150,000 ($1,500,000 note × 10% interest) as interest income from the financing. Thus, the total revenue for Year 4 from this transaction is $250,000 ($100,000 + $150,000).
Answer (B) is incorrect because $150,000 excludes the realized gross profit. Answer (C) is incorrect because $120,000 is 10% of the seller's carrying amount. Answer (D) is incorrect because $100,000 excludes the interest income.

37. Several of Fox, Inc.'s customers are having cash flow problems. Information pertaining to these customers for the years ended March 31, Year 7 and Year 8 follows:

	3/31/Yr 7	3/31/Yr 8
Sales	$10,000	$15,000
Cost of sales	8,000	9,000
Cash collections		
on Year 7 sales	7,000	3,000
on Year 8 sales	--	12,000

If the cost-recovery method is used, what amount would Fox report as gross profit from sales to these customers for the year ended March 31, Year 8?

A. $2,000

B. $3,000

C. $5,000

D. $15,000

Answer (C) is correct. *(CPA, adapted)*
REQUIRED: The gross profit from sales if the cost-recovery method is used.
DISCUSSION: The cost-recovery method recognizes profit only after collections exceed the cost of the item sold, that is, when the full cost has been recovered. Subsequent amounts collected are treated entirely as revenue (debit cash and deferred gross profit, credit the receivable and realized gross profit). The sum of collections in excess of costs to be recognized as gross profit is $5,000 {[$3,000 Year 8 collections on Year 7 sales – ($8,000 cost – $7,000 Year 7 collections on Year 7 sales)] + ($12,000 collections on Year 8 sales – $9,000 cost)}.
Answer (A) is incorrect because $2,000 excludes the profit on Year 8 sales. Answer (B) is incorrect because $3,000 excludes the profit on Year 7 sales. Answer (D) is incorrect because $15,000 equals Year 8 sales.

3.7 Consignment Accounting

38. Garnett Co. shipped inventory on consignment to Hart Co. that originally cost $50,000. Hart paid $1,200 for advertising that was reimbursable from Garnett. At the end of the year, 40% of the inventory was sold for $32,000. The agreement stated that a commission of 10% will be provided to Hart for all sales. What amount should Garnett report as net income for the year?

A. $0

B. $7,600

C. $10,800

D. $12,000

Answer (B) is correct. *(CPA, adapted)*
REQUIRED: The net income reported by the consignor.
DISCUSSION: A consignor ships goods to the consignee, who acts as a sales agent. They remain in the consignor's inventory. Sales revenue and cost of goods sold are recognized when the consignor receives notice of the sale of the consigned goods. Thus, assuming that notice has been received, Garnett should recognize a $12,000 gross profit on the sale of consigned goods [$32,000 revenue – ($50,000 total cost × 40%)]. Its pretax net income equals gross profit minus the selling expenses (always a period cost according to ARB 43, Ch. 4) for which it is liable, or $7,600 [$12,000 – $1,200 for advertising – ($32,000 × 10%) commission payable to the consignee].
Answer (A) is incorrect because $0 is based on the unreasonable assumption that the consignor has received no notice of the consignment by year-end. Answer (C) is incorrect because $10,800 excludes the consignee's commission. Answer (D) is incorrect because $12,000 is the gross profit.

39. During the year just ended, Kam Co. began offering its goods to selected retailers on a consignment basis. The following information for the year was derived from Kam's accounting records:

Beginning inventory	$122,000
Purchases	540,000
Freight-in	10,000
Transportation to consignees	5,000
Freight-out	35,000
Ending inventory	
--held by Kam	145,000
--held by consignees	20,000

In its income statement for the year, what amount should Kam report as cost of goods sold?

A. $507,000

B. $512,000

C. $527,000

D. $547,000

Answer (B) is correct. *(CPA, adapted)*
REQUIRED: The total cost of goods sold.
DISCUSSION: Cost of goods sold is equal to the cost of goods available for sale minus the ending inventory. Cost of goods available for sale is equal to beginning inventory, plus purchases, plus additional costs (such as freight-in and transportation to consignees) that are necessary to prepare the inventory for sale. The cost of goods sold for Kam Co. is $512,000 [($122,000 beginning inventory + $540,000 purchases + $10,000 freight-in + $5,000 transportation to consignees) – ($145,000 Kam's ending inventory + $20,000 consignee ending inventory)]. Freight-out is a selling cost and is not included in cost of goods sold.
Answer (A) is incorrect because $507,000 does not include $5,000 for transportation to consignees. Answer (C) is incorrect because $527,000 does not include $5,000 for transportation to consignees or reflect the $20,000 of inventory held by consignees. Answer (D) is incorrect because $547,000 includes $35,000 of freight-out.

40. Southgate Co. paid the in-transit insurance premium for consignment goods shipped to Hendon Co., the consignee. In addition, Southgate advanced part of the commissions that will be due when Hendon sells the goods. Should Southgate include the in-transit insurance premium and the advanced commissions in inventory costs?

	Insurance Premium	Advanced Commissions
A.	Yes	Yes
B.	No	No
C.	Yes	No
D.	No	Yes

Answer (C) is correct. *(CPA, adapted)*
   REQUIRED: The item(s) included in a consignor's inventory costs.
   DISCUSSION: Inventoriable costs include all costs of making the inventory ready for sale. Costs incurred by a consignor on the transfer of goods to a consignee are costs necessary to make the inventory ready for sale. Consequently, they are inventoriable. Thus, the in-transit insurance premium is inventoried. The advanced commissions constitute a receivable or prepaid expense, not an element of inventory cost.
   Answer (A) is incorrect because the advanced commissions constitute a receivable, not an element of inventory cost. Answer (B) is incorrect because the in-transit insurance premium is inventoried. Answer (D) is incorrect because the in-transit insurance premium is inventoried, but the advanced commissions constitute a receivable, not an element of inventory cost.

41. On December 1, Alt Department Store received 505 sweaters on consignment from Todd. Todd's cost for the sweaters was $80 each, and they were priced to sell at $100. Alt's commission on consigned goods is 10%. At December 31, 5 sweaters remained. In its December 31 balance sheet, what amount should Alt report as payable for consigned goods?

A. $49,000

B. $45,400

C. $45,000

D. $40,400

Answer (C) is correct. *(CPA, adapted)*
   REQUIRED: The payable reported by the consignee for consigned goods.
   DISCUSSION: Consignment-in is a receivable/payable account used by consignees. It is the amount payable to the consignor if it has a credit balance. The amount of the payable equals total sales minus 10% commission on the goods sold, or $45,000 [(500 × $100) sales – (500 × $100 × 10%)].
   Answer (A) is incorrect because $49,000 equals sales minus 10% of total gross margin [500 × ($100 – $80) = $10,000]. Answer (B) is incorrect because $45,400 equals the cost of the 505 sweaters, plus the markup on the sweaters sold, minus commissions. Answer (D) is incorrect because $40,400 is the cost of 505 sweaters.

Use Gleim's *CPA Test Prep* CD-Rom/Pocket PC for interactive testing with over 4,000 additional questions!

3.8 PRACTICE SIMULATION

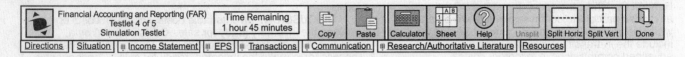

| Financial Accounting and Reporting (FAR) Testlet 4 of 5 Simulation Testlet | Time Remaining 1 hour 45 minutes | Copy | Paste | Calculator | Sheet | Help | Unsplit | Split Horiz | Split Vert | Done |

Directions | Situation | ⊪ Income Statement | ⊪ EPS | ⊪ Transactions | ⊪ Communication | ⊪ Research/Authoritative Literature | Resources

1. Directions

In the following simulation, you will be asked to complete various tasks. You may use the content in the **Information Tabs** to complete the tasks in the **Work Tabs**.

Information Tabs:

FIG 1

- Go through each of the **Information Tabs** to familiarize yourself with the simulation content
- The **Resources** tab will contain information, including formulas and definitions, that may help you to complete the tasks
- Your simulation may have more **Information Tabs** than those shown in Fig. 1

Work Tabs:

FIG. 2

- **Work Tabs**, to the right of **Information Tabs**, contain the tasks for you to complete
- **Work Tabs** contain directions for completing each task - be sure to read these directions carefully
- The tab names in Fig. 2 are for illustration only - yours may differ
- Once you complete any part of a task, the pencil for that tab will be shaded (see **Communication** in Fig. 2)
- The shaded pencil does **NOT** indicate that you have completed the entire task
- You must complete all of the tasks in the **Work Tabs** to receive full credit

Research/Authoritative Literature Tab:

| ⊪ Research/Authoritative Literature |

FIG. 3

- This tab contains both the Research task and the Authoritative Literature
- Detailed instructions for completing the Research task, and for using the Authoritative Literature, appear on this tab
- You may use the Authoritative Literature as a resource for completing other tasks

NOTE: If you believe you have encountered a software malfunction, report it to the test center staff immediately.

2. Situation

Pucket Corp. is in the process of preparing its financial statements for the year ended December 31, Year 4. Before closing the books, it prepared the following:

Condensed Trial Balance
December 31, Year 4

	Debit	Credit
Total assets	$ 7,082,500	
Total liabilities		$ 1,700,000
Common stock		1,250,000
Additional paid-in capital		2,097,500
Donated capital		90,000
Retained earnings, 1/1/Year 4		1,650,000
Net sales		6,250,000
Cost of sales	3,750,000	
Selling and administrative expenses	1,212,500	
Interest expense	122,500	
Gain on sale of long-term investments		130,000
Income tax expense	300,000	
Loss on disposition of plant assets	225,000	
Loss due to earthquake damage	475,000	
	$13,167,500	$13,167,500

Other financial data for the year ended December 31, Year 4:

- Sales returns and allowances equaled $215,000, and sales discounts taken were $95,000.

- Estimated federal income tax payments were $200,000, and accrued federal income taxes equaled $100,000. The total charged to income tax expense does not properly reflect current or deferred income tax expense or interperiod income tax allocation for income statement purposes. The enacted tax rate on all types of taxable income for the current and future years is 30%. The alternative minimum tax is less than the regular income tax.

- Interest expense includes 6% interest on 20-year bonds issued at their face amount of $1,500,000.

- A $90,000 excess of carrying amount over tax basis in depreciable assets arose from receipt of a contribution of equipment by a local government on December 31, Year 4. It is expected to be depreciated over 5 years beginning in Year 5. There were no temporary differences prior to Year 5.

- Officers' life insurance expense (not tax deductible) is $70,000.

- The earthquake damage is considered unusual and infrequent, but the disposition of plant assets is considered infrequent but not unusual. Moreover, the disposition of plant assets was not a disposal of a component of an entity.

- The shares of common stock ($5 par) traded on a national exchange:

Outstanding at 1/1/Year 4	200,000
Issued on 3/30/Year 4 as a 10% stock dividend	20,000
Issued shares for $25 per share on 6/30/Year 4	30,000
Outstanding at 12/31/Year 4	250,000

- Pucket declared a $1.25 common stock dividend on December 28, Year 4.

3. Income Statement

This type of question is presented in a spreadsheet format that requires you to fill in the correct response in the shaded cells provided. Using the information provided below, complete the multiple-step income statement for Pucket Corporation. Write your answers for the income statement line classifications in the shaded areas.

Pucket Corporation Income Statement For the Year Ended December 31, Year 4		
Net sales		$
Cost of sales		
Gross profit		
Selling and administrative expenses		
Income from operations		
Other revenues and gains:		
Gain on sale of long-term investments		
Other expenses and losses:		
Interest expense	$	
Loss on disposition of plant assets		
Income from continuing operations before income tax		
Income tax expense:		
Current tax expense		
Deferred tax expense		
Income before extraordinary item		
Extraordinary item-loss from earthquake (net of applicable taxes)		
Net income		$

4. EPS

This type of question is presented in a spreadsheet format that requires you to fill in the correct response in the shaded cells provided. Based on the information provided in the situation, complete the EPS calculation as follows. Write your answer in the shaded boxes provided.

Basic EPS	Answer
1. Income before extraordinary items	
2. Extraordinary items	
3. Net income	

5. Classification of Transactions

This set of questions has a matching format. Select the BEST match for each numbered item from the terms in the drop-down list and write its letter in the column provided. Each choice may be used once, more than once, or not at all.

Transaction	Answer
1. An increase in the unrealized holding loss for trading securities.	
2. An increase in the unrealized holding loss for available-for-sale securities.	
3. Income from operations of an operating segment in the segment's disposal year. The operations and cash flows of the segment can be clearly distinguished from the rest of the entity for operational and financial reporting purposes.	
4. A gain on remeasuring a foreign subsidiary's financial statements from the local currency into the functional currency.	
5. A loss on translating a foreign subsidiary's financial statements from the functional local currency into the reporting currency.	
6. A loss caused by a major earthquake in an area previously considered to be subject only to minor tremors.	
7. The probable receipt of $1 million from a pending lawsuit.	
8. The purchase of research and development services. There were no other research and development activities.	

Choices
A) Income from continuing operations, with no separate disclosure
B) Income from continuing operations, with separate disclosure
C) Extraordinary items
D) Other comprehensive income
E) None of the other categories

6. Communication

Please write a memorandum explaining the characteristics of extraordinary items. Also, provide examples of items that are not considered extraordinary and describe the exceptional circumstances in which they may be extraordinary.

REMINDER: Your response will be graded for both technical content and writing skills. Technical content will be evaluated for information that is helpful to the intended reader and clearly relevant to the issue. Writing skills will be evaluated for development, organization, and the appropriate expression of ideas in professional correspondence. Use a standard business memo or letter format with a clear beginning, middle, and end. Do not convey information in the form of a table, bullet point list, or other abbreviated presentation.

```
To:        File
From:      CPA
Subject:   Extraordinary Items
```

---

7. Research/Authoritative Literature

See page 12 in the Introduction of this book for a detailed explanation of the AICPA's new Research/Authoritative Literature work tab as well as a screenshot of how the tab will actually look on your exam.

Research and cite the statement in the FASB Current Text or Original Pronouncements that deals with the recognition and measurement of impairment losses.

Unofficial Answers

3. Income Statement (16 Gradable Items)

Pucket Corporation Income Statement For the Year Ended December 31, Year 4		
Net sales		$6,250,000 [1]
Cost of sales		3,750,000 [2]
Gross profit		2,500,000 [3]
Selling and administrative expenses		1,212,500 [4]
Income from operations		1,287,500 [5]
Other revenues and gains:		
Gain on sale of long-term investments		130,000 [6]
Other expenses and losses:		
Interest expense	(122,500) [7]	
Loss on disposition of plant assets	($225,000) [8]	(347,500) [9]
Income from continuing operations before income tax		1,070,000 [10]
Income tax expense:		
Current tax expense	342,000 [11]	
Deferred tax expense	27,000 [12]	369,000 [13]
Income before extraordinary item		701,000 [14]
Extraordinary item-loss from earthquake (net of applicable taxes)		332,500 [15]
Net income		$368,500 [16]

Explanation of amounts

[1] Net sales equals $6,250,000 as provided in the situation.

[2] Cost of sales equals $3,750,000 as provided in the situation.

[3] Gross profit is $2,500,000 ($6,250,000 net sales – $3,750,000 cost of sales).

[4] Selling and administrative expenses equal $1,212,500 as provided in the situation.

[5] Income from operations is $1,287,500 ($2,500,000 gross profit – $1,212,500 selling and administrative expenses).

[6] The gain on the sale of long-term investments is considered an infrequent but not unusual event. Thus, this gain must be reported in the other revenues and gains section.

[7] Interest expense equals $122,500 as provided in the situation. Interest expense is generally presented in the other expenses and losses section.

[8] The loss on the disposition of plant assets is considered an infrequent but not unusual event. Thus, this gain must be reported in the other expenses and losses section.

[9] The total of other expenses and losses is $347,500 ($122,500 interest expense + $225,000 loss on disposition of plant assets).

[10] Income from continuing operations before income tax is $1,070,000 ($1,287,500 operating income + $130,000 other revenues and gains − $347,500 other expenses and losses).

[11]
Income before income taxes and extraordinary item	$1,070,000
Plus officers' life insurance expense (nondeductible)	70,000
Income subject to tax	1,140,000
Income tax rate	× 30%
Income taxes excluding extraordinary item	$ 342,000

[12]
Excess of carrying amount over tax basis in depreciable assets (expected to reverse equally over next 5 years)	$90,000
Deferred income tax liability, 12/31/Year 4 ($90,000 × 30%)	$27,000
Minus beginning balance, 1/1/Year 4	0
Net change in deferred tax liability for Year 4	$27,000

[13]
Current tax expense	$342,000
Plus deferred tax expense	27,000
Total income tax expense	$369,000

[14] Income before extraordinary item is $701,000 ($1,070,000 income from continuing operations before income tax − $369,000 income tax expense).

[15]
Extraordinary loss from earthquake damage	$475,000
Minus income tax benefit ($475,000 × 30%)	142,500
Net of income tax effect	$332,500

[16] Net income is $368,500 ($701,000 income before extraordinary item − $332,500 extraordinary loss).

4. EPS (3 Gradable Items)

1. **$2.98.** The weighted-average number of shares outstanding is 235,000 {200,000 + 20,000 + [30,000 × (6 ÷12)]}. Basic EPS before extraordinary item is $2.98 ($701,000 income before extraordinary item ÷ 235,000 shares).

2. **$(1.41).** Basic loss per share for the extraordinary item (net of tax effect) is $(1.41) ($332,500 ÷ 235,000 shares).

3. **$1.57.** Net income is $368,500 ($701,000 − $332,500). Basic EPS for net income is $1.57 ($368,500 ÷ 235,000 shares).

5. Classification of Transactions (8 Gradable Items)

1. B) - An unrealized holding loss (a decline in fair value) on trading securities must be recognized in earnings. The change in net unrealized holding gain or loss included in earnings for the period must be disclosed.

2. D) - An unrealized holding loss on available-for-sale securities is excluded from earnings and reported in other comprehensive income until realized. SFAS 115 requires a variety of disclosures regarding available-for-sale securities.

3. E) - The operating segment meets the criteria for classification as a component of an entity. Thus, its operating results should be reported in discontinued operations provided that (1) its operations and cash flows will be or have been eliminated from the ongoing operations of the entity as a result of the disposal and (2) the entity will have no significant continuing involvement after the disposal.

4. A) - Remeasurement gains and losses are included in income from continuing operations. SFAS 52, *Foreign Currency Translation*, is silent regarding remeasurement disclosures.

5. D) - Translation adjustments are reported in other comprehensive income. They are not reported in earnings until the entity is sold or liquidated.

6. C) - Because the area has previously been subject to minor tremors only, the loss caused by the major earthquake is unusual and infrequent in the environment in which the entity operates. Hence, the loss meets the criteria of an extraordinary item.

7. E) - A gain contingency is not recognized until realized, but it should be disclosed. However, care should be taken to avoid misleading implications about the likelihood of realization.

8. B) - The costs of R&D contract services are included in R&D costs. These costs are reported under continuing operations with separate disclosure.

6. Communication (5 Gradable Items; for grading information, please refer to page 12.)

To: File
From: CPA
Subject: Extraordinary Items

According to APB Opinion 30, a material transaction or event that is unusual in nature and infrequent in occurrence in the environment in which the entity operates should be reported as an extraordinary item. These criteria, however, do not apply when a pronouncement specifically defines certain gains and losses as extraordinary items. A transaction or event is unusual if it has a high degree of abnormality and is of a type clearly unrelated to, or only incidentally related to, the ordinary and typical activities of the entity. A transaction or event is infrequent if it is not reasonably expected to recur in the foreseeable future; e.g., earthquakes are extraordinary in Florida, not Japan.

APB Opinion 30 gives specific examples of items that are not extraordinary, subject to certain exceptions. The following are classes of items that are not extraordinary: (1) write-downs of receivables, inventories, and intangible assets; (2) gains and losses from exchange or translation of foreign currencies, including those resulting from major devaluations and revaluations; (3) gains and losses on disposal of a component of an entity; (4) other gains and losses from sale or abandonment of property, plant, and equipment used in the business; (5) effects of strikes, including those against competitors and major suppliers; and (6) adjustments of accruals on long-term contracts.

In rare cases, however, an event or transaction that is material, unusual, and infrequent may result in an extraordinary gain or loss that includes one or more of the gains or losses listed above. In those cases, gains and losses, for example, from writedowns or from sale or abandonment of property used in the business, should be included in the extraordinary item if they directly resulted from (1) a major casualty, (2) an expropriation, or (3) a prohibition under a newly enacted law or regulation. Any portion of the losses that would have resulted from valuation of assets on a going-concern basis (such as the loss from writing down assets to fair value) is not included in the extraordinary item.

7. Research/Authoritative Literature (1 Gradable Item)

Answer: FAS 144, Par. 7

FAS 144 -- *Accounting for the Impairment or Disposal of Long-Lived Assets*
Long-Lived Assets to Be Held and Used
Recognition and Measurement of an Impairment Loss

7. For purposes of this Statement, *impairment* is the condition that exists when the carrying amount of a long-lived asset (asset group) exceeds its fair value. An impairment loss shall be recognized only if the carrying amount of a long-lived asset (asset group) is not recoverable and exceeds its fair value. The carrying amount of a long-lived asset (asset group) is not recoverable if it exceeds the sum of the undiscounted cash flows expected to result from the use and eventual disposition of the asset (asset group). That assessment shall be based on the carrying amount of the asset (asset group) at the date it is tested for recoverability, whether in use (paragraph 19) or under development (paragraph 20). An impairment loss shall be measured as the amount by which the carrying amount of a long-lived asset (asset group) exceeds its fair value.

Scoring Schedule:

	Correct Responses		Gradable Items		Weights		
Tab 3	_____	÷	16	×	20%	=	_____
Tab 4	_____	÷	3	×	15%	=	_____
Tab 5	_____	÷	8	×	20%	=	_____
Tab 6	_____	÷	5	×	30%	=	_____
Tab 7	_____	÷	1	×	15%	=	_____
							¯¯¯¯¯¯¯¯
							(Your Score)

Use Gleim's **CPA Gleim Online** to practice more simulations in a realistic environment.

STUDY UNIT FOUR
FINANCIAL STATEMENT DISCLOSURE

(16 pages of outline)

According to the **full disclosure principle**, understandable information capable of affecting user decisions should be reported. The financial statements are the primary means of disclosure. However, almost all accounting pronouncements require additional disclosures in the notes. Because memorizing them is virtually impossible, candidates should anticipate the disclosure requirements before reading the summary, outline, or actual pronouncement. The appropriate perspective is that of an informed creditor or investor.

The study unit begins with significant accounting policies to set the tone for the types of disclosures required by GAAP.

4.1 SIGNIFICANT ACCOUNTING POLICIES

Definition

1. **Accounting policies** are the specific principles and methods used by the reporting entity. Management selects these policies as the most appropriate for presentation of financial statements fairly, in all material respects, in accordance with GAAP.

Scope

2. APB Opinion 22, *Disclosure of Accounting Policies*, requires **business and not-for-profit** entities to disclose all significant accounting policies as an **integral part** of the financial statements.

   a. But it does **not** require disclosure of accounting policies in **unaudited interim financial statements** when the reporting entity has not changed its policies since the end of the preceding fiscal year.

Presentation

3. The preferred presentation is a **summary of accounting policies** in a separate section preceding the notes or in the initial note.

4. The disclosure should include **accounting principles adopted** and the **methods** of applying them that materially affect the financial statements. Disclosure extends to accounting policies that involve

   a. A selection from existing acceptable alternatives,

   b. Policies unique to the industry in which the entity operates, even if they are predominantly followed in that industry, and

   c. GAAP applied in an unusual or innovative way.

5.   Certain disclosures about policies of **business entities** are **commonly required**.

    a.   These items include (1) the basis of consolidation, (2) depreciation methods, (3) amortization of intangible assets (excluding goodwill, which is not amortizable), (4) inventory pricing, (5) recognition of profit on long-term construction-type contracts, and (6) recognition of revenue from franchising and leasing operations.

    b.   Disclosure of accounting policies should **not duplicate details** presented elsewhere. For example, the summary of significant policies should not contain the composition of plant assets, the composition of inventories, or the maturity dates of long-term debt.

        1)   However, in some cases, the summary should refer to details about these matters presented elsewhere in the financial statements.

6.   An entity must disclose its policy for determining which items are cash equivalents.

Stop and review! You have completed the outline for this subunit. Study multiple-choice questions 1 through 3 on page 161.

4.2 SEGMENT REPORTING

Scope

1.   SFAS 131, *Disclosures about Segments of an Enterprise and Related Information*, applies to the interim financial reports and annual financial statements of **public business entities**.

    a.   Such an entity must (1) have issued securities traded in a public market, (2) be required to file with the SEC, or (3) provide financial statements for the purpose of publicly issuing securities.

Objective

2.   The objective is to provide information about the different types of business activities of the entity and the economic environments in which it operates.

    a.   Ordinarily, information is to be reported on the basis that it is **used internally for evaluating performance and making resource allocation decisions** (the management approach).

    b.   Disclosure of information is not required if it is not prepared for internal use, and reporting it would not be feasible.

Operating Segment Approach

3.   This approach matches external and internal reporting. Segmentation is based on internal organizational structure and the availability of separate financial information. An **operating segment** has three characteristics:

    a.   It is a business component of the entity that may earn revenues and incur expenses.

    b.   Its operating results are regularly reviewed by the entity's **chief operating decision maker (CODM)** for the purpose of resource allocation and performance assessment.

    c.   Its separate financial information is available.

Aggregation Criteria

4.   Operating segments may be aggregated if (a) doing so is consistent with the **objective**; (b) they have similar economic characteristics; and (c) they have similar products and services, production processes, classes of customers, distribution methods, and regulatory environments.

Reportable Segments

5. These are operating segments (or an aggregation) that also must meet one of the **quantitative thresholds** given below. The amounts of reported segment items used in the thresholds are the measures that are reviewed by the CODM. Furthermore, if an operating segment does not meet any of the thresholds, management may report it if such information would be useful to readers of the statements.

    a. **Revenue test.** Reported revenue, including sales to external customers and intersegment sales or transfers, is at least 10% of the combined revenue of all operating segments.

    b. **Asset test.** Assets are at least 10% of the combined assets of all operating segments.

    c. **Profit (loss) test.** The absolute amount of reported profit or loss is at least 10% of the greater, in absolute amount, of either the combined reported **profit** of all operating segments that did **not** report a loss, or the combined reported **loss** of all operating segments that **did** report a loss.

6. Information about operating segments **not** meeting the quantitative thresholds may be **combined** to produce a reportable segment only if the operating segments share a **majority of the aggregation criteria**.

7. If the **total external revenue** of the operating segments meeting the quantitative thresholds is **less than 75%** of consolidated revenue, additional operating segments are identified as reportable until the 75% level is reached.

8. Information about nonreportable activities and segments is combined and disclosed in an **"all other" category** as a reconciling item.

9. As the number of reportable segments increases above 10, the entity may decide that it has reached a practical limit.

Disclosures

10. Disclosures include the following:

    a. **General information**, such as the factors used to identify the reportable segments, including the basis of organization, and the types of revenue-generating products and services for each reportable segment.

    b. A **measure of profit or loss and total assets** for each reportable segment. Moreover, if the amounts are included in the measure of profit or loss reviewed by the CODM or are otherwise regularly provided to that person, other disclosures include the following: (1) revenues from external customers and other operating segments, (2) interest revenue and expense, (3) depreciation, (4) depletion, (5) amortization, (6) unusual items, (7) equity in the net income of equity-based investees, (8) income tax expense or benefit, (9) extraordinary items, and (10) other significant noncash items.

    c. The investment in **equity-based investees** and total expenditures for additions to most **long-lived assets** for each reportable segment if they are included in the segment assets reviewed by the CODM.

Interest

11. A segment's **interest revenue** and **interest expense** are reported separately. However, a majority of a segment's revenues may be from interest, with net interest revenue the primary basis for assessing its performance and the resources allocated to it. In this case, **net interest revenue** may be reported given proper disclosure.

Measurement

12. The external information reported is measured in the same way as the internal information used to evaluate a segment's performance and allocate assets to it. The amount of a reported segment item, such as assets, is the measure reported to the CODM for purposes of resource allocation and performance evaluation. The specific elements used in the measure are determined by the reporting entity.

    a. If the CODM uses **more than one measure** of a segment's profit or loss or assets, the reported measures are those most consistent with the consolidated statements.

    b. **Explanations of the measurements** of segment profit or loss and segment assets should be given for each reportable segment.

Reconciliations

13. Reconciliations to the **consolidated amounts** must be provided for the **total reportable segments'** amounts for significant items of information disclosed.

    a. Significant reconciling items should be separately identified and described.

    b. However, reconciliations of **balance sheet items** are required only for years in which a balance sheet is presented.

Interim Period Information

14. This information is disclosed for each reportable segment in **condensed financial statements**. Disclosures include (a) external revenues; (b) intersegment revenues; (c) a measure of segment profit or loss; (d) total assets that have materially changed since the last annual report; (e) differences from the last annual report in the basis of segmentation or of segment profit or loss; and (f) a reconciliation of the total reportable segments' profit or loss to consolidated pretax income and its components.

Restatements

15. Restatement of **previously reported information** is required if changes in internal organization cause the **composition of reportable segments** to change. However, an entity must restate only items of disclosure that it can feasibly restate.

    a. The entity may choose **not to restate** segment information for earlier periods, including interim periods. Segment information for the year of the change then must be disclosed under the **old basis and the new basis** of segmentation if feasible.

Entity-Wide Disclosures

16. Such disclosures must be provided only if they are not given in the reportable operating-segment information.

    a. Revenues from external customers for **each product and service** (or each group of similar products and services) are reported if feasible based on the financial information used to produce the general-purpose financial statements.

    b. The following information about **geographic areas** is also reported if feasible: (1) external revenues attributed to the home country and to all foreign countries, (2) material external revenues attributed to an individual foreign country, (3) the basis for attributing revenues from external customers, and (4) certain information about assets.

    c. If **10% or more** of revenue is derived from sales to any **single customer**, (1) that fact, (2) the amount from each such customer, and (3) the segment(s) reporting the revenues must be disclosed. Single customers include entities under common control and each federal, state, local, or foreign government.

Stop and review! You have completed the outline for this subunit. Study multiple-choice questions 4 through 10 beginning on page 162.

4.3 INTERIM FINANCIAL REPORTING

Scope

1. APB Opinion 28, *Interim Financial Reporting*, does not require reporting of interim information, but it applies whenever entities issue such information. Furthermore, this pronouncement states minimum disclosure requirements when **publicly traded entities** issue **summarized interim information**.

    a. An issuer of securities required to register with the SEC must file quarterly reports on **Form 10-Q**. These reports include data similar to that in annual reports.

    b. For many reasons, the usefulness of interim financial information is limited. Hence, their best qualitative characteristic is **timeliness**.

Modification of GAAP

2. Each interim period is treated primarily as an **integral part of an annual period**. Ordinarily, the results for an interim period should be based on the same accounting principles the entity uses in preparing annual statements.

    a. Certain principles and practices used for annual reporting may require modification at interim dates. Interim reports will then relate more closely to the results of operations for the annual period.

Revenue and Associated Costs

3. **Revenue**, e.g., from long-term construction contracts, should be recognized as earned during an interim period on the same basis as followed for the full year.

4. **Costs associated with revenue** are treated similarly for annual and interim reporting. However, some exceptions are appropriate for **inventory accounting** at interim dates.

    a. The **gross profit method** may be used for estimating cost of goods sold and inventory. A physical count at the interim date may not be feasible. See Study Unit 7.

    b. Use of **LIFO** at an interim date may cause a partial liquidation of the base period inventory level. If the decline is temporary and the partial liquidation will be replaced prior to year-end, no effect is given to the LIFO liquidation.

       1) **Cost of goods sold** for the interim period should include the expected cost of replacing the liquidated LIFO base.

    c. An inventory loss from a **market decline** may be deferred if no loss is reasonably anticipated for the year.

       1) Inventory losses from **nontemporary market declines**, however, must be recognized at the interim date. If the loss is recovered during the fiscal year (in another quarter), it is treated as a **change in estimate**. The price recovery recognized is limited to the losses previously recognized.

    d. Entities using **standard costing** ordinarily should follow the same procedures for reporting variances at interim dates as at year-end. But **planned variances** are deferred if they are expected to be absorbed in subsequent interim periods of a year.

       1) Unanticipated variances are recognized in the interim period when incurred.

All Other Costs and Expenses

5. Costs and expenses **other than product costs** are either charged to income in interim periods as incurred or allocated among interim periods. The **allocation** is based on the (a) benefits received, (b) estimates of time expired, or (c) activities associated with the period. If an item expensed for annual reporting periods benefits more than one interim period, it should be allocated.

    a. **Gains and losses** that are similar to gains and losses that would not be deferred at year-end are not deferred to later interim periods. For example, an **extraordinary gain** is recorded in full in the quarter in which it occurs.

    b. **Annual major repairs** are expensed in annual statements but should be allocated to the interim periods that are clearly benefited.

    c. **Quantity discounts** based on annual sales volume should be charged to interim periods based on periodic sales.

    d. **Interest, rent, and property taxes** may be accrued or deferred at interim dates to provide an appropriate cost in each period.

EXAMPLE

On March 15 of the current year, Chen Company paid property taxes of $120,000 on its factory building for the current calendar year. On April 1, Chen made $240,000 in unanticipated repairs to its equipment. The repairs will benefit operations for the remainder of the calendar year.

The benefit from the payment of the property taxes relates to all four quarters of the current year and should be prorated at $30,000 ($120,000 ÷ 4) per quarter. The benefit from the unanticipated repairs to plant equipment relates to the second, third, and fourth quarters. It should be spread evenly over these quarters at $80,000 ($240,000 ÷ 3) per quarter.

---

    e. **Advertising costs** may be deferred within a fiscal year if the benefits clearly extend beyond the interim period of the expenditure.

    f. Certain costs and expenses, such as (1) inventory shrinkage, (2) allowance for bad debts, (3) allowance for quantity discounts, and (4) discretionary bonuses, are subject to **year-end adjustment**. To the extent possible, these adjustments should be estimated and assigned to interim periods.

Seasonality

6. If interim information is issued, certain **disclosures** are mandatory for businesses that have **material seasonal fluctuations**. These fluctuations cannot be smoothed in interim information.

    a. Accordingly, reporting entities must disclose the seasonal nature of their activities. They also should consider supplementing interim reports with information for the 12-month period that ended at the interim date for the current and preceding years.

Income Taxes

7. At the end of each interim period, the entity should **estimate the annual effective tax rate**. This rate is used in providing for income taxes on a current year-to-date basis.

    a. FASB Interpretation No. 18, *Accounting for Income Taxes in Interim Periods*, specifies that **interim period tax expense (benefit)** equals the **estimated annual effective tax rate**, times year-to-date "ordinary" income (loss), minus the tax expense (benefit) recognized in previous interim periods.

        1) **"Ordinary"** in this context means excluding unusual or infrequent items, extraordinary items, and results of discontinued operations.

b. The **estimated annual effective tax rate** is based on the statutory rate adjusted for the current year's expected conditions. These include (1) anticipated tax credits, (2) foreign tax rates, (3) capital gains rates, and (4) other tax planning alternatives.

   1) The rate also includes the effect of any expected **valuation allowance** at year-end for **deferred tax assets** related to deductible temporary differences and carryforwards arising during the year.

   2) The rate is determined without regard to significant unusual or extraordinary items to be reported separately or reported net of tax effect. However, such items are recognized in the interim period when they occur. The method of **intraperiod tax allocation** described in Study Unit 10 is used.

c. A **tax benefit** is recognized for a **loss** early in the year if the benefits are expected to be realized during the year or recognizable as a deferred tax asset at year-end.

   1) A **valuation allowance** must be recognized if it is **more likely than not** that a deferred tax asset will not be fully realized. Accordingly, the tax benefit of an "ordinary" loss early in the year is not recognized to the extent that this criterion is met.

   a) However, no income tax expense is recognized for subsequent "ordinary" income until the earlier unrecognized tax benefit is used.

   2) The foregoing principles are applied in determining the estimated tax benefit of an "ordinary" loss for the fiscal year used to calculate (a) the annual effective tax rate and (b) the year-to-date tax benefit of a loss.

EXAMPLE

The following information was used in preparing quarterly income statements during the first half of the current year:

Quarter	Income Before Income Taxes	Estimated Effective Annual Income Tax Rate
1	$80,000	45%
2	70,000	45%
3	50,000	40%

The tax expense for the third quarter equals the estimated annual effective tax rate determined at the end of the third quarter times the cumulative year-to-date "ordinary" income (loss), minus the cumulative tax expense for the first two quarters. At the end of the third quarter, the year-to-date "ordinary" income is $200,000 ($80,000 + $70,000 + $50,000), and the cumulative tax expense is $80,000 ($200,000 × 40%). Because the cumulative tax expense at the end of the second quarter was $67,500 [($80,000 + $70,000) × 45%], $12,500 ($80,000 – $67,500) should be reported as income tax expense in the income statement for the third quarter.

---

d. Taxes on all items other than continuing operations are determined at incremental rates. Thus, their **marginal effect on taxes** is calculated.

8. **Accounting Changes in Interim Periods**

a. SFAS 154, *Accounting Changes and Error Corrections*, applies to interim as well as annual periods. A change in **accounting principle** is retrospectively applied unless it is **impracticable** to determine the cumulative or period-specific effects of the change. However, the impracticability exception does not apply to **prechange interim periods** of the fiscal year of change. When application to prechange interim periods is impracticable, the change is made at the **beginning of the next annual period**.

   1) The **cumulative effect** of the change on periods prior to those presented is reflected in the carrying amounts of assets, liabilities, and retained earnings (or other appropriate components of equity or net assets) at the beginning of the first period presented.

2)   All periods presented must be adjusted for **period-specific effects**.

EXAMPLE

The following information is applicable to a change in accounting principle made in the second quarter of the year from FIFO to LIFO. The new principle can be applied retrospectively. For all relevant periods, prices have risen. The effect of the change is limited to the effects on the inventory balance and income tax provisions (a 40% tax rate).

Period	Net Income on the Basis of FIFO	Gross Effect of Changes	Gross Effect Minus Income Taxes
Prior to 1st Qtr	$6,262,000	$300,000	$180,000
1st Qtr	1,032,400	60,000	36,000
2nd Qtr	1,282,400	60,000	36,000
3rd Qtr	1,298,600	90,000	54,000
4th Qtr	1,164,800	120,000	72,000

Given the period-specific effects for the first quarter, net income based on retrospective application is $996,400 ($1,032,400 – $36,000 gross after-tax effect of applying the new principle). Changing to LIFO when prices are rising decreases net income.

---

b.   A **change in an accounting estimate**, including a change in the estimated effective annual tax rate, is accounted for in the interim period in which the change is made and in future periods. Prior-period information is not retrospectively adjusted.

Prior Interim Period Adjustments

9.   SFAS 16, *Prior Period Adjustments*, applies to adjustment or settlement of (a) litigation, (b) income taxes (except for the effects of retroactive tax legislation), (c) renegotiation proceedings, or (d) utility revenue under rate-making processes.

a.   All or part of the adjustment or settlement must relate specifically to a **prior interim period of the current year**. Moreover, its effect must be material, and the amount must have become reasonably estimable only in the current interim period.

b.   If an **item of profit or loss** occurs in other than the first interim period and meets the criteria for an adjustment, the portion of the item allocable to the current interim period is included in net income for that period.

1)   The financial statements for the prior interim periods are **restated** to include their allocable portions of the adjustment.

2)   The portion of the adjustment directly related to **prior fiscal years** is included in net income of the **first interim period** of the current fiscal year.

EXAMPLE

On June 1, Year 5, a calendar-year entity settled a patent infringement lawsuit. The court awarded it $3,000,000 in damages. Of this amount, $1,000,000 related to Year 3, $1,000,000 to Year 4, and $500,000 to each of the first two quarters in Year 5. The applicable tax rate is 40%. Prior interim periods should be restated to include their allocable portions of the adjustment. Accordingly, $500,000 of the settlement should be included in earnings for the second quarter. Given a tax rate of 40%, the settlement increases net income of the second quarter by $300,000.

Summarized Financial Information

10. Publicly traded companies may report **information at interim dates** that is less detailed than information in annual statements. The required **minimum disclosures** when such reports are issued include

    a. Sales or gross revenues, provision for income taxes, extraordinary items, net income, and comprehensive income
    b. Basic and diluted EPS for each period presented
    c. Seasonal revenues, costs, or expenses
    d. Significant changes in estimates or provisions for income taxes
    e. Disposal of a component of an entity and unusual or infrequent items
    f. Contingent items
    g. Changes in accounting principles or estimates
    h. Significant changes in financial position

       1) Reporting of balance sheet and cash flow data is encouraged. If this information is not presented, significant changes in liquid assets, net working capital, long-term liabilities, or equity should be disclosed.

    i. Certain information about reportable operating segments
    j. Certain information about defined benefit postretirement benefit plans

       1) Net periodic benefit cost, with separate disclosures of its components and the gain (loss) due to settlement or curtailment
       2) Total employer's contributions paid and expected to be paid in the current year if significantly different from amounts previously disclosed

    k. Certain information about fair value measurement of assets and liabilities

11. When **summarized quarterly data** are regularly reported, the information for the current quarter and the current year to date (or the last 12 months to date) should be provided along with comparable data for the preceding year.

Disclosures

12. The following are separately disclosed, included in interim-period net income, and not prorated over the year:

    a. **Extraordinary items**
    b. Gains or losses from disposal of a **component of an entity**
    c. Material **unusual or infrequent items**

13. Disclosures of **contingencies** are the same for interim and annual periods.

14. **Unusual seasonal results** and **business combinations** also should be disclosed.

15. If an **accounting change** is made in an interim period, the entity must make all disclosures in the **period of change** that are required for annual reporting. They include the nature of, and reason for, the change.

    a. In a **postchange** interim period of the fiscal year of the change, the effect on (1) income from continuing operations, (2) net income (or other appropriate captions), and (3) related per-share amounts must be disclosed for that interim period.

16. In the financial reports of the interim period when the adjustment occurs, the entity discloses the effect on (a) income from continuing operations, (b) net income, and (c) related per-share amounts for each prior interim period of the current year and for each prior interim period restated.

17. When interim data are **not reported separately for the fourth quarter**, certain disclosures must be made in a note. They are less extensive than the minimum information required when an entity chooses to report at interim dates.

    a. The disclosures must include (1) disposals of components of an entity; (2) extraordinary, unusual, or infrequent items; and (3) the aggregate effect of material year-end adjustments.

    b. If an **accounting change** is made in the fourth quarter, the appropriate disclosures about accounting changes also must be included in the note.

Stop and review! You have completed the outline for this subunit. Study multiple-choice questions 11 through 15 beginning on page 164.

4.4 RELATED PARTY DISCLOSURES

1. SFAS 57, *Related Party Disclosures*, requires the disclosure of material related party transactions other than (a) compensation arrangements (officers' salaries and expenses), (b) expense allowances, and (c) other similar items in the ordinary course of business. Related parties include

    a. A parent and its subsidiaries.
    b. Subsidiaries of a common parent.
    c. An entity and employee trusts managed by or under the trusteeship of the entity's management.
    d. An entity and its principal owners, management, or members of their immediate families. **Principal owners** are owners of record or known beneficial owners of more than 10% of the voting interests of the entity.
    e. Affiliates. An affiliate controls, is controlled by, or is under common control with an entity.
    f. An entity and (1) its equity-based investees or (2) other investees that would be accounted for by the equity method if the **fair value option** had not been elected (see Subunit 5.2).
    g. An entity and any other entity if one party can significantly influence the other to the extent that one party may be prevented from fully pursuing its interests.
    h. A party that can significantly influence the transacting parties or has an ownership interest in one and can significantly influence the other.

2. Related party transactions that are eliminated in the preparation of **consolidated or combined financial statements**, such as intraentity sales or loans, are not required to be disclosed in those statements.

3. Transactions between an entity and its management, such as borrowings and lendings, must be disclosed.

NOTE: The **Sarbanes-Oxley Act of 2002** generally prohibits an issuer, as defined by federal securities law, from extending credit to its directors and officers.

4. **Disclosures** required include

   a. The **nature of the relationship** involved

   b. A description of the **transactions** for each period an **income statement** is presented and such other information as is deemed necessary to an understanding of the effects of the transactions

   c. The **dollar amounts** of transactions for each period an **income statement** is presented and the effects of any change in the method of establishing their terms

   d. **Amounts due from or to related parties** at the date of each **balance sheet**, including the terms of settlement

   e. Certain **tax information** if the entity is part of a group that files a consolidated tax return, such as (1) aggregate current and deferred tax expense, (2) tax-related amounts due to or from affiliates, and (3) the method used to allocate consolidated current and deferred tax expense to group members

5. Disclosure of the effect on the **cash flow statement** for each period a cash flow statement is presented is not required.

Stop and review! You have completed the outline for this subunit. Study multiple-choice questions 16 through 19 beginning on page 166.

4.5 UNCONDITIONAL PURCHASE OBLIGATIONS

1. SFAS 47, *Disclosure of Long-Term Obligations*, requires disclosure of commitments "to transfer funds in the future for fixed or minimum amounts or quantities of goods or services at fixed or minimum prices."

   a. A **take-or-pay contract** requires one party to purchase a certain number of goods from the other party or else pay a penalty. A **throughput contract** requires one party to purchase a certain amount of services.

      1) **Sinking-fund requirements** for the retirement of long-term debt are also affected by the provisions of this pronouncement.

   b. A purchase obligation is considered **unconditional** if it

      1) Is either noncancelable or cancelable **only** (a) upon the happening of a remote contingency, (b) with the permission of the other party, or (c) under terms that make continuation or replacement (but not cancelation) of the agreement reasonably assured.

         a) A purchase obligation cancelable upon the payment of a **nominal penalty is not unconditional**.

      2) Was negotiated as part of the **financing arrangement for facilities** that will provide contracted goods or services.

      3) Has a remaining term of **more than 1 year**.

Disclosure – Recorded Obligations

2. **Disclosure** of the following information is required for **recorded obligations** for each of the 5 years following the date of the latest balance sheet presented:

   a. The aggregate amount of **payments** for unconditional purchase obligations

   b. The aggregate amount of **maturities** and **sinking-fund requirements** for all long-term borrowings

Disclosure – Unrecorded Obligations

3.   If an unconditional purchase obligation is **not recorded**, certain **disclosures** are required. They include the following:

    a.   The **nature and term** of the obligation

    b.   The **variable components** of the obligation

    c.   The **amounts purchased** under the obligation for each period an income statement is presented

    d.   Amount of the **fixed and determinable portion** of the obligation at the latest balance sheet date and, if determinable, for each of the 5 succeeding fiscal years

4.   When an unconditional purchase obligation is **not recorded**, the disclosure of the amount of **imputed interest** necessary to reduce the unconditional purchase obligation to its present value is encouraged.

    a.   If known by the purchaser, the rate should be the **initial effective interest rate** of the debt that financed the facilities providing the contracted goods or services.

        1)   If the rate **cannot** be determined by the purchaser, the **purchaser's incremental borrowing rate** should be used.

Stop and review! You have completed the outline for this subunit. Study multiple-choice questions 20 through 22 beginning on page 167.

4.6 SIGNIFICANT RISKS AND UNCERTAINTIES

1.   AICPA SOP 94-6, *Disclosure of Certain Significant Risks and Uncertainties*, requires disclosures at the balance sheet date about certain items that could significantly affect reported amounts in the near term, that is, within 1 year of the balance sheet date.

Nature of Operations

2.   One set of disclosures concerns risks and uncertainties relating to the nature of operations. Thus, entities must disclose their (a) major products or services, (b) principal markets, and (c) the locations of those markets. They also should disclose (a) all industries in which they operate; (b) the relative importance of each; and (c) the basis for determining the relative importance, e.g., assets, revenue, or earnings. However, this set of disclosures need not be quantified.

Use of Estimates

3.   A second type of disclosures concerns the use of estimates in the preparation of financial statements. Financial statements should explain that conformity with GAAP requires management to use numerous estimates.

Significant Estimates

4.   A third category of disclosures concerns certain significant estimates used to value assets, liabilities, or contingencies. Disclosures are required when the estimated effects of a condition, situation, or set of circumstances at the balance sheet date are subject to a **reasonable possibility** of change in the near term and the effects will be material.

    a.   The effect of using a different estimate determines **materiality**.

    b.   The nature of the uncertainty, that it is reasonably possible, and that the estimate may change in the near term are to be disclosed.

    c.   If an estimate is of a **loss contingency**, the disclosure should include the estimated range of loss or a statement that an estimate cannot be made.

    d.   Factors making an estimate sensitive to change may be, but need not be, disclosed.

    e.   If an entity is not required to make disclosures about certain significant estimates because it has employed **risk-reduction techniques**, it is encouraged to disclose the uncertainty and the risk-reduction techniques.

Concentrations

5. A fourth set of disclosures concerns **current vulnerability due to concentrations**, for example, when entities fail to diversify.

   a. Disclosure is necessary if management knows prior to issuance of the statements that

      1) The concentration **exists** at the balance sheet date,
      2) It makes the entity vulnerable to a near-term **severe impact**, and
      3) Such impact is at least **reasonably possible** in the near term.

   b. **Disclosable concentrations** include those in

      1) The volume of business with a given customer, supplier, lender, grantor, or contributor;
      2) Revenue from given products, services, or fund-raising events;
      3) The available suppliers of materials, labor, services, or rights (e.g., licenses) used in operations; and
      4) The market or geographic area where the entity operates.

   c. A **severe impact** may result from (1) loss of all or a part of a business relationship, (2) price or demand changes, (3) loss of a patent, (4) changes in the availability of a resource or right, or (5) the disruption of operations in a market or geographic area.

      1) Furthermore, it is always reasonably possible in the near term that (a) any customer, grantor, or contributor will be lost, and (b) operations located in another country will be disrupted.

   d. For concentrations of labor subject to **collective bargaining**, disclosure should include the percentage of employees covered by a collective bargaining agreement and the percentage covered by an agreement that will expire within 1 year.

      1) For concentrations of operations in **another country**, disclosure should include the carrying amounts of net assets and the areas where they are located.

Stop and review! You have completed the outline for this subunit. Study multiple-choice question 23 on page 168.

4.7 SUBSEQUENT EVENTS

1. AICPA AU 560, *Subsequent Events*, applies to certain material events or transactions that occur **after the balance sheet date** and **prior to the issuance of the financial statements**. These events and transactions require adjustment of, or disclosure in, the statements.

2. One type of subsequent event provides additional evidence about **conditions at the date of the balance sheet**. It affects the estimates inherent in statement preparation. An example is a loss on an uncollectible receivable as a result of a customer's bankruptcy.

   a. The financial statements should be **adjusted** for any resulting changes in estimates.

3. Subsequent events affecting the **realization of assets** (such as receivables and inventories) or the **settlement of estimated liabilities** ordinarily require **adjustment**. They usually reflect the resolution of conditions that existed over a relatively long period.

4. A second type of subsequent event provides evidence about **conditions that did not exist at the date of the balance sheet**. Some of these events require **disclosure** but not adjustment.

    a. Examples of subsequent events requiring **only disclosure** include

        1) Sale of a bond or capital stock issue

        2) Purchase of a business

        3) Settlement of litigation when the event resulting in the claim occurred after the balance sheet date

        4) Loss of plant or inventories as a result of fire or flood

        5) Losses on receivables resulting from conditions (e.g., a customer's major casualty) arising after the balance sheet date

    b. Some events of the second type may be so significant that the most appropriate disclosure is to supplement the historical statements with **pro forma financial data**.

    c. Subsequent events requiring only disclosure normally do not require modification of the auditor's report.

Stop and review! You have completed the outline for this subunit. Study multiple-choice questions 24 and 25 on page 169.

4.8 FINANCIAL INSTRUMENT DISCLOSURES

Definition

1. A **financial instrument** is cash, evidence of an ownership interest in an entity, or a contract that both

    a. Imposes on one entity a contractual obligation to

        1) Deliver cash or another financial instrument to a second entity or

        2) Exchange other financial instruments on potentially unfavorable terms with the second entity, and

    b. Conveys to that second entity a contractual right to

        1) Receive cash or another financial instrument from the first entity or

        2) Exchange other financial instruments on potentially favorable terms with the first entity.

2. SFAS 107, *Disclosures about Fair Value of Financial Instruments*, requires certain entities to disclose the **fair value** of financial instruments. This rule applies whether or not they are recognized if (a) it is feasible to estimate such fair values, and (b) the aggregated fair value is material.

    a. If estimating fair value is not feasible, disclosures include information pertinent to estimating fair value, such as the carrying amount, effective interest rate, and maturity. The reasons that estimating the fair value is not feasible also should be disclosed.

    b. SFAS 157, *Fair Value Measurements*, provides the framework for determining fair values, including approaches to measurement and a hierarchy of inputs to those approaches. See Study Unit 1.

    c. Ordinarily, disclosures should not net the fair values of instruments even if they are of the same class or are related, e.g., by a risk management strategy.

3. **Credit risk** is the risk of accounting loss from an instrument because of the possible failure of another party to perform.

    a. With certain exceptions, for example, (1) instruments of pension plans, (2) certain insurance contracts, (3) warranty obligations and rights, and (4) unconditional purchase obligations, an entity must disclose all significant **concentrations of credit risk** arising from instruments, whether from one counterparty or groups.

        1) **Group concentrations** arise when multiple counterparties have similar activities and economic characteristics that cause their **ability to meet obligations** to be similarly affected by changes in conditions.

    b. **Disclosures** (in the body of the statements or the notes) should include

        1) Information about the shared activity, region, or economic characteristic that identifies the concentration.

        2) The **maximum loss** due to credit risk if parties failed completely to perform and the security, if any, proved to be of no value.

        3) The **policy of requiring collateral** or other security, information about access to that security, and the nature and a brief description of the security.

        4) The policy of entering into **master netting arrangements** to mitigate the credit risk; information about them; and a description of the terms, including the extent to which they reduce the maximum amount of loss.

    c. An entity is encouraged, but not required, to disclose quantitative information about the **market risks** of instruments that is consistent with the way the entity manages those risks.

Derivatives and Hedging

4. **SFAS 161**, *Disclosures about Derivative Instruments and Hedging Activities*, applies to all entities and all derivatives and hedged items. Its objective is to help users understand (a) the reasons for using derivatives, (b) how they are used, (c) the accounting methods applied, and (d) their effect.

    a. The following are the disclosures for every reporting period for which **statements of financial position and performance** are issued:

        1) Objectives of **hedging instruments**; their context, including each instrument's **primary risk exposure**; and the entity's related strategies

            a) A distinction must be made between instruments (whether or not hedges) used for (1) risk management and (2) other purposes. The entity must disclose which **hedging instruments** are hedges of fair value, cash flows, or the net investment in a foreign operation. If derivatives are **not hedges**, their purpose must be described.

        2) Information about the **volume** of derivatives

        3) Optional qualitative disclosures in the form of discussion of **overall risk exposures** (interest rate, exchange rate, commodity price, equity price, and credit risks), even if not managed by using derivatives

        4) **Location** and **gross fair values** of reported derivatives

            a) These amounts are separately reported as **assets** and **liabilities** and classified as hedges and nonhedges. Within these classes, amounts are separately reported by **type of derivative**. The entity also must disclose the **line items** where the fair value amounts for the classes are reported.

5) Location and amounts of **gains and losses** on derivatives and hedged items

   a) This information includes **separate disclosures** for (1) fair value hedges (hedging instruments and hedged items), (2) **effective portions** of gains and losses on cash flow hedges and hedges of net investments that are currently recognized in OCI or reclassified from accumulated OCI, (3) **ineffective portions** and amounts excluded from the assessment of the effectiveness of cash flow hedges and hedges of net investments, and (4) derivatives that are **not** used as hedges.

   b) The information is separately reported by **type of derivative**, with identification of **line items**.

   c) An entity may include nonhedging derivatives in its **trading activities**. In this case, separate gain/loss disclosures for such instruments is **not** required if information about the trading activities is disclosed.

6) **Fair value hedging** instruments and hedged items. The entity discloses the **net gain (loss) reported in earnings** that results from

   a) Hedge ineffectiveness and the part of the derivatives' gain/loss not included in the assessment of hedge effectiveness.

   b) A **hedged firm commitment's** no longer qualifying as a fair value hedge.

7) **Cash flow hedging** instruments and hedged transactions. The entity discloses

   a) Transactions that will result in **reclassification into earnings** from accumulated OCI and the net amount estimated to be reclassified in the next 12 months.

   b) The maximum period for hedging of **forecasted transactions** (other than those related to current payment of variable interest).

   c) Amounts reclassified into earnings because of the **discontinuance of cash flow hedges** of forecasted transactions when it becomes probable they will not occur within the specified period.

  b. Disclosures for every reporting period for which a **statement of financial position** is issued are made for derivatives (and hedging nonderivatives) with **contingent features** that are related to **credit risk**.

   1) Nature of the features, how they may be activated in derivatives that are in a **net liability position**, and the aggregate fair values of such instruments

   2) An aggregate fair value of posted **collateral**, potentially required collateral, and immediate settlement amounts

Stop and review! You have completed the outline for this subunit. Study multiple-choice questions 26 through 28 beginning on page 169.

QUESTIONS

4.1 Significant Accounting Policies

1. Which of the following facts concerning fixed assets should be included in the summary of significant accounting policies?

	Depreciation Method	Composition
A.	No	Yes
B.	Yes	Yes
C.	Yes	No
D.	No	No

Answer (C) is correct. *(CPA, adapted)*
REQUIRED: The fact(s) concerning fixed assets disclosed in the summary of significant accounting policies.
DISCUSSION: APB Opinion 22 requires disclosure of significant accounting policies when (1) a selection has been made from existing acceptable alternatives; (2) a policy is unique to the industry in which the entity operates, even if the policy is predominantly followed in that industry; and (3) GAAP have been applied in an unusual or innovative way. A depreciation method is a selection from existing acceptable alternatives and should be included in the summary of significant accounting policies. APB Opinion 22 further recognizes that financial statement disclosure of accounting policies should not duplicate details presented elsewhere in the financial statements, such as composition of plant assets.

2. The summary of significant accounting policies should disclose the

A. Reasons that retrospective application of a change in an accounting principle is impracticable.

B. Basis of profit recognition on long-term construction contracts.

C. Adequacy of pension plan assets in relation to vested benefits.

D. Future minimum lease payments in the aggregate and for each of the 5 succeeding fiscal years.

Answer (B) is correct. *(CPA, adapted)*
REQUIRED: The item disclosed in the summary of significant accounting policies.
DISCUSSION: APB Opinion 22 lists certain items as commonly required disclosures in a summary of significant accounting policies: (1) the basis of consolidation, (2) depreciation methods, (3) amortization of intangible assets (excluding goodwill), (4) inventory pricing, (5) recognition of profit on long-term construction-type contracts, and (6) recognition of revenue from franchising and leasing operations.
Answer (A) is incorrect because, if retrospective application of a change in accounting principle is impracticable, SFAS 154 requires disclosure of the reasons and the alternative method of reporting the change. The reasons are not policies. Answer (C) is incorrect because the adequacy of pension plan assets in relation to vested benefits is not a disclosure required by APB Opinion 22 or SFAS 132(R). Answer (D) is incorrect because the future minimum lease payments in the aggregate and for each of the 5 succeeding fiscal years should be disclosed but not in the summary of significant accounting policies.

3. Which of the following items should be included in Melay, Inc.'s summary of significant accounting policies for the current year?

A. Property, plant, and equipment is recorded at cost with depreciation computed principally by the straight-line method.

B. During the current year, the Delay Segment was sold.

C. Business segment sales for the current year are Alay $1M, Belay $2M, and Celay $3M.

D. Future common share dividends are expected to approximate 60% of earnings.

Answer (A) is correct. *(CPA, adapted)*
REQUIRED: The item properly disclosed in the summary of significant accounting policies.
DISCUSSION: APB Opinion 22 lists certain items as commonly required disclosures in a summary of significant accounting policies: (1) the basis of consolidation, (2) depreciation methods, (3) amortization of intangible assets (excluding goodwill), (4) inventory pricing, (5) recognition of profit on long-term construction-type contracts, and (6) recognition of revenue from franchising and leasing operations. Hence, the summary of significant accounting policies should include information about property, plant, and equipment depreciated by the straight-line method.
Answer (B) is incorrect because the sale of a segment is a transaction, not an accounting principle. It is reflected in the discontinued operations section on the income statement. Answer (C) is incorrect because specific segment information does not constitute an accounting policy. An accounting policy is a specific principle or a method of applying it. Answer (D) is incorrect because future dividend policy is a financial management policy.

4.2 Segment Reporting

4. Which of the following qualifies as a reportable operating segment?

A. Corporate headquarters, which oversees $1 billion in sales for the entire company.

B. North American segment, whose assets are 12% of the company's assets of all segments, and management reports to the chief operating officer.

C. South American segment, whose results of operations are reported directly to the chief operating officer, and has 5% of the company's assets, 9% of revenues, and 8% of the profits.

D. Eastern Europe segment, which reports its results directly to the manager of the European division, and has 20% of the company's assets, 12% of revenues, and 11% of profits.

Answer (B) is correct. *(CPA, adapted)*
REQUIRED: The reportable operating segment.
DISCUSSION: An operating segment engages in business activities, is reviewed by the company's chief operating decision maker, and has discrete financial information available. For an operating segment to be reportable, it must meet one or more of the following quantitative thresholds: (1) reported revenue is at least 10% of the combined revenue of all operating segments; (2) reported profit or loss is at least 10% of the greater (in absolute amount) of the combined reported profit of all operating segments that did not incur a loss, or the combined reported loss of all operating segments that did report a loss; or (3) its assets are at least 10% of the combined assets of all operating segments (SFAS 131). North American segment holds 12% of the company's assets and reports to the chief operating officer, so it meets the requirements of an operating segment.
Answer (A) is incorrect because a corporate headquarters is not an operating segment. Any revenues it earns are incidental to the entity's activities. Answer (C) is incorrect because this segment does not meet the asset, revenue, or profit (or loss) quantitative threshold to qualify as an operating segment. Answer (D) is incorrect because this segment does not report to the chief operating decision maker.

5. In financial reporting for operating segments of a public business entity, which of the following must be included in the reported amount of a reportable operating segment's assets?

	Accumulated Depreciation	Marketable Securities Valuation Allowance
A.	No	No
B.	No	Yes
C.	Yes	Yes
D.	Yes	No

Answer (A) is correct. *(CPA, adapted)*
REQUIRED: The items to be included in computing the assets of a reportable operating segment.
DISCUSSION: The amount of a reported segment item, such as assets, is the measure reported to the chief operating decision maker for purposes of making resource allocation and performance evaluation decisions regarding the segment. Thus, if accumulated depreciation and a marketable securities valuation allowance are not included in that measure, they need not be included in the reported amount of the operating segment's assets.

6. Terra Co.'s total revenues from its three operating segments were as follows:

Segment	Sales to External Customers	Inter-segment Sales	Total Revenues
Lion	$ 70,000	$ 30,000	$100,000
Monk	22,000	4,000	26,000
Nevi	8,000	16,000	24,000
Combined	$100,000	$ 50,000	$150,000
Elimination	--	(50,000)	(50,000)
Consolidated	$100,000	$ --	$100,000

Which operating segment(s) is(are) deemed to be (a) reportable segment(s)?

A. None.

B. Lion only.

C. Lion and Monk only.

D. Lion, Monk, and Nevi.

Answer (D) is correct. *(CPA, adapted)*
REQUIRED: The reportable operating segments in conformity with the revenue test.
DISCUSSION: For the purpose of identifying reportable operating segments, SFAS 131 defines revenue to include sales to external customers and intersegment sales or transfers. In accordance with the revenue test, a reportable operating segment has revenue equal to 10% or more of the total combined revenue, internal and external, of all of the entity's operating segments. Given combined revenues of $150,000, Lion, Monk, and Nevi all qualify because their revenues are at least $15,000 ($150,000 × 10%).

7. Correy Corp. and its divisions are engaged solely in manufacturing operations. The following data (consistent with prior years' data) pertain to the industries in which operations were conducted for the year ended December 31, Year 2:

Operating Segment	Total Revenue	Profit	Assets at 12/31/Yr2
A	$10,000,000	$1,750,000	$20,000,000
B	8,000,000	1,400,000	17,500,000
C	6,000,000	1,200,000	12,500,000
D	3,000,000	550,000	7,500,000
E	4,250,000	675,000	7,000,000
F	1,500,000	225,000	3,000,000
	$32,750,000	$5,800,000	$67,500,000

In its segment information for Year 2, how many reportable segments does Correy have?

A. Three.

B. Four.

C. Five.

D. Six.

Answer (C) is correct. *(CPA, adapted)*
REQUIRED: The number of reportable operating segments.
DISCUSSION: Four operating segments (A, B, C, and E) have revenue equal to or greater than 10% of the $32,750,000 total revenue of all operating segments. These four segments also have profit equal to or greater than 10% of the $5,800,000 total profit. Five segments (A, B, C, D, and E) have assets greater than 10% of the $67,500,000 total assets. Because an operating segment is reportable if it meets one or more of the three tests established by SFAS 131, Correy Corp. has five reportable segments for Year 2.

8. Hyde Corp. has three manufacturing divisions, each of which has been determined to be a reportable operating segment. In Year 4, Clay division had sales of $3 million, which was 25% of Hyde's total sales, and had traceable operating costs of $1.9 million. In Year 4, Hyde incurred operating costs of $500,000 that were not directly traceable to any of the divisions. In addition, Hyde incurred interest expense of $300,000 in Year 4. The calculation of the measure of segment profit or loss reviewed by Hyde's chief operating decision maker does not include an allocation of interest expense incurred by Hyde. However, it does include traceable costs. It also includes nontraceable operating costs allocated based on the ratio of divisional sales to aggregate sales. In reporting segment information, what amount should be shown as Clay's operating profit for Year 4?

A. $875,000

B. $900,000

C. $975,000

D. $1,100,000

Answer (C) is correct. *(CPA, adapted)*
REQUIRED: The amount to be shown as profit for a reportable operating segment.
DISCUSSION: The amount of a segment item reported, such as profit or loss, is the measure reported to the chief operating decision maker for purposes of making resource allocation and performance evaluation decisions regarding the segment. However, SFAS 131 does not stipulate the specific items included in the calculation of that measure. Consequently, allocation of revenues, expenses, gains, and losses are included in the determination of reported segment profit or loss only if they are included in the measure of segment profit or loss reviewed by the chief operating decision maker. Given that this measure for Clay reflects traceable costs and an allocation of nontraceable operating costs, the profit is calculated by subtracting the $1,900,000 traceable costs and the $125,000 ($500,000 × 25%) of the allocated costs from the division's sales of $3,000,000. The profit for the division is $975,000.

Sales	$ 3,000,000
Traceable costs	(1,900,000)
Allocated costs (25%)	(125,000)
Profit	$ 975,000

Answer (A) is incorrect because no amount of interest expense should be included in the calculation. Answer (B) is incorrect because Clay's share of interest expense ($300,000 × 25% = $75,000) is excluded from the calculation of profit. Answer (D) is incorrect because the allocated nontraceable operating costs must also be subtracted.

9. Bean Co. included interest expense and transactions classified as extraordinary items in its determination of segment profit, which Bean's chief financial officer considered in determining the segment's operating budget. Bean is required to report the segment's financial data under SFAS 131, *Disclosures about Segments of an Enterprise and Related Information.* Which of the following items should Bean disclose in reporting segment data?

	Interest expense	Extraordinary items
A.	No	No
B.	No	Yes
C.	Yes	No
D.	Yes	Yes

Answer (D) is correct. *(CPA, adapted)*
   REQUIRED: The items disclosed in segment data.
   DISCUSSION: The objective of SFAS 131 is to provide information about the different types of business activities of the entity and the economic environments in which it operates. Disclosures include a measure of profit or loss and total assets for each reportable segment. Items that are typically included are revenues from external customers and other operating segments, interest revenue and expense, depreciation, depletion, amortization, unusual items, equity in the net income of equity-based investees, income tax expense or benefit, extraordinary items, and other significant noncash items.
   Answer (A) is incorrect because items that contribute to the profit and loss of a segment should be disclosed in the segment's data. Answer (B) is incorrect because interest expense affects the profit and loss of a business segment and should be reported. Answer (C) is incorrect because extraordinary items affect the profit and loss of a business segment and should be reported.

10. Opto Co. is a publicly-traded, consolidated entity reporting segment information. Which of the following items is a required entity-wide disclosure regarding external customers?

A. The fact that transactions with a particular external customer constitute more than 10% of the total entity revenues.

B. The identity of any external customer providing 10% or more of a particular operating segment's revenue.

C. The identity of any external customer considered to be "major" by management.

D. Information on major customers is not required in segment reporting.

Answer (A) is correct. *(CPA, adapted)*
   REQUIRED: The entity-wide disclosure about external customers.
   DISCUSSION: Information about products and services and geographical areas is reported if it is feasible to do so. If 10% or more of revenues is derived from one external customer, (1) that fact, (2) the amount from each such customer, and (3) the segment(s) reporting the revenues must be disclosed (SFAS 131).
   Answer (B) is incorrect because the identity of the segment(s) reporting the revenues must be disclosed, not that of the customer. Answer (C) is incorrect because the identity of any external customer, regardless of whether it meets the revenue criterion or is considered to be "major" by management, does not have to be disclosed. Answer (D) is incorrect because the entity must disclose information about each major customer, that is, one providing at least 10% of revenues.

4.3 Interim Financial Reporting

11. Conceptually, interim financial statements can be described as emphasizing

A. Timeliness over reliability.

B. Reliability over relevance.

C. Relevance over comparability.

D. Comparability over neutrality.

Answer (A) is correct. *(CPA, adapted)*
   REQUIRED: The emphasis of interim statements.
   DISCUSSION: Interim financial statements cover periods of less than one year. Because of the seasonality of some businesses, the need for increased use of estimates, the need for allocations of costs and expenses among interim periods, and other factors, the usefulness of the information provided by interim financial statements may be limited. Hence, they emphasize timeliness over reliability.

12. In general, an enterprise preparing interim financial statements should

    A. Defer recognition of seasonal revenue.

    B. Disregard permanent decreases in the market value of its inventory.

    C. Allocate revenues and expenses evenly over the quarters, regardless of when they actually occurred.

    D. Use the same accounting principles followed in preparing its latest annual financial statements.

Answer (D) is correct. *(CPA, adapted)*
REQUIRED: The method of preparing interim financial statements.
DISCUSSION: APB Opinion 28, *Interim Financial Reporting*, views each interim period primarily as an integral part of an annual period. Ordinarily, interim results are based on the same principles applied in annual statements. Certain principles and practices used for annual reporting, however, may require modification so that interim reports may relate more closely to the results of operations for the annual period.
Answer (A) is incorrect because seasonal revenue is not deferred. However, an entity with material seasonal fluctuations must disclose the seasonal nature of its activities and should consider making additional disclosures. Answer (B) is incorrect because inventory losses from nontemporary market declines must be recognized at the interim date. Recovery during the fiscal year is treated as a change in estimate. Answer (C) is incorrect because revenue is recognized as earned during an interim period on the same basis followed for the annual period.

13. Because of a decline in market price in the second quarter, Petal Co. incurred an inventory loss, but the market price was expected to return to previous levels by the end of the year. At the end of the year, the decline had not reversed. When should the loss be reported in Petal's interim income statements?

    A. Ratably over the second, third, and fourth quarters.

    B. Ratably over the third and fourth quarters.

    C. In the second quarter only.

    D. In the fourth quarter only.

Answer (D) is correct. *(CPA, adapted)*
REQUIRED: The true statement about reporting inventory at interim dates when a market decline is expected to reverse by year-end but does not.
DISCUSSION: A market decline reasonably expected to be restored within the fiscal year may be deferred at an interim reporting date because no loss is anticipated for the year. Inventory losses from nontemporary market declines, however, must be recognized at the interim reporting date. Consequently, Petal would not have reported the market decline until it determined at the end of the fourth quarter that the expected reversal would not occur.

14. An inventory loss from a market price decline occurred in the first quarter. The loss was not expected to be restored in the fiscal year. However, in the third quarter the inventory had a market price recovery that exceeded the market decline that occurred in the first quarter. For interim financial reporting, the dollar amount of net inventory should

    A. Decrease in the first quarter by the amount of the market price decline and increase in the third quarter by the amount of the market price recovery.

    B. Decrease in the first quarter by the amount of the market price decline and increase in the third quarter by the amount of decrease in the first quarter.

    C. Decrease in the first quarter by the amount of the market price decline and not be affected in the third quarter.

    D. Not be affected in either the first quarter or the third quarter.

Answer (B) is correct. *(CPA, adapted)*
REQUIRED: The proper interim financial reporting of a market decline and a market price recovery.
DISCUSSION: APB Opinion 28 requires that a market price decline in inventory be recognized in the interim period in which it occurs unless it is expected to be temporary, i.e., unless the decline is expected to be restored by the end of the fiscal year. This loss was not expected to be restored in the fiscal year, and the company should report the dollar amount of the market price decline as a loss in the first quarter. When a market price recovery occurs in an interim period, it should be treated as a change in estimate. The market price recovery recognized in the third quarter is limited, however, to the extent of losses previously recognized, whether in a prior interim or annual period. Accordingly, the inventory should never be written up to an amount above its original cost.
Answer (A) is incorrect because the recovery recognized in the third quarter is limited to the amount of the losses previously recognized. Answer (C) is incorrect because, assuming no market price decline had been recognized prior to the current year, the first quarter loss and the third quarter recovery would be offsetting. The recognized third quarter gain is limited to the amount of the first quarter loss, and the year-end results would not be affected. Answer (D) is incorrect because the inventory amount is affected in both the first and third quarters.

15. During the first quarter of Year 4, Tech Co. had income before taxes of $200,000, and its effective income tax rate was 15%. Tech's Year 3 effective annual income tax rate was 30%, but Tech expects its Year 4 effective annual income tax rate to be 25%. In its first quarter interim income statement, what amount of income tax expense should Tech report?

A. $0

B. $30,000

C. $50,000

D. $60,000

Answer (C) is correct. *(CPA, adapted)*
REQUIRED: The provision for income taxes for the first interim period.
DISCUSSION: At the end of each interim period, the entity should estimate the annual effective tax rate. This rate is used in providing for income taxes on a current year-to-date basis. Tech's ordinary income before taxes for the first quarter is $200,000, and the estimated annual effective tax rate for Year 4 is 25%. The provision for income taxes for the first interim period is therefore $50,000 ($200,000 × 25%).
Answer (A) is incorrect because $0 excludes any income tax expense. Answer (B) is incorrect because $30,000 uses Tech's quarterly effective income tax rate. Answer (D) is incorrect because $60,000 uses Tech's Year 3 effective annual income tax rate.

4.4 Related Party Disclosures

16. Dex Co. has entered into a joint venture with an affiliate to secure access to additional inventory. Under the joint venture agreement, Dex will purchase the output of the venture at prices negotiated on an arm's-length basis. Which of the following is(are) required to be disclosed about the related party transaction?

I.   The amount due to the affiliate at the balance sheet date.

II.   The dollar amount of the purchases during the year.

A. I only.

B. II only.

C. Both I and II.

D. Neither I nor II.

Answer (C) is correct. *(CPA, adapted)*
REQUIRED: The disclosures for a related party transaction.
DISCUSSION: SFAS 57 requires disclosure of (1) the nature of the relationship involved; (2) a description of the transactions for each period an income statement is presented and such other information as is deemed necessary to an understanding of the effects of the transactions; (3) the dollar amounts of transactions for each period an income statement is presented and the effects of any change in the method of establishing their terms; (4) amounts due from or to related parties as of the date of each balance sheet, including the terms of settlement; and (5) certain tax information required by SFAS 109 if the entity is part of a group that files a consolidated tax return.

17. Lemu Co. and Young Co. are under the common management of Ego Co. Ego can significantly influence the operating results of both Lemu and Young. While Lemu had no transactions with Ego during the year, Young sold merchandise to Ego under the same terms given to unrelated parties. In the notes to their respective financial statements, should Lemu and Young disclose their relationship with Ego?

	Lemu	Young
A.	Yes	Yes
B.	Yes	No
C.	No	Yes
D.	No	No

Answer (A) is correct. *(CPA, adapted)*
REQUIRED: The disclosure(s), if any, by entities under common management regarding an entity that can significantly influence them.
DISCUSSION: According to SFAS 57, financial statements should disclose material related party transactions. A related party is essentially any party that controls or can significantly influence the management or operating policies of the reporting entity. Moreover, two or more entities may be under common ownership or management control such that the results of the reporting entity might vary significantly from those obtained if the entities were autonomous. In these circumstances, the relationship should be disclosed even though no transactions occurred between the parties.

18. Dean Co. acquired 100% of Morey Corp. prior to Year 6. Dean and Morey are not issuers. During Year 6, they included in their separate financial statements the following:

	Dean	Morey
Officers' salaries	$ 75,000	$50,000
Officers' expenses	20,000	10,000
Loans to officers	125,000	50,000
Intercompany sales	150,000	--

The amount reported as related party disclosures in the notes to Dean's Year 6 consolidated statements is

A. $150,000

B. $155,000

C. $175,000

D. $330,000

19. Which of the following payments by a company should be disclosed in the notes to the financial statements as a related party transaction?

I. Royalties paid to a major shareholder as consideration for patents purchased from the shareholder.

II. Officers' salaries.

A. I only.

B. II only.

C. Both I and II.

D. Neither I nor II.

4.5 Unconditional Purchase Obligations

20. SFAS 47, *Disclosure of Long-Term Obligations*, does not apply to an unconditional purchase obligation that is cancelable under which of the following conditions?

A. Upon the occurrence of a remote contingency.

B. With the permission of the other party.

C. Under a replacement agreement signed by the same parties.

D. Upon payment of a nominal penalty.

Answer (C) is correct. *(CPA, adapted)*
REQUIRED: The amount of related party disclosures.
DISCUSSION: SFAS 57 requires the disclosure of material related party transactions other than (1) compensation arrangements, (2) expense allowances, and (3) other similar items in the ordinary course of business. Related party transactions that are eliminated in consolidated or combined statements also are not required to be disclosed in those statements. Accordingly, the compensation arrangements (officers' salaries and expenses) and the intercompany sales, which will be eliminated in the consolidated statements, need not be disclosed. However, other transactions between an entity and its management, such as borrowings and lendings, must be disclosed. Dean should therefore report as related party disclosures the $175,000 ($125,000 + $50,000) of loans to officers. The Sarbanes-Oxley Act of 2002 generally prohibits an issuer, as defined by federal securities law, from extending credit to its directors and officers.
Answer (A) is incorrect because $150,000 equals the interentity sales. Answer (B) is incorrect because $155,000 equals the officers' salaries and expenses. Answer (D) is incorrect because $330,000 equals the officers' salaries and expenses plus the loans to officers.

Answer (A) is correct. *(CPA, adapted)*
REQUIRED: The payment(s), if any, disclosed as related party items.
DISCUSSION: SFAS 57 requires the disclosure of material related party transactions other than compensation arrangements (officers' salaries), expense allowances, and other similar items in the ordinary course of business. However, royalties paid to a major shareholder must be disclosed because the shareholder may have considerable influence over the corporation, and the transaction may not be made at arm's length.

Answer (D) is correct. *(Publisher, adapted)*
REQUIRED: The condition excluding unconditional purchase obligation coverage by SFAS 47.
DISCUSSION: SFAS 47 provides the standards of accounting for an unconditional purchase obligation that (1) was negotiated as part of the financing arrangement for (a) facilities that will provide contracted goods or services or (b) the related costs, (2) has a remaining term of more than 1 year, and (3) is either noncancelable or cancelable only under specific terms that make continuation or replacement (but not cancelation) of the agreement reasonably assured. A purchase obligation cancelable upon the payment of a nominal penalty is not unconditional.

21. If an unconditional purchase obligation is not presented in the balance sheet, certain disclosures are required. A disclosure that is not required is

A. The nature and term of the obligation.

B. The variable components of the obligation.

C. The imputed interest necessary to reduce the unconditional purchase obligation to its present value.

D. The amounts purchased under the obligation for each period an income statement is presented.

Answer (C) is correct. *(Publisher, adapted)*
REQUIRED: The item not required to be disclosed if an unconditional purchase obligation is not recognized.
DISCUSSION: When an unconditional purchase obligation is not recognized, SFAS 47 encourages, but does not require, the disclosure of the amount of imputed interest necessary to reduce the unconditional purchase obligation to its present value. Disclosure of the other items is required when an unconditional purchase obligation is not recognized. Moreover, SFAS 47 requires disclosure of the amount of the fixed and determinable portion of the obligation in the aggregate as of the latest balance sheet date. If determinable, the amounts due in each of the next 5 years also should be disclosed.

22. Witt Corp. has outstanding at December 31, Year 6, two long-term borrowings with annual sinking-fund requirements and maturities as follows:

	Sinking-Fund Requirements	Maturities
Year 7	$1,000,000	$ --
Year 8	1,500,000	2,000,000
Year 9	1,500,000	2,000,000
Year 10	2,000,000	2,500,000
Year 11	2,000,000	3,000,000
	$8,000,000	$9,500,000

In the notes to its December 31, Year 6, balance sheet, how should Witt report the above data?

A. No disclosure is required.

B. Only sinking-fund payments totaling $8,000,000 for the next 5 years detailed by year need be disclosed.

C. Only maturities totaling $9,500,000 for the next 5 years detailed by year need be disclosed.

D. The combined aggregate of $17,500,000 of maturities and sinking-fund requirements detailed by year should be disclosed.

Answer (D) is correct. *(CPA, adapted)*
REQUIRED: The required disclosure of sinking fund payments and maturities for long-term borrowings.
DISCUSSION: In addition to the disclosures required by other official pronouncements, SFAS 47 requires the disclosure of the following information for each of the 5 years following the date of the latest balance sheet presented: (1) the aggregate amount of payments for unconditional purchase obligations and (2) the aggregate amount of maturities and sinking-fund requirements for all long-term borrowings. Thus, Witt Corp. should disclose in the notes to the December 31, Year 6, balance sheet the combined aggregate of $17,500,000 ($8,000,000 + $9,500,000) of maturities and sinking-fund requirements detailed by year.

4.6 Significant Risks and Uncertainties

23. According to AICPA SOP 94-6, *Disclosure of Certain Significant Risks and Uncertainties*, financial statements must disclose significant risks and uncertainties. The required disclosures include

A. Quantified comparisons of the relative importance of the different businesses in which the entity operates.

B. Information about a significant estimate used to value an asset only if it is probable that the financial statement effect of a condition existing at the balance sheet date will change materially in the near term.

C. Risk-reduction techniques that have successfully mitigated losses.

D. Vulnerability due to a concentration if a near-term severe impact is at least reasonably possible.

Answer (D) is correct. *(Publisher, adapted)*
REQUIRED: The required disclosure.
DISCUSSION: The current vulnerability due to concentrations must be disclosed if certain conditions are met. Disclosure is necessary if management knows prior to issuance of the statements that the concentration exists at the balance sheet date, it makes the entity vulnerable to a near-term severe impact, and such impact is at least reasonably possible in the near term. A severe impact may result from loss of all or a part of a business relationship, price or demand changes, loss of a patent, changes in the availability of a resource or right, or the disruption of operations in a market or geographic area.
Answer (A) is incorrect because disclosures about the nature of operations need not be quantified. Answer (B) is incorrect because a material financial statement effect need only be reasonably possible in the near term. Answer (C) is incorrect because the criteria for required disclosures about significant estimates may not be met if the entity has successfully employed risk-reduction techniques. In these circumstances, disclosure of those techniques is encouraged but not required.

4.7 Subsequent Events

24. On January 15, Year 2, before the Mapleview Co. released its financial statements for the year ended December 31, Year 1, it settled a long-standing lawsuit. A material loss resulted and no prior liability had been recorded. How should this loss be disclosed or recognized?

    A. The loss should be disclosed in notes to the financial statements, but the financial statements themselves need not be adjusted.

    B. The loss should be disclosed in an explanatory paragraph in the auditor's report.

    C. No disclosure or recognition is required.

    D. The financial statements should be adjusted to recognize the loss.

Answer (D) is correct. *(Publisher, adapted)*
    REQUIRED: The proper disclosure of a material loss on an existing lawsuit after year-end.
    DISCUSSION: Subsequent events that provide additional evidence with the respect to conditions that existed at the balance sheet date and that affect the estimates inherent in the process of preparing the financial statements should be reflected in the current financial statements. Settlement of a lawsuit is indicative of conditions existing at year-end and calls for adjustment of the statements (AU 560, *Subsequent Events*).
    Answer (A) is incorrect because the financial statements should be adjusted to reflect the loss. Answer (B) is incorrect because the audit report need not be modified. Answer (C) is incorrect because failure to adjust the statements for a material loss on an asset that existed at year-end would be misleading.

25. Zero Corp. suffered a loss that would have a material effect on its financial statements on an uncollectible trade account receivable due to a customer's bankruptcy. This occurred suddenly due to a natural disaster ten days after Zero's balance sheet date but one month before the issuance of the financial statements. Under these circumstances,

	The Financial Statements Should Be Adjusted	The Event Requires Financial Statement Disclosure, but No Adjustment	The Auditor's Report Should Be Modified for a Lack of Consistency
A.	Yes	No	No
B.	Yes	No	Yes
C.	No	Yes	Yes
D.	No	Yes	No

Answer (D) is correct. *(CPA, adapted)*
    REQUIRED: The effect on the financial statements and the auditor's report.
    DISCUSSION: Certain subsequent events may provide additional evidence about conditions at the date of the balance sheet and affect estimates inherent in the preparation of statements. These events require adjustment by the client in the financial statements at year-end. Other subsequent events provide evidence about conditions not existing at the date of the balance sheet but arising subsequent to that date and affecting the interpretation of the year-end financial statements. These events may require disclosure in notes to the financial statements but do not require adjustment of the financial statement balances. Thus, Zero's financial statements should not be adjusted, but disclosure should be made in the notes. The auditor's report is unaffected.

4.8 Financial Instrument Disclosures

26. Whether recognized or unrecognized in an entity's financial statements, disclosure of the fair values of the entity's financial instruments is required when

    A. It is feasible to estimate those values and aggregated fair values are material to the entity.

    B. The entity maintains accurate cost records and aggregated fair values are material to the entity.

    C. Aggregated fair values are material to the entity and credit risk has been appropriately hedged.

    D. Individual fair values are material to the entity or any of the instruments are accounted for as derivatives.

Answer (A) is correct. *(CPA, adapted)*
    REQUIRED: The circumstance in which disclosure of the fair values of the entity's financial instruments is required.
    DISCUSSION: Certain entities must disclose the fair value of financial instruments, whether or not they are recognized in the balance sheet, if it is feasible to estimate such fair values and aggregated fair values are material to the entity. If estimating fair value is not feasible, disclosures include information pertinent to estimating the fair value of the financial instrument or class of financial instruments, such as the carrying amount, effective interest rate, and maturity. The reasons that estimating the fair value is not feasible also should be disclosed.

27. Disclosure of information about significant concentrations of credit risk is required for

A. Most financial instruments.

B. Financial instruments with off-balance-sheet credit risk only.

C. Financial instruments with off-balance-sheet market risk only.

D. Financial instruments with off-balance-sheet risk of accounting loss only.

Answer (A) is correct. *(CPA, adapted)*
   REQUIRED: The financial instruments for which disclosure of significant concentrations of credit risk is required.
   DISCUSSION: SFAS 107 requires the disclosure of information about the fair value of financial instruments, whether recognized or not (certain nonpublic entities and certain instruments, such as leases and insurance contracts, are exempt from the disclosure requirements). In accordance with an amendment by SFAS 133, SFAS 107 also requires disclosure of all significant concentrations of credit risk for most financial instruments (except for obligations for deferred compensation, certain instruments of a pension plan, insurance contracts, warranty obligations and rights, and unconditional purchase obligations).

28. Where in its financial statements should a company disclose information about its concentration of credit risks?

A. No disclosure is required.

B. The notes to the financial statements.

C. Supplementary information to the financial statements.

D. Management's report to shareholders.

Answer (B) is correct. *(CPA, adapted)*
   REQUIRED: The method of disclosure about concentration of credit risk.
   DISCUSSION: According to SFAS 107, *Disclosures about Fair Value of Financial Instruments*, an entity must disclose significant concentrations of risk arising from most instruments. These disclosures should be made in the basic financial statements, either in the body of the statements or in the notes.
   Answer (A) is incorrect because disclosure in the basic statements is required. Answer (C) is incorrect because disclosure in supplementary information is normally done when certain entities are excluded from the scope of the requirements. However, the disclosures required by SFAS 107 are to be made by all entities. Answer (D) is incorrect because management's report to shareholders is not part of the basic statements.

Use Gleim's *CPA Test Prep* CD-Rom/Pocket PC for interactive testing with over 4,000 additional questions!

4.9 PRACTICE SIMULATION

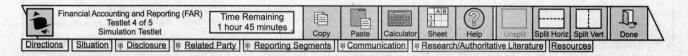

---

1. Directions

In the following simulation, you will be asked to complete various tasks. You may use the content in the **Information Tabs** to complete the tasks in the **Work Tabs**.

Information Tabs:

| Directions | Resources |

FIG 1

- Go through each of the **Information Tabs** to familiarize yourself with the simulation content
- The **Resources** tab will contain information, including formulas and definitions, that may help you to complete the tasks
- Your simulation may have more **Information Tabs** than those shown in Fig. 1

Work Tabs:

| SysTrust | Engagement Letter | Authoritative Sources | Communication |

FIG. 2

- **Work Tabs**, to the right of **Information Tabs**, contain the tasks for you to complete
- **Work Tabs** contain directions for completing each task - be sure to read these directions carefully
- The tab names in Fig. 2 are for illustration only - yours may differ
- Once you complete any part of a task, the pencil for that tab will be shaded (see **Communication** in Fig. 2)
- The shaded pencil does **NOT** indicate that you have completed the entire task
- You must complete all of the tasks in the **Work Tabs** to receive full credit

Research/Authoritative Literature Tab:

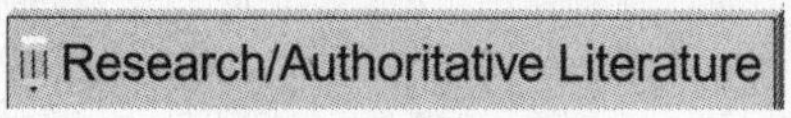

| Research/Authoritative Literature |

FIG. 3

- This tab contains both the Research task and the Authoritative Literature
- Detailed instructions for completing the Research task, and for using the Authoritative Literature, appear on this tab
- You may use the Authoritative Literature as a resource for completing other tasks

NOTE: If you believe you have encountered a software malfunction, report it to the test center staff immediately.

2. Situation

In the audit of Recycling Corporation, you are assigned the task of assessing the required financial statement disclosures.

The corporation has several material related-party transactions as well as segment reporting issues. Moreover, it is heavily involved in hedging activities using financial instruments. The entity also has large unconditional obligations to purchase recycled paper and plastic. The corporation's controller is unfamiliar with these kinds of disclosures. In this simulation, you will determine which items are to be disclosed in both interim and annual financial statements.

3. Disclosure

This type of question will be presented in a check-the-box format that requires you to select the correct response from a given list.

For items 1 through 8, check the box beside the number if disclosure is required. If disclosure is not required, DO NOT check the box.

Disclosure Required	Accounting Issue
☐	1. Material related-party transactions
☐	2. The amount of imputed interest necessary to reduce an unconditional purchase obligation, which is not recorded in the balance sheet, to its present value
☐	3. The prior-interim-period adjustment effect on income from continuing operations for each prior interim period of the current year
☐	4. The effect of a change in accounting principle on EPS amounts for interim periods after the change is made
☐	5. The accounting policies reflected in unaudited interim financial statements when the policies have not changed since the end of the preceding fiscal year
☐	6. A reportable operating segment's carrying amounts of identifiable assets
☐	7. Certain information about sales to a single external customer when it accounts for 5% of revenue
☐	8. Segment information in interim statements of public business entities

4. Related Party

This type of question will be presented in a check-the-box format that requires you to select the correct response from a given list.

From the list of items below, choose the parties that are related according to **SFAS 57**, *Related Party Disclosures*. If it is not a related party, DO NOT check the box.

Related Party	*Entities*
☐	1. A parent and its subsidiaries
☐	2. An entity and a 1% shareholder
☐	3. Subsidiaries of a common parent
☐	4. An entity and its vendors
☐	5. An entity and its customers
☐	6. An entity and employee trusts managed by, or under the trusteeship of, the entity's management
☐	7. An entity and members of the immediate families of its management
☐	8. Affiliates
☐	9. An entity and its nonmanagement employees
☐	10. An entity and its equity-based investees
☐	11. An entity and any other entity that can significantly influence it
☐	12. A party that can significantly influence the parties to a transaction

5. Reporting Segments

This set of questions has a matching format. Select the best match for each numbered item from the terms in the drop-down list and write its letter in the column provided. Each choice may be used once, more than once, or not at all.

Reportable segments are those that have been identified in accordance with certain requirements and also meet one of the quantitative thresholds. For each quantitative test below, choose the correct percentage.

Quantitative Tests for Reportable Segments	*Answers*
1. Revenue test	
2. Asset test	
3. Profit (loss) test	

Percentages
A) At least 5% of the combined amount
B) At least 10% of the combined amount
C) At least 20% of the combined amount
D) At least 25% of the combined amount

6. Communication

Prepare a memo to the board of directors of XYZ Corporation, an entity with over $500 million in assets. The memo should address disclosures about the fair value of XYZ's substantial holdings of financial instruments. The memo should discuss the definition of a financial instrument, the best evidence of fair value, netting, and the required disclosures for concentrations of credit risk and for market risk.

REMINDER: Your response will be graded for both technical content and writing skills. Technical content will be evaluated for information that is helpful to the intended reader and clearly relevant to the issue. Writing skills will be evaluated for development, organization, and the appropriate expression of ideas in professional correspondence. Use a standard business memo or letter format with a clear beginning, middle, and end. Do not convey information in the form of a table, bullet point list, or other abbreviated presentation.

> To: Board of directors, XYZ Corporation
> From: CPA
> Reference: Disclosure of the fair value

7. Research/Authoritative Literature

See page 12 in the Introduction of this book for a detailed explanation of the AICPA's new Research/Authoritative Literature work tab as well as a screenshot of how the tab will actually look on your exam.

Certain items are explicitly listed in APB Opinion 22 as commonly required disclosures in a summary of significant accounting policies. Research and cite the specific paragraph in APB Opinion 22 that lists these items.

Unofficial Answers

3. Disclosure (8 Gradable Items)

1. ✓ SFAS 57, *Related Party Disclosures*, requires the disclosure of material related-party transactions. Exceptions are compensation arrangements, expense allowances, and similar items in the ordinary course of business. Transactions eliminated in the preparation of consolidated or combined financial statements also need not be disclosed.

2. If an unconditional purchase obligation is not recorded in the balance sheet, SFAS 47, *Disclosure of Long-Term Obligations*, encourages, but does not require, disclosure of the imputed interest used to reduce the obligation to its present value.

3. ✓ In the financial reports of the interim period when the adjustment occurs, SFAS 16, *Prior Period Adjustments*, requires disclosure of the effect on income from continuing operations, net income, and related per-share amounts for each prior interim period of the current year and for each prior interim period restated.

4. ✓ SFAS 154, *Accounting Changes and Error Corrections*, requires certain disclosures in postchange interim periods after an entity adopts a new accounting principle. These disclosures include the effect of the change on income from continuing operations, net income, and related EPS amounts.

5. APB Opinion 22, *Disclosure of Accounting Policies*, requires that all significant accounting policies be disclosed. However, when accounting policies have not changed, disclosure is not required for unaudited interim financial statements.

6. SFAS 131, *Disclosures about Segments of an Enterprise and Related Information*, requires disclosure of total assets for each reportable segment. Disclosure is also required of the amount of investment in equity-based investees and total expenditures for additions to most long-lived assets for each reportable segment if they are included in segment assets reviewed by the chief operating decision maker.

7. Under SFAS 131, if 10% or more of revenue is derived from sales to any single customer, it must be disclosed. The amount of revenue from each such customer and the segment(s) reporting the revenues must also be disclosed. Single customers include entities under common control and each federal, state, local, or foreign government.

8. ✓ According to SFAS 131, interim period information is disclosed for each reportable segment in condensed financial statements. Disclosures include external revenues, intersegment revenues, a measure of segment profit or loss, total assets that have materially changed since the last annual report, differences from the last annual report in the basis of segmentation or of segment profit or loss, and a reconciliation of the total reportable segments' profit or loss to consolidated pretax income and its components.

4. Related Party (12 Gradable Items)

1. ✓ SFAS 57 requires disclosure. By definition, a parent can control its subsidiaries. Thus, they are affiliates.

2. SFAS 57 requires disclosure if the shareholder is a principal (more than 10%) owner.

3. ✓ SFAS 57 requires disclosure. Subsidiaries of a common parent are affiliates because they are under common control.

4. SFAS 57 does not require disclosure unless one party can significantly influence the other.

5. SFAS 57 does not require disclosure unless one party can significantly influence the other.

6. ✓ SFAS 57 requires disclosure. Examples of these trusts are pension and profit-sharing trusts.

7. ✓ SFAS 57 requires disclosure of transactions between the entity and its principal owners, management, or members of their immediate families.

8. ✓ SFAS 57 requires disclosure. An affiliate controls, is controlled by, or is under common control with an entity.

9. SFAS 57 does not require disclosure. Management consists of persons responsible for achieving entity objectives (e.g., directors, the CEO, the COO, etc.).

10. ✓ SFAS 57 requires disclosure. An equity-based investee can be significantly influenced by the investor.

11. ✓ SFAS 57 requires disclosure of transactions between an entity and any other entity if one party can significantly influence the other to the extent that one party may be prevented from fully pursuing its interests.

12. ✓ SFAS 57 requires disclosure. A party is a related party if it can significantly influence the management or operating policies of the transacting parties.

5. Reporting Segments (3 Gradable Items)

1.   B). **Revenue test.** Reported revenue, including sales to external customers and intersegment sales or transfers, is at least 10% of the combined revenue of all operating segments.

2.   B). **Asset test.** Assets are at least 10% of the combined assets of all operating segments.

3.   B). **Profit (loss) test.** The absolute amount of reported profit or loss is at least 10% of the greater, in absolute amount, of either the combined reported profit of all operating segments that did not report a loss, or the combined reported loss of all operating segments that did report a loss.

6. Communication (5 Gradable Items; for grading instructions, please refer to page 12.)

Certain entities must disclose the fair value of financial instruments, whether or not they are recognized, if it is feasible to estimate such fair values. A financial instrument is cash, evidence of an ownership interest in an entity, or a contract that both (1) imposes on one entity a contractual obligation to deliver cash or another financial instrument to a second entity or exchange other financial instruments on potentially unfavorable terms with the second entity, and (2) conveys to that second entity a contractual right to receive cash or another financial instrument from the first entity or exchange other financial instruments on potentially favorable terms with the first entity.

Ordinarily, disclosures should not net the fair values of instruments even if they are of the same class or are related, e.g., by a risk management strategy. However, exceptions are made for rights of setoff and for master netting arrangements.

An entity ordinarily must disclose significant concentrations of credit risk arising from most instruments, whether from one counterparty or groups. Group concentrations arise when multiple counterparties have similar activities and economic characteristics that cause their ability to meet obligations to be similarly affected by changes in conditions. Disclosures include (1) information about the shared activity, region, or economic characteristic that identifies the concentration; (2) the maximum loss due to credit risk if parties failed completely to perform and the security, if any, proved to be of no value; (3) the policy of requiring collateral or other security, information about access to that security, and the nature and a brief description of the security; and (4) the policy of entering into master netting arrangements to mitigate the credit risk, information about them, and a description of the terms (including the extent to which they reduce the maximum amount of loss).

Disclosure of quantitative information about the market risks of instruments that is consistent with the way an entity manages those risks is encouraged, not required.

7. Research/Authoritative Literature (1 Gradable Item)

Answer: APB Opinion 22, Par. 13

APB Opinion 22 -- *Disclosure of Accounting Policies*

13. Examples of disclosures by a business entity commonly required with respect to accounting policies would include, among other things, those relating to basis of consolidation, depreciation methods, amortization of intangible assets, inventory pricing, accounting, recognition of profit on long-term construction-type contracts, and recognition of revenue from franchising and leasing operations. This list of examples is not all-inclusive.

Scoring Schedule:

	Correct Responses		Gradable Items		Weights		
Tab 3	_____	÷	8	×	20%	=	_____
Tab 4	_____	÷	12	×	25%	=	_____
Tab 5	_____	÷	3	×	10%	=	_____
Tab 6	_____	÷	5	×	30%	=	_____
Tab 7	_____	÷	1	×	15%	=	_____
							_____
							(Your Score)

Use Gleim's ***CPA Gleim Online*** to practice more simulations in a realistic environment.

STUDY UNIT FIVE
CASH AND INVESTMENTS

(18 pages of outline)

The first subunit concerns **cash**, the most liquid of assets. It includes **cash equivalents**, a special category of assets so close to conversion to cash that they are classified with cash on the balance sheet. **Securities held as investments** are reported in three classifications on the balance sheet. Other matters, such as the **equity method** of accounting for investments in common stock and **bond** investments, also are discussed.

5.1 CASH

Nature of Cash

1. Cash is ready money, the most liquid of assets. Because of that liquidity and the ability to transfer it electronically, internal control of cash must be strong.

2. As the customary **medium of exchange**, it also provides the standard of value (the unit of measurement) of the transactions that are reported in the financial statements.

   a. "Money (cash, including deposits in banks) is valuable because of what it can buy. It can be exchanged for virtually any good or service or it can be saved and exchanged for them in the future. Money's 'command over resources' -- its purchasing power -- is the basis of its value and future economic benefits (SFAC 6, *Elements of Financial Statements*)."

   b. For the sake of simplicity, the changes in that purchasing power over time are not recognized in standard financial statements. **Nominal units of money** provide the measurement scale.

   c. Because cash is the standard medium of exchange, its effective management is vital. Economic entities must plan to hold sufficient cash (have adequate liquidity) to execute transactions. The amount held should be limited, however, because cash usually does not increase in value (appreciate) unless invested.

   d. Cash is a **current asset** unless it is used in the near term for such purposes as payments to sinking funds.

Items of Cash

3.   To be classified as cash, an asset must be readily available for use by the business. The use should not be restricted.

    a.   The cash account on the balance sheet should consist of

        1)   Coin and currency on hand, including petty cash and change funds
        2)   Demand deposits (checking accounts)
        3)   Time deposits (savings accounts)

            a)   Although technically subject to a bank's right to demand notice before withdrawal, savings accounts are treated as cash because the right is seldom exercised.

        4)   Near-cash assets

            a)   They include many **negotiable instruments**, such as money orders, bank drafts, certified checks, cashiers' checks, and personal checks.
            b)   They are usually in the process of being deposited **(deposits in transit)**.
            c)   They must be depositable. They **exclude** unsigned or postdated checks.
            d)   Checks written to creditors but not mailed or delivered at the balance sheet date should be included in the payor's cash account (not considered cash payments at year-end).

4.   **Restricted cash** is not actually set aside in special accounts. However, it is designated for special uses and should be separately presented.

    a.   Examples are bond sinking funds and new building funds.
    b.   The nature of the use will determine whether such an amount will be classified as current or noncurrent.

        1)   A **bond sinking fund** to redeem noncurrent bond debt is noncurrent, but a fund to be used to redeem bonds currently redeemable is a current asset.

    c.   Restricted cash in **foreign banks** should be reported as a receivable (current or noncurrent), but unrestricted deposits are classified as cash.

5.   **Compensating balances.** As part of an agreement regarding either an existing loan or the provision of future credit, a borrower may keep an average or minimum amount on deposit with the lender. This compensating balance **increases the effective rate** of interest paid by the borrower. It also creates a disclosure issue because the full amount reported as cash might not be available to meet general obligations. The **SEC's** recommended solution depends on the duration of the lending arrangement and the nature of the restriction.

    a.   If the balance relates to a **short-term agreement** and is **legally restricted**, it is separately reported among the cash and cash equivalent items as a current asset.
    b.   If the agreement is **long-term**, the legally restricted balance is noncurrent. It should be treated as an investment or other asset.
    c.   If the use of the compensating balance is **not restricted**, full disclosure but not separate classification is required.

Cash Equivalents

6.   They are short-term, highly liquid investments. Common examples are Treasury bills, money market funds, and commercial paper. Cash equivalents are

    a.   Readily convertible to known amounts of cash.
    b.   So near maturity that interest rate risk is insignificant.

        1)   Thus, only investments with an original maturity **to the holder** of 3 months or less qualify.

Noncash Items

7. NSF checks, postdated checks, and IOUs should be treated as receivables. Advances for expenses to employees may be classified as receivables (if expected to be paid by employees) or as prepaid expenses.

8. Postage stamps are accounted for as prepaid expenses or office supplies.

9. An **overdraft** is a current liability unless the entity has sufficient funds in another account in the same bank to cover it.

    a. If an entity has separate accounts in one bank, an overdraft will usually be subject to a **right of offset**: The funds in another account may be legally transferred by the bank to cover the shortage.

        1) This right does not exist when the accounts are in different institutions. Thus, the overdraft must be reported as a liability, not netted.

10. **Noncash short-term investments** are usually substantially restricted and thus not readily available for use by the entity. They should be classified as short-term investments or temporary investments, not cash. However, they may qualify as cash equivalents if the above conditions apply.

    a. **Money market funds** are essentially mutual funds that have portfolios of commercial paper and Treasury bills. However, a money market fund with a usable **checking feature** might be better classified as cash.

    b. **Commercial paper** (also known as negotiable instruments) consists of short-term (no more than 270 days) corporate obligations.

    c. **Treasury bills** are short-term guaranteed U.S. government obligations. In contrast, an **obligation of a federal agency** is guaranteed only by the agency, not by the U.S. government.

    d. **Certificates of deposit** are formal debt instruments issued by a bank or other financial institution and are subject to penalties for withdrawal before maturity.

Internal Controls Over Cash

11. **Cash accounts** may be represented by a general ledger control account, with a subsidiary ledger of accounts for each bank account. An alternative is a series of general ledger accounts.

    a. On the balance sheet, only one cash account is presented. It reflects all unrestricted cash.

    b. Each transfer of cash from one account to another requires an entry.

    c. At the end of each period, a **schedule of transfers** should be prepared and reviewed to make certain all cash transfers are counted only once.

12. An **imprest petty cash system** sets aside a specific amount of money, e.g., $400 in the care of a custodian to pay office expenses that are too small to pay by check or to record in the accounting system as they occur. The entry to establish the fund is

Petty cash	$400	
Cash		$400

    a. Periodically, the fund is reimbursed for all expenditures based on expense receipts, and journal entries are made to reflect the transactions. However, entries are made to petty cash only to (1) establish the fund, (2) change its amount, or (3) adjust the balance if it has not been reimbursed at year-end.

    b. The **cash over and short account** is a nominal account for errors in petty cash. It is used when the total of the expense receipts and the cash remaining does not equal the amount that should be in the petty cash fund (the imprest amount). An **overage is a credit**, and a **shortage is a debit**. The amount is classified on the income statement as a miscellaneous revenue or expense, respectively.

13. A **bank reconciliation** is a schedule comparing the entity's cash balance per books with the balance **shown** on the bank statement (usually received monthly). The most common approach is to **reconcile from the bank balance and the book balance to the true balance**.

    a.   Because the bank and book balances usually vary, this schedule permits the entity to determine whether the difference is attributable to normal conditions, errors, or fraud. It is also a basis for entries to adjust the books to reflect unrecorded items.

    b.   **Common reasons for differences.** The bank and the entity inevitably record many transactions at different times. Both also may make errors.

        1)   **Outstanding checks.** The books may reflect checks written by the entity that have not yet cleared the bank. These amounts are subtracted from the bank balance to arrive at the true balance.

        2)   **Deposits in transit.** A time lag may occur between deposit of receipts and the bank's recording of the transaction. Thus, receipts placed in a night depository on the last day of the month would be reflected only in the next month's bank statement. These receipts are added to the bank balance to arrive at the true balance.

        3)   **Amounts added by the bank.** Interest income added to an account may not be included in the book balance. Banks may act as collection agents, for example, for notes on which the depositor is the payee. If the depositor has not learned of a collection, it will not be reflected in its records.

            a)   These amounts are added to the book balance to arrive at the true balance.

            b)   They should be recorded on the entity's books, after which they are not reconciling items.

        4)   **Amounts subtracted (or not added) by the bank.** These amounts generally include service charges and customer checks returned for insufficient funds **(NSF checks)**. Service charges cannot be recorded in the books until the bank statement is received. Customer checks returned for insufficient funds are not added to the bank balance but are still included in the book balance.

            a)   These amounts are subtracted from the book balance to arrive at the true balance.

            b)   They should be recorded on the entity's books, after which they are not reconciling items.

        5)   **Errors.** If the bank has wrongly charged or credited the entity's account (or failed to record a transaction at all), the error may be detected in the process of preparing the reconciliation. Book errors may likewise be discovered.

c.   **Bank Reconciliation**

EXAMPLE

Raughley Company's bank statement on March 31 indicated a balance of $6,420. The book balance on that date was $7,812. The bank balance did not include $3,229 of receipts for March 31 that were deposited on that day but were not recorded until April 1 by the bank. It also did not include $450 of checks written in March that did not clear until April. The March bank statement revealed that (1) the bank had collected $1,500 in March on a note owed to Raughley, (2) a $160 customer check had been returned for insufficient funds, and (3) service charges totaled $7. Finally, a check for $60 written by Raughley cleared the bank for $6.

Bank Reconciliation

Book balance – March 31		$7,812
Add items on bank statement not on books:		
$60 check cleared for $6	$ 54	
Note proceeds	1,500	1,554
Subtract items on bank statement not on books:		
Service charges	$ (7)	
Deposited check returned NSF	(160)	(167)
True cash balance – March 31		**$9,199**
Bank balance – March 31		$6,420
Add items on books not on bank statement:		
Deposits in transit	$ 3,229	3,229
Subtract items on books not on bank statement:		
Outstanding checks	$ (450)	(450)
True cash balance – March 31		**$9,199**

Stop and review! You have completed the outline for this subunit. Study multiple-choice questions 1 through 3 beginning on page 196.

5.2 FAIR VALUE OPTION (FVO)

Scope

1.   **Accounting mismatches** arise when related financial assets and liabilities are measured using different attributes. The results may be excessive variability in earnings and amounts that are not representationally faithful.

     a.   The FASB issued SFAS 159, *The Fair Value Option for Financial Assets and Financial Liabilities*, to provide for greater **consistency** in accounting.

     b.   Furthermore, it permits an entity to avoid the cost and complexity of **hedge accounting** (see Study Unit 16) by electing fair value treatment for items that would otherwise be hedged.

2.   SFAS 159 allows entities to (a) measure most financial instruments at **fair value** and (b) report unrealized gains and losses in **earnings**. In effect, the FVO permits an entity to account for eligible items in the same way as trading securities (at fair value through earnings).

     a.   An entity **may elect** the **FVO** for the following:

          1)   Most recognized financial assets and liabilities.

          2)   Firm commitments that meet two criteria:

               a)   They would not otherwise be recorded at the time of the agreement.

               b)   They involve only financial instruments. For example, a forward purchase contract for a loan that is not easily convertible to cash is not initially recognized because it is not a derivative. Also, it has no element that is not an instrument.

3)   A written loan commitment.

4)   Insurance contracts and warranties that are not financial instruments (because they require or permit settlement in goods or services instead of cash settlement) but permit payment to a third party to provide the goods or services.

5)   A host instrument that is part of a nonfinancial instrument and is accounted for separately from an embedded nonfinancial derivative. An example is a combination of a derivative payable in cash, goods, or services and a liability payable only in cash.

b.   The FVO **may not be elected** for the following:

1)   An investment in a subsidiary or an interest in a variable interest entity (VIE) that must be consolidated (i.e., the FVO is not an alternative to consolidation)

2)   Obligations for (or assets for overfunded positions in) postretirement employee benefits and other deferred compensation

3)   Most financial assets and liabilities under leases

4)   Demand deposit liabilities

5)   Financial instruments at least partly classified in equity

Election of the FVO

3.   The decision whether to elect the FVO is made **irrevocably** at an **election date** (unless a new election date occurs).

a.   The decision is ordinarily made **instrument by instrument** and only for an **entire instrument**. Thus, the FVO generally need **not be applied to all instruments** in a single transaction. For example, it might be applied only to some of the shares or bonds issued or acquired in a transaction. But an instrument that constitutes one legal contract is indivisible for FVO purposes.

1)   The following are **exceptions**:

a)   An investment otherwise accounted for under the equity method. (All eligible interests in the investee, debt and equity, must be accounted for using the FVO.)

b)   Multiple advances made to one debtor under one contract that are part of a larger balance. (The FVO must be applied to the larger balance.)

c)   An eligible insurance contract. (If the FVO applies to the whole contract, it applies to all claims and obligations under the contract.)

d)   An insurance contract with integrated or nonintegrated features or coverages. (If the FVO applies to the whole contract, it applies to the features and coverages.) Moreover, the entity cannot choose the FVO solely for nonintegrated items.

4.   The following are **election dates**:

a.   Initial recognition of an eligible item

b.   Making an eligible firm commitment

c.   A change in accounting for an investment in another entity because it becomes subject to the equity method

d.   Deconsolidation of a subsidiary or a VIE (with retention of an interest)

e.   An event that causes financial assets (previously measured at fair value through earnings because of a specialized accounting principle) no longer to qualify for such accounting treatment

f.   An event requiring fair value measurement when it occurs but not subsequently (excluding recognition of nontemporary impairment, e.g., of inventory or long-lived assets)

5. Examples of **events requiring either remeasurement at fair value or initial recognition** (or both) of eligible items and that result in an election date are a

    a. Business combination,
    b. Consolidation or deconsolidation, or
    c. Significant modification of debt.

Glossary

6. **Fair value** is an exit price. It equals what "price that would be received to sell an asset or paid to transfer a liability in an orderly transaction between market participants at the measurement date" (SFAS 157, *Fair Value Measurements*).

7. A **financial asset** is cash, "evidence of an ownership interest in an entity, or a contract that conveys to one entity a right (a) to receive cash or another financial instrument from a second entity or (b) to exchange other financial instruments on potentially favorable terms with the second entity."

    a. A **financial liability** is a "contract that imposes on one entity an obligation (1) to deliver cash or another financial instrument to a second entity or (2) to exchange other financial instruments on potentially unfavorable terms with the second entity" (adapted from the definition of a **financial instrument** in SFAS 107, *Disclosures about Fair Value of Financial Instruments*).

8. A **firm commitment** is made with an unrelated party and is mutually binding. It is ordinarily enforceable by legal means but need not be. Moreover, the important terms (a fixed price, when performance will occur, and quantities involved) are stated, and breach of the agreement is not probable (SFAS 133, *Accounting for Derivative Instruments and Hedging Activities*).

Financial Statement Presentation

9. **Balance sheet.** Assets and liabilities measured using the FVO are reported in a way that **separates their fair values** from the carrying amounts of similar items measured using another attribute, e.g., amortized cost.

10. **Income statement. Unrealized gains and losses** on items measured using the FVO are recognized at subsequent reporting dates. **Upfront costs and fees** related to those items are recognized as incurred.

11. **Statement of cash flows.** Cash flows related to items measured at fair value are classified according to their nature and purpose.

Stop and review! You have completed the outline for this subunit. Study multiple-choice questions 4 through 7 beginning on page 197.

5.3 CLASSIFICATION OF INVESTMENTS

Investments in Debt and Equity Securities

1. Investments are made to obtain a return in the form of interest, dividends, or appreciation. SFAS 115, *Accounting for Certain Investments in Debt and Equity Securities*, applies to most investments.

2. A **security** is an interest in property (or an enterprise or obligation of the issuer) that is (a) registered by or for the issuer or represented by an instrument, (b) commonly traded in securities markets or (in instrument form) commonly recognized as a means of investment, and (c) one of a class or series or divisible into a class or series.

    a. This definition excludes trade receivables and consumer, commercial, and real estate loans receivable resulting from lending by financial institutions (unless securitized).

b. An **equity security** is an **ownership** interest in an entity or a right to acquire or dispose of such an interest.

    1) SFAS 115 does not apply to equity securities that do not have **readily determinable fair values**, i.e., when quoted market prices are unavailable.

        a) When fair value is not readily determinable, the securities are measured using the **cost method**. Such equity securities are reported at historical cost until sold, at which time realized gains and losses are recognized.

    2) Convertible debt securities are not equity.

c. A **debt security** represents a **creditor** relationship with the issuer.

    1) This definition includes mandatorily redeemable preferred stock and collateralized mortgage obligations. It excludes leases, options, financial futures contracts, and forward contracts.

3. SFAS 115 applies to the following investments for which the FVO has **not** been elected:

    a. Equity securities with **readily determinable fair values** and
    b. All investments in debt securities.

4. SFAS 115 does **not** apply to the following:

    a. Investments for which the entity has elected the FVO.
    b. Investments in equity securities that, absent election of the FVO, are accounted for using the equity method,
    c. Investments in consolidated subsidiaries,
    d. Entities with specialized accounting practices that include accounting for all investments at fair or market value,
    e. Not-for-profit organizations, and
    f. Most derivative instruments. If the host instrument of an embedded derivative subject to SFAS 133 would otherwise be within the scope of SFAS 115, the host will be accounted for under SFAS 115.

5. The securities to which SFAS 115 applies are classified at acquisition into one of **three categories**. The classification is reassessed at each reporting date.

Category	Criteria
Held-to-maturity	Debt securities that the reporting entity has the positive intent and ability to hold to maturity
Trading	Intended to be sold in the near term
Available for sale	Not classified as held-to-maturity or trading

Held-to-Maturity Securities

6. An investment in a debt security is classified as held-to-maturity when the holder has both the **positive intent** and the **ability** to hold the security until its maturity date.

    a. If the investing entity intends to hold the security for an **indefinite period** or the possibility exists that it may need to be **sold before maturity** (to supply needed cash, avoid interest rate risk, etc.), the security cannot be classified as held-to-maturity.

        1) If circumstances change, however, **an entity can change its intent** with respect to a given debt security "without calling into question the intent to hold other debt securities to maturity in the future."

2) If a **sale before maturity** takes place, the security can still be deemed to have been held-to-maturity if

    a) Sale is near enough to the maturity or call date (e.g., within 3 months) so that **interest rate risk** (change in the market rate) does not have a significant effect on fair value, **or**

    b) Sale is after collection of 85% or more of the principal.

b. A security is not held-to-maturity if it can **contractually be prepaid or otherwise settled** under terms that preclude the holder from substantially recovering its recorded investment.

1) Such a security may therefore need to be **reclassified** and measured as an available-for-sale or trading security. It also should be examined to determine whether it contains an **embedded derivative** requiring separate accounting.

c. Held-to-maturity securities are reported at **amortized cost**. Fair value is irrelevant because the securities are not intended to be traded.

1) The purchase of held-to-maturity securities is recorded as follows:

Held-to-maturity securities	$XXX	
Cash		$XXX

2) Because held-to-maturity securities are not periodically measured, they do not contribute to the volatility of earnings.

7. **Financial statement presentation:**

a. **Balance sheet.** Held-to-maturity securities are presented net of any unamortized premium or discount. **No valuation account** is used.

1) Amortization of any discount (premium) is reported by a debit (credit) to held-to-maturity securities and a credit (debit) to interest income.

2) Individual securities are presented as **current or noncurrent**.

b. **Income statement.** Realized gains and losses and interest income (including amortization of premium or discount) are included in **earnings**.

c. **Cash flow statement.** Cash flows are from **investing activities**.

Trading Securities

8. Trading securities are bought and held primarily for sale in the near term. They are purchased and sold frequently.

a. Each trading security is initially recorded at **cost** (including brokerage commissions and taxes).

Trading securities	$XXX	
Cash		$XXX

b. At each balance sheet date, trading securities are **remeasured at fair value**.

1) Quoted market prices in active markets for identical assets are easy to obtain and are the most reliable and verifiable measure of fair value.

    a) See the fair value measurement framework in Subunit 1.7.

9. **Unrealized holding gains and losses** on trading securities are included in **earnings**. A holding gain or loss is the net change in fair value during the period, not including recognized dividends or interest not received.

a. To retain historical cost in the accounts while reporting changes in the carrying amount arising from changes in fair value, a **valuation allowance** may be established. For example, the entry below debits an allowance for an increase in the fair value of trading securities.

Securities fair value adjustment (trading)	$XXX	
Unrealized holding gain – earnings		$XXX

10. **Financial statement presentation:**

    a. **Balance sheet.** The balances of the securities and valuation accounts are netted. **One amount** is displayed for fair value.

        1) Assets similar to those classified as trading that are **not measured subsequently** at fair value are reported separately.

        2) Individual securities are presented as **current or noncurrent**.

    b. **Income statement.** Unrealized as well as realized holding gains and losses, dividends, and interest income (including premium or discount amortization) are included in earnings.

    c. **Cash flow statement.** Classification of cash flows depends on the nature of the securities and the purpose of their acquisition.

Available-for-Sale Securities

11. Securities that are not classified as held-to-maturity or trading are considered available-for-sale. The accounting is similar to that for trading securities.

    a. The **initial acquisition** is recorded at cost by a debit to available-for-sale securities and a credit to cash.

    b. **Amortization** of any discount (premium) is reported by a debit (credit) to available-for-sale securities or a valuation account and a credit (debit) to interest income.

    c. Receipt of **cash dividends** is recorded by a debit to cash and a credit to dividend income.

    d. The difference is that unrealized **holding gains and losses** are reported in **other comprehensive income (OCI)**, not earnings.

Unrealized holding loss – OCI	$XXX	
Securities fair value adjustment		
(available-for-sale)		$XXX

        1) **Tax effects** are debited or credited directly to OCI.

        2) All or part of unrealized gains and losses for an available-for-sale security designated and qualifying as the **hedged item in a fair value hedge** are recognized in earnings (SFAS 133).

12. **Financial statement presentation:**

    a. **Balance sheet.** The balances of the securities and valuation accounts are netted. **One amount** is displayed for fair value.

        1) Assets similar to those classified as available-for-sale that are **not measured subsequently** at fair value are reported separately.

        2) Individual securities are presented as **current or noncurrent**.

        3) In the equity section, unrealized holding gains and losses are reported in **accumulated OCI** (the real account to which OCI is closed).

    b. **Income statement.** Realized gains and losses, dividends, and interest income (including premium or discount amortization) are included in earnings.

    c. **Cash flow statement.** Cash flows are from **investing activities**.

    d. **Statement of comprehensive income.** Unrealized holding gains and losses are included in comprehensive income.

        1) **Reclassification adjustments** also must be made for each component of OCI. Their purpose is to avoid double counting when an item included in net income also was included in OCI for the same or a prior period. For example, if a gain on available-for-sale securities is realized in the current period, the prior-period recognition of an unrealized holding gain must be eliminated by debiting OCI and crediting a gain.

Transfers Between Categories

13. Transfers between categories are accounted for at transfer-date fair value. The following describes the treatment of **unrealized holding gains and losses** at that date:

    a. **From trading to any category.** Amounts already recognized in earnings are not reversed.

    b. **To trading from any category.** Amounts not already recognized in earnings are recognized in earnings.

    c. **To available-for-sale from held-to-maturity.** Amounts are recognized in OCI.

    d. **To held-to-maturity from available-for-sale.** Amounts recognized in OCI are not reversed but are amortized in the same way as premium or discount.

        1) This amortization at least partly offsets the earnings effect of the amortization of the premium or discount. Fair value accounting may result in recognition of a premium or discount when a debt security is transferred to the held-to-maturity category.

    e. Transfers **from held-to-maturity** or **into or from trading** should be rare.

From	To	Earnings Recognition
Trading	Any category	Already recognized, not reversed
Any category	Trading	If not already recognized
Held-to-maturity	Available-for-sale	Unrealized gain (loss) recognized in OCI
Available-for-sale	Held-to-maturity	Amounts in OCI not reversed but are amortized in same way as premium (discount)

Dividends and Interest Income

14. SFAS 115 does not change the recognition and measurement principles for **dividends and interest**, such as amortization of premium or discount using the effective interest method.

    a. Thus, dividend income and interest income for all categories of securities continue to be included in earnings.

    b. **Realized gains** on available-for-sale and held-to-maturity securities also continue to be included in earnings.

Impairment

15. Unrealized changes in fair value are recognized if they represent nontemporary declines.

    a. The **amortized cost basis** is used to calculate the amount of any impairment. It should be distinguished from fair value, which equals the cost basis plus or minus the net unrealized holding gain or loss.

    b. If a decline in fair value of an individual **held-to-maturity or available-for-sale** security below its amortized cost basis is **other than temporary**, the amortized cost basis is written down to fair value as a **new cost basis**.

        1) However, if a security has been the hedged item in a **fair value hedge**, its amortized cost basis will reflect adjustments in its carrying amount for changes in fair value attributable to the hedged risk.

    c. The impairment is a **realized loss** included in **earnings**.

        1) The new cost basis is not affected by recoveries in fair value.

        2) Subsequent changes in fair value of **available-for-sale securities** are included in OCI, except for other-than-temporary declines.

Summary Tables

16. The following table summarizes the provisions of SFAS 115 when the fair value option has not been elected:

Category	Held-to-maturity		Trading		Available-for-sale	
Definition	Debt securities which the entity has the ability and intent to hold until maturity		Bought and held for near-term sale		All securities not in the other two categories	
Type of security	Debt	Equity	Debt	Equity	Debt	Equity
Recognize holding G/L?	No	--	Yes	Yes	Yes	Yes
Recognize unrealized holding G/L in	--	--	Earnings	Earnings	OCI	OCI
Measured at	Amortized cost	--	Fair value	Fair value	Fair value	Fair value

Stop and review! You have completed the outline for this subunit. Study multiple-choice questions 8 through 15 beginning on page 198.

5.4 EQUITY METHOD

Significant Influence

1. An investment in common stock enabling the investor to exercise **significant influence** over the investee should be accounted for by the **equity method** (APB Opinion 18, *The Equity Method of Accounting for Investments in Common Stock*) (assuming no FVO election).

2. The **accounting method** used by the investor depends on the influence presumed to be conferred by the percentage of the investee's total equity held. This diagram depicts the three possibilities:

% Ownership	Presumed Influence	Accounting Method
100%	Control	Consolidation
50%	Significant	Equity Method or FVO
20%	Little or none	Fair Value Method
0%		

a. The **FVO**, which may be elected when the investor does not have control, is discussed in Subunit 5.2. The fair value method, used when the investor has not elected the FVO and does not have significant influence, is discussed in Subunit 5.3.

b. The **equity method**, used when the investor has significant influence and has not elected the FVO, is discussed in this subunit.

c. **Consolidation**, required when the investor owns more than 50% of the outstanding voting interests, is discussed in Study Unit 15.

1) Consolidation is not required if control **does not rest with the majority owner**.

Applying the Equity Method

3. Under the equity method, the investor's **share of the investee's earnings or losses** is adjusted to eliminate interentity profits and losses not realized in third-party transactions. It is also reduced by any **dividends on cumulative preferred stock**, whether or not declared. The adjusted share of the investee's earnings is a debit (losses and dividends are credits) to the carrying amount of the investment.

   a. The receipt of a **cash dividend** from the investee is treated as a return of an investment. Thus, it is credited to the investment but does not affect equity-based earnings. The following are typical entries to recognize the acquisition of the investment, the share of the investee's earnings, and receipt of cash dividends:

Investment in X Co.	$XXX	
Cash		$XXX
Investment in X Co.	XXX	
Revenue -- equity in X Co. earnings		XXX
Cash -- X Co. dividends	XXX	
Investment in X Co.		XXX

4. The difference between the cost of the investment and the underlying equity in the investee's net assets is treated "as if the investee were a consolidated subsidiary." Thus, **goodwill** may be associated with an equity method investment. Furthermore, the difference also affects the investor's share of the investee's earnings or losses.

   a. This difference may be related wholly or in part to specific accounts, such as assets not recorded at **fair value**.

      1) For example, if the investee's **depreciable assets** are understated, amortization of the excess of the fair value over the carrying amount must be recognized by the following entry:

Revenue -- equity in X Co. earnings	$XXX	
Investment in X Co.		$XXX

      2) Similarly, the investee's **sale of land or inventory** with a fair value in excess of the carrying amount requires an adjustment to prevent double-counting. The excess fair value is already reflected in the investment balance. It should not be counted when the investor's share of the investee's earnings is debited to the investment. The entry is the following:

Revenue -- equity in X Co. earnings	$XXX	
(excess profit)		
Investment in X Co.		$XXX

5. The difference between cost and the underlying equity in the investee's net assets may not be attributable wholly or in part to specific accounts. Accordingly, the difference that is not attributable to specific accounts is treated as **goodwill**.

   a. This amount is **not** amortized. The **equity method investment** (but not the equity method goodwill itself, which is inseparable from the investment) is tested for **impairment** under SFAS 142.

6. The investor's shares of the investee's extraordinary items and prior-period adjustments are classified similarly by the investor if material.

7. Use of the equity method is discontinued when the **investment is reduced to zero** by investee losses, unless the investor has committed to provide additional financial support to the investee.

Change to the Equity Method

8.   When ownership of the **voting stock** of an investee rises to the level of **significant influence**, the investor must adopt the equity method or the FVO. A **20% or greater** ownership interest is rebuttably presumed to permit such influence. The presumption of significant influence is overcome only by predominant contrary evidence (FASB Interpretation No. 35, *Criteria for Applying the Equity Method*).

    a.   The investor must **retroactively adjust** (1) the carrying amount of the investment, (2) results of operations for current and prior periods presented, and (3) retained earnings. The adjustment is made as if the equity method had been in effect during all of the previous periods in which any percentage was held.

    b.   When the change is **from the fair value method**, the entity must eliminate the effects of recognition of unrealized holding gains and losses on available-for-sale securities: (1) their classification as available for sale, (2) accumulated OCI, and (3) the amount included in the allowance account.

    c.   **Deconsolidation.** When the investor **no longer has control** of the investee but retains significant influence, it may choose the **FVO or the equity method**. The new method is applied only from the deconsolidation date.

Change from the Equity Method

9.   If an investor can no longer be presumed to exert significant influence, it ceases to recognize its share of the undistributed earnings or losses of the investee. This **change from the equity method** is not a basis for the FVO election or any retroactive adjustment. The shares retained ordinarily will be accounted for as available-for-sale or trading securities.

    a.   The **carrying amount** of the investment is unchanged except for a fair-value adjustment at the next balance sheet date (assuming the fair value is readily determinable).

    b.   **Subsequent dividends** are accounted for as dividend income unless they are liquidating dividends.

    c.   **Amortization** of the excess of the fair value over the carrying amount of depreciable assets is no longer recognized.

Cost Method

10.   Under the **fair value** method, equity securities are accounted for based on fair values if the equity method is not appropriate. However, if such equity securities do **not have readily determinable fair values**, they are accounted for after acquisition using the cost method.

    a.   Under the **cost method**, an investment in stock is initially recorded at cost, but subsequent unrealized changes in fair value are not recognized unless they are **nontemporary declines**.

    b.   Under the **cost and fair-value methods**,

        1)   **Dividends** are accounted for by the investor as dividend income unless a liquidating dividend is received.

        2)   **Interentity transactions** should be accounted for separately and in full.

Stop and review! You have completed the outline for this subunit. Study multiple-choice questions 16 through 22 beginning on page 201.

5.5 INVESTMENTS IN BONDS

Definition and Classification

1. A **bond** is a formal contractual agreement by an issuer to pay an amount of money (face amount) at the maturity date plus interest at the stated rate at specific intervals. All terms are stated in a document called an **indenture**.

   a. An investment in a bond is a **financial asset**. Thus, the investor may elect the FVO.

   b. Absent this election (or proper classification as a trading security), a bond is classified as held to maturity or available for sale.

      1) If the reporting entity has the positive intent and ability to hold a bond to maturity, it is classified as **held-to-maturity**.

      2) If the bond does not qualify as held-to-maturity, and the entity has not elected the FVO, it is classified as **available for sale**.

      3) Neither an FVO election nor classification as available for sale affects the customary calculation and recognition of **interest revenue** (including premium or discount amortization).

   c. For a listing of the types of bonds, see Study Unit 12.

Carrying Amount

2. In principle, long-term debt securities (e.g., bonds) should be recorded at the present value of the future cash flows discounted at the market rate. In practice, they are recorded at their **historical cost** (including brokerage fees but excluding accrued interest at purchase). Any **discount or premium** (difference between the purchase price and maturity amount) is amortized over the remaining life of the debt.

   a. A separate premium or discount account is seldom used.

      1) The carrying amount (excluding brokerage fees) for a held-to-maturity security equals the face amount plus any unamortized premium or minus any unamortized discount.

      2) If **unrealized gains or losses** are recognized, they are debited (credited) to a valuation account. The adjusted face amount (the held-to-maturity amount) remains the basis for calculating amortization of premium or discount using the effective interest method.

Effective Interest Method

3. This method of amortizing discount or premium results in a constant rate of return on a receivable or payable. Under this method, the effective rate of interest at the transaction date is applied to the carrying amount (adjusted face amount) of the receivable or payable to determine **interest revenue** or **interest expense**.

   a. The effective interest method must be used unless the straight-line method gives results that do not differ materially.

   b. The **effective interest rate** is the rate the instrument was issued to yield. If it is greater than the stated rate, issuance is at a **discount**. If the effective rate is lower than the stated rate, issuance is at a **premium**.

   c. If the instrument was issued at a **discount or premium**, interest revenue or expense will be more or less, respectively, than nominal (cash) interest.

d.   The **amount amortized** is the difference between interest revenue or expense and the actual cash received or paid based on the **nominal rate of interest**.

   1)   Amortization increases from period to period, regardless of whether a **discount or premium** is being amortized. The reason is that the carrying amount increases or decreases from period to period as discount or premium, respectively, is amortized.

   a)   **Issuance at a premium.** The constant cash interest exceeds interest revenue or expense, an amount that decreases over time.

   b)   **Issuance at a discount.** The constant cash interest is less than interest revenue or expense, an amount that increases over time.

e.   Amortization results in the carrying amount of the asset (liability) being adjusted over time, reaching the **face amount at maturity**.

f.   **Amortizing a discount (stated rate less than effective rate).**

EXAMPLE

Assume an investor records a 6%, 5-year, $5,000 bond classified as held-to-maturity (interest received annually at year-end), with an 8% effective rate.

		Times:	Equals:	Minus:	Equals:	
Year	Beginning Net Carrying Amount	Effective Rate	Interest Revenue	Cash Received	Discount Amortized	Ending Carrying Amount
1	$4,601	8%	$368	$300	$68	$4,669
2	$4,669	8%	$374	$300	$74	$4,743
3	$4,743	8%	$379	$300	$79	$4,822
4	$4,822	8%	$386	$300	$86	$4,908
5	$4,908	8%	$393	$300	$93	$5,000

---

   1)   The proceeds paid to the debtor (the issuer) equal the bond's present value and fair value at the time of issue. The gross amount recorded for the bond is its face amount at maturity. To report the bond at present value, the discount (an allowance account) may be recognized separately. The journal entry (using an allowance account for illustrative purposes) is

Bond receivable	$5,000	
Cash		$4,601
Discount on bond receivable		399

   2)   At the end of the first year, the journal entry is

Cash	$300	
Discount on bond receivable	68	
Interest revenue		$368

   a)   Unlike the **balance sheet presentation** of accounts receivable, the allowance (the discount) is not separately displayed.

Bond receivable	$4,669	

   3)   At the end of the fifth year, the journal entries are

Cash	$300	
Discount on bond receivable	93	
Interest revenue		$393
Cash	$5,000	
Bond receivable		$5,000

g.   **Amortizing a premium (stated rate greater than effective rate).**

EXAMPLE

Assume an investor records an 8%, 5-year, $5,000 bond classified as held-to-maturity (interest received annually at year-end), with a 6% effective rate.

	Beginning Net Carrying	Times: Effective	Equals: Interest	Minus: Cash	Equals: Premium	Ending Carrying
Year	Amount	Rate	Revenue	Received	Amortized	Amount
1	$5,421	6%	$325	$400	($75)	$5,346
2	$5,346	6%	$321	$400	($79)	$5,267
3	$5,267	6%	$316	$400	($84)	$5,183
4	$5,183	6%	$311	$400	($89)	$5,094
5	$5,094	6%	$306	$400	($94)	$5,000

1)   The proceeds paid to the debtor (the issuer) equal the bond's present value (and fair value) at the time of issue. The gross amount recorded for the bond is its face amount at maturity. To report the bond at present value, the premium (an allowance account) may be recognized. The journal entry (again using the allowance account for illustration) is

Bond receivable	$5,000	
Premium on bond receivable	421	
Cash		$5,421

2)   At the end of the first year, the journal entry is

Cash	$400	
Interest revenue		$325
Premium on bond receivable		75

a)   Unlike the **balance sheet presentation** of accounts receivable, the allowance (the premium) is not separately displayed.

Bond receivable	$5,346

3)   At the end of the fifth year, the journal entries are

Cash	$400	
Interest revenue		$306
Premium on bond receivable		94
Cash	$5,000	
Bond receivable		$5,000

Cash Paid

4.   Cash paid to the issuer includes **interest accrued** since the last payment date.

a.   Interest accrued at the date of purchase may be debited to interest receivable or to interest revenue.

Fair Value

5.   To **adjust the yield to the market rate**, the price of the bond must fluctuate inversely with the market rate because the nominal interest rate is fixed.

a.   For example, as described above, bonds selling at a premium have a nominal rate in excess of the market rate. If the market rate subsequently increases, the price of the bonds must decrease to provide a yield equal to the new market rate.

Detachable Warrants

6. When debt securities with detachable stock warrants are purchased, the price should be allocated between the warrants and the securities based upon their **relative fair values** at issuance.

   a. The amount debited to investment in stock warrants relative to the total amount paid increases the discount or decreases the premium on the investment.

Sinking Funds

7. A bond indenture may require a sinking fund (a long-term investment). The objective of making payments into the fund is to segregate and accumulate sufficient assets to pay bond interest and principal. The amounts transferred plus the revenue earned on the investments provide the necessary funds.

Stop and review! You have completed the outline for this subunit. Study multiple-choice questions 23 through 28 beginning on page 203.

5.6 CASH SURRENDER VALUE

1. The cash surrender value of **life insurance** policies on **key executives** is shown in the **noncurrent asset** section of the balance sheet. The policy typically contains a schedule specifying the cash surrender value and loan value for each year.

2. The annual premium for life insurance is allocated between expense and the cash surrender value.

   a. The **life insurance expense** recognized equals the difference between the (1) premiums paid (cash), and (2) the sum of the cash surrender value and dividends received on the policy.

   b. Thus, an increase in the policy's cash surrender value decreases insurance expense.

Cash surrender value	$XXX	
Insurance expense	XXX	
Cash		$XXX

3. If the company is the **beneficiary**, the premiums are not deductible on the tax return, and the proceeds of the policy are not taxable.

4. When **proceeds** from the policy are received, the entry is

Cash	$XXX	
Cash surrender value		$XXX
Insurance income		XXX

Stop and review! You have completed the outline for this subunit. Study multiple-choice questions 29 through 31 on page 205.

**Page
Intentionally
Left Blank**

QUESTIONS

5.1 Cash

1. Burr Company had the following account balances at December 31, Year 1:

Cash in banks	$2,250,000
Cash on hand	125,000
Cash legally restricted for additions to plant (expected to be disbursed in Year 2)	1,600,000

Cash in banks includes $600,000 of compensating balances related to short-term borrowing arrangements. The compensating balances are not legally restricted as to withdrawal by Burr. In the current assets section of Burr's December 31, Year 1, balance sheet, total cash should be reported at

- A. $1,775,000
- B. $2,250,000
- C. $2,375,000
- D. $3,975,000

Answer (C) is correct. *(CPA, adapted)*
REQUIRED: The total cash reported in current assets given legal restrictions and compensating balance requirements.
DISCUSSION: Compensating balances against short-term borrowing arrangements that are legally restricted should be reported separately among the cash and cash equivalents in the current assets section. Legally restricted amounts related to long-term arrangements should be classified separately as noncurrent. Thus, the amount restricted for additions should be classified as noncurrent because it relates to a plant asset. Total cash reported as current assets therefore equals $2,375,000 ($2,250,000 + $125,000).
Answer (A) is incorrect because $1,775,000 results from subtracting the $600,000 of compensating balances from cash in banks. Answer (B) is incorrect because cash on hand should be included in the current assets section. Answer (D) is incorrect because the legally restricted cash related to a long-term arrangement should be classified as noncurrent.

2. Ral Corp.'s checkbook balance on December 31, Year 7, was $5,000. In addition, Ral held the following items in its safe on that date:

Check payable to Ral Corp., dated January 2, Year 8, in payment of a sale made in December Year 7, not included in December 31 checkbook balance	$2,000
Check payable to Ral Corp., deposited December 15 and included in December 31 checkbook balance, but returned by Bank on December 30 stamped "NSF." The check was redeposited on January 2, Year 8, and cleared on January 9	500
Check drawn on Ral Corp.'s account, payable to a vendor, dated and recorded in Ral's books on December 31, but not mailed until January 10, Year 8	300

The proper amount to be shown as cash on Ral's balance sheet at December 31, Year 7, is

- A. $4,800
- B. $5,300
- C. $6,500
- D. $6,800

Answer (A) is correct. *(CPA, adapted)*
REQUIRED: The amount to be recorded as cash on the year-end balance sheet.
DISCUSSION: The December 31 checkbook balance is $5,000. The $2,000 check dated January 2, Year 8, is properly not included in this balance because it is not negotiable at year-end. The $500 NSF check should not be included in cash because it is a receivable. The $300 check that was not mailed until January 10 should be added to the balance. This predated check is still within the control of the company and should not decrease the cash account. Consequently, the cash balance to be reported on the December 31, Year 7, balance sheet is $4,800.

Balance per checkbook	$5,000
Add: Predated check	300
Deduct: NSF check	(500)
Cash balance 12/31/Year 7	$4,800

Answer (B) is incorrect because $5,300 does not include the NSF check. Answer (C) is incorrect because $6,500 includes the postdated check but not the predated check. Answer (D) is incorrect because $6,800 includes the postdated check.

3. The following information pertains to Grey Co. at December 31, Year 4:

Checkbook balance	$12,000
Bank statement balance	16,000
Check drawn on Grey's account, payable to a vendor, dated and recorded 12/31/Yr 4 but not mailed until 1/10/Yr 5	1,800

On Grey's December 31, Year 4, balance sheet, what amount should be reported as cash?

- A. $12,000
- B. $13,800
- C. $14,200
- D. $16,000

Answer (B) is correct. *(CPA, adapted)*
REQUIRED: The amount of cash that should be reported on the balance sheet.
DISCUSSION: The cash account on the balance sheet should consist of (1) coin and currency on hand, (2) demand deposits (checking accounts), (3) time deposits (savings accounts), and (4) near-cash assets (e.g., deposits in transit or checks written to creditors but not yet mailed). Thus, the cash balance should be $13,800 ($12,000 checkbook balance + $1,800 check drawn but not mailed). The checkbook balance is used instead of the bank balance in the calculation. It more closely reflects the amount of cash that is unrestricted at the balance sheet date.
Answer (A) is incorrect because $12,000 excludes the check that was recorded but not mailed. Answer (C) is incorrect because $14,200 equals the bank statement balance minus the check not mailed. Answer (D) is incorrect because $16,000 is the bank statement balance.

5.2 Fair Value Option (FVO)

4. According to SFAS 159, *The Fair Value Option for Financial Assets and Liabilities*, election of the fair value option (FVO)

- A. Permits only for-profit entities to measure eligible items at fair value.
- B. Results in recognition of unrealized gains and losses in earnings of a business entity.
- C. Requires deferral of related upfront costs.
- D. Results in recognition of unrealized gains and losses in other comprehensive income of a business entity.

Answer (B) is correct. *(Publisher, adapted)*
REQUIRED: The accounting for the FVO.
DISCUSSION: A business measures at fair value the eligible items for which the FVO election was made at a specified election date. The unrealized gains and losses on those items are reported in earnings at each subsequent reporting date.
Answer (A) is incorrect because the FVO may be elected by all entities. Answer (C) is incorrect because upfront costs and fees are recognized in earnings of a business as they are incurred if they relate to eligible items for which the FVO election was made. Answer (D) is incorrect because the unrealized gains and losses are recognized in earnings, not OCI.

5. Which of the following is an election date for the purpose of determining whether to elect the fair value option (FVO)?

- A. The accounting treatment of an equity investment changes because it is no longer subject to equity-method accounting.
- B. The entity enters into a firm commitment to purchase soybeans in three months.
- C. The accounting for an equity investment changes because the entity no longer consolidates a subsidiary.
- D. The entity recognizes an other than temporary impairment of long-lived assets.

Answer (C) is correct. *(Publisher, adapted)*
REQUIRED: The election date.
DISCUSSION: An entity may choose the FVO only on an election date. For example, an election date occurs when the accounting for an equity investment in another entity changes because the investor retains an interest but no longer consolidates a subsidiary or a variable interest entity.
Answer (A) is incorrect because an election date occurs when the accounting changes because the investment becomes subject to equity-method accounting, not when the investment no longer is subject to equity-method accounting. Answer (B) is incorrect because a firm commitment is not an eligible item unless it involves financial instruments only. Answer (D) is incorrect because an election date occurs when an event requires an eligible item to be measured at fair value at the time of the event but not subsequently. However, an exception to this rule is recognition of impairment for a nontemporary impairment. Another situation in which no election date occurs is recognition of impairment when writing down inventory to the lower of cost or market.

6. The decision whether to elect the fair value option (FVO)

    A. Is irrevocable until the next election date, if any.

    B. May be applied to a portion of a financial instrument.

    C. Must be applied only to classes of financial instruments.

    D. Must be applied to all instruments issued in a single transaction.

Answer (A) is correct. *(Publisher, adapted)*
    REQUIRED: The scope of the decision to elect the FVO.
    DISCUSSION: The decision whether to elect the FVO is final and cannot be revoked unless a new election date occurs. For example, an election date occurs when an entity recognizes an investment in equity securities with readily determinable fair values issued by another entity. A second election date occurs when the accounting changes because the investment later becomes subject to equity-method accounting. An original decision to classify the equity securities as available-for-sale may then be revoked at the second election date by choosing the FVO instead of the equity method.
    Answer (B) is incorrect because the decision whether to elect the FVO applies "only to an entire instrument and not to only specified risks, specific cash flows, or portions of that instrument" (SFAS 159). Answer (C) is incorrect because the decision whether to elect the FVO may be applied to individual eligible items. Thus, identical items may be treated differently. However, certain exceptions apply. For example, the FVO may be applied to an investment to which the equity method would otherwise apply. This election must be applied to all financial interests held by the investor in the investee that are eligible items. Answer (D) is incorrect because, with certain exceptions (e.g., multiple advances to one debtor under a single construction loan that merge into a larger balance), the FVO need not be applied to all eligible items acquired or issued in the same transaction. For example, an acquirer of registered bonds may apply the FVO to only some of the bonds.

7. The reporting entity may elect the fair value option (FVO) for

    A. An investment consisting of more than 50% of the outstanding voting interests of another entity.

    B. An interest in a variable interest entity (VIE) if the reporting entity is the primary beneficiary.

    C. Its obligation for pension and other postretirement employee benefits.

    D. A forward purchase contract for a loan that is not readily convertible to cash.

Answer (D) is correct. *(Publisher, adapted)*
    REQUIRED: The item eligible for the FVO election.
    DISCUSSION: The FVO may be elected for a firm commitment that (1) would not otherwise be recognized at its inception and (2) involves only financial instruments. A forward purchase contract for a loan that is not readily convertible to cash meets the criteria for a firm commitment: (1) an agreement with an unrelated party that is binding on both parties, (2) specifications of all significant terms (including a fixed price), and (3) a disincentive for nonperformance (e.g., damages for breach of contract) that makes performance probable. Moreover, the forward purchase contract (1) is not a derivative and would not otherwise be recognized and (2) involves only a loan and cash (only financial instruments).
    Answer (A) is incorrect because an investment in a subsidiary required to be consolidated is not an eligible item. Answer (B) is incorrect because the primary beneficiary must consolidate the VIE. Thus, the interest in the VIE is not an eligible item. Answer (C) is incorrect because items eligible for the FVO election do not include employers' and plans' obligations for (1) employee pension benefits, (2) other postretirement employee benefits, (3) postemployment benefits, (4) employee stock option and stock purchase plans, and (5) other deferred compensation.

5.3 Classification of Investments

8. Kale Co. purchased bonds at a discount on the open market as an investment and has the intent and ability to hold these bonds to maturity. Kale should account for these bonds at

    A. Cost.

    B. Amortized cost.

    C. Fair value.

    D. Lower of cost or market.

Answer (B) is correct. *(CPA, adapted)*
    REQUIRED: The proper recording of held-to-maturity securities.
    DISCUSSION: SFAS 115 requires that investments in debt securities be classified as held-to-maturity and measured at amortized cost in the balance sheet if the reporting entity has the positive intent and ability to hold them to maturity.
    Answer (A) is incorrect because the discount will be amortized over the term of the bonds. Answer (C) is incorrect because trading and available-for-sale securities are accounted for at fair value. Answer (D) is incorrect because inventory is accounted for at lower of cost or market.

9. On December 31, Ott Co. had investments in trading securities as follows:

	Cost	Fair Value
Man Co.	$10,000	$ 8,000
Kemo, Inc.	9,000	11,000
Fenn Corp.	11,000	9,000
	$30,000	$28,000

Ott's December 31 balance sheet should report the trading securities as

A. $26,000

B. $28,000

C. $29,000

D. $30,000

Answer (B) is correct. *(CPA, adapted)*
REQUIRED: The amount at which the trading securities should be reported.
DISCUSSION: Trading securities are reported at fair value, and unrealized holding gains and losses are included in earnings. Consequently, the securities should be reported as $28,000.
Answer (A) is incorrect because $26,000 is the lower of cost or fair value determined on an individual security basis. Answer (C) is incorrect because $29,000 is the average of the aggregate cost and aggregate fair value. Answer (D) is incorrect because $30,000 is the aggregate cost.

10. On July 2, Year 4, Wynn, Inc. purchased as a short-term investment a $1 million face value Kean Co. 8% bond for $910,000 plus accrued interest to yield 10%. The bonds mature on January 1, Year 11, and pay interest annually on January 1. On December 31, Year 4, the bonds had a fair value of $945,000. On February 13, Year 5, Wynn sold the bonds for $920,000. In its December 31, Year 4, balance sheet, what amount should Wynn report for the bond if it is classified as an available-for-sale security?

A. $910,000

B. $920,000

C. $945,000

D. $950,000

Answer (C) is correct. *(CPA, adapted)*
REQUIRED: The amount to be reported for a bond classified as an available-for-sale security.
DISCUSSION: Available-for-sale securities should be measured at fair value in the balance sheet. Hence, the bond should be reported at its fair value of $945,000 to reflect the unrealized holding gain (change in fair value).
Answer (A) is incorrect because $910,000 is the cost (accrued interest is not recorded as part of the cost but as an adjustment of interest income). Answer (B) is incorrect because $920,000 is the sale price. Answer (D) is incorrect because $950,000 equals the cost plus accrued interest (the total price paid) on July 2, Year 4.

11. The following information pertains to Lark Corp.'s available-for-sale securities:

| | December 31 ||
	Year 2	Year 3
Cost	$100,000	$100,000
Fair value	90,000	120,000

Differences between cost and fair values are considered to be temporary. The decline in fair value was properly accounted for at December 31, Year 2. Ignoring tax effects, by what amount should other comprehensive income (OCI) be credited at December 31, Year 3?

A. $0

B. $10,000

C. $20,000

D. $30,000

Answer (D) is correct. *(CPA, adapted)*
REQUIRED: The credit to OCI if fair value exceeds cost.
DISCUSSION: Unrealized holding gains and losses on available-for-sale securities, including those classified as current assets, are not included in earnings but ordinarily are reported in OCI, net of tax effects (ignored in this question). At December 31, Year 2 (assuming the securities are not designated as being hedged in a fair value hedge), OCI should have been debited for $10,000 for the excess of cost over fair value to reflect an unrealized holding loss. At December 31, Year 3, OCI should be credited to reflect a $30,000 unrealized holding gain ($120,000 fair value at 12/31/Year 3 – $90,000 fair value at 12/31/Year 2).
Answer (A) is incorrect because unrealized holding gains on available-for-sale securities are recognized. Answer (B) is incorrect because $10,000 is merely the recovery of the previously recognized unrealized holding loss. The recognition of gain is not limited to that amount. Answer (C) is incorrect because $20,000 is merely the excess of fair value over cost.

12. The following information was extracted from Gil Co.'s December 31 balance sheet:

Noncurrent assets:
  Available-for-sale securities
    (carried at fair value) $96,450
Equity:
  Accumulated other comprehensive
    income (OCI)
      Unrealized gains and losses on
        available-for-sale securities   (19,800)

Historical cost of the available-for-sale securities was

A. $63,595

B. $76,650

C. $96,450

D. $116,250

Answer (D) is correct. *(CPA, adapted)*
REQUIRED: The historical cost of the available-for-sale securities.
DISCUSSION: The existence of an equity account with a debit balance signifies that the available-for-sale securities are reported at fair value that is less than historical cost. The difference is the net unrealized loss balance. Hence, historical cost must have been $116,250 ($96,450 available-for-sale securities at fair value + $19,800 net unrealized loss).
Answer (A) is incorrect because $63,595 is a nonsense figure. Answer (B) is incorrect because $76,650 results from subtracting the unrealized loss instead of adding. Answer (C) is incorrect because $96,450 ignores the unrealized loss balance.

13. During Year 6, Wall Co. purchased 2,000 shares of Hemp Corp. common stock for $31,500 that are classified as trading securities. The fair value of this investment was $29,500 at December 31, Year 6. Wall sold all of the Hemp common stock for $14 per share on December 15, Year 7, incurring $1,400 in brokerage commissions and taxes. In its income statement for the year ended December 31, Year 7, Wall should report a recognized loss of

A. $4,900

B. $3,500

C. $2,900

D. $1,500

Answer (C) is correct. *(CPA, adapted)*
REQUIRED: The realized loss on the sale of trading securities.
DISCUSSION: A realized loss or gain is recognized when an individual security is sold or otherwise disposed of. Under SFAS 115, Wall would have included the $2,000 ($31,500 – $29,500) decline in the fair value of the trading securities (an unrealized holding loss) in earnings at 12/31/Yr 6. Consequently, the realized loss on disposal at 12/15/Yr 7 is $2,900 {$29,500 carrying amount – [(2,000 shares × $14) – $1,400]}.
Answer (A) is incorrect because $4,900 is the sum of the recognized losses for Year 6 and Year 7. Answer (B) is incorrect because $3,500 is the sum of the recognized losses for Year 6 and Year 7 without regard to the commissions and taxes. Answer (D) is incorrect because $1,500 ignores the commissions and taxes.

14. The following pertains to Smoke, Inc.'s investment in equity securities:

● On December 31, Year 3, Smoke reclassified a security acquired during the year for $70,000. It had a $50,000 fair value when it was reclassified from trading to available-for-sale.

● An available-for-sale security costing $75,000, written down to $30,000 in Year 2 because of an other-than-temporary impairment of fair value, had a $60,000 fair value on December 31, Year 3.

What is the net effect of the above items on Smoke's net income for the year ended December 31, Year 3?

A. No effect.

B. $10,000 increase.

C. $20,000 decrease.

D. $30,000 increase.

Answer (C) is correct. *(CPA, adapted)*
REQUIRED: The effect on net income of a reclassification and a recovery in value of an impaired security.
DISCUSSION: Unrealized holding gains and losses on trading securities are included in earnings, and reclassification is at fair value. Furthermore, "for a security transferred from the trading category, the unrealized holding gain or loss at the date of transfer will have already been recognized in earnings and shall not be reversed" (SFAS 115). Hence, Smoke should include a $20,000 ($70,000 cost – $50,000 fair value at 12/31/Yr 3) unrealized holding loss in the determination of net income. After an available-for-sale security has been written down to reflect an other-than-temporary decline in fair value, with the loss included in earnings, subsequent increases in its fair value are included in OCI (assuming it is not designated as being hedged in a fair value hedge). Thus, the appreciation of this security has no effect on Year 3 net income.

15. When the fair value of an investment in debt securities exceeds its amortized cost, how should each of the following debt securities be reported at the end of the year?

Debt Securities Classified As

	Held-to-Maturity	Available-for-Sale
A.	Amortized cost	Amortized cost
B.	Amortized cost	Fair value
C.	Fair value	Fair value
D.	Fair value	Amortized cost

Answer (B) is correct. *(CPA, adapted)*
REQUIRED: The reporting of debt securities classified as held-to-maturity and available-for-sale.
DISCUSSION: SFAS 115 requires that investments in debt securities be classified as held-to-maturity and measured at amortized cost in the balance sheet if the reporting entity has the positive intent and ability to hold them to maturity. Under SFAS 115, marketable equity securities can be classified as either trading or available-for-sale. Equity securities that are not expected to be sold in the near term should be classified as available-for-sale. These securities should be reported at fair value, with unrealized holding gains and losses (except those on securities designated as being hedged in a fair value hedge) excluded from earnings and reported in OCI.

5.4 Equity Method

16. Birk Co. purchased 30% of Sled Co.'s outstanding common stock on December 31 for $200,000. On that date, Sled's equity was $500,000, and the fair value of its net assets was $600,000. On December 31, what amount of goodwill should Birk attribute to this acquisition?

A. $0
B. $20,000
C. $30,000
D. $50,000

Answer (B) is correct. *(CPA, adapted)*
REQUIRED: The amount of goodwill attributable to a purchase of 30% of the investee's common stock.
DISCUSSION: When an investment in voting interests enables the investor to exercise significant influence over the investee, even when the amount held is 50% or less of such interests, the investment should be accounted for under the equity method. Significant influence is presumed when the investment, whether direct or indirect, is at least 20% of the voting interests. Moreover, if the carrying amount of the investment ($200,000) differs from the underlying equity in net assets ($150,000) of the investee, and the difference cannot be related to specific accounts of the investee, the difference is equity method goodwill (APB Opinion 18). Because the fair value of the net assets was $100,000 ($600,000 – $500,000) greater than their carrying amount, $30,000 [($600,000 – $500,000) × 30%] of the acquisition differential was attributable to specific accounts. Accordingly, on the date of purchase, equity method goodwill was $20,000 ($200,000 purchase price – $150,000 – $30,000).
Answer (A) is incorrect because equity method goodwill exists if the cost of the investment exceeds the fair value of the net assets acquired. Answer (C) is incorrect because $30,000 equals 30% of the difference between the carrying amount of the investee's equity and the fair value of the net assets. Answer (D) is incorrect because $50,000 is the difference between 30% of the equity and the investment cost.

17. On January 2, Well Co. purchased 10% of Rea, Inc.'s outstanding common shares for $400,000, which equaled the carrying amount and the fair value of the interest purchased in Rea's net assets. Well is the largest single shareholder in Rea, and Well's officers are a majority on Rea's board of directors. Rea reported net income of $500,000 for the year and paid dividends of $150,000. In its December 31 balance sheet, what amount should Well report as investment in Rea?

A. $450,000
B. $435,000
C. $400,000
D. $385,000

Answer (B) is correct. *(CPA, adapted)*
REQUIRED: The amount reported in the investment account.
DISCUSSION: The equity method should be used because Well Co. exercises significant influence over Rea. The investment in Rea equals $435,000 [$400,000 investment + ($500,000 net income × 10%) – ($150,000 of dividends × 10%)].
Answer (A) is incorrect because $450,000 does not deduct Well's dividends. Answer (C) is incorrect because $400,000 does not include Well's share of net income or deduct Well's dividends. Answer (D) is incorrect because $385,000 does not include Well's share of net income.

Questions 18 through 20 are based on the following information. Grant, Inc. acquired 30% of South Co.'s voting stock for $200,000 on January 2, Year 1. The price equaled the carrying amount and the fair value of the interest purchased in South's net assets. Grant's 30% interest in South gave Grant the ability to exercise significant influence over South's operating and financial policies. During Year 1, South earned $80,000 and paid dividends of $50,000. South reported earnings of $100,000 for the 6 months ended June 30, Year 2, and $200,000 for the year ended December 31, Year 2. On July 1, Year 2, Grant sold half of its stock in South for $150,000 cash. South paid dividends of $60,000 on October 1, Year 2.

18. Before income taxes, what amount should Grant include in its Year 1 income statement as a result of the investment?

A. $15,000

B. $24,000

C. $50,000

D. $80,000

Answer (B) is correct. *(CPA, adapted)*
REQUIRED: The income statement amount derived from an equity-based investment.
DISCUSSION: Under the equity method, Grant's share of South's revenue reported in the income statement is $24,000 ($80,000 × 30%). The cash dividends received are recorded as a decrease in the investment's carrying amount.
Answer (A) is incorrect because $15,000 equals Grant's share of the cash dividends. Answer (C) is incorrect because $50,000 is the amount of cash dividends South paid. Answer (D) is incorrect because $80,000 is the amount of South's Year 1 earnings.

19. In Grant's December 31, Year 1, balance sheet, what should be the carrying amount of this investment?

A. $200,000

B. $209,000

C. $224,000

D. $230,000

Answer (B) is correct. *(CPA, adapted)*
REQUIRED: The carrying amount of an equity-based investment.
DISCUSSION: Grant acquired the investment for $200,000. The investment was debited for $24,000, Grant's share of South's income, and credited for $15,000, Grant's share of cash dividends.
Answer (A) is incorrect because $200,000 was the original carrying amount. Answer (C) is incorrect because $224,000 does not reflect cash dividends received. Answer (D) is incorrect because $230,000 equals $200,000 plus the difference between South's Year 1 earnings and the cash dividends it paid.

20. In its Year 2 income statement, what amount should Grant report as gain from the sale of half of its investment?

A. $24,500

B. $30,500

C. $35,000

D. $45,500

Answer (B) is correct. *(CPA, adapted)*
REQUIRED: The gain reported from the sale of half of the investment.
DISCUSSION: At the end of December Year 1, the carrying amount of the investment is $209,000 ($200,000 + $24,000 – $15,000). At June 30, Year 2, the investment is increased to $239,000 by the $30,000 share of South's income. Half of the new carrying amount is $119,500. Grant received $150,000, so the gain is $30,500 ($150,000 – $119,500).
Answer (A) is incorrect because $24,500 is based on a carrying amount of $251,000. Answer (C) is incorrect because $35,000 is based on a carrying amount of $230,000. Answer (D) is incorrect because $45,500 is based on a carrying amount of $209,000, which does not include the $30,000 of Year 2 income.

21. Park Co. uses the equity method to account for its January 1 purchase of Tun, Inc.'s common stock. On January 1, the fair values of Tun's FIFO inventory and land exceeded their carrying amounts. How do these excesses of fair values over carrying amounts affect Park's reported equity in Tun's earnings for the year?

	Inventory Excess	Land Excess
A.	Decrease	Decrease
B.	Decrease	No effect
C.	Increase	Increase
D.	Increase	No effect

Answer (B) is correct. *(CPA, adapted)*
REQUIRED: The effect on equity in investee earnings of the excess of the fair values of the investee's FIFO inventory and land over their carrying amounts.
DISCUSSION: The equity method of accounting requires the investor's proportionate share of the investee's reported net income to be adjusted for acquisition differentials. Thus, the difference at the date of acquisition of the investee's stock between the fair value and carrying amount of inventory is such an adjustment when the inventory is sold. A similar adjustment for land is required when the land is sold. Assuming that the FIFO inventory was sold during the year and the land was not, Park's proportionate share of Tun's reported net income is decreased by the inventory differential allocated at the date of acquisition.

22. Plack Co. purchased 10,000 shares (2% ownership) of Ty Corp. on February 14. Plack received a stock dividend of 2,000 shares on April 30, when the market value per share was $35. Ty paid a cash dividend of $2 per share on December 15. In its income statement for the year, what amount should Plack report as dividend income?

A. $20,000

B. $24,000

C. $90,000

D. $94,000

Answer (B) is correct. *(CPA, adapted)*

REQUIRED: The amount of dividend income to be reported.

DISCUSSION: Plack Co. owns 2% of the stock of Ty Corp. Accordingly, this investment should be accounted for using the fair value method. If the fair value of the stock is not readily determinable, the cost method is used. Under either method, dividends from an investee are accounted for by the investor as dividend income unless a liquidating dividend is received. The recipient of a stock dividend does not recognize income. Thus, Plack should report dividend income of $24,000 [(10,000 shares + 2,000 shares received as a stock dividend on April 30) × $2 per share dividend].

Answer (A) is incorrect because $20,000 does not include the dividends received on the 2,000 shares from the April 30 stock dividend. Answer (C) is incorrect because $90,000 equals the sum of the $2 per share cash dividend on 10,000 shares and the April 30 market value of the 2,000-share stock dividend. However, the recipient of a stock dividend does not recognize income. Answer (D) is incorrect because $94,000 equals the sum of the $2 per share cash dividend on 12,000 shares and the April 30 market value of the 2,000-share stock dividend. However, the recipient of a stock dividend does not recognize income.

5.5 Investments in Bonds

23. An investor purchased a bond as a long-term investment between interest dates at a premium. At the purchase date, the cash paid to the seller is

A. The same as the face amount of the bond.

B. The same as the face amount of the bond plus accrued interest.

C. More than the face amount of the bond.

D. Less than the face amount of the bond.

Answer (C) is correct. *(CPA, adapted)*

REQUIRED: The cash paid for a bond issued at a premium.

DISCUSSION: At the date of purchase, the cash paid to the seller is equal to interest accrued since the last interest date, plus the face amount of the bonds, plus the premium. The face amount of the bonds plus the premium (the carrying amount) is equal to the present value of the cash flows associated with the bond discounted at the market rate of interest (yield).

24. An investor purchased a bond classified as a long-term investment between interest dates at a discount. At the purchase date, the carrying amount of the bond is more than the

	Cash Paid to Seller	Face Amount of Bond
A.	No	Yes
B.	No	No
C.	Yes	No
D.	Yes	Yes

Answer (B) is correct. *(CPA, adapted)*

REQUIRED: The carrying amount of a bond purchased at a discount between interest dates.

DISCUSSION: At the date of purchase, the carrying amount of the bond equals its face amount minus the discount. The cash paid equals the initial carrying amount plus accrued interest. Hence, the initial carrying amount is less than the cash paid by the amount of the accrued interest.

25. Jent Corp. purchased bonds at a discount of $10,000. Subsequently, Jent sold these bonds at a premium of $14,000. During the period that Jent held this investment, amortization of the discount amounted to $2,000. What amount should Jent report as gain on the sale of bonds?

A. $12,000

B. $22,000

C. $24,000

D. $26,000

Answer (B) is correct. *(CPA, adapted)*

REQUIRED: The amount reported as gain on the sale of bonds.

DISCUSSION: The gain equals the sale price (face amount + $14,000 premium) minus the carrying amount [face amount – ($10,000 original discount – $2,000 amortization)]. Consequently, the gain is $22,000 (face amount + $14,000 – face amount + $8,000).

Answer (A) is incorrect because $12,000 assumes a carrying amount equal to face amount plus the amortization. Answer (C) is incorrect because $24,000 ignores the amortization. Answer (D) is incorrect because $26,000 results from increasing the discount by the amortization.

26. On July 1, Year 4, Pell Co. purchased Green Corp. 10-year, 8% bonds with a face amount of $500,000 for $420,000. The bonds mature on June 30, Year 14, and pay interest semiannually on June 30 and December 31. Using the interest method, Pell recorded bond discount amortization of $1,800 for the 6 months ended December 31, Year 4. From this long-term investment, Pell should report Year 4 revenue of

A. $16,800

B. $18,200

C. $20,000

D. $21,800

Answer (D) is correct. *(CPA, adapted)*
REQUIRED: The interest revenue when amortization of bond discount is known.
DISCUSSION: Interest income for a bond issued at a discount is equal to the sum of the periodic cash flows and the amount of bond discount amortized during the interest period. The periodic cash flows are equal to $20,000 ($500,000 face amount × 8% coupon rate × 1/2 year). The discount amortization is given as $1,800. Thus, revenue for the 6-month period from July 1 to December 31, Year 4, is $21,800 ($20,000 + $1,800).
Answer (A) is incorrect because $16,800 is 50% of 8% of $420,000. Answer (B) is incorrect because $18,200 equals the cash flow minus discount amortization. Answer (C) is incorrect because $20,000 equals the cash flow.

27. The following information relates to noncurrent investments that Fall Corp. placed in trust as required by the underwriter of its bonds:

Bond sinking-fund balance, 1/1	$ 450,000
Additional investment during year	90,000
Dividends on investments	15,000
Interest revenue	30,000
Administration costs	5,000
Carrying amount of bonds payable	1,025,000

What amount should Fall report in its December 31 balance sheet related to its noncurrent investment for bond sinking-fund requirements?

A. $585,000

B. $580,000

C. $575,000

D. $540,000

Answer (B) is correct. *(CPA, adapted)*
REQUIRED: The amount reported for bond sinking-fund requirements on the year-end balance sheet.
DISCUSSION: The year-end balance for the bond sinking fund is the sum of its beginning balance plus any additional deposits and earnings (i.e., interest and dividends), net of expenses. Consequently, Fall should report a year-end balance of $580,000 ($450,000 beginning balance + $90,000 investment + $15,000 dividends received + $30,000 interest earned – $5,000 costs) on its December 31 balance sheet.
Answer (A) is incorrect because $585,000 does not subtract administrative costs. Answer (C) is incorrect because $575,000 does not include dividends received and adds, rather than subtracts, administrative costs. Answer (D) is incorrect because $540,000 does not include dividends received or interest revenue and does not subtract administrative costs.

28. In its financial statements, Prak, Inc. uses the cost method of accounting for its 15% ownership of Sabe Co. because the fair value of the shares is not readily determinable. At December 31, Prak has a receivable from Sabe. How should the receivable be reported in Prak's December 31 balance sheet?

A. The total receivable should be reported separately.

B. The total receivable should be included as part of the investment in Sabe, without separate disclosure.

C. Eighty-five percent of the receivable should be reported separately, with the balance offset against Sabe's payable to Prak.

D. The total receivable should be offset against Sabe's payable to Prak, without separate disclosure.

Answer (A) is correct. *(CPA, adapted)*
REQUIRED: The amount of a receivable from an investee to be reported on the balance sheet.
DISCUSSION: No presumption of an ability to exercise significant influence over the investee arises when the investor holds less than 20% of the outstanding voting common stock of the investee. Thus, the equity method should not be used to account for the investment. Furthermore, the fair-value method is not used when equity securities do not have readily determinable fair values. Accordingly, the cost method is appropriate. Under this method, interentity receivables should be accounted for separately and in full.

5.6 Cash Surrender Value

29. On January 2, Year 4, Beal, Inc. acquired a $70,000 whole-life insurance policy on its president. The annual premium is $2,000. The company is the owner and beneficiary. Beal charged officer's life insurance expense as follows:

Year 4	$2,000
Year 5	1,800
Year 6	1,500
Year 7	1,100
Total	$6,400

In Beal's December 31, Year 7, balance sheet, the investment in cash surrender value should be

A. $0

B. $1,600

C. $6,400

D. $8,000

Answer (B) is correct. *(CPA, adapted)*
REQUIRED: The investment in cash surrender value.
DISCUSSION: Cash surrender value is the loan value or surrender value of a whole-life insurance policy. It is equal to the difference between the premiums paid and the life insurance expense recognized. Because the total of premiums paid is $8,000 ($2,000 × 4 years) and the total life insurance expense is $6,400, the investment in cash surrender value is $1,600. This amount is classified as a noncurrent asset on a classified balance sheet because management purchases life insurance policies for the life insurance aspect rather than as a short-term investment.
Answer (A) is incorrect because the excess of the premiums over the expenses is the cash surrender value. Answer (C) is incorrect because $6,400 is the total insurance expense for 4 years. Answer (D) is incorrect because $8,000 is the sum of the premiums for 4 years.

30. Upon the death of an officer, Jung Co. received the proceeds of a life insurance policy held by Jung on the officer. The proceeds were not taxable. The policy's cash surrender value had been recorded on Jung's books at the time of payment. What amount of revenue should Jung report in its statements?

A. Proceeds received.

B. Proceeds received less cash surrender value.

C. Proceeds received plus cash surrender value.

D. None.

Answer (B) is correct. *(CPA, adapted)*
REQUIRED: The revenue reported from life insurance proceeds.
DISCUSSION: When life insurance proceeds are received, cash is debited for the amount received. Cash surrender value is credited for the amount of the asset on the books, and the balancing credit is to insurance income (a revenue account).

31. In Year 1, Chain, Inc. purchased a $1 million life insurance policy on its president, of which Chain is the beneficiary. Information regarding the policy for the year ended December 31, Year 6, follows:

Cash surrender value, 1/1/Yr 6	$ 87,000
Cash surrender value, 12/31/Yr 6	108,000
Annual advance premium paid 1/1/Yr 6	40,000

During Year 6, dividends of $6,000 were applied to increase the cash surrender value of the policy. What amount should Chain report as life insurance expense for Year 6?

A. $40,000

B. $21,000

C. $19,000

D. $13,000

Answer (C) is correct. *(CPA, adapted)*
REQUIRED: The life insurance expense to be reported.
DISCUSSION: Life insurance expense is equal to the excess of the premiums paid over the increase in cash surrender value and dividends received. However, the dividends were applied to increase the cash surrender value and were therefore not received. Hence, Chain's life insurance expense is $19,000.

Premium	$40,000
Minus:	
Increase in cash surrender value ($108,000 – $87,000)	(21,000)
Life insurance expense	$19,000

Answer (A) is incorrect because $40,000 is the premium paid. Answer (B) is incorrect because $21,000 is the change in the cash surrender value. Answer (D) is incorrect because $13,000 results from subtracting the dividends applied.

Page
Intentionally
Left Blank

5.7 PRACTICE SIMULATION

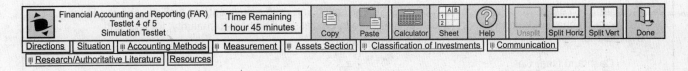

| Financial Accounting and Reporting (FAR) Testlet 4 of 5 Simulation Testlet | Time Remaining 1 hour 45 minutes | Copy | Paste | Calculator | Sheet | Help | Unsplit | Split Horiz | Split Vert | Done |

Directions | Situation | Accounting Methods | Measurement | Assets Section | Classification of Investments | Communication
Research/Authoritative Literature | Resources

1. Directions

In the following simulation, you will be asked to complete various tasks. You may use the content in the **Information Tabs** to complete the tasks in the **Work Tabs**.

Information Tabs:

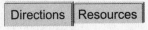

Directions | Resources

FIG 1

- Go through each of the **Information Tabs** to familiarize yourself with the simulation content
- The **Resources** tab will contain information, including formulas and definitions, that may help you to complete the tasks
- Your simulation may have more **Information Tabs** than those shown in Fig. 1

Work Tabs:

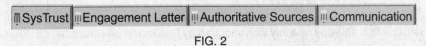

SysTrust | Engagement Letter | Authoritative Sources | Communication

FIG. 2

- **Work Tabs**, to the right of **Information Tabs**, contain the tasks for you to complete
- **Work Tabs** contain directions for completing each task - be sure to read these directions carefully
- The tab names in Fig. 2 are for illustration only - yours may differ
- Once you complete any part of a task, the pencil for that tab will be shaded (see **Communication** in Fig. 2)
- The shaded pencil does **NOT** indicate that you have completed the entire task
- You must complete all of the tasks in the **Work Tabs** to receive full credit

Research/Authoritative Literature Tab:

Research/Authoritative Literature

FIG. 3

- This tab contains both the Research task and the Authoritative Literature
- Detailed instructions for completing the Research task, and for using the Authoritative Literature, appear on this tab
- You may use the Authoritative Literature as a resource for completing other tasks

NOTE: If you believe you have encountered a software malfunction, report it to the test center staff immediately.

2. Situation

At the end of Year 8, Boomtown Co. (EIN 59-123456) held cash and cash equivalents as well as various securities that were purchased during Year 8. These securities are to be classified as held-to-maturity, trading, and available-for-sale.

Cash and Near Cash

Checking	$100,000
Savings	$250,000
CD - 90-day maturity due January 20, Year 9	$300,000
CD - 180-day maturity due March 15, Year 9	$500,000

Securities	Cost	Fair Value 12/31/Year 7	Year 8 Activity: Purchase	Year 8 Activity: Sales	Fair Value 12/31/Year 8
Held-to-Maturity					
ABC			$100,000		$95,000
Trading					
DEF	$150,000	$160,000			$155,000
Available-for-Sale					
GHI	$190,000	$165,000		$175,000	
JKL	$170,000	$175,000			$160,000

1. Boomtown Co's policy is to classify short-term securities with a maturity of 90 days or less as a cash equivalent. In addition, the CD with a 180-day maturity was acquired by Boomtown on November 15, Year 8. It will not be resold.

2. Security JKL is an equity instrument that is expected to be sold within one year but not in the near term.

3. Security ABC matures in 5 years. It was purchased at its face amount.

4. Security GHI was purchased on 01/01/Year 6 and was sold on 12/31/Year 8. No costs were associated with the sale except for the cost basis.

3. Accounting Methods

This set of questions has a matching format. Select the best match for each numbered item from the terms in the drop-down list and write its letter in the column provided. Each choice may be used once, more than once, or not at all. For each of the explanations in the table below, identify the most appropriate category.

Explanation	Answer		Category
1. Holding gains or losses are not recognized.			A) Cash
2. Holding gains or losses are recognized in earnings.			B) Restricted cash
3. Holding gains or losses are recognized in a separate component of equity.			C) Held-to-maturity securities
4. Common examples are Treasury bills and money market funds.			D) Available-for-sale securities
5. Generally investments with a maturity of 3 to 12 months.			E) Trading securities
6. The customary medium of exchange and unit of measurement.			F) Cash equivalents

4. Measurement

This type of question is presented in a spreadsheet format that requires you to fill in the correct response in the shaded cells provided. Enter the amount that should be listed on the financial statement for each security, as well as the applicable unrealized/realized gain or loss. Fill in the numbered items only.

Security	Amount Recorded on Financial Statement for Year 8	Net Unrealized Gain or Loss	Realized Gain or (Loss)
ABC	1		
DEF	2		5
GHI			6
JKL	3	4	

5. Assets Section

This type of question is presented in a spreadsheet format that requires you to fill in the correct response in the shaded cells provided. Determine the amounts that should be reported in the assets portion of the balance sheet for Boomtown Co. in Year 8.

	A	B
	Current assets	
1	Cash and cash equivalents	
2	Held-to-maturity securities	
3	Trading securities	
4	Available-for-sale securities	
5	Total current assets	
	Noncurrent assets	
	Available-for-sale securities	
6	Held-to-maturity securities	

6. Classification of Investments

This type of question is presented in a check-the-box format that requires you to select the correct response from a given list. Select the appropriate category for the investment based upon the description. Make only one choice for each item.

	Held-to-Maturity	Available-For-Sale	Trading
1. Debt securities bought and held for the purpose of selling in the near future	☐	☐	☐
2. U.S Treasury bonds that Boomtown has both the positive intent and ability to hold until maturity	☐	☐	☐
3. $3 million debt security bought and held for the purpose of selling in 3 years to finance payment of Boomtown's $2 million long-term note payable when it matures	☐	☐	☐
4. Convertible preferred stock with a readily determinable fair value that Boomtown does not intend to sell in the near term	☐	☐	☐

7. Communication

Prepare a brief memorandum to a client discussing when an investment in common stock should be accounted for using the equity method without consolidating the investee. Also discuss the investor's accounting for investee earnings and losses, dividends paid or declared but not paid, and differences between the cost of the investment and the underlying equity in the net assets of the investee.

REMINDER: Your response will be graded for both technical content and writing skills. Technical content will be evaluated for information that is helpful to the intended reader and clearly relevant to the issue. Writing skills will be evaluated for development, organization, and the appropriate expression of ideas in professional correspondence. Use a standard business memo or letter format with a clear beginning, middle, and end. Do not convey information in the form of a table, bullet point list, or other abbreviated presentation.

> To: Client
> From: CPA
> Subject: Equity Method

8. Research/Authoritative Literature

See page 12 in the Introduction of this book for a detailed explanation of the AICPA's new Research/Authoritative Literature work tab as well as a screenshot of how the tab will actually look on your exam.

Research and cite the specific paragraph in SFAS 95 that defines a cash equivalent.

Unofficial Answers

3. Accounting Methods (6 Gradable Items)

1.   C) <u>Held-to-maturity securities</u>. Unrealized holding gains or losses are not recognized on held-to-maturity securities.

2.   E) <u>Trading securities</u>. Unrealized holding gains or losses on trading securities are included in earnings.

3.   D) <u>Available-for-sale securities</u>. Unrealized holding gains or losses are recognized for available-for-sale securities in other comprehensive income, a separate component of equity.

4.   F) <u>Cash equivalents</u>. These are short-term, highly liquid investments that are both readily convertible to cash and so near their maturity date that they do not present significant risk of changes in interest rates.

5.   B) <u>Restricted cash</u>. Cash amounts designated for special uses should be separately presented. Examples are bond sinking funds and new building funds.

6.   A) <u>Cash</u>. Cash is ready money, the most liquid of assets. As the customary medium of exchange, it also provides the standard of value (the unit of measurement) of the transactions that are reported in the financial statements.

4. Measurement (6 Gradable Items)

1. <u>$100,000.</u> Held-to-maturity securities are reported at amortized cost. Security ABC was not purchased at a premium or discount. Hence, no amortization was required. The correct amount to report is ABC's cost of $100,000.

2. <u>$155,000.</u> Trading securities are measured at fair value as of the balance sheet date. Any unrealized holding gains or losses are included in earnings. Thus, Security DEF should be reported at $155,000.

3. <u>$160,000.</u> Trading securities and available-for-sale securities are measured at fair value at the balance sheet date. Any unrealized holding gains or losses related to available-for-sale securities are reported in other comprehensive income. Security JKL should be reported at $160,000.

4. <u>$(10,000).</u> Any unrealized holding gains or losses on available-for-sale securities are netted and reported in OCI. As of 12/31/Year 7, the unrealized holding loss on the two available-for-sale securities (GHI and JKL) was $20,000. During Year 8, the sale of Security GHI resulted in the elimination of its unrealized holding loss of $25,000, leaving a $5,000 unrealized holding gain recognized by a credit to OCI. At 12/31/Year 8, Security JKL had a fair value of $160,000. Thus, the balance in OCI pertaining to available-for-sale securities at 12/31/Year 8 was a $10,000 debit, representing a $10,000 unrealized holding loss.

5. <u>$0.</u> As of 12/31/Year 7, Security DEF (a trading security) had a fair value of $160,000. At the end of Year 8, the fair value was $155,000. This decline represents a $5,000 unrealized holding loss that is recognized in the Year 8 income statement. No realized loss was recorded for Security DEF because it was not disposed of.

6. <u>$(15,000).</u> Previous adjustments in the carrying amounts of available-for-sale securities do not affect the amount of recognized gain or loss on subsequent sales. Accordingly, the recognized loss on the sale of Security GHI is $15,000 ($190,000 cost – $175,000 sales price).

5. Assets Section (6 Gradable Items)

1. <u>$650,000.</u> Cash and cash equivalents include checking, savings, and the 90-day CD that matures by January 20, Year 9, and therefore had an original maturity to the holder of no more than 90 days ($100,000 + $250,000 + $300,000 = $650,000).

2. <u>$500,000.</u> Current held-to-maturity securities include the CD (a debt security that will not be resold) that matures by March 15, Year 9. It was not a cash equivalent because it had an original maturity to the holder exceeding 3 months ($500,000).

3. <u>$155,000.</u> Trading securities include the fair value of the DEF security ($155,000).

4. <u>$160,000.</u> Current available-for-sale securities include the fair value of the JKL security ($160,000).

5. <u>$1,465,000.</u> Total current assets include cash and cash equivalents, certain held-to-maturity securities, certain trading securities, and certain available-for-sale securities ($650,000 + $500,000 + $155,000 + $160,000 = $1,465,000).

6. <u>$100,000.</u> Noncurrent held-to-maturity securities include the cost of the ABC security ($100,000).

6. Classification of Investments (4 Gradable Items)

1. <u>Trading Securities.</u> Trading securities are held with the intention of selling them in the near term. Both debt and equity instruments may qualify as trading securities.

2. <u>Held-to-maturity.</u> Debt securities are classified as held-to-maturity and measured at amortized cost only if the holder has the positive intent and ability to hold the securities to maturity.

3. <u>Available-for-sale.</u> The holder intends to sell this debt security in the future. Thus, it should not be classified as held-to-maturity. Because Boomtown intends to sell in 3 years, it should be classified as available-for-sale, not trading.

4. <u>Available-for-sale.</u> Available-for-sale securities include equity securities with readily determinable fair values (e.g., preferred stock) that are not classified as trading securities (e.g., because they are not to be sold in the near term).

7. Communication (5 Gradable Items; for grading instructions, please refer to page 12.)

Under APB Opinion 18, *The Equity Method of Accounting for Investments in Common Stock*, an investment in common stock enabling the investor to exercise significant influence over the operations and management of the investee should be accounted for by the equity method if the fair value option (FVO) has not been elected. A 20% or greater ownership interest is rebuttably presumed to permit such influence. However, if ownership by one entity, directly or indirectly, exceeds 50% of the outstanding voting interests of another entity, consolidated statements ordinarily should be prepared unless **control** does not rest with the majority owner (SFAS 94).

Under the equity method, the investor's share of the investee's earnings or losses is adjusted to eliminate interentity profits and losses not realized in third-party transactions. It is also reduced by any dividends on cumulative preferred stock, whether or not declared. The adjusted share of the investee's earnings is accounted for as a debit (losses and dividends are credits) to the carrying amount of the investment on the investor's books. The receipt of a cash dividend from the investee is treated as a return of an investment. Thus, it is credited to the investment account but does not affect equity-based earnings.

Amortization of any difference between the cost of the investment and the underlying equity in the investee's net assets at the acquisition date also affects the investor's share of the investee's earnings or losses. This difference may be related wholly or in part to specific accounts, such as assets not recorded at fair value. For example, if depreciable assets are undervalued, amortization of the excess of the fair value over the carrying amount must be recognized by a debit to investment income and a credit to the investment account. Similarly, the investee's sale of land or inventory with a fair value in excess of the carrying amount requires an adjustment to prevent double counting. The excess fair value is already reflected in the investment balance and should not be counted again when the investor's share of the investee's earnings is debited to the investment account. The entry is to debit investment income for the excess profit and to credit the investment account. The difference between cost and the carrying amount may not be attributable wholly or in part to specific accounts. Accordingly, the excess of cost over the underlying equity in net assets that is not attributable to specific accounts should be treated as goodwill. This amount is not amortized. The equity method investment (but not the equity method goodwill itself, which is inseparable from the investment) is tested for impairment under SFAS 142.

8. Research/Authoritative Literature (1 Gradable Item)

Answer: FAS 95, Par. 8

SFAS 95 -- *Statement of Cash Flows*

Focus on Cash and Cash Equivalents

--**8.** For purposes of the statement, cash equivalents are short-term, highly liquid investments that are both:

A) Readily convertible to known amounts of cash.

B) So near their maturity that they present insignificant risk of changes in value because of changes in interest rates.

Generally, only investments with original maturities of three months or less qualify under that definition.

Scoring Schedule:

	Correct Responses		Gradable Items		Weights		
Tab 3	_____	÷	6	×	10%	=	_____
Tab 4	_____	÷	6	×	15%	=	_____
Tab 5	_____	÷	6	×	15%	=	_____
Tab 6	_____	÷	4	×	15%	=	_____
Tab 7	_____	÷	5	×	30%	=	_____
Tab 8	_____	÷	1	×	15%	=	_____
							_____
							(Your Score)

Use Gleim's *CPA Gleim Online* to practice more simulations in a realistic environment.

STUDY UNIT SIX
RECEIVABLES

(16 pages of outline)

This study unit primarily covers **accounts and notes receivable**, assets that rank in liquidity below available-for-sale securities but above inventories. Short-term receivables are measured at **net realizable value**, and long-term receivables are measured at the **net present value** of the future cash flows.

6.1 RECEIVABLES – FUNDAMENTALS

Definition

1. A receivable is an asset recognized to reflect a claim against another party for the receipt of money, goods, or services. For most accounting purposes, the claim is one expected to be settled in cash.

   a. The recording of a receivable, which often coincides with **revenue recognition**, is consistent with **accrual accounting**.

Classification

2. **Current vs. Noncurrent**

   a. A receivable is a **current** asset if it is reasonably expected to be collected within the longer of 1 year or the entity's normal operating cycle.

   b. Otherwise, it should be classified as **noncurrent**.

3. **Trade vs. Nontrade**

   a. **Trade receivables**, the majority of receivables, are current assets arising from credit sales to customers in the normal course of business and due in customary trade terms. They result in contracts evidenced by sales orders, invoices, or delivery contracts.

      1) They are normally **unsecured** and most often noninterest-bearing, but charges are added to revolving charge accounts and installment receivables.

      2) **Forfeiture of a cash discount** because of delayed payment is an implicit means of charging interest on trade receivables.

   b. **Nontrade receivables** are all other receivables. They may include

      1) Lease receivables
      2) Deposits to guarantee payment or to cover possible loss
      3) Advances to shareholders, directors, officers, etc.
      4) Subscriptions for the entity's securities
      5) Tax refunds
      6) Claims for insurance proceeds or amounts arising from litigation
      7) Interest, dividends, rent, or royalties accrued

4.   **Accounts vs. notes.** Trade receivables are further classified into accounts and notes.

    a.   **Accounts receivable** are often short-term, unsecured, and informal credit arrangements (open accounts). Most trade receivables are accounts.

        1)   However, **installment accounts receivable** may involve long-term arrangements and be evidenced by formal promissory notes.

    b.   **Notes receivable** are evidenced by a formal instrument, such as a **promissory note**. A formal document provides its holder with a stronger legal status than does an account receivable.

        1)   In a **note**, the maker (debtor) usually promises to pay to the order of a second party (creditor) a fixed amount of money at a definite time.

        2)   Most notes bear **interest** (explicitly or implicitly) because they represent longer-term borrowings than accounts receivable. Notes often are given when an extension of the payment period for an account receivable is sought or when the fair value of what is sold is relatively high.

5.   One type of claim that is not a receivable is for unsold goods on **consignment**.

    a.   The consignor retains title to these goods and should report them in inventory at cost, not in receivables at their sales price.

Stop and review! You have completed the outline for this subunit. Study multiple-choice questions 1 through 3 beginning on page 228.

6.2 ACCOUNTS RECEIVABLE – DISCOUNTS AND RETURNS

Trade Discounts

1.   Trade discounts adjust the **gross (list) price** for different buyers, quantities, and costs. In this way, entities avoid having to reprint catalogs or publish separate price lists. **Net price after the trade discount** is the basis for recognition.

> #### EXAMPLE
> An item with a list price of $1,000 may be subject to a 40% trade discount in sales to wholesalers. Thus, $400 is subtracted from the list price in arriving at the actual selling price of $600. Only the $600 is recorded. The accounts do not reflect trade discounts.

2.   Some sellers offer **chain-trade discounts**, such as 40%, 10%, which means certain buyers receive both a 40% discount and a 10% discount.

> #### EXAMPLE
> In the previous example, a further discount of $60 reduces the actual selling price to $540. All journal entries by the buyer and seller are for $540, with no recognition of the list price or the discount.

3.   Trade discounts are solely a means of calculating the sales price. They are not recorded.

Cash Discounts

4.   Cash discounts (sales discounts) accelerate cash collection by rewarding customers for early payment.

5.   The **gross method** accounts for receivables at their **face amount**. It is used when customers are not expected to pay soon enough to take the discount.

    a.   If the customer pays within the discount period, the discount is recognized as an item contra to sales in the income statement.

6. The **net method** records receivables **net of the cash discount** for early payment. It is used when customers are expected to pay within the discount period.

   a. If the payment is not received during the discount period, a miscellaneous revenue, such as **sales discounts forfeited**, is credited when the payment is received.

EXAMPLE

An item is sold with terms of 2/10, n/30 (2% discount if paid within 10 days, entire balance due in 30 days).

	Gross Method	Net Method
Accounts receivable	$1,000	$980
Sales	$1,000	$980

Payment is received **within the discount period**.

	Gross Method	Net Method
Cash	$ 980	$980
Sales discounts	20	
Accounts receivable	$1,000	$980

Payment is received **after the discount period**.

	Gross Method	Net Method
Cash	$1,000	$980
Accounts receivable	$1,000	$980
Cash		$ 20
Sales discounts forfeited		$ 20

Sales Returns and Allowances

7. A provision must be made for the return of merchandise because of product defects, customer dissatisfaction, etc.

8. If returns are **immaterial**, the usual accounting is to debit sales returns and allowances (a contra-revenue) and credit accounts receivable at the time of the adjustment.

   a. This method is disallowed for tax purposes.

9. If returns are **material**, the method described above will be inconsistent with the matching principle when the sale and the return occur in **different periods**.

   a. Accordingly, an **allowance** should be established at the end of the period for material sales returns that can be reasonably estimated.

EXAMPLE

Assume that Company Q has $500,000 of sales in Year 1, its first year of operations. Actual sales returns and allowances equal $8,000. Q also estimates that total sales returns and allowances are 2% of sales. In Year 2, the estimate proves correct. Returns and allowances on Year 1 sales in Year 2 are $2,000. The entries are

Year 1: Sales returns and allowances	$8,000	
Accounts receivable		$8,000
Year 1: Sales returns and allowances [($500,000 × 2%) − $8,000]	2,000	
Allowance for sales returns and allowances		2,000
Year 2: Allowance for sales returns and allowances	2,000	
Accounts receivable		2,000

---

10. The **income statement presentation** is

Gross sales	$X,XXX
Minus: sales returns and allowances	(XXX)
Net sales	$X,XXX

11. The **balance sheet presentation** is

Accounts receivable	$X,XXX
Minus: allowance for sales returns and allowances	(XXX)
Net accounts receivable	$X,XXX

Right of Return

12. SFAS 48, *Revenue Recognition When Right of Return Exists*, prescribes the accounting when returns are expected to be material. It does not apply to the return of defective goods, such as under a warranty.

   a. If revenue is to be recognized at the time of sale despite the existence of a right of return, any costs or losses anticipated are to be accounted for in accordance with SFAS 5, *Accounting for Contingencies*. Revenue and cost of sales are to be reduced to reflect expected returns.

   b. Revenue may not be recognized at the time of sale when a right of return exists unless **six conditions** are met. Revenue recognition is deferred until they are met or the return privilege expires.

   1) The seller's price is substantially fixed or determinable.
   2) The buyer has paid or is obligated to pay, and the obligation is not contingent on resale.
   3) The buyer's obligation is not changed if the product is stolen, damaged, or destroyed.
   4) The buyer has economic substance apart from the seller.
   5) The seller is not substantially obligated to directly bring about resale.
   6) The amount of future returns can be reasonably estimated.

Costs of Collection and Freight Charges

13. The expenses of collecting receivables, such as legal fees, may be accounted for using the **allowance method**. Freight charges paid by customers and subtracted from their remittances also may be accounted for by accruing an expense and an allowance if receivables and sales are recorded at their **gross amounts**.

   a. The adjusting entry at the end of a period is

Collection expense (or freight-out)	$XXX	
Allowance for collection expense (or freight-out)		$XXX

   1) The allowance is subtracted from receivables on the **balance sheet**.
   2) **Tax law** does not permit accrual of collection costs and freight charges. If these amounts are immaterial or are stable from period to period, recording at the time of sale is acceptable under GAAP. Most entities choose this method.

Sales and Excise Taxes

14. The imposition of a tax on some or all sales requires entities to collect and remit taxes to the government.

   a. Different accounting methods are possible. The best approach when such taxes are treated as separate components of the price is to recognize a **liability** at the **time of sale** to avoid misclassifying the tax as revenue.

Deposits

15. Customers are often charged for deposits, such as those on reusable containers. When **cash deposits** are received, a **liability** must be established. When the containers are returned, the deposit is refunded and the liability debited.

    a. If they are not returned, the entry is

Deposit liability	$XXX	
Inventory		$XXX
Gain or loss (cr or dr)		XXX

16. Deposits are sometimes debited to **trade receivables** as part of the amounts due from customers. Because of the uncertainty about collection, the deposit receivable should be separately reported.

Finance Charges

17. Finance charges may be imposed for **late payment**.

    a. For example, payment within 30 days of a receivable with terms of net 30 incurs no interest charge. Payment beyond the agreed period, however, will be subject to interest charges.

18. Finance charges are **added to receivable balances** with appropriate **credits** to the allowance for uncollectible accounts and a revenue account.

    a. Finance charges on **overdue accounts** may not be collected if the **underlying accounts** are uncollectible.

19. **Unearned** discounts, finance charges, and interest included in the face amount of receivables should be shown as items contra to the face amounts of the related receivables (APB Opinion 6, *Status of Accounting Research Bulletins*).

Stop and review! You have completed the outline for this subunit. Study multiple-choice questions 4 through 8 beginning on page 229.

6.3 ACCOUNTS RECEIVABLE – MEASUREMENT

1. These current, noninterest-bearing assets are reported at **net realizable value**. Thus, **interest recognition** (except for late payment) and **present value** calculations are not relevant.

    a. The principal measurement issue for accounts receivable is the estimation of **uncollectible accounts expense** (a loss contingency). The two approaches to accounting for bad debts are the direct write-off method and the allowance method.

Direct Write-Off Method

2. The direct write-off method expenses bad debts when they are determined to be uncollectible. It is **not acceptable under GAAP** because

    a. The direct write-off method is subject to manipulation. Timing is at the discretion of management.

    b. It does not match revenue and expense when the receivable and the write-off are recorded in different periods.

    c. It does not state receivables at net realizable value.

Allowance Method

3. The allowance method attempts to **match bad debt expense with the related revenue** and to determine the net realizable value of the accounts receivable. This method systematically records bad debt expense as a percentage of either sales or the level of accounts receivable on an annual basis. The allowance method is **acceptable under GAAP**.

    a. The periodic journal entry to **record bad debt expense** is

Bad debt expense	$XXX	
Allowance for doubtful accounts		$XXX

    b. As accounts receivable are written off, they are charged to the allowance account.

Allowance for doubtful accounts	$XXX	
Accounts receivable		$XXX

    1) The write-off of a particular bad debt has **no effect on expenses**. Write-offs do not affect the carrying amount of net accounts receivable because the reductions of gross accounts receivable and the allowance are the same. Thus, they also have **no effect on working capital**.

4. **Two approaches** to calculating the amount charged to bad debt expense are the income-statement approach and the balance-sheet approach.

Income-Statement Approach

5. The income-statement approach embodies the **matching principle**. It treats bad debts as a function of sales on account.

    a. Periodic bad debt expense is a **percentage of sales**.

EXAMPLE

Midburg Co. has the following account balances at year-end:

Accounts receivable	$100,000 Dr.
Allowance for doubtful accounts	1,600 Dr.
Sales on credit	500,000 Cr.

Based on its experience, Midburg expects bad debts to average 2% of credit sales. Hence, the estimated expense is $10,000 ($500,000 × 2%). The year-end adjusting entry is

Bad debt expense	$ 10,000	
Allowance for doubtful accounts		$ 10,000

Because the allowance previously had a debit balance, the new credit balance is $8,400. The balance sheet presentation is

Accounts receivable (gross)	$100,000	
Minus: allowance for doubtful accounts	(8,400)	
Accounts receivable (net)		$ 91,600

Balance-Sheet Approach

6. Under this approach, bad debt expense is a function of both **sales and collections**, reporting accounts receivable at their net realizable value.

    a. The allowance is periodically adjusted to reflect a **percentage of accounts receivable**.

    b. An entity rarely experiences a single rate of uncollectibility on all its accounts. For this reason, entities using the balance-sheet approach to estimate bad debt expense generally prepare an **aging schedule** of accounts receivable.

EXAMPLE

Midburg prepares the following aging schedule of its accounts receivable:

Balance Range	Less than 30 Days	31 – 60 Days	61 – 90 Days	Over 90 Days	Total Balances
$0 - $100	$ 5,000	$ 200	$ 100	$ 100	$ 5,400
$100 - $1,000	8,000	3,800			11,800
$1,000 - $5,000	20,000	2,000	1,900		23,900
$5,000 - $10,000	38,000		8,000	900	46,900
Over $10,000		12,000			12,000
Totals	$71,000	$18,000	$10,000	$1,000	$100,000

Midburg then applies an appropriate percentage to each stratum based on experience:

Aging Intervals	Balance	Estimated Uncollectible	Ending Allowance
Less than 30 days	$ 71,000	2%	$1,420
30 - 60 days	18,000	12%	2,160
61 - 90 days	10,000	15%	1,500
Over 90 days	1,000	20%	200
Total	$100,000		$5,280

Because the allowance currently has a debit balance of $1,600, the following journal entry is required to establish the proper measurement:

Bad debt expense	$ 6,880	
Allowance for doubtful accounts		$ 6,880

The balance sheet presentation is

Accounts receivable (gross)	$100,000	
Minus: allowance for doubtful accounts	(5,280)	
Accounts receivable (net)		$94,720

Accounts Previously Written Off

7.   Occasionally a customer will pay on an **account previously written off**.

    a.   The first entry is to reestablish the account for the amount the customer has agreed to pay (any remainder remains written off):

Accounts receivable	$XXX	
Allowance for doubtful accounts		$XXX

    b.   The second entry records the receipt of cash.

Cash	$XXX	
Accounts receivable		$XXX

    c.   The net effect of these entries is to return the amount written off to the allowance to absorb future write-offs.

        1)   The assumption is that the original write-off was in error and that another account(s) is(are) uncollectible.

Stop and review! You have completed the outline for this subunit. Study multiple-choice questions 9 through 11 beginning on page 231.

6.4 TRANSFERS OF RECEIVABLES AND OTHER FINANCIAL ASSETS

1.   Entities often use their receivables as financing tools, either selling them to improve cash flow or as collateral for loans.

Factoring

2.   **Factoring** is a transfer of receivables to a third party (a factor) who assumes the responsibility of collection.

3.   According to SFAS 140, *Accounting for Transfers and Servicing of Financial Assets and Extinguishments of Liabilities*, factoring is a means of discounting receivables on a **nonrecourse, notification basis**. Thus, payments by the debtors on the transferred accounts will be made directly to the factor. If the transferor (or seller) surrenders **control**, the transaction is accounted for as a **sale**.

      a.   If a sale is **with recourse**, the transferor (or seller) may be required to make payments to the transferee or to buy back receivables in specified circumstances. For example, the seller usually becomes liable for defaults up to a given percentage of the transferred receivables.

      b.   If a sale is **without recourse**, the transferee (or credit agency) assumes all the risks and rewards of collection.

4.   The transferor receives money that can be immediately reinvested. The entity can offset the fee charged by eliminating its bad debts, credit department, and receivables staff.

5.   A factor usually receives a high financing fee, plus a fee for collection. Furthermore, the factor often operates more efficiently than its clients because of the specialized nature of its services.

EXAMPLE

A factor charges a 2% fee plus an interest rate of 18% on all cash advanced to a transferor of accounts receivable. Monthly sales are $100,000, and the factor advances 90% of the receivables submitted after deducting the 2% fee and the interest. Credit terms are net 60 days. What is the cost to the transferor of this arrangement?

Amount of receivables submitted	$100,000
Minus: 10% reserve	(10,000)
Minus: 2% factor's fee	(2,000)
Amount accruing to the transferor	$ 88,000
Minus: 18% interest for 60 days	(2,640)
Amount to be received immediately	$ 85,360

The transferor also will receive the $10,000 reserve at the end of the 60-day period if it has not been absorbed by sales returns and allowances. Thus, the total cost to the transferor to factor the receivables for the month is $4,640 ($2,000 factor fee + interest of $2,640). Assuming that the factor has approved the customers' credit in advance (the sale is without recourse), the transferor will not absorb any bad debts. The journal entry to record the preceding transaction is

Cash	$85,360	
Equity in factored receivables	10,000	
Factor fee expense	2,000	
Prepaid interest	2,640	
Accounts receivable		$100,000

6. One common form of factoring is the **credit card sale**. The retailer benefits by prompt receipt of cash and avoidance of bad debts and other costs. In return, the credit card company charges a fee.

    a. Two methods of accounting for credit card sales may be necessary depending upon the reimbursement method used.

        1) If payment is **after submission of credit card receipt**s, the retailer initially records a receivable. After payment, the entry is

Cash	$XXX	
Service charge expense	XXX	
Receivable		$XXX

        2) If the retailer's checking account is increased by the **direct deposit of credit card receipts**, no receivable is recognized. The entry is to credit sales instead of a receivable.

Secured Borrowings

7. A secured borrowing is a formal borrowing arrangement. The borrower signs a promissory note and financing agreement, and specific receivables are pledged as **collateral**.

    a. The loan is at a specified percentage of the face amount of the collateral, and interest and service fees are charged to the borrower.

8. The collateral may be **segregated** from other receivables on the balance sheet.

Accounts receivable assigned	$XXX	
Accounts receivable		$XXX

    a. The note payable is reported as a **liability**.

Securitization

9. Securitization is (a) the transfer of a portfolio of financial assets (e.g., trade receivables, mortgage loans, automobile loans, or credit card receivables) to a **special-purpose entity (SPE)**, often a trust, and (b) the sale of beneficial interests in the SPE to investors.

    a. The proceeds are paid to the transferor. Interest and principal collected on the securitized assets are paid to the investors in accordance with the legal agreement that established the SPE.

Transfers of Financial Assets -- SFAS 140

10. Transfers and servicing of financial assets are accounted for using a financial-components approach based on whether the seller retains control. The transfer is accounted for as a sale or secured borrowing.

    a. A **transfer** includes (1) the sale of a receivable, (2) its placement in a securitization trust, or (3) its pledge as collateral. It excludes origination or settlement of a receivable.

    b. After a transfer, the **financial-components approach** is applied.

        1) The entity recognizes the financial and servicing assets it controls and the liabilities it has incurred.

        2) The entity derecognizes the financial assets it no longer controls and extinguished liabilities.

        3) If the transfer qualifies as a sale, the entity initially measures the assets obtained and liabilities incurred at fair value and recognizes any gain or loss in earnings.

11. A transfer of financial assets over which the transferor relinquishes control is a **sale**.

    a. The transferor relinquishes **control** only if certain conditions are met:

        1) The transferred assets are beyond the reach of the transferor and its creditors.
        2) Transferees may pledge or exchange the assets or interests received.
        3) The transferor does not maintain effective control through

            a) An agreement at the time of the transfer to repurchase or redeem substantially the same assets before their maturity, or

            b) The ability unilaterally to cause the holder to return specific assets.

    b. The transferor may have **continuing involvement** with the assets transferred or the transferee, whether or not the transfer is a sale. For example, such involvement may arise from a (1) recourse provision, (2) servicing arrangement, (3) repurchase agreement, or (4) pledge of collateral.

12. **If the transfer does not meet the criteria for a sale**, the parties treat the transferor as a debtor and the transferee as a creditor in possession of collateral. The transaction is then accounted for as a **secured borrowing**.

    a. If the transferee **may sell or repledge** the collateral, the transferor **reclassifies and separately reports** that asset.

    b. If the transferee **sells** the collateral, it recognizes the proceeds (debits assets obtained and credits liabilities incurred) and credits a **liability** to return the collateral. This sale itself is a transfer.

Asset	$XXX	
Liability – sale		$XXX
Liability – collateral		XXX

    c. If the transferor **defaults** and no longer has the right of redemption, it derecognizes (credits) the pledged asset. The transferee initially recognizes (debits) an asset at fair value or derecognizes (credits) the liability to return the collateral.

    d. Thus, absent default, the collateral is an **asset of the transferor**.

Servicing Assets

13. A servicing asset is a contract under which future revenues from servicing fees, late charges, etc., are expected to more than adequately compensate the servicer.

    a. A **servicing liability** arises when such compensation is inadequate.

    b. Agreements by transferors to service transferred mortgage loans, credit card receivables, and other financial assets are common.

14. **Servicing assets and liabilities** always are measured initially at **fair value**.

    a. **Subsequent measurement.** For each class of separately recognized servicing assets or liabilities, the entity may elect (1) the amortization method or (2) the fair value method.

15. The following summarizes **transferor accounting**:

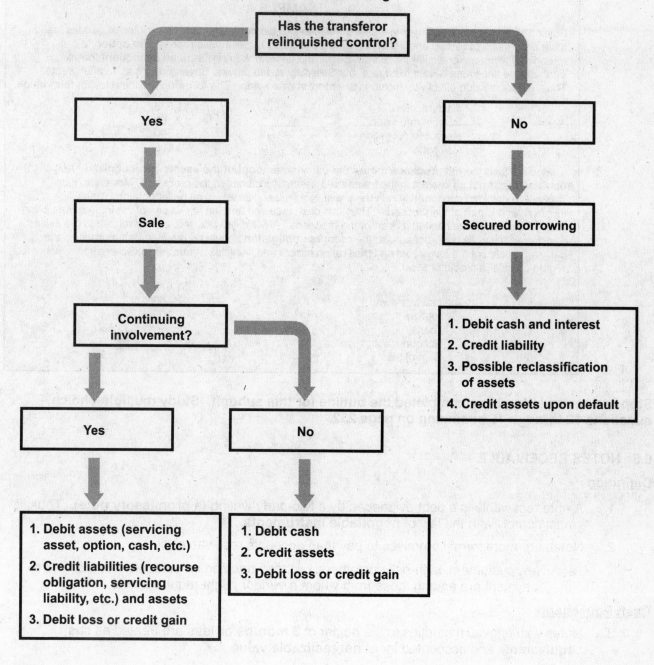

Has the transferor relinquished control?

Yes → **No**

Sale (from Yes)

Secured borrowing (from No)

Continuing involvement? (from Sale)

1. Debit cash and interest
2. Credit liability
3. Possible reclassification of assets
4. Credit assets upon default

Yes → **No** (from Continuing involvement?)

1. Debit assets (servicing asset, option, cash, etc.)
2. Credit liabilities (recourse obligation, servicing liability, etc.) and assets
3. Debit loss or credit gain

1. Debit cash
2. Credit assets
3. Debit loss or credit gain

EXAMPLE

Seller transferred loans to Buyer in a sale transaction. It did not retain a servicing interest. These loans have a fair value of $1,650 and a carrying amount of $1,500. Seller also received an **option** to call (purchase) the same or similar loans from Buyer and undertook to **repurchase delinquent loans**. Furthermore, the loans have a fixed rate, but Seller agreed to provide Buyer a return at a variable rate. Thus, the transaction effectively included an **interest rate swap**. The following are the relevant **fair values**:

Cash received	$1,575
Interest rate swap	60
Recourse obligation	90
Call option	105

The gain equals the **net proceeds minus the carrying amount of the assets derecognized**. Any asset obtained that is not an interest in the transferred assets is included in the proceeds. Moreover, any **derivative** obtained concurrently with the transfer of financial assets is an asset obtained (or liability incurred) and is part of the proceeds. Thus, the cash received and the fair values of the interest rate swap and the call option are debited as part of the proceeds. Any liability incurred, even if related to the assets transferred, reduces the proceeds, so the **recourse obligation** should be credited. After crediting the carrying amount of the loans sold and measuring assets and liabilities at **fair value**, Seller should recognize a **gain** on sale (a credit) of $150.

Cash	$1,575	
Interest rate swap	60	
Call option	105	
Loans		$1,500
Recourse obligation		90
Gain of sale		150

Stop and review! You have completed the outline for this subunit. Study multiple-choice questions 12 through 15 beginning on page 232.

6.5 NOTES RECEIVABLE

Definition

1. A note receivable is a debt evidenced by a two-party writing (a **promissory note**). Thus, it must comply with the law of **negotiable instruments**.

2. Notes are more formal promises to pay than accounts receivable.

   a. New customers, high-risk customers, or those needing an extension for the time of payment are among those from whom a vendor might require a note.

Cash Equivalents

3. Notes with original maturities to the holder of **3 months or less** are treated as **cash equivalents** and accounted for at **net realizable value**.

   a. These notes are usually recorded at **face amount minus allowances**. Because the interest implicit in the maturity amount is immaterial, no interest revenue is recognized.

4. Notes with maturities **longer than 3 months** are not cash equivalents. The creditor must recognize **interest revenue** unless an exception applies.

   a. Receivables are recorded at the **present value of the expected future cash flows**. Any difference between the proceeds and the face amount, if material, must be recognized as a premium or discount and amortized (APB Opinion 21, *Interest on Receivables and Payables*).

5. The accounting and reporting requirements of APB Opinion 21 **do not apply** to

    a. Payables and receivables arising from transactions with suppliers and customers in the normal course of business that are due in customary trade terms in less than 1 year

    b. Amounts that do not require repayment in the future

    c. Transactions whose interest rates are legally fixed

    d. Amounts serving as collateral

    e. Customary transactions of entities whose primary business is lending money

    f. Transactions between parents and subsidiaries

    g. Contingent claims, such as warranties

Effective Interest Method

6. The outline and examples in Subunit 5.5 apply to notes receivable as well as to bonds receivable and are not repeated here.

Noninterest-Bearing Notes

7. Sometimes notes are issued with no stated rate and an **unknown effective rate**. In these cases, the rate must be **imputed** from other facts surrounding the transaction, e.g., the marketability of the note and the debtor's creditworthiness.

8. Certain notes differ from the customary instruments that explicitly bear interest at a reasonable rate. They are discussed in the following outlines.

9. A note may bear no explicit interest because interest is included in the amount to be paid at maturity. The proper accounting treatment is to debit notes receivable for its face (maturity) amount, credit cash (or other appropriate account), and credit a discount account. The discount is amortized to interest revenue.

    a. The entry for initial recognition is

Notes receivable	$XXX	
Cash		$XXX
Discount on note		XXX

    b. At the end of the period, the discount is amortized to interest revenue. The entry for recognition of interest is

Discount on note	$XXX	
Interest revenue		$XXX

    c. When the note arises in the ordinary course of business and is "due in customary trade terms not exceeding approximately 1 year," the interest element need not be recognized (APB Opinion 21).

Unreasonable Interest

10. The term "noninterest-bearing" is confusing because it is used not only when a note bears implicit interest but also when no actual interest is charged (the cash proceeds equal the face amount).

    a. When a note is noninterest-bearing in the second sense, or it bears interest at a rate that is unreasonable in the circumstances, **imputation (estimation)** of an interest rate is necessary. A note that requires imputation of interest also gives rise to amortization of discount or premium.

    b. When a **note is exchanged solely for cash**, and no other right or privilege is exchanged, the proceeds are assumed to reflect the present value of the note. The effective interest rate is therefore the interest rate implicit in that present value.

    c.   When a **note is exchanged for property, goods, or services**, the interest rate determined by the parties in an arm's-length transaction is **presumed to be fair**.

        1)   That presumption is overcome when (a) no interest is stated, (b) the stated rate is unreasonable, or (c) the nominal amount of the note materially differs from the cash sales price of the item or the market value of the note.

            a)   In these circumstances, the transaction should be recorded at the more clearly determinable of

                i)   The fair value of the property, goods, or services or
                ii)   A reasonable approximation of the market value of the note.

            b)   Absent established exchange prices or evidence of the note's market value, the present value of a note with no stated rate or an unreasonable rate should be determined by **discounting future payments using an imputed rate**. The prevailing rate for similar instruments of issuers with similar credit ratings normally helps determine the appropriate rate. The purpose is to approximate the rate in a similar transaction between independent parties.

    d.   The stated interest rate may be less than the effective rate applicable in the circumstances because the lender has received **other stated (or unstated) rights and privileges** as part of the bargain.

        1)   The difference between the respective present values of the note computed at the stated rate and at the effective rate should be accounted for as the cost of the rights or privileges obtained.

Stop and review! You have completed the outline for this subunit. Study multiple-choice questions 16 through 21 beginning on page 233.

6.6 NOTES RECEIVABLE – DISCOUNTING

Nature of Discounting

    1.   When a note receivable is **discounted** (**sold**, usually at a bank), the gain or loss on disposition of the note must be calculated.

    2.   The **holder** of the note receives the maturity amount (principal + interest at maturity) of the note minus the bank's discount. The bank usually collects the maturity amount from the **maker of the note**.

Process of Discounting

    3.   The steps in discounting are to compute the

        a.   Total interest receivable on the note (face amount × stated rate × note term).
        b.   Maturity amount (face amount + total interest receivable).
        c.   Accrued interest receivable (face amount × stated rate × note term elapsed).
        d.   Bank's discount (maturity amount × bank's discount rate × note term remaining).
        e.   Cash proceeds (maturity amount – bank's discount).
        f.   Carrying amount of the note (face amount + accrued interest receivable).
        g.   Gain or loss (proceeds – carrying amount).

            1)   If a gain results, the entry is

Cash	$XXX	
Gain on sale of note receivable		$XXX
Note receivable		XXX
Interest receivable		XXX

2) If a loss results, the entry is

Cash	$XXX	
Loss on sale of note receivable	XXX	
Note receivable		$XXX
Interest receivable		$XXX

4. If a note is discounted **with recourse**, the note must be disclosed as a **contingent liability**.

    a. If the maker dishonors the note, the bank will collect from the entity that discounted the note.

        1) The credit in the previous entry is sometimes made to **notes receivable discounted**, a contra-asset account.

5. When computing yearly interest, the day the note is received, made, etc., is not included, but its maturity date is counted.

EXAMPLE

A 30-day note dated January 17 matures on February 16. Because 14 days (31 − 17) remain in January, 16 days must be counted in February.

Stop and review! You have completed the outline for this subunit. Study multiple-choice questions 22 through 24 beginning on page 235.

6.7 AFFILIATED COMPANY RECEIVABLES

1. A receivable from a related party should be separately and fully disclosed. **Related parties** include affiliates, which are parties "that, directly or indirectly, through one or more intermediaries, control, are controlled by, or are under common control with, an enterprise" (SFAS 57, *Related Party Disclosures*).

2. In **consolidated and combined financial statements**, reciprocal balances, such as receivables and payables, should be eliminated in their entirety.

    a. However, these transactions should not be eliminated from the separate financial statements of the affiliated entities.

    b. Transactions between an investor and a fair-value-based or cost-based investee are not eliminated.

Stop and review! You have completed the outline for this subunit. Study multiple-choice questions 25 through 27 beginning on page 236.

6.8 BALANCE SHEET PRESENTATION

1. **Material receivables** should be segregated. Among the usual categories are

    a. Notes receivable (with disclosure of the effective interest rates)
    b. Trade receivables
    c. Installment receivables
    d. Nontrade receivables

2. Receivables should be separated into **current and noncurrent** portions.

3. **Allowances** should be presented contra to the related accounts receivable.

4. **Discount or premium** resulting from a present value measurement directly decreases or increases the face amount of a note. Thus, notes receivable are reported at present value without a separate allowance.

5.   **Disclosure** should be made of

    a.   Related party receivables, e.g., those arising from loans to employees or affiliates

    b.   Loss contingencies, such as those from transfers with recourse

        1)   When a transfer with recourse is made in a sales transaction, disclosure should be made, if possible, of proceeds and of amounts uncollected for each income statement and balance sheet, respectively.

    c.   Pledged or assigned receivables

    d.   Concentrations of credit risk (see Subunit 4.5)

Stop and review! You have completed the outline for this subunit. Study multiple-choice question 28 on page 237.

QUESTIONS

6.1 Receivables – Fundamentals

1. The following information relates to Jay Co.'s accounts receivable for the year just ended:

Accounts receivable, 1/1	$ 650,000
Credit sales for the year	2,700,000
Sales returns for the year	75,000
Accounts written off during the year	40,000
Collections from customers during the year	2,150,000
Estimated future sales returns at 12/31	50,000
Estimated uncollectible accounts at 12/31	110,000

What amount should Jay report for accounts receivable, before allowances for sales returns and uncollectible accounts, at December 31?

    A. $1,200,000

    B. $1,125,000

    C. $1,085,000

    D. $925,000

Answer (C) is correct. *(CPA, adapted)*
REQUIRED: The year-end balance in accounts receivable.
DISCUSSION: The $1,085,000 ending balance in accounts receivable is equal to the $650,000 beginning debit balance, plus debits for $2,700,000 of credit sales, minus credits for $2,150,000 of collections, $40,000 of accounts written off, and $75,000 of sales returns. The $110,000 of estimated uncollectible receivables and the $50,000 of estimated sales returns are not relevant because they affect the allowance accounts but not gross accounts receivable.

Accounts Receivable (in 000s)

1/1	$ 650	$ 75	Sales returns
Credit sales	2,700	2,150	Collections
		40	Write-offs
12/31	$1,085		

Answer (A) is incorrect because $1,200,000 does not subtract write-offs and sales returns from accounts receivable. Answer (B) is incorrect because $1,125,000 does not subtract sales returns from accounts receivable. Answer (D) is incorrect because estimated future sales returns and uncollectible accounts affect their respective allowance accounts, not gross accounts receivable.

2. On Merf's April 30, Year 4, balance sheet, a note receivable was reported as a noncurrent asset, and its accrued interest for 8 months was reported as a current asset. Which of the following terms would fit Merf's note receivable?

    A. Both principal and interest amounts are payable on August 31, Year 4, and August 31, Year 5.

    B. Principal and interest are due December 31, Year 4.

    C. Both principal and interest amounts are payable on December 31, Year 4, and December 31, Year 5.

    D. Principal is due August 31, Year 5. Interest is due August 31, Year 4, and August 31, Year 5.

Answer (D) is correct. *(CPA, adapted)*
REQUIRED: The terms explaining classification of a note receivable as a noncurrent asset and its accrued interest as a current asset.
DISCUSSION: A noncurrent note receivable is one that is not expected to be converted into cash within 1 year or 1 operating cycle, whichever is longer. Because the principal is due more than 1 year from the balance sheet date, it must be regarded as noncurrent. However, the accrued interest is a current asset because it is due in 4 months.

3. In its December 31 balance sheet, Butler Co. reported trade accounts receivable of $250,000 and related allowance for uncollectible accounts of $20,000. What is the total amount of risk of accounting loss related to Butler's trade accounts receivable, and what amount of that risk is off-balance sheet risk?

	Risk of Accounting Loss	Off-Balance Sheet Risk
A.	$0	$0
B.	$230,000	$0
C.	$230,000	$20,000
D.	$250,000	$20,000

Answer (B) is correct. *(CPA, adapted)*
REQUIRED: The total amount of risk of accounting loss related to trade accounts receivable and the amount that is off-balance-sheet risk.
DISCUSSION: Butler's risk of accounting loss is measured by the net receivables balance ($250,000 accounts receivable – $20,000 allowance for uncollectible accounts = $230,000). Accounting loss is the loss that may have to be recognized due to credit and market risk as a direct result of the rights and obligations of a financial instrument. However, assuming that the carrying amount of these trade receivables approximates their fair value, the accounting loss cannot exceed the amount recognized as an asset. No off-balance-sheet risk of accounting loss results from reported accounts or notes receivable. Off-balance-sheet risk arises because of the existence of conditional rights and obligations that may expose the entity to a risk of accounting loss exceeding the amount recognized in the balance sheet, for example, recourse obligations on receivables sold.

6.2 Accounts Receivable – Discounts and Returns

4. On June 1, Pitt Corp. sold merchandise with a list price of $5,000 to Burr on account. Pitt allowed trade discounts of 30% and 20%. Credit terms were 2/15, n/40 and the sale was made FOB shipping point. Pitt prepaid $200 of delivery costs for Burr as an accommodation. On June 12, Pitt received from Burr a remittance in full payment amounting to

A. $2,744

B. $2,912

C. $2,944

D. $3,112

Answer (C) is correct. *(CPA, adapted).*
REQUIRED: The amount of the full payment.
DISCUSSION: A trade discount is a means of establishing a price for a certain quantity, for a particular class of customers, or to avoid having to reprint catalogs whenever prices change. Neither the buyer nor the seller reflects trade discounts in the accounts. Assuming that the 30% discount is applied first, the initial discount is $1,500 ($5,000 × 30%), and the second discount is $700 [($5,000 – $1,500) × 20%]. Hence, the base price is $2,800. (If both discounts apply, it makes no difference which is taken first.) Because the buyer paid within the discount period, the cash equivalent price is $2,744 ($2,800 × 98%). Given that the goods were shipped FOB shipping point, title passed when they were put in the possession of the carrier, and the buyer is responsible for payment of delivery costs. Accordingly, the full amount owed by the buyer was $2,944 ($2,744 + $200 delivery costs).
Answer (A) is incorrect because $2,744 does not include the delivery costs. Answer (B) is incorrect because $2,912 assumes that the delivery costs are part of the list price. It also ignores the cash discount. Answer (D) is incorrect because $3,112 assumes that the delivery costs are part of the list price. It also ignores the cash discount but adds back the delivery costs.

5. Delta, Inc. sells to wholesalers on terms of 2/15, n/30. Delta has no cash sales, but 50% of Delta's customers take advantage of the discount. Delta uses the gross method of recording sales and trade receivables. An analysis of Delta's trade receivables balances at December 31 revealed the following:

Age	Amount	Collectible
0-15 days	$100,000	100%
16-30 days	60,000	95%
31-60 days	5,000	90%
Over 60 days	2,500	20%
	$167,500	

In its December 31 balance sheet, what amount should Delta report for allowance for discounts?

A. $1,000

B. $1,620

C. $1,675

D. $2,000

Answer (A) is correct. *(CPA, adapted)*
REQUIRED: The amount to be reported as an allowance for discounts.
DISCUSSION: The allowance for discounts should include an estimate of the expected discount based on the eligible receivables. According to the analysis, receivables equal to $100,000 are still eligible. Based on past experience, 50% of the customers take advantage of the discount. Thus, the allowance should be $1,000 [$100,000 × 50% × 2% (the discount percentage)].
Answer (B) is incorrect because $1,620 assumes that 50% of all collectible amounts are eligible for the discount. Answer (C) is incorrect because $1,675 assumes that 50% of the total gross receivables are eligible for the discount. Answer (D) is incorrect because $2,000 assumes 100% of eligible customers will take the discount.

Questions 6 and 7 are based on the following information. ECG Company recorded two sales on March 1 of $20,000 and $30,000 under credit terms of 3/10, n/30. Payment for the $20,000 sale was received March 10. Payment for the $30,000 sale was received on March 25.

6. Under the gross method and the net method, net sales in ECG's March income statement are reported at which amounts?

	Gross Method	Net Method
A.	$48,500	$48,500
B.	$48,500	$49,400
C.	$49,400	$48,500
D.	$49,400	$49,400

Answer (C) is correct. *(Publisher, adapted)*
REQUIRED: The amounts of net sales under the gross and the net methods.
DISCUSSION: The gross method accounts for receivables at their face amount. If a discount is taken, a sales discount is recorded and classified as an offset to sales in the income statement to yield net sales.
The expression "3/10, n/30" means that a 3% discount can be taken if payment is made within 10 days of the invoice. The $20,000 payment was received during this period. The $30,000 payment was not. Under the gross method, a $600 sales discount offsets the $50,000 of gross sales to give net sales of $49,400.
The net method records receivables net of the applicable discount. If the payment is not received during the discount period, an interest revenue account, such as sales discounts forfeited, is credited at the end of the discount period or when the payment is received. Consequently, both sales are recorded net of discount ($48,500), and $900 ($30,000 × 3%) is recorded as interest income.
The income effect of both methods is the same. The difference is in how the items are presented in the income statement.

7. At what amounts are ECG's gross sales reported for the month of March under the gross method and the net method?

	Gross Method	Net Method
A.	$50,000	$50,000
B.	$50,000	$48,500
C.	$49,400	$48,500
D.	$48,500	$50,000

Answer (B) is correct. *(Publisher, adapted)*
REQUIRED: The gross sales for the month.
DISCUSSION: The gross method records March sales at the gross amount ($50,000). Because the $20,000 receivable was paid within the discount period, sales discount is debited for $600 at the payment date. The net method records March sales at the net amount [$50,000 × (1.0 – .03) = $48,500]. The $30,000 receivable was not paid within the discount period, and the following entry also must be made:

Accounts receivable $900
    Sales discounts forfeited $900

8. Lin Co., a distributor of machinery, bought a machine from the manufacturer in November for $10,000. On December 30, Lin sold this machine to Zee Hardware for $15,000 under the following terms: 2% discount if paid within 30 days, 1% discount if paid after 30 days but within 60 days, or payable in full within 90 days if not paid within the discount periods. However, Zee has the right to return this machine to Lin if Zee is unable to resell the machine before expiration of the 90-day payment period, in which case Zee's obligation to Lin is canceled. In Lin's net sales for the year ended December 31, how much should be included for the sale to Zee?

A. $0

B. $14,700

C. $14,850

D. $15,000

Answer (A) is correct. *(CPA, adapted)*
REQUIRED: The sales revenue to be recognized when a right of return exists.
DISCUSSION: SFAS 48, *Revenue Recognition When Right of Return Exists*, states that the sale may be recognized at the time of sale only if all of the following conditions are met:

1. The seller's price is substantially fixed or determinable.

2. The buyer has paid the seller, or the buyer is obligated to pay, and the obligation is not contingent on resale.

3. The buyer's obligation to the seller is unchanged by damage to, theft of, or destruction of the product.

4. The buyer has economic substance apart from the seller.

5. The seller does not have any significant obligations regarding resale of the product by the buyer.

6. The amount of future returns can be reasonably estimated.

The buyer has the right to return the machine to the seller, and the obligation to pay is contingent on resale. Thus, the second condition is not met, and no recognition of sales revenue and cost of sales is allowable.

6.3 Accounts Receivable – Measurement

9. In its December 31, Year 3, balance sheet, Fleet Co. reported accounts receivable of $100,000 before allowance for uncollectible accounts of $10,000. Credit sales during Year 4 were $611,000, and collections from customers, excluding recoveries, totaled $591,000. During Year 4, accounts receivable of $45,000 were written off and $17,000 were recovered. Fleet estimated that $15,000 of the accounts receivable at December 31, Year 4, were uncollectible. In its December 31, Year 4, balance sheet, what amount should Fleet report as accounts receivable before allowance for uncollectible accounts?

A. $58,000

B. $67,000

C. $75,000

D. $82,000

Answer (C) is correct. *(CPA, adapted)*
REQUIRED: The balance of accounts receivable.
DISCUSSION: The beginning balance in the accounts receivable account is $100,000, credit sales equal $611,000, collections equal $591,000, write-offs equal $45,000, and $17,000 of accounts written off were recovered (debit accounts receivable and credit the allowance, then debit cash and credit accounts receivable). Thus, the ending balance in the accounts receivable account is $75,000.

Accounts Receivable (in 000s)

1/1/Yr 4	$100	$591	Collections
Sales	611	45	Write-offs
Recoveries	17	17	Recoveries
12/31/Yr 4	$ 75		

Answer (A) is incorrect because $58,000 results from subtracting the recovered accounts. The collection of written-off accounts has no effect on the ending balance of accounts receivable. Answer (B) is incorrect because $67,000 equals the ending accounts receivable balance, plus the amount recovered, minus the beginning balance of the allowance for uncollectible accounts, minus the estimated uncollectible accounts at year-end. Answer (D) is incorrect because $82,000 is calculated by adding the recovered accounts and subtracting the allowance for uncollectible accounts from Year 3.

10. An internal auditor is deriving cash flow data based on an incomplete set of facts. Bad debt expense was $2,000. Additional data for this period follows:

Credit sales	$100,000
Gross accounts receivable -- beginning balance	5,000
Allowance for bad debts -- beginning balance	(500)
Accounts receivable written off	1,000
Increase in net accounts receivable (after subtraction of allowance for bad debts)	30,000

How much cash was collected this period on credit sales?

A. $64,000

B. $68,000

C. $68,500

D. $70,000

Answer (B) is correct. *(CIA, adapted)*
REQUIRED: The cash collected on credit sales.
DISCUSSION: The beginning balance of gross accounts receivable (A/R) was $5,000 (debit). Thus, net beginning A/R was $4,500 ($5,000 – $500 credit in the allowance for bad debts). The allowance was credited for the $2,000 bad debt expense. Accordingly, the ending allowance (credit) was $1,500 ($500 – $1,000 write-off + $2,000). Given a $30,000 increase in net A/R, ending net A/R must have been $34,500 ($4,500 beginning net A/R + $30,000), with ending gross A/R of $36,000 ($34,500 + $1,500). Collections were therefore $68,000 ($5,000 beginning gross A/R – $1,000 write-off + $100,000 credit sales – $36,000 ending gross A/R).

Gross A/R

$ 5,000	Beg. Bal.	$ 1,000	Write-off
100,000	Cr. Sales	68,000	Collections
$ 36,000	End. Bal.		

Answer (A) is incorrect because $64,000 equals credit sales minus the ending gross accounts receivable. Answer (C) is incorrect because $68,500 equals credit sales, minus the increase in net accounts receivable, minus the ending allowance. Answer (D) is incorrect because $70,000 equals credit sales minus the increase in net accounts receivable.

11. Wren Company had the following account balances at December 31:

Accounts receivable	$ 900,000
Allowance for uncollectible accounts (before any provision for the year uncollectible accounts expense)	16,000
Credit sales for the year	1,750,000

Wren is considering the following methods of estimating uncollectible accounts expense for the year:

- Based on credit sales at 2%
- Based on accounts receivable at 5%

What amount should Wren charge to uncollectible accounts expense under each method?

	Percentage of Credit Sales	Percentage of Accounts Receivable
A.	$51,000	$45,000
B.	$51,000	$29,000
C.	$35,000	$45,000
D.	$35,000	$29,000

Answer (D) is correct. *(CPA, adapted)*
REQUIRED: The amount charged to uncollectible accounts expense under each method.
DISCUSSION: Uncollectible accounts expense is estimated in two ways. One emphasizes asset valuation, the other income measurement. The first is based on an aging of the receivables to determine the balance in the allowance for uncollectible accounts. Bad debt expense is the amount necessary to adjust the allowance account to this estimated balance. The second recognizes bad debt expense as a percentage of sales. The corresponding credit is to the allowance for uncollectible accounts. Under the first method, if uncollectible accounts are estimated to be 5% of gross accounts receivable, the allowance account should have a balance of $45,000 ($900,000 × 5%), and the entry is to debit uncollectible accounts expense and credit the allowance for $29,000 ($45,000 – $16,000 existing balance). Under the second method, bad debt expense is $35,000 ($1,750,000 × 2%).
Answer (A) is incorrect because $51,000 equals 2% of credit sales plus the balance of the allowance account, and $45,000 equals 5% of gross accounts receivable. Answer (B) is incorrect because $51,000 equals 2% of credit sales plus the balance of the allowance account. Answer (C) is incorrect because $45,000 equals 5% of gross accounts receivable.

6.4 Transfers of Receivables and Other Financial Assets

12. Gar Co. factored its receivables without recourse with Ross Bank. Gar received cash as a result of this transaction, which is best described as a

A. Loan from Ross collateralized by Gar's accounts receivable.

B. Loan from Ross to be repaid by the proceeds from Gar's accounts receivable.

C. Sale of Gar's accounts receivable to Ross, with the risk of uncollectible accounts retained by Gar.

D. Sale of Gar's accounts receivable to Ross, with the risk of uncollectible accounts transferred to Ross.

Answer (D) is correct. *(CPA, adapted)*
REQUIRED: The effect of factoring receivables without recourse.
DISCUSSION: When receivables are factored without recourse, the transaction is treated as a sale and the buyer accepts the risk of collectibility. The seller bears no responsibility for credit losses. A sale without recourse is not a loan. In a sale without recourse, the buyer assumes the risk of uncollectible accounts.

13. In accounting for the transfer of financial assets, which of the following is the approach underlying the accounting prescribed by SFAS 140, *Accounting for Transfers and Servicing of Financial Assets and Extinguishments of Liabilities*?

A. Financial-components approach.

B. The risks-and-rewards approach.

C. Inseparable-unit approach.

D. Linked-presentation approach.

Answer (A) is correct. *(Publisher, adapted)*
REQUIRED: The conceptual approach underlying the accounting for transfers of financial assets.
DISCUSSION: SFAS 140, *Accounting for Transfers and Servicing of Financial Assets and Extinguishments of Liabilities*, adopts a financial-components approach based on control. After a transfer, an entity recognizes the financial and servicing assets it controls and the liabilities it has incurred; derecognizes financial assets it no longer controls; derecognizes extinguished liabilities; and, if the transfer qualifies as a sale, recognizes any gain or loss in earnings.
Answer (B) is incorrect because the risks-and-rewards approach was rejected by the FASB. It is consistent with viewing each financial asset as an indivisible unit. Answer (C) is incorrect because the inseparable-unit approach was rejected by the FASB. It is consistent with viewing each financial asset as an indivisible unit. Answer (D) is incorrect because the linked-presentation approach was rejected by the FASB. It is consistent with viewing each financial asset as an indivisible unit.

14. A transfer of financial assets in accordance with SFAS 140, *Accounting for Transfers and Servicing of Financial Assets and Extinguishments of Liabilities*, may be treated as a sale if the transferor surrenders control of the assets. Which of the following is one of the criteria that must be met before control is deemed to be surrendered?

A. The transferred assets are isolated from the transferor and its creditors except in bankruptcy.

B. The transferee cannot pledge or exchange the transferred assets.

C. The transferor is not a party to an agreement that both entitles and obligates it to repurchase or redeem the securities prior to maturity.

D. The consideration received by the transferor consists solely of beneficial interests in the transferred assets.

Answer (C) is correct. *(Publisher, adapted)*
REQUIRED: The criterion that must be met before control over transferred financial assets is deemed to be surrendered.
DISCUSSION: Three criteria must be met: (1) The transferred assets are isolated from the transferor and its creditors even in bankruptcy or other receivership; (2) each regular transferee (or the holder of a beneficial interest in a qualifying SPE that is a transferee) has the right to pledge or exchange the assets or interests, and no condition limits the exercise of that right and provides more than a trivial benefit to the transferor; and (3) the transferor does not maintain effective control of the transferred assets through (a) an agreement that entitles and obligates the transferor to repurchase or redeem the transferred assets prior to maturity or (b) an ability unilaterally to cause the holder to return specific assets (other than through a cleanup call).
Answer (A) is incorrect because control is not surrendered if the transferor's creditors can reach the assets in bankruptcy. Answer (B) is incorrect because the transferee is able to pledge or exchange the assets if control is surrendered. Answer (D) is incorrect because the transfer is accounted for as a sale only to the extent consideration other than beneficial interests in the assets is received by the transferor.

15. Lender Bank made a large loan to a major borrower and then transferred an undivided interest in this loan to Student Union Bank. The transfer was on a nonrecourse basis, and Lender continued to service the loan. Student Union is not a major competitor of Lender. Lender should account for this transfer as a secured borrowing if the participation agreement

A. Allows Student Union Bank to pledge its participation interest.

B. Does not grant Lender the right of first refusal on the sale of Student Union's participation interest.

C. Does not allow Student Union to sell its participation interest.

D. Prohibits Student Union from selling its participation interest to banks that are direct, major competitors of Lender.

Answer (C) is correct. *(Publisher, adapted)*
REQUIRED: The condition under which a loan participation should be accounted for as a secured borrowing.
DISCUSSION: A transfer of financial assets, such as a loan participation agreement, should be accounted for as a sale if the transferor (originating lender) surrenders control over the participation interest transferred to the transferee (participating bank). If control is not surrendered, the transfer should be accounted for as a secured borrowing. Control is not surrendered if the participation agreement prevents the participating bank from pledging or exchanging its participation interest.
Answer (A) is incorrect because the right to exchange or pledge participation interests is consistent with the relinquishment of control. Answer (B) is incorrect because failing to grant Lender the right of first refusal on the sale of Student Union's participation interest is not a constraint on the transferee that permits the transferor to retain control. Indeed, a right of first refusal is not such a constraint. Answer (D) is incorrect because a prohibition on sale to the transferor's competitors is not a constraint on the transferee if other willing buyers exist.

6.5 Notes Receivable

16. On August 15, Benet Co. sold goods for which it received a note bearing the market rate of interest on that date. The 4-month note was dated July 15. Note principal, together with all interest, is due November 15. When the note was recorded on August 15, which of the following accounts increased?

A. Unearned discount.

B. Interest receivable.

C. Prepaid interest.

D. Interest revenue.

Answer (B) is correct. *(CPA, adapted)*
REQUIRED: The account that increased when the note was recorded.
DISCUSSION: Because the note bears interest at a reasonable rate, its present value at the date of issuance is the face amount. Hence, the note should be recorded at this amount. Interest receivable may also be debited and unearned interest revenue credited, although the simple alternative is to debit cash and credit interest revenue when payment is received.
Answer (A) is incorrect because the note bears interest at the market rate. Thus, no discount from its face amount is recorded. Answer (C) is incorrect because no prepayment of interest has been made. Answer (D) is incorrect because interest revenue has not yet been earned.

17. On December 1, Year 4, Tigg Mortgage Co. gave Pod Corp. a $200,000, 12% loan. Pod received proceeds of $194,000 after the deduction of a $6,000 nonrefundable loan origination fee. Principal and interest are due in 60 monthly installments of $4,450, beginning January 1, Year 5. The repayments yield an effective interest rate of 12% at a present value of $200,000 and 13.4% at a present value of $194,000. What amount of accrued interest receivable should Tigg include in its December 31, Year 4, balance sheet?

    A. $4,450

    B. $2,166

    C. $2,000

    D. $0

Answer (C) is correct. *(CPA, adapted)*
    REQUIRED: The accrued interest receivable at year-end.
    DISCUSSION: Accrued interest receivable is always equal to the face amount times the nominal rate for the period of the accrual. Hence the accrued interest receivable is $2,000 [$200,000 × 12% × (1 ÷ 12)].
    Answer (A) is incorrect because $4,450 is the monthly installment. It includes principal as well as interest. Answer (B) is incorrect because $2,166 is based on a present value of $194,000 and an effective rate of 13.4%. It is the interest revenue from the loan. Answer (D) is incorrect because 1 month's interest should be accrued.

18. On December 1, Year 4, Money Co. gave Home Co. a $200,000, 11% loan. Money paid proceeds of $194,000 after the deduction of a $6,000 nonrefundable loan origination fee. Principal and interest are due in 60 monthly installments of $4,310, beginning January 1, Year 5. The repayments yield an effective interest rate of 11% at a present value of $200,000 and 12.4% at a present value of $194,000. What amount of income from this loan should Money report in its Year 4 income statement?

    A. $0

    B. $1,833

    C. $2,005

    D. $7,833

Answer (C) is correct. *(CPA, adapted)*
    REQUIRED: The amount of income from the loan at year-end.
    DISCUSSION: Under the effective-interest method, the effective rate of interest is applied to the net carrying amount of the receivable to determine the interest revenue. Thus, interest revenue from the loan, for the month of December, equals $2,005 [$194,000 × 12.4% × (1 ÷ 12)].
    Answer (A) is incorrect because one month's interest should be accrued. Answer (B) is incorrect because $1,833 is the accrued interest receivable, which equals the face amount times the nominal rate for the period [$200,000 × 11% × (1 ÷ 12)]. Answer (D) is incorrect because $7,833 equals the $6,000 origination fee plus the accrued interest receivable of $1,833.

19. On January 1, Year 3, Mill Co. exchanged equipment for a $200,000, noninterest-bearing note due on January 1, Year 6. The prevailing rate of interest for a note of this type at January 1, Year 3, was 10%. The present value of $1 at 10% for three periods is 0.75. What amount of interest revenue should be included in Mill's Year 4 income statement?

    A. $0

    B. $15,000

    C. $16,500

    D. $20,000

Answer (C) is correct. *(CPA, adapted)*
    REQUIRED: The interest income from a noninterest-bearing note received for property.
    DISCUSSION: When a noninterest-bearing note is exchanged for property, and neither the note nor the property has a clearly determinable exchange price, the present value of the note should be determined by discounting all future payments using an appropriately imputed interest rate. Mill Company will receive $200,000 cash in 3 years. Assuming that 10% is the appropriate imputed rate of interest, the present value (initial carrying amount) of the note at January 1, Year 3, was $150,000 ($200,000 × 0.75). Interest revenue for Year 3 was $15,000 ($150,000 × 10%), and the entry was to debit the discount and credit interest revenue for that amount. Thus, the carrying amount of the note at January 1, Year 4, was $165,000 ($200,000 face amount – $35,000 unamortized discount). Interest revenue for Year 4 is therefore $16,500 ($165,000 carrying amount × 10% interest rate).
    Answer (A) is incorrect because interest should be recognized equal to the imputed rate times the carrying amount of the note. Answer (B) is incorrect because $15,000 was interest income for Year 3. Answer (D) is incorrect because $20,000 is 10% of the face amount of the note.

Questions 20 and 21 are based on the following information. On January 2, Year 4, Emme Co. sold equipment with a carrying amount of $480,000 in exchange for a $600,000 noninterest-bearing note due January 2, Year 7. There was no established exchange price for the equipment. The prevailing rate of interest for a note of this type at January 2, Year 4, was 10%. The present value of 1 at 10% for three periods is 0.75.

20. In Emme's Year 4 income statement, what amount should be reported as interest income?

A. $15,000

B. $45,000

C. $48,000

D. $60,000

Answer (B) is correct. *(CPA, adapted)*
REQUIRED: The interest income from a noninterest-bearing note received for property.
DISCUSSION: When a noninterest-bearing note is exchanged for property, and neither the note nor the property has a clearly determinable exchange price, the present value of the note should be the basis for recording the transaction. The present value is determined by discounting all future payments using an appropriately imputed interest rate. Emme Co. will receive $600,000 cash in 3 years. Assuming that 10% is the appropriate imputed rate of interest, the present value (initial carrying value) of the note at January 2, Year 4, was $450,000 ($600,000 × 0.75). Under the interest method, interest income for Year 4 was $45,000 ($450,000 × 10%), and the entry is to debit the discount and credit interest income for that amount.
Answer (A) is incorrect because $15,000 is the difference between 10% of the face amount and 10% of the carrying amount. Answer (C) is incorrect because interest income is based on the present value of the note, not the carrying amount of the equipment. Answer (D) is incorrect because interest income is based on the carrying amount of the note, not the face amount.

21. In Emme's Year 4 income statement, what amount should be reported as gain (loss) on sale of equipment?

A. $(30,000)

B. $30,000

C. $120,000

D. $150,000

Answer (A) is correct. *(CPA, adapted)*
REQUIRED: The amount reported as gain (loss) on the sale of machinery.
DISCUSSION: Emme Co. sold equipment with a carrying amount of $480,000 and received a note with a present value of $450,000 ($600,000 × .75). Thus, Emme should report a $30,000 loss ($480,000 – $450,000).
Answer (B) is incorrect because the present value of the note is $30,000 less than the carrying amount surrendered. Answer (C) is incorrect because $120,000 is the difference between the face amount of the note and the carrying amount of the equipment. Answer (D) is incorrect because $150,000 is the discount (face amount – present value).

6.6 Notes Receivable – Discounting

22. Leaf Co. purchased from Oak Co. a $20,000, 8%, 5-year note that required five equal annual year-end payments of $5,009. The note was discounted to yield a 9% rate to Leaf. At the date of purchase, Leaf recorded the note at its present value of $19,485. What should be the total interest revenue earned by Leaf over the life of this note?

A. $5,045

B. $5,560

C. $8,000

D. $9,000

Answer (B) is correct. *(CPA, adapted)*
REQUIRED: The total interest revenue earned on a discounted note receivable.
DISCUSSION: Leaf Co. will receive cash of $25,045 ($5,009 × 5). Hence, interest revenue is $5,560 ($25,045 – $19,485 present value).
Answer (A) is incorrect because $5,045 does not include the discount amortization. Answer (C) is incorrect because $8,000 equals $20,000 times 8% nominal interest for 5 years. Answer (D) is incorrect because $9,000 equals $20,000 times the 9% yield rate for 5 years.

23. On July 1, Year 3, Kay Corp. sold equipment to Mando Co. for $100,000. Kay accepted a 10% note receivable for the entire sales price. This note is payable in two equal installments of $50,000 plus accrued interest on December 31, Year 3, and December 31, Year 4. On July 1, Year 4, Kay discounted the note at a bank at an interest rate of 12%. Kay's proceeds from the discounted note were

A. $48,400

B. $52,640

C. $52,250

D. $51,700

Answer (D) is correct. *(CPA, adapted)*
REQUIRED: The proceeds from a discounted note.
DISCUSSION: Following the receipt of $50,000 plus accrued interest on December 31, Year 3, the remaining balance was $50,000. Because the second installment is due 1 year after the first, the interest attributable to this balance is $5,000 ($50,000 principal × 10% × 1 year). On July 1, Year 4, the $55,000 maturity value ($50,000 note + $5,000 interest) is discounted at 12% for the remaining 6 months of the term of the note. The discount fee charged would be $3,300 [$55,000 maturity amount × 12% × (6 ÷ 12)]. The net proceeds are equal to the $55,000 maturity value minus the $3,300 discount fee, or $51,700.

$50,000 × 10% × 1 year = $5,000 interest
$55,000 × 12% × (6 ÷ 12) = $3,300 discount fee

Answer (A) is incorrect because $48,400 results from charging a discount fee for a full year. Answer (B) is incorrect because $52,640 assumes the nominal interest rate is also 12%. Answer (C) is incorrect because $52,250 assumes the discount rate is also 10%.

24. Roth, Inc. received from a customer a 1-year, $500,000 note bearing annual interest of 8%. After holding the note for 6 months, Roth discounted the note at Regional Bank at an effective interest rate of 10%. What amount of cash did Roth receive from the bank?

A. $540,000

B. $528,400

C. $513,000

D. $486,000

Answer (C) is correct. *(CPA, adapted)*
REQUIRED: The amount of cash received when a note is discounted.
DISCUSSION: The maturity amount of the note is $540,000 [$500,000 face value + ($500,000 × 8%)]. The discount is $27,000 [$540,000 × 10% × (6 ÷ 12)]. Consequently, the proceeds equal $513,000 ($540,000 − $27,000).
Answer (A) is incorrect because $540,000 is the maturity value. Answer (B) is incorrect because $528,400 assumes a nominal rate of 10% and a discount rate of 8%. Answer (D) is incorrect because $486,000 results from discounting the note for 1 year.

6.7 Affiliated Company Receivables

25. In its financial statements, Pulham Corp. uses the equity method of accounting for its 30% ownership of Angles Corp. At December 31, Year 4, Pulham has a receivable from Angles. How should the receivable be reported in Pulham's Year 4 financial statements?

A. None of the receivable should be reported, but the entire receivable should be offset against Angles's payment to Pulham.

B. 70% of the receivable should be separately reported, with the balance offset against 30% of Angles's payment to Pulham.

C. The total receivable should be disclosed separately.

D. The total receivable should be included as part of the investment in Angles, without separate disclosure.

Answer (C) is correct. *(CPA, adapted)*
REQUIRED: The method of reporting a receivable from a related party.
DISCUSSION: According to SFAS 57, *Related Party Disclosures*, related parties include an entity and its equity-based investees. A receivable from a related party should be separately and fully disclosed. Indeed, nontrade receivables generally are subject to separate treatment.
Answer (A) is incorrect because elimination of interentity transactions is inappropriate except in the case of combined or consolidated statements. Answer (B) is incorrect because none of the receivable should be separately reported or offset. Answer (D) is incorrect because the investment balance equals cost plus the investor's share of earnings and losses, minus any return of the investment. Also, adjustments may be necessary for acquisition differentials. Furthermore, separate disclosure is required.

26. Shep Co. has a receivable from its parent, Pep Co. Should this receivable be separately reported in Shep's balance sheet and in Pep's consolidated balance sheet?

	Shep's Balance Sheet	Pep's Consolidated Balance Sheet
A.	Yes	No
B.	Yes	Yes
C.	No	No
D.	No	Yes

Answer (A) is correct. *(CPA, adapted)*
REQUIRED: The treatment of an intercompany receivable in the balance sheet of a subsidiary and in the consolidated balance sheet.
DISCUSSION: In a consolidated balance sheet, reciprocal balances, such as receivables and payables, between a parent and a consolidated subsidiary should be eliminated in their entirety regardless of the portion of the subsidiary's stock held by the parent. However, intercompany transactions should not be eliminated from the separate financial statements of the entities.

27. Mr. and Mrs. Dart own a majority of the outstanding capital stock of Wall Corp., Black Co., and West, Inc. During Year 4, Wall advanced cash to Black and West in the amount of $50,000 and $80,000, respectively. West advanced $70,000 in cash to Black. At December 31, Year 4, none of the advances was repaid. In the combined December 31, Year 4, balance sheet of these companies, what amount would be reported as receivables from affiliates?

A. $200,000

B. $130,000

C. $60,000

D. $0

Answer (D) is correct. *(CPA, adapted)*
REQUIRED: The amount to be reported in the combined balance sheet as receivables from affiliates.
DISCUSSION: Consolidated financial statements are presented when one entity (the parent) owns the majority of the outstanding voting interests of another entity (a subsidiary). According to ARB 51, combined financial statements are issued when a relationship such as common ownership or common management exists for two or more entities. Thus, combined statements may be used to present the results of operations of both unconsolidated subsidiaries and entities under common management. Interentity transactions and profits or losses are eliminated from combined statements, and problems with a minority interest, foreign operations, different fiscal periods, and taxes are treated in the same way as in consolidated statements. Consequently, the receivables among the combined entities should be eliminated. The amount of receivables from affiliates is $0.
Answer (A) is incorrect because $200,000 is the total of the amounts advanced by the affiliated entities to each other. Answer (B) is incorrect because $130,000 is the sum of the advances made by Wall. Answer (C) is incorrect because $60,000 is the sum of the advances made by Wall minus the advance made by Black.

6.8 Balance Sheet Presentation

28. Which one of the following is false in regards to the balance sheet presentation?

A. Disclosures are never made of related party transactions or contingencies.

B. Valuation accounts should be separated into current and noncurrent sections.

C. Receivables should be separated into current and noncurrent sections.

D. Material receivables should be segregated.

Answer (A) is correct. *(Publisher, adapted)*
REQUIRED: The false statement regarding balance sheet presentation.
DISCUSSION: Disclosures should be made of related party transactions, such as loans to employees or affiliates. In addition, disclosures should be made for loss contingencies, such as from transfers with recourse.
Answer (B) is incorrect because valuation accounts should be separated into current and noncurrent sections. Answer (C) is incorrect because receivables should be separated into current and noncurrent sections. Answer (D) is incorrect because material receivables should be segregated.

Use Gleim's *CPA Test Prep* CD-Rom/Pocket PC for interactive testing with over 4,000 additional questions!

6.9 PRACTICE SIMULATION

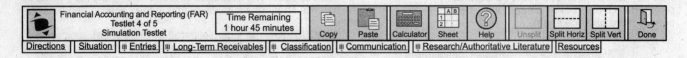

Financial Accounting and Reporting (FAR)
Testlet 4 of 5
Simulation Testlet

Time Remaining
1 hour 45 minutes

Copy | Paste | Calculator | Sheet | Help | Unsplit | Split Horiz | Split Vert | Done

Directions | Situation | ▥ Entries | ▥ Long-Term Receivables | ▥ Classification | ▥ Communication | ▥ Research/Authoritative Literature | Resources

1. Directions

In the following simulation, you will be asked to complete various tasks. You may use the content in the **Information Tabs** to complete the tasks in the **Work Tabs**.

Information Tabs:

| Directions | Resources |

FIG 1

- Go through each of the **Information Tabs** to familiarize yourself with the simulation content
- The **Resources** tab will contain information, including formulas and definitions, that may help you to complete the tasks
- Your simulation may have more **Information Tabs** than those shown in Fig. 1

Work Tabs:

| ▥ SysTrust | ▥ Engagement Letter | ▥ Authoritative Sources | ▥ Communication |

FIG. 2

- **Work Tabs**, to the right of **Information Tabs**, contain the tasks for you to complete
- **Work Tabs** contain directions for completing each task - be sure to read these directions carefully
- The tab names in Fig. 2 are for illustration only - yours may differ
- Once you complete any part of a task, the pencil for that tab will be shaded (see **Communication** in Fig. 2)
- The shaded pencil does **NOT** indicate that you have completed the entire task
- You must complete all of the tasks in the **Work Tabs** to receive full credit

Research/Authoritative Literature Tab:

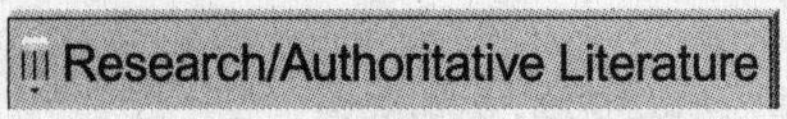

| ▥ Research/Authoritative Literature |

FIG. 3

- This tab contains both the Research task and the Authoritative Literature
- Detailed instructions for completing the Research task, and for using the Authoritative Literature, appear on this tab
- You may use the Authoritative Literature as a resource for completing other tasks

NOTE: If you believe you have encountered a software malfunction, report it to the test center staff immediately.

2. Situation

Kern, Inc., which is not a public company (an issuer under federal securities laws), had the following long-term receivable account balances at December 31, Year 4:

Note receivable from the sale of an idle building $750,000
Note receivable from an officer $200,000

Transactions during Year 5 and other information relating to Kern's receivables follow:

- The $750,000 note receivable is dated May 1, Year 4, bears interest at 9%, and represents the balance of the consideration Kern received from the sale of its idle building to Able Co. Principal payments of $250,000 plus interest are due annually beginning May 1, Year 5. Able made its first principal and interest payment on May 1, Year 5. Collection of the remaining note installments is reasonably assured.

- The $200,000 note receivable is dated December 31, Year 2, bears interest at 8%, and is due on December 31, Year 7. The note is due from Frank Black, president of Kern, Inc., and is collateralized by 5,000 shares of Kern's common stock. Interest is payable annually on December 31, and all interest payments were made through December 31, Year 5. The quoted market price of Kern's common stock was $45 per share on December 31, Year 5.

- On April 1, Year 5, Kern sold a patent to Frey Corp. in exchange for a $100,000 noninterest-bearing note due on April 1, Year 7. There was no established exchange price for the patent, and the note had no ready market. The prevailing interest rate for this type of note was 10% at April 1, Year 5. The present value of $1 for two periods at 10% is 0.826. The patent had a carrying amount of $40,000 at January 1, Year 5, and the amortization for the year ended December 31, Year 5, was $8,000. Kern is reasonably assured of collecting the note receivable from Frey.

- On July 1, Year 5, Kern sold a parcel of land to Barr Co. for $400,000 under an installment sale contract. Barr made a $120,000 cash down payment on July 1, Year 5, and signed a 4-year, 10% note for the balance. The equal annual payments of principal and interest on the note will be $88,332, payable on July 1 of each year from Year 6 through Year 9. The fair value of the land at the date of sale was $400,000. The cost of the land to Kern was $300,000. Collection of the remaining note installments is reasonably assured.

- Kern Company has significant amounts of trade accounts receivable. In March of Year 5, Kern assigned specific trade accounts receivable to Herb Finance Company on a with-recourse, nonnotification basis as collateral for a loan. Kern signed a note and received 70% of the amount assigned. Kern was charged a 5% finance fee and agreed to pay interest at 12% on the unpaid balance. Some specific accounts of the assigned receivables were written off as uncollectible. The remainder of the trade accounts receivable assigned were collected by Kern in March and April. Kern paid Herb Finance in full at the end of April of Year 5.

- Kern also sold some special order merchandise and received a 90-day, 15% interest-bearing note receivable on July 1 of Year 5. On July 31, the note was discounted with recourse at 18% at a bank. The transaction was treated as a borrowing, and the bank has the right to sell the collateral.

3. Entries

This question is presented in a check-the-box format that requires you to select the correct response from a given list. Check the appropriate box for each item. Based on the information provided, indicate whether each account should be debited or credited by Kern to account for the transaction listed.

	Debit	Credit
Transaction: Assignment of trade accounts receivable		
1. Trade accounts receivable assigned	☐	☐
2. Trade accounts receivable	☐	☐
Transaction: Giving a note payable with the assigned receivables as collateral		
3. Notes payable	☐	☐
4. Finance fee expense	☐	☐
5. Cash	☐	☐
Transaction: Subsequent collections on the trade accounts receivable assigned		
6. Cash	☐	☐
7. Trade accounts receivable assigned	☐	☐
Transaction: Write-off of specific uncollectible accounts		
8. Trade accounts receivable assigned	☐	☐
9. Allowance for uncollectible accounts	☐	☐
Transaction: Payment of the note payable		
10. Interest expense	☐	☐
11. Cash	☐	☐
12. Notes payable	☐	☐
Transaction: Recognizing accrued interest		
13. Interest receivable	☐	☐
14. Interest revenue	☐	☐
Transaction: Accounting for collateral		
15. Notes receivable	☐	☐
16. Notes receivable held by bank	☐	☐

4. Long-Term Receivables

This question is presented in a spreadsheet format that requires you to fill in the correct response in the shaded cells provided. Calculate the long-term receivables that should be reported on Kern's December 31, Year 5, balance sheet. Write the calculated amounts in the shaded cells.

Long-term portion of 9% note receivable at 12/31/Year 5	*Amount*
Face amount, 5/1/Year 4	
Minus installment received 5/1/Year 5	
Balance, 12/31/Year 5	
Minus installment due 5/1/Year 6	
Long-term portion, 12/31/Year 5	
Noninterest-bearing note, net of imputed interest at 12/31/Year 5	
Face amount, 4/1/Year 5	
Minus imputed interest	
Balance, 4/1/Year 5	
Plus interest earned to 12/31/Year 5	
Balance, 12/31/Year 5	
Long-term portion of installment contract receivable at 12/31/Year 5	
Contract selling price, 7/1/Year 5	
Minus cash down payment	
Balance, 12/31/Year 5	
Minus installment due 7/1/Year 6	
Long-term portion, 12/31/Year 5	
Long-term 8% note receivable due 12/31/Year 7	

5. Classification of Receivables

This set of questions has a matching format. Select the best match for each numbered item from the terms in the drop-down list, and write its letter in the column provided. Select the answers for 1. and 2. from choices A) and B), for 3. through 6. from C) and D), and for 7. through 10. from E) and F). Each choice may be used once, more than once, or not at all. Determine the most clearly evident additional classification for each of the following items.

Item	Answer	Classification
1. Trade account receivable due within 11 months		A) Current asset
2. Nontrade note receivable due within two years		B) Noncurrent asset

Item	Answer	Classification
3. Noncurrent notes receivable for advances to shareholders, directors, and officers		C) Trade receivable
4. Current note receivable for insurance proceeds		D) Nontrade receivable
5. Current account receivable from credit sales		
6. Current note receivable for rent		

Item	Answer	Classification
7. Unsecured current trade receivable not evidenced by a formal instrument		E) Note receivable
8. Long-term, interest-bearing receivable payable in a single sum		F) Accounts receivable
9. Noncurrent trade receivable evidenced by a formal instrument		
10. Current trade open accounts		

6. Communication

In a memorandum to a client, describe the two basic approaches to estimating uncollectible accounts receivable. Include the rationale for each approach, whether it is acceptable for GAAP purposes, entries, and how it is applied.

REMINDER: Your response will be graded for both technical content and writing skills. Technical content will be evaluated for information that is helpful to the intended reader and clearly relevant to the issue. Writing skills will be evaluated for development, organization, and the appropriate expression of ideas in professional correspondence. Use a standard business memo or letter format with a clear beginning, middle, and end. Do not convey information in the form of a table, bullet point list, or other abbreviated presentation.

> To: Client
> From: CPA
> Subject: Estimating uncollectible accounts

---

7. Research/Authoritative Literature

See page 12 in the Introduction of this book for a detailed explanation of the AICPA's new Research/Authoritative Literature work tab as well as a screenshot of how the tab will actually look on your exam.

A transfer of financial assets (or all or a portion of a financial asset) in which the transferor surrenders control over those financial assets is accounted for as a sale to the extent that consideration other than beneficial interests in the transferred assets is received in exchange. Research and cite the specific paragraph in the FASB Current Text or Original Pronouncements that gives the conditions that must be met to show that the transferor has surrendered control over transferred assets.

Unofficial Answers

3. Entries (16 Gradable Items)

1. <u>Debit</u> Trade accounts receivable assigned. Assigned accounts receivable should be segregated.

2. <u>Credit</u> Trade accounts receivable. Assigned accounts receivable should be segregated.

3. <u>Credit</u> Notes payable. The loan is reported as a liability.

4. <u>Debit</u> Finance fee expense. These finance fees are charged to the assignor-debtor as a reduction of the loan proceeds.

5. <u>Debit</u> Cash. The assignor-debtor receives the cash it borrowed.

6. <u>Debit</u> Cash. The assignor-debtor receives the cash collected because the assignment was on a nonnotification basis.

7. <u>Credit</u> Trade accounts receivable assigned. The assigned receivables are removed from the books when collected.

8. <u>Credit</u> Trade accounts receivable assigned. The assigned receivables are removed from the books when determined to be uncollectible.

9. <u>Debit</u> Allowance for uncollectible accounts. A write-off of an uncollectible account reduces the allowance.

10. <u>Debit</u> Interest expense. The assignor-debtor agreed to pay interest in addition to the initial finance fee.

11. <u>Credit</u> Cash. Cash is paid to settle the liability.

12. <u>Debit</u> Notes payable. The liability is removed when settled.

13. <u>Debit</u> Interest receivable. The creditor customarily accrues interest on its nontrade receivables.

14. <u>Credit</u> Interest revenue. Interest is accrued as a revenue when earned but not yet received.

15. <u>Credit</u> Notes receivable. A note receivable assigned as collateral in a borrowing should be segregated.

16. <u>Debit</u> Notes receivable held by bank. A note receivable assigned as collateral in a borrowing should be segregated.

4. Long-Term Receivables (16 Gradable Items)

Long-term portion of 9% note receivable at 12/31/Year 5	
Face amount, 5/1/Year 4	$750,000
Minus installment received 5/1/Year 5	250,000
Balance, 12/31/Year 5	$500,000
Minus installment due 5/1/Year 6 (current portion)	250,000
Long-term portion, 12/31/Year 5	$250,000
Noninterest-bearing note, net of imputed interest at 12/31/Year 5	
Face amount, 4/1/Year 5	$100,000
Minus imputed interest [$100,000 – ($100,000 × 0.826 factor for the PV of $1 for 2 periods at 10%)]	17,400
Balance, 4/1/Year 5	$ 82,600
Plus interest earned to 12/31/Year 5 [$82,600 × 10% × (9 ÷ 12)]	6,195
Balance, 12/31/Year 5	$ 88,795
Long-term portion of installment contract receivable at 12/31/Year 5	
Contract selling price, 7/1/Year 5	$400,000
Minus cash down payment	120,000
Balance, 12/31/Year 5	$280,000
Minus installment due 7/1/Year 6 [$88,332 – ($280,000 × 10%)]	60,332
Long-term portion, 12/31/Year 5	$219,668
Long-term 8% note receivable due 12/31/Year 7	$200,000

5. Classification (10 Gradable Items)

1. A) - Current asset. A receivable is a current asset if it is reasonably expected to be collected within the longer of 1 year or the entity's normal operating cycle. Otherwise it should be classified as noncurrent.

2. B) - Noncurrent asset. A receivable is a current asset if it is reasonably expected to be collected within the longer of 1 year or the entity's normal operating cycle. Otherwise it should be classified as noncurrent.

3. D) - Nontrade receivables. Typical nontrade receivables are reported for advances to shareholders, directors, officers, other employees, affiliates, or customers.

4. D) - Nontrade receivable. Nontrade receivables may include claims for insurance proceeds or amounts arising from litigation.

5. C) - Trade receivables. Most receivables arise from credit sales to customers as part of the ordinary revenue-producing activities of an entity. These trade receivables represent contractual undertakings usually evidenced by sales orders, invoices, or delivery contracts.

6. D) - Nontrade receivable. Nontrade receivables may include interest, dividends, rent, or royalties accrued.

7. F) - Accounts receivable. Accounts receivable are often short-term, unsecured, and informal credit arrangements (open accounts). They constitute the largest portion of trade receivables.

8. E) - Note receivable. In a note, the maker (debtor) usually promises to pay to the order of a second party (creditor) a fixed amount of money at a definite time. This item also is not an installment account because payment is in a lump sum.

9. E) - Note receivable. Notes receivable are evidenced by a formal instrument, such as a promissory note. A formal document provides its holder with a stronger legal status than does an account receivable.

10. F) - Accounts receivable. Accounts receivable are often short-term, unsecured, and informal credit arrangements (open accounts). They constitute the largest portion of trade receivables.

6. Communication (5 Gradable Items; for grading instructions, please refer to page 12.)

The principal valuation issue for accounts receivable is the estimation of uncollectible accounts expense. The two approaches to determining this expense are the direct write-off method and the allowance method.

The direct write-off method debits bad debt expense and credits accounts receivable at the time the uncollectibility of a specific account is established. This method is convenient but is not acceptable under GAAP because it neither (1) matches revenue and expense when the receivable and the write-off are recorded in different periods nor (2) states receivables at net realizable value.

The allowance method attempts both to match bad debt expense with the related revenue and to determine the net realizable value of the accounts receivable. It is acceptable under GAAP. Based on an estimate of uncollectible accounts for a period, bad debt expense is debited and an allowance account is credited. A subsequent write-off will result in a debit to the allowance and a credit to accounts receivable. When accounts are written off, no immediate debit is made to expense. The allowance is a contra-asset account subtracted from accounts receivable on the balance sheet. Hence, write-offs do not affect the carrying amount of net accounts receivable because gross accounts receivable and the allowance are reduced by the same amounts.

Under the allowance method, bad debt expense reported on the income statement can be estimated by applying a percentage (usually based on past bad debt losses) to credit sales (also reported on the income statement). This process results in an adjusting entry that debits bad debt expense and credits the allowance without regard to the existing balances. Use of total sales may also be acceptable if a company has a stable mix of cash and credit sales over the years.

Other allowance methods emphasize the NRV of the receivables to be reported on the balance sheet. One way to estimate the allowance is to apply a single percentage to the accounts receivable balance at the end of the period. This technique does NOT directly estimate bad debt expense. Instead, it indicates the amount to which the existing balance must be adjusted. The adjustment is the bad debt expense. A more sophisticated method of estimating the desired allowance for bad debts is to apply different percentages to blocks of receivables classified according to how long they have been outstanding, a practice known as aging of receivables.

If a company finds that its estimates of bad debt expense are inaccurate, it may change the percentage(s) used or its method of estimation. In either case, the change should be treated as a change in accounting estimate and accounted for currently and prospectively. No prior period adjustment is needed.

If the company collects previously written-off accounts, the proper procedure is to reestablish the account by debiting accounts receivable and crediting the allowance and then to debit cash and credit accounts receivable for the amount recovered.

7. Research/Authoritative Literature (1 Gradable Item)

Answer: FAS 140, Par. 9

FAS 140 -- *Accounting for Transfers and Servicing of Financial Assets and Extinguishments of Liabilities*
Standards of Financial Accounting and Reporting
Accounting for Transfers and Servicing of Financial Assets

9. A transfer of financial assets (or all or a portion of a financial asset) in which the transferor surrenders control over those financial assets shall be accounted for as a sale to the extent that consideration other than beneficial interests in the transferred assets is received in exchange. The transferor has surrendered control over transferred assets if, and only if, all of the following conditions are met:

a) The transferred assets have been isolated from the transferor--put presumptively beyond the reach of the transferor and its creditors, even in bankruptcy or other receivership.

b) Each transferee (or, if the transferee is a qualifying SPE, each holder of its beneficial interests) has the right to pledge or exchange the assets (or beneficial interests) it received, and no condition both constrains the transferee (or holder) from taking advantage of its right to pledge or exchange and provides more than a trivial benefit to the transferor.

c) The transferor does not maintain effective control over the transferred assets through either (1) an agreement that both entitles and obligates the transferor to repurchase or redeem them before their maturity or (2) the ability to unilaterally cause the holder to return specific assets, other than through a cleanup call.

Scoring Schedule:

	Correct Responses		Gradable Items		Weights		
Tab 3	_____	÷	16	×	20%	=	_____
Tab 4	_____	÷	16	×	20%	=	_____
Tab 5	_____	÷	10	×	15%	=	_____
Tab 6	_____	÷	5	×	30%	=	_____
Tab 7	_____	÷	1	×	15%	=	_____
							_____
							(Your Score)

Use Gleim's **CPA Gleim Online** to practice more simulations in a realistic environment.

STUDY UNIT SEVEN
INVENTORIES

(24 pages of outline)

Inventory consists of the tangible goods intended to be sold to produce revenue. The cost of inventory is a deferral because it is not included in earnings until the reporting period in which the inventory is sold (produces revenue). Many methods of costing inventory are acceptable. Inventory and related concepts are always tested on the CPA exam.

7.1 INVENTORY FUNDAMENTALS

Definition

1. Inventory is "the aggregate of those items of tangible personal property that

    a. Are held for sale in the ordinary course of business,

    b. Are in process of production for such sale, or

    c. Are to be currently consumed in the production of goods or services to be available for sale" (ARB 43, Ch. 4, "Inventory Pricing").

2. Inventory does not include long-term assets subject to depreciation.

Sources of Inventories

3. **Retailing.** A trading (retailing) entity purchases merchandise to be resold without substantial modification.

    a. Such entities also may maintain supplies inventories.

    b. For a retailer, **cost of goods sold** essentially equals beginning merchandise inventory, plus purchases for the period, minus ending merchandise inventory (purchases adjusted for the change in inventory).

4. **Manufacturing.** An entity that acquires goods for conversion into substantially different products has inventories of goods consumed directly or indirectly in production (direct materials and supplies), goods in the course of production (work-in-process), and goods awaiting sale (finished goods).

    a. For a manufacturer, **cost of goods sold** essentially equals beginning finished goods inventory, plus the cost of goods manufactured, minus ending finished goods inventory.

    b. **Cost of goods manufactured** equals beginning-work-in-process, plus current manufacturing costs (direct materials + direct labor + production overhead), minus ending-work-in-process (current manufacturing costs adjusted for the change in work-in-process).

Inventory Accounting Systems

5. Entities that have no need to monitor inventory continuously use a periodic system. Entities that require continuous monitoring use a perpetual system.

    a. **Purchases**

        1) In a **periodic system**, the beginning inventory balance is maintained throughout the period. Acquisitions are debited to purchases.

        2) In a **perpetual system**, acquisitions are added to inventory as they occur.

Periodic		Perpetual	
Purchases	$x,xxx	Inventory	$x,xxx
Accounts payable	$x,xxx	Accounts payable	$x,xxx

    b. **Sales**

        1) In a **periodic system**, changes in inventory and cost of goods sold are recorded only at the end of the period.

        2) In a **perpetual system**, inventory and cost of goods sold are adjusted as sales occur.

Periodic		Perpetual	
Accounts receivable	$x,xxx	Accounts receivable	$x,xxx
Sales	$x,xxx	Sales	$x,xxx
No entry		Cost of goods sold	$x,xxx
		Inventory	$x,xxx

    c. **Closing**

        1) A physical inventory count must be taken at specified intervals, regardless of which system is used.

        2) In a **periodic system**, the physical count must be taken at the end of each reporting period. It allows (a) the inventory balance to be adjusted to match the physical count and (b) cost of goods sold to be calculated.

        3) In a **perpetual system**, the physical count is needed to detect material misstatements in the perpetual records.

            a) **Inventory over-and-short** is debited (credited) when the physical count is less (greater) than the balance in the perpetual records.

                i)   This account is either closed to cost of goods sold or reported separately under other revenues and gains or other expenses and losses.

        4) In normal circumstances, the following are the closing entries:

Periodic		Perpetual	
Inventory (physical count)	$x,xxx	Inventory over-and-short (DR, CR)	$xx
Cost of goods sold	x,xxx	Inventory (correction) (CR, DR)	$xx
Purchases (total for period)	$x,xxx		
Inventory (beginning balance)	x,xxx		

Items Counted in Inventory

6. **Items in transit -- FOB terms** (FOB means free on board). Not all inventory is on hand.

    a. In practice, most sales are recorded by the seller at the time of shipment and the buyer at the time of receipt. But, at year-end, this procedure may misstate inventory, receivables, payables, and earnings.

        1) Thus, a proper cut-off is observed by determining when legal title has passed under the terms of the contract.

            a) **FOB shipping point** means the seller bears the risk and expense of putting the goods in the possession of the carrier. When the seller completes performance by physical delivery to the carrier, title to the goods and risk of loss pass to the buyer, who then may include them in inventory.

            b) **FOB destination** means the seller bears the risk and expense of transporting goods to the destination and appropriately tendering delivery of them. Title and risk of loss pass upon tender of delivery at the destination, and the seller should include them in inventory until that time.

7. **Installment sales.** Because of the greater risk of loss in these transactions, the seller often retains title to the goods until full payment has been made. Nevertheless, these items should not be counted in the seller's inventory if uncollectible accounts expense can be reasonably estimated.

    a. Despite retention of title by the seller, the substance of the transaction is that control of the goods has passed to the buyer, assuming a reasonable expectation of payment in the ordinary course of business.

8. **Consignments.** In a consignment, the consignor ships merchandise to the consignee, who acts as agent for the consignor in selling the goods.

    a. The goods are held by the consignee but remain the property of the consignor and are **included in the consignor's inventory** at cost.

        1) Costs incurred by a consignor on the transfer of goods to a consignee are costs necessary to their sale. Thus, the costs are inventoriable.

            a) Because consigned goods remain in the consignor's inventory, shipping costs, in-transit insurance premiums, etc., should be debited to **consignment-out** (inventory on consignment).

            b) When goods are shipped on consignment, consignment-out is debited and inventory is credited.

    b. Sales revenue and the related cost of goods sold from consigned goods should only be recognized by the consignor when notification is received that the consignee has sold the goods.

    c. The basic account used in consignee accounting is **consignment-in**, a receivable/payable. Its balance is the amount payable to the consignor (a credit) or the amount receivable from the consignor (a debit).

        1) Before consigned goods are sold, expenses chargeable to the consignor are recorded in the consignment-in account as a receivable. After the consigned goods are sold, the consignee's net liability to the consignor is reflected in the account.

9. **Product Financing Arrangements**

a. One type of **product financing arrangement (PFA)** involves an apparent sale of inventory by a **sponsor** (a party seeking financing), coupled with a repurchase agreement (SFAS 49, *Accounting for Product Financing Arrangements*).

b. The PFA also may involve a purchase by another party **(other entity)** from a third entity, coupled with a purchase agreement by the sponsor.

c. In either case, a PFA exists if the sponsor **controls** the disposition of the product by the other entity.

   1) In essence, the future repurchase is a return of collateral upon payment of a debt.

d. The PFA may consist of the **sale** of a product subject to repurchase of

   1) The product,
   2) A substantially identical product, or
   3) Processed goods of which the product is a component.

e. The PFA is a **borrowing** if

   1) It requires the sponsor to purchase at **specified prices** over **specified periods** (or provide resale price guarantees), and

   2) The payments will be adjusted as needed to cover substantially all of the **purchasing and holding costs** (including interest) incurred by the other entity.

      a) This provision indicates that, in a PFA, the risks and rewards of ownership remain with the sponsor.

f. The sponsor accounts for the money received as a **liability** rather than as revenue from a sale if the criteria above are met.

   1) The sponsor also continues to recognize the inventory.

g. If the other entity purchases inventory from a third party for repurchase by a sponsor, the sponsor-repurchaser should record an **asset and a liability** when the other entity makes the purchase.

10. **Right of Return**

a. When sales are made with the understanding that unsatisfactory goods may be returned, revenue and cost of goods sold may be recognized and inventory may be credited when certain conditions exist (SFAS 48, *Revenue Recognition When Right of Return Exists*).

   1) These conditions are listed in Subunit 6.2.

b. If the conditions are met, a sale is recorded in the usual way. In addition, estimated returns (a contra revenue account) is debited and cost of goods sold and deferred gross profit are credited.

   1) Inventory and deferred gross profit are debited and accounts receivable (or cash) is credited when returns are made.

c. If the conditions are not met, revenue and cost of goods sold are not recognized until the right of return expires.

   1) The initial entry is to debit accounts receivable (or cash) and to credit inventory and deferred gross profit. Returns result in a reversal of this entry.

Purchase Commitments

11. A commitment to acquire goods in the future is not recorded at the time of the agreement, e.g., by debiting an asset and crediting a liability. But GAAP require a **recognition in earnings of a loss** on goods subject to a firm purchase commitment if their market price declines below the commitment price.

    a. The reason for current loss recognition is the same as that for inventory. A decrease (not an increase) in the future benefits of the commitment should be recognized when it occurs, even though the contract is executory on both sides. Thus, the LCM rule is followed.

       1) If material losses are expected to arise from **firm, noncancelable, and unhedged commitments** for the future purchase of inventory, they should be measured in the same way as inventory losses, recognized, and separately disclosed.

          a) However, a commitment is **not impaired** and no loss occurs if the amounts to be realized from the disposition of the future inventory are protected by a firm sales contract or if other circumstances reasonably assure against loss.

    b. The entry is

Unrealized holding loss – earnings	$XXX	
Liability – purchase commitment		$XXX

    ### EXAMPLE

    During the year, the Lisbon Company signed a noncancelable contract to purchase 2,000 pounds of a raw material at $64 per pound during the forthcoming year. On December 31, the market price of the raw material is $52 per pound, and the selling price of the finished product is expected to decline accordingly. The financial statements prepared for the year should report a loss of $24,000 in the income statement.

    GAAP requires recognition in the income statement of a material loss on a purchase commitment as if the inventory were already owned. Losses on firm purchase commitments are measured in the same way as inventory losses. If the cost is $128,000 and the market price is $104,000, a $24,000 loss should be disclosed.

    ---

    c. A **firm commitment** is "an agreement with an unrelated party, binding on both parties and usually legally enforceable, with the following characteristics:

       1) The agreement specifies all significant terms, including the quantity to be exchanged, the fixed price, and the timing of the transaction. The fixed price may be expressed as a specified amount of an entity's functional currency or of a foreign currency. It may also be expressed as a specified interest rate or specified effective yield.

       2) The agreement includes a disincentive for nonperformance that is sufficiently large to make performance probable" (SFAS 133, *Accounting for Derivative Instruments and Hedging Activities*).

    d. When a previously unrecognized firm commitment is designated as a **hedged item**, an **asset or liability** is recognized related to the recognition of the gain or loss on the commitment.

Inventory Errors

12. These errors may have a material effect on current assets, working capital (current assets – current liabilities), cost of goods sold, net income, and equity. A common error is inappropriate timing of the recognition of transactions.

    a.   If a purchase on account is not recorded, and the goods are not included in ending inventory, cost of goods sold (BI + purchases – EI) and net income are unaffected. But current assets and current liabilities are understated.

    b.   If purchases and beginning inventory are properly recorded but items are excluded from ending inventory, cost of goods sold is overstated. Net income, inventory, retained earnings, working capital, and the current ratio are understated.

    c.   If the goods are properly included in ending inventory but the purchase is not recorded, net income is overstated because cost of goods sold is understated. Also, current liabilities are understated and working capital overstated.

    d.   Errors arising from recording transactions in the wrong period may reverse in the subsequent period.

        1)   If ending inventory is overstated, the overstatement of net income will be offset by the understatement in the following year that results from the overstatement of beginning inventory.

EXAMPLE

An overstatement error in year-end inventory of the current year will be reflected on the financial statements of two different years.

The **first year's** effects can be depicted as follows:

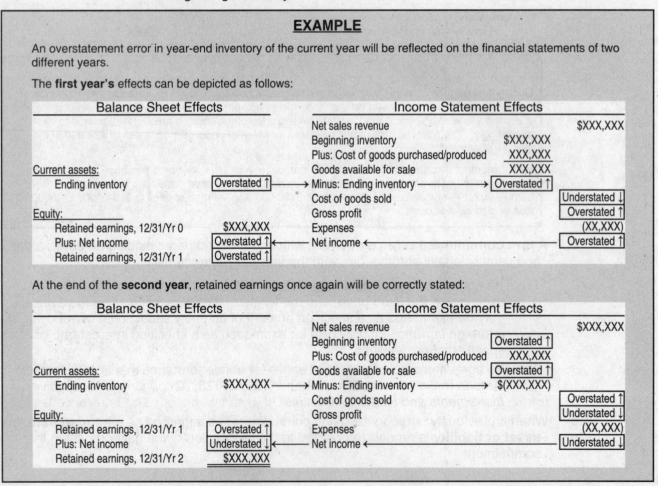

At the end of the **second year**, retained earnings once again will be correctly stated:

Stop and review! You have completed the outline for this subunit. Study multiple-choice questions 1 through 7 beginning on page 271.

7.2 COST ACCOUNTING FOR INVENTORY

Cost Basis

1. Inventory is primarily accounted for at cost, which is "the price paid or consideration given to acquire an asset. As applied to inventories, cost means in principle the sum of the applicable expenditures and charges directly or indirectly incurred in bringing an article to its existing condition and location" (ARB 43).

   a. Many considerations are involved in determining this acquisition and production cost, especially with regard to costing work-in-process and finished goods (SFAS 151, *Inventory Costs*).

      1) Thus, **variable overheads** are allocated based on actual usage of facilities, and **fixed overheads** are allocated based on **normal capacity** (the range of production expected over multiple periods under normal circumstances, including planned maintenance).

         a) When production is **abnormally high**, the per-unit allocation of fixed overhead must be reduced to avoid overstating inventory cost. But if production is **abnormally low** or if facilities are idle, the allocation to inventoriable cost is not increased.

         b) **Unallocated overheads** and **abnormal** freight, handling costs, spoilage, and similar items are expensed as incurred.

   b. **General and administrative expenses**, in most cases, should be classified as **period costs**, except for the portion clearly related to production.

   c. **Selling expenses** and **freight-out** are **not** part of inventory costs.

   d. Exclusion of all overheads from inventory is **not** acceptable.

Product Costs vs. Period Costs

2. Product (inventoriable) costs are incurred to produce or acquire units of inventory and are deferred to the extent they are not sold.

   a. Inventoriable costs are expensed in the period the product is sold.

      1) Product costs include direct materials, direct labor, and production overhead.
      2) The price and the other costs of acquisition, such as freight-in, are inventoried.

   b. Period costs are charged to expense as incurred and not to a particular product.

      1) Period costs are revenue expenditures or capital expenditures.

         a) **Revenue (income) expenditures**, e.g., advertising and officers' salaries, are expensed when incurred. They usually do not benefit future periods.

         b) **Capital expenditures**, e.g., depreciation, are initially recorded as assets and then expensed as they are consumed, used, or disposed of.

      2) A period cost cannot feasibly be related to acquisition or production of inventory. The costs of establishing the relationship would exceed the benefit.

   c. **Interest** is ordinarily not capitalized as part of inventory because its incurrence is relatively remote from the purchase or manufacture of products.

   d. **R&D** costs are customarily **not** inventoried.

Measurement of Purchases

3. Purchased inventory is measured at invoice cost.

   a. **Trade discounts** are usually subtracted prior to invoicing. They allow sellers to change prices without reprinting catalogs or to charge different prices to different customers.

      1) A **chain discount** applies more than one trade discount. The first discount is applied to the list price, the second to the resulting amount, etc.

   b. The buyer's **transportation costs** for purchased goods are inventoried.

      1) In a **perpetual system**, these costs can be assigned to specified purchases.

      2) In a **periodic system**, transportation costs are usually debited to transportation-in (freight-in). Ordinarily, this balance is closed to cost of goods sold (although allocation to cost of goods sold and ending inventory is preferable).

   c. In a periodic system, **purchase returns and allowances** are debited to accounts payable or a receivable and credited to a contra-asset. In a perpetual system, they are credited to inventory.

      1) A return is recognized for goods returned to the seller.

      2) Purchase returns and allowances is a nominal account closed at year-end.

   d. **Cash discounts** are offered to induce early payment and improve cash flow. Two methods of accounting for them are in general use.

      1) The **net method** is theoretically correct. It records the cash price at the date of sale.

         a) **Purchase discounts lost** (a financing expense) is debited when payment is not made within the discount period.

            i) This treatment applies in a periodic or perpetual system.

      2) The **gross method** ignores cash discounts. It is more popular than the net method because of its simplicity (no adjusting entries are needed).

         a) Discounts not taken are not recognized.

         b) If payment is made within the discount period, **purchase discounts** are credited in a periodic system. **Inventory** is credited in a perpetual system.

EXAMPLE

Inventory accounted for using the perpetual method is purchased with terms of 2/10, n/30 (2% discount within 10 days, entire balance due in 30 days).

	Gross Method		Net Method	
Inventory	$1,000		$980	
Accounts payable		$1,000		$980

Payment is made **within the discount period**.

	Gross Method		Net Method	
Accounts payable	$1,000		$980	
Cash		$980		$980
Inventory		20		

Payment is made **after the discount period**.

	Gross Method		Net Method	
Accounts payable	$1,000		$980	
Cash		$1,000		$980
Purchase discounts lost			$20	
Cash				$20

3) If a **periodic system** is used with the **gross method**, cost of goods sold is calculated as follows:

Goods available for sale:		
Beginning inventory	$XXX	
Purchases (net of trade discounts)	XXX	
Purchase discounts	(XXX)	
Purchase returns and allowances	(XXX)	
Transportation-in	XXX	$XXX
Ending inventory		(XXX)
Cost of goods sold		$XXX

Stop and review! You have completed the outline for this subunit. Study multiple-choice questions 8 through 11 beginning on page 273.

7.3 COST FLOWS -- AVERAGE COST, FIFO, AND LIFO

Cash Flow Assumptions

1. The assumption selected should be the one that most clearly reflects periodic income.

2. **Specific identification** requires determining which specific items are sold and thus reflects the actual physical flow of goods. It can be used for blocks of investment securities or special inventory items, such as automobiles or heavy equipment.

   a. This method permits manipulation of income. More (less) costly inventory could be sold if profit is to be decreased (increased).

   b. A second theoretical problem arises when an allocation, e.g., of transportation-in, storage costs, and discounts, must be made to inventory. An exact matching of cost and revenue may not be possible.

   c. A practical weakness of specific identification is the need for detailed records.

3. **Average cost.** The assumption in an average cost system is that goods are indistinguishable and are therefore measured at an average of the costs incurred.

   a. The **moving-average** method requires determination of a new weighted-average cost after each purchase and thus is used only in a **perpetual system**.

EXAMPLE

A new average cost is calculated after each purchase. This cost is used for every sale until the next purchase and recalculation.

	Units	Times: Price	Equals: Additions	Equals: Reductions	Inventory Balance	Divided By: Total Units	Equals: Per Unit Cost
Mar. 31 inventory	1,000	$12.50	$12,500		$12,500	1,000	$12.50
Apr. 14 purchase	2,000	12.20	24,400		36,900	3,000	12.30
Apr. 20 sale	(1,800)	12.30		$(22,140)	14,760	1,200	12.30
Apr. 24 purchase	3,200	12.60	40,320		55,080	4,400	12.52
Apr. 28 sale	(800)	12.52		(10,015)	45,065	3,600	12.52
Total available			$77,220				

Cost of goods sold is calculated as follows:

Goods available for sale	$77,220
Minus: ending inventory	(45,065)
Cost of goods sold	**$32,155**

---

b. The **weighted-average** method determines an average cost only once (at the end of the period) and is therefore applicable in a **periodic system**.

1) It may be used in a perpetual system that records only inventory quantities.

EXAMPLE

Because perpetual records are not kept, purchases and sales for the period are aggregated.

	Units	Times: Price	Equals:
Mar. 31 inventory	1,000	$12.50	$12,500
Apr. 14 purchase	2,000	12.20	24,400
Apr. 24 purchase	3,200	12.60	40,320
Total available	6,200		$77,220
Apr. 20 sale	(1,800)		
Apr. 28 sale	(800)		
Ending inventory	3,600		

A single per-unit cost is calculated for the entire period.

Average per unit cost = $77,220 ÷ 6,200 = $12.4548

Cost of goods sold can then be calculated.

Goods available for sale	$77,220
Minus: ending inventory (3,600 units × $12.4548)	(44,837)
Cost of goods sold	**$32,383**

---

4. **First-in, first-out (FIFO).** This method assumes that the first goods purchased are the first sold. Thus, ending inventory consists of the latest purchases.

a. **Cost of goods sold** includes goods purchased at the beginning of the current period and in prior periods.

b. Ending inventory is measured at the cost of the latest purchases.

c. The measurement will be the same regardless of whether the inventory is recorded at the end of the period (a periodic system) or on a perpetual basis.

EXAMPLE

	Units	Times: Price	Equals: Purchases		Inventory Consists of: Units	Per Unit Cost	Balance
Mar. 31 inventory	1,000	$12.50	$12,500	Beg. layer	1,000	$12.50	$12,500
				Beg. layer	1,000	12.50	12,500
Apr. 14 purchase	2,000	12.20	24,400	Apr. 14 layer	2,000	12.20	24,400
				Inventory bal.	3,000		$36,900
Apr. 20 sale	(1,800)			Beg. layer	0	12.50	0
From Mar. 31 layer	1,000			Apr. 14 layer	1,200	12.20	14,640
From Apr. 14 layer	800			Inventory bal.	1,200		$14,640
				Apr. 14 layer	1,200	12.20	$14,640
Apr. 24 purchase	3,200	12.60	40,320	Apr. 24 layer	3,200	12.60	40,320
				Inventory bal.	4,400		$54,960
Apr. 28 sale	(800)			Apr. 14 layer	400	12.20	$ 4,880
From Apr. 14 layer	800			Apr. 24 layer	3,200	12.60	40,320
From Apr. 24 layer	0			Inventory bal.	3,600		$45,200
Total available			$77,220				

Cost of goods sold is calculated as follows:

Goods available for sale	$77,220
Minus: ending inventory	(45,200)
Cost of goods sold	**$32,020**

d. Advantages and disadvantages of FIFO

   1) One advantage is that FIFO somewhat approximates the specific identification method's matching of cost flow and physical flow.

      a) A disadvantage for the reporting entity is that it does not have the same potential for manipulation.

   2) Another advantage is that ending inventory approximates current replacement cost.

      a) A disadvantage is that current revenues are matched with older costs.

5.   **Last-in, first-out (LIFO).** This method expenses the latest purchases first.

    a.   **LIFO Fundamentals**

        1)   In a time of inflation, this method results in the highest cost of goods sold.

            a)   LIFO reduces income, defers income tax, and improves cash flow, thereby **reducing net income and tax liability**.

            b)   It also defers or avoids the recognition of holding gains or losses arising from specific price changes.

        2)   If fewer units are purchased than sold,

            a)   The beginning inventory is partially or fully liquidated,

            b)   Old costs are matched against current revenues in the year's income statement, and

            c)   LIFO income will usually exceed that for FIFO or average cost (assuming rising prices).

        3)   Another consequence is that management can affect net income with an end-of-period purchase that immediately alters cost of goods sold.

            a)   A last-minute FIFO purchase included in the ending inventory has no such effect.

        4)   Increasing inventory results in the creation of **LIFO layers**. Whenever sales exceed purchases, older layers are partially or fully liquidated.

            a)   Management can manipulate earnings through inventory purchases.

    b.   **Periodic vs. perpetual.** LIFO cost of goods sold varies with the system chosen.

        1)   In a periodic system, a purchases account is used, and the beginning inventory remains unchanged during the accounting period.

            a)   At year-end, cost of goods sold equals goods available for sale (beginning inventory + purchases) minus ending inventory.

            b)   Cost of goods sold is determined only at year-end.

        2)   In a perpetual system, purchases are directly recorded in the inventory account, and cost of goods sold is determined as the goods are sold.

    c.   **Initial Adoption**

        1)   Unless an entity applies LIFO when it begins operations, initial adoption requires a **change in accounting principle**. With certain exceptions, the new principle is retrospectively applied to all prior periods. Only the **direct effects** of the change are included in the adjustments (SFAS 154, *Accounting Changes and Error Corrections*). See Study Unit 3.

        2)   LIFO inventory measurements often cannot be determined retrospectively. Information about the composition of inventory throughout the history of the entity and all unit prices usually cannot be reconstructed.

    d.   **LIFO conformity rule.** An IRS regulation requires LIFO to be used for financial reporting if it is used in the tax return.

        1)   LIFO must be used to report "income, profit, or loss" in the income statement. It need not be used to report inventory amounts in the balance sheet if a **LIFO valuation allowance** is shown.

        2)   Entities may make supplemental disclosures about net income computed on a basis other than LIFO, but not on the income statement.

e.   **LIFO Layers and Pools**

	EXAMPLE		
	Units	Times: Price	Equals: Extended
Year 5 layer	1,600	$74.25	$118,800
Year 4 layer	1,500	59.40	89,100
Year 3 layer	1,350	49.50	66,825
Year 2 layer	1,200	45.00	54,000
Year 1 (base) layer	1,000	40.00	40,000
Year 6 beg. inventory	6,650		$368,725

1)   **LIFO liquidation.** When sales exceed purchases or production, older layers are reduced.

a)   Distortions in net income can result from matching current revenues against the older, lower costs.

b)   To offset LIFO liquidation (and simplify the accounting), an entity may treat substantially identical items of inventory as a single accounting unit called a **pool**. See Subunit 7.4.

f.   **LIFO allowance.** Entities may use another basis internally.

1)   To adjust the inventory to LIFO, an allowance, sometimes called the **LIFO reserve**, is created. This account is contra to inventory. It is the difference between

a)   Lower of LIFO cost or market and

b)   Replacement cost **or** the lower of

i)   Cost determined under an acceptable method (e.g., FIFO) or

ii)   Market.

2)   The accounting profession disapproves of the term "reserve" because no reserve is actually created.

3)   At period end, this allowance is adjusted to reflect the difference between LIFO and the internal costing method.

Cost of goods sold	$XXX
Allowance to reduce inventory to LIFO	$XXX

g.   **LIFO and Interim Reporting**

1)   Interim accounting ordinarily should be based on the principles used in preparing annual statements.

2)   Certain principles and practices used for annual reporting, however, may require modification at interim dates so interim reports may relate more closely to the results of operations for the annual period.

a)   A **temporary LIFO liquidation** need not be given effect in the interim statements.

i)   The cost of goods sold for the interim period should include the expected cost of replacement of the liquidated base.

ii)   The entry to record cost of goods sold is

Cost of goods sold (replacement cost)	$XXX
Inventory (liquidated layer)	$XXX
Liability	XXX

•   This liability does not appear in the annual statements because, by year-end, the true inventory position will be known.

3) Another difficulty of reporting on the LIFO basis at interim dates is that the year-end LIFO allowance must be estimated.

    a) The annual adjustment necessary to reach that balance must be allocated to the interim period being reported on.

h. **LIFO Periodic**

EXAMPLE

Goods available for sale for the period is calculated:

	Units	Times: Price	Equals: Purchases
Mar. 31 inventory	1,000	$12.50	$12,500
Apr. 14 purchase	2,000	12.20	24,400
Apr. 24 purchase	3,200	12.60	40,320
Total available	6,200		$77,220

The period's unit sales are determined:

Apr. 20 sale	(1,800)
Apr. 28 sale	(800)
Sales for month	(2,600)

Sales are removed from the various layers:

	Units in Layer	Units Sold	End. Units	Per-Unit Cost	Balance
Apr. 24 layer	3,200	(2,600)	600	$12.60	$ 7,560
Apr. 14 layer	2,000	0	2,000	12.20	24,400
Mar. 31 layer	1,000	0	1,000	12.50	12,500
Totals	6,200	(2,600)	3,600		$44,460

Cost of goods sold is calculated as follows:

Goods available for sale	$77,220
Minus: ending inventory	(44,460)
Cost of goods sold	**$32,760**

---

i. **LIFO Perpetual**

EXAMPLE

	Times:	Equals:		Inventory Consists of:		
	Units	Price	Purchases		Units	Per-Unit Cost	Balance
Mar. 31 inventory	1,000	$12.50	$12,500	Beg. layer	1,000	$12.50	$12,500
				Beg. layer	1,000	12.50	$12,500
Apr. 14 purchase	2,000	12.20	24,400	Apr. 14 layer	2,000	12.20	24,400
				Inventory bal.	3,000		$36,900
Apr. 20 sale	(1,800)			Beg. layer	1,000	12.50	$12,500
From Mar. 31 layer	0			Apr. 14 layer	200	12.20	2,440
From Apr. 14 layer	1,800			Inventory bal.	1,200		$14,940
				Beg. layer	1,000	12.50	$12,500
				Apr. 14 layer	200	12.20	2,440
Apr. 24 purchase	3,200	12.60	40,320	Apr. 24 layer	3,200	12.60	40,320
				Inventory bal.	4,400		$55,260
Apr. 28 sale	(800)						
From Mar. 31 layer	0			Beg. layer	1,000	12.50	$12,500
From Apr. 14 layer	0			Apr. 14 layer	200	12.20	2,440
From Apr. 24 layer	800			Apr. 24 layer	2,400	12.60	30,240
				Inventory bal.	3,600		$45,180
Total available			$77,220				

Cost of goods sold is calculated as follows:

Goods available for sale	$77,220
Minus: ending inventory	(45,180)
Cost of goods sold	**$32,040**

j. A **comparison** of the results of the five methods other than specific identification reveals that ending inventory and cost of goods sold vary:

	Goods Available for Sale	Ending Inventory	Cost of Goods Sold
Weighted average	$77,220	$(44,837)	$32,383
Moving average	77,220	(45,065)	32,155
FIFO	77,220	(45,200)	32,020
LIFO periodic	77,220	(44,460)	32,760
LIFO perpetual	77,220	(45,180)	32,040

Stop and review! You have completed the outline for this subunit. Study multiple-choice questions 12 through 16 beginning on page 274.

7.4 DOLLAR-VALUE LIFO

Pools of Specific Goods

1. The previous discussion of LIFO has assumed that the method is applied to specific units of inventory with specific unit costs.

    a. However, LIFO may be applied to **groups (pools)** of inventory items that are substantially identical.

2. Record keeping is simplified because all goods in a beginning inventory pool are presumed to have been acquired on the same date and at the same cost.

    a. Using the pooling method, **beginning inventory** is costed at a weighted-average unit price (total cost ÷ unit quantity).

    b. Usually, **purchases** of goods in a pool also are recorded at a weighted-average cost (total cost ÷ unit quantity).

        1) If the quantity of units in the pool increases during the year, a **new LIFO layer** will be formed at the new weighted-average cost.

    c. Because a pool consists of more than one kind of item, erosion of LIFO layers is less likely than if the specific-goods approach is used.

        1) An increase in the quantity of one item may offset a decrease of another item.

3. The disadvantage of pooling specific goods is that the pools may need to be **redefined**.

    a. If an entity discontinues sales of one product and adds another, inventory pools may change if the new product is **not substantially identical**. The result may be the liquidation of base layers of inventory.

Dollar-Value LIFO

4. Because dollar-value pools may embrace more goods, dollar-value LIFO avoids the cost and inconvenience of redefining pools of specific goods and reduces the likelihood of a LIFO liquidation.

    a. It also eliminates much of the detailed record keeping associated with other methods.

5. Dollar-value LIFO accumulates inventoriable costs of **similar (not identical) items**. These items should be similar in the sense of (a) being interchangeable, (b) having similar uses, (c) belonging to the same product line, or (d) constituting the raw materials for a given product.

    a. Changes in inventory are measured in terms of dollars of **constant purchasing power** rather than units of physical inventory. This calculation uses a **specific price index** for each year.

        1) The **ending inventory** is stated at current (year-end acquisition) costs and is then **deflated** by the current-year index to base-year cost.

            a) This amount is then compared with the **beginning inventory** stated at base-year cost to determine what layers are to be in the ending inventory based on a LIFO flow assumption.

            b) Each layer is then **inflated** (weighted) by the price index applicable to the year in which the layer was added. The result is the aggregate ending inventory valuation.

6. **Price Indexes**

    a. The indexes used may be determined in various ways.

        1) Internal indexes may be calculated by the entity itself, for example, using the double-extension method.

2) The U.S. government prepares **external indexes**. For example, the Consumer Price Index for All Urban Consumers and the Producer Price Index.

3) Trade associations also prepare indexes.

b. **Double-Extension Method**

1) Under this method, the quantity of each item in the inventory pool at the close of the year is multiplied twice, once by the **base-year unit cost** and once by the **current-year unit cost**. The respective extensions at the two costs are then each totaled.

a) The first total gives the amount of the current inventory at base-year cost, and the second total gives the amount of such inventory at current-year cost.

2) The index computed under the double-extension method is simply the **ratio** of the **total current-year cost** of the ending inventory pool to the **total base-year cost**. The **LIFO layer for the year** at **base-year cost** is multiplied by this ratio to determine the LIFO inventory.

3) A base-year unit cost must be found for each item entering a pool for the first time subsequent to the beginning of the base year. In such a case, the base-year unit cost is the current-year cost unless the entity can reconstruct or otherwise establish a different cost.

EXAMPLE

Each period's ending inventory is restated at its equivalent base-year amount (Year 1 is the base year). The effects of inflation have been exaggerated for clarity.

	At End-of-Year Price	Divided by: Price Index	At Base-Year Amount
Year 1 ending inventory	$300,000	1.00	$300,000
Year 2 ending inventory	$374,000	1.10	$340,000
Year 3 ending inventory	$384,000	1.20	$320,000
Year 4 ending inventory	$455,000	1.30	$350,000

The LIFO cost basis is determined for each year's component of the ending balances.

Year 1 Calculation:	At Base-Year Price	Times: Price Index	At LIFO Cost
Year 1 layer	$300,000	1.00	$300,000
Year 1 ending inventory	$300,000		$300,000

Year 2 Calculation:	At Base-Year Price	Times: Price Index	At LIFO Cost
Year 1 layer	$300,000	1.00	$300,000
Year 2 layer	40,000	1.10	44,000
Year 2 ending inventory	$340,000		$344,000

In any year when the balance declines, a portion of the most recent year's layer must be removed and cannot be replaced.

Year 3 Calculation:	At Base-Year Price	Times: Price Index	At LIFO Cost
Year 1 layer	$300,000	1.00	$300,000
Year 2 layer	20,000	1.10	22,000
Year 3 ending inventory	$320,000		$322,000

Year 4 Calculation:	At Base-Year Price	Times: Price Index	At LIFO Cost
Year 1 layer	$300,000	1.00	$300,000
Year 2 layer	20,000	1.10	22,000
Year 4 layer	30,000	1.30	39,000
Year 4 ending inventory	$350,000		$361,000

7.   **Dollar-value LIFO retail.** This variant is discussed later in this study unit.

Stop and review! You have completed the outline for this subunit. Study multiple-choice questions 17 through 20 beginning on page 276.

7.5 LOWER OF COST OR MARKET (LCM)

Statement of Rule

1.   Inventory must be written down to market subsequent to acquisition if its utility is no longer as great as its cost.

   a.   The difference should be recognized as a **loss** of the current period.

      1)   Thus, a loss should be recognized whenever the utility of goods is impaired by damage, deterioration, obsolescence, changes in price levels, changes in demand, style changes, or other causes.

   b.   But the LCM rule is applicable only to goods that will be sold in the **ordinary course of business**.

      1)   Damaged or deteriorated goods are usually carried at net realizable value in a separate account.

Market

2.   Market is the current cost to replace inventory, subject to certain limitations.

   a.   Market should not exceed a **ceiling** equal to **net realizable value (NRV)**. This is the **estimated selling price** in the ordinary course of business minus reasonably predictable **costs of completion and disposal**.

      1)   **Replacement cost** does not accurately measure utility if it exceeds NRV. In that case, the NRV more appropriately measures utility.

         a)   Reporting inventory above NRV overstates its utility and will result in a loss at the time of sale.

   b.   Market should not be less than a **floor** equal to NRV reduced by an allowance for an approximately **normal profit margin**.

      1)   If the inventory were written down to a replacement cost below this amount, an abnormal profit margin (NRV – normal profit – replacement cost) would be included in revenue at the time of sale.

      2)   If cost will be recovered with an approximately normal profit upon sale in the ordinary course of business, **no loss** should be recognized even though replacement or production costs are lower.

   c.   Thus, current replacement cost (CRC) is not to be greater than NRV or less than NRV minus a normal profit (NRV – P).

MARKET (M)

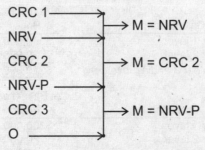

Applying LCM

3. Depending on the character and composition of the inventory, the LCM rule may be applied either directly to **each item** or to the **aggregate total** of the inventory (or, in some cases, to the total of the components of each major category).

    a. The method should be the one that most clearly reflects periodic income.

    b. Once inventory is written down, the reduced amount is the **new cost basis**, and a write-up ordinarily will not be permitted if prices increase.

4. LCM by item always will be equal to or less than the other LCM measurements, and LCM in total always will be equal to or greater than the other LCM measurements.

5. Most entities use LCM by item. This method is required for **tax purposes**.

    a. If **dollar-value LIFO** is used, LCM should be applied to pools of items.

    b. An entity may not use LCM with LIFO for tax purposes.

EXAMPLE

Replacement cost	$22
Cost	23
Selling price	38
Disposal (selling) costs	4
Normal profit	15

Market is the replacement cost of $22 subject to a ceiling of NRV ($38 selling price – $4 disposal costs = $34) and a floor of NRV minus normal profit ($34 – $15 = $19). Because replacement cost of $22 is within this range ($34 to $19), it equals market. Market is therefore lower than the $23 cost, and LCM is $22.

EXAMPLE

	Historical Cost	Replacement Cost	NRV	NRV – Normal Profit	Market	LCM
Dowel screws	**$12.45**	$13.60	$14.40	$14.00	$14.00	$12.45
Drywall screws	15.15	12.00	**11.55**	11.35	**11.55**	11.55
Machine screws	16.00	**14.10**	15.00	13.80	**14.10**	14.10
Metal screws	10.30	**8.75**	9.20	8.45	**8.75**	8.75
Wood screws	8.90	**7.85**	8.20	7.65	**7.85**	7.85

Recording LCM

6. **Direct reduction.** If inventory is written down to market, the unrealized holding loss can be directly credited to inventory and debited to cost of goods sold.

    a. This method has the theoretical drawback of debiting a holding loss to an account that includes the costs of selling goods.

    b. Also, inventory will be presented at LCM rather than at cost net of write-downs.

7. **Allowance method.** Debiting a holding loss and crediting an allowance (contra asset) is preferred.

    a. The unit costs in the subsidiary ledger need not be changed to agree with the control account.

LCM at Interim Dates

8. **Nontemporary** market declines are recognized in the interim periods when they occur.

    a. **Recoveries** of these losses on the same inventory later in the fiscal year are recognized as gains (but only to the extent of the previously recognized losses).

    b. If market declines can reasonably be expected to be restored by year-end, they are not recognized.

Stop and review! You have completed the outline for this subunit. Study multiple-choice questions 21 through 24 beginning on page 277.

7.6   ESTIMATING INVENTORY

Gross Profit Method (GPM)

1. The estimated GPM is used to determine inventory for **interim statements**. Adequate **disclosure** is required of (a) the method used and (b) any significant adjustments that result from reconciliations with the annual physical inventory at year-end.

2. Because of its imprecision, GAAP and federal tax law do **not** permit use of the GPM at **year-end**. But other applications are possible.

    a. If inventory is destroyed, the method may be used to estimate the loss.

    b. External auditors apply the GPM as an analytical procedure to determine the fairness of the ending inventory balance.

    c. The method may be used internally to generate estimates of inventory throughout the year, e.g., as a verification of perpetual records.

3. The GPM calculates ending inventory at a given time by subtracting an **estimated cost of goods sold** from the sum of beginning inventory and purchases (or cost of goods manufactured).

    a. The estimated cost of goods sold equals sales minus the gross profit.

        1) The gross profit equals sales multiplied by the gross profit percentage, an amount ordinarily computed on a historical basis.

> ### EXAMPLE
>
> | | | |
> |---|---:|---:|
> | Beginning inventory | | $60,000 |
> | Purchases | | 20,000 |
> | Goods available for sale | | $80,000 |
> | Sales (at selling price) | $50,000 | |
> | Gross profit (20% of sales) | (10,000) | |
> | Sales (at cost) | | 40,000 |
> | Approximate inventory at cost | | $40,000 |

        2) A simple way to apply this method is to prepare the cost of goods sold section of an income statement and solve algebraically for the amounts not known.

Retail Method

4. Some entities, such as major retailers, have a high volume of transactions in relatively low-cost merchandise. They often use the retail method because it is applied to the dollar amounts of goods, not quantities. The result is easier and less expensive estimates of **ending inventory and cost of goods sold**.

    a. Records of the **beginning inventory** and **net purchases** are maintained at both cost and retail. Sales at retail and any other appropriate items are subtracted from goods available for sale at retail (the sum of beginning inventory and net purchases at retail) to provide ending inventory at retail.

1) This amount is adjusted to determine estimated ending inventory at cost using a **cost-retail ratio**.

	Cost	Retail
Beginning inventory (known)	$XX,XXX	$XX,XXX
Add: Purchases (known)	XX,XXX	XX,XXX
Goods available for sale (GAS)	$XX,XXX	$XX,XXX
Sales (at retail)		(XX,XXX)
Ending inventory at retail		$XX,XXX

Cost-retail ratio = GAS at cost ÷ GAS at retail

Ending inventory at cost = ending inventory at retail × cost-retail ratio

5. The following **records** must be available to implement the retail method:

   a. Beginning inventory at cost and retail
   b. Purchases at cost and retail
   c. Markups, markdowns, cancelations, and employee discounts
   d. Other adjustments, such as sales returns and allowances; transportation-in (freight-in); purchase discounts; purchase returns and allowances; and losses on damaged, stolen, obsolete, or deteriorated goods
   e. Sales

6. **Uses** of the retail inventory method:

   a. Interim and annual financial reporting in accordance with GAAP
   b. Federal income tax reporting
   c. Verifying year-end inventory and cost of goods sold data, e.g., as an analytical procedure by an independent auditor
   d. Simplifying the physical count at year-end

      1) Goods may be marked with sales prices only, and time is saved by not referring to specific purchase records.

   e. Estimating inventory to determine insurance settlements after a casualty

7. Retail Terminology

   a. Markup: an increase in the original retail price
   b. Net markup: additional markups minus markup cancelations
   c. Markdown: amount subtracted from original retail price
   d. Net markdown: markdowns minus markdown cancelations

Other Factors in Applying the Retail Method

8. The various retail inventory methods make different adjustments to determine the ending inventory.

   a. **Transportation-in (freight-in)** is an addition to the **cost** of purchases but does not directly affect the retail measure used in the calculation.

      1) Initial sales prices consider these costs. An addition to the retail measure would therefore overstate goods available at retail.

   b. **Purchase allowances** are price reductions agreed to by a supplier because goods are nonconforming, e.g., as a result of slight damage incurred in shipment.

      1) Purchase allowances are subtracted from purchases stated at **cost** but not at retail. The reasons for the allowances ordinarily are considered in setting initial retail prices.

c. **Purchase discounts** taken are recognized when purchases are recorded at gross amounts, and early payment is made to take advantage of cash discounts.

   1) These reduce **cost** of purchases but ordinarily do not affect purchases at retail.

d. **Purchase returns** require reductions of the **cost and retail** measures of purchases. They decrease goods available for sale.

e. **Sales returns and allowances** decrease gross sales, which in turn reduce goods available at retail.

f. **Sales discounts** offered for early payment ordinarily are not subtracted from gross sales for retail inventory method purposes.

   1) The reason is that sales discounts taken by customers are a **financing expense** incurred to obtain early payment, not an adjustment of the original markup.

      a) Sales discounts are subtracted from gross sales on the income statement.

g. **Employee and special customer discounts** are subtracted from goods available for sale at **retail** after the cost-retail ratio is calculated.

   1) These discounts do not reflect declines in fair value and thus differ from markdowns.

h. **Normal shortage** (spoilage, breakage, etc.) is anticipated in setting retail prices.

   1) Hence, it is **not** considered in the calculation of the cost-retail ratio.

   2) However, normal shortage reduces goods available for sale. It is therefore subtracted from the **retail** measure in the same manner as sales.

i. **Abnormal shortage** (spoilage, breakage, etc.) is neither a cost of the good units nor anticipated in setting retail prices.

   1) It decreases **cost and retail** in arriving at goods available for sale. This treatment is justified because

      a) The goods are not available for sale.

      b) The cost-retail ratio will not reflect the normal relationship if the costs and prices of abnormal shortage are included in its computation.

j. **Transferred-in goods** from other departments are treated as if they were purchases.

Specific Cost Flow Techniques

9. **FIFO cost** is the most straightforward of the retail inventory methods.

   a. The cost-retail ratio is computed for **adjusted purchases**, not goods available for sale. Ending inventory is assumed to include only goods from **current purchases**. Beginning inventory is assumed to be sold first.

      1) To approximate cost, net markups are added to and net markdowns are subtracted from purchases at retail to determine the ratio.

      2) **Cost-retail ratio:** (cost measure of net purchases) ÷ (retail measures of net purchases + net markups – net markdowns).

10. **FIFO** also may be applied to approximate **lower of cost or market**.

   a. By including net markups but not net markdowns in adjusted purchases at retail, a lower cost-retail ratio is derived. Excluding markdowns results in a greater denominator.

   b. Because markdowns reflect a decline in the utility of goods, they should be treated as if they were losses in the current period.

      1) The lower ratio used in the LCM calculation gives a lower inventory cost which effectively includes the loss.

      2) **Cost-retail ratio:** (cost measure of net purchases) ÷ (retail measures of net purchases + net markups)

11. **Average cost** is a straightforward method.

    a.   The only difference between average cost and FIFO cost is that the cost-retail ratio for average cost is based on **goods available for sale** (beginning inventory + purchases), not adjusted purchases.

        1)   The assumption is that beginning inventory and purchases have been combined and are indistinguishable for purposes of determining cost of goods sold and ending inventory.

        2)   **Cost-retail ratio:** (cost measures of beginning inventory + net purchases) ÷ (retail measures of beginning inventory + net purchases + net markups – net markdowns)

12. **LACM (lower of average cost market)** is a popular method also known as the conventional retail inventory method.

    a.   LACM uses the LCM feature (inclusion of markups but not markdowns in the cost-retail ratio). However, it also achieves the weighted-average effect by including the beginning inventories at cost and retail in the ratio.

        1)   **Cost-retail ratio:** (cost measures of beginning inventory + net purchases) ÷ (retail measures of beginning inventory + net purchases + net markups)

13. Many entities use **LIFO retail** to obtain tax benefits as well as to match current costs with current revenues.

    a.   The computation begins in the same way as **FIFO cost**.

        1)   **Beginning inventory is excluded** from the cost-retail ratio. The current-year ratio is applied only to the layer of inventory added in that year.

            a)   However, LIFO retail varies from FIFO cost because a different ratio is used for **each annual layer**. Thus, only adjusted purchases at cost and retail are used to determine the year's ratio.

            b)   **LCM** may **not** be used in any of the LIFO retail methods. Net markups and markdowns are considered in computing the ratio.

            c)   **Cost-retail ratio:** (cost measure of net purchases) ÷ (retail measures of net purchases + net markups – net markdowns)

    b.   LIFO retail in this form also assumes **no adjustment** for changes in the unit of measure. The general price level is assumed to be stable, and any increase in the dollar measure of inventory is attributable to an increase in quantity.

14. The **dollar-value LIFO retail** variant of the retail inventory method is essentially the dollar-value LIFO method with an adjustment from retail to cost.

    a.   Dollar-value LIFO retail is a **cost** (not an average-cost or LCM) method.

        1)   It excludes beginning inventory from, but includes net markups and markdowns in, the calculation of the cost-retail ratio.

    b.   The key feature is that **inventory layers** are adjusted for **changes in price levels** to determine whether actual changes in quantities have occurred.

        1)   Ending inventory at retail is divided by the **current year's price index** for restatement at **base-date prices**.

            a)   This computation reveals whether a new layer has been added or an old layer(s) has been wholly or partially eliminated.

            b)   The index may be a quotient of price indexes. For example, the base-date price index might be 1.25 and the current-date price index 1.50, yielding an index (or conversion factor) of 1.20 (1.50 ÷ 1.25).

2) Each layer stated at retail in base-date prices is **inflated** to the price level in effect when it was added. It is multiplied by the price index in effect for that year.

3) The final step is to multiply each layer by the cost-retail ratio for the year it was added, which reduces it to an estimate of cost.

EXAMPLE

	Cost	Retail	Cost Ratio
Beginning inventory	$12,000	$ 16,800	$12,000 ÷ $ 16,800 = 71.43%
Purchases	70,000	100,000	$70,000 ÷ $100,000 = 70%
Sales		90,000	
Ending inventory		$ 26,800	

The beginning price index was 100%. The year-end index is 134%.

The year-end inventory at base-date prices is $20,000 ($26,800 ÷ 1.34).

The increment is $3,200 ($20,000 – $16,800).

Each layer is inflated to the relevant price level, retail prices are converted to cost, and the layers are added.

$16,800 × 1.00 (price index) × 71.43% (cost ratio) = $12,000.24
$3,200 × 1.34 (price index) × 70.00% (cost ratio) =   3,001.60
$15,001.84

COMPARATIVE EXAMPLE

	Cost	Retail
Beginning inventory	$ 90,000	$130,000
Purchases	330,000	460,000
Markups		10,000
Markdowns		40,000
Sales		480,000

Ending inventory at retail is $80,000 ($130,000 + $460,000 + $10,000 – $40,000 – $480,000).

The cost-retail ratio for the **average cost** retail method is $420,000 ÷ $560,000. Markups and markdowns are included in goods available at retail.

The cost-retail ratio for the **FIFO cost** retail method is $330,000 ÷ $430,000. The assumptions are that (1) all markups and markdowns applied to goods purchased this period, and (2) all inventory is from current-period purchases.

The cost-retail ratio for the **LACM** retail method is $420,000 ÷ $600,000. Markups, but not markdowns, are included in goods available at retail. This method is typically used if LIFO is not used.

The cost-retail ratio for the **LIFO** retail method (given stable prices) is $90,000 ÷ $130,000 (the prior year's ratio) because ending inventory of $80,000 retail is less than beginning inventory of $130,000. If an increase in inventory had occurred, the increment would be measured using a cost-retail ratio of $330,000 ÷ $430,000.

Stop and review! You have completed the outline for this subunit. Study multiple-choice questions 25 through 29 beginning on page 279.

QUESTIONS

7.1 Inventory Fundamentals

1. In a periodic inventory system that uses the weighted-average cost flow method, the beginning inventory is the

A. Net purchases minus the ending inventory.

B. Net purchases minus the cost of goods sold.

C. Total goods available for sale minus the net purchases.

D. Total goods available for sale minus the cost of goods sold.

Answer (C) is correct. *(CPA, adapted)*
REQUIRED: The beginning inventory in a periodic system using weighted average cost.
DISCUSSION: In a periodic inventory system, the beginning inventory is equal to the total goods available for sale minus the net purchases, regardless of the cost flow method used.
Answer (A) is incorrect because it states the difference between the beginning inventory and the cost of goods sold. Answer (B) is incorrect because this difference is the change in inventory valuation during the period. Answer (D) is incorrect because goods available minus cost of sales equals ending inventory.

2. Jel Co., a consignee, paid the freight costs for goods shipped from Dale Co., a consignor. These freight costs are to be deducted from Jel's payment to Dale when the consignment goods are sold. Until Jel sells the goods, the freight costs should be included in Jel's

A. Cost of goods sold.

B. Freight-out costs.

C. Selling expenses.

D. Accounts receivable.

Answer (D) is correct. *(CPA, adapted)*
REQUIRED: The consignee's classification of freight costs paid by the consignee on behalf of the consignor.
DISCUSSION: The consignee should debit consignment-in for the freight costs. Consignment-in is a receivable/payable account used by consignees. It represents the amount payable to the consignor if it has a credit balance. If it has a debit balance, it reflects the amount receivable from the consignor. Before consigned goods are sold, expenditures chargeable to the consignor are recorded in the consignment-in account as a receivable. After the consigned goods are sold, the consignee's net liability to the consignor is reflected in the account.

3. Mare Co.'s December 31 balance sheet reported the following current assets:

Cash	$ 70,000
Accounts receivable	120,000
Inventories	60,000
Total	$250,000

An analysis of the accounts disclosed that accounts receivable consisted of the following:

Trade accounts	$ 96,000
Allowance for uncollectible accounts	(2,000)
Selling price of Mare's unsold goods out on consignment, at 130% of cost, not included in Mare's ending inventory	26,000
Total	$120,000

At December 31, the total of Mare's current assets is

A. $224,000

B. $230,000

C. $244,000

D. $270,000

Answer (C) is correct. *(CPA, adapted)*
REQUIRED: The amount of total current assets to be reported at year-end.
DISCUSSION: Under a consignment sales agreement, the goods are in the physical possession of the consignee but remain the property of the consignor and are included in the consignor's inventory. Thus, unsold consigned goods should be included in inventory at cost ($26,000 ÷ 130% = $20,000), not in receivables at their sale price. Current assets should therefore be $244,000 ($70,000 cash + $94,000 net receivables + $80,000 inventory).
Answer (A) is incorrect because $224,000 does not include the cost of the consigned goods in inventory. Answer (B) is incorrect because $230,000 results from subtracting the cost of the consigned goods from the total reported current assets. Answer (D) is incorrect because $270,000 results from adding the cost of the consigned goods to the total reported current assets.

4. The following information pertained to Azur Co. for the year:

Purchases	$102,800
Purchase discounts	10,280
Freight-in	15,420
Freight-out	5,140
Beginning inventory	30,840
Ending inventory	20,560

What amount should Azur report as cost of goods sold for the year?

A. $102,800

B. $118,220

C. $123,360

D. $128,500

Answer (B) is correct. *(CPA, adapted)*
REQUIRED: The cost of goods sold reported for the year.
DISCUSSION: Cost of goods sold equals beginning inventory, plus net purchases, plus freight-in, minus ending inventory. Freight-out is a cost of selling the goods rather than a cost of acquiring the goods. Thus, cost of goods sold is $118,220 [$30,840 + ($102,800 − $10,280) + $15,420 − $20,560].
Answer (A) is incorrect because $102,800 is the amount of gross purchases. Answer (C) is incorrect because $123,360 treats freight-out as a cost of goods sold. Answer (D) is incorrect because $128,500 omits purchase discounts from the calculation.

5. During Year 4, R Corp., a manufacturer of chocolate candies, contracted to purchase 100,000 pounds of cocoa beans at $1.00 per pound, delivery to be made in the spring of Year 5. Because a record harvest is predicted for Year 5, the price per pound for cocoa beans had fallen to $.80 by December 31, Year 4. Of the following journal entries, the one that would properly reflect in Year 4 the effect of the commitment of R Corp. to purchase the 100,000 pounds of cocoa is

A. Cocoa inventory $100,000
        Accounts payable $100,000

B. Cocoa inventory $80,000
    Loss on purchase
        commitments $20,000
        Accounts payable $100,000

C. Loss on purchase
        commitments $20,000
        Accrued loss on
          purchase
          commitments $20,000

D. No entry is necessary in Year 4.

Answer (C) is correct. *(CPA, adapted)*
REQUIRED: The journal entries to reflect the purchase commitment.
DISCUSSION: ARB 43, Ch. 4, requires recognition of the loss in the income statement and accrual of a liability in Year 4 (assuming the purchase commitment is noncancelable). The loss on purchase commitment is an expense account. Accrued loss on purchase commitment is a liability account.
Answer (A) is incorrect because the entry does not recognize a loss and improperly records an asset. Answer (B) is incorrect because the entry prematurely records the cocoa as an asset prior to acquisition. The loss on purchase commitments is an expense account. Answer (D) is incorrect because an entry is needed to recognize the loss.

6. On January 1, Year 4, Card Corp. signed a 3-year, noncancelable purchase contract that allows Card to purchase up to 500,000 units of a computer part annually from Hart Supply Co. The price is $.10 per unit, and the contract guarantees a minimum annual purchase of 100,000 units. During Year 4, the part unexpectedly became obsolete. Card had 250,000 units of this inventory at December 31, Year 4, and believes these parts can be sold as scrap for $.02 per unit. What amount of probable loss from the purchase commitment should Card report in its Year 4 income statement?

A. $24,000

B. $20,000

C. $16,000

D. $8,000

Answer (C) is correct. *(CPA, adapted)*
REQUIRED: The amount of probable loss from the purchase commitment.
DISCUSSION: ARB 43, Ch. 4, requires the accrual of a loss in the current year's income statement on goods subject to a firm purchase commitment if the market price of these goods declines below the commitment price. This loss should be measured in the same manner as inventory losses. Disclosure of the loss is also required. Consequently, given that 200,000 units must be purchased over the next 2 years for $20,000 (200,000 × $.10), and the parts can be sold as scrap for $4,000 (200,000 × $.02), the amount of probable loss for Year 4 is $16,000 ($20,000 − $4,000).
Answer (A) is incorrect because $24,000 includes the purchase commitment for the current year. Answer (B) is incorrect because $20,000 excludes the net realizable value of the parts from the calculation. Answer (D) is incorrect because $8,000 excludes the probable loss expected in the last year of the purchase commitment.

7. During December of Year 1, Nile Co. incurred special insurance costs but did not record these costs until payment was made during the following year. These insurance costs related to inventory that had been sold by December 31, Year 1. What is the effect of the omission on Nile's accrued liabilities and retained earnings at December 31, Year 1?

	Accrued Liabilities	Retained Earnings
A.	No effect	No effect
B.	No effect	Overstated
C.	Understated	Overstated
D.	Understated	No effect

Answer (C) is correct. *(CPA, adapted)*
REQUIRED: The effect on accrued liabilities and retained earnings of omitting insurance costs of inventory.
DISCUSSION: A liability must be recognized when (1) an item meets the definition of a liability (probable future sacrifice of economic benefits arising from a current obligation of the entity as a result of a past event or transaction), (2) it is measurable, and (3) the information about it is relevant and reliable. These criteria were met in Year 1 with respect to the insurance obligation. The insurance is a cost of inventory and theoretically should be accounted for as a product cost. Thus, the entry in Year 1 should have been to debit inventory and credit a liability. The omission of this entry understated accrued liabilities. Given that the related inventory was sold in Year 1, it also overstated net income and retained earnings by understating cost of goods sold. Moreover, the same effects would occur if the insurance costs were chargeable to expense as a period cost.

7.2 Cost Accounting for Inventory

8. How should the following costs affect a retailer's inventory?

	Freight-in	Interest on Inventory Loan
A.	Increase	No Effect
B.	Increase	Increase
C.	No effect	Increase
D.	No effect	No effect

Answer (A) is correct. *(CPA, adapted)*
REQUIRED: The effect of certain costs on inventory.
DISCUSSION: ARB 43, Ch. 4, "Inventory Pricing," states that cost is "the sum of the applicable expenditures and charges directly or indirectly incurred in bringing an article to its existing condition and location." Freight costs are therefore an inventoriable cost to the extent they are not abnormal (SFAS 151). However, interest cost for inventories is not capitalized. Interest cost is capitalized only for assets produced for an enterprise's own use or for sale or lease as discrete projects (SFAS 34, *Capitalization of Interest Cost*).

9. Application rates for production overhead best reflect anticipated fluctuations in sales over a cycle of years when they are computed under the concept of

A. Maximum capacity.

B. Normal capacity.

C. Practical capacity.

D. Expected actual capacity.

Answer (B) is correct. *(CPA, adapted)*
REQUIRED: The concept of capacity for best applying overhead over a cycle of years.
DISCUSSION: Normal capacity is the output that will approximate demand over a period of years that includes seasonal, cyclical, and trend variations. Deviations in one year will be offset in other years.
Answer (A) is incorrect because maximum (theoretical or ideal) capacity is the level at which output is maximized assuming perfectly efficient operations at all times. This level is impossible to maintain and results in underapplied overhead. Answer (C) is incorrect because practical capacity is the maximum level at which output is produced efficiently. It usually also results in underapplied overhead. Answer (D) is incorrect because expected actual capacity is a short-run output level. It minimizes under- or overapplied overhead but does not provide a consistent basis for assigning overhead cost. Per-unit overhead will fluctuate because of short-term changes in the expected production level.

10. The following information applied to Fenn, Inc. for the year just ended:

Merchandise purchased for resale	$400,000
Freight-in	10,000
Freight-out	5,000
Purchase returns	2,000

Fenn's inventoriable cost for the year was

A. $400,000

B. $403,000

C. $408,000

D. $413,000

Answer (C) is correct. *(CPA, adapted)*
REQUIRED: The amount of inventoriable cost for the year.
DISCUSSION: Inventoriable cost is the sum of the applicable expenditures and charges directly or indirectly incurred in bringing all items of inventory to their existing condition and location. Thus, inventoriable cost includes the $400,000 cost of the merchandise purchased, plus the $10,000 of freight-in, minus the $2,000 of purchase returns. Freight-out is not a cost incurred in bringing the inventory to a salable condition. Consequently, the inventoriable cost for Fenn was $408,000 ($400,000 + $10,000 − $2,000).
Answer (A) is incorrect because $400,000 excludes freight-in and purchase returns. Answer (B) is incorrect because $403,000 excludes freight-in. Answer (D) is incorrect because $413,000 includes freight-out.

11. West Retailers purchased merchandise with a list price of $20,000, subject to trade discounts of 20% and 10%, with no cash discounts allowable. West should record the cost of this merchandise as

A. $14,000

B. $14,400

C. $15,600

D. $20,000

Answer (B) is correct. *(CPA, adapted)*
   REQUIRED: The amount to be recorded as cost of inventory subject to trade discounts.
   DISCUSSION: When inventory is subject to cash discounts, the purchases may be reflected either net of these discounts or at the gross prices. However, purchases should always be recorded net of trade discounts. A chain discount is the application of more than one trade discount to a list price. Chain discounts should be applied in steps as indicated below.

List price	$20,000
20% discount	(4,000)
	$16,000
10% discount	(1,600)
Cost of merchandise	$14,400

   Answer (A) is incorrect because $14,000 results from applying both discount percentages to the list price. Answer (C) is incorrect because $15,600 results from applying the second discount percentage to the first discount amount. Answer (D) is incorrect because purchases should be recorded net of trade discounts.

7.3 Cost Flows -- Average Cost, FIFO, and LIFO

12. Thread Co. is selecting its inventory system in preparation for its first year of operations. Thread intends to use either the periodic weighted-average method or the perpetual moving-average method, and to apply the lower-of-cost-or-market rule either to individual items or to the total inventory. Inventory prices are expected to generally increase throughout the year, although a few individual prices will decrease. What inventory system should Thread select if it wants to maximize the inventory carrying amount at December 31?

	Inventory Method	Cost or Market Application
A.	Perpetual	Total inventory
B.	Perpetual	Individual item
C.	Periodic	Total inventory
D.	Periodic	Individual item

Answer (A) is correct. *(CPA, adapted)*
   REQUIRED: The inventory system that maximizes the inventory carrying amount at year-end.
   DISCUSSION: Weighted-average inventory pricing is applicable to a periodic inventory system. The weighted-average unit cost is equal to the total cost of goods available for sale divided by the number of units available for sale. The moving-average system is only applicable to perpetual inventories. It requires that a new weighted average be computed after every purchase. This moving average is based on remaining inventory held and the new inventory purchased. In a period of rising prices, the moving-average method results in a higher unit and total inventory cost because the most recent purchases are given greater weight in the calculation. ARB 43, Ch. 4, permits application of the lower-of-cost-or-market rule either to each item in the inventory or to the inventory as a whole. Applying the LCM rule to the total inventory will maximize the carrying amount because the reduction in the inventory will equal only the excess of aggregate cost over aggregate market. LCM applied on an individual item basis recognizes all of the inventory declines but none of the gains.

13. The UNO Company was formed on January 2, Year 1, to sell a single product. Over a 2-year period, UNO's costs increased steadily. Inventory quantities equaled 3 months' sales at December 31, Year 1, and zero at December 31, Year 2. Assuming a periodic system and no accounting changes, the inventory cost method that reports the highest amount for each of the following is

	Inventory 12/31/Year 1	Cost of Sales Year 2
A.	LIFO	FIFO
B.	LIFO	LIFO
C.	FIFO	FIFO
D.	FIFO	LIFO

Answer (C) is correct. *(CPA, adapted)*
   REQUIRED: The method resulting in the highest beginning inventory and cost of sales given zero ending inventory.
   DISCUSSION: In a period of rising prices, FIFO inventory will be higher than LIFO inventory. FIFO assumes that the latest and therefore the highest priced goods purchased are in inventory, whereas LIFO assumes that these goods were the first to be sold. Accordingly, the inventory valuation at December 31, Year 1 (beginning inventory for Year 2), would be higher for FIFO than LIFO. Given zero inventory at December 31, Year 2, the units sold in Year 2 must have equaled the sum of Year 2 purchases and beginning inventory. Because beginning inventory for Year 2 would be reported at a higher amount under FIFO than LIFO, the result is a higher cost of goods sold under FIFO.

Questions 14 and 15 are based on the following information. During January, Metro Co., which maintains a perpetual inventory system, recorded the following information pertaining to its inventory:

	Units	Unit Cost	Total Cost	Units On Hand
Balance on 1/1	1,000	$1	$1,000	1,000
Purchased on 1/7	600	3	1,800	1,600
Sold on 1/20	900			700
Purchased on 1/25	400	5	2,000	1,100

14. Under the moving-average method, what amount should Metro report as inventory at January 31?

A. $1,300

B. $2,640

C. $3,225

D. $3,900

Answer (C) is correct. *(CPA, adapted)*
REQUIRED: The ending inventory using the moving-average method.
DISCUSSION: The moving-average system is only applicable to perpetual inventories. It requires that a new weighted average be computed after every purchase. This moving average is based on remaining inventory held and the new inventory purchased. Based on the calculations below, the moving-average cost per unit for the 1/20 sale is $1.75, and the cost of goods sold (CGS) for January is $1,575 (900 units sold × $1.75). Thus, ending inventory is $3,225 ($1,000 beginning balance + $1,800 purchase on 1/7 – $1,575 CGS on 1/20 + $2,000 purchase on 1/25).

	Units	Moving-Average Cost/Unit	Total Cost
Balance 1/1	1,000	$1.00	$1,000
Purchase 1/7	600	3.00	1,800
	1,600	$1.75	$2,800

Answer (A) is incorrect because $1,300 is based on the periodic LIFO method. Answer (B) is incorrect because $2,640 is based on the weighted-average method. Answer (D) is incorrect because $3,900 is based on the FIFO method.

15. Under the LIFO method, what amount should Metro report as inventory at January 31?

A. $3,225

B. $1,300

C. $2,700

D. $3,900

Answer (C) is correct. *(CPA, adapted)*
REQUIRED: The value of ending inventory using a perpetual LIFO system.
DISCUSSION: In a perpetual inventory system, purchases are directly recorded in the inventory account, and cost of goods sold (CGS) is determined as the goods are sold. Under LIFO, the latest goods purchased are assumed to be the first to be sold. Using LIFO perpetual, 600 of the 900 units sold on 1/20 are assumed to have come from the last purchase. Their cost was $1,800 (600 × $3). The remaining 300 came from the beginning balance at a cost of $300 (300 × $1). Hence, the total CGS for January was $2,100, and ending inventory must equal $2,700 ($1,000 beginning inventory + $1,800 purchase on 1/7 + $2,000 purchase on 1/25 – $2,100 CGS).
Answer (A) is incorrect because $3,225 is based on the moving average method. Answer (B) is incorrect because $1,300 is based on the periodic LIFO method. Answer (D) is incorrect because $3,900 is based on the periodic FIFO method.

16. Drew Co. uses the average cost inventory method for internal reporting purposes and LIFO for financial statement and income tax reporting. At December 31, the inventory was $375,000 using average cost and $320,000 using LIFO. The unadjusted credit balance in the LIFO reserve account on December 31 was $35,000. What adjusting entry should Drew record to adjust from average cost to LIFO at December 31?

		Debit	Credit
A.	Cost of goods sold	$55,000	
	Inventory		$55,000
B.	Cost of goods sold	$55,000	
	LIFO reserve		$55,000
C.	Cost of goods sold	$20,000	
	Inventory		$20,000
D.	Cost of goods sold	$20,000	
	LIFO reserve		$20,000

Answer (D) is correct. *(CPA, adapted)*
REQUIRED: The journal entry to adjust from average cost to LIFO.
DISCUSSION: The LIFO reserve account is an allowance that adjusts the inventory balance stated according to the method used for internal reporting purposes to the LIFO amount appropriate for external reporting. If the LIFO effect is $55,000 ($375,000 average cost – $320,000 LIFO cost) and the account has a $35,000 credit balance, it must be credited for $20,000, with a corresponding debit to cost of goods sold.
Answer (A) is incorrect because the balance in the reserve account should equal $55,000, and inventory should not be adjusted. Answer (B) is incorrect because the balance in the reserve account should be $55,000. Answer (C) is incorrect because inventory should not be adjusted.

7.4 Dollar-Value LIFO

17. Estimates of price-level changes for specific inventories are required for which of the following inventory methods?

A. Conventional retail.

B. Dollar-value LIFO.

C. Weighted-average cost.

D. Average cost retail.

Answer (B) is correct. *(CPA, adapted)*
REQUIRED: The inventory method for which estimates of price-level changes for specific inventories are required.
DISCUSSION: Dollar-value LIFO accumulates inventoriable costs of similar (not identical) items. These items should be similar in the sense of being interchangeable, having similar uses, belonging to the same product line, or constituting the raw materials for a given product. Dollar value LIFO determines changes in ending inventory in terms of dollars of constant purchasing power rather than units of physical inventory. This calculation uses a specific price index for each year.
Answer (A) is incorrect because the conventional retail method calculates ending inventory at retail and then adjusts it to cost by applying a cost-retail ratio. Answer (C) is incorrect because the weighted-average method determines an average cost that is not adjusted for general price-level changes. Answer (D) is incorrect because the average cost retail method calculates ending inventory at retail and then adjusts it to cost by applying a cost-retail ratio.

18. Bach Co. adopted the dollar-value LIFO inventory method as of January 1, Year 4. A single inventory pool and an internally computed price index are used to compute Bach's LIFO inventory layers. Information about Bach's dollar-value inventory follows:

	Inventory:	
Date	At Base-Year Cost	At Current-Year Cost
1/1/Year 4	$90,000	$90,000
Year 4 layer	20,000	30,000
Year 5 layer	40,000	80,000

What was the price index used to compute Bach's Year 5 dollar-value LIFO inventory layer?

A. 1.09

B. 1.25

C. 1.33

D. 2.00

Answer (C) is correct. *(CPA, adapted)*
REQUIRED: The price index used to compute the current year dollar-value LIFO inventory layer.
DISCUSSION: To compute the ending inventory under dollar-value LIFO, the ending inventory stated in year-end or current-year cost must be restated at base-year cost. The layers at base-year cost are computed using a LIFO flow assumption and then weighted (multiplied) by the relevant indexes to price the ending inventory. A price index for the current year may be calculated by dividing the ending inventory at current-year cost by the ending inventory at base-year cost. This index is then applied to the current-year inventory layer stated at base-year cost. Thus, the Year 5 index (rounded) is 1.33 {[($90,000 + $30,000 + $80,000) EI at current-year cost] ÷ [($90,000 + $20,000 + 40,000) EI at base-year cost]}.
Answer (A) is incorrect because 1.09 is the price index for Year 4. Answer (B) is incorrect because 1.25 is calculated by dividing the difference in the current-year cost of inventory layers for Year 4 and Year 5 by the Year 5 base-year cost. Answer (D) is incorrect because 2.00 equals the current year cost of the Year 5 layer divided by its base-year.

19. Walt Co. adopted the dollar-value LIFO inventory method as of January 1, when its inventory was measured at $500,000. Walt's entire inventory constitutes a single pool. Using a relevant price index of 1.10, Walt determined that its December 31 inventory was $577,500 at current-year cost, and $525,000 at base-year cost. What was Walt's dollar-value LIFO inventory at December 31?

A. $525,000

B. $527,500

C. $552,500

D. $577,500

Answer (B) is correct. *(CPA, adapted)*
REQUIRED: The dollar-value LIFO inventory cost reported in the balance sheet.
DISCUSSION: A price index for the current year may be calculated by dividing the ending inventory at current-year cost by the ending inventory at base-year cost. This index is then applied to the current-year inventory layer stated at base-year cost. Consequently, the index is 1.10 ($577,500 ÷ $525,000), and the dollar-value LIFO cost at December 31 is $527,500 {$500,000 base layer + [1.10 × ($525,000 − $500,000)]}.
Answer (A) is incorrect because $525,000 is the base-year cost. Answer (C) is incorrect because $552,500 results from using $525,000 as the base layer. Answer (D) is incorrect because $577,500 is the year-end inventory at current cost.

20. On January 1, Year 7, Poe Company adopted the dollar-value LIFO inventory method. Poe's entire inventory constitutes a single pool. Inventory data for Year 7 and Year 8 are as follows:

Date	Inventory at Current-Year Cost	Inventory at Base-Year Cost	Relevant Price Index
01/01/Yr 7	$150,000	$150,000	1.00
12/31/Yr 7	220,000	200,000	1.10
12/31/Yr 8	276,000	230,000	1.20

Poe's dollar-value LIFO inventory at December 31, Year 8, is

A. $230,000

B. $241,000

C. $246,000

D. $276,000

Answer (B) is correct. *(CPA, adapted)*
REQUIRED: The ending inventory under the dollar-value LIFO method.
DISCUSSION: By using price indexes, dollar-value LIFO implements LIFO without the necessity of monitoring the prices of individual items. To compute the ending inventory under dollar-value LIFO, the ending inventory stated in year-end or current-year cost must be restated at base-year cost. The layers at base-year cost are computed using a LIFO flow assumption and then weighted (multiplied) by the relevant indexes to price the ending inventory. The inventory at the end of Year 8 in base-year cost is $230,000. This inventory is composed of a $150,000 base layer, a $50,000 ($200,000 − $150,000) Year 7 layer, and a $30,000 ($230,000 − $200,000) Year 8 layer. Each of these layers, as indicated below, is multiplied by the relevant price index to translate from base-year cost to the price in effect when the layer was added. The result is a December 31, Year 8, inventory value of $241,000.

Base layer	$150,000	× 1.0	=	$150,000
Year 7 layer	50,000	× 1.1	=	55,000
Year 8 layer	30,000	× 1.2	=	36,000
	$230,000			$241,000

Answer (A) is incorrect because $230,000 is the inventory at base-year cost. Answer (C) is incorrect because $246,000 assumes an $80,000 layer was added in Year 8 and none in Year 7. Answer (D) is incorrect because $276,000 is the inventory at current-year cost.

7.5 Lower of Cost or Market (LCM)

21. Which of the following statements are true when an entity applying the lower-of-cost-or-market method reports its inventory at replacement cost?

I. The original cost is less than replacement cost.

II. The net realizable value is equal to or greater than replacement cost.

A. I only.

B. II only.

C. Both I and II.

D. Neither I nor II.

Answer (B) is correct. *(CPA, adapted)*
REQUIRED: The measure(s) of inventory under the lower of cost or market rule.
DISCUSSION: ARB 43, Ch. 4, "Inventory Pricing," defines market as current replacement cost subject to a maximum and a minimum. The maximum is net realizable value, and the minimum is net realizable value minus normal profit. When replacement cost is within this range, it is used as market. Consequently, only statement II is correct.

22. Based on a physical inventory taken on December 31, Chewy Co. determined its chocolate inventory on a FIFO basis at $26,000 with a replacement cost of $20,000. Chewy estimated that, after further processing costs of $12,000, the chocolate could be sold as finished candy bars for $40,000. Chewy's normal profit margin is 10% of sales. Under the lower-of-cost-or-market rule, what amount should Chewy report as chocolate inventory in its December 31 balance sheet?

    A. $28,000

    B. $26,000

    C. $24,000

    D. $20,000

Answer (C) is correct. *(CPA, adapted)*
REQUIRED: The LCM value of inventory.
DISCUSSION: Market equals current replacement cost subject to maximum and minimum values. The maximum is NRV, and the minimum is NRV minus normal profit. When replacement cost is within this range, it is used as market. Cost is given as $26,000. NRV is $28,000 ($40,000 selling price – $12,000 additional processing costs), and NRV minus a normal profit equals $24,000 [$28,000 – ($40,000 × 10%)]. Because the lowest amount in the range ($24,000) exceeds replacement cost ($20,000), it is used as market. Because market value ($24,000) is less than cost ($26,000), it is also the inventory amount.
    Answer (A) is incorrect because $28,000 is the NRV. Answer (B) is incorrect because $26,000 is the cost. Answer (D) is incorrect because $20,000 is the replacement cost.

23. The lower-of-cost-or-market rule for inventories may be applied to total inventory, to groups of similar items, or to each item. Which application usually results in the lowest inventory amount?

    A. All applications result in the same amount.

    B. Total inventory.

    C. Groups of similar items.

    D. Separately to each item.

Answer (D) is correct. *(CPA, adapted)*
REQUIRED: The application of the LCM rule that usually results in the lowest amount.
DISCUSSION: Applying the LCM rule to each item of inventory produces the lowest amount for each item and therefore the lowest and most conservative measurement for the total inventory. The reason is that aggregating items results in the inclusion of some items at amounts greater than LCM. For example, if item A (cost $2, market $1) and item B (cost $3, market $4) are aggregated for LCM purposes, the inventory measurement is $5. If the rule is applied separately to A and B, the LCM measurement is $4.
    Answer (A) is incorrect because each application results in a different amount. Answer (B) is incorrect because grouping all items results in a higher measurement than applying the LCM rule to individual items. Answer (C) is incorrect because grouping some items results in a higher measurement than applying the LCM rule to individual items.

24. Rose Co. sells one product and uses the last-in, first-out method to determine inventory cost. Information for the month of January follows:

	Total Units	Unit Cost
Beginning inventory, 1/1	8,000	$8.20
Purchases, 1/5	12,000	7.90
Sales	10,000	

Rose has determined that at January 31, the replacement cost of its inventory was $8 per unit and the net realizable value was $8.80 per unit. Rose's normal profit margin is $1 per unit. Rose applies the lower of cost or market rule to total inventory and records any resulting loss. At January 31, what should be the net carrying amount of Rose's inventory?

    A. $79,000

    B. $78,000

    C. $80,000

    D. $81,400

Answer (C) is correct. *(CPA, adapted)*
REQUIRED: The net carrying amount of LIFO–based inventory.
DISCUSSION: Subject to certain restrictions, inventory is valued at the lower of cost or market. Because Rose uses the LIFO method to determine inventory cost, the 10,000 units sold are treated as coming from the purchases made on 1/5. Thus, 2,000 units remain from the purchase and 8,000 units from beginning inventory. The average cost of the remaining 10,000 units is $8.14 {[(8,000 × $8.20) + (2,000 × $7.90)] ÷ 10,000}. The replacement cost of $8, which exceeds NRV minus a normal profit ($8.80 – $1.00 = $7.80) but is lower than NRV ($8.80), is lower than the average cost of $8.14. Consequently, ending inventory on a LIFO–LCM basis is $80,000 (10,000 units × $8 replacement cost).
    Answer (A) is incorrect because $79,000 is the FIFO–LCM amount. Answer (B) is incorrect because $78,000 equals 10,000 units times $7.80 (NRV – a normal profit). Answer (D) is incorrect because $81,400 is based on the assumption that average unit cost is below the unit replacement cost.

7.6 Estimating Inventory

25. Which of the following methods of inventory valuation is allowable at interim dates but not at year-end?

A. Weighted average.

B. Estimated gross profit.

C. Retail method.

D. Specific identification.

Answer (B) is correct. *(CPA, adapted)*
REQUIRED: The inventory valuation method permitted at interim dates but not at year-end.
DISCUSSION: APB Opinion 28, *Interim Financial Reporting*, permits using the estimated gross profit method to determine inventory for interim statements provided that adequate disclosure is made of reconciliations with the annual physical inventory at year-end. Any other method allowable at year-end is also allowable at an interim date.
Answer (A) is incorrect because weighted average is allowable at year-end. Answer (C) is incorrect because retail method is allowable at year-end. Answer (D) is incorrect because specific identification is allowable at year-end.

26. The following information was obtained from Smith Co.:

Sales	$275,000
Beginning inventory	30,000
Ending inventory	18,000

Smith's gross margin is 20%. What amount represents Smith purchases?

A. $202,000

B. $208,000

C. $220,000

D. $232,000

Answer (B) is correct. *(CPA, adapted)*
REQUIRED: The amount of purchases given the gross margin.
DISCUSSION: Gross margin equals sales minus cost of goods sold. If it is 20% of sales, cost of goods sold equals $220,000 [$275,000 × (1.0 – 0.2)]. Cost of goods sold equals beginning inventory, plus purchases, minus ending inventory. Thus, purchases equals $208,000 ($220,000 CGS – $30,000 BI + $18,000 EI).
Answer (A) is incorrect because $202,000 equals cost of goods sold minus ending inventory. Answer (C) is incorrect because $220,000 equals cost of goods sold. Answer (D) is incorrect because $232,000 equals cost of goods sold plus beginning inventory, minus ending inventory.

27. Union Corp. uses the first-in, first-out retail method of inventory valuation. The following information is available:

	Cost	Retail
Beginning inventory	$12,000	$ 30,000
Purchases	60,000	110,000
Net additional markups		10,000
Net markdowns		20,000
Sales revenue		90,000

If the lower-of-cost-or-market rule is disregarded, what would be the estimated cost of the ending inventory?

A. $24,000

B. $20,000

C. $19,200

D. $18,000

Answer (A) is correct. *(CPA, adapted)*
REQUIRED: The ending inventory using the FIFO version of the retail inventory method.
DISCUSSION: Under FIFO, ending inventory consists of purchases because beginning inventory is assumed to be sold first. Both markdowns and markups are used to calculate the cost-retail ratio because LCM is not being approximated.

	Cost	Retail
Purchases	$60,000	$110,000
Markups		10,000
Markdowns		(20,000)
Adjusted purchases	$60,000	$100,000
Beg. inv. 1/1	12,000	30,000
Goods available	$72,000	$130,000
Sales		(90,000)
Ending inventory–retail		$ 40,000
Cost-retail ratio ($60,000 ÷ $100,000)		× .6
Ending inventory–FIFO		$ 24,000

Answer (B) is incorrect because $20,000 results from applying the LCM rule (not deducting markdowns in determining the cost-retail ratio) and using the FIFO version of the retail method. Answer (C) is incorrect because $19,200 results from applying the approximate LCM (conventional) retail method. Answer (D) is incorrect because $18,000 results from applying the LIFO retail method (assuming stable prices).

28. At December 31, the following information was available from Huff Co.'s accounting records:

	Cost	Retail
Inventory, 1/1	$147,000	$ 203,000
Purchases	833,000	1,155,000
Additional markups	--	42,000
Available for sale	$980,000	$1,400,000

Sales for the year totaled $1,106,000. Markdowns amounted to $14,000. Under the approximate lower-of-average-cost-or-market retail method, Huff's inventory at December 31 was

A. $280,000

B. $197,160

C. $196,000

D. $194,854

29. On December 31, Year 3, Jason Company adopted the dollar-value LIFO retail inventory method. Inventory data for Year 4 are as follows:

	LIFO Cost	Retail
Inventory, 12/31/Year 3	$360,000	$500,000
Inventory, 12/31/Year 4	?	660,000
Increase in price level for Year 4		10%
Cost-retail ratio for Year 4		70%

Under the dollar-value LIFO retail method, Jason's inventory at December 31, Year 4, is

A. $437,000

B. $462,000

C. $472,000

D. $483,200

Answer (C) is correct. *(CPA, adapted)*
REQUIRED: The estimated inventory using the approximate lower-of-average-cost-or-market retail method.
DISCUSSION: The LACM retail method includes net markups but not net markdowns in the determination of goods available for sale. The approximate LACM (conventional) retail method is a weighted-average method. Accordingly, the numerator of the cost-retail ratio is the sum of the beginning inventory at cost plus purchases at cost, and the denominator is the sum of beginning inventory at retail, purchases at retail, and net markups.

	Cost	Retail
Beginning inventory	$147,000	$ 203,000
Purchases	833,000	1,155,000
Markups, net		42,000
Goods available	$980,000	$1,400,000
Sales		(1,106,000)
Markdowns, net		(14,000)
Ending inventory–retail		$ 280,000
Cost-retail ratio ($980 ÷ $1,400)		× .7
Ending inventory at cost		$ 196,000

Answer (A) is incorrect because $280,000 is the ending inventory at retail. Answer (B) is incorrect because $197,160 (rounded) is the ending inventory using the FIFO version of the retail method without regard to the LCM rule. Answer (D) is incorrect because $194,854 (rounded) is the ending inventory using the LCM rule and the FIFO version of the retail method.

Answer (A) is correct. *(CPA, adapted)*
REQUIRED: The ending inventory under the dollar-value LIFO retail inventory method.
DISCUSSION: The ending inventory at retail end-of-year prices must first be transformed to ending inventory at retail base year prices to determine whether a liquidation has occurred or a layer has been added. The layers are then restated by multiplying each by its specific price index. Finally, these amounts are transformed from retail prices to estimated cost prices by multiplying the layers by the appropriate cost-retail ratios. The 12/31/Year 4 inventory in base year (Year 3) prices is $600,000 ($660,000 ÷ 1.10). Thus, a $100,000 layer was added in Year 4.

Layers at Retail		Specific Price Index		Cost-Retail Ratio		Layers at Cost
$500,000	×	1.0	×	($360 ÷ 500)	=	$360,000
$100,000	×	1.1	×	70%	=	77,000
Ending inventory						$437,000

Answer (B) is incorrect because $462,000 equals 70% of inventory on 12/31/Year 4. Answer (C) is incorrect because $472,000 assumes the Year 4 layer is $160,000 and that no price-index adjustment is made. Answer (D) is incorrect because $483,200 assumes the Year 4 layer is $160,000.

Use Gleim's *CPA Test Prep* CD-Rom/Pocket PC for interactive testing with over 4,000 additional questions!

7.7 PRACTICE SIMULATION

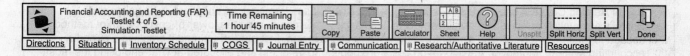

| Financial Accounting and Reporting (FAR) Testlet 4 of 5 Simulation Testlet | Time Remaining 1 hour 45 minutes | Copy | Paste | Calculator | Sheet | Help | Unsplit | Split Horiz | Split Vert | Done |

Directions | Situation | ⫼ Inventory Schedule | ⫼ COGS | ⫼ Journal Entry | ⫼ Communication | ⫼ Research/Authoritative Literature | Resources

---

1. Directions

In the following simulation, you will be asked to complete various tasks. You may use the content in the **Information Tabs** to complete the tasks in the **Work Tabs**.

Information Tabs:

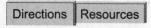

| Directions | Resources |

FIG 1

- Go through each of the **Information Tabs** to familiarize yourself with the simulation content
- The **Resources** tab will contain information, including formulas and definitions, that may help you to complete the tasks
- Your simulation may have more **Information Tabs** than those shown in Fig. 1

Work Tabs:

| ⫼SysTrust | ⫼Engagement Letter | ⫼Authoritative Sources | ⫼Communication |

FIG. 2

- **Work Tabs**, to the right of **Information Tabs**, contain the tasks for you to complete
- **Work Tabs** contain directions for completing each task - be sure to read these directions carefully
- The tab names in Fig. 2 are for illustration only - yours may differ
- Once you complete any part of a task, the pencil for that tab will be shaded (see **Communication** in Fig. 2)
- The shaded pencil does **NOT** indicate that you have completed the entire task
- You must complete all of the tasks in the **Work Tabs** to receive full credit

Research/Authoritative Literature Tab:

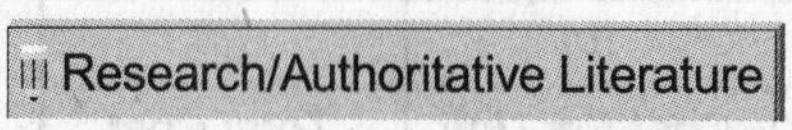

| ⫼ Research/Authoritative Literature |

FIG. 3

- This tab contains both the Research task and the Authoritative Literature
- Detailed instructions for completing the Research task, and for using the Authoritative Literature, appear on this tab
- You may use the Authoritative Literature as a resource for completing other tasks

NOTE: If you believe you have encountered a software malfunction, report it to the test center staff immediately.

2. Situation

Bristol Heating Co. sells one product (heating oil), which it purchases from various suppliers in 10-gallon units. Bristol's accounting policy is to report inventory in its financial statements using the lower-of-cost-or-market method applied to total inventory. Bristol's inventory flow assumption is last-in, first-out (LIFO), and it employs a periodic accounting system. Moreover, transportation costs are debited to freight-in and allocated at year-end using the most popular accounting practice. Cash discounts are recorded using the gross method. Bristol has determined that, at December 31, Year 5, the replacement cost of the inventory was $8 per unit, and the net realizable value was $8.80 per unit. The normal profit margin is $1.05 per unit. Bristol uses the direct method of reporting losses from write-downs of inventory to market. The trial balance at December 31, Year 5, included the following accounts:

Sales (33,000 units × $16)	$528,000
Sales discounts	7,500
Purchases	368,900
Purchase discounts	18,000
Freight-in	5,000
Freight-out	11,000

Bristol's inventory purchases during Year 5 were as follows:

	Units	Cost per Unit
Beginning inventory, January 1	8,000	$8.20
Purchases, quarter ended March 31	12,000	8.25
Purchases, quarter ended June 30	15,000	7.90
Purchases, quarter ended September 30	13,000	7.50
Purchases, quarter ended December 31	7,000	7.70
	55,000	

3. Inventory Schedule

This question is presented in a spreadsheet format that requires you to fill in the correct response in the shaded cells provided.

Use the form below to prepare a schedule of ending inventory.

Bristol Heating Co.
Supporting Schedule of Ending Inventory
December 31, Year 5

Inventory at cost (LIFO)	(a)	(b)	(c)
Inventory Layer	**Units**	**Cost Per Unit**	**Total Cost**
1. Beginning inventory, January 1			
2. Purchases, quarter ended March 31			
3. Purchases, quarter ended June 30			
4. Purchases, quarter ended September 30			
5. Purchases, quarter ended December 31			

4. Cost of Goods Sold Schedule

This set of questions has a matching format. Select the best match for each numbered item from the terms in the drop-down list and write its letter in the column provided. Each choice may be used once, more than once, or not at all.

Use the form below to prepare a schedule of cost of goods sold.

Bristol Heating Co.
Schedule of Cost of Goods Sold
For the Year Ended December 31, Year 5

Accounts	Amounts
1. Beginning inventory	
2. Purchases	
3. Purchase discounts	
4. Freight in	
5. Goods available for sale	
6. Ending inventory	
7. Cost of goods sold	

Choices
A) 528,000
B) 368,900
C) 5,000
D) 421,500
E) 515,000
F) (5,000)
G) 18,000
H) (18,000)
I) 11,000
J) (11,000)
K) 65,600
L) 176,000
M) (176,000)
N) 245,500
O) 317,000

5. Journal Entry

This question is presented in a spreadsheet format that requires you to fill in the correct response in the shaded cells provided.

Bristol uses a FIFO costing system for internal reporting purposes. Ending inventory per FIFO is $225,000. Indicate in the boxes below what the journal entry should be to recognize the difference between Bristol's internal inventory costing method and LIFO.

Account Title	Type of Account	Debit/Credit	Amount
1) Cost of goods sold			
2) Allowance to adjust inventory to LIFO			

6. Communication

In a brief memorandum to a client, describe the general application and advantages of the pooling of LIFO inventory items, including the dollar-value LIFO method. Do not describe the formulation of indexes. Type your communication in your word processor program and print out the copy in a memorandum-style format.

REMINDER: Your response will be graded for both technical content and writing skills. Technical content will be evaluated for information that is helpful to the intended reader and clearly relevant to the issue. Writing skills will be evaluated for development, organization, and the appropriate expression of ideas in professional correspondence. Use a standard business memo or letter format with a clear beginning, middle, and end. Do not convey information in the form of a table, bullet point list, or other abbreviated presentation.

To: Client
From: CPA
Subject: Advantages and application of dollar-value LIFO method

7. Research/Authoritative Literature

See page 12 in the Introduction of this book for a detailed explanation of the AICPA's new Research/Authoritative Literature work tab as well as a screenshot of how the tab will actually look on your exam.

Research and cite the appropriate accounting standard in the FASB Current Text or Original Pronouncements that describes the three types of agreements that qualify as product financing arrangements.

Unofficial Answers

3. Inventory Schedule (15 Gradable Items)

1. (a) 8,000.   Based on a LIFO periodic assumption, ending inventory consists of 22,000 units (55,000 purchased – 33,000 sold) with no liquidation of the 8,000 units in beginning inventory.
    (b) 8.20.   Given.
    (c) 65,600. The total cost of this layer is $65,600 (8,000 × $8.20).
2. (a) 12,000. Based on a LIFO periodic assumption, ending inventory consists of 22,000 units (55,000 purchased – 33,000 sold) with no liquidation of the 12,000 units in the first quarter layer.
    (b) 8.25.   Given.
    (c) 99,000. The total cost of this layer is $99,000 (12,000 × $8.25).
3. (a) 2,000.   Based on a LIFO periodic assumption, the ending inventory consists of 22,000 units (55,000 purchased – 33,000 sold) or (8,000 BI + 12,000 first quarter + 2,000 second quarter).
    (b) 7.90.   Given.
    (c) 15,800. The total cost of this layer is $15,800 (2,000 × $7.90).
4. (a) 0.   Based on a LIFO periodic assumption, the third quarter layer was completely liquidated.
    (b) 7.50.   Given.
    (c) 0.   The total cost of this layer is $0.
5. (a) 0.   Based on a LIFO periodic assumption, the fourth quarter layer was completely liquidated.
    (b) 7.70.   Given.
    (c) 0.   The total cost of this layer is $0.

4. Cost of Goods Sold Schedule (14 Gradable Items)

1. K) 65,600.   The beginning inventory was $65,600 (8,000 × $8.20).
2. B) 368,900.   Given. Bristol records purchases at gross amounts.
3. H) (18,000). Given. In a periodic system used in conjunction with the gross method, the amount of purchase (cash) discounts is subtracted to determine goods available for sale.
4. C) 5,000.   Given. In a periodic system, freight-in is an addition to goods available for sale. Ordinarily, it is not allocated to cost of goods sold and ending inventory.
5. D) 421,500.   Goods available for sale is the sum of beginning inventory, net purchases, and freight-in.
6. M) (176,000). Bristol applies the LCM method to total inventory. Per-unit replacement cost ($8) is the per-unit market amount because it is less than NRV ($8.80) and greater than NRV minus a normal profit margin ($8.80 – $1.05 = $7.75). Total inventory at market is therefore $176,000 [(55,000 units purchased – 33,000 units sold) × $8]. Because the ending inventory is assumed to consist of 8,000 units from beginning inventory, 12,000 units from the first quarter layer, and 2,000 units from the second quarter layer, total inventory at cost is therefore $180,400 [($8,000 × $8.20) + (12,000 × $8.25) + (2,000 × $7.90)]. Under the direct method, the $4,400 loss ($176,000 – $180,400) is debited to CGS and credited to inventory.
7. N) 245,500.   Cost of goods sold equals goods available for sale minus ending inventory adjusted for the direct writedown to market.

5. Journal Entry (6 Gradable Items)

1. Expense; Debit;   Companies often use LIFO for external reporting purposes to increase cost of goods sold and
    $49,000.   reduce net income, thereby reducing (or delaying) income taxes. Thus, when another costing method is used for internal reporting, its cost of goods sold is usually lower than that calculated under LIFO. This is the case with Bristol. In order to bring the internal FIFO cost of goods sold into line with the figure calculated for external reporting under LIFO, cost of goods sold must be debited for the difference of $49,000 ($225,000 FIFO – $176,000 LIFO).
2. Contra-asset;   The credit is to a valuation account that reduces the value of ending inventory.
    Credit; $49,000.

6. Communication (5 Gradable Items; for grading instructions, please refer to page 12.)

LIFO may be applied to groups (pools) of inventory items that are substantially identical. Record keeping is simplified because all goods in a beginning inventory pool are presumed to have been acquired on the same date and at the same cost. Using the pooling method, beginning inventory is costed at a weighted-average unit price (total cost ÷ unit quantity). Usually, purchases of goods in a pool are also recorded at a weighted-average cost (total cost ÷ unit quantity). If the quantity of units in the pool increases during the year, a new LIFO layer will be formed at the new weighted-average cost. Because a pool consists of more than one kind of item, erosion of LIFO layers is less likely than if the specific-goods approach is used. An increase in the quantity of one item may offset a decrease of another item.

The disadvantage of pooling specific goods is that the pools may need to be redefined. If an entity discontinues sales of one product and adds another, inventory pools may change if the new product is not substantially identical. The result may be the liquidation of base layers of inventory. Because dollar-value pools may embrace more goods, dollar-value LIFO avoids the cost and inconvenience of redefining pools of specific goods and reduces the likelihood of a LIFO liquidation. It also eliminates much of the detailed record keeping associated with other methods. Dollar-value LIFO accumulates inventoriable costs of similar (not identical) items. These items should be similar in the sense of being interchangeable, having similar uses, belonging to the same product line, or constituting the raw materials for a given product.

Dollar-value LIFO determines changes in inventory in terms of dollars of constant purchasing power rather than units of physical inventory. This calculation uses a specific price index for each year. The ending inventory is stated at current (year-end acquisition) costs and is then deflated by the current-year index to base-year cost. This amount is then compared with the beginning inventory stated at base-year cost to determine what layers are to be in the ending inventory based on a LIFO flow assumption. Each layer is then inflated (weighted) by the price index applicable to the year in which the layer was added. The result is the aggregate ending inventory valuation.

7. Research/Authoritative Literature (1 Gradable Item)

Answer: FAS 49, Par. 3

FAS 49 -- *Accounting for Product Financing Arrangements*

Applicability and Scope

3. Product financing arrangements include agreements in which a sponsor (the enterprise seeking to finance product pending its future use or resale):

a.   Sells the product to another entity (the enterprise through which the financing flows), and in a related transaction agrees to repurchase the product (or a substantially identical product);

b.   Arranges for another entity to purchase the product on the sponsor's behalf and, in a related transaction, agrees to purchase the product from the other entity; or

c.   Controls the disposition of the product that has been purchased by another entity in accordance with the arrangements described in either (a) or (b) above.

In all of the foregoing cases, the sponsor agrees to purchase the product, or processed goods of which the product is a component, from the other entity at specified prices over specified periods or, to the extent that it does not do so, guarantees resale prices to third parties.

Scoring Schedule:

	Correct Responses		Gradable Items		Weights		
Tab 3	_____	÷	15	×	20%	=	_____
Tab 4	_____	÷	14	×	20%	=	_____
Tab 5	_____	÷	6	×	15%	=	_____
Tab 6	_____	÷	5	×	30%	=	_____
Tab 7	_____	÷	1	×	15%	=	_____
							_____
							(Your Score)

Use Gleim's *CPA Gleim Online* to practice more simulations in a realistic environment.

STUDY UNIT EIGHT
PROPERTY, PLANT, EQUIPMENT, AND DEPLETABLE RESOURCES

(23 pages of outline)

This study unit covers tangible fixed assets. The next study unit addresses intangible assets. Depreciation and depletion are included in this study unit because income statement accounts are traditionally discussed together with the related balance sheet accounts.

8.1 INITIAL MEASUREMENT OF PROPERTY, PLANT, AND EQUIPMENT (PPE)

Definition

1. **Definition.** These assets are known variously as property, plant, and equipment; fixed assets; or plant assets. They provide benefits from their use in the production of goods and services, not in their consumption.

    a. PPE are tangible. They have physical existence.

    b. PPE may be either **personal property** (something movable, e.g., equipment) or **real property** (such as land or a building).

    c. PPE are used in the **ordinary operations** of an entity and are not held primarily for investment, resale, or inclusion in another product. But they are often sold.

        1) Land held for development may be classified as an investment or inventory.
        2) Intangible assets and natural resources also are operating assets.

    d. PPE are **long-term**. They are not expected to be used up within 1 year or the normal operating cycle of the business, whichever is longer.

        1) The **cost** of using up the service potential of PPE (except land) is systematically and rationally allocated by means of **depreciation**.

            a) However, land may sustain a material loss in fair value, e.g., through soil erosion of agricultural property or a natural disaster (flood or earthquake).

        2) Intangible assets and natural resources also are wasting assets. Allocation of their costs is amortization and depletion, respectively.

Types of PPE

2. **Types of PPE**, in addition to land and buildings, include

    a. **Land improvements**, such as landscaping, drainage, streets, street lighting, sewers, sidewalks, parking lots, driveways, fences, and rights-of-way

        1) Temporary improvements are depreciable.

    b. **Machinery and equipment**, such as furniture, **fixtures** (personal property permanently attached to real property, such as a central heating system), and vehicles

    c.   **Leasehold improvements**, such as buildings constructed on, and other modifications made to, the leased property by a lessee

    d.   **Internally constructed assets**

    e.   **Miscellaneous items**, e.g., tools, patterns and dies, and returnable containers

Relevant Accounting Principles

3.   **Historical cost.** PPE "are reported at their historical cost, which is the amount of cash or its equivalent paid to acquire an asset" (SFAC 5).

    a.   The historical cost of an asset also has been defined to include "the costs necessarily incurred to bring it to the condition and location necessary for its intended use" (SFAS 34, *Capitalization of Interest Cost*).

    b.   Historical cost is adjusted for changes in utility, e.g., depreciation and impairment.

    c.   **Capital (asset) expenditures** for acquisition or subsequent enhancement of service potential are included in the historical cost. They benefit more than one period.

        1)   **Revenue expenditures** (e.g., for repairs) are expensed (matched with revenue). They benefit only the period in which they are made.

    d.   The **price** bargained for by the buyer and seller, however, is not the only component of historical cost. Under the **full-cost principle**, the initial measurement embraces all other costs to acquire PPE, transport them to the sites of their intended use, and prepare them for operations.

        1)   Freight-in (transportation-in), installation charges, renovation or reconditioning costs, expenses of tests or trial runs, and insurance and taxes during the preoperations period are capitalizable.

            a)   But **depreciation** is not recognized until PPE are placed in operation and begin to contribute economic benefits, that is, to participate in generating the revenues with which such costs should be matched.

4.   **Matching.** In general, expenses, such as the decline in service potential of PPE, should be recognized at the time related revenues are earned.

    a.   No direct relationship ordinarily exists between the consumption of service potential and specific revenues. Thus, the expense (depreciation) must be **systematically and rationally allocated** to periods expected to be benefited.

5.   **Use of estimates.** Initial measurement and subsequent determination of the carrying amount of PPE inevitably require the use of judgment.

6.   **Nonrecognition of unrealized gains.** "Property, plant, and equipment should not be written up by an entity to reflect appraisal, market, or current values that are above cost to the entity" (APB Opinion 6, *Status of Accounting Research Bulletins*).

Initial Costs of Specific PPE

7.   **Land.** The costs of acquiring and preparing land for its expected use are capitalized.

    a.   The price should include not only the cash price but also any **encumbrances assumed** (such as mortgages or tax liens).

    b.   The cost of land also includes **transaction costs**, e.g., surveying costs, legal fees, brokers' commissions, title insurance, and escrow fees.

    c.   The **cost of an option** to buy land that is subsequently purchased is capitalized.

        1)   But the costs of options, surveys, and other items related to land not purchased should be expensed.

    d.   **Site preparation costs** [clearing, draining, filling, leveling the property, and razing existing buildings, minus any proceeds (such as timber sales)] are costs of the land, not of the building to be constructed on the land.

e. Certain **permanent improvements** made by the entity, such as landscaping, have **indefinite lives** and are debited to the land account.

f. Other improvements (sidewalks, roads, street lights, and sewers) may be paid for through **special assessments** imposed by local governments, which undertake to maintain and replace them. These assessments should be debited to land cost because depreciation will not be recognized.

g. Taxes, insurance costs, etc., incurred while holding land for **investment** should be capitalized if the asset is not generating revenue and expensed if it is.

8. **Land improvements.** If driveways, parking lots, sidewalks, roads, fences, rights-of-way, etc., have limited lives and must be maintained and replaced by the owner, they should be debited to land improvements and depreciated.

9. **Buildings.** The costs that are necessary to the purchase or construction of a building and that will result in future economic benefits should be capitalized. These include

   a. The **purchase price**, including any liens assumed by the purchaser, etc.

   b. Costs of **renovating and preparing the structure** for its expected use

   c. Costs of **building permits** for renovation or construction

   d. The expenses of **excavating the site** to build the foundation (but not site preparation costs)

      1) The **costs of razing an old building** are either debited to the land account or treated as an adjustment of a gain or loss on disposal. The accounting depends on whether the land was purchased as a site for the new structure or the old building was previously used in the entity's operations.

      2) The **carrying amount of an existing building** previously used in the entity's operations is not included in the cost of the new structure. It will not produce future benefits.

   e. The materials, labor, and overhead **costs of construction**

10. **Machinery and Equipment**

    a. **Costs** include

       1) Purchase price (including sales taxes)
       2) Freight-in, handling, insurance, and storage until use begins
       3) Preparation, installation, and start-up costs, such as testing and trial runs
       4) Reconditioning used assets

    b. **Proper categorization** of these assets is important because of differences in depreciation methods and useful lives (especially for **federal tax** purposes).

       1) For example, a common error is to include **fixtures** in the building account rather than the equipment account.

11. **Leasehold improvements**, such as buildings constructed on leased land, are accounted for by the lessee in the same way as property to which title is held. However, the term of the lease may limit the depreciation period.

    a. If the **useful life** of the asset extends beyond the lease term and lease **renewal is likely**, the amortization period may include all or part of the renewal period. If **renewal is uncertain**, the useful life is the remaining term.

12. **Miscellaneous PPE.** Many other assets are long-term, tangible assets used in operations and thus are classifiable as PPE.

    a. **Returnable containers.** If containers (e.g., drums) are expected to be returned but no deposit is charged, the usual accounting is to debit the asset for the acquisition cost and to credit the asset for any reduction indicated by a physical count.

b.   **Tools.** Because depreciation is not feasible, tools and other items classified as PPE that are held in large numbers and have low per-unit costs may be accounted for in the same way as containers.

1)   Another possibility is to expense them when they are acquired, especially if their value is not material.

c.   **Patterns and dies.** These are used to shape, form, or finish a material or to create impressions on objects or material.

1)   Patterns and dies are capitalized and depreciated in the normal manner. If they apply only to a specific job, they should be debited to that job.

Other Factors Affecting Initial Measurement

13.   **Cash discounts.** The issue is whether the discount should be considered in recording the cost, that is, whether the transaction should be recorded at its net or gross amount.

a.   The **net method** is preferable because cost will reflect the cash price.

1)   A discount not taken will be charged to **discounts lost**.

b.   Under the **gross method**, discounts taken (but not lost) will be recorded.

14.   **Acquisition in exchange for a long-term obligation.** If a note, mortgage, or other long-term obligation is given for an item of PPE, the fundamental accounting problem is to distinguish **financing charges** (interest expense) from the recorded **cost of the asset** (the cash-equivalent price).

15.   **Basket (lump-sum) purchases.** When two or more assets with varying estimated useful lives are acquired for a single price, allocation of the cost is required.

a.   Only the **common cost** is allocated. Capital expenditures related to a particular asset should be debited to that asset.

1)   For example, if inventory and equipment are purchased, the start-up costs for the equipment should not be allocated to the inventory.

b.   The basis of allocation is **relative fair value**.

16.   **Issuance of an entity's own securities for PPE.** The usual basis for measurement of this transaction is the fair value of the stock or other securities.

17.   **Donated assets.** In general, **contributions received** should be recognized as (a) revenues or gains in the period of receipt and (b) assets, decreases in liabilities, or expenses (SFAS 116, *Accounting for Contributions Received and Contributions Made*). They are measured at fair value.

a.   **Contributions made** are recognized as expenses and as increases of liabilities or decreases in assets. Contributions made also are measured at fair value.

b.   SFAS 116 does not apply to **contributions by governmental units** to businesses or to tax exemptions, incentives, or abatements. Accordingly, a business may credit a contribution from a governmental unit to donated capital.

1)   However, SFAS 116 does **not prohibit** treating contributions by governmental units as **revenues or gains**. Such treatment is consistent with the accounting for contributions by nongovernmental entities. It is also consistent with the definition of comprehensive income: all changes in equity during a period except those from investments by owners and distributions to owners.

Stop and review! You have completed the outline for this subunit. Study multiple-choice questions 1 through 5 beginning on page 310.

8.2 SPECIAL MEASUREMENT ISSUE -- INTERNALLY CONSTRUCTED ASSETS (ICAs)

Initial Costs of an ICA

1. The costs capitalized when productive assets are constructed may be direct (direct materials and direct labor) or indirect (overhead items, e.g., utilities, depreciation, insurance, taxes, and supplies).

   a. Disagreement exists about **allocation of overhead**, especially those costs that are unaffected by production of an ICA. Widely used methods are to (1) capitalize the incremental increase in variable overhead associated with the construction or (2) allocate total overhead based on cost drivers in the same manner as in other manufacturing processes.

   b. An ICA should be capitalized at the **lower of its fair value or its cost**.

      1) **No gain** is recognized in the year of construction because the acquisition of assets is ordinarily not considered the culmination of an earning process.

      2) If cost exceeds fair value, however, the excess is **expensed immediately** to avoid overstating the asset.

Reason for Capitalization

2. The costs necessary to bring an asset to the condition and location of its intended use are part of the historical cost. **Interest incurred during construction** is such a necessary cost. An imputed cost of equity capital is **not** recognized (SFAS 34, *Capitalization of Interest Cost*).

Qualifying Assets

3. These include

   a. Assets produced by the entity for its own use.
   b. Assets produced for the entity by others for which deposits or progress payments have been made.
   c. Assets produced for sale or lease as separate projects, such as real estate developments or ships.
   d. Equity-based investments. **The investor** may capitalize interest on the investment if **the investee** (1) has activities in progress necessary to commence its planned principal operations and (2) is expending funds to obtain qualifying assets for its operations (SFAS 58, *Capitalization of Interest Cost in Financial Statements That Include Investments Accounted for by the Equity Method*).

Nonqualifying Assets

4. These include

   a. Inventories routinely produced in large quantities on a repetitive basis.
   b. Assets in use or ready for their intended use in earning activities.
   c. Assets not being used in earning activities that are not undergoing the activities necessary to ready them for use.
   d. Idle land.

Capitalization (Acquisition) Period

5.   This period is the time required to carry out the activities necessary to bring a qualifying asset to the condition and location necessary for its intended use.

    a.   **The period begins and continues** as long as

        1)   Expenditures for a qualifying asset are being made,

        2)   Activities necessary to make the asset ready for its intended use are in progress, and

        3)   Interest cost is being incurred.

    b.   Interest **capitalization must cease** if substantially all asset-related activities are suspended.

    c.   **Capitalization ends** "when the asset is substantially complete and ready for its intended use."

    d.   Interest capitalization does not end merely because the asset must be measured at an amount lower than acquisition cost, e.g., because of recognition of an **impairment loss**.

Limitation on Capitalized Interest

6.   Interest cost includes interest (a) on obligations with explicit interest rates (including amortization of issue costs and discount or premium), (b) imputed on certain payables under APB Opinion 21, and (c) on a capital lease.

7.   Capitalizable interest is limited to the **amount theoretically avoidable** if expenditures for ICAs had not been made. For example, if the entity had not incurred costs for ICAs, it might have used the funds to repay debt or to avoid issuing new debts.

8.   Interest capitalized may **not** exceed the actual total incurred during the period.

9.   **Interest earned** on borrowed funds is ordinarily **not** offset against interest cost to determine either capitalization rates or limitations on interest costs to be capitalized. Such income relates to investment, not acquisition, decisions.

Amount of Interest to be Capitalized

10.   Capitalized interest equals the weighted **average accumulated expenditures (AAE)** for the qualifying asset during the capitalization period times the interest rate(s). The weighting is based on the time expenditures incurred interest.

11.   If a **specific new borrowing** outstanding during the period can be identified with the asset, the **rate** on that obligation may be applied to the extent that the AAE **do not exceed the amount borrowed**.

12.   To the extent that AAE exceed the amount of specific new borrowings, a **weighted-average rate** must be applied that is based on other borrowings outstanding during the period.

    a.   However, a weighted average of rates on all borrowings may be applied to the entire amount of AAE.

EXAMPLE

Lyssa Co. constructed a building for its own use. The capitalization period began on 10/1/Year 1, and ended on 9/30/Year 2. The AAE are based on the following **construction-related expenditures** and the amounts of time they incurred interest:

		AAE
10/1/Year 1	$500,000 × (12 ÷ 12) =	$ 500,000
1/1/Year 2	$400,000 × (9 ÷ 12) =	300,000
4/1/Year 2	$600,000 × (6 ÷ 12) =	300,000
7/1/Year 2	$400,000 × (3 ÷ 12) =	100,000
9/30/Year 2	$900,000 × (0 ÷ 12) =	0
		$1,200,000

On 10/1/Year 1, Lyssa **specifically borrowed** $1,000,000 at a rate of 10% to finance the construction. Its **other borrowings** outstanding during the entire construction period consisted of the following bond issues:

$2,000,000 principal, 8% interest rate
$6,000,000 principal, 9% interest rate

All interest is paid at fiscal year-end. Accordingly, the **weighted-average rate on other borrowings** is 8.75%.

		Interest	Principal	Rate
($2,000,000 × 8%)	=	$160,000	$2,000,000	
($6,000,000 × 9%)	=	540,000	6,000,000	
		$700,000	÷ $8,000,000	8.75%

Total actual interest cost for the fiscal year is $800,000.

$1,000,000 × 10%	=	$100,000
$2,000,000 × 8%	=	160,000
$6,000,000 × 9%	=	540,000
		$800,000

Avoidable interest is $117,500.

$1,000,000 × 10%	=	$100,000
($1,200,000 − $1,000,000) × 8.75%	=	17,500
		$117,500

This amount is capitalized because it is less than actual interest.

Interest expense is $682,500 ($800,000 − $117,500).

Disposition of Capitalized Interest

13. **Subsequent to capitalization**, interest is not treated differently from other component costs of an ICA. For example, it is not amortized over a period different from that used to depreciate the ICA.

Disclosures

14. If **no interest cost** is capitalized, the amount incurred and expensed during the period should be reported. If **some interest cost** is capitalized, the total incurred and the amount capitalized should be disclosed.

Stop and review! You have completed the outline for this subunit. Study multiple-choice questions 6 through 9 beginning on page 311.

8.3 SUBSEQUENT EXPENDITURES FOR PPE

Accounting Issues

1. The issues are to determine whether subsequent expenditures should be capitalized or expensed and the accounting methods to be used.

   a. **Capital expenditures** provide additional benefits by improving the quality of services rendered by the asset, extending its useful life, or increasing its output.

      1) These expenditures are matched through changes in depreciation schedules with revenues of the future periods expected to be benefited.

   b. **Revenue expenditures** (expenses) maintain an asset's normal service capacity.

      1) These costs are recurring, not expected to benefit future periods, and expensed when incurred.

      2) An entity usually specifies a materiality threshold below which all costs are expensed, thereby avoiding the burden of depreciating immaterial amounts.

Additions

2. Substantial expenditures for extensions or expansions of existing assets are capitalized. An example is an additional story for a building.

   a. If the addition is essentially a **separate asset**, it is recorded in a separate account and depreciated over its own useful life.

      1) Otherwise, the addition should be debited to the **original asset account** and depreciated over the life of that asset.

   b. If the original asset was constructed **in anticipation of the addition**, the costs related to changes in that asset should be capitalized.

      1) However, costs of alterations in the original asset should be expensed if they could have been avoided by proper planning at an earlier time.

   c. The basic entry is

Asset (new or old)	$XXX	
Cash, etc.		$XXX

Replacements and Improvements (Betterments)

3. A **replacement** substitutes a new component of an asset for a similar one, for example, a tile roof for a tile roof. But an **improvement** substitutes a better component, such as a more efficient heating system.

   a. **Substitution method.** Given accounting recognition of the old component, e.g., recording a central air conditioning system separately from the building, the procedure is to remove it from the ledger, along with accumulated depreciation, and to **substitute the cost of the new component**. A gain or loss may be recognized.

      1) The new component will be depreciated over the shorter of its useful life or that of the entire asset.

      2) The basic entry is

New asset	$XXX	
Accumulated depreciation	XXX	
Old asset		$XXX
Gain (or debit a loss)		XXX
Cash, etc.		XXX

b. If (1) the component replaced or improved has **not been separately accounted for**, or (2) **the old component has been modified**, the substitution method is **not** used.

   1) If the replacement or improvement increases the asset's **service potential** but does not extend its estimated useful life, the **asset is debited**.

   a) The carrying amount of the old component is not removed. However, this amount ordinarily is not material because the transaction will most often occur when the component is almost fully depreciated.

   2) If the replacement or improvement primarily **extends the useful life without enhancing service potential**, the entry is to **debit accumulated depreciation**. The expenditure is a recovery of depreciation, not an increase in the quality of service.

Rearrangements, Reinstallations, Relocations

4. Rearranging the configuration of plant assets, reinstalling such assets, or relocating operations may require material outlays that are separable from recurring expenses and provide probable future benefits.

   a. The **substitution method** of accounting for these costs may be used if the original installation costs and accumulated depreciation **are known**.

   b. Otherwise, if these costs are material, they should be **debited to a new account and amortized** over the (usually brief) period benefited.

   c. **Relocation (moving) costs** are often expensed as incurred.

   1) But if these costs are incurred because of an unusual and infrequent event, such as a natural disaster, they may be included in an extraordinary loss.

Repairs and Maintenance

5. Routine, minor expenditures made to maintain the operating efficiency of PPE are **ordinarily expensed as incurred**. However, as the amounts involved become more significant and the benefits to future periods increase, treatment of a **major repair** as an addition, etc., may be more appropriate.

   a. Although a repair or maintenance cost ordinarily should be allocated to a single annual period only, its full recognition at the interim date when incurred may distort the **interim statements**.

   1) Accordingly, a repair or maintenance cost may be accounted for using an **allowance method** for interim reporting. This method involves

   a) Estimating the annual cost

   b) Allocating an amount to each interim period

Repairs and maintenance expense	$XXX	
Allowance		$XXX

   c) Recording amounts actually expended

Allowance	$XXX	
Cash, etc.		$XXX

   d) Making an adjustment in the final interim period to reduce the year-end allowance to zero

   e) Presenting the allowance in the interim statements as an addition to or subtraction from the related asset, i.e., as a valuation account

Summary

6. The following table summarizes the accounting for subsequent expenditures for PPE:

Action	Accounting Treatment	
Additions	Debit separate asset or debit old asset	
Replacements/Improvements – Carrying Amount Known	Substitution method	
Replacements/Improvements – Carrying Amount Not Known	Increase service potential only: debit asset	Extend useful life only: debit acc. deprec.
Rearrangements/Reinstallations	Cost known: substitution method	Otherwise, material costs debited to new asset
Repairs	Minor: expense	Major: treatment as addition, etc.

Stop and review! You have completed the outline for this subunit. Study multiple-choice questions 10 through 14 beginning on page 313.

8.4 DISPOSALS OTHER THAN BY EXCHANGE

1. Whatever the means of disposition, the procedures below must be followed:

   a. **Depreciation** is recorded up to the time of disposal so that periodic depreciation expense is not understated and the carrying amount of the asset is not overstated.

   b. The asset's **carrying amount** is removed from the accounts by eliminating the asset, its accumulated depreciation, and any other valuation account.

   c. Any **consideration (proceeds) received** is debited appropriately.

   d. **Gain or loss** is usually included in the results of continuing operations as an ordinary item unless the disposal is reported in discontinued operations.

Sale

2. Accounting for a **cash sale** of PPE (including a scrap sale) is straightforward.

   a. Depreciation, if any, is recognized to the date of sale, the carrying amount is removed from the books, the proceeds are recorded, and any gain or loss is recognized.

Abandonment

3. An asset to be abandoned is disposed of when it is no longer used (SFAS 144, *Accounting for the Impairment and Disposal of Long-Lived Assets*).

   a. If the asset to be abandoned is **still in use**, an immediate writedown to zero is usually not done. Continued use indicates that the asset has service potential. However, **depreciation estimates** should be revised to account for the reduced service period.

      1) A long-lived asset that is **temporarily idled** is not treated as abandoned.

   b. An abandonment may sometimes involve receipt of **scrap value**.

Contributions

4. Contributions made do not involve an exchange. They are recorded at **fair value**. A gain or loss is recognized.

Nonreciprocal Transfers to Owners

5. The accounting is based on the **recorded amount** (after recognition of impairment loss) in a distribution of nonmonetary assets **to owners** in a **spinoff** or other similar transaction (APB Opinion 29, *Accounting for Nonmonetary Transactions*).

Involuntary Conversion

6. An item of PPE is involuntarily converted when it is (a) lost through a casualty (flood, earthquake, fire, etc.), (b) expropriated (seized by a foreign government), or (c) condemned (through the governmental power of eminent domain).

   a. The accounting is the same as for other nonexchange dispositions.

   b. The **gain or loss** on an involuntary conversion is reported in a separate caption of the income statement as an **extraordinary item** net of tax **only** if it is unusual and infrequent in the environment in which the entity operates.

   c. If a nonmonetary asset has been involuntarily converted to monetary assets (e.g., insurance proceeds), **tax law** may treat the gain as an adjustment of the basis of replacement property rather than as a currently taxable amount.

   d. Gain or loss recognition is required even though the entity reinvests or is required to reinvest the proceeds in replacement nonmonetary assets (FASB Interpretation No. 30, *Accounting for Involuntary Conversions of Nonmonetary Assets to Monetary Assets*).

      1) Hence, the **replacement property should be recorded at its cost**. The involuntary conversion and replacement are not viewed as equivalent to a single exchange transaction between entities.

EXAMPLE

A state government condemned Owner Co.'s parcel of real estate. Owner will receive $1,500,000 for this property, which has a carrying amount of $1,150,000. Owner incurred the following costs as a result of the condemnation:

Appraisal fees to support a $1,500,000 value	$5,000
Attorney fees for the closing with the state	7,000
Attorney fees to review contract to acquire replacement property	6,000
Title insurance on replacement property	8,000

What amount of cost should Owner use to determine the gain on the condemnation? Gain or loss must be recognized even though the entity reinvests or is obligated to reinvest the monetary assets in replacement nonmonetary assets. The determination of the gain is based on the carrying amount ($1,150,000) and the costs incurred as a direct result of the condemnation ($5,000 appraisal fees and $7,000 attorney fees), a total of $1,162,000. Because the recipient is not obligated to reinvest the condemnation proceeds in other nonmonetary assets, the costs associated with the acquisition of the replacement property (attorney fees and title insurance) should be treated as part of the consideration paid for that property.

Stop and review! You have completed the outline for this subunit. Study multiple-choice questions 15 through 18 beginning on page 314.

8.5 EXCHANGES OF NONMONETARY ASSETS

1. **Nonmonetary exchanges** are **reciprocal transfers** of nonmonetary assets that leave the transferor with no substantial continuing involvement in the assets given up. Thus, the usual risks and rewards of ownership are transferred.

   a. The amounts of **monetary assets and liabilities** are fixed in terms of units of currency. Cash and payables are examples. **Nonmonetary items** are all other items.

   b. **Monetary exchanges** are measured at the **fair value** of the assets involved, with gain or loss recognized immediately. **Fair value of the assets given up** generally is used unless the fair value of the assets received is more evident.

   c.   **Nonmonetary exchanges** also are measured at **fair value**. However, the accounting should be based on the **carrying amount** of the assets given up when

      1) Neither the fair value of the assets given up nor the fair value of the assets received is reasonably determinable,

      2) The exchange involves inventory sold in the same line of business that facilitates sales to customers not parties to the exchange, or

      3) The exchange lacks **commercial substance**, that is, when an entity's cash flows are not expected to change significantly (APB Opinion 29, *Accounting for Nonmonetary Transactions*, and SFAS 153, *Exchanges of Nonmonetary Assets*).

Boot

2.   In an exchange of nonmonetary assets that is not accounted for at fair value, if partial **monetary consideration (boot)** is received, a **proportionate amount of gain** is recognized by the recipient. However, the full amount of any **loss** is recognized as an adjustment of the carrying amount (the carryover basis).

   a.   The **entity paying the boot** does not recognize gain. The new asset should be recorded at the carrying amount of the asset given plus the boot paid.

      1) However, when this amount exceeds the fair value of the assets received, the assets received should be recorded at fair value, with the difference recognized as a **loss**.

   b.   The **recipient of boot** should recognize a gain to the extent that boot exceeds a proportionate share of the carrying amount of the assets surrendered.

      1) The gain recognized equals the **total potential gain** (boot + fair value of assets received − carrying amount given up) times the ratio of

$$\frac{Boot}{Boot + Fair\ value\ of\ nonmonetary\ assets\ received}$$

   c.   This treatment of boot **does not apply** if it is at least 25% of the fair value of the exchange. In such a transaction, **both parties** should record a **monetary exchange** at fair value, with gains and losses recognized in full (Emerging Issues Task Force Issue 01-2).

3.   The following table summarizes gain or loss recognition in nonmonetary exchanges:

Exchange	Gain	Loss
Has commercial substance	Full	Full
Lacks commercial substance – no boot received	None	Full
Lacks commercial substance – boot received	Partial	Full

EXAMPLE

Jayhawk Co. traded a building and $25,000 cash for a building owned by Phog Corp. in an exchange that lacks commercial substance. The following information relates to the accounting for the buildings on the exchange date:

	Carrying Amount	Fair Value
Old building	$130,000	$250,000
New building	$140,000	$275,000

Jayhawk Co.'s Journal Entry

PPE	$155,000	
Cash		$ 25,000
PPE		130,000

Phog Corp.'s Recognized Gain

$$(\$25,000 + \$250,000 - \$140,000) \times \left(\frac{\$25,000}{\$25,000 + \$250,000} \right) = \$135,000 \times .091$$

$$= \$12,285$$

Phog Corp.'s Journal Entry

Cash	$ 25,000	
PPE	127,285	
Gain		$ 12,285
PPE		140,000

Stop and review! You have completed the outline for this subunit. Study multiple-choice questions 19 through 23 beginning on page 316.

8.6 IMPAIRMENT OF LONG-LIVED ASSETS

1. Occasionally, a long-lived asset will experience a permanent **impairment** in value (see item 3. below). An entity may choose to keep and use such impaired assets, or dispose of them (SFAS 144, *Accounting for the Impairment or Disposal of Long-Lived Assets*).

2. This pronouncement also applies to a long-lived asset(s) included in a **group with other assets and liabilities** not subject to SFAS 144. The **unit of accounting** for such a long-lived asset is the group.

   a. If a long-lived asset(s) is to be held and used, the **asset group** is the lowest level at which identifiable cash flows are largely independent of those of other groups.

   b. If a long-lived asset(s) is to be disposed of, the **disposal group** consists of assets to be disposed of together in one transaction and directly associated liabilities to be transferred in the same transaction (for example, warranties associated with an acquired customer base).

Long-Lived Assets to Be Held and Used

3. **Measurement of impairment.** A long-lived asset (asset group) is impaired when its **carrying amount is greater than its fair value**. However, a loss equal to this excess is recognized for the impairment **only** when the carrying amount is **not recoverable**.

   a. **Recoverability test.** The carrying amount is not recoverable when it **exceeds the sum of the undiscounted cash flows** expected from the use and disposition of the asset (asset group).

    b.   The assessment is based on the carrying amount at the time of the **recoverability test**.

        1)   Testing should occur when **events or changes in circumstances** indicate that the carrying amount may not be recoverable, for example, when

            a)   Market price has decreased significantly, or

            b)   The use or physical condition of the asset (asset group) has changed significantly and adversely.

        2)   The **entry** for an impairment of a depreciable asset is

Impairment loss	$XXX	
Accumulated depreciation		$XXX

        3)

Determination of an Impairment Loss
1. Events or changes in circumstances indicate a possible loss
2. Carrying amount > sum of undiscounted cash flows
3. Loss = carrying amount − fair value

    c.   **Estimates of future cash flows employed in the recoverability test** include only those directly associated with and expected to arise as a direct result of the use and disposition of the asset (asset group). However, the estimates do not include interest that will be recognized as an expense when incurred.

        1)   The estimates must be based on the entity's own reasonable **assumptions** about its use of the asset (asset group) and all available evidence.

            a)   A **probability-weighted approach** may be helpful when different courses of action may be taken.

        2)   The estimates are made for the **remaining useful life** as determined from the perspective of the entity. The remaining useful life is that of the **primary asset** of the group, that is, the principal depreciable tangible asset or amortizable intangible asset that is the most significant component of the asset group for generating cash flows.

        3)   The estimates of future cash flows are based on the **existing service potential** at the time of the recoverability test.

Asset Groups

    4.   If in a rare case a long-lived asset (e.g., a corporate headquarters) does not have identifiable cash flows that are largely independent, the asset group for that asset includes **all of the entity's assets and liabilities**.

        a.   **Goodwill** is included in an asset group only if the group is or includes a **reporting unit** (an operating segment or one level below). Estimated future cash flows used to test a lower-level asset group for recoverability are not adjusted for the exclusion of goodwill.

        b.   The **carrying amounts** of assets (other than goodwill) and liabilities not covered by SFAS 144 that are part of an asset group are adjusted in accordance with other relevant GAAP prior to a test for recoverability.

    5.   An **impairment loss** decreases only the carrying amounts of the **long-lived assets in the group** on a pro rata basis according to their relative carrying amounts. However, the carrying amount of a given long-lived asset is **not reduced below fair value** if it is determinable without undue cost and effort.

    6.   The carrying amount of a long-lived asset adjusted for an impairment loss is its **new cost basis**. A previously recognized impairment loss may not be reversed.

7. **Fair value.** If a long-lived asset (asset group) has uncertainties about the timing and amounts of cash flows, an **expected present value** technique is often an appropriate estimator of fair value.

Reporting

8. An impairment loss is reported in **income from continuing operations**. If a subtotal for "income from operations" is reported, the impairment loss is included.

Disclosures

9. The following items are disclosed for an **impairment loss**:

   a. A description of the asset (asset group) and the circumstances of the impairment
   b. The amount of the loss (if not shown on the face of the relevant statement) and the caption in the statement that includes the loss
   c. The methods used to measure fair value
   d. The segment, if any, in which the impaired asset (asset group) is reported

Long-Lived Assets to Be Disposed of

10. If disposition is to be **other than by sale**, for example, by abandonment, exchange, or a distribution to owners in a spinoff, the asset is classified as **held and used** until disposal. It will continue to be depreciated or amortized.

11. **Long-Lived Assets to Be Disposed of by Sale**

    a. An asset (disposal group) is classified as **held for sale** when six conditions are met:

       1) Management has committed to a **plan to sell**.
       2) The asset is **available for immediate sale** in its current condition on usual and customary terms.
       3) Actions (such as actively seeking a buyer) have begun to complete the plan.
       4) Completion of sale **within 1 year is probable**.

          a) This condition need not be met if certain events or circumstances occur that the entity cannot control, e.g., when circumstances arise that previously were deemed to be unlikely, the entity takes steps to respond on a timely basis, and a favorable resolution is anticipated.

       5) The asset is **actively marketed** at a price reasonably related to current fair value.
       6) There is little likelihood of significant change in, or withdrawal of, the plan.

    b. Whenever the conditions are not met, the asset or disposal group must be **reclassified** as held and used.

    c. A **newly acquired** asset (disposal group) is classified as held for sale at the acquisition date only if

       1) The 1-year limit is satisfied (if applicable under the 1-year limit conditions), and
       2) Satisfaction of any of the other recognition criteria not satisfied at the acquisition date is probable within a short time (usually within 3 months).

    d. When the recognition criteria for held-for-sale assets are met **only after the balance sheet date**, a long-lived asset is classified as held and used. However, disclosures about the expected disposal are still required.

       1) Any **recoverability test** should be on a **held-and-used basis** as of the **balance sheet date**. Thus, the estimates of future cash flows and an impairment loss, if any, are determined as of the balance sheet date.

Measurement

12. Assets held for sale are measured at the **lower of carrying amount or fair value minus cost to sell**. If the asset (disposal group) is newly acquired, the carrying amount is the fair value minus cost to sell at the acquisition date.

    a. An asset classified as held for sale is **not depreciated or amortized**, but expenses related to the liabilities of a disposal group are accrued.

    b. **Costs to sell** are the incremental direct costs. Examples are brokers' commissions, legal and title transfer fees, and closing costs, but not future operating losses expected to be incurred.

        1) The **cost to sell is discounted** when the sale will occur in more than 1 year in the circumstances described for the 1-year condition.

    c. A disposal group classified as held for sale may include **goodwill and other assets not covered by SFAS 144**. Their carrying amount should be adjusted in accordance with relevant GAAP before determining the fair value minus cost to sell of the group. **Goodwill** is not included among the assets of a group that is not a business.

13. A **loss** is recognized for a write-down to fair value minus cost to sell. A **gain** is recognized for any subsequent increase but only to the extent of previously recognized losses for write-downs.

    a. The loss or gain adjusts only the **carrying amount of a long-lived asset** even if it is included in a disposal group.

14. A gain or loss from the sale is **recognized at the date of sale**.

Changes to a Plan of Sale

15. Such changes may occur because of circumstances (previously regarded as unlikely) that result in a decision not to sell. In these circumstances, the asset (disposal group) is **reclassified as held and used**.

    a. A reclassified long-lived asset is **measured** individually at the lower of

        1) **Carrying amount** before the asset (disposal group) was classified as held for sale, **minus any depreciation (amortization)** that would have been recognized if it had always been classified as held and used, or

        2) **Fair value** at the date of the decision not to sell.

Reporting

16. A **reclassification adjustment** to the carrying amount is included in **income from continuing operations** in the period of a decision not to sell. It is reported in the **same income statement caption** used to report a disposal loss, if any, recognized for an asset (disposal group) classified as held for sale that is **not** a component of an entity.

17. When a **component of an entity** is reclassified as held and used, its results of operations previously reported in **discontinued operations** are reclassified and included in **income from continuing operations** for all periods presented.

18. If a **long-lived asset** is held for sale, it is reported separately.

    a. If a **disposal group** is held for sale, its assets and liabilities are reported separately in the balance sheet and are not presented as one amount.

        1) The major classes of assets and liabilities held for sale are separately **disclosed** on the face of the balance sheet or in the notes.

Stop and review! You have completed the outline for this subunit. Study multiple-choice questions 24 through 27 beginning on page 317.

8.7 DEPRECIATION

Definition

1. Depreciation systematically and rationally allocates the historical cost of the productive capacity of a tangible capital asset to the periods benefited.

    a. It is not a process of valuation.

    b. The periodic charge for depreciation is offset by a credit to **accumulated depreciation**, a contra-asset. This account is **not a reserve** because it does not set aside assets.

Allocation

2. SFAC 6 defines allocation broadly as "the accounting process of assigning or distributing an amount according to a plan or formula." Allocation includes **amortization**, "the accounting process of reducing an amount by periodic payments or write-downs."

    a. Amortization is the process of accounting for **prepayments and deferrals**.

        1) Common examples of amortizations are **depreciation and depletion**.

        2) In practice, the term amortization is used more narrowly to describe the write-down of intangible assets, such as a patent.

3. **The allocation process** is systematic and rational. Allocation is used when an asset benefits more than one period, but a direct means of **associating cause and effect** is not available. "Allocation is applied if causal relations are generally, not specifically, identified" (SFAC 6).

Noncash Expense

4. Depreciation is **not a cash expense** and therefore does not provide resources for the replacement of assets.

    a. Except to the extent that depreciation is tax deductible and therefore reduces cash outlays for taxes, it does not affect an entity's **cash flows**.

        1) Hence, in a **reconciliation** of net income to net cash flow, depreciation is added to net income.

    b. The resources required to replace assets must come from the entity's earnings, borrowings, or contributions by owners.

Capitalization of Depreciation

5. Depreciation is not always expensed. Periodic depreciation may be recognized in full only over multiple periods.

    a. Thus, under the **full-cost method** required by GAAP, depreciation on a factory building and machinery used in production of inventory is charged to overhead, which in turn is applied to work-in-process.

Elements of Depreciation

6.   The **depreciable base** is estimated at the beginning of the **depreciation period**. It is the portion of the historical cost that will be expensed over the estimated useful life of the asset. It equals the historical or original cost recorded minus the **salvage value** (a residual amount).

   a.   The historical cost itself may result from various assumptions and estimates.

7.   The **estimated useful life** is the service or economic life of a productive asset. It depends on the causes of depreciation and the owner's intended use and maintenance policies.

   a.   The length of time the asset will be held by a future owner, its use by that party, or its potential employment for an alternative purpose are **not** considered.

   b.   The **consumption of the economic benefits** represented by an asset's recorded amount follows a pattern that is unique to each asset. The following are the most common factors to which that **consumption pattern** may be related:

      1)   Passage of time (months or years)
      2)   Units of production (e.g., units of output by a machine)
      3)   Amount of service (such as hours of operation or miles driven)

   c.   The estimated useful life may be expressed not only in units of time but also in terms of such variables as machine hours or units of output.

Methods of Allocating the Depreciable Base

8.   The **straight-line** method is time-based. Depreciation expense is a **constant amount** (depreciable base ÷ estimated useful life) for each period.

   a.   It ignores fluctuations in usage and in maintenance charges. The **carrying amount** is dependent upon the time the asset is held, not its use.

9.   **Accelerated methods** were popularized when they became allowable on **tax returns**. But the same method need not be used for tax and financial statement purposes.

   a.   Accelerated methods are **time-based**. They result in decreasing depreciation charges over the life of the asset.

   b.   **Declining balance (DB)** determines depreciation expense by multiplying the carrying amount (**not** a depreciable base equal to cost – salvage value) at the beginning of each period by some percentage (e.g., 200% or 150%) of the straight-line rate of depreciation.

      1)   The carrying amount decreases by the depreciation recognized. The result is the use of a **constant rate** against a **declining balance**.

      2)   **Salvage value** is ignored in determining the carrying amount, but the asset is **not** depreciated below salvage value.

EXAMPLE

Jayhawk Co. recently acquired a robot to be used in its fully automated factory.

Cost of robot	$1,000,000
Estimated useful life	5 years
Estimated salvage value	$100,000

The following is the depreciation schedule using the double-declining-balance (DDB) method:

Depreciable amount	=	($1,000,000 – $100,000)	= $900,000
Straight-line amount per year	=	$900,000 ÷ 5	= $180,000
Straight-line rate	=	$180,000 ÷ $900,000	= 20%
DDB rate	=	200% × 20%	= 40%

Year	Carrying Amount, First of Year	DDB Rate	Depreciation Expense	Balance, Accumulated Depreciation	Carrying Amount, End of Year
1	$1,000,000	40%	$400,000	$400,000	$600,000
2	600,000	40%	240,000	640,000	360,000
3	360,000	40%	144,000	784,000	216,000
4	216,000	40%	86,400	870,400	129,600
5	129,600	40%	29,600	900,000	100,000

Year 5 depreciation expense is $29,600 because the carrying amount cannot be less than salvage value.

---

c. **Sum-of-the-years' digits (SYD)** multiplies not the carrying amount but a **constant depreciable base** (cost – salvage value) by a declining fraction. It is a **declining-rate, declining-charge** method.

1) The SYD fraction's **numerator** is the number of years of the useful life (n) minus the prior years elapsed.

2) The formula to compute the **denominator** is

$$\frac{n\ (n + 1)}{2}$$

EXAMPLE

See the Jayhawk Co. fact statement. The denominator of the SYD fraction is 15 {[5 × (5 + 1)] ÷ 2}, and the depreciation base is $900,000 ($1,000,000 – $100,000). Thus, the following is the depreciation schedule using the SYD method:

Year	Numerator in Years	Depreciation Base × Fraction	Expense	Accumulated Depreciation	Carrying Amount, Year-End
1	5	$900,000 × (5 ÷ 15)	$300,000	$300,000	$700,000
2	4	$900,000 × (4 ÷ 15)	240,000	540,000	460,000
3	3	$900,000 × (3 ÷ 15)	180,000	720,000	280,000
4	2	$900,000 × (2 ÷ 15)	120,000	840,000	160,000
5	1	$900,000 × (1 ÷ 15)	60,000	900,000	100,000

Usage-Centered Activity Methods

10. **Usage-centered activity** methods calculate depreciation as a function of an asset's use rather than the time it has been held.

    a. The **units-of-output** method allocates cost based on production. As production varies, so will the credit to accumulated depreciation.

        1) **Each unit** is charged with a **constant amount of depreciation** equal to cost minus salvage value, divided by the total units expected to be produced.

        2) This technique is appropriate if obsolescence is not a cause of depreciation and the asset's output can be reasonably estimated.

11. A variation is **modified units of production (MUP)**. It combines the straight-line and units-of-output methods.

    a. If depreciation is a function of output but a reasonable estimate of total output cannot be made, the expense may be calculated using the straight-line method. However, the estimate of the useful life employed each period will vary inversely with periodic output.

12. **Services used.** The reduction in service potential of an asset may be most clearly related to a measure of input or services used, e.g., machine hours.

    a. This technique is appropriate when output is indeterminable because specific output cannot be identified or when the total cannot be estimated.

    b. Like the units-of-output method, the services used method calculates a variable depreciation expense based on a **fixed charge per unit of activity**.

EXAMPLE

The following information is for a truck purchased by Ice Trucking Co. on January 1, Year 1:

Estimated cost	$50,000
Useful life in years	5
Useful life in miles	100,000
Estimated salvage value	$10,000
Actual miles driven: Years 1–4	90,000

No estimates were changed during the life of the asset. Using the services-used method, what was Year 5 depreciation expense? Under the services-used method, periodic depreciation is based on the proportion of expected total activity. For Years 1 through 4, the total depreciation was $36,000 [($50,000 – $10,000) × (90,000 miles ÷ 100,000 miles)]. Hence, the remaining depreciable base was $4,000 ($50,000 cost – $10,000 salvage – $36,000). Given that the 12,000 miles driven in Year 5 exceeded the remaining estimated activity of 10,000 miles (100,000 – 90,000), only the $4,000 of the remaining depreciable base should be recognized in Year 5.

Group and Composite Depreciation

13. These methods use **straight-line** techniques for an aggregate of assets. The composite method applies to groups of **dissimilar assets** with varying useful lives and the group method to **similar assets**. They provide an efficient way to account for large numbers of depreciable assets. They also result in offsetting of under- and overstated depreciation estimates.

    a. Each method calculates (1) **total depreciable cost** (total acquisition cost – salvage value) for all the assets debited to a control account, (2) **weighted-average estimated useful life** (total depreciable cost ÷ total annual straight-line depreciation), and (3) **weighted-average depreciation rate** based on cost (total annual straight-line depreciation ÷ **total acquisition cost**). One accumulated depreciation account also is maintained.

b. **Early and late retirements** are expected to offset each other.

    1) Thus, gains and losses on retirements of single assets are not recognized but are treated as adjustments of accumulated depreciation. The **entry** is

Cash (proceeds)	$XXX	
Asset (cost)		$XXX
Accumulated depreciation (dr or cr)		XXX

    2) **Periodic depreciation** equals the weighted-average rate times the beginning balance of the asset account for the period. Thus, depreciation is calculated based on the cost of assets in use during the period. **Prior-period retirements** are reflected in this balance.

EXAMPLE

For its first year of operations, Argent Co. used the composite method of depreciation and prepared the following schedule of machinery owned:

	Total Cost	Estimated Salvage Value	Estimated Life in Years
Machine X	$550,000	$50,000	20
Machine Y	200,000	20,000	15
Machine Z	40,000	--	5

Argent computes depreciation on the straight-line method. Based upon the information presented, the composite life of these assets (in years) should be 16.0. The composite or average useful life of the assets is essentially a weighted average. As illustrated below, the annual straight-line depreciation for each asset should be calculated. The total cost, estimated salvage value, and depreciable base of the assets should then be computed. Dividing the composite depreciable base ($720) by the total annual straight-line depreciation ($45) gives the composite life (16 years) of these assets.

	Total Cost	Salvage Value	Dep. Base	Est. Life	Annual S-L Dep.
X	$550	$50	$500	20	$25
Y	200	20	180	15	12
Z	40	0	40	5	8
	$790	$70	$720		$45

Depreciation for a Fractional Period

14. Because an asset is most likely to be acquired or disposed of other than at the beginning or end of a fiscal year, depreciation may need to be computed for a fraction of a period. Time-based methods most often compute depreciation to the nearest month of a partial year, but other conventions also are permitted.

    a. A **full year's** depreciation may be recognized in the year of acquisition and none in the year of disposal or vice versa.

    b. Depreciation may be recognized to the **nearest full-year** or the **nearest half-year**.

    c. A **half-year's** depreciation may be recognized in both the year of acquisition and the year of disposal.

Disclosure

15. Full disclosure should be made of **depreciation methods and practices** (APB Opinion 12, *Omnibus Opinion – 1967*), including

    a. Depreciation expense for the period
    b. Balances of major classes of depreciable assets by nature or function
    c. Accumulated depreciation either by major class or in total
    d. Description of depreciation methods for each major class of assets

Stop and review! You have completed the outline for this subunit. Study multiple-choice questions 28 through 34 beginning on page 319.

8.8 DEPLETION

1. **Natural resources** (wasting assets) are held for direct resale or consumption in other products. Examples are petroleum, gold, silver, timber, iron ore, gravel, and coal.

    a. Natural resources differ from depreciable assets because they

        1) Lose their separate character during extraction and consumption
        2) Are produced only by natural processes
        3) Are recorded as **inventory** after extraction

            a) The **entry** to record the inventory and the depletion of the natural resource is

Inventory	$XXX	
Accumulated depletion (a contra account)		$XXX

            b) But some entities credit the natural resource account directly.

2. **Depletion** is similar to depreciation. It is an accounting process of allocating the **historical cost of a tangible asset** to the periods benefited by its uses.

The Depletion Base

3. The **cost subject to depletion is the depletion base**. Accounting for depletion is complicated by the need to capitalize costs other than those incurred for acquisition.

    a. One component of the depletion base is the **cost of purchasing** already discovered natural resources or of obtaining the right to search for them. It includes costs normally incurred to purchase land, such as legal fees and closing costs.

    b. Two methods of accounting for **exploration costs** are permitted.

        1) The **successful-efforts method** capitalizes only those exploration costs that lead to the location of resources that can be feasibly developed.

            a) In the **oil and gas industry**, the cost of an exploratory well is temporarily capitalized until it is determined whether the effort is successful. An entity using the successful-efforts method would then charge these costs to expense if production proves not to be feasible.

        2) The **full-cost method** capitalizes the costs of both successful and unsuccessful efforts. Both are deemed necessary to discovery of productive resources.

4. **Development costs** for extraction of natural resources must be incurred to construct buildings, drill wells or mine shafts, buy equipment, etc.

   a. **Intangible costs** (e.g., for wells and shafts) are part of the depletion base.

   b. **Tangible assets**, such as equipment, are needed to exploit natural resources. These assets are separately capitalized and depreciated over the shorter of their estimated useful lives or the life of the resource if their **usefulness is limited** to the extraction of the particular resource.

      1) Tangible assets **not limited in use** to the exploitation of a particular resource should be depreciated over their useful lives.

      2) The cost of either kind of tangible asset, however, is ordinarily **not** included in the depletion base.

5. The **residual value** of the property from which the natural resource is extracted is also a factor in calculating the depletion base. But any **costs of restoring the property** before sale reduce the residual value (and increase the depletion base).

   a. The amount included in the depletion base for restoration is the **fair value of the liability** (the **asset retirement obligation**).

6. **Production costs** for extracting the resource (e.g., labor, materials, and overhead) are **not** included in the depletion base.

Calculating Depletion

7. Depletion is similar to usage-centered depreciation because it is most often determined by applying the **units-of-output (production)** method.

   a. The **depletion base** (capitalized costs of acquisition, exploration, and development, minus residual value adjusted for restoration costs) is divided by the units estimated to be economically recoverable to determine the **per-unit depletion rate**.

   b. **Units extracted times the depletion rate equals periodic depletion.**

      1) To the extent that extracted units are sold, cost of goods sold is debited.
      2) Unsold units remain in inventory.

   c. The calculation of depletion is straightforward, but **estimating the amount of the recoverable resource** is often extremely difficult. Changes in estimates may be frequent because price movements and new technology will affect the amounts that can be profitably extracted.

EXAMPLE

Jayhawk Co. leased the right to use 1,000 acres of land in Wyoming to drill for oil. The lease cost is $100,000, and the related exploration costs are $150,000. Developmental costs incurred are $750,000. The company estimates that the land will provide approximately 1,000,000 barrels of oil. Moreover, the expected residual value minus restoration costs is $0.

The **depletion cost per unit** (depletion rate) is

$$\frac{\text{Total cost} - \text{Residual value}}{\text{Total estimated units available}} = \text{Depletion cost per barrel of oil}$$

$$\frac{\$1,000,000 - 0}{1,000,000} = \$1 \text{ per barrel}$$

Thus, if Jayhawk extracts 200,000 barrels of oil in the first year, the credit to accumulated depletion is $200,000 for the year.

Stop and review! You have completed the outline for this subunit. Study multiple-choice questions 35 and 36 on page 321.

QUESTIONS

8.1 Initial Measurement of Property, Plant, and Equipment (PPE)

1. Land was purchased to be used as the site for the construction of a plant. A building on the property was sold and removed by the buyer so that construction on the plant could begin. The proceeds from the sale of the building should be

A. Classified as other income.

B. Deducted from the cost of the land.

C. Netted against the costs to clear the land and expensed as incurred.

D. Netted against the costs to clear the land and amortized over the life of the plant.

Answer (B) is correct. *(CPA, adapted)*
REQUIRED: The treatment of proceeds from the sale of a building removed to prepare for construction.
DISCUSSION: Land obtained as a plant site should be recorded at its acquisition cost. This cost includes the purchase price of the land and any additional expenses such as legal fees, title insurance, recording fees, assumption of encumbrances on the property, and any other costs incurred in preparing the property for its intended use. Because the intended use of the land was as a site for the construction of a plant, the proceeds from the sale of the building removed to prepare the land for construction should be deducted from the cost of the land.

2. Merry Co. purchased a machine costing $125,000 for its manufacturing operations and paid shipping costs of $20,000. Merry spent an additional $10,000 testing and preparing the machine for use. What amount should Merry record as the cost of the machine?

A. $155,000

B. $145,000

C. $135,000

D. $125,000

Answer (A) is correct. *(CPA, adapted)*
REQUIRED: The amount to be recorded as the acquisition cost.
DISCUSSION: The amount to be recorded as the acquisition cost of a machine includes all costs necessary to prepare it for its intended use. Thus, the cost of a machine used in the manufacturing operations of a company includes the cost of testing and preparing the machine for use and the shipping costs. The acquisition cost is $155,000 ($125,000 + $20,000 + $10,000).
Answer (B) is incorrect because $145,000 does not include the $10,000 cost of testing and preparation. Answer (C) is incorrect because $135,000 does not include the shipping costs. Answer (D) is incorrect because $125,000 does not include the shipping, testing, and preparation costs.

3. During the year just ended, Burr Co. had the following transactions pertaining to its new office building:

Purchase price of land	$ 60,000
Legal fees for contracts to purchase land	2,000
Architects' fees	8,000
Demolition of the old building on site	5,000
Sale of scrap from old building	3,000
Construction cost of new building (fully completed)	350,000

In Burr's December 31 balance sheet, what amounts should be reported as the cost of land and cost of building?

	Land	Building
A.	$60,000	$360,000
B.	$62,000	$360,000
C.	$64,000	$358,000
D.	$65,000	$362,000

Answer (C) is correct. *(CPA, adapted)*
REQUIRED: The amounts reported as the cost of land and cost of building.
DISCUSSION: The cost of the land should include the purchase price of the land and such additional expenses as legal fees, title insurance, recording fees, subsequent assumption of encumbrances on the property, and the costs incurred in preparing the property for its intended use. Because the land was purchased as the site of an office building, the cost of razing the old building, minus any proceeds received from the sale of salvaged materials, should be capitalized as part of the land account. Thus, land should be reported as $64,000 ($60,000 + $2,000 + $5,000 − $3,000). The architect's fees are included in the cost of the building, which should be reported as $358,000 ($350,000 + $8,000).
Answer (A) is incorrect because a $60,000 land cost omits the legal fees and the net demolition cost, and a $360,000 building cost improperly includes the legal fees. Answer (B) is incorrect because a $62,000 land cost omits the legal fees or the net demolition cost, and a $360,000 building cost improperly includes the legal fees. Answer (D) is incorrect because a $65,000 land cost includes the gross demolition cost but not the legal fees. A $362,000 building cost includes the legal fees and the net demolition cost.

4. On July 1, Casa Development Co. purchased a tract of land for $1.2 million. Casa incurred additional costs of $300,000 during the remainder of the year in preparing the land for sale. The tract was subdivided into residential lots as follows:

Lot Class	Number of Lots	Sales Price per Lot
A	100	$24,000
B	100	16,000
C	200	10,000

Using the relative sales value method, what amount of costs should be allocated to the Class A lots?

A. $300,000

B. $375,000

C. $600,000

D. $720,000

Answer (C) is correct. *(CPA, adapted)*
REQUIRED: The amount of costs allocated using the relative sales value method.
DISCUSSION: The relative sales value method allocates cost based on the relative value of assets in a group. The total sales value of the lots is $6,000,000 [(100 × $24,000) + (100 × $16,000) + (200 × $10,000)]. Class A represents 40% of the total value ($2,400,000 ÷ $6,000,000). Total costs equal $1,500,000 ($1,200,000 + $300,000). Thus, the amount of costs allocated to Class A is $600,000 ($1,500,000 × .40).
Answer (A) is incorrect because $300,000 equals the additional costs incurred. Answer (B) is incorrect because $375,000 equals 25% of the total cost. Class A represents 25% of the lots but 40% of the total value. Answer (D) is incorrect because $720,000 equals 48% of the total cost. Class A's sales price per lot is 48% of the sum of the unit sales prices of Classes A, B, and C.

5. During January, Yana Co. incurred landscaping costs of $120,000 to improve leased property. The estimated useful life of the landscaping is 15 years. The remaining term of the lease is 8 years, with an option to renew for an additional 4 years. However, Yana has not reached a decision with regard to the renewal option. In Yana's December 31 balance sheet, what should be the net carrying amount of landscaping costs?

A. $0

B. $105,000

C. $110,000

D. $112,000

Answer (B) is correct. *(CPA, adapted)*
REQUIRED: The net amount of leasehold improvements reported in the balance sheet.
DISCUSSION: General improvements to leased property should be capitalized as leasehold improvements and amortized in accordance with the straight-line method over the shorter of their expected useful life or the lease term. However, if the useful life of the asset extends beyond the lease term and renewal of the lease is likely, the amortization period may include all or part of the renewal period. If renewal is uncertain, the useful life is the remaining term, and the salvage value is the amount, if any, to be paid by the lessor to the lessee at the expiration of the lease. Consequently, the amortization period is the 8-year lease term, and the net carrying amount at December 31 of the landscaping costs incurred in January is $105,000 [$120,000 × (7 years ÷ 8 years)].
Answer (A) is incorrect because land improvements with limited lives should be capitalized. Answer (C) is incorrect because $110,000 assumes that renewal for 4 years is likely. Answer (D) is incorrect because $112,000 assumes amortization over 15 years.

8.2 Special Measurement Issue -- Internally Constructed Assets (ICAs)

6. On January 2, Year 1, Cruises, Inc. borrowed $3 million at a rate of 10% for three years and began construction of a cruise ship. The note states that annual payments of principal and interest in the amount of $1.3 million are due every December 31. Cruises used all proceeds as a down payment for construction of a new cruise ship that is to be delivered two years after start of construction. What should Cruises report as interest expense related to the note in its income statement for Year 2?

A. $0

B. $300,000

C. $600,000

D. $900,000

Answer (A) is correct. *(CPA, adapted)*
REQUIRED: The interest reported in Year 2.
DISCUSSION: An asset produced by an entity for its own use qualifies for interest capitalization. Capitalized interest is limited to the amount theoretically avoidable if expenditures for the asset had not been made. It is also limited to the interest incurred for the period. Interest capitalized equals average accumulated expenditures (AAE) for the qualifying asset times the appropriate interest rate(s). The capitalization period (e.g., two years for the cruise ship beginning January 2 of Year 1) is the time required to carry out the activities necessary to bring the asset to the condition and location necessary for its intended use. Accordingly, no interest expense related to the note is recognized in the second year. The 10% interest rate on the note, a specific new borrowing outstanding during the capitalization period and identified with the qualifying asset, may be used as the capitalization rate to the extent that AAE do not exceed the amount of the new borrowing. Given that the $3 million of proceeds were used as a down payment, the total interest on the note (the carrying amount of the note for Year 2 × 10%) qualifies for capitalization. Thus, the AAE are at least equal to the carrying amount of the note for the second year. A weighted-average rate must be applied to the amount exceeding the specified new borrowings (SFAS 34).

7. Cole Co. began constructing a building for its own use in January. During the year, Cole incurred interest of $50,000 on specific construction debt and $20,000 on other borrowings. Interest computed on the weighted-average amount of accumulated expenditures for the building during the year was $40,000. What amount of interest cost should Cole capitalize?

A. $20,000

B. $40,000

C. $50,000

D. $70,000

Answer (B) is correct.   *(CPA, adapted)*
REQUIRED: The amount of interest capitalized.
DISCUSSION: Material interest costs incurred for the construction of certain assets for internal use are capitalized. The interest to be capitalized is determined by applying an appropriate rate to the average qualifying expenditures accumulated during a given period. However, the interest capitalized may not exceed the amount incurred during the period. Thus, $40,000 of the interest incurred on the construction is capitalized.
Answer (A) is incorrect because $20,000 equals interest on other borrowings. Answer (C) is incorrect because $50,000 equals the total interest on specific construction debt. Answer (D) is incorrect because $70,000 equals the sum of interest on other borrowings and the total interest on specific construction debt.

8. A company is constructing an asset for its own use. Construction began in Year 3. The asset is being financed entirely with a specific new borrowing. Construction expenditures were made in Year 3 and Year 4 at the end of each quarter. The total amount of interest cost capitalized in Year 4 should be determined by applying the interest rate on the specific new borrowing to the

A. Total accumulated expenditures for the asset in Year 3 and Year 4.

B. Average accumulated expenditures for the asset in Year 3 and Year 4.

C. Average expenditures for the asset in Year 4.

D. Total expenditures for the asset in Year 4.

Answer (B) is correct.   *(CPA, adapted)*
REQUIRED: The expenditures used in determining the capitalizable interest.
DISCUSSION: An asset constructed for an entity's own use qualifies for capitalization of interest if (1) relevant expenditures have been made, (2) activities necessary to prepare the asset for its intended use are in progress, and (3) interest is being incurred. The capitalized amount is determined by applying an interest rate to the average qualifying expenditures accumulated during the period. These expenditures in any given period include those incurred in that period plus those incurred in the construction of the asset in all previous periods. Thus, the total interest cost capitalized in Year 4 equals the interest rate on the specific new borrowing times the average accumulated expenditures for the asset in Year 3 and Year 4.
Answer (A) is incorrect because the basis is an average for Year 3 and Year 4, not the total. Answer (C) is incorrect because the basis includes expenditures during the entire construction period. Answer (D) is incorrect because the basis is an average for Year 3 and Year 4.

9. Clay Company started construction of a new office building on January 1, Year 8, and moved into the finished building on July 1, Year 9. Of the building's $2.5 million total cost, $2 million was incurred in Year 8 evenly throughout the year. Clay's incremental borrowing rate was 12% throughout Year 8, and the total amount of construction-related interest incurred by Clay during Year 8 was $102,000. What amount should Clay report as capitalized interest at December 31, Year 8?

A. $102,000

B. $120,000

C. $150,000

D. $240,000

Answer (A) is correct.   *(CPA, adapted)*
REQUIRED: The amount of interest to be capitalized as a cost of an asset.
DISCUSSION: The new office building qualifies for capitalization of interest cost because (1) the asset is being constructed for the entity's own use, (2) expenditures relative to the qualifying asset have been made, (3) activities necessary to prepare the asset for its intended use are in progress, and (4) interest cost is being incurred. The amount capitalized is determined by applying an interest rate to the average accumulated expenditures (AAE) for the period. The AAE equals the simple average of any cost that is incurred evenly throughout the year. Here, the AAE are $1,000,000 ($2,000,000 × .5). The amount of interest to be capitalized is the $1,000,000 AAE times the rate of interest paid during Year 8, which is given as 12%. Because the $120,000 result ($1,000,000 × 12%) exceeds the $102,000 total amount of interest incurred, $102,000 is the maximum amount of interest that can be capitalized during the period ending 12/31/Year 8.

8.3 Subsequent Expenditures for PPE

10. An expenditure to install an improved electrical system is a

	Capital Expenditure	Revenue Expenditure
A.	No	Yes
B.	No	No
C.	Yes	No
D.	Yes	Yes

Answer (C) is correct. *(CPA, adapted)*
REQUIRED: The nature of an expenditure to install an improved electrical system.
DISCUSSION: A betterment (improvement) occurs when a replacement asset is substituted for an existing asset, and the result is increased productivity, capacity, or expected useful life. If the improvement benefits future periods, it should be capitalized.

11. A building suffered uninsured fire damage. The damaged portion of the building was refurbished with higher-quality materials. The cost and related accumulated depreciation of the damaged portion are identifiable. The owner should

A. Reduce accumulated depreciation equal to the cost of refurbishing.

B. Record a loss in the current period equal to the sum of the cost of refurbishing and the carrying amount of the damaged part of the building.

C. Capitalize the cost of refurbishing and record a loss in the current period equal to the carrying amount of the damaged part of the building.

D. Capitalize the cost of refurbishing by adding the cost to the carrying amount of the building.

Answer (C) is correct. *(CPA, adapted)*
REQUIRED: The proper accounting for a substitution.
DISCUSSION: When a substantial portion of a productive asset is replaced and the cost and related accumulated depreciation associated with the old component are identifiable, the substitution method of accounting is used. Under this approach, the asset account and accumulated depreciation should be reduced by the appropriate amounts and a gain or loss recognized. In this instance, the damages were uninsured, and a loss equal to the carrying amount of the damaged portion of the building should be recognized. In addition, the cost of refurbishing should be capitalized in the asset account.

12. On June 18, Dell Printing Co. incurred the following costs for one of its printing presses:

Purchase of collating and stapling attachment	$84,000
Installation of attachment	36,000
Replacement parts for overhaul of press	26,000
Labor and overhead in connection with overhaul	14,000

The overhaul resulted in a significant increase in production. Neither the attachment nor the overhaul increased the estimated useful life of the press. What amount of the above costs should be capitalized?

A. $0

B. $84,000

C. $120,000

D. $160,000

Answer (D) is correct. *(CPA, adapted)*
REQUIRED: The amount of costs to be capitalized.
DISCUSSION: Expenditures that increase the quality or quantity of a machine's output should be capitalized whether or not its useful life is extended. Thus, the amount of the cost to be capitalized equals $160,000 ($84,000 + $36,000 + $26,000 + $14,000).
Answer (A) is incorrect because $0 omits all of the listed capital expenditures. Answer (B) is incorrect because the installation and overhaul costs are capitalized. Answer (C) is incorrect because $120,000 excludes the overhaul costs.

13. Tomson Co. installed new assembly line production equipment at a cost of $175,000. Tomson had to rearrange the assembly line and remove a wall to install the equipment. The rearrangement cost $12,000, and the wall removal cost $3,000. The rearrangement did not increase the life of the assembly line, but it did make it more efficient. What amount of these costs should be capitalized by Tomson?

A. $175,000

B. $178,000

C. $187,000

D. $190,000

Answer (D) is correct. *(CPA, adapted)*
REQUIRED: The capitalized cost of a new assembly line.
DISCUSSION: The initial measurement equals the sum of the cost to acquire the equipment and the costs necessarily incurred to bring it to the condition and location necessary for its intended use. A rearrangement is the movement of existing assets to provide greater efficiency or to reduce production costs. If the rearrangement expenditure benefits future periods, it should be capitalized. If the wall removal costs likewise improve future service potential, they too should be capitalized. Thus, the capitalized cost is $190,000 ($175,000 + $12,000 + $3,000).
Answer (A) is incorrect because the amount capitalized must include all costs incurred to bring the equipment to use. Answer (B) is incorrect because the rearrangement cost must be included in the amount capitalized. If this cost was incurred for the benefit of existing equipment, different rules apply. Answer (C) is incorrect because cost of removal of the wall is capitalized.

14. During the year just ended, Fox Company made the following expenditures relating to plant machinery and equipment:

- Renovation of a group of machines at a cost of $50,000 to secure greater efficiency in production over their remaining 5-year useful lives. The project was completed on December 31.
- Continuing, frequent, and low-cost repairs at a cost of $35,000.
- A broken gear on a machine was replaced at a cost of $5,000.

What total amount should be charged to repairs and maintenance?

A. $35,000

B. $40,000

C. $85,000

D. $90,000

Answer (B) is correct. *(CPA, adapted)*
REQUIRED: The amount to be charged to repair and maintenance expense.
DISCUSSION: Repair and maintenance costs are incurred to maintain plant assets in operating condition. The continuing, frequent, and low-cost repairs and the replacement of a broken gear meet the definition of repairs and maintenance expense. Accordingly, the amount that should be charged to repairs and maintenance is $40,000 ($35,000 + $5,000). The renovation cost increased the quality of production during the expected useful life of the group of machines. Hence, this $50,000 cost should be capitalized.
Answer (A) is incorrect because $35,000 excludes the gear replacement. Answer (C) is incorrect because $85,000 includes the renovation cost but not the gear replacement. Answer (D) is incorrect because $90,000 includes the renovation cost.

8.4 Disposals Other Than by Exchange

15. An entity disposes of a nonmonetary asset in a nonreciprocal transfer. A gain or loss should be recognized on the disposition of the asset when the fair value of the asset transferred is determinable and the nonreciprocal transfer is to

	Another Entity	A Shareholder of the Entity
A.	No	Yes
B.	No	No
C.	Yes	No
D.	Yes	Yes

Answer (D) is correct. *(CPA, adapted)*
REQUIRED: The circumstances under which gain or loss should be recorded in a nonreciprocal transfer.
DISCUSSION: A nonreciprocal transfer is a transfer of assets or services in one direction. A nonreciprocal transfer of a nonmonetary asset to a shareholder or to another entity should be recorded at the fair value of the asset transferred. A gain or loss should be recognized on the transfer. However, an exception to this general rule is provided for distributions of nonmonetary assets to owners in (1) a spin-off or other form of reorganization or liquidation or (2) a plan that is in substance the rescission of a prior business combination.

16. A state government condemned Cory Co.'s parcel of real estate. Cory will receive $750,000 for this property, which has a carrying amount of $575,000. Cory incurred the following costs as a result of the condemnation:

Appraisal fees to support a $750,000 value	$2,500
Attorney fees for the closing with the state	3,500
Attorney fees to review contract to acquire replacement property	3,000
Title insurance on replacement property	4,000

What amount of cost should Cory use to determine the gain on the condemnation?

- A. $581,000
- B. $582,000
- C. $584,000
- D. $588,000

Answer (A) is correct. *(CPA, adapted)*
REQUIRED: The amount of cost used to determine the gain on the condemnation.
DISCUSSION: FASB Interpretation No. 30 requires that gain or loss be recognized on an involuntary conversion. The determination of the gain is based on the carrying amount ($575,000) and the costs incurred as a direct result of the condemnation ($2,500 appraisal fees and $3,500 attorney fees), a total of $581,000. Because the recipient is not obligated to reinvest the condemnation proceeds in other nonmonetary assets, the costs associated with the acquisition of the replacement property (attorney fees and title insurance) should be treated as part of the consideration paid for that property.
Answer (B) is incorrect because $582,000 includes the costs associated with the replacement property but not the costs incurred as a direct result of the condemnation. Answer (C) is incorrect because $584,000 includes the attorney fees associated with the replacement property. Answer (D) is incorrect because $588,000 includes the costs associated with the replacement property.

17. On July 1, one of Rudd Co.'s delivery vans was destroyed in an accident. On that date, the van's carrying value was $2,500. On July 15, Rudd received and recorded a $700 invoice for a new engine installed in the van in May and another $500 invoice for various repairs. In August, Rudd received $3,500 under its insurance policy on the van, which it plans to use to replace the van. What amount should Rudd report as gain (loss) on disposal of the van in its income statement for the year?

- A. $1,000
- B. $300
- C. $0
- D. $(200)

Answer (B) is correct. *(CPA, adapted)*
REQUIRED: The gain (loss) on disposal of the van.
DISCUSSION: Gain (loss) is recognized on an involuntary conversion equal to the difference between the proceeds and the carrying amount. The carrying amount includes the carrying value at July 1 ($2,500) plus the capitalizable cost ($700) of the engine installed in May. This cost increased the carrying amount because it improved the future service potential of the asset. Ordinary repairs, however, are expensed. Consequently, the gain is $300 [$3,500 – ($2,500 + $700)].
Answer (A) is incorrect because $1,000 results from expensing the cost of the engine. Answer (C) is incorrect because gain (loss) is recognized on an involuntary conversion. Answer (D) is incorrect because $(200) assumes the cost of repairs increased the carrying amount.

18. Ocean Corp.'s comprehensive insurance policy allows its assets to be replaced at current value. The policy has a $50,000 deductible clause. One of Ocean's waterfront warehouses was destroyed in a winter storm. Such storms occur approximately every 4 years. Ocean incurred $20,000 of costs in dismantling the warehouse and plans to replace it. The following data relate to the warehouse:

Current carrying amount	$ 300,000
Replacement cost	1,100,000

The gain Ocean should report as a separate component of income before extraordinary items is

- A. $1,030,000
- B. $780,000
- C. $730,000
- D. $0

Answer (C) is correct. *(CPA, adapted)*
REQUIRED: The gain reported as a separate component of income before extraordinary items.
DISCUSSION: To be classified as an extraordinary item, a transaction must be both unusual in nature and infrequent in occurrence within the environment in which the business operates. If an item meets one but not both of these criteria, it should be presented separately as a component of income from continuing operations. The gain is presumably infrequent but is not unusual in the entity's operating environment. The gain does not possess a high degree of abnormality and is not clearly unrelated to, or only incidentally related to, the entity's ordinary and typical activities. Hence, Ocean should separately recognize a gain from continuing operations equal to $730,000 ($1,100,000 current value – $50,000 deductible – $300,000 carrying amount – $20,000 costs of dismantling).
Answer (A) is incorrect because $1,030,000 disregards the $300,000 carrying amount. Answer (B) is incorrect because $780,000 omits the deductible. Answer (D) is incorrect because a gain (loss) should be recognized for an involuntary conversion.

8.5 Exchanges of Nonmonetary Assets

19. Iona Co. and Siena Co. exchanged goods, held for resale, with equal fair values. Each will use the other's goods to promote its own products. The retail price of the wickets that Iona gave up is less than the retail price of the wombles received. What gain should Iona recognize on the nonmonetary exchange?

A. A gain is not recognized.

B. A gain equal to the difference between the retail prices of the wombles received and the wickets.

C. A gain equal to the difference between the retail price and the cost of the wickets.

D. A gain equal to the difference between the fair value and the cost of the wickets.

Answer (D) is correct. *(CPA, adapted)*
REQUIRED: The gain to be recognized on a nonmonetary exchange of inventory.
DISCUSSION: The accounting for a nonmonetary transaction should be based on the carrying amount of the asset given up in an exchange of goods held for sale in the ordinary course of business for goods to be sold in the same line of business. The exchange also must be designed to facilitate sales to customers other than the parties to the exchange. Because Iona will use the wombles to promote its own product, the requirement that the product be used to facilitate sales to customers other than Iona or Siena is not met. Facilitation entails, for example, meeting immediate inventory needs or reducing transportation costs. Hence, Iona should record a gain equal to the difference between the fair value (the same for both assets) and the cost (carrying amount) of the asset surrendered.
Answer (A) is incorrect because a gain should be recognized. Answer (B) is incorrect because fair value, not retail prices, is the appropriate basis at which the asset received should be recognized. Answer (C) is incorrect because fair value, not retail prices, is the appropriate basis at which the asset received should be recognized.

20. Departure from the use of fair values in accounting for a nonmonetary exchange transaction is acceptable when there is an insignificant difference between the

I. Risk, timing, and amount of the future cash flows of the asset(s) received and the risk, timing, and amount of the future cash flows of the asset(s) transferred.

II. Entity-specific value of the asset(s) received and the entity-specific value of the asset(s) transferred.

A. Both I and II.

B. I only.

C. II only.

D. Neither I nor II.

Answer (A) is correct. *(Publisher, adapted)*
REQUIRED: The appropriate departures, if any, from fair value in accounting for a nonmonetary exchange.
DISCUSSION: Accounting for both monetary and nonmonetary transactions generally should be based on fair value of the assets involved, with gain or loss recognized immediately. However, accounting for nonmonetary transactions should be based on the carrying amount of the asset given up when the transaction is an exchange that lacks commercial substance. An exchange lacks commercial substance when an entity's cash flows are not expected to change significantly. Cash flows do not change significantly when (1) the configuration (risk, timing, and amount) of the future cash flows of the asset(s) received does not significantly differ from the future cash flows of the asset(s) transferred or (2) the entity-specific value of the asset(s) received does not significantly differ from the entity-specific value of the asset(s) transferred. Entity-specific value is determined in the context of the entity's use of the assets.

21. Hagen Co. exchanged a truck with a carrying amount of $12,000 and a fair value of $20,000 for a truck and $5,000 cash. The fair value of the truck received was $15,000. The exchange was not considered to have commercial substance. At what amount should Hagen record the truck received in the exchange?

A. $7,000

B. $9,000

C. $12,000

D. $15,000

Answer (D) is correct. *(CPA, adapted)*
REQUIRED: The amount at which a nonmonetary asset should be recorded in a transaction involving boot.
DISCUSSION: A transaction involving nonmonetary assets and boot is monetary if the boot equals or exceeds 25% of the fair value of the exchange. In this exchange, the $5,000 of boot equals 25% of the $20,000 ($5,000 + $15,000) fair value of the exchange. Thus, the exchange is monetary. Accounting for monetary transactions should be based on the fair value of the assets involved, with gain or loss recognized immediately. Hagen should record the truck received at its $15,000 fair value. It also should record an $8,000 gain equal to the difference between the $20,000 fair value received and the $12,000 carrying amount of the truck given up.
Answer (A) is incorrect because $7,000 is equal to the $12,000 carrying amount of the asset given up minus the $5,000 boot received. Answer (B) is incorrect because $9,000 is equal to the $12,000 carrying amount of the truck given up, minus the $5,000 boot received, plus the $2,000 ($8,000 × 25%) proportionate gain that would have been recognized had the transaction been nonmonetary. Answer (C) is incorrect because $12,000 is equal to the carrying amount of the truck given up.

22. Minor Baseball Company had a player contract with Doe that was recorded in its accounting records at $145,000. Better Baseball Company had a player contract with Smith that was recorded in its accounting records at $140,000. Minor traded Doe to Better for Smith by exchanging player contracts. The fair value of each contract was $150,000. Evidence suggested that the contract exchange lacked commercial substance. At what amount should the contracts be valued in accordance with generally accepted accounting principles at the time of the exchange of the player contracts?

	Minor	Better
A.	$140,000	$140,000
B.	$140,000	$145,000
C.	$145,000	$140,000
D.	$150,000	$150,000

Answer (C) is correct. *(CPA, adapted)*

REQUIRED: The amount at which to record an asset received in a nonmonetary exchange transaction that lacked commercial substance.

DISCUSSION: The accounting for a nonmonetary transaction should be based on the carrying amount of the asset(s) given up when the exchange lacks commercial substance. An exchange lacks commercial substance when an entity's cash flows are not expected to change significantly. Thus, Minor should record its contract with Smith at $145,000, and Better should record its contract with Doe at $140,000.

Answer (A) is incorrect because Minor should record its contract with Smith at $145,000, its previously recorded (carryover) amount for its contract with Doe. Answer (B) is incorrect because Minor should record its contract with Smith at $145,000, and Better should record its contract with Doe at $140,000. Answer (D) is incorrect because $150,000, the fair value of each contract, should be recorded if the exchange has commercial substance.

23. UVW Broadcast Co. entered into a contract to exchange unsold advertising time for travel and lodging services with Hotel Co. As of June 30, advertising commercials of $10,000 were used. However, travel and lodging services were not provided. How should UVW account for advertising in its June 30 financial statements?

A. Revenue and expense is recognized when the agreement is complete.

B. An asset and revenue for $10,000 is recognized.

C. Both the revenue and expense of $10,000 are recognized.

D. Not reported.

Answer (B) is correct. *(CPA, adapted)*

REQUIRED: The accounting for advertising broadcast in exchange for services not yet received.

DISCUSSION: Under SFAS 63, *Financial Reporting by Broadcasters*, broadcasters frequently barter unsold advertising time for products or services. Barter revenue should be recognized in appropriate amounts when the commercials are broadcast. The amounts should be reported at the estimated fair value of the product or service received in accordance with APB Opinion 29. Revenue is not earned until the commercials are broadcast. The merchandise or services need not be resold for revenue to be recognized. An asset should be recognized if the commercials are broadcast before the merchandise or services are received. A liability should be recognized if the merchandise or services are received before the commercials are broadcast. Under APB Opinion 29, the measurement of the asset and revenue may be based on the fair value ($10,000) of commercials broadcast if that amount is more clearly determinable than the fair value of the services to which the entity has become entitled.

Answer (A) is incorrect because the "agreement is complete" when a contract has been formed. In this type of arrangement, the contract is formed prior to performance by either party. An executory contract (one not performed by either party) does not (1) complete an earning process (revenue) or (2) use up economic benefits (expense). Answer (C) is incorrect because the expense should not be recognized until the prepaid services are used. Answer (D) is incorrect because revenue is realizable and has been earned, and an asset should be debited.

8.6 Impairment of Long-Lived Assets

24. SFAS 144, *Accounting for the Impairment or Disposal of Long-Lived Assets*, requires testing for possible impairment of a long-lived asset (asset group) that an entity expects to hold and use

A. At each interim and annual balance sheet date.

B. At annual balance sheet dates only.

C. Periodically.

D. Whenever events or changes in circumstances indicate that its carrying amount may not be recoverable.

Answer (D) is correct. *(Publisher, adapted)*

REQUIRED: The appropriate time for testing impairment of a long-lived asset (asset group) to be held and used.

DISCUSSION: A long-lived asset (asset group) to which SFAS 144 applies is tested for recoverability whenever events or changes in circumstances indicate that its carrying amount may not be recoverable. The carrying amount is not recoverable when it exceeds the sum of the undiscounted cash flows expected to result from the use and disposition of the asset (asset group). If the carrying amount is not recoverable, an impairment loss is recognized equal to the excess of the carrying amount over the fair value.

25. Measuring the impairment loss on a long-lived asset (asset group) to be held and used requires a determination of its fair value. This fair value may in appropriate circumstances be based on

I.   The sum of the individual fair values of the assets and liabilities of the asset group

II. The prices of similar assets or groups

III. Present value estimates

    A. I and III only.

    B. I and II only.

    C. II and III only.

    D. I, II, and III.

Answer (C) is correct. *(Publisher, adapted)*
REQUIRED: The possible bases for a fair value estimate.
DISCUSSION: Quoted market prices in active markets are the best evidence of fair value but may not be available for a long-lived asset (asset group). Thus, fair value may need to be estimated. Such estimates should be based on the best information available, such as prices for similar assets (asset groups) and the results of other valuation methods. The present value methods described in SFAC 7 are often the best available means of estimating fair value. In particular, the expected present value method may be the most appropriate when the cash flows of a long-lived asset (asset group) are uncertain as to timing and amount.

26. An impairment loss on a long-lived asset (asset group) to be held and used is reported by a business enterprise in

    A. Discontinued operations.

    B. Extraordinary items.

    C. Other comprehensive income.

    D. Income from continuing operations.

Answer (D) is correct. *(Publisher, adapted)*
REQUIRED: The reporting of an impairment loss on a long-lived asset (asset group) to be held and used.
DISCUSSION: An impairment loss is included in income from continuing operations before income taxes by a business enterprise (income from continuing operations in the statement of activities by a not-for-profit organization). When a subtotal for "income from operations" is reported, the impairment loss is included.
Answer (A) is incorrect because a long-lived asset (asset group) to be held and used is not a discontinued operation. Answer (B) is incorrect because an impairment loss does not meet the criteria for an extraordinary item (unusual in nature and infrequent in the environment in which the entity operates). Answer (C) is incorrect because an impairment loss is reported in the income statement. Items reported in OCI have bypassed the income statement.

27. If a long-lived asset satisfies the criteria for classification as held for sale,

    A. Its carrying amount is the cost at the acquisition date if the asset is newly acquired.

    B. It is not depreciated.

    C. Interest attributable to liabilities of a disposal group to which the asset belongs is not accrued.

    D. It is classified as held for sale even if the criteria are not met until after the balance sheet date but before issuance of the financial statements.

Answer (B) is correct. *(Publisher, adapted)*
REQUIRED: The treatment of a long-lived asset that meets the criteria for classification as held for sale.
DISCUSSION: A long-lived asset is not depreciated (amortized) while it is classified as held for sale and measured at the lower of carrying amount or fair value minus cost to sell. The reason is that depreciation (amortization) would reduce the carrying amount below fair value minus cost to sell. Furthermore, fair value minus cost to sell must be evaluated each period, so any future decline will be recognized in the period of decline.
Answer (A) is incorrect because the carrying amount of a newly acquired long-lived asset classified as held for sale is its fair value minus cost to sell at the acquisition date. Answer (C) is incorrect because interest and other expenses attributable to liabilities of a disposal group to which the asset belongs are accrued. Answer (D) is incorrect because, if the criteria are not met until after the balance sheet date but before issuance of the financial statements, the long-lived asset continues to be classified as held and used in those statements.

8.7 Depreciation

28. Ichor Co. reported equipment with an original cost of $379,000 and $344,000, and accumulated depreciation of $153,000 and $128,000, respectively, in its comparative financial statements for the years ended December 31, Year 2 and Year 1. During Year 2, Ichor purchased equipment costing $50,000 and sold equipment with a carrying amount of $9,000. What amount should Ichor report as depreciation expense for Year 2?

A. $19,000

B. $25,000

C. $31,000

D. $34,000

Answer (C) is correct. *(CPA, adapted)*
REQUIRED: The depreciation given comparative information and a purchase and a sale of equipment.
DISCUSSION: The reported equipment cost increased by $35,000 ($379,000 – $344,000), and the reported accumulated depreciation increased by $25,000 ($153,000 – $128,000) from December 31, Year 1, to December 31, Year 2. Given that the equipment purchased had a cost of $50,000, the cost of the equipment sold must have been $15,000 ($50,000 – $35,000 increase in the equipment cost balance). Given also that the equipment sold had a carrying amount of $9,000, the accumulated depreciation removed from the books must have been $6,000 ($15,000 cost – $9,000). Accordingly, the depreciation expense for Year 2 must have been $31,000 ($25,000 net increase in accumulated depreciation + $6,000).
Answer (A) is incorrect because $19,000 equals the $10,000 increase in the net equipment balance ($35,000 increase in cost – $25,000 increase in accumulated depreciation) plus $9,000. Answer (B) is incorrect because $25,000 is the increase in accumulated depreciation. Answer (D) is incorrect because $34,000 equals the increase in accumulated depreciation plus $9,000.

29. On January 1, Year 5, Crater, Inc. purchased equipment having an estimated salvage value equal to 20% of its original cost at the end of a 10-year life. The equipment was sold December 31, Year 9, for 50% of its original cost. If the equipment's disposition resulted in a reported loss, which of the following depreciation methods did Crater use?

A. Double-declining balance.

B. Sum-of-the-years'-digits.

C. Straight-line.

D. Composite.

Answer (C) is correct. *(CPA, adapted)*
REQUIRED: The method that would result in a reported loss upon disposition.
DISCUSSION: The straight-line method of depreciation yields the lowest amount of depreciation for the early part of the depreciable life of the asset. Because only 50% of the original cost was received and straight-line accumulated depreciation equaled 40% of cost {[(100% – 20%) ÷ 10 years] × 5 years} at the time of sale, a 10% loss [50% – (100% – 40%)] results.
Answer (A) is incorrect because the DDB method results in 5-year accumulated depreciation that is greater than 50% of cost. Answer (B) is incorrect because the SYD method results in 5-year accumulated depreciation that is greater than 50% of cost. Answer (D) is incorrect because the composite method of depreciation applies to the weighted average of multiple useful lives of assets, whereas only one asset is mentioned in this question. Moreover, it recognizes no gain or loss on disposition.

30. On January 2, Year 1, Union Co. purchased a machine for $264,000 and depreciated it by the straight-line method using an estimated useful life of 8 years with no salvage value. On January 2, Year 4, Union determined that the machine had a useful life of 6 years from the date of acquisition and will have a salvage value of $24,000. An accounting change was made in Year 4 to reflect the additional data. The accumulated depreciation for this machine should have a balance at December 31, Year 4, of

A. $179,000

B. $160,000

C. $154,000

D. $146,000

Answer (D) is correct. *(CPA, adapted)*
REQUIRED: The accumulated depreciation for a machine given changes in estimates.
DISCUSSION: A change in the estimates for depreciation is accounted for prospectively. The new estimates are used in the year of the change. For Year 1–Year 3, the amount of depreciation was $33,000 per year ($264,000 ÷ 8). In Year 4, the new estimates change annual depreciation to $47,000 [($264,000 – $99,000 previous depreciation – $24,000) ÷ 3 years remaining]. Thus, accumulated depreciation for Year 4 is $146,000 ($99,000 + $47,000).
Answer (A) is incorrect because $179,000 does not reflect subtraction of prior depreciation in calculating depreciation for Year 4. Answer (B) is incorrect because $160,000 would be the accumulated depreciation if the revised estimates had been used from the beginning. Answer (C) is incorrect because $154,000 does not reflect subtraction of the salvage value in calculating depreciation for Year 4.

31. Rye Co. purchased a machine with a four-year estimated useful life and an estimated 10% salvage value for $80,000 on January 1, Year 6. In its income statement, what should Rye report as the depreciation expense for Year 8 using the double-declining-balance (DDB) method?

A. $9,000

B. $10,000

C. $18,000

D. $20,000

Answer (B) is correct. *(CPA, adapted)*
REQUIRED: The DDB depreciation expense.
DISCUSSION: Under the DDB method, a constant rate is applied to a declining carrying amount of an asset. Salvage value is ignored except that the asset is not depreciated below salvage value. The constant rate for the DDB method is twice the straight-line rate [(100% ÷ 4 *years*) × 2 = 50%].

Year 6: $80,000 × .50 = $40,000 *depreciation expense*
Year 7: $40,000 × .50 = $20,000 *depreciation expense*
Year 8: $20,000 × .50 = $10,000 *depreciation expense*

Answer (A) is incorrect because $9,000 includes the $8,000 residual value in the calculation. Answer (C) is incorrect because $18,000 is the Year 7 depreciation expense if the residual value is included in the calculation. Answer (D) is incorrect because $20,000 is the depreciation expense for Year 7.

32. In which of the following situations is the units-of-production method of depreciation most appropriate?

A. An asset's service potential declines with use.

B. An asset's service potential declines with the passage of time.

C. An asset is subject to rapid obsolescence.

D. An asset incurs increasing repairs and maintenance with use.

Answer (A) is correct. *(CPA, adapted)*
REQUIRED: The situation in which the units-of-production method of depreciation is most appropriate.
DISCUSSION: The units-of-production depreciation method allocates asset cost based on the level of production. As production varies, so will the credit to accumulated depreciation. Consequently, when an asset's service potential declines with use, the units-of-production method is the most appropriate method.

Answer (B) is incorrect because the straight-line method is appropriate when an asset's service potential declines with the passage of time. Answer (C) is incorrect because an accelerated method is best when an asset is subject to rapid obsolescence. Answer (D) is incorrect because the units-of-production method does not allow for increasing repairs and maintenance.

33. Which of the following uses the straight-line depreciation method?

	Group Depreciation	Composite Depreciation
A.	No	No
B.	Yes	No
C.	Yes	Yes
D.	No	Yes

Answer (C) is correct. *(CPA, adapted)*
REQUIRED: The method(s) using straight-line depreciation.
DISCUSSION: Both composite and group depreciation use the straight-line method. Both methods aggregate groups of assets. The composite method is used for a collection of dissimilar assets with varying useful lives, whereas the group method deals with similar assets. Each method involves the calculation of a total depreciable cost for all the assets included in one account and of a weighted-average estimated useful life.

34. A company using the composite depreciation method for its fleet of trucks, cars, and campers retired one of its trucks and received cash from a salvage company. The net carrying amount of these composite asset accounts was decreased by the

A. Cash proceeds received and original cost of the truck.

B. Cash proceeds received.

C. Original cost of the truck minus the cash proceeds.

D. Original cost of the truck.

Answer (B) is correct. *(CPA, adapted)*
REQUIRED: The effect of a retirement on the net carrying amount of a composite asset account.
DISCUSSION: Because both composite and group methods use weighted averages of useful lives and depreciation rates, early and late retirements are expected to offset each other. Consequently, gains and losses on retirements of single assets are treated as adjustments of accumulated depreciation. The entry is to credit the asset at cost, debit cash for any proceeds received, and debit accumulated depreciation for the difference. Thus, the net carrying amount of the composite asset accounts is decreased by the amount of cash received. The net carrying amount of total assets is unchanged.

8.8 Depletion

35. In January, Vorst Co. purchased a mineral mine for $2,640,000 with removable ore estimated at 1.2 million tons. After it has extracted all the ore, Vorst will be required by law to restore the land to its original condition at an estimated cost of $180,000. Vorst believes it will be able to sell the property afterwards for $300,000. During the year, Vorst incurred $360,000 of development costs preparing the mine for production and removed and sold 60,000 tons of ore. In its income statement for the year, what amount should Vorst report as depletion?

A. $135,000

B. $144,000

C. $150,000

D. $159,000

Answer (B) is correct. *(CPA, adapted)*
REQUIRED: The amount of depletion to be reported.
DISCUSSION: The depletion base is the purchase price of the land ($2,640,000), minus the value of the land after restoration ($300,000 − $180,000 = $120,000), plus any costs necessary to prepare the property for the extraction of ore ($360,000). This depletion base must be allocated over the 1.2 million tons of ore that the land is estimated to yield. Accordingly, Vorst's depletion charge per ton is $2.40 [($2,640,000 − $120,000 + $360,000) ÷ 1,200,000]. Vorst should report $144,000 (60,000 tons sold × $2.40) as depletion in its income statement for the year.
Answer (A) is incorrect because $135,000 does not include the $180,000 restoration costs. Answer (C) is incorrect because $150,000 does not consider the restoration costs and the residual value of the land. Answer (D) is incorrect because $159,000 adds the $180,000 restoration cost instead of deducting the $120,000 net residual value of the land.

36. WD Mining Company purchased a section of land for $600,000 in Year 1 to develop a zinc mine. The mine began operations in Year 9. At that time, management estimated that the mine would produce 200,000 tons of quality ore. A total of 100,000 tons of ore were mined and processed from Year 9 through December 31, Year 16. During January Year 17, a very promising vein was discovered. The revised estimate of ore still to be mined was 250,000 tons. Estimated salvage value for the mine land was $100,000 in both Year 9 and Year 17. Assuming that 10,000 tons of ore were mined in Year 17, what amount should WD Mining Company report as depletion in Year 17?

A. $14,286

B. $11,111

C. $10,000

D. $7,142

Answer (C) is correct. *(CMA, adapted)*
REQUIRED: The depletion recorded after allowing for a change of estimate.
DISCUSSION: The original cost of the land was $600,000. The estimated salvage value in both Year 9 and Year 17 was $100,000. The depletion base in Year 9 was therefore $500,000 ($600,000 − $100,000). Half of the estimated 200,000 tons of quality ore were mined in the period Year 9 through Year 16. Thus, $250,000 would have been allocated to the 100,000 tons mined, and the depletion base in January Year 17 would have been $250,000 ($600,000 − $100,000 − $250,000) before the change in estimate. This amount should be allocated over the 250,000-ton revised estimate of available ore. Multiplying by the 10,000 tons actually mined in Year 17 gives the amount of depletion to record of $10,000.
Answer (A) is incorrect because the revised estimate of 250,000 tons of ore is not included, and the amount of the depletion base already depleted is not included. Answer (B) is incorrect because the $250,000 allocated to the 100,000 tons mined is not subtracted from the numerator, and the denominator should equal the 250,000-ton revised estimate. Answer (D) is incorrect because the denominator should equal the 250,000-ton revised estimate.

Use Gleim's ***CPA Test Prep*** CD-Rom/Pocket PC for interactive testing with over 4,000 additional questions!

8.9 PRACTICE SIMULATION

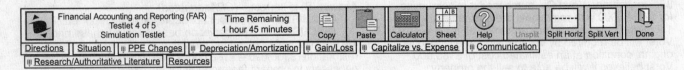

Directions | Situation | PPE Changes | Depreciation/Amortization | Gain/Loss | Capitalize vs. Expense | Communication
Research/Authoritative Literature | Resources

1. Directions

In the following simulation, you will be asked to complete various tasks. You may use the content in the **Information Tabs** to complete the tasks in the **Work Tabs**.

Information Tabs:

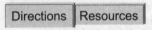

FIG 1

- Go through each of the **Information Tabs** to familiarize yourself with the simulation content
- The **Resources** tab will contain information, including formulas and definitions, that may help you to complete the tasks
- Your simulation may have more **Information Tabs** than those shown in Fig. 1

Work Tabs:

FIG. 2

- **Work Tabs**, to the right of **Information Tabs**, contain the tasks for you to complete
- **Work Tabs** contain directions for completing each task - be sure to read these directions carefully
- The tab names in Fig. 2 are for illustration only - yours may differ
- Once you complete any part of a task, the pencil for that tab will be shaded (see **Communication** in Fig. 2)
- The shaded pencil does **NOT** indicate that you have completed the entire task
- You must complete all of the tasks in the **Work Tabs** to receive full credit

Research/Authoritative Literature Tab:

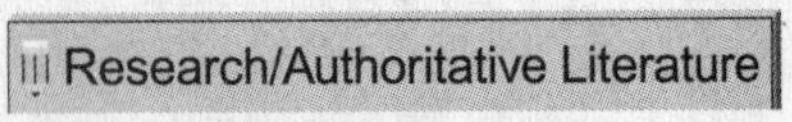

Research/Authoritative Literature

FIG. 3

- This tab contains both the Research task and the Authoritative Literature
- Detailed instructions for completing the Research task, and for using the Authoritative Literature, appear on this tab
- You may use the Authoritative Literature as a resource for completing other tasks

NOTE: If you believe you have encountered a software malfunction, report it to the test center staff immediately.

2. Situation

Yankee Co.'s property, plant, and equipment and accumulated depreciation and amortization balances at December 31, Year 4, are

Asset	Cost	Accumulated Depreciation
Land	$ 275,000	---
Buildings	2,800,000	$ 672,900
Machinery and equipment	1,380,000	367,500
Automobiles and trucks	210,000	114,326
Leasehold improvements	432,000	108,000
Totals	$5,097,000	$1,262,726

Depreciation and amortization methods and useful lives

Buildings	150% declining balance; 25 years
Machinery and equipment	Straight-line; 10 years
Automobiles and trucks	150% declining balance; 5 years, all acquired after 1999
Leasehold improvements	Straight-line

- Depreciation is computed to the nearest month.
- Salvage values of depreciable assets are immaterial except for automobiles and trucks, which have estimated salvage values equal to 15% of cost.

Other additional information

- Yankee entered into a 12-year operating lease starting January 1, Year 2. The leasehold improvements were completed on December 31, Year 1, and the facility was occupied on January 1, Year 2.
- On January 6, Year 5, Yankee completed its self-construction of a building on its own land. Direct costs of construction were $1,095,000. Construction of the building required 15,000 direct labor hours. Yankee's construction department has an overhead allocation system for outside jobs based on an activity denominator of 100,000 direct labor hours, budgeted fixed costs of $2.5 million, and budgeted variable costs of $27 per direct labor hour.
- On July 1, Year 5, machinery and equipment were purchased at a total invoice cost of $325,000. Additional costs of $23,000 to repair damage on delivery and $18,000 for concrete embedding of machinery were incurred. A wall had to be demolished for a large machine to be moved into the plant. The wall demolition cost $7,000, and rebuilding the wall cost $19,000.
- On August 30, Year 5, Yankee purchased a new automobile for $25,000.
- On September 30, Year 5, a truck with a cost of $48,000 and a carrying amount of $30,000 on December 31, Year 4, was sold for $23,500.
- On November 4, Year 5, Yankee purchased a tract of land for investment purposes for $700,000. Yankee may use the land as a future building site.
- On December 20, Year 5, a machine with a cost of $17,000, a carrying amount of $2,975 on the date of disposition, and a fair value of $4,000 was given to a corporate officer in partial liquidation of a debt.

3. PPE Changes

This question is presented in a spreadsheet format that requires you to fill in the correct responses in the shaded cells provided. Enter the appropriate monetary amounts in the Increase, Decrease, and Balance columns for items properly classified as PPE. Do not consider accumulated depreciation. If there is no increase or decrease, leave those columns empty.

Yankee Co.
**ANALYSIS OF CHANGES IN PROPERTY,
PLANT, AND EQUIPMENT**
For the Year Ended December 31, Year 5

	Balance 12/31/Year 4	Increase	Decrease	Balance 12/31/Year 5
1. Land				
2. Buildings				
3. Machinery and equipment				
4. Automobiles and trucks				
5. Leasehold improvements				

4. Depreciation/Amortization

This question is presented in a spreadsheet format that requires you to fill in the correct responses in the shaded cells provided. Enter the appropriate monetary values in the Increase, Decrease, and Balance columns. If there is no increase or decrease, leave those columns empty. Answers are based on calculations required to draft a schedule of depreciation and amortization expense.

Yankee Co.
**ANALYSIS OF CHANGES IN ACCUMULATED
DEPRECIATION AND AMORTIZATION**
For the Year Ended December 31, Year 5

	Balance 12/31/Year 4	Increase	Decrease	Balance 12/31/Year 5
1. Buildings				
2. Machinery and equipment				
3. Automobiles and trucks				
4. Leasehold improvements				

5. Gain/Loss

This question is presented in a spreadsheet format that requires you to fill in the correct responses in the shaded cells provided. Enter the appropriate monetary amounts.

Yankee Co.
GAIN ON DISPOSITION OF PROPERTY, PLANT, AND EQUIPMENT
For the Year Ended December 31, Year 5

	Selling Price	Carrying Amount	Gain
1. Sale of truck			
2. Machine exchanged for debt			
3. Totals			

6. Capitalize vs. Expense

The following items represent expenditures for goods held for resale and equipment. Determine whether the expenditure for each item should be capitalized or expensed as a period cost. Check the box to the right of the description if the item should be capitalized.

Expenditure	Capitalize
1. Freight charges paid for goods held for resale	
2. In-transit insurance on goods held for resale purchased FOB shipping point	
3. Interest on note payable for goods held for resale	
4. Installation of equipment	
5. Testing of newly purchased equipment	
6. Cost of current-year service contract on equipment	

7. Communication

Yankee Co. has asked you for advice regarding financial reporting for some of its property, plant, and equipment. Yankee Co. purchased land as a site for construction of a factory. Outside contractors were engaged to

- Construct the factory
- Grade and pave a parking lot adjacent to the factory for the exclusive use of the factory workers

Operations at the new location began during the year, and normal factory maintenance costs were incurred after production began.

Compose a memo to Yankee Co. explaining how to account for and report each of the following expenditures at the time incurred and in subsequent accounting periods:

- Purchase of land
- Construction of factory
- Grading and paving of parking lot
- Payment of normal factory maintenance costs

Describe how to distinguish between capital and revenue expenditures. Do not discuss capitalization of interest during construction. Type your communication in your word processor program and print the copy in a memorandum-style format.

REMINDER: Your response will be graded for both technical content and writing skills. Technical content will be evaluated for information that is helpful to the intended reader and clearly relevant to the issue. Writing skills will be evaluated for development, organization, and the appropriate expression of ideas in professional correspondence. Use a standard business memo or letter format with a clear beginning, middle, and end. Do not convey information in the form of a table, bullet point list, or other abbreviated presentation.

To: Client
From: CPA
Subject: Financial Reporting for Property, Plant, and Equipment

---

8. Research/Authoritative Literature

See page 12 in the Introduction of this book for a detailed explanation of the AICPA's new Research/Authoritative Literature work tab as well as a screenshot of how the tab will actually look on your exam.

Research and cite the appropriate financial accounting pronouncement in the FASB Current Text or Original Pronouncements that states the general rule for determining the end of an interest capitalization period.

Unofficial Answers

3. PPE Changes (15 Gradable Items)

Yankee Co.
ANALYSIS OF CHANGES IN PROPERTY,
PLANT, AND EQUIPMENT
For the Year Ended December 31, Year 5

	Balance 12/31/Year 4	Increase	Decrease	Balance 12/31/Year 5
1. Land	$ 275,000	$	$	$ 275,000
2. Buildings	2,800,000	1,875,000 [a]		4,675,000
3. Machinery and equipment	1,380,000	369,000 [b]	17,000	1,732,000
4. Automobiles and trucks	210,000	25,000	48,000	187,000
5. Leasehold improvements	432,000			432,000

Explanation of Amounts:

[a] Construction cost of building
Direct costs $1,095,000
Overhead costs
Fixed   [15,000 hours × ($2,500,00 ÷ 100,000 DLH)] $375,000
Variable (15,000 hours × $27)   405,000   780,000
     $1,875,000

[b] Machinery and equipment purchased
Invoice cost $ 325,000
Installation cost (concrete embedding)   18,000
Cost of gaining access to factory ($19,000 + $7,000)   26,000
     Total acquisition cost $ 369,000

[c] The land purchased as an investment should be reported in an investment account, not PPE, because it is not used in the entity's ordinary operations.

4. Depreciation/Amortization (14 Gradable Items)

Yankee Co.
ANALYSIS OF CHANGES IN ACCUMULATED
DEPRECIATION AND AMORTIZATION
For the Year Ended December 31, Year 5

	Balance 12/31/Year 4	Increase	Decrease	Balance 12/31/Year 5
1. Buildings	$672,900	$240,126 [a]	$	$913,025
2. Machinery and equipment	367,500	156,450 [b]	14,025 [e]	509,925
3. Automobiles and trucks	114,326	28,952 [c]	24,750 [f]	118,528
4. Leasehold improvements	108,000	36,000 [d]		144,000

Explanation of Amounts:

Increases

[a]	Buildings		
	Carrying amount, 1/1/Year 5 ($2,800,000 – $672,900)		$2,127,100
	Building completed 1/6/Year 5		1,875,000
	Total subject to depreciation		$4,002,100
	150% declining balance [(100% ÷ 25) × 1.5]		× 6%
	Depreciation for Year 5		$ 240,126

[b]	Machinery and equipment		
	Balance, 1/1/Year 5	$1,380,000	
	Straight-line (100% ÷ 10)	× 10%	$ 138,000
	Purchased 7/1/Year 5	$ 369,000	
	Straight-line [10% × (6 ÷ 12)]	× 5%	18,450
	Depreciation for Year 5		$ 156,450

[c]	Automobiles and trucks		
	Carrying amount, 1/1/Year 5 ($210,000 – $114,326)	$ 95,674	
	Minus carrying amount, 1/1/Year 5 on truck sold 9/30/Year 5	(30,000)	
	Amount subject to depreciation	$ 65,674	
	150% declining balance [(100% ÷ 5) × 1.5]	× 30%	$ 19,702
	Automobile purchased 8/30/Year 5	$ 25,000	
	150% declining balance [30% × (4 ÷ 12)]	× 10%	2,500
	Truck sold 9/30/Year 5 – depreciation for Year 5 (1/1 to 9/30/Year 5) [$30,000 × 30% × (9 ÷ 12)]		6,750
	Depreciation for Year 5		$ 28,952

[d]	Leasehold improvements	
	Amortization for Year 5 ($432,000 ÷ 12 years)	$ 36,000

Decreases

[e]	Machinery and equipment	
	Cost	$ 17,000
	Carrying amount	(2,975)
	Accumulated depreciation	$ 14,025

[f]	Automobiles and trucks	
	Cost	$ 48,000
	Carrying amount ($30,000 – $6,750)	(23,250)
	Accumulated depreciation	$ 24,750

5. Gain/Loss (6 Gradable Items)

Yankee Co.
GAIN ON DISPOSITION OF PROPERTY, PLANT, AND EQUIPMENT
For the Year Ended December 31, Year 5

	Selling Price	Carrying Amount	Gain
1. Sale of truck	$23,500	$23,250	$ 250
2. Machine given to extinguish debt	4,000	2,975	1,025
3. Totals	$27,500	$26,225	$1,275

6. Capitalize vs. Expense (6 Gradable Items)

1. <u>Capitalize.</u> Expenditures may be capitalized as inventory if they are directly or indirectly incurred in bringing items of inventory to their existing condition and location. Freight charges are therefore an inventoriable cost and should be capitalized.

2. <u>Capitalize.</u> Expenditures are inventoriable and should be capitalized if they are incurred directly or indirectly in bringing items of inventory to their existing condition and location. The cost of insurance for in-transit goods held for resale is an inventoriable cost because the goods were purchased FOB shipping point. Because title and risk of loss pass at the point of shipment, shipping costs are the responsibility of the purchaser.

3. <u>Expense.</u> Interest cost is capitalized only for assets produced for an enterprise's own use or for sale or lease as discrete projects. Interest cost for inventories is not capitalized. Hence, the interest on the note for goods held for resale should be expensed.

4. <u>Capitalize.</u> The initial measurement of property, plant, and equipment includes all costs to acquire these assets, transport them to the sites of their intended use, and prepare them for operations. The installation of equipment should therefore be capitalized.

5. <u>Capitalize.</u> The initial measurement of property, plant, and equipment includes all costs to acquire these assets, transport them to the sites of their intended use, and prepare them for operations. Hence, the costs of testing newly purchased equipment should be capitalized.

6. <u>Expense.</u> The cost of a current-year service contract on equipment should be expensed. Routine expenditures that maintain the normal service capacity of an asset do not benefit future periods and are not capitalized.

7. Communication (5 Gradable Items; for grading instructions, please refer to page 12.)

To: Client
From: CPA
Subject: Financial Reporting for Property, Plant, and Equipment

The purpose of this memo is to explain the proper accounting treatment for the activities involved in the construction of your new factory. Capital expenditures for acquisition or subsequent enhancement of service potential are included in the historical cost of an asset because they benefit more than one period. A revenue expenditure (e.g., for routine maintenance) is excluded because it is deemed to benefit only the period in which it was made.

The purchase price of the land should be capitalized. The land should be shown as a noncurrent asset on the balance sheet at its original cost. It is not subject to depreciation.

The costs necessary to the purchase or construction of a building that will result in future economic benefits should be capitalized, e.g., the price, costs of preparing the structure for its intended use, permits, materials, labor, and overhead. The cost of constructing the factory should be capitalized and depreciated over its expected life. The depreciation should be added to the cost of inventory through the application of factory overhead as goods are produced. It is expensed as cost of sales as goods are sold. The factory expenditures, net of accumulated depreciation, should be reported as a noncurrent asset on the balance sheet. Inventory should be reported as a current asset on the balance sheet, and cost of sales should be reported as an expense on the income statement.

If driveways, parking lots, sidewalks, roads, fences, rights-of-way, etc., have limited lives and must be maintained and replaced by the owner, they should be debited to land improvements and depreciated. Thus, the cost of grading and paving the parking lot should be capitalized and depreciated over the expected life of either the factory or parking lot, whichever is shorter. The depreciation should be added to cost of inventory through the application of factory overhead as goods are produced. It is expensed as cost of sales as goods are sold. The land improvement expenditures, net of accumulated depreciation, should be reported as a noncurrent asset on the balance sheet. Inventory should be reported as a current asset on the balance sheet, and cost of sales should be reported as an expense on the income statement.

Routine, minor expenditures made to maintain the operating efficiency of PPE are ordinarily expensed as incurred, but as the amounts involved become more significant and the benefits to future periods increase, treatment of a major repair as a replacement, etc., may be more appropriate. Accordingly, the cost of maintaining the factory once production has begun is a revenue expenditure. However, because it is a factory cost, it should be added to cost of inventory through the application of factory overhead as goods are produced. It is expensed as cost of sales as goods are sold. Inventory should be reported as a current asset on the balance sheet, and cost of sales should be reported as an expense on the income statement.

8. Research/Authoritative Literature (1 Gradable Item)

Answer: FAS 34, Par. 16

FAS 34 -- *Capitalization of Interest Cost*

The Capitalization Period

18. The capitalization period shall end when the asset is substantially complete and ready for its intended use. Some assets are completed in parts, and each part is capable of being used independently while work is continuing on other parts. An example is a condominium. For such assets, interest capitalization shall stop on each part when it is substantially complete and ready for use. Some assets must be completed in their entirety before any part of the asset can be used. An example is a facility designed to manufacture products by sequential processes. For such assets, interest capitalization shall continue until the entire asset is substantially complete and ready for use. Some assets cannot be used effectively until a separate facility has been completed. Examples are the oil wells drilled in Alaska before completion of the pipeline. For such assets, interest capitalization shall continue until the separate facility is substantially complete and ready for use.

Scoring Schedule:

	Correct Responses		Gradable Items		Weights		
Tab 3	_____	÷	15	×	15%	=	_____
Tab 4	_____	÷	14	×	15%	=	_____
Tab 5	_____	÷	6	×	15%	=	_____
Tab 6	_____	÷	6	×	10%	=	_____
Tab 7	_____	÷	5	×	30%	=	_____
Tab 8	_____	÷	1	×	15%	=	_____
							_____
							(Your Score)

Use Gleim's **CPA Gleim Online** to practice more simulations in a realistic environment.

STUDY UNIT NINE
INTANGIBLE ASSETS AND
OTHER CAPITALIZATION ISSUES

(20 pages of outline)

This is the last study unit covering the asset side of the balance sheet. The first four were Cash and Investments; Receivables; Inventories; and Property, Plant, Equipment, and Depletable Resources.

9.1 GOODWILL AND OTHER INTANGIBLE ASSETS

1. **Intangible Assets**

    a. They **lack physical substance**.

        1) Intangible assets may convey to the holder a contractual or legal right to receive future economic benefits (e.g., patents, leaseholds, or franchises).

        2) Another type of intangible asset reflects costs not assignable to specific products or services but that are expected to have future economic benefits (e.g., customer lists, noncontractual customer relationships, and unpatented technology).

    b. They **are not financial assets**.

        1) A **financial asset** is cash, "evidence of an ownership interest in an entity, or a contract that conveys to a second entity a right (1) to receive cash or another financial instrument from a second entity or (2) to exchange other financial instruments on potentially favorable terms with the first entity" (adapted from the definition of a **financial instrument** in SFAS 107, *Disclosures about Fair Value of Financial Instruments*).

    c. The term **intangible assets** as used in this study unit **excludes goodwill**.

        1) Thus, intangible assets do **not** include such items as (a) cash, (b) equity investments, (c) accounts and notes receivable, or (d) bonds receivable.

Initial Recognition

2. An intangible asset must meet the **recognition criteria** in SFAC 5. If it is acquired individually or with other assets but **not in a business combination**, it is initially recognized and measured at **fair value** (SFAS 142, *Goodwill and Other Intangible Assets*).

    a. The cost of a group of assets acquired other than in a business combination is allocated based on **relative fair values**. Goodwill is **not** recognized.

    b. **Cost** is normally the more reliably measurable of (1) the fair value of the consideration given or (2) the fair value of the net assets acquired.

3. The costs of **internally developed intangible assets** and goodwill are expensed when incurred if they

    a. Are not specifically identifiable,

    b. Have indeterminate lives, or

    c. Are inherent in a continuing business and related to the entity as a whole.

Accounting for Intangible Assets Subsequent to Recognition

4. The useful life of an asset is the period during which it is expected to contribute either directly or indirectly to the **future cash flows** of the reporting entity.

   a. Considerations in estimating **useful life** are the entity's expected use of the asset and

      1) The useful life of a related asset or group of assets
      2) Provisions based on law, regulation, or contract that may limit the useful life or that may permit renewal or extension without substantial cost
      3) Economic factors, such as obsolescence, demand, or competition
      4) Expenditures for maintenance

5. An intangible asset with a **finite useful life** to the reporting entity is **amortized** over that useful life. If the useful life is finite but not precisely known, the amortization period is the best estimate of the useful life.

   a. The **useful life** should be reevaluated each reporting period. A change in the estimate results in a prospective change in amortization.

6. Amortization is based on the **pattern of consumption of economic benefits**, if reliably determinable. The **straight-line method** must be used in other cases.

   a. An intangible asset is not written down in the period of acquisition if it is not impaired.

   b. The **amortizable amount** equals the amount initially assigned minus the residual value. The **residual value** is the estimated fair value to the entity at the end of the asset's useful life, minus disposal costs. This amount is **zero** unless

      1) A **third party** has committed to purchase the asset, or
      2) It can be determined from an exchange transaction in an **existing market** for the asset that is expected to exist at the end of the useful life.

7. If a subsequent determination is made that the asset has an **indefinite useful life**, it is no longer amortized and is tested for impairment.

EXAMPLE

An intangible asset was purchased on the first day of the fiscal year for $1,000,000. Its useful life is 5 years, and it has a residual value of $100,000. However, its pattern of consumption of economic benefits is not reliably determinable. The year-end amortization entry is

Intangible asset amortization	$180,000	
Accumulated amortization		$180,000

[($1,000,000 – $100,000) ÷ 5 years = $180,000 straight-line amortization]

---

8. An amortized intangible asset is **reviewed for impairment** when **events or changes in circumstances** indicate that its carrying amount may not be recoverable. An impairment loss is recognized only if the carrying amount is **not recoverable** and is greater than the asset's fair value.

   a. Thus, the impairment test is met if the **sum of the undiscounted expected future cash flows** from the asset is less than the carrying amount. The **loss recognized** is the excess of that carrying amount over the fair value. This loss is nonreversible, so the adjusted carrying amount is the new accounting basis.

Determination of an Impairment Loss
1. Events or changes in circumstances indicate a possible loss.
2. Carrying amount > sum of undiscounted cash flows
3. Loss = carrying amount – fair value

9. An intangible asset with an **indefinite useful life** is **not amortized**.

   a. However, the useful life should be reevaluated each period. If it is found to be finite, a test for impairment is performed. The asset is then **amortized prospectively** and otherwise accounted for as an amortized asset.

   b. A nonamortized intangible asset is **reviewed for impairment** at least annually. It is tested more often if events or changes in circumstances suggest that the asset may be impaired. However, this impairment test does **not consider recoverability**.

      1) If the **carrying amount exceeds the fair value**, the asset is impaired, and the excess is the recognized loss. This loss is nonreversible, so the adjusted carrying amount is the new accounting basis.

Determination of an Impairment Loss
1. Review for impairment
2. Loss = carrying amount − fair value

Goodwill

10. **Goodwill** is recognized **only** in a business combination. It includes acquired intangible assets not meeting the criteria in SFAS 141 for asset recognition distinct from goodwill. [SFAS 141 has been superseded by a new pronouncement that will not be testable until July 2009. If you plan to take FAR during Q3 or Q4 2009, please go to www.gleim.com/updates for a revised outline relating to goodwill under SFAS 141(R).]

   a. A **business combination** is an entity's acquisition of net assets constituting a business or of controlling equity interest of one or more other entities.

   b. Goodwill arises from **cost allocation** by the acquiring entity in a business combination. The allocation is to the elements of an asset (net asset) group based on their **fair values**.

      1) The cost of the group acquired may be greater than the sum of the fair values assigned to the acquired assets (tangible assets, financial assets, and separately recognized intangible assets), minus the sum of the fair values assigned to the liabilities assumed. This difference is **goodwill**.

Accounting for Goodwill Subsequent to Recognition

11. **Goodwill is not amortized.**

12. Goodwill of a reporting unit is **tested for impairment each year** at the same time. But different reporting units may be tested at different times. Furthermore, additional testing also may be indicated.

   a. A **reporting unit** is an **operating segment** or one of its components. An entity must identify its operating segments (see Study Unit 4.2) even if it is not required to report segment information.

      1) A **component** qualifies as a reporting unit if (a) it is a **business** for which discrete financial information is available, and (b) segment management regularly reviews its operating results. However, similar components are aggregated.

13. As part of **testing goodwill for impairment**, acquired assets and assumed liabilities **must be assigned to reporting units**. Also, assets and liabilities considered by the reporting entity to be part of its **corporate assets and liabilities** are assigned.

    a. The assignment is made at the acquisition date to the reporting unit if the assets and liabilities relate to its operations and are included in its fair value.

    b. The amounts of assets relating to **multiple reporting units** are assigned based on a reasonable, supportable, and consistently applied method.

14. **Assignment of goodwill to reporting units. All** goodwill is assigned to the reporting units that will **benefit from the business combination**. The method used should be reasonable, supportable, consistently applied, and consistent with the objectives of the assignment.

    a. The assignment, in principle, should be done **in the same manner as the determination of goodwill** in a business combination. Thus, **the fair value of the acquired business** included in the reporting unit is determined.

        1) An **excess** of this amount over the fair value of the net assets assigned to the reporting unit is the goodwill assigned.

        2) If **no assets or liabilities are assigned** to a reporting unit, the goodwill to be assigned might equal the **change in the fair value** of the reporting unit as a result of the combination.

Goodwill Assigned to a Reporting Unit
FV of reporting unit – FV of net assets assigned

15. **Measuring fair value of a reporting unit.** The **best evidence of fair value** is a quoted market price in an active market. Such prices should be used, if available.

    a. However, the **market capitalization** of a reporting unit may not reflect its fair value. Because of the synergies and other benefits of control, an investor may be willing to pay a **control premium**.

    b. Another valuation method is estimation of fair value based on **multiples of a performance measure**, such as earnings or revenue. This method may be appropriate when information (observable fair value and multiples) about an entity comparable to the reporting unit is known.

16. **Potential impairment** of goodwill is deemed to exist only if the **carrying amount** (including goodwill) of a reporting unit is greater than its **fair value**. Thus, accounting for goodwill is based on the units of the combined entity into which the acquired entity was absorbed.

    a. If a potential impairment is found, the **carrying amount of reporting-unit goodwill is compared with its implied fair value**. An impairment loss not exceeding the carrying amount of goodwill is then recognized equal to any excess of that carrying amount over the implied fair value. This loss is nonreversible.

        1) The **implied fair value** of reporting-unit goodwill is estimated by assigning the fair value of the reporting unit to its assets and liabilities (including unrecognized intangible assets). The excess of that fair value over the amounts assigned equals the implied fair value.

            a) The sole purpose of the assignment is to test impairment of goodwill.

Determination of Impairment Loss
1. Carrying amount of reporting unit > its fair value
2. Carrying amount of reporting unit goodwill > its implied fair value
3. Loss = excess in 2

EXAMPLE

On January 1, Year 1, Apogee Co. purchased Perigee Co. for $200,000,000 and recognized $20,000,000 of goodwill. It properly classifies Perigee as a reporting unit. On December 31, Year 2, Apogee's fiscal year-end, the following information is available about Perigee:

Carrying amount of net assets (including goodwill)	$190,000,000
Fair value	$150,000,000
Fair value of net assets (excluding goodwill)	$135,000,000

The carrying amount ($190,000,000) exceeds the fair value ($150,000,000). Thus, goodwill may be impaired.

The implied fair value of goodwill is $15,000,000 ($150,000,000 – $135,000,000).

The impairment loss is $5,000,000 ($20,000,000 carrying amount of goodwill – $15,000,000 implied fair value).

---

17. **Disposal of a reporting unit.** In the calculation of the gain or loss on disposal of a reporting unit, goodwill is included as part of its carrying amount.

    a. If only **part of the reporting unit** is to be disposed of, and that part constitutes a **business**, the goodwill related to the business is included in the carrying amount. The included goodwill of the business and the portion retained by the reporting unit are determined based on **relative fair values**.

       1) When a partial assignment of goodwill is made to a business to be disposed of, the remaining reporting-unit goodwill is **tested for impairment**.

       2) An acquired business **may not have been integrated** with the other activities of the reporting unit. Thus, the total carrying amount of the goodwill acquired with the business should be included in the carrying amount of the business.

Equity Method Goodwill

18. The difference between the cost of an investment and the investor's underlying equity in the net assets of the investee (stated at its carrying amount) is allocated between two elements: **goodwill** and the difference between the carrying amounts and fair values that can be related to **specific accounts** at the acquisition date (APB Opinion 18, *The Equity Method of Accounting for Investments in Common Stock*).

    a. Equity method **investments** are reviewed for impairment under APB Opinion 18. However, equity method goodwill itself is **not** reviewed for impairment because it is **not separable** from the investment. Furthermore, it is not amortized.

Presentation in the Financial Statements

19. In the **balance sheet**, **intangible assets** are required to be presented, at a minimum, as a single aggregated line item. But individual intangible assets or classes of these assets may be separately presented.

    a. **Goodwill** is presented in the aggregate as a separate line item.

20. In the **income statement**, **amortization expense** and **impairment losses** related to intangible assets are presented as line items under **continuing operations**.

    a. The aggregate **goodwill impairment loss** is presented as the last separate line item before the subtotal income from continuing operations

    b. However, if a **discontinued operation** is reported, a loss related to impairment of goodwill associated with that operation is presented net of tax within the discontinued operations caption.

Stop and review! You have completed the outline for this subunit. Study multiple-choice questions 1 through 6 beginning on page 350.

9.2 INTANGIBLE ASSETS DISTINCT FROM GOODWILL

1. SFAS 141(R) contains a partial list of **intangible assets distinct from goodwill** that meet the criteria (contractual-legal or separability) for recognition. Below are the five categories of items listed. Most meet the **contractual-legal criterion**. Those meeting the **separability** but not the contractual-legal criterion are marked with an S.

    a. **Marketing-related**

        1) Trademarks, tradenames
        2) Service marks, collective marks, certification marks
        3) Trade dress (unique color, shape, or package design)
        4) Newspaper mastheads
        5) Internet domain names
        6) Noncompetition agreements

    b. **Customer-related**

        1) Customer lists (S)
        2) Order or production backlog
        3) Customer contracts and related customer relationships
        4) Noncontractual customer relationships (S)

    c. **Artistic-related**

        1) Plays, operas, ballets
        2) Books, magazines, newspapers, other literary works
        3) Musical works, such as compositions, song lyrics, and advertising jingles
        4) Pictures, photographs
        5) Video and audiovisual material, including motion pictures, music videos, television programs

    d. **Contract-based**

        1) Licensing, royalty, standstill agreements
        2) Advertising, construction, management, service, or supply contracts
        3) Lease agreements
        4) Construction permits
        5) Franchise agreements
        6) Operating and broadcast rights
        7) Use rights, such as drilling, water, air, mineral, timber-cutting, and route authorities
        8) Servicing contracts, such as mortgage servicing contracts
        9) Employment contracts

    e. **Technology-based**

        1) Patented technology
        2) Computer software and mask works
        3) Unpatented technology (S)
        4) Databases, including title plants (S)
        5) Trade secrets, such as secret formulas, processes, recipes

Sources

2. These assets may be acquired from others or developed internally.

    a. Internally developed intangible assets generally are not capitalized.

    b. Intangible personal property includes **intellectual property**. The law protects those who engage in creative or learned endeavors, including R&D, or who invest resources in establishing goodwill signified by various trade symbols.

Patents

3. A patent is a right conferred upon application to and approval by the federal government **(U.S. Patent and Trademark Office)** for the exclusive use of an invention.

    a. The **Constitution** (Article I, Sec. 8) permits Congress to enact legislation "to promote the progress of science and useful arts by securing for limited times to authors and inventors the exclusive right to their respective writings and discoveries."

        1) Under the **Patent Act**, "Whoever invents or discovers any new and useful process, machine, manufacture, or composition of matter, or any new and useful improvement thereof, may obtain a patent therefor."

            a) Thus, an invention must (1) be for a patentable subject, (2) have utility, and (3) be novel and not obvious to a knowledgeable person.

    b. The right is given for a nonrenewable period, but an effective extension can sometimes be provided by obtaining a new patent that involves slight modifications of the old.

        1) **Utility patents** (the most common category) have a legal life ending 20 years after the application was filed.

            a) A **design patent** (as opposed to an invention) has a duration of 14 years.

        2) **Business methods** also may be patented.

            a) A controversial development is the patenting of **tax minimization strategies**. For example, a tax strategy for conversion of a traditional IRA to a Roth IRA has been patented.

    c. The **fair value** of a patent derives from the monopoly of a product or process.

        1) The advantage of a patent right is that it may increase earnings by allowing sale at a higher price, manufacture at a lower cost, or the exclusive distribution of a product or service.

    d. The **amortization period** for a patent is the shorter of its useful life or the legal life remaining after acquisition.

        1) The useful life may be substantially shorter than the legal life because of changes in consumer tastes, delays in marketing the product or service, and development of substitutes or improvements.

    e. Patents may be sold outright or temporarily licensed.

    f. Patents may be purchased or developed internally.

        1) The initial capitalized cost of a **purchased patent** is normally the fair value of the consideration given, that is, its purchase price plus incidental costs, such as registration and attorneys' fees.

        2) **Internally developed patents** are less likely to be capitalized because related R&D costs must be expensed when incurred.

            a) Thus, only relatively minor costs can be capitalized, for example, patent registration fees and legal fees.

    g.   Subsequent to the grant of a patent, its owner may need to bring or defend a **suit for patent infringement**.

        1)   The government does not prosecute such cases but merely provides a forum (federal courts) in which the owner may assert its rights.

        2)   The **unrecovered costs of successful litigation are capitalized** because they will benefit future periods.

            a)   They are **amortized** over the shorter of the remaining legal life or the estimated useful life of the patent.

        3)   The **costs of unsuccessful litigation** (damages, attorneys' fees) are **expensed**.

            a)   An unsuccessful suit also indicates that the unamortized cost of the patent has no value and should be recognized as a loss.

Copyrights

4.   The **Copyright Act** provides broad rights to intellectual property consisting of "original works of authorship in any tangible medium of expression, now known or later developed." An **author's copyright** is for life plus 70 years. A **publisher's copyright** is for the earlier to expire of 95 years from publication or 120 years from creation.

    a.   The Copyright Act is based on specific authority granted in the **Constitution**.

    b.   Among the **works protected** are literary, musical, and dramatic works; sound recordings; motion pictures and other audiovisual works; and computer software.

    c.   The copyright holder has **exclusive rights** to reproduce, distribute, perform, display, and prepare derivative works from copyrighted material.

    d.   **Limited exceptions** are allowed for library or archive reproduction and fair use for purposes of comment, criticism, news coverage, teaching, scholarship, or research.

    e.   The Copyright Act does **not** protect ideas, processes, discoveries, principles, etc.

    f.   A copyright provides automatic protection once it is in **tangible form**.

        1)   **Registration** with the federal **Copyright Office** is necessary only to give a copyright owner standing to sue in federal court for infringement.

        2)   Furthermore, a **notice of copyright** is **not** required to be placed on the work.

    g.   Ordinarily, the **estimated useful life** of a copyright is substantially less than its legal life. However, some exceptions are well-known, e.g., classic films.

    h.   Copyrights are similar to patents in that they **can be sold**.

        1)   Moreover, rights under copyrights and patents can be **licensed**.

        2)   Another similarity to patents is that legal fees, registration fees, litigation costs, and the purchase price can be **capitalized**. But internal **R&D costs cannot**.

Trademarks and Similar Property

5.   A trademark or other mark (e.g., a service mark or certification mark) is a distinctive design, word, symbol, mark, picture, etc. It is affixed to a product or placed on a tag, label, container, or associated display and adopted by the seller or manufacturer to identify it.

    a.   A **trade name** is usually regarded as referring to a business and the goodwill it has generated, for example, Exxon.

6.   In general, **no legal protection** is given to something that is **generic or commonly descriptive**. It must be distinctive or have acquired a secondary meaning.

    a.   For example, "light" has been used in the beer industry for years to describe a certain set of characteristics. Thus, it is not protected.

    b.   But "Coke" is a nickname associated in the public mind with the products of a particular entity. It has acquired a secondary meaning that is protected from infringement.

    c.   Moreover, even common personal names or place names can be trademarked if accompanied by a distinctive design or logo.

7.   Under the **Lanham Act**, trademarks (but not trade names unless they also are trademarks or service marks) can be registered with the U.S. Patent and Trademark Office for **renewable periods** of 10 years. However, the first renewal must be between the fifth and sixth years after initial registration.

    a.   Trademarks and related property are safeguarded as long as they are **used continuously**. Their wrongful use is a deceptive appropriation of the goodwill and reputation of competitors.

    b.   **Registration** requires that the trademark be in use or that the registrant intend to put it in use within 6 months.

8.   Trademarks and related property are **not as readily transferable** as patents and copyrights.

    a.   Their use with goods or services having qualities other than those with which they are commonly associated may be confusing to consumers.

        1)   Hence, uncontrolled licensing is contrary to the spirit of the law.

    b.   A trademark or similar intangible asset may be sold only in connection with the goodwill of the entity it represents.

9.   **Capitalizable costs** include attorneys' fees, registration fees, design costs, and the costs of successfully defending the intangible asset. These costs do not include advertising and R&D expenditures.

Trade Secrets

10.   A trade secret is information of economic value to a business that the business wishes to keep confidential.

11.   The law protects this interest from **discovery by improper means** even when the trade secret cannot be copyrighted or patented.

    a.   A competitor is not prevented from **obtaining the knowledge by lawful means**. Examples are independent research, purchase of the product, or the entity's voluntary disclosure or failure to take reasonable precautions.

12.   Trade secrets **cannot be registered unless they are patentable**.

    a.   However, if an entity makes **reasonable efforts** to protect its secret information, such as processes, formulas, and customer lists, it will receive legal protection.

    b.   Under the **Economic Espionage Act of 1996**, theft of trade secrets is a federal crime. Furthermore, most states have adopted the **Uniform Trade Secrets Act**, which prohibits misappropriation of trade secrets.

13.   Trade secrets are recognized as a legal **form of property** that may be transferred.

14.   **Costs** associated with trade secrets, which are usually recognized only as a result of a business combination, are **amortized** over their estimated useful life if it is finite.

    a.   **R&D costs** incurred to develop a trade secret are **expensed** as incurred.

Franchises

15. A franchise is a contractual agreement by a **franchisor** (grantor of the franchise) to permit a **franchisee** (purchaser) to operate a certain business.

   a. Thus, an exclusive right may be granted to sell a specified product or service in a given geographical area and to use trademarks, patents, trade secrets, etc.

   1) Also, **governments** grant franchises to **public utilities** that provide services to the public, e.g., communications, electricity, gas, and transportation.

   a) The governmental grant may permit the use of public property (such as rights of way), confer other privileges (possibly a monopoly), and impose regulations (including those on rates of return).

   2) Familiar franchises in the private sector include those for retailing and fast food.

16. **Franchisee accounting.** The franchisee should capitalize the costs of acquiring the franchise.

   a. The **capitalizable amount** includes the initial fee and other expenditures, e.g., legal fees, necessary to acquire the franchise that will provide future benefits.

   1) Future payments based on a percentage of revenues or for franchisor services are expensed as incurred. They benefit only the period of payment.

   b. Franchise cost is **amortized** over its **estimated useful life** if such life is **finite**.

17. **Franchisor accounting.** Franchise fee revenue ordinarily should be recognized with a provision for uncollectible amounts. **Recognition** is at the earliest time when the franchisor has substantially performed (SFAS 45, *Accounting for Franchise Fee Revenue*).

   a. The **earliest time** usually is the beginning of operations by the franchisee unless substantial performance of all obligations occurred previously.

   b. **Substantial performance** occurs when

   1) The franchisor has no remaining obligation or intent to refund any cash or to forgive any debt,

   2) The franchisor has performed substantially all of the initial services contracted for, and

   3) No other relevant material obligations or conditions exist.

   c. The **installment and cost recovery methods** are appropriate only when the franchise fees are to be collected over an extended period and collectibility cannot be reasonably estimated.

   d. **Initial fees are deferred** if they are large in relation to subsequent **continuing fees** or if future related services are promised, e.g., if bargain purchase prices exist for supplies.

   1) Deferral is indicated when it is probable that continuing fees will not cover the **cost** of continuing services and provide a **reasonable profit**. The deferral should cover those amounts.

   2) Continuing fees are recognized as **revenue** when they are **earned and become receivable**.

   3) The portion of the initial franchise fee applicable to any **tangible assets** provided to the franchisee is recognized based on the fair values.

e. **Repossession** of the franchise or **refund** of the franchise fee is a reduction of revenue in the current period.

1) If a refund is made to the franchisee, previously recognized revenue is a **contra revenue** in the current period.

2) If no refund is made, bad debt and other expenses are recognized, and associated deferred revenues should be recognized in the current period.

EXAMPLE

On December 31, Year 1, Sigrid Corp. authorized Vortigern to operate as a franchisee for an initial franchise fee of $300,000. Of this amount, $120,000 was received upon signing the agreement, and the balance, represented by a note, is due in three annual payments of $60,000 each, beginning December 31, Year 2. The present value on December 31, Year 1, of the three annual payments appropriately discounted is $144,000. According to the agreement, the nonrefundable down payment is a fair measure of the services already performed by Sigrid. However, substantial future services are required of Sigrid. Collectibility of the note is reasonably certain. Accordingly, Sigrid's entry is

Note receivable	$180,000	
Cash	120,000	
Unearned revenue		$144,000
Franchise fee revenue		120,000
Discount on note receivable		36,000

Because the down payment is the agreed amount paid for services already performed, Sigrid should recognize $120,000 of revenue. The note is a long-term receivable that should be reported at its present value. However, this amount ($144,000) should be recorded as unearned revenue because the franchisor has not substantially performed (completed the earning process).

Licensing Agreements

18. These permit an entity to engage in a given activity, such as selling a well-known product or to use rights (e.g., a patent) owned by others.

a. For example, a broadcaster may secure the FCC's permission (classified by some authors as a franchise) to transmit on a given frequency within a certain area.

1) **Network affiliation agreements** are valuable because they permit a station to obtain programming more cheaply than its unaffiliated competitors. **Licenses to use copyrighted program material**, such as films, are other examples of intangible assets recognized in the broadcast industry.

b. The **amortization period** is the useful life of the agreement if it is **finite**.

1) The **legal life** of the agreement may be **indefinite**. For example, an FCC license is granted for a limited period of years but is ordinarily renewable an unlimited number of times. Thus, such a license may not be amortizable.

c. These intangible assets should be written down to reflect any **permanent impairment**.

19. The matching principle applies to **royalty revenues and expenses** arising from licenses. Thus, revenues should be recognized when the earning process has been completed. Expenses should be recognized as the economic benefits of the asset are consumed.

Start-Up Costs and Organization Costs

20. Costs incurred in the formation of a business entity include payments to promoters, legal and accounting fees, and costs of registering with the state of incorporation.

21. The start-up costs and organization costs of all nongovernmental entities must be **expensed as incurred** (AICPA SOP 98-5, *Reporting on the Costs of Start-up Activities*).

    a. This treatment differs from that for **tax purposes**. A taxpayer may elect to deduct up to $5,000 of **business start-up costs**. The deduction is reduced dollar-for-dollar by the amount by which they exceed $50,000. Any remaining start-up costs are amortized over a minimum of 180 months (15 years), beginning with the month in which the active trade or business begins.

        1) The same rule applies to start-up expenditures of corporations and partnerships.

            a) Corporations and partnerships also may elect to deduct up to $5,000 of **organizational expenditures**, subject to the limits imposed on immediate deduction and subsequent amortization described above.

Leases

22. Leases have been variously classified as PPE, intangible assets, and deferred charges.

Stop and review! You have completed the outline for this subunit. Study multiple-choice questions 7 through 12 beginning on page 352.

9.3 RESEARCH AND DEVELOPMENT

1. R&D costs must be **expensed as incurred** (SFAS 2, *Accounting for Research and Development Costs*).

    a. This rule does not apply to R&D activities **conducted for others**.
    b. This rule also does not apply to assets (tangible or intangible) acquired in a **business combination** that are used in R&D activities. Such assets are initially recognized and measured at fair value even if they have no alternative use.

2. **Research** is planned search or critical investigation aimed at discovery of new knowledge with the hope that it will be useful in developing a new (or significantly improving an existing) product, service, process, or technique **(product or process)**.

3. **Development** is translation of research findings or other knowledge into a plan or design for a new or improved product or process.

    a. It includes conceptual formulation, design, and testing of product alternatives; prototype construction; and operation of pilot plants.
    b. Development does **not** include routine alterations to existing products, production lines, processes, and other ongoing operations.

        1) Market research or testing also is excluded.

R&D Activities

4. SFAS 2 gives the following examples of activities typically included in R&D unless conducted for others under a contract (reimbursable costs are not expensed):

    a. Laboratory research aimed at discovery of new knowledge
    b. Searching for applications of new research findings or other knowledge
    c. Conceptual formulation and design of possible product or process alternatives
    d. Testing in search for, or evaluation of, product or process alternatives
    e. Modification of the formulation or design of a product or process
    f. Design, construction, and testing of preproduction prototypes and models
    g. Design of tools, jigs, molds, and dies involving new technology

h. Design, construction, and operation of a pilot plant that is not of a scale economically feasible to the entity for commercial production

i. Engineering activity required to advance the design of a product until it meets specific functional and economic requirements and is ready for manufacture

Activities Not Classified as R&D

5. SFAS 2 gives the following examples of activities that typically are not classified as R&D:

    a. Engineering follow-through in an early phase of commercial production

    b. Quality control during commercial production, including routine testing of products

    c. Troubleshooting in connection with breakdowns during commercial production

    d. Routine, ongoing efforts to refine, enrich, or otherwise improve upon the qualities of an existing product

    e. Adaptation of an existing capability to a particular requirement or customer's need as part of a continuing commercial activity

    f. Seasonal or other periodic design changes to existing products

    g. Routine design of tools, jigs, molds, and dies

    h. Activity, including design and construction engineering, related to the construction, relocation, rearrangement, or start-up of facilities or equipment other than pilot plants and facilities or equipment whose sole use is for a particular R&D project

    i. Legal work in connection with patent applications or litigation and the sale or licensing of patents

Elements of R&D Costs

6. The following cost elements are associated with R&D:

    a. **Materials, equipment, and facilities.** The costs of such items acquired or constructed for R&D and having **alternative future uses** are **capitalized** as tangible assets.

        1) The **costs** of materials consumed in R&D and the **depreciation** of equipment or facilities used in R&D are R&D costs and are expensed when incurred.

        2) The costs of materials, equipment, or facilities acquired (but not in a business combination) or constructed for a **particular project** and having **no alternative future uses** (and no separate economic values) are R&D costs and are expensed when incurred.

    b. **Personnel.** Salaries, wages, and other related costs of personnel engaged in R&D are included in R&D costs and are expensed when incurred.

    c. **Intangible assets purchased from others.** The costs of intangible assets purchased from others for use in R&D and having **alternative future uses** are capitalized as intangible assets. They are amortized if their useful lives are finite.

        1) The **amortization** of those intangible assets is an R&D cost.

        2) The costs of intangible assets purchased from others (but not in a business combination) for a particular project and having **no alternative future uses** (and no separate economic values) are R&D costs and are expensed when incurred.

    d. **Contract services.** The costs of services performed by others in connection with the R&D activities of an entity, including R&D conducted by others on behalf of the entity, are R&D costs and are expensed when incurred.

    e. **Indirect costs.** R&D costs include a reasonable allocation of indirect costs, which also are expensed.

        1) General and administrative costs not clearly related to R&D are excluded.

7. Disclosure is made in the financial statements of the total R&D costs charged to expense in each period for which an income statement is presented.

R&D Funded by Others

8. Sometimes an entity's R&D is funded wholly or partly by others.

    a. If the entity is **obligated to repay** any of the funds provided by the other party regardless of the outcome of the project, it recognizes a **liability**.

    b. If repayment depends **solely on the results** of the R&D having future economic benefit, the entity accounts for its obligation as a contract to perform R&D for others.

        1) Thus, an advance is accounted for as deferred contract revenue.

    c. Repayment of a **loan or advance to others** may depend on whether the R&D will have future economic benefits. In this case, the loan or advance is debited to R&D expense unless it relates to another activity (SFAS 68, *Research and Development Arrangements*).

Stop and review! You have completed the outline for this subunit. Study multiple-choice questions 13 through 15 on page 354.

9.4 PREPAYMENTS

1. "Future economic benefit is the essence of an asset" (**SFAC 6**, *Elements of Financial Statements*). If a cash payment is made in one period and the recognition of the related expense (receipt of the benefit) is not appropriate until a later period, the **deferred cost** is recorded as an **asset**.

    a. Examples include prepaid insurance, rent, interest, and income taxes.

    b. The amount of the prepaid expense that will be used up within the longer of 1 year or the next operating cycle of the entity is classified as a **current asset**.

    c. If the payment is **initially recorded as an asset**, the year-end **adjusting entry** will credit the asset and debit an expense for the expired portion.

        1) If the payment is **initially recorded as an expense**, the year-end **adjusting entry** will debit an asset and credit expense for the unexpired portion.

Stop and review! You have completed the outline for this subunit. Study multiple-choice questions 16 through 18 on page 355.

9.5 COMPUTER SOFTWARE

1. SFAS 86, *Accounting for the Costs of Computer Software to Be Sold, Leased, or Otherwise Marketed*, applies to software to be "sold, leased, or otherwise marketed as a separate product or as part of a product or process."

    a. The **reporting entity** may

        1) Develop and produce the software internally
        2) Purchase the software from an external source

    b. A **computer software product** is either a

        1) Computer software program or group of programs or a
        2) **Product enhancement.** Such an improvement extends the life or improves marketability of the original. It usually requires a product design or possibly a redesign.

            a) The **product design** should suffice to provide product specifications.
            b) The **detail program design** "takes product function, feature, and technical requirements to their most detailed, logical form and is ready for coding."

        3) SFAS 86 does **not** apply to (a) costs of software that an entity develops for its own use or contractually for others or (b) to revenue recognition for marketed software.

R&D Costs of Computer Software

2. R&D costs are all costs to establish technological feasibility. **They are expensed when incurred.**

   a. **Technological feasibility** is established when the entity has taken the necessary steps so that "the product can be produced to meet its design specifications including functions, features, and technical performance requirements." The following is the **minimum required evidence** of technological feasibility:

      1) The **detail program design and the product design must be complete**. The entity must establish that it has access to the skills, hardware, and software needed for production.

         a) The detail program design and the product design **must be consistent**. Consistency is confirmed by program documentation and comparison with product specifications.

         b) In addition, the detail program design must by evaluated for **high-risk development issues**. Any **uncertainties** should be resolved.

      2) If software is written **without the detail program design working model**,

         a) It must have a completed product design and a **working model**, and

         b) The completeness of the model and its consistency with the product design must be tested.

Production Costs of Computer Software

3. The entity **must capitalize** production costs of product masters, including coding and testing costs, if they are incurred after technological feasibility is determined.

   a. A **product master** is complete and ready for copying. It includes documentation and training materials.

   b. The entity **must not capitalize** production costs for software that are an integral part of a product or process until it has

      1) Established technological feasibility and
      2) Completed all R&D for the rest of the product or process.

   c. Once the product is available for **general release**, software costs are **not capitalized**.

      1) Maintenance and customer support costs, including costs of routine software modifications, are **expensed at the earlier of** recognition of related revenue or incurrence of such costs.

Purchased Computer Software

4. If purchased software to be marketed has **no alternative future use**, the entity accounts for its cost as if it had been developed internally to be sold, leased, or otherwise marketed.

   a. If purchased software to be marketed **has an alternative future use**, the entity **capitalizes** the costs when it purchases the software and accounts for it according to use.

Amortization of Capitalized Software Costs

5. The general rule is to amortize capitalized software costs separately for each product.

   a. **For each product**, the annual amortization is the **GREATER** of the amount determined using

      1) The **ratio** of current gross revenues to the sum of current gross revenues and anticipated future gross revenues, or

      2) The **straight-line method** over the remaining estimated economic life, including the current reporting period.

   b. Amortization begins when the product is **available for general release**.

Inventory Costs

6. Inventory costs include packaging costs and the costs of duplicating from the product masters the (a) software, (b) documentation, and (c) training materials.

   a. They are inventoried on a **unit-specific** basis. These costs are then **charged to cost of goods sold** when revenue from sales of those units is recognized.

Evaluation of Capitalized Software Costs

7. At year-end, the unamortized cost of each software product must be **compared with the net realizable value (NRV)** of that software product.

   a. Any **excess of unamortized cost** over NRV must be written off.

   b. The **NRV for each product** is estimated future gross revenues, minus estimated future completion and disposal costs, minus maintenance and customer support costs.

   c. After a write-down, the product's carrying amount is the NRV recorded at year-end. The write-down cannot later be reversed.

EXAMPLE

On December 31, Year 7, Byte Co. had capitalized software costs of $600,000 with an economic life of four years. Sales for Year 8 were 10% of expected total sales of the software. At December 31, Year 8, the software had a net realizable value of $480,000. In its December 31, Year 8, balance sheet, Byte should report $450,000 of net capitalized cost of computer software. At year-end, the unamortized cost of each software product must be compared with the NRV of that software product. Any excess of unamortized cost over NRV must be written off. The amount of amortization under the straight-line method is used because it is greater than the amount determined using the 10% ratio of current sales to expected total sales. Thus, Byte Co. had an unamortized cost of software of $450,000 [$600,000 capitalized cost – ($600,000 ÷ 4)] at December 31, Year 8. The $450,000 unamortized cost is lower than the $480,000 NRV, so $450,000 is the amount reported in the year-end balance sheet.

Software Developed for Internal Use

8. Software is for **internal use** if (a) it is intended solely to meet the entity's internal needs, and (b), during its development or modification, no substantive plan exists for its external marketing. A joint development agreement is not a substantive marketing plan.

   a. Software costs in the **preliminary project stage** are expensed as incurred. Once the capitalization criteria have been met, (1) external direct costs of materials and services, (2) payroll costs directly associated with the project (to the extent of the direct time spent), and (3) interest costs are capitalized. Training costs and data conversion costs (except costs of software that permits access to new data by old systems) are expensed as incurred.

   b. During the **application development stage**, internal and external costs are capitalized.

   c. During the **post-implementation/operation stage**, internal and external training costs and maintenance costs are expensed as incurred (AICPA SOP 98-1, *Accounting for the Costs of Computer Software Developed or Obtained for Internal Use*).

9. **Internal costs** for **upgrades and enhancements** are expensed or capitalized in accordance with the foregoing sections.

   a. If internal costs cannot be separated on a reasonably cost-effective basis between **maintenance** and **minor upgrades and enhancements**, such costs are expensed as incurred.

10. **External costs** under agreements related to **specified upgrades and enhancements** are also expensed or capitalized as previously indicated. But external costs for (a) maintenance, (b) unspecified upgrades and enhancements, and (c) costs under agreements combining such services are expensed over the contract period on a **straight-line basis** unless another systematic and rational basis is more representative.

    a. Capitalization of the costs of specified upgrades and enhancements requires that the **additional functionality** resulting from such expenditures be **probable**.

11. **Capitalization** begins when the **preliminary project stage** (conceptual formulation and evaluation of alternatives, determination of existence of needed technology, and final selection of alternatives) is **completed**.

    a. Management, with the relevant authority, must implicitly or explicitly authorize and commit to funding the computer software project.

    b. Moreover, it must be **probable** that the project will be completed and the software will be used to perform the function intended.

12. When **completion is no longer probable**, capitalization ceases and impairment is recognized and measured under the provisions of SFAS 144.

13. **Capitalization ends** when the project is substantially complete and ready for its intended use.

14. When **new software replaces old software**, unamortized costs of the old software are expensed.

15. Capitalized costs are **amortized on a straight-line basis** over the useful life of the software unless another systematic and rational basis is more representative.

16. If, after the development of the software is completed, the entity **decides to market the software**, proceeds received from its licensing, net of direct incremental costs of marketing, are reductions of the carrying amount.

EXAMPLE

Yellow Co. spent $12,000,000 during the current year developing its new software package. Of this amount, $4,000,000 was spent before it was at the application development stage, and the package was only to be used internally. The package was completed during the year and is expected to have a four-year useful life. Yellow has a policy of taking a full-year's amortization in the first year. After the development stage, $50,000 was spent on training employees to use the program. Yellow reports $6,050,000 of expense for the current year. Software costs in the preliminary project stage are expensed as incurred. During the application development stage, internal and external costs are capitalized. However, training costs are expensed. Accordingly, $8,000,000 ($12,000,000 total – $4,000,000 spent before application development) of the development cost was capitalized. Amortization is on a straight-line basis over the four-year useful life of the software. Thus, given that a full-year's amortization is recognized in year one, the expense for the year is $6,050,000 [$4,000,000 preliminary project expense + ($8,000,000 ÷ 4) amortization + $50,000 training cost].

Software Revenue Recognition

17.   Special accounting treatment applies to sales, leases, licenses, or other means of marketing software that is not incidental to another product or service as a whole.

   a.   If a software arrangement does **not** require significant production, modification, or customization, **revenue is recognized** when

      1)   Persuasive evidence of an arrangement exists,
      2)   Delivery has occurred,
      3)   The vendor's fee is fixed or determinable, and
      4)   Collectibility is probable (AICPA SOP 97-2, *Software Revenue Recognition*).

18.   If a software arrangement **requires significant production, modification, or customization**, the accounting for long-term construction contracts (e.g., percentage-of-completion) ordinarily should be used. Thus, **separate accounting for different elements is not permitted** unless an exception applies.

19.   Software arrangements may have **multiple elements**, for example, other software, upgrades or enhancements, **postcontract customer support (PCS)**, or services. Moreover, some elements may be deliverable only on a **when-and-if-available** basis.

   a.   If long-term construction contract accounting is **not** used, the vendor's fee is allocated to the elements based on **vendor-specific objective evidence of fair values**. If sufficient evidence of this kind does not exist, all revenue is deferred until sufficient evidence exists or all elements have been delivered.

      1)   **Certain exceptions apply.** For example, if the only undelivered element is PCS or services not requiring significant production, etc., the entire fee is recognized ratably over the contract period or over the period the services are to be performed, respectively. Complex rules beyond the scope of this outline also provide an exception when fees are based on the number of **copies**.

      2)   **Evidence of fair value** consists only of the price when an element is sold separately or, if it is not, the price determined by management.

      3)   If a delivered element is sold only with another element(s) qualifying for separate accounting and evidence of fair value exists for each undelivered element but not for a delivered element(s), **residual accounting** is used.

         a)   This method is appropriate if all other recognition criteria are met and the fair value of all undelivered elements is less than the arrangement fee. Residual accounting **defers the total fair value of the undelivered elements**. It recognizes the difference between the fee and the deferred amount as revenue.

EXAMPLE

Software is sold with a year of PCS for one amount ($300,000), with a provision for annual renewal of PCS for one year at an additional stated amount ($60,000). Assuming other recognition criteria are met, and no evidence of fair value exists for the delivered element, the amount deferred equals the PCS renewal price ($60,000). The balance of the fee ($240,000) is recognized as revenue when the software is delivered.

---

      4)   **Delivery** is deemed not to have occurred if an **undelivered element** is essential to the use of a delivered element. Furthermore, the **collectibility of the fee** is deemed not to be probable if the amount allocable to delivered elements is subject to forfeiture, refund, or other concession if an undelivered element is not delivered.

      5)   Regardless of whether contract accounting is used, a **service element** must be separately accounted for when the services are

          a)   Not essential to the functionality of another element and are

          b)   Described in the contract so that the total price is expected to vary with the inclusion or exclusion of the services.

Stop and review! You have completed the outline for this subunit. Study multiple-choice questions 19 through 21 beginning on page 356.

9.6 SPECIAL ISSUES

Deferred Charges

1.   Deferred charges **(other assets)** is a catchall category. It includes long-term prepayments and any noncurrent asset not classified elsewhere.

    a.   Such a classification has been criticized because many assets (e.g., PPE) are deferred charges. Thus, they are long-term prepayments that will be depreciated or amortized.

Development Stage Enterprises (DSEs)

2.   **DSEs** (a) are devoting substantially all of their efforts to establishing the business and (b) have not begun principal operations or have not earned significant revenues from those operations.

    a.   Financial statements of DSEs must be presented in accordance with the same GAAP applicable to established operating entities (SFAS 7, *Accounting and Reporting by Development Stage Enterprises*).

3.   The following additional information must be **disclosed**:

    a.   The **deficit accumulated** during the development stage should be presented in the equity section of the **balance sheet**. The **income statement and statement of cash flows** should include not only amounts for each period for which an income statement is presented but also **cumulative amounts from the entity's inception**.

        1)   This disclosure is accomplished by placing a cumulative amount column to the right of the current period's amounts.

    b.   During the development stage, an entity's financial statements should be **identified as those of a DSE**, and the nature of the development stage activities should be disclosed.

    c.   When the development stage has been completed, the statements **for the next fiscal year** must disclose that, in prior years, the entity had been in the development stage. No further disclosure is required.

4.   The development stage is considered to be complete when **significant revenue** is generated from the planned principal operations.

5.   **Cost deferral** is permitted to DSEs only to the same extent as to established operating entities under GAAP.

Advertising Costs

6.   Advertising costs should be expensed, either **as incurred** or **when advertising first occurs**. The primary costs are production and communication. **Production** includes idea development, copywriting, artwork, printing, hiring personnel (e.g., audio and video crews and actors), etc. **Communication** requires use of the Internet, newspapers, magazines, radio, television, billboards, etc. (AICPA SOP 93-7, *Reporting on Advertising Costs*).

   a.   However, certain **direct response advertising** costs should be capitalized (deferred).

      1)   Capitalization is appropriate if

         a)   The primary purpose is to generate sales from customers who respond specifically to the advertising, and

         b)   Probable future economic benefits result.

      2)   An entity that wishes to capitalize the costs of direct response advertising must document that **customers have specifically responded** to the advertising. It also must document the benefits from prior direct response advertising.

      3)   The deferral of advertising costs is appropriate for both **interim and year-end** financial reporting if their benefits clearly apply to more than one period.

         a)   Moreover, if a cost that would be fully expensed in an annual report benefits more than one interim period, it may be allocated to those interim reports.

   b.   A second exception to the rule of recognition of advertising expense as incurred or when advertising first occurs is for expenditures **subsequent to recognition** of related revenue.

      1)   An example is a manufacturer's obligation to repay retailers for costs of advertising that involve the manufacturer's products. This type of cost should be accrued and expensed **when related revenues are recognized**.

Stop and review! You have completed the outline for this subunit. Study multiple-choice questions 22 through 25 beginning on page 357.

QUESTIONS

9.1 Goodwill and Other Intangible Assets

1. On June 30, Year 5, Finn, Inc. exchanged 2,000 shares of Edlow Corp. $30 par value common stock for a patent owned by Bisk Co. The Edlow stock was acquired in Year 1 at a cost of $50,000. At the exchange date, Edlow common stock had a fair value of $40 per share, and the patent had a net carrying amount of $100,000 on Bisk's books. Finn should record the patent at

A. $50,000

B. $60,000

C. $80,000

D. $100,000

Answer (C) is correct. *(CPA, adapted)*
REQUIRED: The amount at which a patent should be recorded.
DISCUSSION: When an intangible asset is acquired externally, it should be recorded at its cost at the date of acquisition. In an exchange transaction, cost is measured by the cash paid. Otherwise, the fair value of the more clearly evident of the consideration given or the asset acquired is the basis for measurement. The fair value of the assets given in return for the patent was $80,000 (2,000 shares of stock × $40 per share fair value). The $30 par value, the $25 per share ($50,000 ÷ 2,000 shares) acquisition cost, and the net carrying amount of the patent are not considered in determining fair value.
Answer (A) is incorrect because $50,000 is the acquisition cost of the stock. Answer (B) is incorrect because $60,000 is the par value of the stock. Answer (D) is incorrect because $100,000 is the net carrying amount of the patent.

2. Tech Co. bought a trademark on January 2, two years ago. Tech accounted for the trademark as instructed under the provisions of FASB Statement No. 142, *Goodwill and Other Intangible Assets*, during the current year. The intangible was being amortized over 40 years. The carrying amount at the beginning of the year was $38,000. It was determined that the cash flow will be generated indefinitely at the current level for the trademark. What amount should Tech report as amortization expense for the current year?

A. $0

B. $922

C. $1,000

D. $38,000

Answer (A) is correct. *(CPA, adapted)*
REQUIRED: The amortization expense for a purchased trademark.
DISCUSSION: The useful life of an asset is the period during which it is expected to contribute directly or indirectly to the reporting entity's future cash flow. An intangible asset with a finite useful life to the reporting entity is amortized over that useful life. However, an intangible asset with an indefinite useful life to the reporting entity is not amortized. Thus, because the trademark will generate cash flows indefinitely, it will not be amortized.

3. In accordance with generally accepted accounting principles, which of the following methods of amortization is required for amortizable intangible assets if the pattern of consumption of economic benefits is not reliably determinable?

A. Sum-of-the-years'-digits.

B. Straight-line.

C. Units-of-production.

D. Double-declining-balance.

Answer (B) is correct. *(CPA, adapted)*
REQUIRED: The method of amortization of intangible assets if the pattern of consumption of economic benefits is not reliably determinable.
DISCUSSION: The default method of amortization of intangible assets is the straight-line method (SFAS 142).
Answer (A) is incorrect because sum-of-the-years'-digits may be used only if it is reliably determined to reflect the pattern of consumption of the economic benefits of the intangible asset. Answer (C) is incorrect because units-of-production may be used only if it is reliably determined to reflect the pattern of consumption of the economic benefits of the intangible asset. Answer (D) is incorrect because double-declining-balance may be used only if it is reliably determined to reflect the pattern of consumption of the economic benefits of the intangible asset.

4. Which of the following is not a consideration in determining the useful life of an intangible asset?

A. Legal, regulatory, or contractual provisions.

B. Provisions for renewal or extension.

C. Expected actions of competitors.

D. Initial cost.

Answer (D) is correct. *(CPA, adapted)*
REQUIRED: The consideration not used in determining the useful life of an intangible asset.
DISCUSSION: Initial cost is not a factor relevant to estimating the useful life because it has no causal connection with the asset's contribution to the future cash flows of the reporting entity. Among the relevant factors are the expected use of the asset; the useful life of a related asset or assets; legal, regulatory, or contractual provisions that may limit the useful life or that may permit renewal or extension without substantial cost; economic factors (e.g., obsolescence, competition, or demand); and expenditures for maintenance (SFAS 142).

5. On January 2, Paye Co. acquired Shef Co. in a business combination that resulted in recognition of goodwill of $200,000 having an expected benefit period of 10 years. Shef is treated as a reporting unit, and the entire amount of the recognized goodwill is assigned to it. During the first quarter of the year, Shef spent an additional $80,000 on expenditures designed to maintain goodwill. Due to these expenditures, at December 31 Shef estimated that the benefit period of goodwill was 40 years. In its consolidated December 31 balance sheet, what amount should Paye report as goodwill?

A. $180,000

B. $200,000

C. $252,000

D. $280,000

Answer (B) is correct. *(CPA, adapted)*
REQUIRED: The amount of goodwill in the balance sheet.
DISCUSSION: Goodwill is not recorded except in a business combination. Thus, only the $200,000 recognized at the acquisition date should be recorded as goodwill. It should not be amortized but should be tested for impairment at the reporting-unit level. The facts given suggest that the fair value of the reporting unit (Shef) is not less than its carrying amount. Hence, no impairment of goodwill has occurred, and goodwill is unchanged at $200,000. Moreover, the cost of internally developing, maintaining, or restoring intangible assets (including goodwill) that are not specifically identifiable, have indeterminate useful lives, or are inherent in a continuing business and related to an entity as a whole should be expensed as incurred.
Answer (A) is incorrect because $180,000 results when goodwill is amortized on the straight-line basis over 10 years. Answer (C) is incorrect because $252,000 results from amortizing an additional $80,000 of expenditures to maintain goodwill over 10 years. Answer (D) is incorrect because $280,000 results from adding $80,000 of expenditures for the maintenance of goodwill.

6. Which of the following costs of goodwill should be capitalized and amortized?

	Maintaining Goodwill	Developing Goodwill
A.	Yes	No
B.	No	No
C.	Yes	Yes
D.	No	Yes

Answer (B) is correct. *(CPA, adapted)*
REQUIRED: The costs of goodwill that should be capitalized and amortized.
DISCUSSION: SFAS 141, *Business Combinations*, requires that goodwill arising from a business combination be capitalized. SFAS 142 prohibits amortization of goodwill. Moreover, the cost of developing, maintaining, or restoring intangible assets (including goodwill) that are not specifically identifiable, have indeterminate useful lives, or are inherent in a continuing business and related to an entity as a whole should be expensed as incurred.

9.2 Intangible Assets Distinct from Goodwill

7. Under a royalty agreement with another company, Wand Co. will pay royalties for the assignment of a patent for 3 years. The royalties paid should be reported as expense

A. In the period paid.

B. In the period incurred.

C. At the date the royalty agreement began.

D. At the date the royalty agreement expired.

Answer (B) is correct. *(CPA, adapted)*
REQUIRED: The period in which royalties paid are reported as expense.
DISCUSSION: Royalty expense is recognized when it is incurred as determined by a contractual arrangement. The basic principles of accrual accounting regarding the matching of revenues and expenses are applicable. Thus, the expense should be recognized as the economic benefits of the assets are consumed.

8. During the year just ended, Jase Co. incurred research and development costs of $136,000 in its laboratories relating to a patent that was granted on July 1. Costs of registering the patent equaled $34,000. The patent's legal life is 20 years, and its estimated economic life is 10 years. In its December 31 balance sheet, what amount should Jase report for the patent, net of accumulated amortization?

A. $32,300

B. $33,150

C. $161,500

D. $165,000

Answer (A) is correct. *(CPA, adapted)*
REQUIRED: The amount reported for the patent, net of accumulated amortization.
DISCUSSION: R&D costs are expensed as incurred. However, SFAS 2 specifically excludes legal work in connection with patent applications or litigation and the sale or licensing of patents from the definition of R&D. Hence, the legal costs of filing a patent should be capitalized. The patent should be amortized over its estimated economic life of 10 years. Amortization for the year equals $1,700 [($34,000 ÷ 10) × (6 ÷ 12)]. Thus, the reported amount of the patent at year-end equals $32,300 ($34,000 − $1,700).
Answer (B) is incorrect because $33,150 results from using the 20-year legal life of the patent. Answer (C) is incorrect because the $136,000 of R&D costs should not be capitalized. Answer (D) is incorrect because the R&D costs should not be capitalized, and the useful life, not the legal life, should be used.

9. Gray Co. was granted a patent on January 2, Year 5, and appropriately capitalized $45,000 of related costs. Gray was amortizing the patent over its estimated useful life of 15 years. During Year 8, Gray paid $15,000 in legal costs in successfully defending an attempted infringement of the patent. After the legal action was completed, Gray sold the patent to the plaintiff for $75,000. Gray's policy is to take no amortization in the year of disposal. In its Year 8 income statement, what amount should Gray report as gain from sale of patent?

A. $15,000

B. $24,000

C. $27,000

D. $39,000

Answer (B) is correct. *(CPA, adapted)*
REQUIRED: The amount reported as gain from the sale of a patent.
DISCUSSION: The patent was capitalized at $45,000 in Year 5. Annual amortization of $3,000 ($45,000 ÷ 15 years) for Year 5, Year 6, and Year 7 reduced the carrying amount to $36,000. The $15,000 in legal costs for successfully defending an attempted infringement may be capitalized, which increases the carrying amount of the patent to $51,000 ($36,000 + $15,000). Accordingly, the gain from the sale is $24,000 ($75,000 − $51,000).
Answer (A) is incorrect because $15,000 is the amount of legal costs for defending the patent. Answer (C) is incorrect because $27,000 assumes amortization in the year of disposal. Answer (D) is incorrect because $39,000 results from not capitalizing the $15,000 in legal costs.

10. On January 2, Boulder Co. assigned its patent to Castle Co. for royalties of 10% of patent-related sales. The assignment is for the remaining four years of the patent's life. Castle guaranteed Boulder a minimum royalty of $100,000 over the life of the patent and paid Boulder $50,000 against future royalties during the year. Patent-related sales for the year were $300,000. In its income statement for the year, what amount should Boulder report as royalty revenue?

  A. $25,000

  B. $30,000

  C. $50,000

  D. $100,000

Answer (B) is correct. *(CPA, adapted)*
  REQUIRED: The amount of royalty revenue to recognize.
  DISCUSSION: Patent fee revenue should be recognized when an earning process has been completed. That process is complete when patent-related sales are made by the assignee or the four-year period has expired. Boulder is guaranteed at least $100,000 over the life of the patent. However, it must recognize the royalty revenue when it is earned over the four-year useful life of the patent. For the year, Boulder should report $30,000 ($300,000 × 10%) of the patent revenue as earned.
  Answer (A) is incorrect because $30,000 of patent revenue was earned, and Boulder is allowed to recognize it. Answer (C) is incorrect because the $50,000 advance payment against future royalties will not be fully earned until Boulder makes additional sales or the four-year period expires. Answer (D) is incorrect because the $100,000 has neither been received nor earned.

11. Helsing Co. bought a franchise from Anya Co. on January 1 for $204,000. An independent consultant retained by Helsing estimated that the remaining useful life of the franchise was a finite period of 50 years and that the pattern of consumption of benefits of the franchise is not reliably determinable. Its unamortized cost on Anya's books on January 1 was $68,000. What amount should be amortized for the year ended December 31, assuming no residual value?

  A. $5,100

  B. $4,080

  C. $3,400

  D. $1,700

Answer (B) is correct. *(CPA, adapted)*
  REQUIRED: The first-year amortization expense of the cost of a franchise.
  DISCUSSION: A franchise is an intangible asset. The initial measurement of an intangible asset acquired other than in a business combination is at fair value. Thus, the "cost" to be amortized should be based on the more reliably measurable of the fair value of the consideration given or the fair value of the assets acquired. If the useful life is finite, the intangible asset is amortized over that period. Moreover, if the consumption pattern of benefits of the intangible asset is not reliably determinable, the straight-line method of amortization is used. Accordingly, given no residual value, the amortization expense is $4,080 ($204,000 consideration given ÷ 50-year finite useful life).
  Answer (A) is incorrect because $5,100 is based on a 40-year period. Answer (C) is incorrect because $3,400 is the difference between the $204,000 franchise price and Anya's $68,000 unamortized cost, divided by 40 years. Answer (D) is incorrect because $1,700 equals the unamortized cost on Anya's books amortized over 40 years.

12. Neue Co., a developmental stage enterprise, incurred the following costs during its first year of operations:

Legal fees for incorporation and other related matters	$55,000
Underwriters' fees for initial stock offering	40,000
Exploration costs and purchases of mineral rights	60,000

Neue had no revenue during its first year of operation. What amount must Neue expense as organizational costs?

  A. $155,000

  B. $100,000

  C. $95,000

  D. $55,000

Answer (D) is correct. *(CPA, adapted)*
  REQUIRED: The organizational costs to be expensed.
  DISCUSSION: Organization costs are those incurred in the formation of a business entity. For financial accounting purposes, AICPA SOP 98-5 requires nongovernmental entities to expense all start-up and organization costs as incurred. Thus, the legal fees ($55,000) should be expensed because they are organization costs. Fees for an initial stock offering are customarily treated as a reduction in the proceeds rather than as organization costs, and exploration costs and purchases of mineral rights are capitalizable items that are not organization costs.

9.3 Research and Development

13. During the year just ended, Orr Co. incurred the following costs:

Research and development services performed by Key Corp. for Orr	$150,000
Design, construction, and testing of preproduction prototypes and models	200,000
Testing in search for new products or process alternatives	175,000

In its income statement for the year, what should Orr report as research and development expense?

- A. $150,000
- B. $200,000
- C. $350,000
- D. $525,000

Answer (D) is correct. *(CPA, adapted)*
REQUIRED: The R&D expense.
DISCUSSION: Research is planned search or critical investigation aimed at discovery of new knowledge useful in developing a new product, service, process, or technique, or in bringing about a significant improvement to an existing product, etc. Development is translation of research findings or other knowledge into a plan or design for a new or improved product or process. R&D expenses include R&D performed under contract by others; design, construction, and testing of prototypes; and testing in search for new products (SFAS 2).
Answer (A) is incorrect because $150,000 does not include design, construction, and testing of preproduction prototypes or testing in search of new products. Answer (B) is incorrect because $200,000 does not include R&D performed under contract by others or testing in search for new products. Answer (C) is incorrect because $350,000 does not include testing in search for new products.

14. West, Inc. made the following expenditures relating to Product Y:

- Legal costs to file a patent on Product Y -- $10,000. Production of the finished product would not have been undertaken without the patent.
- Special equipment to be used solely for development of Product Y -- $60,000. The equipment has no other use and has an estimated useful life of 4 years.
- Labor and material costs incurred in producing a prototype model -- $200,000.
- Cost of testing the prototype $80,000.

What is the total amount of costs that will be expensed when incurred?

- A. $280,000
- B. $295,000
- C. $340,000
- D. $350,000

Answer (C) is correct. *(CPA, adapted)*
REQUIRED: The total amount of costs that will be expensed when incurred.
DISCUSSION: R&D costs are expensed as incurred. However, SFAS 2 specifically excludes legal work in connection with patent applications or litigation and the sale or licensing of patents from the definition of R&D. The legal costs of filing a patent should be capitalized. West's R&D costs include those incurred for the design, construction, and testing of preproduction prototypes. Moreover, the cost of equipment used solely for a specific project is also expensed immediately. Thus, the total amount of costs that will be expensed when incurred is $340,000.
Answer (A) is incorrect because $280,000 omits the cost of the special equipment. Answer (B) is incorrect because $295,000 includes 1 year's straight-line depreciation on the special equipment instead of the full cost. Answer (D) is incorrect because $350,000 includes the legal costs of filing a patent.

15. In the year just ended, Ball Labs incurred the following costs:

Direct costs of doing contract R&D work for the government to be reimbursed by governmental unit	$400,000

R&D costs not included above were

Depreciation	$300,000
Salaries	700,000
Indirect costs appropriately allocated	200,000
Materials	180,000

What was Ball's total R&D expense for the year?

- A. $1,080,000
- B. $1,380,000
- C. $1,580,000
- D. $1,780,000

Answer (B) is correct. *(CPA, adapted)*
REQUIRED: The total R&D expense.
DISCUSSION: Under SFAS 2, materials used in R&D, compensation costs of personnel, and indirect costs appropriately allocated are R&D costs that should be expensed immediately. The costs of equipment and facilities that are used for R&D activities and have alternative future uses, whether for other R&D projects or otherwise, are to be capitalized as tangible assets when acquired or constructed. Thus, the depreciation is also expensed immediately. However, SFAS 2 does not apply to R&D activities conducted for others. Hence, the reimbursable costs are not expensed. Ball's total R&D expense is therefore $1,380,000 ($300,000 + $700,000 + $200,000 + $180,000).
Answer (A) is incorrect because $1,080,000 omits depreciation. Answer (C) is incorrect because $1,580,000 includes the reimbursable costs of R&D conducted for others but omits the indirect costs. Answer (D) is incorrect because $1,780,000 includes the reimbursable costs of R&D conducted for others.

9.4 Prepayments

16. On January 1, Sip Co. signed a 5-year contract enabling it to use a patented manufacturing process beginning in the year just ended. A royalty is payable for each product produced, subject to a minimum annual fee. Any royalties in excess of the minimum will be paid annually. On the contract date, Sip prepaid a sum equal to 2 years' minimum annual fees. During the year, only minimum fees were incurred. The royalty prepayment should be reported in Sip's December 31 financial statements as a(n)

A. Expense only.

B. Current asset and an expense.

C. Current asset and noncurrent asset.

D. Noncurrent asset.

Answer (B) is correct. *(CPA, adapted)*
REQUIRED: The proper reporting of a royalty prepayment.
DISCUSSION: Current assets include prepaid expenses, such as royalty prepayments, that are expected to be realized in cash, sold, or consumed within the longer of 1 year or the normal operating cycle of the business. At December 31, the entity should therefore recognize an expense for the first year's royalties and a current asset (a deferred cost) for the second year's royalties.
Answer (A) is incorrect because an asset should be recognized for the unexpired portion of the prepayment. Answer (C) is incorrect because the company should recognize an expense for the expired portion of the prepayment. Answer (D) is incorrect because the unexpired portion of the prepayment will be consumed within 1 year. Thus, it should be classified as current.

17. An analysis of Thrift Corp.'s unadjusted prepaid expense account at December 31, Year 4, revealed the following:

- An opening balance at $1,500 for Thrift's comprehensive insurance policy. Thrift had paid an annual premium of $3,000 on July 1, Year 3.
- A $3,200 annual insurance premium payment made July 1, Year 4.
- A $2,000 advance rental payment for a warehouse Thrift leased for 1 year beginning January 1, Year 5.

In its December 31, Year 4, balance sheet, what amount should Thrift report as prepaid expenses?

A. $5,200

B. $3,600

C. $2,000

D. $1,600

Answer (B) is correct. *(CPA, adapted)*
REQUIRED: The amount reported for prepaid expenses.
DISCUSSION: The $1,500 beginning balance of prepaid insurance expired on 6/30/Yr 4, leaving a $0 balance. The $3,200 annual insurance premium paid on 7/1/Yr 4 should be allocated equally to Year 4 and Year 5, leaving a $1,600 prepaid insurance balance. The $2,000 advance rental payment is an expense that is wholly deferred until Year 5. Consequently, the total of prepaid expenses at year-end is $3,600 ($1,600 + $2,000).
Answer (A) is incorrect because half of the $3,200 of prepaid insurance should be expensed in Year 4. Answer (C) is incorrect because only half of the $3,200 of prepaid insurance should be expensed in Year 4. Answer (D) is incorrect because the prepaid rent is deferred until Year 5.

18. Roro, Inc. paid $7,200 to renew its only insurance policy for 3 years on March 1, Year 4, the effective date of the policy. At March 31, Year 4, Roro's unadjusted trial balance showed a balance of $300 for prepaid insurance and $7,200 for insurance expense. What amounts should be reported for prepaid insurance and insurance expense in Roro's financial statements for the 3 months ended March 31, Year 4?

	Prepaid Insurance	Insurance Expense
A.	$7,000	$300
B.	$7,000	$500
C.	$7,200	$300
D.	$7,300	$200

Answer (B) is correct. *(CPA, adapted)*
REQUIRED: The amounts reported for prepaid insurance and insurance expense.
DISCUSSION: The entry to record the insurance renewal included a debit to insurance expense for $7,200, and the balance in prepaid insurance has expired. At year-end, the expense and prepaid insurance accounts should be adjusted to reflect the expired amounts. The 3-year prepayment is amortized at $200 per month ($7,200 ÷ 36 months). Consequently, insurance expense for the period should be $500 ($300 prepaid insurance balance + $200 amortization of the renewal amount). The $7,000 unexpired amount should be debited to prepaid insurance.
Answer (A) is incorrect because $300 does not include the $200 expense for March. Answer (C) is incorrect because neither the prepaid insurance nor the insurance expense amounts have been adjusted for the $200 expense for March. Answer (D) is incorrect because prepaid insurance includes $300 that should be expensed.

9.5 Computer Software

Questions 19 and 20 are based on the following information. During the year just ended, Pitt Corp. incurred costs to develop and produce a routine, low-risk computer software product, as follows:

Completion of detail program design	$13,000
Costs incurred for coding and testing to establish technological feasibility	10,000
Other coding costs after establishment of technological feasibility	24,000
Other testing costs after establishment of technological feasibility	20,000
Costs of producing product masters for training materials	15,000
Duplication of computer software and training materials from product masters (1,000 units)	25,000
Packaging product (500 units)	9,000

SFAS 86, *Accounting for the Costs of Computer Software to Be Sold, Leased, or Otherwise Marketed*, applies.

19. In Pitt's December 31 balance sheet, what amount should be capitalized as software cost subject to amortization?

A. $54,000

B. $57,000

C. $59,000

D. $69,000

Answer (C) is correct. *(CPA, adapted)*
REQUIRED: The amount capitalized as software cost subject to amortization.
DISCUSSION: Costs incurred internally in creating a computer software product are expensed when incurred as research and development until technological feasibility has been established for the product. Afterward, all software production costs incurred until the product is available for general release to customers are capitalized and amortized separately for each product. Subsequently, the lower of unamortized cost or net realizable value at the end of the period is reported in the balance sheet. Hence, (1) the costs of completing the detail program design and establishing technological feasibility are expensed; (2) the costs of duplicating software, documentation, and training materials and packaging the product are inventoried; and (3) the costs of coding and other testing after establishing technological feasibility and the costs of producing product masters are capitalized and amortized. The amount capitalized as software cost subject to amortization is therefore $59,000 ($24,000 + $20,000 + $15,000).
Answer (A) is incorrect because $54,000 equals inventoriable costs plus the other testing costs. Answer (B) is incorrect because $57,000 is the sum of the costs expensed and the costs inventoried. Answer (D) is incorrect because $69,000 assumes the costs of coding and testing to establish feasibility are capitalized and amortized.

20. In Pitt's December 31 balance sheet, what amount should be reported in inventory?

A. $25,000

B. $34,000

C. $40,000

D. $49,000

Answer (B) is correct. *(CPA, adapted)*
REQUIRED: The amount reported in inventory.
DISCUSSION: Costs incurred internally in creating a computer software product are expensed when incurred as R&D until technological feasibility has been established. Afterward, all software production costs incurred until the product is available for general release to customers shall be capitalized and amortized. The costs of (1) duplicating the software, documentation, and training materials from the product masters and (2) physically packaging the product for distribution are capitalized as inventory. Hence, inventory should be reported at $34,000 ($25,000 duplication costs + $9,000 packaging costs).
Answer (A) is incorrect because $25,000 excludes packaging costs. Answer (C) is incorrect because $40,000 excludes packaging costs but includes costs of producing product masters. Answer (D) is incorrect because $49,000 includes costs of producing product masters.

21. On December 31, Year 7, Byte Co. had capitalized software costs of $600,000 with an economic life of four years. Sales for Year 8 were 10% of expected total sales of the software. At December 31, Year 8, the software had a net realizable value of $480,000. In its December 31, Year 8, balance sheet, what amount should Byte report as net capitalized cost of computer software?

- A. $432,000
- B. $450,000
- C. $480,000
- D. $540,000

Answer (B) is correct. *(CPA, adapted)*
REQUIRED: The net capitalized cost of computer software at year-end.
DISCUSSION: Under SFAS 86, *Accounting for the Costs of Computer Software to Be Sold, Leased, or Otherwise Marketed*, the annual amortization is the greater of the amount determined using (1) the ratio of current gross revenues to the sum of current gross revenues and anticipated future gross revenues, or (2) the straight-line method over the remaining estimated economic life, including the current reporting period. At year-end, the unamortized cost of each software product must be compared with the net realizable value (NRV) of that software product. Any excess of unamortized cost over NRV must be written off. The amount of amortization under the straight-line method is used because it is greater than the amount determined using the 10% ratio of current sales to expected total sales. Thus, Byte Co. had an unamortized cost of software of $450,000 [$600,000 capitalized cost – ($600,000 ÷ 4)] at December 31, Year 8. The $450,000 unamortized cost is lower than the $480,000 NRV, so $450,000 is the amount reported in the year-end balance sheet.
Answer (A) is incorrect because $432,000 equals the NRV at December 31, Year 8, minus amortization calculated as 10% of NRV. Answer (C) is incorrect because $480,000 is the NRV at December 31, Year 8. Answer (D) is incorrect because $540,000 assumes amortization at 10% with no adjustment for NRV.

9.6 Special Issues

22. A development stage enterprise should use the same generally accepted accounting principles that apply to established operating enterprises for

	Revenue Recognition	Deferral of Expenses
A.	Yes	Yes
B.	Yes	No
C.	No	No
D.	No	Yes

Answer (A) is correct. *(CPA, adapted)*
REQUIRED: The item(s) for which development stage enterprises should use standard GAAP.
DISCUSSION: SFAS 7, *Accounting and Reporting by Development Stage Enterprises*, requires development stage enterprises to use the same GAAP that apply to established operating enterprises. Thus, the accounting treatment of revenues and expenses should be governed by the same principles whether or not the reporting entity is a development stage enterprise.

23. Direct response advertising costs are capitalized (deferred) to provide an appropriate expense in each period for

	Interim Financial Reporting	Year-End Financial Reporting
A.	Yes	No
B.	Yes	Yes
C.	No	No
D.	No	Yes

Answer (B) is correct. *(CPA, adapted)*
REQUIRED: The type(s) of reporting in which direct response advertising costs may be accrued or deferred.
DISCUSSION: Direct response advertising costs are capitalized (deferred) if the primary purpose is to make sales to customers who respond specifically to the advertising, and probable future economic benefits result. An entity that capitalizes these costs must document that customers have specifically responded to the advertising. It also must document the benefits from prior direct response advertising (AICPA SOP 93-7, *Reporting on Advertising Costs*). The deferral of advertising costs is appropriate for both interim and year-end financial reporting if their benefits clearly apply to more than one period. Moreover, if a cost that would be fully expensed in an annual report benefits more than one interim period, it may be allocated to those interim periods.

24. Lex Corp. was a development stage enterprise from October 10, Year 2, (inception) through December 31, Year 3. The year ended December 31, Year 4, was the first year in which Lex qualified as an established operating enterprise. The following are among the costs incurred by Lex:

	For the Period 10/10/Yr 2- 12/31/Yr 3	For the Year Ended 12/31/Yr 4
Leasehold improvements, equipment, and furniture	$1,000,000	$ 300,000
Security deposits	60,000	30,000
Research and development	750,000	900,000
Laboratory operations	175,000	550,000
General and administrative	225,000	685,000
Depreciation	25,000	115,000
	$2,235,000	$2,580,000

From its inception through the period ended December 31, Year 4, what is the total amount of costs incurred by Lex that should be charged to operations?

A. $3,425,000

B. $2,250,000

C. $1,775,000

D. $1,350,000

Answer (A) is correct. *(CPA, adapted)*
REQUIRED: The total amount of costs that a development stage enterprise should charge to operations.
DISCUSSION: SFAS 7 requires development stage enterprises to use the same GAAP as established operating enterprises. An established operating enterprise would have capitalized the entire $1.3 million of leasehold improvements, equipment, and furniture, as well as the $90,000 of security deposits. Consequently, Lex Corp., a development stage enterprise, should also capitalize these costs. An established operating enterprise would have expensed the $1,650,000 of research and development costs, the $725,000 of laboratory operations costs, the $910,000 of general and administrative costs, and the $140,000 of depreciation. Lex Corp. should also expense these costs. The total to be expensed by Lex therefore equals $3,425,000 ($1,650,000 + $725,000 + $910,000 + $140,000).
Answer (B) is incorrect because $2,250,000 equals costs incurred in Year 4 minus security deposits and leasehold improvements, equipment, and furniture. Answer (C) is incorrect because $1,775,000 excludes R&D costs. Answer (D) is incorrect because $1,350,000 equals costs incurred during the development stage, minus leasehold improvements, equipment, and furniture, plus Year 4 depreciation.

25. A statement of cash flows for a development stage enterprise

A. Is the same as that of an established operating enterprise and, in addition, shows cumulative amounts from the enterprise's inception.

B. Shows only cumulative amounts from the enterprise's inception.

C. Is the same as that of an established operating enterprise, but does not show cumulative amounts from the enterprise's inception.

D. Is not presented.

Answer (A) is correct. *(CPA, adapted)*
REQUIRED: The true statement about a statement of cash flows for a development stage enterprise.
DISCUSSION: A development stage enterprise must present financial statements in conformity with GAAP together with certain additional information accumulated since its inception. Cumulative net losses must be disclosed in the equity section of the balance sheet, cumulative amounts of revenue and expense in the income statement, cumulative amounts of cash inflows and outflows in the statement of cash flows, and information about each issuance of stock in the statement of equity.
Answer (B) is incorrect because the statement of cash flows also must conform with GAAP. Answer (C) is incorrect because the statement of cash flows also must show cumulative amounts from the enterprise's inception. Answer (D) is incorrect because a statement of cash flows is required as part of a full set of financial statements.

Use Gleim's *CPA Test Prep* CD-Rom/Pocket PC for interactive testing with over 4,000 additional questions!

9.7 PRACTICE SIMULATION

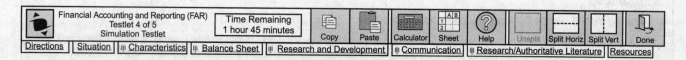

1. Directions

In the following simulation, you will be asked to complete various tasks. You may use the content in the **Information Tabs** to complete the tasks in the **Work Tabs**.

Information Tabs:

Directions	Resources

FIG 1

- Go through each of the **Information Tabs** to familiarize yourself with the simulation content
- The **Resources** tab will contain information, including formulas and definitions, that may help you to complete the tasks
- Your simulation may have more **Information Tabs** than those shown in Fig. 1

Work Tabs:

FIG. 2

- **Work Tabs**, to the right of **Information Tabs**, contain the tasks for you to complete
- **Work Tabs** contain directions for completing each task - be sure to read these directions carefully
- The tab names in Fig. 2 are for illustration only - yours may differ
- Once you complete any part of a task, the pencil for that tab will be shaded (see **Communication** in Fig. 2)
- The shaded pencil does **NOT** indicate that you have completed the entire task
- You must complete all of the tasks in the **Work Tabs** to receive full credit

Research/Authoritative Literature Tab:

⫶ Research/Authoritative Literature

FIG. 3

- This tab contains both the Research task and the Authoritative Literature
- Detailed instructions for completing the Research task, and for using the Authoritative Literature, appear on this tab
- You may use the Authoritative Literature as a resource for completing other tasks

NOTE: If you believe you have encountered a software malfunction, report it to the test center staff immediately.

2. Situation

During Year 5, Broca Co. had the following transactions:

- On January 2, Broca purchased the net assets of Amp Co. for $360,000. The fair value of Amp's acquired net assets (the net of the amounts assigned to assets acquired and liabilities assumed) was $172,000. Broca believes that, due to the popularity of Amp's consumer products, the life of the resulting goodwill is 15 years.

- On February 1, Broca purchased a franchise to operate a ferry service from the state government for $60,000 and an annual fee of 1% of ferry revenues. The franchise expires after five years. Ferry revenues were $20,000 during Year 5. Broca projects future revenues of $40,000 in Year 6 and $60,000 per annum for the following three years.

- On April 5, Broca was granted a patent that had been applied for by Amp. During Year 5, Broca incurred legal costs of $51,000 to register the patent and an additional $85,000 to successfully prosecute a patent infringement suit against a competitor. Broca estimates the patent's economic life to be ten years. When Broca purchased AMP's net assets, it properly did not assign an amount to the possible grant of a patent.

- Broca incurred organization costs of $98,000 for incorporation, state and local licensing fees and permits, training of new employees, feasibility studies, and attorneys' and accountants' fees.

- At December 31, Year 5, Broca had prepaid rent (1 year) and insurance (2 years) balances of $60,000 and $24,000, respectively.

Broca's accounting policy is to amortize all intangible assets on the straight-line basis over the maximum period permitted by generally accepted accounting principles, taking a full year's amortization in the year of acquisition.

3. Characteristics

This set of questions has a matching format. Select the best match for each numbered item from the terms in the drop-down list and write its letter in the column provided. Each choice may be used once, more than once, or not at all. Choose the intangible asset that best matches the following characteristics.

Characteristic	Answer
1. Grants an exclusive right given to the holder to use, produce, and sell a product or process for a period specified by law without interference or infringement by others	
2. May arise from a superior management team, high standing in the community, or good labor relations	
3. Granted for the life of the author plus 70 years	
4. Can be renewed for 10-year periods indefinitely	
5. Permits an entity to use rights owned by others	
6. Grants the right to sell certain products or services within a designated area using a certain trademark or trade name	
7. May include underwriter's fees, legal fees, and incorporation fees	

Choices
A) Copyright
B) Goodwill
C) Franchise
D) Patent
E) Trademark
F) Organization costs
G) Licensing agreement
H) Trade secrets
I) Leaseholds

4. Balance Sheet

This question is presented in a spreadsheet format that requires you to fill in the correct responses in the shaded cells provided. Calculate the amounts to be recorded on the intangible assets section of the balance sheet for Broca Co. Use the information provided in the situation tab to complete this section.

Balance Sheet Item	Calculated Amounts
Goodwill:	
Cash paid	
Value of net assets	
Goodwill	
Amortization	
Balance 12/31/Year 5	
Franchise:	
Franchise	
Amortization	
Balance 12/31/Year 5	
Patent:	
Legal costs	
Amortization	
Balance 12/31/Year 5	

5. Research and Development Activities

Check the boxes corresponding to the items that are research and development activities.

Activity	R&D
1. Quality control during commercial production, including routine testing of products	
2. Laboratory research aimed at discovery of new knowledge	
3. Seasonal or other periodic design changes to existing products	
4. Design of tools, jigs, molds, and dies involving new technology	
5. Searching for applications of new research findings or other knowledge	
6. Routine design of tools, jigs, molds, and dies	
7. Modification of the formulation or design of a product or process	
8. Adaptation of an existing capability to a particular requirement or customer's need as part of a continuing commercial activity	
9. Troubleshooting in connection with breakdowns during commercial production	
10. Engineering follow-through in an early phase of commercial production	
11. Engineering activity required to advance the design of a product until it meets specific functional and economic requirements and is ready for manufacture	
12. Design, construction, and testing of preproduction prototypes and models	
13. Conceptual formulation and design of possible product or process alternatives	
14. Testing in search for or evaluation of product or process alternatives	
15. Legal work in connection with patent applications or litigation and the sale or licensing of patents	

6. Communication

Discuss the accounting for intangible assets after recognition. Issues addressed should include factors used to determine an asset's useful life, the amortization method and amount, and impairment. The communication also should discuss accounting for intangible assets with indefinite useful lives.

REMINDER: Your response will be graded for both technical content and writing skills. Technical content will be evaluated for information that is helpful to the intended reader and clearly relevant to the issue. Writing skills will be evaluated for development, organization, and the appropriate expression of ideas in professional correspondence. Use a standard business memo or letter format with a clear beginning, middle, and end. Do not convey information in the form of a table, bullet point list, or other abbreviated presentation.

To: Client
From: CPA
Subject: Intangible assets subsequent to recognition

---

7. Research/Authoritative Literature

See page 12 in the Introduction of this book for a detailed explanation of the AICPA's new Research/Authoritative Literature work tab as well as a screenshot of how the tab will actually look on your exam.

Research and cite the appropriate pronouncement in the FASB Current Text or Original Pronouncements that governs the amortization of capitalized costs incurred to purchase or internally produce computer software.

Unofficial Answers

3. Characteristics (7 Gradable Items)

1. D) Patent. Utility patents granted by the U.S. have a legal life of 20 years. A patent is an exclusive right to use, manufacture, and sell a product or process.

2. B) Goodwill. Goodwill consists of the favorable characteristics of a business enterprise that are intangible and cannot be separately identified and valued. Such characteristics include a superior management team, high standing in the community, and good labor relations.

3. A) Copyright. A copyright is the exclusive right to reproduce and sell an artistic or literary work. The U.S. grants author copyrights for life plus 70 years.

4. E) Trademark. Trademarks are words, symbols, or other devices that identify particular products. The common law recognizes the right to exclusive use of a trademark or similar property as long as it is used by the original holder. A trademark also may be protected by registration with the U.S. Patent and Trademark Office. This registration can be renewed for an indefinite number of 10-year periods (with the initial renewal made between the fifth and sixth years after initial registration) as long as the trademark is used continuously.

5. G) Licensing agreement. Licensing agreements are contractual agreements that permit an enterprise (the licensee) to engage in a given activity, such as selling a well-known product, or to use rights (e.g., a patent) owned by others.

6. C) Franchise. A franchise is an agreement in which one party provides another party with the exclusive right to market a product or service within a designated territory.

7. F) Organization costs. Organization costs are costs incurred in the formation of a business entity before operations commence and during their early stages. They include legal fees, accounting fees, underwriter's fees, incorporation fees, taxes, and promotional costs. They must be expensed when incurred by nongovernmental entities (AICPA SOP 98-5). However, for federal income tax purposes, organization costs that are not deductible may be amortized over not less than 15 years.

4. Balance Sheet (11 Gradable Items)

Balance Sheet Item	Calculated Amounts
Goodwill	
Cash paid	$ 360,000
Fair value of net assets	(172,000)
Goodwill	188,000
Amortization	0
Balance 12/31/Year 5	$ 188,000
Franchise	
Franchise	$ 60,000
Amortization	(12,000)
Balance 12/31/Year 5	$ 48,000
Patent	
Legal costs	$ 136,000
Amortization	(13,600)
Balance 12/31/Year 5	$ 122,400

5. Research and Development Activities (15 Gradable Items)

1) Not R&D
2) R&D
3) Not R&D
4) R&D
5) R&D
6) Not R&D
7) R&D
8) Not R&D
9) Not R&D
10) Not R&D
11) R&D
12) R&D
13) R&D
14) R&D
15) Not R&D

6. Communication (5 Gradable Items; for grading instructions, please refer to page 12.)

The useful life of an asset is the period during which it is expected to contribute either directly or indirectly to the future cash flows of the reporting entity. Among the considerations in estimating useful life are (1) the reporting entity's expected use of the asset; (2) the useful life of a related asset or group of assets; (3) provisions based on law, regulation, or contract that may limit the useful life or that may permit renewal or extension without substantial cost; (4) economic factors, such as obsolescence, demand, or competition; and (5) expenditures for maintenance.

An intangible asset with a finite useful life to the reporting entity is amortized over that useful life. If the useful life is finite but not precisely known, the amortization period should be the best estimate of the useful life.

The pattern of consumption of economic benefits, if it can be reliably ascertained, is reflected in the method of amortization. Otherwise, the straight-line method is required. However, an intangible asset is not written down in the period of acquisition if it is not impaired.

The amortizable amount equals the amount initially assigned minus the residual value, which is the estimated fair value to the entity at the end of the asset's useful life, minus disposal costs. The residual value is zero unless (1) a third party has committed to purchase the asset or (2) it can be ascertained from an exchange transaction in an existing market for the asset that is expected to exist at the end of the useful life.

The useful life should be reevaluated each reporting period. A change in the estimate results in a prospective change in amortization. If a subsequent determination is made that the asset has an indefinite useful life, it is no longer amortized and is tested for impairment.

An amortized intangible asset is reviewed for impairment when events or changes in circumstances indicate that its carrying amount may not be recoverable. An impairment loss is recognized only if the carrying amount is not recoverable and is greater than the asset's fair value. Thus, the impairment test is met if the sum of the undiscounted expected future cash flows from the asset is less than the carrying amount. The loss recognized is the excess of that carrying amount over the fair value. This loss is nonreversible, so the adjusted carrying amount is the new accounting basis.

An intangible asset with an indefinite useful life is not amortized. However, the useful life should be reevaluated each period. If it is found to be finite, a test for impairment is performed. The asset is then amortized prospectively and otherwise accounted for as an amortized asset.

A nonamortized intangible asset is reviewed for impairment at least annually. It is tested more often if events or changes in circumstances suggest that the asset may be impaired. However, the impairment test does not consider recoverability. If the carrying amount exceeds the fair value, the asset is impaired, and the excess is the recognized loss. This loss is nonreversible, so the adjusted carrying amount is the new accounting basis.

7. Research/Authoritative Literature (1 Gradable Item)

Answer: FAS 86, Par. 43

FAS 86 -- *Accounting for the Costs of Computer Software to be Sold, Leased, or Otherwise Marketed*

Amortization of Capitalized Costs

43. A key objective in requiring the capitalization of certain costs incurred to purchase or internally produce computer software is to recognize the asset representing future economic benefits created by incurring those costs. Because a net realizable value test, which considers future revenues and costs, must be applied to capitalized costs, the Board concluded that amortization should be based on estimated future revenues. In recognition of the uncertainties involved in estimating revenue, the Board further concluded that amortization should not be less than straight-line amortization over the product's remaining estimated economic life. The Board also concluded that amortization expense should be computed on a product-by-product basis and that amortization should begin when the product is available for general release to customers.

Scoring Schedule:

	Correct Responses		Gradable Items		Weights		
Tab 3	_____	÷	7	×	15%	=	_____
Tab 4	_____	÷	11	×	20%	=	_____
Tab 5	_____	÷	15	×	20%	=	_____
Tab 6	_____	÷	5	×	30%	=	_____
Tab 7	_____	÷	1	×	15%	=	_____
							_____
							(Your Score)

Use Gleim's **CPA Gleim Online** to practice more simulations in a realistic environment.

STUDY UNIT TEN
PAYABLES AND TAXES

(16 pages of outline)

This introductory study unit is the first of four on the liability section of the balance sheet. The subject matter is straightforward because it applies basic accrual accounting procedures. The remaining subunits address income tax accounting.

10.1 ACCOUNTS PAYABLE

Definition

1. Accounts payable (trade accounts payable) are **liabilities**. They reflect the obligations to sellers that are incurred when an entity purchases inventory, supplies, or services on credit.

2. Accounts payable should be recorded at **net settlement value**. Thus, they are measured at the undiscounted amounts of cash (or the equivalent) expected to be paid to liquidate an obligation in the due course of business.

3. Accounts payable do not usually provide for a periodic payment of interest unless the accounts are not settled when due or payable. Thus, accounts payable are **non-interest-bearing** and are not within the scope of APB Opinion 21, *Interest on Receivables and Payables*.

    a. They also are usually **not** secured by collateral.

Current Liabilities

4. ARB 43, Ch. 3A, "Current Assets and Current Liabilities," defines a current liability as an obligation that will be either liquidated using current assets or replaced by another current liability.

5. SFAS 78, *Classification of Obligations That Are Callable by the Creditor*, classifies the following as current liabilities: (a) obligations that, by their terms, are or will be due on demand within 1 year (or the operating cycle if longer), and (b) obligations that are or will be callable by the creditor within 1 year because of a violation of a debt covenant.

    a. But noncurrent debt need not be reclassified if

        1) It is probable that a violation at the balance sheet date will be cured within a specified grace period,

        2) The creditor formally waives the right to demand repayment for a period of more than a year from the balance sheet date, or

        3) The debtor expects and has the ability to refinance the obligation on a long-term basis.

6. **Checks** written before the end of the period, but not mailed to creditors, should not be accounted for as cash payments for the period. The amounts remain current liabilities until control of the checks has been surrendered.

Gross Method vs. Net Method

7. Purchases and related accounts payable may be recorded using the gross method or the net method.

8. The **gross method** accounts for payables at their face amount. It is used when the purchaser does not expect to pay soon enough to take the discount.

   a. In a **periodic system**, inventory purchases are initially debited to a **purchases** account that is closed at the end of the period. **Purchase discounts taken** are credited to a contra purchases account and closed to cost of goods sold. In a **perpetual system**, entries are made directly to inventory.

9. The **net method** records payables net of the cash (sales) discount for early payment. It is used when the purchaser expects to pay within the discount period.

   a. Its advantage is that it isolates **purchase discounts lost**, which are treated as financing charges.

EXAMPLE

An entity using a **perpetual system** purchases materials under terms of 2/10, n/30 (2% discount for payment within 10 days, entire balance due in 30 days).

	Gross Method		Net Method	
Inventory	$1,000		$980	
Accounts payable		$1,000		$980

Payment is made within the discount period.

	Gross Method		Net Method	
Accounts payable	$1,000		$980	
Cash		$980		$980
Inventory		20		

Payment is made after the discount period.

	Gross Method		Net Method	
Accounts payable	$1,000		$980	
Cash		$1,000		$980
Purchase discounts lost			$20	
Cash				$20

Shipping Terms

10. The timing of recognition of accounts payable may depend on the shipping terms.

11. When goods are shipped **FOB shipping point**, title and risk of loss pass to the buyer at the time and place of shipment. Thus, the buyer records inventory and a payable at the time of shipment.

12. When goods are shipped **FOB destination**, title and risk of loss do not pass until the goods are duly tendered to the buyer at the destination. Hence, the buyer does not record inventory and a payable until that time.

EXAMPLE

Kew Co.'s accounts payable balance at December 31, Year 3, was $2.2 million before considering the following:

- Goods shipped to Kew **FOB shipping point** on December 22, Year 3, were lost in transit. The invoice cost of $40,000 was not recorded by Kew. On January 7, Year 4, Kew filed a $40,000 claim against the common carrier.

- On December 27, Year 3, a vendor authorized Kew to return, for full credit, goods shipped and billed at $70,000 on December 3, Year 3. The returned goods were shipped by Kew on December 28, Year 3. A $70,000 credit memo was received and recorded by Kew on January 5, Year 4.

- Goods shipped to Kew **FOB destination** on December 20, Year 3, were received on January 6, Year 4. The invoice cost was $50,000.

When goods are shipped FOB shipping point, title and risk of loss pass to the buyer at the time and place of shipment. Hence, Kew should currently recognize a $40,000 payable for the goods lost in transit. The $70,000 purchase return should be recognized currently because the seller authorized the credit on December 27. However, the goods shipped FOB destination and not received until January should be excluded. Title did not pass to Kew until receipt of the goods. Accordingly, the ending accounts payable balance is $2,170,000 ($2,200,000 + $40,000 − $70,000).

Stop and review! You have completed the outline for this subunit. Study multiple-choice questions 1 and 2 on page 382.

10.2 ACCRUED EXPENSES

Definition

1. Ordinarily, accrued expenses meet **recognition criteria** in the current period but have **not been paid** as of year-end. They are accounted for using basic accrual entries.

Reversing Entries

2. These may be used to facilitate accounting for accrued expenses in the next period. For example, if wages payable are accrued at year-end, the **adjusting entry** is

Wages expense	$XXX	
Wages payable		$XXX

    a. The **reversing entry** at the beginning of the next period is

Wages payable	$XXX	
Wages expense		$XXX

    1) No allocation between the liability and wages expense is needed when wages are paid in the subsequent period. All expenses paid in the next period can be charged to expense. The entry will simply be

Wages expense	$XXX	
Cash		$XXX

    b. If **reversing entries are not made**, either of the following methods is used in the next period:

    1) The **liability is debited** when the accrued expense is actually paid. For example, the entry for the first wages payment of the year is

Wages expense	$XXX	
Wages payable	XXX	
Cash		$XXX

    a) This entry will differ from subsequent entries recording the payment of wages.

2)   Payments are recorded by **debiting expense for the full amounts** paid. At year-end, the liability is adjusted to the balance owed at that date. For example, if the liability for accrued wages has decreased, the adjusting entry is

Wages payable	$XXX	
Wages expense		$XXX

Effects of Nonaccrual

3.   If an entity fails to accrue expenses at year-end, **income** is overstated in that period and understated in the next period (when they are paid and presumably expensed).

a.   Moreover, expenses incurred but unpaid and not recorded result in understated **accrued liabilities** and possibly understated assets (for example, if the amounts should be inventoried). In addition, working capital (current assets – current liabilities) will be overstated, but cash flows will not be affected.

EXAMPLE

Windy Co. must determine the December 31, Year 2, year-end accruals for advertising and rent expenses. A $500 advertising bill was received January 7, Year 3. It related to costs of $375 for advertisements in December Year 2 and $125 for advertisements in January Year 3. A lease, effective December 16, Year 1, calls for fixed rent of $1,200 per month, payable beginning 1 month from the effective date. In addition, rent equal to 5% of net sales over $300,000 per calendar year is payable on January 31 of the following year. Net sales for Year 2 were $550,000.

The $375 of advertising expense should be accrued in Year 2 because this amount can be directly related to events in that period. The $125 amount is related to events in Year 3 and should not be accrued in Year 2.

The fixed rental is due at mid-month. Thus, the fixed rental for the last half month of Year 2 ($1,200 ÷ 2 = $600) and the rental based on annual sales [($550,000 – $300,000) × 5% = $12,500] also should be accrued.

In its December 31, Year 2, balance sheet, Windy should report accrued liabilities of $13,475 ($375 + $600 + $12,500).

Stop and review! You have completed the outline for this subunit. Study multiple-choice questions 3 through 5 on page 383.

10.3 CERTAIN TAXES PAYABLE

1.   **Federal unemployment tax** and the employer's share of **FICA taxes** are expenses incurred as employees earn wages. But they are paid only on a periodic basis to the federal government. Accordingly, liabilities should be accrued for both expenses, as well as for wages earned but not paid.

a.   Income taxes withheld and the employees' share of FICA taxes are accrued as **withholding taxes** (payroll deductions), not as employer payroll taxes.

2.   **Property taxes** are usually expensed by monthly accrual over the fiscal period of the taxing authority.

3.   **Sales taxes** are levied on certain types of merchandise by most states. Ordinarily, the tax is paid by the customer purchasing the merchandise but is collected and remitted by the seller. Most states require quarterly or monthly filing of sales tax returns and remittance of taxes collected.

Stop and review! You have completed the outline for this subunit. Study multiple-choice questions 6 through 9 beginning on page 384.

10.4 DEPOSITS AND OTHER ADVANCES

1. A deposit or other advance is a **liability**. It does not qualify for revenue recognition because an earning process is not substantially complete.

2. An issue is whether deposits/advances are classified as **current or noncurrent**. They are current if they will be liquidated using current assets or replaced by another current liability.

3. The sale of a **gift certificate** creates an inflow of cash and a liability for the seller. The seller debits cash and credits deferred revenue.

4. Cash received from customers for **magazine subscriptions** creates a liability for unearned subscription revenue.

EXAMPLE

Nepal Co. requires advance payments with special orders for machinery constructed to customer specifications. These advances are nonrefundable. Information for Year 2 is as follows:

Customer advances--balance 12/31/Year 1	$236,000
Advances received with orders in Year 2	368,000
Advances applied to orders shipped in Year 2	328,000
Advances applicable to orders canceled in Year 2	100,000

In Nepal's December 31, Year 2, balance sheet, the amount reported as a current liability is $176,000 ($236,000 beginning balance + $368,000 advances received – $328,000 advances credited to revenue after shipment of orders – $100,000 for canceled orders) for customer advances. Deposits or other advance payments are liabilities because they involve a probable future sacrifice of economic benefits arising from a current obligation. The advances applicable to canceled orders are not refundable. Thus, no future sacrifice of economic benefits is necessary. The nonrefundable advances applicable to canceled orders qualify for revenue recognition (debit the liability, credit revenue) because the entity's earning process is complete.

Stop and review! You have completed the outline for this subunit. Study multiple-choice questions 10 through 12 beginning on page 385.

10.5 COUPONS AND PREMIUMS

1. Many sellers include stamps, coupons, special labels, etc., with merchandise that can be redeemed for premiums (cash or goods). The purpose is to increase sales.

2. In accordance with the **matching principle**, the expense associated with premium offers is recognized in the same period as the related revenue. Moreover, (a) the premiums must be purchased and recorded as inventory, (b) the expense of redemptions must be debited, and (c) a liability for estimated redemptions must be credited at the end of the accounting period.

3. The following are **typical entries** to account for an offer to provide a toy in exchange for a sum of cash and a label from a box of the seller's primary product:

   a. To record inventory

Inventory of toys	$XXX	
Cash or accounts payable		$XXX

   b. To record sales of the primary product

Cash	$XXX	
Sales		$XXX

   c. To record redemptions when cash is received

Cash	$XXX	
Premium expense	XXX	
Inventory of toys		$XXX

d. To record the estimated liability at the end of the period

Premium expense	$XXX	
Estimated liability		$XXX

EXAMPLE

In packages of its products, the Lilac Company includes coupons that may be presented to grocers for discounts of certain products on or before a stated expiration date. The grocers are reimbursed when they send the coupons to Lilac. In Lilac's experience, 40% of such coupons are redeemed, and 1 month usually elapses between the date a grocer receives a coupon from a consumer and the date Lilac receives it. During Year 1, Lilac issued two series of coupons as follows:

Date Issued	Total Face Amount	Consumer Expiration Date	Amount Disbursed as of 12/31/Year 1
1/1/Year 1	$100,000	6/30/Year 1	$34,000
7/1/Year 1	120,000	12/31/Year 1	40,000

No liability should be reported for unredeemed coupons at December 31 with regard to the coupons issued on 1/1/Year 1 because more than 1 month has elapsed since their expiration date. The total estimated liability for the coupons issued on 7/1/Year 1 is $48,000 ($120,000 total face amount of coupons issued × 40%) minus the $40,000 disbursed as of 12/31/Year 1. Consequently, the liability at December 31 is $8,000 ($48,000 – $40,000).

Stop and review! You have completed the outline for this subunit. Study multiple-choice questions 13 and 14 beginning on page 386.

10.6 WARRANTIES

Definition

1. A warranty is a **written guarantee** of the integrity of a product or service. It is also an undertaking by the seller to repair or replace a product, refund all or part of the price, or provide additional service. A warranty is customarily offered for a limited time, such as 90 days. It **may or may not be separable** from the product or service.

2. A warranty creates a **loss contingency**. Thus, if incurrence of warranty expense is probable, the amount can be reasonably estimated, and the amount is material, **accrual accounting** should be used. If these criteria are not met, warranty expense should be recorded as incurred, that is, on the **cash basis**. This basis must be used for **tax purposes**.

Inseparable Warranties

3. The following are **accrual-basis** entries for warranty expense estimated as a percentage of sales when the **warranty is not separable**:

a. To record a sale of product

Cash or accounts receivable	$XXX	
Sales revenue		$XXX

b. To record related warranty expense accrued and incurred for the current period

Warranty expense	$XXX	
Estimated liability		$XXX
Cash, inventory, wages payable, etc.		XXX

c. To record the costs incurred for prior period sales

Estimated liability	$XXX	
Cash, inventory, wages payable, etc.		$XXX

Separable Warranties

4. The accounting for separately extended warranty and product maintenance contracts applies when the contract is separately priced. **Revenue is deferred** and is ordinarily recognized on the **straight-line basis** over the term of the contract.

    a. **Costs** are deferred and amortized only when they are directly related to, and vary with, the sale of the warranty. The primary example of such a cost is a commission.

        1) Furthermore, if service costs are **not incurred on a straight-line basis**, revenue recognition over the contract's term should be proportionate to the estimated service costs.

Disclosures

5. Only the disclosure provisions of FASB Interpretation No. 45, *Guarantor's Accounting and Disclosure Requirements for Guarantees, Including Indirect Guarantees of the Indebtedness of Others*, apply to **product warranties** issued by the guarantor (whether or not separable and whether payable in services or cash). Thus, the **guarantor** must **disclose** (a) its accounting policy, (b) its method of calculating the product warranty liability, and (c) a reconciliation of the changes in the total for the period.

    a. Also, the guarantor must make the other disclosures required by the Interpretation (nature of the guarantee, etc.) **except** for the maximum potential amount of future payments.

Stop and review! You have completed the outline for this subunit. Study multiple-choice questions 15 through 17 beginning on page 387.

10.7 SCOPE AND PRINCIPLES OF INCOME TAX ACCOUNTING

Scope

1. The **asset and liability method** is used to account for income taxes (SFAS 109, *Accounting for Income Taxes*). It establishes standards of accounting and reporting for income taxes currently payable and for the tax consequences of

    a. Revenues, expenses, gains, and losses included in **taxable income (loss)** of an earlier or later year than the year in which they are recognized in income for financial reporting purposes.

    b. Other events that create **differences between the tax bases** of assets and liabilities and their **amounts for financial reporting purposes**.

    c. Operating loss or tax credit carrybacks for refunds of taxes paid in prior years and carryforwards to reduce taxes payable in future years.

2. SFAS 109 applies to

    a. Domestic federal income taxes

    b. Foreign, state, and local taxes based on income

    c. An entity's domestic and foreign operations that are consolidated, combined, or accounted for by the equity method

    d. Foreign entities in preparing statements based on U.S. GAAP

Objectives

3. Accrual accounting should recognize taxes currently payable or refundable.

4. It also should recognize deferred tax liabilities and assets for the future tax consequences of events that have been previously recognized in the entity's financial statements or tax returns.

Interperiod Tax Allocation

5. **Taxes currently payable or refundable** for a particular year include the tax consequences of most events recognized in the financial statements for the same year.

6. However, certain **significant exceptions** exist. As a result, the **tax consequences** of some transactions or events may be recognized in taxes currently payable or refundable in a year different from that in which their **financial-statement effects** are recognized.

   a. Moreover, some transactions or events may have tax consequences or financial-statement effects but never both.

7. Because of the differences between tax consequences and financial-statement effects, income taxes currently payable or refundable **may differ from** income tax expense or benefit.

   a. The accounting for these differences is **interperiod tax allocation**.

Basic Definitions

8. **Income tax expense or benefit** is the sum of the current tax expense or benefit and deferred tax expense or benefit.

9. **Current tax expense or benefit** is the amount of taxes paid or payable (or refundable) for the year as determined by applying the enacted tax law to the taxable income or excess of deductions over revenues for that year.

10. **Current tax liability** is equal to taxable income times the applicable tax rate.

11. **Deferred tax expense or benefit** is the net change during the year in an entity's deferred tax liabilities and assets.

12. A **deferred tax liability** records the deferred tax consequences attributable to taxable temporary differences. It is measured using the applicable enacted tax rate and provisions of the enacted tax law.

13. A **deferred tax asset** records the deferred tax consequences attributable to deductible temporary differences and carryforwards. It is measured using the applicable enacted tax rate and provisions of the enacted tax law.

Basic Principles of Income Tax Accounting

14. A **current tax liability or asset** is recognized for the estimated taxes payable or refundable on current-year tax returns.

15. A **deferred tax liability or asset** is recognized for the estimated future tax effects attributable to temporary differences and carryforwards.

16. **Measurement** of tax liabilities and assets is based on **enacted tax law**. The effects of future changes in that law are not anticipated.

17. A deferred tax asset is reduced by a **valuation allowance** if it is more likely than not that some portion will not be realized.

Stop and review! You have completed the outline for this subunit. Study multiple-choice questions 18 through 20 beginning on page 388.

10.8 TEMPORARY AND PERMANENT DIFFERENCES

Definitions

1. Income reported under **GAAP** (accrual basis) differs from income reported for **tax purposes** (modified cash basis). Under the asset-and-liability approach, future income statement (and tax) consequences arise from balance sheet measurements.

    a. A **temporary difference (TD)** results when the GAAP basis and the tax basis of an asset or liability differ. The effect is that a taxable or deductible amount will occur in future years when the asset is recovered or the liability is settled.

    b. A **permanent difference** is an event that is recognized either in pretax financial income or in taxable income but never in both. It does not result in a deferred tax asset or liability.

2. Temporary differences have balance sheet consequences. Permanent differences do not.

Temporary Differences

3. **Deferred tax liabilities** arise when TDs will result in **future taxable amounts**. Taxable TDs occur when

    a. **Revenues or gains** are included in taxable income after they are recognized under GAAP.

        1) An example is income recognized under the **equity method** for financial statement purposes and at the time of distribution in taxable income. Another example is sales revenue **accrued** for financial reporting and recognized on the **installment basis** for tax purposes.

    b. **Expenses or losses** are deductible for tax purposes before they are recognized under GAAP.

        1) An example is accelerated tax depreciation of property.

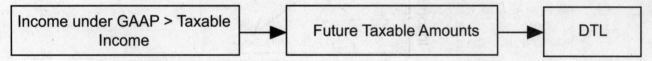

4. **Deferred tax assets** arise when TDs will result in **future deductible amounts**. Deductible TDs occur when

    a. **Revenues or gains** are included in taxable income before they are recognized under GAAP.

        1) An example is subscription revenue received in advance.

    b. **Expenses or losses** are deductible for tax purposes after they are recognized under GAAP.

        1) Examples include bad debt expense recognized under the allowance method and warranty costs.

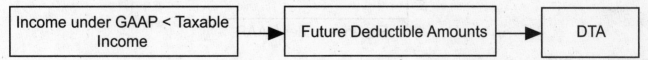

5. Some TDs result from assets or liabilities that are recognized for tax purposes but not for financial reporting purposes. The following are examples of **future deductible amounts** that arise from such circumstances:

    a. **Organization costs** are deferred and amortized for tax purposes. Under AICPA SOP 98-5, they must be expensed when incurred for financial reporting purposes.

    b. **Operating loss carryforwards** are carried forward as deductions in future years for tax purposes. They must be recognized immediately under GAAP.

6. A deferred tax liability must be recognized for the taxable TD arising from tax deductions for **goodwill**, which is not amortizable for financial statement purposes.

    a. This treatment is required even though the deferred tax liability will not be settled until some indefinite future period when goodwill is impaired, sold, or otherwise disposed of. The same treatment applies to **other intangible assets** that are not amortizable because their useful lives are indefinite.

7. In some future period, TDs will reverse. The following are examples:

    a. Accelerated tax depreciation

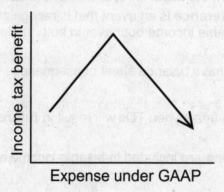

    b. Prepaid expenses

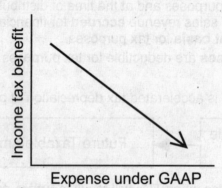

    c. Investments accounted for by the equity method

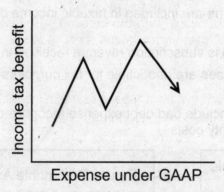

Permanent Differences

8. Permanent differences between taxable income and net income arise from transactions or events that are recognized in one and never the other.

    a. Permanent differences do **not** result in a deferred tax asset or liability. Thus, they have no balance sheet consequences.

9. One category of permanent differences consists of income items included in **net income** but not taxable income.

   a. Examples include state and municipal bond interest and proceeds from life insurance on key employees.

10. Another category of permanent differences consists of items subtracted in arriving at net income but not taxable income.

    a. Examples include premiums paid for life insurance on key employees and fines resulting from a violation of law.

11. A third category of permanent differences consists of items deducted in arriving at taxable income but not net income.

    a. Examples include percentage depletion of natural resources and the dividends received deduction.

Stop and review! You have completed the outline for this subunit. Study multiple-choice questions 21 through 23 beginning on page 389.

10.9 RECOGNITION AND MEASUREMENT OF DEFERRED INCOME TAXES

1. Because recovery of assets and settlement of liabilities are inherent assumptions of GAAP, accrual accounting must recognize deferred tax consequences of TDs.

Valuation Allowance

2. This account is contra to a **deferred tax asset**. It reduces a deferred tax asset if the weight of the available evidence, positive and negative, indicates that it is **more likely than not** (the probability is more than 50%) that some portion will not be realized. The allowance should be sufficient to reduce the deferred tax asset to the amount that is more likely than not to be realized.

3. Future **realization of the tax benefit** represented by a deferred tax asset ultimately depends on the existence of sufficient taxable income of the proper **character** (ordinary income or capital gain) within the **carryback and carryforward period**.

   a. For example, federal corporate tax law permits **net operating losses** to be carried back 2 years (earlier year first) and then forward 20 years. Alternatively, an entity may choose the carryforward only.

4. The following are the **sources of taxable income** permitting realization of the tax benefit of a deferred tax asset and therefore eliminating or reducing the need for a valuation allowance:

   a. Reversals of taxable TDs
   b. Future taxable income without regard to reversing differences and carryforwards
   c. Taxable income in the carryback period
   d. **Tax-planning strategies**, for example, those that accelerate taxable amounts to (1) permit use of an expiring carryforward, (2) change the character of income or loss, or (3) switch from tax-exempt to taxable items of income

      1) Significant expenses or net losses from implementing a strategy are included in the allowance.
      2) A strategy is a prudent and feasible action taken to prevent a carryforward from expiring unused.

Determination of Deferred Taxes

5.   The process below is followed for each taxpaying entity in each tax jurisdiction:

   a.   Identify TDs (types and amounts) and operating loss and tax credit carryforwards for tax purposes (nature and amounts, and length of the remaining carryforward period).

   b.   Measure the total deferred tax liability for taxable TDs using the applicable tax rate.

   c.   Measure the total deferred tax asset for deductible TDs and operating loss carryforwards using the applicable tax rate.

   d.   Measure deferred tax assets for each type of tax credit carryforward.

   e.   Recognize a valuation allowance if necessary.

Applicable Tax Rates

6.   A deferred tax liability or asset is measured using the **enacted tax rate(s)** expected to apply when the liability or asset is expected to be settled or realized. In the U.S., the **applicable tax rate** is the **regular rate**.

   a.   The tax rate used in the measurement of deferred tax liabilities and assets is, in essence, a flat rate if graduated rates are **not** significant to the entity. Otherwise, an **average** of the applicable graduated rates is used.

The Basic Entry

7.   The basic entry to record taxes in accordance with the asset and liability method required by SFAS 109 is

Income tax expense (or benefit)	debit (or credit)
Income tax payable (or refundable)	credit (or debit)
Deferred income tax liability (or asset)	credit (or debit)

Stop and review! You have completed the outline for this subunit. Study multiple-choice questions 24 through 29 beginning on page 390.

10.10 ADDITIONAL INCOME TAX ISSUES

Intraperiod Tax Allocation

1.   Intraperiod tax allocation **is required**. Income tax expense (benefit) is allocated to (a) continuing operations, (b) discontinued operations, (c) extraordinary items, (d) other comprehensive income, and (e) items debited or credited directly to equity.

   a.   The tax benefits of most operating loss carryforwards and carrybacks are reported in the same manner as the source of the income or loss in the current year.

Enacted Changes in Law or Rates

2.   Such changes require an adjustment of a deferred tax liability or asset in the period of the enactment of the tax law or rate. The effect is included in the amount of income tax expense or benefit allocated to continuing operations.

Change in Tax Status

3.   The resulting effect on deferred taxes is recognized as follows:

   a.   When an entity changes from **nontaxable to taxable**, a deferred tax amount reflecting TDs at the time of the change is recognized.

   b.   When an entity changes its status **from taxable to nontaxable**, any existing deferred tax liability or asset is ordinarily eliminated at the date of the change.

c. For an **elective change**, the effect is recognized on the approval date (or on the filing date if approval is not needed).

1) If the change in status results from a **change in tax law**, the effect is recognized on the enactment date.

d. The effect of recognizing or eliminating the deferred tax liability or asset is included in the amount of income tax expense or benefit allocated to **continuing operations**.

Business Combinations

4. Deferred tax liabilities or assets are recognized for the TDs (taxable or deductible) that arise because the assigned amounts and the tax bases of assets and liabilities acquired in a business combination may differ.

a. This rule does not apply to nondeductible goodwill, leveraged leases, and certain other items.

NOTE: If you plan to take FAR during Q3 or Q4 2009, please go to www.gleim.com/support/updates and download a revised outline. SFAS 141(R) will be testable in July 2009, and this section of our outline will be superseded.

Financial Statement Presentation

5. Deferred tax liabilities and assets should be separated into **current and noncurrent** components. Whether an item is current or noncurrent usually depends on the **classification of the related asset or liability**.

a. If a deferred tax item, including a deferred tax asset related to a carryforward, is not related to an asset or liability for financial reporting, it is classified based on the **expected reversal date** of the TD.

b. A **valuation allowance** for a particular tax jurisdiction is allocated pro rata between current and noncurrent deferred tax assets.

c. For a given tax-paying entity and within a specific jurisdiction, current deferred tax assets and liabilities are **netted**. Noncurrent deferred tax assets and liabilities are also offset and shown as a single amount.

Disclosures

6. The following are required disclosures:

a. Total deferred tax liabilities and total deferred tax assets

1) The manner of reporting the tax benefit of an operating loss carryforward or carryback is determined by the source of the income or loss in the current year.

b. Total valuation allowance and the annual change in it

c. Tax effect of each TD or carryforward resulting in a significant deferred tax amount **(by public entities only)**

1) A nonpublic entity must disclose only the types of significant TDs and carryforwards.

Accounting for Uncertainty in Income Taxes

7. FASB Interpretation No. 48, *Accounting for Uncertainty in Income Taxes*, applies to tax positions accounted for under SFAS 109.

a. A **tax position** is one taken or to be taken in a **tax return**. It is reflected in financial statement measurements of tax assets and liabilities, whether current or deferred.

1) For example, tax positions may include (a) decisions not to file, (b) income exclusions, (c) transaction exemptions, (d) income characterizations, or (e) shifts of income among jurisdictions.

8.   The evaluation of a tax position is a two-stage procedure:

a.   **Recognition.** The financial statement effects are initially recognized if it is **more likely than not** (a probability greater than 50%) that the position will be **sustained on review**.

1)   A tax position also may be recognized upon **effective settlement**. This involves considering whether (a) the taxing authority has completed its examination procedures, (b) the entity does not intend to litigate the matter, and (c) the probability is remote that the taxing authority will examine any aspect of the position.

a)   Thus, the position need **not** be specifically reviewed or examined by the taxing authority.

b.   **Measurement.** The entity recognizes the largest benefit that is **more than 50% likely** to be realized.

9.   Applying this Interpretation may result in recognition of a tax benefit in the balance sheet different from the amount in the current tax return. Thus, **unrecognized tax benefits** are differences between a tax position taken (or to be taken) in a tax return and the benefits recognized and measured under the Interpretation. The result is a **liability** (or reduction of a loss carryforward or refund). This result reflects the entity's possible future tax obligation arising because of an unrecognized tax position.

a.   The entity ordinarily recognizes one or both of the following:

1)   An increased liability for taxes payable or a reduced refund receivable
2)   A decreased deferred tax asset or increased deferred tax liability

b.   A tax position recognized under this Interpretation may affect the **tax bases** of assets or liabilities and change (or create) **temporary differences**.

Basic Examples

EXAMPLE -- Deferred Tax Liability

Pitou Co. disposed of certain property in Year 1 in transactions accounted for using the installment method for tax purposes and the accrual method for financial reporting purposes. Pitou does not regularly dispose of such property on the installment plan and is therefore not a dealer with respect to that property. For Year 1, Pitou Co.'s pretax financial income is $520,000, and its taxable income is $500,000. The $20,000 difference is attributable solely to recognition of earned revenue from installment sales that will result in future taxable amounts when the receivables are collected. Pitou's applicable tax rate is 34%. Thus, the deferred tax liability is $6,800 ($20,000 taxable TD × 34%), and the deferred tax expense is also $6,800 ($6,800 year-end deferred tax liability – $0 balance at the beginning of the year). Income tax payable (current tax expense) is $170,000 ($500,000 taxable income × 34%). Accordingly, income tax expense is $176,800 ($170,000 current tax expense + $6,800 deferred tax expense). The year-end entry is

Income tax expense	$176,800	
Income tax payable		$170,000
Deferred income tax liability		6,800

For Year 2, Pitou Co. has taxable income of $450,000, which includes the collection of $8,000 of installment receivables previously recognized in financial accounting income. There is no other difference between pretax financial income and taxable income. Hence, the taxable TD is reduced to $12,000 ($20,000 – $8,000), the year-end deferred tax liability is $4,080 ($12,000 × 34%), and the decrease in the deferred tax liability (the deferred tax benefit arising from reduction in the liability) is $2,720 ($6,800 at the beginning of the year – $4,080 at year-end). Current tax expense (tax payable) is $153,000 ($450,000 taxable income × 34%). Consequently, total income tax expense for the year is $150,280 ($153,000 current tax expense – $2,720 deferred tax benefit). The year-end entry is

Income tax expense	$150,280	
Deferred income tax liability	2,720	
Income tax payable		$153,000

EXAMPLE -- Deferred Tax Asset

Lunes Co. began operations in the year just ended. It has taxable income of $400,000 and pretax financial income of $385,000. The difference is solely attributable to receipt of unearned subscription revenue (a liability) that was included as revenue in the tax return in the year of collection. Lunes will recognize $9,000 of this unearned revenue as earned in its second year of operations and $6,000 in the third year. The applicable tax rate is 34%. Thus, the deferred tax asset is $5,100 ($15,000 deductible TD × 34%), and the deferred tax benefit is also $5,100 ($5,100 year-end deferred tax asset – $0 balance at the beginning of the year). Income tax payable (current tax expense) is $136,000 ($400,000 taxable income × 34%). Accordingly, income tax expense is $130,900 ($136,000 current tax expense – $5,100 deferred tax benefit). Based on the evidence (taxable income), no valuation allowance is required for the deferred tax asset. Thus, the year-end entry is

Income tax expense	$130,900	
Deferred income tax asset	5,100	
Income tax payable		$136,000

In its second year of operations, Lunes has taxable income of $600,000, with income tax payable (current tax expense) of $204,000 ($600,000 × 34%). Taxable income and pretax financial income differ only in that $9,000 of unearned revenue collected in the preceding year is included in the determination of pretax financial income. At the end of the second year, the deferred tax asset is therefore $2,040 [($15,000 – $9,000) × 34%], and the deferred tax expense (the decrease in the deferred tax asset) is $3,060 ($5,100 – $2,040). Total income tax expense is $207,060 ($204,000 current tax expense + $3,060 deferred tax expense). Based on the evidence (taxable income), no valuation allowance is required for the deferred tax asset. Thus, the year-end entry is

Income tax expense	$207,060	
Income tax payable		$204,000
Deferred income tax asset		3,060

EXAMPLE -- Deferred Tax Asset - Valuation Allowance

Mardi Co. has a $6,000 deductible TD at the end of its current year. The applicable tax rate is 34%. Consequently, Mardi recorded a deferred tax asset of $2,040 ($6,000 × 34%). However, after weighing all the evidence, Mardi Co. has decided that it is more likely than not (more than 50% probable) that $4,000 of the deductible temporary difference will not be realized. To reflect this determination, a valuation allowance (a contra account) should be credited. The offsetting debit is to income tax expense. The amount of the valuation allowance should be sufficient to reduce the deferred tax asset to the amount that is more likely than not to be realized. Accordingly, Mardi should recognize a $1,360 valuation allowance to reduce the $2,040 deferred tax asset to $680 ($2,000 × 34%). The entry is

Income tax expense	$1,360	
Deferred tax asset -- valuation allowance		$1,360

EXAMPLE -- Tax Position

An entity expects to claim a $5 million energy credit on its federal income tax return ($1 million for each of five distinct projects). It is more likely than not that the tax benefit finally sustained will be $3,600,000 ($800,000 for each of four projects and $400,000 for the fifth). When evaluating the amount to be recognized, management concludes that the **unit of account** for the tax position is each project. Information is accumulated, and tax authority review will occur at the project level. In evaluating the tax position at the project level, the entity determines that it is more likely than not that the tax benefit with respect to the fifth project ultimately will be sustained in the amount of $200,000. The total tax benefit recognized is therefore $3,400,000. The determination for the fifth project is based on the computation below. The largest benefit that is more than 50% likely to be realized upon ultimate settlement is $200,000.

Possible Outcome 000 Omitted	Probability	Cumulative Probability
$1,000	0%	0%
800	10%	10%
600	10%	20%
500	10%	30%
400	15%	45%
200	25%	70%
0	30%	100%

Stop and review!   You have completed the outline for this subunit. Study multiple-choice questions 30 through 35 beginning on page 392.

QUESTIONS

10.1 Accounts Payable

1. Which of the following is usually associated with payables classified as accounts payable?

	Periodic Payment of Interest	Secured by Collateral
A.	No	No
B.	No	Yes
C.	Yes	No
D.	Yes	Yes

Answer (A) is correct. *(CPA, adapted)*
REQUIRED: The characteristic(s) usually associated with accounts payable.
DISCUSSION: Accounts payable, commonly termed trade accounts payable, are liabilities reflecting the obligations to sellers that are incurred when an entity purchases inventory, supplies, or services on credit. Accounts payable should be recorded at their settlement value. Short-term liabilities, such as accounts payable, do not usually provide for a periodic payment of interest unless the accounts are not settled when due or payable. They also are usually not secured by collateral.

2. Lyle, Inc. is preparing its financial statements for the year ended December 31, Year 3. Accounts payable amounted to $360,000 before any necessary year-end adjustment related to the following:

- At December 31, Year 3, Lyle has a $50,000 debit balance in its accounts payable to Ross, a supplier, resulting from a $50,000 advance payment for goods to be manufactured to Lyle's specifications.

- Checks in the amount of $100,000 were written to vendors and recorded on December 29, Year 3. The checks were mailed on January 5, Year 4.

What amount should Lyle report as accounts payable in its December 31, Year 3, balance sheet?

A. $510,000

B. $410,000

C. $310,000

D. $210,000

Answer (A) is correct. *(CPA, adapted)*
REQUIRED: The amount of accounts payable reported after year-end adjustments.
DISCUSSION: The ending accounts payable balance should include amounts owed as of December 31, Year 3, on trade payables. Although Lyle wrote checks for $100,000 to various vendors, that amount should still be included in the accounts payable balance because the company had not surrendered control of the checks at year-end. The advance to the supplier was erroneously recorded as a reduction of (debit to) accounts payable. This amount should be recorded as a prepaid asset, and accounts payable should be credited (increased) by $50,000. Thus, accounts payable should be reported as $510,000 ($360,000 + $50,000 + $100,000).
Answer (B) is incorrect because $410,000 does not include the $100,000 in checks not yet mailed at year-end. Answer (C) is incorrect because $310,000 does not include the $100,000 in checks, and it reflects the subtraction, not the addition, of the $50,000 advance. Answer (D) is incorrect because $210,000 results from subtracting the advance payment and the checks.

10.2 Accrued Expenses

3. In its Year 4 financial statements, Cris Co. reported interest expense of $85,000 in its income statement and cash paid for interest of $68,000 in its cash flow statement. There was no prepaid interest or interest capitalization at either the beginning or the end of Year 4. Accrued interest at December 31, Year 3, was $15,000. What amount should Cris report as accrued interest payable in its December 31, Year 4, balance sheet?

A. $2,000

B. $15,000

C. $17,000

D. $32,000

Answer (D) is correct. *(CPA, adapted)*
REQUIRED: The accrued interest payable at year-end.
DISCUSSION: The cash paid for interest was $68,000, including $15,000 of interest paid for Year 3. Consequently, $53,000 ($68,000 – $15,000) of the cash paid for interest related to Year 4. Interest payable is therefore $32,000 ($85,000 – $53,000).
Answer (A) is incorrect because $2,000 results from adding the $15,000 to $68,000 and subtracting that sum from the $85,000 interest expense. Answer (B) is incorrect because $15,000 is the interest paid for Year 3. Answer (C) is incorrect because $17,000 is the difference between the interest expense and cash paid out.

4. Ross Co. pays all salaried employees on a Monday for the 5-day workweek ended the previous Friday. The last payroll recorded for the year ended December 31, Year 4, was for the week ended December 25, Year 4. The payroll for the week ended January 1, Year 5, included regular weekly salaries of $80,000 and vacation pay of $25,000 for vacation time earned in Year 4 not taken by December 31, Year 4. Ross had accrued a liability of $20,000 for vacation pay at December 31, Year 3. In its December 31, Year 4, balance sheet, what amount should Ross report as accrued salary and vacation pay?

A. $64,000

B. $69,000

C. $84,000

D. $89,000

Answer (D) is correct. *(CPA, adapted)*
REQUIRED: The accrued salary and vacation pay.
DISCUSSION: The salary accrual at December 31, Year 4, was for a 4-day period (December 28-31). Thus, the accrued salary (amount earned in Year 4 but not paid until Year 5) should be $64,000 [$80,000 in salaries for a 5-day week × (4 days ÷ 5 days)]. Vacation pay ($25,000) for time earned but not taken in Year 4 was not paid until Year 5. Hence, $25,000, not $20,000, should have been accrued at year-end. The total accrual is $89,000.
Answer (A) is incorrect because $64,000 does not include vacation pay. Answer (B) is incorrect because $69,000 results from erroneously deducting $20,000. Answer (C) is incorrect because $84,000 assumes accrued vacation pay is $20,000.

5. On December 31, Year 4, Deal, Inc. failed to accrue the December Year 4 sales salaries that were payable on January 6, Year 5. What is the effect of the failure to accrue sales salaries on working capital and cash flows from operating activities in Deal's Year 4 financial statements?

	Working Capital	Cash Flows from Operating Activities
A.	Overstated	No effect
B.	Overstated	Overstated
C.	No effect	Overstated
D.	No effect	No effect

Answer (A) is correct. *(CPA, adapted)*
REQUIRED: The effect of the failure to accrue sales salaries on working capital and cash flows from operating activities.
DISCUSSION: The effect is to overstate working capital (current assets – current liabilities) because of the failure to accrue a current liability by a debit to salaries expense and a credit to salaries payable. The error has no effect on cash flows because an accrual does not involve a cash payment or receipt.
Answer (B) is incorrect because cash flows are unaffected. Answer (C) is incorrect because cash flows are unaffected, but working capital is overstated. Answer (D) is incorrect because working capital is overstated.

10.3 Certain Taxes Payable

6. Bloy Corp.'s payroll for the pay period ended October 31, Year 4, is summarized as follows:

Department Payroll	Total Wages	Federal Income Tax Withheld	Amount of Wages Subject to Payroll Taxes FICA	Amount of Wages Subject to Payroll Taxes Unemployment
Factory	$ 60,000	$ 7,000	$56,000	$18,000
Sales	22,000	3,000	16,000	2,000
Office	18,000	2,000	8,000	--
	$100,000	$12,000	$80,000	$20,000

Assume the following payroll tax rates:

FICA for employer and employee	7% each
Unemployment	3%

What amount should Bloy accrue as its share of payroll taxes in its October 31, Year 4, balance sheet?

- A. $18,200
- B. $12,600
- C. $11,800
- D. $6,200

7. Lime Co.'s payroll for the month ended January 31, Year 4, is summarized as follows:

Total wages	$10,000
Federal income tax withheld	1,200

All wages paid were subject to FICA. FICA tax rates were 7% each for employee and employer. Lime remits payroll taxes on the 15th of the following month. In its financial statements for the month ended January 31, Year 4, what amounts should Lime report as total payroll tax liability and as payroll tax expense?

	Liability	Expense
A.	$1,200	$1,400
B.	$1,900	$1,400
C.	$1,900	$700
D.	$2,600	$700

8. Under state law, Acme may pay 3% of eligible gross wages or it may reimburse the state directly for actual unemployment claims. Acme believes that actual unemployment claims will be 2% of eligible gross wages and has chosen to reimburse the state. Eligible gross wages are defined as the first $10,000 of gross wages paid to each employee. Acme had five employees, each of whom earned $20,000 during Year 4. In its December 31, Year 4, balance sheet, what amount should Acme report as accrued liability for unemployment claims?

- A. $1,000
- B. $1,500
- C. $2,000
- D. $3,000

Answer (D) is correct. *(CPA, adapted)*
REQUIRED: The amount to be accrued for payroll taxes.
DISCUSSION: The amount of wages subject to payroll taxes for FICA purposes is $80,000. At a 7% rate, the employer's share of FICA taxes equals $5,600 ($80,000 × 7%). Wages subject to unemployment payroll taxes are $20,000. At a 3% rate, unemployment payroll taxes equal $600 ($20,000 × 3%). Consequently, the total of payroll taxes is $6,200 ($5,600 + $600). A 7% employee rate also applies to the wages subject to FICA taxes. This amount ($80,000 × 7% = $5,600) should be withheld from the employee's wages and remitted directly to the federal government by the employer, along with the $6,200 in employer payroll taxes. The employee's share, however, should be accrued as a withholding tax (an employee payroll deduction) and not as an employer payroll tax.
Answer (A) is incorrect because $18,200 includes the federal income tax withheld. Answer (B) is incorrect because $12,600 is the sum of the federal income tax withheld and the unemployment tax. Answer (C) is incorrect because $11,800 includes the FICA employee taxes.

Answer (D) is correct. *(CPA, adapted)*
REQUIRED: The amounts reported as total payroll tax liability and as payroll tax expense.
DISCUSSION: The payroll liability is $2,600 ($1,200 federal income tax withheld + $700 employer's FICA + $700 employees' FICA). The payroll tax expense consists of the employer's share of FICA. The employees' share is considered a withholding, not an expense.
Answer (A) is incorrect because $1,200 does not include employer and employee shares of current FICA taxes, and $1,400 includes the employees' share of FICA taxes. Answer (B) is incorrect because $1,900 does not include $700 of FICA taxes, and $1,400 includes the employees' share of FICA taxes. Answer (C) is incorrect because $1,900 does not include $700 of FICA taxes.

Answer (A) is correct. *(CPA, adapted)*
REQUIRED: The accrued liability for unemployment claims.
DISCUSSION: A contingent liability should be accrued when it is probable that a liability has been incurred and the amount can be reasonably estimated. Thus, Acme should accrue a liability for $1,000 [(5 × $10,000) eligible wages × 2%].
Answer (B) is incorrect because $1,500 is based on a 3% rate. Answer (C) is incorrect because $2,000 is based on the total wages paid to the employees. Answer (D) is incorrect because $3,000 is based on a 3% rate and the total wages paid to the employees.

9. On July 1, Year 4, Ran County issued realty tax assessments for its fiscal year ended June 30, Year 5. The assessments are to be paid in two equal installments. On September 1, Year 4, Day Co. purchased a warehouse in Ran County. The purchase price was reduced by a credit for accrued realty taxes. Day did not record the entire year's real estate tax obligation, but instead records tax expenses at the end of each month by adjusting prepaid real estate taxes or real estate taxes payable, as appropriate. On November 1, Year 4, Day paid the first installment of $12,000 for realty taxes. What amount of this payment should Day record as a debit to real estate taxes payable?

    A. $4,000

    B. $8,000

    C. $10,000

    D. $12,000

Answer (B) is correct. *(CPA, adapted)*
    REQUIRED: The amount to be debited to real estate taxes payable.
    DISCUSSION: The credit balance in real estate taxes payable at November 1, Year 4, is $8,000. This amount reflects accrued real estate taxes of $2,000 a month [(2 × $12,000) ÷ 12 months] for 4 months (July through October). This payable should be debited for $8,000 when the real estate taxes are paid.
    Answer (A) is incorrect because the $4,000 includes real estate taxes for September and October only. Answer (C) is incorrect because $10,000 includes real estate taxes for November. Answer (D) is incorrect because $12,000 equals 6 months of real estate taxes.

10.4 Deposits and Other Advances

10. Barnel Corp. owns and manages 19 apartment complexes. On signing a lease, each tenant must pay the first and last months' rent and a $500 refundable security deposit. The security deposits are rarely refunded in total, because cleaning costs of $150 per apartment are almost always deducted. About 30% of the time, the tenants are also charged for damages to the apartment, which typically cost $100 to repair. If a 1-year lease is signed on a $900 per month apartment, what amount would Barnel report as refundable security deposit?

    A. $1,400

    B. $500

    C. $350

    D. $320

Answer (B) is correct. *(CPA, adapted)*
    REQUIRED: The amount of the refundable security deposit.
    DISCUSSION: The refundable security deposit is a liability because it involves a probable future sacrifice of economic benefits arising from a current obligation of a particular entity to transfer assets or provide services to another entity in the future as a result of a past transaction (SFAC 6). The reported amount of the liability for the refundable security deposit should be $500 because that is the probable future sacrifice of economic benefits, whether in the form of (a) a $500 refund or (b) the sum of an estimated $320 refund, $150 of cleaning costs, and $30 of damages.
    Answer (A) is incorrect because $1,400 equals the deposit plus the last month's rent, an amount that is not refundable. Answer (C) is incorrect because $350 does not reflect the expected value of damages. Answer (D) is incorrect because the probable future economic sacrifice is $500.

11. Buc Co. receives deposits from its customers to protect itself against nonpayments for future services. These deposits should be classified by Buc as

    A. A liability.

    B. Revenue.

    C. A deferred credit deducted from accounts receivable.

    D. A contra account.

Answer (A) is correct. *(CPA, adapted)*
    REQUIRED: The nature of customer deposits.
    DISCUSSION: A customer deposit is a liability because it involves a probable future sacrifice of economic benefits arising from a current obligation of a particular entity to transfer assets or provide services to another entity in the future as a result of a past transaction (SFAC 6).
    Answer (B) is incorrect because a revenue is not recognized until it is earned. Answer (C) is incorrect because GAAP ordinarily prohibit offsetting assets and liabilities (APB Opinion 10). Most deferred credits are liabilities. Answer (D) is incorrect because a contra account is a valuation account.

12. Marr Co. sells its products in reusable containers. The customer is charged a deposit for each container delivered and receives a refund for each container returned within 2 years after the year of delivery. Marr accounts for the containers not returned within the time limit as being retired by sale at the deposit amount. Information for Year 4:

Container deposits at December 31, Year 3, from deliveries in

Year 2	$150,000	
Year 3	430,000	$580,000

Deposits for containers delivered in Year 4 $780,000

Deposits for containers returned in Year 4 from deliveries in

Year 2	$ 90,000	
Year 3	250,000	
Year 4	286,000	$626,000

In Marr's December 31, Year 4, balance sheet, the liability for deposits on returnable containers should be

- A. $494,000
- B. $584,000
- C. $674,000
- D. $734,000

Answer (C) is correct. *(CPA, adapted)*
REQUIRED: The liability for deposits on returnable containers at year-end.
DISCUSSION: At the beginning of Year 4, the liability for returnable containers is given as $580,000. This liability is increased by $780,000 attributable to containers delivered in Year 4. The liability is decreased by the $626,000 attributable to containers returned in Year 4. Moreover, the 2-year refund period for Year 2 deliveries has expired. Accordingly, the liability should also be decreased for $60,000 ($150,000 − $90,000) worth of containers deemed to be retired. As indicated below, the liability for returnable containers at December 31, Year 4, is $674,000.

Deposits on Returnable Containers

Containers		$580,000	12/31/Yr3
returned	$626,000	780,000	Year 4 Containers
Year 2 retired	60,000		delivered
		$674,000	12/31/Yr4

Answer (A) is incorrect because $494,000 is the difference between total deposits for containers delivered in Year 4 and Year 4 deposits returned. Answer (B) is incorrect because $584,000 assumes that all Year 2 containers were retired. Answer (D) is incorrect because $734,000 omits the Year 2 containers retired by sale from the calculation.

10.5 Coupons and Premiums

13. Dunn Trading Stamp Company records stamp service revenue and provides for the cost of redemptions in the year stamps are sold to licensees. Dunn's past experience indicates that only 80% of the stamps sold to licensees will be redeemed. Dunn's liability for stamp redemptions was $6 million at December 31, Year 3. Additional information for Year 4 is as follows:

Stamp service revenue from stamps sold to licensees	$4,000,000
Cost of redemptions (stamps sold prior to 1/1/Yr4)	2,750,000

If all the stamps sold in Year 4 were presented for redemption in Year 5, the redemption cost would be $2,250,000. What amount should Dunn report as a liability for stamp redemptions at December 31, Year 4?

- A. $7,250,000
- B. $5,500,000
- C. $5,050,000
- D. $3,250,000

Answer (C) is correct. *(CPA, adapted)*
REQUIRED: The reported liability for stamp redemptions at year-end.
DISCUSSION: The liability for stamp redemptions at the beginning of Year 4 is given as $6 million. This liability would be increased in Year 4 by $2,250,000 if all stamps sold in Year 4 were presented for redemption. However, because only 80% are expected to be redeemed, the liability should be increased by $1,800,000 ($2,250,000 × 80%). The liability was decreased by the $2,750,000 attributable to the costs of redemptions. Thus, the liability for stamp redemptions at December 31, Year 4, is $5,050,000 ($6,000,000 + $1,800,000 − $2,750,000).
Answer (A) is incorrect because $7,250,000 equals the beginning balance, plus stamp service revenue, minus redemptions of stamps sold before Year 4. Answer (B) is incorrect because $5,500,000 is based on an expected 100% redemption rate. Answer (D) is incorrect because $3,250,000 assumes that no stamps were sold in Year 4.

14. In December Year 4, Mill Co. began including one coupon in each package of candy that it sells and offering a toy in exchange for $.50 and five coupons. The toys cost Mill $.80 each. Eventually, 60% of the coupons will be redeemed. During December, Mill sold 110,000 packages of candy and no coupons were redeemed. In its December 31, Year 4, balance sheet, what amount should Mill report as estimated liability for coupons?

A. $3,960

B. $10,560

C. $19,800

D. $52,800

Answer (A) is correct. *(CPA, adapted)*
REQUIRED: The amount to be reported as a liability for unredeemed coupons at year-end.
DISCUSSION: The liability for coupon redemptions is $3,960 {[(110,000 coupons issued ÷ 5 per toy) × 60% redemption rate] × ($.80 – $.50) set cost per toy}.
Answer (B) is incorrect because $10,560 does not include the $.50 paid by customers for the toy. Answer (C) is incorrect because $19,800 assumes one coupon can be redeemed for a toy. Answer (D) is incorrect because $52,800 assumes one coupon can be redeemed for a toy, and it excludes the $.50 that customers must pay per toy.

10.6 Warranties

15. Vadis Co. sells appliances that include a 3-year warranty. Service calls under the warranty are performed by an independent mechanic under a contract with Vadis. Based on experience, warranty costs are estimated at $30 for each machine sold. When should Vadis recognize these warranty costs?

A. Evenly over the life of the warranty.

B. When the service calls are performed.

C. When payments are made to the mechanic.

D. When the machines are sold.

Answer (D) is correct. *(CPA, adapted)*
REQUIRED: The proper recording of warranty costs.
DISCUSSION: Under the accrual method, a provision for warranty costs is made when the related revenue is recognized.
Answer (A) is incorrect because the accrual method matches the costs and the related revenues. Answer (B) is incorrect because, when the warranty costs can be reasonably estimated, the accrual method should be used. Recognizing the costs when the service calls are performed is the cash basis. Answer (C) is incorrect because recognizing costs when paid is the cash basis.

16. During Year 3, Rex Co. introduced a new product carrying a 2-year warranty against defects. The estimated warranty costs related to dollar sales are 2% within 12 months following sale and 4% in the second 12 months following sale. Sales and actual warranty expenditures for the years ended December 31, Year 3 and Year 4, are as follows:

	Sales	Actual Warranty Expenditures
Year 3	$ 600,000	$ 9,000
Year 4	1,000,000	30,000
	$1,600,000	$39,000

At December 31, Year 4, Rex should report an estimated warranty liability of

A. $0

B. $39,000

C. $57,000

D. $96,000

Answer (C) is correct. *(CPA, adapted)*
REQUIRED: The estimated warranty liability at the end of the second year.
DISCUSSION: Because this product is new, the beginning balance in the estimated warranty liability account at the beginning of Year 3 is $0. For Year 3, the estimated warranty costs related to dollar sales are 6% (2% + 4%) of sales or $36,000 ($600,000 × 6%). For Year 4, the estimated warranty costs are $60,000 ($1,000,000 sales × 6%). These amounts are charged to warranty expense and credited to the estimated warranty liability account. This liability account is debited for expenditures of $9,000 and $30,000 in Year 3 and Year 4, respectively. Hence, the estimated warranty liability at 12/31/Yr4 is $57,000.

Estimated Warranty Liability			
		$ 0	1/1/Yr3
Year 3 expenditures	$ 9,000	36,000	Year 3 expense
Year 4 expenditures	30,000	60,000	Year 4 expense
		$57,000	12/31/Yr4

Answer (A) is incorrect because all warranties have not expired. Answer (B) is incorrect because $39,000 equals the total warranty expenditures to date. Answer (D) is incorrect because $96,000 equals the total warranty expense to date.

17. Oak Co. offers a 3-year warranty on its products. Oak previously estimated warranty costs to be 2% of sales. Due to a technological advance in production at the beginning of Year 4, Oak now believes 1% of sales to be a better estimate of warranty costs. Warranty costs of $80,000 and $96,000 were reported in Year 2 and Year 3, respectively. Sales for Year 4 were $5 million. What amount should be disclosed in Oak's Year 4 financial statements as warranty expense?

A. $ 50,000

B. $ 88,000

C. $100,000

D. $138,000

Answer (A) is correct. *(CPA, adapted)*
REQUIRED: The amount of warranty expense reported.
DISCUSSION: The change affects only Year 4 sales. No change in the previously recorded estimates is necessary. Thus, the debit to warranty expense is $50,000 ($5,000,000 sales × 1%). Estimated liability under warranties is credited for $50,000.
Answer (B) is incorrect because $88,000 is the average of Year 2 and Year 3 costs. Answer (C) is incorrect because $100,000 results from using 2% instead of 1%. Answer (D) is incorrect because $138,000 includes $88,000, which is the average of Year 2 and Year 3 costs.

10.7 Scope and Principles of Income Tax Accounting

18. The provisions of SFAS 109, *Accounting for Income Taxes*, are applicable to

A. All foreign, state, and local taxes.

B. Foreign, state, and local taxes based on income.

C. An enterprise's foreign operations accounted for by the cost method.

D. Financial statements of foreign enterprises required to pay U.S. federal income taxes.

Answer (B) is correct. *(Publisher, adapted)*
REQUIRED: The applicability of SFAS 109.
DISCUSSION: The principles and requirements of SFAS 109 are applicable not only to domestic federal income taxes but also foreign, state, and local taxes based on income.
Answer (A) is incorrect because SFAS 109's provisions are applicable to domestic federal income taxes and foreign, federal, state, and local taxes that are based on income. Answer (C) is incorrect because the provisions are applicable only to an enterprise's domestic and foreign operations that are consolidated, combined, or accounted for by the equity method. Answer (D) is incorrect because foreign enterprises are affected only if they report based on U.S. GAAP.

19. Under current generally accepted accounting principles, which approach is used to determine income tax expense?

A. Asset and liability approach.

B. "With and without" approach.

C. Net-of-tax approach.

D. Deferred approach.

Answer (A) is correct. *(CPA, adapted)*
REQUIRED: The current approach used to determine income tax expense.
DISCUSSION: The asset and liability approach accrues liabilities or assets (taxes payable or refundable) for the current year. It also recognizes deferred tax amounts for the future tax consequences of events previously recognized in the financial statements or tax returns. These liabilities and assets recognize the effects of temporary differences measured using the tax rate(s) expected to apply when the liabilities and assets are expected to be settled or realized. Accordingly, deferred tax expense (benefit) is determined by the change during the period in the deferred tax assets and liabilities. Income tax expense (benefit) is the sum of current tax expense (benefit), that is, the amount paid or payable, and the deferred tax expense (benefit).
Answer (B) is incorrect because the "with and without" approach was an element of the deferred approach followed by APB Opinion 11 (superseded by SFAS 109). APB Opinion 11 stated that the tax effect of a timing difference should "be measured by the differential between income taxes computed with and without inclusion of the transaction creating the difference between taxable income and pretax accounting income." Answer (C) is incorrect because the net-of-tax approach accounts for the effects of taxability or deductibility on assets and liabilities as reductions in their reported amounts. Answer (D) is incorrect because the deferred method used in APB Opinion 11 (superseded by SFAS 109) determined income tax expense by multiplying pretax financial income by the current tax rate. The difference between taxes payable (refundable) and income tax expense (benefit) was recorded as a deferred credit or charge.

20. SFAS 109 establishes standards of financial accounting and reporting for income taxes that are currently payable and for

A. The tax consequences of revenues and expenses included in taxable income in a different year from the year in which they are recognized for financial reporting purposes.

B. The method of accounting for the U.S. federal investment tax credit.

C. The discounting of income taxes.

D. The accounting for income taxes in general in interim periods.

Answer (A) is correct. *(Publisher, adapted)*
REQUIRED: The applicability of SFAS 109.
DISCUSSION: The scope of SFAS 109 extends to the tax consequences of (1) revenues, expenses, gains, and losses included in taxable income of a year other than the year when they are recognized in income for financial reporting purposes; (2) other events that create differences between the tax bases of assets and liabilities and their amounts for financial reporting purposes; and (3) operating loss or tax credit carrybacks for refunds of taxes paid in prior years and carryforwards to reduce taxes payable in future years.
Answer (B) is incorrect because the method of accounting for the U.S. investment tax credit is excluded from the scope of SFAS 109. Answer (C) is incorrect because the discounting of income taxes is excluded from the scope of SFAS 109. Answer (D) is incorrect because, with certain exceptions, SFAS 109 does not address accounting for income taxes in interim periods.

10.8 Temporary and Permanent Differences

21. Temporary differences arise when expenses are deductible for tax purposes

	After They Are Recognized in Financial Income	Before They Are Recognized in Financial Income
A.	No	No
B.	No	Yes
C.	Yes	Yes
D.	Yes	No

Answer (C) is correct. *(CPA, adapted)*
REQUIRED: The situations in which temporary differences arise.
DISCUSSION: A temporary difference exists when (1) the reported amount of an asset or liability in the financial statements differs from the tax basis of that asset or liability, and (2) the difference will result in taxable or deductible amounts in future years when the asset is recovered or the liability is settled at its reported amount. A temporary difference may also exist although it cannot be identified with a specific asset or liability recognized for financial reporting purposes. Temporary differences most commonly arise when either expenses or revenues are recognized for tax purposes either earlier or later than in the determination of financial income.

22. Orleans Co., a cash-basis taxpayer, prepares accrual-basis financial statements. In its current year balance sheet, Orleans's deferred income tax liabilities increased compared with those reported for the prior year. Which of the following changes would cause this increase in deferred income tax liabilities?

I. An increase in prepaid insurance
II. An increase in rent receivable
III. An increase in warranty obligations

A. I only.

B. I and II only.

C. II and III only.

D. III only.

Answer (B) is correct. *(CPA, adapted)*
REQUIRED: The change(s) causing an increase in deferred income tax liabilities.
DISCUSSION: An increase in prepaid insurance signifies the recognition of a deduction on the tax return of a cash-basis taxpayer but not in the accrual-basis financial statements. The result is a temporary difference giving rise to taxable amounts in future years when the reported amount of the asset is recovered. An increase in rent receivable involves recognition of revenue in the accrual-basis financial statements but not in the tax return of a cash-basis taxpayer. This temporary difference also will result in future taxable amounts when the asset is recovered. A deferred tax liability records the tax consequences of taxable temporary differences. Hence, these transactions increase deferred tax liabilities. An increase in warranty obligations is a noncash expense recognized in accrual-basis financial statements but not on a modified-cash-basis tax return. The result is a deductible temporary difference and an increase in a deferred tax asset.

23. In its Year 4 income statement, Cere Co. reported income before income taxes of $300,000. Cere estimated that, because of permanent differences, taxable income for Year 4 would be $280,000. During Year 4, Cere made estimated tax payments of $50,000, which were debited to income tax expense. Cere is subject to a 30% tax rate. What amount should Cere report as income tax expense?

A. $34,000

B. $50,000

C. $84,000

D. $90,000

Answer (C) is correct. *(CPA, adapted)*
REQUIRED: The amount to be reported for income tax expense.
DISCUSSION: A permanent difference does not result in a change in a deferred tax asset or liability, that is, in a deferred tax expense or benefit. Thus, income tax expense equals current income tax expense, which is the amount of taxes paid or payable for the year. Income taxes payable for Year 4 equal $84,000 ($280,000 taxable income × 30%).
Answer (A) is incorrect because $34,000 equals the $84,000 of income taxes payable minus the $50,000 of income taxes paid. Answer (B) is incorrect because $50,000 equals income taxes paid, not the total current income tax expense. Answer (D) is incorrect because $90,000 is equal to the reported income of $300,000 times the tax rate.

10.9 Recognition and Measurement of Deferred Income Taxes

24. On its December 31, Year 2, balance sheet, Shin Co. had income taxes payable of $13,000 and a current deferred tax asset of $20,000 before determining the need for a valuation account. Shin had reported a current deferred tax asset of $15,000 at December 31, Year 1. No estimated tax payments were made during Year 2. At December 31, Year 2, Shin determined that it was more likely than not that 10% of the deferred tax asset would not be realized. In its Year 2 income statement, what amount should Shin report as total income tax expense?

A. $8,000

B. $8,500

C. $10,000

D. $13,000

Answer (C) is correct. *(CPA, adapted)*
REQUIRED: The total income tax expense.
DISCUSSION: The deferred tax expense or benefit recognized is the sum of the net changes in the deferred tax assets and deferred tax liabilities. It is aggregated with the current tax expense or benefit to determine the income tax expense for the year. The amount of income taxes payable (current tax expense) is given as $13,000. The deferred tax asset increased by $5,000, but $2,000 ($20,000 × 10%) was determined to be an appropriate credit to an allowance account. Thus, income tax expense for Year 2 is $10,000 [$13,000 current tax expense – ($5,000 increase in the deferred tax asset – $2,000 credit to an allowance account) deferred tax benefit].
Answer (A) is incorrect because $8,000 ignores the balance in the valuation account. Answer (B) is incorrect because $8,500 assumes the balance in the valuation account equals 10% of the Year 2 increase in the deferred tax asset. Answer (D) is incorrect because $13,000 is the amount of current income taxes payable.

25. West Corp. leased a building and received the $36,000 annual rental payment on June 15, Year 4. The beginning of the lease was July 1, Year 4. Rental income is taxable when received. West's tax rates are 30% for Year 4 and 40% thereafter. West had no other permanent or temporary differences. West determined that no valuation allowance was needed. What amount of deferred tax asset should West report in its December 31, Year 4, balance sheet?

A. $5,400

B. $7,200

C. $10,800

D. $14,400

Answer (B) is correct. *(CPA, adapted)*
REQUIRED: The amount of deferred tax asset reported at year-end.
DISCUSSION: The $36,000 rental payment is taxable in full when received in Year 4, but only $18,000 [$36,000 × (6 ÷ 12)] should be recognized in financial accounting income for the year. The result is a deductible temporary difference (deferred tax asset) arising from the difference between the tax basis ($0) of the liability for unearned rent and its reported amount in the year-end balance sheet ($36,000 – $18,000 = $18,000). The income tax payable for Year 4 based on the rental payment is $10,800 ($36,000 × 30% tax rate for Year 4), the deferred tax asset is $7,200 ($18,000 future deductible amount × 40% enacted tax rate applicable after Year 4 when the asset will be realized), and the income tax expense is $3,600 ($10,800 current tax expense – $7,200 deferred tax benefit). The deferred tax benefit equals the net change during the year in the enterprise's deferred tax liabilities and assets ($7,200 deferred tax asset recognized in Year 4 – $0).
Answer (A) is incorrect because $5,400 is based on a 30% tax rate. Answer (C) is incorrect because $10,800 is the income tax payable. Answer (D) is incorrect because $14,400 would be the income tax payable if the 40% tax rate applied in Year 4.

26. Miro Co. began business on January 2, Year 1. Miro used the double-declining balance method of depreciation for financial statement purposes for its building, and the straight-line method for income taxes. On January 16, Year 3, Miro elected to switch to the straight-line method for both financial statement and tax purposes. The building cost $240,000 in Year 1. It had an estimated useful life of 15 years and no salvage value. Information related to the building is as follows:

Year	Double-declining balance depreciation	Straight-line depreciation
1	$30,000	$16,000
2	20,000	16,000

Miro's tax rate is 40%.

Which of the following statements is correct?

A. There should be no reduction in Miro's deferred tax liabilities or deferred tax assets in Year 3.

B. Miro's deferred tax liability should be reduced by $7,200 in Year 3.

C. Miro's deferred tax asset should be reduced by $554 in Year 3.

D. Miro's deferred tax asset should be reduced by $7,200 in Year 3.

Answer (C) is correct. *(CPA, adapted)*
REQUIRED: The accounting for deferred taxes.
DISCUSSION: The difference between the tax basis and the carrying amount of a depreciable asset is a temporary difference (TD). This TD will result in future deductible amounts after Year 2 because more depreciation was recognized in Year 1 and Year 2 for financial-statement purposes than for tax purposes. Thus, after Year 2, the tax basis of the building was $208,000 ($240,000 – $16,000 – $16,000), and its carrying amount was $190,000 ($240,000 – $30,000 – $20,000), a difference of $18,000. The result was a deferred tax asset of $7,200 ($18,000 future deductible amount × 40% tax rate). However, Miro changed to the straight-line depreciation method for tax and financial statements purposes at the beginning of Year 3. Under SFAS 154, *Accounting Changes and Error Corrections*, a change in a method of depreciation is accounted for prospectively as a change in estimate because the change in principle is inseparable from the change in estimate. Hence, Miro will recognize $190,000 of depreciation in its financial statements for the remainder of the building's estimated useful life (13 years, starting in Year 3). During the same period, Miro will deduct $208,000 on its tax return (assuming sufficient taxable income). Miro's depreciation expense for Year 3 is $14,615 ($190,000 ÷ 13 years). The excess tax deduction (assuming sufficient taxable income) is $1,385 ($16,000 – $14,615), so the reduction in the deferred tax asset is $554 ($1,385 × 40%).

Answer (A) is incorrect because use of prospective accounting for the change in depreciation method means that depreciation expense will be less than the tax deduction (assuming sufficient taxable income) for each remaining year of the estimated useful life. The effect in Year 3 is a partial reversal of the deductible TD and a reduction in the deferred tax asset. Answer (B) is incorrect because Miro recognized a deferred tax asset. Answer (D) is incorrect because, prior to SFAS 154, a change in depreciation methods would have been accounted for by a cumulative-effect adjustment recognized through the income statement (debit accumulated depreciation for $18,000, credit deferred tax asset for $7,200, and credit cumulative-effect adjustment for $10,800). Under SFAS 154, however, the carrying amount of the building is not adjusted, and the deferred tax asset is not eliminated.

27. According to SFAS 109, which of the following items should affect current income tax expense for Year 3?

A. Interest on a Year 1 tax deficiency paid in Year 3.

B. Penalty on a Year 1 tax deficiency paid in Year 3.

C. Change in income tax rate for Year 3.

D. Change in income tax rate for Year 4.

Answer (C) is correct. *(CPA, adapted)*
REQUIRED: The item that affects current income tax expense for Year 3.
DISCUSSION: Current tax expense is the amount of income taxes paid or payable for a year as determined by applying the provisions of the enacted tax law to the taxable income for that year.

Answer (A) is incorrect because interest on a Year 1 tax deficiency paid in Year 3 is applicable to Year 1. Answer (B) is incorrect because penalty on a Year 1 tax deficiency paid in Year 3 is applicable to Year 1. Answer (D) is incorrect because a change in income tax rate for Year 4 would affect the deferred tax expense or benefit for Year 3, assuming scheduled effects of a temporary difference will occur in Year 4.

28. Mobe Co. reported the following amounts of taxable income (operating loss) for its first 3 years of operations:

Year 2	$ 300,000
Year 3	(700,000)
Year 4	1,200,000

For each year, Mobe had no temporary differences, and its effective income tax rate was 30% at all relevant times. In its Year 3 income tax return, Mobe elected to carry back the maximum amount of loss possible. Furthermore, Mobe determined that it was more likely than not that the full benefit of any loss carryforward would be realized. In its Year 4 income statement, what amount should Mobe report as total income tax expense?

A. $120,000

B. $150,000

C. $240,000

D. $360,000

Answer (D) is correct. *(CPA, adapted)*
REQUIRED: The total income tax expense.
DISCUSSION: A net operating loss (NOL) may be carried back 2 years (earlier year first) and forward 20 years. Alternatively, the taxpayer may elect to carry the NOL forward only. Given that Mobe's first year of operations was Year 2 and that it elected to carry the NOL back, it could apply $300,000 of the loss (equal to the taxable income for Year 2) to Year 2 and the remaining $400,000 to Year 4. As a result, a deferred tax asset would have been recognized for the future tax benefit of the NOL, but no valuation allowance was necessary because it was not likely that some or all of the tax benefit would not be realized. Thus, in Year 3, Mobe recognized a deferred tax asset (a debit) of $120,000 [($700,000 – $300,000 NOL carryback) NOL carryforward × 30%], a tax refund receivable (a debit) of $90,000 ($300,000 NOL carryback × 30%), and a tax benefit (a credit) of $210,000 ($120,000 + $90,000). In Year 4, Mobe's income tax payable equals $240,000 [($1,200,000 – $400,000 NOL carryforward) × 30%]. Because the benefit of the deferred tax asset is fully realized in Year 4, it is credited for $120,000. Consequently, total income tax expense (the sum of the change in the deferred tax amounts and the current tax paid or payable) is $360,000 ($120,000 + $240,000).

Income tax expense	$360,000	
Income tax payable		$240,000
Deferred tax asset		120,000

Answer (A) is incorrect because $120,000 is the tax benefit (the credit to the deferred tax asset). Answer (B) is incorrect because $150,000 is the income tax payable if the loss is carried forward only. Answer (C) is incorrect because $240,000 is the income tax payable.

29. Rein, Inc. reported deferred tax assets and deferred tax liabilities at the end of both Year 3 and Year 4. According to SFAS 109, for the year ended in Year 4, Rein should report deferred income tax expense or benefit equal to the

A. Sum of the net changes in deferred tax assets and deferred tax liabilities.

B. Decrease in the deferred tax assets.

C. Increase in the deferred tax liabilities.

D. Amount of the income tax liability plus the sum of the net changes in deferred tax assets and deferred tax liabilities.

Answer (A) is correct. *(CPA, adapted)*
REQUIRED: The method of determining deferred income tax expense or benefit.
DISCUSSION: The deferred tax expense or benefit recognized is the sum of the net changes in the deferred tax assets and deferred tax liabilities. The deferred income tax expense or benefit is aggregated with the income taxes currently payable or refundable to determine the amount of income tax expense or benefit for the year to be recorded in the income statement.
Answer (B) is incorrect because the deferred tax liabilities must also be considered. Answer (C) is incorrect because the deferred tax assets must also be considered. Answer (D) is incorrect because this calculation determines the income tax expense or benefit for the year.

10.10 Additional Income Tax Issues

30. Intraperiod income tax allocation arises because

A. Items included in the determination of taxable income may be presented in different sections of the financial statements.

B. Income taxes must be allocated between current and future periods.

C. Certain revenues and expenses appear in the financial statements either before or after they are included in taxable income.

D. Certain revenues and expenses appear in the financial statements but are excluded from taxable income.

Answer (A) is correct. *(CPA, adapted)*
REQUIRED: The accounting reason for intraperiod allocation of income taxes.
DISCUSSION: To provide a fair presentation, SFAS 109 requires that income tax expense for the period be allocated among continuing operations, discontinued operations, extraordinary items, other comprehensive income, and items debited or credited directly to equity.
Answer (B) is incorrect because allocation among periods is interperiod tax allocation. Answer (C) is incorrect because differences in the timing of revenues and expenses for financial statement and tax return purposes create the need for interperiod income tax allocation. Answer (D) is incorrect because permanent differences do not create a need for tax allocation.

31. Last year, before providing for taxes, Ajax Company had income from continuing operations of $930,000 and an extraordinary gain of $104,000. The current effective tax rate on continuing operations income was 40% and the total tax liability was $398,000 ignoring any temporary differences. The amount of the extraordinary gain net of tax effect was

A. $41,600

B. $62,400

C. $78,000

D. $104,000

Answer (C) is correct. *(Publisher, adapted)*
REQUIRED: The extraordinary gain net of tax effect.
DISCUSSION: Given that the effective tax rate for continuing operations was 40%, the related tax expense was $372,000 ($930,000 × 40%). Because the total tax liability was $398,000, $26,000 ($398,000 – $372,000) was applicable to the extraordinary item. Accordingly, the extraordinary gain net of tax effect was $78,000 ($104,000 – $26,000).
Answer (A) is incorrect because $41,600 results from multiplying the extraordinary gain times the effective tax rate. Answer (B) is incorrect because $62,400 results from subtracting the extraordinary gain times the effective tax rate from the extraordinary gain. Answer (D) is incorrect because $104,000 results from not accounting for the tax effect.

32. On September 15, Year 4, the county in which Spirit Company operates enacted changes in the county's tax law. These changes are to become effective on January 1, Year 5. They will have a material effect on the deferred tax accounts that Spirit reported in accordance with SFAS 109. In which of the following interim and annual financial statements issued by Spirit should the effect of the changes in tax law initially be reported?

A. The interim financial statements for the 3-month period ending September 30, Year 4.

B. The annual financial statements for the year ending December 31, Year 4.

C. The interim financial statements for the 3-month period ending March 31, Year 5.

D. The annual financial statements for the year ending December 31, Year 5.

Answer (A) is correct. *(Publisher, adapted)*
REQUIRED: The financial statements in which the effects of a change in tax law should initially be reported.
DISCUSSION: When a change in the tax law or rates occurs, the effect of the change on a deferred tax liability or asset is recognized as an adjustment in the period that includes the enactment date of the change. The adjustment is allocated to income from continuing operations in the first financial statements issued for the period that includes the enactment date.

33. The manner of reporting the tax benefit of an operating loss carryforward or carryback is determined by the source of the

A. Income or loss in the current year.

B. Expected future income that will result in realization of a deferred tax asset for an operating loss carryforward from the current year.

C. Operating loss carryforward in a prior year.

D. Taxes paid in a prior year.

Answer (A) is correct. *(Publisher, adapted)*
REQUIRED: The reporting of a loss carryforward or carryback.
DISCUSSION: For purposes of intraperiod tax allocation, SFAS 109, with certain exceptions, requires that the tax benefit of an operating loss carryforward be reported in the same manner as the source of the income offset by the carryforward in the current year. Similarly, the tax benefit of an operating loss carryback is reported in the same manner as the source of the current-year loss.

34. Because Jab Co. uses different methods to depreciate equipment for financial statement and income tax purposes, Jab has temporary differences that will reverse during the next year and add to taxable income. Deferred income taxes that are based on these temporary differences should be classified in Jab's balance sheet as a

A. Contra account to current assets.

B. Contra account to noncurrent assets.

C. Current liability.

D. Noncurrent liability.

Answer (D) is correct. *(CPA, adapted)*
REQUIRED: The classification of deferred income taxes based on temporary differences.
DISCUSSION: These temporary differences arise from use of an accelerated depreciation method for tax purposes. Future taxable amounts reflecting the difference between the tax basis and the reported amount of the asset will result when the reported amount is recovered. Accordingly, Jab must recognize a deferred tax liability to record the tax consequences of these temporary differences. This liability is noncurrent because the related asset (equipment) is noncurrent (SFAS 109).
Answer (A) is incorrect because a liability is not shown as an offset to assets and it is not current. Answer (B) is incorrect because a liability is not shown as an offset to assets. Answer (C) is incorrect because the classification of a deferred tax liability should not be determined by the reversal date of the temporary differences unless it is not related to an asset or liability for financial reporting.

35. Thorn Co. applies SFAS 109. At the end of Year 4, the tax effects of temporary differences were as follows:

	Deferred Tax Assets (Liabilities)	Related Asset Classification
Accelerated tax depreciation	($75,000)	Noncurrent asset
Additional costs in inventory for tax purposes	25,000	Current asset
	($50,000)	

A valuation allowance was not considered necessary. Thorn anticipates that $10,000 of the deferred tax liability will reverse in Year 5. In Thorn's December 31, Year 4, balance sheet, what amount should Thorn report as noncurrent deferred tax liability?

A. $40,000

B. $50,000

C. $65,000

D. $75,000

Answer (D) is correct. *(CPA, adapted)*
REQUIRED: The noncurrent deferred tax liability.
DISCUSSION: In a classified balance sheet, deferred tax assets and liabilities are separated into current and noncurrent amounts. Classification as current or noncurrent is based on the classification of the related asset or liability. Because the $75,000 deferred tax liability is related to a noncurrent asset, it should be classified as noncurrent.
Answer (A) is incorrect because $40,000 equals the $50,000 net deferred tax liability minus the $10,000 expected to reverse in Year 5. Answer (B) is incorrect because $50,000 equals the net deferred tax liability. Answer (C) is incorrect because $65,000 equals the $75,000 noncurrent deferred tax liability minus the $10,000 expected to reverse in Year 5.

Use Gleim's **CPA Test Prep** CD-Rom/Pocket PC for interactive testing with over 4,000 additional questions!

10.11 PRACTICE SIMULATION

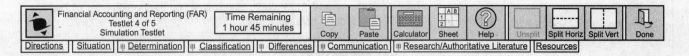

Financial Accounting and Reporting (FAR) Testlet 4 of 5 Simulation Testlet	Time Remaining 1 hour 45 minutes	Copy Paste Calculator Sheet Help Unsplit Split Horiz Split Vert Done

Directions | Situation | ‖ Determination | ‖ Classification | ‖ Differences | ‖ Communication | ‖ Research/Authoritative Literature | Resources

1. Directions

In the following simulation, you will be asked to complete various tasks. You may use the content in the **Information Tabs** to complete the tasks in the **Work Tabs**.

Information Tabs:

Directions	Resources

FIG 1

- Go through each of the **Information Tabs** to familiarize yourself with the simulation content
- The **Resources** tab will contain information, including formulas and definitions, that may help you to complete the tasks
- Your simulation may have more **Information Tabs** than those shown in Fig. 1

Work Tabs:

‖ SysTrust | ‖ Engagement Letter | ‖ Authoritative Sources | ‖ Communication

FIG. 2

- **Work Tabs**, to the right of **Information Tabs**, contain the tasks for you to complete
- **Work Tabs** contain directions for completing each task - be sure to read these directions carefully
- The tab names in Fig. 2 are for illustration only - yours may differ
- Once you complete any part of a task, the pencil for that tab will be shaded (see **Communication** in Fig. 2)
- The shaded pencil does **NOT** indicate that you have completed the entire task
- You must complete all of the tasks in the **Work Tabs** to receive full credit

Research/Authoritative Literature Tab:

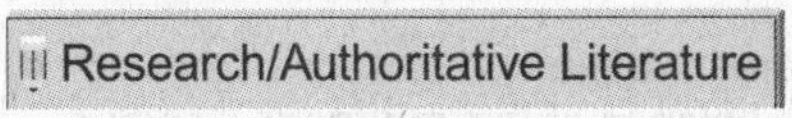

‖ Research/Authoritative Literature

FIG. 3

- This tab contains both the Research task and the Authoritative Literature
- Detailed instructions for completing the Research task, and for using the Authoritative Literature, appear on this tab
- You may use the Authoritative Literature as a resource for completing other tasks

NOTE: If you believe you have encountered a software malfunction, report it to the test center staff immediately.

2. Situation

Presented below is the unaudited balance sheet as of December 31, Year 2, as prepared by the bookkeeper of Zed Manufacturing Corp., a firm not required to report under federal securities law.

Zed Manufacturing Corp.
BALANCE SHEET
For the Year Ended December 31, Year 2

Assets		Liabilities and Equity	
Cash	$ 225,000	Accounts payable	$ 133,800
Accounts receivable (net)	345,700	Mortgage payable	900,000
Inventories	560,000	Notes payable	500,000
Prepaid income taxes	40,000	Lawsuit liability	80,000
Investments	57,700	Income taxes payable	61,200
Land	450,000	Deferred tax liability	28,000
Building	1,750,000	Accumulated depreciation	420,000
Machinery and equipment	1,964,000	Total liabilities	$2,123,000
Goodwill	37,000	Common stock, $50 par;	
Total assets	$5,429,400	40,000 shares issued	2,231,000
		Retained earnings	1,075,400
		Total equity	$3,306,400
		Total liabilities and equity	$5,429,400

Your firm has been engaged to perform an audit, during which the following data are found:

- Checks totaling $14,000 in payment of accounts payable were mailed on December 30, Year 2, but were not recorded until Year 3. Late in December Year 2, the bank returned a customer's $2,000 check, marked "NSF," but no entry was made. Cash includes $100,000 restricted for building purposes.

- Included in accounts receivable is a $30,000 note due on December 31, Year 5, from Zed's president.

- During Year 2, Zed purchased 500 shares of common stock of a major corporation that supplies Zed with raw materials. Total cost of this stock was $51,300, and fair value on December 31, Year 2, was $47,000. The decline in fair value is considered temporary. Zed plans to hold these shares indefinitely.

- Treasury stock was recorded at cost when Zed purchased 200 of its own shares for $32 per share in May Year 2. This amount is included in investments.

- On December 30, Year 2, Zed borrowed $500,000 from a bank in exchange for a 10% note payable, maturing December 30, Year 7. Equal principal payments are due December 30 of each year, beginning in Year 3. This note is collateralized by a $250,000 tract of land acquired for speculative purposes. This tract is included in the land account.

- The mortgage payable requires $50,000 principal payments, plus interest, at the end of each month. Payments were made on January 31 and February 28, Year 3. The balance of this mortgage was due June 30, Year 3. On March 1, Year 3, prior to issuance of the audited financial statements, Zed consummated a noncancelable agreement with the lender to refinance this mortgage. The new terms require $100,000 annual principal payments, plus interest, on February 28 of each year, beginning in Year 4. The final payment is due February 28, Year 11.

- The lawsuit liability will be paid in Year 3.

- The following is an analysis of the deferred tax liability at December 31, Year 2:

Deferred tax liability -- depreciation	$48,000
Deferred tax asset -- lawsuit liability	(20,000)
Net deferred tax liability	$28,000

$25,000 of the deferred taxes related to depreciation will reverse in Year 3.

- The current income tax expense reported in Zed's Year 2 income statement was $61,200.

- The company was authorized to issue 100,000 shares of $50 par value common stock.

Additional Information:

One of Zed's manufacturing plants is located in a foreign country. This plant is threatened with expropriation. Expropriation is deemed to be reasonably possible. Any compensation from the foreign government would be less than the carrying amount of the plant.

3. Determination of Balances

This question is presented in a spreadsheet format that requires you to fill in the correct responses in the shaded cells provided. For each of the following accounts, calculate the amount that Zed Manufacturing Corp. will report on its corrected classified balance sheet as of December 31, Year 2.

Account	Amount
1. Cash	
2. Accounts receivable	
3. Long-term investments	
4. Land	
5. Accounts payable	
6. Income taxes payable	
7. Common stock	
8. Deferred tax liability	
9. Cost of treasury stock	

4. Classification

This set of questions has a matching format. Select the best match for each numbered item from the terms in the drop-down list and write its letter in the column provided. Each choice may be used once, more than once, or not at all. Indicate whether each of the following is a current liability, noncurrent liability, or other item.

Item	Answer
1. An appropriation of retained earnings	
2. A long-term obligation that will become callable by the creditor within 1 year because of a violation of a debt covenant	
3. Current maturity of a long-term debt	
4. Pension benefits to be paid at the beginning of the next period from the pension fund	
5. Short-term obligations to be refinanced, given an ability to consummate the refinancing	
6. Trade accounts payable	
7. An accommodation endorsement on a demand note issued by an affiliated entity	
8. A cash dividend declared before the balance sheet date when the date of record is subsequent to the balance sheet date	
9. Unfunded past service costs of a pension plan to the extent that the benefits have not vested and the costs have not been charted to operations	
10. Dividends in arrears on cumulative preferred stock	

Choices
A) Current liability
B) Noncurrent liability
C) Other item

5. Temporary and Permanent Differences

This question is presented in a check-the-box format that requires you to select the correct responses from a given list. For each of the following, determine whether the explanation of the situation results in a temporary or permanent difference for the purpose of accounting for income taxes.

	Difference	
Situation	**Temporary**	**Permanent**
1. A warranty liability recognized as an expense in financial income when a product is sold and recognized in taxable income when the expenditures are made in a future period.		
2. A receivable from a nondealer installment sale recognized at the time of sale in financial income and at the time of collection in taxable income.		
3. An asset depreciates more quickly for tax purposes than for financial reporting purposes.		
4. Percentage depletion of certain natural resources.		
5. The insurance premiums paid by a beneficiary entity on policies covering its corporate officers.		
6. Subscriptions revenue received in advance that is recognized in taxable income when received and in financial income when earned in a later period.		

6. Communication

In a memorandum to your client, explain the rationale for interperiod tax allocation and the nature of temporary and permanent differences. Contrast intraperiod tax allocation. Type your communication in your word processor program and print out the copy in a memorandum-style format.

REMINDER: Your response will be graded for both technical content and writing skills. Technical content will be evaluated for information that is helpful to the intended reader and clearly relevant to the issue. Writing skills will be evaluated for development, organization, and the appropriate expression of ideas in professional correspondence. Use a standard business memo or letter format with a clear beginning, middle, and end. Do not convey information in the form of a table, bullet point list, or other abbreviated presentation.

     To: Client
     From: CPA
     Subject: Interperiod and intraperiod tax allocation

---

7. Research/Authoritative Literature

See page 12 in the Introduction of this book for a detailed explanation of the AICPA's new Research/Authoritative Literature work tab as well as a screenshot of how the tab will actually look on your exam.

Research and cite the paragraph in the FASB Current Text or Original Pronouncements that explains which principles apply to the classification of obligations that are callable by the creditor.

Unofficial Answers

3. Determination of Balances (9 Gradable Items)

1. **$109,000.**

Cash (unaudited)	$ 225,000
Unrecorded checks in payment of accounts payable	(14,000)
NSF check not recorded	(2,000)
Cash restricted for building purposes (should be reported in other assets)	(100,000)
Corrected balance	$ 109,000

2. **$317,700.**

Net accounts receivable (unaudited)	$345,000
Charge-back for NSF check	2,000
Officer's note receivable (should be reported in other assets)	(30,000)
Corrected balance	$317,700

3. **$297,000.**

Investments (unaudited)	$ 57,700
Land acquired for speculation	250,000
Treasury stock (should be reported as a deduction from total equity)	(6,400)
Unrealized holding loss ($51,300 – $47,000)	
(erroneously reported in accumulated other comprehensive income)	(4,300)
Corrected balance	$297,000

4. **$200,000.**

Land (unaudited)	$ 450,000
Land acquired for speculation (should be reported in investments)	(250,000)
Corrected balance	$ 200,000

5. **$119,800.**

Accounts payable (unaudited)	$133,800
Unrecorded payments (checks mailed 12/30/Year 2)	(14,000)
Corrected balance	$119,800

6. **$21,200.**

Income taxes payable (unaudited)	$ 61,200
Prepaid income taxes	(40,000)
Corrected balance	$ 21,200

7. **$2,000,000.**

Common stock (unaudited)	$2,231,000
Additional paid-in capital in excess of par value	(231,000)
Corrected balance	$2,000,000

8. **$48,000.** The deferred tax liability is noncurrent because it relates to a depreciable (noncurrent) asset. Current and noncurrent deferred tax amounts are not offset.

9. **$(6,400).** Treasury stock (properly reported as a reduction of total equity).

4. Classification (10 Gradable Items)

1. C) Other Item. An appropriation of retained earnings is presented in an equity account. Its sole purpose is disclosure. The account is established with a credit, and retained earnings is debited. The effect is to reduce retained earnings available for dividend payments.

2. A) Current liability. Current liabilities include an obligation that is or will be callable by the creditor within 1 year because a violation of a debt covenant makes it callable, or because the violation, if not cured, will make it callable. However, if cure is probable or the creditor has lost the right to demand repayment, classification as current may not be appropriate.

3. A) Current liability. Current maturity of a long-term debt customarily requires expenditure of current assets. Thus, it is treated as a current liability with certain exceptions; e.g., it is to be retired using assets accumulated for that purpose that are not classified as current, or it is to be refinanced.

4. C) Other Item. Future payments from a pension fund are not reflected as liabilities. They are recorded as decreases in the fund balance of the pension fund, a separate accounting entity.

5. B) Noncurrent liability. The portion of debt scheduled to mature in the following fiscal year ordinarily should be classified as a current liability. However, if an enterprise intends to refinance short-term obligations on a long-term basis and demonstrates an ability to consummate the refinancing, the obligation should be excluded from current liabilities and classified as noncurrent.

6. A) Current Liability. Trade accounts payable that will require the use of current assets or the creation of other current liabilities are current liabilities. In general, current liabilities include obligations for items that have entered into the operating cycle.

7. C) Other Item. An endorsement would not give rise to a liability until the maker of the note defaulted.

8. A) Current Liability. A cash dividend that is declared and will be paid in the subsequent year is a current liability. It will decrease current assets.

9. C) Other Item. Such pension costs are not expensed or otherwise recorded as liabilities. As they are expensed, they become liabilities that are usually noncurrent.

10. C) Other Item. Preferred dividends in arrears are not accrued as a liability until they have been declared.

5. Temporary and Permanent Differences (6 Gradable Items)

1. Temporary. The reported amount of the warranty liability exceeds its tax basis. The result will be a deductible amount in the future when the liability is settled. This deductible temporary difference results in a deferred tax asset.

2. Temporary. The reported amount of the asset exceeds its tax basis. The result will be a taxable amount when the asset is recovered. This taxable temporary difference results in a deferred tax liability.

3. Temporary. The reported amount of a depreciable asset subject to accelerated tax depreciation exceeds its tax basis. The result will be a future taxable amount when the asset is recovered. This taxable temporary difference results in a deferred tax liability.

4. Permanent. Cost depletion, which is a function of the cost basis of the asset, is permitted on the tax return and the financial statements. Percentage depletion is an additional deduction that is a function of the gross income from the property. It is recognized in the determination of taxable income but is never recognized in the determination of financial income. Because percentage depletion has no deferred tax consequences, it results in a permanent difference, and no deferred tax asset or liability arises.

5. Permanent. Insurance premiums paid by a beneficiary entity on policies covering its corporate officers are not deductible for tax purposes. Hence, the difference is permanent.

6. Temporary. A future deductible amount relating to a revenue or gain that is taxable before it is recognized in net income is a temporary difference resulting in a deferred tax asset.

6. Communication (5 Gradable Items; for grading instructions, please refer to page 12.)

Tax consequences are a transaction's or an event's effects on current and deferred income taxes. Income taxes currently payable or refundable for a particular year usually include the tax consequences of most of the events recognized in the financial statements for the same year. However, certain significant exceptions exist. As a result, the tax consequences of some transactions or events may be recognized in income taxes currently payable or refundable in a year different from that in which their financial-statement effects are recognized. The reason for these temporary differences is that the accrual basis of accounting is used in financial statements and the modified cash basis is used on income tax returns. Moreover, some transactions or events result in permanent differences because they have tax consequences or financial-statement effects but never both. Because of these differences, income taxes currently payable or refundable may differ from (exceed or be less than) income tax expense or benefit. The accounting for these differences is interperiod tax allocation.

Accordingly, accrual accounting should recognize taxes payable or refundable for the current year. It also should recognize deferred tax liabilities and assets for the future tax consequences of events that have been previously recognized in the enterprise's financial statements or tax returns.

A temporary difference (TD) is the difference between the tax basis of an asset or liability and its reported amount in the financial statements that will result in taxable or deductible amounts in future years. This definition rests on the assumption that the assets and liabilities reported in conformity with GAAP will ultimately be recovered or settled, respectively. For example, a future taxable amount and a taxable TD will result from recovery of an asset related to a revenue or gain that is taxable subsequent to being recognized in financial income. A future taxable amount also results from the recovery of an asset related to any expense or loss that is deductible for tax purposes prior to being recognized in financial income. A future deductible amount and a deductible TD results from the settlement of a liability related to an expense or loss that is deductible for tax purposes subsequent to being recognized in financial income. A future deductible amount also results from the settlement of a liability related to a revenue or gain that is taxable prior to being recognized in financial income. TDs also may result from events that have been recognized in the financial statements and will result in taxable or deductible amounts in future years but that cannot be identified with a particular asset or liability for financial reporting purposes. A TD relates to an asset or liability if its reduction causes reversal of the TD.

A permanent difference is an event that is recognized either in pretax financial income or in taxable income but never in both. It does not result in a deferred tax asset or liability.

SFAS 109 requires intraperiod tax allocation. Income tax expense (benefit) is allocated to continuing operations, discontinued operations, extraordinary items, other comprehensive income, and items debited or credited directly to equity. Unlike interperiod tax allocation, intraperiod tax allocation does not affect income tax expense or benefit for the year.

7. Research/Authoritative Literature (1 Gradable Item)

Answer: FAS 78, Par. 5

FAS 78 -- *Classification of Obligations That Are Callable by the Creditor*

5. The following sentences and footnotes are added to the end of paragraph 7 of ARB 43, Ch. 3A:

The current liability classification is also intended to include obligations that, by their terms, are due on demand or will be due on demand within one year (or operating cycle, if longer) from the balance sheet date, even though liquidation may not be expected within that period. It is also intended to include long-term obligations that are or will be callable by the creditor either because the debtor's violation of a provision of the debt agreement at the balance sheet date makes the obligation callable or because the violation, if not cured within a specified grace period, will make the obligation callable. Accordingly, such callable obligations shall be classified as current liabilities unless one of the following conditions is met:

a.   The creditor has waived or subsequently lost the right to demand repayment for more than one year (or operating cycle, if longer) from the balance sheet date.

b.   For long-term obligations containing a grace period within which the debtor may cure the violation, it is probable that the violation will be cured within that period, thus preventing the obligation from becoming callable.

If an obligation under (b) above is classified as a long-term liability (or, in the case of an unclassified balance sheet, is included as a long-term liability in the disclosure of debt maturities), the circumstances shall be disclosed. Short-term obligations that are expected to be refinanced on a long-term basis, including those callable obligations discussed herein, shall be classified in accordance with SFAS 6, *Classification of Short-Term Obligations Expected to be Refinanced*.

Scoring Schedule

	Correct Responses		Gradable Items		Weights		
Tab 3	_____	÷	9	×	20%	=	_____
Tab 4	_____	÷	10	×	20%	=	_____
Tab 5	_____	÷	6	×	15%	=	_____
Tab 6	_____	÷	5	×	30%	=	_____
Tab 7	_____	÷	1	×	15%	=	_____
							(Your Score)

Use Gleim's *CPA Gleim Online* to practice more simulations in a realistic environment.

STUDY UNIT ELEVEN
EMPLOYEE BENEFITS

(16 pages of outline)

This study unit emphasizes accounting for pensions. Postretirement benefits other than pensions are accounted for in a very similar manner. The remainder of the study unit addresses compensated absences and share-based payment.

11.1 PENSIONS

Types of Plans

1. Pension cost is a component of employee compensation. SFAS 87, *Employers' Accounting for Pensions*, defines accounting for pension expense. It was amended by SFAS 158, *Employers' Accounting for Defined Benefit Pension and Other Postretirement Plans*. A **pension plan** is a separate accounting entity to which a sponsoring employer makes contributions. It invests the assets and makes payments to beneficiaries (but the assets and liabilities are the employer's). The following are the two basic types of pension plans:

   a. In a **defined contribution plan**, the employer makes no guarantee as to the amount of benefits the employee will receive during retirement. The employer only makes periodic deposits into an investment of the employee's choosing during the period of employment. The ultimate benefits received by the retiree are based on his or her investment decisions. The accounting for a defined contribution plan is simple.

      1) The employer's **annual pension cost** is the amount paid into the employee pension trust. The employer reports an asset only if the contribution is greater than the defined, required contribution. The employer reports a liability only if the contribution is less than the required amount.

   b. In a **defined benefit plan**, the employer guarantees to all qualifying employees upon retirement a certain periodic payment based on the employee's salary history. Because the exact amount of the future payouts is unknown, estimates must be made. The accounting for a defined benefit plan is complex.

      1) The defined benefit plan is a **separate accounting entity** with its own set of books. Each year, entities with defined benefit plans must recognize pension expense, the funding provided, and any unfunded liability.

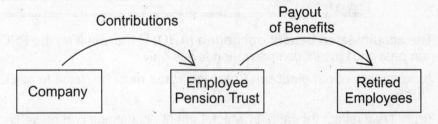

Employers' Accounting for Pensions (SFAS 87)

2. SFAS 87 applies to any arrangement that is similar in substance to a pension plan. It applies regardless of form, the method of financing, or whether the plan is written or implied by the well-defined practice of paying postretirement benefits.

3. The fundamental assumption is that a defined benefit pension plan is part of an **employee's compensation** incurred when the services provided to the employer by the employee are rendered.

4. The defined pension benefit is provided in the form of **deferred payments** that are not precisely determinable.

   a. These payments can only be estimated based on the plan benefit formula and relevant future events, such as future compensation levels, mortality rates, ages at retirement, and vesting considerations.

5. SFAS 87 permits the delayed recognition of certain events, the reporting of a net cost, and the offsetting of assets and liabilities.

   a. **Delayed recognition** means that certain changes in the pension obligation and in the value of the plan assets are not recognized as they occur. They are recognized on a systematic and gradual basis over subsequent accounting periods.

   b. Reporting of **net cost** means that various pension costs are reflected in the income statement as one annual pension expense.

   c. The **offsetting** feature means that the recognized values of the plan assets contributed to the plan are offset in the statement of financial position against the recognized liabilities.

Pension Benefit Obligations

6. The **vested benefit obligation (VBO)** is the actuarial present value of pension benefits employees have a right to receive regardless of future employment or future salary levels.

7. The **projected benefit obligation (PBO)** as of a certain date is equal to the actuarial present value of all benefits attributed by the **pension benefit formula** to employee services rendered prior to that date. The **measurement date** for benefit obligations and plan assets is generally the balance sheet date. The PBO is measured using assumptions about future as well as past and current salary levels.

   a. The **PBO at the end of a period** equals the following:

   $$
   \begin{array}{l}
   + \text{ Beginning PBO} \\
   + \text{ Service cost} \\
   + \text{ Interest cost} \\
   + \text{ Prior service cost} \\
   - \text{ Prior service credit} \\
   - \text{ Benefits paid} \\
   \pm \text{ Changes in the PBO resulting from (a) experience different from that assumed or} \\
   \quad \text{ (b) changes in assumptions} \\
   \hline
   \text{Ending PBO}
   \end{array}
   $$

8. The **accumulated benefit obligation (ABO)** is the same as the PBO except that it is based on past and current compensation levels only.

9. Assumptions about **discount (interest) rates** must be made to calculate the PBO and the ABO.

   a. They reflect the rates at which benefit obligations can be settled. In estimating these rates, it is appropriate to consider current prices of **annuity contracts** that could be used to settle pension obligations as well as the rates on high-quality fixed investments.

Plan Assets

10. These assets are invested by a trustee and are not reported on the employer's balance sheet.

11. Plan assets change as a result of

    a. The return on investments
    b. Benefit payments
    c. Contributions from the employer

Pension Expense

12. One objective of accounting for defined benefit pensions is to recognize the expense of providing these postretirement benefits over employees' service periods. Another objective is to relate that expense more directly to the terms of the pension plan.

13. The **required minimum** annual pension expense consists of the following elements:

+	Service cost
+	Interest cost
−	**Expected** return on plan assets
−/+	**Amortization** of net gain or loss
−/+	**Amortization** of prior service cost or credit
	Pension expense

    a. **Service cost** is the present value of the future benefits earned by the employees in the current period (as calculated according to the plan's benefit formula). This amount is a portion of the PBO and is calculated by the plan's actuary. (It will always be given on the exam.) It is unaffected by the funded status of the plan.

       1) Service cost for the year increases pension expense.

    b. **Interest cost** is the increase in the PBO resulting from the passage of time. It is determined by multiplying the PBO at the beginning of the year by the **current discount rate** (e.g., the interest rate at which annuities could be purchased to settle pension obligations).

       1) This discount rate may change with changes in interest rates.
       2) The PBO and the discount rate are provided by the plan's actuary.
       3) Interest cost increases pension expense.

    c. **Return on Plan Assets**

       1) The return on plan assets (if positive) **decreases pension expense**.
       2) The **actual return on plan assets** is based on the **fair value of the plan assets** at the beginning and end of the accounting period, with adjustments for contributions and payments.

+	Fair value – end of period
−	Fair value – beginning of period
−	Contributions to plan assets
+	Benefits paid
	Actual return on plan assets

       3) The **expected return on plan assets** is the **market-related value of plan assets (MRV)** at the beginning of the period multiplied by the **expected long-term rate of return**.

          Expected return = MRV × Long-term rate

          a) MRV may be either **fair value or a calculated value** that recognizes changes in fair value systematically and rationally over not more than 5 years, such as a 5-year moving average.

    b)   Spreading recognition of the changes in fair value over as long as 5 years reduces the volatility of pension expense. For example, an employer may recognize 20% of the last 5 years' gains and losses each year.

4)   The **differences** between the actual and expected returns are **asset gains and losses**. They are not required to be amortized until they are included in MRV.

    a)   **Gains and losses** (including asset gains and losses not in MRV) are **not required** to be recognized in pension expense of the **period in which they occur**.

5)   Thus, the required minimum pension expense reflects the **expected**, not the actual, **return on plan assets**. The current asset gain or loss, that is, the difference between the actual and expected returns, may be deferred.

6)   The following is the entry to record annual service cost, interest cost, and expected return on plan assets (assuming service cost and interest cost are unfunded and their sum is greater than the expected return):

Pension expense	$XXX	
Deferred tax asset	XXX	
Deferred tax benefit – net income		$XXX
Pension liability		XXX

d.   **Gains and losses** may be realized or unrealized. They arise from changes in the amount of the PBO or plan assets that result from (1) experience different from that expected (asset gains and losses) and (2) changes in actuarial assumptions (what actuaries call **liability gains and losses**).

1)   Gains and losses not recognized in pension expense must be recognized in **other comprehensive income (OCI)**, net of tax, when they occur. (**NOTE:** OCI is a nominal account that is closed to accumulated OCI, a real account, at the end of the period.)

    a)   For example, a loss not recognized in pension expense is recorded as follows:

OCI	$XXX	
Deferred tax asset	XXX	
Deferred tax benefit – OCI		$XXX
Pension liability		XXX

2)   SFAS 87 adopts a **corridor approach** to reduce the volatility of the pension expense caused by gains and losses.

    a)   The **net gain or loss included in accumulated OCI** (excluding asset gains and losses not reflected in MRV) is subject to **required amortization** in pension expense. However, only the amount that exceeds (at the beginning of the year) 10% of the greater of the PBO or the MRV must be amortized.

b) The minimum required amortization equals the excess described above divided by the **average remaining service period** of active employees expected to receive benefits.

EXAMPLE

At January 1, Year 1, Penco's PBO was $1,200,000, and the market-related value of plan assets (MRV) was $880,000. The MRV reflected 80% of the $200,000 net asset loss included in accumulated OCI, and the average remaining service period is 10 years. Amortization is calculated as follows:

Net asset loss at 1/1/Year 1	$ 200,000
Asset loss not in MRV at 1/1/Year 1	
[$200,000 × (1.0 − .8)]	(40,000)
Amortizable asset loss	$ 160,000
Corridor (10% of greater of PBO	
or MRV at 1/1/Year 1	(120,000)
Net loss outside of corridor	$ 40,000
1 ÷ 10 years	× .1
Amortization	$ 4,000

---

c) Amortization of a net gain (loss) decreases (increases) pension expense.

d) OCI is debited (credited), net of tax, each period for required amortization of net gain (loss) arising in prior periods. The following is the entry for **amortization of a net loss** arising in a prior period [see 13.d.1)a) on the previous page]:

Pension expense	$XXX	
Deferred tax benefit – OCI	XXX	
Deferred tax benefit – net income		$XXX
OCI		XXX

e. **Amortization of prior service cost or credit.** If a plan is amended to grant **additional benefits** for past service, the cost is allocated to the future periods of service of employees active at the date of the amendment who are expected to receive benefits.

1) The cost of retroactive benefits is an **increase in the PBO**. This cost is **debited to OCI**, net of tax, at the amendment date. The entry is

OCI	$XXX	
Deferred tax asset	XXX	
Deferred tax benefit – OCI		$XXX
Pension liability		XXX

2) **Prior service cost** is amortized as part of pension expense by assigning an equal amount to each future period of service of each qualifying employee. OCI is credited, net of tax, each period for **required amortization** of prior service cost. The entry is

Pension expense	$XXX	
Deferred tax benefit – OCI	XXX	
Deferred tax benefit – net income		$XXX
OCI		XXX

3) To reduce the burden of allocation computations, any **alternative approach** (e.g., straight-line) that more rapidly amortizes the cost is acceptable. This alternative must be applied consistently.

EXAMPLE

At the start of its current fiscal year, Cannon Co. amended its defined benefit pension plan, resulting in an increase of $200,000 in the PBO. Cannon had 20 employees on the date of the amendment. Five employees are expected to leave at the end of each of the next 4 years (including the current year). Hence, the total service years expected to be rendered during the 4-year period equal 50 (20 + 15 + 10 + 5). The amortization fraction for the first year is therefore 20 ÷ 50. The minimum amortization equals the amount of the increase in the PBO multiplied by the amortization fraction. Accordingly, Cannon's minimum amortization for the first year is $80,000 [$200,000 × (20 ÷ 50)].

---

4) A plan amendment that retroactively reduces benefits decreases the PBO. This decrease **(prior service credit)** is **credited to OCI**, net of tax.

a) First, it is used to reduce any prior service cost in accumulated OCI.

b) Second, any remaining prior service credit is amortized as part of pension expense on the same basis as prior service cost.

Recognition of Funded Status

14. If the **PBO is overfunded** (fair value of plan assets > PBO), the excess must be recognized in the balance sheet as an **asset**.

15. If the **PBO is underfunded** (PBO > fair value of plan assets), the deficit must be recognized in the balance sheet as a **liability**.

16. If the employer has **multiple plans**, the aggregate overfunding for the **overfunded plans** is recognized as a noncurrent asset. The aggregate underfunding for all **underfunded plans** is recognized as a liability as follows:

a. A **current liability** is recognized for the amount by which the benefits payable by an underfunded plan over the next 12 months (or longer operating cycle) exceed the fair value of plan assets. The remainder is a noncurrent liability.

17. A **temporary difference** may arise from recognition of an asset or liability reflecting the funded status of a plan. Any **deferred tax effects** are recognized in income tax expense (benefit) and allocated to OCI and other financial statement components.

18. The balances of net gains (losses), prior service costs (credits), and the net transition amount in **accumulated OCI** are adjusted and reported in **OCI** when

a. The net gains (losses), etc., are amortized as part of pension expense, or

b. A new determination of funded status of the plan is made

19. **Not-for-profit organizations.** The foregoing outlines also apply to NPOs or other entities that do not report OCI.

a. Thus, the **funded status** of an employer-NPO's plan should be recognized as an asset or liability. Changes in the funded status are recognized as changes in the NPO's **unrestricted net assets**.

Pension Accounting under SFAS 87 and SFAS 158

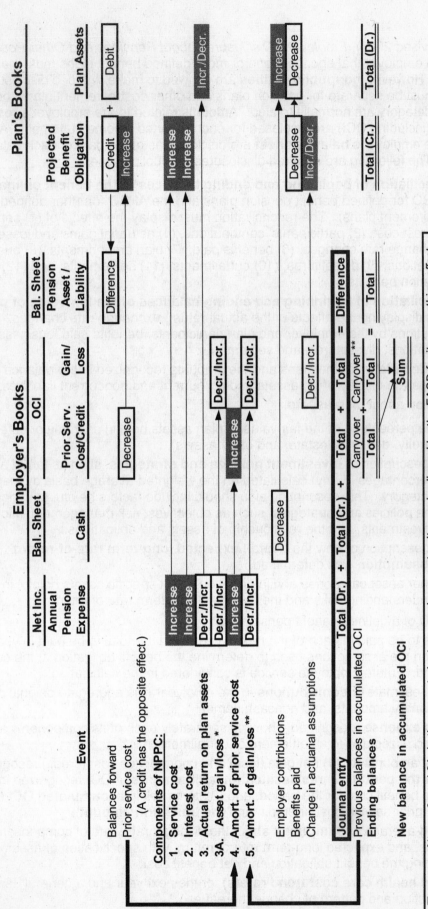

Disclosures

20. **SFAS 132 (revised 2003),** *Employers' Disclosures about Pensions and Other Postretirement Benefits.* An employer that sponsors one or more defined benefit plans must make certain disclosures. However, **nonpublic entities** are allowed to make reduced disclosures. Disclosure must be separate for pension plans and other postretirement plans, but amounts within each category are normally totaled. Amounts related to the employer's **results of operations** (including OCI) are disclosed for each reported income statement. Amounts related to the employer's **balance sheet** are disclosed as of the date of each balance sheet presented. The following are required disclosures for public entities:

   a. A **reconciliation of beginning and ending balances of the benefit obligation** (the PBO for defined benefit pension plans and the APBO for other defined benefit postretirement plans). The reconciliation must display the effects of (1) service cost, (2) interest cost, (3) participants' contributions, (4) actuarial gains and losses, (5) exchange rate changes, (6) benefits paid, (7) plan amendments, (8) business combinations, (9) divestitures, (10) curtailments, (11) settlements, and (12) special termination benefits.

   b. A **reconciliation of beginning and ending balances of the fair value of plan assets** displaying the effects of the actual return, exchange rate changes, contributions by the employer and plan participants, benefits paid, business combinations, divestitures, and settlements.

   c. The **funded status** of the plans and the amounts recognized in the balance sheet, with separate display of (1) assets and (2) current and noncurrent liabilities.

   d. Information about **plan assets**.

      1) The percentage of the fair value of plan assets held in each major category (e.g., equity, debt, real estate, and other assets).

      2) A description of **investment policies and strategies**, such as target allocation percentages (if any) calculated on the weighted-average basis by major asset category. This description also should include factors helpful to understanding the policies and strategies, such as objectives, risk management, allowable investments, and the relationship of assets and obligations.

      3) A description of how the **overall expected long-term rate-of-return assumption** was determined.

      4) Other asset categories and information about specific assets helpful in understanding risks and the expected long-term rate of return.

   e. The **ABO** of a defined benefit pension plan.

   f. **Benefits** to be paid in each of the next 5 years and the total to be paid in years 6-10 based on the assumptions used to determine the benefit obligation at the current year-end. Future employee service is considered in the calculation.

   g. The best estimate of **contributions** in the next year (the aggregate of legal mandates, discretionary amounts, and noncash items).

   h. **Pension expense** recognized, showing separately each of its components and gain or loss recognized due to a settlement or curtailment.

   i. Separate amounts for (1) net gain (loss) and prior service cost (credit) recognized in **OCI for the period**, (2) **reclassification adjustments** of OCI recognized in net periodic benefit cost for the period, and (3) items still in **accumulated OCI** (net gain or loss, prior service cost or credit, and **the transition amount**).

   j. Weighted-average **assumptions** about the discount rate, rate of compensation increase, and expected long-term rate of return, with specification of assumptions for calculating the benefit obligation and net benefit cost.

   k. Assumed **health care cost trend rate(s)** for the next year and a general description of the direction and pattern of change thereafter.

l. The effect of a one-percentage-point increase or decrease in the assumed health care cost trend rates on the

    1) Total of the service and interest cost elements of the NPPBC for health care and
    2) APBO for health care.

m. **Securities of the employer** and related parties included in plan assets, the approximate future annual benefits covered by insurance, and significant transactions between the employer or related parties and the plan.

n. Alternative amortization methods for prior service amounts or net gains and losses.

o. Any substantive commitment used to calculate the benefit obligation.

p. Cost of special or contractual **termination benefits** and a description of the event.

q. Any significant change in the benefit obligation or plan assets not otherwise apparent.

r. Amounts in OCI expected to be recognized in net periodic benefit cost in the next year.

s. Plan assets expected to be returned to the employer in the next year.

Settlements, Curtailments, and Terminations

21. SFAS 88, *Employers' Accounting for Settlements and Curtailments of Defined Benefit Pension Plans and for Termination Benefits*, applies within the SFAS 87 framework.

22. A **settlement** is an irrevocable action that relieves the employer (or the plan) of the primary responsibility for a PBO. It eliminates significant risks related to the pension obligation and the assets used to effect the settlement. Recognition of a settlement gain or loss is mandatory if the cost of all settlements in a year exceeds the sum of the interest and service cost components of pension expense.

23. A **curtailment** significantly reduces the expected years of future service of current employees. An event also may be a curtailment if it eliminates the accrual of defined benefits for some or all future service for a significant number of employees.

24. **Termination benefits** are provided to employees in connection with their termination of employment. **Special** termination benefits are offered only for a short period. **Contractual** termination benefits are required by the terms of a pension plan only if a specified event occurs.

Stop and review! You have completed the outline for this subunit. Study multiple-choice questions 1 through 9 beginning on page 419.

11.2 POSTRETIREMENT BENEFITS OTHER THAN PENSIONS

Definition

1. SFAS 106 applies principles very similar to those of pension accounting. It emphasizes an employer's accounting for a single-employer plan that defines the postretirement benefits other than pensions to be provided to employees (**other postretirement employee benefits** or **OPEB**).

    a. The OPEB are defined in terms of monetary amounts (e.g., a given dollar value of life insurance) or benefit coverage (e.g., amounts per day for hospitalization).

        1) The amount of benefits depends on such factors as (a) the benefit formula, (b) the life expectancy of the retiree and any beneficiaries and covered dependents, and (c) the frequency and significance of events (e.g., illnesses) requiring payments.

        2) **Measurements** of plan assets and benefit obligations are generally made as of the balance sheet date.

b. The costs are expensed over **the attribution period**, which begins on the **date of hire** unless the plan's benefit formula grants credit for service only from a later date. The end of the period is the full eligibility date.

Expected Postretirement Benefit Obligation

2. A **basic element** of accounting for OPEB is the expected postretirement benefit obligation (EPBO). It equals the accumulated postretirement benefit obligation (APBO) after the full eligibility date. Do not confuse EPBO with PBO.

3. The **EPBO** for an employee is the actuarial present value at a given date of the OPEB expected to be paid. Its measurement depends on (a) the anticipated amounts and timing of future benefits, (b) the costs to be incurred to provide those benefits, and (c) the extent the costs are shared by the employee and others (such as governmental programs).

4. The **APBO** for an employee is the actuarial present value at a given date of the future benefits attributable to the employee's service as of that date.

    a. Unlike the ABO described in SFAS 87, the APBO (as well as the EPBO and service cost) implicitly includes the consideration of **future salary progression**.

    b. An employer's obligation for OPEB must be **fully accrued** by the full eligibility date for all benefits. This rule applies even if the employee is expected to render additional service.

        1) The **full eligibility date** is reached when the employee has rendered all the services necessary to earn all of the expected benefits.

        2) Prior to that date, the EPBO exceeds the APBO.

Current employees not yet eligible for benefits

Current employees eligible for benefits

EPBO

APBO

Retirees and dependents currently receiving benefits

Funded Status

5. The funded status of the plan must be recognized in the balance sheet as the difference between the fair value of plan assets and the APBO. An employer must apply SFAS 109, *Accounting for Income Taxes*, to determine the tax effects of recognizing the following:

    a. Funded status of the plan;

    b. Gains (losses) and prior service costs (credits) arising in the current period but included in OCI; and

    c. Reclassification adjustments for gains (losses), prior service costs (credits), and any transition amount included in accumulated OCI but amortized in the current period.

Net Periodic Postretirement Benefit Cost

6. The possible components included in **net periodic postretirement benefit cost (NPPBC)** of an employer sponsoring a defined benefit postretirement plan are

    a. Service cost
    b. Interest on the APBO
    c. Actual return on plan assets

        1)   However, gains and losses normally are **not** required to be recognized in NPPBC in the period when they are incurred. Thus, the amount that must be included in this component of NPPBC is the expected return for the period.

    d.   Amortization of any prior service cost or credit included in accumulated OCI

    e.   Amortization of any transition obligation or asset included in accumulated OCI

    f.   Gain or loss **component**

7.   **Service cost** increases NPPBC. It is the part of the **EPBO** attributed to services by employees during the period and is not affected by the level of funding.

8.   **Interest cost** increases NPPBC. It is the change in the **APBO** during the period resulting solely from the passage of time. It equals the APBO at the beginning of the period times the **assumed discount rate** used in determining the present value of future cash outflows currently expected to be required to satisfy the obligation.

9.   **Prior service cost** is the cost of benefit improvements incurred due to a **plan amendment**. It provides benefits to employees in exchange for prior service. This increase in the APBO is debited to OCI, net of tax, at the amendment date.

    a.   Prior service cost generally should be recognized in NPPBC by assigning an equal amount to each remaining year of service to the full eligibility date of each participant active at the amendment date who was not yet fully eligible. OCI is credited, net of tax, as prior service cost is included in NPPBC.

10.   A **prior service credit** retroactively reduces benefits and the APBO. The credit to OCI, net of tax, first reduces any prior service cost still in accumulated OCI. It then reduces any transition obligation in accumulated OCI. The remainder is amortized as part of NPPBC on the same basis as prior service cost.

    a.   The remaining prior service credit must not be recognized in full immediately.

11.   The **gain or loss component** equals any gain (loss) immediately recognized in NPPBC or the amortization of the net gain (loss) from prior periods that was recognized in OCI. Moreover, the employer may use a systematic method of amortizing net gain or loss included in accumulated OCI **other than the corridor approach** described in SFAS 87.

    a.   The alternative is allowable if it results in amortization at least equal to the minimum determined using the corridor approach.

    b.   If an enterprise consistently recognizes gains and losses immediately, gains (losses) that do not offset previously recognized losses (gains) must first reduce any transition obligation (asset) included in accumulated OCI.

Substantive Plan

12.   The substantive plan is the plan as understood by the parties, as opposed to the existing written plan.

13.   **A gain or loss from a temporary deviation** from the **substantive plan** is immediately recognized in income.

    a.   For example, under a plan's terms, an excess of benefit payments over the sum of the employer's cost and the employees' contributions for a year may be recovered from increased employees' contributions in the subsequent year. However, for the current year only, the employer may decide not to adjust contributions.

    b.   Delayed recognition is not appropriate because the effect of a temporary deviation is not deemed to provide future economic benefits and relates to benefits already paid.

    c.   The deviation may be other than temporary. If the employer decides to continue to bear the increased costs, the implication is that the **substantive plan** has been amended. An **amendment** requires accounting for prior service cost.

Stop and review! You have completed the outline for this subunit. Study multiple-choice questions 10 through 15 beginning on page 422.

11.3 COMPENSATED ABSENCES AND POSTEMPLOYMENT BENEFITS

Compensated Absences

1. SFAS 43, *Accounting for Compensated Absences*, applies to employees' rights to receive compensation for future absences, such as vacations. It requires an accrual of a liability when four criteria are met:

    a. The payment of compensation is probable.
    b. The amount can be reasonably estimated.
    c. The benefits either vest or accumulate.

        1) Rights **vest** if they are not contingent on future service.
        2) They **accumulate** if earned, but unused rights may be carried forward to subsequent periods.

    d. The compensation relates to employees' services that have already been rendered.

2. However, **sick pay benefits** that meet the criteria above are accrued only if the rights vest.

Postemployment Benefits

3. SFAS 112, *Employers' Accounting for Postemployment Benefits*, states the accounting standards for employers who provide benefits to former or inactive employees after employment but before retirement.

4. **Postemployment benefits** are all benefits provided to former or inactive employees, their beneficiaries, and covered dependents. Examples are salary continuation, supplemental unemployment benefits, severance benefits, disability-related benefits (including workers' compensation), job training and counseling, and continuation of such benefits as health care and life insurance coverage.

5. However, SFAS 112 does not apply to pensions, postretirement benefit plans, certain deferred compensation arrangements, special or contractual termination agreements, and stock compensation plans addressed by SFAS 123(R).

6. An employer should accrue a liability for postemployment benefits if all four criteria stated in SFAS 43 are met.

EXAMPLE

Papina Co. developed reasonable estimates of its obligations for $450,000 in severance pay and $150,000 in job training benefits. Payment is probable, and the benefits relate to employees' services previously rendered. The job training benefits vest, and the severance pay benefits accumulate. Because all the criteria are met, Papina should accrue a liability of $600,000 for postretirement benefits.

---

7. If postemployment benefits are within the scope of SFAS 112 but do not meet the criteria stated in SFAS 43, they are accounted for in accordance with the principles governing **loss contingencies** stated in SFAS 5.

8. If an obligation for postemployment benefits is not accrued solely because the amount cannot be reasonably estimated, the statements should disclose that fact.

Stop and review! You have completed the outline for this subunit. Study multiple-choice questions 16 through 19 beginning on page 424.

11.4 SHARE-BASED PAYMENT

Stock Option Plans

1. In lieu of cash payments, corporations often **grant options to purchase shares** of the firm's stock to certain employees.

    a. The FASB requires that these share-based payments be recorded at the **fair value** of the shares on the **grant date** [SFAS 123(R), *Share-Based Payment*].

        1) Fair value is determined using an **option-pricing model** (such as the Black-Scholes model), not the market price of the stock on the grant date.

        2) The **vesting date** is the first day on which the options can be exercised. Unless stated otherwise, vesting in options is immediate (that is, the employees are vested on the grant date).

EXAMPLE

On January 1, Year 1, a corporation grants its top five executives options to purchase 10,000 shares each of the firm's $1 par value common stock at $40 per share. The executives must work at least another two years to be vested in the options and must exercise them within 10 years of the grant date.

On the grant date, the company's option pricing model determines that the total fair value of the options is $620,000. The stock's market price on that day is $50. Since no time has passed, no services associated with the options have been performed yet, and no compensation expense is recognized.

January 1, Year 1:
No entry

---

    b. The total compensation expense associated with share-based payments must be **allocated over the service period** of the employees receiving the shares, that is, the time period during which the company expects to receive the benefit of the employees' services.

EXAMPLE

At the end of each of the next 10 years, one year of compensation expense associated with the options must be recognized.

December 31, Year 1:
Compensation expense	$62,000	
Paid-in capital – stock options ($620,000 ÷ 10)		$62,000

---

    c. If a covered employee **separates** from the company **before the vesting date**, the compensation expense associated with that employee recognized thus far is **reversed**.

EXAMPLE

After one year, one of the executives leaves the company. This executive is associated with 20% (1 ÷ 5) of the compensation expense recognized thus far.

January 1, Year 2:
Paid-in capital – stock options ($62,000 × 20% × 1 year)	$12,400	
Compensation expense		$12,400

---

        1) If a covered employee **separates** from the company **after the vesting date but before exercise**, the compensation expense associated with that employee recognized thus far **remains** on the books.

2) Periodic compensation expense recognized over the remaining service period must be adjusted following either of these events.

EXAMPLE

Periodic compensation expense is adjusted to recognize services from only four executives.

December 31, Year 2:
Compensation expense	$56,000	
Paid-in capital – stock options ($560,000 ÷ 10)		$56,000

---

d. The **exercise date** is the date (on or after the vesting date) on which a particular employee chooses to exercise his/her options.

EXAMPLE

Two and a half years after the grant date, two of the executives (50% of those remaining) choose to exercise their options. Note that total compensation expense is unaffected and that the market price of the stock is irrelevant (it is assumed to be higher than the exercise price). First, a half-year's compensation expense must be recognized.

July 1, Year 3:
Compensation expense	$28,000	
Paid-in capital – stock options ($56,000 ÷ 2)		28,000

The balance in paid-in capital – stock options is now $133,600.

Cash (10,000 shares × 4 executives × $40)	$160,000	
Paid-in capital – stock options ($133,600 × 50%)	66,800	
Common stock (40,000 shares × $1 par value)		$ 40,000
Additional paid-in capital – common stock		186,800

---

e. The **expiration date** is the date after which options can no longer be exercised.

EXAMPLE

After 10 years, the other two executives still have not exercised their options. The expiration is recorded this way:

December 31, Year 10:
Paid-in capital – stock options	$280,000	
Paid-in capital – expired stock options ($560,000 × 50%)		$280,000

---

2. Certain stock option plans have **performance conditions** imposed, not on the covered employees, but on the price of the stock. The accounting for these plans depends on whether the company believes that the target will be met.

a. If a company **believes** that the target will be met, compensation expense is recognized the same as in a regular stock option plan (shown in item 1).

1) If the company **does not believe** the target can be met, no compensation expense is recognized.

b. Once it becomes clear that the company has misjudged its ability to meet the target, it changes the estimate.

1) When a company **previously believed that it could** meet the target and later determines that it cannot, the previous compensation expense entries can be **reversed**.

2) When a company **previously believed that it could not** meet the target and later determines that it can, a **catch-up** entry is recorded in that year.

3. In the rare cases in which a firm **cannot reasonably estimate** the fair value of equity instruments at the grant date, the measurement is based on **intrinsic value** (market price of an underlying share – exercise price of an option).

Other Types of Compensation Plans

4. A **stock award plan** is a compensatory stock plan in which employees are granted shares of stock from the company to sell on their own behalf.

   a. Shares granted under the stock award plan are usually **restricted** by the issuing firm, i.e., the employees are vested in the shares but are prohibited from selling them before rendering services to the company for a specified period.

   b. The price per share of the restricted stock is the same as the price per share of unrestricted stock on the grant date.

5. **Stock appreciation rights** allow employees to receive the increase in value of the shares directly from the employer rather than having to purchase the shares and sell them to receive the benefit.

   a. The covered employee receives the **appreciation of the market price** on the exercise date over the option price.

      1) The award can be distributed with cash or shares of the company's stock.

   b. If the employer has the right to pay the award in stock, it is considered an **equity transaction**.

      1) The fair value of the SARs is measured at the grant date in the same way as stock options, and the compensation expense is recognized over the service period.

   c. If the employee has the right to **choose to receive cash** on the exercise date, the SARs are considered to be a **liability**.

      1) The liability is estimated at the grant date but continually adjusted to show the fair value of the liability at the balance sheet date.

   d. Compensation expense is recognized every year of the service period as a fraction of total compensation expense. The estimate of total compensation expense changes every year, so amounts from previous years should be subtracted out in order to obtain the appropriate balance in the liability account.

6. **Employee share purchase plans** are classified one of two ways.

   a. A plan is **compensatory** if an employee has an option to buy at the

      1) Lower of the market price at the grant date or the purchase date or

      2) Market price at the grant date and to cancel and receive a refund before the purchase date.

   b. A plan is considered **noncompensatory** when certain conditions are met:

      1) Either (a) the terms of the plan do not favor participants over other holders of the shares, or (b) purchase discounts do not exceed per share issuance costs in a significant public offering (5% or less always complies with this condition);

      2) All employees satisfying limited qualification criteria may enroll; and

      3) The plan has essentially no option features.

Employee Stock Ownership Plans (ESOPs)

7.   An ESOP is defined as a stock bonus plan, or a combination stock bonus and money purchase pension plan, designed to invest primarily in the employer's stock.

8.   **Leveraged ESOPs** are allowed to borrow, either from the sponsor with or without an outside loan or directly from an outside lender, to acquire employer securities, with the shares usually serving as collateral.

   a.   These shares are held in a suspense account until the debt is repaid, ordinarily from employer contributions and dividends. As the debt is repaid, the shares are released and allocated to individual accounts. Any outside loan is usually guaranteed by the employer-sponsor.

9.   The employer records a **debit to unearned ESOP shares** (a contra equity account) when shares are issued or treasury shares are sold to the ESOP.

   a.   Even if the ESOP buys on the market, the employer debits unearned shares and credits cash or debt, depending on whether the ESOP is internally or externally leveraged (AICPA SOP 93-6, *Employer's Accounting for Employee Stock Ownership Plans*).

10.   When ESOP shares are **committed to be released**, unearned shares is credited at cost and, depending on the purpose of the release, compensation cost, dividends payable, or compensation liability is debited for the fair value of the shares. The difference between cost and fair value is ordinarily an adjustment of additional paid-in capital.

   a.   **Dividends** on unallocated shares reduce liabilities or serve as compensation to participants. Dividends on allocated shares are debited to retained earnings.

   b.   **Redemptions** of ESOP shares, whether the ESOP is internally or externally leveraged, are treasury stock purchases.

   c.   If the ESOP has a **direct outside loan**, the sponsor reports a liability for the loan. It also accrues interest cost. Furthermore, it reports cash payments to the ESOP to be used for debt service as reductions of the debt and accrued interest.

      1)   If the ESOP has an **indirect loan** (a loan from the sponsor, which in turn has an outside loan), essentially the same accounting is followed.

      2)   If an employer loan is made to the ESOP **without an outside loan**, the employer does not record the ESOP's note payable, the employer's note receivable, interest cost, or interest income.

11.   If the **ESOP is not leveraged**, shares must be allocated at fiscal year-end. Employer compensation cost is reported equal to the cash or shares (at fair value) contributed or committed to be contributed as provided for in the plan. Dividends are debited to retained earnings.

Stop and review! You have completed the outline for this subunit. Study multiple-choice questions 20 through 26 beginning on page 425.

QUESTIONS

11.1 Pensions

1. Visor Co. maintains a defined benefit pension plan for its employees. The service cost component of Visor's pension expense is measured using the

A. Unfunded accumulated benefit obligation.

B. Unfunded vested benefit obligation.

C. Projected benefit obligation.

D. Expected return on plan assets.

Answer (C) is correct. *(CPA, adapted)*
REQUIRED: The item that is used to measure the service cost component of the pension expense.
DISCUSSION: The service cost is the actuarial present value of benefits attributed by the pension benefit formula to services rendered during the accounting period. It is a component of the projected benefit obligation. The PBO as of a date is equal to the actuarial present value of all benefits attributed by the pension benefit formula to employee service rendered prior to that date. The PBO is measured using assumptions as to future salary levels.
Answer (A) is incorrect because the accumulated benefit obligation is based on current salaries without assumptions about future salaries. Answer (B) is incorrect because service cost includes nonvested benefits. Answer (D) is incorrect because the expected return on plan assets is not a cost.

2. The following information pertains to Seda Co.'s pension plan:

Actuarial estimate of projected benefit obligation at 1/1/Year 1	$72,000
Assumed discount rate	10%
Service cost for Year 1	18,000
Pension benefits paid during Year 1	15,000

If no change in actuarial estimates occurred during Year 1, Seda's PBO at December 31, Year 1, was

A. $67,800

B. $75,000

C. $79,200

D. $82,200

Answer (D) is correct. *(CPA, adapted)*
REQUIRED: The projected benefit obligation at the end of the year.
DISCUSSION: The ending balance of the PBO is the beginning balance plus the service cost and interest cost components, minus the benefits paid. The interest cost component is equal to the PBO's beginning balance times the discount rate.

Beginning PBO balance	$ 72,000
Service cost	18,000
Interest cost ($72,000 × 10%)	7,200
Benefits paid	(15,000)
Ending PBO balance	$ 82,200

Answer (A) is incorrect because $67,800 results from subtracting interest cost. Answer (B) is incorrect because $75,000 excludes interest cost. Answer (C) is incorrect because $79,200 ignores service costs and benefits paid.

3. On January 2, Year 1, Loch Co. established a noncontributory defined-benefit pension plan covering all employees and contributed $400,000 to the plan. At December 31, Year 1, Loch determined that the Year 1 service and interest costs on the plan were $720,000. The expected and the actual rate of return on plan assets for Year 1 was 10%. Loch's pension expense has no other components. What amount should Loch report in its December 31, Year 1, balance sheet as liability for pension benefits?

A. $280,000

B. $320,000

C. $360,000

D. $720,000

Answer (A) is correct. *(CPA, adapted)*
REQUIRED: The accrued pension liability.
DISCUSSION: Service and interest costs and the return on plan assets are the entity's only components of pension expense in the plan's first year. The return on plan assets for Year 1 is $40,000 ($400,000 contributed to the plan × 10%). The pension expense is therefore $680,000 ($720,000 service and interest costs – $40,000 actual and expected return on plan assets). Because the actual and expected returns were the same, no gain or loss occurred in Year 1. The funded status of the plan is the difference between plan assets at fair value ($400,000 + $40,000 = $440,000 at year-end) and the projected benefit obligation ($720,000 service and interest costs, given no prior service cost or credit). Consequently, the liability recognized to record the unfunded status of the plan at year-end is $280,000 ($720,000 – $440,000).
Answer (B) is incorrect because $320,000 is the result if the return on plan assets is not added to plan assets at year-end. Answer (C) is incorrect because $360,000 results when the return on plan assets is subtracted from plan assets at year-end. Answer (D) is incorrect because $720,000 is the sum of service and interest costs.

4. Effective January 1, Year 1, Flood Co. established a defined benefit pension plan with no retroactive benefits. The first of the required equal annual contributions was paid on December 31, Year 1. A 10% discount rate was used to calculate service cost, and a 10% rate of return was assumed for plan assets. All information on covered employees for Year 1 and Year 2 is the same. How should the service cost component of pension expense for Year 2 compare with Year 1, and should the Year 1 balance sheet report a pension asset or liability?

	Service Cost for Year 2 Compared with Year 1	Pension Amount Reported on the Year 1 Balance Sheet
A.	Equal to	Liability
B.	Equal to	Asset
C.	Greater than	Liability
D.	Greater than	Asset

Answer (D) is correct. *(CPA, adapted)*
REQUIRED: The relation of Year 2 and Year 1 service cost and the reporting of Year 1 pension cost.
DISCUSSION: Service cost equals the actuarial present value of benefits attributed by the benefit formula to services rendered by employees during the period. Service cost is unaffected by the funded status of the plan. The minimum pension expense for Year 1 will be equal to the service cost. Any gain or loss arising in Year 1 will be amortized in the minimum pension expense in subsequent periods. No prior service cost is amortized because no retroactive benefits were granted at the inception of the plan. No interest cost is included because the PBO on 1/1/Year 1 was $0 (no benefits had been earned at that date). No expected return on plan assets is recognized because no plan assets existed during the period (the first contribution was on 12/31/Year 1). Because the information on the covered employees for both Year 1 and Year 2 is the same, the actual benefits to be paid attributable to each of these years also will be the same. Thus, service cost for Year 1 will be less than for Year 2 because the present value of the same future benefits will be based on a discount period that is 1 year longer. It is given that the company makes required equal annual contributions to the plan. Accordingly, the contribution in Year 1 will exceed pension expense in Year 1 (the plan will be overfunded). A pension asset should be reported in Year 1 on the balance sheet to recognize the funded status of the plan.

5. Jan Corp. amended its defined benefit pension plan, granting a total credit of $100,000 to four employees for services rendered prior to the plan's adoption. The employees, A, B, C, and D, are expected to retire from the company as follows:

"A" will retire after three years.
"B" and "C" will retire after five years.
"D" will retire after seven years.

What is the amount of prior service cost amortization in the first year?

A. $0

B. $5,000

C. $20,000

D. $25,000

Answer (C) is correct. *(CPA, adapted)*
REQUIRED: The prior service cost amortization in the first year after amendment of a defined benefit pension plan.
DISCUSSION: The cost of retroactive benefits is the increase in the PBO at the date of the amendment (debit OCI, net of tax, and credit pension liability or asset). It should be amortized by assigning an equal amount to each future period of service of each employee active at the date of the amendment who is expected to receive benefits under the plan. However, to reduce the burden of these allocation computations, any alternative amortization approach (e.g., averaging) that more rapidly reduces the unrecognized prior service cost is acceptable provided that it is applied consistently. The total service years to be rendered by the employees equals 20 (3 + 5 + 5 + 7). Hence, the amortization percentage for the first year is 20% (4 ÷ 20), and the minimum amortization is $20,000 (20% × $100,000).
Answer (A) is incorrect because amortization of prior service cost is a component of pension expense. Answer (B) is incorrect because $5,000 is the amount assigned to each period of service by each employee. Answer (D) is incorrect because $25,000 results from assigning an equal amount to each employee.

6. The following information pertains to Gali Co.'s defined benefit pension plan for Year 1:

Fair value of plan assets, beginning of year	$350,000
Fair value of plan assets, end of year	525,000
Employer contributions	110,000
Benefits paid	85,000

In computing pension expense, what amount should Gali use as actual return on plan assets?

A. $65,000

B. $150,000

C. $175,000

D. $260,000

Answer (B) is correct. *(CPA, adapted)*
REQUIRED: The actual return on plan assets.
DISCUSSION: The actual return on plan assets is based on the fair value of plan assets at the beginning and end of the accounting period adjusted for contributions and payments during the period. The actual return for Gali is $150,000 ($525,000 − $350,000 − $110,000 + $85,000).
Answer (A) is incorrect because $65,000 results when benefits paid to employees are not included. Answer (C) is incorrect because $175,000 is the change in the fair value of plan assets without adjustment for contributions or benefits paid. Answer (D) is incorrect because $260,000 does not deduct employer contributions.

7. The following information pertains to Lee Corp.'s defined benefit pension plan for Year 1:

Service cost	$160,000
Actual and expected gain on plan assets	35,000
Unexpected loss on plan assets related to a Year 1 disposal of a subsidiary	40,000
Amortization of prior service cost	5,000
Annual interest on pension obligation	50,000

What amount must Lee report as pension expense in its Year 1 income statement?

   A. $250,000

   B. $220,000

   C. $210,000

   D. $180,000

Answer (D) is correct. *(CPA, adapted)*
REQUIRED: The pension expense for the year.
DISCUSSION: The components of the required minimum pension expense are (1) service cost, (2) interest cost, (3) return on plan assets, (4) amortization of the net gain or loss recognized in accumulated OCI, and (5) amortization of any prior service cost or credit. Accordingly, the service cost, actual and expected gain on plan assets, interest cost, and amortization of prior service cost are included in the computation. Gains and losses arising from changes in the PBO or plan assets resulting from experience different from that assumed and from changes in assumptions about discount rates, life expectancies, etc., are not required to be included in the calculation of the required minimum pension expense when they occur. Accordingly, the unexpected Year 1 loss on plan assets is included in the gain or loss recognized in OCI (debit OCI, net of tax, and credit pension liability or asset). It must be amortized beginning in Year 2. Pension expense is therefore $180,000 ($160,000 service cost – $35,000 actual and expected return on plan assets + $5,000 prior service cost amortization + $50,000 interest cost).
Answer (A) is incorrect because $250,000 results from adding, not subtracting, the expected gain on plan assets. Answer (B) is incorrect because $220,000 includes the unexpected loss. Answer (C) is incorrect because $210,000 includes the unexpected loss and subtracts instead of adding the amortization of prior service cost.

8. The following is the only information pertaining to Kane Co.'s defined benefit pension plan:

Pension asset, January 1, Year 1	$ 2,000
Service cost	19,000
Interest cost	38,000
Actual and expected return on plan assets	22,000
Amortization of prior service cost arising in a prior period	52,000
Employer contributions	40,000

In its December 31, Year 1, balance sheet, what amount should Kane report as the unfunded or overfunded projected benefit obligation (PBO)?

   A. $7,000 overfunded.

   B. $15,000 underfunded.

   C. $45,000 underfunded.

   D. $52,000 underfunded.

Answer (A) is correct. *(CPA, adapted)*
REQUIRED: The unfunded or overfunded PBO.
DISCUSSION: The employer must recognize the funded status of the plan as the difference between the fair value of plan assets and the PBO. That amount is an asset or a liability. Current service cost and interest cost increase the PBO. The return on plan assets and contributions increase plan assets. Amortization of prior service cost arising in a prior period and recognized in accumulated OCI has no additional effect on the PBO or plan assets. However, it is a component of pension expense. The PBO was overfunded by $2,000 on January 1. It increased during the year by $57,000 ($19,000 + $38,000). Plan assets increased by $62,000 ($22,000 + $40,000). Accordingly, the plan is overfunded by $7,000 [$2,000 + ($62,000 – $57,000)] at year-end. Kane should recognize a pension asset of $7,000 at year-end.
Answer (B) is incorrect because the return on plan assets should be added to plan assets. Answer (C) is incorrect because $45,000 underfunded includes prior service cost amortization. Prior service cost that arose in a prior period was reflected in the asset or liability recognized for the funded status of the plan at the beginning of the year. When prior service cost arises, the entry is to debit OCI, net of tax, and credit pension liability. Answer (D) is incorrect because $52,000 is the prior service cost amortization.

9. A public entity that sponsors a defined benefit pension plan must disclose in the notes to its financial statements a reconciliation of

   A. The vested and nonvested benefit obligation of its pension plan with the accumulated benefit obligation.

   B. The accrued or prepaid pension cost reported in its balance sheet with the pension expense reported in its income statement.

   C. The accumulated benefit obligation of its pension plan with its projected benefit obligation.

   D. The beginning and ending balances of the projected benefit obligation.

Answer (D) is correct. *(CPA, adapted)*
REQUIRED: The employer disclosures required for a defined benefit pension plan.
DISCUSSION: Under SFAS 132(R), one of the required disclosures by a public entity with a defined benefit pension plan is a reconciliation of the beginning and ending balances of the PBO. It should display separately the effects during the period of (1) service cost, (2) interest cost, (3) participants' contributions, (4) actuarial gains and losses, (5) foreign currency exchange rate changes, (6) benefits paid, (7) plan amendments, (8) business combinations, (9) divestitures, (10) curtailments, (11) settlements, and (12) special termination benefits.
Answer (A) is incorrect because vested and nonvested amounts need not be disclosed. Answer (B) is incorrect because the employer must disclose the full funded status of the plan. Accrued/prepaid pension cost measures the extent of the funding of net period pension cost. Answer (C) is incorrect because the ABO must be disclosed but not with the PBO.

11.2 Postretirement Benefits Other Than Pensions

10. Bounty Co. provides postretirement health care benefits to employees who have completed at least 10 years service and are aged 55 years or older when retiring. Employees retiring from Bounty have a median age of 62, and no one has worked beyond age 65. Fletcher is hired at 48 years old. The attribution period for accruing Bounty's expected postretirement health care benefit obligation to Fletcher is during the period when Fletcher is aged

    A. 48 to 65.

    B. 48 to 58.

    C. 55 to 65.

    D. 55 to 62.

Answer (B) is correct. *(CPA, adapted)*
    REQUIRED: The attribution period for accruing the expected postretirement health care benefit obligation to an employee.
    DISCUSSION: The attribution period begins on the date of hire unless the plan's benefit formula grants credit for service only from a later date. The end of the period is the full eligibility date. If the exception does not apply, Fletcher's attribution period is from age 48, the date of hire, to age 58, the date of full eligibility.

11. SFAS 106 emphasizes an employer's accounting for a single-employer plan that defines the postretirement employee benefits other than pensions (OPEB) to be provided to employees. The OPEB are defined in terms of monetary amounts (e.g., a given dollar value of life insurance) or benefit coverage (e.g., amounts per day for hospitalization). The amount of benefits depends on such factors as the benefit formula, the life expectancy of the retiree and any beneficiaries and covered dependents, and the frequency and significance of events (e.g., illnesses) requiring payments. The basic elements of accounting for OPEB include

    A. The expected postretirement benefit obligation (EPBO), which equals the accumulated postretirement benefit obligation (APBO) after the full eligibility date.

    B. The APBO, which is the actuarial present value at a given date of the benefits projected to be earned after the full eligibility date.

    C. Required recognition of a minimum liability for any excess of the EPBO over the APBO.

    D. The projected benefit obligation (PBO) and the vested benefit obligation (VBO).

Answer (A) is correct. *(Publisher, adapted)*
    REQUIRED: The true statement about the elements of accounting for OPEB.
    DISCUSSION: The EPBO for an employee is the actuarial present value at a given date of the OPEB expected to be paid. Its measurement depends on the anticipated amounts and timing of future benefits, the costs to be incurred to provide those benefits, and the extent the costs are shared by the employee and others (such as governmental programs). The APBO for an employee is the actuarial present value at a given date of the future benefits attributable to the employee's service as of that date. Unlike the calculation of the ABO described in SFAS 87, the determination of the APBO (as well as of the EPBO and service cost) implicitly includes the consideration of future salary progression to the extent the benefit formula defines benefits as a function of future compensation levels. The full eligibility date is reached when the employee has rendered all the services necessary to earn all of the benefits expected to be received by that employee. After the full eligibility date, the EPBO and APBO are equal. Prior to that date, the EPBO exceeds the APBO.
    Answer (B) is incorrect because the APBO for an employee is the actuarial present value at a given date of the future benefits attributable to the employee's service as of that date, not as of the full eligibility date. Answer (C) is incorrect because the full funded status must be recognized in the balance sheet. Answer (D) is incorrect because these terms relate to pension accounting only.

12. The service cost component of the NPPBC is

    A. Included in the APBO but not in the EPBO.

    B. Defined as the portion of the EPBO attributed to employee service for a period.

    C. Included in the EPBO but not the APBO.

    D. Measured using implicit and explicit actuarial assumptions and present value techniques.

Answer (B) is correct. *(Publisher, adapted)*
    REQUIRED: The definition of the service cost component of the NPPBC.
    DISCUSSION: Service cost is defined as the actuarial present value of benefits attributed to services rendered by employees during the period. It is the portion of the EPBO attributed to service in the period and is not affected by the level of funding.
    Answer (A) is incorrect because the service cost for the most recently completed period is included in the EPBO as well as the APBO. Answer (C) is incorrect because the service cost for the most recently completed period is included in the APBO as well as the EPBO. Answer (D) is incorrect because SFAS 106 requires the use of explicit (not implicit) assumptions, each of which is the best estimate of a particular event.

13. The interest cost component of the NPPBC is the

    A. Increase in the EPBO because of the passage of time.

    B. Increase in the APBO because of the passage of time.

    C. Product of the market-related value of plan assets and the expected long-term rate of return on plan assets.

    D. Change in the APBO during the period.

Answer (B) is correct. *(Publisher, adapted)*
    REQUIRED: The definition of the interest cost component of the NPPBC.
    DISCUSSION: Interest cost reflects the change in the APBO during the period resulting solely from the passage of time. It equals the APBO at the beginning of the period times the assumed discount rate used in determining the present value of future cash outflows currently expected to be required to satisfy the obligation.
    Answer (A) is incorrect because interest cost is a function of the APBO. Answer (C) is incorrect because the expected return on plan assets is the product of the market-related value of plan assets and the expected long-term rate of return on plan assets. Answer (D) is incorrect because the change in the obligation reflects many factors, of which interest cost is one.

14. The gain or loss components of net periodic postretirement benefit cost (SFAS 106) and pension expense (SFAS 87) are calculated similarly. Under either pronouncement, an employer may use a systematic method of amortizing net gain or loss included in accumulated OCI other than the corridor approach described in each pronouncement. The alternative is allowable if it results in amortization at least equal to the minimum determined using that approach. Under SFAS 106, however, if an enterprise consistently recognizes gains and losses immediately,

    A. Any net loss in excess of a net gain previously recognized first offsets any prior service cost remaining in accumulated OCI.

    B. Any net gain in excess of a net loss previously recognized first offsets any transition asset remaining in accumulated OCI.

    C. Any net loss in excess of a net gain previously recognized first offsets any transition obligation remaining in accumulated OCI.

    D. Any net gain in excess of a net loss previously recognized first offsets any transition obligation remaining in accumulated OCI.

Answer (D) is correct. *(Publisher, adapted)*
    REQUIRED: The proper treatment of gains or losses recognized immediately.
    DISCUSSION: Under either SFAS 87 or SFAS 106, gains and losses may be recognized immediately or delayed. But SFAS 106 also provides that immediately recognized gains (losses) that do not offset previously recognized losses (gains) must first reduce any transition obligation (asset) remaining in accumulated OCI. The transition obligation (asset) represents an underlying unfunded (overfunded) APBO. The FASB believes that gains (losses) should not be recognized until the unfunded (overfunded) APBO is recognized.

15. Employer Co. maintains a postretirement health care plan for its employees. Under the plan's terms, an excess of benefit payments over the sum of the employer's cost and the employees' contributions for a year will be recovered from increased employees' contributions in the subsequent year. However, for the current year only, Employer has decided not to adjust contributions. Employer should

    A. Delay recognition of the loss by using the corridor approach.

    B. Apply any systematic and rational delayed recognition approach to accounting for the loss.

    C. Immediately recognize the loss in income.

    D. Adjust the transition asset.

Answer (C) is correct. *(Publisher, adapted)*
    REQUIRED: The treatment of a loss resulting from a temporary deviation from the plan.
    DISCUSSION: A gain or loss from a temporary deviation from the substantive plan is immediately recognized in income. No delayed recognition method is appropriate because the effect of a temporary deviation (1) is not deemed to provide future economic benefits and (2) relates to benefits already paid. If the deviation is other than temporary, that is, if the employer decides to continue to bear the burden of increased costs, the implication is that the substantive plan (the plan as understood by the parties as opposed to the extant written plan) has been amended. An amendment would require accounting for prior service cost.

11.3 Compensated Absences and Postemployment Benefits

16. If the payment of employees' compensation for future absences is probable, the amount can be reasonably estimated, and the obligation relates to rights that vest, the compensation should be

    A. Recognized when paid.

    B. Accrued if attributable to employees' services whether or not already rendered.

    C. Accrued if attributable to employees' services already rendered.

    D. Accrued if attributable to employees' services not already rendered.

Answer (C) is correct. *(CPA, adapted)*
    REQUIRED: The additional criterion to be met to accrue an expense for compensated absences.
    DISCUSSION: SFAS 43, *Accounting for Compensated Absences*, requires an accrual when four criteria are met: (1) the payment of compensation is probable, (2) the amount can be reasonably estimated, (3) the benefits either vest or accumulate, and (4) the compensation relates to employees' services that have already been rendered.

17. At December 31, Year 2, Taos Co. estimates that its employees have earned vacation pay of $100,000. Employees will receive their vacation pay in Year 3. Should Taos accrue a liability at December 31, Year 2, if the rights to this compensation accumulated over time or if the rights are vested?

	Accumulated	Vested
A.	Yes	No
B.	No	No
C.	Yes	Yes
D.	No	Yes

Answer (C) is correct. *(CPA, adapted)*
    REQUIRED: The effect of accumulation and vesting on accrual of a liability for vacation pay.
    DISCUSSION: SFAS 43 requires an accrual for compensated services when the compensation relates to services previously provided, the benefits either vest or accumulate, and payment is both probable and reasonably estimable. The single exception is for sick pay benefits, which must be accrued only if the rights vest.
    Answer (A) is incorrect because vesting meets one of the criteria for accrual of a liability. Answer (B) is incorrect because either vesting or accumulation meets one of the criteria for accrual of a liability. Answer (D) is incorrect because accumulation meets one of the criteria for accrual of a liability.

18. Gavin Company grants all employees 2 weeks of paid vacation for each full year of employment. Unused vacation time can be accumulated and carried forward to succeeding years and will be paid at the salaries in effect when vacations are taken or when employment is terminated. There was no employee turnover in Year 4. Additional information relating to the year ended December 31, Year 4, is as follows:

Liability for accumulated vacations at 12/31/Year 3	$35,000
Pre-Year 4 accrued vacations taken from 1/1/Year 4 to 9/30/Year 4 (the authorized period for vacations)	20,000
Vacations earned for work in Year 4 (adjusted to current rates)	30,000

Gavin granted a 10% salary increase to all employees on October 1, Year 4, its annual salary increase date. For the year ended December 31, Year 4, Gavin should report vacation pay expense of

    A. $45,000

    B. $34,500

    C. $31,500

    D. $30,000

Answer (C) is correct. *(CPA, adapted)*
    REQUIRED: The amount of vacation pay expense.
    DISCUSSION: SFAS 43 requires an accrual for vacation pay when the compensation relates to services previously provided, the benefits either vest or accumulate, and payment is both probable and reasonably estimable. Gavin Co. pays salaries at the amount in effect when the vacations are taken, and the amount estimated should be based on this provision. At 9/30/Year 4, the liability for accumulated vacations is equal to $15,000 ($35,000 beginning balance – $20,000 attributable to vacations taken). This balance must be adjusted by $1,500 to reflect the 10% salary increase. Consequently, vacation pay expense to be reported in Year 4 is equal to the $30,000 attributable to vacations earned for work in Year 4 (adjusted to current rates) plus the $1,500 attributable to the adjustment of the pre-Year 4 liability, a total of $31,500.
    Answer (A) is incorrect because $45,000 equals vacation pay earned in Year 4 plus the liability at 9/30/Year 4 before adjustment for the salary increase. Answer (B) is incorrect because $34,500 assumes the vacation pay earned in Year 4 has not been adjusted to current rates. Answer (D) is incorrect because $30,000 omits the adjustment of the remaining liability for pre-Year 4 accrued vacation pay.

19. The following information relating to compensated absences was available from Graf Company's accounting records at December 31, Year 4:

- Employees' rights to vacation pay vest and are attributable to services already rendered. Payment is probable, and Graf's obligation was reasonably estimated at $110,000.

- Employees' rights to sick pay benefits do not vest but accumulate for possible future use. The rights are attributable to services already rendered, and the total accumulated sick pay was reasonably estimated at $50,000.

What amount is Graf required to report as the liability for compensated absences in its December 31, Year 4, balance sheet?

- A. $160,000
- B. $110,000
- C. $50,000
- D. $0

Answer (B) is correct. *(CPA, adapted)*
REQUIRED: The amount to be reported as a liability for compensated absences at year-end.
DISCUSSION: In general, SFAS 43 requires an accrual for compensated services when the compensation relates to services previously provided, the benefits either vest or accumulate, and payment is both probable and reasonably estimable. An exception is made for sick pay benefits, which must be accrued only if the rights vest. Because Graf's obligation for sick pay benefits relates to benefits that do not vest, no accrual for the $50,000 in accumulated sick pay should be recognized. Consequently, only the $110,000 obligation for employee rights to vacation pay should be recognized as part of the liability for compensated absences in the year-end balance sheet.
Answer (A) is incorrect because $160,000 includes the nonvesting sick pay benefits. Answer (C) is incorrect because $50,000 includes the nonvesting sick pay benefits but excludes the vacation pay. Answer (D) is incorrect because $0 excludes the vacation pay.

11.4 Share-Based Payment

20. SFAS 123 (revised 2004), *Share-Based Payment*, normally requires entities to account for share-based employee compensation awards classified as equity in accordance with which of the following methods?

	Fair-Value Method	Intrinsic-Value Method
A.	Yes	Yes
B.	Yes	No
C.	No	Yes
D.	No	No

Answer (B) is correct. *(Publisher, adapted)*
REQUIRED: The method(s) prescribed for accounting for share-based employee compensations awards.
DISCUSSION: Entities must account for share-based payments classified as equity in accordance with the fair-value method except in the rare cases in which a nonpublic entity cannot reasonably estimate the fair value of the equity instruments at the grant date. In these cases, entities must account for such payments in accordance with the intrinsic-value method.
Answer (A) is incorrect because the pronouncement superseded by SFAS 123(R) permitted either method. However, an award classified as equity now must be measured at fair value except in rare cases. Answer (C) is incorrect because the pronouncement superseded by SFAS 123(R) permitted either method. However, an award classified as equity now must be measured at fair value except in rare cases. Answer (D) is incorrect because SFAS 123(R) prescribes the fair-value method except in rare cases.

21. On January 2, Year 1, Kine Co. granted Morgan, its president, fully vested share options to buy 1,000 shares of Kine's $10 par common stock. The options have an exercise price of $20 per share and are exercisable for 3 years following the grant date. Morgan exercised the options on December 31, Year 1. The market price of the shares was $50 on January 2, Year 1, and $70 on the following December 31. If the fair value of the options is not reasonably estimable at the grant date, by what net amount should equity increase as a result of the grant and exercise of the options?

- A. $20,000
- B. $30,000
- C. $50,000
- D. $70,000

Answer (A) is correct. *(CIA, adapted)*
REQUIRED: The amount equity increases as a result of the grant and exercise of share options.
DISCUSSION: In the rare cases in which an entity cannot reasonably estimate the fair value of equity instruments at the grant date, the measurement is based on intrinsic value (market price of an underlying share – exercise price of an option). On the grant date, the intrinsic value of the options is $30,000 [1,000 shares × ($50 market price – $20 option price)]. This $30,000 will be recorded as both compensation expense and options outstanding. The net effect on equity is $0. When the options are exercised, the $20,000 (1,000 shares × $20 exercise price) cash received and the $30,000 of options outstanding will be allocated to share capital as $10,000 common stock and $40,000 additional paid-in capital. Moreover, compensation expense will be debited and additional paid-in capital will be credited for $20,000 to reflect the final measure of intrinsic value. The net effect on equity will be a $20,000 increase.
Answer (B) is incorrect because $30,000 is the amount of the initial debit to compensation expense and credit to options outstanding. Answer (C) is incorrect because $50,000 is the final measure of intrinsic value. Answer (D) is incorrect because $70,000 is the market price of the shares issued on the settlement date.

Questions 22 through 26 are based on the following information. On December 21, Year 1, the board of directors of Oak Corporation approved a plan to award 600,000 share options to 20 key employees as additional compensation. Effective January 1, Year 2, each employee was granted the option to purchase 30,000 shares of the company's $2 par value stock at an exercise price of $36 per share. The market-price on that date was $32 per share. All share options vest at December 31, Year 4, the end of the 3-year requisite service period. They expire on December 31, Year 11. Based on an appropriate option-pricing formula, the fair value of the options on the grant date was estimated at $12 per option.

22. What amount of compensation expense should Oak Corporation recognize in accordance with the provisions of SFAS 123(R) in its annual income statement for the year ended December 31, Year 2?

    A. $7,200,000

    B. $6,400,000

    C. $2,400,000

    D. $1,200,700

Answer (C) is correct. *(Publisher, adapted)*
REQUIRED: The compensation expense recognized in Year 2.
DISCUSSION: Total compensation cost recognized during the requisite service period should equal the grant-date fair value of all share options for which the requisite service is rendered. SFAS 123(R) requires an entity to (1) estimate the number of share options for which the requisite service is expected to be rendered, (2) measure the cost of employee services received in exchange for those options at their fair value on the grant date, and (3) allocate that cost to the requisite service period. Given that all options vest at the same time (known as cliff vesting), the $7,200,000 (600,000 shares × $12 estimated fair value) total compensation cost should be allocated proportionately to the 3-year requisite service period. Thus, $2,4000,000 ($7,200,200 ÷ 3) should be expensed in the annual income statement for the year ended December 31, Year 2.
Answer (A) is incorrect because $7,200,000 is the total estimated compensation cost for the entire requisite service period. Answer (B) is incorrect because $6,400,000 is total compensation expense based on the $32 market price. Answer (D) is incorrect because $1,200,000 is 600,000 shares times the $2 par value.

23. On January 1, Year 2, 5 key employees left Oak Corporation. What amount of previously recognized compensation expense should Oak Corporation remove from its books in accordance with the provisions of SFAS 123(R) in the year ended December 31, Year 2?

    A. $2,400,000

    B. $1,800,000

    C. $1,200,000

    D. $600,000

Answer (D) is correct. *(Publisher, adapted)*
REQUIRED: The compensation expense removed from the books in Year 2.
DISCUSSION: Five of the 20 covered key employees separated from Oak on January 1, Year 2. Since those employees left the company before vesting in the stock option plan, all compensation expense associated with them must be removed from the books. The cumulative compensation expense recognized as of _____ was $2,400,000 (600,000 options × $12 fair value ÷ 3 year requisite service period × 1 year). Of this amount, the portion associated with the 5 former employees is $600,000 [$2,400,000 × (5 ÷ 20)].
Answer (A) is incorrect because $2,400,000 is total compensation expense recognized so far. Answer (B) is incorrect because $1,800,000 is the amount of compensation that should remain on the books after the adjustment for the 5 former employees. Answer (C) is incorrect because $1,200,000 is the difference between the amount of compensation expense that should remain on the books and the amount that should be removed.

24. On January 1, Year 2, 5 key employees left Oak Corporation. What amount of compensation expense should Oak report in the income statement for the year ended December 31, Year 3?

    A. $5,400,000

    B. $3,600,000

    C. $2,400,000

    D. $1,800,000

Answer (D) is correct. *(Publisher, adapted)*
REQUIRED: The compensation expense to be recognized in Year 3.
DISCUSSION: Fifteen key employees are now covered by the stock option plan. The total compensation expense for these employees is $5,400,000](30,000 options × 15 employees) × $12 fair value]. The amount to be recognized each year of the requisite service period is thus $1,800,000 ($5,400 ÷ 3).
Answer (A) is incorrect because $5,400,000 is the total compensation expense for the entire requisite service period. Answer (B) is incorrect because $3,600,000 is the total compensation expense that should be recognized in Years 3 and 4 combined. Answer (C) is incorrect because $2,400,000 is based on the assumption that all 20 key employees remain employed.

25. On January 1, Year 2, 5 key employees left Oak Corporation. During the period from January 1, Year 5, through December 31, Year 11, 400,000 of the share options that vested were exercised. At the end of this period, the cumulative amount that should have been credited to additional paid-in capital is

A. $19,200,000

B. $18,400,000

C. $13,600,000

D. $4,000,000

Answer (B) is correct. *(Publisher, adapted)*
REQUIRED: The credit to additional paid-in capital at the end of the period.
DISCUSSION: Additional paid-in capital–stock options was credited for $5,400,000 (450,000 × $12) as compensation expense was recognized during the requisite service period. During the period from January 1, Year 5, through December 31, Year 11, 400,000 options were exercised. Hence, additional paid-in capital should be credited for $18,400,000 [400,000 shares × ($36 exercise price + $12 previously credited to additional paid-in capital–stock options − $2 par value allocated to common stock)].
Answer (A) is incorrect because $19,200,000 includes the $2 par value allocated to the common stock account. Answer (C) is incorrect because $13,600,000 does not include the $12 fair value of the options determined at the grant date. Answer (D) is incorrect because $4,000,000 does not include the $36 exercise price.

26. On January 1, Year 2, 5 key employees left Oak Corporation. During the period from January 1, Year 5, through December 31, Year 11, 400,000 of the share options that vested were exercised. The remaining options were not exercised. What amount of the previously recognized compensation expense should be adjusted upon expiration of the stock options?

A. $2,400,000

B. $2,300,000

C. $100,000

D. $0

Answer (D) is correct. *(Publisher, adapted)*
REQUIRED: The adjustment to previously recognized compensation expense when share options are not exercised.
DISCUSSION: Total compensation expense for the requisite service period is not adjusted for expired options.
Answer (A) is incorrect because $2,400,000 is the annual compensation expense recognized during each of the years of the requisite service period. Answer (B) is incorrect because $2,300,000 is the amount that would have been credited to additional paid-in capital if the 50,000 expired options had been exercised. Answer (C) is incorrect because $100,000 is the amount that would have been credited to common stock if the 50,000 expired options had been exercised.

11.5 PRACTICE SIMULATION

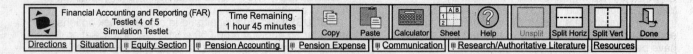

Financial Accounting and Reporting (FAR) Testlet 4 of 5 Simulation Testlet	Time Remaining 1 hour 45 minutes	Copy Paste Calculator Sheet Help Unsplit Split Horiz Split Vert Done

Directions | Situation | Equity Section | Pension Accounting | Pension Expense | Communication | Research/Authoritative Literature | Resources

1. Directions

In the following simulation, you will be asked to complete various tasks. You may use the content in the **Information Tabs** to complete the tasks in the **Work Tabs**.

Information Tabs:

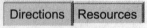

Directions | Resources

FIG 1

- Go through each of the **Information Tabs** to familiarize yourself with the simulation content
- The **Resources** tab will contain information, including formulas and definitions, that may help you to complete the tasks
- Your simulation may have more **Information Tabs** than those shown in Fig. 1

Work Tabs:

SysTrust | Engagement Letter | Authoritative Sources | Communication

FIG. 2

- **Work Tabs**, to the right of **Information Tabs**, contain the tasks for you to complete
- **Work Tabs** contain directions for completing each task - be sure to read these directions carefully
- The tab names in Fig. 2 are for illustration only - yours may differ
- Once you complete any part of a task, the pencil for that tab will be shaded (see **Communication** in Fig. 2)
- The shaded pencil does **NOT** indicate that you have completed the entire task
- You must complete all of the tasks in the **Work Tabs** to receive full credit

Research/Authoritative Literature Tab:

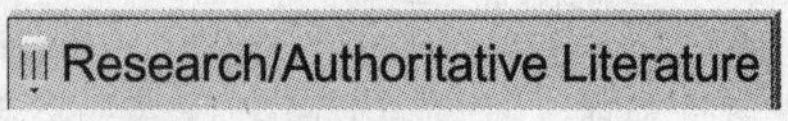

Research/Authoritative Literature

FIG. 3

- This tab contains both the Research task and the Authoritative Literature
- Detailed instructions for completing the Research task, and for using the Authoritative Literature, appear on this tab
- You may use the Authoritative Literature as a resource for completing other tasks

NOTE: If you believe you have encountered a software malfunction, report it to the test center staff immediately.

2. Situation

Field Co's equity account balances at December 31, Year 2, were as follows:

Common stock	$ 800,000
Additional paid-in capital	1,600,000
Retained earnings	1,845,000

The following Year 3 transactions and other information relate to the equity accounts:

- Field had 400,000 authorized shares of $5 par common stock, of which 160,000 shares were issued and outstanding.

- On March 5, Year 3, Field acquired 5,000 shares of its common stock for $10 per share to hold as treasury stock. The shares were originally issued at $15 per share. Field uses the cost method to account for treasury stock. Treasury stock is permitted in Field's state of incorporation.

- On July 15, Year 3, Field declared and distributed a property dividend of inventory. The inventory had a $75,000 carrying amount and a $60,000 fair value.

- On January 2, Year 1, Field granted share options to employees to purchase 20,000 shares of Field's common stock at $18 per share, the market price on that date. The options have a grant-date fair value of $10 per option and a 2-year requisite service period. They may be exercised within a 3-year period beginning January 2, Year 3. No forfeitures were expected, and tax effects should be ignored. On October 1, Year 3, employees exercised all 20,000 options. Field issued new shares to settle the transaction.

- Field's net income for Year 3 was $240,000. It included $50,000 of unrealized holding gains on trading securities.

- Field intends to issue new share options to key employees in Year 4. Field's management is aware that Statement of Financial Accounting Standards 123(R), *Share-Based Payment*, discusses both the "intrinsic value" method and the "fair value" method of accounting for share options. Field's management is unsure of the application of the two methods.

Additional Information

- The following information pertains to Field Co.'s defined-benefit pension plan at December 31, Year 3:

Projected benefit obligation	$150,000
Service cost	6,000
Amortization of prior service cost in accumulated OCI	2,000
Fair value of plan assets	160,000
Unamortized prior service cost	12,000
Expected return on plan assets	5,000
Amortization of net gain in accumulated OCI	8,000
Interest cost	10,000

3. Equity Section

This question is presented in a spreadsheet format that requires you to fill in the correct responses in the shaded cells provided. Define the amount to be listed on the equity section of Field's December 31, Year 3, balance sheet. Support all computations.

Field Co.
EQUITY SECTION OF
BALANCE SHEET
December 31, Year 3

Common stock		
Additional paid-in capital		
Retained earnings:		
Beginning balance		
Add: Net Income		
Minus: Property dividend distributed		
Minus: Common stock in treasury		
Total equity		

4. Pension Accounting

This question has a multiple-choice format that requires you to select the correct response from a drop-down list. Select the correct answer from the answer choices and write the answer in the answer column next to the item or question.

		Answer	Choices
1.	At December 31, Year 3, what amount should Field record as a pension asset or liability?		A) $8,000 B) $12,000 C) $10,000
2.	In its December 31, Year 3, statement of income, what amount should Field report as the required minimum pension expense?		A) $5,000 B) $10,000 C) $18,000
3.	Field Co. must disclose in the notes to its financial statements a reconciliation of		A) The beginning and ending balances of the projected benefit obligation. B) The accumulated benefit obligation of its pension plan with its projected benefit obligation. C) The vested and nonvested benefit obligation of its pension plan with the accumulated benefit obligation.
4.	SFAS 88, *Employers' Accounting for Settlements and Curtailments Defined Benefit Pension Plans and for Termination Benefits*, provides that, in a settlement,		A) The unrecognized transition net asset or obligation is included in the calculation of the maximum gain or loss. B) The cost of a participation right reduces the maximum gain or loss subject to recognition. C) A transaction must eliminate significant risks related to the obligation and the assets involved.

5. Pension Expense

Identify the elements that are factors in calculating the minimum required pension expense.

		Element of Pension Expense	Non-Element
1.	Asset gain or loss occurring in current period	☐	☐
2.	Amortization of gain or loss consisting of the difference between the actual and expected return on plan assets	☐	☐
3.	Interest cost	☐	☐
4.	Underfunded projected benefit obligation	☐	☐
5.	Service cost	☐	☐
6.	Cost of termination benefits	☐	☐
7.	Amortization of unrecognized prior service cost	☐	☐
8.	Market-related value of plan assets	☐	☐

6. Communication

In a memo to Field's management, explain how compensation cost is measured under both the fair-value method and the intrinsic-value method of accounting for share-based payment. Also explain the accounting for awards of equity and liability instruments.

REMINDER: Your response will be graded for both technical content and writing skills. Technical content will be evaluated for information that is helpful to the intended reader and clearly relevant to the issue. Writing skills will be evaluated for development, organization, and the appropriate expression of ideas in professional correspondence. Use a standard business memo or letter format with a clear beginning, middle, and end. Do not convey information in the form of a table, bullet point list, or other abbreviated presentation.

```
To:        Management, Field Co.
From:      CPA
Subject:   Share-Based Payment
```

---

7. Research/Authoritative Literature

See page 12 in the Introduction of this book for a detailed explanation of the AICPA's new Research/Authoritative Literature work tab as well as a screenshot of how the tab will actually look on your exam.

Research and cite the annual financial statements and information from either the FASB Current Text or Original Pronouncements that must be reported by a defined benefit pension plan.

Unofficial Answers

3. Equity Section (8 Gradable Items)

Field Co.
EQUITY SECTION OF
BALANCE SHEET
December 31, Year 3

Common stock		$ 900,000 [1]
Additional paid-in capital		2,060,000 [2]
Retained earnings:		
Beginning balance	$1,845,000 [3]	
Add: Net Income	240,000 [4]	
Minus: Property dividend distributed	(60,000) [5]	2,025,000 [6]
		4,985,000 [7]
Minus: Common stock in treasury		(50,000) [8]
Total equity		$4,935,000

[1] [(160,000 + 20,000) shares issued × $5] = $900,000

[2] Additional paid-in capital: $1,600,000 + [20,000 × ($18 + $10 − $5)] = $1,600,000 + $460,000 = $2,060,000

[3] Provided in situation

[4] Provided in situation

[5] $60,000 was the fair value of the property distributed on July 15, Year 3.

[6] Current year retained earnings adjustments: $1,845,000 + $240,000 − $60,000 = $2,025,000

[7] [6] above + Common stock of $900,000 + Additional paid in capital of $2,060,000 = $4,985,000

[8] 5,000 shares re-acquired in Year 5 at a cost of $10 per share: 5,000 × $10 = $50,000

4. Pension Accounting (4 Gradable Items)

1. C) $10,000. The PBO is overfunded by $10,000 ($160,000 fair value of plan assets – $150,000 PBO).

2. A) $5,000. The required minimum pension expense equals $5,000 ($6,000 service cost + $2,000 amortization of prior service cost in accumulated OCI + $10,000 interest cost – $5,000 expected return on plan assets – $8,000 amortization of net gain in accumulated OCI).

3. A) The beginning and ending balances of the projected benefit obligation. Under SFAS 132(R), one of the required disclosures by a company with a defined benefit pension plan is a reconciliation of the beginning and ending balances of the PBO. It should display separately the effects during the period of service cost, interest cost, participants' contributions, actuarial gains and losses, foreign currency exchange rate changes, benefits paid, plan amendments, business combinations, divestitures, curtailments, settlements, and special termination benefits.

4. C) A transaction must eliminate significant risks related to the obligation and the assets involved to constitute a settlement. A settlement is an irrevocable action that relieves the employer (or the plan) of the primary responsibility for a PBO and eliminates significant risks related to the pension obligation and the assets used to effect the settlement.

5. Pension Expense (8 Gradable Items)

1. Non-Element. Asset gains and losses are differences between the actual and expected returns. They are included in the gain or loss component of pension expense. Gains and losses (including asset gains and losses) are not required to be recognized in pension expense of the period in which they occur. Thus, the required minimum pension expense reflects the amount of the expected, not the actual, return on plan assets. The current asset gain or loss, that is, the difference between the actual and expected returns, may be deferred.

2. Element of Pension Expense. The cumulative unrecognized net gain or loss at the beginning of the year (excluding the asset gains and losses not reflected in market-related value) is subject to required amortization in pension expense. However, only the amount exceeding 10% of the greater of the PBO or the market-related value of plan assets must be amortized.

3. Element of Pension Expense. Interest cost is the increase in the projected benefit obligation (PBO) determined by multiplying the PBO at the beginning of the year by the current discount rate (e.g., the interest rate at which annuities could be purchased to settle pension obligations).

4. Non-Element. An underfunded PBO is recognized as a liability, not as an element of pension expense.

5. Element of Pension Expense. Service cost is the present value of the future benefits earned by the employees in the current period (as calculated according to the plan's benefit formula). This amount is a portion of the PBO and is calculated by the plan's actuary. It is unaffected by the funded status of the plan.

6. Non-Element. Termination benefits are provided to employees in connection with their termination of employment. Special termination benefits are offered for a short period. Contractual termination benefits are required by the terms of a pension plan only if a specified event occurs.

7. Element of Pension Expense. If a plan is amended to grant additional benefits for past service, the cost is allocated to future periods of service.

8. Element of Pension Expense. The expected return on plan assets is the market-related value of the plan assets at the beginning of the period multiplied by the expected long-term rate of return. The expected return (given that it is positive) decreases pension expense. Market-related value may be either fair value or a calculated value that recognizes changes in fair value systematically and rationally over not more than 5 years, such as a 5-year moving average.

6. Communication (5 Gradable Items; for grading instructions, please refer to page 12.)

Compensation cost for an award classified as equity is recognized over the requisite service period (RSP). The credit is usually to paid-in capital. This period is the period during which employees must perform services. It is most often the vesting period. The requisite service period begins at the service inception date. The service required is called the requisite service. Total compensation cost at the end of the RSP is based on the number of equity instruments for which the requisite service was completed. The entity must estimate this number when initial accruals are made. Changes in the estimate result in recognition of the cumulative effect on prior and current periods in the calculation of compensation cost for the period of change. Compensation cost is not recognized when employees do not perform the requisite service or meet other stated conditions.

The cost of employee services performed in exchange for awards of share-based compensation normally is measured at the (1) grant-date fair value of the equity instruments issued or (2) fair value of the liabilities incurred. Such liabilities are remeasured at each reporting date. The fair value of employee services is reduced by any amounts an employee must pay. At the grant date, the employer and employee must have reached "a mutual understanding of the key terms and conditions of a share-based payment award." Also, necessary approvals (other than those that are formalities) must have been received. Moreover, the employer becomes obligated to make share-based payments to employees who render the requisite service. For an award of equity instruments, the grant date is when an employee begins to be affected by changes in the price of the shares.

When a nonpublic entity cannot reasonably estimate the fair value of equity instruments at the grant date, the accounting is based on intrinsic value (fair value of an underlying share - exercise price of an option). Remeasurement is required at each reporting date and on final settlement. Periodic compensation cost is based on the change in intrinsic value. The final measure of compensation cost is the intrinsic value on the settlement date.

The criteria for liability classification in SFAS 150, *Accounting for Certain Financial Instruments with Characteristics of both Liabilities and Equity*, are generally applicable to freestanding financial instruments given to employees in SBPTs. The measurement date for liabilities is the settlement date. Thus, after initial recognition, liabilities are remeasured at each reporting date. A public entity remeasures liabilities based on their fair values. Periodic compensation cost depends on the change (or part of the change, depending on the requisite service performed to date) in fair value. A nonpublic entity may elect to measure all such liabilities at fair value or intrinsic value. However, fair value is preferable for the purpose of justifying a change in accounting principle. The percentage of fair value or intrinsic value accrued as compensation cost equals the percentage of required service rendered to date.

7. Research/Authoritative Literature (1 Gradable Item)

Answer: FAS 35, Par. 6

FAS 35 -- *Accounting and Reporting by Defined Benefit Pension Plans*

6. The annual financial statements of a plan shall include:

a. A statement that includes information regarding the net assets available for benefits as of the end of the plan year

b. A statement that includes information regarding the changes during the year in the net assets available for benefits

c. Information regarding the actuarial present value of accumulated plan benefits as of either the beginning or the end of the plan year

d. Information regarding the effects, if significant, of certain factors affecting the year-to-year change in the actuarial present value of accumulated plan benefits.

Scoring Schedule:

	Correct Responses		Gradable Items		Weights		
Tab 3	_____	÷	8	×	20%	=	_____
Tab 4	_____	÷	4	×	20%	=	_____
Tab 5	_____	÷	8	×	15%	=	_____
Tab 6	_____	÷	5	×	30%	=	_____
Tab 7	_____	÷	1	×	15%	=	_____
							_____
							(Your Score)

Use Gleim's **CPA Gleim Online** to practice more simulations in a realistic environment.

STUDY UNIT TWELVE
NONCURRENT LIABILITIES

(15 pages of outline)

This study unit covers traditional noncurrent liabilities (bonds and notes). Unless the **fair value option** (see Study Unit 5) is elected, they are measured and accounted for in accordance with APB Opinion 21, *Interest on Receivables and Payables*. The topics in this study unit are frequently tested.

12.1 TYPES OF BOND LIABILITIES

Classification of Bonds

1. A **bond** is a formal contractual agreement to pay an amount of money (face amount) at the maturity date plus interest at the stated rate at specific intervals. All of the terms of the agreement are stated in a document called an **indenture**.

2. Bonds may be classified as follows:

    a. Securitization

        1) **Mortgage bonds** are backed by specific assets, usually real estate.
        2) **Debentures** are backed by the borrower's general credit but not by specific collateral.
        3) **Collateral trust bonds** are backed by specific securities.
        4) **Guaranty bonds** are guaranteed by a third party, e.g., the parent of the subsidiary that issued the bonds.

    b. Maturity Pattern

        1) A **term bond** has a single maturity date at the end of its term.
        2) A **serial bond** matures in stated amounts at regular intervals.

    c. Ownership

        1) **Registered bonds** are issued in the name of the owner. Interest payments are sent directly to the owner. When the owner sells registered bonds, the bond certificates must be surrendered and new certificates issued.
        2) **Bearer bonds**, also called coupon bonds, are bearer instruments. Whoever presents the periodic interest coupons is entitled to payment.

    d. Priority

        1) **Subordinated debentures** and **second mortgage bonds** are junior securities with claims inferior to those of senior bonds.

e. Repayment Provisions

1) **Income bonds** pay interest contingent on the debtor's profitability.

2) **Revenue bonds** are issued by governmental units and are payable from specific revenue sources.

3) **Participating bonds** share in excess earnings of the debtor as defined in the bond indenture.

f. Valuation

1) **Variable rate bonds** pay interest that is dependent on market conditions.

2) **Zero-coupon** or **deep-discount bonds** are noninterest-bearing. Because they are sold at less than their face amount, an interest rate is imputed.

3) **Commodity-backed bonds** are payable at prices related to a commodity such as gold.

g. Redemption Provisions

1) **Callable bonds** may be repurchased by the issuer before maturity.

2) **Redeemable bonds** may be presented for payment by the creditor prior to the maturity date. The bonds usually are redeemable only after a specified period.

3) **Convertible bonds** may be converted into equity securities of the issuer at the option of the holder (buyer) under the conditions specified in the bond indenture.

3. A bond indenture may require a **bond sinking fund** (a long-term investment). The objective of making payments into the fund is to segregate and accumulate sufficient assets to pay a bond liability. The amounts transferred plus the revenue earned on the investments provide the necessary funds.

Stop and review! You have completed the outline for this subunit. Study multiple-choice questions 1 through 3 on page 450.

12.2 ISSUANCE OF BONDS AT A PREMIUM OR DISCOUNT

Proceeds

1. The issue price of a bond is a function of the market interest rate and reflects the bond's fair value.

2. The **proceeds received** from the sale of a bond equal the sum of the **present values** of the **face amount** and the **interest payments** (if the bond is interest-bearing).

a. When bonds are issued between interest payment dates, the buyer includes **accrued interest** in the purchase price.

3. When the **proceeds differ from the face amount**, the difference is a premium or discount.

a. Bonds are sold at a **premium** when the stated (contract) interest rate exceeds the market (effective) interest rate. The entry is

Cash	$XXX	
Premium on bonds payable		$XXX
Bonds payable		XXX

b. Bonds are sold at a **discount** when the stated interest rate is less than the market (effective) interest rate. The entry is

Cash	$XXX	
Discount on bonds payable	XXX	
Bonds payable		$XXX

Effective Interest Method

4. Bond discount or premium must be amortized using the **effective interest method**, also known as the **interest method** (unless the results of another method are not materially different).

    a. Under the interest method, interest expense changes every period, but the interest rate is constant.

    b. For a comprehensive illustration of the interest method, see Subunit 5.5.

Periodic Payments

5. **Interest expense** for a period is equal to the **carrying amount** of the bonds at the beginning of the period (face amount – unamortized discount or + unamortized premium) times the yield (market) interest rate.

6. The **cash paid** for periodic interest is equal to the face amount of the bonds times the stated rate. It remains constant over the life of the bonds.

7. The difference between interest expense and cash interest paid is the discount or premium **amortization**.

    a. Discount amortized, total interest expense, and the carrying amount of the bonds **increase** each period when amortizing a **discount**. The journal entry is

Interest expense	$XXX	
Discount on bonds payable		$XXX
Cash		XXX

    b. Premium amortized, total interest expense, and the carrying amount of the bonds **decrease** each period when amortizing a **premium**. The journal entry is

Interest expense	$XXX	
Premium on bonds payable	XXX	
Cash		$XXX

EXAMPLE

Amortizing a discount (stated rate less than effective rate). Assume issuance of a 6%, 5-year, $5,000 bond (interest paid at the end of each annual period) with an 8% effective rate.

Year	Beginning Net Carrying Amount	Times: Effective Rate	Equals: Interest Expense	Minus: Cash Paid	Equals: Discount Amortized	Ending Net Carrying Amount
1	$4,601	8%	$ 368	$ 300	$ 68	$4,669
2	4,669	8%	374	300	74	4,743
3	4,743	8%	379	300	79	4,822
4	4,822	8%	386	300	86	4,908
5	4,908	8%	393	300	93	5,000
			$1,899	$1,500	$399	

EXAMPLE

Amortizing a premium (stated rate greater than effective rate). Assume issuance of an 8%, 5-year, $5,000 bond (interest paid at the end of each annual period) with a 6% effective rate.

Year	Beginning Net Carrying Amount	Times: Effective Rate	Equals: Interest Expense	Minus: Cash Paid	Equals: Premium Amortized	Ending Net Carrying Amount
1	$5,421	6%	$ 325	$ 400	$ (75)	$5,346
2	5,346	6%	321	400	(79)	5,267
3	5,287	6%	316	400	(84)	5,183
4	5,183	6%	311	400	(89)	5,094
5	5,094	6%	306	400	(94)	5,000
			$1,579	$2,000	$(421)	

c. At the **maturity date**, the discount or premium will be **fully amortized** to zero, and the net carrying amount of the bonds will equal the face amount.

Display

8. Bond discount or premium is a direct subtraction from or addition to, respectively, the face amount of the bonds payable in the **balance sheet** (APB Opinion 21).

Stop and review! You have completed the outline for this subunit. Study multiple-choice questions 4 through 8 beginning on page 451.

12.3 DEBT ISSUE COSTS

1. Issue costs are incurred to bring debt to market. They include (a) printing and engraving costs, (b) legal fees, (c) accountants' fees, (d) underwriters' commissions, (e) registration fees, and (f) promotion costs.

2. SFAC 6, *Elements of Financial Statements*, states that debt issue costs do not constitute an asset because they provide no future economic benefit. Instead, their effect is to reduce the proceeds of the borrowing and increase the effective interest rate.

    a. Hence, SFAC 6 suggests that issue costs may be treated either as **an expense** or as **a reduction in the net carrying amount** of the related debt liability (as an increase in discount or a decrease in premium).

    b. While this treatment is theoretically superior, it is not generally accepted.

3. Issue costs should be reported in the balance sheet as **deferred charges** and amortized over the life of the debt, not commingled with premium or discount (APB Opinion 21).

    a. Because APB Opinions have the status of GAAP, the deferred charge method is the most prevalent in practice.

Cash	$9,225,000	
Discount on debt payable	500,000	
Unamortized issue costs	275,000	
Debt payable		$10,000,000

    b. Although the interest method is theoretically preferable, issue costs may be amortized on a straight-line basis if the results are not materially different.

Debt issue expense ($275,000 ÷ 10 years)	$27,500	
Unamortized issue costs		$27,500

Stop and review! You have completed the outline for this subunit. Study multiple-choice questions 9 through 11 beginning on page 452.

12.4 CONVERTIBLE DEBT

Definition

1. Convertible bonds can be exchanged for shares in the issuer.

2. APB Opinion 14, *Accounting for Convertible Debt and Debt Issued with Stock Purchase Warrants*, states that the debt and equity aspects of convertible debt are inseparable. The **entire proceeds** (usually cash) should be accounted for and reported as **debt** (a liability) until conversion.

   a. However, the bond's issue price (fair value) is affected by the conversion feature.

Cash	$XXX	
Premium on bonds payable		$XXX
Bonds payable		XXX

Market Value Method

3. The market-value method of recording the conversion of bonds into common stock can be used when the market value of the bonds or of the stock is readily determinable. A **gain or loss** is recognized.

Bonds payable	$XXX	
Unamortized premium on bonds payable	XXX	
Loss on redemption of bonds payable	XXX	
Common stock		$XXX
Additional paid-in capital		XXX

Book-Value Method

4. The book-value method is more common in practice and must be used when no market value can be readily determined for the bonds or the stock. **No gain or loss** is recognized.

Bonds payable	$XXX	
Unamortized premium on bonds payable	XXX	
Common stock		$XXX
Additional paid-in capital		XXX

Carrying Amount

5. The carrying amount of convertible debt is affected by all related accounts.

   a. Unamortized premium or discount, unamortized issue costs, and conversion costs all affect the net carrying amount.

   b. Consequently, these items are adjustments of additional paid-in capital when the book-value method is used.

Induced Conversion

6. To reduce interest costs or total debt, an issuer of convertible debt may **induce conversion**. This is accomplished by offering cash, additional securities, or other consideration as an incentive.

7. SFAS 84, *Induced Conversions of Convertible Debt*, requires the additional consideration to be reported as an ordinary expense.

8. The amount equals the fair value of the consideration transferred in excess of the fair value of the securities that would have been issued under the original conversion privilege.

Bonds payable	$XXX	
Debt conversion expense	XXX	
Common stock		$XXX
Additional paid-in capital		XXX
Cash		XXX

9.   The treatment of **gains or losses** from early extinguishment of convertible debt is the same as for the retirement of ordinary debt.

Stop and review! You have completed the outline for this subunit. Study multiple-choice questions 12 through 14 beginning on page 453.

12.5 STOCK WARRANTS

Detachable vs. Nondetachable

1.   Like convertible debt, **warrants** allow a bondholder to obtain common shares. Unlike convertible debt, warrants require the bondholder to pay an additional amount to receive the shares.

2.   APB Opinion 14, *Accounting for Convertible Debt and Debt Issued with Stock Purchase Warrants*, distinguishes detachable and nondetachable warrants.

   a.   When warrants are **nondetachable**, their conversion feature is considered to be **inseparable** from the underlying debt, and the entire proceeds are attributed to debt.

3.   When debt is issued with **detachable** warrants, the proceeds must be **allocated** between the underlying debt and the warrants based on their **relative fair values** at the time of issuance.

   a.   Allocate the proceeds to the bonds

$$Cash\ proceeds\ received\ \times\ \left(\frac{FV\ of\ bonds}{FV\ of\ bonds\ +\ warrants}\right)$$

   b.   Record the issuance of the bonds:

Cash (calculated in a.)	$XXX	
Discount on bonds payable	XXX	
Bonds payable		$XXX

   c.   Allocate the proceeds to the warrants:

$$Cash\ proceeds\ received\ \times\ \left(\frac{FV\ of\ warrants}{FV\ of\ bonds\ +\ warrants}\right)$$

   d.   Record the issuance of the warrants:

Cash (calculated in c.)	$XXX	
Paid-in capital -- warrants		$XXX

   e.   When the fair value of the warrants but not the bonds is known, **additional paid-in capital from warrants** should be credited (increased) for the fair value of the warrants. The remainder is credited to the bonds.

4.   When the warrants are exercised, the journal entry is

Cash	$XXX	
Paid-in capital -- warrants	XXX	
Common stock		$XXX
Additional paid-in capital		XXX

EXAMPLE

On January 2, Matrix Co. issued $1,000,000 of 9% bonds for $1,040,000. Each $1,000 bond had 20 detachable warrants. Each warrant was redeemable for one share of Matrix $10 par value stock at a price of $30. Directly after the issuance, the warrants were trading for $5 each.

The fair value of the 20,000 warrants [($1,000,000 ÷ $1,000) bonds × 20] was $100,000 (20,000 warrants × $5). Given that the fair value of the bonds is not known, the warrants are credited for $100,000. The remainder of the proceeds ($1,040,000 – $100,000 = $940,000) is assigned to the bonds.

To record the issuance of the bonds:

Cash	$940,000	
Discount on bonds payable	60,000	
Bonds payable		$1,000,000

To record the issuance of the warrants:

Cash	$100,000	
Paid-in capital--warrants		$100,000

To record the exercise of the warrants:

Cash (20,000 × $30)	$600,000	
Paid-in capital--warrants	100,000	
Common stock (20,000 × $10)		$200,000
Additional paid-in capital		400,000

Stop and review! You have completed the outline for this subunit. Study multiple-choice questions 15 through 18 beginning on page 454.

12.6 EXTINGUISHMENT OF DEBT

Early Extinguishment

1. Issuers sometimes retire debt before maturity, for example, to eliminate high-interest debt in a time of falling interest rates or to improve debt ratios.

2. APB Opinion 26, *Early Extinguishment of Debt*, applies to all extinguishments, regardless of the means used. It states that all extinguishments of debt before scheduled maturities are **fundamentally alike** and should be accounted for similarly.

    a. SFAS 140, *Accounting for Transfers and Servicing of Financial Assets and Extinguishments of Liabilities*, defines the transactions that extinguish liabilities.

3. The **net carrying amount** is the amount due at maturity, adjusted for unamortized premium or discount, and unamortized issue costs.

4. The **reacquisition price** is the amount paid on extinguishment, including any call premium and miscellaneous costs of reacquisition.

    a. If extinguishment is by a direct exchange of new securities (a refunding), the reacquisition price is equal to the total present value of the new securities.

Gains or Losses

5.   Gains or losses are recognized in earnings in the period of extinguishment. They are presumed to be ordinary.

a.   The gain or loss is measured by the difference between the reacquisition price (including any call premium and miscellaneous costs of reacquisition) and the carrying amount of the debt.

Debt payable	$XXX	
Loss on redemption of debt (face amount)	XXX	
Unamortized premium on debt payable (carrying amount – debt payable)	XXX	
Cash		$XXX
Unamortized issue costs		XXX

Extinguishment

6.   A debtor derecognizes a liability only if it has been extinguished. **Extinguishment** results only if (a) the debtor pays the creditor and is relieved of its obligation with respect to the liability, or (b) the debtor is legally released from being the primary obligor, either judicially or by the creditor.

Stop and review! You have completed the outline for this subunit. Study multiple-choice questions 19 through 23 beginning on page 456.

12.7 REFINANCING OF SHORT-TERM OBLIGATIONS

Ability to Refinance

1.   When an entity (a) **intends to refinance** short-term obligations on a **long-term basis** and (b) demonstrates an ability to consummate such refinancing, SFAS 6, *Classification of Short-term Obligations Expected to Be Refinanced*, allows the obligation to be reclassified from current liabilities to noncurrent.

a.   The **ability to consummate** the refinancing may be demonstrated by a post-balance-sheet-date issuance of a long-term obligation or equity securities prior to the issuance of the balance sheet. It also may be demonstrated by a **financing agreement** prior to the issuance of the balance sheet that meets the following criteria:

1)   The agreement does not expire within the longer of 1 year or the operating cycle.
2)   It is noncancelable by the lender.
3)   No violation of the agreement exists at the balance sheet date.
4)   The lender is financially capable of honoring the agreement.

Balance Sheet Classification

2.   The amount excluded from current liabilities must not exceed the proceeds from the new obligation or equity securities issued.

a.   The amount excluded may be further reduced by the amount of proceeds not expected to be available for refinancing.

3.   Sometimes a current liability is **repaid after year-end** and refinanced by long-term debt **before the balance sheet is issued**. Because this retirement requires the use of current assets, the liability must be classified as current in the balance sheet.

4.   Under SFAS 78, *Classification of Obligations That Are Callable by the Creditor*, long-term obligations that are callable by the creditor because of the debtor's **violation of the debt agreement** at the balance sheet date are classified as **current liabilities**.

5.   Notes to the financial statements should include a general description of the financing agreement and the terms of any new obligation incurred or securities issued.

Stop and review! You have completed the outline for this subunit. Study multiple-choice questions 24 and 25 beginning on page 457.

12.8 NONCURRENT NOTES PAYABLE

<u>Definition</u>

1. **Notes payable** are essentially the same as bonds. However, a note is payable to a single creditor, and bonds are payable to many creditors. In practice, notes are usually of shorter duration than bonds.

   a. Noncurrent notes, such as **mortgage notes**, that are payable in installments are classified as current to the extent of any payments due in the coming year. Payments not due in the current year are classified as noncurrent.

2. APB Opinion 21, *Interest on Receivables and Payables*, applies. For a full outline, see Subunit 6.5.

EXAMPLE

An entity agrees to give, in return for merchandise, a 3-year, $100,000 note bearing 8% interest paid annually. The effective interest rate is 6%. Because the note's stated rate exceeds the effective rate, the note will be issued at a premium.

The entity records the note at the present value of (a) a single payment of $100,000 in 3 years and (b) three interest payments of $8,000 each. These payments are discounted at the effective rate (five decimal places are used for increased accuracy).

Present value of principal ($100,000 × 0.83962)	$ 83,962
Present value of interest ($8,000 × 2.67301)	21,384
Present value of note	$105,346

The entry to record the note is

Inventory	$105,346	
Premium on note payable		$ 5,346
Note payable		100,000

<u>Discount or Premium</u>

3. Discount or premium, loan origination fees, etc. are amortized in accordance with the effective-interest method to arrive at a periodic interest expense that reflects a constant rate of interest when applied to the beginning balance.

4. Discount or premium is not an asset or liability separable from the related note. A discount or premium is therefore reported in the balance sheet as a direct deduction from, or addition to, the face amount of the note (APB Opinion 21).

Stop and review! You have completed the outline for this subunit. Study multiple-choice questions 26 through 30 beginning on page 458.

12.9 TROUBLED DEBT RESTRUCTURING

Definition

1. Under SFAS 15, *Accounting by Debtors and Creditors for Troubled Debt Restructurings*, a troubled debt restructuring (TDR) occurs when "the creditor for economic or legal reasons related to the debtor's financial difficulties grants a concession to the debtor that it would not otherwise consider."

   a. A TDR can consist of either a **settlement of the debt in full** or a continuation of the debt with a **modification in terms**.

   b. TDRs almost always involve a **loss** to the creditor and a **gain** to the debtor.

Settlement in Full with a Transfer of Assets

2. The **creditor** recognizes a **loss** equal to the difference between the fair value of the assets received and the carrying amount of the receivable. Thus, if the allowance method is used for recording bad debts, the loss is net of the previously recognized bad debt expense related to the debt.

EXAMPLE

Debtor gave a mortgage on its building to Creditor. The principal amount of Creditor's mortgage receivable is $5,000,000 (the recorded investment), and it has credited the related allowance for uncollectible accounts for $200,000. Thus, the carrying amount of the receivable is $4,800,000. Assume (for computational simplicity) that the carrying amount of Debtor's mortgage is $5,000,000. The building's fair value is $4,500,000, and its carrying amount on Debtor's balance sheet is $6,000,000. If Debtor transfers the building to Creditor in full settlement of the debt, Creditor's entry is:

Building (fair value)	$4,500,000	
Loss on receivable	300,000	
Allowance for uncollectible accounts	200,000	
Mortgage receivable (principal)		$5,000,000

---

   a. If the creditor receives **long-lived assets to be sold** in full satisfaction, the assets are recorded at **fair value minus cost to sell**.

3. The **debtor** recognizes a **gain** when the **carrying amount** of the debt exceeds the **fair value** of the asset(s) given.

EXAMPLE

The debtor also recognizes a **gain (loss)** equal to the difference between the fair value of the assets given and their carrying amount. Debtor's entry in the example is

Mortgage payable (carrying amount)	$5,000,000	
Loss on disposition of building (carrying amount – fair value)	1,500,000	
Building (carrying amount)		$6,000,000
Gain on restructuring (debt settled – fair value of building)		500,000

---

4. The **creditor's total loss (bad debt expense previously recognized + current loss) equals the debtor's gain**.

Settlement in Full with a Transfer of an Equity Interest

5.   The **creditor** again recognizes a **current loss** equal to the difference between the assets received and the carrying amount of the receivable.

> ### EXAMPLE
>
> In the previous example, assume that Creditor receives Debtor common stock (100,000 shares at $10 par) with a fair value of $4,800,000. Because the fair value received ($4,800,000) equals the carrying amount ($5,000,000 – $200,000 allowance), Creditor recognizes no current loss. Creditor's entry is
>
> | | | |
> |---|---:|---:|
> | Investment in debtor (fair value) | $4,800,000 | |
> | Allowance for uncollectible accounts | 200,000 | |
> | Mortgage receivable (principal) | | $5,000,000 |
>
> The **debtor** recognizes a **gain** only on the restructuring. Debtor's entry after the transfer of the equity interest is
>
> | | | |
> |---|---:|---:|
> | Mortgage payable (carrying amount) | $5,000,000 | |
> | Common stock (100,000 shares at $10 par) | | $1,000,000 |
> | Additional paid-in capital (fair value of stock – total par value) | | 3,800,000 |
> | Gain on restructuring (debt settled – fair value of stock) | | 200,000 |

    a.   As in the previous case, the **creditor's total loss equals the debtor's gain**.

Modification of Terms when Future Cash Flows Exceed the Carrying Amount

6.   Three changes in the terms of the loan are common.

    a.   A reduction in the principal
    b.   An extension of the maturity date
    c.   A lowering of the interest rate

7.   The debtor will recognize a gain if the total of the cash flows associated with the modified terms is less than the carrying amount of the troubled debt. **The recording of this event does not consider the time value of money.**

8.   When a TDR involves a modification of terms and the **undiscounted total future cash flows (UCF)** that the debtor has committed to pay are **greater than** the carrying amount of the debt, the **debtor** recognizes **no gain**.

> ### EXAMPLE
>
> Instead of a full settlement as illustrated above, the creditor agrees that (a) the mortgage principal will be reduced from $5,000,000 to $4,000,000, (b) the final maturity will be extended from 1 year to 5 years, and (c) the interest rate will be reduced from 8% to 6%. Interest continues to be paid at year-end.
>
> The new principal of $4,000,000 plus interest of $1,200,000 ($4,000,000 × 6% × 5 years) yields a UCF of $5,200,000.
>
> Because the UCF exceeds the carrying amount of the debt ($5,200,000 > $5,000,000), the debtor recognizes no gain. It continues making journal entries to record periodic interest payments and retirement of debt.

9. The **creditor's** accounting is governed by SFAS 114, *Accounting by Creditors for Impairment of a Loan.* A creditor must recognize the impairment of a loan when it is probable that the creditor will not be able to collect all amounts (principal and interest) due in accordance with the original terms of the loan. The total impairment recognized is based on the **recorded investment** in the loan, **not** the carrying amount.

    a. In the revised example, the **current impairment loss** is the difference between (1) the discounted cash flows **(DCF)** reflecting an effective rate based on the **original contractual rate** (8%) and (2) the carrying amount of the receivable.

EXAMPLE

The present value of the new principal discounted at 8% for 5 years is $2,722,320 ($4,000,000 × .68058).

The present value of the new annual interest payments discounted at 8% for 5 years is $958,250 ($4,000,000 × 6% × 3.99271).

Mortgage receivable (principal)	$5,000,000
Minus: discounted principal	(2,722,320)
Minus: discounted interest payments	(958,250)
Total impairment of receivable	$1,319,430

Given an existing credit in the allowance account of $200,000, the creditor records the current impairment loss as follows:

Bad debt expense ($1,319,430 – $200,000)	$1,119,430	
Allowance for uncollectible accounts		$1,119,430

---

    b. Because the creditor uses the time value of money in this calculation, its impairment loss **does not equal** the debtor's gain. (The debtor may have no gain.)

    c. A creditor measures **impairment** of the recorded investment based on the present value of expected future cash flows discounted at the loan's effective rate based on the original contractual rate.

        1) An alternative is to use the loan's **observable market price** or the **fair value of the collateral** if the loan is collateral dependent.

        2) If **foreclosure** is probable, impairment is based on the fair value of the collateral.

Modification of Terms when Future Cash Flows are Less Than the Carrying Amount

10. When a TDR involves a modification of terms and the UCF are **less than** the carrying amount of the debt, the **debtor** recognizes a **gain**.

    a. In the revised example, instead of reducing the principal to $4,000,000, the creditor agrees to reduce the principal to $3,000,000.

EXAMPLE

The principal of $3,000,000 plus interest of $900,000 ($3,000,000 × 6% × 5 years) yields UCF of $3,900,000.

Because the UCF are less than the carrying amount of the debt ($3,900,000 < $5,000,000), the debtor recognizes a gain equal to the difference.

Mortgage payable	$1,100,000	
Gain on restructuring		$1,100,000

---

11. In the second version of the revised example, the **creditor's current impairment loss** is the difference between the DCF and the carrying amount of the receivable.

EXAMPLE

The present value of the principal discounted at 8% for 5 years is $2,041,740 ($3,000,000 × .68058).

The present value of the new annual interest payments discounted at 8% for 5 years is $718,688 ($3,000,000 × 6% × 3.99271).

Mortgage receivable (carrying amount)	$5,000,000
Minus: discounted principal	(2,041,740)
Minus: discounted interest payments	(718,688)
Total impairment of receivable	$2,239,572

Given an existing credit in the allowance account of $200,000, the creditor records the current impairment loss as follows:

Bad debt expense ($2,239,572 – $200,000)	$2,039,572	
Allowance for uncollectible accounts		$2,039,572

---

12. The creditor's impairment loss **does not equal** the debtor's gain (if any).

13. As a result of an amendment by SFAS 118, *Accounting by Creditors for Impairment of a Loan-Income Recognition and Disclosures*, SFAS 114 does not address the issues of recognition, measurement, or display of interest income derived from an impaired loan.

14. **Debt restructuring expenses** are expensed as incurred, except by debtors issuing equity securities (restructuring expenses reduce paid-in capital from these securities).

Stop and review! You have completed the outline for this subunit. Study multiple-choice questions 31 through 33 on page 460.

12.10 ASSET RETIREMENT OBLIGATIONS

Definition

1. Certain long-lived tangible assets, such as mines or nuclear power plants, incur significant costs after the end of their productive lives. SFAS 143, *Accounting for Asset Retirement Obligations*, applies to all such assets and all entities.

2. An **asset retirement obligation (ARO)** reflects a legal obligation arising from acquisition, construction, development, or normal operation of an asset. A legal obligation is one arising from an existing or enacted law, statute, ordinance, or contract.

3. The ARO is recognized at **fair value** when incurred. An **expected present value** technique ordinarily should be used to estimate the fair value of an ARO. A **credit-adjusted risk-free rate (CARF)** is the appropriate discount rate.

4. An ARO has an associated **asset retirement cost (ARC)**. This cost is added to the carrying amount of the tangible long-lived asset when an ARO is recognized.

5. SFAS 143 does not apply if the obligation arises

   a. Solely form a plan to sell or otherwise dispose of a long-lived asset covered by SFAS 144, *Accounting for the Impairment or Disposal of Long-Lived Assets*, or

   b. From the improper operation of an asset.

6.   An ARO may be **conditional**, e.g., because a governmental unit has the right to decide in the future whether to require an asset retirement activity. Nevertheless, the entity has a **legal obligation** to be ready to perform.

EXAMPLE

A mining entity is required by law to restore land used in its operations.

The entity estimates that a new mine will be productive for 12 years. The adjusted expected cash flows for reclamation costs equal $4,000,000:

The entity's **CARF** is 8%.

The expected present value of the reclamation costs, discounted at 8% for 12 years, is $1,588,455 ($4,000,000 × .3971138).

The ARC is added to the carrying amount of the long-lived asset, and the ARO is credited.

Mine - ARC	$1,588,455	
Asset retirement obligation		$1,588,455

The entity allocates this initial ARC to expense using the straight-line method over the life of the mine.

Depreciation expense ($1,588,455 ÷ 12)	$132,371	
Accumulated depreciation		$132,371

The entity amortizes the difference between the maturity amount and the carrying amount of the ARO by annual recognition of **accretion expense**.

Year	Beginning Net Carrying Amount	Times: Discount Rate	Equals: Dr. Accretion Expense, Cr. ARO	Ending Net Carrying Amount
1	$1,588,455	8%	$127,076	$1,715,531
2	1,715,531	8%	137,243	1,852,774
3	1,852,774	8%	148,222	2,000,996
4	2,000,996	8%	160,080	2,161,075
5	2,161,075	8%	172,886	2,333,962
6	2,333,962	8%	186,717	2,520,678
7	2,520,678	8%	201,652	2,722,333
8	2,722,333	8%	217,787	2,940,119
9	2,940,119	8%	235,210	3,175,329
10	3,175,329	8%	254,026	3,429,355
11	3,429,355	8%	274,348	3,703,704
12	3,703,704	8%	296,296	4,000,000

The first-year journal entry is

Accretion expense	$127,076	
Asset retirement obligation		$127, 076

At the end of the mine's service life, the entity may incur costs to reclaim the land exceeding the initial estimate. The journal entry is

Asset retirement obligation	$4,000,000	
Loss on settlement of ARO	125,000	
Cash		$4,125,000

Stop and review! You have completed the outline for this subunit. Study multiple-choice questions 34 through 36 on page 461.

12.11 COSTS ASSOCIATED WITH EXIT OR DISPOSAL ACTIVITIES

Definition

1. SFAS 146, *Accounting for Costs Associated with Exit or Disposal Activities*, states that a **liability** for exit or disposal costs is ordinarily recognized and measured at **fair value** when the liability is incurred.

   a. The liability is incurred when a present obligation to others exists. A **present obligation** exists when the entity has little discretion to avoid a future transfer of assets in settlement.

   b. The commitment to an exit or disposal plan does not, by itself, create the required present obligation.

2. An **exit activity** includes an activity involving any entity recently acquired through a business combination.

   a. Among the activities included in the definition are **restructurings**. These are programs planned and controlled by management that materially alter either the scope of the business or how it is conducted.

   b. Costs subject to SFAS 146 include **certain one-time termination benefits**; **contract termination costs** other than those for a capital lease; and **other costs**, such as facilities consolidation and employee relocation costs.

3. **Changes in the liability** are recorded using the **CARF rate** on which the initial measurement was based.

One-Time Termination Benefits

4. **One-time termination benefits** are paid under a one-time benefit arrangement based on a **plan of termination** for a specified termination event or future period

   a. The arrangement exists when the plan has been **communicated** to employees and certain other requirements are met.

   b. Timing of recognition and the fair value (FV) measurement of the liability depend on whether employees must provide services until terminated. If so, a second issue is whether employees will be retained beyond a **minimum retention period (MRP)**, which cannot exceed 60 days.

      1) **No required service to termination or no retention beyond MRP**

         a) Recognition: On communication date (CD)
         b) Measurement: At FV on the CD

      2) **Required service to termination and retention beyond MRP**

         a) Recognition: Proportionately over the future service period
         b) Measurement: On CD at FV on termination date

Contract Termination Costs

5. Such costs (other than those for a capital lease) are of two types: (a) costs to terminate **prior to completion** of the contract's term and (b) contract costs that will continue to be incurred without economic benefit **(continuing costs)**.

Reporting

6. Costs covered by SFAS 146 are included in **income from continuing operations** (before income taxes for a business entity).

   a. If these costs involve a **discontinued operation**, they are included in the results of discontinued operations.

Stop and review! You have completed the outline for this subunit. Study multiple-choice questions 37 through 39 beginning on page 462.

QUESTIONS

12.1 Types of Bond Liabilities

1. Bonds payable issued with scheduled maturities at various dates are called

	Serial Bonds	Term Bonds
A.	No	Yes
B.	No	No
C.	Yes	No
D.	Yes	Yes

Answer (C) is correct. *(CPA, adapted)*
REQUIRED: The definition of bonds issued with scheduled maturities at various dates.
DISCUSSION: Serial bonds are bond issues that mature in installments at various dates. Term bonds mature on a single date.

2. Hancock Co.'s December 31, Year 4, balance sheet contained the following items in the long-term liabilities section:

Unsecured
9.375% registered bonds ($25,000
  maturing annually beginning in Year 8) $275,000
11.5% convertible bonds, callable
  beginning in Year 13, due Year 24   125,000

Secured
9.875% guaranty security bonds, due
  Year 24 $250,000
10.0% commodity backed bonds ($50,000
  maturing annually beginning in Year 8)   200,000

What are the total amounts of serial bonds and debenture bonds?

	Serial Bonds	Debenture Bonds
A.	$475,000	$400,000
B.	$475,000	$125,000
C.	$450,000	$400,000
D.	$200,000	$650,000

Answer (A) is correct. *(CPA, adapted)*
REQUIRED: The total amounts of serial bonds and debenture bonds.
DISCUSSION: Serial bonds mature in installments at various dates. Debentures are unsecured bonds. The commodity-backed bonds and the registered bonds are serial bonds. They total $475,000 ($275,000 + $200,000). The registered bonds and the convertible bonds are debentures. They total $400,000 ($275,000 + $125,000).
  Answer (B) is incorrect because the registered bonds are also debentures. Answer (C) is incorrect because the registered bonds, not the guaranty security bonds, are serial bonds. Answer (D) is incorrect because the registered bonds are serial bonds and the guaranty security bonds are not debentures.

3. Blue Corp.'s December 31, Year 4, balance sheet contained the following items in the long-term liabilities section:

9 3/4% registered debentures, callable in
  Year 15, due in Year 20 $700,000
9 1/2% collateral trust bonds, convertible
  into common stock beginning in Year 13,
  due in Year 23   600,000
10% subordinated debentures ($30,000
  maturing annually beginning in Year 10)   300,000

What is the total amount of Blue's term bonds?

- A. $600,000
- B. $700,000
- C. $1,000,000
- D. $1,300,000

Answer (D) is correct. *(CPA, adapted)*
REQUIRED: The total amount of term bonds.
DISCUSSION: Term bonds mature on a single date. Hence, the registered bonds and the collateral trust bonds are term bonds, a total of $1,300,000 ($700,000 + $600,000).
  Answer (A) is incorrect because the registered bonds are also term bonds. Answer (B) is incorrect because the collateral trust bonds are also term bonds. Answer (C) is incorrect because the collateral trust bonds, not the subordinated debentures, are term bonds.

12.2 Issuance of Bonds at a Premium or Discount

4. The market price of a bond issued at a discount is the present value of its principal amount at the market (effective) rate of interest

    A. Minus the present value of all future interest payments at the market (effective) rate of interest.

    B. Minus the present value of all future interest payments at the rate of interest stated on the bond.

    C. Plus the present value of all future interest payments at the market (effective) rate of interest.

    D. Plus the present value of all future interest payments at the rate of interest stated on the bond.

Answer (C) is correct. *(CPA, adapted)*
    REQUIRED: The market price of a bond issued at a discount.
    DISCUSSION: The cash flows associated with a bond are the amount due at the end of the life of the bond (its face value) and the periodic payments. These cash flows must be allocated between principal and interest so that the interest reflects the prevailing market rate. Allocation is based on the present value method. The sum of the present value of the amount due at the end of the bond's term plus the present value of the periodic interest payments, each discounted at the prevailing market rate, is the market value. The difference between the cash flows and the market value is interest. This difference should then be allocated to the interest periods during the life of the bond so that it is recognized at a constant rate (the effective-interest method). This valuation method is applicable whether the bond is issued at a discount, a premium, or face amount.

5. The following information pertains to Camp Corp.'s issuance of bonds on July 1, Year 4:

Face amount	$800,000
Term	10 years
Stated interest rate	6%
Interest payment dates	Annually on July 1
Yield	9%

	At 6%	At 9%
Present value of 1 for 10 periods	0.558	0.422
Future value of 1 for 10 periods	1.791	2.367
Present value of ordinary annuity of 1 for 10 periods	7.360	6.418

What should the issue price be for each $1,000 bond?

    A. $1,000

    B. $943

    C. $864

    D. $807

Answer (D) is correct. *(CPA, adapted)*
    REQUIRED: The issue price for each bond.
    DISCUSSION: The issue price for each bond reflects the fair value. It equals the sum of the present values of the future cash flows (principal + interest). This amount is $807 [($1,000 face amount × .422 PV of 1 for 10 periods at 9%) principal + ($1,000 face amount × 6% stated rate × 6.418 PV of an ordinary annuity for 10 periods at 9%) interest].
    Answer (A) is incorrect because $1,000 is the face amount. Answer (B) is incorrect because $943 is the result of discounting the interest payments at 9% and the face amount at 6%. Answer (C) is incorrect because $864 is the result of discounting the interest payments at 6% and the face amount at 9%.

6. A bond issued on June 1, Year 4, has interest payment dates of April 1 and October 1. Bond interest expense for the year ended December 31, Year 4, is for a period of

    A. Three months.

    B. Four months.

    C. Six months.

    D. Seven months.

Answer (D) is correct. *(CPA, adapted)*
    REQUIRED: The bond interest expense for the year.
    DISCUSSION: The price of a bond issued between payment dates includes the amount of accrued interest. Thus, this bond will include 2 months of accrued interest, which will be recorded either as a payable or a decrease in interest expense. As a result, interest expense for the year will be reported only for the period the bond is outstanding or 7 months (June-December).
    Answer (A) is incorrect because 3 months is the period for which interest is accrued at year-end. Answer (B) is incorrect because 4 months is the period for which interest expense is recorded on October 1. Answer (C) is incorrect because 6 months is the period between payment dates.

7. On June 30, Year 4, Huff Corp. issued one thousand of its 8%, $1,000 bonds at 99. The bonds were issued through an underwriter to whom Huff paid bond issue costs of $35,000. On June 30, Year 4, Huff should report the bond liability at

A. $955,000

B. $990,000

C. $1,000,000

D. $1,025,000

Answer (B) is correct. *(CPA, adapted)*
REQUIRED: The amount of the bond liability at the issue date.
DISCUSSION: APB Opinion 21, *Interest on Receivables and Payables*, requires that bond discount or premium appear as a direct subtraction from or addition to the face amount of the bond payable to report the effective liability for the bonds. Hence, the bond liability is shown net of unamortized discount. At the issue date, no amortization has occurred. Consequently, the carrying amount (bond liability) equals the face amount minus the total discount ($1,000 × 1,000 × 99% = $990,000).
Answer (A) is incorrect because $955,000 equals the net proceeds (assuming no accrued interest was received). Answer (C) is incorrect because $1,000,000 is the face amount. Answer (D) is incorrect because $1,025,000 is the sum of the net liability and the issue costs.

8. Album Co. issued 10-year $200,000 debenture bonds on January 2. The bonds pay interest semiannually. Album uses the effective interest method to amortize bond premiums and discounts. The carrying amount of the bonds on January 2 was $185,953. A journal entry was recorded for the first interest payment on June 30, debiting interest expense for $13,016 and crediting cash for $12,000. What is the annual stated interest rate for the debenture bonds?

A. 6%

B. 7%

C. 12%

D. 14%

Answer (C) is correct. *(CPA, adapted)*
REQUIRED: The annual stated interest rate for bonds.
DISCUSSION: Under the effective-interest method, bond interest expense equals the carrying amount ($185,953) of the bonds at the beginning of the period times the effective interest rate. The Album Co. bonds must have been issued at a discount given an initial carrying amount lower than their face amount (debit cash for $185,953, debit discount for $14,047, credit bonds payable for $200,000). Bond discount amortization is then determined by comparing the bond interest expense with the interest to be paid. The bonds were sold at a discount, allowing the bond holder to earn the market rate of interest rather than the lower nominal rate. The nominal (annual stated) rate is 12% [2 × ($12,000 semiannual interest paid ÷ $200,000 face amount of the bonds)]. Accordingly, the journal entry to record the first interest payment is

Bond interest expense	$13,016	
Discount on bonds payable		$ 1,106
Cash		12,000

Answer (A) is incorrect because 6% is half of the annual stated rate. The first interest payment is one of two semi-annual payments. Answer (B) is incorrect because 7% is half of the annual effective rate. Answer (D) is incorrect because 14% is the annual effective rate [2 × ($13,016 ÷ $185,953)].

12.3 Debt Issue Costs

9. During Year 4, Eddy Corp. incurred the following costs in connection with the issuance of bonds:

Printing and engraving	$ 30,000
Legal fees	160,000
Fees paid to independent accountants for registration information	20,000
Commissions paid to underwriter	300,000

What amount should be recorded as a deferred charge to be amortized over the term of the bonds?

A. $510,000

B. $480,000

C. $300,000

D. $210,000

Answer (A) is correct. *(CPA, adapted)*
REQUIRED: The amount to be recorded as a deferred charge.
DISCUSSION: APB Opinion 21, *Interest on Receivables and Payables*, states that issue costs should be reported in the balance sheet as deferred charges to be amortized over the life of the bonds. They should not be commingled with bond premium or discount. Issue costs are incurred to bring a bond to market. They include lawyers', accountants', and underwriters' fees; engraving and printing costs; registration costs; and promotion costs. In this case, they include the $30,000 of printing and engraving costs, the $160,000 of legal fees, the $20,000 of accountants' fees, and the $300,000 of underwriter's commissions. Hence, the amount that should be recorded as a deferred charge to be amortized over the term of the bonds is equal to $510,000.
Answer (B) is incorrect because $480,000 omits the printing and engraving costs. Answer (C) is incorrect because $300,000 includes the commissions only. Answer (D) is incorrect because $210,000 excludes the commissions.

10. On January 2, Year 3, Gill Co. issued $2 million of 10-year, 8% bonds at par. The bonds, dated January 1, Year 3, pay interest semiannually on January 1 and July 1. Bond issue costs were $250,000. What amount of bond issue costs are unamortized at June 30, Year 4?

A. $237,500

B. $225,000

C. $220,800

D. $212,500

Answer (D) is correct. *(CPA, adapted)*
    REQUIRED: The amount to be recorded as unamortized bond issue costs.
    DISCUSSION: Bond issue costs are customarily amortized using the straight-line method over the term of the bonds. The amortization is $25,000 per year ($250,000 ÷ 10 years). Because the bond has been held for 18 months, $37,500 ($25,000 + $12,500) of issue costs have been amortized by June 30, Year 4. The unamortized issue costs are $212,500 ($250,000 – $37,500).
    Answer (A) is incorrect because an additional full year of amortization should have been claimed. Answer (B) is incorrect because 6 more months of issue costs should have been amortized for the time between January 1 and June 30, Year 4. Answer (C) is incorrect because $220,800 results from amortization using the interest method. Although the interest method is theoretically superior, issue costs are customarily amortized using the straight-line method.

11. Perk, Inc. issued $500,000, 10% bonds to yield 8%. Bond issuance costs were $10,000. How should Perk calculate the net proceeds to be received from the issuance?

A. Discount the bonds at the stated rate of interest.

B. Discount the bonds at the market rate of interest.

C. Discount the bonds at the stated rate of interest and deduct bond issuance costs.

D. Discount the bonds at the market rate of interest and deduct bond issuance costs.

Answer (D) is correct. *(CPA, adapted)*
    REQUIRED: The net proceeds to be received from the issuance.
    DISCUSSION: Bonds are sold at the sum of the present values of the maturity amount and the interest payments (if interest-bearing). The difference between the face amount and the selling price of bonds is either a discount or a premium. Bonds are sold at a discount when they sell for less than face amount, that is, when the contract (stated) interest rate is less than the market (effective) interest rate. Bonds are sold at a premium (in excess of face amount) when the stated rate exceeds the effective rate. To determine the present value of the bonds' future cash flows, the market rate of interest is used as the discount rate. The result is the market price of the bonds at the issue date. The net proceeds equal the price of the bonds minus the issue costs. Issue costs are incurred to bring a bond to market and include printing and engraving costs, legal fees, accountants' fees, underwriters' commissions, registration fees, and promotion costs.
    Answer (A) is incorrect because the bonds should be discounted at the market rate, and the net proceeds equal the price (cash flows discounted at the market rate) minus the issue costs. Answer (B) is incorrect because the net proceeds equal the price (cash flows discounted at the market rate) minus the issue costs. Answer (C) is incorrect because the bonds should be discounted at the market rate.

12.4 Convertible Debt

12. Which of the following statements characterizes convertible debt?

A. The holder of the debt must be repaid with shares of the issuer's stock.

B. No value is assigned to the conversion feature when convertible debt is issued.

C. The transaction should be recorded as the issuance of stock.

D. The issuer's stock price is **less** than market value when the debt is converted.

Answer (B) is correct. *(CPA, adapted)*
    REQUIRED: The characteristic of convertible debt.
    DISCUSSION: APB Opinion 14, *Accounting for Convertible Debt and Debt issued with Stock Purchase Warrants*, states that the debt and equity aspects of convertible debt are inseparable. The entire proceeds should be accounted for as debt until conversion.
    Answer (A) is incorrect because the holder of the debt has an option to receive (1) the face or redemption amount of the security or (2) common shares. Answer (C) is incorrect because the entire proceeds should be accounted for as debt until conversion. Answer (D) is incorrect because conversion is favorable to the holder when the market value of the issuer's common stock is greater than the conversion price. (The conversion price exceeds market value upon initial issuance.)

13. On January 2, Year 1, Chard Co. issued 10-year convertible bonds at 105. During Year 4, these bonds were converted into common stock having an aggregate par value equal to the total face amount of the bonds. At conversion, the market price of Chard's common stock was 50% above its par value. Depending on whether the book-value method or the market-value method was used, Chard should have recognized gains or losses on conversion when using the

	Book-Value Method	Market-Value Method
A.	Either gain or loss	Gain
B.	Either gain or loss	Loss
C.	Neither gain nor loss	Loss
D.	Neither gain nor loss	Gain

Answer (C) is correct. *(CPA, adapted)*
REQUIRED: The accounting method(s) that recognizes gains or losses on the conversion of convertible bonds.
DISCUSSION: Under the book-value method for recognizing the conversion of outstanding bonds payable to common stock, the stock issued is recorded at the carrying amount of the bonds with no recognition of gain or loss. Under the market-value method, the stock is recorded at the market value of the stock (or of the bonds). A gain or loss is recognized equal to the difference between the market value recorded and the carrying amount of the bonds payable. At the time of the conversion, Chard's common stock had an aggregate par value equal to the total face amount of the bonds, and the market price of the stock was 50% above its par value. Thus, a loss should have been recognized upon conversion in accordance with the market-value method. The total of the credits to equity accounts exceeds the total of the debits to bonds payable and unamortized premium. The difference is the loss.
Answer (A) is incorrect because use of the book-value method results in neither a gain nor a loss, and use of the market-value method results in a loss. Answer (B) is incorrect because use of the book-value method results in neither a gain nor a loss. Answer (D) is incorrect because use of the market-value method results in a loss.

14. On March 31, Year 4, Ashley, Inc.'s bondholders exchanged their convertible bonds for common stock. The carrying amount of these bonds on Ashley's books was less than the market value but greater than the par value of the common stock issued. If Ashley used the book-value method of accounting for the conversion, which of the following statements accurately states an effect of this conversion?

A. Equity is increased.

B. Additional paid-in capital is decreased.

C. Retained earnings is increased.

D. An extraordinary loss is recognized.

Answer (A) is correct. *(CPA, adapted)*
REQUIRED: The effect of converting bonds to common stock when using the book-value method.
DISCUSSION: Under the book-value method for recognizing the conversion of outstanding bonds payable to common stock, the stock issued is recorded at the carrying amount of the bonds with no recognition of gain or loss. Because the carrying amount of the bonds is greater than the par value of the common stock, the conversion will record common stock at par value and additional paid-in capital for the remainder of the carrying amount of the bonds. Ashley will decrease its liabilities (debit bonds payable) and increase its equity (credit common stock and additional paid-in capital).
Answer (B) is incorrect because additional paid-in capital will increase. Answer (C) is incorrect because retained earnings is not directly affected. Answer (D) is incorrect because no loss is associated with the conversion.

12.5 Stock Warrants

15. When bonds are issued with stock purchase warrants, a portion of the proceeds should be allocated to additional paid-in capital for bonds issued with

	Detachable Stock Purchase Warrants	Nondetachable Stock Purchase Warrants
A.	No	Yes
B.	Yes	Yes
C.	Yes	No
D.	No	No

Answer (C) is correct. *(CPA, adapted)*
REQUIRED: The warrants receiving an allocation of bond proceeds.
DISCUSSION: APB Opinion 14, *Accounting for Convertible Debt and Debt Issued with Stock Purchase Warrants*, requires the proceeds from debt securities issued with detachable warrants to be allocated between the debt securities and the warrants based on their relative fair values at the time of issuance. The portion allocated to the warrants should be accounted for as additional paid-in capital. However, when debt securities are issued with nondetachable warrants, no part of the proceeds should be allocated to the warrants.

16. Bonds with detachable stock warrants were issued by Flack Co. Immediately after issue, the aggregate market value of the bonds and the warrants exceeds the proceeds. Is the portion of the proceeds allocated to the warrants less than their market value, and is that amount recorded as contributed capital?

	Less Than Warrants' Market Value	Contributed Capital
A.	No	Yes
B.	Yes	No
C.	Yes	Yes
D.	No	No

Answer (C) is correct. *(CPA, adapted)*
REQUIRED: The allocation of proceeds to detachable warrants and the recording of the allocation.
DISCUSSION: APB Opinion 14, *Accounting for Convertible Debt and Debt Issued with Stock Purchase Warrants*, requires the proceeds from debt securities issued with detachable warrants to be allocated between the debt securities and the warrants based on their relative fair values at the time of issuance. The portion allocated to the warrants should be accounted for as paid-in capital. Assuming that the market values of both the bonds and the warrants are known, and that the proceeds are less than their sum, the allocation process must result in crediting additional paid-in capital from stock warrants (stock warrants outstanding) for less than their market value. If the market value of the bonds is not known, the warrants will be credited at their market value.
Answer (A) is incorrect because the warrants will be credited at less than market value. Answer (B) is incorrect because the amount allocated to the warrants is credited to paid-in (contributed) capital. Answer (D) is incorrect because the warrants will be credited at less than market value and the amount allocated to the warrants is credited to paid-in (contributed) capital.

17. On December 30, Year 4, Fort, Inc. issued 1,000 of its 8%, 10-year, $1,000 face value bonds with detachable stock warrants at par. Each bond carried a detachable warrant for one share of Fort's common stock at a specified option price of $25 per share. Immediately after issuance, the market value of the bonds without the warrants was $1,080,000 and the market value of the warrants was $120,000. In its December 31, Year 4 balance sheet, what amount should Fort report as bonds payable?

A. $1,000,000

B. $975,000

C. $900,000

D. $880,000

Answer (C) is correct. *(CPA, adapted)*
REQUIRED: The amount reported for bonds payable with detachable stock warrants.
DISCUSSION: The issue price of the bonds is allocated between the bonds and the detachable stock warrants based on their relative fair values. The market price of bonds without the warrants is $1,080,000, which is 90% [$1,080,000 ÷ ($1,080,000 + $120,000)] of the total fair value. Consequently, 90% of the issue price should be allocated to the bonds, and they should be reported at $900,000 ($1,000,000 × 90%) in the balance sheet.
Answer (A) is incorrect because $1,000,000 equals the total proceeds. Answer (B) is incorrect because $975,000 is the result of deducting the option price of the stock from the issue price. Answer (D) is incorrect because $880,000 is the result of deducting the fair value of the warrants from the issue price.

18. On July 28, Vent Corp. sold $500,000 of 4%, eight-year subordinated debentures for $450,000. The purchasers were issued 2,000 detachable warrants, each of which was for one share of $5 par common stock at $12 per share. Shortly after issuance, the warrants sold at a market price of $10 each. What amount of discount on the debentures should Vent record at issuance?

A. $50,000

B. $60,000

C. $70,000

D. $74,000

Answer (C) is correct. *(CPA, adapted)*
REQUIRED: The discount on bonds issued with detachable warrants.
DISCUSSION: When detachable warrants are issued with bonds, the proceeds must be allocated between the debt and the warrants based on their relative fair values at the time of issuance. But if the fair value of the warrants but not the debt is known, additional paid-in capital is credited for the fair value of the warrants. The fair value of the warrants is $20,000. Vent received $450,000 for the bonds and warrants. Accordingly, the amount assigned to the debt is $430,000 ($450,000 proceeds – $20,000 FV of the warrants). The discount is $70,000 ($500,000 face amount – $430,000).
Answer (A) is incorrect because $50,000 equals the face amount ($500,000) of the bonds minus the proceeds ($450,000). Answer (B) is incorrect because $60,000 is based on the assumption that the fair value of the warrants is $10,000 (2,000 warrants × $5). Answer (D) is incorrect because $74,000 is based on the assumption that the fair value of the warrants is $24,000 (2,000 warrants × $12).

12.6 Extinguishment of Debt

19. On March 1, Year 1, Somar Co. issued 20-year bonds at a discount. By September 1, Year 6, the bonds were quoted at 106 when Somar exercised its right to retire the bonds at 105. How should Somar report the bond retirement on its Year 6 income statement?

A. A gain in continuing operations.

B. A loss in continuing operations.

C. An extraordinary gain.

D. An extraordinary loss.

Answer (B) is correct. *(CPA, adapted)*
REQUIRED: The proper accounting for the retirement of a bond.
DISCUSSION: All extinguishment of debt before scheduled maturities are fundamentally alike and should be accounted for similarly. Gains or losses from early extinguishment should be recognized in income of the period of extinguishment (APB Opinion 26). Because the bonds were issued at a discount and were retired early for more than the carrying amount, a loss was incurred. Under APB Opinion 30, an event or transaction is perceived to be ordinary and usual absent clear evidence to the contrary. No such evidence is presented, and Somar should recognize an ordinary loss.
Answer (A) is incorrect because the amount paid exceeded the carrying amount. Thus, an ordinary loss is recognized. Answer (C) is incorrect because the bond retirement resulted in a loss that, absent contrary evidence, should be classified as ordinary. Answer (D) is incorrect because the loss is presumptively ordinary absent contrary evidence.

20. A 15-year bond was issued in Year 1 at a discount. During Year 10, a 10-year bond was issued at face amount with the proceeds used to retire the 15-year bond at its face amount. The net effect of the Year 10 bond transactions was to increase long-term liabilities by the excess of the 10-year bond's face amount over the 15-year bond's

A. Face amount.

B. Carrying amount.

C. Face amount minus the deferred loss on bond retirement.

D. Carrying amount minus the deferred loss on bond retirement.

Answer (B) is correct. *(CPA, adapted)*
REQUIRED: The net effect of the bond transactions.
DISCUSSION: The 10-year bond was issued at its face amount, that is, at neither a premium nor a discount. Its face amount, therefore, equaled its proceeds, which were used to retire the 15-year bond at its face amount. The 15-year bond was carried at a discount (face amount – unamortized discount). Consequently, net long-term liabilities must have increased by the amount of the unamortized discount on the 15-year bond, which is the excess of the 10-year bond's face amount over the carrying amount of the 15-year bond.
Answer (A) is incorrect because the face amount of the 10-year bond equaled the face amount of the 15-year bond. Answer (C) is incorrect because the carrying amount of the 15-year bond should be used, and the loss is not deferred. Answer (D) is incorrect because the loss on early extinguishment is not deferred.

21. On July 31, Year 4, Dome Co. issued $1,000,000 of 10%, 15-year bonds at par and used a portion of the proceeds to call its 600 outstanding 11%, $1,000 face amount bonds, due on July 31, Year 14, at 102. On that date, unamortized bond premium relating to the 11% bonds was $65,000. In its Year 4 income statement, what amount should Dome report as gain or loss from retirement of bonds?

A. $53,000 gain.

B. $0

C. $(65,000) loss.

D. $(77,000) loss.

Answer (A) is correct. *(CPA, adapted)*
REQUIRED: The amount to be reported for the retirement of bonds.
DISCUSSION: The excess of the net carrying amount of the bonds over the reacquisition price is a gain from extinguishment. The carrying amount of the bonds equals $665,000 ($600,000 face amount + $65,000 unamortized premium). The reacquisition price is $612,000 (600 × $1,000 × 1.02). Thus, the gain from extinguishment is $53,000 ($665,000 – $612,000).
Answer (B) is incorrect because the excess of the carrying amount over the reacquisition cost is a gain. Answer (C) is incorrect because $65,000 is the unamortized premium. Answer (D) is incorrect because $77,000 equals the reacquisition price of $612,000, minus the face amount of $600,000, plus $65,000 unamortized premium.

22. In open market transactions, Gold Corp. simultaneously sold its long-term investment in Iron Corp. bonds and purchased its own outstanding bonds. The broker remitted the net cash from the two transactions. Gold's gain on the purchase of its own bonds exceeded its loss on the sale of the Iron bonds. Gold should report the

A. Net effect of the two transactions as an extraordinary gain.

B. Net effect of the two transactions in income before extraordinary items.

C. Gain on its purchase in income before extraordinary items and the loss on the sale as an extraordinary loss.

D. Gain on its purchase as an extraordinary gain and the loss on the sale in income before extraordinary items.

Answer (B) is correct. *(CPA, adapted)*
REQUIRED: The reporting of the sale of a long-term investment in bonds and an extinguishment of debt.
DISCUSSION: APB Opinion 26 requires that differences between the reacquisition prices and the net carrying amounts of extinguished debt be recognized currently as gains or losses in income of the period of extinguishment. Transactions are presumed to be ordinary and usual unless a pronouncement specifically states otherwise or the evidence clearly supports classification as extraordinary. No currently effective pronouncement classifies these transactions as extraordinary, and no evidence clearly supports that classification. The sale of securities and the extinguishment of debt are not clearly infrequent and unusual in the environment in which the entity operates. Thus, the gain on the bond purchase and the loss on the sale of bonds should be reported in income before extraordinary items.

23. On December 31, Marcar Co. placed cash of $430,000 in an irrevocable trust. The trust's assets are to be used solely for satisfying scheduled payments of both interest and principal on Marcar's $550,000 bond payable. The possibility that Marcar will be required to make future payments with respect to that debt is remote. Marcar has not been legally released from its obligations under the bond agreement. On December 31, the bond's carrying amount was $520,000, and its present value was $400,000. Disregarding income taxes, what amount of gain (loss) should Marcar report in its income statement for the year?

A. $0

B. $90,000

C. $120,000

D. $150,000

Answer (A) is correct. *(Publisher, adapted)*
REQUIRED: The amount of extraordinary gain (loss) on an in-substance defeasance.
DISCUSSION: In accordance with SFAS 140, *Accounting for Transfers and Servicing of Financial Assets and Extinguishments of Liabilities*, an in-substance defeasance is not considered to be an extinguishment of debt. A debtor may derecognize a liability only if it has been extinguished. An extinguishment occurs only if the debtor (1) pays the creditor and is relieved of the obligation or (2) is legally released from being the primary obligor. Hence, the liability has not been extinguished, and no gain or loss should be recognized.
Answer (B) is incorrect because $90,000 is the gain if the debt is considered to be extinguished. Answer (C) is incorrect because $120,000 is the difference between the face amount and the proceeds paid. Answer (D) is incorrect because $150,000 is the difference between the face amount and the present value.

12.7 Refinancing of Short-Term Obligations

24. Verona Co. had $500,000 in short-term liabilities at the end of the current year. Verona issued $400,000 of common stock subsequent to the end of the year, but before the financial statements were issued. The proceeds from the stock issue were intended to be used to pay the short-term debt. What amount should Verona report as a short-term liability on its balance sheet at the end of the current year?

A. $0

B. $100,000

C. $400,000

D. $500,000

Answer (B) is correct. *(CPA, adapted)*
REQUIRED: The amount of the short-term liability.
DISCUSSION: The portion of debt scheduled to mature in the following fiscal year ordinarily should be classified as a current liability. However, if an entity intends to refinance short-term obligations on a long-term basis and demonstrates an ability to consummate the refinancing, the obligation should be excluded from current liabilities and classified as noncurrent. One method of demonstrating the ability to refinance is to issue long-term obligations or equity securities after the balance sheet date but before the financial statements are issued (SFAS 6). Verona demonstrated an ability to refinance $400,000 of the short-term liabilities by issuing common stock. Hence, it should report a short-term liability of $100,000 ($500,000 – $400,000).
Answer (A) is incorrect because Verona did not demonstrate an ability to refinance the full amount of the short-term liabilities. Answer (C) is incorrect because $400,000 equals the proceeds from the issuance of stock. Answer (D) is incorrect because $500,000 is based on the assumption that the entity's intent to refinance has not been demonstrated.

25. On December 31, Year 4, Largo, Inc. had a $750,000 note payable outstanding due July 31, Year 5. Largo borrowed the money to finance construction of a new plant. Largo planned to refinance the note by issuing long-term bonds. Because Largo temporarily had excess cash, it prepaid $250,000 of the note on January 12, Year 5. In February Year 5, Largo completed a $1.5 million bond offering. Largo will use the bond offering proceeds to repay the note payable at its maturity and to pay construction costs during Year 5. On March 3, Year 5, Largo issued its Year 4 financial statements. What amount of the note payable should Largo include in the current liabilities section of its December 31, Year 4, balance sheet?

A. $750,000

B. $500,000

C. $250,000

D. $0

Answer (C) is correct. *(CPA, adapted)*
REQUIRED: The amount that should be classified as short-term obligations.
DISCUSSION: The portion of debt scheduled to mature in the following fiscal year ordinarily should be classified as a current liability. However, if an entity intends to refinance short-term obligations on a long-term basis and demonstrates an ability to consummate the refinancing, the obligation should be excluded from current liabilities and classified as noncurrent. One method of demonstrating the ability to refinance is to issue long-term obligations or equity securities after the balance sheet date but before the financial statements are issued (SFAS 6). Largo demonstrated an intention to refinance $500,000 of the note payable. Thus, the portion prepaid ($250,000) is a current liability, and the remaining $500,000 should be classified as noncurrent.
Answer (A) is incorrect because $750,000 includes the $500,000 that was refinanced. Answer (B) is incorrect because $500,000 is the amount that should be reclassified as noncurrent. Answer (D) is incorrect because $250,000 should be classified as a current liability.

12.8 Noncurrent Notes Payable

Questions 26 and 27 are based on the following information. House Publishers offered a contest in which the winner would receive $1 million, payable over 20 years. On December 31, Year 4, House announced the winner of the contest and signed a note payable to the winner for $1 million, payable in $50,000 installments every January 2. Also on December 31, Year 4, House purchased an annuity for $418,250 to provide the $950,000 prize monies remaining after the first $50,000 installment, which was paid on January 2, Year 5.

26. In its December 31, Year 4, balance sheet, at what amount should House measure the note payable, net of current portion?

A. $368,250

B. $418,250

C. $900,000

D. $950,000

Answer (B) is correct. *(CPA, adapted)*
REQUIRED: The amount at which the note payable should be measured.
DISCUSSION: Noninterest-bearing notes payable should be measured at their present value rather than their face amount. Thus, the measure of the note payable, net of the current portion, which has a nominal amount equal to its present value at December 31, Year 4, of $50,000, is its present value of $418,250 (debit annuity cost $418,250, debit discount $531,750, credit note payable $950,000). Under APB Opinion 21, the present value of the noncurrent portion of the note is assumed to be the cash given for the annuity ($418,250) because no other right or privilege was exchanged.
Answer (A) is incorrect because $368,250 includes a reduction of $50,000 for the first installment. Answer (C) is incorrect because $900,000 equals the face amount of the note payable minus two installments. Answer (D) is incorrect because $950,000 equals the face amount of the note payable minus the first installment.

27. In its Year 4 income statement, what should House report as contest prize expense?

A. $0

B. $418,250

C. $468,250

D. $1,000,000

Answer (C) is correct. *(CPA, adapted)*
REQUIRED: The contest prize expense.
DISCUSSION: The contest prize expense equals $468,250 ($418,250 cost of the annuity + $50,000 first installment).
Answer (A) is incorrect because $0 does not include the purchase of the annuity or the first installment as an expense in Year 4. Answer (B) is incorrect because $418,250 does not include the $50,000 installment due in Year 5. Answer (D) is incorrect because $1,000,000 is the face amount of the note.

28. On December 31, Year 4, Roth Co. issued a $10,000 note payable to Wake Co. in exchange for services rendered to Roth. The transaction was not in the normal course of business. The note, made at usual trade terms, is due in 9 months and bears interest, payable at maturity, at the annual rate of 3%, a rate that is unreasonable in the circumstances. The market interest rate is 8%, the prevailing rate for similar instruments of issuers with similar credit ratings. The compound interest factor of $1 due in 9 months at 8% is .944. At what amount should the note payable be credited in Roth's December 31, Year 4, balance sheet?

A. $10,300

B. $10,000

C. $9,652

D. $9,440

Answer (C) is correct. *(CPA, adapted)*
REQUIRED: The amount credited for a note payable.
DISCUSSION: APB Opinion 21, *Interest on Receivables and Payables*, applies to this short-term payable because the transaction was not in the ordinary course of business. Thus, the payable is measured at present value. Moreover, absent evidence of the market value of the note or an established exchange price for the services, the present value of a note with an interest rate that is clearly unreasonable is determined by discounting the payments at an imputed rate. The prevailing rate for issuers with similar credit ratings normally helps determine the appropriate rate. Assuming that 8% is the best approximation of the rate that would have resulted in a similar transaction between independent parties, the note payable should be credited at its present value of $9,652 {($10,000 × .944) + [$10,000 × 3% × .944 × (9 ÷ 12)]}.
Answer (A) is incorrect because $10,300 is the sum of the face amount of the note and annual 3% interest. Answer (B) is incorrect because $10,000 is the face amount of the note. Answer (D) is incorrect because $9,440 is the present value of the principal of the note.

29. On March 1, Year 3, Fine Co. borrowed $10,000 and signed a 2-year note bearing interest at 12% per annum compounded annually. Interest is payable in full at maturity on February 28, Year 5. What amount should Fine report as a liability for accrued interest at December 31, Year 4?

A. $0

B. $1,000

C. $1,200

D. $2,320

Answer (D) is correct. *(CPA, adapted)*
REQUIRED: The amount of accrued interest liability.
DISCUSSION: Given annual compounding, interest for the second year is calculated based on a carrying amount equal to the $10,000 principal plus the $1,200 ($10,000 × 12%) of first-year interest. Thus, accrued interest for the next 10 months is $1,120 [($10,000 + $1,200) × 12% × (10 months ÷ 12 months)]. Total accrued interest after 22 months is $2,320 ($1,200 + $1,120).
Answer (A) is incorrect because interest is accrued annually. Answer (B) is incorrect because $1,000 is the Year 3 interest accrual. Answer (C) is incorrect because $1,200 is the interest for the first 12 months.

30. A company issued a current note payable with a stated 12% rate of interest to a bank. The bank charged a .5% loan origination fee and remitted the balance to the company. The effective interest rate paid by the company in this transaction is

A. Equal to 12.5%.

B. More than 12.5%.

C. Less than 12.5%.

D. Independent of 12.5%.

Answer (B) is correct. *(CPA, adapted)*
REQUIRED: The effective interest rate paid by the company.
DISCUSSION: The proceeds received by the company equaled the face amount minus the loan origination fee, but interest is calculated on the face amount, and the company must repay the face amount. Thus, the effective rate paid by the company equals the sum of the fee and the interest, divided by the proceeds, a rate that must exceed 12.5%. For example, if the note is for $200, the nominal rate is 12%, and the lender charges a fee of .5%, the proceeds will be $199 [$200 – (.005 × $200)], the sum of the interest and the fee will be $25 [(.12 × $200) + (.005 × $200)], and the effective interest rate will be 12.5628% ($25 ÷ $199).

12.9 Troubled Debt Restructuring

31. For a troubled debt restructuring involving only a modification of terms, which of the following items specified by the new terms would be compared with the carrying amount of the debt to determine whether the debtor should report a gain on restructuring?

A. The total future cash payments.

B. The present value of the debt at the original interest rate.

C. The present value of the debt at the modified interest rate.

D. The amount of future cash payments designated as principal repayments.

Answer (A) is correct. *(CPA, adapted)*
REQUIRED: The item used to determine the debtor's gain on a troubled debt restructuring.
DISCUSSION: Under SFAS 15, *Accounting by Debtors and Creditors for Troubled Debt Restructurings*, when a troubled debt restructuring includes a modification of terms that results in future undiscounted cash flows less than the carrying amount of the debt, the debtor recognizes a gain equal to the difference. If the future undiscounted cash flows are greater than the carrying amount of the debt, the difference is recognized as interest using a new effective interest rate that equates the future cash payments with the carrying amount.

32. Ace Corp. entered into a troubled debt restructuring agreement with National Bank. National agreed to accept land with a carrying amount of $75,000 and a fair value of $100,000 in exchange for a note with a carrying amount of $150,000. Disregarding income taxes, what amount should Ace report as extraordinary gain in its income statement?

A. $0

B. $25,000

C. $50,000

D. $75,000

Answer (A) is correct. *(CPA, adapted)*
REQUIRED: The amount reported by the debtor as an extraordinary gain in a troubled debt restructuring.
DISCUSSION: The debtor must recognize a gain as a result of the extinguishment of debt because the creditor settled the debt by accepting assets with a fair value less than the carrying amount of the debt. However, no extraordinary gain is recognized. An event or transaction is presumed to be ordinary and usual absent clear evidence to the contrary (APB Opinion 30). Accordingly, Ace should recognize an ordinary gain of $75,000 attributable to the $25,000 appreciation of the land ($100,000 fair value – $75,000 carrying amount) and the $50,000 excess of the carrying amount of the debt over the fair value of the land ($150,000 – $100,000).

33. On December 30, Year 4, Hale Corp. paid $400,000 cash and issued 80,000 shares of its $1 par value common stock to its unsecured creditors on a pro rata basis pursuant to a reorganization plan under Chapter 11 of the bankruptcy statutes. Hale owed these unsecured creditors a total of $1.2 million. Hale's common stock was trading at $1.25 per share on December 30, Year 4. As a result of this transaction, Hale's total equity had a net increase of

A. $1,200,000

B. $800,000

C. $100,000

D. $80,000

Answer (B) is correct. *(CPA, adapted)*
REQUIRED: The net increase in equity immediately after the Chapter 11 reorganization.
DISCUSSION: According to SFAS 15, a debtor that grants an equity interest in full settlement of a payable should account for the equity interest at fair value. The difference between the fair value of the equity interest and the carrying amount of the payable is a gain. The appropriate accounting for this troubled debt restructuring is to debit liabilities for $1,200,000 and to credit cash for $400,000, common stock at its par value of $80,000 (80,000 shares × $1), additional paid-in capital for $20,000 [80,000 shares × ($1.25 fair value per share – $1 par)], and a gain for $700,000. Accordingly, the net increase in total equity is $800,000 ($80,000 + $20,000 + $700,000).
Answer (A) is incorrect because $1,200,000 is the amount of the debt. Answer (C) is incorrect because $100,000 is the increase in contributed capital. Answer (D) is incorrect because $80,000 is the increase in common stock.

12.10 Asset Retirement Obligations

34. SFAS 143, *Asset Retirement Obligations*, prescribes the accounting for obligations related to the retirement of long-lived tangible assets. A liability for an asset retirement obligation (ARO) within the scope of SFAS 143 may arise solely from

A. A plan to sell a long-lived asset.

B. The improper operation of a long-lived asset.

C. The temporary idling of a long-lived asset.

D. The acquisition, construction, development, or normal operation of a long-lived asset.

Answer (D) is correct. *(Publisher, adapted)*
REQUIRED: The source of a liability for an ARO.
DISCUSSION: An ARO is recognized for a legal obligation relating to the retirement of a tangible long-lived asset. This obligation results from the acquisition, construction, development, or normal operation of such an asset.
Answer (A) is incorrect because the scope of SFAS 143 does not extend to obligations arising solely from a plan to sell or otherwise dispose of a long-lived asset covered by SFAS 144. Answer (B) is incorrect because the scope of SFAS 143 does not extend to obligations arising from the improper operation of an asset. Answer (C) is incorrect because retirement is the nontemporary removal of the asset from service, for example, by sale, abandonment, or recycling.

35. An entity is most likely to account for an asset retirement obligation (ARO) by

A. Recognizing the fair value of the liability using an expected present value technique.

B. Recognizing a liability equal to the sum of the net undiscounted future cash flows associated with the ARO.

C. Decreasing the carrying amount of the related long-lived asset.

D. Decreasing the liability for the ARO to reflect the accretion expense.

Answer (A) is correct. *(Publisher, adapted)*
REQUIRED: The proper accounting for an ARO.
DISCUSSION: The fair value of the ARO liability is recognized when incurred. If a reasonable estimate of the fair value cannot be made at that time, the ARO will be recognized when such an estimate can be made. An expected present value technique ordinarily should be used to estimate the fair value. A credit-adjusted risk-free rate is the appropriate discount rate (SFAS 146 as amended by SFAS 157).
Answer (B) is incorrect because a present value method may be used to estimate fair value. Probability-weighted present values, not undiscounted amounts, are ordinarily used to measure the ARO. Answer (C) is incorrect because the associated asset retirement cost (ARC) is added (debited) to the carrying amount of the tangible long-lived asset when the ARO is recognized (credited). Answer (D) is incorrect because accretion expense is debited when the ARO is credited to reflect its increase due to passage of time.

36. On January 1, 10 years ago, Andrew Co. created a subsidiary for the purpose of buying an oil tanker depot at a cost of $1,500,000. Andrew expected to operate the depot for 10 years, at which time it is legally required to dismantle the depot and remove underground storage tanks. It was estimated that it would cost $150,000 to dismantle the depot and remove the tanks at the end of the depot's useful life. However, the actual cost to demolish and dismantle the depot and remove the tanks in the tenth year is $155,000. What amount of loss should Andrew recognize in its financial statements in Year 10?

A. None.

B. $5,000

C. $150,000

D. $155,000

Answer (B) is correct. *(CPA, adapted)*
REQUIRED: The settlement loss for an asset retirement obligation.
DISCUSSION: The asset retirement obligation (ARO) is recognized at fair value when incurred. An expected present value technique ordinarily is used to estimate the fair value. An amount equal to the ARO is the associated asset retirement cost (ARC). It is debited to the long-lived asset when the ARO is credited. The ARC is allocated to expense using the straight-line method over the life of the underlying asset (debit depreciation expense-ARC, credit accumulated depreciation). Furthermore, the entity recognizes accretion expense as an allocation of the difference between the maturity amount and the carrying amount of the ARO. Accretion expense for a period equals the beginning carrying amount of the ARO times the credit-adjusted risk-free interest rate. This amount is debited to accretion expense and credited to the ARO. At the end of the useful life of the underlying asset (the depot), the ARO should equal its maturity amount ($150,000). Moreover, the carrying amount of the ARC is zero. The credit balance in accumulated depreciation-ARC equals the initial debit to record the ARC. Accordingly, given that the ARO liability after 10 years is $150,000, and the settlement cost is $155,000, the entry to record the settlement is to debit the ARO for $150,000, debit a loss for $5,000, and credit cash (or other accounts) for $155,000.
Answer (A) is incorrect because the actual settlement cost exceeded the ARO. Answer (C) is incorrect because $150,000 is the maturity amount of the ARO. Answer (D) is incorrect because $155,000 equals the actual settlement cost.

12.11 Costs Associated with Exit or Disposal Activities

Questions 37 and 38 are based on the following information. Employer plans to close a plant in 18 months. All of the employees of the plant will be terminated at the time of closing. Because of its need to retain employees until closing, Employer defines a one-time benefit arrangement in a plan of termination that meets the criteria established by GAAP, including communication to employees. Under the plan, each employee who provides services for the entire 18-month period will receive a bonus of $5,000 payable 6 months after termination. An employee who leaves voluntarily prior to closing will receive no part of the bonus. The expected value of the cash outflow for this one-time termination benefit is $2,000,000. Employer's credit-adjusted risk-free (CARF) rate is 3% semiannually. Potentially relevant interest factors for the present value of $1 include the following:

3% for	1 period	.971
	2 periods	.943
	3 periods	.915
	4 periods	.888

37. What is the amount of the liability recognized by Employer in the first month of the future service period?

A. $98,667

B. $107,889

C. $1,776,000

D. $1,942,000

Answer (B) is correct. *(Publisher, adapted)*
REQUIRED: The liability recognized in the first month of the future service period.
DISCUSSION: Employees may be required to provide services until terminated and be retained beyond the minimum retention period. Hence, an exchange transaction (promise of one-time benefits for rendition of services beyond a minimum period) is involved, and no present obligation exists at the communication date. In these circumstances, initial measurement of the liability is at the communication date in an amount equal to the fair value on the termination date. The liability is recognized proportionately over the future service period, that is, as employees provide services over the future service period. The termination date is 18 months after the communication date and 6 months before payment must be made. Using expected present value to estimate fair value, the initial measurement of the fair value at the termination date equals $2,000,000 discounted at the CARF rate of 3% for one semiannual period, or $1,942,000 ($2,000,000 × .971). Accordingly, the monthly liability recognized ratably over the future service period is $107,889 ($1,942,000 ÷ 18 months).
Answer (A) is incorrect because $98,667 results from using the present value at the communication date. Answer (C) is incorrect because $1,776,000 is the present value at the communication date. Answer (D) is incorrect because $1,942,000 is the present value at the termination date calculated at the measurement date.

38. Assume that, after 6 months, Employer revises its expected value of the cash outflow for the bonus to $1,600,000 because fewer employees are likely to remain for the full service period. What is the amount of the cumulative-effect change, if any, required to reflect this revised estimate?

A. $86,311

B. $129,467

C. $517,867

D. $647,334

Answer (B) is correct. *(Publisher, adapted)*
REQUIRED: The amount of the cumulative effect change.
DISCUSSION: The timing or amount of estimated cash flows may be revised. Any revisions must be measured using the CARF rate on which the initial measurement was based. The cumulative effect of this accounting change adjusts the liability in the period of change. The new expected present value estimate of the fair value of the one-time termination benefit at the termination date is $1,553,600 ($1,600,000 × .971 interest factor for 3% and one semiannual period). The liability that should have been recognized for the first 6 months is $517,867 [($1,553,600 ÷ 18 months) × 6 months]. The liability recognized would have been $647,334 ($107,889 recognized per month under the original estimate × 6 months). Thus, the reduction in the liability (the cumulative-effect change) is $129,467 ($647,334 − $517,867).
Answer (A) is incorrect because $86,311 is the monthly amount of the liability that should be recognized given the new estimate. Answer (C) is incorrect because $517,867 is the liability that should have been recognized for the first 6 months given the new estimate. Answer (D) is incorrect because $647,334 is the liability recognized for the first 6 months under the initial estimate.

39. Grand Corporation has decided to close its plant in Littleville. Accordingly, it will terminate the 50 employees who work at the plant. Grand gives the employees 60 days' notice on March 1 that it will close the plant on April 30. It will pay each employee $3,000 at the time (s)he stops providing services during the retention period. This one-time benefit arrangement is defined in a plan of termination that meets the criteria established by GAAP, including communication to employees. Grand should account for the one-time termination benefits by recognizing a liability

A. At the communication date at either fair value on that date or $150,000.

B. At the termination date for $150,000.

C. At the communication date at fair value on the termination date.

D. Ratably over the future service period.

Answer (A) is correct. *(Publisher, adapted)*
REQUIRED: The accounting for one-time termination benefits payable if employees will receive those benefits whenever they stop providing services.
DISCUSSION: Under SFAS 146, *Costs Associated with Exit or Disposal Activities*, one-time termination benefits are paid under a one-time benefit arrangement based on a plan of termination for a specified termination event or future period. If employees need not provide services until terminated to receive the benefits, or if they will not be retained beyond the minimum retention period, the liability is recognized at the communication date. The reason is that a present obligation exists at that time. Measurement is at fair value on the communication date. However, use of estimates and computational shortcuts consistent with measurement at fair value is permitted. Thus, given the brevity of the discount period, the total of the undiscounted cash payments of $150,000 (50 employees × $3,000) is a reasonable estimate of the fair value.

Answer (B) is incorrect because the liability is recognized at the communication date if employees need not provide services until they are terminated to qualify for the benefits or if they will not be retained beyond the minimum retention period. No exchange of benefits for future services exists in this case. Answer (C) is incorrect because recognition and measurement are at fair value (or $150,000) on the communication date. Answer (D) is incorrect because, if employees must provide services until terminated and will be retained beyond the minimum retention period, the liability is recognized ratably over the future service period.

Use Gleim's **CPA Test Prep** CD-Rom/Pocket PC for interactive testing with over 4,000 additional questions!

12.12 PRACTICE SIMULATION

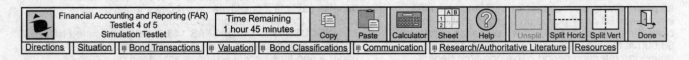

1. Directions

In the following simulation, you will be asked to complete various tasks. You may use the content in the **Information Tabs** to complete the tasks in the **Work Tabs**.

Information Tabs:

| Directions | Resources |

FIG 1

- Go through each of the **Information Tabs** to familiarize yourself with the simulation content
- The **Resources** tab will contain information, including formulas and definitions, that may help you to complete the tasks
- Your simulation may have more **Information Tabs** than those shown in Fig. 1

Work Tabs:

FIG. 2

- **Work Tabs**, to the right of **Information Tabs**, contain the tasks for you to complete
- **Work Tabs** contain directions for completing each task - be sure to read these directions carefully
- The tab names in Fig. 2 are for illustration only - yours may differ
- Once you complete any part of a task, the pencil for that tab will be shaded (see **Communication** in Fig. 2)
- The shaded pencil does **NOT** indicate that you have completed the entire task
- You must complete all of the tasks in the **Work Tabs** to receive full credit

Research/Authoritative Literature Tab:

| Research/Authoritative Literature |

FIG. 3

- This tab contains both the Research task and the Authoritative Literature
- Detailed instructions for completing the Research task, and for using the Authoritative Literature, appear on this tab
- You may use the Authoritative Literature as a resource for completing other tasks

NOTE: If you believe you have encountered a software malfunction, report it to the test center staff immediately.

2. Situation

On January 2, Year 1, Dru, Inc. issued bonds payable with a face amount of $480,000 at a discount. The bonds are due in 10 years, and interest is payable semiannually every June 30 and December 31. On June 30, Year 1, and on December 31, Year 1, its fiscal year-end, Dru made the semiannual interest payments due and recorded interest expense and amortization of bond discount.

Dru, Inc.'s $50 par value common stock has always traded above par.

During Year 1, Dru had several transactions that affected the following balance sheet accounts: bond discount, bond premium, and bonds payable.

- Dru issued bonds payable with a nominal rate of interest that was less than the market rate of interest.
- Dru issued bonds convertible to common stock for an amount in excess of the bonds' face amounts.
- Dru issued common stock when the convertible bonds were submitted for conversion. Each $1,000 bond was converted into 20 common shares. The book-value method was used for the early conversion.
- Dru issued bonds, with detachable stock warrants, for an amount equal to the face amount of the bonds. The stock warrants have a determinable value.
- Dru declared and issued a 2% stock dividend.

On December 31, Year 1, Dru had short-term obligations that it intends to refinance on a long-term basis, including $100,000 of commercial paper and a $200,000 construction loan. To refinance the commercial paper, Dru issued equity securities on January 10, Year 1. To refinance the construction loan, Dru entered into a financing agreement on January 15, Year 1, that will expire on December 31, Year 2.

3. Bond Transactions

This set of questions has a matching format. Select the best match for each numbered item from the terms in the drop-down list and write it in the column provided. Each choice may be used once, more than once, or not at all.

Determine whether the transaction increased, decreased, or had no effect on the balances of bond discount, bond premium, and bonds payable.

Transaction	Bond Discount	Bond Premium	Bonds Payable
1. Dru issued bonds payable with a nominal rate of interest that was less than the market rate of interest.			
2. Dru issued bonds convertible to common stock for an amount in excess of the bonds' face amount.			
3. Dru issued common stock when the convertible bonds described in item 2 were submitted for conversion. Each $1,000 bond was converted into 20 common shares. The book-value method was used for the early conversion.			
4. Dru issued bonds with detachable stock warrants for a total amount equal to the face amount of the bonds. The stock warrants have a determinable value.			
5. Dru declared and issued a 2% stock dividend.			

Choices
Increased
Decreased
No effect

4. Valuation

This question is presented in a spreadsheet format that requires you to fill in the correct responses in the shaded cells provided. Given the information in the situation, fill in the numbered boxes with the appropriate amounts or rates.

	Cash	Interest Expense	Amortization	Discount	Carrying Amount
1/2/Year 1					[1]
6/30/Year 1	[3]	$18,000	$3,600	[2]	$363,600
12/31/Year 1	$14,400	[6]	[7]		

Interest Rates	
Stated	[4]
Effective	[5]

5. Bond Classifications

This set of questions has a matching format. Select the best match for each numbered item from the terms in the drop-down list and write its letter in the column provided. Each choice may be used once, more than once, or not at all. Given the description of each specific bond, select its most likely type.

Description	Answer
1. Backed by the borrower's general credit only.	
2. Usually backed by real estate.	
3. Usually bearer instruments.	
4. May be retired before maturity.	
5. Payable at prices related to gold.	
6. Issued by governmental units.	
7. Pays interest only at maturity.	

Choices
A) Debentures
B) Mortgage bonds
C) Term bonds
D) Coupon bonds
E) Income bonds
F) Deep discount bonds
G) Commodity-backed bonds
H) Revenue bonds
I) Callable bonds
J) Collateral trust bonds
K) Convertible bonds
L) Serial bonds

6. Communication

In a brief memorandum to a client, explain the nature of a troubled debt restructuring and how a creditor accounts for it after receipt of assets, a modification of terms, or a combination of the two. Type your communication in your word processor program and print out the copy in a memorandum-style format.

REMINDER: Your response will be graded for both technical content and writing skills. Technical content will be evaluated for information that is helpful to the intended reader and clearly relevant to the issue. Writing skills will be evaluated for development, organization, and the appropriate expression of ideas in professional correspondence. Use a standard business memo or letter format with a clear beginning, middle, and end. Do not convey information in the form of a table, bullet point list, or other abbreviated presentation.

To:	Client
From:	CPA
Subject:	Troubled debt restructuring

7. Research/Authoritative Literature

See page 12 in the Introduction of this book for a detailed explanation of the AICPA's new Research/Authoritative Literature work tab as well as a screenshot of how the tab will actually look on your exam.

APB Opinion 26, *Early Extinguishment of Debt*, applies to all extinguishments except troubled debt restructurings. Research and cite the paragraph that explains how gains and losses from extinguishment should be recognized.

Unofficial Answers

3. Bond Transactions (15 Gradable Items)

	Bond Discount	Bond Premium	Bonds Payable
1. Dru issued bonds payable with a nominal rate of interest that was less than the market rate of interest.	Increased	No effect	Increased
2. Dru issued bonds convertible to common stock for an amount in excess of the bonds' face amount.	No effect	Increased	Increased
3. Dru issued common stock when the convertible bonds described in item 2 were submitted for conversion. Each $1,000 bond was converted into 20 common shares. The book-value method was used for the early conversion.	No effect	Decreased	Decreased
4. Dru issued bonds with detachable stock warrants for a total amount equal to the face amount of the bonds. The stock warrants have a determinable value.	Increased	No effect	Increased
5. Dru declared and issued a 2% stock dividend.	No effect	No effect	No effect

1.   Bonds are sold at a discount when they sell for less than their face amount, that is, when the contract (stated) interest rate is less than the market (effective) interest rate. The entry is to debit cash and a discount and to credit bonds payable.

2.   APB Opinion 14, *Accounting for Convertible Debt and Debt Issued with Stock Purchase Warrants*, states that the debt and equity aspects of convertible debt are inseparable. The entire proceeds (usually cash) should be accounted for as debt (a liability) until conversion. Because the proceeds exceeded the face amount, the entry is to debit cash and credit a premium and bonds payable.

3.   Under the book-value method for recognizing the conversion of outstanding bonds payable to common stock, the stock issued is recorded at the carrying amount of the bonds (credit common stock and additional paid-in capital, debit the payable) at the time of issuance, with no recognition of gain or loss. This method is the most common and is deemed to be the generally accepted approach. The entry is to debit the premium and bonds payable and to credit common stock and additional paid-in capital.

4.   The proceeds from debt securities issued with detachable warrants are allocated between the debt securities and the warrants based on their relative fair values at the time of issuance. The bonds are then recorded in the customary way (debit cash, credit bonds payable at face amount, and debit discount or credit premium). Because the bonds and warrants were issued at the face amount of the bonds, and the warrants have a determinable value, the entry is to debit cash and a discount and to credit bonds payable and paid-in capital from warrants.

5.   The entry is to debit retained earnings and credit common stock and additional paid-in capital for the fair value of the shares.

4. Valuation (7 Gradable Items)

1. $360,000. The original carrying amount was $360,000 ($363,600 carrying amount on 6/30/Year 1 – $3,600 discount amortization on 6/30/Year 1).

2. $116,400. The original discount was $120,000 ($480,000 face amount – $360,000 original carrying amount). Thus, the discount at 6/30/Year 1 was $116,400 ($120,000 – $3,600 amortization).

3. $14,400. The semiannual credit to cash for interest paid does not change. The amount paid on 12/31/Year 1 ($14,400) is the same as that paid on 6/30/Year 1.

4.   6%. The stated annual interest rate equals cash paid ($14,400 × 2 = $28,800) divided by the face amount ($480,000), or 6%.

5.   10%. The semiannual effective interest rate equals interest expense ($18,000) divided by the carrying amount ($360,000), or 5%. Hence, the annual rate is 10% (2 × 5%).

6. $18,180. Interest expense equals the semiannual effective interest rate (5%) times the carrying amount at the beginning of the period ($363,600), or $18,180.

7. $3,780. The amortization equals the difference between interest expense ($18,180) and cash paid ($14,400), or $3,780.

5. Bond Classification (7 Gradable Items)

1. A) <u>Debentures</u> are backed by the borrower's general credit but not by specific collateral.

2. B) <u>Mortgage bonds</u> are backed by specific assets, usually real estate.

3. D) <u>Coupon bonds</u> are usually bearer instruments. Whoever presents the periodic interest coupons is entitled to payment.

4. I) <u>Callable bonds</u> may be redeemed by the issuer and retired before maturity.

5. G) <u>Commodity-backed bonds</u> are payable at prices related to a commodity, such as gold. They are also known as asset-linked bonds.

6. H) <u>Revenue bonds</u> are issued by governmental units and are payable from specific revenue sources.

7. F) <u>Deep-discount bonds</u> (zero-interest debentures or zero-coupon bonds) provide capital appreciation, not periodic interest income.

6. Communication (5 Gradable Items; for grading instructions, please refer to page 12.)

SFAS 15, *Accounting by Debtors and Creditors for Troubled Debt Restructurings*, is the applicable pronouncement. A TDR occurs when "a creditor for economic or legal reasons related to the debtor's financial difficulties grants a concession to the debtor that it would not otherwise consider."

If assets are received in full payment of a debt, a creditor accounts for them at fair value. The gain or loss equals the difference between the fair value received and the recorded investment. If the creditor receives long-lived assets to be sold from the debtor in full satisfaction of the debt, those assets should be accounted for at fair value minus cost to sell.

SFAS 114, *Accounting by Creditors for Impairment of a Loan*, applies to a TDR involving a modification of terms. All such loans are to be measured under SFAS 114. A loan is impaired if it is probable that the creditor will not collect all amounts due under the contractual terms of the original loan agreement. The impairment is measured based on the present value of the expected future cash flows discounted at the loan's effective interest rate. Based on the original contractual rate, a creditor also is permitted to measure impairment based on a loan's observable market price or the fair value of the collateral if the loan is collateral dependent. If foreclosure is probable, impairment is based on the fair value of the collateral. If the recorded investment in the loan exceeds the present value of the expected future cash flows (or an alternative measure), the creditor debits bad-debt expense and credits an allowance account. An existing allowance is adjusted appropriately, with a corresponding debit or credit to bad-debt expense.

SFAS 114 does not address the issues of recognition, measurement, or display of interest income derived from an impaired loan.

A TDR may involve a receipt of assets in partial satisfaction of a receivable and a modification of terms of the remainder. The creditor accounts for the assets received as described above. The creditor also reduces the recorded investment by the fair value minus cost to sell of the assets received. The creditor then accounts for the remaining portion under SFAS 114.

7. Research/Authoritative Literature (1 Gradable Item)

APB Opinion 26 -- *Early Extinguishment of Debt*

5. Differences on nonrefunding extinguishments are generally treated currently in income as losses or gains. Three basic methods are generally accepted to account for the differences on refunding transactions.

   a. Amortization over the remaining original life of the extinguished issue
   b. Amortization over the life of the new issue
   c. Recognition currently in income as a loss or gain

Each method has been supported in court decisions, in rulings of regulatory agencies, and in accounting literature.

Scoring Schedule:

	Correct Responses		Gradable Items		Weights		
Tab 3	_____	÷	15	×	20%	=	_____
Tab 4	_____	÷	7	×	20%	=	_____
Tab 5	_____	÷	7	×	15%	=	_____
Tab 6	_____	÷	5	×	30%	=	_____
Tab 7	_____	÷	1	×	15%	=	_____
							_____
							(Your Score)

Use Gleim's **CPA Gleim Online** to practice more simulations in a realistic environment.

STUDY UNIT THIRTEEN
LEASES AND CONTINGENCIES

(12 pages of outline)

A **lease** is a long-term, contractual agreement in which the **lessor** (owner) conveys to the **lessee** the right to use **specific property** for a stated period in exchange for a stated payment. The basic pronouncement applicable to leases is SFAS 13, *Accounting for Leases* (as amended). The complex accounting rules for leases attempt to remove subjectivity from the classification of the transactions. The fundamental issue is whether a lease is a long-term rental contract or a purchase-and-financing agreement. **Lessees** have an incentive to avoid capitalizing leases because such contracts require recognition of debt on the balance sheet. However, **lessors** may benefit, although the matter is more complex. For example, the lessee, not the lessor, depreciates a leased asset for financial statement purposes. Also, the financing aspect of the transaction may be at a favorable rate.

13.1 LESSEE ACCOUNTING FOR CAPITAL LEASES

Classification

1. Leases are classified in one of two ways.

    a. Substantially all of the benefits and risks of ownership remain with the lessor under an **operating lease**. Such a lease is a simple rental arrangement.

    b. Substantially all of the benefits and risks of ownership are transferred to the lessee under a **capital lease**. Such a lease is a purchase-and-financing arrangement.

2. A lease is classified as a capital lease by the **lessee** if, at its inception, **one of four criteria** is satisfied.

    a. The presence of **any one** of the following indicates that substantially all of the benefits and risks of ownership have been transferred:

        1) The lease provides for the **transfer of ownership**.
        2) The lease contains a **bargain purchase option (BPO)**.
        3) The lease term is **75% or more of the estimated economic life** of the leased property.

            a) This criterion is inapplicable if the beginning of the lease term falls within the last 25% of the property's total estimated economic life.

        4) The **present value of the minimum lease payments** (excluding executory costs) is **at least 90%** of the fair value of the leased property to the lessor at the inception of the lease.

            a) This criterion is inapplicable if the beginning of the lease term falls within the last 25% of the property's total estimated economic life.

    b. If a lease covers **only land** and it provides for either a transfer of ownership at the end of its term or a BPO, the lessee capitalizes the lease. Otherwise, it is accounted for as an **operating lease**.

Discount Rate

3. The lessee must record a capital lease as an asset and an obligation at an amount equal to the **present value of the minimum lease payments**.

Leased property	$XXX
Lease obligation	$XXX

4. The **discount rate** used by the lessee in calculating the present value of the minimum lease payments is the lower of

    a. The lessor's implicit rate if it is known to the lessee or
    b. The lessee's incremental borrowing rate.

5. If the lessor's implicit rate is unknown to the lessee, the lessor and the lessee may use **different rates**. The higher the rate used, the lower the present value of the minimum lease payments and the less likely that the fourth capitalization criterion will be met.

    a. Thus, if the lessee and lessor use **different rates**, one might recognize an operating lease and the other a capital lease.

6. The amount recorded for the present value of the minimum lease payments **cannot exceed** the fair value of the leased property at the inception of the lease.

Lessee's Minimum Lease Payments

7. **Minimum rental payments** are the periodic amounts owed by the lessee, minus any **executory costs** (such as insurance, maintenance, or taxes) that will be paid by the lessor.

8. A **BPO** gives the lessee the right to purchase the leased property for a price lower than its expected fair value at the date the BPO becomes exercisable. To qualify as a BPO, the option price must be sufficiently low that exercise "appears, at the inception of the lease, to be reasonably assured."

9. **Guaranteed residual value.** The residual value is generally the estimated fair value of the leased property upon expiration of the lease. All or part of this amount may be guaranteed by the lessee (or by an unrelated third party). Any amount guaranteed by the lessee is in effect a final payment to the lessor.

    a. FASB Interpretation No. 19, *Lessee Guarantee of the Residual Value of Leased Property*, states that the amount of guaranteed residual value to be **included** in the lessee's minimum lease payments is the **maximum** amount the lessee is obligated to pay.
    b. A guarantee of residual value may be obtained by the lessee from an **unrelated third party for the benefit of the lessor**. This third-party guarantee is specifically **excluded** from the lessee's minimum lease payments, if the lessor explicitly releases the lessee from liability on a **residual value deficiency**.

        1) Furthermore, amounts paid as consideration for this third-party guarantee are treated as executory costs and also are excluded.

10. A **nonrenewal penalty** is a required payment by the lessee upon failure to renew or extend the lease at the end of the lease term.

11. Minimum lease payments do **not** include **contingent rentals** (SFAS 29).

Calculation of the Minimum Lease Payments

12. Given a BPO, minimum lease payments have two components: (a) minimum rental payments (excluding executory costs) and (b) the amount of the BPO.

EXAMPLE

On January 2, Year 1, Cottle, Inc. leased a machine for 3 years from Crimson, LLC. Cottle must pay Crimson $100,000 at the end of each year. The machine's useful life is 4 years, and the estimated residual value at the end of 3 years is $50,000. The lease allows Cottle to purchase the machine at the end of the lease for $10,000. Cottle's incremental borrowing rate is 15%, but the rate implicit in the lease is 10%, which is known to Cottle. The present value factor for an ordinary annuity at 10% for three periods is 2.4869. The present value of $1 at 10% for three periods is .7513.

PV of minimum rental payments	=	$100,000 × 2.4869	=	$248,690
PV of BPO	=	$ 10,000 × .7513	=	7,513
		PV of minimum lease payments	=	$256,203

Leased machine	$256,203	
Lease obligation		$256,203

---

13. If no such BPO exists, the **present value of the minimum lease payments** equals the sum of the present values of (a) the minimum rental payments, (b) the amount of residual value guaranteed by the lessee, and (c) any nonrenewal penalty imposed.

EXAMPLE

In the previous example, assume no BPO. Instead, Cottle must guarantee that the residual value of the machine will be $50,000.

PV of minimum rental payments	=	$100,000 × 2.4869	=	$248,690
PV of guaranteed residual value	=	$ 50,000 × .7513	=	37,565
		PV of minimum lease payments	=	$286,255

Leased machine	$286,255	
Lease obligation		$286,255

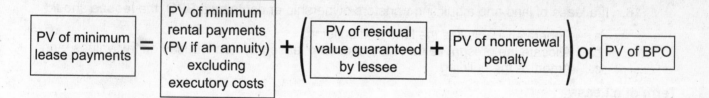

Lease Payments

14. Each periodic lease payment made by the lessee has two components: interest and the reduction of the lease obligation.

15. The **effective-interest method** is required. It applies the appropriate interest rate to the carrying amount of the lease obligation at the beginning of each period to calculate **interest expense**. The effect is to produce a constant periodic rate of interest on the remaining balance.

    a. The portion of the minimum lease payment in excess of interest expense reduces the lease liability.

    b. In a classified balance sheet, the lease liability must be allocated between **current and noncurrent** portions. The current portion at a balance sheet date is the reduction of the lease liability in the forthcoming year.

EXAMPLE

Assume the previous example with no BPO.

Date	Lease Obligation	Times: Effective Rate	Equals: Interest Expense	Cash Payment	Difference: Reduction of Lease Obligation	Lease Obligation
1/2/Year 1						$286,255
12/31/Year 1	$286,255	10%	$28,626	$100,000	$(71,374)	214,881
12/31/Year 2	214,881	10%	21,488	100,000	(78,512)	136,369
12/31/Year 3	136,369	10%	13,637	100,000	(86,363)	50,005

Journal Entries 12/31/Year 1

Interest expense	$28,626	
Interest payable		$28,626
Interest payable	$28,626	
Lease obligation	71,374	
Cash		$100,000

Lease of Land and a Building

16. If a lease of land and a building transfers ownership or contains a BPO, the **lessee** should

    a. Separately capitalize the land and building,
    b. Allocate the present value of the minimum lease payments based on fair values, and
    c. Amortize the building.

Term of a Lease

17. The term of a lease may not extend beyond the date a BPO becomes exercisable. In the absence of a BPO, the term of the lease includes the fixed, noncancelable lease term and any additional periods.

    a. Covered by bargain renewal options
    b. Covered by ordinary renewal options preceding the date at which a BPO is exercisable
    c. Covered by ordinary renewal options during which a guarantee by the lessee of the lessor's debt or a loan from the lessee to the lessor related to the leased property is expected to be in effect
    d. For which failure to renew the lease imposes a penalty on the lessee in an amount such that renewal appears to be reasonably assured
    e. Representing renewals or extensions of the lease at the lessor's option

Depreciation of Leased Assets

18. An asset recorded under a capital lease by the lessee should be depreciated in a manner consistent with the lessee's **normal depreciation policy**.

    a. Thus, the lease obligation is accounted for under lease accounting. However, the depreciation of the asset is the same as if the lessee owned the asset.

19. If the lease is capitalized because the lease either **transfers ownership** to the lessee by the end of the lease term (criterion 1) or contains a **BPO** (criterion 2), the depreciation of the asset is over its entire estimated **economic life**.

20. If the third capitalization criterion (lease term) or the fourth criterion (PV of minimum lease payments) is met, the asset is depreciated over the **lease term** to its expected value to the lessee, if any, at the end of that term.

    a. For example, if the lessee has guaranteed a residual value and has no interest in any excess that might be realized, the maximum expected value to the lessee is the amount of the guarantee.

21. Assets that are recorded under an operating lease are **not** depreciated.

    a. However, general improvements to leased property should be capitalized as leasehold improvements and amortized in accordance with the straight-line method over the shorter of their expected useful life or the lease term.

EXAMPLE

Using the information in the example under 15.b., Cottle will depreciate the machine using the same depreciation method (straight-line) that Cottle uses with other machines.

Depreciation expense [($286,255 − $50,000) ÷ 3]	$78,752	
Accumulated depreciation		$78,752

Operating Leases

22. **Rent** is reported as an expense by the **lessee** in accordance with the lease agreement.

23. If rental payments vary from a straight-line basis, e.g., if the first month is free, **rent expense** should be recognized over the full lease term on the **straight-line basis**. However, another systematic and rational basis may be used if it is more representative of the time pattern in which the benefit of the property is reduced.

Disclosures

24. **Future minimum lease payments** as of the latest balance sheet presented must be disclosed in the aggregate and for each of the 5 succeeding fiscal years. This disclosure is required whether the lease is a capital or an operating lease.

Stop and review! You have completed the outline for this subunit. Study multiple-choice questions 1 through 9 beginning on page 483.

13.2 LESSOR ACCOUNTING FOR CAPITAL LEASES

Classification

1. Lease classification is **more complex** for the lessor.

   a. For the lessor to treat a lease as a **capital lease**, the lease must first meet one of the four capitalization criteria described in Subunit 13.1, and **two** additional criteria must then be met:

      1) **Collectibility** of the remaining payments is reasonably predictable, **and**
      2) No material **uncertainties** exist regarding unreimbursable costs to be incurred by the lessor.

2. If the lease is to be capitalized, the lessor also must determine whether it is a direct financing or sales-type lease.

   a. If the asset's fair value at the inception of the lease **is equal** to its carrying amount, the lease is a **direct financing lease**.

   b. If the asset's fair value at the inception of the lease **is not equal** to its carrying amount, the lease is a **sales-type lease**.

Direct Financing Leases

3. In a direct financing lease, the lessor does **not** recognize a **manufacturer's or dealer's profit (loss)**. The lessor's economic interest is financing the purchase, not promoting the sale of its product. Thus, the lessor will **debit a lease receivable and credit the asset leased**.

4. The fair value of the leased property and its cost or carrying amount are the same at the inception of the lease. The difference between the **gross investment** (minimum lease payments + unguaranteed residual value) and the cost or carrying amount is recorded as **unearned income**.

5. **Initial direct costs** include the lessor's costs to originate a lease incurred in dealings with independent third parties that directly result from, and are essential to, the acquisition of the lease.

   a. They also include certain costs directly related to specified activities performed for that lease, e.g., (1) evaluating lessee financial condition and security arrangements, (2) negotiating terms, (3) preparing documents, and (4) closing.

6. The unearned income and the initial direct costs of a direct financing lease are amortized to income over the lease term using the interest method so as to produce a constant rate of return on the **net investment** (gross investment + unamortized initial direct costs − unearned income).

EXAMPLE

On January 2, Year 1, Cottle, Inc. leased a machine for 3 years from Crimson, LLC. Cottle must pay Crimson $100,000 at the end of each year. The machine has zero residual value after 3 years. The rate implicit in the lease is 10%. The present value factor for an ordinary annuity at 10% for three periods is 2.4869. The present value of $1 at 10% for three periods is .7513.

> PV of minimum rental payments = PV of minimum lease payments
> = $100,000 × 2.4869 = $248,690

Crimson's journal entry on January 2, Year 1:

Lease payments receivable*	$300,000	
Asset		$248,690
Unearned interest income		51,310

*This entry records the gross receivable. An alternative is to debit the receivable for an amount net of unearned interest.

Crimson's journal entry on December 31, Year 1:

Cash	$100,000	
Lease payments receivable		$100,000
Unearned interest income	$24,869	
Interest income		$24,869

Date	Lease Receivable	Times: Effective Rate	Equals: Interest Income	Cash Receipt	Difference: Reduction of Lease Receivable	Lease Receivable
1/2/Year 1						$248,690
12/31/Year 1	$248,690	10%	$24,869	$100,000	$(75,131)	173,559
12/31/Year 2	173,559	10%	17,356	100,000	(82,644)	90,915
12/31/Year 3	90,915	10%	9,091	100,000	(90,915)	0

Sales-Type Leases

7. In a **sales-type lease**, the lessor recognizes a **manufacturer's or dealer's profit (loss)**. The fair value of the leased property at the lease's inception differs from its cost or carrying amount.

8. In the entry for a sales-type lease,

   a. **Cost of goods sold** is debited for the cost or carrying amount, plus any initial direct costs, minus the present value of any unguaranteed residual value (a continuing investment of the lessor).

   b. **Lease payments receivable** is debited for the gross investment.

   c. The **asset** is credited for its cost or carrying amount.

   d. **Sales revenue** (price) is credited for the present value of the minimum lease payments.

   e. **Unearned interest income** is credited for the difference between the gross investment (lease payments receivable) and the sum of the present values of its components discounted at the rate implicit in the lease.

9. Assuming no initial direct costs, the **gross profit** on the sale will equal the sales revenue minus cost of goods sold.

10. Profit is not affected if **residual value is unguaranteed**. In that case, the present value of the residual value is not included in the present value of the minimum lease payments. As a result, both cost of goods sold and sales revenue are lower. Minimum lease payments include any residual value guaranteed by the lessee.

11. The **minimum lease payments** calculated by the **lessor** are the same as those for the lessee except that they include any residual value or rental payments beyond the lease term guaranteed by a financially capable third party unrelated to the lessor or the lessee.

> Lessor's PV of Minimum　=　Lessee's PV of Minimum　+　Amounts Guaranteed by
> 　　Lease Payments　　　　　　　　Lease Payments　　　　　　Lessee or Independent
> 　　　　　　　　　　　　　　　　　　　　　　　　　　　　　　　　　　　3rd Party

   a.　The effect of this difference may be that the fourth capitalization criterion is met by the lessor but not the lessee.

   b.　Assume a leased asset with a guaranteed residual value of $20,000 and a fair value of $15,000 at the end of the lease term. The lessor's entry at this time is

Leased asset	$15,000	
Cash	5,000	
Lease receivable		$20,000

12. The unearned income is amortized to income over the lease term using the **interest method** so as to produce a constant rate of return on the **net investment**. In the case of a sales-type lease, it equals the **gross investment minus unearned income**.

13. The **estimate of residual value** is reviewed at least annually. A nontemporary decrease results in revision of the accounting for the transaction and recognition of a nonreversible loss because of the reduction in the net investment.

EXAMPLE

In the continuing example, assume that Crimson produced the machine, which has a carrying amount of $200,000. No direct costs were associated with the lease of the machine to Cottle.

Crimson's journal entry on January 2, Year 1:

Cost of goods sold	$200,000	
Lease payments receivable	300,000	
Leased asset		$200,000
Sales revenue		248,690
Unearned interest income		51,310

Crimson's journal entry on December 31, Year 1:

Cash	$100,000	
Lease payments receivable		$100,000
Unearned interest income	$24,869	
Interest income		$24,869

EXAMPLE

In the continuing example, assume that Cottle guarantees a residual value of $20,000.

PV of minimum rental payments	=	$100,000 ×	2.4869 =	$248,690
PV of guaranteed residual value	=	$ 20,000 ×	.7513 =	$15,026
PV of minimum lease payments	=	$248,690 +	$15,026 =	$263,716

Cost of goods sold	$200,000	
Lease payments receivable	320,000	
Leased asset		$200,000
Sales revenue		263,716
Unearned interest income		56,284

Crimson's journal entry on December 31, Year 1:

Cash	$100,000	
Lease payments receivable		$100,000
Unearned interest income	$26,372	
Interest interest income		$26,372

14.

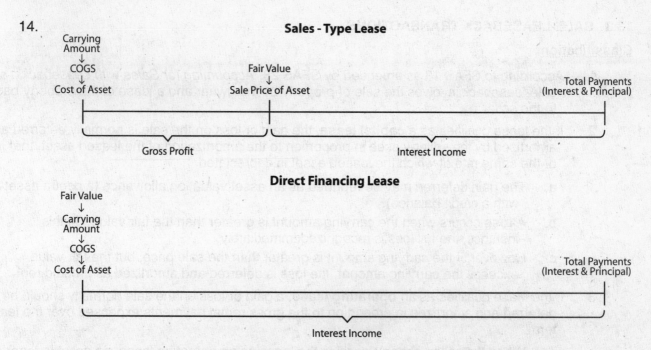

Sales - Type Lease

Direct Financing Lease

15. Selling or assigning a sales-type or financing lease or property subject to such a lease does not change the original accounting. Moreover, any transfer of minimum lease payments under, or residual values guaranteed at the inception of, such a lease is governed by SFAS 140.

Operating Leases

16. Operating leases do not meet the criteria for capitalization. They are transactions in which lessees rent the right to use lessor assets without acquiring a substantial portion of the benefits and risks of ownership. Thus, the **lessor** does not record a sale or financing.

17. **Rent** is reported as **revenue** by the lessor in accordance with the lease agreement.

   a. If rental payments vary from a straight-line basis, e.g., if the first month is free, rental revenue should be recognized over the full lease term on the straight-line basis. However, another systematic and rational basis may be used if it is more representative of the time pattern in which the use benefit from the property is reduced.

      1) Nonrefundable lease bonuses also should be recognized as rental revenue on a straight-line basis over the lease term.

18. The lessor should report the leased property near **property, plant, and equipment** in the balance sheet.

   a. It should depreciate the property according to its normal depreciation policy for owned assets.

19. **Initial direct costs**, such as realtor fees, should be deferred and amortized by the lessor over the lease term in proportion to the recognition of rental income.

Stop and review! You have completed the outline for this subunit. Study multiple-choice questions 10 through 12 on page 486.

13.3 SALE-LEASEBACK TRANSACTIONS

Classification

1. According to SFAS 13 as amended by SFAS 28, *Accounting for Sales with Leasebacks*, a sale-leaseback involves the sale of property by the owner and a lease of the property back to the seller.

2. If the lease qualifies as a **capital lease**, the gain or loss on the sale is normally deferred and amortized by the seller-lessee in proportion to the amortization of the leased asset, that is, at the same rate at which the leased asset is depreciated.

   a. The gain deferred may be reported as an asset valuation allowance (a contra asset with a credit balance).

   b. A **loss** occurs when the carrying amount is greater than the fair value. In this instance, the full loss is recognized immediately.

   c. However, if the carrying amount is greater than the sale price, but the fair value exceeds the carrying amount, the loss is deferred and amortized as prepaid rent.

3. If the lease qualifies as an **operating lease**, a gain or loss on the sale normally should be deferred and amortized in proportion to the gross rental payments expensed over the lease term.

   a. When the seller-lessee classifies the lease as an operating lease, no asset is reported on the balance sheet. Thus, the deferral cannot be presented as a contra asset. Accordingly, the usual practice is to report the gain (loss) as a deferred credit (debit).

Exceptions

4. One exception applies when the seller-lessee retains **more than a minor part** (more than 10%) but **less than substantially all** (less than 90%) of the use of the property through the leaseback.

   a. The **excess profit** is recognized at the date of the sale if the seller-lessee in this situation realizes a profit on the sale in excess of either

      1) The present value of the minimum lease payments over the lease term if the leaseback is an operating lease, or

      2) The recorded amount of the leased asset if the leaseback is classified as a capital lease.

   b. "Substantially all" has essentially the same meaning as the "90% test" used in determining whether a lease is a capital or operating lease (the present value of the lease payments is 90% or more of the fair value of the leased property). "Minor" refers to a transfer of 10% or less of the use of the property in the lease.

5. Another exception applies when the seller-lessee **relinquishes the right to substantially all** of the remaining use of the property sold and retains only a minor portion of such use.

   a. This exception is indicated if the present value of a reasonable amount of rentals for the leaseback represents a minor part of the use of the property (10% or less of the fair value of the asset sold). In this case, the seller-lessee should account for the sale and the leaseback as separate transactions based upon their respective terms.

6. The third exception is for **an indicated loss** measured by the excess of the carrying amount of the asset sold over its fair value.

Purchaser-Lessor Accounting

7. The purchaser-lessor accounts for a sale-leaseback transaction as a purchase and a direct financing lease if the capitalization criteria are satisfied. If these criteria are not met, the lessor records a purchase and an operating lease.

Stop and review! You have completed the outline for this subunit. Study multiple-choice questions 13 through 15 beginning on page 487.

13.4 CONTINGENCIES

Definition

1. SFAS 5, *Accounting for Contingencies*. A contingency is "an existing condition, situation, or set of circumstances involving uncertainty as to possible gain (a **gain contingency**) or loss (a **loss contingency**) to an enterprise that will ultimately be resolved when one or more future events occur or fail to occur."

   a. An **estimate** should not be confused with a contingency. Thus, the estimated depreciation for the period is not consistent with the definition of a contingency because it is certain that the utility of a depreciable asset will expire.

2. A contingency may be

   a. **Probable.** Future events are likely to occur.

   b. **Reasonably possible.** The chance of occurrence is more than remote but less than probable.

   c. **Remote.** The chance of occurrence is slight.

Probable Loss Contingencies

3. A **contingent loss** must be accrued (debit loss, credit liability or asset valuation allowance) when, based on information available prior to the issuance of the financial statements, two conditions are met: (a) It is **probable** that, at a balance sheet date, an asset has been impaired or a liability has been incurred, and (b) the amount of the loss can be **reasonably estimated**.

   a. If the loss is probable and can be reasonably estimated, it should be accrued if the amount is **material**.

4. According to FASB Interpretation No. 14, *Reasonable Estimation of the Amount of a Loss*, if the **estimate is stated within a range** and no amount within that range appears to be a better estimate than any other, the minimum should be accrued.

5. **Disclosure** of the nature of the accrual and, in some cases, the amount or the range of loss may be required to prevent the financial statements from being misleading.

Reasonably Possible Loss Contingencies

6. If both conditions are not met but the probability of the loss is at least **reasonably possible**, the nature of the contingency must be described. Also, an estimate of the amount or the range of loss must be disclosed, or a statement must be included indicating that an estimate cannot be made.

Remote Loss Contingencies

7. Normally, loss contingencies are not disclosed when their probability of occurrence is **remote**.

8. However, a **guarantee** (e.g., of the indebtedness of another or to repurchase receivables) must be disclosed even if the probability of loss is remote. The disclosure should include the nature and amount of the guarantee.

   a. This disclosure is required whether the guarantee is **direct or indirect** (FASB Interpretation No. 45, *Guarantor's Accounting and Disclosure Requirements for Guarantees, Including Indirect Guarantees of Indebtedness of Others*).

b.   The essence of a guarantee is a **noncontingent obligation** to perform after the occurrence of a triggering event or condition. It is coupled with a **contingent obligation** to make payments if such an event or condition occurs. Thus, **recognition of a liability** at the inception of a guarantee is required even when it is not probable that payments will be made.

1)   The **initial measurement** of a noncontingent obligation ordinarily is at **fair value**. If a contingent loss and liability also are required to be recognized, the liability recognized by the guarantor is the greater of the fair value measurement or the contingent liability amount. However, the Interpretation does not address **subsequent measurement**.

2)   Examples of a noncontingent obligation are a standalone guarantee given for a premium (debit cash or a receivable), a standalone guarantee to an unrelated party without consideration (debit expense), or an operating lessee's guarantee of residual value (debit prepaid rent).

9.   Other remote loss contingencies that should be disclosed are obligations of commercial banks under standby letters of credit and guarantees to repurchase receivables (or the related property) that were sold or assigned.

10.   No accrual is permitted for **general or unspecified business risks**, for example, those related to national and international economic conditions. No disclosure is required.

Gain Contingencies

11.   Gain contingencies are **recognized only when realized**. For example, an award of damages in a lawsuit is not realized if it is being appealed.

12.   A gain contingency must be adequately disclosed, but misleading implications about realization must be avoided.

Stop and review! You have completed the outline for this subunit. Study multiple-choice questions 16 through 20 beginning on page 488.

QUESTIONS

13.1 Lessee Accounting for Capital Leases

1. Crane Mfg. leases a machine from Frank Leasing. Ownership of the machine returns to Frank after the 15-year lease expires. The machine is expected to have an economic life of 17 years. At this time, Frank is reasonably capable of estimating the collectibility of the lease payments to be received from Crane. The present value of the minimum lease payments exceeds 90% of the fair value of the machine. What is the appropriate classification of this lease for Crane?

A. Operating.

B. Leveraged.

C. Capital.

D. Installment.

Answer (C) is correct. *(CPA, adapted)*
REQUIRED: The criteria for properly classifying leases.
DISCUSSION: A lease is classified as a capital lease by the lessee if, at its inception, any one of the following four criteria is satisfied: (1) The lease provides for the transfer of ownership of the leased property, (2) the lease contains a bargain purchase option, (3) the lease term is 75% or more of the estimated economic life of the leased property, and (4) the present value of the minimum lease payments is at least 90% of the fair value of the leased property to the lessor. Because the lease is for 75% or more of the estimated economic life of the leased property, Crane must capitalize the lease.
Answer (A) is incorrect because the lease is for 75% or more of the estimated economic life of the leased property. It must be capitalized. Answer (B) is incorrect because a lessee accounts for leveraged and nonleveraged leases in the same manner. Furthermore, a leveraged lease involves at least three parties (lessee, long-term creditor, and lessor), financing provided by the creditor that is nonrecourse with respect to the general credit of the lessor, and a substantial degree of leverage. Absent a third party, this transaction cannot be recorded as a leveraged lease even by the lessor. Answer (D) is incorrect because an installment lease is a lease contract that authorizes or requires the delivery of goods in separate lots to be separately accepted.

2. Beal, Inc. intends to lease a machine from Paul Corp. Beal's incremental borrowing rate is 14%. The prime rate of interest is 8%. Paul's implicit rate in the lease is 10%, which is known to Beal. Beal computes the present value of the minimum lease payments using

A. 8%

B. 10%

C. 12%

D. 14%

Answer (B) is correct. *(CPA, adapted)*
REQUIRED: The discount rate used by the lessee in determining the present value of minimum lease payments.
DISCUSSION: According to SFAS 13, a lessee should compute the present value of the minimum lease payments using its incremental borrowing rate unless

1. The lessee knows the lessor's implicit rate.

2. The implicit rate is less than the lessee's incremental borrowing rate.

If both conditions are met, the lessee must use the implicit rate. The 10% implicit rate is less than Beal's 14% incremental borrowing rate, and Beal has this information, so the rate to be used is 10%.
Answer (A) is incorrect because the prime rate (8%) is irrelevant. Answer (C) is incorrect because 12% is merely the average of the implicit rate and the incremental rate. Answer (D) is incorrect because the implicit rate is known and is lower than the incremental rate (14%).

3. Neal Corp. entered into a 9-year capital lease on a warehouse on December 31, Year 4. The land and building are capitalized as a single unit. Lease payments of $52,000, which include real estate taxes of $2,000, are due annually, beginning on December 31, Year 5, and every December 31 thereafter. Neal does not know the interest rate implicit in the lease; Neal's incremental borrowing rate is 9%. The rounded present value of an ordinary annuity for 9 years at 9% is 5.6. What amount should Neal report as capitalized lease liability at December 31, Year 4?

A. $280,000

B. $291,200

C. $450,000

D. $468,000

Answer (A) is correct. *(CPA, adapted)*
REQUIRED: The amount reported as capitalized lease liability.
DISCUSSION: For a capital lease, the present value of the minimum lease payments should be recorded at the inception date. The minimum lease payments exclude executory costs, such as insurance, maintenance, and taxes. The capitalized lease liability is therefore $280,000 [($52,000 – $2,000) × 5.6].
Answer (B) is incorrect because $291,200 is based on a $52,000 annual payment. Answer (C) is incorrect because $450,000 is the total undiscounted amount of the minimum lease payments. Answer (D) is incorrect because $468,000 is the total undiscounted amount of the minimum lease payments plus real estate taxes.

4. A 6-year capital lease entered into on December 31, Year 4, specified equal minimum annual lease payments due on December 31 of each year. The first minimum annual lease payment, paid on December 31, Year 4, consists of which of the following?

	Interest Expense	Lease Liability
A.	Yes	Yes
B.	Yes	No
C.	No	Yes
D.	No	No

Answer (C) is correct. *(CPA, adapted)*
REQUIRED: The item(s) included in a lease payment made at the inception of the lease.
DISCUSSION: Under the effective-interest method, interest is recognized to account for a change in value due to the passage of time. Given that the first payment is made at the inception of the lease, no time has passed. Thus, the first payment reduces the lease liability, but no interest is recognized.

5. At the inception of a capital lease, the guaranteed residual value should be

A. Included as part of minimum lease payments at present value.

B. Included as part of minimum lease payments at future value.

C. Included as part of minimum lease payments only to the extent that guaranteed residual value is expected to exceed estimated residual value.

D. Excluded from minimum lease payments.

Answer (A) is correct. *(CPA, adapted)*
REQUIRED: The treatment of guaranteed residual value at the inception of a capital lease.
DISCUSSION: A capital lease is recorded at the present value of the minimum lease payments. Minimum lease payments from the lessee's perspective include the minimum rental payments (excluding executory costs) required during the lease term and the amount of a bargain purchase option. If no such option exists, the minimum lease payments equal the sum of (1) the minimum rental payments, (2) the amount of residual value guaranteed by the lessee, and (3) any nonrenewal penalty imposed. From the lessor's perspective, minimum lease payments also include residual value guaranteed by a financially capable third party unrelated to the lessee or lessor.
Answer (B) is incorrect because minimum lease payments are recorded at present value. Answer (C) is incorrect because the full guaranteed residual value is included in the minimum lease payments. At the end of the lease, any difference between the guaranteed residual value and the fair value is recognized as a gain or loss. Answer (D) is incorrect because minimum lease payments include guaranteed residual value.

6. On January 1, Year 4, Day Corp. entered into a 10-year lease agreement with Ward, Inc. for industrial equipment. Annual lease payments of $10,000 are payable at the end of each year. Day knows that the lessor expects a 10% return on the lease. Day has a 12% incremental borrowing rate. The equipment is expected to have an estimated useful life of 10 years. In addition, a third party has guaranteed to pay Ward a residual value of $5,000 at the end of the lease.

The present value of an ordinary annuity of $1 at

> 12% for 10 years is 5.6502
> 10% for 10 years is 6.1446

The present value of $1 at

> 12% for 10 years is .3220
> 10% for 10 years is .3855

In Day's October 31, Year 4, balance sheet, the principal amount of the lease obligation was

A. $63,374

B. $61,446

C. $58,112

D. $56,502

Answer (B) is correct. *(CPA, adapted)*
REQUIRED: The amount of the lease obligation recorded at the end of the fiscal year.
DISCUSSION: This lease qualifies as a capital lease because the 10-year lease term is greater than 75% of the 10-year estimated useful life of the equipment. The lessee should record the present value of the minimum lease payments at the lower of the lessee's incremental borrowing rate or the lessor's implicit rate if known to the lessee. Because the 10% implicit rate (the lessor's expected return on the lease) is less than the 12% incremental borrowing rate, the lease obligation should be recorded on 1/1/Year 4 at $61,446 ($10,000 periodic payment × 6.1446). The end of the fiscal year (10/31/Year 4) is 10 months after the inception of the lease, but the annual lease payments are payable at the end of the calendar year. Hence, the lease obligation recorded at the inception of the lease has not yet been reduced by the first payment. Moreover, given that the residual value of $5,000 is guaranteed by a third party, it is not included in the minimum lease payments by the lessee.
Answer (A) is incorrect because $63,374 includes the PV of $1 calculated at 10% for 10 years of the residual value guaranteed by a third party. Answer (C) is incorrect because $58,112 is based on the interest factor for the PV of an ordinary annuity of $1 at 12% for 10 years. It also includes the PV of $1 calculated at 12% for 10 years of the residual value guaranteed by a third party. Answer (D) is incorrect because $56,502 is based on the interest factor for the PV of an ordinary annuity of $1 at 12% for 10 years.

7. On January 1, Year 4, Harrow Co. as lessee signed a 5-year noncancelable equipment lease with annual payments of $100,000 beginning December 31, Year 4. Harrow treated this transaction as a capital lease. The five lease payments have a present value of $379,000 at January 1, Year 4, based on interest of 10%. What amount should Harrow report as interest for the year ended December 31, Year 4?

A. $37,900

B. $27,900

C. $24,200

D. $0

Answer (A) is correct. *(CPA, adapted)*
REQUIRED: The interest to be recognized in the first year of a capital lease.
DISCUSSION: The lease liability at the inception of the lease is $379,000. Under the effective-interest method, the lease liability balance (the carrying amount) at the beginning of each year should be multiplied by the implicit interest rate to determine interest for that year. Accordingly, the interest expense for the first year is $37,900 ($379,000 × 10%).
Answer (B) is incorrect because $27,900 assumes the initial payment was made immediately. Answer (C) is incorrect because $24,200 is one-fifth of the total interest ($500,000 – $379,000 PV). Answer (D) is incorrect because interest must be accrued.

8. In the long-term liabilities section of its balance sheet at December 31, Year 3, Mene Co. reported a capital lease obligation of $75,000, net of current portion of $1,364. Payments of $9,000 were made on both January 2, Year 4, and January 2, Year 5. Mene's incremental borrowing rate on the date of the lease was 11% and the lessor's implicit rate, which was known to Mene, was 10%. In its December 31, Year 4, balance sheet, what amount should Mene report as capital lease obligation, net of current portion?

A. $66,000

B. $73,500

C. $73,636

D. $74,250

Answer (B) is correct. *(CPA, adapted)*
REQUIRED: The capital lease obligation, net of current portion.
DISCUSSION: The total lease obligation on 12/31/Year 3 was $76,364 ($75,000 + $1,364 current portion). After the Year 4 payment, which included the current portion, the lease obligation was $75,000. Consequently, the Year 5 payment included interest of $7,500 ($75,000 carrying amount during Year 4 × 10% lessor's implicit rate, which is both known to the lessee and lower than the lessee's incremental borrowing rate) and a principal component of $1,500 ($9,000 – $7,500 interest). The latter is the current portion of the lease obligation on 12/31/Year 4. The capital lease obligation, net of current portion, is therefore $73,500 ($75,000 – $1,500).
Answer (A) is incorrect because $66,000 results from treating the full $9,000 payment made in Year 5 as principal. Answer (C) is incorrect because $73,636 assumes the current portion is the same as the previous years'. Answer (D) is incorrect because $74,250 is based on an 11% rate.

9. On January 1 of the current year, Tell Co. leased equipment from Swill Co. under a nine-year sales-type lease. The equipment had a cost of $400,000 and an estimated useful life of 15 years. Semiannual lease payments of $44,000 are due every January 1 and July 1. The present value of lease payments at 12% was $505,000, which equals the sales price of the equipment. Using the straight-line method, what amount should Tell recognize as depreciation expense on the equipment in the current year?

A. $26,667

B. $33,667

C. $44,444

D. $56,111

Answer (D) is correct. *(CPA, adapted)*
REQUIRED: The depreciation expense for a lease.
DISCUSSION: The lessee capitalizes the lease because the present value of the minimum lease payments (excluding executory costs) is at least equal to 90% of the excess of the fair value of the leased property to the lessor at the inception of the lease over any related investment tax credit (ITC). The fair value to the lessor is presumably the sales price, and no ITC is stated. Given that the sale price equals the present value of the minimum lease payments, the latter amount equals 100% of the excess of the lessor's fair value over the ITC ($0). Thus, the lessee records an asset and an obligation for $505,000. The lessee should amortize the asset in a manner consistent with its normal depreciation policy. Given straight-line depreciation, annual depreciation expense is $56,111 ($505,000 ÷ 9 years). The estimated useful life is used only if a bargain purchase option exists and most likely will be exercised.
Answer (A) is incorrect because $26,667 is based on the equipment's cost and estimated useful life. Answer (B) is incorrect because $33,667 is based on the lease term, not the estimated useful life. Answer (C) is incorrect because $44,444 is based on the equipment's cost.

13.2 Lessor Accounting for Capital Leases

10. Glade Co. leases computer equipment to customers under direct-financing leases. The equipment has no residual value at the end of the lease, and the leases do not contain bargain purchase options. Glade wishes to earn 8% interest on a 5-year lease of equipment with a fair value of $323,400. The present value of an annuity due of $1 at 8% for 5 years is 4.312. What is the total amount of interest revenue that Glade will earn over the life of the lease?

A. $51,600

B. $75,000

C. $129,360

D. $139,450

Answer (A) is correct. *(CPA, adapted)*
REQUIRED: The interest revenue earned over the life of a lease.
DISCUSSION: To earn 8% interest over the lease term, the annual payment must be $75,000 ($323,400 fair value at the inception of the lease ÷ 4.312 annuity factor). Given no residual value and no bargain purchase option, total lease payments will be $375,000 ($75,000 payment × 5 years). Because no profit is recognized on a direct-financing lease, the fair value is presumably the carrying amount. The difference between the gross lease payments received and their present value is interest revenue of $51,600 ($375,000 − $323,400).

11. Farm Co. leased equipment to Union Co. on July 1, Year 4, and properly recorded the sales-type lease at $135,000, the present value of the lease payments discounted at 10%. The first of eight annual lease payments of $20,000 due at the beginning of each year was received and recorded on July 3, Year 4. Farm had purchased the equipment for $110,000. What amount of interest revenue from the lease should Farm report in its Year 4 income statement?

A. $0

B. $5,500

C. $5,750

D. $6,750

Answer (C) is correct. *(CPA, adapted)*
REQUIRED: The interest income recognized by the lessor in the first year of a sales-type lease.
DISCUSSION: Under the effective-interest method, interest revenue equals the carrying amount of the net investment in the lease at the beginning of the interest period multiplied by the interest rate used to calculate the present value of the lease payments. The present value of $135,000 is reduced by the $20,000 payment made at the inception of the lease, leaving a carrying amount of $115,000. Interest revenue for Year 4 is therefore $5,750 ($115,000 × 10% × 6/12).
Answer (A) is incorrect because interest income for Year 2 is $5,750. Answer (B) is incorrect because $5,500 equals ($110,000 × 10% × 6/12). Answer (D) is incorrect because $6,750 equals ($135,000 × 10% × 6/12).

12. Howe Co. leased equipment to Kew Corp. on January 2, Year 4, for an 8-year period expiring December 31, Year 11. Equal payments under the lease are $600,000 and are due on January 2 of each year. The first payment was made on January 2, Year 4. The list selling price of the equipment is $3,520,000, and its carrying cost on Howe's books is $2.8 million. The lease is appropriately accounted for as a sales-type lease. The present value of the lease payments at an imputed interest rate of 12% (Howe's incremental borrowing rate) is $3.3 million. What amount of profit on the sale should Howe report for the year ended December 31, Year 4?

A. $720,000

B. $500,000

C. $90,000

D. $0

Answer (B) is correct. *(CPA, adapted)*
REQUIRED: The amount of profit on a sales-type lease.
DISCUSSION: Howe Co., the lessor, should report a profit from a sales-type lease. The gross profit equals the difference between the sales price (present value of the minimum lease payments) and the cost. The cost for a sales-type lease is not the same as the fair value. Consequently, the profit on the sale equals $500,000 ($3,300,000 − $2,800,000).
Answer (A) is incorrect because $720,000 is the result of using the list selling price instead of the present value of the lease payments. Answer (C) is incorrect because $90,000 is one-eighth of the difference between the list price and the cost. Answer (D) is incorrect because a profit of $500,000 should be reported.

13.3 Sale-Leaseback Transactions

13. On December 31, Year 4, Bain Corp. sold a machine to Ryan and simultaneously leased it back for 1 year. Pertinent information at this date follows:

Sales price	$360,000
Carrying amount	330,000
Present value of reasonable lease rentals ($3,000 for 12 months at 12%)	34,100
Estimated remaining useful life	12 years

In Bain's December 31, Year 4, balance sheet, the deferred revenue from the sale of this machine should be

A. $34,100

B. $30,000

C. $4,100

D. $0

Answer (D) is correct. *(CPA, adapted)*

REQUIRED: The deferred revenue to be reported from a sale-leaseback transaction.

DISCUSSION: The general rule is that profit or loss on the sale in a sale-leaseback transaction is deferred and amortized over the life of the lease. However, SFAS 28 provides for certain exceptions. One exception applies when the seller-lessee relinquishes the right to substantially all of the remaining use of the property sold and retains only a minor portion of such use. This exception is indicated if the present value of a reasonable amount of rentals for the leaseback represents 10% or less of the fair value of the asset sold. In this case, the seller-lessee should account for the sale and the leaseback as separate transactions based upon their respective terms. Because the $34,100 present value of the reasonable lease rentals is less than 10% of the $360,000 sales price (the fair value), Bain should recognize the entire $30,000 difference between the $360,000 sales price and the $330,000 carrying amount as a gain from the sale. The leaseback should then be accounted for as if it were unrelated to the sale, because the leaseback is considered to be minor.

Answer (A) is incorrect because $34,100 is the present value of reasonable lease rentals. Answer (B) is incorrect because $30,000 is the profit recognized. Answer (C) is incorrect because $4,100 is the excess of the present value of reasonable lease rentals over the profit recognized.

14. On December 31, Year 4, Dirk Corp. sold Smith Co. two airplanes and simultaneously leased them back. Additional information pertaining to the sale-leasebacks follows:

	Plane #1	Plane #2
Sales price	$600,000	$1,000,000
Carrying amount, 12/31/Year 4	$100,000	$ 550,000
Remaining useful life, 12/31/Year 4	10 years	35 years
Lease term	8 years	3 years
Present value of annual lease payments	$500,000	$ 100,000

In its December 31, Year 4, balance sheet, what amount should Dirk report as deferred gain on these transactions?

A. $950,000

B. $500,000

C. $450,000

D. $0

Answer (B) is correct. *(CPA, adapted)*

REQUIRED: The amount to be recorded as deferred gain in a sale and leaseback.

DISCUSSION: The lease of Plane #1 is a capital lease because its 8-year term exceeds 75% of the 10-year estimated remaining economic life of the plane. In a sale and leaseback transaction, any profit or loss on the sale is ordinarily required to be deferred and amortized in proportion to the amortization of the leased asset if the lease is a capital lease. The amortization is in proportion to the gross rental payments expensed over the lease term if the lease is an operating lease. At the inception of this lease, the $500,000 gain ($600,000 sales price – $100,000 carrying amount) should be deferred.

The lease of Plane #2 is an operating lease that falls under an exception provided by SFAS 28. When the seller-lessee retains only a minor part of the asset sold, i.e., when the present value of reasonable minimum lease payments is no more than 10% of the fair value of the asset sold, the sale and the leaseback are accounted for separately. Dirk retained only a minor part of Plane #2 [($100,000 PV of lease payments ÷ $1,000,000 FV of asset sold) = 10%]. Thus, the $450,000 gain on Plane #2 will be recognized on the date of sale.

Answer (A) is incorrect because $950,000 includes the gain on Plane #2. Answer (C) is incorrect because $450,000 equals the gain on Plane #2. Answer (D) is incorrect because the gain on Plane #1 should be deferred.

15. On January 1, Year 4, Hooks Oil Co. sold equipment with a carrying amount of $100,000 and a remaining useful life of 10 years to Maco Drilling for $150,000. Hooks immediately leased the equipment back under a 10-year capital lease with a present value of $150,000. It will depreciate the equipment using the straight-line method. Hooks made the first annual lease payment of $24,412 in December Year 4. In Hooks's December 31, Year 4, balance sheet, the unearned gain on the equipment sale should be

- A. $50,000
- B. $45,000
- C. $25,588
- D. $0

Answer (B) is correct. *(CPA, adapted)*
REQUIRED: The unearned gain on the equipment sale 1 year after a sale-leaseback transaction.
DISCUSSION: A profit or loss on the sale in a sale-leaseback transaction is ordinarily deferred and amortized in proportion to the amortization of the leased asset if the leaseback is classified as a capital lease. At 12/31/Year 4, a gain proportionate to the lease amortization will be recognized [($150,000 – $100,000) ÷ 10 years = $5,000]. Hence, the deferred gain will be $45,000 ($50,000 – $5,000).
Answer (A) is incorrect because $50,000 is the total deferred gain at the inception of the lease. Answer (C) is incorrect because $25,588 is the difference between the total deferred gain and the periodic lease payment. Answer (D) is incorrect because the seller-lessee has retained substantially all of the use of the property and should therefore defer gain.

13.4 Contingencies

16. Invern, Inc. has a self-insurance plan. Each year, retained earnings is appropriated for contingencies in an amount equal to insurance premiums saved minus recognized losses from lawsuits and other claims. As a result of a Year 4 accident, Invern is a defendant in a lawsuit in which it will probably have to pay damages of $190,000. What are the effects of this lawsuit's probable outcome on Invern's Year 4 financial statements?

- A. An increase in expenses and no effect on liabilities.
- B. An increase in both expenses and liabilities.
- C. No effect on expenses and an increase in liabilities.
- D. No effect on either expenses or liabilities.

Answer (B) is correct. *(CPA, adapted)*
REQUIRED: The effect on the financial statements of litigation with a probable unfavorable outcome.
DISCUSSION: A loss contingency is an existing condition, situation, or set of circumstances involving uncertainty as to the impairment of an asset's value or the incurrence of a liability as of the balance sheet date. Resolution of the uncertainty depends on the occurrence or nonoccurrence of one or more future events. A loss should be debited and either an asset valuation allowance or a liability credited when the loss contingency is both probable and reasonably estimable. Thus, the company should accrue a loss and a liability.

17. Wyatt Co. has a probable loss that can only be reasonably estimated within a range of outcomes. No single amount within the range is a better estimate than any other amount. The loss accrual should be

- A. Zero.
- B. The maximum of the range.
- C. The mean of the range.
- D. The minimum of the range.

Answer (D) is correct. *(CPA, adapted)*
REQUIRED: The contingent loss that should be accrued when a range of estimates is provided.
DISCUSSION: Because the loss is probable and can be reasonably estimated, it should be accrued if the amount is material. According to FASB Interpretation No. 14, *Reasonable Estimation of the Amount of a Loss*, if the estimate is stated within a given range and no amount within that range appears to be a better estimate than any other, the minimum of the range should be accrued.

18. Bell Co. is a defendant in a lawsuit that could result in a large payment to the plaintiff. Bell's attorney believes that there is a 90% chance that Bell will lose the suit and estimates that the loss will be anywhere from $5,000,000 to $20,000,000 and possibly as much as $30,000,000. No estimate is better than the others. What liability should Bell report on its balance sheet related to the lawsuit?

A. $0

B. $5,000,000

C. $20,000,000

D. $30,000,000

Answer (B) is correct. *(CPA, adapted)*
REQUIRED: The liability of a defendant in a lawsuit.
DISCUSSION: A loss contingency is accrued by a debit to expense and a credit to a liability if it is probable that a loss will occur and the loss can be reasonably estimated. The $5,000,000 estimated loss is reported on the balance sheet, and the range of the contingent loss is disclosed in the notes. The loss is probable (likely to occur) given expert opinion that the chance of loss is 90%. When no amount within a reasonable estimated range is a better estimate than any other, the minimum is accrued (FASB Interpretation No. 14).

19. In Year 4, hail damaged several of Toncan Co.'s vans. Hailstorms had frequently inflicted similar damage to Toncan's vans. Over the years, Toncan had saved money by not buying hail insurance and either paying for repairs or selling damaged vans and then replacing them. In Year 4, the damaged vans were sold for less than their carrying amount. How should the hail damage cost be reported in Toncan's Year 4 financial statements?

A. The actual Year 4 hail damage loss as an extraordinary loss, net of income taxes.

B. The actual Year 4 hail damage loss in continuing operations, with no separate disclosure.

C. The expected average hail damage loss in continuing operations, with no separate disclosure.

D. The expected average hail damage loss in continuing operations, with separate disclosure.

Answer (B) is correct. *(CPA, adapted)*
REQUIRED: The reporting of hail damage costs when a company is uninsured and sells the damaged item for a loss.
DISCUSSION: Because Toncan sold its damaged vans for less than their carrying amount, the company suffered a loss. The actual loss should be reported even though the company is uninsured against future hail damage and a contingency exists as defined by SFAS 5. With respect to future hailstorms, no asset has been impaired and no contingent loss should be recorded. Furthermore, this occurrence is not unusual or infrequent, and a separate disclosure is not needed.
Answer (A) is incorrect because hail damage is a frequent occurrence and does not meet the definition of an extraordinary item. Answer (C) is incorrect because Toncan should report the actual loss incurred in Year 4. Answer (D) is incorrect because Toncan should report the actual loss, and a separate disclosure is not needed.

20. Seller-Guarantor sold an asset with a carrying amount at the time of sale of $500,000 to Buyer for $650,000 in cash. Seller also provided a guarantee to Guarantee Bank of the $600,000 loan that Guarantee made to Buyer to finance the sale. The probability that Seller will become liable under the guarantee is remote. In a stand-alone arm's-length transaction with an unrelated party, the premium required by Seller to provide the same guarantee would have been $40,000. The entry made by Seller at the time of the sale should include a

A. Gain of $150,000.

B. Noncontingent liability of $40,000.

C. Contingent liability of $600,000.

D. Loss of $450,000.

Answer (B) is correct. *(Publisher, adapted)*
REQUIRED: The entry made to reflect sale of an asset and the seller's guarantee of the buyer's debt.
DISCUSSION: No contingent liability results because the likelihood of payment by the guarantor is remote. However, a noncontingent liability is recognized at the inception of the seller's obligation to stand ready to perform during the term of the guarantee. This liability is initially measured at fair value. In a multiple-element transaction with an unrelated party, the fair value is estimated, for example, as the premium required by the guarantor to provide the same guarantee in a stand-alone arm's-length transaction with an unrelated party. The amount of that premium is given as $40,000. Hence, Seller debits cash for the total received ($650,000), credits the asset sold for its carrying amount ($500,000), credits the noncontingent liability for its estimated fair value ($40,000), and credits a gain for $110,000 ($650,000 – $500,000 – $40,000).
Answer (A) is incorrect because a gain of $150,000 assumes neither a noncontingent nor a contingent liability is recognized. Answer (C) is incorrect because no contingent liability is recognized. The likelihood of payment is remote, not probable. Answer (D) is incorrect because a loss of $450,000 assumes recognition of a contingent liability of $600,000.

Use Gleim's *CPA Test Prep* CD-Rom/Pocket PC for interactive testing with over 4,000 additional questions!

13.5 PRACTICE SIMULATION

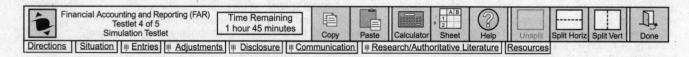

| Financial Accounting and Reporting (FAR) Testlet 4 of 5 Simulation Testlet | Time Remaining 1 hour 45 minutes | Copy | Paste | Calculator | Sheet | Help | Unsplit | Split Horiz | Split Vert | Done |

Directions | Situation | ⅲ Entries | ⅲ Adjustments | ⅲ Disclosure | ⅲ Communication | ⅲ Research/Authoritative Literature | Resources

1. Directions

In the following simulation, you will be asked to complete various tasks. You may use the content in the **Information Tabs** to complete the tasks in the **Work Tabs**.

Information Tabs:

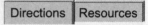

Directions | Resources

   FIG 1

- Go through each of the **Information Tabs** to familiarize yourself with the simulation content
- The **Resources** tab will contain information, including formulas and definitions, that may help you to complete the tasks
- Your simulation may have more **Information Tabs** than those shown in Fig. 1

Work Tabs:

ⅲ SysTrust | ⅲ Engagement Letter | ⅲ Authoritative Sources | ⅲ Communication

   FIG. 2

- **Work Tabs**, to the right of **Information Tabs**, contain the tasks for you to complete
- **Work Tabs** contain directions for completing each task - be sure to read these directions carefully
- The tab names in Fig. 2 are for illustration only - yours may differ
- Once you complete any part of a task, the pencil for that tab will be shaded (see **Communication** in Fig. 2)
- The shaded pencil does **NOT** indicate that you have completed the entire task
- You must complete all of the tasks in the **Work Tabs** to receive full credit

Research/Authoritative Literature Tab:

ⅲ Research/Authoritative Literature

   FIG. 3

- This tab contains both the Research task and the Authoritative Literature
- Detailed instructions for completing the Research task, and for using the Authoritative Literature, appear on this tab
- You may use the Authoritative Literature as a resource for completing other tasks

NOTE: If you believe you have encountered a software malfunction, report it to the test center staff immediately.

2. Situation

On January 2, Year 4, Drake Co. leased equipment from Brewer, Inc. Lease payments are $100,000, payable annually every December 31 for 20 years. Title to the equipment passes to Drake at the end of the lease term. The lease is noncancelable.

Additional Facts:

- The equipment has a $750,000 carrying amount on Brewer's books. Its estimated economic life was 25 years on January 2, Year 4.
- The rate implicit in the lease, which is known to Drake, is 10%. Drake's incremental borrowing rate is 12%.
- Drake normally uses the straight-line method of depreciation for equipment.

The rounded present value factors of an ordinary annuity for 20 years are as follows:

12%	7.5
10%	8.5

3. Entries

This question is presented in a spreadsheet format that requires you to fill in the correct responses in the shaded cells provided. Fill in the amounts for the necessary journal entries to be recorded by Drake.

	Debits	Credits
1. January 2, Year 4		
Leased equipment		
Capital lease liability		
2. December 31, Year 4		
Capital lease liability		
Cash		
3. December 31, Year 4		
Depreciation expense		
Accumulated depreciation		
4. December 31, Year 4		
Interest expense		
Capital lease liability		

4. Adjustments

Each numbered item describes an amount(s) not reflected in the financial statements. This set of questions has a matching format. Select the best match for each numbered item from the terms in the drop-down list and write its letter in the column provided. Each choice may be used once, more than once, or not at all. For each of the following items, determine the amount, if any, required to be recognized in Drake's financial statements based on a calendar year for Year 4.

Description	Answer
1. Drake owns a small warehouse located on the banks of a river in which it stores inventory worth approximately $500,000. Drake is not insured against flood losses. The river last overflowed its banks 20 years ago.	
2. During Year 4, Drake began offering certain healthcare benefits to its eligible retired employees. Drake's net periodic postretirement benefit cost (NPPBC) is $150,000.	
3. Drake offers an unconditional warranty on its toys. Based on past experience, Drake estimates its warranty expenses to be 1% of sales. Sales during Year 4 were $10 million.	
4. On October 20, Year 4, a safety hazard related to one of Drake's toy products was discovered. It is probable that Drake will be liable for an amount in the range of $100,000 to $500,000. No amount in the range is a better estimate than any other.	
5. On November 22, Year 4, Drake initiated a lawsuit seeking $250,000 in damages from patent infringement.	
6. On December 17, Year 4, a former employee filed a lawsuit seeking $100,000 for unlawful dismissal. Drake's attorneys believe the suit is without merit. No court date has been set.	
7. On December 15, Year 4, Drake guaranteed a bank loan to a related entity for $1,000,000. It is not likely that payments will be made. The fair value of the guarantee is $250,000.	
8. On December 31, Year 4, Drake's board of directors voted to sell its computer games division, which qualifies as a component of an entity held for sale. The division was sold on February 15, Year 5. On December 31, Year 4, Drake estimated that losses from operations, net of tax, for the period January 1, Year 5, through February 15, Year 5, would be $400,000 and that the gain from the sale of the division's assets, net of tax, would be $250,000. These estimates were materially correct.	
9. On January 5, Year 5, a warehouse containing a substantial portion of Drake's inventory was destroyed by fire. Drake expects to recover the entire loss, except for a $250,000 deductible, from insurance.	
10. On January 4, Year 5, inventory purchased FOB shipping point on December 30, Year 4, from a foreign country was detained at that country's border because of political unrest. The shipment is valued at $150,000. Drake's attorneys have stated that it is probable that Drake will be able to obtain the shipment.	
11. On January 30, Year 5, Drake issued $10 million of bonds at a premium of $500,000.	

Choices

A) No adjustment is required

B) $100,000

C) $150,000

D) $250,000

E) $400,000

F) $500,000

5. Disclosure

This question is presented in a check-the-box format that requires you to select the correct responses from a given list. For each of the following, determine whether an additional disclosure is required by placing a check in the box. If no additional disclosure is required, leave the box blank.

Description	*Additional Disclosure*
1. Drake owns a small warehouse located on the banks of a river in which it stores inventory worth approximately $500,000. Drake is not insured against flood losses. The river last overflowed its banks 20 years ago.	
2. During Year 4, Drake began offering certain healthcare benefits to its eligible retired employees. Drake's net periodic postretirement benefit cost (NPPBC) is $150,000.	
3. Drake offers an unconditional warranty on its toys. Based on past experience, Drake estimates its warranty expenses to be 1% of sales. Sales during Year 4 were $10 million.	
4. On October 20, Year 4, a safety hazard related to one of Drake's toy products was discovered. It is probable that Drake will be liable for an amount in the range of $100,000 to $500,000. No amount in the range is a better estimate than any other.	
5. On November 22, Year 4, Drake initiated a lawsuit seeking $250,000 in damages from patent infringement.	
6. On December 17, Year 4, a former employee filed a lawsuit seeking $100,000 for unlawful dismissal. Drake's attorneys believe the suit is without merit. No court date has been set.	
7. On December 15, Year 4, Drake guaranteed a bank loan to a related entity for $1,000,000. It is not likely that payments will be made. The fair value of the guarantee is $250,000.	
8. On December 31, Year 4, Drake's board of directors voted to sell its computer games division, which qualifies as a component of an entity held for sale. The division was sold on February 15, Year 5. On December 31, Year 4, Drake estimated that losses from operations, net of tax, for the period January 1, Year 5, through February 15, Year 5, would be $400,000 and that the gain from the sale of the division's assets, net of tax, would be $250,000. These estimates were materially correct.	
9. On January 5, Year 5, a warehouse containing a substantial portion of Drake's inventory was destroyed by fire. Drake expects to recover the entire loss, except for a $250,000 deductible, from insurance.	
10. On January 4, Year 5, inventory purchased FOB shipping point on December 30, Year 4, from a foreign country was detained at that country's border because of political unrest. The shipment is valued at $150,000. Drake's attorneys have stated that it is probable that Drake will be able to obtain the shipment.	
11. On January 30, Year 5, Drake issued $10 million of bonds at a premium of $500,000.	

6. Communication

Prepare a brief memorandum to your client, Drake Co., discussing the theoretical basis for requiring lessees to capitalize certain long-term leases and how the lessee initially measures the asset and the obligation.

REMINDER: Your response will be graded for both technical content and writing skills. Technical content will be evaluated for information that is helpful to the intended reader and clearly relevant to the issue. Writing skills will be evaluated for development, organization, and the appropriate expression of ideas in professional correspondence. Use a standard business memo or letter format with a clear beginning, middle, and end. Do not convey information in the form of a table, bullet point list, or other abbreviated presentation.

To:	Drake Co.
From:	CPA
Subject:	Capitalization of long-term leases

7. Research/Authoritative Literature

See page 12 in the Introduction of this book for a detailed explanation of the AICPA's new Research/Authoritative Literature work tab as well as a screenshot of how the tab will actually look on your exam.

Research and cite the paragraph either in the FASB Current Text or Original Pronouncements that details how a lessor should account for an operating lease.

Unofficial Answers

3. Entries (8 Gradable Items)

	Debits		Credits	
1. January 2, Year 4				
Leased equipment	[1]	850,000		
Capital lease liability			[1]	850,000
2. December 31, Year 4				
Capital lease liability	[2]	100,000		
Cash			[2]	100,000
3. December 31, Year 4				
Depreciation expense	[3]	34,000		
Accumulated depreciation			[3]	34,000
4. December 31, Year 4				
Interest expense	[4]	85,000		
Capital lease liability			[4]	85,000

1. The lessee capitalizes the lease because the lease transfers ownership. Also, the lease term is 75% or more (20 years ÷ 25 years = 80%) of the estimated economic life of the leased asset. The capitalized amount is $850,000 ($100,000 annual payment × 8.5 PV factor for an ordinary 20-year annuity and an interest rate of 10%, the lower of the implicit rate or the lessee's incremental borrowing rate).

2. The annual lease payment is $100,000.

3. The lease transfers ownership, so the leased asset is depreciated over its 25-year estimated economic life using the lessee's normal depreciation policy (straight-line). Accordingly, depreciation expense is $34,000 ($850,000 ÷ 25 years).

4. The appropriate interest rate is 10%. Thus, interest expense for the lease's first year is $85,000 ($850,000 balance at the beginning of the period × 10%), and the net decrease in the liability is $15,000 ($100,000 annual payment – $85,000 interest expense), which is the result of combining entries 2. and 4.

4. Adjustments (11 Gradable Items)

1. A) No adjustment is required. Contingent losses for which occurrence of the future event is not probable require no accrual. The river last overflowed 20 years ago; the possibility that it will occur is no more than reasonably possible.

2. C) $150,000. Under SFAS 106, the NPPBC should be recognized.

3. B) $100,000. Under SFAS 5, if incurrence of warranty expense is probable and the amount can be reasonably estimated, accrual of the liability is appropriate. The estimate for warranties of 1% of sales is reasonable.

4. B) $100,000. If a loss contingency is considered probable and can be reasonably estimated, the loss should be accrued. When a range is estimated, the minimum amount of loss should be accrued if no other amount is a better estimate.

5. A) No adjustment is required. A gain contingency should not be recognized until it is realized.

6. A) No adjustment is required. When a loss contingency is not probable, no accrual is required.

7. D) $250,000. Assuming the loss contingency arising from the guarantee of the loan is considered either reasonably possible or remote, no accrual is required. However, Drake must recognize the $250,000 fair value of the noncontingent guarantee obligation.

8. A) No adjustment is required. When a component is classified as held for sale, its operating results are reported in discontinued operations in the period(s) in which they occur.

9. A) No adjustment is required. A subsequent event providing evidence about conditions not existing at the balance sheet date may require disclosure but not adjustment of the statements. Examples of subsequent events requiring disclosure only are sale of a bond or stock issue and loss of a plant or inventories due to fire or flood.

10. A) No adjustment is required. Because the receipt of the shipment is probable, no accrual is necessary.

11. A) No adjustment is required. A subsequent event providing evidence about conditions not existing at the balance sheet date may require disclosure but not adjustment of the statements. Examples of subsequent events requiring disclosure only are sale of a bond or stock issue and loss of a plant or inventories due to fire or flood.

5. Disclosure (11 Gradable Items)

1. <u>No disclosure required.</u> If the probability of a contingent loss not arising from a guarantee is remote, no disclosure is required.

2. <u>Disclosure required.</u> SFAS 132 (revised), *Employers' Disclosures about Pensions and Other Postretirement Benefits*, requires numerous standardized employer disclosures about pension and other postretirement benefits.

3. <u>Disclosure required.</u> FASB Interpretation No. 45 applies to guarantor's accounting and disclosure requirements. Product warranties are not subject to its initial recognition and measurement provisions. However, the guarantor must make the disclosures required by the Interpretation (nature of the guarantee, etc.) except for the maximum potential amount of future payments. In lieu of this information, the guarantor must disclose (1) its accounting policy and methods used to determine its warranty liability and (2) a reconciliation of changes in the total warranty liability for the period.

4. <u>Disclosure required.</u> If disclosure is necessary to prevent financial statements from being misleading, the nature and, possibly, the amount of the accrual should be disclosed. Moreover, if it is at least reasonably possible that the loss may exceed the accrual, the disclosure of the nature of the contingency and the additional exposure to loss is required.

5. <u>Disclosure required.</u> A gain contingency must be adequately disclosed, but misleading implications about realization must be avoided.

6. <u>No disclosure required.</u> If the probability of a contingent loss not arising from a guarantee is remote, no disclosure is required.

7. <u>Disclosure required.</u> Disclosure is required because of the nature of the contingency even if the likelihood of loss is remote.

8. <u>Disclosure required.</u> SFAS 144, *Accounting for the Impairment or Disposal of Long-Lived Assets*, requires disclosures about a long-lived asset or disposal group that has been sold or meets the criteria for classification as held for sale. Examples are the circumstances leading to expected disposal, any loss on the writedown to fair value minus cost to sell, and amounts reported in discontinued operations.

9. <u>Disclosure required.</u> A subsequent event providing evidence about conditions not existing at the balance sheet date may require disclosure but not adjustment of the statements. Examples of subsequent events requiring disclosure only are sale of a bond or stock issue and loss of a plant or inventories due to fire or flood.

10. <u>No disclosure required.</u> Because the receipt of the shipment is probable, no disclosure is necessary.

11. <u>Disclosure required.</u> A subsequent event providing evidence about conditions not existing at the balance sheet date may require disclosure but not adjustment of the statements. Examples of subsequent events requiring disclosure only are sale of a bond or stock issue and loss of a plant or inventories due to fire or flood.

6. Communication (5 Gradable Items; for grading instructions, please refer to page 12.)

The economic effects of a long-term capital lease on the lessee are similar to those of an equipment purchase using installment debt. Such a lease transfers substantially all of the benefits and risks incident to the ownership of property to the lessee and obligates the lessee in much the same way as when funds are borrowed. To enhance comparability between a firm that purchases an asset on a long-term basis and a firm that leases an asset under substantially equivalent terms, the lease should be capitalized.

The lessee must record a capital lease as an asset and an obligation at an amount equal to the present value of the minimum lease payments. The discount rate used by the lessor is the rate implicit in the lease. It is the rate at which the present value of the minimum lease payments and the unguaranteed residual value at the beginning of the lease term equals the fair value of the leased property at the inception of the lease, minus any investment tax credit expected to be realized by the lessor. However, the lessee must use the lower of the lessor's implicit rate (if known) or the lessee's incremental borrowing rate. The higher the rate used, the lower the present value of the minimum lease payments, and the less likely that the capitalization criteria will be met. Thus, if a lessee and a lessor use different rates, one may recognize an operating lease, and the other may recognize a capital lease. The present value cannot exceed the fair value of the leased property at the inception of the lease.

Minimum lease payments include the minimum rental payments (excluding executory costs such as insurance, maintenance, and taxes) required during the lease term and the payment called for by a bargain purchase option. If no such option exists, the lessee's minimum lease payments equal the sum of the minimum rental payments, the amount of residual value guaranteed by the lessee, and any nonrenewal penalty imposed. Hence, the amount capitalized will be lower if no residual value is guaranteed. Minimum lease payments do not include contingent rentals.

7. Research/Authoritative Literature (1 Gradable Item)

Answer: FAS 13, Par. 19

FAS 13 -- *Accounting for Leases (Amended)*

Operating Leases

19. Operating leases shall be accounted for by the lessor as follows:

    a.   The leased property shall be included with or near property, plant, and equipment in the balance sheet. The property shall be depreciated following the lessor's normal depreciation policy, and in the balance sheet the accumulated depreciation shall be deducted from the investment in the leased property.

    b.   Rent shall be reported as income over the lease term as it becomes receivable according to the provisions of the lease. However, if the rentals vary from a straight-line basis, the income shall be recognized on a straight-line basis unless another systematic and rational basis is more representative of the time pattern in which use benefit from the lease property is diminished, in which case that basis shall be used.

    c.   Initial direct costs shall be deferred and allocated over the lease term in proportion to the recognition of rental income. However, initial direct costs may be charged to expense as incurred if the effect is not materially different from that which would have resulted from the use of the method prescribed in the preceding sentence.

    d.   If, at the inception of the lease, the fair value of the property in an operating lease involving real estate that would have been classified as a sales-type lease except that it did not meet the criterion in paragraph 7(a) [transfer of ownership] is less than its cost or carrying amount, if different, then a loss equal to that difference shall be recognized at the inception of the lease.

Scoring Schedule:

	Correct Responses		Gradable Items		Weights		
Tab 3	_____	÷	8	×	15%	=	_____
Tab 4	_____	÷	11	×	20%	=	_____
Tab 5	_____	÷	11	×	20%	=	_____
Tab 6	_____	÷	5	×	30%	=	_____
Tab 7	_____	÷	1	×	15%	=	_____
							(Your Score)

Use Gleim's **CPA Gleim Online** to practice more simulations in a realistic environment.

STUDY UNIT FOURTEEN
EQUITY

(27 pages of outline)

Corporate equity is more complex than partner or proprietor equity. Its major components are contributed capital, retained earnings, and accumulated other comprehensive income.

14.1 EQUITY

Display

1. The following is an **illustrative equity section** of a balance sheet:

Preferred stock	$XXX	
Additional paid-in capital	XXX	$XXX
Donated capital		XXX
Common (preferred) stock subscribed	$XXX	
Additional paid-in capital	XXX	XXX
Common stock dividends distributable	$XXX	
Additional paid-in capital	XXX	XXX
Stock warrants outstanding		XXX
Common stock	$XXX	
Additional paid-in capital	XXX	XXX
Total contributed capital		$XXX
Appropriation of retained earnings	$XXX	
Unappropriated retained earnings	XXX	
Total retained earnings		XXX
Accumulated other comprehensive income		XXX
Subscriptions receivable		(XXX)
Treasury stock (at cost)		(XXX)
Total equity		$XXX

Par or Stated Value

2. An important concept is **legal capital**, which in many states is the par or stated value of preferred and common stock.

3. **Par or stated value** is a designated amount per share established in the articles of incorporation.

4. Legal capital cannot be distributed to shareholders as dividends.

Common Stock

5.   The most widely used classes of stock are common and preferred. Common shareholders are entitled to receive **liquidating distributions** only after all other claims have been satisfied, including those of preferred shareholders.

    a.   Common shareholders are not entitled to **dividends**. A corporation may choose not to declare dividends.

    b.   State statutes typically permit different classes of common stock with different rights or privileges, e.g., class A common with voting rights and class B common with no voting rights.

    c.   If only one class of stock is issued, it is treated as common, and each shareholder must be treated equally.

    d.   Common shareholders elect directors to the board.

Preferred Stock

6.   Preferred shareholders have the right to receive (a) dividends at a specified rate (before common shareholders may receive any) and (b) distributions before common shareholders (but after creditors) upon **liquidation** or bankruptcy. But they tend not to have voting rights or to enjoy the same capital gains as the common shareholders when **the entity is successful**.

    a.   If a board issues preferred stock, it may establish different classes or series. Each may be assigned independent rights, dividend rates, and redemption prices.

    b.   Holders of **convertible preferred stock** have the right to convert the stock into shares of another class (at a predetermined ratio set forth in the articles or bylaws).

       1)   Moreover, some types of preferred stock may be convertible into shares of another entity.

    c.   **Callable preferred stock** is issued with the condition that it may be **called** (redeemed or repurchased) by the issuer at a stated price and time. Issuers may establish a **sinking fund** for this purpose.

    d.   Holders of preferred stock also may have a right to compel **redemption**.

       1)   The **SEC** prohibits the combining of common and preferred stock and of redeemable and nonredeemable preferred stock in financial statements.

       2)   Moreover, equity may not include redeemable preferred stock.

       3)   Accordingly, redeemable preferred stock, especially **transient preferred stock** (redeemable within a relatively short period, such as 5 to 10 years), may be similar to debt.

          a)   The FASB requires that **mandatorily redeemable financial instruments (MRFI)** be accounted for as liabilities unless the redemption is required only upon the liquidation or termination of the entity. MRFIs are redeemable shares that embody an unconditional obligation to transfer assets at a fixed or determinable time or upon an event certain to occur.

Stock Warrants

7.   A stock warrant is a certificate evidencing a **right** to purchase shares of stock at a specified price within a specified period. Thus, it is an equity security. Warrants are usually attached to other securities.

Equity Accounts

8. **Contributed capital** (paid-in capital) represents amounts invested by owners in exchange for stock (common or preferred).

   a. The **stated capital** (capital stock) shows the par or stated value of all shares issued and outstanding. If stock has no par or stated value, the amount received is presented.

      1) Amounts for common and preferred stock are separately listed.
      2) Stated capital can be affected by treasury stock transactions.

   b. **Additional paid-in capital** (paid-in capital in excess of par or stated value) consists of the sources of contributed capital in excess of legal capital. Sources include

      1) Amounts in excess of par or stated value received for the entity's stock
      2) A debit item for receipts that are less than par or stated value, for example, discount on common stock
      3) Transfers at fair value from retained earnings upon the declaration of stock dividends
      4) Stock subscriptions defaults (if forfeiture is allowed by law and corporate policy)
      5) Amounts attributable to treasury stock transactions

9. **Retained earnings** is increased by net income and quasi-reorganization and decreased by (a) net losses, (b) cash or property dividends, (c) scrip dividends, (d) stock dividends, (e) split-ups effected in the form of a dividend, and (f) certain treasury stock transactions.

   a. **Prior-period adjustments** (essentially, error corrections) also are made directly to retained earnings.

   b. A **change in accounting principle** is applied retrospectively. The cumulative effect on all prior periods is reflected in the opening balances of assets, liabilities, and retained earnings (or other appropriate components of equity) for the first period presented.

10. **Treasury stock** consists of the entity's own stock reacquired for various purposes, e.g., (a) mergers, (b) share options, (c) stock dividends, (d) tax advantages (favorable capital gains rates) to shareholders, (e) an increase in EPS and other ratios, (f) avoidance of a hostile takeover, or (g) elimination of a particular ownership interest.

    a. It is most commonly accounted for at cost. Under the **cost method**, treasury stock is reported as an unallocated amount contra to the sum of the stock accounts and retained earnings (APB Opinion 6).

    b. Treasury stock is not an asset, and dividends are not paid on such stock.

11. **Accumulated other comprehensive income** is a separate component of equity that includes items excluded from net income. Items in that component should be classified according to their nature. Study Unit 2 includes a listing of classifications under existing accounting standards.

Stop and review! You have completed the outline for this subunit. Study multiple-choice questions 1 through 3 on page 526.

14.2 ISSUANCE OF STOCK

Articles of Incorporation

1. The articles of incorporation (charter) filed with the secretary of state of the state of incorporation indicates the **classes of stock** that may be issued and their **authorized amounts** in terms of shares or total dollar value.

2. When authorized shares are issued, the effect is to increase the amount of that class of stock outstanding.

3. If an entity does not hold any treasury stock, the number of shares of each type of stock may be determined by dividing the value allocated to each stock account by the related par value or stated value.

Issuance of Stock

4. Upon issuance of stock, cash is debited and common (preferred) stock is credited for the par or stated value. The difference is credited to **additional paid-in capital**.

Cash	$XXX	
Common stock (par value)		$XXX
Additional paid-in capital		XXX

   a. **Direct issuance costs** of equity (underwriting, legal, accounting, tax, registration, etc.) are debited to additional paid-in capital. Indirect costs of issuance, records maintenance, and ownership transfers (e.g., a stock transfer agent's fees) are expensed.

5. A discount is unlikely but would be debited to stock discount.

6. Issuance of stock may be subject to a **preemptive right**. Existing shareholders may have the right, not the obligation, to purchase enough shares to maintain their proportional ownership.

Stock Subscription

7. A stock subscription is a contractual arrangement to sell a specified number of shares at a specified price at some future date. When stock is subscribed, the corporation recognizes an obligation to issue stock, and the subscriber undertakes the legal obligation to pay for the shares subscribed. A down payment is usually paid at the inception of the agreement. Payments are then made (often on an installment basis) until the stock is fully paid for, and the buyer is granted full ownership.

8. At the inception of the subscription, if collection of the price is reasonably assured, the corporation makes the following entry:

Subscriptions receivable	$XXX	
Common (preferred) stock subscribed		$XXX
Additional paid-in capital		XXX

   a. The **SEC** requires that **subscriptions receivable** be reported as a contra equity account unless collection has occurred before issuance of the financial statements. In that case, the account may be reported as an asset.

9. When the subscription price is paid and the stock is issued, the corporation makes the following entry:

Cash	$XXX	
Common (preferred) stock subscribed	XXX	
Subscriptions receivable		$XXX
Common (preferred) stock		XXX

   a. Thus, additional paid-in capital is increased when the stock is subscribed and is not affected when the stock is subsequently issued.

10. When a subscriber **defaults**, the entry to record the subscription must be reversed.

    a. State laws and corporate policies vary with regard to defaults. The possibilities range from complete refund to complete forfeiture.

    b. To the extent that payment has been received and is forfeited, additional paid-in capital from stock subscription default is credited for the amount forfeited.

Issuance for Property or Services

11. Stock may be issued in exchange for property or services as well as for cash.

12. The transaction should be recorded at the more clearly determinable of the **fair values** of the stock or the property or services received.

13. The fair value used is that in effect at the date of the agreement.

14. If the property or services are assigned an excessive valuation by the board, the stock is said to be **watered**.

15. If the property or services are understated, the result is a **secret reserve**.

Donated Assets

16. In general, SFAS 116, *Accounting for Contributions Received and Contributions Made*, requires that contributions received be recognized as revenues or gains in the period of receipt. They should be measured at fair value.

17. **Contributions of the donee's stock.** APB Opinion 9, *Reporting the Results of Operations*, states that transactions in an entity's own stock do not affect net income or the results of operations. Thus, the receipt of a contribution of an entity's own stock is recorded at fair value as increases in both **contributed capital and treasury stock**. Because these accounts offset, the transaction has no net effect on equity.

18. **Contributions by governmental entities.** SFAS 116 does not apply to tax exemptions, abatements, or incentives, or to transfers of assets from a government to a business entity. Hence, a credit to **donated capital** may be appropriate in these cases.

    a. Nevertheless, SFAS 116 does not prohibit treating contributions by governmental entities as **revenues or gains**. Such treatment is consistent with the accounting for contributions by nongovernmental entities. It is also consistent with the definition of comprehensive income given in SFAC 6. Comprehensive income includes all changes in equity during a period except those resulting from investments by owners and distributions to owners.

Conversion of Convertible Securities

19. Stock may be issued upon the conversion of convertible securities such as bonds or preferred stock.

20. The customary accounting method for the conversion of convertible debt is commonly referred to as the **book value method**. It records the newly issued stock at the carrying amount of the converted securities.

    a. No gain or loss is recognized, but a gain or loss would be recognized under the **market-value method**, which records the transaction at market value.

21. When **preferred stock** is converted to common stock, no gain or loss is recognized because the transaction is with holders of equity. Accordingly, the transaction must be recorded using the book value method.

Combined Issuance

22. The proceeds of the combined issuance of different classes of securities are allocated based on the relative fair values of the securities.

23. If the fair value of one of the classes of securities is not known, the **incremental method** is used. The other securities are recorded at their fair values. The remaining proceeds are credited to the securities for which the fair value is not determinable.

Stop and review! You have completed the outline for this subunit. Study multiple-choice questions 4 through 7 beginning on page 527.

14.3 RETIREMENT

1. When stock is retired, cash (or treasury stock) is credited. The stock account is debited for the par or stated value. Additional paid-in capital is debited to the extent additional paid-in capital exists from the original stock issuance.

    a. Any remainder is debited to retained earnings or credited to additional paid-in capital from stock retirement.

2. As previously noted, no gain or loss is reported on transactions involving an entity's own stock.

    a. However, the transfer of **nonmonetary assets** in exchange for stock requires recognition of any holding gain or loss on the nonmonetary assets.

3. Preferred stock may be subject to a **call provision**, that is, mandatory redemption at the option of the issuer at a specified price.

Stop and review! You have completed the outline for this subunit. Study multiple-choice questions 8 through 10 beginning on page 528.

14.4 CASH DIVIDENDS

Recording Dividend Payments

1. Unlike stock dividends, cash dividends cannot be rescinded. Thus, a liability to the shareholders is created because the dividends must be paid once declared.

    a. At the **declaration date**, retained earnings must be decreased.

Retained earnings	$XXX
Dividends payable	$XXX

        1) An alternative is to debit a nominal account, **dividends declared**, that will be closed to retained earnings at year-end.

    b. When cash dividends are paid, dividends payable is debited and cash credited. At the **payment date**, retained earnings is not affected.

Dividends payable	$XXX
Cash	$XXX

Preferred Stock Dividends

2. If **preferred stock is cumulative**, dividends in arrears and the preferred dividends for the current period must be paid before common shareholders may receive dividends.

    a. **Dividends in arrears** are not recognized as a liability until they are declared. However, the aggregate and per share amounts of dividends in arrears are disclosed on the face of the balance sheet or in the notes.

3. Preferred stock may be **fully participating**. It may share equally in a cash dividend after a basic return has been paid to holders of both common and preferred stock at the preference rate for the preferred.

    a. Preferred stock also may be **partially participating**, for example, up to a ceiling rate or only after a specified higher rate has been paid to the common shareholders.

Stop and review! You have completed the outline for this subunit. Study multiple-choice questions 11 through 13 beginning on page 529.

14.5 PROPERTY DIVIDENDS

Definition

1. APB Opinion 29, *Accounting for Nonmonetary Transactions*, requires that certain nonreciprocal transfers of nonmonetary assets to owners be based on the **recorded amount** of the assets given up.

    a. These transfers are made "in a spinoff or other form of reorganization or liquidation or in a plan that is in substance the rescission of a prior business combination."

2. The recorded amount is determined after recognition of any **impairment loss**. SFAS 144, *Accounting for the Impairment or Disposal of Long-Lived Assets*, prescribes the impairment accounting for assets it covers.

3. Other nonreciprocal transfers of nonmonetary assets to owners are recorded at the **fair value** of the assets transferred.

Example

4. For example, if the property has appreciated, it is written up to fair value.

Property A	$XXX	
Gain on disposition		$XXX

5. The dividend is then recognized as a decrease in retained earnings and a corresponding increase in a dividend payable.

Retained earnings	$XXX	
Property dividend payable		$XXX

6. The distribution of the property dividend is recognized as follows:

Property dividend payable	$XXX	
Property A		$XXX

Stop and review! You have completed the outline for this subunit. Study multiple-choice questions 14 and 15 on page 530.

14.6 SCRIP DIVIDENDS

Definition

1. Scrip dividends may be declared when a corporation has sufficient retained earnings but is short of cash. Scrip is a form of note payable.

    a. When a scrip dividend is declared, retained earnings is debited and scrip dividend payable is credited.

    b. When the scrip dividend is paid, scrip dividend payable and interest expense are debited, and cash is credited. Interest is incurred for the period from declaration to payment.

Stop and review! You have completed the outline for this subunit. Study multiple-choice question 16 on page 531.

14.7 LIQUIDATING DIVIDENDS

1.   Liquidating dividends are repayments of capital. They are distributions in excess of the corporation's retained earnings.

2.   Because the effect of a liquidating dividend is to decrease contributed capital, additional paid-in capital is debited first to the extent available before the other contributed capital accounts are charged.

   a.   Thus, declaration of a dividend, a portion of which is liquidating, may decrease both additional paid-in capital and retained earnings.

Stop and review! You have completed the outline for this subunit. Study multiple-choice questions 17 through 19 beginning on page 531.

14.8 STOCK DIVIDENDS AND SPLITS

Definitions

1.   Stock dividends and stock splits are distributions of an entity's own stock to current shareholders for **no consideration**. But the financial substance of the two transactions differs.

   a.   In a **stock dividend**, a portion of retained earnings is capitalized.

   1)   The **par or stated value** of the shares is unchanged.

   2)   An issuance of shares of **less than 20% to 25%** of the outstanding common shares usually should be recognized as a **stock dividend**.

   a)   The **SEC requires** an issuance of less than 25% by a public entity to be treated as a stock dividend.

   3)   An issuance of shares of **more than 20% to 25%** of the outstanding common shares (25% or more for public entities) is considered to more closely resemble a **split** than a dividend.

   a)   The reason is that the effect of such a distribution is to increase the marketability of the stock.

   b.   In a **stock split**, no journal entry is made other than a memorandum entry.

   1)   The **par or stated value** of the shares is reduced.

2.   Stock dividends and stock splits do not affect the fair value of a shareholder's interest or the proportionate amount of that interest. Thus, the effect is simply a reclassification of equity.

   a.   However, because more shares are outstanding, the fair value (and market price) of a share is reduced.

Stock Dividends

3. The **primary purpose** is to provide shareholders with additional evidence of their interests in the retained earnings of the business without distribution of cash or other assets.

4. The par or stated value of each common share is unaffected. Thus, a stock dividend increases permanent capitalization but **does not affect total equity**. According to ARB 43, Ch. 7B, "Stock Dividends and Stock Split-Ups," a stock dividend is recognized by **capitalizing retained earnings** in an amount equal to the **fair value** of the additional shares distributed.

EXAMPLE

Pine Company has 100,000 shares of $100 par value common stock outstanding and retained earnings of $5,000,000. Pine declares a 15% stock dividend when the fair value of the stock is $140 per share.

The entry on the date of declaration is

Retained earnings (15,000 × $140)	$2,100,000	
Common stock dividend distributable (15,000 × $100)		$1,500,000
Additional paid-in capital (difference)		600,000

The entry on the date of distribution is

Common stock dividend distributable	$1,500,000	
Common stock		$1,500,000

---

5. Stock dividends often require the issuance of **fractional share rights**.

   a. When they are issued as part of a stock dividend, retained earnings is debited and stock rights outstanding is credited.

   b. If the stock rights are **forfeited**, the entry is to debit stock rights outstanding and credit additional paid-in capital from forfeiture of stock rights.

6. Stock dividends are **revocable**. Nevertheless, undistributed stock dividends are normally reported in the equity section.

Stock Split-Ups in the Form of a Dividend

7. The amount capitalized ordinarily is based on **par value**.

EXAMPLE

Pine Company declares a 35% stock dividend on its $100 par common stock when its fair value is $140 per share.

The entry on the date of declaration is

Retained earnings (35,000 × $100)	$3,500,000	
Common stock dividend distributable		$3,500,000

The entry on the date of distribution is

Common stock dividend distributable	$3,500,000	
Common stock		$3,500,000

---

8. In some circumstances, legal requirements of the state of incorporation may require the capitalization of retained earnings when a stock split in the form of a dividend occurs.

   a. Under these circumstances, the par or stated value per share is not changed. Retained earnings should be capitalized in an amount equal to the **legal requirement**, usually the par or stated value of the additional shares distributed.

   b. Furthermore, the term "dividend" should be avoided in referring to a stock split. When this usage is legally required, the transaction should be described as a **split-up effected in the form of a dividend**.

Stock Splits

9.   The **primary purpose of** a stock split is to improve the stock's marketability by reducing its market price and increasing the number of shares outstanding.

10.   A stock split is recognized by a decrease in the par or stated value of each common share, accompanied by a proportionate **increase in the number of shares** outstanding.

   a.   Thus, a stock split does not increase permanent capitalization and **does not affect total equity**.

EXAMPLE

Pine Company declares a 2-for-1 stock split of its $100 par common stock when the fair value is $140 per share. The number of shares outstanding increases to 200,000, and the par value of each share is reduced to $50. A memorandum entry is recorded in Pine's books.

The firm's total permanent capital is unchanged:

$$100{,}000 \text{ shares} \times \$100 \text{ par} = 200{,}000 \text{ shares} \times \$50 \text{ par}$$

---

11.   A **reverse stock split** reduces the number of shares outstanding, which serves to increase the fair value per share of those shares still outstanding.

Other Issues

12.   The **recipient** of a stock dividend or stock split should **not recognize income**. After receipt, the shareholder has the same proportionate interest in the corporation and the same total carrying amount as before the declaration.

13.   **Treasury stock** may be adjusted for stock dividends and splits depending on the intended use of the treasury stock. Thus, the adjustment is more likely if the stock is held to meet obligations under an employee stock ownership plan. If the stock has no designated purpose, no adjustment is made. However, **some states prohibit** the payment of stock dividends on treasury stock.

Stop and review! You have completed the outline for this subunit. Study multiple-choice questions 20 through 23 beginning on page 532.

14.9 APPROPRIATIONS OF RETAINED EARNINGS

1.   Retained earnings is sometimes **appropriated** (restricted) to a special account to disclose that earnings retained in the business (not paid out in dividends) are being used for special purposes. Purposes include (a) compliance with the terms of a bond indenture (bond contract), (b) retention of assets for internally financed expansion, (c) anticipation of losses, or (d) adherence to legal restrictions. For example, a state law may restrict retained earnings by an amount equal to the cost of treasury stock.

2.   The appropriation **does not set aside assets**. Rather, it limits the amount available for **dividends**. A formal entry (debit retained earnings, credit retained earnings appropriated) may be used, or the restriction may be disclosed in a note.

3.   According to APB Opinion 9, *Reporting the Results of Operations*, transfers to and from have no effect on appropriated retained earnings net income.

   a.   SFAS 5, *Accounting for Contingencies*, permits an appropriation of retained earnings if it is displayed within equity and is clearly identified. Costs and losses are not debited to an appropriation, and no amount of the appropriation is transferred to income.

Stop and review! You have completed the outline for this subunit. Study multiple-choice questions 24 through 26 beginning on page 533.

14.10 TREASURY STOCK – COST METHOD

Acquisition

1. When the cost method of accounting for treasury stock transactions is used, the acquisition of treasury stock is recorded as a debit to treasury stock and a credit to cash. No other accounts are affected.

2. Treasury stock is a **contra equity account**.

    a. Treasury stock accounted for at cost on the balance sheet is a reduction of the sum of the stock accounts and retained earnings.

3. **Transactions** in treasury stock, including gifts received, are excluded from net income.

    a. Donated treasury stock may be accounted for using the cost or the par value method.

Reissue in Excess of Cost

4. The difference between the cash received and the carrying amount (acquisition cost) of the treasury stock is credited to an account titled **paid-in capital from treasury stock** (or additional paid-in capital from treasury stock transactions), not to "additional paid-in capital."

Reissue at Less than Cost

5. The difference between the acquisition cost and the reissue price is debited to paid-in capital from treasury stock.

    a. After paid-in capital from treasury stock has been reduced to a zero balance, the remaining debit is to retained earnings.

Stop and review! You have completed the outline for this subunit. Study multiple-choice questions 27 through 29 beginning on page 534.

14.11 TREASURY STOCK – PAR VALUE METHOD

Acquisition

1. The par value method treats the **acquisition** of treasury stock as a **constructive retirement** and the resale as a new issue. Upon acquisition, the entry originally made to issue stock is effectively reversed. **Treasury stock at par value** is recorded as an offset to the contributed capital account representing issued stock of the same type. The additional paid-in capital recorded when the stock was originally issued is removed.

    a. Any difference between the original issue price and the acquisition price is ordinarily adjusted through paid-in capital accounts and retained earnings.

    b. An excess of the original price over the acquisition price is credited to **paid-in capital from treasury stock**. Any excess acquisition price is debited to the same account but only to the extent of the credit balance from prior transactions.

        1) If the credit balance in the account is insufficient to absorb the excess acquisition price, **retained earnings** will be debited for the remainder.

Reissue

2. Subsequent reissue removes the treasury stock at par value and reestablishes additional paid-in capital for any excess of the reissue price over par value.

    a. If the reissue price is less than par, the debit is to a paid-in capital account or to retained earnings.

Cost Method vs. Par Value Method

EXAMPLE

Rhone Company has the following balances in its equity section on December 31, Year 1:

Common stock, $20 par value, 300,000 shares outstanding	$6,000,000
Additional paid-in capital ($2 per share)	$600,000
Retained earnings	$2,000,000

The following transactions occurred in Year 2. The entries (assuming no prior treasury stock transactions) are shown below.

1) Reacquired 50,000 shares for $2,000,000 ($40 per share)
2) Reissued 10,000 shares of treasury stock for $30 per share
3) Retired the 40,000 shares remaining in treasury stock

Cost

1)	Treasury stock (cost)	$2,000,000	
	Cash		$2,000,000
2)	Cash	$300,000	
	Retained earnings	100,000	
	Treasury stock (10,000 × $40)		$400,000
3)	Common stock (40,000 × $20)	$800,000	
	Additional paid-in capital (40,000 × $2)	80,000	
	Retained earnings	720,000	
	Treasury stock (cost) (40,000 × $40)		$1,600,000

Par Value

1)	Treasury stock (par value) (50,000 × $20)	$1,000,000	
	Additional paid-in capital (50,000 × $2)	100,000	
	Retained earnings	900,000	
	Cash		$2,000,000
2)	Cash	$300,000	
	Treasury stock at par value (10,000 × $20)		$200,000
	Paid-in capital from treasury stock		100,000
3)	Common stock	$800,000	
	Treasury stock (par value)		$800,000

Stop and review! You have completed the outline for this subunit. Study multiple-choice questions 30 and 31 beginning on page 535.

14.12 STOCK RIGHTS

Preemptive Right

1. The **preemptive right** safeguards a shareholder's proportionate ownership. Thus, it is the right to purchase a pro rata amount of a new issuance of the same class of stock. However, many entities have eliminated the preemptive right because it may inhibit the large issuances of stock that are often needed in business combinations.

Right Offering

2. In a **rights offering**, each shareholder is issued a certificate or **warrant** that is an option to buy a certain number of shares at a fixed price.

    a. If the **rights are exercised** and stock is issued, the issuer will reflect the proceeds received as a credit to (an increase in) common (preferred) stock at par value, with any remainder credited to additional paid-in capital.

    b. When rights are **issued for no consideration**, the issuer makes only a memorandum entry. If the rights previously issued without consideration are allowed to lapse, contributed capital is unaffected.

3. From the time the rights offering is announced to the issue date, the stock trades **rights-on**. After the issue date, it trades **ex-rights** because the rights can be sold separately.

4. The recipient of stock rights must **allocate the carrying amount of the shares owned** between the shares and rights based on their **relative fair values** at the time the rights are received. An example entry is to debit available-for-sale securities (rights) and credit available-for-sale securities. The recipient then has three options:

   a. If the rights are **exercised**, the amount allocated to them becomes part of the carrying amount of the acquired shares.

   b. If the rights are **sold**, their carrying amount is credited, cash is debited, and a gain (loss) is credited (debited).

   c. If the rights **expire**, a loss is recorded.

5. Stock rights with **readily determinable fair values** are equity securities that are classified as available-for-sale or trading.

6. **Transaction costs** associated with the redemption of stock rights reduce equity.

Stop and review! You have completed the outline for this subunit. Study multiple-choice questions 32 through 34 beginning on page 536.

14.13 PROPRIETORSHIPS AND PARTNERSHIPS

Sole Proprietorships

1. **Sole proprietorships** are business entities owned by individuals. A sole proprietorship is not a separate legal entity. It is an extension of the owner. A sole proprietor has unlimited liability for business debts.

2. A single **capital (equity) account** is customarily used to account for all equity transactions of a sole proprietorship.

3. A sole proprietorship does not pay income taxes. Rather, any profit or loss flows through to the owner who reports the amounts in his/her individual tax return.

4. Relevant GAAP ordinarily apply regardless of the form of business organization.

Partnerships Defined

5. A partnership, as defined by the **Revised Uniform Partnership Act (RUPA)**, is an association of two or more persons to carry on, as co-owners, a business for profit.

6. Unlike corporations, general partnerships do not insulate a partner from liability to creditors. Each general partner has **unlimited liability** for partnership debts.

   a. The general partners may agree among themselves to limit a partner's liability, but such a provision cannot limit direct liability to creditors.

Partnership Formation

7.   Partners contribute cash and other property as the basis of their equity in a partnership. Cash is recorded at its nominal amount and property at its fair value.

EXAMPLE

Gilda Rosecrans, Bill Bragg, and Tim Thomas agree to form Chickamauga Partners. Besides cash, each partner contributes tangible property consisting of a building, inventory, and equipment, respectively. Rosecrans' building is subject to a $45,000 mortgage. The values of the contributions on the date of formation are as follows:

Partner	Cash	Property at Carrying Amount	Property at Fair Value
Rosecrans	$ 20,000	$ 80,000	$110,000
Bragg	55,000	18,000	15,000
Thomas	40,000	30,000	20,000
	$115,000	$128,000	$145,000

The journal entry to record the formation of the partnership is

Cash	$115,000	
Inventory	15,000	
Equipment	20,000	
Building	110,000	
Mortgage payable		$45,000
Bragg, capital ($55,000 + $15,000)		70,000
Rosecrans, capital ($20,000 + $110,000 – $45,000)		85,000
Thomas, capital ($40,000 + $20,000)		60,000

---

8.   **Capital accounts.** Partnerships provide only a limited amount of equity disclosure. Thus, the equity section of the partnership balance sheet includes only the partners' (or class of partners') capital accounts.

9.   **Intangible contributions.** The partners may decide that a given partner's contribution exceeds the value of cash and tangible property contributed, e.g., a special talent or an established customer list. Two accounting treatments are available.

    a.   Under the **bonus method**, only the values of cash and tangible property contributed are recorded on the partnership's books. The partners then apportion the capital accounts to reflect a partner's special contribution.

EXAMPLE

Dick McPherson and Josh Logan contribute $90,000 and $10,000, respectively, to their new partnership. Under normal circumstances, the journal entry is

Cash	$100,000	
McPherson, capital		$90,000
Logan, capital		10,000

However, the two partners agree that Logan's extensive contacts in the field in which the partnership will do business are worth more than the cash he is contributing. Their agreement results in a 60:40 apportionment.

Cash	$100,000	
McPherson, capital		$60,000
Logan, capital		40,000

---

b. Under the **goodwill method**, the partners create an asset account to hold the perceived value of the intangible benefit contributed by a given partner. In practice, no objective basis is needed for this measure of the goodwill.

EXAMPLE

McPherson and Logan acknowledge the worth of Logan's professional contacts by creating a goodwill account. Their 60:40 apportionment of equity results in the following journal entry:

Cash	$100,000	
Goodwill	30,000	
McPherson, capital		$78,000
Logan, capital		52,000

Additions and Withdrawals of Capital

10. Existing partners may make **additional contributions** to the partnership. The appropriate asset account is debited for the nominal amount of cash or fair value of property, and that partner's capital account is credited. No reapportionment of equity among the partners is performed.

11. Partners occasionally **withdraw funds** from the partnership. These transactions are recorded in **drawing accounts**.

EXAMPLE

Rosecrans and Thomas make a withdrawal of cash from Chickamauga Partners:

Rosecrans, drawing	$10,000	
Thomas, drawing	5,000	
Cash		$15,000

Drawing accounts are **nominal accounts** that are closed to partnership capital at the end of each period.

Rosecrans, capital	$10,000	
Thomas, capital	5,000	
Rosecrans, drawing		$10,000
Thomas, drawing		5,000

Partnership Income and Loss – Simple

12.   Profit and loss are distributed equally among partners unless the partnership agreement provides otherwise.

   a.   The equal distribution is based on the number of partners, not capital balances.

   b.   If the partnership agreement specifies how profits are to be shared, but is silent with respect to losses, losses are divided in the same manner as profits.

EXAMPLE

Chickamauga Partners' agreement is that net income will be distributed 50% to Rosecrans and 25% each to Bragg and Thomas. The partnership's net income for the period is $60,000.

Income summary	$60,000	
Bragg, capital		$15,000
Rosecrans, capital		30,000
Thomas, capital		15,000

The distribution of profit and loss is **not** based on the relative proportions of the partners' capital balances, but only on the contractual agreement entered into by the partners at the time of formation.

Had Chickamauga Partners lacked such an agreement, profits and losses would have been distributed **equally**. Given three partners, each would have received 33 1/3% of the net income.

The statement of partners' capital can be prepared once the books are closed:

	Bragg	Rosecrans	Thomas	Totals
Capital balances, beginning of year	$70,000	$ 85,000	$60,000	$215,000
Add: Allocation of net income	15,000	30,000	15,000	60,000
Minus: Drawings	0	(10,000)	(5,000)	(15,000)
Capital balances, end of year	$85,000	$105,000	$70,000	$260,000

Partnership Income and Loss – Complex

13.   Partners often find that a division of profits based on a simple formula (e.g., 40%:30%:30%) is not adequate to reflect the business dynamics of the partnership.

   a.   A typical arrangement calls for either or both of the following provisions:

   1)   The **accrual of interest** on each partner's capital balance
   2)   A **bonus** to one or more of the partners

b.   Any remaining profit is then divided among the partners according to the agreed-upon ratio.

EXAMPLE

The McPherson and Logan partnership has $100,000 of net income for the year.

The partners have agreed to the following provisions for the division of profits:

1)   Both partners will be allocated 15% interest on their average monthly capital balances for the year
2)   Logan will receive a bonus of 10% of net income after deduction of the interest allocation
3)   Any remainder will be divided according to the agreed-upon ratio of 60% to McPherson and 40% to Logan.

McPherson's and Logan's average monthly capital balances for the year were $60,000 and $40,000, respectively. The allocation of the year's net income is as follows:

	McPherson	Logan	Totals
Interest on capital	$ 9,000	$ 6,000	$ 15,000
Bonus		8,500	8,500
Residual net income	45,900	30,600	76,500
Allocated net income	$54,900	$45,100	$100,000

Sale of a Partnership Interest

14.   When **an existing partner sells** his/her interest in a partnership to an outside party, the new partner is entitled to share in the partnership's profits and losses but is not allowed to participate in management decisions until the remaining partners agree to admit the new partner to the partnership.

EXAMPLE

Bill Bragg sells his interest in Chickamauga Partners to Jenna Longstreet for $100,000, an amount greater than Bragg's capital balance.

Bragg, capital	$85,000	
Longstreet, capital		$85,000

The cash exchanged between Bragg and Longstreet is irrelevant to partnership accounting.

Longstreet now shares in the partnership's profits and losses. She owns Bragg's partnership interest but may not participate in management.

Addition of a New Partner

15. New partners may contribute cash, property, or service. A partner's tangible and intangible contributions are subject to **four possible accounting treatments**.

16. **Bonus credited to the original partners.** The fair value of the new partner's contribution exceeds the amount credited to his/her capital account. The excess is considered a bonus to the existing partners.

EXAMPLE

Instead of buying out Bragg, Longstreet contributes $80,000 in cash to the partnership. The three existing partners agree to assign her a 20% interest in the partnership's capital.

Longstreet's contribution of $80,000 increases the total capital of the partnership to $340,000. Her capital account is credited for the agreed-upon 20% interest in the new partnership's total capital ($68,000).

The existing partners split the bonus ($80,000 – $68,000) in proportion to their contractual profit-loss allocation.

Cash	$80,000	
Bragg, capital ($12,000 × 25%)		$ 3,000
Longstreet, capital ($340,000 × 20%)		68,000
Rosecrans, capital ($12,000 × 50%)		6,000
Thomas, capital ($12,000 × 25%)		3,000

---

17. **Goodwill credited to the original partners.** The original partners wish to recognize an increase in total partnership capital in excess of the new partner's contribution. The excess is debited to goodwill.

EXAMPLE

The original partners have assigned Longstreet a 20% interest in return for $80,000, implying a fair value of $400,000 for the partnership as a whole ($80,000 ÷ 20%).

Goodwill is recorded for the $60,000 difference in the valuation of the partnership ($400,000 – $260,000 – $80,000).

Cash	$80,000	
Longstreet, capital		$80,000
Goodwill	$60,000	
Bragg, capital ($60,000 × 25%)		$15,000
Rosecrans, capital ($60,000 × 50%)		30,000
Thomas, capital ($60,000 × 25%)		15,000

---

18. **Revaluation of current assets.** The existing partners reassess the fair values of the partnership assets and recognize any increase as a bonus in their respective capital accounts.

EXAMPLE

Before admitting Longstreet, the partners revalue their identifiable assets. They determine that the building and equipment are each worth $10,000 more than their carrying amounts. This revaluation is allocated to the existing partners' capital accounts.

Equipment	$10,000	
Building	10,000	
Bragg, capital ($20,000 × 25%)		$ 5,000
Rosecrans, capital ($20,000 × 50%)		10,000
Thomas, capital ($20,000 × 25%)		5,000

The partnership's total capital is now $360,000 ($260,000 + $20,000 + $80,000 cash from Longstreet).

Longstreet's capital account is credited for 20% of the new total ($72,000). The bonus ($80,000 – $72,000) is allocated among the existing partners in proportion to their profit-and-loss percentages.

Cash	$80,000	
Bragg, capital ($8,000 × 25%)		$ 2,000
Longstreet, capital ($360,000 × 20%)		72,000
Rosecrans, capital ($8,000 × 50%)		4,000
Thomas, capital ($8,000 × 25%)		2,000

---

19. **Bonus or goodwill credited to the new partner.** The existing partners acknowledge an intangible benefit brought to the partnership in addition to cash or property.

EXAMPLE

The existing partners wish to recognize the leadership that Longstreet brings to the business by crediting her with a 25% interest in the partnership.

A 25% interest in the resulting $340,000 total partnership capital ($260,000 existing + $80,000 contributed by Longstreet) is $85,000. The excess of Longstreet's capital over her cash contribution is a reduction in the existing partners' capital accounts.

Cash	$80,000	
Bragg, capital ($5,000 × 25%)	1,250	
Rosecrans, capital ($5,000 × 50%)	2,500	
Thomas, capital ($5,000 × 25%)	1,250	
Longstreet, capital		$85,000

Withdrawal of a Partner

20. When a partner withdraws, the transaction is in essence a buy-out by the remaining partners.

21. An appraisal is performed to determine the fair values of the partnership assets. **Three accounting treatments** of the results are available.

    a. In each case, the withdrawing partner is given cash or other property equal to his/her capital account after the appraisal.

22. **Bonus method.** The results of the appraisal are not formally recognized on the partnership's books.

EXAMPLE

Bragg decides that he wants to leave Chickamauga Partners without bringing in another partner to replace him.

An appraisal of the business concludes that the building and equipment are each worth $10,000 more than their carrying amounts and that the partnership has generated $10,000 of goodwill during its time in operation. Bragg is entitled to a distribution that includes his proportionate share of these valuations ($30,000 × 25% = $7,500).

The apportionment of Bragg's share of the revaluation and recognition of the new goodwill is subtracted from the remaining partners' capital accounts, based on the relative profit-and-loss percentages (Rosecrans: 50% ÷ 75% or 66 2/3%, Thomas: 25% ÷ 75% or 33 1/3%).

Bragg, capital	$85,000	
Rosencrans, capital ($7,500 × 66 2/3%)	5,000	
Thomas, capital ($7,500 × 33 1/3%)	2,500	
Cash		$92,500

---

23. **Goodwill method.** Tangible assets are formally revalued on the partnership's books, and any goodwill is recognized.

EXAMPLE

The appraisal referred to on the previous page results in the asset accounts being adjusted. Bragg's capital account is removed from the books and the appropriate amount of cash is distributed to him.

Building	$10,000	
Equipment	10,000	
Goodwill	10,000	
Bragg, capital ($30,000 × 25%)		$ 7,500
Rosecrans, capital ($30,000 × 50%)		15,000
Thomas, capital ($30,000 × 25%)		7,500
Bragg, capital	$92,500	
Cash		$92,500

---

24. **Hybrid method.** Tangible assets are formally revalued on the partnership's books, but goodwill is not recognized.

EXAMPLE

The appraisal referred to on the previous page results in the asset accounts being adjusted but not in the recognition of goodwill. Bragg's capital account is removed from the books, and the appropriate amount of cash is distributed to him.

Building	$10,000	
Equipment	10,000	
Bragg, capital ($20,000 × 25%)		$ 5,000
Rosecrans, capital ($20,000 × 50%)		10,000
Thomas, capital ($20,000 × 25%)		5,000
Bragg, capital	$90,000	
Cash		$90,000

Liquidation of a Partnership – Process

25. Once the partners decide to dissolve their partnership, the process of liquidating noncash assets and settling liabilities begins. The liquidation process almost always involves incurring losses and proceeds through four steps:

    a. First, any **gain or loss** realized from the actual sale of assets is allocated to the partners' capital accounts in accordance with the profit-and-loss ratio.

    b. Second, **remaining assets** are assumed to have a fair value of $0, which results in an assumed loss equal to their carrying amounts. This amount is allocated to the partners' accounts in accordance with the profit-and-loss ratio.

    c. Third, if at least one of the partners' capital accounts has a **deficit balance**, the deficit is allocated to the remaining partners' accounts.

    d. Fourth, the **final balances** in the partnership accounts equal the amounts of cash, if any, that may be distributed to the partners.

26. Creditors are paid in full before any distributions are made to partners. However, **partners who are creditors** share equally with nonpartner creditors under the RUPA. In practice, because partners are liable for all partnership debts, partnership creditors are paid first.

27. After payment of creditors, any surplus is paid **in cash** to the partners. A partner has no right to a **distribution in kind** and is not required to accept a distribution in kind.

28. To settle **partnership accounts** with credit balances, each partner receives a distribution equal to the excess of credits over debits to his/her account. Thus, no distinction is made between distributions of capital and of profits.

    a. Profits and losses from liquidation of assets are credits and debits, respectively.

    b. Prior credits to an account include contributions made and the partner's share of profits.

    c. Prior debits include distributions received and the partner's share of losses.

29. If the account has a debit balance, the partner is liable to **contribute** the amount of the balance.

a. If a partner does not make a required contribution, the other partners must pay the difference in the same proportion in which they share losses.

b. A partner making an excess contribution may recover the excess from the other partners.

c. Moreover, the representative of creditors of the partnership or of a partner (e.g., a trustee in bankruptcy) may enforce the obligation to contribute.

d. One effect of these rules is that, consistent with the federal **Bankruptcy Code**, partnership creditors

1) Have priority in partnership assets and
2) Share equally with creditors of a partner in the partner's separate assets.

Liquidation of a Partnership – Cash Predistribution Plan

30. To avoid the inconvenience of constantly preparing new schedules after each transaction during the liquidation period, a schedule of possible losses, called a **cash predistribution plan**, is prepared at the beginning of the liquidation process.

a. The plan tracks a projected series of incremental losses incurred during liquidation to indicate the amount of loss, called the **maximum loss allowable**, that would eliminate each partner's capital account in sequence.

b. The purpose of the cash predistribution plan is to determine the amount of **cash that can safely be distributed** to the partners.

EXAMPLE

After several years of operation, Rosecrans, Bragg, and Thomas decide to dissolve Chickamauga Partners. At the time, the partnership's balance sheet is as follows:

Assets		Liabilities and Equity	
Cash	$ 20,000	Accounts payable	$ 20,000
Inventory	4,000	Loan from Rosecrans	40,000
Equipment	6,000	Bragg, capital	20,000
Building	110,000	Rosecrans, capital	60,000
		Thomas, capital	10,000
Total	$140,000	Total	$140,000

The maximum loss that would eliminate each partner's capital balance is calculated.

	Capital Balances at Beginning of Liquidation	Profit/Loss Allocation	Maximum Absorbable Loss (Balance ÷ Allocation %)
Bragg, capital	$20,000	25%	$ 80,000
Rosecrans, capital	60,000	50%	120,000
Thomas, capital	10,000	25%	40,000

Tim Thomas is in the most vulnerable position. A loss of $40,000 eliminates his interest in the partnership. This amount is the Step 1 Loss.

	Bragg, Capital	Rosecrans, Capital	Thomas, Capital
Beginning balances	$20,000	$60,000	$ 10,000
Assumed $40,000 loss	(10,000)	(20,000)	(10,000)
Balances after Step 1	$10,000	$40,000	$ 0

EXAMPLE – *continued*

The next maximum loss allowable is then calculated. Bragg's share is now 33% (25% ÷ 75%) and Rosecrans' is 67% (50% ÷ 75%).

	Capital Balances at Beginning of Step 2	New Profit/ Loss Allocation	Maximum Absorbable Loss (Balance ÷ Allocation %)
Bragg, capital	$10,000	33%	$30,303
Rosecrans, capital	40,000	67%	59,701

Bragg is in the next most vulnerable position. A further loss of $30,303 eliminates his interest.

	Bragg, Capital	Rosecrans, Capital
Beginning balances	$10,000	$40,000
Assumed $30,303 loss	(10,000)	(20,303)
Balances after Step 2	$ 0	$19,697

Given three partners, only three incremental losses will eliminate the partnership's capital. The Step 3 Loss is the amount of capital remaining to the third partner after the first two steps. The following is a complete schedule:

	Bragg, Capital	Rosecrans, Capital	Thomas, Capital
Beginning balances	$20,000	$60,000	$10,000
Assumed $40,000 loss	(10,000)	(20,000)	(10,000)
Balances after Step 1	$10,000	$40,000	$ 0
Assumed $30,303 loss	(10,000)	(20,303)	
Balances after Step 2	$ 0	$19,697	
Assumed $19,697 loss		(19,697)	
Final balance		$ 0	

If each successive loss in reverse does not materialize, that amount of cash may safely be distributed to the partners. As cash becomes available after the partnership's liabilities are settled, it is safe to distribute the first $19,697 to Rosecrans. If a further $30,303 becomes available, it can be distributed $20,303 to Rosecrans and $10,000 to Bragg. Any additional cash may be distributed to all three partners.

The following is the cash predistribution plan:

Outside creditors	$20,000	
Liquidation expenses	14,000	
First distribution		$34,000
Loan from Rosecrans	40,000	
Second distribution		40,000
To Rosecrans	19,697	
Third distribution		19,697
To Bragg	10,000	
To Rosecrans	20,303	
Fourth distribution		30,303
All further distributions:		
Bragg -- 25%		
Rosecrans -- 50%		
Thomas -- 25%		

Incorporation of a Partnership

31. When a partnership incorporates, the transfer of the net assets, including goodwill, should be at fair value. Thus, **contributed capital** will equal the fair value of the assets transferred minus the fair value of the liabilities assumed.

Stop and review! You have completed the outline for this subunit. Study multiple-choice question 35 on page 537.

14.14 BANKRUPTCY AND REORGANIZATION

Bankruptcy Accounting

1. Because a bankrupt entity about to be liquidated is not a **going concern**, the appropriate financial statement is not a balance sheet but a **statement of affairs**. This statement is prepared as of a specific date to present assets and liabilities of the debtor at **liquidation values**. Carrying amounts are shown on a memorandum basis. See the example on the following page.

2. The statement of affairs uses a classification scheme based on the **Federal Bankruptcy Code's** priorities and rankings of claims, not the current-noncurrent categories of the balance sheet.

    a. The **asset section** has columns for liquidation values and realizable amounts. Assets are presented as

        1) Pledged for fully secured liabilities
        2) Pledged for partially secured liabilities
        3) Available for priority and other unsecured creditors (free assets)

    b. The **liability section** lists liabilities for priority claims and liabilities offset by secured amounts, with the amounts unsecured and without priority presented in a separate column. Liabilities are shown as

        1) Priority liabilities
        2) Fully secured liabilities
        3) Partially secured liabilities
        4) Unsecured liabilities without priority

    c. An offsetting technique is used to determine the **estimated amount realizable from each asset**. For example, the amount of a mortgage on land is subtracted from the asset's liquidation value on the statement of affairs to determine the amount shown in the amounts realizable column.

        1) Similarly, the amounts owed to priority creditors are subtracted in arriving at the amount realizable for payment to unsecured creditors.

    d. The preparation of a statement of affairs results in either an **estimated deficiency** or an **estimated amount available** to shareholders. This example resulted in an estimated deficiency. It is equal to the excess of unsecured claims without priority ($100,000) over the amount available to pay such claims ($89,400).

EXAMPLE

THE GULF COMPANY
Statement of Affairs
March 31, Year 1

Carrying Amounts	Assets			Realizable Amounts
	Pledged with fully secured creditors			
$ 8,000	Land	$10,000		
102,000	Building	90,000	$100,000	
	Notes payable	$70,000		
	Accrued interest	1,600	71,600	$ 28,400
	Pledged with partially secured creditors			
4,800	Arco common stock		$ 10,150	
	Bank loan -- First State Bank	$20,000		
	Accrued interest	1,700	21,700	
	Free assets			
2,300	Cash			2,300
13,500	Accounts receivable			10,000
22,400	Notes receivable			14,400
38,000	Inventory			24,100
40,000	Equipment			15,000
	Realizable amount of unpledged assets			94,200
	Liabilities having priority			4,800
	Net free assets			89,400
	Estimated deficiency to unsecured creditors			10,600
$231,000				$100,000

Carrying Amounts	Liabilities			Unsecured
	Priority liabilities			
$ 4,800	Wages and salaries		$ 4,800	
	Fully secured liabilities			
70,000	Notes payable		$70,000	
1,600	Accrued interest		1,700	
	Partially secured liabilities			
	Bank loan -- First State Bank			
20,000	Principal		$20,000	
1,700	Accrued interest		1,700	
	Arco common stock		10,150	$ 11,550
	Unsecured liabilities			
88,450	Accounts payable			88,450
	Equity			
120,000	Capital stock			
(75,550)	Retained earnings (deficit)			
$231,000				$100,000

3. When the trustee takes control of the assets of the debtor, (s)he is likely to continue use of the entity's accounting records in a **reorganization**.

4. In a **liquidation**, the trustee may choose to establish a new set of books for the bankruptcy estate. A trustee in these circumstances may adopt various methods of accounting.

    a. One possibility is to record assets (without valuation accounts) and liabilities at their carrying amounts on the debtor's books.

        1) Gains and losses on realization, the expenses of liquidation, and any unrecorded items discovered by the trustee are taken directly to estate equity.

    b. A **statement of realization and liquidation** is often submitted to the court to reflect the trustee's progress toward liquidation. However, the statement is not required, and the judge in the case prescribes the form of the information required to be presented.

Quasi-Reorganizations

5. Quasi-reorganizations are undertaken by corporations with **negative retained earnings**. In many states, such entities are **not permitted to pay dividends**. Accordingly, a corporation that has begun to be profitable may nevertheless not be able to pay dividends because of accumulated losses reflected in retained earnings.

6. In this situation, a quasi-reorganization may be permitted to reduce the deficit in retained earnings to zero. However, the **shareholders must approve**.

    a. ARB 43, Ch. 7A, "Quasi-Reorganization or Corporate Readjustment," requires that a quasi-reorganization be accomplished first by restating assets to fair values and liabilities to present values. This process (an **accounting reorganization**) usually increases the deficit in retained earnings. But the restatement must not result in a writeup of net assets.

        1) **Additional paid-in capital** or its equivalent then must be available or be created to provide a source of capital against which the deficit may be written off.

        2) This result is usually accomplished by reducing **par or stated value**, with a debit to common stock and a credit to additional paid-in capital. The latter is then debited to enable the retained earnings balance to be reduced to zero. However, additional paid-in capital need not be eliminated.

b. If only a deficit in retained earnings is eliminated, the procedure is called a **deficit reclassification**.

EXAMPLE

Tabitha Company has the following items on its books on December 31, Year 1.

*   Property, plant, and equipment recorded at $1,000,000
*   Common stock, par value $30 per share, 50,000 shares outstanding recorded at $1,500,000
*   Additional paid-in capital recorded at $500,000
*   Retained earnings (deficit) ($100,000)
*   Property, plant, and equipment's fair value recorded at $400,000
*   The par value of the common stock reduced to $10 per share

The effects of a quasi-reorganization in the form of an **accounting reorganization** are as follows:

1) Restate assets

Retained earnings	$600,000	
Property, plant, and equipment		$600,000

2) Adjust common stock

Common stock		
[50,000 shares × ($30 – $10)]	$1,000,000	
Additional paid-in capital		$1,000,000

3) Write-off deficit

Additional paid-in capital	$700,000	
Retained earnings		$700,000

4) Present the new equity section as follows:

Common stock, par value $10 per share, 50,000 shares outstanding	$ 500,000
Additional paid-in capital ($500,000 – $700,000 + $1,000,000)	800,000
Retained earnings (after quasi-reorganization dated December 31, Year 1)	0
	$1,300,000

---

7. ARB 46, *Discontinuance of Dating Earned Surplus*, requires that, after a quasi-reorganization, the retained earnings account be dated for a period of 10 years. Dating discloses the quasi-reorganization and when it occurred.

Stop and review! You have completed the outline for this subunit. Study multiple-choice questions 36 and 37 on page 537.

QUESTIONS

14.1 Equity

1. During the prior year, Brad Co. issued 5,000 shares of $100 par convertible preferred stock for $110 per share. One share of preferred stock can be converted into three shares of Brad's $25 par common stock at the option of the preferred shareholder. On December 31 of the current year, when the market value of the common stock was $40 per share, all of the preferred stock was converted. What amount should Brad credit to common stock and to additional paid-in capital -- common stock as a result of the conversion?

	Common Stock	Additional Paid-in Capital
A.	$375,000	$175,000
B.	$375,000	$225,000
C.	$500,000	$50,000
D.	$600,000	$0

Answer (A) is correct. *(CPA, adapted)*
REQUIRED: The amounts credited to common stock and additional paid-in capital.
DISCUSSION: Brad received $550,000 (5,000 × $110) for the preferred stock converted to common stock. The par value of the 15,000 shares (5,000 × 3) of common stock is $375,000 (15,000 × $25). The remaining $175,000 ($550,000 – $375,000) is credited to additional paid-in capital.
Answer (B) is incorrect because $175,000 is credited to additional paid-in capital ($550,000 – $375,000). Answer (C) is incorrect because $500,000 is the par value of the preferred stock, not the common stock. Answer (D) is incorrect because $600,000 equals the fair value of the common stock at the date of conversion.

2. Data regarding Ball Corp.'s available-for-sale securities follow:

	Cost	Fair Value
December 31, Year 3	$150,000	$130,000
December 31, Year 4	150,000	160,000

Differences between cost and fair values are considered temporary. The decline in fair value was considered temporary and was properly accounted for at December 31, Year 3. Ball's Year 4 statement of changes in equity should report an increase of

A. $30,000

B. $20,000

C. $10,000

D. $0

Answer (A) is correct. *(CPA, adapted)*
REQUIRED: The increase reported in the statement of changes in equity because of a change in the fair value of available-for-sale securities.
DISCUSSION: Unrealized holding gains and losses on available-for-sale securities that are deemed to be temporary are ordinarily excluded from earnings. They are reported in other comprehensive income. At 12/31/Year 4, the fair value was greater than the cost. Consequently, the net amount reported for these securities (an unrealized net holding gain) is a credit of $10,000 ($160,000 fair value – $150,000 cost). At 12/31/Year 3, the net amount reported (an unrealized holding loss) was a debit of $20,000 ($150,000 cost – $130,000 fair value). Thus, the change from a debit of $20,000 to a credit of $10,000 increases total equity by $30,000.
Answer (B) is incorrect because $20,000 is the excess of cost over fair value on 12/31/Year 3. Answer (C) is incorrect because $10,000 is the excess of fair value over cost on 12/31/Year 4. Answer (D) is incorrect because equity increases when the unrealized holding gain is reported in other comprehensive income.

3. On December 30, Year 1, Hale Corp. paid $400,000 cash and issued 80,000 shares of its $1 par value common stock to its unsecured creditors on a pro rata basis pursuant to a reorganization plan under Chapter 11 of the bankruptcy statutes. Hale owed these unsecured creditors a total of $1.2 million. Hale's common stock was trading at $1.25 per share on December 30, Year 1. As a result of this transaction, Hale's total equity had a net increase of

A. $1,200,000

B. $800,000

C. $100,000

D. $80,000

Answer (B) is correct. *(CPA, adapted)*
REQUIRED: The net increase in equity immediately after a Chapter 11 reorganization.
DISCUSSION: According to SFAS 15, a debtor that grants an equity interest in full settlement of a payable should account for the equity interest at fair value. The difference between the fair value of the equity interest and the carrying amount of the payable is a gain. The appropriate accounting for this troubled debt restructuring is to debit liabilities for $1.2 million and to credit cash for $400,000, common stock at its par value of $80,000 (80,000 shares × $1), additional paid-in capital for $20,000 [80,000 shares × ($1.25 fair value per share – $1 par)], and a gain for $700,000. Accordingly, the net increase in total equity is $800,000 ($80,000 + $20,000 + $700,000).
Answer (A) is incorrect because $1,200,000 is the amount of the debt. Answer (C) is incorrect because $100,000 is the increase in contributed capital. Answer (D) is incorrect because $80,000 is the increase in common stock.

14.2 Issuance of Stock

4. When collectibility is reasonably assured, the excess of the subscription price over the stated value of no-par common stock subscribed should be recorded as

   A. No-par common stock.

   B. Additional paid-in capital when the subscription is recorded.

   C. Additional paid-in capital when the subscription is collected.

   D. Additional paid-in capital when the common stock is issued.

Answer (B) is correct. *(CPA, adapted)*
   REQUIRED: The recording of the excess of the subscription price over the stated value of no-par common stock subscribed.
   DISCUSSION: The accounting for subscriptions of no-par stock with a stated value is the same as for par value stock. When stock is subscribed, the corporation recognizes an obligation to issue stock and the subscriber undertakes the legal obligation to pay for the shares subscribed. If collectibility of the subscription price is reasonably assured on the date the subscription is received, the issuing corporation should recognize the cash collected and a subscription receivable for the remainder. In addition, the common stock subscribed account should be credited for the stated value of the shares subscribed, with the excess of the subscription price over the stated value recognized as additional paid-in capital.
   Answer (A) is incorrect because the credit is to additional paid-in capital. Answer (C) is incorrect because additional paid-in capital is credited when the subscription is recorded. Answer (D) is incorrect because the recording of additional paid-in capital is not dependent on when the stock is issued.

5. East Co. issued 1,000 shares of its $5 par common stock to Howe as compensation for 1,000 hours of legal services performed. Howe usually bills $160 per hour for legal services. On the date of issuance, the stock was trading on a public exchange at $140 per share. By what amount should the additional paid-in capital account increase as a result of this transaction?

   A. $135,000

   B. $140,000

   C. $155,000

   D. $160,000

Answer (A) is correct. *(CPA, adapted)*
   REQUIRED: The increase in additional paid-in capital.
   DISCUSSION: When stock is issued for property or services, the transaction is recorded at the fair value of the stock or of the property or services received. In this case, the value of the stock is used because it is more definite. The $140,000 should be allocated as follows: $5,000 (1,000 shares × $5 par) to common stock and $135,000 to additional paid-in capital.
   Answer (B) is incorrect because $5,000 should be allocated to common stock. Answer (C) is incorrect because the value of the stock should be used to record the transaction. Answer (D) is incorrect because $5,000 should be allocated to common stock, and because the value of the stock should be used to record the transaction.

6. On July 1, Year 4, Cove Corp., a closely held corporation, issued 6% bonds with a maturity value of $60,000, together with 1,000 shares of its $5 par value common stock, for a combined cash amount of $110,000. The market value of Cove's stock cannot be ascertained. If the bonds were issued separately, they would have sold for $40,000 on an 8% yield to maturity basis. What amount should Cove record for additional paid-in capital on the issuance of the stock?

   A. $75,000

   B. $65,000

   C. $55,000

   D. $45,000

Answer (B) is correct. *(CPA, adapted)*
   REQUIRED: The amount allocated to additional paid-in capital together with bonds.
   DISCUSSION: The proceeds of the combined issuance of different classes of securities should be allocated based on the relative fair values of the securities. However, the fair value of the stock is not known. Accordingly, the bonds should be recorded at their fair value ($40,000), with the remainder of the proceeds ($110,000 – $40,000 = $70,000) credited to common stock at par value ($5 × 1,000 shares = $5,000) and additional paid-in capital ($70,000 – $5,000 par = $65,000).
   Answer (A) is incorrect because $75,000 results from adding the par value to the total allocable to the stock. Answer (C) is incorrect because $55,000 is based on an allocation of $60,000 to the stock. Answer (D) is incorrect because $45,000 is based on an allocation of $60,000 (maturity value) to the bonds.

7. On February 1, Hyde Corp., a newly formed company, had the following stock issued and outstanding:

- Common stock, no par, $1 stated value, 10,000 shares originally issued for $15 per share
- Preferred stock, $10 par value, 3,000 shares originally issued for $25 per share

Hyde's February 1 statement of equity should report

	Common Stock	Preferred Stock	Additional Paid-in Capital
A.	$150,000	$30,000	$45,000
B.	$150,000	$75,000	$0
C.	$10,000	$75,000	$140,000
D.	$10,000	$30,000	$185,000

Answer (D) is correct. *(CPA, adapted)*
REQUIRED: The amounts of common stock, preferred stock, and additional paid-in capital to be reported in the statement of equity.
DISCUSSION: The common stock was issued for a total of $150,000 (10,000 shares × $15). Of this amount, $10,000 (10,000 shares × $1 stated value) should be allocated to the common stock, with the remaining $140,000 ($150,000 – $10,000) credited to additional paid-in capital. The preferred stock was issued for $75,000 (3,000 shares × $25), of which $30,000 (3,000 shares × $10 par value) should be allocated to the preferred stock and $45,000 ($75,000 – $30,000) to additional paid-in capital. In the statement of equity, Hyde therefore should report $10,000 in the common stock account, $30,000 in the preferred stock account, and $185,000 ($140,000 + $45,000) as additional paid-in capital.

14.3 Retirement

8. In Year 2, Fogg, Inc. issued $10 par value common stock for $25 per share. No other common stock transactions occurred until March 31, Year 4, when Fogg acquired some of the issued shares for $20 per share and retired them. Which of the following statements accurately states an effect of this acquisition and retirement?

A. Year 4 net income is decreased.

B. Year 4 net income is increased.

C. Additional paid-in capital is decreased.

D. Retained earnings is increased.

Answer (C) is correct. *(CPA, adapted)*
REQUIRED: The effect of the acquisition and retirement of a company's stock for less than the issue price.
DISCUSSION: When shares of common stock are reacquired and retired, contributed capital should be debited for the amount that was credited upon the issuance of the securities. In addition, because the acquisition of a company's own shares is an equity transaction, no gain or loss should be reflected in the determination of income. The entry is to debit common stock at par (number of shares × $10) and additional paid-in capital [number of shares × ($25 – $10)], and to credit additional paid-in capital from retirement of common stock [number of shares × ($25 – $20)] and cash (number of shares × $20). The net effect is to decrease total additional paid-in capital.
Answer (A) is incorrect because net income is not affected. Answer (B) is incorrect because net income is not affected. Answer (D) is incorrect because retained earnings is only affected when a company retires its stock at a higher price than the original issue price.

9. Cross Corp. had outstanding 2,000 shares of 11% preferred stock, $50 par. These shares were not mandatorily redeemable. On August 8, Cross redeemed and retired 25% of these shares for $22,500. On that date, Cross's additional paid-in capital from preferred stock totaled $30,000. To record this transaction, Cross should debit (credit) its capital accounts as follows:

	Preferred Stock	Additional Paid-in Capital	Retained Earnings
A.	$25,000	$7,500	$(10,000)
B.	$25,000	--	$ (2,500)
C.	$25,000	$7,500	--
D.	$22,500	--	--

Answer (C) is correct. *(CPA, adapted)*
REQUIRED: The accounting for redemption and retirement of preferred stock.
DISCUSSION: Under the cost method, the entry to record a treasury stock purchase is to debit treasury stock at cost ($22,500) and credit cash. The entry to retire this stock is to debit preferred stock at par [(2,000 shares × 25%) × $50 = $25,000], debit additional paid-in capital from the original issuance ($30,000 × 25% = $7,500), credit treasury stock at cost ($22,500), and credit additional paid-in capital from stock retirement ($10,000). No entry to retained earnings is necessary.

10. The following were among the accounts on Luna Corp.'s year-end balance sheet:

Securities (fair value $150,000)	$ 80,000
Preferred stock, $20 par value 20,000 shares issued and outstanding	400,000
Additional paid-in capital on preferred stock	30,000
Retained earnings	900,000

On January 20, Luna exchanged all of the securities for 5,000 shares of Luna's preferred stock, which were not mandatorily redeemable. Fair values at the date of the exchange were $150,000 for the securities and $30 per share for the preferred stock. The 5,000 shares were retired immediately. The journal entry is

	Debit	Credit
A. Preferred stock	$100,000	
Additional paid-in capital	7,500	
Retained earnings	42,500	
Securities		$80,000
Gain		70,000
B. Preferred stock	100,000	
Additional paid-in capital	30,000	
Securities		80,000
Additional paid-in capital		50,000
C. Preferred stock	150,000	
Securities		80,000
Additional paid-in capital		70,000
D. Preferred stock	150,000	
Securities		80,000
Gain		70,000

Answer (A) is correct. *(CPA, adapted)*
REQUIRED: The journal entry to record the reacquisition of preferred stock in exchange for appreciated securities.
DISCUSSION: The reacquisition and retirement of the preferred stock result in debits to preferred stock at par (5,000 shares × $20 = $100,000) and additional paid-in capital [(5,000 ÷ 20,000 shares) × $30,000 = $7,500]. The transfer of the nonmonetary asset to a shareholder should be recorded at the fair value of the asset transferred, and a gain should be recognized in accordance with APB Opinion 29 (credit securities at their $80,000 carrying amount and credit a gain for the $70,000 excess of fair value over the carrying amount). The balancing debit is to retained earnings for $42,500.
Answer (B) is incorrect because a gain should be recognized for the appreciation of the securities, and only a proportionate amount of the additional paid-in capital should be removed from the accounts. Answer (C) is incorrect because the preferred stock should be debited at par and only a proportionate amount of the additional paid-in capital should be removed from the accounts. Answer (D) is incorrect because preferred stock should be debited at par.

14.4 Cash Dividends

11. On January 15, Year 5, Rico Co. declared its annual cash dividend on common stock for the year ended January 31, Year 5. The dividend was paid on February 9, Year 5, to shareholders of record as of January 28, Year 5. On what date should Rico decrease retained earnings by the amount of the dividend?

A. January 15, Year 5.

B. January 31, Year 5.

C. January 28, Year 5.

D. February 9, Year 5.

Answer (A) is correct. *(CPA, adapted)*
REQUIRED: The date to decrease retained earnings by the amount of the dividend.
DISCUSSION: Unlike stock dividends, cash dividends cannot be rescinded. A liability to the shareholders is created because the dividends must be paid once they are declared. At the declaration date, retained earnings must be debited, resulting in a decrease.

Retained earnings	$XXX	
Dividends payable		$XXX

The declaration date was January 15.

12. At December 31, Year 3 and Year 4, Apex Co. had 3,000 shares of $100 par, 5% cumulative preferred stock outstanding. No dividends were in arrears as of December 31, Year 2. Apex did not declare a dividend during Year 3. During Year 4, Apex paid a cash dividend of $10,000 on its preferred stock. Apex should report dividends in arrears in its Year 4 financial statements as a(n)

A. Accrued liability of $15,000.

B. Disclosure of $15,000.

C. Accrued liability of $20,000.

D. Disclosure of $20,000.

Answer (D) is correct. *(CPA, adapted)*
REQUIRED: The amount and means of reporting preferred dividends in arrears.
DISCUSSION: Dividends in arrears on preferred stock are not an obligation of the company and are not recognized in the financial statements. However, the aggregate and per-share amounts of arrearages in cumulative preferred dividends should be disclosed on the face of the balance sheet or in the notes (APB Opinion 10). The aggregate amount in arrears is $20,000 [(3,000 shares × $100 par × 5% × 2 years) – $10,000 paid in Year 4].

13. Arp Corp.'s outstanding capital stock at December 15, Year 4, consisted of the following:

- 30,000 shares 5% cumulative preferred stock, par value $10 per share, fully participating as to dividends. No dividends were in arrears.
- 200,000 shares of common stock, par value $1 per share

On December 15, Year 4, Arp declared dividends of $100,000. What was the amount of dividends payable to Arp's common shareholders?

- A. $10,000
- B. $34,000
- C. $40,000
- D. $60,000

Answer (C) is correct. *(CPA, adapted)*
REQUIRED: The dividends to common shareholders.
DISCUSSION: The stated rate of dividends must be paid to preferred shareholders before any amount is paid to common shareholders. Given no dividends in arrears, this amount is $15,000 (30,000 shares × $10 par × 5%). The preferred stock will also participate equally in the cash dividend after a 5% return is paid on the common. The basic return to common shareholders is $10,000 (200,000 shares × $1 par × 5%). The remaining $75,000 ($100,000 – $15,000 – $10,000) will be shared in proportion to the par values of the shares outstanding.
The aggregate par value of the preferred is $300,000 (30,000 shares × $10 par). The aggregate par value of the common is $200,000 (200,000 shares × $1 par). The distribution will therefore be in the ratio of 3:2, and $45,000 ($75,000 × 60%) is the participating share of the preferred shareholders. The balance of $30,000 ($75,000 – $45,000) will be paid to the common shareholders. The total dividends on the common stock is $40,000 ($10,000 + $30,000).
Answer (A) is incorrect because $10,000 is the basic return to common shareholders. Answer (B) is incorrect because $34,000 results from assuming that no basic return is paid to the common shareholders. Answer (D) is incorrect because $60,000 is paid to the preferred shareholders.

14.5 Property Dividends

14. On December 1, Year 4, Pott Co. declared and distributed a property dividend when the fair value exceeded the carrying amount. As a consequence of the dividend declaration and distribution, what are the accounting effects?

	Property Dividends Recorded at	Retained Earnings
A.	Fair value	Decreased
B.	Fair value	Increased
C.	Cost	Increased
D.	Cost	Decreased

Answer (A) is correct. *(CPA, adapted)*
REQUIRED: The effects of a property dividend.
DISCUSSION: A nonreciprocal transfer of nonmonetary assets to owners is customarily recorded at the fair value of the asset transferred on the declaration date. As a consequence of the dividend declaration, the property should first be written up to its fair value and a gain recognized. The dividend should then be recognized as a decrease in (debit to) retained earnings and a corresponding increase in (credit to) a dividend payable. The distribution of the property dividend is recognized by a debit to property dividend payable and a credit to the property account.

15. On December 1, Year 4, Nilo Corp. declared a property dividend to be distributed on December 31, Year 4, to shareholders of record on December 15, Year 4. On December 1, Year 4, the property to be transferred had a carrying amount of $60,000 and a fair value of $78,000. What is the effect of this property dividend on Nilo's Year 4 retained earnings, after all nominal accounts are closed?

- A. $0
- B. $18,000 increase.
- C. $60,000 decrease.
- D. $78,000 decrease.

Answer (C) is correct. *(CPA, adapted)*
REQUIRED: The effect of the property dividend on retained earnings after all nominal accounts are closed.
DISCUSSION: A nonreciprocal transfer of nonmonetary assets to owners ordinarily should be recorded at the fair value of the asset transferred on the declaration date. As a consequence of the declaration, the property should be written up to its fair value and a gain recognized. The dividend should then be debited to retained earnings and credited to a dividend payable. The distribution is recognized by a debit to property dividend payable and a credit to the property. The net effect of recognition of the gain and the declaration of the dividend is a $60,000 decrease in retained earnings ($78,000 fair value of the property dividend – $18,000 gain).
Answer (A) is incorrect because the dividend must be charged to retained earnings. Answer (B) is incorrect because $18,000 is the gain recognized. Answer (D) is incorrect because $78,000 is the fair value of the shares.

14.6 Scrip Dividends

16. East Corp., a calendar-year company, had sufficient retained earnings in Year 4 as a basis for dividends but was temporarily short of cash. East declared a dividend of $100,000 on April 1, Year 4, and issued promissory notes to its shareholders in lieu of cash. The notes, which were dated April 1, Year 4, had a maturity date of March 31, Year 5, and a 10% interest rate. How should East account for the scrip dividend and related interest?

A. Debit retained earnings for $110,000 on April 1, Year 4.

B. Debit retained earnings for $110,000 on March 31, Year 5.

C. Debit retained earnings for $100,000 on April 1, Year 4, and debit interest expense for $10,000 on March 31, Year 5.

D. Debit retained earnings for $100,000 on April 1, Year 4, and debit interest expense for $7,500 on December 31, Year 4.

Answer (D) is correct. *(CPA, adapted)*
REQUIRED: The accounting for a scrip dividend and its related interest.
DISCUSSION: When a scrip dividend is declared, retained earnings should be debited and scrip dividends (or notes) payable should be credited for the amount of the dividend ($100,000) excluding interest. Interest accrued on the scrip dividend is recorded as a debit to interest expense up to the balance sheet date with a corresponding credit for interest payable. Thus, interest expense will be debited and interest payable credited for $7,500 [$100,000 × 10% × (9 ÷ 12)] on 12/31/Year 4.
Answer (A) is incorrect because interest expense is recognized on the balance sheet date and on the date of payment, not on the date of declaration. Answer (B) is incorrect because $7,500 of the $10,000 interest expense should be recognized at year-end, and retained earnings should be debited on the date of declaration. Answer (C) is incorrect because $7,500 of the $10,000 interest expense should be recognized at year-end.

14.7 Liquidating Dividends

17. A corporation declared a dividend, a portion of which was liquidating. How does this declaration affect each of the following?

	Additional Paid-in Capital	Retained Earnings
A.	Decrease	No effect
B.	Decrease	Decrease
C.	No effect	Decrease
D.	No effect	No effect

Answer (B) is correct. *(CPA, adapted)*
REQUIRED: The effect of a dividend, a portion of which was liquidating, on additional paid-in capital and retained earnings.
DISCUSSION: When cash dividends are declared, a liability to the shareholders is created because the dividends must be paid once they are declared. At the declaration date, the portion of cash dividends that is not liquidating is debited to (decreases) retained earnings. The portion that is liquidating results in a distribution in excess of the corporation's retained earnings. The effect of a liquidating dividend is to decrease contributed capital. Additional paid-in capital is debited first to the extent available before other contributed capital accounts are charged. Thus, declaration of a cash dividend, a portion of which was liquidating, decreases additional paid-in capital and retained earnings.

18. On January 2, Year 5, Lake Mining Co.'s board of directors declared a cash dividend of $400,000 to shareholders of record on January 18, Year 5, payable on February 10, Year 5. The dividend is permissible under law in Lake's state of incorporation. Selected data from Lake's December 31, Year 4, balance sheet are as follows:

Accumulated depletion	$100,000
Capital stock	500,000
Additional paid-in capital	150,000
Retained earnings	300,000

The $400,000 dividend includes a liquidating dividend of

A. $0

B. $100,000

C. $150,000

D. $300,000

Answer (B) is correct. *(CPA, adapted)*
REQUIRED: The amount of a liquidating dividend.
DISCUSSION: A common practice of companies whose major activity is the exploitation of depletable resources is to pay dividends in amounts up to the sum of retained earnings and accumulated depletion. However, any distribution by a corporation to its shareholders in excess of the dollar balance in the retained earnings account is considered a liquidating dividend and return of capital to the shareholders. Consequently, the liquidating dividend equals $100,000 ($400,000 dividend − $300,000 retained earnings).
Answer (A) is incorrect because the company paid a liquidating dividend. Answer (C) is incorrect because $150,000 is the additional paid-in capital. Answer (D) is incorrect because $300,000 equals retained earnings.

19. Ole Corp. declared and paid a liquidating dividend of $100,000. This distribution resulted in a decrease in Ole's

	Paid-in Capital	Retained Earnings
A.	No	No
B.	Yes	Yes
C.	No	Yes
D.	Yes	No

Answer (D) is correct. *(CPA, adapted)*
REQUIRED: The effect of the distribution of a liquidating dividend.
DISCUSSION: When cash dividends are declared, a liability to the shareholders is created because the dividends must be paid once they are declared. At the declaration date, the portion of cash dividends that is not liquidating is debited to (decreases) retained earnings. The portion that is liquidating results in a distribution in excess of the corporation's retained earnings. The effect of a liquidating dividend is to decrease contributed capital. Thus, by definition, declaration and payment of a liquidating dividend does not affect retained earnings.

14.8 Stock Dividends and Splits

Questions 20 and 21 are based on the following information. The format displayed is used by Gee, Inc. for its Year 4 statement of changes in equity. When both the 100% and the 5% stock dividends were declared, Gee's common stock was selling for more than its $1 par value.

	Common Stock $1 par	Additional Paid-in Capital	Retained Earnings
Balance at 1/1/Year 4	$90,000	$800,000	$175,000
Additions and deductions:			
100% stock dividend			
5% stock dividend			
Balance at 12/31/Year 4			

20. How would the 100% stock dividend affect the additional paid-in capital and retained earnings amounts reported in Gee's Year 4 statement of changes in equity?

	Additional Paid-in Capital	Retained Earnings
A.	Increase	Increase
B.	Increase	Decrease
C.	No change	Increase
D.	No change	Decrease

Answer (D) is correct. *(CPA, adapted)*
REQUIRED: The effect of a 100% stock dividend on additional paid-in capital and retained earnings.
DISCUSSION: Given that an issuance of common shares exceeds 20% to 25% of the outstanding shares and that it is to be effected in the form of a dividend, ARB 43, Ch. 7B, requires a debit to retained earnings at least equal to the legal requirement in the state of incorporation (usually the par or stated value of the shares). Thus, if retained earnings is debited for the par value of the shares, additional paid-in capital will be unaffected although retained earnings will decrease.

21. How would the 5% stock dividend affect the additional paid-in capital and retained earnings amounts reported in Gee's Year 4 statement of equity?

	Additional Paid-in Capital	Retained Earnings
A.	Increase	Decrease
B.	Increase	Increase
C.	No change	Decrease
D.	No change	Increase

Answer (A) is correct. *(CPA, adapted)*
REQUIRED: The effect of a 5% stock dividend on additional paid-in capital and retained earnings.
DISCUSSION: ARB 43, Ch. 7B, states that a stock dividend, which usually consists of fewer than 20% to 25% of the common shares outstanding, should be accounted for by debiting retained earnings for the fair value of the stock and crediting a capital stock account for the par or stated value. A difference between the fair value and the par or stated value is credited to an additional paid-in capital account. Hence, additional paid-in capital increases and retained earnings decreases.

22. Universe Co. issued 500,000 shares of common stock in the current year. Universe declared a 30% stock dividend. The market value was $50 per share, the par value was $10, and the average issue price was $30 per share. By what amount will Universe decrease shareholders' equity for the dividend?

A. $0

B. $1,500,000

C. $4,500,000

D. $7,500,000

Answer (A) is correct. *(CPA, adapted)*
REQUIRED: The decrease in equity after declaration of a stock dividend.
DISCUSSION: A stock dividend is recognized by capitalizing retained earnings equal to the fair value of the shares distributed. The result is a debit to retained earnings and credits to common stock and additional paid-in capital. Moreover, the par or stated value of each common share is unaffected. Thus, a stock dividend increases permanent capitalization, but it does not affect total equity or the proportionate interests of shareholders. The entity's description of the intent of the distribution normally determines whether it should be accounted for as a stock dividend. However, an issuance of shares less than 20% or 25% of the previously outstanding shares usually should be recognized as a stock dividend. Moreover, the SEC requires an issuance of less than 25% by a public company to be treated as a stock dividend.

23. Band Co. uses the equity method to account for its investment in Guard, Inc. common stock. How should Band record a 2% stock dividend received from Guard?

A. As dividend revenue at Guard's carrying amount of the stock.

B. As dividend revenue at the market value of the stock.

C. As a reduction in the total cost of Guard stock owned.

D. As a memorandum entry reducing the unit cost of all Guard stock owned.

Answer (D) is correct. *(CPA, adapted)*
REQUIRED: The entry to record a stock dividend received from an equity investee.
DISCUSSION: No entries are made to record the receipt of stock dividends. However, a memorandum entry should be made in the investment account to record additional shares owned. This treatment applies whether the investment is accounted for by the fair-value method, the equity method, or the cost method.
Answer (A) is incorrect because the receipt of a stock dividend is not a revenue. The shareholder has the same proportionate interest in the investee. Answer (B) is incorrect because the stock dividend does not result in revenue. Answer (C) is incorrect because the cost per share, not the total cost, is reduced.

14.9 Appropriations of Retained Earnings

24. A retained earnings appropriation can be used to

A. Absorb a fire loss when a company is self-insured.

B. Provide for a contingent loss that is probable and reasonable.

C. Smooth periodic income.

D. Restrict earnings available for dividends.

Answer (D) is correct. *(CPA, adapted)*
REQUIRED: The use of a retained earnings appropriation.
DISCUSSION: According to APB Opinion 9, *Reporting the Results of Operations*, "transfers to and from accounts properly designated as appropriated retained earnings (such as general purpose contingency reserves or provisions for replacement costs of fixed assets)" are always excluded from the determination of net income. However, SFAS 5, *Accounting for Contingencies*, permits appropriation of retained earnings if it is shown within the equity section and is clearly identified. The effect of the appropriation is to restrict the amount of retained earnings available for dividends, not to set aside assets.

25. At December 31, Year 3, Eagle Corp. reported $1,750,000 of appropriated retained earnings for the construction of a new office building, which was completed in Year 4 at a total cost of $1.5 million. In Year 4, Eagle appropriated $1.2 million of retained earnings for the construction of a new plant. Also, $2 million of cash was restricted for the retirement of bonds due in Year 5. In its Year 4 balance sheet, Eagle should report what amount of appropriated retained earnings?

    A. $1,200,000

    B. $1,450,000

    C. $2,950,000

    D. $3,200,000

Answer (A) is correct. *(CPA, adapted)*
REQUIRED: The amount of appropriated retained earnings reported.
DISCUSSION: Appropriating retained earnings is a formal way of marking a portion of retained earnings for other uses. A journal entry is used to move the amount from one account to the other. When the appropriation is no longer necessary, the entry is reversed, even if the full appropriation is not needed. Eagle appropriated only $1.2 million. The cash restriction is not included in appropriated retained earnings. If the amount is material, the restriction will require separate reporting of the cash item in the balance sheet, disclosure in the notes, and, possibly, reclassification as noncurrent.
Answer (B) is incorrect because $1,450,000 includes the previous year's excess of appropriated retained earnings over the actual cost. Answer (C) is incorrect because $2,950,000 includes the cash restriction and subtracts the previous year's excess of appropriated retained earnings over the actual cost. Answer (D) is incorrect because $3,200,000 includes the $2 million restriction on cash for bond retirement.

26. The following information pertains to Meg Corp.:

- Dividends on its 1,000 shares of 6%, $10 par value cumulative preferred stock have not been declared or paid for 3 years.
- Treasury stock that cost $15,000 was reissued for $8,000.

What amount of retained earnings should be appropriated as a result of these items?

    A. $0

    B. $1,800

    C. $7,000

    D. $8,800

Answer (A) is correct. *(CPA, adapted)*
REQUIRED: The amount of retained earnings that should be appropriated.
DISCUSSION: An appropriation is a discretionary reclassification of retained earnings. Its purpose is to restrict the amount of retained earnings available for dividends. Undeclared cumulative preferred dividends are not recognized in the accounts. The loss on the sale of treasury stock is charged to additional paid-in capital from treasury stock transactions to the extent it has a credit balance, or to retained earnings. Hence, these transactions do not result in appropriated retained earnings. However, state law may have required an appropriation of the cost of the treasury stock.
Answer (B) is incorrect because $1,800 is the amount of cumulative preferred dividends in arrears. Answer (C) is incorrect because $7,000 is the loss on the treasury stock. Answer (D) is incorrect because $8,800 equals the proceeds from the treasury stock.

14.10 Treasury Stock – Cost Method

27. Grid Corp. acquired some of its own common shares at a price greater than both their par value and original issue price but less than their book value. Grid uses the cost method of accounting for treasury stock. What is the impact of this acquisition on total equity and the book value per common share?

	Total Equity	Book Value per Share
A.	Increase	Increase
B.	Increase	Decrease
C.	Decrease	Increase
D.	Decrease	Decrease

Answer (C) is correct. *(CPA, adapted)*
REQUIRED: The impact of the acquisition on total equity and the book value per common share.
DISCUSSION: Under the cost method, the acquisition of treasury stock is recorded as a debit to treasury stock and a credit to cash equal to the amount of the purchase price. This transaction results in a decrease in both total assets and total equity because treasury stock is a contra-equity account. Moreover, if the acquisition cost is less than book value, the book value per share will increase. For example, if equity is $100, 10 shares are outstanding, and 5 shares are purchased for $45, the book value per share will increase from $10 ($100 ÷ 10) to $11 [($100 – $45) ÷ 5].

28. Selected information from the accounts of Row Co. at December 31, Year 4, follows:

Total income since incorporation	$420,000
Total cash dividends paid	130,000
Total value of property dividends distributed	30,000
Excess of proceeds over cost of treasury stock sold, accounted for using the cost method	110,000

In its December 31, Year 4, financial statements, what amount should Row report as retained earnings?

   A. $260,000

   B. $290,000

   C. $370,000

   D. $400,000

Answer (A) is correct. *(CPA, adapted)*
REQUIRED: The amount to be reported as retained earnings.
DISCUSSION: Retained earnings is increased by net income and decreased by net losses, dividends, and certain treasury stock transactions. Thus, retained earnings is $260,000 ($420,000 – $130,000 – $30,000). Because Row uses the cost method to account for treasury stock, the $110,000 excess of proceeds over the cost of treasury stock sold does not affect retained earnings. Under the cost method, the excess should be credited to additional paid-in capital.
Answer (B) is incorrect because $290,000 fails to subtract the $30,000 in property dividends. Answer (C) is incorrect because $370,000 includes the $110,000 excess of proceeds over cost of treasury stock. Answer (D) is incorrect because $400,000 includes the $110,000 excess of proceeds over cost of treasury stock and does not subtract the $30,000 value of property dividends distributed.

29. On December 1, Year 4, Line Corp. received a contribution of 2,000 shares of its $5 par value common stock from a shareholder. On that date, the stock's fair value was $35 per share. The stock was originally issued for $25 per share. By what amount will this contribution cause total equity to decrease if Line accounts for treasury stock using the cost method?

   A. $70,000

   B. $50,000

   C. $20,000

   D. $0

Answer (D) is correct. *(CPA, adapted)*
REQUIRED: The decrease in equity from receipt of a donation of the company's own stock.
DISCUSSION: Contributions received ordinarily are recorded as revenues or gains when received (SFAS 116). However, APB Opinion 9, *Reporting the Results of Operations*, states that "adjustments or charges or credits resulting from transactions in the company's own capital stock" are excluded from net income or the results of operations. Thus, the receipt of a contribution of a company's own stock is recorded at fair value as increases in both contributed capital and treasury stock. Because these accounts offset, the net effect on equity is $0.
Answer (A) is incorrect because $70,000 records an effect equal to the current market price. Answer (B) is incorrect because $50,000 records an effect equal to the original issuance price. Answer (C) is incorrect because $20,000 records an effect equal to the difference between the current market price and the original issuance price.

14.11 Treasury Stock – Par Value Method

30. On incorporation, Dee, Inc. issued common stock at a price in excess of its par value. No other stock transactions occurred except that treasury stock was acquired for an amount exceeding this issue price. If Dee uses the par value method of accounting for treasury stock appropriate for retired stock, what is the effect of the acquisition on the following?

	Net Common Stock	Additional Paid-in Capital	Retained Earnings
A.	No effect	Decrease	No effect
B.	Decrease	Decrease	Decrease
C.	Decrease	No effect	Decrease
D.	No effect	Decrease	Decrease

Answer (B) is correct. *(CPA, adapted)*
REQUIRED: The effects of a purchase of treasury stock accounted for under the par value method.
DISCUSSION: Under the par value method, treasury stock is debited at par value, and the amount is reported as a reduction of common stock. The purchase also results in the removal of the additional paid-in capital associated with the original issue of the shares. Given that no other stock transactions occurred and that treasury stock was acquired for an amount exceeding the issue price, the balancing debit for the excess of the acquisition price over the issue price is to retained earnings. If paid-in capital from treasury stock had been previously recorded, the balancing debit would be to that account but only to the extent of its credit balance. Thus, retained earnings is also decreased.

31. Asp Co. was organized on January 2, Year 4, with 30,000 authorized shares of $10 par common stock. During Year 4, the corporation had the following capital transactions:

January 5	--	Issued 20,000 shares at $15 per share
July 14	--	Purchased 5,000 shares at $17 per share
December 27	--	Reissued the 5,000 shares held in treasury at $20 per share

Asp used the par value method to record the purchase and reissuance of the treasury shares. It had no prior treasury stock transactions. In its December 31, Year 4, balance sheet, what amount should Asp report as additional paid-in capital?

A. $100,000

B. $125,000

C. $140,000

D. $150,000

Answer (B) is correct. *(CPA, adapted)*
REQUIRED: The additional paid-in capital reported under the par value method.
DISCUSSION: Under the par value method, additional paid-in capital is debited for $25,000 (5,000 shares × $5 excess of the issue price over par) when the treasury stock is acquired. Treasury stock is debited for the $50,000 par value (5,000 shares × $10), and retained earnings is debited for $10,000 [5,000 shares × ($17 – $15)]. When the stock is reissued, additional paid-in capital is credited for $50,000 (5,000 shares × $10 excess over par). Thus, ending additional paid-in capital is $125,000 ($100,000 – $25,000 + $50,000).
Answer (A) is incorrect because $100,000 does not reflect the acquisition and reissuance of treasury stock. Answer (C) is incorrect because $140,000 does not include the $25,000 debit to additional paid-in capital but does include the $10,000 amount that should be debited to retained earnings. Answer (D) is incorrect because $150,000 does not reflect the $25,000 debit resulting from the purchase of treasury stock.

14.12 Stock Rights

32. Blue Co. issued preferred stock with detachable common stock warrants at a price that exceeded both the par value and the fair value of the preferred stock. At the time the warrants are exercised, Blue's total equity is increased by the

	Cash Received Upon Exercise of the Warrants	Carrying Amount of the Warrants
A.	Yes	No
B.	Yes	Yes
C.	No	No
D.	No	Yes

Answer (A) is correct. *(CPA, adapted)*
REQUIRED: The effect of the exercise of warrants on total equity.
DISCUSSION: When shares of preferred stock with detachable common stock warrants are issued at a price that exceeds both the par value and the fair value of the preferred stock, the consideration received must be allocated between the preferred stock and the detachable warrants. The amount allocated to the stock warrants outstanding should be recorded in the equity section as contributed capital. At the time the warrants are exercised, contributed capital will reflect both the cash received upon the exercise of the warrants and the carrying amount of the warrants. Total equity, however, will be increased only by the amount of cash received because the carrying amount of the warrants is already included in total equity.

33. On January 2, Year 4, Kine Co. granted Morgan, its president, compensatory stock options to buy 1,000 shares of Kine's $10 par common stock. The options call for a price of $20 per share and are exercisable for 3 years following the grant date. Kine accounts for the transaction using APB Opinion 25, *Accounting for Stock Issued to Employees*. Morgan exercised the options on December 31, Year 4. The market price of the stock was $50 on January 2, Year 4, and $70 on December 31, Year 4. By what net amount should equity increase as a result of the grant and exercise of the options?

A. $20,000

B. $30,000

C. $50,000

D. $70,000

Answer (A) is correct. *(CPA, adapted)*
REQUIRED: The increase in equity as a result of the grant and exercise of a compensatory stock option.
DISCUSSION: The change in equity equals the cash received (1,000 × $20 = $20,000).
Answer (B) is incorrect because $30,000 is the amount of compensation expense. Answer (C) is incorrect because $50,000 is the increase in the shareholders' equity without regard to the compensation expense. Answer (D) is incorrect because $70,000 calculates the increase in equity using the stock price on the exercise date and excludes the decrease in retained earnings.

34. On March 4, Year 4, Evan Co. purchased 1,000 shares of LVC common stock at $80 per share. On September 26, Year 4, Evan received 1,000 stock rights to purchase an additional 1,000 shares at $90 per share. The stock rights had an expiration date of February 1, Year 5. On September 26, Year 4, LVC's common stock had a fair value, ex-rights, of $95 per share, and the stock rights had a fair value of $5 each. What amount should Evan record on September 26, Year 4, for investment in stock rights?

A. $4,000

B. $5,000

C. $10,000

D. $15,000

Answer (A) is correct. *(CPA, adapted)*
REQUIRED: The amount to be recorded for the investment in stock rights on the balance sheet.
DISCUSSION: The $80 original cost of each share should be allocated between the share and the stock right based on their relative fair values at the time the rights are received.

Stock:	[$95 ÷ ($95 + $5)] × $80 cost	=	$76
Right:	[$5 ÷ ($95 + $5)] × $80 cost	=	4
			$80

Thus, the stock rights should be recorded at $4,000 (1,000 rights × $4) on the balance sheet.
Answer (B) is incorrect because $5,000 is the fair value of the rights. Answer (C) is incorrect because $10,000 is the difference between the cost of the 1,000 shares and the exercise price for an additional 1,000 shares. Answer (D) is incorrect because $15,000 is the difference between the cost of the 1,000 shares and their fair value.

14.13 Proprietorships and Partnerships

35. Which of the following business enterprises are distinct legal entities separate from their owners?

	Corporations	Sole Proprietorships	Partnerships
A.	Yes	Yes	Yes
B.	Yes	Yes	No
C.	Yes	No	Yes
D.	No	No	No

Answer (C) is correct. *(Publisher, adapted)*
REQUIRED: The business enterprises that are distinct legal entities.
DISCUSSION: Sole proprietorships are business entities owned by individuals. A sole proprietorship is not a legal entity in and of itself. It is an extension of its owner. A sole proprietorship has unlimited liability for business debts. Corporations and partnerships, however, have a distinct legal existence.

14.14 Bankruptcy and Reorganization

36. Barb, Inc. has been forced into bankruptcy and has begun to liquidate. Unsecured claims will be paid at the rate of 40 cents on the dollar. Yola Co. holds a noninterest-bearing note receivable from Barb in the amount of $100,000, collateralized by machinery with a liquidation value of $25,000. The total amount to be realized by Yola on this note receivable is

A. $25,000

B. $40,000

C. $55,000

D. $65,000

Answer (C) is correct. *(CPA, adapted)*
REQUIRED: The total amount of cash to be realized from a partially unsecured claim.
DISCUSSION: Yola has a secured claim for the $25,000 liquidation value of the machinery. The remaining $75,000 unsecured claims will be paid at the rate of 40 cents on the dollar. Yola will receive $30,000 ($75,000 × 40%) from its unsecured claim. The total amount to be realized is $55,000 ($25,000 + $30,000).
Answer (A) is incorrect because $25,000 is the amount of the secured claim. Answer (B) is incorrect because $40,000 is the amount Yola would receive if the note were not collateralized. Answer (D) is incorrect because $65,000 equals the amount of the secured claim plus the amount Yola would receive if the note were not collateralized.

37. The primary purpose of a quasi-reorganization is to give a corporation the opportunity to

A. Obtain relief from its creditors.

B. Revalue understated assets to their fair values.

C. Eliminate a deficit in retained earnings.

D. Distribute the stock of a newly created subsidiary to its shareholders in exchange for part of their stock in the corporation.

Answer (C) is correct. *(CPA, adapted)*
REQUIRED: The purpose of a quasi-reorganization.
DISCUSSION: A quasi-reorganization is undertaken to reduce a deficit in retained earnings to zero. The purpose is to permit the corporation to pay dividends in the near future.
Answer (A) is incorrect because a quasi-reorganization is an accounting adjustment. Answer (B) is incorrect because assets are usually written down to fair value. Answer (D) is incorrect because a quasi-reorganization does not entail an exchange of stock.

14.15 PRACTICE SIMULATION

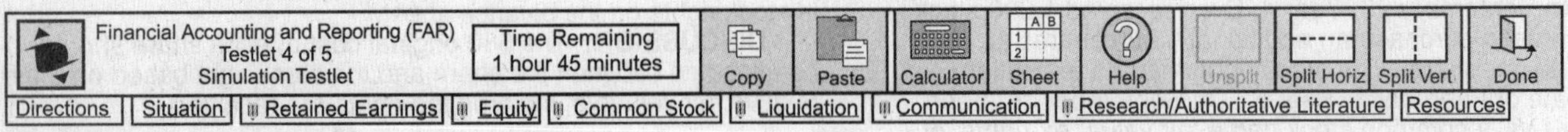

Financial Accounting and Reporting (FAR) Testlet 4 of 5 Simulation Testlet	Time Remaining 1 hour 45 minutes	Copy	Paste	Calculator	Sheet	Help	Unsplit	Split Horiz	Split Vert	Done

Directions | Situation | Retained Earnings | Equity | Common Stock | Liquidation | Communication | Research/Authoritative Literature | Resources

1. Directions

In the following simulation, you will be asked to complete various tasks. You may use the content in the **Information Tabs** to complete the tasks in the **Work Tabs**.

Information Tabs:

| Directions | Resources |

FIG 1

- Go through each of the **Information Tabs** to familiarize yourself with the simulation content
- The **Resources** tab will contain information, including formulas and definitions, that may help you to complete the tasks
- Your simulation may have more **Information Tabs** than those shown in Fig. 1

Work Tabs:

| SysTrust | Engagement Letter | Authoritative Sources | Communication |

FIG. 2

- **Work Tabs**, to the right of **Information Tabs**, contain the tasks for you to complete
- **Work Tabs** contain directions for completing each task - be sure to read these directions carefully
- The tab names in Fig. 2 are for illustration only - yours may differ
- Once you complete any part of a task, the pencil for that tab will be shaded (see **Communication** in Fig. 2)
- The shaded pencil does **NOT** indicate that you have completed the entire task
- You must complete all of the tasks in the **Work Tabs** to receive full credit

Research/Authoritative Literature Tab:

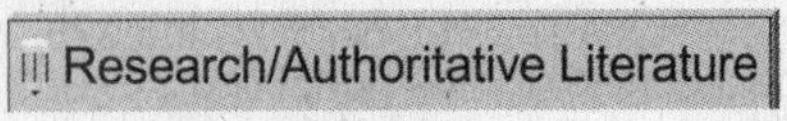

| Research/Authoritative Literature |

FIG. 3

- This tab contains both the Research task and the Authoritative Literature
- Detailed instructions for completing the Research task, and for using the Authoritative Literature, appear on this tab
- You may use the Authoritative Literature as a resource for completing other tasks

NOTE: If you believe you have encountered a software malfunction, report it to the test center staff immediately.

2. Situation

Mart, Inc. is a public company whose shares are traded in the over-the-counter market. At December 31, Year 2, Mart had 6 million authorized shares of $5 par value common stock, of which 2 million shares were issued and outstanding. The equity accounts at December 31, Year 2, had the following balances:

Common stock	$10,000,000
Additional paid-in capital	7,500,000
Retained earnings	3,250,000

Transactions during Year 3 and other information relating to Mart's equity accounts were as follows:

- On January 5, Year 3, Mart issued 100,000 shares of $50 par value, 9% cumulative, convertible preferred stock at $54 per share. Each share of preferred stock is convertible, at the option of the holder, into two shares of common stock. Mart had 250,000 authorized shares of preferred stock. The preferred stock has a liquidation value of $55 per share.

- On February 1, Year 3, Mart reacquired 20,000 shares of its common stock for $16 per share. Mart uses the cost method to account for treasury stock.

- On March 15, Year 3, Mart paid $200,000 for 10,000 shares of common stock of Lew, Inc., a public company whose stock is traded on a national stock exchange. This stock was 1% of the outstanding common stock of Lew. It was acquired for long-term investment purposes and had a fair value of $15 per share on December 31, Year 3. This decline in fair value was not considered permanent.

- On April 30, Year 3, Mart had completed an additional public offering of 500,000 shares of its $5 par value common stock. The stock was sold to the public at $12 per share, net of offering costs.

- On June 17, Year 3, Mart declared a cash dividend of $1 per share of common stock, payable on July 10, Year 3, to shareholders of record on July 1, Year 3.

- On November 6, Year 3, Mart sold 10,000 shares of treasury stock for $21 per share.

- On December 7, Year 3, Mart declared the yearly cash dividend on preferred stock, payable on January 7, Year 4, to shareholders of record on December 31, Year 3.

- On January 17, Year 4, before the books were closed for Year 3, Mart became aware that the ending inventories at December 31, Year 2, were overstated by $200,000. The tax rate applicable to Year 2 net income was 30%. The appropriate correcting entry was recorded the same day.

- After correction of the beginning inventories, net income for Year 3 was $2,250,000.

3. Retained Earnings

This question is presented in a spreadsheet format that requires you to fill in the correct responses in the shaded cells provided. Calculate the amounts to be reported on Mart's statement of retained earnings for the year ended December 31, Year 3.

Mart, Inc.
Statement of Retained Earnings
For the Year Ended December 31, Year 3

Balance on December 31, Year 2		
As originally reported		
Prior-period adjustment from error overstating inventories at December 31, Year 2		
Income tax effect		
Net income for Year 3		
Cash dividends on		
Preferred stock		
Common stock		
Balance on December 31, Year 3		

4. Equity

This question is presented in a spreadsheet format that requires you to fill in the correct responses in the shaded cells provided. Calculate the amounts to be reported in the equity section of Mart's balance sheet on December 31, Year 3.

Mart, Inc.
Balance Sheet - Equity
December 31, Year 3

1. Preferred stock	
2. Common stock	
3. Additional paid-in capital	
4. Retained earnings	
5. Accumulated other comprehensive income – Unrealized holding loss on available-for-sale securities	
6. Common stock in treasury	
7. Total equity	

5. Common Stock

This set of questions has a matching format. Select the best match for each numbered item from the terms in the drop-down list and write its letter in the column provided. Each choice may be used once, more than once, or not at all. For each of the following, determine what effect (increase, decrease, or no effect) the transaction will have on the Mart's common stock account. The state in which Mart is incorporated requires capitalization of retained earnings in the amount of the par value of the shares issued when a stock split in the form of a dividend occurs.

Transaction	Answer		Choices
1. Mart declares a 10% stock dividend.			A) Increase
2. Mart retires 5,000 of its outstanding shares of common stock.			B) Decrease
3. Mart acquires its own stock to hold as treasury stock using the cost method.			C) No effect
4. Mart issues a 3-for-1 stock split.			
5. Mart issues 1,000 previously unissued common shares at $25 per share.			
6. Mart declares a 30% stock dividend.			
7. Mart distributes a dividend of $1,200,000. Only $900,000 is in retained earnings to distribute as a cash dividend.			

6. Liquidation

This question is presented in a check-the-box format that requires you to select the correct responses from a given list of responses. Listed below are the four steps that must be taken in distributing partnership assets to partners pursuant to a liquidation of the partnership. A is the first step and D is the fourth.

A	B	C	D	Steps during liquidation
				1. Remaining assets are assumed to have a fair value of $0.
				2. Any deficit balance in a partner's account is allocated.
				3. Any gain or loss realized from the actual sale of assets is allocated.
				4. Cash is distributed.

7. Communication

In a memorandum to Client, briefly discuss the accounting for stock dividends and stock splits. Type your communication in your word processor program and print out the copy in a memorandum-style format.

REMINDER: Your response will be graded for both technical content and writing skills. Technical content will be evaluated for information that is helpful to the intended reader and clearly relevant to the issue. Writing skills will be evaluated for development, organization, and the appropriate expression of ideas in professional correspondence. Use a standard business memo or letter format with a clear beginning, middle, and end. Do not convey information in the form of a table, bullet point list, or other abbreviated presentation.

TO: Client
FROM: CPA
Subject: Accounting for stock dividends and stock splits

8. Research/Authoritative Literature

See page 12 in the Introduction of this book for a detailed explanation of the AICPA's new Research/Authoritative Literature work tab as well as a screenshot of how the tab will actually look on your exam.

Research and cite from either the FASB current text or original pronouncements the conditions under which an appropriation of retained earnings is allowed.

Unofficial Answers

3. Retained Earnings (4 Gradable Items)

Mart, Inc.
Statement of Retained Earnings
For the Year Ended December 31, Year 3

Balance on December 31, Year 2		
As originally reported		$ 3,250,000
Prior-period adjustment for error overstating inventories at December 31, Year 2	$ (200,000)	
Income tax effect	60,000	(140,000) [1]
Net income for Year 3		$ 2,250,000 [2]
Cash dividends on		
Preferred stock	$ (450,000) [3]	
Common stock	$(2,480,000) [4]	(2,930,000)
Balance on December 31, Year 3		$ 2,430,000

Explanation of Amounts

[1] The overstatement of ending inventories had the effect of understating cost of goods sold and overstating net income and retained earnings reported in the December 31, Year 2, financial statements. The correction of this error requires a debit to beginning retained earnings for Year 3 of $140,000 [$200,000 × (1.0 − .30 tax rate)].

[2] Net income for Year 3 is given.

[3] **Preferred stock dividend**
Par value of all outstanding preferred stock shares $5,000,000
Dividend rate   9%
Dividends paid on preferred stock $ 450,000

[4] **Common stock dividend**
Number of common stock shares outstanding, 12/31/Year 2 $2,000,000
Number of common stock shares issued, 4/30/Year 3   500,000
Total common stock shares issued   2,500,000
Minus treasury stock shares acquired 2/1/Year 3   (20,000)
Shares outstanding, 7/1/Year 3 $2,480,000
Dividends paid (2,480,000 × $1) $2,480,000

4. Equity (7 Gradable Items)

Mart, Inc.
Balance Sheet - Equity
December 31, Year 3

1. Preferred stock, $50 par value, 9% cumulative, convertible; 250,000 shares authorized; 100,000 shares issued and outstanding	$5,000,000 [1]
2. Common stock, $5 par value; 6,000,000 authorized; 2,500,000 shares issued, of which 10,000 shares are held in treasury	$12,500,000 [2]
3. Additional paid-in capital	$11,450,000 [3]
4. Retained earnings	$2,430,000 [4]
5. Accumulated other comprehensive income – Unrealized holding loss on available-for-sale security	$(50,000) [5]
6. Common stock in treasury, 10,000 shares	$(160,000) [6]
7. Total equity	$31,170,000 [7]

[1] The par value of the preferred stock is $5,000,000 (100,000 shares issued × $50).

[2] The par value of the common stock is $12,500,000 (2,500,000 shares issued × $5). When treasury stock is accounted for by the cost method, the common stock account is unaffected.

[3] Additional paid-in capital equals $11,450,000 {$7,500,000 at 12/31/Year 2 + [100,000 preferred shares issued × ($54 – $50)] + [500,000 common shares issued × ($12 – $5)] + [10,000 treasury shares sold × ($21 – $16)]}. Additional paid-in capital is unaffected by the treasury stock purchase accounted for at cost.

[4] This amount was calculated in Tab 3.

[5] The Lew, Inc. stock is accounted for at fair value as available-for-sale securities. They are not trading securities because they are intended to be held, and the equity method does not apply because a 1% holding does not imply significant influence. Hence, the $50,000 unrealized holding loss [10,000 shares × ($20 – $15)] is a debit to other comprehensive income.

[6] The treasury stock was debited for its cost of $160,000 [(20,000 – 10,000) shares × $16].

[7] Accumulated OCI and treasury stocks are subtracted to arrive at this amount.

5. Common Stock (7 Gradable Items)

1. <u>A) - Increase</u>. A 10% stock dividend is accounted for at fair value by debiting retained earnings and crediting common stock and additional paid-in capital.

2. <u>B) - Decrease</u>. When stock is retired, cash (or treasury stock) is credited. The stock account is debited for the par or stated value. Additional paid-in capital is debited to the extent additional paid-in capital exists from the original stock issuance. Any remainder is debited to retained earnings or credited to additional paid-in capital from stock retirement.

3. <u>C) - No effect</u>. The entry is to debit treasury stock and credit cash.

4. <u>C) - No effect</u>. A stock split is recognized by a decrease in the par or stated value of each common share, resulting in a proportionate increase in the number of shares outstanding. Thus, a stock split does not change the aggregate par or stated value of shares outstanding.

5. <u>A) - Increase</u>. The entry is to debit cash for $25,000, credit the par value of common stock for $5,000, and credit additional paid-in capital for $20,000.

6. <u>A) - Increase</u>. According to SEC rules, this distribution is a split-up effected in the form of a dividend. The issuance is of 25% or more of the previously outstanding shares of a public company. Accordingly, Mart capitalizes retained earnings for the par value as required by applicable state law.

7. <u>C) - No effect</u>. The entry is to debit retained earnings for $900,000, debit additional paid-in capital for $300,000, and credit cash for $1,200,000.

6. Liquidation (4 Gradable Items)

1. <u>B) - Second Step</u>. The second step in the liquidation of a partnership is to assume that the remaining assets have a fair value of $0, which results in an assumed loss equal to their carrying amount. This assumed loss is allocated to the partners' capital accounts in accordance with the profit and loss ratio.

2. <u>C) - Third Step</u>. The third step in the liquidation of a partnership is, if at least one of the partners' capital accounts has a deficit balance, to allocate the deficit to the remaining partners' accounts.

3. <u>A) - First Step</u>. The first step in the liquidation of a partnership is to allocate any gain or loss realized from the actual sale of assets to the partners' capital accounts in accordance with the profit and loss ratio.

4. <u>D) - Fourth Step</u>. The last step in the liquidation of a partnership is to ensure that the final balances in the partnership accounts equal the amounts of cash, if any, that may be distributed to the partners.

7. Communication (5 Gradable Items; for grading instructions, please refer to page 12.)

A stock dividend is recognized by capitalizing retained earnings in an amount equal to the fair value of the additional shares distributed. Capitalizing retained earnings results in a debit to retained earnings and credits to common stock and additional paid-in capital. Moreover, the par or stated value of each common share is unaffected. Thus, a stock dividend increases the aggregate par or stated value of shares outstanding.

A stock split is recognized by a decrease in the par or stated value of each common share, resulting in a proportionate increase in the number of shares outstanding. Thus, a stock split does not change the aggregate par or stated value of shares outstanding.

In some circumstances, legal requirements of the state of incorporation may require the capitalization of retained earnings when a stock split in the form of a dividend occurs. Under these circumstances, the par or stated value per share is not changed. Retained earnings should be capitalized in an amount equal to the legal requirement, usually the par or stated value of the additional shares distributed. Furthermore, the term "dividend" should be avoided in referring to a stock split. When this usage is legally required, the transaction should be described as a split-up effected in the form of a dividend.

The enterprise's description of the intent of the distribution normally determines whether the distribution should be accounted for as a stock dividend. However, an issuance of shares less than 20% to 25% of the previously outstanding shares usually should be recognized as a stock dividend. Moreover, the SEC provides that an issuance of less than 25% by a public company should be treated as a stock dividend.

The recipient of a stock dividend or stock split should not recognize income. After receipt, the shareholder has the same proportionate interest in the corporation and the same total carrying amount as before the declaration of the stock dividend or stock split.

8. Research/Authoritative Literature (1 Gradable Item)

Answer: FAS 5, Par. 15

FAS 5 -- *Accounting for Contingencies*

Appropriation of Retained Earnings

15. Some enterprises have classified a portion of retained earnings as "appropriated" for loss contingencies. In some cases, the appropriation has been shown outside the stockholders' equity section of the balance sheet. Appropriation of retained earnings is not prohibited by this Statement provided that it is shown within the stockholders' equity section of the balance sheet and is clearly identified as an appropriation of retained earnings. Costs or losses shall not be charged to an appropriation of retained earnings, and no part of the appropriation shall be transferred to income.

Scoring Schedule:

	Correct Responses		Gradable Items		Weights		
Tab 3	_____	÷	4	×	15%	=	_____
Tab 4	_____	÷	7	×	15%	=	_____
Tab 5	_____	÷	7	×	10%	=	_____
Tab 6	_____	÷	4	×	15%	=	_____
Tab 7	_____	÷	5	×	30%	=	_____
Tab 8	_____	÷	1	×	15%	=	_____
							_____
							(Your Score)

Use Gleim's *CPA Gleim Online* to practice more simulations in a realistic environment.

STUDY UNIT FIFTEEN
BUSINESS COMBINATIONS

(15 pages of outline)

A **business combination** is an entity's acquisition of net assets constituting a business or of controlling equity interests of one or more other entities. The governing pronouncement is SFAS 141, *Business Combinations*. It applies when (1) entities are merged or become subsidiaries, (2) one entity's net assets or equity interests are transferred to another entity, or (3) net assets or equity interests of the existing entities are transferred to a newly formed entity. SFAS 141 also applies regardless of the nature of the consideration given or whether the owners of a combining entity have a majority of the voting rights of the combined entity. However, combinations of not-for-profit organizations or of mutual enterprises are not currently subject to SFAS 141. Acquisitions of for-profit businesses by not-for-profit organizations also are not within its scope.

An exchange of businesses qualifies as a business combination. Joint ventures, the acquisition of noncontrolling interests in a subsidiary (a minority interest), and exchange of equity interests (or transfers of net assets) between entities under common control are not business combinations.

NOTE: The FASB has issued SFAS 141 (revised 2007), *Business Combinations*, and SFAS 160, *Noncontrolling Interests in Consolidated Financial Statements*. These pronouncements, which are not testable until July 2009, will require substantial revision of this study unit. Accordingly, an update reflecting the changes will be available in May 2009 on our website at www.gleim.com/update/. If you will be taking FAR in the third quarter or the fourth quarter, it is imperative that you study the update instead of this study unit.

15.1 PURCHASE ACCOUNTING

Historical-Cost Accounting

1. The customary principles relevant to initial recognition and measurement of assets, liabilities, and equity interests issued; cost allocation; and subsequent accounting also apply to business combinations.

   a. **Initial recognition** of assets, liabilities, and equity interests ordinarily results from exchange transactions. Assets surrendered are derecognized, and liabilities assumed or equity interests issued are recognized, at the acquisition date.

   b. **Initial measurement** of exchange transactions is at fair value, and the assumption is that the fair values exchanged are equal.

      1) Accordingly, the cost of an acquisition equals the fair value of the consideration given, and gain or loss is not recognized unless

         a) The carrying amount of noncash assets surrendered differs from their fair value, or

         b) The fair value of net assets acquired exceeds cost, and the excess is not fully allocated.

      2) If the consideration given is cash, an exchange transaction is measured based on the amount paid. Otherwise, the fair value of the more clearly evident of the consideration given or the asset (net assets) acquired is the basis for measurement.

    c.   **Cost allocation** to the elements of an asset (net asset) group is based on their fair values. The cost of the group acquired in a business combination may be greater than the sum of the fair values assigned to the acquired assets (tangible assets, financial assets, and separately recognized intangible assets), minus the liabilities assumed. This difference is recognized as **goodwill**. It is tested for impairment but not amortized.

    d.   **Post-acquisition accounting** for an asset ordinarily is determined by its nature, not the method of acquisition or the basis for initial measurement.

    e.   The **fair value option (FVO)** applies to most financial assets and financial liabilities. The FVO permits an entity to measure eligible items at fair value and report unrealized gains and losses in earnings.

        1)   The decision to elect the FVO is made only at an election date. Election dates include, among others, the date of

            a)   Initial recognition of an eligible item or

            b)   An event requiring fair value measurement when it occurs but not subsequently.

        2)   A business combination is among the events requiring either fair value remeasurement or initial recognition. Hence, it results in an election date for FVO purposes.

2.   A business combination subject to SFAS 141 is accounted for using the **purchase method**. An acquisition of a **minority interest** is also accounted for in this way.

3.   The **acquiring entity** must be identified. Thus, when no equity interests are exchanged, the entity that distributes cash or other assets or incurs liabilities is the acquiring entity.

    a.   However, if a business combination results from an **exchange of equity interests**, the determination is often more difficult. Neither the issuer of equity interests nor the larger entity is necessarily the acquirer. Thus, all facts and circumstances should be considered, such as

        1)   Relative voting rights in the combined entity,

        2)   The presence of a large minority interest when other voting interests are fragmented,

        3)   The ability to determine the voting majority of the combined entity's board,

        4)   Domination of senior management of the combined entity, and

        5)   Which party paid a premium for the equity securities of the other(s).

    b.   **Three or more entities** may be involved. In this case, additional factors to be considered are the initiator of the combination and whether one entity has significantly greater assets, revenues, and earnings than the other combining entities.

    c.   If a **new entity** is created to issue equity securities, one existing entity must be designated as the acquiring entity.

Cost of the Acquired Entity

4.   **Issuance of Equity Securities**

    a.   The **fair value of preferred shares** that are more nearly akin to debt often may be determined on the same basis as debt securities. Thus, the determination may be by comparison of their terms (e.g., dividend and redemption provisions) with those of comparable securities and by considering market factors. This method differs from the usual practice of recording the fair value of the consideration received as the initial carrying amount of shares issued.

b. The **quoted market price of equity securities** issued in a business combination ordinarily is more clearly evident than the fair value of the acquired entity. Hence, it is the usual basis for estimating that fair value. The market price for a reasonable time before and after the announcement of the terms of the combination should be considered. It is adjusted for such factors as the quantity traded and issue costs.

    1) If the quoted market price is not the fair value, the consideration received must be estimated. The extent of the adjustment to the quoted market price and the net assets received are considered. The net assets received include goodwill. The negotiations and all other facets of the combination should be evaluated, and independent appraisals may be obtained. Moreover, the other consideration paid may be evidence of the total fair value received.

5. **Costs of the business combination** are accounted for as follows:

    a. **Direct costs** include finders' and consultants' fees, as well as legal and accounting fees. They are treated as costs of the acquired entity.

    b. The fair value of securities issued is reduced by their **registration and issuance costs**. The reduction is ordinarily charged to additional paid-in capital.

    c. **Indirect and general expenses** are expensed as incurred.

6. **Contingent consideration.** An issuance of securities or the payment of other consideration may be contingent upon specified future events or transactions. A typical practice is to place part of the consideration in escrow, with its disposition determined by subsequent specified events.

    a. The **cost of the acquired entity** includes the determinable amount of contingent consideration at the acquisition date. Other contingent amounts are disclosed but not recorded as liabilities or outstanding securities until the contingency is resolved beyond a reasonable doubt.

    b. When resolution of a contingency based on **future earnings** levels results in the issuance or issuability of additional consideration, its current fair value should be treated as an additional cost of the acquired entity.

    c. Resolution of a contingency based on **security prices** does not result in an adjustment of the cost of the acquired entity. The additional consideration currently distributable because of failure to achieve or maintain a security price is recorded at current fair value. Securities previously issued at the acquisition date are reduced to the lower current fair value.

        1) The reduction of the fair value of previously issued debt securities results in a discount that is amortized from the time of issuance of additional securities.

        2) The foregoing principles provide guidance applicable to other circumstances involving contingent consideration. An example is a contingency that involves both earnings and security prices.

        3) If the contingent consideration relates to future settlement of a contingency, any increase in the cost of the acquired assets may be amortizable over the useful lives of those assets, depending on their nature.

    d. The accounting for **interest and dividends** on securities held in escrow depends on the accounting for the securities, which is dependent on the resolution of the contingency. Pending that resolution, no interest expense or dividend distributable is recorded for payments into escrow.

        1) Later distributions from escrow to former shareholders are added to the cost of the acquired assets at the distribution date.

    e. **Imputed interest** on contingently issuable shares that reduces taxes also reduces the recorded contingent consideration based on earnings. Moreover, it increases the additional capital resulting from contingent consideration based on security prices.

    f. Contingent consideration is **expensed** if it is given as compensation for services or use of property or profit sharing.

Purchase Price Allocation

7. The general principles of historical-cost accounting apply. Thus, the cost of the acquired entity is determined at the acquisition date. It is allocated to the assets acquired and liabilities assumed in accordance with their fair values at the acquisition date. However, before this step, the noncash purchase consideration should be reviewed to determine that it has been properly valued. Also, all of the assets acquired (possibly including intangible assets not on the acquired entity's balance sheet) and liabilities assumed should be identified.

    a. Estimated fair values may be based on independent appraisals, actuarial valuations, or other sources of relevant information. The tax bases of assets or liabilities are not appropriate estimates.

    b. SFAS 141 provides the following guidance for assigning amounts to the assets (excluding goodwill) acquired and liabilities assumed by the acquiring entity:

        1) **Marketable securities** at fair values.

        2) **Receivables** at present values based on current interest rates, minus allowances for uncollectibility and collection costs.

        3) **Finished goods and merchandise** at estimated selling prices minus disposal costs and a reasonable profit allowance for the selling effort of the acquiring entity.

        4) **Work-in-process** inventory at estimated selling prices minus costs to complete, disposal costs, and a reasonable profit allowance for the completing and selling effort of the acquiring entity.

        5) **Raw materials** at current replacement costs.

        6) **Plant and equipment to be used** at current replacement costs for similar capacity unless expected use indicates a lower value to the acquirer.

        7) **Plant and equipment to be sold** at fair values minus costs to sell.

        8) **Intangible assets** meeting the recognition criteria at estimated fair values.

        9) **Other assets**, such as land, natural resources, and nonmarketable securities, at appraised values.

        10) A liability for the **projected benefit obligation in excess of plan assets** or an asset for the **excess of plan assets over the PBO** of a single-employer defined-benefit pension plan. After the employer is acquired, the amount is determined in accordance with the provisions in SFAS 87 for the calculation of such liability or asset.

        11) A liability for the **accumulated postretirement benefit obligation in excess of the fair value of plan assets** or an asset for the **fair value of the plan assets in excess of the APBO** of a single-employer defined-benefit postretirement plan. After the employer is acquired, the amount is determined in accordance with the provisions in SFAS 106 for the calculation of such liability or asset.

        12) Amounts for **preacquisition contingencies** as determined in e. on the following page.

        13) **Other liabilities, accruals, and commitments** at present values of amounts to be paid based on current interest rates.

    c. **Preacquisition goodwill and deferred tax amounts** on the acquired entity's balance sheet are not recognized. However, the acquiring entity should recognize deferred tax amounts for differences between assigned amounts and tax bases of assets acquired and liabilities assumed.

d. An **intangible asset distinct from goodwill** is recognized if it arises from contractual or other legal rights even if it is not transferable or separable. If this criterion is not met, an intangible asset distinct from goodwill may still be recognized if it is separable.

1) Examples of intangible assets meeting the **contractual-legal criterion** include trade names and trademarks, Internet domain names, noncompetition agreements, order or production backlogs, artistic works, licensing agreements, service or supply contracts, leases, broadcast rights, franchises, patents, computer software, and trade secrets.

2) The **separability criterion** may be met even if the intangible asset is not individually separable if it can be sold, transferred, licensed, rented, or exchanged along with a related item.

3) Examples of intangible assets meeting the separability criterion include customer lists, noncontractual customer relationships, unpatented technology, and databases.

4) An assembled workforce is an example of an item not recognizable as an intangible asset distinct from goodwill.

5) The criteria for recognition of intangible assets apply only to those acquired in a business combination.

6) **Subsequent accounting** for goodwill and other intangible assets acquired in a business combination is prescribed by SFAS 142, *Goodwill and Other Intangible Assets*.

e. A **preacquisition contingency** is a contingent asset, liability, or impairment of an asset of the acquired entity that existed before the business combination. It is normally included in the allocation of the purchase price. However, it is excluded if it consists of (1) possible income tax effects (accounted for under SFAS 109) of temporary differences and carryforwards or (2) uncertainties concerning the acquisition (e.g., whether the tax basis of an asset will be accepted by the tax authorities).

1) A preacquisition contingency is included in the purchase price allocation at fair value if the fair value is determinable during the **allocation period**. This period ends when the acquiring entity no longer is waiting for information it has arranged to obtain and that is available or obtainable. The period for identifying assets and liabilities and measuring fair values ordinarily is not more than 1 year after the combination is consummated.

2) If the fair value is not determinable during the allocation period, the allocation is based on the following:

a) Given information available before the allocation period ends, it is probable that an asset existed, a liability was incurred, or an asset was impaired when the combination was consummated, and

b) The amount is capable of reasonable estimation. (SFAS 5 and FASB Interpretation No. 14 are pertinent to applying the foregoing criteria.)

3) After the allocation period, an adjustment for a preacquisition contingency (other than a loss carryforward, which is accounted for under SFAS 109) is included in net income when determined.

f. Amounts assigned to assets used in a particular R&D project and having no alternative future use are expensed at the acquisition date.

g. **Goodwill** includes acquired intangible assets that do not satisfy either the contractual-legal or the separability recognition criterion.

h.   The total amount assigned to assets acquired and liabilities assumed may exceed the cost of the acquired entity. This **excess over cost**, also known as **negative goodwill**, is allocated proportionately to reduce the amounts assignable to certain acquired assets.

1)   Before the excess over cost is allocated, the acquiring entity should

a)   Reevaluate whether all assets and liabilities have been identified and

b)   Remeasure the consideration paid, assets acquired, and liabilities assumed.

2)   The acquired assets to which the excess over cost is **not** allocated are

a)   Financial assets (excluding equity-method investments)
b)   Assets to be disposed of by sale
c)   Deferred tax assets
d)   Prepaid assets of postretirement benefit plans, including pension plans
e)   Other current assets

3)   The excess over cost may not be fully allocated. A partial allocation may have reduced to zero the amounts assignable to specified types of acquired assets. The **remaining excess over cost** is treated as an **extraordinary gain** in accordance with APB Opinion 30 when the combination is completed.

a)   An extraordinary gain recognized during the allocation period may require subsequent adjustment because of changes in the purchase price allocation. Such an adjustment is an extraordinary item.

EXAMPLE

Parent purchased 100% of Subsidiary (Sub) for $100,000. Sub's assets and liabilities had the following fair values at the acquisition date:

Financial assets	$ 200,000	
Deferred tax assets	100,000	
Other current assets	300,000	
Noncurrent assets	1,000,000	
Liabilities		$400,000

The fair value of the net assets acquired is $1,200,000 ($200,000 + $100,000 + $300,000 + $1,000,000 – $400,000). The excess over cost is therefore $1,100,000 ($1,200,000 – $100,000). The financial assets, deferred tax assets, and other current assets cannot be allocated any portion of the excess over cost. Accordingly, the noncurrent assets must be reduced to zero. The remaining excess over cost ($1,100,000 – $1,000,000 allocated = $100,000) is credited to an extraordinary gain. Parent's entry is

Financial assets	$200,000	
Deferred tax assets	100,000	
Other current assets	300,000	
Liabilities		$400,000
Cash		100,000
Extraordinary gain		100,000

Acquisition Date

8. The **acquisition date** may for the sake of convenience be specified as the end of an accounting period between the initiation and the consummation of the combination. For accounting purposes, this date is appropriate if a written agreement transfers control on that date, subject only to restrictions needed to protect the owners of the acquired entity.

   a. Specifying an acquisition date that is not the date of consummation necessitates adjustment of the cost of the acquired entity and net income otherwise reported. This adjustment compensates for recognizing income prior to transfer of consideration.

      1) Accordingly, **imputed interest** at an appropriate current rate is recognized on the consideration transferred (assets surrendered, liabilities assumed or incurred, or preferred shares issued). The effect is to reduce the cost of the acquired entity and net income.

   b. For the period of the business combination, the acquiring entity recognizes the acquired entity's income after the acquisition date. However, these revenues and expenses are based on the acquiring entity's cost incurred.

Documentation

9. Under SFAS 142, assets and liabilities must be assigned to reporting units. Hence, the determination of the purchase price of the acquired entity and related factors (e.g., reasons for the acquisition) should be documented at the acquisition date.

Stop and review! You have completed the outline for this subunit. Study multiple-choice questions 1 through 14 beginning on page 559.

15.2 CONSOLIDATION

Criteria for Consolidation

1. A parent **must consolidate** all entities over which it has a **controlling financial interest** through direct or indirect majority ownership, i.e., over 50% of the outstanding voting interests (SFAS 94, *Consolidation of All Majority-Owned Subsidiaries – an amendment of ARB No. 51*).

   a. However, consolidation is not required if control does not rest with the majority owner. For example, the subsidiary may be in bankruptcy or in legal reorganization or be subject to foreign exchange restrictions or other government-imposed restrictions that preclude exercise of control.

   b. If the conditions dictating consolidation are met, subsidiaries should be reported on a consolidated basis with the parent.

      1) The **fair value option** (see Study Unit 5) is **not** an alternative to consolidation.

2. Consolidation is an **accounting process** to prepare statements for a business combination when the combined entities remain **legally separate**. It should not be confused with a business combination effected as a consolidation, that is, one in which a new entity is formed to account for the assets and liabilities of the combining entities.

3.   Consolidated statements present the results of operations, financial position, and cash flows of a parent and its subsidiaries as if they constituted a **single economic entity**. Accounting information pertains to an entity, the boundaries of which are not necessarily those of the legal entity.

    a.   The normal procedure is to start with the output of the formal accounting systems of the parent and the subsidiary(ies). On a worksheet only, the informal adjusting and elimination entries are then prepared.

        1)   These consolidating adjusting entries must be cumulative. Previous worksheet entries were not recorded in the accounts of either the parent or the subsidiary.

        2)   The working papers can be based on balances after year-end closing or on trial balances before closing. Thus, the latter include revenue and expense accounts.

Consolidation Procedures

4.   The guidance provided by authoritative pronouncements regarding consolidations is not extensive. However, ARB 51 gives the following description of the general consolidation procedures:

    a.   **Parent-subsidiary balances and transactions**, such as open account balances (receivables and payables), the parent's investment in the subsidiary, sales and purchases, interest, holdings of securities, and dividends, are **eliminated in full** even if a minority interest exists.

        1)   Elimination means debits are credited and credits are debited.

        2)   Retained earnings or deficit of a purchased subsidiary at the date of acquisition is excluded from consolidated retained earnings in the entry eliminating the parent's investment account and the subsidiary's equity accounts.

        3)   Shares of the parent held by a subsidiary should not be treated as outstanding in the consolidated balance sheet. They are eliminated by debiting treasury stock and crediting the subsidiary's investment account.

    b.   **Profits and losses** on transactions within the consolidated entity (intraentity) are completely eliminated, but the procedure varies with the direction of the sale.

        1)   **Parent to subsidiary (downstream):** The entire unrealized profit or loss is subtracted from the parent's income.

            a)   The minority interest is unaffected by the elimination.

        2)   **Subsidiary to parent (upstream):** The entire unrealized profit or loss is subtracted from the subsidiary's income.

            a)   In the upstream case, the effect is to allocate the elimination of the unrealized profit or loss between the parent (or consolidated entity) and the minority interest.

            b)   The upstream case is only relevant if the subsidiary has a minority interest.

    c.   The amount of the **minority interest** recognized at the date of the combination equals a proportionate share of the subsidiary's carrying amount.

        1)   Subsequently, the minority interest is adjusted for its share of the subsidiary's income and dividends.

            a)   On consolidating worksheets, an adjustment to minority interest is also needed for unrealized profits and losses on upstream sales of inventory and fixed assets and purchases of combining entity debt.

d.   In the **income statement**, the minority interest's adjusted share of the subsidiary's income is usually subtracted in arriving at consolidated income.

1)   The parent's investment account and its proportionate share of the subsidiary's equity accounts, which include retained earnings, are eliminated in a consolidation. The remainder of the subsidiary's equity is reported separately as the minority interest.

e.   The consolidated net income equals the **parent's net income** because the parent should account for the investment using the **equity method**.

1)   **Consolidated net income** is also equal to the parent's net income, plus subsidiary net income, minus minority interest net income, minus adjustments for unrealized profit. The latter involve inventory, fixed assets, and debt.

2)   In **combined statements**, no parent-subsidiary relationship exists, but some or all of the combining entities may have a minority interest and unrealized profit transactions (inventory, fixed assets, or debt).

3)   A subsidiary may be purchased during the year being reported on. Under the purchase method, income of the acquiring entity includes its share of the earnings of the acquired entity after acquisition (cash flows are also consolidated after acquisition). Under ARB 51, when a subsidiary is purchased, the preferred method of presenting the results of operations is to include the subsidiary's operations in consolidated income as though it had been acquired at the beginning of the year and to subtract the preacquisition earnings from the total earnings. The minority interest income for the entire year is also subtracted. Thus, the results of operations for the year of combination do not equal the combined results for the entire year unless the acquisition date is the first day of the fiscal year.

f.   In the consolidated balance sheet, the **equity section** should reflect the parent's equity section. The placement of the minority interest is in dispute, although SFAC 6 indicates a preference for treating it as part of equity.

Entries

5.   **Consolidating Journal Entries**

a.   **Basic elimination entry.** This entry eliminates the investment account and subsidiary equity accounts attributable to the parent.

Common stock (sub)	$XXX	
Additional paid-in capital (sub)	XXX	
Retained earnings (sub)	XXX	
Dividends declared (sub)		$XXX
Investment (parent)		XXX
Minority interest		XXX

The subsidiary's net assets are allocated between the parent's "investment in subsidiary" account and the minority interest.

b.   **Elimination of directly offsetting intraentity accounts.** They are reciprocal and do not affect consolidated net income or minority interest.

Sales	$XXX	
Cost of sales		$XXX
Payables	$XXX	
Receivables		$XXX
Interest income	$XXX	
Interest expense		$XXX

c. **Elimination of unrealized profit from inventory.** If ending inventory of a combining entity includes purchased goods from another combining entity that were sold at a profit, unrealized profit exists from a consolidated perspective because the goods have not been sold outside the consolidated group.

Cost of sales	$XXX	
Inventory		$XXX

This entry writes the inventory down to cost and decreases consolidated net income. Part of this reduction of income should be allocated to the minority interest if the sale is upstream (sale by a combining entity with a minority interest).

d. **Elimination of Unrealized Profit in Fixed Asset Purchase/Sale Transactions**

1) In the period of the purchase/sale, any gain recognized on the sale of a **fixed asset** between combining entities should be eliminated.

Gain on sale	$XXX	
Fixed asset		$XXX

2) **Depreciation** taken by the purchaser may differ from the amount that would have been recognized if the seller had retained and depreciated the fixed asset. This difference should be eliminated.

Accumulated depreciation (Dr or Cr)	$XXX	
Depreciation expense (Cr or Dr)		$XXX

3) In subsequent periods, the **previously reported gain** included in retained earnings should be eliminated. The **excess depreciation** taken in the period and in all prior periods (i.e., a cumulative adjustment) should then be eliminated.

Retained earnings	$XXX	
Fixed asset		$XXX
Accumulated depreciation	$XXX	
Depreciation expense		$XXX
Retained earnings		XXX

4) If the seller has a **minority interest**, minority interest and minority interest income should be adjusted as appropriate. However, all adjustments for unrealized profit elimination flow through to consolidated totals unless explicitly taken to the minority interest.

e. **Elimination of Intraentity Debt Transactions**

1) The debt issued by a combining entity of a consolidated group may be purchased by another combining entity of the group from a third party so that the debt accounts are not reciprocal. Thus, the purchase price may not be equal to the carrying amount of the debt on the books of the issuer, another combining entity.

2) The gain or loss on **extinguishment of debt** from a consolidated perspective must be recognized in the period the debt is purchased by a combining entity. The following are the accounting issues:

a) Maturity or face amount of the debt
b) Interest receivable/payable at period-end
c) Interest income/expense based on maturity amount and stated rate
d) Discount or premium on the books of the issuer (debtor)
e) Discount or premium on the books of the purchaser (creditor)

3) The maturity amount, interest receivable/payable, and interest income/expense are direct eliminations.

4) The **premium or discount** on the debtor's and creditor's books and any related amortization should be eliminated and recognized as a gain or loss on extinguishment in the period of purchase. Retained earnings is adjusted in each subsequent period.

    a) The **"investment in debt"** account of the investor/creditor is debited or credited to reduce the balance to zero (after the maturity amount is eliminated). Any amortization of that balance that was an adjustment of interest income during the period also should be eliminated.

        i) If the purchase was at a premium (discount), amortization required a debit (credit) to interest income. Thus, the elimination entry is to credit (debit) interest income.

        ii) The balance of the entry recognizes gain or loss in the period of debt acquisition and adjusts retained earnings in all remaining periods.

    b) The premium or discount on the books of the debtor is debited or credited. Any related amortization of premium or discount that was an adjustment of interest expense during the period should be eliminated.

        i) If the purchase was at a premium (discount), amortization results in a credit (debit) to interest expense that must be reversed.

        ii) The balance of the entry recognizes gain or loss in the period of debt acquisition and adjusts retained earnings in all remaining periods.

    c) The cumulative adjustments to **retained earnings** in the elimination entry decrease over the life of the debt. The gain or loss realized when one affiliate acquired the debt of another affiliate is periodically amortized.

f. All **upstream intraentity profit or loss items** require an adjustment to minority interest.

1) Adjustments are made to retained earnings and current minority interest income.

2) In the preceding journal entries, adjustments to retained earnings can individually be made pro rata to retained earnings and minority interest; e.g., if the minority interest is 10%, 10% of every entry to retained earnings is made to minority interest instead of retained earnings.

    a) An alternative is to make one summary entry to retained earnings to adjust minority interest (established with the first elimination entry).

3) All entries to **nominal accounts** involving upstream transactions (those from combining entities with minority interest) require an adjustment to minority interest income.

    a) The entry to establish minority interest net income is to debit a contra consolidated net income account and credit minority interest income.

Consolidated net income	$XXX	
Minority interest income		$XXX

    b) The amount is the minority interest percentage times the subsidiary's/ combining entity's net income adjusted for any upstream transactions.

    c) For example, if inventory, which includes $1,000 of gross profit sold upstream by a 10% minority interest combining entity, has not been resold out of the consolidated group, the previous minority interest entry is reduced by $100 ($1,000 × 10%) in the period of the sale.

Variable Interest Entities

6.   The accounting scandals of 2001-2002 led the FASB to address the abuse of **off-balance-sheet arrangements** with FASB Interpretation No. 46 (revised December 2003), Consolidation of Variable Interest Entities.

    a.   **A variable interest entity (VIE)** is an off-balance-sheet arrangement that may take any legal form (e.g., corporation, partnership, limited liability company, or trust). Moreover, a VIE either has insufficient equity or its equity investors lack one of the specified characteristics of financial control. An enterprise first determines whether an entity is a VIE when it **becomes involved** with the entity.

        1)   However, this determination is unnecessary if the enterprise

            a)   Has an insignificant interest and

            b)   Is not, along with its related parties (including de facto agents), a significant participant in the entity's design.

        2)   **Reconsideration** of whether an entity is a VIE is required when certain events occur, for example, events that increase (decrease) the VIE's expected losses or alter the nature or sufficiency of the equity at risk. A **troubled debt restructuring** is not such an event.

    b.   **Variable interests** are ownership, contractual, or monetary interests that vary with changes in the **fair value of the VIE's net assets** (excluding variable interests). Examples are equity investments in a VIE that are at risk, subordinated debt or beneficial interests issued by the VIE, and guarantees of the VIE's assets or liabilities.

    c.   The **primary beneficiary (PB)** consolidates a VIE. An enterprise determines whether it is the PB when it **becomes involved** with the VIE. The PB is an entity with variable interests that absorb a majority of the expected losses or receive a majority of the expected residual returns of the VIE. If different enterprises qualify under this criterion, the one that absorbs the majority of the expected losses is the PB.

        1)   **Reconsideration** of the decision to consolidate is indicated when, for example, expected losses or residual returns have been reallocated among the PB and unrelated parties, the PB disposes of its variable interests to unrelated parties, or the VIE issues new variable interests.

    d.   Calculation of expected losses and residual returns begins with **expected cash flow** as defined in SFAC 7. It results from multiplying the possible estimated cash flows by their probabilities and adding the products.

        1)   An **expected loss** is the expected negative variability in the fair value of the VIE's net assets (excluding variable interests). An **expected residual return** is the expected positive variability in that fair value. The sum of the absolute values of these amounts is the total **expected variability**.

            a)   Expected negative (positive) variability is determined for the cases in which the estimated cash flows are less (greater) than the expected cash flow.

        2)   Assuming the present value of expected cash flow equals the fair value of the VIE's net assets (excluding variable interests), the following is one computational technique:

            a)   Determine each possible estimated cash flow and its probability.

            b)   Calculate the expected cash flow.

            c)   Determine the difference between each estimated cash flow and the expected cash flow.

        d)   Multiply each difference by the probability of the estimated cash flow. Each product is then discounted and adjusted for market factors and assumptions.

        e)   Add the negative (positive) amounts to determine the expected loss (residual return) based on fair value.

e.   If an enterprise holds a variable interest in any entity, a variable interest in that entity held by a **related party** is attributed to the enterprise. Related parties are those defined in SFAS 57, *Related Party Disclosures*, and certain de facto agents or principals of the enterprise. An example of a de facto agent is an undercapitalized VIE of which the enterprise is the PB.

    1)   Related parties may hold variable interests in a VIE that together would qualify a party to be the PB. In this situation, the party in the group that is **most closely associated** with the VIE is the PB.

f.   An entity must be consolidated as a VIE if, **by design**, any of three conditions exist.

    1)   The VIE is not properly capitalized. Its **equity investment at risk** is insufficient to finance its operations without additional **subordinated financial support** from any parties.

        a)   Equity at risk equal to **less than 10%** of the VIE's total assets is rebuttably presumed to be insufficient. However, an entity may require equity at risk exceeding 10% of total assets to finance operations, e.g., if it faces high risk. Thus, the sufficiency threshold may exceed 10%.

        b)   A **development stage enterprise** does not meet the equity insufficiency criterion if its equity investment suffices for current activities and additional investment is permitted.

    2)   As a group, the holders of equity at risk **lack** any one of the following characteristics of a **controlling financial interest**:

        a)   The ability based on voting or similar rights to make decisions significantly affecting the VIE's success,

        b)   An obligation to absorb expected losses, or

        c)   The right to receive expected residual returns.

    3)   Equity investors as a group lack the **voting rights** characteristic if

        a)   Voting rights of some investors are disproportionate to their obligations to absorb expected losses or their rights to receive expected returns of the VIE, and

        b)   Substantially all of the VIE's activities involve or are performed for an investor with disproportionately few voting rights.

g.   An enterprise may have a **variable interest in specified assets** (VISA) of a VIE. An example is the guarantee of the residual value of leased property.

    1)   The VISA is considered to be a **variable interest** in the VIE only when

        a)   The fair value of the specified assets exceeds 50% of the fair value of the VIE's assets, or

        b)   The enterprise has a variable interest in the whole VIE. However, this interest must not be either insignificant or have little variability.

    2)   Only when the VISA is a variable interest in the VIE are its expected losses and residual returns considered to be those of the VIE.

3) The specified assets must be more than 50% of the assets of the VIE if the **expected losses** associated with the VISA are to be treated as expected losses of the VIE for the following purposes:

   a) Assessing the adequacy of the equity at risk in the VIE.
   b) Determining the PB.

4) Part of a VIE may be treated as a separate VIE when

   a) The enterprise has a VISA of the overall VIE, and
   b) The specified assets (and any associated credit enhancements) are substantially the sole source of payment of a specified interest (e.g., a liability).

5) When part of a VIE has been consolidated as a separate VIE, that part should not be treated by other holders of variable interests as included within the larger VIE.

h. The PB's **initial measurement** of the VIE's assets, liabilities, and noncontrolling interests is at **fair value** on the date the enterprise becomes the PB (the first date at which it would consolidate the VIE if it issued statements).

   1) However, initial measurement is at the **carrying amount** on the books of the controlling enterprise if the PB and VIE are **under common control**.

   2) Transfers of assets or liabilities to the VIE by the PB made shortly before, at, or any time after the date when the enterprise became the PB are measured as if they had not been transferred. Thus, these transfers do not result in gain or loss.

   3) A loss from initial measurement is an **extraordinary item** if the VIE is not a business or **goodwill** if it is a business. A **gain** is **allocated** to reduce assets as described in SFAS 141, *Business Combinations*.

      a) A gain is the excess of

         i) The sum of the fair values of the consolidated assets of the VIE and the reported amounts of assets transferred by the PB over

         ii) The sum of the consideration given (measured at fair value), the reported amounts of interests in the VIE previously held, and the fair value of the VIE's consolidated liabilities and noncontrolling interests.

      b) Goodwill (if the VIE is a business) or an extraordinary loss is recognized for any excess of ii) over i). For the purpose of this calculation, only **identifiable assets** consolidated or transferred are included in i).

   4) **Subsequent accounting** follows the principles that apply to ordinary consolidations.

i. **Disclosures -- PB.** A PB of a VIE that does not have a majority voting interest must disclose

   1) The nature, purpose, size, and activities of the VIE.
   2) Information about consolidated assets that are collateral for the VIE's liabilities.
   3) Whether the VIE's creditors have recourse to the PB's general credit.

j. **Disclosures -- non-PB.** A non-PB holder of a significant variable interest in a VIE should make disclosures about the nature of its involvement; maximum exposure to loss; and the nature, purpose, size, and activities of the VIE.

Stop and review! You have completed the outline for this subunit. Study multiple-choice questions 15 through 25 beginning on page 566.

15.3 COMBINED FINANCIAL STATEMENTS

1. According to ARB 51, consolidated statements should be prepared only when the controlling financial interest is held by one of the consolidated entities. When consolidated statements are not prepared, combined statements may be more meaningful than the separate statements of commonly controlled entities.

   a. For example, they are useful when one individual owns a controlling interest in several entities with related operations.

   b. They are also used to present the financial position, results of operations, and cash flows of a group of unconsolidated subsidiaries and to combine the statements of entities under common management.

2. Combined statements are prepared in much the same manner as consolidated statements.

   a. Intraentity ownership and the related portion of equity must be eliminated.

   b. According to ARB 51, when combined statements are prepared for a group of related entities, e.g., a group of unconsolidated subsidiaries or a group of commonly controlled entities, such matters as minority interests, foreign operations, different fiscal periods, and income taxes should be treated in the same manner as in consolidated statements.

Stop and review! You have completed the outline for this subunit. Study multiple-choice questions 26 through 31 beginning on page 569.

QUESTIONS

15.1 Purchase Accounting

1. In the period when a material business combination occurs, what supplemental information should be disclosed on a pro forma basis in the notes to the financial statements of a combined entity that is a public business enterprise?

A. Contingent payments, options, or commitments specified in the acquisition agreement.

B. If comparative statements are presented, the results of operations for all periods reported as though the combination had been completed at the beginning of the earliest period.

C. If comparative financial statements are presented, the results of operations for the comparable prior period as though the combination had been completed at the beginning of that period.

D. The period for which the results of operations of the acquired entity are included in the income statement of the combined entity.

Answer (C) is correct. *(Publisher, adapted)*
   REQUIRED: The pro forma disclosure required.
   DISCUSSION: SFAS 141, *Business Combinations*, requires pro forma disclosure of the results of operations (1) for the current period, as though the combination had been completed at the beginning of the period, unless the acquisition was at or near the beginning of the period, and (2) for the comparable prior period, as though the combination had been completed at the beginning of that period, if comparative financial statements are presented. However, pro forma disclosures for nonpublic entities are not required.
   Answer (A) is incorrect because contingent payments, options, and commitments are required disclosures of actual data. Answer (B) is incorrect because disclosure is required only for the comparable prior period. Answer (D) is incorrect because the period for which the results are included is a required disclosure of actual data.

2. To effect a business combination initiated on July 1, Year 4, Proper Co. acquired all the outstanding common shares of Scapula Co. for cash equal to the carrying amount of Scapula's net assets. The carrying amounts of Scapula's assets and liabilities approximated their fair values, except that the carrying amount of its building was more than fair value. In preparing Proper's December 31, Year 4, consolidated income statement, what is the effect of recording the assets acquired and liabilities assumed at fair value, and should goodwill amortization be recognized?

	Depreciation Expense	Goodwill Amortization
A.	Lower	Yes
B.	Higher	Yes
C.	Lower	No
D.	Higher	No

3. Zuider Corp. acquired 100% of the outstanding common stock of Zee Corp. in a business combination initiated in September Year 4. The cost of the acquisition exceeded the fair value of the acquired net assets. The general guidelines for assigning amounts to the inventories acquired provide for

A. Raw materials to be valued at original cost.

B. Work-in-process to be valued at the estimated selling prices of finished goods, minus both costs to complete and costs of disposal.

C. Finished goods to be valued at replacement cost.

D. Finished goods to be valued at estimated selling prices, minus both costs of disposal and a reasonable profit allowance.

4. Dire Co., in a business combination initiated and completed in October Year 4, purchased Wall Co. at a cost that resulted in recognition of goodwill having an expected 10-year benefit period. However, Dire plans to make additional expenditures to maintain goodwill for a total of 40 years. What costs should be capitalized, and over how many years should they be amortized?

	Costs Capitalized	Amortization Period
A.	Acquisition costs only	0 years
B.	Acquisition costs only	40 years
C.	Acquisition and maintenance costs	10 years
D.	Acquisition and maintenance costs	40 years

Answer (C) is correct. *(CPA, adapted)*
REQUIRED: The adjustments made in preparing the consolidated income statement.
DISCUSSION: A business combination is accounted for as a purchase regardless of the form of consideration given. Under purchase accounting, assets acquired and liabilities assumed should be recorded at their fair values. The differences between fair values and carrying amounts will affect net income when related expenses are incurred. The effect of recording the building at fair value in the consolidated balance sheet instead of its higher carrying amount on Scapula's books will be to decrease future depreciation. If the building is to be used, fair value is its current replacement cost for similar capacity unless expected use indicates a lower value to the acquirer. If the building is to be sold, it should be reported at fair value minus cost to sell. The excess of the cost over fair value of the net assets acquired will be recognized as goodwill, but, under SFAS 142, *Goodwill and Other Intangible Assets*, this amount will be tested for impairment but not amortized.

Answer (D) is correct. *(CPA, adapted)*
REQUIRED: The proper accounting for inventories when the cost of the acquisition exceeds the fair value of the net assets acquired.
DISCUSSION: Finished goods and merchandise should be assigned amounts equal to estimated selling prices minus the sum of (1) costs of disposal and (2) a reasonable profit allowance for the selling effort of the acquiring entity.
Answer (A) is incorrect because raw materials should be valued at current replacement cost. Answer (B) is incorrect because work-in-process should be valued at estimated selling prices of finished goods minus the sum of (1) costs to complete, (2) costs of disposal, and (3) a reasonable profit allowance for the completing and selling effort of the acquiring entity based on profit for similar finished goods. Answer (C) is incorrect because finished goods are valued at estimated selling prices minus the sum of (1) costs of disposal and (2) a reasonable profit allowance.

Answer (A) is correct. *(CPA, adapted)*
REQUIRED: The costs to be capitalized and the amortization period.
DISCUSSION: SFAS 141, *Business Combinations*, requires that goodwill (the excess of the cost of the acquired entity over the fair value of the acquired net assets) from a business combination be capitalized. Subsequent accounting for goodwill is governed by SFAS 142, *Goodwill and Other Intangible Assets*, which provides that goodwill is tested for impairment but not amortized. In contrast, the cost of developing, maintaining, or restoring intangible assets that (1) are not specifically identifiable, (2) have indeterminate lives, or (3) are inherent in a continuing business and related to an enterprise as a whole should be expensed as incurred.

Questions 5 and 6 are based on the following information. On January 1, Year 1, Pathan Corp. purchased 80% of Samoa Corp.'s $10 par common stock for $975,000 in a business combination initiated after June 30, Year 1. On this date, the carrying amount of Samoa's net assets was $1 million. The fair values of the assets acquired and liabilities assumed were the same as their carrying amounts on Samoa's balance sheet except for plant assets (net), the fair value of which was $100,000 in excess of the carrying amount. For the year ended December 31, Year 1, Samoa had net income of $190,000 and paid cash dividends totaling $125,000.

5. The goodwill recognized at the date of the Pathan/Samoa business combination is

A. $0

B. $75,000

C. $95,000

D. $175,000

Answer (C) is correct. *(CPA, adapted)*
REQUIRED: The goodwill to be recorded at the date of the business combination.
DISCUSSION: A business combination is accounted for as a purchase. The excess of the cost of the acquired entity over the fair value of the acquired net assets is goodwill. As indicated below, the fair value of 80% of the net assets of the acquired entity is $880,000. Goodwill is therefore $95,000.

Cost	$975,000
Fair value of acquired net assets:	
Carrying amount: $1,000,000 × 80%	(800,000)
Undervalued plant: $100,000 × 80%	(80,000)
Goodwill	$ 95,000

Answer (A) is incorrect because the cost exceeds the fair value of the net assets acquired. Hence, goodwill should be recognized. Answer (B) is incorrect because $75,000 assumes that 100% of the undervaluation is included in Pathan's 80% interest. Answer (D) is incorrect because $175,000 equals the $975,000 cost of the interest acquired minus 80% of the carrying amount ($1,000,000 × 80% = $800,000) of the acquiree's net assets.

6. In the December 31, Year 1, consolidated balance sheet for Pathan/Samoa, the minority interest should be reported at

A. $200,000

B. $213,000

C. $220,000

D. $233,000

Answer (B) is correct. *(CPA, adapted)*
REQUIRED: The minority interest to be reported in the consolidated balance sheet at year-end.
DISCUSSION: The minority interest is equal to the 20% (100% – 80%) interest in Samoa not held by Pathan (the parent). Whereas the parent's interest reflects the fair value of the net assets acquired at the date of purchase, the minority interest should be recorded at the carrying amount recorded on the subsidiary's books. As indicated below, the minority interest to be reported in the year-end balance sheet equals 20% of the equity (net assets) at the beginning of the year, plus 20% of the net income, minus 20% of the dividends. Thus, the minority interest should be reported at $213,000.

	20% Minority Interest
Equity at 1/1/Year 1	$200,000
Net income ($190,000 × 20%)	38,000
Dividends ($125,000 × 20%)	(25,000)
Minority interest at 12/31/Year 1	$213,000

Answer (A) is incorrect because $200,000 was the minority interest at 1/1/Year 1. Answer (C) is incorrect because $220,000 is the minority interest measured at fair value at 1/1/Year 1. Answer (D) is incorrect because $233,000 is the minority interest measured at fair value at 1/1/Year 1, plus its share of net income, minus its share of dividends.

Questions 7 through 10 are based on the following information. The separate condensed balance sheets and income statements of Pater Corp. and its wholly owned subsidiary, Subito Corp., are as follows:

BALANCE SHEETS
December 31, Year 4

Assets	Pater	Subito
Current assets		
Cash	$ 80,000	$ 60,000
Accounts receivable (net)	140,000	25,000
Inventories	90,000	50,000
Total current assets	$ 310,000	$135,000
Property, plant, and equipment (net)	515,000	280,000
Intangible assets	100,000	
Investment in Subito (equity method)	400,000	--
Total assets	$1,325,000	$415,000
Liabilities and Equity		
Current liabilities		
Accounts payable	$ 160,000	$ 95,000
Accrued liabilities	110,000	30,000
Total current liabilities	$ 270,000	$125,000
Equity		
Common stock ($10 par)	$ 300,000	$ 50,000
Additional paid-in capital		10,000
Retained earnings	755,000	230,000
Total equity	$1,055,000	$290,000
Total liabilities and equity	$1,325,000	$415,000

INCOME STATEMENTS
For the Year Ended December 31, Year 4

	Pater	Subito
Sales	$2,000,000	$750,000
Cost of goods sold	1,540,000	500,000
Gross margin	$ 460,000	$250,000
Operating expenses	260,000	150,000
Operating income	$ 200,000	$100,000
Equity in earnings of Subito	70,000	--
Income before income taxes	$ 270,000	$100,000
Provision for income taxes	70,000	30,000
Net income	$ 200,000	$ 70,000

Additional Information:

- On January 1, Year 4, Pater purchased for $360,000 all of Subito's $10 par, voting common stock. On January 1, Year 4, the fair value of Subito's assets and liabilities equaled their carrying amount of $410,000 and $160,000, respectively, except that the fair values of certain items identifiable in Subito's inventory were $10,000 more than their carrying amounts. These items were still on hand at December 31, Year 4. Pater amortizes intangible assets over a 10-year period.

- During Year 4, Pater and Subito paid cash dividends of $100,000 and $30,000, respectively. For tax purposes, Pater receives the 100% exclusion for dividends received from Subito.

- There were no transactions between Pater and Subito, except for Pater's receipt of dividends from Subito and Pater's recording of its share of Subito's earnings.

- No transactions affected other comprehensive income.

- Both Pater and Subito paid income taxes at the rate of 30%.

- Pater treats Subito as a reporting unit, and all goodwill acquired in the business combination is assigned to Subito for the purpose of testing impairment. However, goodwill was not impaired at December 31, Year 4.

7. In the December 31, Year 4, consolidated financial statements of Pater and its subsidiary, total assets should be

A. $1,740,000
B. $1,450,000
C. $1,350,000
D. $1,325,000

Answer (B) is correct. *(CPA, adapted)*
REQUIRED: The consolidated total assets.
DISCUSSION: All of a subsidiary's assets should be included in a consolidated balance sheet after elimination of parent-subsidiary transactions. Given that the only such transaction in Year 4 was the dividend payment, no adjustment is needed. The amount of total assets is determined as follows:

Total assets (12/31/Year 4)		
($1,325,000 + $415,000)		$1,740,000
Minus: Investment in Subito		(400,000)
Add: Increase in inventory and		
unimpaired goodwill:		
Cost of investment	$360,000	
Equity acquired ($410,000 – $160,000)	(250,000)	
Excess	$110,000	
Applied to inventory	(10,000)	10,000
Goodwill	$100,000	
Goodwill impairment	0	100,000
		$1,450,000

Answer (A) is incorrect because $1,740,000 is the unadjusted sum of the assets of Pater and Subito. Answer (C) is incorrect because $1,350,000 is not adjusted for goodwill. Answer (D) is incorrect because $1,325,000 equals the parent's total assets.

8. In the December 31, Year 4, consolidated financial statements of Pater and its subsidiary, total current assets should be

A. $455,000
B. $445,000
C. $310,000
D. $135,000

Answer (A) is correct. *(CPA, adapted)*
REQUIRED: The consolidated total current assets.
DISCUSSION: In a business combination, the excess of the acquisition cost over the subsidiary's equity is allocated to assets acquired and liabilities assumed based on their estimated fair values. Any remaining excess is treated as goodwill. As stated, $10,000 was allocated to inventory items that were still on hand at year-end. Hence, total current assets at year-end equals $455,000 ($310,000 Pater current assets + $135,000 Subito current assets + $10,000 excess fair value attributable to inventory).
Answer (B) is incorrect because $445,000 does not reflect the fair value of the inventory. Answer (C) is incorrect because $310,000 equals the parent's current assets. Answer (D) is incorrect because $135,000 equals the unadjusted current assets of the subsidiary.

9. In the December 31, Year 4, consolidated financial statements of Pater and its subsidiary, total retained earnings should be

A. $985,000
B. $825,000
C. $795,000
D. $755,000

Answer (D) is correct. *(CPA, adapted)*
REQUIRED: The consolidated total retained earnings.
DISCUSSION: Pater acquired Subito in a purchase transaction and properly accounts for the investment using the equity method. Thus, Pater's $755,000 of retained earnings equals consolidated retained earnings.
Answer (A) is incorrect because $985,000 includes the subsidiary's retained earnings. Answer (B) is incorrect because $825,000 includes the subsidiary's net income, an amount already reflected in the parent's retained earnings under the equity method. Answer (C) is incorrect because $795,000 includes the subsidiary's net income minus the dividends paid, an amount already accounted for using the equity method.

10. In the December 31, Year 4, consolidated financial statements of Pater and its subsidiary, net income should be

A. $270,000
B. $200,000
C. $190,000
D. $170,000

Answer (B) is correct. *(CPA, adapted)*
REQUIRED: The consolidated net income.
DISCUSSION: The equity in the earnings of the subsidiary recorded on the parent's income statement is recorded in accordance with the equity method. Thus, the parent's $200,000 of net income equals consolidated net income.
Answer (A) is incorrect because $270,000 equals the sum of the net incomes of Pater and Subito. Answer (C) is incorrect because $190,000 equals Pater's net income minus goodwill amortization ($100,000 ÷ 10 years). However, goodwill is tested for impairment but not amortized. Goodwill was not impaired at December 31, Year 4. Answer (D) is incorrect because $170,000 equals Pater's net income minus the dividend payment, which does not affect equity-based net income.

11. Pellew Corp. paid $600,000 for the outstanding common stock of Stillwell Co. in a business combination initiated and completed in December Year 4. At that time, Stillwell had the following condensed balance sheet:

	Carrying Amounts
Current assets	$ 80,000
Plant and equipment, net	760,000
Liabilities	400,000
Equity	440,000

The fair value of the plant and equipment was $120,000 more than its carrying amount. The fair values and carrying amounts were equal for all other assets and liabilities. What amount of goodwill related to Stillwell's acquisition should Pellew report in its consolidated balance sheet?

- A. $40,000
- B. $80,000
- C. $120,000
- D. $160,000

12. Purchase Corporation purchased for cash at $10 per share all 100,000 shares of the outstanding common stock of Seller Company. The total fair value of the assets acquired minus liabilities assumed of Seller was $1.4 million on the acquisition date, including the fair value of Seller's property, plant, and equipment (its only noncurrent asset) of $250,000. The consolidated financial statements of Purchase Corporation and its wholly owned subsidiary should reflect

- A. A deferred credit of $150,000 on the balance sheet.
- B. Goodwill of $150,000 on the balance sheet.
- C. An extraordinary gain of $150,000 on the income statement.
- D. Goodwill of $400,000 on the balance sheet.

Answer (A) is correct. *(CPA, adapted)*
REQUIRED: The amount of goodwill reported in the consolidated balance sheet.
DISCUSSION: A business combination is accounted for as a purchase regardless of the form of the consideration given. Under purchase accounting, assets acquired and liabilities assumed should be recorded at their fair values. Any excess of cost over the fair value of the net assets acquired is recorded as goodwill. After adjusting the net plant and equipment and given that other items are stated at fair value, the fair value of the net assets acquired is $560,000 [$80,000 current assets + ($760,000 + $120,000) plant and equipment – $400,000 liabilities]. Hence, goodwill is $40,000 ($600,000 cost – $560,000).
Answer (B) is incorrect because $80,000 is the amount of current assets. Answer (C) is incorrect because $120,000 is the amount plant and equipment is undervalued. Answer (D) is incorrect because $160,000 is the difference between the $600,000 cost and the $440,000 carrying amount of the net assets.

Answer (C) is correct. *(CPA, adapted)*
REQUIRED: The accounting treatment of the excess of the fair value of net assets acquired over cost.
DISCUSSION: In a business combination, any excess of the fair value assigned to the net assets acquired over the cost of the purchase must be allocated proportionately to reduce the amounts otherwise assignable to all of the acquired assets except (1) financial assets (excluding equity-method investments), (2) assets to be disposed of by sale, (3) deferred tax assets, (4) prepaid assets relating to postretirement benefit plans, and (5) other current assets. Any remainder after the amounts otherwise assignable to those assets have been reduced to zero is reported as an extraordinary gain (SFAS 141). The excess over cost in this transaction is $400,000 ($1,400,000 fair value – $1,000,000 cash paid). Given that the only assets to which the excess over cost may be allocated are those classified as property, plant, and equipment (all other acquired assets are current), only $250,000 of the excess is allocable. Hence, the excess of $150,000 ($400,000 – $250,000) remaining after allocation is recognized as an extraordinary gain.
Answer (A) is incorrect because a deferred credit is never recognized for the excess of the fair value of acquired net assets over cost. Answer (B) is incorrect because goodwill is recognized when cost exceeds the fair value of acquired net assets. Answer (D) is incorrect because goodwill is recognized when cost exceeds the fair value of acquired net assets, and the amount of gain recognized is reduced by the value of the property, plant, and equipment.

13. On January 1, Year 4, Pane Corp. exchanged 150,000 shares of its $20 par value common stock for all of Sky Corp.'s common stock in a business combination initiated in November Year 3. At that date, the fair value of Pane's common stock issued was equal to the carrying amount of Sky's net assets. Both corporations continued to operate as separate businesses, maintaining accounting records with years ending December 31. Information from separate company operations follows:

	Pane	Sky
Retained earnings – 12/31/Year 3	$3,200,000	$925,000
Net income – 6 mos ended 6/30/Year 4	800,000	275,000
Dividends paid – 3/25/Year 4	750,000	--

What amount of retained earnings should Pane report in its June 30, Year 4, consolidated balance sheet?

    A. $5,200,000

    B. $4,450,000

    C. $3,525,000

    D. $3,250,000

Answer (D) is correct. *(CPA, adapted)*
REQUIRED: The retained earnings at the date of a business combination.
DISCUSSION: The purchase method accounts for a business combination on the basis of the fair values exchanged. Hence, the cost of the acquired entity is allocated to the assets acquired and liabilities assumed based on their fair values, with possible adjustments for goodwill or the excess of fair value over cost. Accordingly, only the cost of the acquired entity is included in a consolidated balance sheet prepared using the purchase method. The equity, including retained earnings of the acquired entity, is excluded. Pane's separate retained earnings is therefore equal to the amount in the consolidated balance sheet, i.e., $3,250,000 ($3,200,000 beginning RE + $800,000 NI – $750,000 dividends).
Answer (A) is incorrect because $5,200,000 includes Sky's retained earnings at 6/30/Year 4 and does not deduct the dividends paid. Answer (B) is incorrect because $4,450,000 equals the consolidated retained earnings if the combination had been accounted for as a pooling, a method no longer acceptable under GAAP. Answer (C) is incorrect because $3,525,000 double counts Sky's net income through 6/30/Year 4. The income statement of the acquiring entity for the period in which a business combination occurs includes the income of the acquired entity after the acquisition date, with revenues and expenses based on the cost to the acquiring entity.

14. On December 31, Year 4, Saxe Corporation was merged into Voe Corporation in a business combination initiated in July Year 4. On December 31, Voe issued 200,000 shares of its $10 par common stock, with a market price of $18 a share, for all of Saxe's common stock. The equity section of each company's balance sheet immediately before the combination was as presented below:

	Voe	Saxe
Common stock	$3,000,000	$1,500,000
Additional paid-in capital	1,300,000	150,000
Retained earnings	2,500,000	850,000
	$6,800,000	$2,500,000

In the December 31, Year 4, consolidated balance sheet, additional paid-in capital should be reported at

    A. $950,000

    B. $1,300,000

    C. $1,450,000

    D. $2,900,000

Answer (D) is correct. *(CPA, adapted)*
REQUIRED: The additional paid-in capital to be reported in the consolidated balance sheet.
DISCUSSION: To effect the acquisition, the 200,000 shares were issued for $3,600,000 (200,000 shares × $18 market price). Of this amount, $2,000,000 (200,000 shares × $10 par) should be allocated to the common stock of Voe, with the remaining $1,600,000 ($3,600,000 – $2,000,000) allocated to additional paid-in capital. The additional paid-in capital recorded on Voe's (the parent company's) books is $2,900,000 ($1,300,000 + $1,600,000). This balance is also reported on the Year 2 consolidated balance sheet.
Answer (A) is incorrect because $950,000 is the additional paid-in capital reported under the pooling-of-interests method, no longer acceptable under GAAP. Answer (B) is incorrect because $1,300,000 is the amount reported by Voe immediately before the combination. Answer (C) is incorrect because $1,450,000 is the sum of the amounts reported by Voe and Saxe immediately before the combination.

15.2 Consolidation

15. Consolidated financial statements are typically prepared when one entity has a majority voting interest in another unless

   A. The subsidiary is a financial institution.

   B. The fiscal year-ends of the two entities are more than 3 months apart.

   C. Control does not rest with the majority owners.

   D. The two entities are in unrelated industries, such as manufacturing and real estate.

Answer (C) is correct. *(CPA, adapted)*
   REQUIRED: The exception to consolidation.
   DISCUSSION: SFAS 94, *Consolidation of All Majority-owned Subsidiaries*, usually requires consolidation when one entity owns, directly or indirectly, more than 50% of the outstanding voting interests of another entity. However, a majority-owned subsidiary is not consolidated if control does not rest with the majority owners.

16. Sun Co. is a wholly owned subsidiary of Star Co. The companies have separate general ledgers and prepare separate financial statements. Sun requires stand-alone financial statements. Which of the following statements is correct?

   A. Consolidated financial statements should be prepared for both Star and Sun.

   B. Consolidated financial statements should only be prepared by Star and not by Sun.

   C. After consolidation, the accounts of both Star and Sun should be changed to reflect the consolidated totals for future ease in reporting.

   D. After consolidation, the accounts of both Star and Sun should be combined into one general-ledger accounting system for future ease in reporting.

Answer (B) is correct. *(CPA, adapted)*
   REQUIRED: The reporting of a parent and a wholly owned subsidiary.
   DISCUSSION: SFAS 94, *Consolidation of All Majority-Owned Subsidiaries*, requires the consolidation of all entities in which a parent has a controlling financial interest through direct or indirect majority ownership (over 50% of the outstanding voting interests). Thus, Star should prepare consolidated financial statements.
   Answer (A) is incorrect because Sun is the subsidiary and does not have majority ownership. Answer (C) is incorrect because the accounts after consolidation remain separate to facilitate preparation of separate statements. Consolidation is done solely for external reporting purposes. Answer (D) is incorrect because the accounts of both companies must retain their individual identities. Consolidation is a process that uses eliminating entries to present results as if the parent and subsidiary were a single economic entity. However, these eliminating entries are done on workpapers that do not affect the general ledger.

17. Penn, Inc., a manufacturing company, owns 75% of the common stock of Sell, Inc., an investment company. Sell owns 60% of the common stock of Vane, Inc., an insurance company. In Penn's consolidated financial statements, should consolidation accounting or equity method accounting be used for Sell and Vane?

   A. Consolidation used for Sell and equity method used for Vane.

   B. Consolidation used for both Sell and Vane.

   C. Equity method used for Sell and consolidation used for Vane.

   D. Equity method used for both Sell and Vane.

Answer (B) is correct. *(CPA, adapted)*
   REQUIRED: The method of accounting used by an entity that has a direct controlling interest in one entity and an indirect interest in another.
   DISCUSSION: SFAS 94, *Consolidation of All Majority-Owned Subsidiaries*, amended ARB 51, *Consolidated Financial Statements*, to require that all entities in which a parent has a controlling financial interest through direct or indirect ownership of a majority voting interest be consolidated. However, a subsidiary is not consolidated when control does not rest with the majority owner. Penn has direct control of Sell and indirect control of Vane and should consolidate both.

18. Perez, Inc. owns 80% of Senior, Inc. During Year 4, Perez sold goods with a 40% gross profit to Senior. Senior sold all of these goods in Year 4. For Year 4 consolidated financial statements, how should the summation of Perez and Senior income statement items be adjusted?

A. Sales and cost of goods sold should be reduced by the intercompany sales.

B. Sales and cost of goods sold should be reduced by 80% of the intercompany sales.

C. Net income should be reduced by 80% of the gross profit on intercompany sales.

D. No adjustment is necessary.

Answer (A) is correct. *(CPA, adapted)*
REQUIRED: The adjustment, if any, to prepare consolidated financial statements given a sale by the parent to the subsidiary.
DISCUSSION: Given that all of the goods were sold, no adjustment is necessary for interentity profit in ending inventory. Accordingly, the parent's cost should be included in consolidated cost of goods sold, and the price received by the subsidiary should be included in consolidated sales. The required adjustment is to eliminate the sale recorded by the parent and the cost of goods sold recorded by the subsidiary.
Answer (B) is incorrect because the elimination is made without regard to the minority interest. Answer (C) is incorrect because no profit should be eliminated. All of the goods sold to Senior have been resold. Answer (D) is incorrect because sales and cost of sales should be reduced.

Questions 19 through 21 are based on the following information.

On January 2, Year 4, Pare Co. purchased 75% of Kidd Co.'s outstanding common stock. Selected balance sheet data at December 31, Year 4, appear to the right. During Year 4, Pare and Kidd paid cash dividends of $25,000 and $5,000, respectively, to their shareholders. There were no other transactions between Pare and Kidd.

	Pare	Kidd
Total assets	$420,000	$180,000
Liabilities	$120,000	$ 60,000
Common stock	100,000	50,000
Retained earnings	200,000	70,000
	$420,000	$180,000

---

19. In its December 31, Year 4, consolidated statement of retained earnings, what amount should Pare report as dividends paid?

A. $5,000

B. $25,000

C. $26,250

D. $30,000

Answer (B) is correct. *(CPA, adapted)*
REQUIRED: The amount reported as dividends paid.
DISCUSSION: In consolidated statements, the amount of dividends paid equals the parent's dividends paid. The subsidiary's dividends paid to the parent ($5,000 × 75% = $3,750) are eliminated. The remaining $1,250 of the subsidiary's dividends reduces the amount reported as the minority interest.
Answer (A) is incorrect because $5,000 is the subsidiary's dividends paid. Answer (C) is incorrect because $26,250 includes the minority interest. Answer (D) is incorrect because $30,000 includes the subsidiary's dividends paid.

---

20. In Pare's December 31, Year 4, consolidated balance sheet, what amount should be reported as minority interest in net assets?

A. $0

B. $30,000

C. $45,000

D. $105,000

Answer (B) is correct. *(CPA, adapted)*
REQUIRED: The minority interest in net assets.
DISCUSSION: Given that 25% of the stock is held by minority interests, $30,000 equals the minority interest in net assets [($180,000 – $60,000) × 25%].

---

21. In its December 31, Year 4, consolidated balance sheet, what amount should Pare report as common stock?

A. $50,000

B. $100,000

C. $137,500

D. $150,000

Answer (B) is correct. *(CPA, adapted)*
REQUIRED: The amount reported as common stock.
DISCUSSION: In consolidated statements, the parent's common stock equals the consolidated common stock.

22. Wagner, a holder of a $1 million Palmer, Inc. bond, collected the interest due on March 31, Year 4, and then sold the bond to Seal, Inc. for $975,000. On that date, Palmer, a 75% owner of Seal, had a $1,075,000 carrying amount for this bond. What was the effect of Seal's purchase of Palmer's bond on the retained earnings and minority interest amounts reported in Palmer's March 31, Year 4, consolidated balance sheet?

	Retained Earnings	Minority Interest
A.	$100,000 increase	$0
B.	$75,000 increase	$25,000 increase
C.	$0	$25,000 increase
D.	$0	$100,000 increase

Answer (A) is correct. *(CPA, adapted)*
REQUIRED: The effect of the purchase by the subsidiary of the parent's debt.
DISCUSSION: The purchase was in substance a retirement of debt by the consolidated entity for less than its carrying amount. The transaction resulted in a constructive gain of $100,000 ($1,075,000 carrying amount – $975,000 price) and therefore a $100,000 increase in consolidated retained earnings. The minority interest was unaffected. The minority interest is based on the subsidiary's carrying amounts adjusted for subsidiary income and dividends. This transaction did not result in gain or loss for Seal.
Answer (B) is incorrect because the gain is not allocated. Answer (C) is incorrect because retained earnings is increased by $100,000, but the minority interest is not affected. Answer (D) is incorrect because all $100,000 is added to retained earnings.

23. Wright Corp. has several subsidiaries that are included in its consolidated financial statement. In its December 31, Year 4, trial balance, Wright had the following interentity balances before eliminations:

	Debit	Credit
Current receivable due from Main Co.	$ 32,000	
Noncurrent receivable from Main	114,000	
Cash advance to Corn Corp.	6,000	
Cash advance from King Co.		$ 15,000
Interentity payable to King		101,000

In its December 31, Year 4, consolidated balance sheet, what amount should Wright report as interentity receivables?

A. $152,000

B. $146,000

C. $36,000

D. $0

Answer (D) is correct. *(CPA, adapted)*
REQUIRED: The interentity receivables reported in a consolidated balance sheet.
DISCUSSION: In a consolidated balance sheet, reciprocal balances, such as receivables and payables, between a parent and a consolidated subsidiary should be eliminated in their entirety regardless of the portion of the subsidiary's stock held by the parent. Thus, Wright should report $0 as interentity receivables.

24. Clark Co. had the following transactions with affiliated parties during Year 4:

- Sales of $50,000 to Dean, Inc., with $20,000 gross profit. Dean had $15,000 of this inventory on hand at year-end. Clark owns a 15% interest in Dean and does not exert significant influence.

- Purchases of raw materials totaling $240,000 from Kent Corp., a wholly owned subsidiary. Kent's gross profit on the sale was $48,000. Clark had $60,000 of this inventory remaining on December 31, Year 4.

Before eliminating entries, Clark had consolidated current assets of $320,000. What amount should Clark report in its December 31, Year 4, consolidated balance sheet for current assets?

A. $320,000

B. $314,000

C. $308,000

D. $302,000

Answer (C) is correct. *(CPA, adapted)*
REQUIRED: The amount reported on the consolidated balance sheet for current assets.
DISCUSSION: When a parent buys inventory from a subsidiary (an upstream transaction), the inventory on the consolidated balance sheet must be adjusted to the price paid by the subsidiary until the inventory is sold to an outside party. Hence, the gross profit made by Kent included in the $60,000 of inventory held by Clark must be reduced by the pro rata share of profit made on the sale by Kent, reducing the inventory to Kent's original cost. The reduction is $12,000 [($60,000 EI ÷ $240,000 purchases) × $48,000 gross profit]. Thus, current assets equal $308,000 ($320,000 – $12,000). Because Kent is wholly owned, no allocation of the reduction in gross profit to a minority interest is necessary. The transaction with Dean requires no elimination. Dean is not consolidated.
Answer (A) is incorrect because $320,000 does not eliminate interentity transactions. Answer (B) is incorrect because $314,000 does not eliminate the effect of the transactions with Kent but deducts the gross profit included in the inventory held by Dean. Answer (D) is incorrect because $302,000 treats the sales to Dean as between a parent and a consolidated subsidiary.

25. Port, Inc. owns 100% of Salem Inc. On January 1, Year 4, Port sold Salem delivery equipment at a gain. Port had owned the equipment for 2 years and used a 5-year straight-line depreciation rate with no residual value. Salem is using a 3-year straight-line depreciation rate with no residual value for the equipment. In the consolidated income statement, Salem's recorded depreciation expense on the equipment for Year 4 will be decreased by

A. 20% of the gain on sale.

B. 33 1/3% of the gain on sale.

C. 50% of the gain on sale.

D. 100% of the gain on sale.

Answer (B) is correct. *(CPA, adapted)*
REQUIRED: The consolidated depreciation expense on equipment sold by a parent to a subsidiary.
DISCUSSION: The effects of parent-subsidiary transactions should be eliminated. Consequently, the equipment and the related depreciation expense should be reported at amounts that exclude the gain on the sale to Salem. Given that the equipment was held by Port for 2 of its 5 years of estimated useful life, that it has no salvage value, and that Salem is depreciating it over 3 years, Salem recognizes as depreciation expense in its separate Year 4 statements 33 1/3% of the acquisition cost, which equals the gain recognized by Port plus Port's carrying amount. Thus, 33 1/3% of the gain is included in the Year 4 depreciation expense recorded on the equipment and should be eliminated.
Answer (A) is incorrect because 20% was the rate used by the parent. Answer (C) is incorrect because 50% is greater than the 1/3 rate used by Salem. Answer (D) is incorrect because not all of the gain is recognized in depreciation expense for Year 4 in Salem's separate statements.

15.3 Combined Financial Statements

26. Combined statements may be used to present the results of operations of

	Entities under Common Management	Commonly Controlled Entities
A.	No	Yes
B.	Yes	No
C.	No	No
D.	Yes	Yes

Answer (D) is correct. *(CPA, adapted)*
REQUIRED: The condition(s) in which combined financial statements are appropriate.
DISCUSSION: ARB 51 states that combined (as distinguished from consolidated) statements of commonly controlled entities may be more meaningful than their separate statements. For example, combined statements may be used (1) when one individual owns a controlling interest in several entities with related operations, (2) to present financial position and results of operations of a group of unconsolidated subsidiaries, or (3) to combine the statements of entities under common management.

27. Selected data for two subsidiaries of Dunn Corp. taken from December 31, Year 4, preclosing trial balances are as follows:

	Banks Co. Debit	Lamm Co. Credit
Shipments to Banks	--	$150,000
Shipments from Lamm	$200,000	--
Interentity inventory profit on total shipments	--	50,000
Additional data relating to the December 31, Year 4, inventory are as follows:		
Inventory acquired from outside parties	$175,000	$250,000
Inventory acquired from Lamm	60,000	--

At December 31, Year 4, the inventory reported on the combined balance sheet of the two subsidiaries should be

A. $425,000

B. $435,000

C. $470,000

D. $485,000

Answer (C) is correct. *(CPA, adapted)*
REQUIRED: The inventory to be reported on the combined balance sheet of two subsidiaries.
DISCUSSION: When combined financial statements are prepared for unconsolidated subsidiaries, interentity profits should be eliminated. The $60,000 of ending inventory acquired by Banks from Lamm is equal to 30% ($60,000 inventory remaining ÷ $200,000 shipments) of the total received from Lamm. Accordingly, $15,000 ($50,000 inventory profit on total shipments × 30%) should be eliminated. Given that $425,000 ($175,000 + $250,000) of the ending inventory held by Banks and Lamm was obtained from outside parties, the combined balance sheet of the two subsidiaries should report inventory of $470,000 ($425,000 + $60,000 − $15,000).
Answer (A) is incorrect because $425,000 is the total inventory acquired from outside parties. Answer (B) is incorrect because $435,000 excludes the profit on inventory acquired from Lamm and subsequently sold. Answer (D) is incorrect because $485,000 does not exclude the interentity inventory profit.

28. Mr. Cord owns four corporations. Combined financial statements are being prepared for these corporations, which have interentity loans of $200,000 and interentity profits of $500,000. What amount of these loans and profits should be included in the combined financial statements?

	Interentity Loans	Profits
A.	$200,000	$0
B.	$200,000	$500,000
C.	$0	$0
D.	$0	$500,000

Answer (C) is correct. *(CPA, adapted)*
REQUIRED: The amount of interentity loans and profits that should be included in combined financial statements.
DISCUSSION: According to ARB 51, combined financial statements are appropriately issued when two or more entities have a common relationship, such as a common ownership interest or common management. When combined financial statements are issued, interentity loans and profits should be eliminated in their entirety. Consequently, $200,000 in loans and $500,000 in profits should not be included in the combined financial statements.

29. At December 31, Year 4, Spud Corp. owned 80% of Jenkins Corp.'s common stock and 90% of Thompson Corp.'s common stock. Jenkins's Year 4 net income was $100,000 and Thompson's Year 4 net income was $200,000. Thompson and Jenkins had no interentity ownership or transactions during Year 4. Combined Year 4 financial statements are being prepared for Thompson and Jenkins in contemplation of their sale to an outside party. In the combined income statement, combined net income should be reported at

A. $210,000

B. $260,000

C. $280,000

D. $300,000

Answer (D) is correct. *(CPA, adapted)*
REQUIRED: The combined net income for the year.
DISCUSSION: Combined financial statements are appropriate when a relationship, such as common management or common ownership, exists for two or more entities not subject to consolidation. Combined net income should be recorded at the total of the net income reported by the combined entities, adjusted for any interentity profits or losses. In the combined income statement issued for Jenkins Corp. and Thompson Corp., net income should be reported at $300,000 ($100,000 + $200,000).
Answer (A) is incorrect because $210,000 is 70% of the combined net income. Answer (B) is incorrect because $260,000 equals 80% of the net income of Jenkins and 90% of the net income of Thompson. Answer (C) is incorrect because $280,000 equals 80% of the net income of Jenkins and 100% of Thompson's net income.

30. Mr. and Mrs. Gasson own 100% of the common stock of Able Corp. and 90% of the common stock of Baker Corp. Able previously paid $4,000 for the remaining 10% interest in Baker. The condensed December 31, Year 4, balance sheets of Able and Baker are as follows:

	Able	Baker
Assets	$600,000	$60,000
Liabilities	$200,000	$30,000
Common stock	100,000	20,000
Retained earnings	300,000	10,000
	$600,000	$60,000

In a combined balance sheet of the two corporations at December 31, Year 4, what amount should be reported as total equity?

A. $430,000

B. $426,000

C. $403,000

D. $400,000

Answer (B) is correct. *(CPA, adapted)*
REQUIRED: The amount reported as total equity.
DISCUSSION: Combined statements are prepared in much the same manner as consolidated statements. Hence, interentity ownership and the related portion of equity must be eliminated. The investment in Baker's account must be credited and equity debited for $4,000. Consequently, the combined total equity is $426,000 [($400,000 common stock and RE of Able + $30,000 common stock and RE of Baker) – $4,000].
Answer (A) is incorrect because $430,000 does not reflect the elimination of the interentity ownership. Answer (C) is incorrect because $403,000 equals Able's equity plus 10% of Baker's. Answer (D) is incorrect because $400,000 equals Able's separate equity.

31. Which of the following items should be treated in the same manner in both combined financial statements and consolidated statements?

	Different Fiscal Periods	Foreign Operations
A.	No	No
B.	No	Yes
C.	Yes	Yes
D.	Yes	No

Answer (C) is correct. *(CPA, adapted)*

REQUIRED: The items treated in the same manner in both combined financial statements and consolidated statements.

DISCUSSION: According to ARB 51, when combined statements are prepared, "if there are problems in connection with such matters as minority interests, foreign operations, different fiscal periods, or income taxes, they should be treated in the same manner as in consolidated statements."

Use Gleim's ***CPA Test Prep*** CD-Rom/Pocket PC for interactive testing with over 4,000 additional questions!

15.4 PRACTICE SIMULATION

| | Financial Accounting and Reporting (FAR) Testlet 4 of 5 Simulation Testlet | Time Remaining 1 hour 45 minutes | Copy | Paste | Calculator | Sheet | Help | Unsplit | Split Horiz | Split Vert | Done |

Directions | Situation | Valuation | Reported Amount | Purchase Accounting | Communication | Research/Authoritative Literature | Resources

1. Directions

In the following simulation, you will be asked to complete various tasks. You may use the content in the **Information Tabs** to complete the tasks in the **Work Tabs**.

Information Tabs:

| Directions | Resources |

FIG 1

- Go through each of the **Information Tabs** to familiarize yourself with the simulation content
- The **Resources** tab will contain information, including formulas and definitions, that may help you to complete the tasks
- Your simulation may have more **Information Tabs** than those shown in Fig. 1

Work Tabs:

| SysTrust | Engagement Letter | Authoritative Sources | Communication |

FIG. 2

- **Work Tabs**, to the right of **Information Tabs**, contain the tasks for you to complete
- **Work Tabs** contain directions for completing each task - be sure to read these directions carefully
- The tab names in Fig. 2 are for illustration only - yours may differ
- Once you complete any part of a task, the pencil for that tab will be shaded (see **Communication** in Fig. 2)
- The shaded pencil does **NOT** indicate that you have completed the entire task
- You must complete all of the tasks in the **Work Tabs** to receive full credit

Research/Authoritative Literature Tab:

| Research/Authoritative Literature |

FIG. 3

- This tab contains both the Research task and the Authoritative Literature
- Detailed instructions for completing the Research task, and for using the Authoritative Literature, appear on this tab
- You may use the Authoritative Literature as a resource for completing other tasks

NOTE: If you believe you have encountered a software malfunction, report it to the test center staff immediately.

2. Situation

Presented below are selected amounts from the separate unconsolidated financial statements of Poe Corp. and its 90%-owned subsidiary, Shaw Co., at December 31, Year 2. Additional information follows:

	Poe	Shaw
Selected income statement amounts		
Sales	$710,000	$530,000
Cost of goods sold	490,000	370,000
Gain on sale of equipment		21,000
Earnings from investment in subsidiary	61,000	
Interest expense		16,000
Depreciation	25,000	20,000
Selected balance sheet amounts		
Cash	$ 50,000	$ 15,000
Inventories	229,000	150,000
Equipment	440,000	360,000
Accumulated depreciation	(200,000)	(120,000)
Investment in Shaw	189,000	
Investment in bonds	100,000	
Discount on bonds	(9,000)	
Bonds payable		(200,000)
Common stock	(100,000)	(10,000)
Additional paid-in capital	(250,000)	(40,000)
Retained earnings	(402,000)	(140,000)
Selected statement of retained earnings amounts		
Beginning balance, December 31, Year 1	$272,000	$100,000
Net income	210,000	70,000
Dividends paid	80,000	30,000

Additional information

- On January 2, Year 2, Poe Corp. purchased 90% of Shaw Co.'s 100,000 outstanding common shares for cash of $155,000. On that date, Shaw's equity accounts equaled $150,000, and the fair values of Shaw's assets and liabilities equaled their carrying amounts.
- On September 4, Year 2, Shaw paid cash dividends of $30,000.
- On December 31, Year 2, Poe recorded its equity in Shaw's earnings.

3. Valuation

This question is presented in a spreadsheet format that requires you to fill in the correct responses in the shaded cells provided.

For each of the following, determine its dollar effect on Year 2 consolidated income before considering the minority interest. Ignore income tax considerations.

Transaction	Amount
1. On January 3, Year 2, Shaw sold equipment with an original cost of $30,000 and a carrying amount of $15,000 to Poe for $36,000. The equipment had a remaining life of 3 years and was depreciated using the straight-line method by both companies.	
2. During Year 2, Shaw sold merchandise to Poe for $60,000, which included a profit of $20,000. At December 31, Year 2, half of this merchandise remained in Poe's inventory.	
3. On December 31, Year 2, Poe paid $91,000 to purchase 50% of the outstanding bonds issued by Shaw. The bonds mature on December 31, Year 8, and were originally issued at their face amount. The bonds pay interest annually on December 31 of each year, and the interest was paid to the prior investor immediately before Poe's purchase of the bonds.	
4. Poe recognized goodwill on January 2, Year 2. It determined on December 31, Year 2, that goodwill was not impaired.	

4. Reported Amount

This set of questions has a matching format. Select the best match for each numbered item from the terms in the drop-down list and write its letter in the column provided. Each answer choice may be used once, more than once, or not at all.

The items in the accounts column may or may not be included in the consolidated financial statements. The list of choices contains descriptions of amounts to be reported in the consolidated financial statements for the year ended December 31, Year 2. Consider all the transactions stated in the VALUATION tab in determining your answers. Ignore income tax considerations.

Accounts	Answers	Choices
1. Cash		A) Sum of amounts on Poe's and Shaw's separate unconsolidated financial statements
2. Equipment		
3. Investment in subsidiary		B) Less than the sum of amounts on Poe's and Shaw's separate unconsolidated financial statements but not the same as the amount on either
4. Bonds payable		
5. Noncontrolling Interest		
6. Common stock		
7. Beginning retained earnings		C) Same as amount for Poe only
8. Dividends paid		D) Same as amount for Shaw only
9. Gain on retirement of bonds		E) Eliminated entirely in consolidation
10. Cost of goods sold		F) Shown in consolidated financial statements but not in separate unconsolidated financial statements
11. Interest expense		
12. Depreciation expense		G) Neither in consolidated nor in separate unconsolidated financial statements

5. Purchase Accounting

This question is presented in a check-the-box format that requires you to select the correct responses from a given list.

Is the statement consistent with purchase accounting, or are the facts insufficient to make this determination?

Item	Yes	No	Facts Insufficient
1. When the investment cost is lower than the carrying amount of the acquired entity's net assets, the acquired entity's assets will be recorded on the books of the combined entity at less than their original carrying amounts.			
2. A combination is finalized within 2 years after the combination plan was initiated.			
3. Results of operations for the year of combination include the combined results of the separate entities for the entire year.			
4. Costs of furnishing information to shareholders related to effecting the business combination are subtracted directly from the combined entity's retained earnings.			
5. When the investment cost is higher than the fair value of the target entity's net assets, goodwill and goodwill amortization may appear in the consolidated financial statements.			

6. Communication

Prepare a memo to Poe Corp. outlining the reasons for preparing consolidated financial statements, the general procedures required, and when consolidation is not necessary. Type your communication in your word processor program and print out the copy in a memorandum-style format.

REMINDER: Your response will be graded for both technical content and writing skills. Technical content will be evaluated for information that is helpful to the intended reader and clearly relevant to the issue. Writing skills will be evaluated for development, organization, and the appropriate expression of ideas in professional correspondence. Use a standard business memo or letter format with a clear beginning, middle, and end. Do not convey information in the form of a table, bullet point list, or other abbreviated presentation.

> To: Poe Corp.
> From: CPA
> Subject: Consolidated financial statements

7. Research/Authoritative Literature

See page 12 in the Introduction of this book for a detailed explanation of the AICPA's new Research/Authoritative Literature work tab as well as a screenshot of how the tab will actually look on your exam.

Research and cite the specific paragraph in the FASB current text or original pronouncements that details the significant differences between SFAS 141, *Business Combinations*, and APB Opinion 16, *Business Combinations*, the pronouncement that SFAS 141 superseded.

Unofficial Answers

3. Valuation (4 Gradable Items)

1. $14,000. The interentity profit to be eliminated is $21,000 ($36,000 sales price – $15,000 carrying amount). Accordingly, the excess depreciation to be eliminated is $7,000 ($21,000 ÷ 3 years). The net adjustment to consolidated net income before considering minority interest and taxes is therefore $14,000 ($21,000 – $7,000).

2. $10,000. The profit on the interentity sale of inventory should be eliminated to the extent that it is unrealized. Thus, the net adjustment to consolidated net income before considering minority interest and taxes is $10,000 ($20,000 profit × 50% inventory still held by Poe).

3. $9,000. This transaction is a retirement of debt by the consolidated entity that resulted in a $9,000 gain before taxes and before considering the minority interest ($100,000 carrying amount on Shaw's books – $91,000 paid by Poe).

4. $0. Poe acquired a 90% interest in Shaw. Hence, goodwill was $20,000 [$155,000 price – ($150,000 balance in equity accounts × 90%)]. However, no Year 2 amortization or impairment loss is recognized. Under SFAS 142, goodwill is not amortized. Moreover, the entity determined at year-end that goodwill was not impaired.

4. Reported Amount (12 Gradable Items)

1.   <u>A) – Sum of amounts on Poe's and Shaw's separate unconsolidated financial statements</u>. Eliminating the effects of interentity transactions does not change the sum of the cash balances in the separate statements.

2.   <u>B) – Less than the sum of amounts on Poe's and Shaw's separate unconsolidated financial statements but not the same as the amount on either</u>. The equipment sold to Poe by Shaw is carried on Poe's books at $24,000 [$36,000 – ($36,000 ÷ 3 years) depreciation]. On the consolidated books, it should be reported at $10,000 ([$15,000 – ($15,000 ÷ 3 years) depreciation]. The balance in the equipment account on the consolidated balance sheet should equal the sum of the balances on the separate books of Poe and Shaw, minus the underappreciated profit on the interentity sale.

3.   <u>E) – Eliminated entirely in consolidation</u>. In a consolidation, interentity balances and transactions are eliminated to avoid double counting. The investment in the subsidiary is eliminated against the equity accounts (net assets) of the subsidiary.

4.   <u>B) – Less than the sum of amounts on Poe's and Shaw's separate unconsolidated financial statements but not the same as the amount on either</u>. Shaw issued $200,000 of bonds at par, and Poe purchased 50% or $100,000 of these bonds at a $9,000 discount. On the consolidated books, this transaction resulted in an extinguishment of part of the debt and a gain. After eliminating the reciprocal bonds payable and receivable balances, the discount, and the discount amortization, the consolidated entity should report bonds payable of $100,000, an amount that is less than the $200,000 carrying amount on Shaw's books and greater than the $91,000 (plus discount amortization) on Poe's books.

5.   <u>F) – Shown in consolidated financial statements but not in separate unconsolidated financial statements</u>. Consolidation is required when a parent owns a majority of voting interest in a subsidiary unless control does not rest with the majority owner. Thus, Poe must consolidate Shaw and report the 10% minority interest. The consolidation process results in a set of statements for the economic entity that must reflect the interest of noncontrolling parties (the minority interest) in the net assets of the subsidiary. Separate unconsolidated statements are presented for a single legal entity, not a combination of entities. Hence, no minority interest is shown.

6.   <u>C) – Same as the amount for Poe only</u>. In a business combination, the consolidated common stock balance equals that of the parent. Because the combination is treated as an acquisition of net assets only, the equity balances of the acquired entity are excluded from the consolidated statements.

7.   <u>C) – Same as the amount for Poe only</u>. In a business combination, the consolidated retained earnings balance equals that of the parent. Because the combination is treated as an acquisition of net assets only, the equity balances of the acquired entity are excluded from the consolidated statements.

8.   <u>C) – Same as the amount for Poe only</u>. In a business combination, the consolidated retained earnings balance equals that of the parent. Because the combination is treated as an acquisition of net assets only, the equity balances of the acquired entity are excluded from the consolidated statements.

9.   <u>F) – Shown in consolidated financial statements but not in separate unconsolidated financial statements</u>. The purchase of Shaw's bonds by Poe effectively retired the bonds from the consolidated perspective. The debt represented by those bonds is now owed to another member of the consolidated group. Thus, the gain on this constructive retirement should be reported in the consolidated statements. In their separate statements, Shaw and Poe will continue to recognize the bond payable and receivable, respectively, and will not report the gain.

10.   <u>B) – Less than the sum of amounts on Poe's and Shaw's separate unconsolidated financial statements but not the same as the amount on either</u>. The effects of Shaw's sale of merchandise to Poe must be eliminated to the extent that Poe's cost of goods sold includes the price paid to Shaw. An elimination is also required to the extent that Shaw's cost of goods sold includes the cost of merchandise not yet sold outside the consolidated group. Hence, consolidated cost of goods sold equals the separate amounts reported for Poe and Shaw, minus the amounts eliminated.

11.   <u>D) – Same as amount for Shaw only</u>. Poe recognized no interest expense. Moreover, Shaw's interest expense must have equaled the interest paid to the outside investor. Poe earned no interest on the Shaw bonds because it purchased half the bonds on the balance sheet date. For the same reason, no discount amortization was recorded. Accordingly, no eliminating entry is needed for interest paid or payable to Poe. Consolidated interest expenses therefore equals the amount reported by Shaw.

12.   <u>B) – Less than the sum of amounts on Poe's and Shaw's separate unconsolidated financial statements but not the same as the amount on either</u>. Depreciation for the consolidated entity is the sum of the separate amounts reported by Poe and Shaw, minus the amount attributable to the profit on the sale of equipment by Shaw to Poe.

5. Purchase Accounting (5 Gradable Items)

1. <u>C) – Facts insufficient</u>. In a business combination, the assets acquired and liabilities assumed are assigned amounts based on their fair values at the acquisition date. If the cost of the acquired net assets exceeds the net amount assigned, goodwill is recognized for the difference. If the net amount assigned exceeds the cost, however, the excess is allocated proportionately to reduce the amounts assignable to certain acquired assets (excluding financial assets not accounted for using the equity method, assets to be sold, deferred tax assets, prepaid assets of postretirement benefit plans, and other noncurrent assets). Any unallocated amount of the excess over cost is recorded as an extraordinary gain. Consequently, it cannot be determined whether the acquired assets will be assigned amounts equal to, less than, or greater than their carrying amounts on the books of the acquired entity. The nature of the assets and their fair values must be known. For example, if the amounts assigned to assets acquired exceed their carrying amounts on the acquired entity's books, but the assets are not the types to which the excess over cost is allocated, the acquired assets may be recorded at amounts in excess of their carrying amounts on the books of the acquired entity.

2. <u>A) – Yes</u>. The purchase method is used regardless of the time between the initiation and consummation of the combination.

3. <u>B) – No</u>. Under the purchase method, income of the acquiring entity includes its share of the earnings of the acquired entity after acquisition (cash flows are also consolidated after acquisition). Under ARB 51, when a subsidiary is purchased, the preferred method of presenting the results of operations is to include the subsidiary's operations in consolidated income as though it had been acquired at the beginning of the year, and to subtract the preacquisition earnings from the total earnings. The minority interest income for the entire year is also subtracted. Thus, the results of operations for the year of combination do not equal the combined results for the entire year unless the acquisition date is the first day of the fiscal year.

4. <u>B) – No</u>. The direct costs of the combination are capitalized as part of the cost of the entity acquired.

5. <u>B) – No</u>. Goodwill is the excess of the cost of an acquired entity over the net of the amounts (fair values) assigned to the assets acquired and liabilities assumed. Goodwill is recognized as an asset but is not amortized. However, it is tested for impairment.

6. Communication (5 Gradable Items; for grading instructions, please refer to page 12.)

> To: Poe Corp.
> From: CPA
> Subject: Consolidated financial statements

Consolidated operating results, cash flows, and financial position are prepared as if a parent and its subsidiaries are a single entity. This procedure reflects the operating results, financial status, and central management ties that bind the entities into a single economic and financial unit. As a result, the information is representationally faithful and without the biases caused by exclusions or netting of data. Also, it is comparable with information about other economic entities regardless of the legal framework of the combining entities. Thus, the information is relevant and complete for investors and other parties basing decisions on the data.

ARB 51 gives a description of the general consolidated procedures. Parent-subsidiary balances and transactions, such as open account balances (receivables and payables), the parent's investment in the subsidiary, sales and purchases, interest, holdings of securities, dividends, etc., are eliminated in full even if a minority interest exists. Profits and losses on transactions within the consolidated entity are completely eliminated, but the procedure varies with the direction of the sale. The amount of the minority interest recognized at the date of the combination equals a proportionate share of the subsidiary's carrying amount. Subsequently, the minority interest is adjusted for its share of the subsidiary's income and dividends. On consolidating worksheets, an adjustment to minority interest is also needed for unrealized profits and losses on sales of inventory and fixed assets to the parent and purchases of combining entity debt. In the income statement, the minority interest's adjusted share of the subsidiary's income is usually subtracted in arriving at consolidated income. The parent's investment in subsidiary account and its proportionate share of the subsidiary's equity accounts, which include retained earnings, are eliminated in a consolidation. The remainder of the subsidiary's equity is reported separately as the minority interest. The consolidated net income equals the parent's net income because the parent should account for the investment using the equity method. In the consolidated balance sheet, the equity section should reflect the parent's equity section. The placement of the minority interest is in dispute, although SFAC 6 indicates a preference for treating it as part of equity.

However, consolidation is not required if control does not rest with the majority owner, for example, because the subsidiary is in bankruptcy or in legal reorganization, or is subject to foreign exchange restrictions or other government-imposed restrictions that preclude exercise of control (ARB 51 as amended by SFAS 94 and SFAS 144).

7. Research/Authoritative Literature (1 Gradable Item)

Answer: FAS 141, Summary

FAS 141 – *Business Combinations*
Differences between This Statement and Opinion 16

This statement changes the accounting for business combinations in Opinion 16 in the following significant respects:

● This statement requires that all business combinations be accounted for by a single method – the purchase method.

● In contrast to Opinion 16, which required separate recognition of intangible assets that can be identified and named, this statement requires that they be recognized as assets apart from goodwill if they meet one of two criteria – the contractual-legal criterion or the separability criterion. To assist in identifying acquired intangible assets, this statement also provides an illustrative list of intangible assets that meet either of those criteria.

● In addition to the disclosure requirements in Opinion 16, this statement requires disclosure of the primary reasons for a business combination and the allocation of the purchase price paid to the assets acquired and liabilities assumed by major balance sheet caption. When the amounts of goodwill and intangible assets acquired are significant in relation to the purchase price paid, disclosure of other information about those assets is required, such as the amount of goodwill by reportable segment and the amount of the purchase price assigned to each major intangible asset class.

Scoring Schedule

	Correct Responses		Gradable Items		Weights		
Tab 3	_____	÷	4	×	20%	=	_____
Tab 4	_____	÷	12	×	20%	=	_____
Tab 5	_____	÷	5	×	15%	=	_____
Tab 6	_____	÷	5	×	30%	=	_____
Tab 7	_____	÷	1	×	15%	=	_____

_____
(Your Score)

Use Gleim's **CPA Gleim Online** to practice more simulations in a realistic environment.

STUDY UNIT SIXTEEN
DERIVATIVES, HEDGING, AND OTHER TOPICS

(21 pages of outline)

This is the last study unit concerning financial accounting for nongovernmental for-profit entities. Foreign currency transactions and translation and financial statement analysis are topics explicitly listed in the AICPA's CSO. Comprehensive bases of accounting other than GAAP also are included in the CSO. Only the price-level basis is covered by a FASB Statement.

16.1 DERIVATIVES AND HEDGING

General Financial Market Terms

1. The following are common financial market terms:

    a. A **call option** is the right to purchase an asset at a fixed price (i.e., the exercise price) on or before a future date (i.e., expiration date).

    b. A **derivative** is an investment transaction in which the buyer purchases the right to a potential gain with a commitment for a potential loss. It is a bet on whether the value of something will go up or down. The purpose is either to speculate (incur risk) or to hedge (avoid risk). A derivative is an unperformed contract that results in cash flow between two counterparties based on the change in some other indicator of value.

    c. **Embedded** means that a derivative is contained within either (1) another derivative or (2) a financial instrument. For example, a mortgage has an embedded option. The mortgagor generally has the option to refinance the mortgage if interest rates decrease.

    d. The **exercise or strike price** is the agreed upon price of exchange in an options contract.

    e. The **expiration date** is the date when the option may no longer be exercised.

    f. A **put option** is the right to sell an asset at a fixed price (i.e., the exercise price) on or before a future date (i.e., expiration date).

    g. An **underlying asset** is the specified asset in an options contract. In practice, it is referred to simply as the "underlying."

Formal Definition of a Derivative

2. SFAS 133, *Accounting for Derivative Instruments and Hedging Activities*, **formally** defines a **derivative** as a financial instrument or other contract with the following characteristics:

    a. A derivative, including one **embedded** in another contract, has at least one **underlying** (interest rate, currency exchange rate, stock index, price of a specific financial instrument, etc.) and at least one **notional amount** (number of units specified in the contract) or payment provision, or both.

    b. No **initial net investment**, or one smaller than that necessary for contracts with similar responses to the market, is required.

    c.   A derivative's terms require or permit net settlement or provide for the equivalent.

          1)   **Net settlement** means that the derivative can be readily settled with only a net delivery of assets. Thus, neither party need deliver (a) an asset associated with its underlying or (b) an asset that has a principal, stated amount, etc., equal to the notional amount (possibly adjusted for discount or premium)

                a)   If one party must deliver such an asset, the net settlement criterion is still met if (1) a **market mechanism** exists to facilitate net settlement, (2) the asset is readily convertible to cash, or (3) it is a derivative.

Hedging

    3.   Hedging is not defined in SFAS 133. However, *The CPA Letter* (October 2000) defines a hedge as "a defensive strategy designed to protect an entity against the risk of adverse price or interest-rate movements on certain of its assets, liabilities, or anticipated transactions. A hedge is used to avoid or reduce risks by creating a relationship by which losses on certain positions are expected to be counterbalanced in whole or in part by gains on separate positions in another market."

        a.   The purchase or sale of a derivative or other instrument is a hedge if it is **expected to neutralize the risk** of (1) a recognized asset or liability, (2) an unrecognized firm commitment, or (3) a forecasted transaction.

          1)   For example, a flour company buys and uses wheat in its product. It may wish to guard against increases in wheat costs when it has committed to sell at a price related to the current cost of wheat. If so, the company will purchase wheat futures contracts that will result in gains if the price of wheat increases (offsetting the actual increased costs).

Typical Derivatives

    4.   The following are examples of derivative instruments:

        a.   A **call option** allows the purchaser to benefit from an increase in price of the underlying. The purchaser pays a premium for the opportunity to benefit from the appreciation in the underlying.

          1)   An **American call option** allows the holder of the option to exercise the option at any date prior to the expiration date.

          2)   A **European call option** permits the holder of the option to exercise the option only on the expiration date.

        b.   A **put option** allows the purchaser to benefit from a decrease in the price of the underlying. The gain is the excess of the exercise price over the market price. The purchaser pays a premium for the opportunity to benefit from the depreciation in the underlying.

          1)   An **American put option** allows the holder of the option to exercise the option at any date prior to the expiration date.

          2)   A **European put option** permits the holder of the option to exercise the option only on the expiration date.

        c.   A **forward contract** is an agreement for the purchase and sale of a stated amount of a commodity, foreign currency, or financial instrument at a stated price. Delivery or settlement is at a stated future date.

          1)   Forward contracts are usually specifically negotiated agreements and are not traded on regulated exchanges. Accordingly, the parties are subject to **default risk** (i.e., that the other party will not perform).

d. A **futures contract** is a forward-based agreement to make or receive delivery or make a cash settlement that involves a specified quantity of a commodity, foreign currency, or financial instrument during a specified time interval.

1) Futures contracts are usually standardized and exchange traded. They are therefore less risky than forward contracts.

2) Another reason for their lesser risk is that they are **marked to market** daily; that is, money must be paid daily to cover any losses as they occur. Thus, the default risk for a futures contract is much less than for a forward contract.

3) Furthermore, unlike forward contracts, futures contracts rarely result in actual delivery. The parties customarily make a **net settlement in cash** on the expiration date.

e. An **interest rate swap** is an exchange of one party's interest payments based on a **fixed rate** for another party's interest payments based on a **variable rate**. The maturity amount may or may not be swapped. Moreover, most interest rate swaps permit **net settlement** because they do not require delivery of interest-bearing assets with a principal equal to the contracted amount.

1) An interest rate swap is appropriate when one counterparty prefers the payment pattern of the other. For example, a firm with **fixed-rate** debt may have revenues that vary with interest rates. It may prefer variable-rate debt so that **its debt service burden will correlate directly with its revenues**.

f. Certain **financial instruments**, e.g., accounts receivable, notes receivable, bonds, preferred stock, and common stock, are not derivatives. However, any of these instruments may be an underlying of a derivative.

Standards for Derivatives and Hedging

5. SFAS 133 (as amended) applies to all entities. It establishes four principles:

a. Derivatives should be recognized as **assets or liabilities**.

b. **Fair value** is the only relevant measure for derivatives. Moreover, adjustments to the carrying amount of a **hedged item** should reflect any changes in its fair value while the hedge is in effect that are attributable to the hedged risk.

1) Derivatives usually have **no initial fair value** but result in positive or negative fair value as the price of the underlying changes.

c. Only items that are assets and liabilities should be recognized as such.

d. **Designated hedged items** should receive special accounting treatment only if they meet qualifying criteria. An example is the likelihood of effectiveness of the hedge in producing offsetting **fair value or cash flow changes** during the term of the hedge for the risk being hedged.

1) At all times, the hedge is expected to be **highly effective**. Effectiveness is the percentage of the gain or loss on the hedged item that is offset by the hedging instrument's loss or gain. Thus, these amounts should be highly correlated.

a) An **assessment of hedge effectiveness** should be made when financial statements or earnings are reported and at least every three months.

Accounting for Derivatives

6. The accounting for changes in fair value of a derivative depends on (a) the **reasons for holding it**, (b) whether the entity has elected to **designate** it as part of a hedging relationship, and (c) whether it meets the **qualifying criteria** for the particular accounting.

a. All or part of a derivative may be designated as a hedging instrument. The proportion must be expressed as a **percentage of the entire derivative**.

     b.   Most qualifying criteria are not reproduced here because they are numerous and complex. For example, they relate to (1) effectiveness; (2) the formal documentation of the hedging relationship; and (3) requirements for particular hedging instruments, hedged items, and transactions.

        1)   An entity that elects hedge accounting must, among other things, formally determine at the **hedge's inception** the methods (consistent with its risk management strategy) for determining the **effectiveness and ineffectiveness** of the hedge. Thus, an entity must specify whether all of the gain or loss on the hedging instrument will be included in the assessment of effectiveness.

            a)   For example, an entity may exclude all or part of the **time value** from the assessment of effectiveness.

        2)   **Special hedge accounting** is not needed or permitted when the hedged item (or forecasted transaction) is (or will be) remeasured, with changes in fair value attributable to the hedged risk recognized in current earnings. An example of such a hedged item is a **trading security**.

7.   **Gains and losses** from changes in the **fair value** of a derivative, whether or not it is designated and qualifies as a hedging instrument, are **included in earnings** in the period of change. **Exceptions** are certain gains and losses on a derivative designated as a (a) cash flow hedge, (b) foreign currency cash flow hedge, or (c) hedge of a net investment in a foreign operation.

Types of Hedges

8.   A **fair value hedge** hedges **changes in the fair value** of a **recognized asset or liability** or of an **unrecognized firm commitment** with fixed cash flows. These changes must be attributable to a specified risk.

     a.   A firm commitment is an agreement with an unrelated party that is binding on both parties and is usually legally enforceable. It specifies all significant terms, and its performance is probable because of the negative consequences of nonperformance.

9.   A **cash flow hedge** hedges the **variability in cash flows** of a **recognized asset or liability** or of a **forecasted transaction** that is attributable to a specified risk.

     a.   A forecasted transaction is probable, i.e., expected to occur, although no firm commitment exists. It does not (1) confer current rights to future benefits or (2) impose a current obligation for future sacrifices of resources because no transaction or event has occurred. When such a transaction or event occurs, it will be at the prevailing market price.

10.   Certain **foreign currency exposures** also may qualify for hedge accounting.

Fair Value Hedges

11.   Examples of hedged items are (a) fixed rate investments and debt and (b) firm commitments to purchase or sell assets or incur liabilities.

12.   The change in fair value of the **hedged item** (the gain or loss) attributable to the risk being hedged is an adjustment to the carrying amount of the item. It is recognized currently in **earnings**.

     a.   This rule applies even if changes in fair value of the hedged item are normally reported in **other comprehensive income (OCI)**. An example is a hedge of an **available-for-sale security**.

     b.   When the hedged item is a **previously unrecognized firm commitment**, the recognition of the gain or loss on the firm commitment includes debiting an asset or crediting a liability, respectively. Accordingly, the phrase "asset and liability" used in SFAS 133 includes a firm commitment.

     c.   The change in fair value of the **hedging instrument** (the loss or gain) also is recognized currently in **earnings**.

13. SFAS 133 permits a **fair value hedge** of certain types of **foreign currency exposures**. If the hedged item is measured in a foreign currency, an entity may designate a fair value hedge of an **unrecognized firm commitment** or a **recognized asset or liability** (including an available-for-sale security).

   a. A **derivative** or a **nonderivative** that may result in a **foreign currency transaction gain or loss** may hedge the changes in fair value of an **unrecognized firm commitment** that are attributable to exchange rates.

   b. A **derivative (not a nonderivative)** may hedge the changes in fair value of a **recognized asset or liability** for which a **foreign currency transaction gain or loss** is recognized.

Cash Flow Hedges

14. Examples are (a) all or certain interest payments on variable rate debt (a recognized liability) or (b) an anticipated purchase or sale (a forecasted transaction).

15. The earnings effect of the hedged item may not occur until a future period. Thus, the **effective** portion of the loss or gain on the hedging instrument is reported in **OCI**. It will be recognized in earnings (**reclassified** from OCI) when the hedged item affects earnings.

   a. The ineffective portion is recognized in earnings immediately.

   b. The entity's specified **risk management strategy** may exclude part of the gain or loss (or related cash flows) from the assessment of effectiveness. These excluded amounts are recognized currently in earnings.

16. A **nonderivative** may **not** hedge a **foreign currency cash flow hedge**. However, a derivative may hedge the foreign currency exposure to variability in the functional-currency-equivalent cash flows of (a) a **forecasted transaction**, (b) a **recognized asset or liability**, (c) an **unrecognized firm commitment**, or (d) a **forecasted intraentity transaction** (e.g., a forecasted sale to a foreign subsidiary).

17. A derivative may hedge the foreign currency exposure of a **net investment in a foreign operation**. Gains and losses on the derivative are reported in the **cumulative translation adjustment in OCI** to the extent the hedge is effective.

   a. If the hedging instrument is a **nonderivative**, the **foreign currency transaction gain or loss** on the instrument is treated in the same manner. [Recall that a nonderivative also may hedge the foreign currency exposure of an unrecognized firm commitment (a fair value hedge).]

   b. SFAS 52, *Foreign Currency Translation*, prescribes accounting rules (other than for hedging, for (1) translation (including remeasurement), (2) transaction gains and losses, and (3) a net investment in a foreign investment. See Subunit 16.2.

Embedded Derivatives

18. A common example is the conversion feature of convertible debt. It is a call option on the issuer's stock. Embedded derivatives must be **accounted for separately** from the host if

   a. The economic characteristics and risks of the embedded derivative are **not clearly and closely related** to the economic characteristics of the host;

   b. The hybrid instrument is **not remeasured at fair value** under otherwise applicable GAAP, with changes in fair value reported in earnings; and

   c. A freestanding instrument with the same terms as the embedded derivative would be **subject to SFAS 133**.

19. If an embedded derivative is accounted for separately, the **host contract** is accounted for based on the accounting standards that apply to instruments of its type. The **separated derivative** should be accounted for under SFAS 133.

   a. If the embedded derivative to be separated is **not reliably identifiable and measurable**, the entire contract must be measured at **fair value**, with gains and losses recognized in **earnings**.

      1) It may not be designated as a hedging instrument because nonderivatives usually do not qualify as hedging instruments.

Not-for-Profit Organizations

20. For a not-for-profit organization or other entity not reporting earnings separately, the change in fair value of hedging instruments and nonhedging derivatives is a **change in net assets** (unless the hedge is of a foreign currency exposure of a net investment in a foreign operation).

   a. In a **fair value hedge**, the change in fair value of the **hedged item** attributable to the risk being hedged is recognized as a change in net assets.

   b. These entities may **not** use cash flow hedge accounting.

Examples of Hedging Transactions

EXAMPLE

Fair value hedge of a recognized asset. A company wishes to hedge the fair value of its investment in an inventory of Commodity A. It sells futures contracts on August 1, Year 1, for delivery on February 1, Year 2, the date on which it intends to sell the inventory. The following information is available about spot and futures prices and estimates of changes in the fair value of the inventory (changes in spot rates adjusted for transportation costs, storage costs, etc.):

	Spot Rate	Futures Rate for February 1 Delivery	Change in Fair Value of Inventory
August 1, Year 1	$.51	$.53	
December 31, Year 1	.49	.51	$(21,000)
February 1, Year 2	.52	.52	32,000

The company sold futures contracts for one million pounds of Commodity A at $.53 per pound. Its inventory had an average cost of $.38 per pound, and it sold the entire inventory of Commodity A on February 1, Year 2, at the spot rate of $.52 per pound. The company also bought offsetting February Year 2 futures contracts on February 1, Year 2, for one million pounds of Commodity A at $.52 per pound. This transaction closed out its futures position. The following journal entries should be made (ignoring the margin deposit with the broker):

August 1, Year 1
The fair value of the futures contracts is zero at the inception date. Thus, no entry is made to record their fair value.

December 31, Year 1

Loss	$21,000	
Inventory -- Commodity A		$21,000

(The company estimates a loss of $21,000.)

Receivable from/liability to broker	$20,000	
Gain on the hedge		$20,000

The gain on the futures contract is $20,000 [1,000,000 pounds × ($.53 futures rate at August 1, Year 1 – $.51 futures rate at December 31, Year 1, for February 1, Year 2, delivery)].

<u>February 1, Year 2</u>

Inventory -- Commodity A	$32,000	
Gain		$32,000

(The company estimates a gain of $32,000.)

Loss on the hedge	$10,000	
Receivable from/liability to broker		$10,000

The loss on the futures contracts is $10,000 [1,000,000 pounds × ($.52 futures rate at February 1, Year 2 – $.51 futures rate at December 31, Year 1, for February 1, Year 2, delivery)].

Cash	$10,000	
Receivable from/liability to broker		$10,000

(This entry records settlement of the futures contracts.)

Accounts receivable	$520,000	
Cost of goods sold	391,000	
Sales		$520,000
Inventory -- Commodity A		391,000

The revenue from the sale equaled $520,000 (1,000,000 pounds × $.52 spot rate). The inventory equaled $391,000 [(1,000,000 pounds × $.38 average cost) – $21,000 fair value loss on December 31, Year 1 + $32,000 fair value gain on February 1, Year 2].

EXAMPLE

Cash flow hedge of a forecasted transaction. At January 2, Year 1, a company determines that it will need to purchase 100,000 pounds of Commodity B in June Year 1. The purchase is expected to be at the spot rate. To hedge this forecasted transaction, the company agrees to purchase futures contracts for 100,000 pounds of Commodity B at the June Year 1 futures price of $3.05 per pound. Hedge effectiveness will be determined by comparing the total change in the fair value of the futures contracts with the changes in the cash flows of the anticipated purchase. In June, the company buys 100,000 pounds of Commodity B at the spot rate of $3.20 per pound. Ignoring the margin deposit for the futures contracts, the following are the journal entries for this transaction:

<u>January Year 1</u>

Because the margin deposit is ignored in this problem, no journal entry is made. The futures contract is not recorded because, at its inception, its fair value is zero.

<u>June Year 1</u>

Inventory -- Commodity B	$320,000	
Cash		$320,000

The price of the quantity purchased was $320,000 (100,000 pounds × $3.20 spot rate).

Futures contracts	$15,000	
Other comprehensive income		$15,000

The gain, which will subsequently be reclassified into earnings when the inventory is sold, equals $15,000 [100,000 pounds × $3.20 spot rate – $3.05 futures contract rate)].

Cash	$15,000	
Futures contracts		$15,000

(This entry records the net cash settlement. In practice, futures contracts are settled daily.)

EXAMPLE

Hedge of a net investment in a foreign operation. Parent, Inc., a U.S. company, has a net investment in its Xenadian subsidiary, Subco. The amount is 100 million foreign currency units (FCU), the subsidiary's functional currency. At November 1, Year 1, Parent sells a forward exchange contract for the delivery of 100 million FCU on February 1, Year 2. This contract is designated as a hedge of the net investment in Subco. The contract rate equals the forward rate at November 1, Year 1, of $1.15 per FCU. On that date, the spot rate is $1.17 per FCU. Parent records the premium on the forward contract [100,000,000 FCU × ($1.17 – $1.15) = $2,000,000] as a translation adjustment. Moreover, Parent records the change in fair value of the forward contract at fair value in its balance sheet. The effective portion of the hedge (100% in this case) is recorded in other comprehensive income (OCI). Parent also translates its net investment in Subco into U.S. dollars, and it reports the effects of changes in exchange rates as a cumulative translation adjustment in OCI.

The following table provides information about exchange rates, the forward contract's changes in fair value, and the translation adjustments (change in spot rates × the notional amount). Measuring the fair value of a foreign currency forward contract requires discounting the estimated future cash flows. This estimate of cash flows is based on the changes in the forward rate, not in the spot rate.

	Gain (Loss) – Forward Contract's Change in Fair Value (Discounted)	Gain (Loss) – Cumulative Translation Adjustment	Spot Rates per FCU	Forward Rates per FCU for 2/1 Delivery
November 1, Year 1			$1.17	$1.15
December 31, Year 1	$3,920,000	$(4,000,000)	1.13	1.11
February 1, Year 2	2,080,000	(4,000,000)	1.09	1.09
	$6,000,000	$(8,000,000)		

<u>November 1, Year 1</u>
No entry is made because the forward rate and the contract rate were the same.

<u>December 31, Year 1</u>

Receivable -- forward contract	$3,920,000	
OCI		$3,920,000

The change in fair value of the contract (discounted future cash flows based on changes in the forward rate) is recorded in OCI in the same manner as a translation adjustment. Parent determined that the estimated change in cash flows equaled $4,000,000 [100,000,000 FCU × ($1.15 forward rate at November 1, Year 1 – $1.11 forward rate at December 31, Year 1)]. It then determined that the present value of that change was $3,920,000 (given).

OCI	$4,000,000	
Net investment -- Subco		$4,000,000

The translation adjustment in accordance with SFAS 52 is $4,000,000 [100,000,000 FCU × ($1.17 spot rate at November 1, Year 1 – $1.13 spot rate at December 31, Year 1)].

February 1, Year 2

Receivable -- forward contract	$2,080,000	
OCI		$2,080,000

The total change in fair value of the contract is a gain of $6,000,000 [100,000,000 FCU × ($1.15 forward rate at November 1, Year 1 – $1.09 forward rate at February 1, Year 2)]. Of this amount, $3,920,000 (discounted) was recognized at December 31, Year 1. Thus, to record the fair value of the contract on the settlement date requires an additional credit to OCI of $2,080,000 ($6,000,000 gain – $3,920,000).

OCI	$4,000,000	
Net investment -- Subco		$4,000,000

The translation adjustment is a loss of $4,000,000 [100,000,000 FCU × ($1.13 spot rate at December 31, Year 1 – $1.09 spot rate at February 1, Year 2)].

Cash	$6,000,000	
Receivable -- forward contract		$6,000,000

This entry reflects the net cash settlement of the foreign currency forward contract.

Hedging Summary

21.

	What is it?	SFAS 133 Requirements	Initial Recognition	
			Hedged Asset, Liability, Forecasted Transaction, or Firm Commitment	Hedging Instrument
1. Cash flow hedge	The hedging instrument must offset the variability of the cash flows of a recognized asset or liability or a forecasted transaction. In a foreign currency cash flow hedge, the hedged item also may be an unrecognized firm commitment.	The hedging instrument must be designated as part of a hedge and meet the criteria for a cash flow hedge.	Recognize receivable or payable.	No journal entry is made. The contract has no initial fair value because it is unperformed at its inception.
Journal entry			A/R $XXX Sales $XXX	
2. Fair value hedge	A fair value hedge must offset the changes in fair value of a recognized asset or liability or an unrecognized firm commitment.	The hedging instrument must be designated as part of a hedge and meet the criteria for a fair value hedge.	Recognize receivable or payable.	No journal entry is made. The contract has no initial fair value because it is unperformed at its inception.
Journal entry			A/R $XXX Sales $XXX	

22.

Balance Sheet Date

	Hedged Asset, Liability, Forecasted Transaction, or Firm Commitment	Hedging Instrument		Amortization of Discount/Premium
1. Cash flow hedge	Adjusted to fair value based on the spot rate. Recognized in earnings.	Adjusted to fair value. An asset/liability is recognized on balance sheet. Offsetting entry is an adjustment to other comprehensive income (OCI).		The discount/premium (forward contract) or the time value (option) must be amortized over the life of the derivative. This amount is recognized in earnings and offset by an entry to OCI.

Journal entry	A/R $XXX
	    Gain $XXX
		OCI $XXX
		    Derivative $XXX
				Discount amortization $XXX
				    OCI $XXX

2. Fair value hedge	Adjusted to fair value based on the spot rate. Offsetting entry is gain/loss and is recognized in earnings.	Adjusted to fair value. An asset/liability is recognized on balance sheet. Offsetting entry is gain/loss and is recognized in earnings.		

Journal entry	A/R $XXX
	    Gain $XXX
		Loss on derivative $XXX
		    Derivative $XXX		

23.

Expiration Date

	Hedged Asset, Liability, Forecasted Transaction, or Firm Commitment	Hedging Instrument	OCI Entry	Amortization of Discount/Premium
1. Cash flow hedge	Adjusted to fair value based on the spot rate. Recognized in earnings.	Adjusted to fair value. The offsetting entry is to OCI.	The adjustment of OCI is transferred to earnings. This allows the gain/loss on the hedged item to be offset by the change in fair value of the derivative.	The discount/premium (forward contract) or the time value (option) must be amortized over the life of the derivative. This amount is recognized in earnings and offset by an entry to OCI.

Journal entry	Loss $XXX
	    A/R $XXX
		Derivative $XXX
		    OCI $XXX
			OCI $XXX
			    Gain on derivative $XXX
				Discount amortization $XXX
				    OCI $XXX

2. Fair value hedge	Adjusted to fair value based on the spot rate. Offsetting entry is to gain/loss recognized in earnings.	Adjusted to fair value. Offsetting entry is to gain/loss recognized in earnings.	N/A	N/A

Journal entry	Loss $XXX
	    A/R $XXX
		Derivative $XXX
		    Gain on derivative $XXX		

Stop and review! You have completed the outline for this subunit. Study multiple-choice questions 1 through 5 beginning on page 599.

16.2 FOREIGN CURRENCY ISSUES

1.   SFAS 52, *Foreign Currency Translation* (as amended by SFAS 133), primarily concerns foreign currency transactions and translation.

Definitions

2.   The following are important to understanding this outline:

    a.   The **reporting currency** is the currency in which an entity prepares its financial statements.

    b.   **Foreign currency translation** expresses in the reporting currency amounts that (1) are denominated in (fixed in units of) a different currency or (2) are measured in a different currency. For example, a U.S. entity may have a liability denominated in (fixed in) euros that it measures in U.S. dollars.

        1)   A consolidated entity may consist of separate entities operating in different economic and currency environments. Translation is necessary in these circumstances so that consolidated amounts are presented in one currency.

    c.   The **functional currency** is the currency of the primary economic environment in which the entity operates. Normally, that environment is the one in which it primarily generates and expends cash. For example, the functional currency of a foreign subsidiary is more likely to be the parent's currency if its cash flows directly and currently affect the parent's cash flows.

    d.   **Foreign currency transactions** are fixed in a currency other than the functional currency. They result when an entity

        1)   Buys or sells on credit;

        2)   Borrows or lends;

        3)   Is a party to a derivative instrument; or,

        4)   For other reasons, acquires or disposes of assets, or incurs or settles liabilities, fixed in a foreign currency.

    e.   A **foreign currency** is any currency other than the entity's functional currency.

    f.   The **current exchange rate** is the rate used for currency conversion.

    g.   The **spot rate** is the rate for immediate exchange of currencies.

    h.   The **transaction date** is the time when a transaction is recorded under GAAP.

    i.   A **transaction gain (loss)** results from a change in exchange rates between the functional currency and the currency in which the transaction is denominated. It is the change in functional currency cash flows

        1)   Actually realized on settlement and

        2)   Expected on unsettled transactions.

Foreign Currency Transactions

3.   Transactions are recorded at the spot rate in effect at the transaction date.

4.   Transaction gains and losses are recorded at each balance sheet date and at the date the receivable or payable is settled. The gains or losses ordinarily are included in the determination of net income.

5. When the amount of the functional currency exchangeable for a unit of the currency in which the transaction is fixed increases, a transaction gain or loss is recognized on a receivable or payable, respectively. The opposite occurs when the exchange rate (functional currency to foreign currency) decreases.

EXAMPLE

JRF Corporation, a U.S. entity, purchases and receives radios from Tokyo Corporation, a Japanese entity, on December 15, Year 1. The transaction is fixed in yen and calls for JRF to pay Tokyo 1.5 million yen on January 15, Year 2. The spot rate for yen is $.01015 at the time of the transaction. The spot rate is $.01010 on December 31, Year 1, and $.01020 on January 15, Year 2. JRF records the transaction as follows:

12/15/Year 1	Inventory	$15,225	
	Accounts payable (yen)		$15,225
	(1,500,000 × $0.01015 spot rate)		
12/31/Year 1	Accounts payable (yen)	75	
	Transaction gain		75
	[$15,225 − (1,500,000 × $.01010) = $75 gain]		
1/15/Year 2	Accounts payable (yen)	15,150	
	Transaction loss	150	
	Cash		15,300
	[(1,500,000 × $.01020) − $15,150 = $150 loss]		

Translation

6. The method used to convert foreign currency amounts into units of the reporting currency is the **functional currency translation approach**.

    a. It is appropriate for use in accounting for and reporting the financial results and relationships of foreign subsidiaries in consolidated statements. This method

        1) Identifies the **functional currency** of the entity (the currency of the primary economic environment in which the foreign entity operates),

        2) Measures all elements of the statements in the functional currency, and

        3) Uses a **current exchange rate** for translation from the functional currency to the reporting currency.

    b. **Assets and liabilities** are translated at the exchange rate at fiscal year-end.

    c. **Revenues, expenses, gains, and losses** should be translated at the rates in effect when they were recognized. However, translation at a **weighted-average rate** for the period may be used for these items.

7. **Foreign currency translation adjustments** for a foreign operation that is relatively self-contained and integrated within its environment do not affect cash flows of the reporting entity. They should be excluded from earnings. Accordingly, translation adjustments are reported in **other comprehensive income** (OCI).

    a. When an operation is relatively self-contained, the cash generated and expended by the entity is normally in the currency of the foreign country. That currency is the operation's functional currency.

    b. A pro rata portion of the accumulated translation adjustment attributable to an investment in a foreign entity is recognized in measuring the gain or loss on the sale (FASB Interpretation No. 37).

    c. The functional currency may **change to the reporting currency**. After the change, translation adjustments are not removed from equity. Also, the translated amounts of nonmonetary assets become the accounting bases for those assets.

        1) If the **change is from the reporting currency to a foreign currency**, the adjustment for translation of nonmonetary assets at the date of change is reported in **OCI**.

8. **Remeasurement.** If the books of a foreign entity are maintained in a currency not the functional currency, foreign currency amounts must be remeasured into the functional currency using the **temporal method**. They are then translated into the reporting currency using the **current-rate method**.

   a. **Nonmonetary** balance sheet items and related revenue, expense, gain, and loss amounts are remeasured at the historical rate.

      1) Examples are (a) marketable securities carried at cost; (b) inventories carried at cost; (c) cost of goods sold; (d) prepaid expenses; (e) property, plant, and equipment; (f) depreciation; (g) intangible assets; (h) amortization of intangible assets; (i) deferred income; (j) common stock; and (k) preferred stock carried at its issuance price.

   b. **Monetary** items are remeasured at the current rate.

      1) Examples of monetary items are (a) receivables, (b) payables, (c) inventories carried at market, and (d) marketable securities carried at fair value.

   c. Any **gain or loss** on remeasurement of monetary assets and liabilities is recognized in current earnings as part of continuing operations. This accounting treatment was adopted because gains or losses on remeasurement affect functional currency cash flows.

   d. The financial statements of a foreign entity in a **highly inflationary economy** are remeasured into the reporting currency using the temporal method. Thus, the reporting currency is treated as if it were the functional currency.

      1) A highly inflationary economy has cumulative inflation of approximately **100% or more** over a 3-year period.

9. **Transaction gains and losses** on the following are excluded from earnings and are reported in the same way as translation adjustments, that is, in **OCI**:

   a. Transactions that are designated and effective as economic hedges of a **net investment in a foreign entity**

   b. Transactions that are in effect **long-term investments** in foreign entities to be consolidated, combined, or accounted for by the equity method

Tax Effects

10. **Tax Consequences of Changes in Exchange Rates**

    a. **Interperiod tax allocation** is necessary when transaction gains and losses result in temporary differences. Moreover, the tax consequences of translation adjustments are accounted for in the same way as temporary differences under SFAS 109.

    b. **Intraperiod tax allocation** is also required. For example, taxes related to transaction gains and losses and translation adjustments reported in OCI should be allocated to those items.

Stop and review! You have completed the outline for this subunit. Study multiple-choice questions 6 through 13 beginning on page 601

16.3 PRICE-LEVEL BASIS OF ACCOUNTING

NOTE: Price-level accounting is not explicitly listed in the AICPA's current content specification outline. However, statements prepared in conformity with a comprehensive basis of accounting other than GAAP (OCBOA) are explicitly included in the CSO. The price-level basis is one such comprehensive basis. Furthermore, the AICPA has released questions on price-level accounting.

1. SFAS 89, *Financial Reporting and Changing Prices*, provides for optional supplementary disclosures of current cost and constant-purchasing power amounts.

Measuring Specific Items

2. Certain assets are to be reported at current cost or lower recoverable amount.

    a. **Current cost** should be based on the types of information appropriate to the entity's unique circumstances. This information may be applied to a category of items or single items. Examples are

        1) Externally generated price indexes
        2) Internally generated price indexes
        3) Direct pricing (e.g., current invoice prices or vendor's price lists)

    b. The **recoverable amount** is the current worth of the net amount of cash expected to be recoverable from the use or sale of an asset.

        1) If the recoverable amount of a group of assets is materially and permanently **lower than current cost**, it is used to measure the assets and the expenses associated with their use or sale.

3. **Inventory** is measured at current cost or lower recoverable amount.

    a. The **current cost** is the cost of purchasing the goods or the current cost of the resources needed to produce the goods.

4. **Property, plant, and equipment (PPE)** is measured at the current cost or lower recoverable amount of the remaining service potential.

    a. The **current cost** is the cost of acquiring the same service potential.

    b. Depreciation, depletion, and amortization expense for PPE is measured on the basis of (1) average current cost of the assets' service potential or (2) lower recoverable amount during the period.

5. **Net assets** on a current cost basis equals (a) net assets in the primary statements, (b) adjusted for the difference between historical cost amounts and (c) the current cost or lower recoverable amounts of **inventory and PPE**.

6. **Cost of goods sold (CGS)** is measured at current cost or lower recoverable amount (a) at the date of sale or (b) when resources are committed to a contract.

    a. The practical approach multiplies units sold times average current cost or lower recoverable amount based on beginning and end-of-period amounts [(current cost at beginning of the year + current cost at year-end) ÷ 2].

    b. Given rapid turnover and no allocation of material amounts of depreciation to inventory, CGS may be measured on a **LIFO basis**. However, the effect of any LIFO liquidations must be excluded.

    c. The **FIFO basis** more closely approximates the current cost of ending inventory purchases that are the last to be sold.

7. **Other revenues, expenses (including income tax), gains, and losses** are measured at the same amounts as in the primary statements.

8. The change **(holding gain or loss)** in the current cost or lower recoverable amounts of **inventory and PPE** is the difference between the measures of the assets at their entry dates and their exit dates.

    a. A holding gain or loss is realized through use, sale, or commitment.

    b. An unrealized holding gain or loss is recognized on assets held at the end of the period.

    c. For the current year, the change in current cost amounts is reported before and after eliminating the effects of general inflation.

Current Cost-Constant Purchasing Power Accounting

9. This method measures "current cost or lower recoverable amount in units of currency, each of which has the same general purchasing power."

    a. It adjusts for **changes in specific prices and in the general price level**.
    b. The following is the adjustment ratio:

$$\frac{Current\ price\ level\ index}{Price\ level\ index\ when\ item\ was\ recognized}$$

Historical Cost-Constant Purchasing Power Accounting

10. This method measures "historical prices in units of a currency, each of which has the same general purchasing power."

    a. It may be used instead of current cost if it does not result in a significantly different number for **income from continuing operations**.
    b. The historical cost principle is retained with restatement of the unit of measure to reflect changes in its general purchasing power. Hence, this method adjusts for **general price level changes but not for changes in specific prices**.

        1) Historical financial statements are restated by adjusting each nonmonetary item by applying the adjustment ratio.

    c. The **sales** ratio is:

$$\frac{Price\ level\ index\ at\ year\text{-}end}{Average\ price\ level\ for\ year}$$

    d. The ratio for **depreciation** is:

$$\frac{Price\ level\ index\ at\ year\text{-}end}{Average\ price\ level\ when\ asset\ was\ purchased}$$

Monetary vs. Nonmonetary Items

11. Calculation of purchasing power gain or loss depends on understanding monetary and nonmonetary items. All items that are not monetary are nonmonetary.

12. A **monetary asset** is either cash or a claim to receive cash. The amount is fixed or determinable without regard to future prices of specific goods or services.

    a. Examples are (1) accounts and notes receivable (including allowance accounts), (2) bond investments, (3) long-term receivables, and (4) demand bank deposits.

13. A **monetary liability** is an obligation to pay cash. The amount is fixed or determinable without regard to future prices of specific goods or services.

    a. Examples are (1) accounts and notes payable, (2) bonds payable, and (3) various accrued payables.

14. **Nonmonetary assets** are held primarily for resale or to provide services for the business. They also may be claims to cash that change in relationship to future prices of specific goods and services. A third category consists of residual rights (e.g., goodwill or common stock not accounted for using the equity method).

    a. Examples are (1) intellectual property (such as patents, copyrights, and trademarks); (2) most inventories; and (3) property, plant, and equipment (including accumulated depreciation).

15. **Nonmonetary liabilities** are obligations to provide goods or services in amounts that are fixed or determinable without regard to price changes. They also may be obligations to pay cash amounts dependent on future prices of specific goods or services.

    a. Examples are (1) deferred revenue (if the obligation is to provide goods or services), (2) pension accruals (but not a fixed payable to a fund), (3) warranties (obligations to provide goods or services at their future price), and (4) minority interests in consolidated subsidiaries.

16. **Purchasing power gains and losses** on **net monetary items** are determined by restating in units of constant purchasing power the opening and closing balances of, and transactions in, monetary assets and liabilities.

    a. During inflationary periods, if balances remain constant, monetary assets will suffer purchasing power losses. Monetary liabilities will enjoy purchasing power gains.

Five-Year Summary

17. SFAS 89 recommends a **5-year summary** of the following:

    a. Net sales and other operating revenue
    b. Income from continuing operations on a current cost basis
    c. Purchasing power gain or loss on net monetary items
    d. Change in the current cost or lower recoverable amount of inventory and PPE, net of inflation
    e. Aggregate foreign currency translation adjustment on a current cost basis
    f. Net assets at year-end on a current cost basis
    g. Income per common share from continuing operations on a current cost basis
    h. Cash dividends declared per common share
    i. Market price per common share at year-end.

18. **One of two methods** must be used to state the information in the 5-year summary:

    a. Average-for-the-year or end-of-year units of constant purchasing power.
    b. Dollars with a purchasing power equal to dollars of the base period used to calculate the **Consumer Price Index**.

Stop and review! You have completed the outline for this subunit. Study multiple-choice questions 14 through 18 beginning on page 604.

16.4 FINANCIAL STATEMENT ANALYSIS

1. One common form of financial statement analysis is **ratio analysis**. Numerous ratios may be calculated, and their forms and names routinely vary.

    a. For example, the cash ratio presented on the next page might be calculated as operating cash flow divided by average current liabilities.

Liquidity Ratios

2. Liquidity (solvency) ratios measure the short-term viability of the business, i.e., its ability to continue in the short term by paying its obligations.

    a. **Current Ratio**

       $$\frac{\textit{Current assets}}{\textit{Current liabilities}}$$

       1) If the current ratio is less than 1.0, a transaction that results in equal increases (decreases) in the numerator and denominator increases (decreases) the ratio.

          a) However, if the current ratio is more than 1.0, equal increases (decreases) in the numerator and denominator decreases (increases) the ratio.

b. **Acid Test or Quick Ratio**

$$\frac{Current\ assets\ -\ Inventory}{Current\ liabilities}$$

c. **Defensive-Interval Ratio**

$$\frac{Defensive\ assets}{Average\ daily\ operating\ costs}$$

1) Defensive assets include cash, short-term marketable securities, and net short-term receivables.

d. **Working Capital**

$$Current\ assets\ -\ Current\ liabilities$$

1) Working capital is the relatively liquid portion of capital available for meeting obligations within the operating cycle.

e. **Current Assets Turnover**

$$\frac{Cost\ of\ goods\ sold\ +\ Operating\ expenses\ +\ Taxes\ -\ Noncash\ expenses}{Current\ assets}$$

f. **Cash Ratio**

$$\frac{Cash\ equivalents\ +\ Marketable\ securities}{Current\ liabilities}$$

Activity Ratios

3. Activity ratios measure the ability to generate revenue and income.

a. **Inventory Turnover**

$$\frac{Cost\ of\ sales}{Average\ inventory}$$

1) A high turnover implies that the entity does not hold excessive inventories that are unproductive and lessen its profitability.

2) A high turnover also implies that the inventory is truly marketable and does not contain obsolete goods.

b. **Number of Days of Inventory**

$$\frac{365,\ 360,\ or\ 300}{Inventory\ turnover}$$

1) The number of days in a year may be 365, 360 (a banker's year), or 300 (number of business days).

c. **Accounts Receivable Turnover**

$$\frac{Net\ revenue}{Average\ net\ accounts\ receivable}$$

1) In principle, the numerator should be net credit sales, but this amount may not be known.

d. **Number of Days of Receivables**

$$\frac{365,\ 360,\ or\ 300}{Accounts\ receivable\ turnover}$$

e. **Operating Cycle**

$$Days\ in\ receivables\ +\ Days\ in\ inventory$$

f. **Asset Turnover**

$$\frac{Net\ revenue}{Average\ total\ assets}$$

g. **Fixed Asset Turnover**

$$\frac{Net\ sales}{Net\ fixed\ assets}$$

Leverage Ratios

4. Leverage ratios measure the use of debt to finance assets and operations.

a. **Debt-to-Equity Ratio**

$$\frac{Total\ liabilities}{Total\ equity}$$

b. **Equity Ratio**

$$\frac{Equity}{Total\ assets}$$

c. **Debt Ratio**

$$\frac{Total\ liabilities}{Total\ assets}$$

d. **Times-Interest-Earned Ratio**

$$\frac{Net\ income\ +\ Interest\ expense\ +\ Income\ tax\ expense}{Interest\ expense}$$

1) If earnings decline sufficiently, no income tax expense will be recognized.

e. **Fixed-Charge Coverage**

$$\frac{Net\ income\ +\ Interest\ expense\ +\ Income\ tax\ expense\ +\ Lease\ obligations}{Interest\ expense\ +\ Lease\ obligations}$$

1) **Trading on the equity (leverage)** is the strategy that uses fixed-charge securities, such as debt or preferred stock, to finance assets. The expectation is that the return on assets will be greater than the fixed charges.

f. **Operating Cash Flow to Total Debt**

$$\frac{Operating\ cash\ flow}{Total\ debt}$$

1) A cash coverage ratio also may be calculated for current debt.

Profitability Ratios

5. Profitability ratios measure income on a relative basis.

a. **Profit Margin on Sales**

$$\frac{Net\ income\ after\ taxes}{Sales}$$

b. **Return on Assets**

$$\frac{Net\ income\ after\ taxes}{Average\ total\ assets}$$

c. **Return on Common Equity**

$$\frac{Net\ income\ after\ taxes}{Average\ common\ equity}$$

d. **Common Stock Dividend Payout Ratio**

$$\frac{Cash\ dividends\ to\ common\ shareholders}{Net\ income\ before\ extraordinary\ items\ -\ Preferred\ dividends}$$

e. **Earnings per Share**

1) Study Unit 3 describes how to calculate basic and diluted earnings per share.

f. **Book Value per Common Share**

$$\frac{Net\ assets\ available\ to\ common\ shareholders}{Shares\ outstanding}$$

1) Assets available to common shareholders are assets, minus liabilities, minus assets required to redeem preferred shareholders' shares.

g. **Price-to-Earnings Ratio**

$$\frac{Price\ per\ common\ share}{EPS}$$

1) P-E ratios tend to be higher for entities that the market expects to grow rapidly.

2) EPS equals net income divided by the shares of stock outstanding during the year. Diluted EPS is the customary denominator measure.

Free Cash Flow

6. Free cash flow is an analytical measure of financial flexibility. It is the cash from operations remaining after subtracting amounts that must be paid to sustain the current level of productive capacity. The elements subtracted, however, vary in practice.

a. Most models subtract all **capital expenditures** to arrive at free cash flow. But some authorities treat capital expenditures to increase capacity as discretionary items and do not subtract them.

b. Some models also subtract **interest, dividends, and taxes** to arrive at free cash flow because these amounts may be viewed as nondiscretionary.

Limitations of Ratio Analysis

7. Although ratio analysis provides useful information about the efficiency of operations and the stability of financial condition, it has inherent limitations.

a. Development of ratios for comparison with **industry averages** is more useful for entities that operate within a particular industry than for conglomerates (entities that operate in a variety of industries).

b. The effects of **inflation** on fixed assets and depreciation, inventory costs, long-term debt, and profitability cause misstatement of the balance sheet and income statement. For example, fixed assets and depreciation will be understated, and inventory also will be understated if LIFO is used.

1) Moreover, the **interest-rate** increases that accompany inflation will decrease the fair value of outstanding long-term debt. Many assets are recorded at historical cost, so their true fair value may not be reflected on the balance sheet.

c. Ratio analysis may be affected by **seasonal factors**. For example, inventory and receivables may vary widely, and year-end balances may not reflect the averages for the period.

    d.   Management has an incentive to **window dress** financial statements to improve results. For example, if the current ratio is greater than 1.0, paying liabilities on the last day of the year will increase it.

    e.   **Comparability** of financial statement amounts and the ratios derived from them is impaired if different entities choose different **accounting policies**. Also, changes in accounting policies may create some distortion in the comparison of the results over a period of years.

    f.   Generalizations about which ratios are strong indicators of **financial position** may change from industry to industry, entity to entity, and division to division.

    g.   Ratios are constructed from **accounting data**, much of which is subject to **estimation**.

    h.   Current performance and trends may be misinterpreted if **sufficient years** of historical analysis are not considered.

    i.   Ratio analysis may be distorted by failing to use an **average or weighted average**.

    j.   Misleading conclusions may result if **improper comparisons** are selected.

    k.   Whether a certain level of a ratio is favorable depends on the **underlying circumstances**. For example, a high quick ratio indicates high liquidity, but it may also imply that excessive cash is being held.

    l.   Different ratios may yield opposite conclusions about financial health. Thus, the **net effects** of a set of ratios should be analyzed.

    m.   Industry averages may include data from capital-intensive and labor-intensive entities. They may also include data from entities with greatly divergent policies regarding **leverage**.

    n.   Some industry averages may be based on **small samples**.

    o.   Different **sources** of information may compute ratios differently.

    p.   Some data may be presented either **before or after taxes**.

    q.   Comparability among entities may be impaired if they have **different fiscal years**.

    r.   The **geographical locations** of firms may affect comparability because of differences in labor markets, price levels, governmental regulation, taxation, and other factors.

    s.   **Size differentials** among firms affect comparability because of differences in access to and cost of capital, economies of scale, and width of markets.

Comparative Analysis

    8.   Comparative analysis involves both horizontal and vertical analysis. **Horizontal (trend) analysis** compares analytical data over a period of time. **Vertical analysis** makes comparisons among a single year's data.

        a.   GAAP recommend that comparative financial statements be prepared for at least the current and the prior year. Firms that report publicly are subject to more stringent **SEC guidelines**. These mandate two years of balance sheets and three years of other statements (income, cash flows, and changes in equity) included in audited statements reported annually on Form 10-K.

        b.   Comparing an entity's performance with respect to its industry may identify strengths and weaknesses. Horizontal analysis of the industry may identify industrywide trends and practices.

        c.   **Common-size financial statements** are used to compare entities of different sizes. Items on common-size financial statements are expressed as percentages of corresponding base amounts. A base amount is assigned the value of 100%.

            1)   The **horizontal** form of common-size analysis is useful for evaluating trends. Each amount for subsequent years is stated as a percentage of a **base-year amount**.

2) **Vertical** common-size analysis presents amounts for a single year expressed as percentages of a base amount on the **balance sheet** (e.g., total assets) and on the **income statement** (e.g., sales). Common-size analysis permits management to compare individual expenses or asset categories with those of other entities and with industry averages.

Stop and review! You have completed the outline for this subunit. Study multiple-choice questions 19 through 28 beginning on page 605.

QUESTIONS

16.1 Derivatives and Hedging

Questions 1 and 2 are based on the following information. As part of its risk management strategy, a copper mining company sells futures contracts to hedge changes in fair value of its inventory. On March 12, the commodity exchange spot price was $0.81/lb., and the futures price for mid-June was $0.83/lb. On that date, the company, which has a March 31 fiscal year-end, sold 200 futures contracts on the commodity exchange at $0.83/lb. for delivery in June. Each contract was for 25,000 lb. The company designated these contracts as a fair-value hedge of 5 million lb. of current inventory for which a mid-June sale is expected. The average cost of this inventory was $0.58/lb. The company documented (1) the hedging relationship between the futures contracts and its inventory, (2) its objectives and strategy for undertaking the hedge, and (3) its conclusion that the hedging relationship will be highly effective. On March 31, the mid-June commodity exchange futures price was $0.85/lb.

1. In the March 31 statement of financial position, the copper mining company should record the futures contracts as a

   A. $100,000 asset.

   B. $100,000 liability.

   C. $4,250,000 liability.

   D. $4,250,000 asset.

Answer (B) is correct. *(Publisher, adapted)*
REQUIRED: The amount at which the futures contracts should be recorded on March 31.
DISCUSSION: SFAS 133 requires that derivative instruments be recorded as assets and liabilities and measured at fair value. At the inception of the futures contracts, their fair value was $0 because the contracts were entered into at the futures price at that date. On March 31, the fair value of the futures contracts is equal to the change in the futures price between the inception price and the March 31 price. Given that the futures contracts created an obligation to deliver 5 million lb. (25,000 lb. × 200 contracts) of copper at $0.83/lb. and that the price had risen to $0.85/lb. at the date of the financial statements, the company should record a loss and a liability of $100,000 [5 million lb. × ($0.83 – $0.85)].

2. If, on March 31, the copper mining company concluded that the hedge was 100% effective, it should record the hedged copper inventory in the March 31 statement of financial position at

   A. $4,350,000

   B. $4,250,000

   C. $3,000,000

   D. $2,900,000

Answer (C) is correct. *(Publisher, adapted)*
REQUIRED: The amount at which the hedged inventory should be recorded on March 31.
DISCUSSION: On March 31, the company recognized a loss and liability for the futures contracts of $100,000 [5 million lb. × ($0.83 contract price – $0.85 futures price)]. If the hedge was completely effective, the loss on the hedging derivatives must have been offset by a $100,000 gain on the hedged item. For a fair-value hedge, changes in the fair value of the hedged item attributable to the hedged risk are reflected as adjustments to the carrying amount of the hedged recognized asset or liability or the previously unrecognized firm commitment. The adjustments to carrying amount are accounted for in the same manner as other components of the carrying amount of the asset or liability. Thus, the inventory should be recorded at $3,000,000 [(5 million lb. × $0.58) original cost + $100,000 gain in fair value].
Answer (A) is incorrect because $4,350,000 equals the fair value of the inventory at the futures price on March 31 plus $100,000. Answer (B) is incorrect because $4,250,000 equals the fair value of the inventory at the futures price on March 31. Answer (D) is incorrect because $2,900,000 is the original cost of the inventory.

3. Garcia Corporation has entered into a binding agreement with Hernandez Company to purchase 400,000 pounds of Colombian coffee at $2.53 per pound for delivery in 90 days. This contract is accounted for as a

A. Financial instrument.

B. Firm commitment.

C. Forecasted transaction.

D. Fair value hedge.

Answer (B) is correct. *(Publisher, adapted)*
REQUIRED: The type of transaction defined.
DISCUSSION: A firm commitment is an agreement with an unrelated party, binding on both parties and usually legally enforceable, that specifies all significant terms and includes a disincentive for nonperformance.
Answer (A) is incorrect because a financial instrument does not involve the delivery of a product. Answer (C) is incorrect because a forecasted transaction is a transaction that is expected to occur for which no firm commitment exists. Answer (D) is incorrect because the purchase commitment is an exposure to risk, not a hedge of an exposure to risk.

4. On October 1, Year 3, Weeks Co., a calendar-year-end U.S. company, forecasts that, near the end of March Year 4, Sullivan Corp., a foreign entity, will purchase 50,000 gallons of Weeks's primary product for FC500,000. Sullivan has not firmly committed to the purchase. However, based on Sullivan's purchasing pattern, Weeks believes that the sale is probable. Weeks's risk-management policy includes avoiding foreign currency exposure through the use of foreign currency forward contracts. Thus, on October 1, Weeks enters into a 6-month foreign currency forward contract to sell FC500,000 to a dealer on March 31. Weeks designates the contract as a hedge and determines that hedge effectiveness will be based on changes in forward rates. The following information is available:

	Value of FC500,000 Based on Spot Rates	Value of FC500,000 Based on Forward Rates for 03/31/Yr4	Incremental Discounted Changes in Value of Forward Contract Based on Changes in Forward Rates
10/01/Yr3	$570,000	$500,000	$0
12/31/Yr3	$540,000	$490,000	$9,800
03/31/Yr4	$475,000	$475,000	$15,200

At what amounts should Weeks record the forward contract on December 31, Year 3, and March 31, Year 4?

	12/31/Yr3	03/31/Yr4
A.	$9,800	$25,000
B.	$10,000	$25,000
C.	$540,000	$475,000
D.	$490,000	$475,000

Answer (A) is correct. *(Publisher, adapted)*
REQUIRED: The amounts at which the forward contract should be recognized.
DISCUSSION: Weeks should record the forward contract as a receivable at fair value. Fair value is based on changes in forward rates discounted on a net present value basis. Thus, the receivable should be recorded at $9,800 on December 31, Year 3, and $25,000 ($9,800 + $15,200) on March 31, Year 4. Because a hedge of the foreign currency exposure of a forecasted transaction is a cash flow hedge, Weeks should also credit these amounts to other comprehensive income. On March 31, the sale should be recorded at $500,000 ($475,000 value based on the spot rate at March 31 + $25,000 balance in other comprehensive income). The amount of cash received also is equal to $500,000 ($475,000 + $25,000 balance in the forward contract receivable).
Answer (B) is incorrect because the change in forward rates should be adjusted for the time value of money. Answer (C) is incorrect because $540,000 and $475,000 reflect the value of FC500,000 at spot rates. Answer (D) is incorrect because $490,000 and $475,000 reflect the value of FC500,000 at forward rates.

5. According to SFAS 133, *Accounting for Derivative Instruments and Hedging Activities*, as amended by SFAS 138, *Accounting for Certain Derivative Instruments and Certain Hedging Activities*, the effective portion of a loss associated with a change in fair value of a derivative instrument should be reported as a component of other comprehensive income only if the derivative is appropriately designated as a

- A. Cash flow hedge of the foreign currency exposure of a forecasted transaction.

- B. Fair value hedge of the foreign currency exposure of an unrecognized firm commitment.

- C. Fair value hedge of the foreign currency exposure of a recognized asset or liability for which a foreign currency transaction gain or loss is recognized in earnings.

- D. Speculation in a foreign currency.

Answer (A) is correct. *(Publisher, adapted)*
    REQUIRED: The derivative for which the effective portion of a loss associated with its change in fair value is reported as a component of other comprehensive income.
    DISCUSSION: The hedge of the foreign currency exposure of a forecasted transaction is designated as a cash flow hedge. The effective portion of gains and losses associated with changes in fair value of a derivative instrument designated and qualifying as a cash flow hedging instrument is reported as a component of other comprehensive income.
    Answer (B) is incorrect because a hedge of the foreign currency exposure of an unrecognized firm commitment may be a cash flow hedge or a fair value hedge. Answer (C) is incorrect because a hedge of the foreign currency exposure of a recognized asset or liability for which a foreign currency transaction gain or loss is recognized in earnings may be a cash flow hedge or a fair value hedge. Answer (D) is incorrect because gains and losses associated with changes in fair value of a derivative used as a speculation in a foreign currency are included in earnings of the period of change.

16.2 Foreign Currency Issues

6. Which of the following statements regarding foreign exchange gains and losses is true?

- A. An exchange gain occurs when the exchange rate increases between the date a payable is recorded and the date of cash payment.

- B. An exchange gain occurs when the exchange rate increases between the date a receivable is recorded and the date of cash receipt.

- C. An exchange loss occurs when the exchange rate decreases between the date a payable is recorded and the date of the cash payment.

- D. An exchange loss occurs when the exchange rate increases between the date a receivable is recorded and the date of the cash receipt.

Answer (B) is correct. *(CPA, adapted)*
    REQUIRED: The true statement about foreign exchange gains and losses.
    DISCUSSION: A foreign currency transaction gain or loss (commonly known as a foreign exchange gain or loss) is recorded in earnings under SFAS 52, *Foreign Currency Translation*. When the amount of the functional currency receivable or payable in exchange for a unit of the currency in which the transaction is denominated increases, the reporting entity recognizes a transaction gain or loss, respectively. The opposite occurs when exchange rates decrease.
    Answer (A) is incorrect because the payable will become more expensive in the functional currency, resulting in a loss. Answer (C) is incorrect because the payable will become less expensive in the functional currency, resulting in a gain. Answer (D) is incorrect because an exchange gain occurs.

7. Fogg Co., a U.S. company, contracted to purchase foreign goods. Payment in foreign currency was due one month after the goods were received at Fogg's warehouse. Between the receipt of goods and the time of payment, the exchange rates changed in Fogg's favor. The resulting gain should be included in Fogg's financial statements as a(n)

- A. Component of income from continuing operations.

- B. Extraordinary item.

- C. Deferred credit.

- D. Item of other comprehensive income.

Answer (A) is correct. *(CPA, adapted)*
    REQUIRED: The accounting treatment of a foreign currency transaction gain.
    DISCUSSION: This foreign currency transaction resulted in a payable denominated in a foreign currency. The favorable change in the exchange rate between the functional currency and the currency in which the transaction was denominated should be included in determining net income for the period in which the exchange rate changed. It should be classified as a component of income from continuing operations because it does not meet the criteria for classification under any other caption in the income statement, for example, as an extraordinary item.
    Answer (B) is incorrect because APB Opinion 30 states that gains or losses from exchange or translation of foreign currencies are not extraordinary items except in rare situations. They are usual in nature and may be expected to recur in the course of customary and continuing business activities. Answer (C) is incorrect because the gain should not be deferred but should be recognized in the period in which the exchange rate changed. Answer (D) is incorrect because translation adjustments, not transaction gains and losses, are included in OCI.

8. On October 1, Year 4, Mild Co., a U.S. company, purchased machinery from Grund, a German company, with payment due on April 1, Year 5. If Mild's Year 4 operating income included no foreign currency transaction gain or loss, the transaction could have

A. Resulted in an extraordinary gain.

B. Been denominated in U.S. dollars.

C. Caused a foreign currency gain to be reported as a contra account against machinery.

D. Caused a foreign currency translation gain to be reported in other comprehensive income.

Answer (B) is correct. *(CPA, adapted)*
REQUIRED: The reason no foreign currency transaction gain or loss occurred.
DISCUSSION: The terms of a foreign currency transaction are denominated in a currency other than the functional currency. A fluctuation in the exchange rate between the functional currency and the other currency is a gain or loss that ordinarily should be included in determining net income when the exchange rate changes. If Mild's functional currency is the U.S. dollar and the transaction was denominated in U.S. dollars, no foreign currency transaction gain or loss occurred.
Answer (A) is incorrect because foreign currency transaction gains and losses are ordinarily operating items. Answer (C) is incorrect because foreign currency transaction gains and losses not included in the determination of net income (certain intercompany transactions and certain hedges) are reported in OCI. Answer (D) is incorrect because translation expresses in the reporting currency amounts denominated in the functional currency. The U.S. dollar is the reporting and functional currency of Mild, so translation is not required.

9. On September 22, Year 2, Yumi Corp. purchased merchandise from an unaffiliated foreign company for 10,000 units of the foreign company's local currency. On that date, the spot rate was $.55. Yumi paid the bill in full on March 20, Year 3, when the spot rate was $.65. The spot rate was $.70 on December 31, Year 2. What amount should Yumi report as a foreign currency transaction loss in its income statement for the year ended December 31, Year 2?

A. $0

B. $500

C. $1,000

D. $1,500

Answer (D) is correct. *(CPA, adapted)*
REQUIRED: The amount of foreign currency transaction loss to be reported in the income statement.
DISCUSSION: SFAS 52, *Foreign Currency Translation*, requires that a receivable or payable denominated in a foreign currency be adjusted to its current exchange rate at each balance sheet date. The resulting gain or loss should ordinarily be included in determining net income. It is the difference between the spot rate on the date the transaction originates and the spot rate at year-end. Thus, the Year 2 transaction loss for Yumi Corp. is $1,500 [($0.55 – $0.70) × 10,000 units].
Answer (A) is incorrect because a loss resulted when the spot rate increased. Answer (B) is incorrect because $500 results from using the spot rates at 12/31/Year 2 and 3/20/Year 3. Answer (C) is incorrect because $1,000 results from using the spot rates at 9/22/Year 2 and 3/20/Year 3.

10. Which of the following is debited to other comprehensive income (OCI)?

A. Discount on convertible bonds that are dilutive potential common stock.

B. Premium on convertible bonds that are dilutive potential common stock.

C. Cumulative foreign currency translation loss.

D. Organizational costs.

Answer (C) is correct. *(CPA, adapted)*
REQUIRED: The item debited to OCI.
DISCUSSION: When the currency used to prepare a foreign entity's financial statements is its functional currency, SFAS 52 specifies that the current rate method be used to translate the foreign entity's financial statements into the reporting currency. The translation gains and losses arising from applying this method are reported in OCI in the consolidated statements and are not reflected in income. Accumulated OCI is a component of equity displayed separately from retained earnings and additional paid-in capital in the statement of financial position (SFAS 130). Because a cumulative foreign currency translation loss reduces the balance, it is a debit item.
Answer (A) is incorrect because a discount on bonds is a contra account to bonds payable in the liability section of the balance sheet. Answer (B) is incorrect because premium on bonds is a contra account to bonds payable in the liability section. Answer (D) is incorrect because organizational costs are expensed when incurred.

11. A wholly owned subsidiary of Ward, Inc. has certain expense accounts for the year ended December 31, Year 4, stated in local currency units (LCU) as follows:

	LCU
Depreciation of equipment (related assets were purchased Jan. 1, Year 2)	120,000
Provision for doubtful accounts	80,000
Rent	200,000

The exchange rates at various dates are as follows:

	Dollar Equivalent of 1 LCU
December 31, Year 4	$.40
Average for year ended 12/31/Yr 4	.44
January 1, Year 2	.50

Assume that the LCU is the subsidiary's functional currency and that the charges to the expense accounts occurred approximately evenly during the year. What total dollar amount should be included in Ward's Year 4 consolidated income statement to reflect these expenses?

A. $160,000

B. $172,000

C. $176,000

D. $200,000

Answer (C) is correct. *(CPA, adapted)*
REQUIRED: The amount of expenses in the consolidated income statement.
DISCUSSION: When the local currency of the subsidiary is the functional currency, translation into the reporting currency is necessary. Assets and liabilities are translated at the exchange rate at the balance sheet date, and revenues, expenses, gains, and losses are usually translated at average rates for the period. Thus, the 400,000 LCU in total expenses should be translated at the average exchange rate of $.44, resulting in expenses reflected in the consolidated income statement of $176,000 (400,000 LCU × $.44).
Answer (A) is incorrect because the average exchange rate, not the current year-end rate, should be used. Answer (B) is incorrect because the average exchange rate, not a combination of rates, should be used. Answer (D) is incorrect because it values all assets at the January 1, Year 2, rate.

12. In preparing consolidated financial statements of a U.S. parent company with a foreign subsidiary, the foreign subsidiary's functional currency is the currency

A. In which the subsidiary maintains its accounting records.

B. Of the country in which the subsidiary is located.

C. Of the country in which the parent is located.

D. Of the environment in which the subsidiary primarily generates and expends cash.

Answer (D) is correct. *(CPA, adapted)*
REQUIRED: The foreign subsidiary's functional currency.
DISCUSSION: The method used to convert foreign currency amounts into units of the reporting currency is the functional currency translation approach. It is appropriate for use in accounting for and reporting the financial results and relationships of foreign subsidiaries in consolidated statements. This method identifies the functional currency of the entity (the currency of the primary economic environment in which the foreign entity operates), measures all elements of the financial statements in the functional currency, and uses a current exchange rate for translation from the functional currency to the reporting currency. The currency in which the subsidiary maintains its accounting records, the currency of the country in which the subsidiary is located, and the currency of the country in which the parent is located may not be the currency indicated by the salient economic indicators, such as cash flows, sales prices, sales markets, expenses, financing, and intercompany transactions.

13. Gains from remeasuring a foreign subsidiary's financial statements from the local currency into its functional currency should be reported

A. As a deferred foreign currency transaction gain.

B. In other comprehensive income.

C. As an extraordinary item, net of income taxes.

D. In current income.

Answer (D) is correct. *(CPA, adapted)*
REQUIRED: The proper reporting of a gain arising from remeasurement.
DISCUSSION: If the books of record of a foreign entity are maintained in a currency other than the functional currency, SFAS 52 requires that the foreign currency amounts first be remeasured into the functional currency using the temporal method and then translated using the current rate method into the reporting currency. The gain arising from remeasurement should be reported in current income.
Answer (A) is incorrect because the gain is not deferred. Answer (B) is incorrect because a gain arising from translation, not remeasurement, is reported in other comprehensive income. Answer (C) is incorrect because the criteria for treatment as an extraordinary item have not been met.

16.3 Price-Level Basis of Accounting

14. A company that wishes to disclose information about the effect of changing prices in accordance with SFAS 89, *Financial Reporting and Changing Prices*, should report this information in

A. The body of the financial statements.

B. The notes to the financial statements.

C. Supplementary information to the financial statements.

D. Management's report to shareholders.

Answer (C) is correct. *(CPA, adapted)*
REQUIRED: The reporting of the effect of changing prices.
DISCUSSION: SFAS 89 encourages, but does not require, disclosure of supplementary current cost/constant purchasing power information.
Answer (A) is incorrect because voluntary disclosures about the effects of changing prices should not be reported in the body of the financial statements. Answer (B) is incorrect because voluntary disclosures about the effects of changing prices should not be reported in the notes to the financial statements. Answer (D) is incorrect because information about the effect of changing prices is meaningful to users of financial statements other than shareholders.

15. Financial statements prepared under which of the following methods include adjustments for both specific price changes and general price-level changes?

A. Historical cost/nominal dollar.

B. Current cost/nominal dollar.

C. Current cost/constant dollar.

D. Historical cost/constant dollar.

Answer (C) is correct. *(CPA, adapted)*
REQUIRED: The method that adjusts for specific price changes and general price level changes.
DISCUSSION: Current cost accounting attempts to present financial statement items on the basis of current value. Thus, it considers the changes in the prices of specific items. Constant dollar (constant purchasing power) accounting reflects changes in the general purchasing power of the unit of measure.
Answer (A) is incorrect because historical cost/nominal dollar accounting does not adjust for specific price changes or general price-level changes. Answer (B) is incorrect because nominal dollar accounting does not adjust for changes in the general price level. Answer (D) is incorrect because historical cost does not adjust for specific price changes.

16. Manhof Co. prepares supplementary reports on income from continuing operations on a current cost basis in accordance with SFAS 89, *Financial Reporting and Changing Prices*. How should Manhof compute cost of goods sold on a current cost basis?

A. Number of units sold times average current cost of units during the year.

B. Number of units sold times current cost of units at year-end.

C. Number of units sold times current cost of units at the beginning of the year.

D. Beginning inventory at current cost, plus cost of goods purchased, minus ending inventory at current cost.

Answer (A) is correct. *(CPA, adapted)*
REQUIRED: The method of computing cost of goods sold on a current cost basis.
DISCUSSION: If an entity provides supplementary information about the effects of changing prices in accordance with SFAS 89 and operating income on a current cost/constant purchasing power basis differs significantly from that reported in the primary statements, it should, among other items, disclose the difference between the cost of goods sold in the primary financial statements and the current cost amount. SFAS 89 calculates the latter by multiplying the units sold during the period by the average of the unit current cost or lower recoverable amount at the beginning and end of the period.

17. In its financial statements, Hila Co. discloses supplemental information on the effects of changing prices in accordance with SFAS 89, *Financial Reporting and Changing Prices*. Hila computed the increase in current cost of inventory as follows:

Increase in current cost (nominal dollars)	$15,000
Increase in current cost (constant dollars)	$12,000

What amount should Hila disclose as the inflation component of the increase in current cost of inventories?

A. $3,000

B. $12,000

C. $15,000

D. $27,000

Answer (A) is correct. *(CPA, adapted)*
REQUIRED: The inflation component of the increase in current cost of inventories.
DISCUSSION: If supplemental information on the effects of changing prices is presented in accordance with SFAS 89, the change in current cost amounts of inventory and property, plant, and equipment is reported both before and after eliminating the effects of general inflation. The inflation component of the increase in current cost (the change attributable to general price-level changes) is the difference between the nominal dollar and constant dollar measures, or $3,000 ($15,000 − $12,000).
Answer (B) is incorrect because $12,000 is the increase in current cost stated in constant dollars. Answer (C) is incorrect because $15,000 is the increase in current cost stated in nominal dollars. Answer (D) is incorrect because $27,000 is the sum of the increase in current cost stated in constant dollars plus the increase in current cost stated in nominal dollars.

18. When computing purchasing power gain or loss on net monetary items, which of the following accounts is classified as nonmonetary?

A. Accumulated depreciation of equipment.

B. Advances to unconsolidated subsidiaries.

C. Allowance for doubtful accounts.

D. Unamortized premium on bonds payable.

Answer (A) is correct.   *(CPA, adapted)*
REQUIRED: The item classified as nonmonetary in historical cost/constant purchasing power accounting.
DISCUSSION: A monetary asset is either money or a claim to receive a sum of money the amount of which is fixed or determinable without reference to future prices of specific goods or services. A monetary liability is an obligation to pay a sum of money the amount of which is fixed or determinable without reference to future prices of specific goods and services. Equipment and the related accumulated depreciation account are an asset and a contra asset, respectively, the value of which will change in relationship to future prices of specific goods and services. Hence, accumulated depreciation is a nonmonetary item.
Answer (B) is incorrect because advances to unconsolidated subsidiaries are monetary assets. Answer (C) is incorrect because the allowance for doubtful accounts is a monetary liability. Answer (D) is incorrect because unamortized premium on bonds payable is a monetary liability.

16.4 Financial Statement Analysis

19. North Bank is analyzing Belle Corp.'s financial statements for a possible extension of credit. Belle's quick ratio is significantly better than the industry average. Which of the following factors should North consider as a possible limitation of using this ratio when evaluating Belle's creditworthiness?

A. Fluctuating market prices of short-term investments may adversely affect the ratio.

B. Increasing market prices for Belle's inventory may adversely affect the ratio.

C. Belle may need to sell its available-for-sale investments to meet its current obligations.

D. Belle may need to liquidate its inventory to meet its long-term obligations.

Answer (A) is correct.   *(CPA, adapted)*
REQUIRED: The possible limitation of using the quick ratio to evaluate creditworthiness.
DISCUSSION: The quick ratio equals current assets minus inventory, divided by current liabilities. Because short-term marketable securities are included in the numerator, fluctuating market prices of short-term investments may adversely affect the ratio if Belle holds a substantial amount of such current assets.
Answer (B) is incorrect because inventory is excluded from the calculation of the quick ratio. Answer (C) is incorrect because, if the available-for-sale securities are not current, they are not included in the calculation of the ratio. If they are classified as current, their sale to meet current obligations is consistent with normal current assets management practices. Answer (D) is incorrect because inventory and long-term obligations are excluded from the calculation of the quick ratio.

20. The following financial ratios and calculations were based on information from Kohl Co.'s financial statements for the current year:

Accounts receivable turnover
Ten times during the year

Total assets turnover
Two times during the year

Average receivables during the year
$200,000

What was Kohl's average total assets for the year?

A. $2,000,000

B. $1,000,000

C. $400,000

D. $200,000

Answer (B) is correct.   *(CPA, adapted)*
REQUIRED: The average total assets.
DISCUSSION: The total assets turnover ratio (given as 2.0) equals net revenue divided by average total assets. The accounts receivable turnover ratio (given as 10.0) equals net revenue divided by average accounts receivable. Given $200,000 of average accounts receivable, net revenue must equal $2,000,000 ($200,000 × 10.0). Accordingly, average total assets equals $1,000,000 ($2,000,000 net revenue ÷ 2.0 total assets turnover).
Answer (A) is incorrect because $2,000,000 equals net revenue. Answer (C) is incorrect because $400,000 equals average accounts receivable times total assets turnover. Answer (D) is incorrect because $200,000 equals average receivables during the year.

Questions 21 through 23 are based on the following information. Selected data pertaining to Lore Co. for the Year 4 calendar year is as follows:

Net cash sales	$ 3,000
Cost of goods sold	18,000
Inventory at beginning of year	6,000
Purchases	24,000
Accounts receivable at beginning of year	20,000
Accounts receivable at end of year	22,000

21. The accounts receivable turnover for Year 4 was 5.0 times. What were Lore's Year 4 net credit sales?

A. $105,000

B. $107,000

C. $110,000

D. $210,000

Answer (A) is correct. *(CPA, adapted)*
REQUIRED: The net credit sales.
DISCUSSION: Credit sales may be determined from the accounts receivable turnover formula (credit sales ÷ average accounts receivable). Credit sales are equal to 5.0 times average receivables [($20,000 + $22,000) ÷ 2], or $105,000.
Answer (B) is incorrect because $107,000 equals ending accounts receivable multiplied by the accounts receivable turnover ratio, minus cash sales. Answer (C) is incorrect because $110,000 equals ending accounts receivable multiplied by the accounts receivable turnover ratio. Answer (D) is incorrect because $210,000 equals beginning accounts receivable plus ending accounts receivable, multiplied by the accounts receivable turnover ratio.

22. What was Lore's inventory turnover for Year 4?

A. 1.2 times.

B. 1.5 times.

C. 2.0 times.

D. 3.0 times.

Answer (C) is correct. *(CPA, adapted)*
REQUIRED: The inventory turnover ratio.
DISCUSSION: Inventory turnover is equal to cost of goods sold divided by average inventory. Ending inventory equals beginning inventory, plus purchases, minus cost of goods sold, or $12,000 ($6,000 + $24,000 – $18,000). Average inventory is $9,000 [($6,000 + $12,000) ÷ 2]. Inventory turnover is 2.0 times ($18,000 cost of goods sold ÷ $9,000 average inventory).
Answer (A) is incorrect because 1.2 times uses the average of beginning inventory and purchases. Answer (B) is incorrect because 1.5 times uses ending inventory instead of average inventory. Answer (D) is incorrect because 3.0 times uses beginning inventory instead of average inventory.

23. Lore would use which of the following to determine the average day's sales in inventory?

	Numerator	Denominator
A.	365	Average inventory
B.	365	Inventory turnover
C.	Average inventory	Sales divided by 365
D.	Sales divided by 365	Inventory turnover

Answer (B) is correct. *(CPA, adapted)*
REQUIRED: The formula to calculate average day's sales in inventory.
DISCUSSION: The average day's sales in inventory is calculated by dividing 365 days by the inventory turnover.

24. Barr Co. has total debt of $420,000 and equity of $700,000. Barr is seeking capital to fund an expansion. Barr is planning to issue an additional $300,000 in common stock and is negotiating with a bank to borrow additional funds. The bank requires a debt-to-equity ratio of .75. What is the maximum additional amount Barr will be able to borrow?

A. $225,000

B. $330,000

C. $525,000

D. $750,000

Answer (B) is correct. *(CPA, adapted)*
REQUIRED: The maximum additional borrowing allowed to satisfy a specific debt-to-equity ratio.
DISCUSSION: Barr will have $1,000,000 ($700,000 + $300,000) in total equity. The debt-to-equity restriction allows up to $750,000 ($1,000,000 × .75) in debt. Barr already has $420,000 in debt, so the additional borrowing cannot exceed $330,000 ($750,000 – $420,000).
Answer (A) is incorrect because $225,000 results from multiplying the $300,000 of additional common stock by the debt-to-equity ratio. Answer (C) is incorrect because $525,000 equals the $700,000 of shareholders' equity times the debt-to-equity ratio. Answer (D) is incorrect because $750,000 is the total debt allowed.

25. The following data pertain to Cowl, Inc., for the year ended December 31, Year 4:

Net sales	$ 600,000
Net income	150,000
Total assets, January 1, Year 4	2,000,000
Total assets, December 31, Year 4	3,000,000

What was Cowl's rate of return on assets for Year 4?

A. 5%

B. 6%

C. 20%

D. 24%

Answer (B) is correct. *(CPA, adapted)*
REQUIRED: The rate of return on assets.
DISCUSSION: Return on assets equals net income divided by average total assets, or 6% ($150,000 ÷ $2,500,000).
Answer (A) is incorrect because 5% results from using ending total assets instead of the average total assets. Answer (C) is incorrect because 20% results from dividing net sales by ending total assets. Answer (D) is incorrect because 24% results from dividing net sales by average total assets.

26. Which of the following is not a limitation of ratio analysis affecting comparability among firms?

A. Different accounting policies.

B. Different fiscal years.

C. Different sources of information.

D. All of the answer choices are limitations of ratio analysis.

Answer (D) is correct. *(Publisher, adapted)*
REQUIRED: The factor that is not a limitation of ratio analysis affecting comparability among firms.
DISCUSSION: Ratio analysis provides useful information regarding the efficiency of operations and the stability of financial condition. Nevertheless, it has several inherent limitations, such as firms using different accounting policies, different fiscal years, and different sources of information. Each of these factors impairs the comparability of financial statement amounts and the ratios derived from them.

27. In financial statement analysis, expressing all financial statement items as a percentage of base-year amounts is called

A. Horizontal common-size analysis.

B. Vertical common-size analysis.

C. Trend analysis.

D. Ratio analysis.

Answer (A) is correct. *(CMA, adapted)*
REQUIRED: The term for expressing all financial statement items as a percentage of base-year amounts.
DISCUSSION: Expressing financial statement items as percentages of corresponding base-year figures is a horizontal form of common-size (percentage) analysis that is useful for evaluating trends. The base amount is assigned the value of 100%, and the amounts for other years are denominated in percentages compared to the base year.
Answer (B) is incorrect because vertical common-size (percentage) analysis presents figures for a single year expressed as percentages of a base amount on the balance sheet (e.g., total assets) and on the income statement (e.g., sales). Answer (C) is incorrect because the term "trend analysis" is most often applied to the quantitative techniques used in forecasting to fit a curve to given data. Answer (D) is incorrect because it is a general term.

28. In assessing the financial prospects for a firm, financial analysts use various techniques. Which of the following is an example of vertical common-size analysis?

A. An assessment of the relative stability of a firm's level of vertical integration.

B. A comparison in financial ratio form between two or more firms in the same industry.

C. A statement that current advertising expense is 2% greater than in the prior year.

D. A statement that current advertising expense is 2% of sales.

Answer (D) is correct. *(CMA, adapted)*
REQUIRED: The example of vertical common-size analysis.
DISCUSSION: Vertical common-size analysis compares the components within a set of financial statements. A base amount is assigned a value of 100%. For example, total assets on a common-size balance sheet and net sales on a common-size income statement are valued at 100%. Common-size statements permit evaluation of the efficiency of various aspects of operations. An analyst who states that advertising expense is 2% of sales is using vertical common-size analysis.
Answer (A) is incorrect because vertical integration occurs when a corporation owns one or more of its suppliers or customers. Answer (B) is incorrect because vertical common-size analysis restates financial statement amounts as percentages. Answer (C) is incorrect because a statement that advertising expense is 2% greater than in the previous year results from horizontal analysis.

16.5 PRACTICE SIMULATION

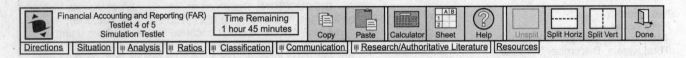

| | Financial Accounting and Reporting (FAR) Testlet 4 of 5 Simulation Testlet | Time Remaining 1 hour 45 minutes | Copy | Paste | Calculator | Sheet | Help | Unsplit | Split Horiz | Split Vert | Done |

Directions | Situation | Analysis | Ratios | Classification | Communication | Research/Authoritative Literature | Resources

1. Directions

In the following simulation, you will be asked to complete various tasks. You may use the content in the **Information Tabs** to complete the tasks in the **Work Tabs**.

Information Tabs:

Directions | Resources

    FIG 1

- Go through each of the **Information Tabs** to familiarize yourself with the simulation content
- The **Resources** tab will contain information, including formulas and definitions, that may help you to complete the tasks
- Your simulation may have more **Information Tabs** than those shown in Fig. 1

Work Tabs:

SysTrust | Engagement Letter | Authoritative Sources | Communication

    FIG. 2

- **Work Tabs**, to the right of **Information Tabs**, contain the tasks for you to complete
- **Work Tabs** contain directions for completing each task - be sure to read these directions carefully
- The tab names in Fig. 2 are for illustration only - yours may differ
- Once you complete any part of a task, the pencil for that tab will be shaded (see **Communication** in Fig. 2)
- The shaded pencil does **NOT** indicate that you have completed the entire task
- You must complete all of the tasks in the **Work Tabs** to receive full credit

Research/Authoritative Literature Tab:

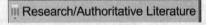

Research/Authoritative Literature

    FIG. 3

- This tab contains both the Research task and the Authoritative Literature
- Detailed instructions for completing the Research task, and for using the Authoritative Literature, appear on this tab
- You may use the Authoritative Literature as a resource for completing other tasks

NOTE: If you believe you have encountered a software malfunction, report it to the test center staff immediately.

2. Situation

Parker, Inc. is consistently profitable. Parker's normal financial statement relationships are as follows:

I.	Current ratio	3 to 1
II.	Inventory turnover	4 times
III.	Total debt-total assets ratio	0.5 to 1
IV.	Acid-test ratio	2 to 1
V.	Working capital	$1,000,000
VI.	Times interest earned	10 times
VII.	Equity ratio	0.5
VIII.	Profit margin on sale	5%
IX.	Return on assets	9%
X.	Return on common equity	15%
XI.	Price-earnings ratio	12%

3. Analysis

This set of questions has a matching format. Select the best match for each numbered item from the terms in the drop-down list and write its letter in the column provided. Each choice may be used once, more than once, or not at all. Determine whether each Year 8 transaction or event increased, decreased, or had no effect on each of the Year 8 ratios given.

Transaction	I.	II.	III.	Answer Choices
1. Parker issued a stock dividend.				A) Increase
2. Parker declared, but did not pay, a cash dividend.				B) Decrease
3. Customers returned invoiced goods for which they had not paid.				C) No effect
4. Accounts payable were paid on December 31, Year 8.				
5. Parker recorded both a receivable from an insurance company and a loss from fire damage to a factory building.				
6. Early in Year 8, Parker increased the selling price of one of its products that had a demand in excess of capacity. The number of units sold and costs incurred in Year 7 and Year 8 were the same.				

4. Ratios

This set of questions has a matching format. Select the best match for each numbered item from the terms in the drop-down list and write its letter in the column provided. Each choice may be used once, more than once, or not at all. For each of the following, determine whether the ratio is a liquidity ratio, activity ratio, leverage ratio, or profitability ratio.

Ratio	Answer
1. Price-earnings ratio	
2. Current ratio	
3. Debt-to-equity ratio	
4. Inventory turnover ratio	
5. Basic earnings per share	
6. Asset turnover	
7. Return on assets	
8. Quick ratio	
9. Debt ratio	
10. Times-interest-earned ratio	
11. Working capital	
12. Accounts receivable turnover	
13. Cash ratio	
14. Profit margin on sales	
15. Fixed asset turnover	

Choices
A) Liquidity ratio
B) Activity ratio
C) Leverage ratio
D) Profitability ratio

5. Classification

This question is presented in a check-the-box format that requires you to select the correct responses from a given list. For each of the following, indicate whether the item is monetary or nonmonetary.

Item	Monetary	Nonmonetary
1. Cash		
2. Patent		
3. Accumulated depreciation		
4. Accounts receivable		
5. Trademark		
6. Accounts payable		
7. Demand bank deposits		
8. Allowance for doubtful accounts		
9. Minority interest from the consolidated entity's perspective		
10. Deferred revenue from sale of goods		

6. Communication

In a memorandum to your client, explain the objectives of translating its foreign subsidiary's financial statements. Also, explain how the adjustments arising from the translation will be measured and reported in its financial statements. This explanation should address the accounting when the books of the subsidiary are and are not maintained in its functional currency. Type your communication in your word processor program and print out the copy in a memorandum-style format.

REMINDER: Your response will be graded for both technical content and writing skills. Technical content will be evaluated for information that is helpful to the intended reader and clearly relevant to the issue. Writing skills will be evaluated for development, organization, and the appropriate expression of ideas in professional correspondence. Use a standard business memo or letter format with a clear beginning, middle, and end. Do not convey information in the form of a table, bullet point list, or other abbreviated presentation.

To:	Client
From:	CPA
Subject:	Foreign currency translation

7. Research/Authoritative Literature

See page 12 in the Introduction of this book for a detailed explanation of the AICPA's new Research/Authoritative Literature work tab as well as a screenshot of how the tab will actually look on your exam.

SFAS 52 identifies economic factors that are to be considered both individually and collectively in determining the functional currency for a consolidated subsidiary. What are the financing indicators to be considered in determining whether the parent's currency or a foreign currency should be identified as the functional currency?

Unofficial Answers

3. Analysis (18 Gradable Items)

1. <u>I: C) No effect; II: C) No effect; III: C) No effect.</u> A stock dividend affects only equity accounts. The current ratio equals current assets over current liabilities, inventory turnover equals the cost of goods sold divided by average inventory, and the debt-to-assets ratio equals total debt over total assets. A stock dividend has no effect on these ratios.

2. <u>I: B) Decrease; II: C) No effect; III: A) Increase.</u> When cash dividends are declared but not yet paid, retained earnings is debited and dividends payable is credited. Because the current ratio equals current assets over current liabilities, the credit to dividends payable increases the denominator and therefore decreases the ratio. The inventory turnover equals the cost of goods sold over average inventory. Hence, a cash dividend declaration has no effect on the ratio. Finally, the debt-to-assets ratio equals total debt over total assets, and an increase in dividends payable increases the numerator and therefore the ratio.

3. <u>I: B) Decrease; II: B) Decrease; III: A) Increase.</u> When invoiced goods that have not been paid for are returned, sales returns is debited, accounts receivable is credited, inventory is debited, and cost of goods sold is credited. A decrease in accounts receivable decreases the numerator of the current ratio, which decreases the ratio. Although the numerator is increased by the increase in inventory (at cost), assuming the goods are sold at a profit, the net effect on the ratio is a decrease. The decrease in cost of goods sold decreases the numerator of the inventory turnover ratio and therefore decreases the ratio. The increase in inventory increases the denominator, which also decreases the ratio. Because this transaction caused a net decrease in total assets, the total-debt-to-total-assets ratio is increased.

4. <u>I: A) Increase; II: C) No effect; III: B) Decrease.</u> When an account payable is settled, accounts payable is debited and cash is credited. When the current ratio is greater than 1.0, equal decreases in the numerator and denominator increase the ratio. The settlement of an account payable has no effect on the inventory turnover ratio. Given that the total debt to total assets ratio is less than 1.0, equal decreases in the numerator and denominator decrease the ratio.

5. <u>I: A) Increase; II: C) No effect; III: A) Increase.</u> Recording a receivable increases current assets, and the loss decreases net income. The numerator of the current ratio increases, which increases the ratio. Because inventory turnover equals cost of goods sold divided by average inventory, an increase in accounts receivable has no effect on the ratio. Debiting accounts receivable increases the denominator of the total debt-total assets ratio, but crediting the carrying amount of the damaged building decreases the denominator. Given that a loss (a debit) was also recorded, the credit must have exceeded the debit, resulting in a net decrease in the denominator and an increase in the ratio.

6. <u>I: A) Increase; II: C) No effect; III: B) Decrease.</u> An increase in the selling price when sales and costs remain constant increases cash and receivables. Accordingly, the current ratio increases because the numerator increases. Cost of goods sold remains constant and inventory turnover is unaffected. The total debt-total assets ratio decreases because total assets increases.

4. Ratios (15 Gradable Items)

1. <u>D) Profitability ratio.</u> The P-E ratio equals price per common share divided by the EPS. Profitability ratios measure income on a relative basis.

2. <u>A) Liquidity ratio.</u> The current ratio equals current assets divided by current liabilities. Liquidity (solvency) ratios measure the short-term viability of the business, i.e., the firm's ability to continue in the short term by paying its obligations.

3. <u>C) Leverage ratio.</u> The debt-equity ratio equals total liabilities divided by total equity. Leverage ratios measure the firm's use of debt to finance assets and operations.

4. <u>B) Activity ratio.</u> Inventory turnover equals cost of sales divided by average inventory. Activity ratios measure the firm's ability to generate revenue and income.

5. <u>D) Profitability ratio.</u> Basic EPS equals earnings available to common shareholders divided by the weighted-average number of shares of common stock outstanding. Profitability ratios measure income on a relative basis.

6. <u>B) Activity ratio.</u> Asset turnover equals net revenue divided by average total assets. Activity ratios measure the firm's ability to generate revenue and income.

7. <u>D) Profitability ratio.</u> Return on assets equals net income divided by average total assets. Profitability ratios measure income on a relative basis.

8. <u>A) Liquidity ratio.</u> The acid-test or quick ratio equals current assets minus inventory, divided by current liabilities. Liquidity (solvency) ratios measure the short-term viability of the business, i.e., the firm's ability to continue in the short term by paying its obligations.

9. <u>C) Leverage ratio.</u> The debt ratio equals total liabilities divided by total assets. Leverage ratios measure the firm's use of debt to finance assets and operations.

10. __C) Leverage ratio.__ The times-interest-earned ratio equals the sum of net income, interest, and income taxes, divided by interest. Leverage ratios measure the firm's use of debt to finance assets and operations.

11. __A) Liquidity ratio.__ Working capital equals current assets minus current liabilities. Liquidity (solvency) ratios measure the short-term viability of the business, i.e., the firm's ability to continue in the short term by paying its obligations.

12. __B) Activity ratio.__ Accounts receivable turnover equals net credit sales divided by average accounts receivable. Activity ratios measure the firm's ability to generate revenue and income.

13. __A) Liquidity ratio.__ The cash ratio equals the sum of cash equivalents and marketable securities, divided by current liabilities. Liquidity (solvency) ratios measure the short-term viability of the business, i.e., the firm's ability to continue in the short term by paying its obligations.

14. __D) Profitability ratio.__ The profit margin on sales equals net income divided by sales. Profitability ratios measure income on a relative basis.

15. __B) Activity ratio.__ Fixed asset turnover equals net assets divided by net fixed assets. Activity ratios measure the firm's ability to generate revenue and income.

5. Classification (10 Gradable Items)

1. __Monetary.__ A monetary asset is either cash or a claim to receive cash.

2. __Nonmonetary.__ Nonmonetary assets are held primarily for resale or to provide services for the business. They also may be claims to cash that change in relationship to future prices of specific goods and services. A third category consists of residual rights (e.g., goodwill or common stock not accounted for using the equity method). Examples are intellectual property (such as patents, copyrights, and trademarks); most inventories; and property, plant, and equipment (including accumulated depreciation).

3. __Nonmonetary.__ Nonmonetary assets are held primarily for resale or to provide services for the business. They also may be claims to cash that change in relationship to future prices of specific goods and services. A third category consists of residual rights (e.g., goodwill or common stock not accounted for using the equity method). Examples are intellectual property (such as patents, copyrights, and trademarks); most inventories; and property, plant, and equipment (including accumulated depreciation).

4. __Monetary.__ A monetary asset is either cash or a claim to receive cash. The amount is fixed or determinable without regard to future prices of specific goods or services.

5. __Nonmonetary.__ Nonmonetary assets are held primarily for resale or to provide services for the business. They also may be claims to cash that change in relationship to future prices of specific goods and services. A third category consists of residual rights (e.g., goodwill or common stock not accounted for using the equity method). Examples are intellectual property (such as patents, copyrights, and trademarks); most inventories; and property, plant, and equipment (including accumulated depreciation).

6. __Monetary.__ A monetary liability is an obligation to pay cash. The amount is fixed or determinable without regard to future prices of specific goods and services. Examples are accounts and notes payable, bonds payable, and various accrued payables.

7. __Monetary.__ A monetary asset is either cash or a claim to receive cash. The amount is fixed or determinable without regard to future prices of specific goods or services.

8. __Monetary.__ A monetary asset is either cash or a claim to receive cash. The amount is fixed or determinable without regard to future prices of specific goods or services. Examples are accounts and notes receivable (including allowance accounts), bond investments, long-term receivables, and demand bank deposits.

9. __Nonmonetary.__ Nonmonetary liabilities are obligations to provide goods or services in amounts that are fixed or determinable without regard to price changes. They also may be obligations to pay cash amounts dependent on future prices of specific goods or services. From the consolidated entity's perspective, the minority interest is a residual that varies with earnings of the subsidiary, dividends, and other transactions affecting equity.

10. __Nonmonetary.__ Nonmonetary liabilities are obligations to provide goods or services in amounts that are fixed or determinable without regard to price changes. They also may be obligations to pay cash amounts dependent on future prices of specific goods or services. An example is deferred revenue if the obligation is to provide goods or services.

6. Communication (5 Gradable Items; for grading instructions, please refer to page 12.)

The objectives of translating a foreign subsidiary's financial statements are to (1) provide information that is generally compatible with the expected economic effects of a rate change on a subsidiary's cash flows and equity and to (2) reflect the subsidiary's financial results and relationships in single currency consolidated financial statements, as measured in its functional currency and in conformity with U.S. GAAP.

The method used to convert foreign currency amounts into units of the reporting currency is the functional currency translation approach. This method (1) identifies the functional currency of the entity (the currency of the primary economic environment in which the foreign entity operates), (2) measures all elements of the financial statements in the functional currency, and (3) uses a current exchange rate for translation from the functional currency to the reporting currency. Assets and liabilities are translated at the exchange rate at the balance sheet date. Revenues, expenses, gains, and losses should be translated at the rates in effect when they were recognized. However, translation at a weighted-average rate for the period may be used for these items.

Foreign currency translation adjustments for a foreign operation that is relatively self-contained and integrated within its environment do not affect cash flows of the reporting enterprise and should be excluded from net income. Accordingly, translation adjustments are reported in other comprehensive income.

If the books of a foreign entity are maintained in a currency not the functional currency, foreign currency amounts must be remeasured into the functional currency using the temporal method. They are then translated into the reporting currency using the current-rate method. Nonmonetary balance sheet items and related revenue, expense, gain, and loss accounts are remeasured at the historical rate. Monetary items are remeasured at the current rate. Any gain or loss on remeasurement is a component of income from continuing operations.

7. Research/Authoritative Literature (1 Gradable Item)

Answer: FAS 52, App. A, Par. 42

FAS 52 -- *Foreign Currency Translation*

Appendix A, 42.

Financing indicators

1) Foreign Currency – Financing is primarily denominated in foreign currency, and funds generated by the foreign entity's operations are sufficient to service existing and normally expected debt obligations.

2) Parent's Currency – Financing is primarily from the parent or other dollar-denominated obligations, or funds generated by the foreign entity's operations are not sufficient to service existing and normally expected debt obligations without the infusion of additional funds from the parent company. Infusion of additional funds from the parent company for expansion is not a factor, provided funds generated by the foreign entity's expanded operations are expected to be sufficient to service that additional financing.

Note: This information can be found in Appendix A, "Determination of the Functional Currency."

Scoring Schedule:

	Correct Responses		Gradable Items		Weights		
Tab 3	_____	÷	18	×	20%	=	_____
Tab 4	_____	÷	15	×	15%	=	_____
Tab 5	_____	÷	10	×	20%	=	_____
Tab 6	_____	÷	5	×	30%	=	_____
Tab 7	_____	÷	1	×	15%	=	_____
							(Your Score)

Use Gleim's *CPA Gleim Online* to practice more simulations in a realistic environment.

STUDY UNIT SEVENTEEN
GOVERNMENTAL ACCOUNTING I

(25 pages of outline)

This study unit and the next one relate to the governmental entities group in the Content Specification Outlines. Study Unit 17 provides an overview of (1) the fundamental concepts underlying state and local governmental accounting and reporting, (2) the importance of budgetary accounting in government, and (3) the recognition rules and journal entries related to governmental financing. Study Unit 18 describes (1) the accounts and journal entries related to transactions specific to governmental entities, (2) the process of defining the governmental reporting entity, (3) the components of the comprehensive annual financial report (CAFR), (4) the reporting requirements for government-wide and fund-based financial statements, and (5) other required information in the CAFR. For GAAP relative to specific types of transactions, events, and entities, study the summaries of currently effective GASB Statements (GASBSs) and Interpretations in Appendix A.

17.1 FUND ACCOUNTING CONCEPTS AND REPORTING

Authoritative Pronouncements

1. **Standard-Setting for Governmental Accounting**

    a. The National Committee on Municipal and Governmental Accounting served from 1934 through 1974.

        1) In 1968, the Committee established principles of accounting and reporting for state and local governments in its publication *Governmental Accounting, Auditing, and Financial Reporting (GAAFR)*.

    b. The National Council on Governmental Accounting (NCGA) served from 1974 through 1984.

        1) In 1979, the Council issued NCGA Statement 1, *Governmental Accounting and Financial Reporting Principles*. Much of this statement remains in effect.

            a) It restated the principles of GAAFR and included some aspects of the relevant AICPA Audit Guides and SOPs. The Council also issued various other pronouncements.

    c. The **Governmental Accounting Standards Board (GASB)**, established in 1984, is the primary standard setter for state and local governmental entities.

        1) The **Financial Accounting Foundation** oversees the GASB and the FASB.

            a) GASBS 1, *Authoritative Status of NCGA Pronouncements and AICPA Industry Audit Guide*, continues these pronouncements in force "until altered, amended, supplemented, revoked, or superseded" by the GASB.

            b) The GASB has issued 53 Statements, 6 Interpretations, and 4 Concepts Statements as of November 1, 2008.

        2) The AICPA Audit and Accounting Guide, *Audits of State and Local Governments*, was cleared by the GASB.

    d.   The most notable GASB pronouncement is **GASBS 34**, *Basic Statements – and Management's Discussion and Analysis – for State and Local Governments.* It **fundamentally changed the governmental accounting and reporting model**.

        1)   Thus, it underlies Study Units 17 and 18.

        2)   The greatest change made by GASBS 34 is the requirement for a reporting unit to issue **government-wide financial statements** (a statement of net assets and a statement of activities). They are included in the **basic financial statements** with the fund financial statements and notes.

   2.   **Applicability of Nongovernmental Pronouncements**

    a.   The **funds and activities** of governmental units should be presented fairly and with full disclosure in **conformity with GAAP**.

        1)   However, if finance-related legal and contractual provisions differ from GAAP, the governmental unit should present the additional schedules and narratives necessary to meet its responsibilities.

        2)   GASBS 35, *Basic Financial Statements – and Management's Discussion and Analysis – for Public Colleges and Universities*, requires governmental colleges and universities to apply the reporting model stated in GASBS 34.

        3)   **Governmental health care providers** should apply the AICPA Audit and Accounting Guide, *Health Care Organizations*, a pronouncement cleared by the GASB.

        4)   On **November 30, 1989**, the date of the **Jurisdictional Determination**, the trustees of the Financial Accounting Foundation reaffirmed the GASB as the standard setter for state and local governments.

           a)   One result was the establishment of GAAP hierarchies. Thus, **pronouncements of the FASB after November 30, 1989**, are not effective for governmental entities absent GASB action.

           b)   The highest level in the state and local governmental hierarchy consists of (1) GASB Statements and Interpretations and (2) AICPA and FASB pronouncements applied to state and local governments by the FASB.

Fund Accounting

   3.   The diversity of governmental activities and the need for legal compliance preclude the use of a single accounting entity. Thus, independent, distinct fiscal and accounting entities called funds are established.

    a.   A **fund** is "a fiscal and accounting entity with a self-balancing set of accounts recording cash and other financial resources, together with all related liabilities and residual equities and balances, and changes therein, which are segregated for the purpose of carrying on specific activities or attaining certain objectives in accordance with special regulations, restrictions, or limitations" (GASBS 1).

    b.   A fund accounting system of a governmental reporting entity must be able to present fairly in **conformity with GAAP** and with full disclosure the financial position and results of operations of the funds. Also, it must determine and demonstrate **compliance with finance-related legal and contractual provisions**.

        1)   No more than the number of funds required by law and efficient financial administration should be created.

   4.   **Funds Used in Governmental Accounting**

    a.   **Governmental funds** account for the nonbusiness activities of government and its current, expendable, general resources (most often **taxes**).

        1)   The **general fund** accounts for all financial resources except those required to be accounted for in another fund. Only one general fund may be reported.

2) **Special revenue funds** account for proceeds of specific revenue sources (other than for certain trusts and major capital projects) that are legally required to be spent for specified purposes.

    a) For example, a government may have a special revenue fund for operation of its municipal auditorium, its zoo, or road maintenance.

    b) Donations provided by benefactors for programs to be administered by the government also are accounted for in special revenue funds.

3) **Capital projects funds** account for financial resources, including general obligation bond proceeds, dedicated to the construction of major capital facilities, such as schools, bridges, or tunnels. But other capital facilities may be financed through proprietary funds or certain trust funds.

    a) The assets themselves are not accounted for in these funds.

4) **Debt service funds** account for resources dedicated to paying the principal and interest on general long-term debt. But these funds do not account for the debt itself.

5) **Permanent funds** account for assets donated by outside parties. The government is allowed to spend income generated by these assets but not the principal. An example is a perpetual-care fund for a public cemetery.

b. **Proprietary funds** account for the **business-type activities** of government. They serve defined **customer** groups and are generally financed through **fees**.

1) **Enterprise funds** account for government activities that benefit outside parties who are willing to pay for them, such as municipal pools, parking garages, and utilities. They are the funds that most closely resemble private businesses.

2) **Internal service funds** account for activities performed primarily for the benefit of other government agencies, such as a centralized information technology department or motor pool.

c. **Fiduciary funds** account for resources held by the government in trust or as an agent for **specific individuals, private organizations, or other governments**. They cannot be used for the reporting entity's purposes.

1) **Pension (and other employee benefit) trust funds** account for employee benefit programs.

2) **Investment trust funds** account for resources held for investment on behalf of other governments in an **investment pool**.

3) **Private-purpose trust funds** account for all other trust arrangements that benefit individuals, private organizations, or other governments.

4) **Agency funds** account for resources held temporarily in a purely custodial capacity, such as tolls that will be remitted to a private business.

5. **Objectives of Governmental Reporting**

a. **"Accountability is the paramount objective of governmental financial reporting – the objective from which all other financial reporting objectives flow."**

1) **Fiscal accountability** is "the responsibility of governments to justify that their actions in the current period have complied with public decisions concerning the raising and spending of public moneys in the **short term**."

2) **Operational accountability** is "governments' responsibility to report the extent to which they have met their accounting objectives efficiently and effectively, using all resources available for that purpose, and whether they can continue to meet their objectives for the **foreseeable future**" (GASBS 34).

b. Governmental reporting traditionally has emphasized fiscal accountability for governmental activities and operational accountability for business-type activities and fiduciary funds.

1) Reporting for governmental bodies was **fundamentally changed** by GASBS 34. Its most important provision was the requirement that governmental entities report **two sets of financial statements**.

c. The fund financial statements of **governmental funds** continue to focus on the fiscal accountability of governmental activities.

1) However, **government-wide financial statements** now provide information about the operational accountability of the governmental activities and business-type activities of the government as a whole.

2) The financial statements of **proprietary funds** and **fiduciary funds** provide information about the operational accountability of those funds.

d. **Interperiod equity** is an important component of accountability that is fundamental to public administration. **Financial resources** received during a period should suffice to pay for the services provided during that period. Moreover, **debt** should be repaid during the probable period of usefulness of the assets acquired.

1) Thus, governmental reporting should help users assess whether **future taxpayers must bear the financial burden** for services already provided.

2) Governmental financial reporting also should assist users (e.g., citizens and legislative and oversight bodies) in making **economic, political, and social decisions**. For example, revenue forecasts may help advocates for increased expenditures for education or transportation (GASB Concepts Statement 1).

Measurement Focus and Basis of Accounting

6. The measurement focus of a set of financial statements refers to what is being **measured or tracked** by the information provided. The basis of accounting refers to the **timing of the recognition** in the financial records of economic events or transactions.

7. The **current financial resources measurement focus** and the **modified accrual basis** of accounting are used to report the **governmental fund** financial statements.

a. This approach emphasizes **short-term** fiscal accountability for expendable available financial resources. The reporting elements are sources, uses, and balances of current financial resources.

b. Under the **modified accrual basis** of accounting, **revenue** or another increase in financial resources (such as bond issue proceeds) is recognized when it is **susceptible to accrual**.

1) Revenue is accrued when it is measurable and **available to finance expenditures of the current period**.

a) **Available** means collectible within the current period or "soon enough thereafter" to be used to pay liabilities of the current period. Ordinarily, material revenues that are otherwise not recorded until received are accrued if receipt is delayed beyond the normal time.

b) For **property tax purposes**, the phrase "soon enough thereafter" means **not more than 60 days after the end of the year**. But in unusual cases, a longer period may be justified. The governmental unit should disclose the period used and the justification for it.

c) Property taxes are measurable when assessed property values can be multiplied by the tax rate to obtain the total tax to be levied.

      2) A charge to operations is normally made when goods or services are acquired. Thus, **expenditures** are usually measurable and should be recognized when the **related liability is incurred**.

      3) However, expenditures for **principal and interest** on **general long-term debt** are usually recognized only when those **amounts are due**. The amount of an expenditure is what is normally liquidated with expendable available financial resources.

      4) For a fuller discussion, see Subunit 17.3.

8.   The **economic resources measurement focus** and the **accrual basis** of accounting are used to report the **government-wide, proprietary fund**, and **fiduciary fund** financial statements.

    a.   This approach provides **longer-term operational accountability** information about economic activity. It measures revenues and expenses in the **same way as in commercial accounting** but without necessarily emphasizing net income. Instead, the emphasis is on a longer-range measure of revenues earned or levied (and accrued immediately if measurable).

      1) Furthermore, the economic resources model focuses on **cost of services**.

    b.   Under the **accrual basis** of accounting, most economic transactions and other events that are feasibly measurable are recognized **without regard to cash flows**. Moreover, a charge is made to operations when goods or services are used or consumed, not when they are acquired. Acquired but unused goods and services are treated as assets.

      1) Thus, revenues, expenses, gains, losses, assets, and liabilities that arise from **exchange or exchange-like transactions** are accrued when the exchange occurs.

      2) Items arising from **nonexchange transactions** are recognized as described in GASBS 33 (see Subunit 17.3).

    c.   The **cash basis** is not used in governmental accounting except for miscellaneous cash items that are not feasibly measurable until cash is received or paid.

    d.   **Transfers** are recognized in all affected funds when the interfund receivable and payable arise.

General Capital Assets and General Long-Term Liabilities

9.   General capital assets are all capital assets **not** reported in the **proprietary funds** or the **fiduciary funds**. Thus, they are not specifically related to activities reported in nongovernmental funds. They usually result from expenditure of governmental fund financial resources.

    a.   They are reported at **historical cost, including ancillary charges** (freight-in, site preparation, etc.), only in the **governmental activities** column of the government-wide statement of net assets.

    b.   In **governmental funds**, the full cost of a capital asset is debited as an expenditure when acquired in accordance with the current financial resources measurement focus.

    c.   **Donated capital assets** are reported at **fair value** (plus ancillary charges).

10. General long-term liabilities are all **unmatured long-term liabilities not** directly related to and expected to be paid from proprietary funds and fiduciary funds. They should be reported only in the **governmental activities** column of the government-wide statement of net assets. General long-term liabilities include

    a.   The unmatured principal amounts of general obligation indebtedness (such as bonds, warrants, and notes);

    b.   Lease-purchase agreements and other commitments not recorded as current liabilities in governmental funds; and

     c.   The noncurrent portions of liabilities for

         1)   Capital leases,
         2)   Operating leases with scheduled rent increases,
         3)   Compensated absences,
         4)   Claims and judgments,
         5)   Pensions,
         6)   Special termination benefits, and
         7)   Landfill closure and postclosure care.

Accounting for Capital Assets and Long-Term Liabilities in Other Fund Types

11.   In **proprietary funds**, the measurement focus is on economic resources. Capital assets and long-term liabilities specifically related to proprietary funds activities are accounted for in the same manner as in a for-profit business. They are reported in those funds and in the government-wide statements.

12.   **Fiduciary funds** contain resources held on behalf of other governments, private organizations, or individuals. Because these resources are held in a trustee capacity and cannot be used to finance the operations of the government, capital assets and long-term liabilities specifically related to fiduciary funds are reported in the fund financial statements but not in the government-wide statements.

Summary

13.   The following table summarizes reporting in the financial statements:

	Governmental Funds Financial Statements	Proprietary Funds Financial Statements	Fiduciary Funds Financial Statements	Government-Wide Financial Statements
Measurement Focus	Current financial resources	Economic resources	Economic resources	Economic resources
Basis of Accounting	Modified accrual	Accrual	Accrual	Accrual
Capital Assets	No	Yes	Trust funds only	Yes
Long-Term Liabilities	No	Yes	Trust funds only	Yes

Stop and review! You have completed the outline for this subunit. Study multiple-choice questions 1 through 9 beginning on page 639.

17.2 BUDGETARY ACCOUNTING AND ENCUMBRANCES

Budgetary Accounting

1.   Budgetary accounting is unique to governmental bodies. A governmental body's formal budget is an expression of **public policy**.

     a.   The budget represents a statement of financial intent indicating how the governmental entity **plans** to raise revenue and expend its resources.

     b.   For most governments, the budget is **legally enforceable** against the financial managers. By law, they cannot exceed the budget without a formally approved budget amendment.

     c.   The budget provides a basis for **evaluating performance**. Actual expenditures and expenses are compared with amounts budgeted for each period.

2.   Because the formally adopted budget has legal implications, most governmental bodies **integrate their budgets into the accounting system**.

     a.   According to GASBS 1, *Authoritative Status of NCGA Pronouncements and AICPA Industry Audit Guide*, this integration should be done for the following:

         1)   The general fund
         2)   Special revenue funds
         3)   Other governmental funds with numerous transactions

b. Integration is usually **unnecessary in debt service funds** because transactions are few and contractual provisions prescribe receipts and expenditures.

c. Some degree of budgetary integration **may be needed** in a **capital projects fund** when many projects are being accounted for in the fund or work is being done by the governmental entity itself.

d. Because flexible rather than fixed budgets are usually prepared for **proprietary funds**, integration of fixed budgetary accounts is **normally inappropriate** for such funds.

e. Budget integration is necessary for **fiduciary funds that are similar to special revenue funds**. It is not necessary for agency funds or for fiduciary funds that are budgeted similarly to proprietary funds.

3. **Common terminology and classifications** must be used consistently throughout the budget, the accounts, and the financial reports of each fund.

   a. The budget(s) to be adopted should encompass every governmental, proprietary, and fiduciary fund of the governmental entity.

   b. The **basis of accounting** for the budget preferably should correspond to the basis of accounting used by the fund for which the budget is being prepared.

   c. However, if the law requires another basis, governmental entities often keep supplemental records that permit reporting in accordance with GAAP.

4. **Budgetary accounts** are used to record the budget at the beginning of the fiscal period.

   a. Despite being formally integrated into the accounting system, the budgetary amounts **are not reported**. The budgetary entries are **separate and distinct** from both the financial statements.

   b. The following are the **principal accounts** used in the entry to record the annual budget:

      1) **Estimated revenues** is an **anticipatory asset** that is debited in the budgetary entry. It reflects the amount expected to be collected from a governmental body's main sources of revenue, such as taxes, fees, and fines.

      2) **Estimated other financing sources** is another anticipatory asset that includes the sources of government financing other than its main revenues. Examples are the face amount of long-term debt, issuance premium, and interfund transfers.

      3) **Estimated other financing uses** is an anticipatory liability used to record an expected flow of resources to another fund. Issuance discount and interfund transfers for debt service are common examples.

      4) **Appropriations** is an **anticipatory liability** reflecting the total amount authorized to be expended by the governmental unit for the fiscal period. It is credited in the budgetary entry.

         a) Unless a balanced budget or deficit is planned, the balance in estimated revenues exceeds that in appropriations control. This allows for some flexibility if revenues prove to be lower, or expenditures prove to be higher, than expected.

      5) **Fund balance** is a real account. It is the difference (fund equity) between the assets and liabilities of a governmental fund.

         a) Some accountants prefer to use a **budgetary fund balance**, a nominal account, rather than unreserved fund balance, a real account, to record the budgeted change in fund balance for the year.

         b) In the context of accounting for and reporting governmental funds, the term **reserve** means that part of the fund balance is not available to be appropriated for expenditure or is legally restricted to a particular use. Examples are reserves for encumbrances, inventories, supplies, and employee benefits.

    c)   Portions of unreserved fund balance may be **designated** to indicate that management has tentative plans for use of the resources. Hence, designated amounts are legally available for other uses.

    d)   Reserves are reported in the fund balance section of a governmental fund's balance sheets.

    e)   **Valuation accounts** are not reserves.

    f)   In **proprietary-fund accounting**, reserves or designations are not recognized. However, restricted net assets is reported on the fund balance sheet.

EXAMPLE

A state adopts its budget for the year. The following entries record the budget for the general fund and one of the special revenue funds:

General fund:

Estimated revenues -- sales taxes	$2,400,000,000	
Estimated other financing sources -- bond proceeds	400,000,000	
Appropriations control .		$2,100,000,000
Estimated other financing uses		
-- transfer to debt service fund		600,000,000
Budgetary fund balance		100,000,000

Special revenue fund -- highway maintenance:

Estimated revenues -- vehicle license fees	$130,000,000	
Appropriations -- salaries		$40,000,000
Appropriations -- wages		20,000,000
Appropriations -- road equipment		40,000,000
Appropriations -- construction materials		20,000,000
Budgetary fund balance		10,000,000

---

    c.   **As conditions change during the year**, a portion of the fund balance can be moved to appropriations. This is the formal acknowledgment in the budget of new circumstances.

EXAMPLE

The state discovers during the course of the year that it has underestimated the amount of materials needed to maintain its roads. The authorization to spend more on materials must be recognized in the budget.

Special revenue fund -- highway maintenance:

Budgetary fund balance	$5,000,000	
Appropriations -- construction materials		$5,000,000

Encumbrances

    5.   Governmental accounting differs from accounting for private entities.

        a.   When a **for-profit** entity arranges to purchase a good or service, no entry is made in the accounting records. A payable is not accrued until the good is delivered or the service performed.

            1)   When a **governmental entity** makes a commitment to expend resources, that is, when a contract is signed or a purchase order approved, the amount is formally entered in the accounting system as an **encumbrance**.

            2)   Encumbrance accounting is used by governmental funds, especially general and special revenue funds.

6. The journal entry debits the **encumbrances control** account and increases a special **fund balance** account that is often called **reserve for encumbrances**. Unlike the budgetary entries, encumbrances **are reported** in the financial statements.

EXAMPLE

The state has contracted to purchase road maintenance equipment. The following entry is made in the **fund financial statements**:

Special revenue fund -- highway maintenance:

Encumbrances control	$750,000	
Fund balance -- reserved for encumbrances		$750,000

---

   a. At any given time, the encumbrances control account summarizes a government's spending commitments.

7. When the good is delivered or the service performed, **two entries are made**.

   a. **The original entry is reversed.**

EXAMPLE

The state takes delivery of the equipment.

Special revenue fund -- highway maintenance:

Fund balance -- reserved for encumbrances	$750,000	
Encumbrances control		$750,000

---

   b. **The legal obligation to pay is recognized.**

      1) Governmental funds report **expenditures** rather than expenses, and credit **vouchers payable** rather than accounts payable.

EXAMPLE

The equipment costs less than anticipated.

Special revenue fund -- highway maintenance:

Expenditures -- road equipment	$745,000	
Vouchers payable		$745,000

---

   c. If the **actual cost** of the good or service is **greater** than the amount of the original encumbrance, the excess is an expenditure of the period in which it is paid.

Year-End Closing

8. **The budgetary entries are reversed.** Note that the mid-year amendment to the budget for construction materials is taken into account in the reversal entry for the special revenue fund.

General fund:

Appropriations control	$2,100,000,000	
Estimated other financing uses		
-- transfer to debt service fund	600,000,000	
Budgetary fund balance	100,000,000	
Estimated revenues -- sales taxes		$2,400,000,000
Estimated other financing sources -- bond proceeds		400,000,000

Special revenue fund -- highway maintenance:

Appropriations -- salaries	$40,000,000	
Appropriations -- wages	20,000,000	
Appropriations -- road equipment	40,000,000	
Appropriations -- construction materials	25,000,000	
Budgetary fund balance	5,000,000	
Estimated revenues -- vehicle license fees		$130,000,000

9.   **Encumbrances are removed from the books.**

> ### EXAMPLE
>
> At year-end, the state has $12,751,215 of outstanding encumbrances.
>
> Fund balance -- reserved for encumbrances $12,751,215
>   Encumbrances control $12,751,215

a.   The common assumption is that (1) all appropriations lapse, but (2) the entity intends to honor its commitments. On this assumption, the accounting treatment is to reduce unreserved fund balance. Thus, a government that **carries encumbrances over** is acknowledging in its financial statements the claim on next period's resources of commitments made in the reporting period.

> ### EXAMPLE
>
> The amount of outstanding encumbrances is **reclassified** on the balance sheet.
>
> Unreserved fund balance $12,751,215
>   Fund balance -- reserved for encumbrances $12,751,215
>
> At the beginning of the next year, the entity restores the accounts to the relationships existing before encumbrances were closed.
>
> Encumbrances control $12,751,215
>   Unreserved fund balance $12,751,215

b.   Common anticipated liabilities, such as wages payable and payroll taxes payable, need not be encumbered because of the controls in place for such expenditures.

Summary

10.   The following table summarizes the use of budgetary and encumbrance accounting:

	Governmental Funds	Proprietary Funds	Fiduciary Funds
Budgetary accounting	General and special revenue funds; other funds with many transactions; rarely in debt service funds	Rarely	If similar to special revenue funds
Outlays encumbered	General and special revenue funds; possibly other funds	No	No

Stop and review! You have completed the outline for this subunit. Study multiple-choice questions 10 through 20 beginning on page 642.

17.3 GOVERNMENTAL SOURCES OF FINANCING

Nonexchange Transactions

1.   **Revenue recognition** for a government is unlike that for a private entity.

a.   A government often does not directly exchange something of value, such as a good or service, for its sources of income. Primary sources of government revenue, therefore, are **nonexchange transactions**.

2.   GASBS 33, *Accounting and Financial Reporting for Nonexchange Transactions*, classified all nonexchange transactions into **four categories**.

a.   **Derived tax revenues** are assessments on underlying exchange transactions. The primary examples are income taxes and sales taxes. Income is earned or a sale is completed and a tax is levied based on the amount involved.

b. **Imposed nonexchange revenues** are assessments on nongovernmental entities, for example, property taxes, forfeitures, or fines. No underlying exchange exists. The assessment is on ownership of property (real estate, automobile, etc.) or the commission of an act (speeding, failing to obtain an occupational license, etc.).

c. **Government-mandated nonexchange transactions** occur when one government provides resources to a government at another level and requires that they be used for a specific purpose. Fulfillment of **eligibility requirements** is essential. An example is federal grant money that state governments are required to expend on primary education.

d. **Voluntary nonexchange transactions** arise from legislative or contractual agreements entered into willingly by the parties. Thus, they are **not** imposed on any party, and fulfillment of **eligibility requirements** is essential. Moreover, one party may be a nongovernmental entity (e.g., an individual). Examples of voluntary nonexchange transactions are certain grants, certain entitlements, and private donations (such as a gift of an art collection to a municipal museum).

3. The **timing of recognition** of assets, liabilities, and expenses or expenditures that arise from nonexchange transactions is not affected by the basis of accounting (accrual or modified accrual).

a. **Revenue recognition** on the **modified accrual basis**, however, requires that the GASBS 33 criteria be met and that the resources be **available**.

1) Accordingly, the revenue recognition criteria described below are those for accrual-basis accounting, but the availability criterion also may need to be met.

b. GASBS 33 does not change the method of accounting for **property taxes** (recognition in the period for which they were levied).

Accounting Procedures

4. **Derived tax revenues. Assets** are recognized when the underlying exchange transaction occurs or resources are received, whichever is earlier.

a. **Revenues** are recognized when the underlying exchange transaction occurs.

1) Resources received before the underlying exchange are **deferred revenues**, that is, **liabilities**.

EXAMPLE

Retail establishments most likely report their sales monthly to the state government.

Receivable -- sales taxes	$100,000,000	
Revenue -- sales taxes		$100,000,000

---

b. In the **governmental fund financial statements**, resources also must be available to qualify for revenue recognition.

5. **Imposed nonexchange revenues. Assets** are recognized when (a) a legal claim to the resources has arisen or (b) resources are received, whichever is earlier.

a. **Revenues** are recognized when the resources are required to be used or when their use is first allowed by the time requirements.

1) Resources received or recognized as receivable before the time requirements are met are **deferred revenues**.

2) If **no time requirements** have been established, then revenue recognition is at the same time as the recognition of the assets.

b. In the **governmental fund financial statements**, resources also must be available to qualify for revenue recognition.

c.   For **property taxes**, revenue is recognized in the period for which they were **levied**.

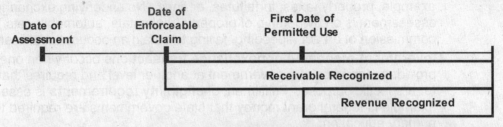

EXAMPLE

On November 1, a city levies $110,000,000 of property taxes that are due December 1 and are to be used in the following calendar year.

November 1:
No entry

The city offers a discount to taxpayers who pay early and a few property owners take advantage of this provision. Any amounts received before they are legally due (December 1) must be recorded as a liability (deferred revenue).

November 30:

Cash	$1,350,000	
Deferred property tax revenues		$1,350,000

On the day when the assessment is legally enforceable, the city recognizes a receivable (reduced by an allowance for uncollectibles) and a liability (deferred revenue).

December 1:

Property taxes receivable	$108,000,000	
Deferred property tax revenues		$100,000,000
Allowance for uncollectible taxes		8,000,000

Once the period when the resources must or may be used begins (the period for which the taxes were levied), the city removes the liability and recognizes the revenue.

January 1:

Deferred property tax revenues	$101,350,000	
Revenues -- property taxes		$101,350,000

6.   **Government-mandated and voluntary nonexchange transactions. Assets** are recognized by recipients and **liabilities** by providers when all eligibility requirements are met or resources are received, whichever is earlier.

a.   **Revenues** are recognized by recipients and **expenses or expenditures** by providers when all eligibility requirements are met. Thus, a provider debits an expense or expenditure and credits a liability or an asset.

1)   A recipient debits an asset or a liability and credits revenue.

2)   In the **governmental funds financial statements**, resources also must be available to qualify for revenue recognition.

b.   If the provider requires the recipient to use the resources in or beginning in the following period, prepaid amounts are recognized as **advances (assets)** by providers and as **deferred revenues (liabilities)** by recipients.

c.   If the provider requires that resources be maintained intact in perpetuity, for a specified number of years, or until a specific event, they should be recognized as **revenues** by the recipient when received and as **expenses or expenditures** by the provider when paid. Examples of such arrangements are permanent endowments and term endowments.

d.   When a provider shares its **derived tax revenues** or **imposed nonexchange revenues** with a recipient, both parties account for the sharing as a voluntary or government-mandated nonexchange transaction, as appropriate (GASBS 36, *Recipient Reporting for Certain Shared Nonexchange Revenues*).

e. **Required characteristics of recipients.** For example, a state may not be able to recognize revenue from a federal law enforcement grant until the state has a certain number of highway patrol officers per mile of highway, as required by the federal legislation establishing the grant.

1) Even if the state already has a sufficient number of patrol officers, it cannot recognize revenue from the grant until the first day specified in the enabling legislation.

f. **Reimbursement.** Some grants are on a reimbursement basis, that is, the recipient spends the money before reimbursement by the grantor. In such cases, the recipient does not recognize revenue until the money has been spent (thereby establishing a receivable).

Summary of Nonexchange Transactions

7. The following table summarizes the recognition criteria for nonexchange transactions:

Category	Timing of Recognition
Derived tax revenues	**Assets** – Earlier of when underlying exchange has occurred or resources are received. **Revenues** – When underlying exchange has occurred (advance receipts are credited to deferred revenues). Resources also should be **available** if resources are accounted for in a governmental fund.
Imposed nonexchange revenues	**Assets** – Earlier of when an enforceable legal claim has arisen or resources are received. **Revenues** – When resources are required to be used or use is first allowed (for property taxes, the period for which levied). Resources also should be **available** if resources are accounted for in a governmental fund. Absent time requirements, asset and revenue recognition are at the same time.
Government-mandated and voluntary nonexchange transactions	**Assets and liabilities** – Earlier of when all eligibility requirements have been met or (for assets) resources are received. **Revenues and expenses or expenditures** – When all eligibility requirements have been met (advance receipts or payments are recorded as deferred revenues or advances, respectively). Given **time requirements**, revenues and expenses or expenditures are recorded when the resources are, respectively, received or paid. The resulting net assets, equity, or fund balance is restricted. Resources also should be **available** if resources are accounted for in a governmental fund.

Bonds

8. **Issuance.** The proceeds of long-term debt are not revenues but are a major source of funding for governmental units.

a. The **government-wide financial statements** report all resources and obligations, regardless of whether they are current or noncurrent.

1) The receipt of cash and the related obligation are recognized. The inflow of financing sources from the bond issue is not.

EXAMPLE

The state issues bonds to finance the construction of a new building.

Cash	$200,000,000	
Bonds payable		$200,000,000

---

2) Any **premium received or discount paid** upon issuance is not recognized in the government-wide financial statements. Premium and discount do not affect the amount of long-term resources that must be expended to retire the bonds.

b.   In the **governmental fund financial statements**, the treatment is different because they have a short-term focus, and bonds are not repaid with current financial resources.

1)   The credit to other financing sources emphasizes that this inflow of resources is not a revenue.

EXAMPLE

The fund out of which the cash will be spent recognizes the receipt of the cash and the related financing sources.

Capital projects fund -- highway patrol headquarters building:
Cash	$202,000,000	
Other financing sources -- bond proceeds		$200,000,000
Other financing sources -- bond issue premium		2,000,000

---

2)   The premium is treated as an inflow of additional resources. It will not be amortized.

9.   **Construction.** Payments for the project are made from the bond proceeds.

a.   In the **government-wide financial statements**, the finished building (or construction-in-progress) is reported as a general capital asset.

b.   In the **governmental fund financial statements**, payments to the contractor are reported as expenditures.

1)   The building itself is not capitalized in the governmental fund financial statements.

EXAMPLE

A progress payment is made for work done during the year.

Capital projects fund -- highway patrol headquarters building:
Expenditures -- capital outlay	$85,000,000	
Cash		$85,000,000

---

10.   **Retirement.** When the bonds are repaid, the entries reflect the same differences in recognition as in the issuance.

a.   The **government-wide financial statements** recognize the reduction in assets and liabilities and the accompanying interest expense.

1)   Just as the receipt of the bond proceeds was not a revenue in the government-wide statements, so the retirement of the principal is not an expenditure.

EXAMPLE

The current portion of the bond principal is retired.

Bonds payable	$10,000,000	
Interest expense	700,000	
Cash		$10,700,000

---

b.   The **governmental fund financial statements** reflect a multi-stage process.

EXAMPLE

General fund resources are earmarked for debt service.

<u>General fund:</u>
Other financing uses -- interfund transfer to
  debt service fund $10,700,000
    Due to debt service fund $10,700,000

<u>Debt service fund:</u>
Due from general fund $10,700,000
    Other financing sources -- interfund transfer
      from general fund $10,700,000

The resources are transferred.

<u>General fund:</u>
Due to debt service fund $10,700,000
    Cash $10,700,000

<u>Debt service fund:</u>
Cash $10,700,000
    Due from general fund $10,700,000

Expenditures are recorded when principal and interest are legally due.

<u>Debt service fund:</u>
Expenditure -- bond principal $10,000,000
Expenditure -- bond interest   700,000
    Bonds payable $10,000,000
    Interest payable   700,000

The current portion of the debt is repaid.

<u>Debt service fund:</u>
Bonds payable $10,000,000
Interest payable   700,000
    Cash $10,700,000

---

c.   The **capital projects fund** records no transactions involving the retirement of debt.

11.   **Anticipation notes.** Governments may issue short-term debt because cash is required before the financing is available. In these cases, bond, tax, or revenue anticipation notes are issued.

a.   In the **government-wide statements**, the notes are reported in two components if average maturities exceed one year (amounts due in one year and amounts due in more than one year).

1)   These liabilities may be reported in either the governmental or business-type activities column.

b.   In the **proprietary funds**, they are reported as long-term if the following criteria for refinancing on a long-term basis have been met:

1)   The government has shown an intent to refinance the notes on a long-term basis, and

2)   The government has demonstrated the ability to consummate such refinancing.

c.   For **governmental funds**, if (1) all legal steps have been taken to refinance the notes, and (2) the intent to refinance is supported by an ability to consummate the refinancing on a long-term basis, they are reported **solely** as **general long-term liabilities** in the government-wide financial statements.

1)   If these criteria are **not** met, bond as well as tax and revenue anticipation notes are reported in the fund receiving the proceeds.

Special Assessments

12. Governments may agree to construct physical improvements that will benefit one or more property owners. The government issues debt, pays for the improvements with the proceeds, then repays the debt with reimbursements from the property owners.

13. In the **government-wide financial statements**, the accounting is straightforward.

EXAMPLE

A city agrees to build roads, install street lights, and lay water and sewer lines for an employer who intends to build a factory. The city is also liable for the special assessment debt. Thus, it recognizes a general long-term liability and a capital asset.

The bonds are issued.

Cash	$10,000,000	
Bonds payable -- special assessment		$10,000,000

The improvements are finished.

Infrastructure assets	$10,000,000	
Cash		$10,000,000

Once the bonds were issued, interest began accruing on them. This amount is added to what the factory owner owes for the improvements.

Special assessment receivable	$10,675,000	
Revenue -- special assessment		$10,675,000

The factory owner pays the assessment.

Cash	$10,675,000	
Special assessment receivable		$10,675,000

The bonds are retired and the portion of the interest that accrued while the project was underway is capitalized.

Bonds payable -- special assessment	$10,000,000	
Infrastructure assets	500,000	
Interest expense	175,000	
Cash		$10,675,000

14. In the **governmental fund financial statements**, the accounting is slightly different. Two funds are involved because resources used for the improvements will be reported in one fund, but the repayment of the bonds will be from another.

EXAMPLE

Certain entries are omitted below. These include entries reflecting the reduction of deferred revenue that initially offset the assessment receivable. (Deferred revenue is reduced as resources become available.)

The bonds are issued.

Capital projects fund:		
Cash	$10,000,000	
Other financing sources -- bonds payable		$10,000,000

The contractor is paid for building the improvements.

Capital projects fund:		
Expenditures -- special assessment	$10,000,000	
Cash		$10,000,000

The factory owner is assessed for the full amount including accrued interest.

Debt service fund:		
Special assessment receivable	$10,675,000	
Revenue -- special assessment		$10,675,000

The factory owner pays the assessment.

Debt service fund:		
Cash	$10,675,000	
Special assessment receivable		$10,675,000

The bonds are retired.

Debt service fund:		
Expenditure -- special assessment bond	$10,000,000	
Expenditure --- interest	675,000	
Cash		$10,675,000

    a.   Also see Appendix A, GASBS 6, *Accounting and Financial Reporting for Special Assessments*.

Interfund Transactions

15. **Transfers of resources.** Transfers from one fund to another are a significant source of financing for governmental units.

    a.   The reporting of transfers is different in the government-wide and fund financial statements.

        1)   Transfers **within the governmental activities section** are not reported in the government-wide statements. These transfers result in no overall change in governmental activities.

        2)   Transfers **between governmental activities and business-type activities** are reported in both the government-wide statements and the fund statements.

3) The following diagram illustrates this difference:

Governmental Activities						Business-Type Activities	

Governmental Funds					Proprietary Funds	Proprietary Funds	
General Fund	Special Revenue Funds	Capital Projects Funds	Debt Service Fund	Permanent Funds	Most Internal Service Funds	Enterprise Funds	Other Internal Service Funds

Transactions within governmental activities:
Fund financial statements **only**

Transactions between activities:
Both fund statements **and** government-wide statements

EXAMPLE

A common interfund transfer is from the general fund to the debt service fund for the repayment of debts. When the transfer is recognized, the transferor establishes a payable and the recipient a receivable.

General fund:
Other financing uses -- transfer to debt service fund	$2,000,000	
Due to debt service fund		$2,000,000

Debt service fund:
Due from general fund	$2,000,000	
Other financing sources -- transfer from general fund		$2,000,000

The following are the entries when the transfer is made:

General fund:
Due to debt service fund	$2,000,000	
Cash		$2,000,000

Debt service fund:
Cash	$2,000,000	
Due from general fund		$2,000,000

---

b. The transfers in and out are reported in the **governmental fund financial statements**.

1) If the transfer is not made in the same period, the payable and receivable also are reported. These transactions are offsetting within governmental activities. Thus, they are not reported in the **government-wide financial statements**.

EXAMPLE

On occasion, a government will transfer resources from the general fund to an enterprise fund for a major upgrade or expansion. When the transfer is recognized, the accounting is identical to that used above.

General fund:
Other financing uses -- transfer to municipal hospital fund	$130,000,000	
Due to municipal hospital fund		$130,000,000

Enterprise fund:
Due from general fund	$130,000,000	
Other financing sources -- transfer from general fund		$130,000,000

The movement of cash is also recorded the same way.

General fund:
Due to municipal hospital fund $130,000,000
    Cash $130,000,000

Enterprise fund:
Cash $130,000,000
    Due from general fund $130,000,000

In the government-wide statements, an additional set of entries is made. Resources have passed not only between funds but also between activities.

Governmental activities:
Transfer to municipal hospital fund $130,000,000
    Cash $130,000,000

Business-type activities:
Cash $130,000,000
    Transfer from general fund $130,000,000

16. **Payment for services.** Governments pay their proprietary funds for services rendered. Enterprise and internal service funds in turn recognize revenue.

   a. In the **fund financial statements**, all transfers (those between activities and those within activities) are recognized.

EXAMPLE

A government pays for unemployment benefit coverage and computer processing time.

General fund:
Expenditures -- unemployment compensation $ 8,500,000
Expenditures -- information services   15,500,000
    Cash $24,000,000

Enterprise fund -- unemployment compensation:
Cash $8,500,000
    Revenues $8,500,000

Internal service fund -- information services:
Cash $15,500,000
    Revenues $15,500,000

---

   b. In the **government-wide financial statements**, however, only the transactions affecting the enterprise fund are recorded.

EXAMPLE

The transactions affecting the internal service fund are entirely within the governmental activities section.

Governmental activities:
Expenses -- unemployment compensation $8,500,000
    Cash $8,500,000

Business-type activities:
Cash $8,500,000
    Revenues $8,500,000

Stop and review! You have completed the outline for this subunit. Study multiple-choice questions 21 through 30 beginning on page 645.

17.4 CHARACTERISTIC TRANSACTIONS OF GOVERNMENTAL ENTITIES

Outlays for Operations vs. Outlays for Capital Assets

1. In the **governmental fund financial statements**, whether an expenditure was for services consumed immediately or for a general capital asset is irrelevant.

   a. The focus of governmental-fund reporting is on the disposition of **current period resources**. Such outlays are thus **expenditures** rather than expenses.

EXAMPLE		
An entry for the purchase of road maintenance equipment is similar to an entry to pay for extra office space.		
General fund:		
Expenditures -- rent	$20,000	
Vouchers payable		$20,000
Special revenue fund -- highway maintenance:		
Expenditures -- road equipment	$745,000	
Vouchers payable		$745,000

2. In the **government-wide financial statements**, all economic resources, both current and long-term, are reported.

   a. The services consumed in the current period are debited to an expense, and the long-lived asset is capitalized.

EXAMPLE		
The entries for road maintenance equipment and rental expense are as follows:		
Rental expense	$20,000	
Vouchers payable		$20,000
Road equipment	$745,000	
Vouchers payable		$745,000

Supplies and Prepaid items

3. In the **governmental fund financial statements**, inventories of supplies and prepaid items present an accounting challenge.

   a. They are not current financial resources because they cannot be expended to acquire other assets or to settle liabilities. But they are not long-lived assets and should not be reported as immediate expenditures.

      1) The **two methods** in common use for accounting for supplies and prepayments are described on the next page.

b.   The **purchases method** is a characteristically governmental accounting treatment. It is used with a periodic system.

EXAMPLE

Supplies and prepayments are recognized as expenditures at the time of purchase.

Expenditures -- supplies	$200,000	
Expenditures -- insurance	400,000	
Vouchers payable		$600,000

Assuming no beginning balances, i.e., increases in inventory and prepaid insurance, the year-end entries are

Inventory of supplies	$ 95,000	
Prepaid insurance	190,000	
Other financing sources -- inventory increase		$ 95,000
Other financing sources -- prepayment increase		190,000
Unreserved fund balance	$285,000	
Fund balance -- reserved for increase in supplies inventory		$ 95,000
Fund balance -- reserved for increase in prepaid insurance		190,000

---

c.   The **consumption method** more closely resembles the treatment by a for-profit business. It is used with a periodic or perpetual system.

EXAMPLE

Using the perpetual system, supplies and prepayments are recognized as assets at the time of purchase.

Inventory of supplies	$200,000	
Prepaid insurance	400,000	
Vouchers payable		$600,000

During the period, issuances of inventory are recognized by debits to expenditures and credits to inventory. At year-end, the following entries recognize an inventory shortage of $5,000 based on a physical count and the expired portion of prepaid insurance ($210,000):

Expenditures control	$215,000	
Inventory of supplies		$ 5,000
Prepaid insurance		210,000

---

4.   In the **government-wide financial statements**, the treatment of supplies and prepaid items parallels the consumption method.

a.   An asset is recognized at the time of purchase, and an expense (rather than an expenditure) is recognized with the usage of the asset or the passage of time.

Capital Leases

5.   The GASB adopted the FASB's guidelines for classifying leases as capital or operating (see Study Unit 13 for a discussion). Thus, when any of the four capitalization criteria is met, a governmental unit must recognize a capital lease.

6.   **Lessee Accounting**

a.   In the **government-wide financial statements** and in the **fund financial statements of proprietary funds**, a capital lease is recognized in the same way as in an outright purchase.

1)   The leased asset is capitalized at the present value of the minimum lease payments and a long-term liability is recognized for any remainder after a cash payment at the lease's inception.

EXAMPLE

A government enters into a long-term capital lease for a piece of equipment. The present value of the minimum lease payments is $120,000.

Equipment -- capital lease	$120,000	
Cash		$ 10,000
Capital lease obligation		110,000

At the end of the first year, a portion of the lease is amortized.

Interest expense	$9,000	
Capital lease obligation	1,000	
Cash		$10,000

---

b. The **fund financial statements of governmental funds**, with their focus on current financial resources, do not recognize the long-term nature of a leased asset and its related obligation.

EXAMPLE

The initiation of the lease is recorded as follows:

Expenditures -- leased assets	$120,000	
Cash		$ 10,000
Other financing sources -- capital lease		110,000

The payment at the end of the first year is recorded as follows:

Expenditures -- interest	$9,000	
Expenditures -- principal	1,000	
Cash		$10,000

---

7. **Lessor Accounting**

   a. A lease receivable is recognized to the extent it represents another financing source that is measurable and available. The rest is deferred.

   b. Furthermore, the noncurrent receivable is not a general capital asset. It is therefore reported in the fund accounting for the lease.

Municipal Solid Waste Landfills

8. Municipalities that operate solid waste landfills are required to recognize the **long-term liability** for closing landfills using an **expected cash flow** measurement.

   a. The **estimated total current cost** of landfill **closure and postclosure care** includes (1) the cost of equipment expected to be installed and (2) facilities expected to be constructed near or after the date that the landfill stops accepting waste and during the postclosure period.

EXAMPLE

A government estimates that its landfill will eventually require $10,000,000 in total costs for closure and environmental protection. At the end of the first year, the landfill is 15% full.

Government-wide financial statements:

Expenditures -- landfill closure	$1,500,000	
Landfill closure liability		$1,500,000

At the end of the first year, a progress payment is made.

Government-wide financial statements:

Landfill closure liability	$300,000	
Cash		$300,000

---

9. If the landfill is operated as a **business-type activity** (i.e., it is accounted for in an enterprise fund), the accounting in the fund financial statements is the same as in the government-wide statements presented on the previous page.

    a. However, if the landfill is operated as a **governmental activity** (i.e., it is accounted for in the general fund), only the effect on current financial resources is recognized. The long-term liability will be disclosed in the summary reconciliation. See Subunit 18.3.

    EXAMPLE

    The long-term liability is not recognized. The first year's progress payment is recorded as follows:

General fund:		
Expenditures -- landfill closure	$300,000	
Cash		$300,000

Compensated Absences

10. When governmental bodies grant their employees paid time off, the salary rate used to calculate the liability should be the rate in effect at the balance sheet date.

    EXAMPLE

    In the financial statements of governmental funds, only the portion of compensated absences that employees will use in the upcoming fiscal period is recognized, i.e., the portion that must be paid with current financial resources.

General fund:		
Expenditures -- compensated absences	$91,000	
Liability -- compensated absences		$91,000

    Government-wide financial statements:
    The entire liability must be recognized.

Expenses -- compensated absences	$750,000	
Liability -- compensated absences		$750,000

Works of Art and Historical Treasures

11. The accounting measurement of a work of art or historic object obtained by a government depends on whether the item is purchased or donated.

    a. If the object is **purchased**, it is recorded at **historical cost**.

    EXAMPLE

    A government pays $12,000,000 for an object for its museum. An identical item had recently sold at auction for $14,000,000.

Government-wide financial statements:		
Museum object -- Ming dynasty vase	$12,000,000	
Cash		$12,000,000

    ---

    1) If the museum in which the object is displayed is operated as an **enterprise fund**, i.e., an admission fee is charged, the asset generates revenue. The above entry is duplicated in the proprietary fund financial statements.

    2) If the museum is accounted for in the **general fund**, the current resources focus requires the transaction to be recorded as an expenditure.

    EXAMPLE

    The government operates its museum as a governmental activity.

General fund:		
Expenditures -- museum object	$12,000,000	
Cash		$12,000,000

    ---

b.   If the object is **donated**, it is recorded at **fair value**.

EXAMPLE

If the government accounts for the museum in an enterprise fund, the following entry is recorded in both the government-wide financial statements and the proprietary fund financial statements:

Museum object -- Ming dynasty vase	$12,000,000	
Revenue -- donation		$14,000,000

If the government accounts for the museum in the general fund, the object is not capitalized, in keeping with the current resources focus.

---

12.   Although GASBS 34 encourages the recognition of works of art and historical treasures as assets, capitalization is **optional** in some circumstances. The GASB adopted the FASB's guidelines for these circumstances.

   a.   A government can record the acquisition (whether by purchase or donation) of a piece of art or historic object as an **expense** if the **collection** to which the object is being added meets these **three criteria**:

   1)   The collection is held for public exhibition, education, or research in furtherance of public service rather than financial gain;

   2)   The collection is protected, kept unencumbered, cared for, and preserved; and

   3)   The collection is subject to an organizational policy that requires the proceeds from sales of collection items to be used to acquire other items for collections.

   b.   A collection or item that is exhaustible is depreciated.

Infrastructure Assets

13.   Infrastructure assets are capital assets that normally are stationary and can be preserved for a longer time than most capital assets. Examples include roads, bridges, tunnels, sidewalks, water and sewer systems, drainage systems, and lighting systems.

14.   The treatment of public infrastructure assets is similar to that for other capital assets.

   a.   In the **government-wide financial statements**, they are reported as assets. In the **financial statements** of **governmental funds**, they are reported as expenditures (they do not constitute current financial resources).

15.   The GASB realized that arriving at historical cost information for **older infrastructure assets** (e.g., bridges and dams built in the 1930s) would be very difficult. For this reason, only major assets meeting **one of the following criteria** need be capitalized:

   a.   The asset was acquired in a fiscal year ending after June 30, 1980, or
   b.   The asset had major renovations, restorations, or improvements after June 30, 1980.

16.   GASBS 34 requires **depreciation** for capital assets except (a) land and (b) art and historic objects that have been deemed inexhaustible. Depreciation is recognized in the **government-wide, proprietary fund, and fiduciary fund statements**.

   a.   Infrastructure assets present a situation similar to the exceptions to the depreciation requirement. Their lives may be so long that they are in effect inexhaustible. For example, parts of the U.S. Interstate Highway System are already fifty years old, and the system as a whole will last for several generations.

b.   The GASB provided an **alternative to depreciation** for very long-lived infrastructure assets.

1)   Under the **modified approach**, infrastructure assets that are part of **a network or subsystem of a network (eligible infrastructure assets)** need not be depreciated. However, the government must use an asset management system with certain characteristics. It also must document that the assets are being preserved approximately at an **established condition level** disclosed by the government.

a)   This method allows a government to **expense maintenance costs** instead of recording depreciation expense.

b)   **Additions and improvements** to infrastructure assets are still **capitalized**.

Stop and review! You have completed the outline for this subunit. Study multiple-choice questions 31 through 36 beginning on page 649.

QUESTIONS

17.1 Fund Accounting Concepts and Reporting

1. Fund accounting is used by governmental units with resources that must be

A.   Composed of cash or cash equivalents.

B.   Incorporated into combined or combining financial statements.

C.   Segregated for the purpose of carrying on specific activities or attaining certain objectives.

D.   Segregated physically according to various objectives.

Answer (C) is correct. *(CPA, adapted)*
REQUIRED: The nature of fund accounting.
DISCUSSION: According to NCGA Statement 1, a fund is "a fiscal and accounting entity with a self-balancing set of accounts recording cash and other financial resources, together with all related liabilities and residual equities or balances, and changes therein, which are segregated for the purpose of carrying on specific activities or attaining certain objectives in accordance with special regulations, restrictions, or limitations."
Answer (A) is incorrect because funds may account for all types of resources, related liabilities, and residuals. Answer (B) is incorrect because the essence of fund accounting is separation of resources into discrete accounting entities. Answer (D) is incorrect because resources must be accounted for separately but need not be physically separated.

2. The government-wide financial statements report capital assets

A.   In the general fixed assets account group.

B.   At historical cost, including ancillary charges.

C.   Only in the notes if they are donated.

D.   At estimated fair value.

Answer (B) is correct. *(Publisher, adapted)*
REQUIRED: The reporting of capital assets in the government-wide financial statements.
DISCUSSION: Capital assets include land, land improvements, easements, buildings, vehicles, machinery, equipment, works of art, historical treasures, infrastructure, and other tangible and intangible operating assets with useful lives greater than one reporting period. They are reported at historical cost, including ancillary charges necessary to put them in their intended location and condition for use. Ancillary charges, e.g., for freight, site preparation, and professional fees, are directly attributable to acquisition of the assets.
Answer (A) is incorrect because presentation of government-wide financial statements eliminates the need for the general fixed assets account group and the general long-term debt account group. Answer (C) is incorrect because capital assets are reported at historical cost, including ancillary charges, in the statements. Answer (D) is incorrect because only donated capital assets are reported at estimated fair value at the time of acquisition plus ancillary charges.

3. Thornton County is required under state law to report its financial statements on a basis that conflicts with generally accepted governmental accounting principles. On which basis of accounting should Thornton County's financial statements be prepared?

A. Generally accepted governmental accounting basis only.

B. State law basis only.

C. State law basis with supplemental disclosure of generally accepted governmental accounting reconciliation schedules.

D. Generally accepted governmental accounting basis with supplemental supporting schedules as necessary to report compliance with state law.

Answer (D) is correct. *(J.P. Trebby)*
REQUIRED: The proper presentation of county financial statements when state law conflicts with GAAP.
DISCUSSION: Certain state laws and regulatory requirements conflict with generally accepted accounting and financial reporting practices. When such a conflict exists, the governmental entity should prepare basic financial statements conforming with GAAP and also present supporting schedules and narrative explanations in the CAFR as necessary to clearly report upon compliance with legal responsibilities.
Answer (A) is incorrect because the financial statements should include supplemental matter to comply with state law. Answer (B) is incorrect because the financial statements should be prepared in accordance with GAAP. Answer (C) is incorrect because the statements should be prepared in accordance with GAAP with supplementary schedules that comply with state law.

4. Kew City received a $15,000,000 federal grant to finance the construction of a center for rehabilitation of drug addicts. The proceeds of this grant should be accounted for in the

A. Special revenue funds.

B. General fund.

C. Capital projects funds.

D. Trust funds.

Answer (C) is correct. *(CPA, adapted)*
REQUIRED: The fund used to account for a federal grant earmarked to finance the construction of a center for rehabilitation of drug addicts.
DISCUSSION: The capital projects fund is used to account for the receipt and disbursement of resources restricted to acquisition of major capital facilities (other than those financed by proprietary and trust funds) through purchase or construction.
Answer (A) is incorrect because this fund does not record resources to be used for major capital facilities. Answer (B) is incorrect because this fund does not record resources to be used for major capital facilities. Answer (D) is incorrect because a grant for a drug rehabilitation center is not accounted for in a trust fund. A trust fund accounts for assets held by a governmental entity in the capacity of a trustee for individuals, private organizations, or other governments.

5. In governmental accounting, a fund is

I.   The basic accounting unit
II. Used to assist in ensuring fiscal compliance

A. I only.

B. II only.

C. Both I and II.

D. Neither I nor II.

Answer (C) is correct. *(CPA, adapted)*
REQUIRED: The nature of a fund.
DISCUSSION: Although government-wide financial statements are also reported, the diversity of governmental activities and the need for legal compliance preclude the use of a single accounting entity. Thus, independent, distinct fiscal and accounting entities called funds are established. A fund accounting system of a governmental reporting entity must be able to present fairly in conformity with GAAP and with full disclosure the financial position and results of operations of the funds. Also, it must determine and demonstrate compliance with finance-related legal and contractual provisions. A fund is "a fiscal and accounting entity with a self-balancing set of accounts recording cash and other financial resources, together with all related liabilities and residual equities and balances, and changes therein, which are segregated for the purpose of carrying on specific activities or attaining certain objectives in accordance with special regulations, restrictions, or limitations" (NCGA Statement 1, *Governmental Accounting and Financial Reporting Principles*).

6. A local governmental unit could use which of the following types of funds?

	Fiduciary	Proprietary
A.	Yes	No
B.	Yes	Yes
C.	No	Yes
D.	No	No

Answer (B) is correct. *(CPA, adapted)*
REQUIRED: The types of funds that could be used by a local governmental unit.
DISCUSSION: Three broad categories and eleven generic fund types can be used by a state or local governmental unit in its fund financial statements.

1) Governmental – general, special revenue, debt service, capital projects,and permanent funds
2) Proprietary – internal service and enterprise funds
3) Fiduciary – pension (and other employee benefit) trust, investment trust, private-purpose trust, and agency funds

GASBS 6, *Accounting and Financial Reporting for Special Assessments*, restricts the use of special assessment funds to internal and compliance reporting. Special assessment funds are not used in the basic financial statements.

7. The focus of accounting and reporting for proprietary funds of governmental units is most likely on

A. Determination of operating income.

B. Project completion.

C. Current financial resources.

D. Adherence to the budget.

Answer (A) is correct. *(CPA, adapted)*
REQUIRED: The accounting focus of proprietary funds.
DISCUSSION: The financial statements of proprietary funds focus on determination of operating income, changes in net assets (or cost recovery), financial position, and cash flows. A proprietary fund accounts for the business-type functions of a government. Users of the financial statements for proprietary funds may find profitability information to be valuable.
Answer (B) is incorrect because projects and programs are entities for which information is accumulated, not measurement models. Answer (C) is incorrect because current financial resources is the measurement focus of governmental funds. Answer (D) is incorrect because governmental funds have a budgetary orientation.

8. Lake County received the following proceeds that are legally restricted to expenditure for specified purposes:

Levies on affected property owners to install sewers	$500,000
Gasoline taxes to finance road repairs	900,000

What amount most likely will be accounted for in Lake's special revenue funds?

A. $1,400,000

B. $900,000

C. $500,000

D. $0

Answer (B) is correct. *(CPA, adapted)*
REQUIRED: The amount to be recorded in special revenue funds.
DISCUSSION: Special assessments for construction activity may be accounted for in a capital projects fund or other appropriate fund. The gasoline taxes are special revenues received from the state government to be expended for a specific purpose and are properly recorded in the special revenue funds. However, special revenue funds need not be used unless they are legally mandated.
Answer (A) is incorrect because $1,400,000 includes the special assessment for a capital project. Answer (C) is incorrect because $500,000 is the amount of the special assessment for a capital project. Answer (D) is incorrect because $0 is based on the assumption that neither revenue source is accounted for in special revenue funds.

9. In the fund financial statements of which of the following fund types of a city government are revenues and expenditures recognized on the same basis of accounting as the general fund?

A. Private-purpose trust.

B. Internal service.

C. Enterprise.

D. Debt service.

Answer (D) is correct. *(CPA, adapted)*
REQUIRED: The fund that recognizes revenues and expenditures in the same manner as the general fund.
DISCUSSION: The debt service fund is the only fund listed that is classified as a governmental fund. The other funds are proprietary or fiduciary. Governmental funds use the modified accrual basis in preparing their fund financial statements, and proprietary and fiduciary funds use the accrual basis.
Answer (A) is incorrect because a private-purpose trust fund is a fiduciary fund. Its financial statements are prepared on the same basis as those of proprietary funds. Answer (B) is incorrect because the internal service fund is a proprietary fund. Its financial statements are prepared using the accrual basis of accounting. Answer (C) is incorrect because the enterprise fund is a proprietary fund. Its financial statements are prepared using the accrual basis of accounting.

17.2 Budgetary Accounting and Encumbrances

10. On what accounting basis does GASB recommend that governmental fund budgets be prepared?

A. Cash.

B. Modified cash.

C. Accrual.

D. Modified accrual.

Answer (D) is correct. *(CPA, adapted)*

REQUIRED: The basis of accounting for a governmental fund.

DISCUSSION: The basis of accounting for a budget preferably should be the same as that used by the fund for which the budget is being prepared. The modified accrual basis of accounting is used to prepare the fund financial statements for all governmental fund types: general, special revenue, capital projects, debt service, and permanent.

Answer (A) is incorrect because the cash basis is used for miscellaneous cash items that are not practicably measurable until cash is received or paid. Answer (B) is incorrect because the modified cash basis is never used. Answer (C) is incorrect because the accrual basis is used in the government-wide statements and in all fund statements other than governmental fund statements.

Questions 11 and 12 are based on the following information. Ridge Township's governing body adopted its general fund budget for the year ended July 31, Year 1, composed of estimated revenues of $100,000 and appropriations of $80,000. Ridge formally integrates its budget into the accounting records.

11. To record the appropriations of $80,000, Ridge should

A. Credit appropriations control.

B. Debit appropriations control.

C. Credit estimated expenditures control.

D. Debit estimated expenditures control.

Answer (A) is correct. *(CPA, adapted)*

REQUIRED: The entry to record appropriations.

DISCUSSION: The basic budgetary entry is:

Estimated revenues control	$X,XXX,XXX	
Estimated other financing sources	X,XXX,XXX	
Appropriations control		$XX,XXX,XXX
Estimated other financing uses		X,XXX,XXX
Budgetary fund balance		XXX,XXX

Thus, Ridge should credit appropriations control for $80,000. It is a control account because it is the summation of numerous individual appropriations. Estimated revenues and estimated other financing sources are anticipatory assets. Appropriations and estimated other financing uses are anticipatory liabilities.

Answer (B) is incorrect because appropriations is credited, not debited. Answer (C) is incorrect because expenditures is not credited in the budgetary entry. Answer (D) is incorrect because expenditures is not debited in the budgetary entry.

12. To record the $20,000 budgeted excess of estimated revenues over appropriations, Ridge should

A. Credit estimated excess revenues control.

B. Debit estimated excess revenues control.

C. Credit budgetary fund balance.

D. Debit budgetary fund balance.

Answer (C) is correct. *(CPA, adapted)*

REQUIRED: The correct entry to record the budgeted excess of estimated revenues over appropriations.

DISCUSSION: The basic budgetary entry is:

Estimated revenues control	$X,XXX,XXX	
Estimated other financing sources	X,XXX,XXX	
Appropriations control		$XX,XXX,XXX
Estimated other financing uses		X,XXX,XXX
Budgetary fund balance		XXX,XXX

Given that estimated revenues exceed appropriations, budgetary fund balance is credited for the $20,000 difference.

13. The estimated revenues control account of a governmental unit is debited when

A. Actual revenues are recorded.

B. Actual revenues are collected.

C. The budget is recorded.

D. The budget is closed at the end of the year.

Answer (C) is correct. *(CPA, adapted)*
REQUIRED: The circumstance in which the estimated revenues control account of a governmental unit is debited.
DISCUSSION: The budgetary accounts are used to record the budget at the beginning of the fiscal period. The basic budgetary entry is:

Estimated revenues control	$X,XXX,XXX	
Estimated other financing sources	X,XXX,XXX	
Appropriations control		$XX,XXX,XXX
Estimated other financing uses		X,XXX,XXX
Budgetary fund balance		XXX,XXX

No other entries are made in these accounts until the end of the fiscal year, at which time they are closed to fund balance.
Answer (A) is incorrect because revenues control is credited and a receivable is debited when actual revenues are recorded. Answer (B) is incorrect because cash is debited when actual revenues are collected. Answer (D) is incorrect because estimated revenues control is credited when the budget is closed at the end of the year.

14. A county's balances in the general fund included the following:

Appropriations	$745,000
Encumbrances	37,250
Expenditures	298,000
Vouchers payable	55,875

What is the remaining amount available for use by the county?

A. $353,875

B. $391,125

C. $409,750

D. $447,000

Answer (C) is correct. *(CPA, adapted)*
REQUIRED: The remaining amount available for use.
DISCUSSION: Appropriations is the account credited in the general fund's budgetary entry. It establishes the total amount available for use during the period. When a commitment is made to expend resources of a governmental unit, the amount of the commitment is encumbered by a journal entry in which the encumbrances account is debited and the reserve for encumbrances account (a fund balance account) is credited for the amount of the purchase order. Comparison of encumbrances, appropriations, and expenditures determines the unencumbered amount of appropriations that may still be expended. The encumbrances account will be decreased when previously ordered items have been received. Expenditures and vouchers payable will be increased for the actual amount to be paid for the items. Accordingly, the remaining amount available for use by the county is $409,750 ($745,000 – $37,250 – $298,000).
Answer (A) is incorrect because $353,875 results from subtracting the vouchers payable balance, the account credited when expenditures is debited. Answer (B) is incorrect because $391,125 results from subtracting vouchers payable instead of encumbrances. Answer (D) is incorrect because $447,000 results from not subtracting encumbrances.

15. During its fiscal year ended June 30, Cliff City issued purchase orders totaling $5 million, which were properly charged to encumbrances at that time. Cliff received goods and related invoices at the encumbered amounts totaling $4.5 million before year-end. The remaining goods of $500,000 were not received until after year-end. Cliff paid $4.2 million of the invoices received during the year. The amount of Cliff's encumbrances outstanding at June 30 was

A. $0

B. $300,000

C. $500,000

D. $800,000

Answer (C) is correct. *(CPA, adapted)*
REQUIRED: The amount of encumbrances outstanding.
DISCUSSION: In fund accounting, when a commitment is made to expend monies, encumbrances is debited and reserve for encumbrances (a fund balance account) is credited. When the goods are received and the liability is recognized, this entry is reversed and an expenditure is recorded. Because goods totaling $500,000 were not received at year-end, encumbrances outstanding total $500,000 ($5,000,000 – $4,500,000).
Answer (A) is incorrect because not all of the goods related to the encumbrance amounts were received during the year. Answer (B) is incorrect because $300,000 is the excess of goods received over the amount actually paid on the invoices during the year. Answer (D) is incorrect because $800,000 is the excess of total encumbrances over the amount paid on the invoices.

16. Park City uses encumbrance accounting and formally integrates its budget into the general fund's accounting records. For the year ending July 31, Year 1, the following budget was adopted:

Estimated revenues	$30,000,000
Appropriations	27,000,000
Estimated transfer to debt service fund	900,000

Park's budgetary fund balance is a

A. $3,000,000 credit balance.

B. $3,000,000 debit balance.

C. $2,100,000 credit balance.

D. $2,100,000 debit balance.

Answer (C) is correct. *(CPA, adapted)*
REQUIRED: The budgetary fund balance when a budget is adopted and recorded.
DISCUSSION: Park City's budgetary entry for the Year 1 fiscal year:

Estimated revenues control	$30,000,000	
Appropriations control		$27,000,000
Estimated other financing uses		
-- transfer to debt service fund		900,000
Budgetary fund balance		2,100,000

Answer (A) is incorrect because the $900,000 estimated transfer to debt service fund must be credited. Answer (B) is incorrect because the estimated revenues must be debited and the transfer to debt service must be credited. Answer (D) is incorrect because the estimated revenues should be debited.

17. Which of the following amount(s) is(are) included in a general fund's encumbrances account?

I. Outstanding vouchers payable amounts

II. Outstanding purchase order amounts

III. Excess of the amount of a purchase order over the actual expenditure for that order

A. I only.

B. I and III only.

C. II only.

D. II and III only.

Answer (C) is correct. *(CPA, adapted)*
REQUIRED: The amounts included in a general fund's encumbrances account.
DISCUSSION: When a purchase order is approved, the following entry is recorded:

Encumbrances control	$XX,XXX	
Fund balance		
-- reserved for encumbrances		$XX,XXX

When the contract is complete or virtually complete, the entry is reversed, effectively eliminating the purchase order amount. Thus, the encumbrance account includes only those amounts that represent outstanding purchase orders.

Answer (A) is incorrect because the encumbrance is eliminated when the expenditure and the voucher payable relating to the purchase order are recorded. Answer (B) is incorrect because the encumbrance includes only outstanding purchase order amounts. Answer (D) is incorrect because, when the contract is complete or virtually complete, the original encumbrance entry is reversed. The actual amount owed is recorded in the expenditures account, so any excess is not reflected in the encumbrance account.

18. Which of the following journal entries should be made in the general fund of a city to record $250,000 for salaries and wages incurred during the month of May?

A. Salaries & wages
expense	$250,000	
Appropriations		$250,000

B. Salaries & wages
expense	$250,000	
Encumbrances		$250,000

C.
Encumbrances	$250,000	
Salaries payable		$250,000

D. Expenditures - salaries
& wages	$250,000	
Salaries payable		$250,000

Answer (D) is correct. *(CPA, adapted)*
REQUIRED: The entry used by a city to record salaries and wages in the general fund.
DISCUSSION: An expenditure is recorded when a current liability is to be liquidated with expendable available current resources. Because wages and salaries have been earned by employees, a liability should be recognized, not an encumbrance. The controls in place for such routine outlays as wages and payroll taxes mean that such liabilities are rarely encumbered.

19. For the budgetary year ending December 31, Maple City's general fund expects the following inflows of resources:

Property taxes, licenses, and fines	$9,000,000
Proceeds of debt issue	5,000,000
Interfund transfers for debt service	1,000,000

In the budgetary entry, what amount should Maple record for estimated revenues?

- A. $9,000,000
- B. $10,000,000
- C. $14,000,000
- D. $15,000,000

Answer (A) is correct. *(CPA, adapted)*
REQUIRED: The amount of estimated revenues.
DISCUSSION: Estimated revenues is an anticipatory asset and is debited for the amount expected to be collected from a governmental body's main source of revenue. In the general fund, the main source of revenue is made up of taxes, fees, penalties, etc. Expected proceeds from the issuance of debt constitute an other financing source. An expected transfer to a different fund is an other financing use.
Answer (B) is incorrect because $10,000,000 incorrectly includes the interfund transfers. Answer (C) is incorrect because $14,000,000 incorrectly includes the debt issue proceeds. Answer (D) is incorrect because $15,000,000 incorrectly includes the debt issue proceeds and interfund transfers.

20. When a snowplow purchased by a governmental unit is received, it should be recorded in the general fund as a(n)

- A. Encumbrance.
- B. Expenditure.
- C. General capital asset.
- D. Appropriation.

Answer (B) is correct. *(CPA, adapted)*
REQUIRED: The effect of receipt of equipment.
DISCUSSION: When previously ordered goods are received, the entry includes a debit to expenditures for the actual amount to be paid. An expenditure is recognized when a liability is incurred, that is, when an executory contract is complete or virtually complete.
Answer (A) is incorrect because an encumbrance is recorded to account for the purchase commitment. Answer (C) is incorrect because general capital assets are reported only in the governmental activities column of the government-wide statement of net assets. Answer (D) is incorrect because appropriations are accounted for when recording the budget.

17.3 Governmental Sources of Financing

21. Property taxes and fines represent which of the following classes of nonexchange transactions for governmental units?

- A. Derived tax revenues.
- B. Imposed nonexchange revenues.
- C. Government-mandated nonexchange transactions.
- D. Voluntary nonexchange transactions.

Answer (B) is correct. *(CPA, adapted)*
REQUIRED: The classification of property taxes and fines assessed by a governmental unit.
DISCUSSION: According to GASBS 33, *Accounting and Financial Reporting for Nonexchange Transactions*, imposed nonexchange revenues arise from assessments on nongovernmental entities, including individuals, other than assessments on exchange transactions. Examples are fines, forfeitures, and property taxes.
Answer (A) is incorrect because derived tax revenues arise from assessments imposed on exchange transactions. Answer (C) is incorrect because government-mandated nonexchange transactions occur when one government provides resources to a government at another level and requires that they be used for a specific purpose. Answer (D) is incorrect because voluntary nonexchange transactions result from legislative or contractual agreements, other than exchanges, entered into willingly.

22. During the current year, Knoxx County levied property taxes of $2,000,000, of which 1% is expected to be uncollectible. The following amounts were collected during the current year

Prior year taxes collected within the first 90 days of the current year	$ 50,000
Prior year taxes collected between 60 and 90 days into the current year	120,000
Current year taxes collected in the current year	1,800,000
Current year taxes collected within the first 60 days of the subsequent year	80,000

What amount of property tax revenue should Knoxx County report in its government-wide statement of activities?

A. $1,800,000

B. $1,970,000

C. $1,980,000

D. $2,000,000

Answer (C) is correct. *(CPA, adapted)*

REQUIRED: The property tax revenue reported in the government-wide statement of activities.

DISCUSSION: Revenue from a property tax assessment is recognized in the period for which it was levied, provided the criteria of being available and measurable are met. (Property taxes are accounted for in governmental funds, which use the modified accrual basis.) Property taxes are measurable when assessed property values can be multiplied by a known tax rate. Available means collectible within the current period or expected to be collected soon enough thereafter to pay current liabilities. Such time may not exceed 60 days for a property tax assessment except in unusual circumstances. However, the accrual basis is used to prepare the entity-wide (government-wide) statement of activities. Accrual basis recognition of property tax revenue (imposed nonexchange revenue) also is in the period for which the taxes are levied, but the availability criterion does not apply. Recognition is net of estimated refunds and uncollectible amounts. Consequently, current-year property tax revenue recognized on the accrual basis is $1,980,000 [$2,000,000 levied × (100% − 1% estimated to be uncollectible)]. The amounts collected currently but levied for a prior year are accrual basis revenue of that year.

Answer (A) is incorrect because $1,800,000 is the amount of the current-year levy collected in the current year. Answer (B) is incorrect because $1,970,000 is the amount collected in the current year. Answer (D) is incorrect because 1% of the total levy is expected to be uncollectible.

23. On March 2, Year 4, the city of Finch issued 10-year general obligation bonds at face amount, with interest payable March 1 and September 1. The proceeds were to be used to finance the construction of a civic center over the period April 1, Year 4, to March 31, Year 5. During the fiscal year ended June 30, Year 4, no resources had been provided to the debt service fund for the payment of principal and interest. On June 30, Year 4, Finch should report the construction in progress for the civic center in the

	Capital Projects Fund	Government-Wide Statement of Net Assets
A.	Yes	Yes
B.	Yes	No
C.	No	No
D.	No	Yes

Answer (D) is correct. *(CPA, adapted)*

REQUIRED: The reporting of construction in progress.

DISCUSSION: Expenditures for the construction project but not the resulting general capital assets should be reported in the capital projects fund. The construction in progress (a general capital asset if it results from expenditure of governmental fund financial resources and is not related to activities reported in nongovernmental funds) and ultimately the completed civic center should be reported in the government-wide statement of net assets at historical cost, including capitalized interest and ancillary charges. They should not be reported in the governmental funds balance sheet.

Answer (A) is incorrect because expenditures but not in-progress assets are reported in the capital projects fund. General capital assets are not reported in governmental funds. Answer (B) is incorrect because the completed and in-progress assets are reported in the government-wide statement of net assets, not in the capital projects fund. Answer (C) is incorrect because the completed and in-progress assets are reported in the government-wide statement of net assets.

24. In which situation(s) should property taxes due to a governmental unit be recorded as deferred revenue?

I. Property taxes receivable are recognized in advance of the year for which they are levied.

II. Property taxes receivable are collected in advance of the year in which they are levied.

A. I only.

B. Both I and II.

C. II only.

D. Neither I nor II.

Answer (B) is correct. *(CPA, adapted)*

REQUIRED: The situation(s) when taxes due should be recorded as deferred revenue.

DISCUSSION: A property tax assessment is made to finance the budget of a specific period. Hence, the revenue produced should be recognized in the period for which the assessment was levied. When property taxes are recognized or collected in advance, they should be recorded as deferred revenue in a governmental fund. They are not recognized as revenue until the year for which they are levied. Under GASBS 33, a property tax assessment is classified as an imposed nonexchange revenue transaction. In such a transaction, assets should be recognized when an enforceable legal claim arises or when resources are received, whichever is earlier. Thus, under GASBS 33, recognition of a receivable in a year prior to that for which the property taxes were levied implies that, under the enabling statute, the enforceable legal claim arose in that prior year.

25. In what fund type should the proceeds from special assessment bonds issued to finance construction of sidewalks in a new subdivision be reported?

A. Agency fund.

B. Special revenue fund.

C. Enterprise fund.

D. Capital projects fund.

26. In Year 8, Menton City received $5,000,000 of bond proceeds to be used for capital projects. Of this amount, $1,000,000 was expended in Year 8 with the balance expected to be expended in Year 9. When should the bond proceeds be recorded in a capital projects fund?

A. $5,000,000 in Year 8.

B. $5,000,000 in Year 9.

C. $1,000,000 in Year 8 and $4,000,000 in Year 9.

D. $1,000,000 in Year 8 and in the general fund for $4,000,000 in Year 8.

27. Wood City, which is legally obligated to maintain a debt service fund, issued the following general obligation bonds on July 1:

Term of bonds	10 years
Face amount	$1,000,000
Issue price	101
Stated interest rate	6%

Interest is payable January 1 and July 1. What amount of bond issuance premium should be amortized in Wood's debt service fund for the year ended December 31?

A. $1,000

B. $500

C. $250

D. $0

Answer (D) is correct. *(CPA, adapted)*
REQUIRED: The fund type that accounts for special assessment bond proceeds used to construct sidewalks.
DISCUSSION: Construction of sidewalks in a new subdivision financed by special assessment bonds is a capital project that results in a general capital asset that will be recognized only in the governmental activities column of the government-wide statement of net assets. If the governmental unit is obligated in some manner on the special assessment debt, this capital improvement may be accounted for in the same way as other capital transactions. Hence, the transactions of the construction phase are reported in a capital projects fund. Transactions of the debt service phase are reported in a debt service fund, if one is required. If the government is not obligated, the construction transactions may still be reported in a capital projects fund, but the debt service transactions are recorded in an agency fund.
Answer (A) is incorrect because agency funds are purely custodial funds. However, an agency fund should report debt service transactions related to special assessment debt if the governmental unit is not obligated in any manner. Answer (B) is incorrect because bond proceeds are not considered revenues of a governmental unit. They must be repaid. Answer (C) is incorrect because enterprise funds account for business-type activities.

Answer (A) is correct. *(CPA, adapted)*
REQUIRED: The date(s) bond proceeds should be recorded in a capital projects fund.
DISCUSSION: The general obligation debt will be reported as a general long-term liability in the governmental activities column of the government-wide statements of net assets, and expenditures will be recorded in Year 8 and Year 9. The face amount of long-term debt, issuance premium or discount, certain payments to escrow agents for bond refundings, transfers, and sales of capital assets not qualifying as special items are reported as other financing sources and uses in the governmental funds statement of revenues, expenditures, and changes in fund balances. Thus, the entry in the capital projects fund in Year 8, the year of receipt, to record the bond proceeds is a debit to cash and a credit to other financing sources -- bond issue proceeds for $5,000,000.

Answer (D) is correct. *(CPA, adapted)*
REQUIRED: The amount of bond premium amortized in the debt service fund.
DISCUSSION: The debt service fund of a governmental unit is a governmental fund used to account for the accumulation of resources for, and the payment of, general long-term debt principal and interest. Bond issuance premium will be accounted for as an other financing source in the fund out of which the proceeds will be spent. Thus, bond issuance premium is not amortized, in the debt service fund or anywhere else.

28. A public school district should recognize revenue from property taxes levied for its debt service fund when

A. Bonds to be retired by the levy are due and payable.

B. Assessed valuations of property subject to the levy are known.

C. Funds from the levy are measurable and available to the district.

D. Proceeds from collection of the levy are deposited in the district's bank account.

Answer (C) is correct. *(CPA, adapted)*
REQUIRED: The timing of property tax recognition.
DISCUSSION: Debt service funds apply the modified accrual basis of accounting. Thus, revenues are recognized when they are measurable and available. Moreover, under GASBS 33, assets from imposed nonexchange revenue transactions, such as property tax levies, should be recognized when an enforceable legal claim arises or the resources are received, whichever is earlier. If the legal claim arises in the period after that for which the property taxes are levied, a receivable is recognized when revenues are recognized. Revenues are recognized in the period for which the taxes are levied if the availability criterion is met. For property taxes, this criterion is met if they are collected within the current period or soon enough thereafter (not exceeding 60 days) to pay current liabilities.
Answer (A) is incorrect because revenues are recognized when property taxes are levied. Answer (B) is incorrect because the assessed valuations are necessary for calculating the amount of tax but do not make the tax revenue available. Answer (D) is incorrect because revenue recognition is not on the cash basis.

29. The renovation of Fir City's municipal park was accounted for in a capital projects fund. Financing for the renovation, which was begun and completed during the current year, came from the following sources:

Grant from state government	$400,000
Proceeds from general obligation bond issue	500,000
Transfer from Fir's general fund	100,000

In its governmental fund statement of revenues, expenditures, and changes in fund balances for the current year, Fir should report these amounts as

	Revenues	Other Financing Sources
A.	$1,000,000	$0
B.	$900,000	$100,000
C.	$400,000	$600,000
D.	$0	$1,000,000

Answer (C) is correct. *(CPA, adapted)*
REQUIRED: The amounts to be reported in the governmental fund statement of revenues, expenditures, and changes in fund balances.
DISCUSSION: Governmental fund revenues are increases in fund financial resources other than from interfund transfers, debt issue proceeds, and redemptions of demand bonds. Thus, revenues of a capital projects fund include grants. Under GASBS 33, the grant (a voluntary nonexchange transaction) is recognized when all eligibility requirements, including time requirements, have been met. When modified accrual accounting is used, as in a capital projects fund, the grant must also be "available." Other financing sources include proceeds from bonds and interfund transfers in. Thus, Fir reports revenues of $400,000 and other financing sources of $600,000 ($500,000 + $100,000) in its governmental fund statement of revenues, expenditures, and changes in fund balances.
Answer (A) is incorrect because the proceeds from the bond issue and the transfer from the general fund should be reported under other financing sources. Answer (B) is incorrect because the proceeds from bond issue should be reported under other financing sources. Answer (D) is incorrect because the grant should be reported under revenues.

30. On January 2, City of Walton issued $500,000, 10-year, 7% general obligation bonds. Interest is payable annually, beginning January 2 of the following year. What amount of bond interest is Walton required to report in the statement of revenue, expenditures, and changes in fund balances of its governmental funds at the close of this fiscal year, September 30?

A. $0

B. $17,500

C. $26,250

D. $35,000

Answer (A) is correct. *(CPA, adapted)*
REQUIRED: The bond interest reported in the governmental funds.
DISCUSSION: The financial statements of governmental funds are prepared using the modified accrual basis of accounting. It recognizes expenditures for principal and interest on general long-term debt only when these amounts are due. Because the fiscal year ends on September 30 and the interest is payable on the following January 2, Walton does not recognize the bond interest.
Answer (B) is incorrect because Walton is not required to report 6 months of interest for the fiscal year, or $17,500 [$500,000 × 7% × (6÷12)]. Answer (C) is incorrect because Walton is not required to report 9 months of interest for the fiscal year, or $26,500 [$500,000 × 7% × (9÷12)]. This amount is recognized in the government-wide statement of activities, which is prepared using the accrual basis. Answer (D) is incorrect because Walton is not required to report 12 months of interest for the fiscal year, or $35,000 [$500,000 × 7% × (12÷12)].

17.4 Characteristic Transactions of Governmental Entities

31. Kingwood Town, at the beginning of the year, paid $22,000 cash for a flatbed trailer to be used in the general operations of the town. The expected useful life of the trailer is 6 years with an estimated $7,000 salvage value. Which of the following amounts should be reported?

A. $15,000 increase in equipment in the general fund.

B. $15,000 increase in general capital assets.

C. $22,000 increase in general capital assets.

D. $22,000 increase in equipment in the general fund.

Answer (C) is correct. *(CPA, adapted)*
REQUIRED: The recording of the purchase of equipment for general operations.
DISCUSSION: Capital assets related to proprietary funds are accounted for in the government-wide financial statements and in the fund financial statements. Capital assets related to fiduciary funds are reported only in the statement of fiduciary net assets. All other capital assets are general capital assets reported only in the governmental activities column in the government-wide statement of net assets. Capital assets are recorded at historical cost or at estimated fair value if donated. Thus, general capital assets should be debited for $22,000, the historical cost of the equipment.
Answer (A) is incorrect because capital assets are not reported in the general fund and the assets are recorded at historical cost. Answer (B) is incorrect because capital assets are reported at historical cost, not historical cost minus salvage value. Answer (D) is incorrect because capital assets are not reported in the general fund.

32. Lys City reports a general long-term compensated absences liability in its financial statements. The salary rate used to calculate the liability should normally be the rate in effect

A. When the unpaid compensated absences were earned.

B. When the compensated absences are to be paid.

C. At the balance sheet date.

D. When the compensated absences were earned or are to be paid, or at the balance sheet date, whichever results in the lowest amount.

Answer (C) is correct. *(CPA, adapted)*
REQUIRED: The salary rate used to calculate the liability for compensated absences.
DISCUSSION: According to GASBS 16, "The compensated absences liability should be calculated based on the pay or salary rates in effect at the balance sheet date. However, if the employer pays employees for their compensated absences at other than their pay or salary rates -- for example, at a lower amount as established by contract, regulation, or policy -- that other rate as of the balance sheet date should be used to calculate the liability."

33. Dayne County's general fund had the following disbursements during the year:

Payment of principal on long-term debt	$100,000
Payments to vendors	500,000
Purchase of a computer	300,000

What amount should Dayne County report as expenditures in its governmental funds statement of revenues, expenditures, and changes in fund balances?

A. $300,000

B. $500,000

C. $800,000

D. $900,000

Answer (D) is correct. *(CPA, adapted)*
REQUIRED: The amount classified as expenditures.
DISCUSSION: Expenditures are recognized in the fund financial statements of a governmental fund under the modified accrual basis. They are decreases in (uses of) expendable available financial resources of a governmental fund. Expenditures are usually measurable and should be recognized when the related liability is incurred. However, expenditures for principal and interest on general long-term debt are usually recognized when those amounts are due. The liabilities for payments to vendors and the computer purchase were most likely incurred in the current year. The liability for payment of the principal on long-term debt was most likely due in the current year. Thus, general fund expenditures equaled $900,000 ($100,000 + $500,000 + $300,000).
Answer (A) is incorrect because the purchase of a computer is not the only expenditure. Answer (B) is incorrect because the payments to vendors are not the only expenditures. Answer (C) is incorrect because the payment on long-term debt also should be considered an expenditure.

34. Expenditures of a government for insurance extending over more than one accounting period

A. Must be accounted for as expenditures of the period of acquisition.

B. Must be accounted for as expenditures of the periods subsequent to acquisition.

C. Must be allocated between or among accounting periods.

D. May be allocated among periods or accounted for as expenditures when acquired.

Answer (D) is correct. *(CPA, adapted)*
REQUIRED: The proper treatment of expenditures extending over more than one period.
DISCUSSION: Under current GAAP, prepaid insurance may be reported by either the purchases method, in which an expenditure is reported when the policy is purchased, or the consumption method, in which an expenditure is reported when the asset is consumed.

35. The City of Bell entered into a capital lease agreement on December 31, Year 4, to acquire a capital asset. Under this agreement, Bell is to make three annual payments of $75,000 each on principal, plus interest of $22,000, $15,000, and $8,000 at the end of Year 5, Year 6, and Year 7, respectively. At the beginning of the lease, what amount should be debited to expenditures control in Bell's general fund?

A. $270,000

B. $225,000

C. $75,000

D. $97,000

Answer (B) is correct. *(CPA, adapted)*
REQUIRED: The amount that should be debited to expenditures control in the general fund.
DISCUSSION: General capital assets that are acquired by capital lease are recorded in the same manner as those acquired by outright purchase. The asset is reported only in the governmental activities column of the government-wide statement of net assets. It is measured in accordance with SFAS 13. In the general fund, when a capital lease represents the acquisition of a general capital asset, the transaction is reported by debiting an expenditure and crediting an other financing sources -- capital lease at the present value of the minimum lease payments ($75,000 annual principal repayment × 3 years = $225,000).
Answer (A) is incorrect because $270,000 includes the interest payments. Answer (C) is incorrect because $75,000 is the amount of one annual payment. Answer (D) is incorrect because $97,000 is the first annual payment plus the first interest payment.

36. Which of the following fund types used by a government most likely would have a fund balance reserved for an inventory of supplies?

A. General.

B. Internal service.

C. Private-purpose trust.

D. Capital projects.

Answer (A) is correct. *(CPA, adapted)*
REQUIRED: The fund type most likely to have a fund balance reserved for an inventory of supplies.
DISCUSSION: Governmental units normally record the purchases of supplies inventory in the general fund. In accounting for supplies, the expenditure account may be debited when the materials and supplies are purchased or when they are consumed. Under either method, the inventory of supplies remaining at year-end must be recorded on the balance sheet as an asset. In addition, under the purchases method, because resources have already been expended to acquire these supplies, a fund balance reserved for inventory of supplies must be credited to indicate the unavailability of resources in this amount for other expenditures.
Answer (B) is incorrect because an internal service fund is a proprietary fund. Thus, net assets, not fund balance, would be reported. Answer (C) is incorrect because a private-purpose trust is a fiduciary fund. Thus, net assets, not fund balance, would be reported. Answer (D) is incorrect because supplies are not generally recognized as an asset of a capital projects fund.

Use Gleim's **CPA Test Prep** CD-Rom/Pocket PC for interactive testing with over 4,000 additional questions!

17.5 PRACTICE SIMULATION

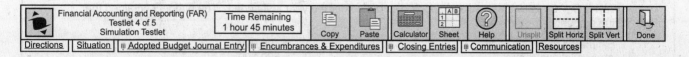

Financial Accounting and Reporting (FAR) Testlet 4 of 5 Simulation Testlet	Time Remaining 1 hour 45 minutes	Copy	Paste	Calculator	Sheet	Help	Unsplit	Split Horiz	Split Vert	Done

Directions | Situation | ✏ Adopted Budget Journal Entry | ✏ Encumbrances & Expenditures | ✏ Closing Entries | ✏ Communication | Resources

1. Directions

In the following simulation, you will be asked to complete various tasks. You may use the content in the **Information Tabs** to complete the tasks in the **Work Tabs**.

Information Tabs:

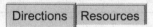

Directions | Resources

    FIG 1

1. Go through each of the **Information Tabs** to familiarize yourself with the simulation content

2. The **Resources** tab will contain information, including formulas and definitions, that may help you to complete the tasks

3. Your simulation may have more **Information Tabs** than those shown in Fig. 1

Work Tabs:

✏ SysTrust | ✏ Engagement Letter | ✏ Authoritative Sources | ✏ Communication

            FIG. 2

1. **Work Tabs**, to the right of **Information Tabs**, contain the tasks for you to complete

2. **Work Tabs** contain directions for completing each task - be sure to read these directions carefully

3. The tab names in Fig. 2 are for illustration only - yours may differ

4. Once you complete any part of a task, the pencil for that tab will be shaded (see **Communication** in Fig. 2)

5. The shaded pencil does **NOT** indicate that you have completed the entire task

6. You must complete all of the tasks in the **Work Tabs** to receive full credit

Research/Authoritative Literature Tab:

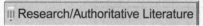

✏ Research/Authoritative Literature

        FIG. 3

1. This tab contains both the Research task and the Authoritative Literature

2. Detailed instructions for completing the Research task, and for using the Authoritative Literature, appear on this tab

3. You may use the Authoritative Literature as a resource for completing other tasks

NOTE: If you believe you have encountered a software malfunction, report it to the test center staff immediately.

2. Situation

The Wayne City Council approved and adopted its budget for the year just ended. The budget contained the following amounts:

Estimated revenues control	$700,000
Appropriations control	660,000
Authorized interfund transfer to the library debt service fund	30,000

During the year, various transactions and events occurred that affected the general fund.

Property taxes assessed	$800,000
Uncollectible taxes	100,000
Interfund transfer to the debt service fund	30,000
Interfund reimbursement received	40,000
Expenditures	700,000

3. Adopted Budget Journal Entry

This question is presented in a spreadsheet format that requires you to fill in the correct responses in the shaded cells provided. Based on the information given in the situation tab, determine which accounts are affected when recording the adopted budget in the general fund. Provide the amount to insert in the debit and credit fields by account. If the account is not affected, leave the corresponding boxes blank.

Account	Debit	Credit
1. Estimated revenues control		
2. Budgetary fund balance		
3. Appropriations control		
4. Estimated other financing uses – interfund transfers		
5. Expenditures control		

4. Encumbrances and Expenditures

This question is presented in a check-the-box format that requires you to select the correct responses from a given list. For each event, determine whether the account listed should be debited, credited, or is not affected.

Event 1: Recording encumbrances in the general fund at the time purchase orders are issued.

Account	Debited	Credited	Not Affected
1. Encumbrances			
2. Reserve for encumbrances			
3. Expenditures			
4. Vouchers payable			
5. Purchases			

Event 2: Recording expenditures that had been previously encumbered in the current year in the general fund.

Account	Debited	Credited	Not Affected
6. Encumbrances			
7. Reserve for encumbrances			
8. Expenditures			
9. Vouchers payable			
10. Purchases			

5. Closing Entries

This question is presented in a check-the-box format that requires you to select the correct responses from a given list. Determine whether each account below will be debited, credited, or not affected when Wayne City Council records, in the general fund, the closing entries (other than encumbrances) for the year just ended.

Account	*Debited*	*Credited*	*Not Affected*
1. Estimated revenues control			
2. Budgetary fund balance			
3. Appropriations control			
4. Estimated other financing uses – interfund transfers			
5. Expenditures control			
6. Revenues control			
7. Other financing uses – interfund transfers			
8. Allowance for uncollectible current taxes			
9. Bad debt expense			
10. Depreciation expense			
11. Interfund reimbursements			

6. Communication

In a brief memorandum to your governmental client, discuss the concepts of fiscal and operational accountability, including interperiod equity. Type your communication in your word processor program and print out the copy in a memorandum-style format.

REMINDER: Your response will be graded for both technical content and writing skills. Technical content will be evaluated for information that is helpful to the intended reader and clearly relevant to the issue. Writing skills will be evaluated for development, organization, and the appropriate expression of ideas in professional correspondence. Use a standard business memo or letter format with a clear beginning, middle, and end. Do not convey information in the form of a table, bullet point list, or other abbreviated presentation.

    TO: Governmental client
    FROM: CPA
    Subject: Accountability

Unofficial Answers

3. Adopted Budget Journal Entry (5 Gradable Items)

Account	Debit	Credit
1. Estimated revenues control	$700,000	
2. Budgetary fund balance		$10,000
3. Appropriations control		$660,000
4. Estimated other financing uses – interfund transfers		$30,000
5. Expenditures control		

1. Estimated revenues control is an anticipatory asset account that is debited in the budgetary entry.

2. Some accountants prefer to use a budgetary fund balance, a nominal account, rather than unreserved fund balance, a real account, to record the budgeted change in fund balance for the year.

3. The total amount authorized to be expended by the governmental unit for the fiscal period is credited in the budgetary entry. Appropriations control is an anticipatory liability account.

4. Estimated other financing sources (uses) include interfund transfers, the face amount of long-term debt, issuance premium or discount, certain payments to escrow agents for bond refundings, and sales of capital assets not qualifying as special items. The budgetary entry may include estimated other financing sources (a debit) or estimated other financing uses (a credit).

5. Expenditures control is not affected by recording the budget. An expenditure is debited when a fund liability is incurred.

4. Encumbrances and Expenditures (10 Gradable Items)

1. Debit. When a commitment is made to expend resources of a governmental unit, the appropriations account is encumbered. The journal entry is to debit the encumbrances account and credit the reserve for encumbrances account (a fund balance account) for the amount of the commitment. Comparison of encumbrances, appropriations, and expenditures determines the unencumbered amount of appropriations that may still be expended.

2. Credit. When a commitment is made to expend resources of a governmental unit, the appropriations account is encumbered. The journal entry is to debit the encumbrances account and credit the reserve for encumbrances account (a fund balance account) for the amount of the commitment. Comparison of encumbrances, appropriations, and expenditures determines the unencumbered amount of appropriations that may still be expended.

3. Not affected. An expenditure is not recognized by a debit until the related liability is incurred.

4. Not affected. Vouchers payable is not recognized by a credit until the related liability is incurred.

5. Not affected. A purchases account is not used to record inventory in a governmental fund.

6. Credit. The encumbrance is reversed and an expenditure is recorded when the related liability is incurred, that is, when an executory contract is complete or virtually completed. Thus, encumbrances is credited.

7. Debit. The reversal of the encumbrance entry requires a debit to reserve for encumbrances, a fund balance account.

8. Debit. An expenditure is recognized (debited) when the related liability is incurred, that is, when the liability is no longer contingent.

9. Credit. Vouchers payable is the liability account credited when the recognition criteria are satisfied.

10. Not affected. A purchases account is not used to record inventory in a governmental fund.

5. Closing Entries (11 Gradable Items)

1. <u>Credit.</u> Estimated revenues control is an anticipatory asset account that is debited in the budgetary entry. It is therefore credited in the closing entry.

2. <u>Debit.</u> Budgetary fund balance (a nominal account) is debited because the budgetary entry is being reversed. Thus, an unreserved fund balance (a real account) should be debited or credited to balance the closing of budgetary and operational accounts.

3. <u>Debit.</u> The total amount authorized to be expended by the governmental unit for the fiscal period is credited in the budgetary entry. Appropriations control is an anticipatory liability account. It is therefore debited in the closing entry.

4. <u>Debit.</u> The budgetary entry may include estimated other financing sources (a debit) or estimated other financing uses (a credit). Estimated other financing uses – interfund transfers is therefore debited in the closing entry.

5. <u>Credit.</u> Expenditures are debited when liabilities are incurred. Expenditures control is therefore credited when operational general-ledger accounts are closed.

6. <u>Debit.</u> Under the modified accrual basis of accounting, revenue is accrued by a credit when it is measurable and available to finance current expenditures. It is therefore debited when operational general-ledger accounts are closed.

7. <u>Credit.</u> Other financing uses – interfund transfer is debited when the interfund transfer is recorded. The account is therefore credited when operational general-ledger accounts are closed.

8. <u>Debit.</u> A year-end reclassification entry is needed for unpaid taxes receivable. This entry debits "property taxes receivable – delinquent" and the "allowance for uncollectibles – current" and credits "property taxes receivable – current" and "allowance for uncollectibles – delinquent."

9. <u>Not affected.</u> Bad debt expense is not recognized in a governmental fund. Revenues are recorded net of estimated bad debts.

10. <u>Not affected.</u> Depreciation expense is not recorded in governmental fund financial statements. Depreciation expense is recorded in proprietary fund financial statements, fiduciary fund financial statements, and the government-wide financial statements.

11. <u>Not affected.</u> Interfund reimbursements are not displayed in the financial statements.

6. Communication (5 Gradable Items; for grading instructions, please refer to page 12.)

Accountability is the paramount and pervasive objective of governmental financial reporting. Financial statements of governments traditionally have emphasized fiscal accountability for governmental activities and operational accountability for business-type and fiduciary activities.

GASBS 34 defines fiscal accountability as "the responsibility of governments to justify that their actions in the current period have complied with public decisions concerning the raising and spending of public moneys in the short term." Operational accountability is "governments' responsibility to report the extent to which they have met their accounting objectives efficiently and effectively, using all resources available for that purpose, and whether they can continue to meet their objectives for the foreseeable future."

The governmental funds financial statements continue to focus on the fiscal accountability of governmental activities. However, government-wide financial statements now provide information about the operational accountability of the governmental activities and business-type activities of the government as a whole. The fiduciary funds financial statements and the proprietary funds financial statements provide information about the operational accountability of the fiduciary funds and the proprietary funds, respectively.

Interperiod equity is an important component of accountability that is fundamental to public administration. Financial resources received during a period should suffice to pay for the services provided during that period. Moreover, debt should be repaid during the probable period of usefulness of the assets required. Thus, financial reporting should help taxpayers assess whether future taxpayers will have to assume burdens for services already provided.

Scoring Schedule:

	Correct Responses		Gradable Items		Weights		
Tab 3	_____	÷	5	×	20%	=	_____
Tab 4	_____	÷	10	×	25%	=	_____
Tab 5	_____	÷	11	×	25%	=	_____
Tab 6	_____	÷	5	×	30%	=	_____

<u>(Your Score)</u>

Use Gleim's *CPA Gleim Online* to practice more simulations in a realistic environment.

STUDY UNIT EIGHTEEN
GOVERNMENTAL ACCOUNTING II

(20 pages of outline)

This study unit is the second related to the governmental entities group in the Content Specification Outlines. It describes (1) the accounts and journal entries related to transactions specific to governmental entities, (2) the process of defining the governmental reporting entity, (3) the components of the comprehensive annual financial report (CAFR), (4) the reporting requirements for government-wide and fund financial statements, and (5) other required information in the CAFR. The presentation assumes knowledge of the information in Study Unit 17.

18.1 THE REPORTING ENTITY AND THE CAFR

Defining the Reporting Entity

1.   The variety of activities in which governments engage, the various funds used for accounting for these activities, and the numerous semi-governmental bodies with which governments interact complicate reporting.

   a.   GASBS 14, *The Financial Reporting Entity*, emphasizes **financial accountability** as the criterion for defining the reporting entity.

2.   The **overall reporting entity** consists of the primary government and its component units.

   a.   The **primary government** is the main portion of the overall reporting entity. It is financially accountable for the entities that make up its legal entity and certain other entities.

      1)   Any state or general-purpose local government qualifies as a primary government.

      2)   A special-purpose local government (such as a school system) also is considered a primary government if it

         a)   Has a separately elected governing body,
         b)   Is legally independent, and
         c)   Is fiscally independent of other state or local governments.

   b.   **Component units** are bodies legally separate from the primary government for which it is financially accountable.

      1)   They also include entities the exclusion of which would cause the financial statements to be misleading or incomplete.

      2)   See GASBS 39 in Appendix A.

    c.   The primary government also is financially accountable when

        1)   The separate body is **fiscally dependent** on the primary government.

            a)   A typical example of a fiscally dependent government is a dependent school district. Although the district may have a separately elected board, it is dependent if a local general-purpose government may approve its budget and levy a property tax on its behalf.

        2)   The officers of the primary government appoint a voting majority of the board of the separate body, and either (1) the primary government can impose its will on the separate body, or (2) the separate body provides a financial benefit or imposes a financial burden on the primary government.

Blended vs. Discretely Presented Component Units

3.   **Blended component units** are, in substance, the same as the primary government and should be reported as a part of it.

    a.   **Blending** is appropriate only if the component unit's governing body is substantially the same as the primary government's, or the component unit exclusively or almost exclusively benefits the primary government.

4.   Blended component-unit **balances and transactions** are reported in a manner similar to the balances and transactions of the primary government.

    a.   Thus, blended component units are reported as part of the primary government in the fund financial statements and the government-wide financial statements.

    b.   The **funds of the component unit** are blended with those of the primary government in the fund statements and combining statements. However, the primary government's **general fund** should be the only general fund reported. Hence, the general fund of the blended component unit should be reported as a **special revenue fund** of the primary government.

5.   The financial statements of the reporting entity should provide an overview of the entity but should **distinguish** between the primary government and its **component units**. Thus, the statements should communicate information about the component units and their relationships with the primary government rather than suggest that these organizations constitute one legal entity. .

    a.   For this purpose, the **government-wide financial statements** should report information about **discretely presented component units** in separate rows and columns. Most component units should be included in the reporting entity in this way.

    b.   Information about **discretely presented component units** that are **fiduciary** in nature is reported only in the fiduciary fund statements of the primary government. No other discretely presented component units are reported in the fund financial statements.

6.   Discrete presentation also includes reporting of **major component unit** information in the basic statements. This requirement, which does not apply to fiduciary component units, may be met by presentation of

    a.   Each major component unit in a separate column in the government-wide statements,

    b.   Combining statements after the fund statements, or

    c.   Condensed statements of net assets and activities in the notes.

7.   The financial statements of the reporting entity should include **data from all of its component units**.

    a.   This data from the component units' statements should be the amounts that would be in the **total columns** of those statements if they had been presented. Moreover, the requirement to use these aggregated totals applies regardless of how the reporting entity presents major component unit information.

The Comprehensive Annual Financial Report (CAFR)

8. The CAFR is a governmental reporting format of long standing. GASBS 34 prescribes the standard content of the CAFR.

    a. The **introductory section** contains:

        1) Letter of transmittal from the appropriate government officials
        2) Organization chart
        3) Names of principal officers

    b. The **financial section** contains:

        1) Independent auditor's report
        2) Management's discussion and analysis (MD&A)
        3) Basic financial statements

            a) **Government-wide financial statements**

                i) Statement of net assets
                ii) Statement of activities

            b) **Fund financial statements**

                i) **Governmental funds financial statements**

                     • Balance sheet (with reconciliation to government-wide statement of net assets)
                     • Statement of revenues, expenditures, and changes in fund balances (with reconciliation to government-wide statement of activities)

                ii) **Proprietary funds financial statements**

                     • Statement of net assets
                     • Statement of revenues, expenses, and changes in fund net assets
                     • Statement of cash flows

                iii) **Fiduciary funds financial statements** (and fiduciary component units)

                     • Statement of fiduciary net assets
                     • Statement of changes in fiduciary net assets

            c) Notes to the financial statements

        4) Required supplementary information (RSI) other than MD&A
        5) Combining statements and individual fund statements and schedules

    c. The **statistical section** is described in GASBS 44 in Appendix A.

9. The following are the minimum elements required for **general-purpose external financial reporting**:

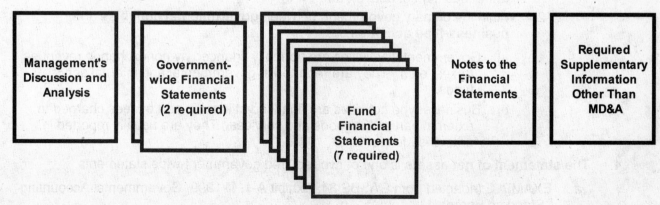

Stop and review! You have completed the outline for this subunit. Study multiple-choice questions 1 through 6 beginning on page 676.

18.2 MD&A AND THE GOVERNMENT-WIDE FINANCIAL STATEMENTS

Management's Discussion and Analysis (MD&A)

1. **MD&A** is part of required supplementary information (RSI). It precedes the basic financial statements and provides an analytical overview of financial activities. It is based on **currently known** facts, decisions, or conditions.

    a. MD&A includes **comparisons** of the current and prior years, with an emphasis on the current year, based on government-wide information. The focus is on the **primary government**, with distinctions between that government and its component units.

2. MD&A requirements are stated in general terms to encourage reporting of only the most relevant information. This information should be confined to the following:

    a. MD&A discusses the **basic financial statements**, including (1) their relationships to each other, (2) differences in the information provided, and (3) analyses of relationships of information in the fund and government-wide statements.

    b. MD&A also analyzes **overall financial position and results of operations** to aid in determining whether the year's activities have resulted in an improvement in that position and those results.

        1) It should discuss **governmental and business-type activities** and the reasons for significant changes.

    c. Moreover, MD&A analyzes significant **budget variances** and changes in balances and transactions of funds. These include limitations on future resource availability.

    d. MD&A describes **capital asset and long-term debt activity**.

        1) A government that uses the modified approach to reporting **infrastructure assets** should discuss (a) significant changes in the assessed condition of eligible assets, (b) how the current assessed condition compares with the established level, and (c) any significant differences between the actual and estimated amounts spent to maintain/preserve the assets.

    e. Another required topic is a description of **currently known** facts, decisions, or conditions expected to affect financial position or results of operations significantly.

Government-Wide Financial Statements

3. These do not display funds or fund types but instead report information about the **government as a whole**.

    a. **Two distinctions** are made in the government-wide financial statements:

        1) Between the **primary government** and its **discretely presented component units** (see item 3. above), and

        2) Within the primary government, between **governmental activities** and **business-type activities**.

            a) Governmental activities are normally financed by nonexchange revenues (taxes, etc.). They are reported in governmental and internal service funds.

            b) Business-type activities are financed at least in part by fees charged to external parties for goods and services. They are usually reported in enterprise funds.

4. The **statement of net assets** is one of two required government-wide statements.

    a. EXAMPLE (adapted from GASBS 34, Exhibit A-1, © 1999, Governmental Accounting Standard Board):

ASSETS	Primary Government			Component Units
	Governmental Activities	Business-type Activities	Total	
Cash and equivalents	$ XX,XXX,XXX	$ XX,XXX,XXX	$ XX,XXX,XXX	$ XXX,XXX
Investments	XX,XXX,XXX	--	XX,XXX,XXX	X,XXX,XXX
Receivables (net)	XX,XXX,XXX	X,XXX,XXX	XX,XXX,XXX	X,XXX,XXX
Internal balances	XXX,XXX	(XXX,XXX)	--	--
Inventories	XXX,XXX	XXX,XXX	XXX,XXX	XX,XXX
Capital assets, net	XXX,XXX,XXX	XXX,XXX,XXX	XXX,XXX,XXX	XX,XXX,XXX
Total assets	**$XXX,XXX,XXX**	**$XXX,XXX,XXX**	**$XXX,XXX,XXX**	**$ XX,XXX,XXX**
LIABILITIES				
Accounts payable	$ X,XXX,XXX	$ XXX,XXX	$ X,XXX,XXX	$ X,XXX,XXX
Deferred revenue	X,XXX,XXX	--	X,XXX,XXX	XX,XXX
Noncurrent liabilities:				
Due within one year	X,XXX,XXX	X,XXX,XXX	XX,XXX,XXX	X,XXX,XXX
Due in more than one year	XX,XXX,XXX	XX,XXX,XXX	XXX,XXX,XXX	XX,XXX,XXX
Total liabilities	**$XXX,XXX,XXX**	**$ XX,XXX,XXX**	**$XXX,XXX,XXX**	**$XXX,XXX,XXX**
NET ASSETS				
Invested in capital assets, net of related debt	$XXX,XXX,XXX	$ XX,XXX,XXX	$XXX,XXX,XXX	$ XX,XXX,XXX
Restricted for:				
Capital projects	XX,XXX,XXX	--	XX,XXX,XXX	XXX,XXX
Debt service	X,XXX,XXX	X,XXX,XXX	X,XXX,XXX	--
Community development projects	X,XXX,XXX	--	X,XXX,XXX	--
Other purposes	X,XXX,XXX	--	X,XXX,XXX	--
Unrestricted (deficit)	(X,XXX,XXX)	XX,XXX,XXX	X,XXX,XXX	X,XXX,XXX
Total net assets	**$XXX,XXX,XXX**	**$ XX,XXX,XXX**	**$XXX,XXX,XXX**	**$ XX,XXX,XXX**

    b.   The statement of net assets reports **all financial and capital resources**.

        1)   No particular format is required, although the GASB prefers the net assets format (assets – liabilities = net assets). Thus, the difference between assets and liabilities is **net assets**, not equity or fund balance.

    c.   Presentation of assets and liabilities in order of relative liquidity is encouraged. A classified statement of net assets is also acceptable.

    d.   **Net assets** should be displayed in **three components**:

        1)   **Invested in capital assets, net of related debt**, includes unrestricted and restricted capital assets, net of accumulated depreciation and related liabilities for borrowings.

            a)   However, **debt** related to significant **unspent proceeds** is classified in the same net assets component as those proceeds, such as restricted for capital projects.

        2)   **Restricted net assets** are subject to constraints imposed by external entities (creditors, grantors, or other governments) or by law (constitutional provisions or **enabling legislation**).

            a)   If permanent endowments or permanent fund principal amounts are included, restricted net assets should be displayed as two additional components: expendable and nonexpendable. **Nonexpendable** means that the net assets are retained in perpetuity.

        3)   **Unrestricted net assets** is a residual category. For example, this category includes items that are merely internally **designated** rather than externally restricted or restricted by enabling legislation. Designations are not reported on the face of the financial statements.

  5.   The **statement of activities** presents operations in a format that displays **net (expense) revenue** for each function.

EXAMPLE

(adapted from GASBS 34, Exhibit A-1, © 1999, Governmental Accounting Standard Board)

Functions/Programs	Expenses	Program Revenues — Charges for Services	Program Revenues — Operating Grants and Contributions	Program Revenues — Capital Grants and Contributions	Net (Expense) Revenue and Changes in Net Assets — Primary Government — Governmental Activities	Net (Expense) Revenue and Changes in Net Assets — Primary Government — Business-type Activities	Net (Expense) Revenue and Changes in Net Assets — Primary Government — Total	Net (Expense) Revenue and Changes in Net Assets — Component Units
Primary government:								
Governmental activities:								
General government	$ X,XXX,XXX	$ X,XXX,XXX	$ XXX,XXX	—	$ (X,XXX,XXX)	—	$ (X,XXX,XXX)	—
Public safety	XX,XXX,XXX	X,XXX,XXX	X,XXX,XXX	XX,XXX	(XX,XXX,XXX)	—	(XX,XXX,XXX)	—
Public works	XX,XXX,XXX	XXX,XXX	—	X,XXX,XXX	(XX,XXX,XXX)	—	(XX,XXX,XXX)	—
Engineering services	X,XXX,XXX	XXX,XXX	—	—	(XXX,XXX)	—	(XXX,XXX)	—
Etc.	X,XXX,XXX	X,XXX,XXX	X,XXX,XXX	X,XXX,XXX	(XX,XXX,XXX)	—	(XX,XXX,XXX)	—
Total governmental activities	$ XXX,XXX,XXX	$ XX,XXX,XXX	$ X,XXX,XXX	$ X,XXX,XXX	$ (XX,XXX,XXX)	—	$ (XX,XXX,XXX)	—
Business-type activities:								
Water	$ X,XXX,XXX	$ X,XXX,XXX	—	$ X,XXX,XXX		$ X,XXX,XXX	$ X,XXX,XXX	—
Sewer	X,XXX,XXX	X,XXX,XXX	—	XXX,XXX		X,XXX,XXX	X,XXX,XXX	—
Parking facilities	X,XXX,XXX	X,XXX,XXX	—	—		(X,XXX,XXX)	(X,XXX,XXX)	—
Total business-type activities	$ XX,XXX,XXX	$ XX,XXX,XXX	—	$ X,XXX,XXX		$ X,XXX,XXX	$ X,XXX,XXX	—
Total primary government	$ XXX,XXX,XXX	$ XX,XXX,XXX	$ X,XXX,XXX	$ X,XXX,XXX	$ (XX,XXX,XXX)	$ X,XXX,XXX	$ (XX,XXX,XXX)	—
Component units:								
Landfill	$ X,XXX,XXX	$ X,XXX,XXX	$ X,XXX,XXX	$ XX,XXX				XXX,XXX
Public school system	XX,XXX,XXX	XXX,XXX	X,XXX,XXX	—				(XX,XXX,XXX)
Total component units	$ XX,XXX,XXX	$ X,XXX,XXX	$ X,XXX,XXX	$ XX,XXX				$ (XX,XXX,XXX)

General revenues:				
		Governmental Activities	Business-type Activities	Total	Component Units
Taxes:				
Property taxes, levied for general purposes	$ XX,XXX,XXX		XX,XXX,XXX	$ XX,XXX,XXX
Property taxes, levied for debt service	X,XXX,XXX		X,XXX,XXX	X,XXX,XXX
Franchise fees	X,XXX,XXX		X,XXX,XXX	X,XXX,XXX
Public service taxes	X,XXX,XXX		X,XXX,XXX	X,XXX,XXX
Payment from City	—		—	$ XX,XXX,XXX
Grants and contributions not restricted to specific programs	X,XXX,XXX		X,XXX,XXX	X,XXX,XXX
Investment earnings	X,XXX,XXX	XXX,XXX	X,XXX,XXX	XXX,XXX
Miscellaneous	XXX,XXX	XXX,XXX	XXX,XXX	XX,XXX
Special item – gain on sale of park land	X,XXX,XXX		X,XXX,XXX	—
Transfers	XXX,XXX	(XXX,XXX)	—	—
Total general revenues, special items, and transfers	$ XX,XXX,XXX	XXX,XXX	XX,XXX,XXX	$ XX,XXX,XXX
Change in net assets	XX,XXX,XXX	X,XXX,XXX	XX,XXX,XXX	XXX,XXX
Net assets — beginning	XXX,XXX,XXX	XX,XXX,XXX	XXX,XXX,XXX	X,XXX,XXX
Net assets — ending	$ XXX,XXX,XXX	$ XX,XXX,XXX	$ XXX,XXX,XXX	$ XX,XXX,XXX

a.   The statement of activities presents operations in a format that displays **net (expense) revenue** for each function.

1)   The purpose is to report the relative financial burden to the taxpayers for that function.

2)   The net (expense) revenue for each governmental or business-type function equals expenses (at a minimum, the **direct expenses** of the function) minus program revenues.

b.   The minimum levels of detail for activities accounted for in governmental funds and in enterprise funds are by **function** and by **different identifiable activities**, respectively.

1)   An **identifiable activity** has a specific revenue stream and related expenses, gains, and losses separately accounted for. Whether it is different ordinarily depends on the goods, services, or programs that the activity provides.

c.   **Direct expenses** must be reported by function. **Indirect expenses** may or may not be allocated. A government may choose to allocate some indirect expenses, to adopt a full-cost allocation approach, or not to allocate.

1)   If indirect expenses are allocated, direct and indirect expenses should be displayed in separate columns.

2)   **Depreciation** specifically identifiable with a function is a direct expense. Depreciation of capital assets **shared by functions** is allocated as a direct expense.

a)   Depreciation of capital assets that **serve all functions** is not required to be included in direct expenses of the functions. It may be displayed on a separate line in the statement of activities or as part of the general government function. It may or may not be allocated.

b)   Depreciation of infrastructure assets is not allocated to other functions.

3)   **Interest on general long-term liabilities** is usually an indirect expense.

d.   **Program revenues** include (1) charges for services, (2) program-specific operating grants and contributions, and (3) program-specific capital grants and contributions.

1)   They also may include (a) earnings on endowments, (b) permanent fund investments, or (c) other investments if such earnings are specifically restricted to a given program. Multiple columns may be used to report a category.

2)   **Charges for services** constitute a category of program revenues resulting from charges to customers, applicants, or others who (a) directly benefit from what is provided (goods, services, or privileges) or (b) are otherwise directly affected.

a)   Thus, **fines and forfeitures** are charges for services because they are paid by persons directly affected by a program or service.

b)   Charges for services are assigned to a given function if the function generates those revenues.

3)   Program revenues in the form of **grants and contributions** are assigned to a given function if the revenues are restricted to it.

e.   **General revenues** are not required to be reported as program revenues. They are reported separately after total net (expense) revenue for all functions. All taxes, including those levied for a special purpose, are general revenues.

1)   General revenues are reported at the bottom of the statement of activities to determine the change in net assets for the period.

f.   The following are reported separately at the bottom of the statement: (1) contributions to endowments, (2) contributions to permanent fund principal, (3) transfers between governmental and business-type activities, and (4) special and extraordinary items.

1)   **Extraordinary items** are unusual in nature and infrequent in occurrence.

        2) **Special items** are significant transactions or other events that are **either** unusual **or** infrequent and are **within the control of management**. They are reported separately after extraordinary items.

6. Government-wide financial statements are prepared using the **economic resources measurement focus** and the **accrual basis of accounting**. They report all of the government's assets, liabilities, revenues, expenses, gains, and losses.

    a. Items arising from **exchange or exchange-like transactions** are recognized when the exchange occurs. Items arising from nonexchange transactions are recognized in accordance with GASBS 33.

    b. The resources of **fiduciary activities** and similar component units (e.g., some public employee retirement systems) are not available to finance the government's programs. Thus, they are reported only in the fund statements (the statements of fiduciary net assets and changes in fiduciary net assets).

7. **Eliminations** and **reclassifications** are necessary to prepare the government-wide statements.

    a. Thus, **interfund receivables and payables** reported in fund balance sheets are eliminated in the governmental and business-type activities columns of the statement of net assets.

        1) Exceptions are net residual amounts due (presented as **internal balances** between the two types of activities). Failing to report residual amounts contradicts the principle requiring separate presentation of governmental and business-type activities. However, the total primary government column excludes internal balances.

    b. Fund receivables from, or payables to, **fiduciary funds** are treated in the statement of net assets as amounts arising from transactions with **external parties**, not as internal balances. The reason is that fiduciary funds only report balances held for individuals, private organizations, and other governments.

    c. The effect of **internal service fund** activity should be eliminated in the statement of activities. Thus, preparation of this statement essentially requires adjusting the internal service fund's change in net assets to zero. The result is a decrease or increase in the charges made to the participating funds or functions. Moreover, similar internal events that are, in effect, allocations of overhead also result in eliminations. Accordingly, only the function to which they were allocated reports them.

    d. Eliminations are not made in the statement of activities for the effects of **interfund services provided and used** between functions (e.g., the sale of power by a utility to the general government).

    e. Flows of resources between **the primary government** and its **blended component units** are reclassified as internal activity based on the requirements for interfund activity.

        1) Flows between the primary government and its **discretely presented component units** (unless they affect the balance sheet only) are treated as **external transactions** (i.e., as revenues and expenses). The payables and receivables are reported on a separate line.

    f. Any balances of **internal service funds** that are not eliminated are usually reported in the governmental activities column. These funds' activities are ordinarily more governmental than business-type. But this presentation is not appropriate if enterprise funds are the predominant participants in the internal service funds.

Stop and review! You have completed the outline for this subunit. Study multiple-choice questions 7 through 17 beginning on page 678.

18.3 GOVERNMENTAL FUNDS REPORTING

Major vs. Nonmajor Fund Reporting

1. The **focus** of governmental and enterprise fund financial statements is on **major funds**.

   a. Aspects of major fund reporting

      1) Each **major fund** is presented in a **separate column**.

         a) The **main operating fund** (the general fund) is **always** reported as a major fund.

      2) **Nonmajor funds** are aggregated in **one column**.
      3) **Combining statements** are not required for nonmajor funds.

   b. Any individual governmental or enterprise fund **must be reported as major if both**

      1) Total assets, liabilities, revenues, or expenditures/expenses (excluding revenues and expenditures/expenses classified as extraordinary) of the fund are **at least 10%** of the corresponding element total (assets, etc.) for all funds of its category or type (i.e., all governmental or all enterprise funds), **and**
      2) An element that met the 10% standard above is **at least 5%** of the corresponding element total for all governmental and enterprise funds.

   c. Any governmental or enterprise fund **believed to be particularly important** to users also may be reported in this way.

   d. Major fund reporting is **not required** for **internal service funds**.

Governmental Funds

2. Governmental funds emphasize sources, uses, and balances of current financial resources.

   a. Expendable assets are assigned to funds based on their intended use, current liabilities are assigned to funds from which they will be paid, and the difference (fund equity) is the fund balance.

   b. Thus, the governmental funds are reported using the **current financial resources measurement focus** and the **modified accrual basis of accounting**.

3. The **general fund** accounts for all resources of the governmental unit not required to be reported elsewhere.

   a. The reporting entity has **only one** general fund.

4. **Special revenue funds** account for the proceeds of special sources of revenue (other than for major capital projects and trusts for individuals, private organizations, and other governments).

   a. The proceeds must be **legally restricted** to expenditure for a particular purpose, such as certain federal grant monies, revenue-sharing funds, and gasoline taxes. However, special revenue funds are **not required** unless legally mandated.

   b. The general fund of a **blended component unit** is reported as a special revenue fund.

5. **Capital projects funds** account for financial resources, including general obligation bond proceeds, to be used for the acquisition or construction of major capital facilities for general government use.

   a. Capital projects financed by proprietary funds or in trust funds for individuals, private organizations, or other governments are accounted for in those funds.

6.   **Debt service funds** account for resources accumulated to pay the principal and interest on general long-term debt.

   a.   They are required if they are legally mandated or if resources are being accumulated for payment of principal and interest in future years.

   b.   If the government has no obligation on a **special assessment issue**, the debt service transactions are accounted for in an **agency fund**.

7.   **Permanent funds** report resources legally restricted so that earnings only, not principal, may be expended to support the government's programs. An example is a perpetual-care fund for a public cemetery.

   a.   Permanent funds are distinct from private-purpose trust funds, which benefit individuals, private organizations, or other governments. Private-purpose trust funds are reported with the other fiduciary funds.

Governmental Funds Financial Statements

8.   A **balance sheet** is required for governmental funds. It should be in balance sheet format (assets = liabilities + fund balances) with a **total column**

   a.   **Fund balances** should be segregated into **reserved** and **unreserved** amounts.

   b.   EXAMPLE (adapted from GASBS 34, Exhibit C-1, © 1999, Governmental Accounting Standard Board):

	General Fund	Major Fund	Major Fund	Major Fund	All Nonmajor Funds	Total Governmental Funds
ASSETS						
Cash	$ XXX,XXX	$ XXX,XXX	$ XXX,XXX	$ XXX,XXX	$ XXX,XXX	$ X,XXX,XXX
Investments	XXX,XXX	XXX,XXX	XXX,XXX	XXX,XXX	XXX,XXX	X,XXX,XXX
Etc.	XXX,XXX	XXX,XXX	XXX,XXX	XXX,XXX	XXX,XXX	X,XXX,XXX
Total assets	**$X,XXX,XXX**	**$X,XXX,XXX**	**$X,XXX,XXX**	**$X,XXX,XXX**	**$X,XXX,XXX**	**$XX,XXX,XXX**
LIABILITIES AND FUND BALANCES						
Liabilities:						
Accounts payable	$ XXX,XXX	$ XXX,XXX	$ XXX,XXX	$ XXX,XXX	$ XXX,XXX	$ X,XXX,XXX
Due to other funds	XXX,XXX	XXX,XXX	XXX,XXX	XXX,XXX	XXX,XXX	X,XXX,XXX
Etc.	XXX,XXX	XXX,XXX	XXX,XXX	XXX,XXX	XXX,XXX	X,XXX,XXX
Total liabilities	$X,XXX,XXX	$X,XXX,XXX	$X,XXX,XXX	$X,XXX,XXX	$X,XXX,XXX	$XX,XXX,XXX
Fund balances:						
Reserved for:						
Inventories	$ XXX,XXX	--	--	--	--	$ XXX,XXX
Encumbrances	XX,XXX	$ XX,XXX	$ XX,XXX	$ XX,XXX	$ XXX,XXX	XXX,XXX
Debt service	--	--	--	--	XXX,XXX	XXX,XXX
Unreserved, reported in:						
General fund	XXX,XXX	--	--	--	--	XXX,XXX
Special revenue funds	--	XXX,XXX	XXX,XXX	--	XXX,XXX	XXX,XXX
Capital projects funds	--	--	--	XXX,XXX	XXX,XXX	XXX,XXX
Total fund balances	$X,XXX,XXX	$ XXX,XXX	$ XXX,XXX	$ XXX,XXX	$X,XXX,XXX	$ X,XXX,XXX
Total liabilities and fund balances	**$X,XXX,XXX**	**$X,XXX,XXX**	**$X,XXX,XXX**	**$X,XXX,XXX**	**$X,XXX,XXX**	**$XX,XXX,XXX**

9.   A **summary reconciliation of total governmental fund balances** to net assets of governmental activities in the government-wide statement of net assets must be prepared. This summary should be presented at the bottom of the statement or in a schedule. Brief explanations on the face of the statement may suffice, but a more detailed explanation in the notes may be necessary.

   a.   **General capital assets and general long-term liabilities** not currently due are reconciling items because they are not reported on the balance sheet. Thus, the **current** financial resources measurement focus of the governmental funds balance sheet is reconciled with the reporting of **all** resources and obligations.

1) EXAMPLE (adapted from GASBS 34, Exhibit C-1, © 1999, Governmental Accounting Standard Board):

Total governmental fund balances	$XX,XXX,XXX
Amounts reported for *governmental activities* in the statement of net assets are different because:	
Capital assets used in governmental activities are not financial resources and therefore are not reported in the funds.	XX,XXX,XXX
Other long-term assets are not available to pay for current-period expenditures and therefore are deferred in the funds.	X,XXX,XXX
Internal service funds are used by management to charge the costs of certain activities, such as insurance and telecommunications, to individual funds. The assets and liabilities of the internal service funds are included in governmental activities in the statement of net assets.	X,XXX,XXX
Long-term liabilities, including bonds payable, are not due and payable in the current period and therefore are not reported in the funds.	(XX,XXX,XXX)
Net assets of governmental activities	**$XX,XXX,XXX**

10. A **statement of revenues, expenditures, and changes in fund balances** is required for governmental funds.

   a. It reports inflows, outflows, and balances of current financial resources. The focus is on major fund reporting.

      1) EXAMPLE (adapted from GASBS 34, Exhibit C-2, © 1999, Governmental Accounting Standard Board):

	General Fund	Major Fund	Major Fund	Major Fund	All Nonmajor Funds	Total Governmental Funds
REVENUES						
Property taxes	$ X,XXX,XXX	--	--	--	$ XXX,XXX	$ X,XXX,XXX
Public service taxes	XXX,XXX	--	--	--	--	XXX,XXX
Fees and fines	XXX,XXX	--	--	--	--	XXX,XXX
Intergovernmental	XXX,XXX	$ XXX,XXX	--	--	XXX,XXX	X,XXX,XXX
Investment earnings	XXX,XXX	XXX,XXX	$ XXX,XXX	$ XXX,XXX	XXX,XXX	X,XXX,XXX
Etc.	XXX,XXX	XXX,XXX	--	XXX,XXX	XXX,XXX	X,XXX,XXX
Total revenues	**$ X,XXX,XXX**	**$X,XXX,XXX**	**$X,XXX,XXX**	**$X,XXX,XXX**	**$ X,XXX,XXX**	**$ XX,XXX,XXX**
EXPENDITURES						
Current:						
General governmental	$ XXX,XXX	--	$ XXX,XXX	$ XXX,XXX	$ XXX,XXX	$ X,XXX,XXX
Public safety	XXX,XXX	--	--	--	XXX,XXX	X,XXX,XXX
Public works	XXX,XXX	--	--	--	XXX,XXX	X,XXX,XXX
Etc.	XXX,XXX	$ XXX,XXX	--	--	XXX,XXX	X,XXX,XXX
Debt service:						
Principal	--	--	--	--	XXX,XXX	XXX,XXX
Interest and other charges	--	--	--	--	XXX,XXX	XXX,XXX
Capital outlay	--	--	XXX,XXX	XXX,XXX	XXX,XXX	X,XXX,XXX
Total expenditures	**$ X,XXX,XXX**	**$X,XXX,XXX**	**$ X,XXX,XXX**	**$ X,XXX,XXX**	**$ X,XXX,XXX**	**$ XX,XXX,XXX**
Excess (deficiency) of revenues over expenditures	**$(X,XXX,XXX)**	**$ (XXX,XXX)**	**$(X,XXX,XXX)**	**$(X,XXX,XXX)**	**$(X,XXX,XXX)**	**$(XX,XXX,XXX)**
OTHER FINANCING SOURCES (USES)						
Proceeds of refunding bonds	--	--	--	--	$XX,XXX,XXX	$XX,XXX,XXX
Proceeds of long-term capital-related debt	--	--	$XX,XXX,XXX	--	X,XXX,XXX	XX,XXX,XXX
Payment to bond refunding escrow agent	--	--	--	--	(XX,XXX,XXX)	(XX,XXX,XXX)
Transfers in	$ XXX,XXX	--	--	--	X,XXX,XXX	X,XXX,XXX
Transfers out	(X,XXX,XXX)	$ (XXX,XXX)	(X,XXX,XXX)	--	(XXX,XXX)	(X,XXX,XXX)
Total other financing sources and uses	**$X,XXX,XXX**	**$X,XXX,XXX**	**$ X,XXX,XXX**	**--**	**$X,XXX,XXX**	**$ XX,XXX,XXX**
SPECIAL ITEM						
Proceeds from sale of park land	$ X,XXX,XXX	--	--	--	--	$ X,XXX,XXX
Net changes in fund balances	**$(X,XXX,XXX)**	**$ (XXX,XXX)**	**$XX,XXX,XXX**	**$(XX,XXX,XXX)**	**$ (XXX,XXX)**	**$ (XXX,XXX)**
Fund balances – beginning	X,XXX,XXX	X,XXX,XXX	XX,XXX	XX,XXX,XXX	XX,XXX,XXX	XX,XXX,XXX
Fund balances – ending	**$ X,XXX,XXX**	**$X,XXX,XXX**	**$XX,XXX,XXX**	**$ X,XXX,XXX**	**$ X,XXX,XXX**	**$ XX,XXX,XXX**

b. **Revenues** are classified in this statement by major source and **expenditures** by, at a minimum, function.

   1) **Debt issue costs** (e.g., underwriter's fees) paid from the proceeds are expenditures. Issue costs (e.g., rating agency fees) paid from existing resources are likewise classified as expenditures (but not until the liability is incurred). ·

c. **Other financing sources and uses** include the face amount of long-term debt, issuance premium or discount, some payments to escrow agents for bond refundings, interfund transfers, and sales of capital assets (unless the sale is a special item).

d. **Special and extraordinary items** are reported separately after other financing sources and uses. A transaction or an event may meet the definition of a special item except that it is **not** within the control of management. Such a transaction or event should be separately identified in the appropriate revenue or expenditure category or disclosed in the notes.

   1) **Debt refundings** in governmental funds are not extraordinary items. They result in other financing sources or uses, not gains or losses.

11. A summary **reconciliation of the net change in governmental fund balances** to the **change in net assets of governmental activities in the government-wide statement of activities** must be prepared. This summary should be presented at the bottom of the statement or in a schedule. Brief explanations on the face of the statement may suffice, but a more detailed explanation in the notes may be necessary.

   a. EXAMPLE (adapted from GASBS 34, Exhibit C-3, © 1999, Governmental Accounting Standard Board):

Net change in fund balances – total governmental funds	$ (XXX,XXX)

Amounts reported for *governmental activities* in the statement of activities are different because:

Governmental funds report **capital outlays** as expenditures. However, in the statement of activities, the cost of those assets is allocated over their estimated useful lives as depreciation expense. This is the amount by which capital outlays exceeded depreciation in the current period.	XX,XXX,XXX
In the statement of activities, only the **gain on the sale of the park land** is reported. But in the governmental funds, the proceeds from the sale increase financial resources. Thus, the change in net assets differs from the change in fund balances by the cost of the land sold.	(XXX,XXX)
Revenues in the statement of activities that do not provide current financial resources are not reported as revenues in the funds.	X,XXX,XXX
Bond proceeds provide current financial resources to governmental funds, but issuing debt increases long-term liabilities in the statement of net assets. Repayment of bond principal is an expenditure in the governmental funds, but the repayment reduces long-term liabilities in the statement of net assets. This is the amount by which proceeds exceeded repayments.	(XX,XXX,XXX)
Some expenses reported in the statement of activities do not require the use of current financial resources and therefore are not reported as expenditures in governmental funds.	(X,XXX,XXX)
Internal service funds are used by management to charge the costs of certain activities, such as insurance and telecommunications, to individual funds. The net revenue (expense) of the internal service funds is reported with governmental activities.	(XXX,XXX)
Change in net assets of governmental activities	**$ (X,XXX,XXX)**

Stop and review! You have completed the outline for this subunit. Study multiple-choice questions 18 through 22 beginning on page 682.

18.4 PROPRIETARY FUNDS REPORTING

Enterprise Funds

1. These funds may be used for any activities for which fees are charged to external users. They need not be used for insignificant activities.

2. An activity must be reported as an enterprise fund if **one of three criteria** is met. These are applied in the context of the activity's **principal revenue sources**. The criteria emphasize **fees charged to external users**.

   a. It is financed with debt and the only security is a pledge of the activity's net revenues from fees and charges.

      1) If the debt is also secured by the full faith and credit of a related governmental entity, this criterion is not met because such debt is not payable solely from the activity's net revenues.

   b. Its capital and other costs of providing services are legally required to be recovered from fees and charges, not taxes or similar revenues.

      1) For example, if a water utility is required by state regulation to recover the costs of its plant from user charges, the utility must be reported as an enterprise fund if the charges are the activity's **principal revenue source**. The legal requirement for cost recovery meets one of the criteria for enterprise fund reporting.

      2) Another example is an unemployment compensation fund.

   c. Its pricing policies set fees and charges to recover capital and other costs.

3. **Examples** of enterprise fund activities are

   a. Public transportation systems
   b. State-run lotteries
   c. Public utilities (water, sewage, electricity)
   d. Unemployment compensation funds
   e. Emergency services
   f. Government-owned healthcare facilities

4. Journal entries are virtually the same as in any business enterprise. Major fund reporting is required for enterprise funds.

Internal Service Funds

5. They may be used for activities that provide goods and services to **other subunits** of the primary government and its component units or to **other governments** on a **cost-reimbursement basis**.

   a. However, if the reporting government is not the predominant participant, the activity should be reported as an **enterprise fund**.

6. **Examples** of the uses of an internal service fund are

   a. Information technology
   b. Central purchasing and warehousing
   c. Motor pool maintenance
   d. Photocopying and printing
   e. Self-insurance for payment of claims and judgments

7. **Billings for goods and services** are recorded as operating revenues. These activities are considered to be **interfund services provided and used**.

8.   **Journal entries** are virtually the same as for any business.

   a.   The initial allocation of resources may come from an interfund transfer, that is, from an amount not to be repaid or an interfund loan.

      1)   To record an interfund transfer from the general fund and an interfund loan from an enterprise fund, the entry might be

Cash	$XXX,XXX	
Interfund transfer from the general fund		$XXX,XXX
Due to enterprise fund		XXX,XXX

9.   **Major fund** reporting is **not** required for internal service funds. Thus, the combined totals for all internal service funds are reported in a separate column (usually labeled as governmental activities) to the right of the total enterprise funds column in each proprietary fund financial statement.

Proprietary Fund Financial Statements

10.   The emphasis of **proprietary funds** is on operating income, changes in net assets (or cost recovery), financial position, and cash flows.

   a.   Moreover, these funds customarily **do not** record a budget and encumbrances.

   b.   The **economic resources measurement focus** and the **accrual basis of accounting** are required in the proprietary fund financial statements.

11.   A **statement of net assets or balance sheet** is required for proprietary funds. Assets and liabilities must be **classified** as current or noncurrent. Either a net assets format (assets – liabilities = net assets) or a balance sheet format (assets = liabilities + net assets) may be used.

   a.   Net assets should be reported in three components (invested in capital assets, net of related debt; restricted; and unrestricted). Moreover, **capital contributions** (such as grants or contributions by developers) should **not** be displayed as a separate component. **Designations** should **not** be shown on the face of the statements.

      1)   **Restricted assets** are subject to use restrictions imposed by external entities or by law that change the nature or normal understanding of the availability of the asset.

      2)   **Capital assets** of proprietary funds and **long-term liabilities** directly related to, and expected to be paid from, proprietary funds are reported in the government-wide statement of net assets and in the proprietary fund statement of net assets.

12.   A **statement of revenues, expenses, and changes in fund net assets or fund equity** (either label may be used) is required for proprietary funds.

   a.   **Revenues** are reported by major source either **net** with disclosure of discounts and allowances or **gross** with discounts and allowances reported beneath the revenue amounts.

b. **Operating and nonoperating** revenues and expenses are distinguished. Separate subtotals are given for operating revenues, operating expenses, and operating income. The sequence of items in the all-inclusive format shown below must be followed in each column of the statement:

	Operating revenues (detailed)
+	Total operating revenues
	Operating expenses (detailed)
−	Total operating expenses
=	**Operating income (loss)**
+/−	Nonoperating revenues and expenses (detailed)
=	Income before other revenues, expenses, gains, losses, and transfers
+/−	Capital contributions, additions to endowments, special and extraordinary items, and interfund transfers
=	**Change in net assets**
+	Net assets − beginning
=	**Net assets − ending**

c. A government should consistently follow appropriate **definitions of operating items**. One consideration in defining these items is the principal purpose of the fund. A second consideration is the presentation of these items in a cash flows statement. Thus, an item not classified as an operating cash flow most likely should be treated as a nonoperating revenue or expense.

d. Recognition of **nonexchange revenues** should be based on GASBS 33.

e. Restricted net assets should be presented in **expendable and nonexpendable components** when additions are made to permanent endowments.

f. **Reconciliation.** Net assets and changes in net assets are reported in the proprietary fund statements for total enterprise funds. They will ordinarily be the same as the corresponding amounts for business-type activities in the government-wide statements. Any differences should be reconciled.

1) For example, although **internal service funds** are proprietary funds, the activities they account for are normally governmental. Thus, they should be included in the governmental activities column in the government-wide statement of activities.

2) However, if enterprise funds are the **predominant participants** in the internal service funds, this presentation is not appropriate. Accordingly, the reclassification of internal service fund transactions from governmental to business-type activities is an item needed to reconcile the amounts for total enterprise funds to amounts in the government-wide statements.

13. A **statement of cash flows** is required for proprietary funds. See the outline of GASBS 9 in Appendix A.

Stop and review! You have completed the outline for this subunit. Study multiple-choice questions 23 through 31 beginning on page 684.

18.5 FIDUCIARY FUNDS REPORTING AND INTERFUND ACTIVITY

Overview

1. **Fiduciary funds** emphasize net assets and changes in net assets. They report assets that cannot be used to support the government's own programs. They are held in trust or in an agency capacity for **specific individuals, private organizations, or other governments**. They are **not** held for other funds or component units of the reporting entity.

   a. A **trust fund** differs from an **agency fund**. The trust agreement determines how long resources are held and the degree of management involvement. The governmental entity serves as a **fiduciary** of a trust. The role of the government is purely **custodial** for resources held in an agency fund.

   b. The **economic resources measurement focus** and the **accrual basis of accounting** are required in the fiduciary fund financial statements.

2. **Fiduciary fund financial statements** include information about all fiduciary funds and similar component units. The statements report information in a separate column for each fund type but **not** by major fund. The notes present financial statements for individual defined benefit pension and other postemployment benefit plans unless separate GAAP reports have been issued.

   a. A **statement of fiduciary net assets** is required for fiduciary funds. It reports assets, liabilities, and net assets for each fiduciary fund type. However, it does not present the three components of net assets reported in the government-wide statement of net assets or in the proprietary fund statement of net assets.

      1) The statement is equivalent to the **statement of plan net assets** required for defined benefit pension and other postemployment benefit plans.

      2) **Capital assets** of fiduciary funds and **long-term liabilities** directly related to, and expected to be paid from, fiduciary funds are reported in the statement of fiduciary net assets. They are **not** reported in the government-wide statement of net assets.

   b. A **statement of changes in fiduciary net assets** is required for fiduciary funds. It reports additions to, subtractions from, and the annual net change in net assets for each fiduciary fund type.

      a) It is equivalent to the **statement of changes in plan net assets** required for defined benefit pension and other postemployment benefit plans.

Fiduciary Fund Types

3. **Pension (and other employee benefit) trust funds** report resources held for members and beneficiaries of pension plans (defined benefit or contribution), other postemployment benefit plans, or other employee benefit plans. They (a) report contributions to such plans to be held in a fiduciary capacity by a governmental entity, (b) track investments in the funds, and (c) calculate and disburse benefits due to members and beneficiaries.

   a. A governmental body with a **defined contribution pension plan** should report a plan description, a summary of significant accounting policies, and information about investment concentrations (GASBS 25, *Financial Reporting for Defined Benefit Pension Plans and Note Disclosures for Defined Contribution Plans*).

      1) The plan description should identify the plan as a defined contribution plan and disclose in the notes to the financial statements the number of participating employers and other contributing entities.

      2) The description also should include the classes of employees covered and the total current membership, a brief description of plan provisions and the authority under which they are established (or may be amended), and contribution requirements.

4. An **investment trust fund** is used by a sponsoring government to report the external portion of an **external investment pool** (the portion belonging to legally separate entities not part of the sponsor's reporting entity). Moreover, the sponsor should report each external pool as a separate fund. Also see GASBS 31 in Appendix A.

    a. The statements required are similar to those for pension trust funds.

5. **Private-purpose trust funds** are used for all other trust arrangements under which the beneficiaries are specific individuals, private organizations, or other governments. An example is a fund for escheat property (see GASBS 21 in Appendix A).

6. **Agency funds** report resources held solely in a custodial capacity. These funds ordinarily account only for the receipt, temporary investment, and payment of resources to **individuals, private organizations, or other governments**.

    a. Agency fund **assets** should equal **liabilities** in the statement of fiduciary net assets. Agency funds are **not** reported in the statement of changes in fiduciary net assets.

        1) Agency funds may account for certain grants and other financial assistance to be transferred to, or spent on behalf of, secondary recipients (individuals, private organizations, or other governments). The agency fund acts purely as a conduit. It receives the resources and passes them through to the ultimate recipients. However, if the recipient has **administrative or direct financial involvement** in the program, the pass-through grant is accounted for in an appropriate governmental, proprietary, or trust fund (GASBS 24).

    b. Thus, agency funds record assets and liabilities only. Net assets (fund equity) does not exist, so **assets equal liabilities**.

        1) Revenues and expenses are not recorded.

    c. **Tax agency funds** are used when a governmental entity is the collection agent of taxes for disbursement to other governmental units, e.g., school districts, city governments, and special taxing districts.

        1) A governmental unit acting as a collection agent for another government usually subtracts administrative fees for the collection services.

            a) The agency fund should recognize a liability owed to the general fund for the amount of the administrative fees.

Interfund Activity

7. **Interfund activity** involves internal events. (A **transaction** is an external event.)

    a. Interfund activities may be reciprocal (analogous to exchange and exchange-like transactions) or nonreciprocal (analogous to nonexchange transactions).

8. **Reciprocal interfund activity.**

    a. **Interfund loans** result in interfund receivables and payables, not financing sources and uses. Any amount not expected to be repaid reduces the interfund balances. It is reported as a transfer.

        1) Liabilities arising from interfund activity are not general long-term liabilities. Thus, they may be reported in governmental funds.

    b. **Interfund services provided and used** are activities involving sales and purchases at prices equivalent to external exchange values. They result in revenues to seller funds and expenditures or expenses to buyer funds. Unpaid amounts are interfund receivables or payables.

        1) However, when the general fund accounts for **risk-financing activity**, charges to other funds are treated as reimbursements (GASBS 10).

9.   **Nonreciprocal interfund activity.**

a.   **Interfund transfers** are one-way asset flows with no repayment required. They must be reported in the basic financial statements separately from revenues and expenditures or expenses.

1)   In a **governmental fund**, a transfer is an other financing use (source) in the transferor (transferee) fund. It is reported after excess (deficiency) of revenues over expenditures in the statement of revenues, expenditures, and changes in fund balances.

2)   In a **proprietary fund**, the statement of revenues, expenses, and changes in fund net assets reports interfund transfers separately after nonoperating revenues and expenses.

b.   **Interfund reimbursements** are repayments by the funds responsible for specific outlays to the payor funds. They are not displayed in the statements.

Stop and review! You have completed the outline for this subunit. Study multiple-choice questions 32 through 43 beginning on page 687.

18.6 OTHER STATEMENTS AND INFORMATION IN THE CAFR

Combining Statements and Individual Fund Statements

1.   Combining statements are included in the CAFR when the primary government has more than one (a) nonmajor governmental or enterprise fund or (b) internal service or fiduciary fund (or fiduciary component unit).

a.   Combining statements also are included when the reporting entity has more than one nonmajor discretely presented component unit.

b.   Individual fund statements are reported when the primary government has just one nonmajor fund of a given type or when prior-year or budgetary comparisons are not included in RSI.

1)   Fund financial statements for individual component units are necessary in the absence of separately issued financial statements of the individual component units.

Notes to the Financial Statements

2.   Notes are an integral part of the basic financial statements. They disclose information essential to fair presentation that is not reported on the face of the statements.

a.   The focus is on the primary government's (1) governmental activities, (2) business-type activities, (3) major funds, and (4) nonmajor funds in the aggregate.

3.   The **summary of significant accounting policies** should make the following **general disclosures** (if applicable):

a.   A description of the government-wide financial statements;

b.   The measurement focus and basis of accounting of the government-wide financial statements;

c.   The policy for eliminating internal activity in the statement of activities;

d.   The policy for applying FASB pronouncements issued after November 30, 1989, to business-type activities and enterprise funds;

e.   The policy for capitalizing assets (including, if applicable, the modified approach to reporting infrastructure assets);

f.   The transactions included in program revenues and the policy for allocating indirect expenses to functions;

  g. The policy for defining operating and nonoperating revenues of proprietary funds; and

  h. The policy regarding whether to use restricted or unrestricted resources first when an expense is recognized.

 4. Required disclosures also include details about (a) capital assets, (b) long-term liabilities, (c) donor-restricted endowments, and (d) segment information for activities that are reported using enterprise fund accounting.

  a. A **segment** is an identifiable activity reported as or within an enterprise fund or another stand-alone entity. It must have debt outstanding with a revenue stream pledged in support.

   1) Also, revenues, expenses, gains, losses, assets, and liabilities must be accounted for separately under an externally imposed requirement (e.g., a bond indenture).

   2) Segment disclosures should be in the form of **condensed statements** of net assets; revenues, expenses and changes in net assets; and cash flows. The goods and services provided also must be disclosed.

  b. For more about note disclosures, see GASBS 38 in Appendix A.

Required Supplementary Information (RSI)

 5. **Budgetary comparison schedules** must be reported for the **general fund and each major special revenue fund with a legally adopted annual budget**.

  a. A schedule includes

   1) The original budgets, that is, the first complete appropriated budgets;

   2) The final appropriated budgets; and

   3) The actual inflows, outflows, and balances stated on the **budgetary basis of accounting**.

  b. A reconciliation of budgetary and GAAP information should be provided.

   1) An excess of expenditures over appropriations for a fund in the budgetary comparison should be disclosed in a note.

  c. A government may elect to report budgetary comparison information in a statement as part of the basic statements.

  d. Under GASBS 41, *Budgetary Comparison Schedules – Perspective Differences*, if a government has **significant budgetary perspective differences** that prevent the presentation of such comparisons, it must use a different format for the comparison schedule. This format is based on the fund, organization, or program structure used in the legally adopted budget. Such a schedule is presented as RSI.

   1) A perspective difference is a difference between the GAAP fund structure and the fund structure in the legally adopted budget.

   2) The difference must be **significant**. It must prevent the association of

    a) Estimated revenues and appropriations in the legally adopted budget with

    b) Major revenue sources and functional expenditures reported in the general fund and major special revenue funds in accordance with GAAP.

   3) For example, assume that (a) a city's budget for a general fund does not use a GAAP fund structure, and (b) comparison schedules cannot be prepared for the general fund. Thus, a comparison schedule must be presented for the budgetary general fund because it is the only fund used to budget the activities reported in the general fund.

6. **Information about infrastructure assets** reported using the modified approach is also RSI.

    a.   It includes

        1)   Schedules presenting the assessed condition of all eligible infrastructure assets for at least the last three complete assessments (done at least every 3 years),

        2)   The amounts needed to maintain the assets at or above the condition level established and disclosed, and

        3)   The amounts actually expensed for each of the last five periods.

    b.   Disclosures in addition to the schedules include (1) the basis for the condition measurement, (2) the measurement scale used, and (3) the condition level at which the government intends to preserve the assets.

7. **Special-purpose governments** are legally separate entities that are component units or other stand-alone governments. If they have governmental and business-type activities or are engaged in two or more governmental programs, they should be reported as **general-purpose governments**.

    a.   If a special-purpose government is engaged in **one governmental program** (e.g., an assessment or drainage district), it may combine the government-wide and fund statements in a format that reconciles individual items of fund data to government-wide data in a separate column. It may also report separate government-wide and fund statements, with the government-wide statement of activities presented in a different format.

    b.   If a special-purpose government is engaged only in **business-type activities**, it should report only the statements required for **enterprise funds**, in addition to MD&A, the notes, and RSI other than MD&A. If it is engaged only in **fiduciary activities**, it should report only the statements required for fiduciary funds, in addition to MD&A and the notes.

        1)   A **public employee retirement system (PERS)** may administer multiple defined benefit pension plans or other postemployment benefit plans. If so, it should present a separate column for each plan in the statements or present combining statements for those plans. However, for other types of plans, a PERS should apply GASBS 34 with regard to measurement focus, basis of accounting, and display. GASBS 34 also encourages, but does not require, combining statements for such plans.

        2)   After the issuance of GASBS 35, **public colleges and universities** must apply GASBS 34. Thus, they follow the guidance for special-purpose governments.

Stop and review! You have completed the outline for this subunit. Study multiple-choice questions 44 through 47 beginning on page 690.

QUESTIONS
18.1 The Reporting Entity and the CAFR

1. What is the basic criterion used to determine the reporting entity for a governmental unit?

    A.   Special financing arrangement.

    B.   Geographic boundaries.

    C.   Scope of public services.

    D.   Financial accountability.

Answer (D) is correct. *(CPA, adapted)*
    REQUIRED: The basic criterion used to determine the reporting entity for a governmental unit.
    DISCUSSION: The financial reporting entity is defined as the primary government, organizations for which the primary government is financially accountable, and other organizations with a relationship with the primary government such that exclusion would cause the reporting entity's basic financial statements to be misleading or incomplete. This definition is based on financial accountability. Separate governmental units may be organized based on special financing arrangements, the nature of services provided, and geographic limits and have apparent legal, financial, and administrative autonomy. Nevertheless, their governing bodies are usually appointed by elected officials of a primary government and therefore should be part of that financial reporting entity.

2. Valley Town's public school system is administered by a separately elected board of education. The board of education is not organized as a separate legal entity and does not have the power to levy taxes or issue bonds. Valley Town's city council approves the school system's budget. How should Valley Town report the public school system's annual financial results?

	Discrete Presentation	Blended
A.	Yes	Yes
B.	Yes	No
C.	No	Yes
D.	No	No

3. The financial statements of the reporting entity of a state or local governmental unit include information about which of the following?

I. The primary government
II. Discretely presented component units
III. Blended component units

A. I only.

B. I and II only.

C. I and III only.

D. I, II, and III.

4. Which of the following statements about the statistical section of the comprehensive annual financial report (CAFR) of a governmental unit is true?

A. Statistical tables may not cover more than two fiscal years.

B. Statistical tables may not include nonaccounting information.

C. The statistical section is not part of the basic financial statements.

D. The statistical section is an integral part of the basic financial statements.

Answer (C) is correct. *(CPA, adapted)*
REQUIRED: The reporting of a public school system's annual financial results.
DISCUSSION: Most component units should be included in the government-wide financial statements of the reporting entity by discrete presentation, that is, by reporting component-unit financial data in rows and columns separate from the financial data of the primary government. Moreover, some component units are, in substance, the same as the primary government and should be reported as a part of it, that is, blended. Valley Town's public school system is part of Valley Town's primary government. Although the board of education is separately elected, the school system is not legally separate and discrete presentation of its results is not appropriate because it does not meet the definition of a component unit. Thus, the annual financial results of the school system should be blended with those of Valley Town.

Answer (D) is correct. *(Publisher, adapted)*
REQUIRED: The organization(s) about which information is included in the financial statements of the reporting entity of a state or local governmental unit.
DISCUSSION: The financial statements of the reporting entity should provide an overview of the entity but should distinguish between the primary government and its component units. Thus, the statements should communicate information about the component units and their relationships with the primary government rather than suggest that these organizations constitute one legal entity. For this purpose, the government-wide financial statements should report information about discretely presented component units in separate rows and columns. Most component units should be included in the reporting entity in this way. Fiduciary component units are reported only in the primary government's fiduciary fund statements. However, the other fund statements report information only for blended (not discretely presented) component units. Discrete presentation also includes reporting of major component unit information in the basic statements. Furthermore, some component units are, in substance, the same as the primary government and should be reported as a part thereof. Blending is appropriate only if the component unit's governing body is substantially the same as the primary government's, or the component unit exclusively or almost exclusively benefits the primary government. Blended component-unit balances and transactions are reported in a manner similar to the balances and transactions of the primary government. Thus, blended component units are reported as part of the primary government in the fund financial statements and the government-wide financial statements.

Answer (C) is correct. *(CPA, adapted)*
REQUIRED: The true statement about the statistical section of the CAFR.
DISCUSSION: State and local governments are required to prepare and publish a comprehensive annual financial report (CAFR). As a minimum, the CAFR should include (1) an introductory section, (2) MD&A, (3) the basic financial statements, (4) required supplementary information in addition to the MD&A, (5) combining and individual fund statements, (6) schedules, (7) narrative explanations, and (8) a statistical section. The basic financial statements should include (1) government-wide financial statements, (2) fund financial statements, and (3) notes to the financial statements. Thus, the statistical section is not a part of the basic financial statements.
Answer (A) is incorrect because statistical tables may cover more than two fiscal years. Answer (B) is incorrect because statistical tables may include nonaccounting information, such as social and economic data and financial trends. Answer (D) is incorrect because the statistical section is not a part of the basic financial statements.

5. Users of a government's financial statements should be able to distinguish between the primary government and its component units. Furthermore, an overview of the discretely presented component units should be provided. According to GASBS 34, *Basic Financial Statements – and Management's Discussion and Analysis – for State and Local Governments,*

    A. The government-wide statements provide discrete presentation of component unit data, including data for fiduciary component units.

    B. Condensed financial statements for major component units must be presented in the notes to the basic statements.

    C. Information about each major component unit must be provided in the reporting entity's basic statements.

    D. Major component unit information must be provided in the form of combining statements.

Answer (C) is correct. *(Publisher, adapted)*
    REQUIRED: The appropriate presentation of component unit data.
    DISCUSSION: To provide an overview of component units, discrete presentation of component unit data is required in the government-wide statements, but fiduciary component units are included only in the fund statements. Blended component units are reported in accordance with GASBS 14. Each major component unit should be reported in the basic statements by presentation (1) in a separate column in the government-wide statements, (2) in combining statements of major component units after the fund statements, or (3) of condensed statements (a statement of net assets and a statement of activities) in the notes. However, major component unit information is not required for fiduciary component units.
    Answer (A) is incorrect because information for fiduciary component units is presented only in the fund financial statements with information for the primary government's fiduciary funds. Answer (B) is incorrect because major component units may also be presented in combining statements after the fund statements or in separate columns in the government-wide statements. Answer (D) is incorrect because major component units may also be presented in separate columns or in condensed statements in the notes.

6. In accordance with GASBS 44, *Economic Condition Reporting: The Statistical Section*, a state or local government that prepares a statistical section should

    A. Report information about the entity's ability to produce its own revenues but not shared revenues and intergovernmental aid.

    B. Exclude information about discretely presented component units.

    C. Present the information in a stand-alone document.

    D. Include 5-year trend information in all categories.

Answer (A) is correct. *(Publisher, adapted)*
    REQUIRED: The true statement regarding GASBS 44.
    DISCUSSION: The statistical section presents information about financial trends, revenue capacity, debt capacity, demographic and economic factors, and operations. Revenue capacity relates to an entity's ability to produce own-source revenues (e.g., taxes but not shared revenues). Subcategories are (1) the revenue base (including the total direct rate applied), (2) revenue rates, (3) principal revenue payers for a 10-year period, and (4) property tax levies and collections.
    Answer (B) is incorrect because the focus of the information is on the primary government (and its blended component units). Nevertheless, information about discretely presented component units may be helpful in evaluating the economic condition of the primary governments. Answer (C) is incorrect because GASBS 44 applies to a statistical section presented with the basic financial statements, rates, and required supplementary information (RSI) of any type of state or local government. Answer (D) is incorrect because the government should provide 10-year information about certain matters, e.g., debt limitations and principal revenue payers.

18.2 MD&A and the Government-Wide Financial Statements

7. Government-wide financial statements are prepared using the

	Economic Resources Measurement Focus	Current Financial Resources Measurement Focus	Accrual Basis	Modified Accrual Basis
A.	Yes	No	Yes	No
B.	No	Yes	No	Yes
C.	Yes	No	No	Yes
D.	No	Yes	Yes	No

Answer (A) is correct. *(Publisher, adapted)*
    REQUIRED: The measurement focus and basis of accounting used in government-wide financial statements.
    DISCUSSION: Government-wide financial statements are prepared using the economic resources measurement focus and the accrual basis of accounting and should report all of the government's assets, liabilities, revenues, expenses, gains, and losses. The economic resources measurement focus differs from the shorter-term flow-of-current-financial-resources approach used in governmental funds. It measures revenues and expenses in the same way as in proprietary funds or commercial accounting but does not necessarily emphasize net income. Instead, the emphasis is on a longer-range measure of revenues earned or levied (and accrued immediately if measurable). Moreover, the economic resources model focuses on cost of services. The accrual basis of accounting recognizes most transactions when they occur, regardless of when cash is received or paid.

8. According to GASBS 34, *Basic Financial Statements – and Management's Discussion and Analysis – for State and Local Governments*, financial reporting by general-purpose governments includes presentation of MD&A as

A. Required supplementary information after the notes to the financial statements.

B. Part of the basic financial statements.

C. A description of currently known facts, decisions, or conditions expected to have significant effects on financial activities.

D. Information that may be limited to highlighting the amounts and percentages of change from the prior to the current year.

Answer (C) is correct. *(Publisher, adapted)*
REQUIRED: The nature of MD&A.
DISCUSSION: Management's discussion and analysis (MD&A) is required supplementary information (RSI) that precedes the basic financial statements and provides an analytical overview of financial activities. It is based on currently known facts, decisions, or conditions and includes comparisons of the current and prior years, with an emphasis on the current year, based on government-wide information. Currently known facts are those of which management is aware at the audit report date.
Answer (A) is incorrect because MD&A precedes the basic financial statements. Answer (B) is incorrect because MD&A is not part of the basic financial statements. Answer (D) is incorrect because MD&A should state the reasons for change from the prior year, not merely the amounts or percentages of change.

9. Government-wide financial statements

A. Display individual funds.

B. Display aggregated information about fund types.

C. Exclude information about discretely presented component units.

D. Use separate columns to distinguish between governmental and business-type activities.

Answer (D) is correct. *(Publisher, adapted)*
REQUIRED: The focus of government-wide financial statements.
DISCUSSION: The basic financial statements include government-wide financial statements, fund financial statements, and the notes to the financial statements. Government-wide financial statements do not display funds or fund types but instead report information about the overall government. They distinguish between the primary government and its discretely presented component units and between the governmental activities and business-type activities of the primary government by reporting such information in separate rows and columns.

10. The portion of capital improvement special assessment debt maturing in 5 years, to be repaid from general resources of the government, should be reported in the

A. General fund.

B. Government-wide statement of net assets.

C. Agency fund.

D. Capital projects fund.

Answer (B) is correct. *(CPA, adapted)*
REQUIRED: The reporting of special assessment debt maturing in 5 years.
DISCUSSION: If the government is obligated in some manner for capital improvement special assessment debt, it should be reported as a general long-term liability only in the governmental activities column of the government-wide statement of net assets (except for any portion related to, and expected to be paid from, proprietary funds). The public benefit portion (the amount repayable from general resources of the government) is treated in the same manner as other general long-term liabilities.
Answer (A) is incorrect because governmental funds have a current resources focus. Answer (C) is incorrect because the debt service transactions of special assessment debt for which the government is not obligated in any manner are reported in an agency fund in the statement of fiduciary net assets. Answer (D) is incorrect because general long-term liabilities are not reported in governmental funds.

11. In the current year, the city of Beech issued $400,000 of bonds, the proceeds of which were restricted to the financing of a major capital project. The bonds will be paid wholly from special assessments against benefited property owners. However, Beech is obligated to provide a secondary source of funds for repayment of the bonds in the event of default by the assessed property owners. In Beech's basic financial statements, this $400,000 special assessment debt should

A. Not be reported.

B. Be reported in the special assessment fund.

C. Be reported as a general long-term liability.

D. Be reported in an agency fund.

Answer (C) is correct. *(CPA, adapted)*
REQUIRED: The proper reporting treatment for special assessment bonds.
DISCUSSION: If the government is obligated in some manner for capital improvement special assessment debt, it should be reported as a general long-term liability only in the governmental activities column of the government-wide statement of net assets (except for any portion related to, and expected to be paid from, proprietary funds). The public benefit portion (the amount repayable from general resources of the government) is treated in the same manner as other general long-term liabilities.
Answer (A) is incorrect because all debt of the governmental unit is required to be reported. Answer (B) is incorrect because special assessment funds are not used for external reporting in the basic financial statements. Answer (D) is incorrect because the debt service transactions of special assessment debt for which the government is not obligated in any manner are reported in an agency fund in the statement of fiduciary net assets.

12. In the government-wide statement of net assets, restricted capital assets should be included in the

A. Expendable component of restricted net assets.

B. Nonexpendable component of restricted net assets.

C. Invested in capital assets, net of related debt, component of net assets.

D. Designated component of net assets.

Answer (C) is correct. *(Publisher, adapted)*
REQUIRED: The classification of restricted capital assets in the statement of net assets.
DISCUSSION: Invested in capital assets, net of related debt, includes unrestricted and restricted capital assets, net of accumulated depreciation and related liabilities for borrowings. However, debt related to significant unspent proceeds is classified in the same net assets component as those proceeds.
Answer (A) is incorrect because restricted net assets are subject to constraints imposed by external entities (creditors, grantors, or other governments) or by law (constitutional provisions or enabling legislation). If permanent endowments or permanent fund principal amounts are included, restricted net assets should be displayed as expendable and nonexpendable. Answer (B) is incorrect because nonexpendable means that the net assets are retained in perpetuity. However, capital assets must be included in the invested in capital assets, net of related debt, component of net assets, even if they are restricted. Answer (D) is incorrect because designations of net assets are not reported on the face of the statement.

13. How are expenses reported in the government-wide statement of activities?

A. Interest on general long-term liabilities is ordinarily treated as a direct expense.

B. At a minimum, direct expenses should be reported for each function.

C. If indirect expenses are allocated, a full-cost approach must be used.

D. Direct and allocated indirect expenses are aggregated in a single column.

Answer (B) is correct. *(Publisher, adapted)*
REQUIRED: The reporting of expenses in the statement of activities.
DISCUSSION: Direct expenses are specifically associated with a service, program, or department. Hence, they are clearly identifiable with a given function. The net (expense) revenue for each function equals expenses (at a minimum, the direct expenses of the function) minus program revenues. However, indirect expenses need not be allocated and included in the determination of net (expense) revenue for each function.
Answer (A) is incorrect because interest on general long-term liabilities is a direct expense only in unusual circumstances, that is, when the borrowing is essential to establishing or maintaining a program and omitting the interest from the program's direct expenses would be misleading. Answer (C) is incorrect because direct expenses must be reported by function, whereas indirect expenses may or may not be allocated. A government may choose to allocate some indirect expenses, to adopt a full-cost allocation approach, or not to allocate. Answer (D) is incorrect because, if indirect expenses are allocated, direct and indirect expenses should be displayed in separate columns.

14. In the government-wide statement of activities, depreciation of

A. Capital assets shared by some of the government's functions is an indirect expense.

B. Capital assets shared by all of the government's functions is not required to be included in the direct expenses of those functions.

C. General infrastructure assets should be allocated to the various functions.

D. General infrastructure assets must be presented as a separate line item.

Answer (B) is correct. *(Publisher, adapted)*
REQUIRED: The treatment of depreciation in the statement of activities.
DISCUSSION: Depreciation of shared capital assets, such as a structure that houses offices for the tax assessor, election supervisor, and building inspector, should be apportioned to, and included in the direct expenses of, the sharing functions. However, if a capital asset, such as a city hall, serves all of the government's functions, depreciation of that asset need not be reported as a direct expense of the various functions. It may be displayed as a separate line item or as part of the general government function and, in either case, may or may not be allocated.
Answer (A) is incorrect because depreciation of shared capital assets should be apportioned to, and included in the direct expenses of, the sharing functions. Answer (C) is incorrect because depreciation of infrastructure assets is not allocated to other functions. Answer (D) is incorrect because depreciation of infrastructure assets is reported either as a separate line item or as a direct expense of the function associated with capital outlays for, and maintenance of, the infrastructure assets.

15. In accordance with GASBS 34, *Basic Financial Statements – and Management's Discussion and Analysis – for State and Local Governments*, general revenues reported in the government-wide statement of activities

A. Include all taxes.

B. Exclude taxes levied for a specific purpose.

C. Are aggregated with contributions, special and extraordinary items, and transfers in a line item.

D. Exclude interest and grants.

Answer (A) is correct. *(Publisher, adapted)*
REQUIRED: The true statement about general revenues.
DISCUSSION: General revenues are revenues not required to be reported as program revenues. They are reported separately after total net (expense) revenue for all functions in the government-wide statement of activities. All taxes, including those levied for a special purpose, are general revenues.
Answer (B) is incorrect because all taxes are general revenues but should be reported by type of tax, e.g., income, sales, and property. Answer (C) is incorrect because contributions to endowments, contributions to permanent fund principal, transfers between governmental and business-type activities, and special and extraordinary items are reported separately in the same manner as general revenues (at the bottom of the statement of activities to determine the change in net assets for the period). Answer (D) is incorrect because general revenues are all revenues not required to be reported as program revenues.

16. Chase City uses an internal service fund for its central motor pool. The assets and liabilities account balances for this fund that are not eliminated normally should be reported in the government-wide statement of net assets as

A. Governmental activities.

B. Business-type activities.

C. Fiduciary activities.

D. Note disclosures only.

Answer (A) is correct. *(CPA, adapted)*
REQUIRED: The reporting of assets and liabilities account balances of an internal service fund in the government-wide statement of net assets.
DISCUSSION: Any balances of internal service funds that are not eliminated are usually reported in the government activities column because these funds' activities are ordinarily more governmental than business-type. However, this presentation is not appropriate if enterprise funds are the predominant participants in the internal service funds.
Answer (B) is incorrect because the activities of internal service funds are normally more governmental than business-type. Answer (C) is incorrect because fiduciary activities are reported only in the fund financial statements. Fiduciary activity resources are not available to finance the government's programs because they are held in trust or in an agency capacity for others. Internal service funds are proprietary funds that provide goods and services to other subunits of the primary government on a cost-reimbursement basis. Answer (D) is incorrect because the asset and liabilities account balances of an internal service fund are required to be reported in the government-wide statement of net assets.

17. If a primary government's general fund has an equity interest in a joint venture, all of this equity interest should be reported in

    A. The government-wide statement of net assets.

    B. The general fund.

    C. An enterprise fund.

    D. An internal service fund.

Answer (A) is correct. *(CPA, adapted)*
    REQUIRED: The reporting of a general fund's equity interest in a joint venture.
    DISCUSSION: An equity interest in a joint venture ordinarily does not meet the definition of a financial resource. For example, the interest in the joint venture usually reflects equity primarily in capital assets. The amount recorded in the governmental fund is limited to that properly recognized under the modified accrual basis. Hence, the entire net investment in the joint venture should not be reported in a governmental fund, e.g., the general fund. However, the entire equity interest should be reported in the government-wide statement of net assets (GASBS 14).
    Answer (B) is incorrect because the general fund reports only the amount recognized under the modified accrual basis. Answer (C) is incorrect because the general fund has the equity interest, not an enterprise fund, which is a proprietary fund. Answer (D) is incorrect because the general fund has the equity interest, not an internal service fund, which is a proprietary fund.

18.3 Governmental Funds Reporting

18. The focus of certain fund financial statements of a local government is on major funds. Accordingly,

    A. Major internal service funds must be presented separately in the statement of net assets for proprietary funds.

    B. The main operating fund is always reported as a major fund.

    C. Combining statements for nonmajor funds are required.

    D. Enterprise funds not meeting the quantitative criteria are not eligible for presentation as major funds.

Answer (B) is correct. *(Publisher, adapted)*
    REQUIRED: The true statement about major fund reporting.
    DISCUSSION: The focus of governmental and proprietary fund financial statements is on major funds (but major fund reporting is not required for internal service funds). Each major fund is presented in a separate column, and nonmajor funds are aggregated in one column. Combining statements are not required for nonmajor funds. The main operating fund (e.g., the general fund) is always reported as a major fund, and any governmental or enterprise fund believed to be particularly important to users also may be reported in this way. Other individual governmental or enterprise funds must be reported as major if they meet the quantitative thresholds.
    Answer (A) is incorrect because major fund reporting requirements apply to governmental and enterprise funds but not to internal service funds. Answer (C) is incorrect because combining statements for nonmajor funds are not required but may be reported as supplementary information. Answer (D) is incorrect because a government may report any governmental or enterprise individual fund as major if it is believed to be particularly important to users.

19. A capital projects fund of a local government must be reported as major if

    A. Total assets of that fund are 5% of the total assets of all governmental funds and 2% of the total assets of all governmental and enterprise funds combined.

    B. Total expenditures of that fund are 10% of the total expenditures of all governmental funds and 2% of the total expenditures of all governmental and enterprise funds combined.

    C. Total liabilities of that fund are 10% of the total liabilities of all governmental funds and 5% of the total liabilities of all governmental and enterprise funds combined.

    D. Total revenues of that fund are 6% of the total revenues of all governmental funds and 3% of the total revenues of all governmental and enterprise funds combined.

Answer (C) is correct. *(Publisher, adapted)*
    REQUIRED: The criteria for requiring major fund reporting.
    DISCUSSION: The main operating fund (e.g., the general fund) is always reported as a major fund, and any governmental or enterprise fund believed to be particularly important to users may also be reported in this way. Moreover, any fund must be reported as major if total revenues, expenditures/expenses, assets, or liabilities (excluding revenues and expenditures/expenses reported as extraordinary items) of the fund are (1) at least 10% of the corresponding element total (assets, etc.) for all funds of the same category or type, that is, for all governmental or all enterprise funds, and (2) the same element that met the 10% standard is at least 5% of the corresponding element total for all governmental and enterprise funds in the aggregate.

20. The measurement focus of the governmental funds of a state or local governmental entity is on the determination of

	Changes in Financial Position	Financial Position
A.	Yes	No
B.	No	Yes
C.	No	No
D.	Yes	Yes

Answer (D) is correct. *(CPA, adapted)*
REQUIRED: The measurement focus of governmental funds.
DISCUSSION: The financial statements of governmental funds measure financial flow data. They focus on reporting the sources, uses, and balances of current financial resources, that is, the determination of financial position and changes therein.

21. A summary reconciliation of the government-wide and fund financial statements

A. Must be presented at the bottom of the fund statements or in an accompanying schedule.

B. Must be presented as required supplementary information.

C. Must be presented in the notes.

D. Is recommended but not required.

Answer (A) is correct. *(Publisher, adapted)*
REQUIRED: The presentation of a summary reconciliation of the government-wide and fund financial statements.
DISCUSSION: A government must provide a summary reconciliation to the government-wide statements at the bottom of the fund statements or in a schedule. Brief explanations on the face of the statements may suffice, but a more detailed explanation in the notes may be necessary.
Answer (B) is incorrect because RSI consists of MD&A, budgetary comparison schedules, and information about infrastructure assets reported using the modified approach. Answer (C) is incorrect because the summary reconciliation must be presented at the bottom of the fund statements or in an accompanying schedule. Additional detail may need to be given in the notes. Answer (D) is incorrect because the summary reconciliation is required.

22. Tree City reported a $1,500 net increase in fund balance for governmental funds for the current year. During the year, Tree purchased general capital assets of $9,000 and recorded depreciation expense of $3,000. What amount should Tree report as the change in net assets for governmental activities?

A. $(4,500)

B. $1,500

C. $7,500

D. $10,500

Answer (C) is correct. *(CPA, adapted)*
REQUIRED: The change in net assets for governmental activities.
DISCUSSION: General capital assets are not reported as assets in the fund financial statements. Moreover, capital assets must be depreciated unless they are infrastructure assets that meet certain requirements. The modified accrual basis of accounting is required for governmental funds, and the accrual basis for the government-wide statements. Thus, the $1,500 net increase in the fund balance for governmental funds reflects a $9,000 expenditure (modified accrual basis) for general capital assets. The effect of the expenditure is a decrease in current financial resources of $9,000. However, the government-wide statements report an expense of $3,000 (accrual basis) for depreciation and a depreciated asset with a carrying amount of $6,000 ($9,000 cost – $3,000 depreciation). The effect is a decrease in economic resources of $3,000. Reconciling the net increase in fund balance to the change in net assets therefore requires adding $6,000 ($9,000 modified accrual basis expenditure – $3,000 accrual basis expense). The change in net assets is $7,500 ($1,500 + $6,000 reconciling item).
Answer (A) is incorrect because $(4,500) is the excess of the expenditure over the sum of the expense and the increase in fund balance. Answer (B) is incorrect because $1,500 is the increase in fund balance. Answer (D) is incorrect because $10,500 assumes depreciation is not recognized.

18.4 Proprietary Funds Reporting

23. A state or local government must present which financial statements for proprietary funds?

I.   A statement of activities
II. A statement in net assets or balance sheet format
III. A statement of cash flows

   A. I only.

   B. I and III only.

   C. II and III only.

   D. I, II, and III.

Answer (C) is correct.   *(Publisher, adapted)*
REQUIRED: The statement(s) required for proprietary funds.
DISCUSSION: Proprietary funds emphasize determination of operating income, changes in net assets (or cost recovery), financial position, and cash flows. A statement of net assets or balance sheet is required for proprietary funds, with assets and liabilities classified as current or noncurrent. Either a net assets format (assets – liabilities = net assets) or a balance sheet format (assets = liabilities + net assets) may be used. A statement of revenues, expenses, and changes in fund net assets or fund equity (either label may be used) is the required operating statement for proprietary funds. A statement of cash flows prepared in accordance with GASBS 9 is also required for proprietary funds. However, GASBS 34 requires that the direct method (including a reconciliation of operating cash flows to operating income) be used. The direct method reports major classes of gross operating cash receipts and payments and their sum (net cash flow from operating activities).

24. The statement of revenues, expenses, and changes in fund net assets (or fund equity) for proprietary funds

   A. Combines special and extraordinary items in a subtotal presented before nonoperating revenues and expenses.

   B. Must report revenues at gross amounts, with discounts and allowances disclosed parenthetically.

   C. Distinguishes between operating and nonoperating revenues and expenses.

   D. Must define operating items in the same way as in the statement of cash flows.

Answer (C) is correct.   *(Publisher, adapted)*
REQUIRED: The true statement about the statement of revenues, expenses, and changes in fund net assets (or fund equity).
DISCUSSION: A statement of revenues, expenses, and changes in fund net assets or fund equity (either label may be used) is the required operating statement for proprietary funds. Operating and nonoperating revenues and expenses should be distinguished, with separate subtotals for operating revenues, operating expenses, and operating income.
Answer (A) is incorrect because nonoperating revenues and expenses are presented immediately after operating income (loss). Moreover, special and extraordinary items are reported separately. Answer (B) is incorrect because revenues are reported by major source either net with disclosure of discounts and allowances or gross with discounts and allowances reported beneath the revenue amounts. Answer (D) is incorrect because a government should consistently follow appropriate definitions of operating items. Considerations in defining these items are (1) the principal purpose of the fund and (2) their presentation in a cash flows statement. However, the categorization of items in the statement of cash flows need not control the definitions of operating items in the statement of revenues, expenses, and changes in fund net assets.

25. With regard to the statement of cash flows for a governmental unit's proprietary funds, items generally presented as cash equivalents are

	2-month Treasury Bills	3-month Certificates of Deposit
A.	No	No
B.	No	Yes
C.	Yes	Yes
D.	Yes	No

Answer (C) is correct.   *(CPA, adapted)*
REQUIRED: The items generally presented as cash equivalents.
DISCUSSION: Cash equivalents are highly liquid investments, readily convertible to known amounts of cash with an original time to maturity at acquisition of 3 months or less. The T-bills and CDs both meet these criteria and are presented as cash equivalents.

26. The GASB has established criteria for the required reporting of activities as enterprise funds. Based on these criteria, and assuming the amounts involved are derived from principal revenue sources, enterprise fund reporting is most likely to be optional if

A. Fees are charged to external users for goods or services.

B. The activity is financed with debt, and the only security is a pledge of the activity's net revenues from fees and charges.

C. The activity's costs are legally required to be recovered from fees and charges.

D. The activity's pricing policies set fees and charges to recover costs.

Answer (A) is correct. *(Publisher, adapted)*
REQUIRED: The circumstances in which enterprise fund reporting may be optional.
DISCUSSION: Enterprise funds need not be used to report insignificant activities. They may be used for activities for which fees are charged to external users, but they must be used if one of three criteria (applied in the context of the activity's principal revenue sources) is satisfied. The criteria primarily emphasize fees charged to external users. The activity should be reported as an enterprise fund if it is financed with debt, and the only security is a pledge of the activity's net revenues from fees and charges. If the debt is also secured by the full faith and credit of a related governmental entity, the debt is not payable solely from the activity's net revenues. The activity also should be reported as an enterprise fund if its costs (including capital costs) of providing services are legally required to be recovered from fees and charges, not taxes or similar revenues. Furthermore, the activity should be reported as an enterprise fund if its pricing policies set fees and charges to recover its costs (including capital costs).

27. On January 2, Basketville City purchased equipment with a useful life of three years to be used by its water and sewer enterprise fund. Which of the following is the correct treatment for the asset?

A. Record the purchase of the equipment as an expenditure.

B. Capitalize; depreciation is optional.

C. Capitalize; depreciation is required.

D. Capitalize; depreciation is not permitted.

Answer (C) is correct. *(CPA, adapted)*
REQUIRED: The accounting for a purchase of equipment to be used by an enterprise fund.
DISCUSSION: An enterprise fund is a proprietary fund. Thus, the economic resources measurement focus and the accrual basis of accounting are required in its financial statements. Capital assets, such as equipment, are reported in the government-wide statement of net assets and in the proprietary fund statement of net assets. They must be depreciated over their estimated useful lives unless they are inexhaustible or are infrastructure assets that meet certain requirements (GASBS 34).
Answer (A) is incorrect because, under the modified accrual basis, the entity must record the purchase of the equipment as an expenditure if it is acquired with governmental fund financial resources. Answer (B) is incorrect because only depreciation is mandatory. Answer (D) is incorrect because only depreciation of inexhaustible assets, such as land and land improvements, is prohibited.

28. The following transactions were among those reported by Corfe City's electric utility enterprise fund for the year just ended:

Capital contributed by subdividers	$ 900,000
Cash received from customer households	2,700,000
Proceeds from sale of revenue bonds	4,500,000

In the proprietary funds statement of cash flows for the year ended December 31, what amount should be reported as cash flows from the electric utility enterprise fund's capital and related financing activities?

A. $4,500,000

B. $5,400,000

C. $7,200,000

D. $8,100,000

Answer (B) is correct. *(CPA, adapted)*
REQUIRED: The amount reported as cash flows from capital and related financing activities.
DISCUSSION: Cash flows should be classified as operating, noncapital financing, capital and related financing, or investing. Operating activities include producing and delivering goods and providing services. Thus, cash from customer households is a revenue item reported under cash flows from operating activities. Capital and related financing activities include acquiring and disposing of capital assets, borrowing and repaying money related to capital asset transactions, etc. Assuming the sale of revenue bonds and the capital contributions by subdividers are for the acquisition or improvement of capital assets, the amount to report under capital and related financing activities is $5,400,000 ($900,000 + $4,500,000).
Answer (A) is incorrect because $4,500,000 omits the capital contributed by subdividers. Answer (C) is incorrect because $7,200,000 includes customer fees revenue and omits capital contributed by subdividers. Answer (D) is incorrect because $8,100,000 includes customer fees.

29. Dogwood City's water enterprise fund received interest of $10,000 on long-term investments. How should this amount be reported on the statement of cash flows?

    A. Operating activities.

    B. Noncapital financing activities.

    C. Capital and related financing activities.

    D. Investing activities.

Answer (D) is correct. *(CPA, adapted)*
    REQUIRED: The classification of interest received on long-term investments in the statement of cash flows.
    DISCUSSION: GASBS 9 requires reporting of cash flows of proprietary funds and entities engaged in business-type activities, e.g., governmental utilities. Cash inflows should be classified as operating, financing, and investing. Investing activities include making and collecting loans (other than program loans) and acquiring and disposing of debt and equity instruments. Cash inflows from investing activities include interest and dividends received as returns on loans (not program loans), debt of other entities, equity securities, and cash management or investment pools.
    Answer (A) is incorrect because operating activities are all transactions and other events that are not classified as either financing or investing activities. In general, operating activities involve transactions and other events the effects of which are included in the determination of operating income. Answer (B) is incorrect because noncapital financing activities include borrowings for purposes other than acquiring, constructing, or improving capital assets and debt. Answer (C) is incorrect because capital and related financing activities include borrowings and repayments of debt related to (1) acquiring, constructing, or improving capital assets; (2) acquiring and disposing of capital assets used to provide goods or services; and (3) paying for capital assets obtained on credit.

30. The billings for transportation services provided to other governmental units are recorded by the internal service fund as

    A. Interfund reimbursements.

    B. Interfund transfers.

    C. Transportation appropriations.

    D. Operating revenues.

Answer (D) is correct. *(CPA, adapted)*
    REQUIRED: The recording of the billings for transportation services provided to other governmental units.
    DISCUSSION: Interfund services provided and used are reciprocal interfund activities. They are sales and purchases at prices equivalent to external exchange values that result in revenues to seller funds and expenditures or expenses to buyer funds. Thus, billings for services provided by an internal service fund are properly considered operating revenues to be reported in the proprietary fund statement of revenues, expenses, and changes in fund net assets (or fund equity).
    Answer (A) is incorrect because interfund reimbursements are repayments by the funds responsible for expenditures or expenses. They are not displayed in the financial statements. Answer (B) is incorrect because interfund transfers are one-way asset flows with no repayment required. Answer (C) is incorrect because an appropriation is recorded as part of a budgetary entry.

31. An unrestricted grant received from another government to support enterprise fund operations should be reported as

    A. Contributed capital.

    B. Nonoperating revenues.

    C. Operating revenues.

    D. Revenues and expenditures.

Answer (B) is correct. *(CPA, adapted)*
    REQUIRED: The classification in an enterprise fund of an unrestricted grant received from another government.
    DISCUSSION: The donation of an unrestricted grant by one government to an enterprise fund of another government is a nonreciprocal transfer and is thus classified as a nonoperating revenue on the enterprise fund statement of revenues, expenses, and changes in fund net assets.
    Answer (A) is incorrect because a state or local governmental entity reports net assets, not contributed capital. Answer (C) is incorrect because the grant is a nonoperating item. Answer (D) is incorrect because the recipient debits an asset or liability and credits revenue.

18.5 Fiduciary Funds Reporting and Interfund Activity

32. Fiduciary fund financial statements report

A. Information by major fund.

B. Three components of net assets.

C. A separate column for each fund type.

D. No separate statements for individual pension plans.

Answer (C) is correct. *(Publisher, adapted)*

REQUIRED: The reporting in fiduciary fund financial statements.

DISCUSSION: Fiduciary fund financial statements include information about all fiduciary funds and similar component units. The statements report information in a separate column for each fund type but not by major fund. The notes present financial statements for individual pension plans and postemployment healthcare plans unless separate GAAP reports have been issued. A statement of fiduciary net assets is required for fiduciary funds. It reports assets, liabilities, and net assets for each fiduciary fund type but does not present the three components of net assets reported in the government-wide statement of net assets or in the proprietary fund statement of net assets.

Answer (A) is incorrect because major funds are reported only in governmental and enterprise fund statements. Answer (B) is incorrect because three components of net assets are reported only in the government-wide statement of net assets and in the proprietary fund statement of net assets. Answer (D) is incorrect because separate financial statements for individual pension plans and postemployment healthcare plans are reported in the notes. However, if separate GAAP financial statements have been issued for such plans, information is given in the notes about how those statements may be obtained.

33. Glen County uses governmental fund accounting and is the administrator of a multiple-jurisdiction deferred compensation plan covering both its own employees and those of other governments participating in the plan. This plan is an eligible deferred compensation plan under the U.S. Internal Revenue Code and Income Tax Regulations, and it meets the criteria for a pension (and other employee benefit) trust fund. Glen has legal access to the plan's $40 million in assets, of which $2 million pertain to Glen and $38 million to the other participating governments. In Glen's balance sheet, what amount should be reported in an agency fund for plan assets and as a corresponding liability?

A. $0

B. $2,000,000

C. $38,000,000

D. $40,000,000

Answer (A) is correct. *(CPA, adapted)*

REQUIRED: The deferred compensation plan assets and liability to record in an agency fund.

DISCUSSION: Under GASBS 32, *Accounting and Financial Reporting for Internal Revenue Code Section 457 Deferred Compensation Plans*, the plan should be reported in a pension (and other employee benefit) trust fund in the statements of fiduciary net assets and changes in fiduciary net assets if it meets the criteria for that fund type. This treatment is in accordance with a 1996 amendment to IRC Section 457 that required all assets and income of the plan to be held in trust for the exclusive benefit of participants and their beneficiaries. Consequently, no amounts should be reported in an agency fund.

34. River City has a defined contribution pension plan. How should River report the pension plan in its financial statements?

A. Amortize any transition asset over the estimated number of years of current employees' service.

B. Disclose in the notes to the financial statements the amount of the pension benefit obligation and the net assets available for benefits.

C. Disclose in the notes to the financial statements the classes of employees covered and the employer's and employees' obligations to contribute to the fund.

D. Accrue a liability for benefits earned but not paid to fund participants.

Answer (C) is correct. *(CPA, adapted)*

REQUIRED: The method for reporting a defined contribution pension plan.

DISCUSSION: GASBS 25, *Financial Reporting for Defined Benefit Pension Plans and Note Disclosures for Defined Contribution Plans*, requires that a defined contribution pension plan report a plan description, a summary of significant accounting policies, and information about investment concentrations. The plan description should identify the plan as a defined contribution plan and disclose the number of participating employers and other contributing entities. The description should also include the classes of employees covered and the total current membership, a brief description of plan provisions and the authority under which they are established (or may be amended), and contribution requirements.

Answer (A) is incorrect because no transition asset arises under a defined contribution plan. Answer (B) is incorrect because a pension benefit obligation arises under a defined benefit pension plan. Answer (D) is incorrect because, under a defined contribution plan, the governmental employer's obligation is for contributions, not benefits.

35. A government may report which fiduciary funds?

    A. Private-purpose trust funds.

    B. Expendable trust funds.

    C. Nonexpendable trust funds.

    D. Permanent funds.

Answer (A) is correct. *(Publisher, adapted)*
    REQUIRED: The fiduciary funds.
    DISCUSSION: Under GASBS 34, fiduciary funds include pension (and other employee benefit) trust funds, investment trust funds, private-purpose trust funds, and agency funds. Pension (and other employee benefit) trust funds report resources held for members and beneficiaries of pension plans (defined benefit or contribution), other postemployment benefit plans, or other employee benefit plans. Investment trust funds are used by a sponsoring government to report the external portions of external investment pools (GASBS 31). Private-purpose trust funds are used for all other trust arrangements, whether the beneficiaries are individuals, private organizations, or other governments.
    Answer (B) is incorrect because expendable trust funds were eliminated by GASBS 34. Answer (C) is incorrect because nonexpendable trust funds were eliminated by GASBS 34. Answer (D) is incorrect because permanent funds are governmental funds.

36. Taxes collected and held by Franklin County for a separate school district are accounted for in which fund?

    A. Special revenue.

    B. Internal service.

    C. Trust.

    D. Agency.

Answer (D) is correct. *(CPA, adapted)*
    REQUIRED: The fund that collects and holds taxes for a separate school district.
    DISCUSSION: Agency funds report resources held solely in a custodial capacity. These funds ordinarily account only for the receipt, temporary investment, and payment of resources to individuals, private organizations, or other governments. Thus, tax agency funds are used when a governmental entity is the collection agent of taxes for disbursement to other governmental units, e.g., school districts or special taxing districts.
    Answer (A) is incorrect because special revenue funds are governmental funds. Special revenue funds account for proceeds of specific revenue sources legally restricted to expenditure for specified purposes. However, a special revenue fund is not required unless legally mandated. Answer (B) is incorrect because internal service funds may be used for activities that provide goods and services to other subunits of the primary government and its component units or to other governments on a cost-reimbursement basis. However, if the reporting government is not the predominant participant, the activity should be reported as an enterprise fund. Answer (C) is incorrect because a trust fund differs from an agency fund because the trust agreement determines how long resources are held and the degree of management involvement.

37. Fish Road property owners in Sea County are responsible for special assessment debt that arose from a storm sewer project. If the property owners default, Sea has no obligation regarding debt service, although it does bill property owners for assessments and uses the monies it collects to pay debt holders. What fund type should Sea use to account for these collection and servicing activities?

    A. Agency.

    B. Debt service.

    C. Special revenue funds.

    D. Capital projects.

Answer (A) is correct. *(CPA, adapted)*
    REQUIRED: The reporting of debt service transactions of a special assessment issue.
    DISCUSSION: When capital improvements are financed by special assessment debt, the "debt service transactions of a special assessment issue for which the government is not obligated in any manner should be reported in an agency fund in the statement of fiduciary net assets rather than a debt service fund, to reflect that the government's duties are limited to acting as an agent for the assessed property owners and the bondholders" (GASBS 6, as amended by GASBS 34).

38. Which of the following is a reporting requirement for agency funds?

A. They should be reported in a statement of fiduciary net assets and a statement of changes in fiduciary net assets.

B. Agency fund assets should equal liabilities in the statement of fiduciary net assets.

C. An agency fund used as a clearing account should report as assets the amounts pertaining to the other funds.

D. An agency fund should not be used as a clearing account.

Answer (B) is correct. *(Publisher, adapted)*
   REQUIRED: The reporting requirement for agency funds.
   DISCUSSION: Agency fund assets should equal liabilities in the statement of fiduciary net assets, but agency funds are not reported in the statement of changes in fiduciary net assets.
   Answer (A) is incorrect because agency funds are not reported in the statement of changes in fiduciary net assets. Answer (C) is incorrect because an agency fund may be used as a clearing account to distribute resources to other funds as well as to other entities, for example, by a county tax collector to distribute taxes to other funds and other governments. Assets pertaining to other funds are reported in those funds, not in the agency fund. Answer (D) is incorrect because an agency fund may be used as a clearing account.

39. An internal service provided and used by a state or local government

A. Is the internal counterpart to a nonexchange transaction.

B. Results in expenditures or expenses to buyer funds and revenues to seller funds.

C. Normally is displayed in the financial statements as a reimbursement.

D. Requires recognition of an other financing source by the transferee fund and an other financing use by the transferor fund.

Answer (B) is correct. *(Publisher, adapted)*
   REQUIRED: The treatment of an internal service provided and used.
   DISCUSSION: Interfund services provided and used are reciprocal interfund activities. They are sales and purchases of goods and services at prices equivalent to external exchange values. Hence, they result in revenues to seller funds and expenditures or expenses to buyer funds. Unpaid amounts are interfund receivables or payables.
   Answer (A) is incorrect because an internal service provided and used is a reciprocal interfund activity, which is analogous to an exchange or an exchange-like transaction. Answer (C) is incorrect because interfund services provided and used normally result in revenues to sellers and expenditures or expenses to buyers. Reimbursements are not displayed in the statements. Answer (D) is incorrect because an interfund transfer (nonreciprocal interfund activity) is an other financing source (use) in a transferee (transferor) governmental fund. An internal service provided and used is reciprocal interfund activity.

40. During the year, a city's electric utility, which is operated as an enterprise fund, rendered billings for electricity supplied to the general fund. Which of the following accounts should be debited by the general fund?

A. Appropriations.

B. Expenditures.

C. Due to electric utility enterprise fund.

D. Other financing uses -- interfund transfer.

Answer (B) is correct. *(CPA, adapted)*
   REQUIRED: The account debited by the general fund for receipt of services supplied by an enterprise fund.
   DISCUSSION: Enterprise funds are used to account for operations similar to those of private businesses. This rendition of services by the enterprise fund to the general fund is presumably at prices equivalent to external exchange values and is classified as an interfund service provided and used. The result is revenue to the seller and an expenditure to the buyer, a governmental fund. Unpaid amounts are interfund receivables or payables. The entry is to debit expenditures control and credit due to enterprise fund.
   Answer (A) is incorrect because appropriations is debited when the budgetary accounts are closed. Answer (C) is incorrect because due to enterprise fund should be credited. Answer (D) is incorrect because this transaction is an interfund service provided and used, not an interfund transfer.

41. An interfund transfer

A. Is the internal counterpart to an exchange or an exchange-like transaction.

B. Results in a receivable and a payable.

C. Is reported in a proprietary fund's statement of revenues, expenses, and changes in fund net assets (or fund equity) after nonoperating revenues and expenses.

D. Is reported in a proprietary fund as an other financing source or use.

Answer (C) is correct. *(Publisher, adapted)*
   REQUIRED: The treatment of an interfund transfer.
   DISCUSSION: Interfund transfers are one-way asset flows with no repayment required. In a governmental fund, a transfer is an other financing use (source) in the transferor (transferee) fund. In a proprietary fund's statement of revenues, expenses, and changes in fund net assets (or fund equity), transfers should be reported separately after nonoperating revenues and expenses in the same component as capital contributions, additions to endowments, and special and extraordinary items.
   Answer (A) is incorrect because nonreciprocal interfund activity is analogous to nonexchange transactions. Answer (B) is incorrect because reciprocal interfund activity results in a receivable and a payable. Answer (D) is incorrect because, in a governmental fund, a transfer is an other financing use (source) in the transferor (transferee) fund.

42. For which of the following funds do interfund transfers affect the results of operations?

	Governmental Funds	Proprietary Funds
A.	No	No
B.	No	Yes
C.	Yes	Yes
D.	Yes	No

Answer (C) is correct. *(CPA, adapted)*
REQUIRED: The fund operating results affected by interfund transfers.
DISCUSSION: Interfund transfers are one-way asset flows with no repayment required. They must be reported in the basic financial statements separately from revenues and expenditures or expenses. In a governmental fund, a transfer is an other financing use (source) in the transferor (transferee) fund. It is reported after excess (deficiency) of revenues over expenditures in the statement of revenues, expenditures, and changes in fund balances. In a proprietary fund's statement of revenues, expenses, and changes in fund net assets (or fund equity), transfers should be reported separately after nonoperating revenues and expenses. Accordingly, the change in fund balances reported in governmental funds and the change in net assets reported in proprietary funds are affected by interfund transfers.

43. Most state and local governmental entities, including external investment pools, report most investments at fair value. Assuming that a governmental entity reports investments at fair value, changes in the fair value of the investments should be recognized as

A. Investment income in the operating statement when they occur.

B. Investment income in the operating statement when they are realized.

C. A component of the operating statement below the excess of revenues over expenditures, or net income.

D. A direct change in a component of equity.

Answer (A) is correct. *(Publisher, adapted)*
REQUIRED: The treatment of changes in the fair value of investments.
DISCUSSION: Fair value is a better measure of a government's investments than cost because it helps to assess investment management and performance and financial position. Furthermore, changes in fair value should be recognized as investment income in the year they occur because they are as relevant as other investment earnings, e.g., dividends and interest, to the foregoing assessment. This approach also avoids the possibility that investment sales might be timed to distort results (GASBS 31).
Answer (B) is incorrect because reporting only realized fair value changes in the operating statement is a historical-cost concept. The effect may be to misstate investments and operating results. Answer (C) is incorrect because changes in fair value are similar to dividends and interest. Answer (D) is incorrect because the operating statement reflects operating results, including changes in fair value of investments.

18.6 Other Statements and Information in the CAFR

44. What approach to presentation of the notes to the financial statements is adopted by GASBS 34?

A. The notes are essential for fair presentation of the statements.

B. The notes are required supplementary information.

C. The notes have the same status as MD&A.

D. The notes give equal focus to the primary government and its discretely presented component units.

Answer (A) is correct. *(Publisher, adapted)*
REQUIRED: The approach to presentation of the notes to the financial statements adopted by GASBS 34.
DISCUSSION: Notes to the financial statements are an integral part of the basic financial statements because they disclose information essential to fair presentation that is not reported on the face of the statements. The focus is on the primary government's governmental activities, business-type activities, major funds, and nonmajor funds in the aggregate.
Answer (B) is incorrect because notes are not merely RSI. Answer (C) is incorrect because RSI mandated by GASBS 34 includes MD&A, budgetary comparison schedules for governmental funds, and information about infrastructure assets reported using the modified approach. Answer (D) is incorrect because the notes focus on the primary government.

45. GASBS 34 requires disclosure of segment information for activities reported using enterprise fund accounting. For this purpose, GASBS 34 defines a segment as

- A. An individual enterprise fund of a state or local government.
- B. A separate major line of business or class of customer.
- C. A component of an enterprise that engages in business activities from which it may earn revenues and incur expenses.
- D. An identifiable activity that has outstanding debt with a revenue stream pledged in support.

Answer (D) is correct. *(Publisher, adapted)*
REQUIRED: The definition of a segment.
DISCUSSION: A segment is an identifiable activity reported as or within an enterprise fund or an other stand-alone entity that has debt (for example, bonds or certificates of participation) outstanding with a revenue stream pledged in support. Also, revenues, expenses, gains, losses, assets, and liabilities must be accounted for separately pursuant to an externally imposed requirement. Segment disclosures should be in the form of condensed statements of net assets, revenues, expenses, and changes in net assets; and cash flows.
Answer (A) is incorrect because NCGA Interpretation 2 (superseded by GASBS 34) defines a segment as an individual enterprise fund of a state or local government. Answer (B) is incorrect because APB Opinion 30 (superseded by SFAS 144) defined a segment of a business as a separate major line of business or class of customer. Answer (C) is incorrect because SFAS 131 defines an operating segment as a component of an enterprise that engages in business activities from which it may earn revenues and incur expenses.

46. GASBS 34 requires that budgetary comparison schedules

- A. Be reported for the general fund and each major special revenue fund with a legally adopted budget.
- B. Be presented instead of budgetary comparison statements included in the basic statements.
- C. Convert the appropriated budget information to the GAAP basis for comparison with actual amounts reported on that basis.
- D. Compare only the final appropriated budget with actual amounts.

Answer (A) is correct. *(Publisher, adapted)*
REQUIRED: The true statement about budgetary comparison schedules.
DISCUSSION: Under GASBS 34, certain information must be presented as RSI in addition to MD&A. Budgetary comparison schedules must be reported for the general fund and each major special revenue fund with a legally adopted annual budget. A schedule includes the original budgets, that is, the first complete appropriated budgets; the final appropriated budgets; and the actual inflows, outflows, and balances stated on the budgetary basis of accounting. Thus, budgetary comparison schedules are not required for proprietary funds, fiduciary funds, and governmental funds other than the general fund and major special revenue funds.
Answer (B) is incorrect because a government may elect to report budgetary comparison information in a statement as part of the basic statements. Answer (C) is incorrect because the budgetary comparison schedules compare the budgets with actual inflows, outflows, and balances stated on the government's budgetary basis. However, a reconciliation to GAAP is required. Answer (D) is incorrect because the original and final appropriated budgets are compared with the actual inflows, outflows, and balances.

47. According to GASBS 34, a government is reported as a special-purpose government if it

- A. Has governmental and business-type activities.
- B. Is engaged in two or more governmental programs.
- C. Is not a legally separate entity.
- D. Is engaged in one governmental program.

Answer (D) is correct. *(Publisher, adapted)*
REQUIRED: The entity that may be reported as a special-purpose government.
DISCUSSION: Special-purpose governments are legally separate entities that are component units or other stand-alone governments. If they have governmental and business-type activities or are engaged in two or more governmental programs, they should be reported as general-purpose governments. If a special-purpose government is engaged in one governmental program, it may combine the government-wide and fund statements in a format that reconciles individual items of fund data to government-wide data in a separate column.
Answer (A) is incorrect because a government that has governmental and business-type activities should be reported in the same manner as a general-purpose government. Answer (B) is incorrect because a government that is engaged in two or more governmental programs should be reported in the same manner as a general-purpose government. Answer (C) is incorrect because a special-purpose government is a legally separate entity.

Use Gleim's *CPA Test Prep* CD-Rom/Pocket PC for interactive testing with over 4,000 additional questions!

18.7 PRACTICE SIMULATION

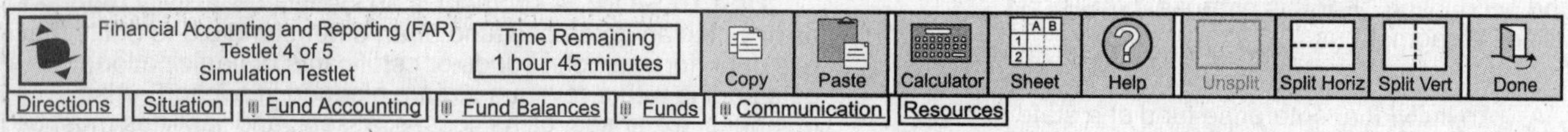
Financial Accounting and Reporting (FAR)
Testlet 4 of 5
Simulation Testlet
Time Remaining
1 hour 45 minutes
Copy
Paste
Calculator
Sheet
Help
Unsplit
Split Horiz
Split Vert
Done
Directions
Situation
Fund Accounting
Fund Balances
Funds
Communication
Resources

1. Directions

In the following simulation, you will be asked to complete various tasks. You may use the content in the **Information Tabs** to complete the tasks in the **Work Tabs**.

Information Tabs:

Directions
Resources

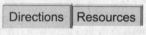

FIG 1

- Go through each of the **Information Tabs** to familiarize yourself with the simulation content
- The **Resources** tab will contain information, including formulas and definitions, that may help you to complete the tasks
- Your simulation may have more **Information Tabs** than those shown in Fig. 1

Work Tabs:

SysTrust
Engagement Letter
Authoritative Sources
Communication

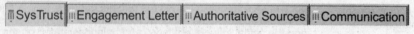

FIG. 2

- **Work Tabs**, to the right of **Information Tabs**, contain the tasks for you to complete
- **Work Tabs** contain directions for completing each task - be sure to read these directions carefully
- The tab names in Fig. 2 are for illustration only - yours may differ
- Once you complete any part of a task, the pencil for that tab will be shaded (see **Communication** in Fig. 2)
- The shaded pencil does **NOT** indicate that you have completed the entire task
- You must complete all of the tasks in the **Work Tabs** to receive full credit

Research/Authoritative Literature Tab:

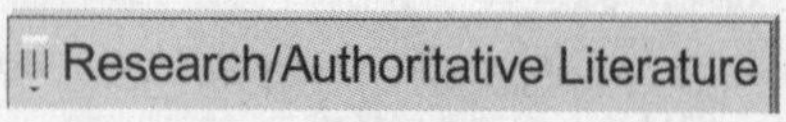
Research/Authoritative Literature

FIG. 3

- This tab contains both the Research task and the Authoritative Literature
- Detailed instructions for completing the Research task, and for using the Authoritative Literature, appear on this tab
- You may use the Authoritative Literature as a resource for completing other tasks

NOTE: If you believe you have encountered a software malfunction, report it to the test center staff immediately.

2. Situation

The following information relates to Bel City. Assume Bel has only the long-term debt specified in the information and only the funds necessitated by the information.

1. *General fund:*

The following selected information is taken from Bel's Year 4 general fund financial records:

	Budget	Actual
Property taxes	$5,000,000	$4,700,000
Other revenues	1,000,000	1,050,000
Total revenues	$6,000,000	$5,750,000
Total expenditures	$5,600,000	$5,700,000
Property taxes receivable – delinquent		$ 420,000
Minus: Allowance for estimated		
uncollectible taxes – delinquent		50,000
		$ 370,000

- There were no amendments to the budget as originally adopted.
- No property taxes receivable have been written off, and the allowance for uncollectibles balance (reclassified as uncollectible taxes–delinquent) is unchanged from the initial entry at the time of the original tax levy. Property taxes collectible not more than 90 days after year-end are deemed to be measurable and available.
- There were no encumbrances outstanding at December 31, Year 5.

2. *Capital projects fund:*

- Financing for Bel's new civic center was provided by a combination of general fund transfers, a state grant, and an issue of general obligation bonds. Any bond premium on issuance is to be used for the repayment of the bonds at their $1.2 million par value. At December 31, Year 4, the capital projects fund for the civic center had the following closing entries:

Revenues	$ 800,000	
Other financing sources – bond proceeds	1,230,000	
Other financing sources – interfund transfers from the general fund	500,000	
Expenditures		$1,080,000
Other financing uses – interfund transfers		30,000
Unreserved fund balance		1,420,000

- Also, at December 31, Year 4, capital projects fund entries reflected Bel's intention to honor the $1.3 million purchase orders and commitments outstanding for the center.
- During Year 4, total capital projects fund encumbrances exceeded the related expenditures by $42,000. All expenditures were previously encumbered.
- During Year 5, the capital projects fund received no revenues and no other financing sources. The civic center building was completed in early Year 5, and the capital projects fund was closed by a transfer of $27,000 to the general fund.

3. *Water utility enterprise fund:*

- Bel issued $4 million of revenue bonds at par. These bonds, together with a $700,000 interfund transfer from the general fund, were used to acquire a water utility. Water utility revenues are to be the sole source of funds to retire these bonds beginning in Year 8.

3. Fund Accounting

This question is presented in a check-the-box format that requires you to select the correct responses from a given list.

For items 1 through 13, indicate whether the answer to each item is yes (Y) or no (N). Items 1 through 8 relate to Bel's general fund. Items 9 through 13 relate to Bel's general capital assets, general long-term liabilities, and funds other than the general fund.

	YES	NO
1. Assuming a budgetary fund balance account was not used, did recording budgetary accounts at the beginning of Year 4 increase the unreserved fund balance by $50,000?		
2. Should the budgetary accounts for Year 4 include an entry for the expected transfer of funds from the general fund to the capital projects fund?		
3. Should the $700,000 payment from the general fund, which was used to help to establish the water utility fund, be reported as an "other financing use – interfund transfers"?		
4. Did the general fund receive the $30,000 bond premium from the capital projects fund?		
5. Should a payment from the general fund for water received for normal civic center operations be reported as an "other financing use – interfund transfers"?		
6. Does the net property taxes receivable of $370,000 include amounts recognized as revenues expected to be collected after March 1, Year 5?		
7. Would closing only the budgetary accounts cause the fund balance to increase by $400,000?		
8. Would the interaction between budgetary and actual amounts cause the fund balance to decrease by $350,000?		
9. Should a debit amount be reported for Year 4 in the government-wide financial statements for the civic center?		
10. Should Bel record depreciation in Year 5 on the civic center?		
11. Should Bel record depreciation on water utility equipment?		
12. Should the capital projects fund be included in Bel's statement of revenues, expenditures, and changes in fund balances?		
13. Should the water utility enterprise fund be included in Bel's governmental funds balance sheet?		

4. Fund Balances

This question is presented in a spreadsheet format that requires you to fill in the correct responses in the shaded cells provided.

Given the information listed in the situation, calculate the amounts required below.

Items	*Amount*
1. What was the amount recorded in the opening entry for appropriations?	
2. What was the total amount debited to property taxes receivable?	
3. What amount should be reported in the government-wide financial statements as a general long-term liability at December 31, Year 4?	
4. What amount should be reported as a general capital asset in the government-wide financial statements at December 31, Year 4?	
5. What was the completed cost of the civic center?	
6. How much was the state capital grant for the civic center?	
7. In the capital projects fund, what was the amount of the total encumbrances recorded during Year 4?	
8. In the capital projects fund, what was the unreserved fund balance reported at December 31, Year 4?	

5. Funds

This set of questions has a matching format. Select the best match for each numbered item from the terms in the drop-down list and write its letter in the column provided. Each choice may be used once, more than once, or not at all.

In the categories of funds listed below, choose the answer that matches the item description.

Aspect	*Governmental Funds*	*Proprietary Funds*	*Fiduciary Funds*
Government-wide financial statements:			
1. Basis of accounting			
2. Measurement focus			
Fund financial statements:			
3. Basis of accounting			
4. Measurement focus			

Choices
A) Cash
B) Modified cash
C) Accrual
D) Modified accrual
E) Current financial resources
F) Economic resources

Aspect	*Governmental Funds*	*Proprietary Funds*	*Fiduciary Funds*
Government-wide financial statements:			
5. Long-term liabilities			
6. Capital assets			
Fund financial statements:			
7. Long-term liabilities			
8. Capital assets			

Choices
G) Yes
H) No

6. Communication

In a brief memorandum to a client, describe the main emphasis of the governmental, proprietary, and fiduciary funds and the related required financial statements. Type your communication in your word processor program and print out the copy in a memorandum-style format.

REMINDER: Your response will be graded for both technical content and writing skills. Technical content will be evaluated for information that is helpful to the intended reader and clearly relevant to the issue. Writing skills will be evaluated for development, organization, and the appropriate expression of ideas in professional correspondence. Use a standard business memo or letter format with a clear beginning, middle, and end. Do not convey information in the form of a table, bullet point list, or other abbreviated presentation.

To:	Client
From:	CPA
Subject:	The Fund Types and Related Statements

Unofficial Answers

3. Fund Accounting (13 Gradable Items)

1. <u>No.</u> In recording the budget, Bel would have debited estimated revenues control for $6 million and credited appropriations control for $5.6 million. The interfund transfer to the capital projects fund would have been budgeted by crediting estimated other financing uses for $500,000, and the interfund transfer to the water utility would have been budgeted by crediting estimated other financing uses for $700,000. Thus, unreserved fund balance would have been debited for $800,000.

2. <u>Yes.</u> When a budget is recorded, anticipated interfund transfers from the general fund to other funds are credited to the estimated other financing uses account.

3. <u>Yes.</u> The purpose of this nonreciprocal interfund activity was to establish the water utility fund. No equivalent asset flow will occur in return, and the amount need not be repaid. Thus, the transaction is debited to other financing use – interfund transfer in the general fund.

4. <u>No.</u> Cash equal to the bond premium would have been transferred to the debt service fund. The entry in that fund was to debit cash and to credit other financing sources – interfund transfers.

5. <u>No.</u> Such a payment from the general fund to an enterprise fund is for an interfund service provided and used. This type of transaction is reported as an expenditure, an expense, or a revenue of the funds involved. In this case, the general fund records an expenditure.

6. <u>Yes.</u> Amounts expected to be collected more than 60 days after year-end ordinarily should be reclassified as deferred revenues (because they do not meet the availability criterion) except in unusual circumstances. However, the selected information indicates that management has decided that the facts justify using a period longer than 60 days. Moreover, the uncollectibles balance has not changed. Thus, the net property taxes receivable of $370,000 is deemed by management to be measurable, available, collectible, and recognizable as revenue.

7. <u>No.</u> The entry to record the general fund budget included a debit to unreserved fund balance of $800,000 (see item 1). Thus, closing only the budgetary accounts (excluding actual amounts) requires a credit to unreserved fund balance (an increase) of $800,000.

8. <u>No.</u> The balancing debit to unreserved fund balance in the budgetary entry was $800,000. Because estimated revenues exceeded actual revenues by $250,000 and expenditures exceeded appropriations by $100,000, the closing of both budgetary and actual accounts requires an additional debit to the fund balance of $350,000. Thus, the general fund's unreserved fund balance has decreased during the year by $1,150,000 ($800,000 + $350,000). This amount equals the total transfers-out ($700,000 + $500,000 = $1,200,000) minus the excess of actual revenues over actual expenditures ($5,750,000 – $5,700,000).

9. <u>Yes.</u> The construction of the civic center results in a general capital asset because it does not relate to a proprietary fund or a fiduciary fund (Bel has no such funds other than the water utility enterprise fund). General capital assets are reported only in the governmental activities column of the government-wide statement of net assets.

10. <u>Yes.</u> Capital assets are depreciated unless they are inexhaustible or are infrastructure assets accounted for using the modified approach. Because buildings are not inexhaustible and are not usually infrastructure assets, they should be depreciated over their estimated useful lives. Depreciation expense is reported in the statement of activities, and accumulated depreciation is reported in the government-wide statement of net assets. However, depreciation is not reported in the fund statements for the civic center because it is a general capital asset.

11. <u>Yes.</u> Capital assets accounted for in a proprietary fund are depreciated unless they are inexhaustible or are infrastructure assets reported using the modified approach. Depreciation expense should be reported in the government-wide statement of activities and in the proprietary fund statement of revenues, expenses, and changes in fund net assets (or fund equity).

12. <u>Yes.</u> Capital projects fund information is reported in the government-wide statements of net assets and activities (but without display of individual funds or fund types) and in the governmental funds balance sheet and statement of revenues, expenditures, and changes in fund balances.

13. <u>No.</u> Enterprise fund information is reported in the government-wide statements of net assets and activities (but without display of individual funds or fund types) and in the proprietary funds statements of net assets (or balance sheet); revenues, expenses, and changes in fund net assets (or fund equity); and cash flows.

4. Fund Balances (8 Gradable Items)

1. $5,600,000. In recording a budget, the appropriations account is credited for the total estimated expenditures for the year.

2. $4,750,000. The allowance for estimated uncollectible taxes is a revenue adjustment account. Because Bel City recorded actual tax revenues of $4,700,000, the debit to taxes receivable was $4,750,000 ($4,700,000 actual tax revenue + $50,000 allowance for estimated uncollectible taxes).

3. $1,200,000. The bond issue should be reported at par value as a general long-term liability in the governmental activities column of the government-wide statement of net assets. General long-term debt is the unmatured principal of bonds, warrants, notes, and other noncurrent general obligation debt that is not a specific liability of any proprietary fund or trust fund.

4. $1,080,000. The civic center is a general capital asset. Capital assets are reported at historical cost. The cost as of December 31, Year 4, equals the expenditures of $1,080,000 made during Year 4. Encumbrances outstanding at year-end do not meet the criteria for expenditures.

5. $2,473,000. The total completed cost of the civic center is represented by the total expenditures recorded, or $2,473,000 ($1,080,000 of Year 4 expenditures + $1,420,000 fund balance at 12/31/Year 4 – $27,000 interfund transfer to the general fund in Year 5).

6. $800,000. Of the fund sources for the civic center, the only one that qualifies as revenue for the capital projects fund is the state grant. Grants from other government entities are government-mandated or voluntary nonexchange transactions. The recipient recognizes revenue when all eligibility requirements are met. The closing entry debits revenues of $800,000.

7. $2,422,000. According to the given information, all expenditures were previously encumbered. To calculate total encumbrances, the outstanding purchase orders and other commitments ($1,300,000), which should have been encumbered, and the excess of encumbrances over related expenditures ($42,000) must be added to total expenditures ($1,080,000). The sum of these amounts is total encumbrances of $2,422,000 ($1,300,000 + $42,000 + $1,080,000).

8. $120,000. The calculation of the unreserved fund balance is illustrated in the following statement of revenues, expenditures, and changes in fund balance for the year ended December 31, Year 4:

Revenues:		
State grant		$ 800,000
Expenditures		(1,080,000)
Deficiency of revenues over expenditures		$ (280,000)
Other financing sources (uses):		
Bond proceeds	$1,230,000	
Interfund transfer from general fund	500,000	
Interfund transfer to debt service fund	(30,000)	1,700,000
Net change in fund balance		$ 1,420,000
Fund balance - beginning		0
		$ 1,420,000
Minus: Reserve for encumbrances		(1,300,000)
Unreserved fund balance, 12/31/Year 4		$ 120,000

5. Funds (24 Gradable Items)

Aspect	Governmental Funds	Proprietary Funds	Fiduciary Funds
Government-wide financial statements:			
1. Basis of accounting	C) Accrual	C) Accrual	
2. Measurement focus	F) Economic resources	F) Economic resources	
Fund financial statements:			
3. Basis of accounting	D) Modified accrual	C) Accrual	C) Accrual
4. Measurement focus	E) Current financial resources	F) Economic resources	F) Economic resources

Aspect	Governmental Funds	Proprietary Funds	Fiduciary Funds
Government-wide financial statements:			
5. Long-term liabilities	G) Yes	G) Yes	H) No
6. Capital assets	G) Yes	G) Yes	H) No
Fund financial statements:			
7. Long-term liabilities	H) No	G) Yes	G) Yes
8. Capital assets	H) No	G) Yes	G) Yes

6. Communication (5 Gradable Items; for grading instructions, please refer to page 12.)

Governmental funds emphasize sources, uses, and balances of current financial resources, often with the use of budgetary accounts. Expendable assets are assigned to funds based on their intended use, current liabilities are assigned to the funds from which they will be paid, and the difference (fund equity) is the fund balance. A balance sheet is required for governmental funds. It should be in balance sheet format (assets = liabilities + fund balances) with a total column and segregation of fund balances into reserved and unreserved amounts. A statement of revenues, expenditures, and changes in fund balances is required for governmental funds. It reports inflows, outflows, and balances of current financial resources for each major fund, for nonmajor funds in the aggregate, and in a total column. Revenues are classified in this statement by major source and expenditures by, at a minimum, function. Other financial sources and uses include the face amount of long-term debt, issuance premium or discount, some payments to escrow agents for bond refundings, interfund transfers, and sales of capital assets (unless the sale is a special item). Special and extraordinary items are reported separately after other financing sources and uses.

The emphasis of proprietary funds is on operating income, changes in net assets (or cost recovery), financial position, and cash flows. Moreover, these funds customarily do not record a budget or encumbrances. The economic resources measurement focus and the accrual basis of accounting are required in the proprietary fund financial statements. A statement of net assets or balance sheet is required for proprietary funds. Assets and liabilities must be classified as current or noncurrent. Either a net assets format (assets – liabilities = net assets) or a balance sheet format (assets = liabilities + net assets) may be used. Net assets should be reported in three components (invested in capital assets, net of related debt; restricted; and unrestricted). Moreover, capital contributions (such as grants or contributions by developers) should not be displayed as a separate component. A statement of revenues, expenses, and changes in fund net assets or fund equity (either label may be used) is required for proprietary funds. Revenues are reported by major source either net with disclosure of discounts and allowances or gross with discounts and allowances reported beneath the revenue amounts. Operating and nonoperating revenues and expenses are distinguished. Separate subtotals are given for operating revenues, operating expenses, and operating income. A separate caption contains capital contributions, additions to permanent and term endowments, special and extraordinary items, and interfund transfers.

Fiduciary funds emphasize net assets and changes in net assets. They report assets that cannot be used to support the government's own programs because they are held in trust or in an agency capacity for others, that is, for specific individuals, private organizations, or other governments and not for other funds or component units of the reporting entity. Fiduciary fund financial statements include information about all fiduciary funds and similar component units. The statements report information in a separate column for each fund type but NOT by major fund. The notes present financial statements for individual pension plans and other postemployment benefit plans unless separate GAAP reports have been issued. A statement of fiduciary net assets (for defined benefit pension plans, equivalent to the statement of plan net assets required by GASB Statement 25) is required for fiduciary funds. It reports assets, liabilities, and net assets for each fiduciary fund type. However, it does not present the three components of net assets reported in the government-wide statement of net assets or in the proprietary fund statement of net assets. A statement of changes in fiduciary net assets (for defined benefit pension plans, equivalent to the statement of changes in plan net assets required by GASB Statement 25) is required for fiduciary funds. It reports additions to, subtractions from, and the annual net change in net assets for each fiduciary fund type.

Scoring Schedule:

	Correct Responses		Gradable Items		Weights		
Tab 3	_____	÷	13	×	25%	=	_____
Tab 4	_____	÷	8	×	20%	=	_____
Tab 5	_____	÷	24	×	25%	=	_____
Tab 6	_____	÷	5	×	30%	=	_____
							_____
							(Your Score)

Use Gleim's **CPA Gleim Online** to practice more simulations in a realistic environment.

STUDY UNIT NINETEEN
NOT-FOR-PROFIT CONCEPTS

(11 pages of outline)

This study unit and the next relate to nongovernmental not-for-profit organizations (NPOs). Among other possibilities, NPOs may be institutions of higher learning, health care organizations, or voluntary health and welfare organizations (VHWOs).

The **operating environments** in which financial reporting occurs are similar for NPOs and business entities. Both use scarce resources to produce and distribute goods and services. Thus, the manner in which resources are obtained is the primary difference between them.

Although governmental bodies share certain characteristics with NPOs, the authoritative accounting literature for governments, with limited exceptions, does not apply to NPOs. NPOs follow the **GAAP hierarchy for nongovernmental entities** (see Subunit 1.8) unless a specific pronouncement exempts NPOs, or it is inapplicable because of its subject matter.

19.1 FRAMEWORK FOR NOT-FOR-PROFIT REPORTING

1. The following are the **distinguishing characteristics** of nonbusiness organizations (SFAC 4, *Objectives of Financial Reporting by Nonbusiness Organizations*):

    a. "Receipts of significant amounts of resources from resource providers who do not expect to receive either repayment or economic benefits proportionate to resources provided"

    1) Nonbusiness organizations have transactions that are infrequent in businesses, such as **grants and contributions**.

    b. "Operating purposes that are other than to provide goods or services at a profit or profit equivalent"

    1) For this reason, nonbusiness organizations have **no single indicator of performance** like net income. Thus, other performance indicators are needed.

    c. "Absence of defined ownership interests that can be sold, transferred, or redeemed, or that convey entitlement to a share of a residual distribution of resources in the event of liquidation of the organization"

    1) Nonbusiness organizations report **net assets** rather than equity.

    2) **Investor-owned entities** and organizations that provide economic benefits directly to owners, members, or participants (e.g., credit unions or employee benefit plans) are **not NPOs**.

2. **Resource providers** to NPOs have **reporting needs** that differ from those of the stakeholders of for-profit entities.

    a. Stakeholders of for-profit entities are primarily concerned about financial return. Resource providers to **not-for-profit entities** are primarily concerned about the **services rendered** and the **continuing ability** to render those services.

    b. An entity may possess **some of the characteristics** of a nonbusiness organization but not others. Examples include private not-for-profit hospitals and schools that receive small amounts of contributions but are essentially dependent on debt issues and user fees.

        1) For such entities, the **reporting objectives of business entities** may be more appropriate.

Financial Reporting Model

3. The **objectives of financial reporting** for NPOs include providing information that

    a. Is **useful** to current and potential resource providers in making resource allocation decisions.

    b. Helps in the **assessment of the service efforts and accomplishments** of a nonbusiness organization and its ability to continue providing services.

    c. Is useful in evaluating how well managers have discharged their **stewardship** responsibilities.

        1) Information on performance is not subject to the test of market competition. Thus, **other controls** are necessary, such as formal budgets and donor restrictions. Information about departures from such mandates is important to assess management's stewardship.

    d. Concerns **economic resources**, liabilities, net resources, and the effects of changes in resources and interests in them.

        1) Information about resources and liabilities often provide indications of **cash flow potential**.

        2) Periodic measurement of changes in the amount and nature of net resources is the most useful **measure of performance** for a nonbusiness organization.

    e. Concerns (1) the sources and uses of cash and other liquid assets, (2) borrowing and repayment activities, and (3) other factors useful in **assessing liquidity**.

4. The FASB identifies **two purposes** for external financial reporting by NPOs. It should help external users assess

    a. The **services** an organization provides and its **ability to continue** to provide those services, and

    b. How managers discharge their **stewardship responsibilities** and other aspects of their performance (SFAS 117, *Financial Statements of Not-for-Profit Organizations*).

5. The FASB adopted a **net assets model** for financial accounting and reporting by NPOs.

    a. This model requires reporting of the amounts of unrestricted, temporarily restricted, and permanently restricted net assets in a **statement of financial position** as of the end of the reporting period.

    b. It also requires that changes in the classes of net assets, including the effects of reclassification, be reported in a **statement of activities** and that a **statement of cash flows** be presented.

6. The net assets model emphasizes **aggregated information** about the entity as a whole, not individual funds.

   a. **Fund accounting is not required** for external reporting, but it may be used for internal purposes. **Disaggregated fund information** may be disclosed in external financial reports if the required aggregated information is reported.

Stop and review! You have completed the outline for this subunit. Study multiple-choice questions 1 through 8 beginning on page 712.

19.2 FINANCIAL STATEMENTS OF NPOs

Statement of Financial Position

1. The statement of financial position reports the organization's total assets, liabilities, and net assets at a moment in time.

EXAMPLE

The American National Red Cross
Consolidated Statement of Financial Position
June 30, 2007 (with comparative information as of June 30, 2006)
(in thousands)

Assets	2007	2006
Current assets:		
Cash and cash equivalents	$ 211,240	$ 427,573
Investments	1,088,021	1,104,975
Trade receivables	104,981	133,748
Contributions receivable	94,532	97,121
Inventories	152,666	121,831
Other current assets	20,505	17,608
Total current assets	$1,671,945	$1,902,856
Investments	1,473,531	1,333,560
Contributions receivable	31,863	23,211
Land, buildings, and other property, net	1,205,898	1,165,790
Other assets	80,186	87,579
Total assets	**$4,463,423**	**$4,512,996**

Liabilities and net assets		
Current liabilities:		
Accounts payable and accrued expenses	$ 369,884	$ 416,299
Current portion of debt	136,400	42,127
Postretirement benefits	6,621	31,302
Other current liabilities	27,789	24,960
Total current liabilities	$ 540,694	$ 514,688
Debt	353,338	389,023
Pension and postretirement benefits	228,001	306,448
Other liabilities	117,087	117,274
Total liabilities	**$1,239,120**	**$1,327,433**
Net assets:		
Unrestricted net assets	$1,801,654	$1,596,067
Temporarily restricted net assets	879,816	1,095,221
Permanently restricted net assets	542,833	494,275
Total net assets	**$3,224,303**	**$3,185,563**
Total liabilities and net assets	**$4,463,423**	**$4,512,996**

---

2. **Assets and liabilities** must be classified into reasonably homogeneous groups.

   a. Assets (including cash) that are **donor-restricted** to long-term use cannot be classified with unrestricted and currently available assets.

3.   **Net assets** must be presented in **three categories**.

    a.   **Unrestricted net assets** arise from providing goods and services and from receipts of contributions and dividends or interest, minus expenses. The only limits are the nature of the organization, its environment, its specified purposes, and contractual agreements.

        1)   These assets may be **board-designated** (internally restricted).

        2)   Significant **contractual limits**, including loan covenants, are described in the notes.

    b.   **Temporarily restricted net assets** result from restrictions removable by the passage of time **(time restrictions)** or by the actions of the NPO **(purpose restrictions)**.

        1)   **Temporary restrictions** may be for support of operating activities, investment for a specified term **(term endowments)**, use in a specified future period, or acquisition of long-lived assets.

        2)   For example, a disease-fighting charity may receive a grant specifying that the amount must be used for vaccinations in Africa for 5 years. Any balance remaining at the end of that time may be used for any purpose the board deems appropriate.

    c.   **Permanently restricted net assets** arise from asset increases and decreases subject to restrictions not removable by passage of time or by the organization's actions. They may result from reclassifications within the classes of net assets created by donor stipulations.

        1)   In the example of the disease-fighting charity, the organization may receive a grant that must be invested in AAA-grade bonds in perpetuity, with the income being spent on vaccinations in Africa (i.e., a permanent endowment fund).

4.   Information about restrictions (donor-imposed, not self-imposed) on net assets is provided either **on the statement or in the notes**.

Statement of Activities and Changes in Net Assets

5.   The **statement of activities** reports information about the ways resources are used in providing programs or services.

    a.   The statement reports the **changes in net assets** and **changes in the categories of net assets**.

        1)   Revenues, expenses, gains, and losses increase or decrease net assets. Other events, e.g., expirations of donor-imposed restrictions, that increase one class of net assets and decrease another **(reclassifications)** are reported separately as net assets released from restrictions.

EXAMPLE

The American National Red Cross
Consolidated Statement of Activities
Year Ended June 30, 2007 (with summarized information for the year ended June 30, 2006)
(in thousands)

	Unrestricted	Temporarily Restricted	Permanently Restricted	Totals 2007	2006
Operating revenues and gains					
Contributions:					
Corporate, foundation, and individual giving	$ 209,798	$ 111,929	$ -	$ 321,727	$2,645,044
United Way and other federated	58,441	100,070	-	158,511	162,300
Legacies and bequests	59,233	10,700	44,573	114,506	92,687
Services and materials	22,180	20,228	-	42,408	238,341
Grants	28,048	40,498	-	68,546	74,452
Products and services:					
Biomedical	2,071,781	-	-	2,071,781	2,165,172
Program materials	157,449	348	-	157,797	141,687
Contracts, including federal government	48,274	(138)	-	48,136	311,435
Investment income	133,274	2,389	-	135,663	109,979
Other revenues	56,166	-	-	56,166	67,528
Net assets released from restrictions	503,162	(503,162)	-	-	-
Total operating revenues and gains	**$3,347,806**	**$ (217,138)**	**$ 44,573**	**$3,175,241**	**$6,008,625**
Operating expenses					
Program services:					
Armed Forces Emergency Services	$ 55,219	$ -	$ -	$ 55,219	$ 54,096
Biomedical services	2,064,355	-	-	2,064,355	2,103,572
Community services	131,214	-	-	131,214	133,467
Domestic disaster services	442,439	-	-	442,439	2,630,766
Health and safety services	243,673	-	-	243,673	224,594
International relief and development services	142,272	-	-	142,272	154,283
Total program services	**$3,079,172**	**-**	**-**	**$3,079,172**	**$5,300,778**
Supporting services:					
Fund raising	142,711	-	-	142,711	140,082
Management and general	229,411	-	-	229,411	187,249
Total supporting services	**$ 372,122**	**$ -**	**$ -**	**$ 372,122**	**$ 327,331**
Total operating expenses	**$3,451,294**	**-**	**-**	**$3,451,294**	**$5,628,109**
Change in net assets from operations	(103,488)	(217,138)	44,573	(276,053)	380,516
Nonoperating gains	182,223	1,733	3,985	187,941	64,456
Additional minimum pension liability	-	-	-	-	94,470
Effect of adoption of recognition provisions of FASB Statement No. 158	126,852	-	-	126,852	-
Change in net assets	**$ 205,587**	**$ (215,405)**	**$ 48,558**	**$ 38,740**	**$ 539,442**
Net assets at beginning of year	1,596,067	1,095,221	494,275	3,185,563	2,646,121
Net assets at end of year	$1,801,654	$ 879,816	$542,833	$3,224,303	$3,185,563

6. **Revenues** are reported as increases in unrestricted net assets unless the use of the assets received is restricted. All **expenses** are reported as **decreases in unrestricted net assets**.

  a. Absent explicit or implicit restrictions, **contributions** are unrestricted revenues or gains **(unrestricted support)**. They increase unrestricted net assets.

     1) Donor-restricted contributions are restricted revenues or gains **(restricted support)**. They increase temporarily restricted net assets or permanently restricted net assets.

  b. **Gains and losses** are changes in unrestricted net assets unless their use is temporarily or permanently restricted explicitly by the donor or by law.

  c. The **gross amounts of revenues and expenses** from the entity's ongoing major or central operations are reported. However, **investment revenues** may be reported net of related expenses if those expenses are disclosed.

     1) **Gains and losses** may be reported as **net amounts** if they result from peripheral or incidental transactions or from other events and circumstances largely beyond the control of management.

7. Certain **other categories** of changes in net assets may be useful.

    a. Such **designations** as (1) operating and nonoperating, (2) recurring and nonrecurring, (3) earned and unearned, and (4) expendable or nonexpendable may be employed.

    b. An **intermediate measure of operations**, such as "excess of operating revenues over expenses," may only be used in a statement that reports the change in unrestricted net assets.

8. When expenses are paid out of **restricted** net assets, the following is an additional reporting requirement:

    a. In the subsection of revenues titled "net assets released from restrictions," the amount of the expense is reported as both an **increase in unrestricted revenues** and a **decrease in restricted revenues**.

9. A statement of activities or the notes should provide information about **expenses reported by functional classification**, e.g., by major classes of program services and supporting services.

EXAMPLE

The American National Red Cross
Statement of Functional Expenses
Year Ended June 30, 2007 (with summarized information for the year ended June 30, 2006)
(in thousands)

	Program Services						
	Armed Forces Emergency Services	Biomedical Services	Community Services	Domestic Disaster Services	Health and Safety Services	Int'l Relief & Development Services	Total Program Services
Salaries and wages	$30,113	$ 863,229	$ 52,544	$103,281	$107,733	$ 19,794	$1,176,694
Employee benefits	8,262	249,246	13,920	28,181	27,967	5,709	333,285
Subtotal	$38,375	$1,112,475	$ 66,464	$131,462	$135,700	$ 25,503	$1,509,979
Travel and maintenance	1,269	31,757	3,137	25,862	4,523	4,242	70,790
Equipment maintenance and rental	1,055	71,830	5,826	14,538	5,293	2,249	100,791
Supplies and materials	2,164	495,982	18,493	23,294	46,749	2,523	589,205
Contractual services	8,675	300,905	19,706	105,412	38,000	8,267	480,965
Financial and material assistance	1,952	3,410	12,046	128,070	4,201	99,174	248,853
Depreciation and amortization	1,729	47,996	5,542	13,801	9,207	314	78,589
Total expenses	**$55,219**	**$2,064,355**	**$131,214**	**$442,439**	**$243,673**	**$142,272**	**$3,079,172**

	Supporting Services			Total Expenses	
	Fund Raising	Management and General	Total Supporting Services	2007	2006
Salaries and wages	$ 52,117	$ 88,325	$140,442	$1,317,136	$1,284,395
Employee benefits	13,942	24,724	38,666	371,951	386,810
Subtotal	$ 66,059	$113,049	$179,108	$1,689,087	$1,671,205
Travel and maintenance	3,419	6,698	10,117	80,907	158,433
Equipment maintenance and rental	1,801	4,223	6,024	106,815	148,922
Supplies and materials	19,254	3,473	22,727	611,932	585,683
Contractual services	40,009	84,425	124,434	605,399	726,994
Financial and material assistance	9,362	3,270	12,632	261,485	2,243,647
Depreciation and amortization	2,807	14,273	17,080	95,669	93,225
Total expenses	**$142,711**	**$229,411**	**$372,122**	**$3,451,294**	**$5,628,109**

---

    a. **Program services** are "the activities that result in goods and services being distributed to beneficiaries, customers, or members that fulfill the purposes or mission for which the organization exists. Those services are the major purpose for and the major output of the organization and often relate to several major programs."

    b. **Supporting services** are "all activities of a not-for-profit organization other than program services. Generally, they include management and general, fund-raising, and membership-development activities."

10. **Voluntary health and welfare organizations (VHWOs)** are **required** to report a **statement of functional expenses**.

   a.   VHWOs are tax-exempt NPOs organized for the benefit of the public and supported by the public through contributions. Examples are the United Way, the Girl Scouts, the Boy Scouts, the American Cancer Society, the YMCA, and the YWCA.

   b.   VHWOs must report information about expenses by **functional classification and natural classification** (salaries, rent, interest, depreciation, etc.) in a matrix format.

   1)   Other NPOs are encouraged but not required to provide information about expenses by natural classification.

Statement of Cash Flows

11. SFAS 117 amends SFAS 95, *Statement of Cash Flows*, to extend it to all nongovernmental NPOs. Moreover, it makes certain **terminology changes**. For example, the terms "income statement" and "net income" apply to "statement of activities" and "change in net assets," respectively.

EXAMPLE

The American National Red Cross
Consolidated Statement of Cash Flows
Year Ended June 30, 2007
(with comparative information for the year ended June 30, 2006)
(in thousands)

	2007	2006
Cash flows from operating activities:		
Change in net assets	$ 38,740	$ 539,442
Adjustments to reconcile change in net assets to net cash provided by operating activities:		
Depreciation and amortization	95,669	93,225
Provision for doubtful accounts receivable	1,600	(3,307)
Provision for obsolete inventory	2,012	(73)
Net gain on sales of property	(33,980)	(53,738)
Net investment and derivative gains	(218,765)	(82,776)
Additional minimum pension liability	--	(94,470)
Effect of adoption of FASB Statement No. 158	(126,852)	--
Permanently restricted contributions	(44,573)	(23,412)
Changes in operating assets and liabilities:		
Receivables	21,104	126,300
Inventories	(32,847)	30,302
Other assets	4,496	(28,331)
Pension intangible asset	--	10,555
Accounts payable and accrued expenses	(46,415)	31,096
Other liabilities	2,938	24,030
Pension and postretirement benefits	23,724	43,310
Net cash (used in) provided by operating activities	**$(313,149)**	**$ 612,153**
Cash flows from investing activities:		
Purchases of property	$(176,897)	$(172,167)
Proceeds from sales of property	75,312	66,068
Purchases of investments	(209,897)	(743,001)
Proceeds from sales of investments	306,071	347,847
Net cash used in investing activities	**$ (5,411)**	**$(501,253)**
Cash flows from financing activities:		
Permanently restricted contributions	$ 43,851	$ 20,694
Proceeds from borrowings	169,398	441,640
Repayments of debt	(111,022)	(438,220)
Net cash provided by financing activities	**$ 102,227**	**$ 24,114**
Net increase (decrease) in cash and cash equivalents	**$(216,333)**	**$ 135,014**
Cash and cash equivalents, beginning of year	427,573	292,559
Cash and cash equivalents, end of year	**$ 211,240**	**$ 427,573**
Supplemental disclosures of cash flow information:		
Cash paid during the year for interest	$ 26,583	$ 21,729
Noncash investing and financing transactions:		
Acquisition of equipment under capital lease agreements	212	338
Donated stock and beneficial interest in perpetual trust	3,386	17,628

a. **Cash inflows from operating activities** include receipts of unrestricted contributions.

   1) NPOs and for-profit entities also treat **interest and dividends** on unrestricted investments as operating cash flows.

   2) Either the **direct or indirect method** of presenting cash flows from operating activities may be used.

   3) Operating activities may include **agency transactions** (AICPA Audit and Accounting Guide, *Not-for-Profit Organizations*).

b. **Cash inflows from investing activities** include receipt of gifts of investment assets (i.e., securities) or buildings.

   1) However, donations for the purpose of **constructing** a building (or another **long-term purpose**) are reported as cash inflows from **financing** activities.

c. **Cash inflows from financing activities** include receipts of resources that are donor-restricted for long-term purposes.

   1) **Interest and dividends** restricted by donor stipulation also are considered financing cash flows.

d. **Noncash** investing and finance activities include receipt of a gift of a building or an investment asset.

Summary of NPO Financial Statements

12. The following table summarizes the financial statements issued by nongovernmental NPOs:

	Non-VHWO NPOs	VHWOs
Statement of financial position	×	×
Statement of activities	×	×
Statement of cash flows	×	×
Statement of functional expenses		×

Stop and review! You have completed the outline for this subunit. Study multiple-choice questions 9 through 15 beginning on page 714.

19.3 CONTRIBUTIONS TO NPOs

Accounting for Contributions

1. SFAS 116, *Accounting for Contributions Received and Contributions Made*, applies to **contributions received or made** by for-profit or not-for-profit entities.

   a. It does not apply to exchange transactions; to transactions in which the entity is an agent, trustee, or intermediary; or to transfers of tax benefits.

      1) A **contribution** is one entity's **unconditional transfer** of assets to another entity (or a settlement of its liabilities). The transfer must be voluntary and nonreciprocal, and the donor entity must not act as an owner. Assets include cash, securities, land, buildings, use of facilities or utilities, materials and supplies, intangible assets, services, and **unconditional promises to give** those items in the future.

         a) A **promise to give** is a written or oral agreement to contribute assets to another entity. Sufficient verifiable documentation must exist before the promise may be recognized (i.e., by debiting a receivable and crediting revenue).

         b) A **donor-imposed condition** specifies a future and uncertain event. Its occurrence or nonoccurrence gives the donor a right of return or releases the donor from an obligation. Thus, it precludes recognition of a contribution. A **donor-imposed restriction** merely limits the use of contributed assets.

2. **Contributions received** are ordinarily accounted for when received at **fair value** as credits to revenues or gains. Debits are to assets, liabilities, or expenses.

    a. If **present value** is used to measure the fair value of an unconditional promise to give cash, later **interest accruals** are recorded as contribution income (expense) by donees (donors).

        1) However, unconditional promises to give, expected to be collected in less than 1 year, may be recognized at **net realizable value** (that is, minus an estimated uncollectible amount).

    b. **Contributions of services** are recognized if they

        1) Create or enhance nonfinancial assets, or

        2) Require special skills, are provided by those having such skills, and would usually be purchased if not obtained by donations.

    c. A contribution of **utilities**, such as electricity, is considered a contribution of **other assets**, not services. A simultaneous receipt and use of utilities should be recognized as both an unrestricted revenue and an expense in the period of receipt and use.

    d. **Contributions of collection items**, such as art works and historical treasures, need not be capitalized and recognized as revenues if they are

        1) Held for public exhibition, education, or research in furtherance of public service rather than financial gain;

        2) Protected, kept unencumbered, cared for, and preserved; and

        3) Subject to a policy that requires the proceeds of their sale to be used to acquire other collection items.

    e. Distinctions should be drawn among contributions that are permanently restricted, temporarily restricted, and unrestricted.

        1) A **temporary restriction** is "a donor-imposed restriction that permits the donee organization to use up or expend the donated assets as specified and is satisfied either by the passage of time or by actions of the organization."

        2) A **permanent restriction** is "a donor-imposed restriction that stipulates that resources be maintained permanently but permits the organization to use up or expend part or all of the income (or other economic benefits) derived from the donated assets."

        3) A **permanent endowment** is a donation restricted by the donor to generate investment income in perpetuity (see Subunit 4).

        4) Revenues or gains from contributions that increase permanently restricted or temporarily restricted net assets are reported as **restricted support**.

        5) A contribution whose restrictions are met in the same period may be reported as **unrestricted support**. This policy must be disclosed and consistently applied.

        6) Revenues or gains from contributions without restrictions constitute **unrestricted support**. They increase unrestricted net assets.

        7) **Unconditional promises to give**, with amounts due in future periods, are reported as restricted support unless the circumstances clearly indicate that the donor intended support for current activities. Thus, unconditional promises of future cash amounts usually increase temporarily restricted net assets.

        8) **Gifts of long-lived assets** (or other assets required to be used to acquire them) may be received without stipulations about their use. In this case, if the entity's choice of accounting policy is to **imply a time restriction** expiring over their useful life, the gifts are reported as restricted support. Because the implied time restriction will expire, it is temporary.

3.   The **expiration of a restriction** is recognized when it expires. Expiration occurs when the stipulated time has elapsed, the purpose of the restriction has been fulfilled, or both. It is reported **separately as a reclassification** in the statement of activities as net assets released from restrictions. The effect is to increase one class of net assets and decrease another.

   a.   For example, an **implied time restriction** on a long-lived depreciable asset expires as the economic benefits are used. Depreciation expense is reported as a decrease in unrestricted net assets.

      1)   However, the reclassified amount and depreciation expense may differ. A time restriction imposed by a donor may be for a period different from the useful life of the asset. In that case, expiration occurs over the period of the restriction, not the useful life.

   b.   An expense may be incurred for a purpose for which **unrestricted and temporarily restricted** net assets are available. Hence, the use of the unrestricted resources may result in expiration of the donor restriction to the extent of the expense incurred. This result follows even if the restricted resources are not used or are used only in part.

      1)   However, this rule does not apply if the expense is for a purpose directly related to **another specific external revenue source**.

4.   **Contributions made** are recognized at **fair value** when made as expenses and as decreases of assets or increases in liabilities.

5.   **Conditional promises to give** are recognized when the conditions are substantially met.

   a.   A conditional promise is considered unconditional if the likelihood is **remote** that the condition will not be met.

   b.   A transfer of assets subject to a conditional promise is treated as a refundable advance (debit an asset, credit a liability) until the conditions are substantially met.

6.   **Recipients of promises to give** must make appropriate disclosures.

Donations on Behalf of a Beneficiary

7.   A **donor** may make a contribution to an NPO that agrees to use it in behalf of a **third party beneficiary**.

   a.   A recipient NPO that accepts **cash** or other **financial assets** recognizes the **fair value** of the assets as a **liability** to the specified beneficiary when it recognizes the assets received from the donor (SFAS 136, *Transfer of Assets to a Not-for-Profit Organization or Charitable Trust That Raises or Holds Contributions for Others*).

      1)   If the assets are **nonfinancial**, such as materials or supplies, the recipient need not recognize the assets and the liability. The recipient NPO must disclose its accounting policy in this regard and apply it consistently.

      2)   If the donor explicitly grants the recipient NPO **variance power**, the recipient recognizes the fair value of any assets received as a contribution.

         a)   Variance power is the unilateral power to redirect the use of the assets to another beneficiary.

Stop and review! You have completed the outline for this subunit. Study multiple-choice questions 16 through 26 beginning on page 716.

19.4 INVESTMENTS HELD BY NPOs

1. According to SFAS 124, *Accounting for Certain Investments Held by Not-for-Profit Organizations*, **equity securities with readily determinable fair values** and **all debt securities** are to be measured at **fair value** in the statement of financial position.

    a. The **total change in fair value** includes the **change in unpaid interest** on debt securities (or unpaid dividends on equity securities until the ex-dividend date) and the **holding gain or loss** (realized or unrealized).

2. **Gains and losses** are reported when they occur. They are included in the statement of activities as changes in unrestricted net assets unless a legal or donor restriction exists.

    a. If **unrealized gains and losses** were recognized in prior periods, gains and losses recognized for a current disposition of the same investments exclude the amounts previously recognized.

3. **Investment income** is reported when earned as increases in unrestricted net assets, barring a donor restriction. It is reported as an increase in temporarily restricted or permanently restricted net assets given a donor-imposed restriction.

4. Gains and income that are donor-restricted to certain uses may be reported as increases in unrestricted net assets if the **restrictions expire** in the period the gains and income are recognized. If the entity adopts this policy, it must apply the same policy to contributions, report consistently, and disclose the accounting policy.

5. A donor may require a gift to be invested permanently or for a specified term. The result is a **donor-restricted endowment fund**. However, absent a legal or donor restriction, gains and losses on investments of a donor-restricted endowment fund are changes in unrestricted net assets.

    a. If a **specific security** is to be held permanently, the gains and losses on that security are assumed to be changes in **permanently restricted net assets** absent a contrary donor instruction.

        1) However, if the donee may **choose investments**, the **gains** are not permanently restricted absent a donor stipulation or legal requirement. Rather, the gains (the net appreciation of the fund investments) are unrestricted or temporarily restricted if the income is unrestricted or temporarily restricted, respectively.

    b. Absent donor stipulations or contrary law, **losses** reduce **temporarily restricted net assets**. This reduction is to the extent that a donor's temporary restriction on net appreciation of the fund has not expired prior to the losses. Any **remaining losses** reduce **unrestricted net assets**.

        1) If losses reduce the fund's assets below the level required by the law or by the donor, gains restoring the fair value to the required level are increases in **unrestricted net assets**.

Stop and review! You have completed the outline for this subunit. Study multiple-choice questions 27 through 30 beginning on page 719.

QUESTIONS

19.1 Framework for Not-for-Profit Reporting

1. The reporting model described in SFAS 117, *Financial Statements of Not-for-Profit Organizations*, applies to

A. Business entities and governmental not-for-profit organizations.

B. Business entities and nongovernmental not-for-profit organizations.

C. Nongovernmental not-for-profit organizations.

D. Governmental not-for-profit organizations that also use proprietary fund accounting.

Answer (C) is correct. *(Publisher, adapted)*
REQUIRED: The entities that use the net assets reporting model.
DISCUSSION: SFAS 117 presents a reporting model for financial accounting and reporting by nongovernmental not-for-profit organizations (NPOs). This approach recognizes that the information needs of resource providers of NPOs differ from those of resource providers of business entities. The latter are primarily concerned about financial return, whereas the former are primarily concerned about the services rendered by the NPO and its continuing ability to render those services.

2. Which of the following is ordinarily not considered one of the major distinguishing characteristics of nonbusiness organizations?

A. Significant amounts of resources are provided by donors in nonreciprocal transactions.

B. There is an absence of defined, transferable ownership interests.

C. Performance indicators similar to a business enterprise's profit are readily available.

D. The primary operating purpose is not to provide goods or services at a profit.

Answer (C) is correct. *(Publisher, adapted)*
REQUIRED: The statement not ordinarily considered a major characteristic of nonbusiness organizations.
DISCUSSION: SFAC 4, *Objectives of Financial Reporting by Nonbusiness Organizations*, states that the objectives of financial reporting are derived from the common interests of those who provide the resources to nonbusiness organizations. Such organizations ordinarily have no single indicator of performance comparable to a business enterprise's profit. Thus, nonbusiness organization performance is usually evaluated in terms of management stewardship.

3. Which of the following is a characteristic of nonbusiness organizations?

A. Noneconomic reasons seldom underlie the decision to provide resources to nonbusiness enterprises.

B. Business and nonbusiness organizations usually obtain resources in the same way.

C. Both nonbusiness and business organizations use scarce resources in the production and distribution of goods and services.

D. The operating environment of nonbusiness organizations ordinarily differs from that of business organizations.

Answer (C) is correct. *(Publisher, adapted)*
REQUIRED: The characteristic of nonbusiness organizations.
DISCUSSION: The operating environments of nonbusiness and business organizations are similar in many ways. Both produce and distribute goods and services using scarce resources.
Answer (A) is incorrect because many noneconomic factors affect decisions to provide resources to nonbusiness enterprises. Answer (B) is incorrect because business organizations obtain resources by providing goods and services. Many nonbusiness organizations obtain resources from contributors and are accountable to the providers of those resources or to their representatives. Answer (D) is incorrect because the operating environments of nonbusiness and business organizations are similar.

4. Net assets is an element of the financial statements of not-for-profit organizations. It

A. Is the residual interest in the assets of a not-for-profit organization after deducting its liabilities.

B. Is the change in equity during a period from transactions and other events and circumstances not involving resource providers.

C. Differs from equity in business enterprises because it is not a residual interest.

D. Consists of the probable future economic benefits obtained or controlled by a particular entity as a result of past transactions or events.

Answer (A) is correct. *(Publisher, adapted)*
REQUIRED: The definition of the net assets element of the financial statements of not-for-profit organizations.
DISCUSSION: Net assets equal the residual interest in the assets of an entity that remains after deducting its liabilities. For a business enterprise, equity (the ownership interest) is the analogue of net assets. In a not-for-profit organization, which has no ownership interest in the same sense as a business enterprise, the net assets element is divided into three classes based on the presence or absence of donor-imposed restrictions.
Answer (B) is incorrect because comprehensive income "is the change in equity of a business enterprise during a period from transactions and other events and circumstances from nonowner sources" (SFAC 6). Answer (C) is incorrect because equity and net assets are residuals. Answer (D) is incorrect because assets, not net assets, are "probable future economic benefits obtained or controlled by a particular entity as a result of past transactions or events" (SFAC 6).

5. The resource providers of not-for-profit organizations have which of the following as their primary concerns?

I.   Financial return on investment

II. Services rendered by the not-for-profit organization

III. The continuing ability of the not-for-profit organization to render services

IV. The avoidance of fraud or embezzlement

   A. I and IV.

   B. II, III, and IV.

   C. I, II, and III.

   D. II and III.

6. All of the following are objectives of financial reporting by nonbusiness organizations except

   A. To provide information that is useful to current and potential resource providers in making resource allocation decisions.

   B. To provide information that concerns the sources and uses of cash and other liquid assets, borrowing and repayment activities, and other factors affecting liquidity.

   C. To provide information that concerns performance, including a single indicator comparable to a business enterprise's net income, that permits resource providers to assess how effectively the entity is competing with others.

   D. To provide information that concerns economic resources, liabilities, net resources, and the effects of changes in resources and interests.

7. Pharm, a nongovernmental not-for-profit organization, is preparing its year-end financial statements. Which of the following statements is required?

   A. Statement of changes in financial position.

   B. Statement of cash flows.

   C. Statement of changes in fund balances.

   D. Statement of revenues, expenses, and changes in fund balances.

Answer (D) is correct. *(Publisher, adapted)*
   REQUIRED: The primary concerns of resource providers of not-for-profit organizations.
   DISCUSSION: Resource providers of not-for-profit organizations have as their primary concerns the services rendered by the organization and the continuing ability of the organization to render those services. These needs differ from the needs of resource providers for business entities, whose primary concern is financial return.

Answer (C) is correct. *(Publisher, adapted)*
   REQUIRED: The objectives of financial reporting by nonbusiness organizations.
   DISCUSSION: Nonbusiness organizations often have no single indicator of performance comparable to a business enterprise's net income. Accordingly, other performance indicators are needed, with the most useful being information measuring the changes in the amount and nature of net resources that is combined with information about service efforts and accomplishments.
   Answer (A) is incorrect because among the objectives of financial reporting by nonbusiness organizations is to provide information that is useful to current and potential resource providers in making resource allocation decisions. Answer (B) is incorrect because among the objectives of financial reporting by nonbusiness organizations is to provide information that concerns the sources and uses of cash and other liquid assets, borrowing and repayment activities, and other factors affecting liquidity. Answer (D) is incorrect because among the objectives of financial reporting by nonbusiness organizations is to provide information that concerns economic resources, liabilities, net resources, and the effects of changes in resources and interests.

Answer (B) is correct. *(CPA, adapted)*
   REQUIRED: The statements required in a complete set of financial statements of not-for-profit organizations.
   DISCUSSION: SFAS 117 states that "a complete set of financial statements of a not-for-profit organization shall include a statement of financial position as of the end of the reporting period, a statement of activities and a statement of cash flows for the reporting period, and accompanying notes to financial statements."
   Answer (A) is incorrect because a statement of changes in financial position is not required for nongovernmental not-for-profit organizations by SFAS 117. Answer (C) is incorrect because a statement of changes in fund balances is not required for nongovernmental not-for-profit organizations by SFAS 117. Answer (D) is incorrect because a statement of revenues, expenses, and changes in fund balances is not required for nongovernmental not-for-profit organizations by SFAS 117.

8. SFAS 117, *Financial Statements of Not-for-Profit Organizations*, focuses on

    A. Basic information for the organization as a whole.

    B. Standardization of funds nomenclature.

    C. Inherent differences of not-for-profit organizations that affect reporting presentations.

    D. Distinctions between current fund and noncurrent fund presentations.

Answer (A) is correct. *(CPA, adapted)*
    REQUIRED: The focus of SFAS 117.
    DISCUSSION: SFAS 117 is intended to promote the relevance, understandability, and comparability of financial statements issued by not-for-profit organizations by requiring that certain basic information be reported. The focus of the financial statements required by SFAS 117 is on the organization as a whole, and on reporting assets, liabilities, and net assets; changes in net assets; flows of economic resources; cash flows, borrowing and repayment of borrowing, and other factors affecting liquidity; and service efforts.

19.2 Financial Statements of NPOs

9. During the current year, Mill Foundation, a nongovernmental not-for-profit organization, received $100,000 in unrestricted contributions from the general public. Mill's board of directors stipulated that $75,000 of these contributions would be used to create an endowment. At the end of the current year, how should Mill report the $75,000 in the net assets section of the statement of financial position?

    A. Permanently restricted.

    B. Unrestricted.

    C. Temporarily restricted.

    D. Donor restricted.

Answer (B) is correct. *(CPA, adapted)*
    REQUIRED: The reporting of unrestricted contributions designated as an endowment.
    DISCUSSION: The Mill Foundation received unrestricted contributions of $100,000. The board then decided to create an endowment. An internal decision to designate a portion of unrestricted net assets as an endowment is not a restriction. If the contributions had been restricted by the donor, the classification of the assets would have been either permanently restricted or temporarily restricted.
    Answer (A) is incorrect because the contributions were not restricted by the donors, the general public. Answer (C) is incorrect because the contributions were not restricted by the donors, the general public. Answer (D) is incorrect because the board of directors, not the general public, designated $75,000 of the contributions as an endowment.

10. A large not-for-profit organization's statement of activities should report the net change for net assets that are

	Unrestricted	Permanently Restricted
A.	Yes	Yes
B.	Yes	No
C.	No	No
D.	No	Yes

Answer (A) is correct. *(CPA, adapted)*
    REQUIRED: The changes in net assets reported in a large not-for-profit organization's statement of activities.
    DISCUSSION: In accordance with SFAS 117, *Financial Statements of Not-for-Profit Organizations*, the statement of financial position should report the amounts of permanently restricted, temporarily restricted, and unrestricted net assets. The statement of activities should report the changes in each category.

11. In the preparation of the statement of activities for a nongovernmental not-for-profit organization, all expenses are reported as decreases in which of the following net asset classes?

    A. Total net assets.

    B. Unrestricted net assets.

    C. Temporarily restricted net assets.

    D. Permanently restricted net assets.

Answer (B) is correct. *(CPA, adapted)*
    REQUIRED: The net asset class in which expenses are recorded by a nongovernmental NPO.
    DISCUSSION: A statement of activities always reports expenses as decreases in unrestricted net assets. Expenses may be classified within unrestricted net assets as operating and nonoperating, recurring and nonrecurring, or in other ways. Moreover, expenses are normally reported as gross amounts. The statement of activities or notes reported by most NPOs also must provide information about expenses reported by their functional classification.
    Answer (A) is incorrect because total net assets is not a category of net assets. Answer (C) is incorrect because revenues, gains, and losses, not expenses, are reported in temporarily restricted net assets in appropriate cases. Answer (D) is incorrect because permanently restricted net assets is decreased only by losses.

12. Forkin Manor, a nongovernmental not-for-profit organization (NPO), wants to reformat its financial statements using terminology that is more readily associated with for-profit entities. The director believes that the term "operating profit" and the practice of segregating recurring and nonrecurring items more accurately depict the NPO's activities. Under what condition will Forkin be allowed to use "operating profit" and to segregate its recurring items from its nonrecurring items in its statement of activities?

A. The NPO reports the change in unrestricted net assets for the period.

B. A parenthetical disclosure in the notes implies that the NPO is seeking for-profit entity status.

C. Forkin receives special authorization from the Internal Revenue Service that this wording is appropriate.

D. At a minimum, the NPO reports the change in permanently restricted net assets for the period.

Answer (A) is correct. *(CPA, adapted)*
REQUIRED: The condition allowing an NPO to use the term "operating profit" and to segregate recurring and nonrecurring items in its statement of activities.
DISCUSSION: In its statement of activities, an NPO classifies revenues, expenses, gains, and losses within the three classes of changes in net assets (permanently restricted, temporarily restricted, and unrestricted). Within a class or classes, other classifications are permitted, for example, operating and nonoperating, expendable and nonexpendable, earned and unearned, and recurring and nonrecurring. Furthermore, a term such as operating income or operating profit is permitted when an intermediate measure of operations is reported. However, this measure must be in a financial statement that reports the change in unrestricted net assets for the period (SFAS 117).
Answer (B) is incorrect because the NPO need not seek for-profit status to report in the described manner. Answer (C) is incorrect because the NPO need not obtain IRS authorization to report in the described manner. Answer (D) is incorrect because the NPO should report the changes in all three classes of net assets regardless of whether additional classifications are included in the statement of activities.

13. In its fiscal year ended June 30, Year 4, Barr College, a large private institution, received $100,000 designated by the donor for scholarships for superior students. On July 26, Year 4, Barr selected the students and awarded the scholarships. How should the July 26 transaction be reported in Barr's statement of activities for the year ended June 30, Year 5?

A. As both an increase and a decrease of $100,000 in unrestricted net assets.

B. As a decrease only in unrestricted net assets.

C. By footnote disclosure only.

D. Not reported.

Answer (A) is correct. *(CPA, adapted)*
REQUIRED: The treatment by a private not-for-profit organization of funds received and used for a designated purpose.
DISCUSSION: When Barr College received the contribution, it should have been classified as temporarily restricted because it was to be used for a specified purpose. Once the purpose has been fulfilled, the temporary restriction expires, and the amount should be reclassified as a decrease in temporarily restricted net assets and an increase in unrestricted net assets. When the scholarships are awarded, unrestricted net assets are decreased.

14. At the beginning of the year, the Baker Fund, a nongovernmental not-for-profit corporation, received a $125,000 contribution restricted to youth activity programs. During the year, youth activities generated revenues of $89,000 and had program expenses of $95,000. What amount should Baker report as net assets released from restrictions for the current year?

A. $0

B. $6,000

C. $95,000

D. $125,000

Answer (C) is correct. *(CPA, adapted)*
REQUIRED: The net assets released from restrictions for the current year.
DISCUSSION: At the time the contribution was made, net restricted assets increased by $125,000. The restriction stated that the funds were to be used for youth activity programs. The amount of actual program expenses for the year is reported under net assets released from restrictions.
Answer (A) is incorrect because the incurrence of program expenses reduced restricted net assets by fulfilling the purpose of the restriction to the extent the resources were used. Answer (B) is incorrect because $6,000 is the excess of program expenses over revenues generated by youth activities. Answer (D) is incorrect because the purpose of the restriction was fulfilled only to the extent the contribution was used for the stated purpose.

15. A nongovernmental not-for-profit organization borrowed $5,000, which it used to purchase a truck. In which section of the organization's statement of cash flows should the transaction be reported?

A. In cash inflow and cash outflow from investing activities.

B. In cash inflow and cash outflow from financing activities.

C. In cash inflow from financing activities and cash outflow from investing activities.

D. In cash inflow from operating activities and cash outflow from investing activities.

Answer (C) is correct. *(CPA, adapted)*
REQUIRED: The section of the statement of cash flows in which the purchase of a truck is reported by a nongovernmental NPO.
DISCUSSION: SFAS 95, *Statement of Cash Flows*, applies to nongovernmental NPOs. Thus, the borrowing is a cash inflow from a financing activity because it arises from issuing debt. The purchase of the truck is a cash outflow from an investing activity because it involves the acquisition of property, plant, or equipment or other productive assets.
Answer (A) is incorrect because the cash inflow is from a financing activity. Answer (B) is incorrect because the cash outflow is from an investing activity. Answer (D) is incorrect because the cash inflow is from a financing activity.

19.3 Contributions to NPOs

16. During the current year, a voluntary health and welfare organization receives $300,000 in unrestricted pledges. Of this amount, $100,000 has been designated by donors for use next year to support operations. If 15% of the unrestricted pledges are expected to be uncollectible, what amount of unrestricted support should the organization recognize in its current-year financial statements?

A. $300,000

B. $270,000

C. $200,000

D. $170,000

Answer (D) is correct. *(CPA, adapted)*
REQUIRED: The current-year unrestricted support to be recognized.
DISCUSSION: Only $200,000 of the pledged total constitutes unrestricted support. These pledges may be recognized at net realizable value (NRV) if their collection is expected in less than one year. The NRV of these pledges is $170,000 [$200,000 × (1.0 – .15 estimated uncollectible)].
Answer (A) is incorrect because $300,000 is the total amount of pledges. Answer (B) is incorrect because $100,000 of the pledges is restricted until the next year. Answer (C) is incorrect because $200,000 does not reflect the estimated uncollectible pledges.

17. The League, a not-for-profit organization, received the following pledges:

Unrestricted	$200,000
Restricted for capital additions	150,000

All pledges are legally enforceable and are expected to be received in the upcoming year. The League's experience indicates that 10% of all pledges prove to be uncollectible. What amount may the League report as a reasonable estimate of the fair value of pledges receivable?

A. $135,000

B. $180,000

C. $315,000

D. $350,000

Answer (C) is correct. *(CPA, adapted)*
REQUIRED: The amount to report as a reasonable estimate of the fair value of pledges receivable.
DISCUSSION: Not-for-profit organizations must recognize unconditional promises to give at fair value. The present value of estimated future cash flows is an appropriate measure of fair value. However, unconditional promises to give and expected to be collected in less than 1 year may be recognized at net realizable value (i.e., less an estimated uncollectible amount). The League may therefore report net pledges receivable of $315,000 [($200,000 + $150,000) × (1.0 – 0.1 estimated uncollectible)].
Answer (A) is incorrect because $135,000 is based on the assumption that only the pledges "restricted for capital additions" are reported as receivables, net of 10% of the amount. Answer (B) is incorrect because $180,000 is based on the assumption that only the unrestricted pledges are reported, net of 10% of that amount. Answer (D) is incorrect because pledges receivable expected to be collected in less than 1 year may be reported at net realizable value.

18. A storm damaged the roof of a new building owned by K-9 Shelters, a not-for-profit organization. A supporter of K-9, a professional roofer, repaired the roof at no charge. In K-9's statement of activities, the damage and repair of the roof should

A. Be reported by note disclosure only.

B. Be reported as an increase in both expenses and contributions.

C. Be reported as an increase in both net assets and contributions.

D. Not be reported.

Answer (B) is correct. *(CPA, adapted)*
REQUIRED: The treatment of services received at no charge by a not-for-profit entity.
DISCUSSION: Contributions of services at fair value are recognized if they require special skills, are provided by individuals having those skills, and would have to be purchased if not received by donation (SFAC 116, *Accounting for Contributions Received and Contributions Made*). Hence, K-9 should report an expense and contribution revenue for the services received.

19. Stanton College, a not-for-profit organization, received a building with no donor stipulations as to its use. Stanton does not have an accounting policy implying a time restriction on donated assets. What type of net assets should be increased when the building was received?

I. Unrestricted

II. Temporarily restricted

III. Permanently restricted

   A. I only.

   B. II only.

   C. III only.

   D. II or III.

Answer (A) is correct. *(CPA, adapted)*
   REQUIRED: The classification of net assets affected by a contribution of a building.
   DISCUSSION: SFAC 116 requires that contributions received by not-for-profit organizations be reported as restricted support or unrestricted support. Contributions with donor-imposed restrictions are reported as restricted support. Restricted support increases permanently restricted net assets or temporarily restricted net assets. Contributions without donor-imposed restrictions are reported as unrestricted support, which increases unrestricted net assets. If Stanton had an accounting policy to imply a time restriction on gifts of long-lived assets, the gift of the building would be reported as temporarily restricted support even though no donor restrictions were imposed.
   Answer (B) is incorrect because temporarily restricted net assets are increased by contributions classified as restricted support. Answer (C) is incorrect because permanently restricted net assets are increased by contributions classified as restricted support. Answer (D) is incorrect because temporarily and permanently restricted net assets are increased by contributions classified as restricted support.

20. The Turtle Society, a nongovernmental not-for-profit organization (NPO), receives numerous contributed hours from volunteers during its busy season. Chris, a clerk at the local tax collector's office, volunteered 10 hours per week for 24 weeks transferring turtle food from the port to the turtle shelter. His rate of pay at the tax office is $10 per hour, and the prevailing wage rate for laborers is $6.50 per hour. What amount of contribution revenue should Turtle Society record for this service?

   A. $0

   B. $840

   C. $1,560

   D. $2,400

Answer (A) is correct. *(CPA, adapted)*
   REQUIRED: The amount of contribution revenue recorded for a volunteer's service.
   DISCUSSION: Contributions of services are recognized if they (1) create or enhance nonfinancial assets, or (2) require special skills, are provided by those having such skills, and would usually be purchased if not obtained by donations. The volunteer's efforts meet neither of these criteria. Thus, no contribution revenue is recognized.
   Answer (B) is incorrect because $840 equals 24 weeks, times 10 hours per week, times $3.50 per hour ($10 – $6.50). Answer (C) is incorrect because $1,560 equals 24 weeks, times 10 hours per week, times $6.50 per hour. Answer (D) is incorrect because $2,400 equals 24 weeks, times 10 hours per week, times $10 per hour.

21. The Pel Museum, a not-for-profit organization, received a contribution of historical artifacts. It need not recognize the contribution if the artifacts are to be sold and the proceeds used to

   A. Support general museum activities.

   B. Acquire other items for collections.

   C. Repair existing collections.

   D. Purchase buildings to house collections.

Answer (B) is correct. *(CPA, adapted)*
   REQUIRED: The circumstance under which a contribution of artifacts to be sold need not be recognized.
   DISCUSSION: Contributions of such items as art works and historical treasures need not be capitalized and recognized as revenues if they are added to collections that are (1) held for public exhibition, education, or research for public service purposes rather than financial gain (SFAS 116, *Accounting for Contributions Received and Contributions Made*); (2) protected, kept unencumbered, cared for, and preserved; and (3) subject to a policy that requires the proceeds of sale of collection items to be used to acquire other collection items.

22. Janna Association, a nongovernmental not-for-profit organization, received a cash gift with the stipulation that the principal be held for at least 20 years. How should the cash gift be recorded?

   A. A temporarily restricted asset.

   B. A permanently restricted asset.

   C. An unrestricted asset.

   D. A temporary liability.

Answer (A) is correct. *(CPA, adapted)*
   REQUIRED: The classification of a cash gift with a time restriction.
   DISCUSSION: Temporarily restricted net assets result from restrictions removable by the passage of time (time restrictions) or by the actions of the NPO (purpose restrictions). A stipulation that the principal be held for at least 20 years is a temporary time restriction.
   Answer (B) is incorrect because, once 20 years pass, the asset is no longer restricted. Answer (C) is incorrect because the asset cash gift is restricted for at least 20 years. Answer (D) is incorrect because cash is an asset.

23. On December 30 of the current year, Leigh Museum, a not-for-profit organization, received a $7 million donation of Day Co. shares with donor-stipulated requirements as follows:

- Shares valued at $5 million are to be sold, with the proceeds used to erect a public viewing building.
- Shares valued at $2 million are to be retained, with the dividends used to support current operations.

As a consequence of the receipt of the Day shares, how much should Leigh report as temporarily restricted net assets on its statement of financial position for the current year?

    A. $0

    B. $2,000,000

    C. $5,000,000

    D. $7,000,000

Answer (C) is correct. *(CPA, adapted)*
    REQUIRED: The amount to report as temporarily restricted net assets.
    DISCUSSION: A temporary restriction permits the donee organization to "expend the donated assets as specified and is satisfied either by the passage of time or by actions of the organization" (SFAS 116). The shares valued at $5 million meet this definition because they are to be sold and used for a specified project. A permanent restriction requires that the "resources be maintained permanently but permits the organization to use up or expend part or all of the income derived" (SFAS 116). The $2 million stock donation meets this definition and should be reported as permanently restricted net assets. Leigh should report $5 million as temporarily restricted net assets.
    Answer (A) is incorrect because the shares valued at $5,000,000 are only temporarily restricted. Answer (B) is incorrect because the shares valued at $2,000,000 are permanently restricted, and the shares valued at $5,000,000 have temporary restrictions. Answer (D) is incorrect because only the shares valued at $5,000,000 have temporary restrictions.

24. In Year 3, Gamma, a not-for-profit organization, deposited at a bank $1 million given to it by a donor to purchase endowment securities. The securities were purchased January 2, Year 4. At December 31, Year 3, the bank recorded $2,000 interest on the deposit. In accordance with the bequest, this $2,000 was used to finance ongoing program expenses in March Year 4. At December 31, Year 3, what amount of the bank balance should be included as current assets in Gamma's classified balance sheet?

    A. $0

    B. $2,000

    C. $1,000,000

    D. $1,002,000

Answer (B) is correct. *(CPA, adapted)*
    REQUIRED: The amount of the bank balance classified as current assets.
    DISCUSSION: In accordance with SFAS 117, a not-for-profit organization may classify its assets and liabilities as current or noncurrent as defined in ARB 43, Ch. 3A. That pronouncement defines current assets as those reasonably expected to be realized in cash, sold, or consumed during the operating cycle or within 1 year, whichever is longer. Accordingly, the $2,000 of interest recorded at December 31, Year 3, should be classified as current because the bequest stipulated that it be used for ongoing program expenses. However, the $1 million restricted to the purchase of endowment securities is not classified as current. SFAS 117 states that assets received with a donor-imposed restriction limiting their use to long-term purposes should not be classified with assets available for current use.

25. On December 31, Year 3, Dahlia, a nongovernmental not-for-profit organization, purchased a vehicle with $15,000 unrestricted cash and received a donated second vehicle having a fair value of $12,000. Dahlia expects each vehicle to provide it with equal service value over each of the next five years and then to have no residual value. Dahlia has an accounting policy implying a time restriction on gifts of long-lived assets. In Dahlia's Year 4 statement of activities, what depreciation expense should be included under changes in unrestricted net assets?

    A. $0

    B. $2,400

    C. $3,000

    D. $5,400

Answer (D) is correct. *(CPA, adapted)*
    REQUIRED: The depreciation expense included under changes in unrestricted net assets.
    DISCUSSION: The expiration of a restriction is recognized when it expires. Expiration occurs when the stipulated time has elapsed, the purpose of the restriction has been fulfilled, or both. It is reported separately as a reclassification in the statement of activities as net assets released from restrictions. The effect is to increase one class of net assets and decrease another. For example, an implied time restriction on a long-lived depreciable asset expires as the economic benefits are used. Depreciation expense is reported as a decrease in unrestricted net assets (SFAS 116). Consequently, Dahlia should record a decrease in unrestricted net assets related to depreciation of $5,400 [$15,000 + $12,000) ÷ 5-year useful life], assuming no residual value.

26. The Bruneski family lost its home in a fire. On December 25, Year 3, a philanthropist sent money to the Amer Benevolent Society to purchase furniture for the Bruneski family. The resource provider did not explicitly grant Amer the unilateral power to redirect the use of the assets. During January Year 4, Amer purchased this furniture for the Bruneski family. Amer, a not-for-profit organization, should report the receipt of the money in its Year 3 financial statements as a(n)

A. Unrestricted contribution.

B. Temporarily restricted contribution.

C. Permanently restricted contribution.

D. Liability.

Answer (D) is correct. *(CPA, adapted)*
REQUIRED: The reporting of a transfer to an NPO with a direction that the assets be used to aid a specific beneficiary.
DISCUSSION: According to SFAS 136, if the recipient and beneficiary are not financially interrelated, the recipient does not recognize a contribution unless the donor of cash or other financial assets explicitly grants the recipient variance power, that is, the unilateral power to redirect the use of the assets to another beneficiary. Because Amer was not explicitly granted variance power, it is a mere agent or trustee acting on behalf of a third-party donee. It has no discretion in use of the cash. Thus, the transfer should be accounted for as a liability, not a contribution.

19.4 Investments Held by NPOs

27. Midtown Church received a donation of equity securities with readily determinable fair values from a church member. The securities had appreciated in value after they were purchased by the donor, and they continued to appreciate through the end of Midtown's fiscal year. At what amount should Midtown report its investment in donated securities in its year-end balance sheet?

A. Donor's cost.

B. Fair value at the date of receipt.

C. Fair value at the balance sheet date.

D. Fair value at either the date of receipt or the balance sheet date.

Answer (C) is correct. *(CPA, adapted)*
REQUIRED: The valuation of donated marketable equity securities.
DISCUSSION: In its statement of financial position, a not-for-profit organization should measure the following investments at fair value: (1) equity securities with readily determinable fair values and (2) debt securities. Thus, the total change in the fair value of the donated securities from the date of receipt to the balance sheet date must be reported in the statement of activities (SFAS 124).

28. RST Charities received equities securities valued at $100,000 as an unrestricted gift. During the year, RST received $5,000 in dividends from these securities; at year end, the securities had a fair market value of $110,000. By what amount did these transactions increase RST's net assets?

A. $100,000

B. $105,000

C. $110,000

D. $115,000

Answer (D) is correct. *(CPA, adapted)*
REQUIRED: The increase in a not-for-profit organization's net assets from an unrestricted contribution of securities that paid dividends and appreciated after receipt.
DISCUSSION: Contributions received are ordinarily accounted for when received at fair value as credits to revenues or gains. Debits are to assets, liabilities, or expenses. Revenues or gains from contributions without restrictions constitute unrestricted support. They increase unrestricted net assets. SFAS 124, *Accounting for Certain Investments Held by Not-for-Profit Organizations*, requires not-for-profit entities to measure investments in equity securities with readily determinable fair values and all investments in debt securities at fair value in the statement of financial position. Unrealized holding gains or losses (changes in fair value) are reported in the statement of activities as changes in unrestricted net assets (barring a legal or donor restriction). Investment income (e.g., dividends) is reported when earned as increases in unrestricted net assets (barring a legal or donor restriction). Accordingly, the donee's unrestricted net assets increased by $115,000 [$100,000 fair value of contribution + $5,000 in dividends + $10,000 ($110,000 − $100,000) unrealized holding gain in fair value].
Answer (A) is incorrect because $100,000 excludes the dividends and the unrealized holding gain. Answer (B) is incorrect because $105,000 excludes the unrealized holding gain. Answer (C) is incorrect because $110,000 excludes the dividends.

29. A not-for-profit voluntary health and welfare organization received a $500,000 permanent endowment. The donor stipulated that the income be used for a mental health program. The endowment fund reported a $60,000 net decrease in fair value and $30,000 of investment income. The organization spent $45,000 on the mental health program during the year. What amount of change in temporarily restricted net assets should the organization report?

A. $75,000 decrease.

B. $15,000 decrease.

C. $0

D. $425,000 increase.

Answer (C) is correct. *(CPA, adapted)*
REQUIRED: The change in temporarily restricted net assets.
DISCUSSION: The contribution to a permanent endowment is an increase in permanently restricted net assets. Income from donor-restricted permanent endowments is an increase in restricted support if the donor restricts its use. However, if the restriction is met in the period the income is recognized, it may be reported as an increase in unrestricted net assets if the entity (1) has a similar policy for reporting contributions received, (2) reports consistently, and (3) makes adequate disclosure. The restriction on the income expired when it was spent (along with an additional $15,000, presumably from other sources). Absent donor stipulation or contrary law, losses on a permanent endowment reduce temporarily restricted net assets to the extent that a temporary restriction on net appreciation has not expired prior to the losses. Any remaining losses reduce unrestricted net assets. Thus, absent such a restriction, the decrease in the fair value of the endowment's investments reduced unrestricted net assets. The effect on temporarily restricted net assets of (1) creation of the endowment, (2) the receipt and expenditure in the same period of income, and (3) the loss on the principal of the endowment (absent a donor restriction) is $0.
Answer (A) is incorrect because $75,000 is the sum of the fair value decrease and the excess of expenditures over income. Answer (B) is incorrect because $15,000 is the excess of the amount spent over the income. Answer (D) is incorrect because $425,000 equals the contribution minus the sum of the fair value decrease and the excess of expenditures over income.

30. A voluntary health and welfare organization received a $700,000 permanent endowment during the year. The donor stipulated that the income and investment appreciation be used to maintain its senior center. The endowment fund reported a net investment appreciation of $80,000 and investment income of $50,000. The organization spent $60,000 to maintain its senior center during the year. What amount of change in temporarily restricted net assets should the organization report?

A. $50,000

B. $70,000

C. $130,000

D. $770,000

Answer (B) is correct. *(CPA, adapted)*
REQUIRED: The change in temporarily restricted net assets reported by a voluntary health and welfare organization that received a permanent endowment with a use restriction on appreciation and income.
DISCUSSION: The contribution to a permanent endowment is an increase in permanently restricted net assets. Income or appreciation from donor-restricted permanent endowments is an increase in restricted support if the donor restricts its use. (However, if the restriction is met in the period the income is recognized, it may be reported as an increase in unrestricted net assets if the entity (1) has a similar policy for reporting contributions received, (2) reports consistently, and (3) makes adequate disclosure.) The temporary restriction on the income and appreciation was met and is deemed to have expired only to the extent it was expended during the year. Accordingly, the change in temporarily restricted net assets was $70,000 ($80,000 appreciation + $50,000 income – $60,000 spent).
Answer (A) is incorrect because $50,000 is the amount of income. Answer (C) is incorrect because $130,000 is the sum of appreciation and income. Answer (D) is incorrect because $770,000 is the sum of the appreciation and the permanent endowment.

19.5 PRACTICE SIMULATION

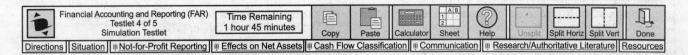

Financial Accounting and Reporting (FAR) Testlet 4 of 5 Simulation Testlet	Time Remaining 1 hour 45 minutes	Copy	Paste	Calculator	Sheet	Help	Unsplit	Split Horiz	Split Vert	Done

Directions | Situation | ⊞ Not-for-Profit Reporting | ⊞ Effects on Net Assets | ⊞ Cash Flow Classification | ⊞ Communication | ⊞ Research/Authoritative Literature | Resources

---

1. Directions

In the following simulation, you will be asked to complete various tasks. You may use the content in the **Information Tabs** to complete the tasks in the **Work Tabs**.

Information Tabs:

Directions	Resources

FIG 1

- Go through each of the **Information Tabs** to familiarize yourself with the simulation content
- The **Resources** tab will contain information, including formulas and definitions, that may help you to complete the tasks
- Your simulation may have more **Information Tabs** than those shown in Fig. 1

Work Tabs:

⊞ SysTrust	⊞ Engagement Letter	⊞ Authoritative Sources	⊞ Communication

FIG. 2

- **Work Tabs**, to the right of **Information Tabs**, contain the tasks for you to complete
- **Work Tabs** contain directions for completing each task - be sure to read these directions carefully
- The tab names in Fig. 2 are for illustration only - yours may differ
- Once you complete any part of a task, the pencil for that tab will be shaded (see **Communication** in Fig. 2)
- The shaded pencil does **NOT** indicate that you have completed the entire task
- You must complete all of the tasks in the **Work Tabs** to receive full credit

Research/Authoritative Literature Tab:

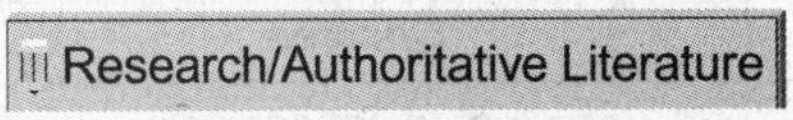

⊞ Research/Authoritative Literature

FIG. 3

- This tab contains both the Research task and the Authoritative Literature
- Detailed instructions for completing the Research task, and for using the Authoritative Literature, appear on this tab
- You may use the Authoritative Literature as a resource for completing other tasks

NOTE: If you believe you have encountered a software malfunction, report it to the test center staff immediately.

---

2. Situation

As a newly hired CPA with a large firm, you have been assigned to an audit of a national not-for-profit organization. You are eager to take on this challenge; however, you are not quite up to speed on certain concepts relating to not-for-profit organizations (NPOs). Thus, you have decided to review the main authoritative sources regarding accounting and reporting by NPOs.

3. Not-for-Profit Reporting

This question is presented in a check-the-box format that requires you to select the correct response from a given list. Designate whether each statement concerning financial reporting by NPOs is true or false.

		TRUE	FALSE
1.	Changes in net assets must be reported in three categories	☐	☐
2.	Balances in net assets must be reported in three categories	☐	☐
3.	Expenses paid from restricted funds reduce overall restricted net assets	☐	☐
4.	Expenses paid from restricted funds reduce overall unrestricted net assets	☐	☐
5.	Board-designated funds are classified as restricted	☐	☐
6.	NPOs must report functional expenses in a statement given equal prominence with the statement of activities	☐	☐
7.	Donated collections must be capitalized and recognized as revenue	☐	☐
8.	Donations held for the benefit of third-parties are recognized as liabilities	☐	☐
9.	Investments in debt and equity securities are reported at historical cost	☐	☐
10.	Income from restricted investments are always recognized as restricted	☐	☐

4. Effects on Net Assets

This set of questions has a matching format. Select the best match for each numbered item from the terms in the drop-down list and write its letter in the column provided. Each choice may be used once, more than once, or not at all. Determine the most likely classification(s) of net assets, if any, that is(are) affected by each transaction of a not-for-profit organization.

Transactions	Answers		Choices
1. Legally restricted gains.			A) Unrestricted net assets
2. Expenses reported by functional classification.			B) Temporarily restricted net assets
3. Contributions of services that do not create or enhance nonfinancial assets or require special skills.			C) Permanently restricted net assets
4. Unrestricted contribution of collection items to be held for financial gain.			D) No effect on net assets
5. Board-designated endowment.			
6. Expenses reported by natural classification.			
7. Conditional promise to give if the likelihood that the condition will not be met is more than remote.			
8. Unconditional promises to give cash with amounts due in future periods.			
9. Receipt of a gift of a long-lived asset for which the entity chooses to imply a time restriction.			
10. Gains and losses on a specific security required by the donor to be held permanently. No donor instruction was made regarding gains and losses.			

5. Cash Flow Classification

This set of questions has a matching format. Select the best match for each numbered item from the terms in the drop-down list and write its letter in the column provided. Each choice may be used once, more than once, or not at all. Choose the proper cash flow classification for each transaction.

Transactions	Answers
1. Purchase of equipment	
2. Insurance proceeds from fire loss on building	
3. Interest paid	
4. Principal payments on long-term debt	
5. Interest and dividend income donor-restricted for long-term purposes	
6. Cash paid to employees and suppliers	
7. Investment of a contribution donor-restricted to acquiring a plant	
8. Investment of a contribution donor-restricted to a term endowment	
9. Cash received from collection of unrestricted contributions receivable	
10. Proceeds from sale of investments	

Choices
A) Cash flows from operating activities
B) Cash flows from investing activities
C) Cash flows from financing activities

6. Communication

In a brief memorandum to a client, describe the requirements of the net assets model and what the model emphasizes. Also describe the main components of net assets. Type your communication in your word processor program and print out the copy in a memorandum-style format.

REMINDER: Your response will be graded for both technical content and writing skills. Technical content will be evaluated for information that is helpful to the intended reader and clearly relevant to the issue. Writing skills will be evaluated for development, organization, and the appropriate expression of ideas in professional correspondence. Use a standard business memo or letter format with a clear beginning, middle, and end. Do not convey information in the form of a table, bullet point list, or other abbreviated presentation.

TO: Client
FROM: CPA
Reference: The net assets model

7. Research/Authoritative Literature

See page 12 in the Introduction of this book for a detailed explanation of the AICPA's new Research/Authoritative Literature work tab as well as a screenshot of how the tab will actually look on your exam.

A not-for-profit organization may receive assets from a donor with the stipulation that they be used on behalf of a specified beneficiary. Research and cite the specific paragraph in either the FASB Current Text or Original Pronouncements that details the circumstances in which the assets should be recorded as a liability by the NPO.

Unofficial Answers

3. Not-for-Profit Reporting (10 Gradable Items)

1. <u>True.</u> SFAS 117, *Financial Statements of Not-for-Profit Organizations*, requires changes in net assets to be reported in all defined three categories: unrestricted, temporarily restricted, and permanently restricted.

2. <u>True.</u> SFAS 117, *Financial Statements of Not-for-Profit Organizations*, requires balances in net assets to be reported in all defined three categories: unrestricted, temporarily restricted, and permanently restricted.

3. <u>True.</u> Expenses paid from restricted funds are reported as reductions to restricted net assets under the subsection of revenues titled "net assets released from restrictions."

4. <u>False.</u> Expenses paid from restricted funds are reported in unrestricted net assets as both increases in revenues and increases in expenses, thus having a zero net effect.

5. <u>False.</u> Funds can only be reported as restricted when the donor places a restriction on their investment or use.

6. <u>False.</u> A statement of activities or the notes should provide information about expense reported by functional classification. However, only voluntary health and welfare organizations (VHWOs) are required to publish this information in the form of a separate statement.

7. <u>False.</u> Contributions of collection items, such as art works and historical treasures, need not be capitalized and recognized as revenues if they are (a) held for public exhibition, education, or research in furtherance of public service rather than financial gain; (b) protected, kept unencumbered, cared for, and preserved; and (c) subject to a policy that requires the proceeds of their sale to be used to acquire other collection items.

8. <u>True.</u> A recipient NPO that accepts cash or other financial assets recognizes the fair value of the assets as a liability to the specified beneficiary when it recognizes the assets received from the donor (SFAS 136, *Transfer of Assets to a Not-for-Profit Organization or Charitable Trust That Raises or Holds Contributions for Others*).

9. <u>False.</u> Equity securities with readily determinable fair values and all debt securities are to be measured at fair value in the statement of financial position.

10. <u>False.</u> Investment income is reported when earned as increases in unrestricted net assets, barring a donor restriction. It is reported as an increase in temporarily restricted or permanently restricted net assets given a donor-imposed restriction.

4. Effects on Net Assets (10 Gradable Items)

1. <u>B) Temporarily restricted net assets or C) Permanently restricted net assets.</u> Gains and losses are increases or decreases in unrestricted net assets unless their use is temporarily or permanently restricted by explicit donor stipulations or by law.

2. <u>A) Unrestricted net assets.</u> A statement of activities or the notes should provide information about expenses reported by functional classification, e.g., by major classes of program services and supporting services. However, whether the classification of expenses is functional or natural (e.g., salaries, rent, depreciation, etc.), they are reported as decreases in unrestricted net assets in the statement of activities.

3. <u>D) No effect on net assets.</u> Contributions of services are recognized if they create or enhance nonfinancial assets, or require special skills, are provided by those having such skills, and would usually be purchased if not obtained by donations.

4. <u>A) Unrestricted net assets.</u> Contributions of collection items, such as art works and historical treasures, need not be capitalized and recognized as revenues if they are held for public exhibition, education, or research in furtherance of public service rather than financial gain; protected, kept unencumbered, cared for, and preserved; and subject to a policy that requires the proceeds of their sale to be used to acquire other collection items.

5. <u>D) No effect on net assets.</u> Unrestricted net assets arise from providing goods and services and from receipts of contributions and dividends or interest, minus expenses. The only limits are the nature of the organization, its environment, its specified purposes, and contractual agreements. Significant contractual limits, including loan covenants, are described in the notes. Self-imposed limits, e.g., voluntary designation of a portion of unrestricted net assets as an endowment (a board-designated endowment), are described in the notes or on the statements. Accordingly, a board-designated endowment does not increase or decrease any component of net assets.

6. <u>A) Unrestricted net assets.</u> Voluntary health and welfare organizations (VHWOs) report information about expenses by functional classification and natural classification (salaries, rent, interest, depreciation, etc.) in a matrix format in a separate statement of functional expenses. Other NPOs are encouraged but not required to provide information about expenses by natural classification. However, whether expenses are classified as functional or natural, they are still decreases in unrestricted net assets.

7. <u>D) No effect on net assets.</u> Conditional promises to give are recognized when the conditions are substantially met. A conditional promise is considered unconditional if the likelihood is remote that the condition will not be met. Consequently, this promise should not be recognized.

8. <u>B) Temporarily restricted net assets.</u> Unconditional promises to give with amounts due in future periods are reported as restricted support unless the circumstances clearly indicate that the donor intended support for current activities. Thus, unconditional promises of future cash amounts usually increase temporarily restricted net assets.

9. <u>B) Temporarily restricted net assets.</u> Gifts of long-lived assets (or other assets required to be used to acquire them) may be received without stipulations about their use. In this case, if the entity's choice of accounting policy is to imply a time restriction expiring over their useful life, the gifts are reported as temporarily restricted support.

10. <u>C) Permanently restricted net assets.</u> If a specific security is to be held permanently, the gains and losses on that security are assumed to be changes in permanently restricted net assets absent a contrary donor instruction.

5. Cash Flow Classification (10 Gradable Items)

1. <u>B) Cash flows from investing activities.</u> Investing activities include making and collecting loans and acquiring and disposing of debt or equity instruments and property, plant, and equipment and other productive assets. These assets are held for or used in the production of goods or services (other than the materials held in inventory). Investing activities exclude transactions in cash equivalents and in certain loans or other debt or equity instruments acquired specifically for resale.

2. <u>B) Cash flows from investing activities.</u> Investing activities include making and collecting loans and acquiring and disposing of debt or equity instruments and property, plant, and equipment and other productive assets. These assets are held for or used in the production of goods or services (other than the materials held in inventory). Investing activities exclude transactions in cash equivalents and in certain loans or other debt or equity instruments acquired specifically for resale.

3. <u>A) Cash flows from operating activities.</u> Operating activities include all transactions and other events not classified as investing and financing activities. They usually include producing and selling goods and providing services. In principle, operating cash flows are the cash effects of items included in the determination of net income or the change in net assets.

4. <u>C) Cash flows from financing activities.</u> Financing activities include the issuance of stock, the payment of dividends, treasury stock transactions, the issuance of debt, and the repayment or other settlement of debt obligations. They also include receiving donor-restricted resources that must be used for long-term purposes, for example, contributions and investment income that are donor-restricted to acquiring, constructing, or improving long-lived assets or to establishing or increasing a permanent or term endowment.

5. <u>C) Cash flows from financing activities.</u> Financing activities include the issuance of stock, the payment of dividends, treasury stock transactions, the issuance of debt, and the repayment or other settlement of debt obligations. They also include receiving donor-restricted resources that must be used for long-term purposes, for example, contributions and investment income that are donor-restricted to acquiring, constructing, or improving long-lived assets or to establishing or increasing a permanent or term endowment.

6. <u>A) Cash flows from operating activities.</u> Operating activities include all transactions and other events not classified as investing and financing activities. They usually include producing and selling goods and providing services. In principle, operating cash flows are the cash effects of items included in the determination of net income or the change in net assets.

7. <u>C) Cash flows from financing activities.</u> Financing activities include the issuance of stock, the payment of dividends, treasury stock transactions, the issuance of debt, and the repayment or other settlement of debt obligations. They also include receiving donor-restricted resources that must be used for long-term purposes, for example, contributions and investment income that are donor-restricted to acquiring, constructing, or improving long-lived assets or to establishing or increasing a permanent or term endowment.

8. <u>C) Cash flows from financing activities.</u> Financing activities include the issuance of stock, the payment of dividends, treasury stock transactions, the issuance of debt, and the repayment or other settlement of debt obligations. They also include receiving donor-restricted resources that must be used for long-term purposes, for example, contributions and investment income that are donor-restricted to acquiring, constructing, or improving long-lived assets or to establishing or increasing a permanent or term endowment.

9. <u>A) Cash flows from operating activities.</u> Operating activities include all transactions and other events not classified as investing and financing activities. They usually include producing and selling goods and providing services. In principle, operating cash flows are the cash effects of items included in the determination of net income or the change in net assets.

10. <u>B) Cash flows from investing activities.</u> Investing activities include making and collecting loans and acquiring and disposing of debt or equity instruments and property, plant, and equipment and other productive assets. These assets are held for or used in the production of goods or services (other than the materials held in inventory). Investing activities exclude transactions in cash equivalents and in certain loans or other debt or equity instruments acquired specifically for resale.

6. Communication (5 Gradable Items; for grading instructions, please refer to page 12.)

The net assets model requires reporting of the amounts of unrestricted, temporarily restricted, and permanently restricted net assets in a statement of financial position as of the end of the reporting period. It also requires changes in the classes of net assets, including the effects of reclassification, to be reported in a statement of activities, and that a statement of cash flows be presented. The net assets model emphasizes aggregated information about the entity as a whole, not individual funds. Consequently, fund accounting is not required for external reporting. However, it may be used for internal record-keeping purposes. Furthermore, disaggregated fund information may be disclosed in external financial reports as long as the required aggregated information is reported.

Permanently restricted net assets arise from asset increases and decreases subject to restrictions not removable by passage of time or by the organization's actions. They may result from reclassifications within the classes of net assets created by donor stipulations. Temporarily restricted net assets result from restrictions removable by the passage of time (time restrictions) or by the actions of the NPO (purpose restrictions).

Information about restrictions is provided either on the statement or in the notes. Restrictions are donor-imposed, not self-imposed. Permanent restrictions on holdings of assets (e.g., land or art works) may arise when they are donated with stipulations that they be used for a specified purpose, be preserved, and not be sold. Donations also may be invested as a permanent source of income (permanent endowment funds). Temporary restrictions may be for support of operating activities, investment for a specified term (term endowments), use in a specified future period, or acquisition of long-lived assets.

Unrestricted net assets arise from providing goods and services and from receipts of contributions and dividends or interest, minus expenses. The only limits are the nature of the organization, its environment, its specified purposes, and contractual agreements. Significant contractual limits, including loan covenants, are described in the notes. Self-imposed limits, e.g., voluntary designation of a portion of unrestricted net assets as an endowment (a board-designated endowment), are described in the notes or on the statements.

7. Research/Authoritative Literature (1 Gradable Item)

Answer: FAS 136, Par. 17.

FAS 136 -- *Transfers of Assets to a Not-for-Profit Organization or Charitable Trust That Raises or Holds Contributions for Others*

Transfers of Assets That Are Not Contributions

17. A transfer of assets to a recipient organization is not a contribution and shall be accounted for as an asset by the resource provider and as a liability by the recipient organization if one or more of the following conditions is present:

a.   The transfer is subject to the resource provider's unilateral right to redirect the use of the assets to another beneficiary.

b.   The transfer is accompanied by the resource provider's conditional promise to give or is otherwise revocable or repayable.

c.   The resource provider controls the recipient organization and specifies an unaffiliated beneficiary.

d.   The resource provider specifies itself or its affiliate as the beneficiary and the transfer is not an equity transaction.

Scoring Schedule:

	Correct Responses		Gradable Items		Weights		
Tab 3	_____	÷	10	×	15%	=	_____
Tab 4	_____	÷	10	×	20%	=	_____
Tab 5	_____	÷	10	×	20%	=	_____
Tab 6	_____	÷	5	×	30%	=	_____
Tab 7	_____	÷	1	×	15%	=	_____
							_____
							(Your Score)

Use Gleim's **CPA Gleim Online** to practice more simulations in a realistic environment.

STUDY UNIT TWENTY
NOT-FOR-PROFIT ACCOUNTING AND REPORTING

(14 pages of outline)

The AICPA has issued audit and accounting guides applicable to nongovernmental not-for-profit organizations (NPOs) and to governmental and nongovernmental health care organizations (HCOs). These guides, which supersede all prior NPO and HCO pronouncements, incorporate certain provisions of the FASB statements applying the net assets model. (See the outlines in Study Unit 19, which should be followed even if other pronouncements address the same classes of transactions.)

The NPO guide has replaced prior specialized guidance on accounting and reporting for nongovernmental colleges and universities, voluntary health and welfare organizations (VHWOs), and other NPOs. The HCO guide applies to (1) for-profit nongovernmental, (2) not-for-profit but business-oriented nongovernmental, and (3) governmental entities.

In addition, nongovernmental NPOs should follow FASB Statements and Interpretations, APB Opinions, ARBs, and certain other applicable guidance included in the GAAP hierarchy (Guides, SOPs, etc.). However, a specific pronouncement may exempt NPOs, or its subject matter may preclude applicability.

20.1 NOT-FOR-PROFIT ORGANIZATIONS (NPOs)

1. The AICPA Audit and Accounting Guide *Not-for-Profit Organizations* applies to an entity that meets the definition of an NPO in SFAS 116:

   An entity that possesses the following characteristics that distinguish it from a business enterprise: (a) contributions of significant amounts of resources from resource providers who do not expect commensurate or proportionate pecuniary return, (b) operating purposes other than to provide goods or services at a profit, and (c) absence of ownership interests like those of business enterprises.

   a. However, an entity may qualify as an NPO without having all three characteristics. For example, an NPO may receive no contributions.

   b. Governmental organizations or entities controlled by governments are excluded.

2. SFAS 117, *Financial Statements of Not-for-Profit Organizations*, which is outlined in Study Unit 19, defines the **basic financial statements**. This study unit will present some additional considerations.

   a. If a prior year's financial information is summarized and does not include the minimum required by GAAP, the nature of the prior-year information should be described using appropriate titles on the face of the financial statements and in a note.

   b. An NPO may not be in compliance with donor-imposed restrictions. The result could be a material contingent liability, a material loss of future revenue, or an inability to continue as a going concern, so disclosure is necessary given at least a reasonable possibility of such a result.

   c. Entities should include in their financial statements information about the nature of their operations, use of estimates, and certain concentrations of risk.

3. **Cash and cash equivalents** should be included as a separate item in a statement of financial position. Cash that is donor-restricted or set aside for long-term purposes should not be classified with current assets.

   a. Information about the nature and amount of limitations on the use of cash should be included on the face of the statements or in the notes. Disclosure should also be made of unusual circumstances or of failure to maintain cash balances to meet donor restrictions.

4. **Contributions received** should be distinguished from other transactions.

   a. A contribution is a voluntary nonowner transfer of resources without direct receipt of something of equal value in exchange. When an entity voluntarily transfers assets to an NPO, the extent of discretion the NPO has over the use of the assets must be determined. If it has little discretion, the transaction is an agency transaction. If it has discretion, the transaction is a contribution, an exchange, or combination of the two.

      1) Amounts received in an **agency transaction** should be reported as increases in assets and liabilities; distributions should be reported as decreases in those accounts. Cash received and paid should be reported in the operating activities section of the statement of cash flows.

      2) **Gifts in kind**, such as property, equipment, and inventory, that can be used or sold should be measured at fair value after considering the quality and quantity of the gifts and any applicable discounts. The difference between the amount ultimately received and the fair value is recognized as an adjustment to the original contributions.

      3) "**Exchange transactions** are reciprocal transfers in which each party receives and sacrifices something of approximately equal value" (SFAS 116). The issue is to distinguish exchanges from contributions.

         a) The cost of premiums given to potential donors in a mass fund-raising appeal is a fund-raising expense related to exchange transactions. The cost of premiums given to acknowledge contributions is also a fund-raising expense, provided the cost is nominal in relation to the contributions.

      4) **Dues** from members may have elements of both a contribution and an exchange if members receive tangible or intangible benefits from membership.

         a) **Revenue** from dues in exchange transactions is recognized over the period to which the dues relate. **Nonrefundable fees** received in exchange transactions are recognized as revenues when they become receivable if future fees are expected to cover the costs of future services to members. If **current fees** are expected to cover those costs, they should be recognized over the average duration of membership, the life expectancy of members, etc.

      5) **Grants, awards, or sponsorships** are contributions if the resource providers receive no value or if the value is incidental to the potential public benefit. The transfers are exchange transactions if the potential public benefit is secondary.

      6) **Resources received in exchange transactions** are classified as **unrestricted** revenues and net assets, even when resource providers limit the use of the resources.

b. **Recognition principles** for contributions depend on whether the donor has imposed conditions, restrictions, or both.

   1) A **promise is unconditional** if the possibility is remote that any condition will not be met.

   2) A **conditional transfer of assets** is accounted for as a refundable advance until the conditions have been substantially met or explicitly waived.

   3) Conditions may be substantially met in **stages**. Thus, part of the contribution should be recognized as revenue as each stage is met.

   4) Contributions may have **donor-imposed restrictions** that are permanent or temporary. They also may be explicit or implicit in the circumstances.

      a) Donors can impose a restriction on a contribution by requiring that the NPO restrict a stated amount of its **unrestricted net assets**.

      b) If an **expense** is incurred for a purpose for which unrestricted and temporarily restricted net assets are available, a restriction is met. However, it is not met if the expense is for a purpose that is **directly attributable** to another specific external source of revenue.

      c) An organization may adopt a **policy of implying time restrictions** on the use of long-lived contributed assets that expire over the expected useful lives. These contributions are restricted support that increases temporarily restricted net assets, depreciation is recorded over the useful lives, and net assets are reclassified from temporarily restricted to unrestricted as depreciation is recognized.

         i) **Gains and losses on disposal** are changes in unrestricted net assets, and a reclassification is reported for any remaining temporarily restricted net assets.

         ii) If an NPO adopts a **policy of not implying time restrictions** in these circumstances, a contribution of long-lived assets without donor-imposed time restrictions is unrestricted.

   5) **Promises to give** are reported as contribution revenue and receivables if they are, in substance, unconditional. The promises need not be legally enforceable.

      a) A **conditional promise** is recognized when the conditions are substantially met. An unconditional promise is recognized when the promise is received.

      b) An **intention to give**, for example, a communication from an individual indicating that the NPO has been included in the individual's will, is not an unconditional promise to give.

   6) **Contributed services** (and the related assets and expenses) are recognized if

      a) Employees of separately governed affiliated organizations regularly perform services under the direction of the recipient NPO and

      b) Recognition criteria are met.

   7) **Contributed use of utilities or long-lived assets** is recognized as contribution **revenue** when the contribution is received. **Expense** is recognized when use occurs.

      a) **Fair value** may be estimated from rate schedules.

      b) If the contribution is an **unconditional promise** to give for a specified period, the promise should be reported as **contributions receivable**. Moreover, it is treated as restricted support that increases temporarily restricted net assets.

    c.   **Measurement principles** for contributions.

         1)   Contribution revenue is measured at **fair value**, but unconditional promises to give expected to be collected within 1 year may be measured at their **net realizable value**.

             a)   The fair value of unconditional promises to give cash expected to be collected in 1 year or more is the **present value** of the estimated future cash flows.

             b)   The fair value of **contributed services** is based on the more readily determinable of the fair value of the services received or the fair value of the assets created.

             c)   Fair value is best measured by **quoted market prices**. If they are not available, measurement is by quoted market prices of similar assets, replacement cost, independent appraisals, or discounted cash flows.

             d)   Fair value should be measured when any **conditions** are met.

             e)   The fair value of **unconditional promises to give noncash assets** is the **present value of the expected fair value** of the underlying assets expected to be received. The assumption is that receipt is 1 year or more after the balance sheet date. The likelihood that the promise will be kept should be considered in determining the expected fair value.

         2)   **Discounting.** The present value of unconditional promises to give is based on the **risk-free rate** appropriate for the expected term of the promise.

             a)   **Discounts** on contributions receivable are amortized using the **interest method**. Amortization is a component of contribution revenue. It is an increase in the net asset class in which the promise was originally reported. **Contributions receivable** is reported net of the discount.

         3)   **Subsequent Measurement**

             a)   **Decreases in fair value** of unconditional promises to give may result from changes in the quantity or nature of assets expected to be received. They are recognized as expenses or losses in the appropriate net asset class when the expectation changes.

                 i)   No increase in net assets is recognized if the **fair value increases**, except for recoveries of previously recognized decreases. Amounts collected, other than such recoveries, in excess of the carrying amount of contributions receivable are contribution revenue.

             b)   The fair value of unconditional promises to give **equity securities with readily determinable fair values or debt securities** may change. Such a change should be reported as an increase or a decrease in contribution revenue when the change occurs.

             c)   Decreases in the fair value of unconditional promises to give other **noncash assets** should be reported as decreases in contribution revenue when the decreases occur. No additional revenue should be recognized if the expected fair value increases.

5.   **Split-Interest Agreements (SIAs)**

    a.   Under trusts or other arrangements, NPOs may share benefits with others.

         1)   SIAs may be **revocable or irrevocable**.

         2)   The **period covered** may be a specific number of years (or in perpetuity) or the remaining life of a designated individual or individuals.

         3)   The assets are invested by the NPO, a trustee, or a fiscal agent. **Distributions** are made to beneficiaries during the term of the agreement.

4) At the end of the agreement, the remaining assets are distributed to or retained by either the NPO or another beneficiary.

5) If the NPO has a **lead interest**, it receives distributions during the agreement's term. If it has a **remainder interest**, the donor (or others designated by the donor) receives those distributions, and the NPO receives all or part of the assets remaining at the end of the agreement.

b. **Recognition and Measurement**

1) Assets received under **irrevocable SIAs** are recorded at fair value. The contribution is recognized as a revenue or gain. Liabilities incurred in the exchange part of an SIA are also recognized.

2) Absent conditions, **contribution revenue and related assets and liabilities** are recognized when an irrevocable SIA naming the NPO trustee or fiscal agent is executed.

a) If a third party acts as trustee or fiscal agent, recognition occurs when the NPO is notified of the agreement.

b) The third party may have **variance power**, or the NPO may have only **conditional rights** to the benefits. In these situations, contribution revenue and related assets and liabilities are not recognized until the NPO has an unconditional right to receive benefits.

3) A **revocable SIA** is accounted for as an intention to give. If an NPO serves as trustee under a revocable SIA, assets received are recognized at fair value when received and as refundable advances.

a) **Contribution revenue** is not recognized until the SIA becomes irrevocable or the assets are distributed to the NPO for its unconditional use.

b) **Income on assets** not available for the NPO's unconditional use and any subsequent adjustments to their carrying amount are treated as adjustments to the assets and as refundable advances.

4) Upon initial recognition of an unconditional irrevocable SIA, contributions are measured at **fair value**.

a) **Changes in fair value** of SIAs are recognized in a statement of activities and classified in the appropriate net assets category.

5) When an SIA **terminates**, related assets and liabilities are closed. Remaining amounts are recognized as changes in the value of SIAs and classified in the appropriate net assets category.

6. **Other Assets**

a. NPOs may sell **inventory** obtained in transactions or from contributions. Contributions of inventory are reported when received at fair value.

b. The recognition and measurement of **prepaid expenses, deferred charges, and similar costs** are based on the same principles used by business organizations.

c. **Collections** are works of art, historical treasures, etc., that meet the criteria in SFAS 116. When an NPO initially adopts SFAS 116, it may choose to capitalize its collections, including all items not previously capitalized; to capitalize only those items acquired after initial adoption of SFAS 116; or not to capitalize collections. Capitalization of part of the collections is not permitted.

1) If an NPO **capitalizes collections**, items acquired in exchange transactions are recognized as assets and measured at cost. Contributed items are recognized as assets and as contributions in the appropriate net asset class and measured at fair value.

2) If an NPO does **not capitalize collections**, no assets or contributions are recognized. Cash flows are reported as investing activities.

   a) The NPO reports costs as a decrease in the appropriate class of net assets; it reports proceeds from sale or from insurance recoveries as an increase.

3) **Contributions** by an NPO of previously recognized collection items are expenses and decreases in assets and may be measured at fair value. A gain or loss may be recognized. Contributions of previously unrecognized collection items are not recognized; disclosure is made in the notes.

4) Works of art, historical treasures, etc., that are not collection items are recognized as assets and disclosed separately.

5) If collections are **capitalized prospectively**, proceeds from sales and insurance recoveries of items not previously capitalized are reported separately from revenues, expenses, gains, and losses.

7. **Investments**

   a. SFAS 124 applies only to investments in debt securities and in equity securities with readily determinable fair values that are not accounted for under the equity method and not consolidated. Moreover, it does not apply to derivatives subject to SFAS 133, *Accounting for Derivative Instruments and Hedging Activities*.

      1) However, if an instrument that is subject to SFAS 124 has an **embedded derivative**, the host instrument is still within the scope of SFAS 124.

      2) An NPO that does not report earnings separately in a statement of financial performance ordinarily reports gain (loss) on a hedging instrument or a nonhedging derivative as a **change in net assets**.

      3) Derivatives are discussed in Study Unit 16. They must be recorded as assets or liabilities and measured at fair value.

   b. **Purchased investments** are initially recorded at acquisition cost. Those received as contributions or through agency transactions are recorded at fair value.

   c. **Investment income** is recognized as earned. The revenue is an increase in the appropriate class of net assets.

      1) A statement of activities ordinarily reports gross amounts of revenues and expenses, but investment revenues may be reported net of related expenses if the amount of expenses is disclosed.

   d. SFAS 124 and SFAS 133 provide for **fair value accounting**, but guidance concerning other investments subsequent to acquisition is varied because measurement principles in these cases have not been changed by the new guide.

   e. **Investment pools** may be created for portfolio management. Ownership interests (units) are assigned to the pool categories (participants) based on the market value of the cash and securities obtained from each participant. Current market value also determines the units allocated to additional assets placed in the pool and the value of withdrawals.

   f. Realized and unrealized losses may be **netted** against realized and unrealized gains.

      1) An NPO may manage investments on a **total return basis**. The emphasis is on the overall return. A spending-rate formula determines how much of the return to use for current operations.

      2) In addition to other disclosures, NPOs should provide information about financial instruments in accordance with **GAAP**.

8. **Property and equipment (P&E)** consist of long-lived tangible assets, including the contributed use of facilities and equipment, except collection items and investment assets.

    a. The **recognition and measurement** principles for P&E obtained in exchange transactions are similar to those of businesses.

    b. P&E used in exchange transactions in which the **provider retains title** should be reported as a contribution only if it is probable that the NPO will keep the assets.

    c. The amount initially recognized for contributed P&E includes all costs incurred to place the assets in use.

    d. Under SFAS 93, *Recognition of Depreciation by Not-for-Profit Organizations*, NPOs recognize **depreciation** for most P&E. Items not depreciated are land used as a building site and certain individual works of art and historical treasures with very long useful lives.

        1) An **art work** or **historical treasure** is nondepreciable only if verifiable evidence supports the conclusions that

            a) It has "cultural, aesthetic, or historical value worth preserving perpetually;" and

            b) The holder has the means of, and is, preserving its full service potential.

        2) Depreciation **decreases unrestricted net assets**.

            a) If contributed P&E have donor-imposed restrictions, temporarily restricted net assets should be **reclassified** as unrestricted as the restrictions expire. The amount reclassified may not be equal to the related depreciation. The amount reclassified is based on the length of the restrictions, whereas depreciation is based on the useful economic life.

        3) Reclassifications are also required when an accounting policy implies a **time restriction** on contributions that expires over the useful life of the contributed assets. Reclassifications are included in net assets released from restrictions in a statement of activities.

    e. Under SFAS 144, *Accounting for the Impairment or Disposal of Long-Lived Assets*, when the carrying amount of a long-lived asset or asset group may not be recoverable, it should be tested for impairment. If the carrying amount exceeds fair value and is not recoverable (future estimated undiscounted cash flows are less than the carrying amount), a loss is recognized for the excess of the carrying amount over fair value.

        1) A long-lived asset (disposal group) not classified as held and used is classified as **held for sale** if the criteria in SFAS 144 are met. It is then measured at the lower of carrying amount or fair value minus cost to sell.

    f. SFAS 143, *Accounting for Asset Retirement Obligations*, applies to an ARO related to a tangible long-lived asset. The associated **asset retirement cost (ARC)** is added to the carrying amount of the tangible long-lived asset when an ARO is recognized. The initial ARC debit equals the initial ARO credit.

        1) An **asset retirement obligation (ARO)** is a legal obligation arising from acquisition, construction, development, or normal operation of an asset.

        2) The **fair value** of the ARO liability is recognized when incurred. If a reasonable estimate of the fair value cannot be made at that time, the ARO will be recognized when such an estimate can be made. If an asset with an ARO is acquired, the acquirer records a liability on the acquisition date as if the ARO had been incurred at that time.

    g. **Gains and losses** on P&E, including impairment losses, are classified as changes in unrestricted net assets, absent a basis for a restriction.

9.   **Debt and Other Liabilities**

    a.   Obligations of NPOs arising from **tax-exempt financing** arranged by state and local authorities are reported as liabilities.

    b.   NPOs are usually tax-exempt but may be taxed on portions of their income. Thus, **current and deferred tax liabilities (and assets)** may also arise.

    c.   **Deferred revenue** is recognized when resources are received in transactions with service beneficiaries for specific activities that have not yet occurred.

    d.   **Advances from third parties**, e.g., government agencies, are liabilities if they are based on estimated costs of providing services to constituents to the extent such services have not yet been performed. Liabilities are also recognized for receipts of resources from third parties for loans to the NPO's constituents.

    e.   An NPO must recognize a liability for an **unconditional promise to give** when it is obligated to transfer the promised asset, ordinarily when the donor approves the specific grant or the donee is notified. Payments to be made over several periods are measured at present value.

        1)   The **interest method** is used to amortize discounts on contributions payable measured at present value.

    f.   **Annuity obligations.** Some contributions received by NPOs create obligations to make future payments to others. These annuity obligations are recognized as liabilities and measured at the present value of the actuarially determined obligations. Revaluations of these liabilities are reported as changes in the appropriate net asset classes.

    g.   Amounts held under **agency transactions** may be liabilities of an NPO. See the outline of SFAS 136 in Study Unit 19.

    h.   **Loss contingencies** may arise from, for example, failure to comply with donor-imposed restrictions or from uncertainties about the NPO's tax-exempt status.

10. NPOs account for **net assets** (a residual interest) in accordance with SFAS 117, which requires that three classes of net assets be reported: unrestricted, temporarily restricted, and permanently restricted.

11. **Revenues and Receivables from Exchange Transactions**

    a.   Exchange transactions resulting in revenues for NPOs usually involve providing goods or services to beneficiaries for a fee.

    b.   Determining whether an increase in net assets is a revenue or a gain is based on the relationship of the transaction to the NPO's activities.

    c.   An NPO's **recognition, measurement, and display** of revenues and related receivables resulting from exchange transactions are usually consistent with the GAAP applicable to for-profit entities. Revenues from exchange transactions are increases in unrestricted net assets. Moreover, classifications in addition to the three net asset classes (for example, operating and nonoperating) may be used in a statement of activities.

12. **Expenses, gains, and losses** of NPOs are similar to those of for-profit entities.

    a.   Some expense recognition issues are unique to NPOs. Thus, expenses are treated as decreases in unrestricted net assets. In addition,

        1)   **Fund-raising costs**, including the cost of special events, are expensed as incurred even if they result in contributions in future periods.

        2)   **Reductions in amounts charged** for goods or services, for example, financial aid provided by an educational institution, are expenses if they are given in an exchange transaction. Reductions given other than in exchange transactions are expenses to the extent the NPO incurs incremental expense; they are discounts if incremental expense is not incurred.

3) **Advertising costs** are expensed either when incurred or when the advertising first occurs, except for direct-response advertising that results in probable future benefits. Such advertising should be capitalized.

    a) Fund-raising is not considered advertising.

4) Start-up costs and organization costs are expensed as incurred.

5) AICPA SOP 98-1, *Accounting for the Costs of Computer Software Developed or Obtained for Internal Use*, describes when software is for internal use and when its costs may be expensed or capitalized.

b. **Gains and Losses**

1) How **costs related to sales** are displayed depends on whether the sales constitute a major activity or an incidental activity. For example, a major fund-raising activity should report and display separately the revenues from sales and the related cost of sales. If sales relate to a program service, the cost of sales is a program expense. In another case, cost of sales could be reported as a separate supporting service.

    a) If sales relate to an **incidental activity**, gains or losses from those sales, and the receipts and related costs, may be offset. Only the net gains or losses are reported.

2) **Investment revenues** may be reported net of related expenses, e.g., custodial costs and internal and external investment advisory costs, given adequate disclosure. Expenses netted against investment revenues are reported by their functional classification. Realized and unrealized investment losses may be netted against realized and unrealized gains.

c. **Expenses** (but not losses) are reported by their **functional classification**.

1) The number of classifications for **program services** varies with the nature of the services. Thus, a university may have programs for student instruction, research, and public service.

    a) The components of total program expenses should be provided on the face of the statement of activities or in the notes. Total program expenses should be reconciled with the amount in the statement of activities.

d. NPOs have various **supporting activities**, e.g., management and general, fund-raising, and membership development. Some industries have **functional categories** of supporting activities. Thus, a college usually has institutional support and institutional development activities. One functional reporting classification usually suffices for each supporting service, but more detailed disaggregated information for each kind of supporting service may be given.

1) **Management and general activities** are not identifiable with a single program, but they are essential to an NPO's existence. These activities include oversight, business management, general record keeping, budgeting, financing, soliciting revenue from exchange transactions, and management and administration except direct conduct of program services or fund-raising.

2) **Fund-raising activities** persuade potential donors to contribute money, services, their time, etc. These activities include fund-raising campaigns, maintaining donor mailing lists, special fund-raising events, and preparing and distributing fund-raising materials.

a) AICPA SOP 98-2, *Accounting for Costs of Activities of Not-for-Profit Organizations and State and Local Governmental Entities That Include Fund Raising*, applies to allocation of **costs of joint activities**. These activities include not only fund-raising but also program or management and general functions. If the criteria of purpose, audience, and content are met, any costs of a joint activity that are **identifiable** with a given function are assigned to that function. The remaining costs of the joint activity **(joint costs)** are allocated on a rational and systematic basis between fund-raising and the given program or management and general function.

i) Thus, the joint activity's **purpose** must include accomplishing program or management and general functions.

ii) The **audience** for the joint activity must not be selected solely for its ability or likelihood to contribute. It must

- Have a reasonable potential for use of the program component of the activity,
- Be able to assist in meeting the program component's goals, or
- Have a reasonable potential for use of the management and general component or be the group toward which that component must be directed.

iii) The **content** of the joint activity must support program or management and general functions.

iv) If all criteria are not met, all costs of the joint activity are treated as fund-raising costs except for costs of goods or services provided in exchange transactions.

3) If no significant benefits accrue to membership, **membership-development activities** may in substance be fund-raising, and the related costs are fund-raising costs. Membership development activities conducted in conjunction with other activities require allocation of costs.

e. Some expenses can be assigned to one major program or service or one supporting activity. Other expenses relate to more than one program or supporting activity, or a combination.

1) **Direct identification** (assignment) of specific expenses with programs, services, or support activities is preferable when feasible. Otherwise, these expenses are allocated. A reasonable allocation should be made on an objective basis.

a) For example, the cost of a direct-mail solicitation may need to be allocated between fund-raising (a supporting service) and the NPO's educational mission (a program service).

f. Payments or other support provided to **affiliated organizations** are reported by functional classification if practicable, even if the entire amount cannot be allocated to functions. Payments that cannot be allocated to functions are considered a separate supporting service and reported separately.

g. **Federated fund-raising organizations** make grants and awards to other NPOs. Their fund-raising activities, including those related to fund-raising for others, are reported as fund-raising expenses.

h. The following diagram summarizes the composition of functional expenses for a not-for-profit organization:

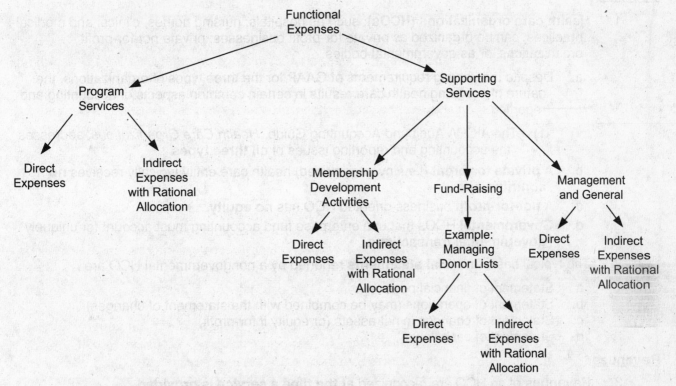

13. **Tax considerations.** NPOs should be aware of relevant tax laws and regulations and their effect on the financial statements. Failure to maintain **tax-exempt status** may have serious tax consequences and affect both the financial statements and related disclosures.

   a. In addition to the tax-exempt entities created by **federal law**, other exemptions may be created by **state law**. NPOs are subject to the laws of the state of incorporation and the laws of states where they conduct significant activities.

   b. The **IRS** may revoke exemptions for any of several reasons. States also have regulatory bodies that can revoke state tax-exempt status without regard to federal tax-exempt status. **Revocation** of an NPO's federal tax-exempt status may be based on, for example,

   1) Material changes in the NPO's character, purpose, or method of operation;
   2) Inappropriate insider transactions;
   3) Private benefit to insiders or outsiders, other than incidental benefits;
   4) Commerciality as the NPO's primary purpose; and
   5) Political campaign activities.

   c. Most tax-exempt organizations, except those with less than $25,000 in gross receipts or churches, must file **annual information returns**. States also have registration and filing requirements, some including audited financial statements.

   d. The IRS considers all **charitable organizations** to be private foundations unless they qualify as public charities. **Private foundations** are subject to numerous restrictions, including an excise tax on net investment income. However, **public charities** are exempt from federal unemployment taxes.

   e. Unrelated business income of NPOs is subject to federal corporate taxes on income, including the alternative minimum tax.

Stop and review! You have completed the outline for this subunit. Study multiple-choice questions 1 through 14 beginning on page 740.

20.2 HEALTH CARE ORGANIZATIONS (HCOs)

Overview

1. **Health care organizations (HCOs)**, such as hospitals, nursing homes, clinics, and medical practices, can be organized as private for-profit businesses; private not-for-profit organizations; or as governmental bodies.

   a. Despite the varying requirements of GAAP for the three types of organizations, the nature of providing health care results in certain common aspects of accounting and reporting.

      1) The AICPA Audit and Accounting Guide, *Health Care Organizations*, addresses the accounting and reporting issues of **all three types**.

   b. A **private for-profit** (i.e., investor-owned) health care entity typically receives **no contributions**.

   c. A **not-for-profit** business-oriented HCO has **no equity**.

   d. **Governmental** HCOs that use enterprise fund accounting must account for uniquely **governmental transactions**.

2. The typical basic **financial statements** reported by a nongovernmental HCO are

   a. Statement of financial position
   b. Statement of operations (may be combined with the statement of changes)
   c. Statement of changes in net assets (or equity if for-profit)
   d. Statement of cash flows

Revenues

3. **Revenues** of an HCO are recognized **at the time a service is provided**.

   a. The **three principal sources of HCO revenue** are patient service revenue, premium revenue, and resident service revenue.

4. **Patient service revenues** are recorded on an accrual basis at the provider's established rates, that is, at their **gross amount**.

   a. A substantial amount of health care is paid for by **third-party payors**, such as insurance companies and the federal government.

      1) Because the collection practices of the two types of payors are so different, they are **recorded separately** in the accounting records.

Accounts receivable – third-party payors	$1,400,000	
Accounts receivable – patients	320,000	
Patient service revenues		$1,720,000

   b. A certain number of patients will prove unable or unwilling to pay the amounts they have been billed. An HCO establishes an **allowance account** in the same manner as a for-profit entity.

Bad debt expense ($320,000 × 5%)	$16,000	
Allowance for uncollectible accounts		$16,000

   c. HCOs acknowledge that certain patients cannot be expected to pay.

      1) These **charity care** amounts cannot justifiably be treated as receivables because, at the time the service is rendered, they are not expected to be paid.

      2) Thus, these amounts are treated as **reductions of revenue and receivables**.

Patient service revenues ($320,000 × 2%)	$6,400	
Accounts receivable – patients		$6,400

    d.   Moreover, HCOs also do not expect to collect the full amount billed to **third-party payors**.

        1)   However, the accounting treatment is not the same. These reductions are the result of **contractual arrangements** already agreed to between the HCO and the payor.

        2)   The HCO can make a **reasonable estimate** of these write-offs because the terms of the contract are known.

Contractual adjustments	$168,000	
Allowance for uncollectible accounts		$168,000

5.   **Premium revenues** are generated by **agreements to provide health care** rather than by actually providing services.

    a.   For example, an integrated delivery system may contract to provide all health-related services for a certain group within its primary service area for a specified amount per member per month.

6.   **Other revenues** may include

    a.   Donated medicine or supplies.

        1)   Occasionally a supplier may cancel an invoice billed to an HCO.

Accounts payable	$10,000	
Other operating revenue		$10,000

    b.   Donated labor.

        1)   Not-for-profit HCOs can recognize revenue from volunteer services if they either

            a)   Create or enhance nonfinancial assets, or

            b)   Require special skills, are provided by those having such skills, and would usually be purchased if not obtained by donations.

    c.   Providing educational programs.

    d.   Proceeds from the sale of cafeteria meals and guest trays.

    e.   Gifts and grants, whether restricted to a specific purpose or not.

7.   Reporting

    a.   **Revenues are reported** on the statement of operations at their **net amounts**:

Unrestricted revenues, gains, and other support:	
Net patient service revenue	$ 875,400
Premium revenue	168,700
Other revenue	1,200
Net assets released from restrictions used for operations *	550
Total unrestricted revenues, gains, and other support	$1,045,850

      * Not-for-profit HCOs only

    b.   The **components of net patient service revenue** are **disclosed** in the **notes** to the financial statements:

Gross patient service revenue:	
Inpatient	$ 700,000
Outpatient	300,000
Total gross patient service revenue	$1,000,000
Allowances for charity care and contractual adjustments	(124,600)
Net patient service revenue	$ 875,400

Expenses

8.   According to the Audit and Accounting Guide,

a.   Expense recognition by for-profit HCOs generally is the same as for other business entities.

b.   A governmental HCO's treatment of expenses resulting from nonexchange transactions depends on the type of transaction (see Subunit 17.3).

Net Assets

9.   Not-for-profit HCOs must **report three categories of net assets** and the **changes** in them during the reporting period.

Stop and review! You have completed the outline for this subunit. Study multiple-choice questions 15 through 25 beginning on page 744.

QUESTIONS

20.1 Not-for-Profit Organizations (NPOs)

1. In Year 3, a not-for-profit trade association enrolled five new member companies, each of which was obligated to pay nonrefundable initiation fees of $1,000. These fees were receivable by the association in Year 4. Three of the new members paid the initiation fees in Year 3, and the other two new members paid their initiation fees in Year 4. Annual dues (excluding initiation fees) received by the association from all of its members have always covered the organization's costs of services provided to its members. It can be reasonably expected that future dues will cover all costs of the organization's future services to members. Average membership duration is 10 years because of mergers, attrition, and economic factors. What amount of initiation fees from these five new members should the association recognize as revenue in Year 4?

A. $5,000

B. $3,000

C. $500

D. $0

Answer (A) is correct. *(CPA, adapted)*
REQUIRED: The amount of initiation fees to be reported as revenue.
DISCUSSION: Membership dues received or receivable in exchange transactions that relate to several accounting periods should be allocated and recognized as revenue in those periods. Nonrefundable initiation and life membership fees are recognized as revenue when they are receivable if future dues and fees can be reasonably expected to cover the costs of the organization's services. Otherwise, they are amortized to future periods. Hence, given that future dues are expected to cover the organization's costs, the $5,000 in nonrefundable initiation fees should be recognized as revenue when assessed and reported as such in the Year 4 statement of activities.

2. In July Year 3, Katie irrevocably donated $200,000 cash to be invested and held in trust by a church. Katie stipulated that the revenue generated from this gift be paid to Katie during Katie's lifetime. After Katie dies, the principal is to be used by the church for any purpose chosen by its governing body. The church received interest of $16,000 on the $200,000 for the year ended June 30, Year 4, and the interest was remitted to Katie. In the church's June 30, Year 4, annual financial statements,

A. $200,000 should be reported as revenue.

B. $184,000 should be reported as revenue.

C. $16,000 should be reported as revenue.

D.   The gift and its terms should be disclosed only in notes to the financial statements.

Answer (A) is correct. *(CPA, adapted)*
REQUIRED: The proper accounting for a split-interest agreement.
DISCUSSION: An NPO should report an irrevocable split-interest agreement. Assets under the control of the NPO are recorded at fair value at the time of initial recognition, and the contribution is recognized as revenue. Because the NPO has a remainder interest, it should not recognize revenue from receipt of the income of the trust. Thus, the NPO should recognize revenue of $200,000 (the presumed fair value of the contributed cash).
Answer (B) is incorrect because the contribution is not reduced by the income paid to the donor. Answer (C) is incorrect because the income paid to the donor is not revenue of the NPO. Answer (D) is incorrect because the contribution should be recognized at fair value.

3. Famous, a nongovernmental not-for-profit art museum, has elected not to capitalize its permanent collections. In Year 3 a bronze statue was stolen. The statue was not recovered, and insurance proceeds of $35,000 were paid to Famous in Year 4. This transaction should be reported in

I. The statement of activities as permanently restricted revenues.

II. The statement of cash flows as cash flows from investing activities.

    A. I only.

    B. II only.

    C. Both I and II.

    D. Neither I nor II.

Answer (B) is correct. *(CPA, adapted)*
    REQUIRED: The reporting by an NPO of insurance proceeds received after theft of an uncapitalized art work.
    DISCUSSION: Contributions of purchases of works of art, historical treasures, and similar assets added to collections that meet the criteria in SFAS 116 need not be capitalized. If they are not capitalized, the entity must report on the face of the statement of activities (separately from revenues, expenses, gains and losses) the costs (proceeds) of collection items purchased (sold) as a decrease (increase) in the appropriate class of net assets. The entity also must disclose the proceeds from insurance recoveries of lost or destroyed collection items as an increase in the appropriate class of net assets. Furthermore, the AICPA Audit and Accounting Guide *Not-for-Profit Organizations* states that cash flows from purchases, sales, and insurance recoveries of uncapitalized collection items are reported in the investing activities section of the statement of cash flows.

4. Lane Foundation received a permanent endowment of $500,000 in Year 3 from Gant Enterprises. The endowment assets were invested in publicly traded securities, and Lane is permitted to choose suitable investments. Gant did not specify how gains and losses from dispositions of endowment assets were to be treated. No restrictions were placed on the use of dividends received and interest earned on fund resources. In Year 4, Lane realized gains of $50,000 on sales of fund investments and received total interest and dividends of $40,000 on fund securities. What amount of these capital gains, interest, and dividends increases unrestricted net assets?

    A. $0

    B. $40,000

    C. $50,000

    D. $90,000

Answer (D) is correct. *(CPA, adapted)*
    REQUIRED: The amount of capital gains, interest, and dividends that increases unrestricted net assets.
    DISCUSSION: Absent an explicit donor stipulation or law to the contrary, assuming the donee is allowed to choose suitable investments, income and gains or losses on a donor-restricted endowment fund's assets are changes in unrestricted net assets. Thus, the increase in unrestricted net assets is $90,000 ($50,000 gains + $40,000 interest and dividends).
    Answer (A) is incorrect because $0 assumes the income and gains are restricted. Answer (B) is incorrect because $40,000 assumes the gains are restricted. Answer (C) is incorrect because $50,000 assumes the income is restricted.

5. Maple Church has cash available for investments from contributions with different restrictions. Maple's policy is to maximize its financial resources. How may Maple pool its investments?

    A. Maple may not pool its investments.

    B. Maple may pool all investments but must equitably allocate realized and unrealized gains and losses among participants.

    C. Maple may pool only unrestricted investments but must equitably allocate realized and unrealized gains and losses among participating funds.

    D. Maple may pool only restricted investments but must equitably allocate realized and unrealized gains and losses among participating funds.

Answer (B) is correct. *(CPA, adapted)*
    REQUIRED: The true statement about pooling of investments by an NPO.
    DISCUSSION: Investment pools, including investments from contributions with different restrictions, are created for portfolio management. Ownership interests are assigned (ordinarily in terms of units) to the pool categories (participants) based on the market value of the cash and securities obtained from each participant. Current market value also determines the units allocated to additional assets placed in the pool and to value withdrawals. Investment income, realized gains and losses, and recognized unrealized gains and losses are allocated based on the units assigned.
    Answer (A) is incorrect because pooling of investments is allowed to obtain investment flexibility and reduce risk. Answer (C) is incorrect because no prohibition exists as to the pooling restricted investments. Answer (D) is incorrect because no prohibition exists as to pooling unrestricted investments.

6. On January 1, Year 4, a not-for-profit botanical society received a gift of an exhaustible fixed asset with an estimated useful life of 10 years and no salvage value. The donor's cost of this asset was $20,000, and its fair value at the date of the gift was $30,000. What amount of depreciation of this asset should the society recognize in its Year 4 financial statements?

A. $3,000

B. $2,500

C. $2,000

D. $0

Answer (A) is correct. *(CPA, adapted)*
REQUIRED: The amount of depreciation to be recognized in the financial statements.
DISCUSSION: SFAS 93 requires not-for-profit organizations to recognize depreciation in the statement of activities. Moreover, contributions are recorded at their fair value when received. Assuming the straight-line method is used, the amount of depreciation that the not-for-profit botanical society should recognize is $3,000 [($30,000 fair value – $0 salvage value) ÷ 10 years].

7. Which of the following assets of a nongovernmental not-for-profit charitable organization must be depreciated?

A. A freezer costing $150,000 for storing food for the soup kitchen.

B. Building costs of $500,000 for construction in progress for senior citizen housing.

C. Land valued at $1 million being used as the site of the new senior citizen home.

D. A bulk purchase of $20,000 of linens for its nursing home.

Answer (A) is correct. *(CPA, adapted)*
REQUIRED: The asset of a nongovernmental not-for-profit charity that must be depreciated.
DISCUSSION: Under SFAS 93, *Recognition of Depreciation by Not-for-Profit Organizations*, NPOs recognize depreciation for most property and equipment. Exceptions are land used as a building site and certain individual works of art and historical treasures with extremely long useful lives. A freezer is a long-lived tangible asset that is depreciable equipment.
Answer (B) is incorrect because construction in progress is inventory. Inventory is not depreciated. Answer (C) is incorrect because land is not depreciated. Answer (D) is incorrect because linens are inventory. Inventory is not depreciated.

8. In a not-for-profit organization, which of the following should be included in total expenses?

	Grants to other organizations	Depreciation
A.	Yes	Yes
B.	Yes	No
C.	No	No
D.	No	Yes

Answer (A) is correct. *(CPA, adapted)*
REQUIRED: The item(s), if any, included in total expenses by an NPO.
DISCUSSION: Under SFAS 93, *Recognition of Depreciation by Not-for-Profit Organizations*, depreciation expense is recognized for most property and equipment. Other types of expenses recognized by NPOs may include (1) salaries, (2) rent, (3) electricity, (4) interest, (5) awards to others, (6) grants to subrecipients, and (7) professional fees. These are natural classifications of expense. But NPOs must report expenses by functional classification (major classes of program services and supporting activities).
Answer (B) is incorrect because an NPO recognizes depreciation expense. Answer (C) is incorrect because an NPO recognizes depreciation and grants to other organizations as expenses. Answer (D) is incorrect because an NPO recognizes expenses for grants to other organizations.

9. For the fall semester of the current year, Ames University assessed its students $3 million for tuition and fees. The net amount realized was only $2.5 million because scholarships of $400,000 were granted to students and tuition remissions of $100,000 were allowed to faculty members' children attending Ames. These amounts were properly classified as expenses. What amount should Ames report for the period as revenues for tuition and fees?

A. $2,500,000

B. $2,600,000

C. $2,900,000

D. $3,000,000

Answer (D) is correct. *(CPA, adapted)*
REQUIRED: The amount reported as revenues for tuition and fees.
DISCUSSION: Revenues from exchange transactions are normally recorded at gross amounts. Thus, in accounting for tuition and fees for colleges and universities, the full amount of the tuition assessed is usually reported as revenue. Tuition waivers, scholarships, and like items are recorded as expenses if given in exchange transactions, for example, as part of a compensation package. However, when the institution regularly provides discounts to certain students, revenues are recognized net of the discounts. Accordingly, given that scholarships and tuition remissions were expenses, revenues should be reported at their gross amount of $3,000,000.
Answer (A) is incorrect because $2,500,000 assumes that only net tuition is recorded. Answer (B) is incorrect because $2,600,000 assumes that scholarships are deducted before recording tuition revenues. Answer (C) is incorrect because $2,900,000 assumes that tuition remissions are deducted before recording tuition revenues.

10. Functional expenses recorded in the general ledger of ABC, a nongovernmental not-for-profit organization, are as follows:

Soliciting prospective members	$45,000
Printing membership benefits brochures	30,000
Soliciting membership dues	25,000
Maintaining donor list	10,000

What amount should ABC report as fund-raising expenses?

    A. $10,000

    B. $35,000

    C. $70,000

    D. $110,000

Answer (A) is correct. *(CPA, adapted)*
    REQUIRED: The fund-raising expenses.
    DISCUSSION: The major functional classes of expenses for an NPO are program services and supporting activities. The latter include management and general, fund-raising, and membership development activities. Fund-raising includes maintaining donor lists ($10,000). Soliciting members and dues and printing membership benefits brochures are membership-development activities.
    Answer (B) is incorrect because $35,000 includes the cost of soliciting dues, a membership-development activity. Answer (C) is incorrect because $70,000 is the cost of soliciting members and dues. Answer (D) is incorrect because only the cost of the donor list is an expense of fund-raising.

11. The following expenditures were made by Green Services, a society for the protection of the environment:

Printing of the annual report	$12,000
Unsolicited merchandise sent to encourage contributions	25,000
Cost of an audit performed by a CPA firm	3,000

What amount should be classified as fund-raising costs in the society's statement of activities?

    A. $37,000

    B. $28,000

    C. $25,000

    D. $0

Answer (C) is correct. *(CPA, adapted)*
    REQUIRED: The amount to be reported as fund-raising costs in the activity statement.
    DISCUSSION: There are two major classifications of expenses for an NPO: program service expenses and supporting services expenses. Program service expenses relate directly to the primary purpose or mission of the organization. Supporting services expenses are further classified as management and general expenses, fund-raising expenses, and membership development costs. The only fund-raising-related cost here is the unsolicited merchandise sent to encourage contributions.
    Answer (A) is incorrect because $37,000 classifies all of the expenses as fund-raising expenses when only the unsolicited merchandise is related to fund-raising. Answer (B) is incorrect because the cost of an audit is a management-related expense. Answer (D) is incorrect because this answer assumes that none of the expenses listed are related to fund-raising when, in fact, the unsolicited merchandise is a fund-raising expense.

12. Cancer Educators, a not-for-profit organization, incurred costs of $10,000 in its combined program services and fund-raising activities. Which of the following cost allocations might Cancer Educators report in its statement of activities?

	Program Services	Fund-Raising	General Services
A.	$0	$0	$10,000
B.	$0	$6,000	$4,000
C.	$6,000	$4,000	$0
D.	$10,000	$0	$0

Answer (C) is correct. *(CPA, adapted)*
    REQUIRED: The allocation of costs for combined functions.
    DISCUSSION: NPOs must provide information about expenses reported by functional classification. The $10,000 of costs should therefore be divided between program services and fund-raising.

13. Molko, a community foundation, incurred $10,000 in management and general expenses during Year 4. In Molko's statement of activities for the year ended December 31, Year 4, the $10,000 should be reported as

    A. A direct reduction of fund balance.

    B. Part of supporting services.

    C. Part of program services.

    D. A contra account to offset revenue.

Answer (B) is correct. *(CPA, adapted)*
    REQUIRED: The expense classification for management and general expenses in the statement of activities.
    DISCUSSION: Two functional categories of expenses for an NPO are program services expenses and supporting services expenses. Supporting services expenses, which do not relate to the primary mission of the organization, may be further subdivided into (1) management and general expenses, (2) fund-raising expenses, and (3) membership development costs.
    Answer (A) is incorrect because a direct reduction of fund balance would be the result of a transfer or a refund to a donor. Moreover, fund accounting information is not required to be externally reported. Answer (C) is incorrect because program services expenses relate directly to the primary mission of the NPO. Answer (D) is incorrect because only costs directly related to a certain source of support, such as a special event or estimated uncollectible pledges, may be offset against revenue.

14. Cura Foundation, a voluntary health and welfare organization supported by contributions from the general public, included the following costs in its statement of functional expenses for the year:

Fund-raising	$500,000
Administrative (including data processing)	300,000
Research	100,000

Cura's functional expenses for program services included

A. $900,000

B. $500,000

C. $300,000

D. $100,000

Answer (D) is correct. *(CPA, adapted)*
REQUIRED: The amount of functional expenses for program services incurred by a VHWO.
DISCUSSION: An NPO's statement of activities or notes thereto should classify expenses by function. The major functional classes include program services and supporting services. Management and general expenses, along with fund-raising expenses, are classified in the supporting services category. Program services expenses are those directly related to the administration of programs. Of the costs given, only the research costs ($100,000) are program services expenses.
Answer (A) is incorrect because $900,000 includes $500,000 of fund-raising expenses and $300,000 of administrative expenses, which should be included in supporting services expenses. Answer (B) is incorrect because $500,000 of fund-raising expenses should be classified as supporting services expenses. Answer (C) is incorrect because $300,000 of administrative expenses should be classified as supporting services expenses.

20.2 Health Care Organizations (HCOs)

15. Palma Hospital's patient service revenue for services provided in Year 4 at established rates amounted to $8 million on the accrual basis. For internal reporting, Palma uses the discharge method. Under this method, patient service revenue is recognized only when patients are discharged, with no recognition given to revenue accruing for services to patients not yet discharged. Patient service revenue at established rates using the discharge method amounted to $7 million for Year 4. According to generally accepted accounting principles, Palma should report patient service revenue for Year 4 of

A. Either $8,000,000 or $7,000,000, at the option of the hospital.

B. $8,000,000

C. $7,500,000

D. $7,000,000

Answer (B) is correct. *(CPA, adapted)*
REQUIRED: The amount of patient service revenue to be reported.
DISCUSSION: Revenue is recognized when the service is provided to a patient. Thus, gross patient service revenue is recorded on the accrual basis at the HCO's established rates, regardless of whether it expects to collect the full amount. Contractual and other adjustments are also recorded on the accrual basis and subtracted from gross patient service revenue to arrive at net patient service revenue, which is the amount reported in the statement of operations. Charity care is excluded from patient service revenue for financial reporting purposes. Thus, the discharge method is not acceptable under GAAP. In its general purpose external financial statements, Palma should report $8 million of patient service revenue based on established rates.
Answer (A) is incorrect because the hospital does not have this option. Answer (C) is incorrect because $7,500,000 is the average of the $8,000,000 accrual basis amount and the $7,000,000 discharge method amount. Answer (D) is incorrect because the $7,000,000 resulting from the discharge method is not acceptable under GAAP.

16. Under Cura Hospital's established rate structure, health care services revenues of $9 million would have been earned for the year ended December 31. However, only $6.75 million was collected because of charity allowances of $1.5 million and discounts of $750,000 to third-party payors. For the year ended December 31, what amount should Cura report as health care services revenues in the statement of operations?

A. $6,750,000

B. $7,500,000

C. $8,250,000

D. $9,000,000

Answer (A) is correct. *(CPA, adapted)*
REQUIRED: The health care services revenues reported in the statement of operations.
DISCUSSION: Gross health care services revenues do not include charity care, which is disclosed separately in the notes to the financial statements. Moreover, such revenues are reported in the financial statements net of contractual and other adjustments. Thus, health care services revenues are recorded in the accounting records at the gross amount (excluding charity care) of 7.5 million but reported in the financial statements at the net realizable value of 6.75 million.
Answer (B) is incorrect because $7,500,000 equals gross revenues. Answer (C) is incorrect because $8,250,000 assumes that charity allowances are included in gross and net revenues. Answer (D) is incorrect because charity care is excluded from gross revenue, and contractual adjustments are subtracted to arrive at net revenue.

17. Terry, an auditor, is performing test work for a not-for-profit hospital. Listed below are components of the statement of operations:

Revenue relating to charity care	$100,000
Bad debt expense	70,000
Net assets released from restrictions used for operations	50,000
Other revenue	80,000
Net patient service revenue (includes revenue related to charity care)	500,000

In accordance with the Audit and Accounting Guide *Health Care Organizations*, what amount would be reported as total revenues, gains, and other support on the statement of operations?

    A. $460,000

    B. $530,000

    C. $580,000

    D. $630,000

Answer (B) is correct. *(CPA, adapted)*
REQUIRED: The total revenues, gains, and other support reported by a not-for-profit hospital.
DISCUSSION: The total revenues, gains, and other support subtotal in the statement of operations of a not-for-profit hospital includes net patient service revenue, premium revenue, other revenue, and net assets released from restrictions used for operations. Net patient service revenue is recognized for fees charged for patient care, minus contractual adjustments and discounts. Reported net patient service revenue does not include charity care. Services performed as charity care are not expected to produce cash inflows and thus do not qualify for recognition as revenue or receivables. Bad debt expense is recognized in total expense, not as a reduction to revenue. Other revenue derives from services not involving providing health care services or coverage to patients, residents, or enrollees (e.g., of a health care delivery plan). Net assets released from restrictions used for operations are reported in the statement of operations when a temporary restriction expires, with a reclassification of net assets to unrestricted net assets. Thus, the total revenues, gains and other support is $530,000 ($500,000 net patient service revenue – $100,000 charity care + $50,000 net assets released from restrictions used for operations + $80,000 other revenue).
    Answer (A) is incorrect because bad debt expense is not a revenue, gain, or other support and does not decrease any such item in this caption of the statement of operations. Answer (C) is incorrect because $580,000 includes charity care but excludes net assets released from restrictions for operations. Answer (D) is incorrect because $630,000 includes charity care.

18. Which of the following should normally be considered ongoing or central transactions for a not-for-profit hospital?

    I. Room and board fees from patients
    II. Recovery room fees

    A. Neither I nor II.

    B. Both I and II.

    C. II only.

    D. I only.

Answer (B) is correct. *(CPA, adapted)*
REQUIRED: The fees, if any, that are ongoing or central transactions for a not-for-profit hospital.
DISCUSSION: Revenues arise from an entity's ongoing major or central operations. Revenues of an HCO include patient service revenue, premium revenue, resident service revenue, and other revenue. Room and board fees and recovery room fees are patient services revenues.

19. Hospital, Inc., a not-for-profit organization with no governmental affiliation, reported the following in its accounts for the current year ended December 31:

Gross patient service revenue from all services provided at the established billing rates of the hospital (note that this figure includes charity care of $25,000)	$775,000
Provision for bad debts	15,000
Difference between established billing rates and fees negotiated with third-party payors (contractual adjustments)	70,000

What amount would the hospital report as net patient service revenue in its statement of operations for the current year ended December 31?

    A. $680,000

    B. $690,000

    C. $705,000

    D. $735,000

Answer (A) is correct. *(CPA, adapted)*
REQUIRED: The net patient service revenue.
DISCUSSION: Total revenues, gains, and other support subtotal in the statement of operations of a not-for-profit health care organization includes net patient service revenue, premium revenue, other revenue, and net assets released from restrictions used for operations. Net patient service revenue is recognized for fees charged for patient care, minus contractual adjustments and discounts. Reported net patient service revenue does not include charity care. Services performed as charity care are not expected to produce cash inflows and thus do not qualify for recognition as revenue or receivables. Bad debt expense, however, is recognized in total expenses. Thus, net patient service revenue equals $680,000 ($775,000 gross revenue – $25,000 charity care – $70,000 contractual adjustments).
    Answer (B) is incorrect because $690,000 includes charity care and subtracts bad debt expense. Answer (C) is incorrect because $705,000 includes charity care. Answer (D) is incorrect because $735,000 subtracts bad debt expense but not the contractual adjustments.

20. In April, Delta Hospital purchased medicines from Field Pharmaceutical Co. at a cost of $5,000. However, Field notified Delta that the invoice was being canceled and that the medicines were being donated to Delta. Delta should record this donation of medicines as

A. A memorandum entry only.

B. A $5,000 credit to nonoperating expenses.

C. A $5,000 credit to operating expenses.

D. Other operating revenue of $5,000.

Answer (D) is correct. *(CPA, adapted)*
   REQUIRED: The accounting for a donation of medicine.
   DISCUSSION: Contributions of noncash assets that are not long-lived are reported at fair value in the statement of operations. Thus, when a supplier cancels an invoice, the HCO removes the payable and recognizes other operating revenue.

21. An organization of high school seniors performs services for patients at Leer Hospital. These students are volunteers and perform services that the hospital would not otherwise provide, such as wheeling patients in the park and reading to patients. They donated 5,000 hours of service to Leer in Year 4. At a minimum wage rate, these services would amount to $18,750, while it is estimated that the fair value of these services was $25,000. In Leer's Year 4 statement of activities, what amount should be reported as nonoperating revenue?

A. $25,000

B. $18,750

C. $6,250

D. $0

Answer (D) is correct. *(CPA, adapted)*
   REQUIRED: The nonoperating revenue to record for services by volunteers.
   DISCUSSION: Contributed services are recognized if they (1) create or enhance nonfinancial assets or (2) require special skills, are provided by persons possessing those skills, and would ordinarily be purchased if not provided by donation. Hence, the hospital should report no revenue. Nonfinancial assets are not involved, and no special skills, such as those of professionals or craftsmen, are required.

22. Monies from educational programs of a hospital normally are included in

A. Premium revenue.

B. Patient service revenue.

C. Nonoperating gains.

D. Other revenue, gains, or losses.

Answer (D) is correct. *(CPA, adapted)*
   REQUIRED: The classification of monies derived from educational programs of a hospital.
   DISCUSSION: Revenues of an HCO include patient service revenue, premium revenue, and other revenue, gains, or losses. Other revenue, gains, or losses derive from services other than providing health care services or coverage to patients. One source is student tuition and fees. Thus, the monies received from an educational program conducted by a hospital should be classified as other revenue.
   Answer (A) is incorrect because premium revenue is derived from a capitation arrangement, that is, from a contract under which a prepaid health care plan pays a per-individual fee to a provider. Answer (B) is incorrect because educational program revenue is not directly related to patient care and is therefore not includible in patient service revenues. Answer (C) is incorrect because nonoperating gains typically arise from activities such as sales of investments or fixed assets.

23. Valley's community hospital normally includes proceeds from the sale of cafeteria meals in

A. Deductions from dietary service expenses.

B. Ancillary service revenues.

C. Patient service revenues.

D. Other revenue, gains, or losses.

Answer (D) is correct. *(CPA, adapted)*
   REQUIRED: The classification of revenue from cafeteria meals.
   DISCUSSION: Other revenue, gains, or losses are derived from services other than providing health care services or coverage to patients. This category includes proceeds from sale of cafeteria meals and guest trays to employees, medical staff, and visitors.
   Answer (A) is incorrect because expenses are not usually netted against revenues. Answer (B) is incorrect because "ancillary service revenues" is not a proper classification of hospital revenues. Answer (C) is incorrect because patient service revenues are derived from fees charged for patient care.

24. Amounts received by a research hospital in the form of grants specified by the donor for research are normally included in

    A. Nonoperating gains.

    B. Other revenue.

    C. Patient service revenue.

    D. Ancillary service revenue.

Answer (B) is correct. *(CPA, adapted)*
    REQUIRED: The correct classification of grants specified for research by the donor.
    DISCUSSION: Revenues derive from the major ongoing or central operations of the entity, e.g., research by a research institution. The two major classes of revenues for hospitals are health care services revenues and other revenues. Other revenues may include research and other gifts or grants.
    Answer (A) is incorrect because gains are incidental to the provider's ongoing major or central operations. Answer (C) is incorrect because patient service revenue includes revenues received only from the direct provision of health care to patients, such as room, board, nursing, and ancillary department fees. Answer (D) is incorrect because ancillary service revenue is not a proper classification.

25. Which of the following normally is included in the other revenue, gains, or losses of a hospital?

	Fees from Educational Programs	Unrestricted Gifts
A.	No	No
B.	No	Yes
C.	Yes	No
D.	Yes	Yes

Answer (D) is correct. *(CPA, adapted)*
    REQUIRED: The items normally included in a hospital's operating revenues.
    DISCUSSION: Other revenue, gains, or losses may appropriately be recognized by a hospital for services other than health care or coverage provided to patients. Other revenue may include donated medicine or supplies, donated labor, fees for educational programs, proceeds from the sale of cafeteria meals, and gifts and grants. Revenue or expense results from an entity's ongoing major or central operations. Gains or losses result from peripheral or incidental transactions and from all transactions and other events and circumstances that do not generate revenue or expense (SFAC 6). Thus, contributions, either unrestricted or for a specific purpose, should be treated as other revenue, gains, or losses unless fund-raising is an ongoing major activity of the hospital. They are recognized at fair value.
    Answer (A) is incorrect because a hospital normally recognizes fees from its educational programs and unrestricted gifts as other revenue, gains, or losses. Answer (B) is incorrect because a hospital normally recognizes fees from its educational programs as other revenue, gains, or losses. Answer (C) is incorrect because unrestricted gifts are usually classified as other revenue, gains, or losses unless fund-raising is an ongoing major activity of the hospital.

Use Gleim's *CPA Test Prep* CD-Rom/Pocket PC for interactive testing with over 4,000 additional questions!

20.3 PRACTICE SIMULATION

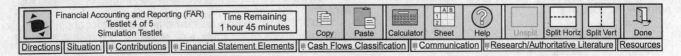

| | Financial Accounting and Reporting (FAR)
Testlet 4 of 5
Simulation Testlet | Time Remaining
1 hour 45 minutes | Copy | Paste | Calculator | Sheet | Help | Unsplit | Split Horiz | Split Vert | Done |

Directions | Situation | ☰ Contributions | ☰ Financial Statement Elements | ☰ Cash Flows Classification | ☰ Communication | ☰ Research/Authoritative Literature | Resources

---

1. Directions

In the following simulation, you will be asked to complete various tasks. You may use the content in the **Information Tabs** to complete the tasks in the **Work Tabs**.

Information Tabs:

| Directions | Resources |

FIG 1

- Go through each of the **Information Tabs** to familiarize yourself with the simulation content
- The **Resources** tab will contain information, including formulas and definitions, that may help you to complete the tasks
- Your simulation may have more **Information Tabs** than those shown in Fig. 1

Work Tabs:

| ☰ SysTrust | ☰ Engagement Letter | ☰ Authoritative Sources | ☰ Communication |

FIG. 2

- **Work Tabs**, to the right of **Information Tabs**, contain the tasks for you to complete
- **Work Tabs** contain directions for completing each task - be sure to read these directions carefully
- The tab names in Fig. 2 are for illustration only - yours may differ
- Once you complete any part of a task, the pencil for that tab will be shaded (see **Communication** in Fig. 2)
- The shaded pencil does **NOT** indicate that you have completed the entire task
- You must complete all of the tasks in the **Work Tabs** to receive full credit

Research/Authoritative Literature Tab:

| ☰ Research/Authoritative Literature |

FIG. 3

- This tab contains both the Research task and the Authoritative Literature
- Detailed instructions for completing the Research task, and for using the Authoritative Literature, appear on this tab
- You may use the Authoritative Literature as a resource for completing other tasks

NOTE: If you believe you have encountered a software malfunction, report it to the test center staff immediately.

2. Situation

Community Service, Inc. is a nongovernmental, not-for-profit voluntary health and welfare calendar-year organization that began operations on January 1, Year 1. It performs voluntary services and derives its revenue primarily from voluntary contributions from the general public. Community implies a time restriction on all promises to contribute cash in future periods. However, no such policy exists with respect to gifts of long-lived assets.

Selected transactions that occurred during Community's Year 2 calendar year:

- Unrestricted written promises to contribute cash--Year 1 and Year 2

Year 1 promises collected in Year 2	$22,000
Year 2 promises collected in Year 2	95,000
Year 2 promises uncollected	28,000

- Written promises to contribute cash restricted to use for community college scholarships--Year 1 and Year 2

Year 1 promises collected and expended in Year 2	10,000
Year 2 promises collected and expended in Year 2	20,000
Year 2 promises uncollected	12,000

- Written promise to contribute $25,000 if matching funds are raised for the capital campaign during Year 2

Cash received in Year 2 from contributor as a good faith advance	25,000
Matching funds received in Year 2	0

- Cash received in Year 1 with donor's only stipulation that a bus be purchased

Expenditure of full amount of donation 7/1/Year 2	37,000

Other selected transactions that occurred during Community's Year 2 calendar year:

- Debt security endowment received in Year 2; income to be used for community services

Face amount	$90,000
Fair value at time of receipt	88,000
Fair value at 12/31/Year 2	87,000
Interest earned in Year 2	9,000

- 10 concerned citizens volunteered to serve meals to the homeless

400 hrs. free; FMV of services $5 per hr.	2,000

- Short-term investment in equity securities in Year 2

Cost	10,000
Fair value 12/31/Year 2	12,000
Dividend income	1,000

- Music festival to raise funds for a local hospital

Admission fees	5,000
Sales of food and drinks	14,000
Expenses	4,000

- Reading materials donated to Community and distributed to the children in Year 2

Fair market value	8,000

- Federal youth training fee for service grant

Cash received during Year 2	30,000
Instructor salaries paid	26,000

- Other cash operating expenses

Business manager salary	60,000
General bookkeeper salary	40,000
Director of community activities salary	50,000
Space rental (75% for community activities, 25% for office activities)	20,000
Printing and mailing costs for pledge cards	2,000

- Interest payment on short-term bank loan in Year 2   1,000

- Principal payment on short-term bank loan in Year 2   20,000

3. Contributions

This set of questions has a matching format. Select the best match for each numbered item from the terms in the drop-down list and write its letter in the column provided. Each choice may be used once, more than once, or not at all. Items 1 through 4 represent the Year 2 amounts that Community reported for selected contribution amounts in its December 31, Year 2, statement of financial position and Year 2 statement of activities. For each item, indicate whether the amount was overstated, understated, or correctly stated. Refer to the selected transactions in the situation tab for each item.

Amounts	Answer
1. Community reported $28,000 as contributions receivable.	
2. Community reported $37,000 as net assets released from restrictions (satisfaction of use restrictions).	
3. Community reported $22,000 as net assets released from restrictions (due to the lapse of time restrictions).	
4. Community reported $97,000 as contributions -- temporarily restricted.	

Choices
A) Overstated
B) Understated
C) Correctly stated

4. Financial Statement Elements

This question is presented in a spreadsheet format that requires you to fill in the correct responses in the shaded cells provided. For items 1 through 7, determine the amounts for the following financial statement elements in the Year 2 statement of activities. Use the information from the other selected transactions that occurred during Community's Year 2 calendar year given in the situation tab.

Financial Statement Elements	Amount
1. Contributions -- permanently restricted	
2. Revenues -- fees	
3. Investment income -- debt	
4. Program expenses	
5. General fund-raising expenses (excludes special events)	
6. Income on long-term investments -- unrestricted	
7. Contributed voluntary services	

5. Cash Flows Classification

This set of questions has a matching format. Select the best match for each numbered item from the terms in the drop-down list and write its letter in the column provided. Each choice may be used once, more than once, or not at all.

Events	Answer
1. Unrestricted Year 1 promises collected	
2. Cash received from a contributor as a good-faith advance on a promise to contribute matching funds	
3. Purchase of bus	
4. Principal payment on short-term bank loan	
5. Purchase of equity securities	
6. Dividend income earned on equity securities	
7. Interest payment on short-term bank loan	
8. Interest earned on endowment	

Choices
A) Cash flows from operating activities
B) Cash flows from investing activities
C) Cash flows from financing activities

6. Communication

In a brief memorandum to a not-for-profit client, describe the nature, structure, and operation of a split-interest agreement. Also describe the recognition and measurement principles applicable to revocable and irrevocable split-interest agreements. Type your communication in your word processor program and print out the copy in a memorandum-style format.

REMINDER: Your response will be graded for both technical content and writing skills. Technical content will be evaluated for information that is helpful to the intended reader and clearly relevant to the issue. Writing skills will be evaluated for development, organization, and the appropriate expression of ideas in professional correspondence. Use a standard business memo or letter format with a clear beginning, middle, and end. Do not convey information in the form of a table, bullet point list, or other abbreviated presentation.

To:	Not-for-profit client
From:	CPA
Re:	Split-interest agreements

---

7. Research/Authoritative Literature

See page 12 in the Introduction of this book for a detailed explanation of the AICPA's new Research/Authoritative Literature work tab as well as a screenshot of how the tab will actually look on your exam.

According to the FASB Current Text or Original Pronouncements, when may a not-for-profit organization not recognize depreciation on an individual work of art?

Unofficial Answers

3. Contributions (4 Gradable Items)

1. **B) Understated.** An unconditional promise to give may be treated as a contribution if it is sufficiently documented. The $28,000 of contributions receivable is understated. It does not include the $12,000 of unconditional but restricted promises made in Year 2 that have not been collected.

2. **B) Understated.** The $37,000 of net assets released as a result of the satisfaction of use restrictions is understated. It does not include the $30,000 of contributions collected and expended in Year 2 for the stipulated purpose of providing scholarships. Note: Although the restriction on the $37,000 received in Year 1 to purchase a bus expired in Year 2 when the funds were used for the stipulated purpose, the restriction would not have expired if additional donor restrictions on the use of the long-lived asset had been stated or if the organization had a policy of implying a time restriction that expired over the life of the donated asset.

3. **C) Correctly stated.** The contributions restricted to use for scholarships and purchase of a bus were not time restricted. However, Community implies a time restriction on promises to contribute cash in future periods. Thus, the only net assets released from time restrictions in Year 2 consisted of the $22,000 collected in Year 2 as a result of Year 1 promises. The Year 2 collections on unrestricted promises made in Year 2 were not subject to the implied restriction, and the uncollected amounts related to Year 2 promises.

4. **A) Overstated.** Restricted contributions include the $28,000 of uncollected Year 2 promises that were not donor restricted but that were subject to an implied time restriction. They also include the $12,000 of uncollected Year 2 promises subject to a donor restriction. The total is therefore only $40,000. The $25,000 of cash received that is conditioned upon the raising of matching funds is treated as arising from a conditional promise to give. It is accounted for as a refundable advance, not a contribution, because the condition has not been substantially met.

4. Financial Statement Elements (7 Gradable Items)

1. **$88,000.** Permanent restrictions are imposed when, for example, assets are donated with stipulations that they provide a permanent source of income. Hence, the endowment is a permanently restricted contribution. A contribution should be measured at fair value ($88,000).

2. **$5,000.** The only fee revenues – fees earned in Year 2 – were the admission fees to the music festival in the amount of $5,000.

3. **$8,000.** The investment income is the $9,000 interest earned on the debt security endowment minus the $1,000 interest payment.

4. **$99,000.** "Program services are the activities that result in goods and services being distributed to beneficiaries, customers, or members that fulfill the purposes or mission for which the organization exists" (SFAS 117). Community's program expenses include the salary of the director of community activities ($50,000), the salaries paid to instructors to provide youth training ($26,000), space rental ($20,000 x 75% for community activities = $15,000), and reading materials distributed to children ($8,000). The services provided by the 10 concerned citizens are not recognized as contribution revenue and expenses because these services did not create or enhance nonfinancial assets or require special skills.

5. **$2,000.** The music festival was a special event. Thus, only the $2,000 for printing and mailing pledge cards qualified as a general fund-raising expense.

6. **$0.** No long-term investments were unrestricted.

7. **$0.** The services are not recognized because they do not create or enhance nonfinancial assets, and they do not require special skills.

5. Cash Flows Classification (8 Gradable Items)

1. <u>A) Cash flows from operating activities.</u> Operating activities include all activities not defined as investing or financing activities. Financing activities include the issuance of stock, the payment of dividends, treasury stock transactions, the issuance of debt, and the repayment or other settlement of debt obligations. They also include receiving contributions and investment income that are donor-restricted to acquiring, constructing, or improving long-lived assets or to establishing or increasing a permanent or term endowment. Because the collections on Year 1 promises were unrestricted, they should be classified as operating cash flows.

2. <u>A) Cash flows from operating activities.</u> Operating activities include all activities not defined as investing or financing activities. Thus, a cash flow from a refundable advance made pursuant to a conditional promise to give is an operating item because no indication is given that it qualifies as an investing or financing cash flow.

3. <u>B) Cash flows from investing activities.</u> Investing activities include making and collecting loans and acquiring and disposing of debt or equity instruments and property, plant, and equipment and other productive assets, that is, assets held for or used in the production of goods or services (other than the materials held in inventory). Thus, a cash outflow for purchase of a bus (equipment) is an investing item.

4. <u>C) Cash flows from financing activities.</u> The repayment or other settlement of debt is a financing activity.

5. <u>B) Cash flows from investing activities.</u> Investing activities include acquiring and disposing of equity instruments.

6. <u>A) Cash flows from operating activities.</u> Cash flows from operating activities include cash receipts from sales of goods and services, from interest on loans, and from dividends on equity securities as well as cash payments to employees and suppliers; to governments for taxes, duties, and fees; and to lenders for interest.

7. <u>A) Cash flows from operating activities.</u> Paying interest on loans is an operating activity, but repayment of principal is ordinarily a financing activity.

8. <u>A) Cash flows from operating activities.</u> In general, cash receipts from returns on loans, other debt instruments of other entities, and equity securities (interest and dividends) are cash inflows from operating activities.

6. Communication (5 Gradable Items; for grading instructions, please refer to page 12.)

Under trusts or other arrangements, NPOs may share benefits with others through split-interest agreements (SIAs). SIAs may be revocable or irrevocable, and the period covered may be a specific number of years (or in perpetuity) or the remaining life of a designated individual or individuals. The assets are invested by the NPO, a trustee, or a fiscal agent, with distributions made to beneficiaries during the term of the agreement. At the end of the agreement, the remaining assets are distributed to or retained by either the NPO or another beneficiary. If the NPO has a lead interest, it receives distributions during the agreement's term. If it has a remainder interest, the donor (or others designated by the donor) receives those distributions, and the NPO receives all or part of the assets remaining at the end of the agreement.

Assets received under irrevocable SIAs are recorded at fair value. The contribution is recognized as a revenue or gain. Also, liabilities incurred in the exchange part of an SIA are recognized.

Absent conditions, contribution revenue and related assets and liabilities are recognized when an irrevocable SIA naming the NPO trustees or fiscal agent is executed. If a third party acts as a trustee or fiscal agent, recognition occurs when the NPO is notified of the agreement. The third party may have variance power, or the NPO may have only conditional rights to the benefits. In these situations, contribution revenue and related assets and liabilities are not recognized until the NPO has an unconditional right to receive benefits.

A revocable SIA is accounted for as an intention to give. If an NPO serves as trustee under a revocable SIA, assets received are recognized at fair value when received and as refundable advances. Contribution revenue is not recognized until the SIA becomes irrevocable, or the assets are distributed to the NPO for its conditional use. Income on assets not available for the NPO's unconditional use and any subsequent adjustments to their carrying amount are treated as adjustments to the assets and as refundable advances.

Upon initial recognition of an unconditional irrevocable SIA, contributions are measured at fair value. Changes in fair value of SIAs are recognized in a statement of activities and classified in the appropriate net assets category.

When an SIA terminates, related assets and liabilities are closed. Remaining amounts are recognized as changes in the value of SIAs and classified in the appropriate net assets category.

7. Research/Authoritative Literature (1 Gradable Item)

Answer: FAS 93, Par. 6

FAS 93 -- *Recognition of Depreciation by Not-for-Profit Organizations*

6. **Recognition and Disclosure.** Consistent with the accepted practice for land used as a building site, depreciation need not be recognized on individual works of art or historical treasures whose economic benefit or service potential is used up so slowly that their estimated useful lives are extraordinarily long. A work of art or historical treasure shall be deemed to have that characteristic only if verifiable evidence exists demonstrating that (a) the asset individually has cultural, aesthetic, or historical value that is worth preserving perpetually and (b) the holder has the technological and financial ability to protect and preserve essentially undiminished the service potential of the asset and is doing that.

Scoring Schedule:

	Correct Responses		Gradable Items		Weights		
Tab 3	_____	÷	4	×	15%	=	_____
Tab 4	_____	÷	7	×	20%	=	_____
Tab 5	_____	÷	8	×	20%	=	_____
Tab 6	_____	÷	5	×	30%	=	_____
Tab 7	_____	÷	1	×	15%	=	_____
							_____
							(Your Score)

Use Gleim's **CPA Gleim Online** to practice more simulations in a realistic environment.

APPENDIX A
PRONOUNCEMENT SUMMARY

This appendix provides summaries of financial accounting pronouncements tested on the Financial Accounting & Reporting section (FAR is the AICPA's acronym).

Throughout this book, the sources of official pronouncements often are cited to document the information provided and to facilitate further study. However, learning their formal titles or numbers is not necessary. Rather, candidates need to understand their content and how to apply it. This understanding is the focus of the study outlines and answer explanations in this book.

Accounting pronouncements may be tested 6 months after their effective date. When early application is permitted, pronouncements may be tested 6 months after the issuance date, but the old rule is also subject to testing until superseded.

The following outlines summarize certain CAP (Committee on Accounting Procedure of the AICPA), APB (Accounting Principles Board of the AICPA), FASB, and GASB pronouncements. Those superseded have been omitted. The unsuperseded Accounting Research Bulletins issued by the CAP are not identified by number or chapter but are summarized in one outline. If a pronouncement of the APB, FASB, or GASB is extensively outlined in the main text, no summary is given.

ACCOUNTING RESEARCH BULLETINS (ARBs)

A. Normally, **gross profit** is recognized at the time a sale in the ordinary course of business occurs, unless collection of the price is not reasonably assured. Sales are recorded when title passes or a service is performed. Related costs are recognized in the same period. If collection is **not reasonably assured**, the installment method or the cost recovery method should be used to account for income.

    1. Under the **installment method**, gross profit is deferred and recognized as cash is collected (e.g., if 30% of a cash sale is collected in one year, 30% of the gross profit would then be recognized).

    2. The **cost recovery method** only recognizes profit after all costs have been recovered.

B. Paid-in capital is charged only for losses (and deficits in retained earnings) in quasi-reorganizations. A **quasi-reorganization** is a statutorily prescribed procedure by which a company may eliminate a deficit in retained earnings by writing down assets to fair values and then charging paid-in capital (and perhaps even reducing the par or stated value of stock). The result is a retained earnings account with a zero balance.

    1. Disclosure of a quasi-reorganization must be made in the notes to the financial statements for the following 10 years.

C. **Current assets** are cash and other assets expected to be realized in cash, sold, or consumed during the normal operating cycle of the business.

    1. **Current liabilities** are obligations requiring the use of current assets or creation of other current liabilities during the operating cycle of the business.

    2. The **operating cycle** is the average time between the expenditure of cash for materials and services and the final realization of cash.

D. **Inventory** consists of finished goods, work-in-process, and raw materials.

    1. Inventory cost includes fixed and variable production overheads.

    2. **Lower of cost or market (LCM)** defines market as replacement cost.

        a. **Replacement cost** cannot be more than net realizable value (upper limit).

            1) Net realizable value is selling price minus cost to complete and disposal costs.

        b. Replacement cost cannot be less than net realizable value minus normal profit (lower limit).

    c.   These limits on replacement cost preclude deferring inventory costs at values that would seriously over- or understate inventory and therefore result in losses or abnormal gains in subsequent periods.

    d.   If inventory has been the **hedged item in a fair value hedge**, its cost basis used in the LCM determination reflects adjustments of its carrying amount for changes in fair value attributable to the hedged risk.

    3.   Inventory may be stated above cost only when there is no basis for cost allocation and both the disposal price and sale are assured.

    4.   Any losses on **purchase commitments** should be recognized when they occur.

E.   A receipt of a **stock dividend** or a **stock split-up** is not a receipt of income.

    1.   The distinction between stock dividends and stock split-ups is usually determined by the intent of the distributing enterprise. However, the magnitude of the increase in the number of shares outstanding is also relevant.

        a.   Increases of less than 20% to 25% are normally considered dividends. Increases in excess of 20% to 25% are stock split-ups. ARB 43 recommends that the term "dividend" be avoided in the latter case. However, if such usage is legally required, the transaction should be described by a term such as "split-up" effected in the form of a dividend.

        b.   Dividends are accounted for by debiting retained earnings and crediting capital stock for the fair value of shares issued.

            1)   For stock dividends of closely held companies and stock split-ups of all companies, only the amount necessary to meet legal requirements must be debited to retained earnings. This amount is usually the par or stated value.

F.   Assets should not be written up to **appraisal values**. But if they are, depreciation should be recorded on the written-up amount.

G.   Real and personal property tax assessment, billing, collection, etc., vary from jurisdiction to jurisdiction. **Tax expense** should be recognized by monthly accrual over the fiscal period of the taxing authority.

H.   **Stock option and stock purchase plans** may involve a measurable amount of compensation to employees, and this cost of services should be accounted for as such. However, it is not recognized if the options are issued either to raise capital or to encourage wider holdings by employees. See also **SFAS 123** (revised 2004), *Share-Based Payment*.

I.   **Accelerated depreciation** (including declining-balance and sum-of-the-years'-digits) is systematic and rational and is acceptable under GAAP.

J.   The **percentage-of-completion method** is recommended (instead of the completed-contract method) when total costs and percentage of completion may be reasonably estimated.

K.   **ARB 51**, as amended by SFAS 94, requires that **consolidated financial statements** be issued when one entity owns over 50% of another, unless control does not rest with the majority owner, e.g., because the subsidiary is in legal reorganization or bankruptcy or operating under foreign exchange restrictions, controls, or severe governmentally imposed uncertainties.

    1.   Differing fiscal periods of parents and subsidiaries of up to 3 months are acceptable; otherwise, interim statements must be used to prepare the consolidated worksheet.

    2.   Intraentity balances and the effects of intraentity transactions should be eliminated in the consolidated statements.

    3.   **SFAS 131**, *Disclosures about Segments of an Enterprise and Related Information*, covers the reporting of revenues from foreign operations and assets located outside the U.S.

ACCOUNTING PRINCIPLES BOARD OPINIONS (APB Opinions)

A. The Accounting Principles Board (APB) was the predecessor of the FASB. It issued 30 Opinions. Those still relevant are outlined below and on the next page or in a study unit.

1. **APB Opinion 4**, *Accounting for the "Investment Credit,"* allows an investment credit to be recognized either as a reduction in federal income taxes in the year when the credit arises (the **flow-through method**) or as a reduction of net income over the productive life of the property. The latter treatment (the **deferral method**) may be accomplished by subtracting the credit from the cost of the asset or by characterizing it as deferred income to be amortized over the useful life of the asset.

   a. An investment credit is reflected in the financial statements to the extent it offsets income taxes otherwise currently payable or to the extent its benefit is recognizable under **SFAS 109**, *Accounting for Income Taxes*.

2. **APB Opinion 6**, *Status of Accounting Research Bulletins*, revised several of the ARBs.

   a. **Accounts and notes receivable** should be reported net of unearned discounts (except for cash and quantity discounts and similar items), finance charges, and interest.

   b. The **equity method** is permitted for substantial intercorporate investments.

   c. APB Opinion 6 describes the accounting and reporting for both **treasury stock** intended to be retired and that acquired for other purposes. For example, "gains" on treasury stock transactions are additional paid-in capital (not income).

      1) "Losses" may be debited to additional paid-in capital, to the extent it exists for that class of stock. Otherwise, retained earnings should be debited.

   d. **Property, plant, and equipment** should not be written up to fair values (but if they have been, depreciation should be based on the written-up values).

3. **APB Opinion 10**, *Omnibus Opinion-1966*, clarifies previously issued pronouncements and addresses miscellaneous matters.

   a. Liabilities and assets are not to be **offset** against each other unless a right of offset exists.

   b. **Revenues** should be recognized when goods are sold unless the collectibility of receivables is in doubt and no reasonable basis exists for estimating the degree of collectibility.

   c. Deferred taxes should not be reported on a **discounted basis**.

4. **APB Opinion 12**, *Omnibus Opinion-1967*, concerns a variety of issues.

   a. Allowances should be deducted from the related assets or groups of assets.

   b. Full disclosure should be made of **depreciation** methods and practices, including

      1) Depreciation expense for the period
      2) Balances of major classes of depreciable assets by nature or function
      3) Accumulated depreciation either by major class or in total
      4) Description of depreciation methods for each major class of assets

   c. **Changes in equity.** Disclosure of changes in all equity accounts and of changes in the number of equity securities should be made in a separate statement, the basic statements, or the notes.

   d. **Deferred compensation contracts** that are equivalent to a postretirement income plan or health or welfare benefit plan should be accounted for in accordance with SFAS 87 or SFAS 106, respectively.

      1) Other deferred compensation contracts should be accounted for individually on an accrual basis and in a systematic and rational manner over the employee's term of service. At the end of that term, the total accrual should equal the present value of the expected benefits.

e.   The **interest method** may be used to amortize debt discount and expense or premium.

5.   **APB Opinion 23**, *Accounting for Income Taxes - Special Areas*, contains certain specialized exceptions to the requirements for recognition of deferred taxes.

STATEMENTS OF FINANCIAL ACCOUNTING STANDARDS (SFASs)

A.   SFASs are the main pronouncements of the FASB. To date, 163 have been issued. Those still in effect and not covered in detail in a study unit are summarized below and on the following pages.

1.   **SFAS 19**, *Financial Accounting and Reporting by Oil and Gas Producing Companies*, **SFAS 25**, *Suspension of Certain Accounting Requirements for Oil and Gas Producing Companies*, and **SFAS 69**, *Disclosures about Oil and Gas Producing Activities*, apply to **oil- and gas-**producing activities that involve exploration, development, production, and the acquisition of mineral interests in properties.

a.   These activities may be accounted for in accordance with either the successful-efforts method or the full-cost method. **Full-cost accounting** capitalizes all costs of acquiring, exploring, and developing properties in a **relatively large geopolitical area** when incurred. They are amortized as mineral reserves are produced. However, capitalized costs must not exceed the value of reserves. **Successful-efforts accounting** capitalizes costs that result directly in the discovery of oil or gas (successful wells). The same costs are expensed for dry holes (unsuccessful wells). Thus, **acquisition costs** are capitalized. Otherwise, capitalization requires a direct relationship between incurrence of cost and discovery of specific reserves.

b.   All entities must **disclose** how costs of oil- and gas-producing activities are accounted for and how capitalized costs are amortized. The following are other required disclosures by **publicly-held** companies if 10% or more of revenues or income (loss) is derived from oil- and gas-producing activities:

1)   Proved oil and gas reserves at beginning and end of year

2)   Aggregate capitalized costs and accumulated depreciation on oil and gas property

3)   Oil and gas costs for the period

4)   Operating results in the aggregate and by each area for which reserve data are disclosed

5)   Discounted future cash flows from proved reserves

2.   **SFAS 22**, *Changes in the Provisions of Lease Agreements Resulting from Refundings of Tax-Exempt Debt*, applies when the lessor refunds tax-exempt debt; the advantages of the refunding are passed through to the lessee; and the lessee classifies the revised agreement as a capital lease, or the lessor classifies it as a direct-financing lease.

3.   **SFAS 23**, *Inception of the Lease*, defines the inception of the lease as occurring at the date of the earlier of the lease agreement or commitment, not at the date that construction is completed or the property is acquired by the lessor. It also redefines the "fair value of the leased property" for a lease with a cost-based or escalator provision.

4.   **SFAS 27**, *Classification of Renewals or Extensions of Existing Sales-Type or Direct Financing Leases*, requires a lessor to classify a renewal or an extension of a sales-type or direct financing lease as a sales-type lease if the lease otherwise qualifies as a sales-type lease and the renewal or extension occurs near the end of the lease term.

5.   **SFAS 29**, *Determining Contingent Rentals*, defines contingent rentals as lease payments based on a factor that does not exist or is not measurable at the inception of the lease. For example, future sales do not exist at the inception of the lease, so lease payments based on future sales are contingent rentals.

6. **SFAS 35**, *Accounting and Reporting by Defined Benefit Pension Plans*, applies to defined benefit plans, whether or not subject to ERISA, except those of state and local governments, which are covered by GASB pronouncements. Thus, it does not provide guidance for employers. It requires that financial statements of these plans be prepared on an accrual basis and that substantial disclosures be made.

    a. **Net assets available for benefits** at year-end with reasonable detail of

        1) Contributions receivable
        2) Investments (at fair value, but see SFAS 110)
        3) Operating assets

    b. **Changes in net assets** during the year

        1) Net appreciation (depreciation) of each class of investment
        2) Investment income
        3) Contributions

            a) Employer
            b) Employee
            c) Other, e.g., government

        4) Benefits paid
        5) Payments to insurance companies
        6) Administrative expenses

    c. **Actuarial present value of benefits** at the beginning or end of the year based on

        1) Employee pay and length of employment
        2) Expected continued employment
        3) Future benefit increases
        4) Other factors affecting future payments

    d. Factors affecting changes in the actuarial present value of plan benefits that are **assumptions** about the future, including

        1) Rate of Return
        2) Inflation
        3) Employee continued service
        4) Investment current value
        5) Method of computing benefit present value

    e. Further description, if applicable, of

        1) The plan agreement
        2) Significant plan amendments
        3) The priority order of participants' claims to the assets of the plan upon plan termination and benefits guaranteed by the **Pension Benefit Guaranty Corporation (PBGC)**
        4) The funding policy and any changes in such policy
        5) The policy regarding purchase of contracts with insurance companies that are excluded from plan assets
        6) The federal income tax status of the plan, if a favorable letter of determination has not been obtained
        7) Investments of 5% or more of the net assets available for benefits
        8) Significant real estate or other transactions with related parties
        9) Significant, unusual, or infrequent events or transactions occurring after the latest information date but before issuance of the statements

7. **SFAS 37**, *Balance Sheet Classification of Deferred Income Taxes*, states that a temporary difference (TD) relates to an asset or liability if reduction of the asset or liability causes the TD to reverse. A deferred tax amount for a TD related to an asset or liability is classified based on the classification of the asset or liability. A deferred tax amount for a TD not related to an asset or liability is classified based on the expected reversal date of the TD.

8. **SFAS 42**, *Determining Materiality for Capitalization of Interest Cost*, amended SFAS 34 to delete ambiguous language that might be construed to allow capitalization of interest to be avoided in some cases and to clarify that SFAS 34 does not establish new tests of materiality.

9. **SFAS 50**, *Financial Reporting in the Record and Music Industry*, requires the owner of a record master or copyright to recognize revenue from a **licensing agreement** that is an outright sale in substance, provided that **collectibility** of the full amount is reasonably assured. The **earning process** is complete if the licensor has (a) signed a noncancelable contract, (b) agreed to a fixed fee, (c) delivered the rights to a licensee who is free to use them, and (4) incurred no significant remaining obligations to provide records or music.

    a. **Minimum guarantees** received in advance by the **licensor** are recorded initially as a liability. They are recognized as revenue when the license fee is earned. If the amount of the fee earned in a period is not determinable, the guarantee is recognized equally over the **performance period** (normally the period of the agreement). **Other fees** are recognized as revenue when reasonable estimates of their amounts can be made or the agreement expires.

    b. **Artists' royalties** (adjusted for expected returns) are expensed when the records are sold. **Advances** are recorded as prepaid assets if a sound basis exists for estimating that they are recoverable. They are expensed as earned by artists or if a loss becomes evident. Amounts are **classified** as current and noncurrent.

    c. The **costs of record masters** are assets if a sound basis exists for estimating that they are recoverable. These amounts are amortized over the estimated useful life by a method reasonably relating amounts to net estimated revenue.

    d. **Minimum guarantees** paid in advance by a **licensee** to a licensor should be capitalized by the licensee and expensed in accordance with the terms of the licensing agreement, unless all or a portion of the guarantee appears nonrecoverable. The amount not recoverable from future use of the license is expensed. **Other fees** are estimated and accrued by the licensee on a per-license basis unless fixed prior to the agreement's expiration.

10. **SFAS 51**, *Financial Reporting by Cable Television Companies*, prescribes accounting by cable TV companies during the **prematurity period** (usually no more than 2 years). This period begins with the first subscriber revenue and ends when (a) a predetermined subscriber level is reached, (b) no additional investment for the cable TV plant is required, or (3) the first major construction period is completed. The period is not changed once established (unless circumstances are very unusual). The portion of a system that is in the prematurity period is separately accounted for if it is clearly distinguishable. Costs of the remainder of the system are charged to the portion in the prematurity period only if such costs are specifically identified with it.

    a. During the prematurity period, the cost of the **cable television plant**, including materials, direct labor, and overhead, must be capitalized in full. **Subscriber-related costs** and **general administrative expenses** should be expensed during, as well as after, the prematurity period. **Programming and other system costs and depreciation and amortization** are expensed according to the relationship of the current level of subscribers to the number expected at the end of the prematurity stage.

    b. **Interest cost** capitalized during the prematurity period is based on **SFAS 34**.

c.   **Initial hookup revenue** is recognized as revenue to the extent that **direct selling costs** are incurred. They include commissions, salespersons' compensation, local advertising, document processing, etc. Any remaining initial hookup revenue should be deferred and amortized over the estimated average period that subscribers are expected to remain connected.

d.   **Initial subscriber installation costs** should be capitalized and depreciated over a period not to exceed the expected useful life of the cable TV plant. The costs of subsequent disconnecting and reconnecting are expensed as incurred.

e.   **Costs of successful franchise applications** are capitalized and amortized in accordance with GAAP for intangible assets. Costs of unsuccessful applications are expensed as incurred.

f.   GAAP for determining **impairment of long-lived assets** apply to cable TV plant and intangible assets.

11.   **SFAS 58**, *Capitalization of Interest Cost in Financial Statements That Include Investments Accounted for by the Equity Method*, amended **SFAS 34** to limit capitalization of consolidated interest to qualifying assets of the parent and consolidated subsidiaries. Investments by the investor qualify if they are accounted for by the equity method during the period that "the investee has activities in progress necessary to commence its planned principal operations provided that the investee's activities include the use of funds to acquire qualifying assets for its operations."

12.   **SFAS 60**, *Accounting and Reporting by Insurance Enterprises*, requires insurance enterprises to classify insurance contracts as short-duration or long-duration. **Short-duration contracts** give protection for a fixed, short period. The insurer may cancel the contract or adjust its terms (e.g., premiums or coverage) at the end of a contract period. Examples are most property and liability contracts and certain term life insurance contracts. **Long-duration contracts** ordinarily are not subject to unilateral changes. They require performance of functions and services over an extended period. Examples are **whole life insurance** (in force for the insured's entire life), **endowment contracts** (the maturity amount, adjusted for any loans and dividends, is paid to the insured if (s)he survives to the maturity date), and **annuity contracts** (payments are made from a specified or contingent date for a specified period).

a.   **Premiums** from **short-duration contracts** ordinarily are recognized as revenue over the period of the contract in proportion to the amount of insurance protection provided. Liabilities for **unpaid claims** (including estimated costs of unreported insured events that have occurred) and **claim adjustment expenses** are credited at the time of insured events. If the **period of risk** differs significantly from the contract period, premium revenue is recognized over the period of risk. If **premiums are adjustable**, a reasonably estimable ultimate premium is recognized over the contract period (but is revised for current experience). The **cost recovery method** or **deposit method** is used if the ultimate premium is not reasonably estimable. A **premium deficiency** is accounted for by expensing any unamortized acquisition costs. A liability is then credited for any excess deficiency. A premium deficiency equals the sum of the following items over the sum of the related unearned premiums:

1)   Expected claim costs,
2)   Expected claim adjustment expenses,
3)   Expected dividends to policyholders,
4)   Unamortized acquisition costs for new and renewal contracts, and
5)   Maintenance costs.

b.   **Premiums** from **long-duration contracts** are recognized as revenue when due from policyholders. A liability for related **expected costs** is accrued over the duration (current and expected renewal periods) of the contracts. A liability for **future policy benefits** (present value of estimated benefits payable – present value of estimated net premiums collectible) is accrued when premium revenue is recognized. **Estimates** are based on **assumptions** made when contracts are formed, for example, (1) investment returns, (2) mortality (rate of deaths for a given place), (3) morbidity (rate of disability from disease or physical impairment, (4) terminations of contracts (e.g., from expiration, maturity, death of insureds, or failure to pay premiums), and (5) expenses.

1)   A **premium deficiency** arises when actual experience indicates that existing liabilities and the present value of future gross premiums are insufficient. A premium deficiency is debited to income. The credit is to unamortized acquisition costs or to the liability for future policy benefits. The following is the calculation based on assumptions revised for actual and expected experience:

> PV of future payments (benefits and costs)
> – PV of future gross premiums
> ——————————————————————
> Liability for future policy benefits (revised)
> – (Liability for future policy benefits at valuation date –
>   unamortized acquisition costs)
> ——————————————————————
> Deficiency

c.   **Acquisition costs** vary with, and are primarily related to, obtaining insurance contracts. Examples are commissions paid to agents and brokers, medical fees, property inspection fees, and certain policy issue costs. Acquisition costs are **capitalized and expensed** in proportion to the recognition of premium revenue. Other costs are **expensed as incurred**.

d.   An insurance enterprise accrues **estimated policyholder dividends**. A limitation may exist on the portion of net income from participating **life insurance contracts** that may be distributed to shareholders. The nondistributable amount is debited to operations and credited to a liability. **Dividends declared or paid** to policyholders decrease the liability.

13. **SFAS 61**, *Accounting for Title Plant*, applies to title insurance enterprises. It defines title plant as a historical record of all matters affecting title to parcels of land in a particular geographic area. It includes (a) indexed and cataloged information concerning ownership and encumbrances on parcels of the land in a geographic area; (b) information relating to persons having an interest in real estate; and (c) maps and plots, copies of prior title insurance contracts, and other documents and records. Updated on a daily or other frequent basis, title plants are maintained for the number of years required by regulation and for the minimum information period considered necessary to issue title insurance policies efficiently. Title plant does not include the building, furniture, or fixtures of the title insurance firm. The **costs of title plants** should be capitalized as they are developed. After completion, they should not be depreciated. All the costs of updating (maintaining) the title plant and doing title searches should be expensed as incurred. Costs of subsequent modernization of the information retrieval system or conversion to another retrieval system should be capitalized and expensed systematically and rationally (i.e., depreciated).

14. **SFAS 62**, *Capitalization of Interest Cost in Situations Involving Certain Tax-Exempt Borrowings and Certain Gifts and Grants*, amended **SFAS 34** to require capitalization of interest cost of restricted tax-exempt borrowings minus interest earned on their temporary investment from the date of borrowing until the qualifying assets are ready for their intended use. It also prohibits capitalization of interest on qualifying assets acquired using restricted gifts or grants.

15. **SFAS 63**, *Financial Reporting by Broadcasters*, requires broadcasters (licensees) to report the rights acquired (an asset) and obligations incurred (a liability) under a **license agreement for program material** when the (a) license period begins, (b) cost of each program is known or determinable, (c) program material has been accepted by the licensee, and (d) program is available for its first viewing or telecast. The **asset** should be allocated in the balance sheet between current and noncurrent based on the **time of usage**. The **liability** should be allocated between current and noncurrent based on **payment terms**. The asset and liability for a broadcast license agreement are reported at either the **present value** of the liability or the **gross amount** of the liability. **Amortization of capitalized costs** is based on one of these methods. Allocation of the costs to programs in a package is according to their **relative value to the broadcaster**, which is usually determined by contract. **Feature programs** are amortized individually. **Program series** and other syndicated products are amortized on a per-series basis. **Accelerated amortization** is used when initial showings are more valuable than reruns.

   a. **Rights to program materials** are reported at the lower of **unamortized cost** or **estimated net realizable value**. Measurement may be by program, series, package, or **daypart** (a group of similar programs, e.g., sports, or those broadcast during a given segment of the day, e.g., in the afternoon).

   b. Broadcasters frequently barter unsold advertising time for products or services. **Barter revenue** should be recognized in appropriate amounts when the commercials are broadcast. The amounts should be reported at the **estimated fair value** of the product or service received in accordance with **APB Opinion 29**. Revenue is not earned until the commercials are broadcast. The merchandise or services need not be resold for revenue to be recognized. An **asset** should be recognized if the commercials are broadcast before the merchandise or services are received. A **liability** should be recognized if the merchandise or services are received before the commercials are broadcast.

   c. **Network affiliation agreements** and similar items are classified as **intangible assets**. They are valuable because they permit a station to obtain programming more cheaply than its unaffiliated competitors. If the agreement is **terminated**, the accounting depends on whether it is immediately replaced or under agreement to be replaced. If not, the unamortized balance is **expensed**. Otherwise, a **loss** is recognized if the new agreement's fair value is less than the carrying amount of the old. However, **no gain** is recognized if that fair value exceeds the carrying amount of the old agreement.

16. **SFAS 65**, *Accounting for Certain Mortgage Banking Activities*, as amended by SFAS 91, *Accounting for Nonrefundable Fees and Costs Associated with Originating or Acquiring Loans and Initial Direct Costs of Leases*, establishes accounting and reporting standards for the mortgage banking industry. It states that mortgage loans and mortgage-backed securities held for sale are reported at lower of cost or market value. If a loan is held for resale, loan origination fees and the direct loan origination costs specified in SFAS 91 are deferred until the related loan is sold. If the loan is held for investment, such fees and costs are deferred and recognized as an adjustment of yield by the interest method. Fees for services performed by third parties and loan placement fees are recognized as revenue when all significant services have been performed.

17. **SFAS 66**, *Accounting for Sales of Real Estate*, addresses recognition of profit or loss on retail and nonretail sales. These sales may involve property improvements or integral equipment, such as refineries, power plants, manufacturing facilities, or office buildings.

   a. Under **FASB Interpretation No. 43**, *Real Estate Sales*, SFAS 66 applies to sales of real estate with **property improvements** or **integral equipment** that cannot be removed without significant cost. However, it is inapplicable to

   1) Separate sales (without the land or a lease of the land) of property improvements or integral equipment;

2) Sales of net assets or stock of a subsidiary or segment unless the substance of the transaction is a real estate sale; or

3) Sales of securities accounted for under SFAS 115.

b. A **retail land sales project** is a homogeneous, reasonably contiguous area of land that may, for development and marketing, be subdivided. A single method should be used to recognize profit from all sales transactions within a retail land sales project. However, when certain conditions change for the entire project, the method of recognizing profit should be changed to reflect the new conditions.

1) The **accrual method** is applied to a retail land sale if

    a) The period of cancelation with refund has expired,

    b) Cumulative payments equal or exceed 10% of the contract sales price,

    c) The receivables are collectible,

    d) The receivables are not subject to subordination, and

    e) The development is complete.

2) If these criteria are not met, the **percentage-of-completion method** is applied if

    a) The accrual method conditions in 1)a) through 1)d) are satisfied,

    b) There has been progress on improvements, and

    c) The development is practical.

3) If the conditions for the accrual and percentage-of-completion methods are not met, the **installment method** is applied if

    a) The conditions in 1)a) and 1)b) are satisfied, and

    b) The seller is financially capable.

4) If no method listed above is appropriate, then the transaction is incomplete, no sale is recorded, and cash received is treated as a deposit (a liability).

c. Profit is recognized in full on **other real estate sales** if the profit is determinable and the earning process is virtually complete.

1) The full **accrual method** may be used to recognize the profit if

    a) The sale is consummated,

    b) The buyer's initial and continuing investment demonstrates a commitment to pay for the property,

    c) The seller's receivable is not subject to future subordination, and

    d) The seller has no substantial continuing involvement with the property.

2) If those conditions are not met, various methods are used. For example, if a sale has not occurred, the **deposit method** is used. Thus, the seller reports cash received as a liability. No revenue or income is recorded.

    a) If the initial investment is insufficient for recognition of profit under the accrual method, either the **installment or the cost-recovery method** is used if recovery of the cost is reasonably assured.

        i) The cost-recovery method recognizes profit only after collections exceed cost.

        ii) The installment method recognizes gross profit each period equal to the gross profit percentage times the cash collected.

    b) If recovery of the cost is not reasonably assured or if cost has been recovered but collection of additional amounts is uncertain, the **cost-recovery or the deposit method** is used.

    c)   If the initial but not the continuing investment is sufficient for use of the accrual method, the **reduced-profit method** is used if each year's payments at least cover interest and principal amortization on the maximum first mortgage obtainable plus interest on the excess of the debt over such a loan. If these criteria are not met, the **installment or cost-recovery method** may be used.

        i)   The reduced-profit method **discounts the receivable** from the buyer using an appropriate rate not less than the contract rate. The annual payments to be discounted are the lowest required by the contract over the maximum period specified in SFAS 66 (20 years for a land sale and the customary term for a first mortgage in other sales). The discount reduces the profit recognized over the maximum period.

    d.   Under **SFAS 152**, *Accounting for Real Estate Time-Sharing Transactions*, time-sharing transactions are accounted for as nonretail land sales.

18.   **SFAS 67**, *Accounting for Costs and Initial Rental Operations of Real Estate Projects*, applies to acquisition, development, construction, selling, and rental costs of such projects.

    a.   **Payments to obtain an option** to acquire real property should be capitalized. **Other preacquisition costs** incurred before the enterprise acquires the property should be expensed, not capitalized, unless the following conditions are met:

        1)   The costs are directly identifiable with a specific property.
        2)   The costs would be capitalized if the property had already been acquired.
        3)   Acquisition of an option to acquire the property is probable.

    b.   **Taxes and insurance costs** are capitalized during periods when activities necessary to get the property ready for its intended use are in progress.

    c.   **Direct costs** of acquiring, developing, and constructing real estate projects and **indirect costs** clearly related to several projects are capitalized.

    d.   If **amenities** are transferred with individual units, their costs in excess of anticipated proceeds are allocated as **common costs**.

        1)   If amenities are sold separately or retained by the developer, their capitalizable costs exceeding fair value are allocated as common costs.
        2)   Costs of amenities are allocated to the parcels benefited.
        3)   Before completion, amenity income (loss) is an adjustment of common costs. Afterward, income and expenses are included in current operating results.

    e.   Incremental revenue in excess of incremental costs of **incidental operations** is a reduction of capitalized costs, but excess incremental costs are expensed.

    f.   Capitalized costs of a real estate project should be allocated to its components by **specific identification**. If that is not practicable, land costs are allocated based on the **relative fair values** of the parcels before construction.

        1)   Construction costs are allocated to units on the basis of **relative sales values**.
        2)   If allocation based on relative value is also not practicable, the capitalized cost is allocated based on an **area method** such as square footage.

    g.   Capitalized costs of **abandoned real estate** are expensed.

        1)   Costs of real estate **donated** to governmental agencies to benefit the project are common costs.
        2)   If a **change in use** is made under a formal plan for a project expected to have a higher yield, costs expensed are limited to the excess of the capitalized costs incurred and to be incurred over the estimated value of the revised project.

h. Reasonably recoverable **costs incurred to sell real estate projects** should be capitalized if they are incurred for (1) tangible assets used directly throughout the selling period to aid in the sale or (2) services needed for regulatory approval.

    1) Other reasonably recoverable selling costs are recorded as prepaid costs if they are directly associated with sales not accounted for by the full accrual method.

i. **Costs incurred to rent a real estate project** should be capitalized if they directly relate to its rental and their recovery is reasonably expected.

j. A real estate project should be considered **substantially completed and held available for occupancy** upon completion of tenant improvements by the developer. This date is no later than 1 year from the end of major construction activity. When the project is substantially complete, costs are expensed as they accrue and previously capitalized costs should be amortized.

    1) Costs related to a rental project for which some portions are substantially completed and others are still under construction should be allocated to each portion. They are then treated as separate projects.

k. If a real estate project (or a part) is substantially complete and is to be sold, **SFAS 144**, *Accounting for the Impairment or Disposal of Long-Lived Assets*, applies to **long-lived assets to be disposed of by sale**. Thus, the project will be measured at the **lower of its carrying amount or fair value minus cost to sell**.

    1) The provisions of SFAS 144 relating to **long-lived assets to be held and used** apply to real estate held for development and to a real estate project that is substantially complete and is to be held and used. Individual projects must be evaluated to determine any impairment loss. If the carrying amount exceeds fair value and is not recoverable from the expected undiscounted cash flows, an **impairment loss** equal to that excess is recognized.

l. SFAS 67 does not apply to (1) costs of selling real estate projects or (2) incidental operations if such costs or operations are related to **time-sharing transactions**.

19. **SFAS 71**, *Accounting for the Effects of Certain Types of Regulation*, applies to the general-purpose financial statements of regulated enterprises. Proprietary activities of state and local governments that meet the criteria in SFAS 71 may apply this statement.

a. **Criteria.** SFAS 71 applies when (1) the enterprise's **rates** are approved by an independent regulator, or its board is authorized by statute or contract to set rates; (2) rates are intended to recover the specific enterprise's **costs** of providing regulated services or products; and (3) given demand and the level of competition, it is reasonable to expect that rates set for cost recovery are **collectible from customers**.

b. SFAS 71 must be applied instead of **conflicting GAAP**. However, accounting prescribed by regulatory agencies should not be considered generally accepted in and of itself. Differences should exist between GAAP for nonrate-regulated enterprises and rate-regulated enterprises. Thus, SFAS 71 applies GAAP in the regulatory environment. For example, some public utilities are permitted to capitalize **interest** during construction based on the cost of debt capital (permitted under **SFAS 34**) and equity capital (not permitted by SFAS 34). In such a case, a utility would apply SFAS 71 instead of SFAS 34. Another example is that rates based on allowable costs may include reasonable **interentity profits**. These profits on **sales to regulated affiliates** are not eliminated if the price is reasonable, and it is probable that the rate-making process will result in future revenue equal to the price.

c. Rate actions by regulators provide assurance of the **existence of an asset**. Hence, **incurred costs** are **capitalized** if it is probable that the capitalized costs will be included in **allowable costs** for rate making, and **future revenue** will be provided by regulators for recovery of incurred costs (not future similar costs). Rate actions also may **eliminate an asset**. Thus, after exclusion of a cost from allowable costs, the carrying amount of the asset is reduced by the amount of the cost. If recovery is allowed for costs not previously allowed, a **new asset** is recognized.

d. Rate actions may impose a **liability** (usually to the enterprise's customers). The regulator may require **refunds** (a possible loss contingency). If current recovery is provided for costs that are expected to be incurred in the future, those **current receipts** should be recognized as liabilities. For example, if it is understood that future rates will be reduced if the costs are not incurred, revenue is not recognized. A **gain or other reduction of net allowable costs** may be amortized over future years by rate reductions. That amount is a liability.

e. **Other Relevant Pronouncements.** SFAS 71 requires recognition of a deferred tax liability or asset for the deferred tax consequences of temporary differences (**SFAS 109**, *Accounting for Income Taxes*). **Refunds to customers** should be recognized in accordance with **SFAS 5**, *Accounting for Contingencies*. **Leases** should be accounted for under **SFAS 13**, *Accounting for Leases*.

20. **SFAS 72**, *Accounting for Certain Acquisitions of Banking or Thrift Institutions*, was amended by **SFAS 147** to restrict its scope to transactions between or among mutual enterprises. SFAS 72 concerns accounting for the excess of the fair value of liabilities assumed over the fair value of tangible and identified intangible assets acquired in an acquisition of a bank or thrift institution. This "excess" (an unidentifiable intangible asset) is amortized by using the interest method. The amortization period is to be no longer than the period over which the discount on the long-term interest-bearing assets acquired is to be recognized as interest income (but not exceeding 40 years).

21. **SFAS 88**, *Employers' Accounting for Settlements and Curtailments of Defined Benefit Pension Plans and for Termination Benefits*, applies within the SFAS 87 framework.

a. A **settlement** is an irrevocable action that relieves the employer (or the plan) of the primary responsibility for a PBO. It eliminates significant risks related to the pension obligation and the assets used to effect the settlement. Recognition of a settlement gain or loss is mandatory if the cost of all settlements in a year exceeds the sum of the interest and service cost components of NPPC.

1) The **maximum potential settlement gain or loss** is the sum of any **net gain or loss** remaining in accumulated OCI plus any **transition asset** remaining in accumulated OCI from initial application of SFAS 87. (Because SFAS 87 became effective after 1986, no transition asset is likely to remain.)

a) The proportion of maximum gain or loss recognized in earnings equals the percentage reduction in the PBO.

b) If the purchase of a participating annuity contract constitutes a settlement, the **maximum gain** is reduced by the cost of the **right to participate** in the experience of the seller. The **maximum loss** is not adjusted.

c) For example, assume that an employer settles 80% of its $100,000 PBO by purchasing a nonparticipating annuity contract for $80,000. The net loss subsequent to transition and remaining in accumulated OCI was $30,000, and none of the remaining asset at transition remains. The **maximum loss** is therefore the $30,000 net loss. The **settlement loss** is $24,000 ($30,000 maximum loss × 80% settlement percentage).

b.   A **curtailment** significantly reduces the expected years of future service of current employees. An event also may be a curtailment if it eliminates the accrual of defined benefits for some or all future service for a significant number of employees.

   1)   A **curtailment net gain or loss** equals the sum of the following:

      a)   The prior service cost included in accumulated OCI associated with service no longer expected to be rendered (a **los**s)

      b)   The decrease in the **PBO** (a **gain**) or the increase in the PBO (a **loss**) that is not the reversal of any net loss or net gain, respectively, included in accumulated OCI.

   2)   In the calculation of curtailment net gain or loss, prior service cost includes any **transition obligation** included in accumulated OCI.

      a)   In the calculation of the PBO gain or loss, any **transition asset** included in accumulated OCI is treated as a net gain. It is combined with any net gain or loss that arose after the transition to SFAS 87. (As explained previously, the existence of a transition amount is now unlikely.)

   3)   **Termination of a plan** is not required for a curtailment.

   4)   A **net loss** is recognized when it is probable that a curtailment will occur and its effects are reasonably estimable.

   5)   A **net gain** is recognized when the related employees terminate their employment or the plan suspension or amendment is adopted.

EXAMPLE

On December 31, Year 5, Curtco curtailed its defined benefit pension plan. The PBO was $2,000,000 before the curtailment, and the reduction in the PBO was $200,000. The amounts included in accumulated OCI are the following:

Prior service cost associated with service no longer expected to be rendered	$200,000
Transition net asset	200,000
Net loss since the transition to SFAS 87	300,000

The curtailment net loss is calculated as follows:

Prior service cost		$(200,000)
PBO decrease	$ 200,000	
Transition net asset	200,000	
Net loss since transition	(300,000)	
Curtailment gain		100,000
Curtailment net loss		$(100,000)

---

c.   **Termination benefits** are provided to employees in connection with their termination of employment. Special termination benefits are offered only for a short period. Contractual termination benefits are required by the terms of a pension plan only if a specified event occurs.

   1)   The liability and loss arising from **special termination benefits** are recognized by an employer when the employees accept the offer and the amount can be reasonably estimated.

   2)   The liability and loss arising from **contractual termination benefits** are recognized when it is probable that employees will be entitled to benefits and the amount can be reasonably estimated.

   3)   The amount includes any lump-sum payments and the present value of any future payments.

d. Certain entities, e.g., **not-for-profit organizations (NPOs)**, do not report OCI. For them, the references above to OCI do not apply. Instead, the following are reported separately in the same line item(s) within **changes in unrestricted net assets**:

1) Gains (losses) and prior service costs (credits) **arising during the period** but not recognized in NPPC.

2) Reclassifications to NPPC of amortizations of amounts **previously recognized** in changes in unrestricted net assets. These amounts would have been recognized when the funded status of the plan was recognized. The reclassifications are of amounts previously reported for

a) Gains (losses)
b) Prior service costs (credits)
c) The transition amount

22. **SFAS 90**, *Regulated Enterprises - Accounting for Abandonments and Disallowances of Plant Costs*, applies to costs of abandoned utility plants and disallowed costs of newly completed plants.

a. **Probable future revenue** from the rate-making process based on recovery of costs of abandoned plants is reported at its **present value**. Any excess of the plant's cost over that present value is a loss.

b. Any **disallowances** in the rate-making process of cost of newly completed plants is recognized as a loss.

c. An **allowance for funds used during construction** is capitalized only if its inclusion in allowable costs for rate-making purposes is probable.

23. **SFAS 91**, *Accounting for Nonrefundable Fees and Costs Associated With Originating or Acquiring Loans and Initial Direct Costs of Leases*, concerns nonrefundable loan fee revenue and loan origination costs applicable to any loan and any lender or purchaser of a loan (banks, S&Ls, insurance companies, etc.).

a. **Loan origination fees and direct loan origination costs** (incremental direct costs and certain costs directly related to specified lender activities) are offset. The net amount is deferred and amortized using the **interest method**.

b. **Estimated prepayments** may not be anticipated in the amortization schedules unless the enterprise holds a large number of similar loans and reasonable estimates of future prepayments can be made.

c. With certain exceptions, **loan commitment fees** are deferred and recognized as additional interest over the life of the loan (under the interest method). Expired unused commitment fees are expensed immediately.

d. A **refinancing** is considered a new loan if terms are as favorable to the lender as the original terms. The unamortized costs (revenues) are included in income when the new loan is granted. If the terms are not as favorable, the unamortized fees or costs are carried forward as part of the new loan basis.

e. Unamortized loan origination, commitment, or other fees and costs and purchase premiums and discounts **amortized under the interest method** should be included in the loan balance.

f. SFAS 91 also applies to **initial direct costs of leases**.

1) Initial direct costs have two components: (a) the lessor's external costs to originate a lease incurred in dealings with independent third parties and (b) the internal costs directly related to specified activities performed by the lessor for that lease, e.g., to evaluate the lessee's financial condition, to evaluate guarantees and collateral (security arrangements), to negotiate lease terms, to prepare and process lease documents, and to close the transaction.

2) Initial direct costs do not include the cost of advertising and other solicitation, servicing of existing leases, establishing and monitoring of credit policies, supervision, and administration.

24. **SFAS 92**, *Regulated Enterprises - Accounting for Phase-in Plans*, specifies the accounting for phase-in plans of regulated enterprises.

    a. A **phase-in plan** is adopted by a regulator when conventional rate-making would provide for a substantial increase in rates upon completion of a new plant. The purpose of the plan is to defer allowable costs that would otherwise be expensed under GAAP to permit graduated rate increases while the utility recovers its costs, including a return on investment. **Allowable costs** are current operating costs, depreciation, interest on borrowings invested in the plant, and an allowance for earnings.

    b. If substantial construction was performed or the plant was completed prior to 1988, all allowable costs deferred by the regulator under the plan should be capitalized as a deferred charge provided (1) costs are deferred under a formal plan accepted by the regulator, (2) the plan states the timing of cost recovery, (3) deferred costs are recovered within 10 years of the time deferrals begin, and (4) the scheduled percentage rate increase for any plan year is not greater than that for the preceding year.

25. **SFAS 97**, *Accounting and Reporting by Insurance Enterprises for Certain Long-Duration Contracts and for Realized Gains and Losses from the Sale of Investments*, applies to new types of insurance policies, e.g., universal life contracts, developed since the issuance of **SFAS 60** (which covered insurance accounting). These policies are beyond the scope of this text. SFAS 97 applies to **realized gains and losses** on most investments (except for investments classified as trading securities and as hedges of a net investment in a foreign operation or as cash flow hedges). These gains and losses are reported pretax as a component of income. They are not deferred but are separately presented in the income statement or disclosed in the notes.

26. **SFAS 101**, *Regulated Enterprises - Accounting for the Discontinuation of Application of FASB Statement No. 71*, specifies how a regulated enterprise that no longer meets the **criteria for applying SFAS 71** should report that event. Regardless of the reason for discontinuation (e.g., deregulation or a change in the competitive environment), the enterprise must eliminate from the balance sheet the effects of regulatory actions inconsistent with GAAP. Nevertheless, the carrying amounts of **plant, equipment, and inventory** are not adjusted unless they are **impaired**. The net **adjustment** is classified as an **extraordinary item**. The enterprise continues to recognize rights to receive payment and obligations to pay resulting solely from past transactions or events.

27. **SFAS 102**, *Statement of Cash Flows - Exemption of Certain Enterprises and Classification of Cash Flows from Certain Securities Acquired for Resale*, states that defined benefit pension plans and certain other employee benefit plans need not provide a statement of cash flows. This exemption also applies to certain highly liquid investment companies. Furthermore, SFAS 102 classifies as operating items cash flows from (a) certain securities and other assets acquired for resale that are carried at market value in a trading accounting or (b) loans acquired for resale that are carried at lower of cost or market.

28. **SFAS 104**, *Statement of Cash Flows - Net Reporting of Certain Cash Receipts and Cash Payments and Classification of Cash Flows from Hedging Transactions*, permits banks, savings institutions, and credit unions to report net amounts for customer time deposits and loans and its own deposits with other institutions.

29. **SFAS 110**, *Reporting by Defined Benefit Pension Plans of Investment Contracts*, amended **SFAS 35** to clarify that all investment contracts of a defined benefit plan are to be reported at fair value. However, insurance contracts (long-duration contracts that incorporate mortality or morbidity risk of the policyholder) are to be presented as specified by ERISA for filings with regulators, i.e., at fair value or at the contract value determined by the insurer.

30. **SFAS 111**, *Rescission of FASB Statement No. 32 and Technical Corrections*, supersedes SFAS 32, *Specialized Accounting and Reporting Principles and Practices in AICPA Statements of Position and Guides on Accounting and Auditing Matters*. The guidance in SFAS 32, which stated that the principles and practices in SOPs and Guides are preferable for purposes of justifying a change in accounting principles, is no longer needed. **SAS 69 (AU 411)**, *The Meaning of "Present Fairly in Conformity With Generally Accepted Accounting Principles,"* now requires an entity to adopt the accounting principles in pronouncements whose effective dates are after March 15, 1992. An entity initially applying an accounting principle after that date (including those making an accounting change) must follow the hierarchy in SAS 69. An entity following an established accounting principle effective as of March 15, 1992, need not change its accounting until a new pronouncement is issued.

31. **SFAS 113**, *Accounting and Reporting for Reinsurance of Short-Duration and Long-Duration Contracts*, addresses accounting by insurance enterprises for the reinsuring (ceding) of insurance contracts.

    a. **Reinsurance** involves the assumption for a premium by one insurer of all or part of a risk originally undertaken by another insurer (the ceding enterprise). However, the ceding enterprise usually remains liable to the insured.

    b. **Reinsurance receivables** (including amounts related to claims incurred but not reported and liabilities for future policy benefits) and prepaid reinsurance premiums should be reported as assets. Estimated reinsurance receivables are recognized in a manner consistent with the liabilities relating to the underlying reinsured contracts.

    c. SFAS 113 states the requirements for a contract with a reinsurer to be accounted for as reinsurance and prescribes standards for those contracts. The accounting treatment depends on whether the contract is long-duration or short-duration. If it is the latter, the accounting also depends on whether it is prospective or retroactive. **Immediate recognition of gains** is precluded unless the ceding enterprise's liability is extinguished.

       1) Contracts that do not result in the **reasonable possibility that the reinsurer may realize a significant loss** from the insurance risk assumed ordinarily do not qualify for reinsurance accounting. They are to be accounted for as **deposits**.

32. **SFAS 120**, *Accounting and Reporting by Mutual Life Insurance Enterprises and by Insurance Enterprises for Certain Long-Duration Participating Contracts*, extends the requirements of **SFAS 60**, **SFAS 97**, and **SFAS 113** to the reporting of insurance and reinsurance activities of mutual life insurance enterprises.

    a. Mutual life insurance enterprises apply SFAS 60 and 97 to participating life insurance contracts unless (1) they are long-duration participating contracts expected to pay dividends to policyholders based on the insurer's actual experience, and (2) such dividends are distributed based on identified divisible surplus in approximately the same proportion that the contracts are deemed to have contributed to the surplus. The accounting for such contracts of mutual life insurance enterprises that meet the two criteria is described in **SOP 95-1**, *Accounting for Certain Insurance Activities of Mutual Life Insurance Enterprises*. Stock life insurance enterprises also are permitted to apply the provisions of the SOP to participating life insurance contracts that meet the conditions.

33. **SFAS 134**, *Accounting for Mortgage-Backed Securities Retained after the Securitization of Mortgage Loans Held for Sale by a Mortgage Banking Enterprise*, requires that the entity classify the mortgage-backed securities or other retained interests in accordance with **SFAS 115** (that is, as held-to-maturity, available-for-sale, or trading). Nevertheless, a mortgage-banking enterprise must designate as trading any mortgage-backed securities that have been committed to be sold before or during the securitization process.

34. **SFAS 135**, *Rescission of FASB Statement No. 75 and Technical Corrections*, rescinded SFAS 75, which deferred the application of **SFAS 35** to pension plans of state and local governments. Because GASB pronouncements now provide guidance about these matters, SFAS 35 no longer applies, and SFAS 75 no longer is necessary. The technical corrections (a) reflect amendments effectively made by new pronouncements that have not previously been made explicit, (b) eliminate inconsistencies, (c) change references, and (d) extend certain provisions to reflect established practice.

35. **SFAS 137**, *Accounting for Derivative Instruments and Hedging Activities--Deferral of the Effective Date of FASB Statement No. 133*, provides that, on the date of initial application of SFAS 133, an entity can either (a) recognize all embedded derivatives to be separated from their host contracts or (b) choose January 1, 1998, or January 1, 1999, as a transition date for such recognition. The choice is on an all-or-none basis.

36. **SFAS 138**, *Accounting for Certain Derivative Instruments and Certain Hedging Activities (an amendment of SFAS 133)*, is a collection of specialized revisions at a level of refinement unlikely to be tested on the CPA examination.

37. **SFAS 139**, *Rescission of FASB Statement No. 53 and amendments to FASB Statements No. 63, 89, and 121*, withdrew SFAS 53, *Financial Reporting by Producers and Distributors of Motion Picture Films*, and made technical corrections to certain other SFASs. SFAS 53 was replaced by AICPA **SOP 00-2**, *Accounting by Producers or Distributors of Films*.

38. **SFAS 145**, *Rescission of FASB Statements No. 4, 44, and 64; Amendment of FASB Statement No. 13; and Technical Corrections*, provides that gains and losses on most debt extinguishments are not automatically to be classified as extraordinary. SFAS 44 was issued to establish accounting requirements for the transition to the implementation of the Motor Carrier Act of 1980 and for the transition to deregulation of intrastate operating rights. These transitions are complete, and SFAS 44 is unnecessary. SFAS 145 further provides that, if the terms of a capital lease are modified and the resulting lease is an operating lease, it should be accounted for under the sale-leaseback provisions of SFAS 98 or SFAS 28.

39. **SFAS 147**, *Acquisitions of Certain Financial Institutions*, primarily amends the scope of **SFAS 72**, *Accounting for Certain Acquisitions of Banking or Thrift Institutions*, to restrict its scope to acquisitions between or among mutual enterprises.

40. **SFAS 149**, *Amendment of Statement 133 on Derivative Instruments and Hedging Activities*, also is a collection of specialized revisions at a level of refinement unlikely to be tested on the CPA examination.

41. **SFAS 150**, *Accounting for Certain Financial Instruments with Characteristics of Both Liabilities and Equity*, classifies certain **freestanding financial instruments**.

    a. A freestanding instrument is separate and legally detachable from other instruments and equity transactions. However, it may consist of **more than one option or forward contract**. An example is a combination consisting solely of a written put option and a purchased call option on the issuer's equity shares.

    b. **Mandatorily redeemable financial instruments (MRFIs)** are liabilities except when redemption is upon termination of the entity. They are instruments **in the form of shares** that **embody unconditional obligations** to **transfer assets** at specified or determinable times or upon an event certain to occur.

        1) **Shares** include ownership and other interests, even if they are liabilities in substance. The term **equity shares** refers to shares accounted for as equity.

        2) An **example** of an MRFI is stock that must be redeemed upon the holder's death, a certain event.

3) However, stock redeemable at a fixed date after a **change in control** of the entity (a type of "poison pill" used to discourage takeovers) is not an MRFI. Such stock is not classified as a liability until a change in control occurs.

    a) The entity must determine at the **reporting date** whether the obligation has become unconditional. Thus, when a change of control occurs, the shares are reclassified as liabilities. They are initially measured at fair value, equity is reduced by that amount, and no gain or loss is recognized.

4) **Preferred stock** that is convertible at the holder's option for a fixed period is not an MRFI during that period.

c. Certain **obligations to repurchase the issuer's equity shares by transferring assets** are treated as liabilities (or, in some cases, as assets).

    1) These instruments are **not outstanding shares**. An instrument in this class has the following characteristics:

        a) It relates to a conditional or unconditional obligation to repurchase the issuer's equity shares.

            i) At inception, the instrument either **embodies that obligation** or is based on variability in the fair value of the obligation (i.e., is **indexed to the obligation**).

        b) The instrument requires or may require settlement by transferring assets.

        c) A typical example is a written put option involving the issuer's equity shares.

            i) If this instrument is freestanding and requires **physical settlement**, it is accounted for as a liability. It **embodies** a conditional obligation to repurchase the issuer's equity shares that will require settlement by transferring assets if the option is "in the money."

            ii) If this instrument is freestanding and requires **net cash settlement**, it is also accounted for as a liability. It is **indexed** to the conditional repurchase obligation and may require settlement by transferring assets.

d. **Certain obligations to issue a variable number of equity shares** are classified as liabilities (or, in some cases, assets) even though they do not meet the current definition of liabilities in SFAC 6.

    1) These instruments **embody conditional or unconditional obligations** that may or must be settled by issuing a variable number of equity shares, not by transferring assets.

    2) If the obligation is **conditional**, the instrument must not be an **outstanding share**. For example, preferred stock convertible to a variable number of shares of the issuer's common stock is not classified as a liability (asset) of the issuer even if it meets the other criteria in this section.

    3) An instrument in this group is classified as a liability (an asset) when its holder is not exposed to an **owner's** risks and benefits. Furthermore, at inception, the **monetary value** of the obligation must be based **solely or predominantly** on one of the following:

        a) A **known fixed monetary amount** (e.g., a payable requiring settlement with equity shares having a fair value equal to the fixed amount).

        b) Variations in something **not the fair value** of the issuer's equity shares (e.g., a stock index).

    c) Variations with an **inverse relation** to the fair value of the issuer's equity shares (e.g., changes in the fair value of a written put option that can be net-share settled). In **net share settlement**, the loss party delivers to the gain party shares of stock with a fair value equal to the gain.

EXAMPLE

An entity receives $250,000 in cash. This amount is in return for its future obligation to issue a variable number of equity shares with a **fixed monetary amount at inception** of $270,000. Accordingly, if the fair value of a share at settlement is $25, the number of shares to be issued is 10,800 ($270,000 ÷ 25). The instrument is classified as a liability because the monetary value received by the holder is **based solely on the fixed monetary amount at inception**.

---

    e.   MRFIs are initially **measured at fair value**.

       1) **Forward contracts requiring physical settlement by repurchase of a fixed number of the issuer's equity shares for cash** are a means of converting the shares into MRFIs. They are initially measured based on the fair value of the shares at inception.

          a)   The measurement is adjusted for any consideration or any unstated rights or privileges. This amount may be determined by reference to the cash to be paid if the shares were immediately repurchased.

42. **SFAS 152**, *Accounting for Real Estate Time-Sharing Transactions*, states that time-sharing transactions are accounted for as nonretail land sales.

    a.   Profit is recognized in full on these sales if the profit is determinable and the earning process is virtually complete.

       1) The full **accrual method** may be used to recognize the profit if certain conditions are met regarding the likelihood of payment.

       2) If those conditions are not met, various methods are used.

43. **SFAS 155**, *Accounting for Certain Hybrid Instruments*, primarily addresses certain highly technical issues regarding the accounting for embedded derivatives.

44. **SFAS 156**, *Accounting for Servicing of Financial Assets*, defines the circumstances in which a servicing asset or liability is recognized.

    a.   It also requires a servicing asset or liability to be **measured initially at fair value**.

    b.   **Subsequent measurement** may be on an amortized basis in proportion to estimated net servicing income (loss), with recognition of impairment or increased obligation. An alternative is fair value measurement, with changes in fair value recognized in earnings.

45. **SFAS 163**, *Accounting for Financial Guarantee Insurance Contracts* (effective December 2008, testable July 2009)

    a.   SFAS 163 requires an insurer to recognize a claim liability under such a contract before an event of default (nonpayment of contractual amounts due by the issuer of an insured obligation). Evidence of credit deterioration in the insured financial obligation must exist. SFAS 163 also clarifies the applicability of **SFAS 60** to such contracts, especially the recognition and measurement of premium revenue and claim liabilities.

GOVERNMENTAL ACCOUNTING PRONOUNCEMENTS

    Statements (GASBSs) and Interpretations are issued by the Governmental Accounting Standards Board. The GASB has issued 53 GASBSs and 6 Interpretations. Those still in effect are summarized here unless outlined in Study Units 17 and 18. The summaries should be read closely because questions may be asked about specialized transactions and events.

GASB STATEMENTS

GASBS 1, *Authoritative Status of NCGA Pronouncements and AICPA Industry Audit Guide*
Standards of the GASB's predecessors ["Governmental Accounting and Financial Reporting Principles Statement 1," issued by the National Council on Governmental Accounting (NCGA); other NCGA statements and interpretations effective at the GASB's inception; and AICPA pronouncements] continue in force until changed by the GASB.

GASBS 3, *Deposits with Financial Institutions, Investments (including Repurchase Agreements), and Reverse Repurchase Agreements*
Carrying amounts and fair value of investments (including repurchase agreements and reverse repurchase agreements) must be disclosed, including contractual and legal requirements for deposits or investments. Also, assets and liabilities of reverse repurchase agreements CANNOT be offset (nor can related interest revenue and expense). Under a **repurchase agreement**, a broker-dealer or financial institution receives cash in exchange for securities transferred to a governmental entity. The transferor promises to repay the cash with interest (to repurchase the securities). Under a **reverse repurchase agreement**, the governmental entity is the seller-borrower. Also see the summaries of **GASBS 31** and **GASBS 40**.

GASBS 6, *Accounting and Financial Reporting for Special Assessments*
This statement applies to financing of services and capital improvements by special assessments. A special assessment fund type is not used in the basic financial statements for this purpose.

1. In the fund statements, **service-type** special assessments are accounted for in the fund type that reflects the nature of the transaction, normally the general fund, a special revenue fund, or an enterprise fund. Revenues are accounted for as if they were user fees, and the basis of accounting for revenues and expenditures (expenses) depends on the fund type.

   a. In the government-wide statements, service-type assessments may be reported as governmental or business-type activities.

2. A government may be primarily liable, be **obligated in some manner**, or not have any liability for special assessment debt related to **capital improvements**. If general obligation debt is to be repaid at least partly from special assessments, it is reported as a **general long-term liability** only in the governmental activities column of the government-wide statement of net assets.

   a. If the government is obligated in some manner, a general long-term liability also is recognized, except for any portion related to, and to be paid from, proprietary funds. (If the government is not obligated in any manner, it merely discloses the special assessment debt.)

   b. If the government is obligated in some manner, it reports **capital assets** under governmental or business-type activities in the government-wide statement of net assets.

   c. When a fund is created to provide for default by the assessed property owners, the transactions and balances should be reported in a **debt service fund**.

3. If the government is obligated in some manner, capital improvements financed by special assessment debt may be accounted for in the **governmental funds** in the same way as other capital improvement and financing transactions, e.g., through use of capital projects and debt service funds, recognition of special assessment receivables offset by deferred revenue, recognition of revenue in accordance with the principles applicable to nonexchange transactions **(GASBS 33)**, reduction of deferred revenue as assessments become measurable and available, and reporting of general capital assets and general long-term liabilities only under governmental activities in the government-wide statement of net assets. If the government is not obligated in some manner, transactions related to construction are reported in a capital projects or other appropriate fund, the capital assets are reported only under the governmental activities column as general capital assets, and debt service transactions are reported in an agency fund.

4. If the special assessment debt on which an entity is obligated in some manner is related to and expected to be paid from **proprietary funds**, capital improvement transactions are reported in the same way as other such transactions of proprietary funds, with revenue and receivables recognized on the accrual basis.

    a. If the entity is not obligated in some manner, it capitalizes amounts in the proprietary fund, accrues equal amounts as capital contributions, and reports them separately after nonoperating revenue.

    b. Only the portion of special assessment debt expected to be repaid from enterprise fund revenues is reported as a liability of that fund. Nevertheless, an enterprise fund may report all of the transactions and balances of a project so as to represent its actual administration.

5. In the **government-wide statements**, a government that is obligated in some manner for capital improvement special assessment debt should report capital assets under governmental or business-type activities. If the government is not obligated in some manner, an amount equal to that capitalized is reported on the accrual basis as program revenue restricted for capital purposes in the government-wide statement of activities.

GASBS 7, *Advance Refundings Resulting in Defeasance of Debt*
This statement provides standards of accounting and reporting for advance and current refundings resulting in defeasance of general long-term debt. A **current refunding** uses the proceeds of new debt to repay the old debt immediately. An **advance refunding** places those proceeds in escrow, with the old debt to be repaid in the future.

1. An advance refunding ordinarily results in either a legal or an **in-substance defeasance**. The latter is defined in the same way as in **SFAS 76**, *Extinguishment of Debt*, a pronouncement that has been withdrawn by the FASB. In the **governmental fund statements**, the proceeds of the new debt are reported in the recipient fund as an other financing source. Payments to an escrow agent are reported as an other financing use. However, payment to an escrow agent from other entity resources are debt service expenditures. If one large issue refunds several smaller ones, allocations are required when some refunded items are general long-term liabilities and some are reported in proprietary or fiduciary fund statements. Also see the summary of GASBS 23.

GASBS 9, *Reporting Cash Flows of Proprietary and Nonexpendable Trust Funds and Governmental Entities That Use Proprietary Fund Accounting* (NOTE: The title is inconsistent with current reporting.)

1. GASBS 9 requires the reporting of cash flows of proprietary funds and entities engaged in business-type activities, e.g., public benefit corporations and authorities, governmental utilities, governmental healthcare providers, and public colleges and universities. However, pension and other trust funds are not required to report a statement of cash flows.

2. A statement of cash flows is reported for each period for which results of operations are presented. It describes the changes in **cash and cash equivalents** during the period. Cash equivalents are short-term, highly liquid investments. Purchases and sales of these investments represent cash management activities. They must be both **readily convertible** to known amounts of cash and so **near their maturity** that they present insignificant risk of changes in value because of changes in interest rates. Generally, cash equivalents include only investments with original maturities of 3 months or less. Examples are Treasury bills, commercial paper, CDs, money market funds, and cash management pools. However, not all short-term, highly liquid investments that qualify must be classified as cash equivalents. An entity should establish and **consistently apply a policy** concerning which qualifying investments are to be treated as cash equivalents. A change in that policy is a change in principle requiring restatement of prior financial statements presented comparatively.

3. In general, information about **gross amounts of cash flows** should be reported. However, items may be **netted** if their turnover is quick, amounts are large, and maturities are short. These items include investments (not qualifying as cash equivalents), loans receivable, and debt with an original asset or liability maturity of no more than 3 months. Netting also is permitted when substantially all of the entity's assets were highly liquid investments, and the entity had little or no debt during the period.

4. Cash flows should be classified as operating, financing, and investing. Moreover, financing cash flows are reported in separate categories. **Noncapital financing activities** include borrowings for purposes other than acquiring, constructing, or improving capital assets and debt. Cash flows may include grants and subsidies received or paid, tax receipts, debt proceeds, and cash received from or paid to other funds (excluding flows from interfund services provided or used). **Capital and related financing activities** include borrowings and repayments of debt related to acquiring, constructing, or improving capital assets; acquiring and disposing of capital assets used to provide goods or services; and paying for capital assets obtained on credit. **Operating activities** are all transactions and other events that are not classified as either financing or investing activities. In general, operating activities involve transactions and other events the effects of which are included in the determination of operating income. They include loan activities not intended as investments (program loans), interfund services provided and used, and providing goods or services. **Investing activities** include making and collecting loans (other than program loans) and acquiring and disposing of debt and equity instruments. In addition, interest income is accounted for in investing activities.

5. The **direct method** (including a reconciliation of operating income to operating cash flows) is used to report operating cash flows. It reports **major classes of gross operating cash receipts and payments** and their sum (net cash flow from operating activities). The minimum classes to be reported are cash receipts from customers, cash receipts from interfund services provided, other operating cash receipts, cash payments to employees for services, cash payments to other suppliers, cash payments for interfund services used, and other operating cash payments. The **reconciliation** adjusts for the effects of depreciation, amortization, other deferrals of past operating cash flows (e.g., changes in inventory and deferred revenue), and accruals of future operating cash flows (e.g., changes in receivables and payables).

6. **Noncash financing, capital, and investing activities** that affect assets or liabilities are reported. These disclosures are presented in a separate schedule in tabular or narrative form. The presentation clearly distinguishes between the cash and noncash aspects of the transactions involving similar items. Examples of noncash financing and investing activities include the acquisition of assets through the assumption of related liabilities, such as the purchase of a building by incurring a mortgage to the seller, the exchange of noncash assets or liabilities for other noncash assets or liabilities, and the capital lease of an asset.

GASBS 10, *Accounting and Financial Reporting for Risk Financing and Related Insurance Issues*
This statement essentially requires public entity risk pools to follow **SFAS 60**, *Accounting and Reporting by Insurance Enterprises*. A public entity risk pool is accounted for in an enterprise fund. It should report only the financial statements appropriate for such a fund.

GASBS 12*, *Disclosure of Information on Postemployment Benefits Other Than Pension Benefits by State and Local Governmental Employers*
All state and local employers that furnish such benefits must describe the benefits provided, the employees covered, and the obligations for contributions of the employer and participants; the authority for establishment of benefit provisions and obligations; accounting and funding policies; and the expenditures/expenses for benefits recognized during the period and certain related data. However, no changes in accounting and financial reporting for these benefits are necessary until the GASB completes its other postemployment benefits project.

*GASBS 12 will be superseded by GASBS 45 over the latter's 3-year phase-in period, which commences with periods beginning after December 15, 2006.

GASBS 13, *Accounting for Operating Leases with Scheduled Rent Increases*

If the payment pattern is systematic and rational, the terms of the lease will control the accounting. But if payment requirements in a year are artificially low, measurement of the lease transactions should be either on a straight-line basis or based on the fair value of the rental. In the latter case, the implicit financing arrangement is accounted for using the **interest method** (a constant rate applied to the outstanding accrued lease receivable or payable). The accrual basis is required for recognition in the government-wide statements and in the proprietary and trust fund statements. Entities reporting these transactions in governmental funds should use the modified accrual basis.

GASBS 16, *Accounting for Compensated Absences*

This statement applies regardless of the reporting model or fund type used by the state or local government to report the transactions.

1. Benefits for **vacation leave** and other similar compensated absences should be accrued as a liability as they are earned if the leave is attributable to past service and if it is probable that the employer will compensate the employees through paid time off or some other means, such as payment at termination or retirement.

2. Benefits for **sick leave** should be accrued as a liability as they are earned but only to the extent it is probable that the employer will compensate the employees through cash payments conditioned on the employees' termination or retirement. An alternative is to measure the liability based on the sick leave accumulated by employees currently eligible to receive termination payments and other employees expected to become eligible. These accumulations should be reduced to the maximum allowed as a termination payment.

3. The compensated absences liability ordinarily is measured using the pay rates in effect at the balance sheet date. Other amounts should be accrued for certain items related to compensated absences, e.g., the employer's share of Social Security and Medicare taxes.

GASBS 18, *Accounting for Municipal Solid Waste Landfill Closure and Postclosure Care Costs*

An EPA rule issued in 1991 established closure requirements for all municipal solid waste landfills (MSWLFs). The rule also established 30-year postclosure care requirements. The effect of the rule and similar laws or regulations is to require owners and operators to perform certain closing functions and postclosure monitoring and maintenance functions. **GASBS 18** applies to state and local governmental entities that are required to incur these **closure and postclosure care (CPC)** costs. The term "costs" applies to amounts determined using an economic or a current financial resources measurement focus.

1. Certain costs are included in the **estimated total current costs (ETCC)** of CPC. They include the cost of equipment and facilities expected to be installed or constructed shortly before or after the time that the MSWLF stops accepting solid waste, the cost of final cover, and the cost of monitoring and maintaining the expected usable MSWLF area. **Current cost** is the amount that would be paid if the components of the estimate were obtained currently. Current cost is adjusted annually for the effects of price-level and other changes. Any change in estimates before the MSWLF stops accepting solid waste is reported primarily in the period of change.

2. If an MSWLF is reported in **proprietary fund financial statements**, part of the ETCC is recognized as an expense and a liability in each period that the MSWLF accepts solid waste. The recognition period extends from the time the MSWLF begins accepting solid waste to the time it stops. ETCC is allocated to periods based on MSWLF use. ETCC is multiplied by the cumulative percentage of the total estimated capacity used. The amount previously recognized is then subtracted from the result. When an element of ETCC is acquired, it is treated as a reduction of the accrued liability for CPC. Moreover, equipment and facilities included in ETCC are not reported as capital assets. Capital assets excluded from the ETCC should be fully depreciated when the MSWLF stops accepting solid waste. Capital assets used for a single cell should be fully depreciated when that cell is closed.

3. MSWLFs reported in **governmental fund financial statements** should recognize a CPC liability measured in the same way as for proprietary funds. MSWLFs should recognize expenditures and liabilities in governmental funds using the modified accrual basis. A long-term liability for CPC of an MSWLF reported in governmental funds is a general long-term liability presented in the governmental activities column of the government-wide statement of net assets. Equipment and facilities are included in CPC expenditures, not capital assets.

4. MSWLFs reported in the **government-wide financial statements** recognize assets, liabilities, revenues, and expenses based on the requirements for proprietary funds.

GASBS 20, *Accounting and Financial Reporting for Proprietary Funds and Other Governmental Entities That Use Proprietary Fund Accounting*

Proprietary funds should be reported based on all applicable GASB pronouncements as well as the following pronouncements issued on or before November 30, 1989, that do not conflict with or contradict GASB pronouncements: FASB Statements and Interpretations, APB Opinions, and Accounting Research Bulletins. An **enterprise fund** also may apply all FASB Statements and Interpretations issued after November 30, 1989, except for those that conflict with or contradict GASB pronouncements or that are limited to, or primarily concern, not-for-profit entities. **SFAS 71**, *Accounting for the Effects of Certain Regulation*, and related pronouncements issued before November 30, 1989, may be applied to enterprise funds that meet the criteria in SFAS 71 and related pronouncements.

GASBS 21, *Accounting for Escheat Property*

Property escheats when it reverts to a governmental entity in the absence of legal claimants. GASBS 21 (as amended) specifies the standards to be used to report such transactions in the government-wide and fund financial statements.

1. In the **fund financial statements**, escheat property is ordinarily reported in the governmental or proprietary fund to which it ultimately reverts (debit an asset and credit revenue). However, revenue is debited and a liability is credited to the extent it is probable that escheat property will be paid to claimants. If escheat property is held for an individual, private organization, or other government, it is reported in a private-purpose trust fund or an agency fund. It may also be reported in the governmental or proprietary fund in which it would otherwise be reported. In the latter case, the escheat property asset is offset by a liability. This liability should equal the best estimate of the amount ultimately to be paid.

2. In the **government-wide financial statements**, escheat-related transactions are reported using the economic resources measurement focus and the accrual basis of accounting. However, escheat transactions reported in private-purpose trust funds or in agency funds are excluded from the government-wide statements.

GASBS 23, *Accounting and Financial Reporting for Refundings of Debt Reported by Proprietary Activities*

This pronouncement is related to **GASBS 7**. It applies to current refundings and advance refundings resulting in defeasance of debt reported by **business-type activities**, i.e., proprietary funds and special-purpose governments that use enterprise fund accounting and financial reporting.

1. GASBS 23 requires that the difference between the reacquisition price and the net carrying amount of the old debt be deferred and amortized as interest expense in a systematic and rational manner over the shorter of the remaining life of the old debt or the life of the new debt. The deferred amount should be reported as a deduction from, or an addition to, the new debt liability. Similar treatment is accorded to refundings of prior refundings.

2. All current and advance refundings, including those involving general long-term debt, are reported in the **government-wide statements** in the same manner as in the proprietary fund statements. Refunding transactions involving general long-term debt are reported in the governmental activities columns of the government-wide statements of net assets and activities.

GASBS 24, *Accounting and Financial Reporting for Certain Grants and Other Financial Assistance*
Recipient governments ordinarily should recognize cash **pass-through grants** as revenue and expenditures or expenses in a governmental, proprietary, or trust fund. However, if the recipient is merely a cash conduit, i.e., has no administrative or direct financial involvement, the grant should be reported in an agency fund.

1. **Food stamp benefits** are recognized as revenues and expenditures in the general fund or a special revenue fund when they are distributed. Food stamp balances are an asset offset by deferred revenue.

2. **On-behalf payments** for fringe benefits and salaries are direct payments made by one entity to a third-party recipient for the employees of another, legally separate, entity. Employer governments must recognize revenue and expenditures or expenses for on-behalf payments. Revenue equals the amounts that third-party recipients have received and that are receivable at year-end. If the employers are not legally responsible for the payments, expenditures or expenses equal revenues. If they are legally responsible, they should follow accounting standards for that type of transaction. On-behalf payments should be classified in the same manner as similar cash grants.

GASBS 25, *Financial Reporting for Defined Benefit Pension Plans and Note Disclosures for Defined Contribution Plans*
GASBS 25 applies when the plan is included as a pension trust fund or fiduciary component unit in the fiduciary financial statements of a plan sponsor or employer, or when the plan statements are included in the stand-alone financial reports of the pension plan or of the **public employee retirement system** that administers it. Reduced disclosures are acceptable when a stand-alone plan financial report is publicly available and contains all required information.

1. Financial reporting for defined benefit pension plans distinguishes between current information about plan assets and financial activities and actuarially determined information, from a long-term perspective, about funded status and the accumulation of assets. Current information is given in a **statement of plan net assets** and a **statement of changes in plan net assets**. The notes should include a plan description, a summary of accounting policies, and information about contributions, legal reserves, and investment concentrations. Actuarial information should be included, for a minimum of 6 years, in supplementary information: a **schedule of funding progress** and a **schedule of employer contributions**. Note disclosures should include the actuarial methods and significant assumptions used. Plans may elect to report one or more years of the information required for the schedules in additional financial statements or in the notes.

2. Reported actuarially determined information must be in accordance with certain **parameters**, including requirements for the frequency and timing of valuations and for the methods and assumptions that are acceptable for financial reporting. When the methods and assumptions that determined funding requirements meet the parameters, they are used for financial reporting by both a plan and its participating employer(s). If they do not, different methods and assumptions that meet the parameters must be used for reporting.

3. The notes to the financial statements of defined contribution plans must include a plan description, a summary of accounting policies, and information about contributions and investment concentrations.

4. GASBS 25 is amended by **GASBS 50**.

GASBS 27, *Accounting for Pensions by State and Local Government Employers*

GASBS 27 provides standards for employer measurement, recognition, and display of pension expenditures or expenses and related liabilities, assets, note disclosures, and, if applicable, required supplementary information.

1. With regard to single-employer and agent multiple-employer defined benefit pension plans, employers must measure and disclose **annual pension cost** on the **accrual basis**, regardless of the amount recognized. Annual pension cost is the **annual required contribution (ARC)**, unless a **net pension obligation (NPO)** for past under- or overcontributions exists (including a transition amount). The ARC is based on certain parameters: requirements for the frequency and timing of actuarial valuations and for the actuarial methods and assumptions acceptable for financial reporting. When the methods and assumptions that determine funding requirements meet the parameters, they are used for financial reporting by a plan and the employer(s). If they do not, different methods and assumptions that meet the parameters must be used for reporting.

2. **Given an NPO, annual pension cost** equals the ARC, one year's interest on the NPO, and an adjustment to the ARC to offset actuarial amortization of past under- or over-contributions. The transition amount is calculated in the same way as the NPO after the effective date.

3. Pension expenditures of **governmental funds** are recognized on the **modified accrual basis**. If the annual pension expenditure is not equal to annual pension cost, the difference is an adjustment of the NPO.

4. A positive NPO at year-end is recognized as a **general long-term liability** in the governmental activities column in the government-wide statement of net assets. A negative year-end NPO results in a reduction to zero of an existing liability to the same plan. Any remaining negative amount is reported as a prepaid expense.

5. Pension expense of **proprietary funds** is recognized on the **accrual basis** in the proprietary fund and government-wide statements. Annual pension expense equals annual pension cost, with an adjustment to the NPO for any difference between contributions and expense. A year-end balance in the NPO is an asset or liability.

6. Employers in **cost-sharing multiple-employer defined benefit pension plans** recognize pension expenditures or expenses for contractually required contributions and a liability (asset) for unpaid (overpaid) contributions. Recognition in the fund financial statements is on the modified accrual or accrual basis depending on the reporting fund. Recognition in the government-wide statements is on the accrual basis. Previously recognized liabilities are adjusted to the transition amount.

7. Employers that participate in **defined contribution plans** recognize pension expenditures or expenses for the required contributions to the plan and a liability (asset) for unpaid (overpaid) contributions. Recognition in the fund financial statements is on the modified accrual or accrual basis depending on the reporting fund. Recognition in the government-wide statements is on the accrual basis.

8. GASBS 27 also includes guidance for employers that participate in insured plans, for entities legally responsible for contributions to plans covering employees of other entities, and for sole and agent employers that elect to apply the pension measurement provisions to postemployment healthcare benefits on an interim basis.

9. GASBS 27 is amended by GASBS 50.

GASBS 28, *Accounting and Financial Reporting for Securities Lending Transactions*

These transactions involve the transfer of the securities of a governmental entity (lender) to broker-dealers and others (borrowers) for collateral, with an agreement to return the collateral for the same securities in the future.

1. The securities lent should be reported as assets in the balance sheet (including the government-wide statement of net assets and the statement of fiduciary net assets. Cash received as collateral and investments made with that cash are also assets. Securities received as collateral are assets if the governmental entity can pledge or sell them without a borrower default.

2. Liabilities resulting from these transactions are reported in the balance sheet. Letters of credit or securities that the governmental entity cannot pledge or sell unless the borrower defaults are not reported as assets and liabilities.

3. The costs of these transactions, e.g., borrower rebates (interest costs) and agent fees, are expenditures or expenses. They are not netted with interest revenue or income from the investment of cash collateral, any other related investments, or loan premiums or fees.

4. If resources from several funds are pooled and the pool has securities lending transactions, the resulting assets and liabilities are assigned to the funds that have the risk of loss on the collateral, often with a pro rata allocation based on pool equity. Income and costs are reported in fund operating statements. However, if the income representing equity of one fund becomes an asset of another fund, the terms of any applicable legal or contractual provision determines the accounting. Otherwise, the fund that reports the equity recognizes income, costs, and an interfund transfer.

GASBS 30, *Risk Financing Omnibus*

This statement is an amendment of **GASBS 10**.

1. The method of calculating a premium deficiency for a public entity risk pool is modified, and a liability and expense must be recognized for the excess of the deficiency over the unamortized acquisition costs.

2. Required disclosures in the notes include the type of reinsurance or excess insurance coverage for certain claims costs, and gross, ceded, and net premiums and claims costs should be presented in the 10-year revenue and claims development information. Claims development information should be reported consistently on an accident-year basis, a report-year basis, or a policy-year basis. Additional percentage information may also be given.

3. Specific, incremental claim adjustment expenditures/expenses and estimated recoveries (e.g., salvage and subrogation) should be included in the determination of the liability for unpaid claims of an entity other than a pool. Whether other claim adjustment expenditures/expenses are included in the liability for unpaid claims must also be disclosed.

GASBS 31, *Accounting and Financial Reporting for Certain Investments and for External Investment Pools*

GASBS 31 applies to all investments by a governmental **external investment pool** (an investing arrangement that commingles monies of legally separate entities not part of the same reporting entity). For entities other than external investment pools and defined benefit pension plans, it requires **fair value accounting** for investments in (a) participating interest-earning investment contracts; (b) external investment pools; (c) open-end mutual funds; (d) debt securities; and (e) equity securities, option contracts, stock warrants, and stock rights with readily determinable fair values.

1. For **defined benefit pension plans** and **Section 457 deferred compensation plans**, GASBS 31 originally provided guidance for applying fair value accounting only to certain investment transactions. However, **GASBS 32** amended GASBS 31 so that it now covers all the investments listed above made by a Section 457 plan.

2. Governmental entities should report investments at fair value in the basic financial statements, but entities other than external investment pools may report certain money market investments at **amortized cost** if the investment has a remaining maturity of 1 year or less at time of purchase. External investment pools may report short-term debt investments at amortized cost if the fair value of those investments is not significantly affected by the impairment of the credit standing of the issuer, etc. Short-term investments are those with remaining maturities of up to 90 days. GASBS 31 also governs the determination of the fair value of investments in open-end mutual funds and external investment pools.

3. **Investment income** (e.g., interest and dividends), including changes in the fair value of investments, is reported as revenue in the operating statement. For internal and external investment pools, the equity position of each fund and component unit of the sponsoring entity must be reported as assets in those funds and component units. GASBS 31 also establishes reporting standards when income from investments associated with one fund is assigned to another fund. Unless the accounting is prescribed by a legal or contractual provision, the income is recorded in the fund that reports the investments. The transfer to the recipient fund is an interfund transfer.

4. An external investment pool that is a **2a7-like** pool is permitted to report investments at amortized cost. A 2a7-like pool is not registered with the SEC as an investment company but follows a policy that it will operate in a manner consistent with the SEC's Rule 2a7 of the Investment Company Act of 1940. This rule allows money market mutual funds to report net assets at amortized cost. Furthermore, GASBS 31 sets minimum requirements for the financial statements and disclosures in the separate financial reports of external investment pools.

5. A sponsoring entity should report the external portion of each external investment pool as an **investment trust fund**. Separate statements of fiduciary net assets and changes in fiduciary net assets should be presented for each such fund. The external portion belongs to legally separate entities not included in the reporting entity. Transactions and balances should be reported based on the **economic resources measurement focus** and the **accrual basis of accounting**. Moreover, GASBS 31 sets minimum requirements for the financial statements and disclosures in the sponsor's report concerning those pools. GASBS 31 also establishes standards for reporting individual investment accounts provided to other entities.

GASBS 32, *Accounting and Financial Reporting for IRC Code Section 457 Deferred Compensation Plans*

A Section 457 deferred compensation plan that meets the criteria for a **pension (and other employee benefit) trust fund** is reported in that fund type in the fiduciary fund financial statements. Entities that report Section 457 plans should apply the valuation provisions of GASBS 31 to the types of plan investments listed in that Statement. Other plan investments are reported at fair value.

GASBS 36, *Recipient Reporting for Certain Shared Nonexchange Revenues*

GASBS 33 required a recipient of **shared nonexchange revenues** to account and report for such revenues in accordance with their original character. However, it required the provider to account for the sharing as a government-mandated or voluntary nonexchange transaction.

1. Because these rules may sometimes require the recipient and provider to recognize the sharing at different times, GASBS 36 states that the recipient should also account for the sharing as a **government-mandated or voluntary nonexchange transaction**.

2. Furthermore, GASBS 36 states that the recipient may use any reasonable estimate of the amount to be accrued if notice by the provider is not timely.

GASBS 38, *Certain Financial Statement Note Disclosures*

1. In the **summary of significant accounting policies**, activities accounted for in the columns for major funds, internal service funds, and fiduciary fund types should be described in ways specific to the particular government.

2. In the governmental fund financial statements, **revenue** is recognized when it is measurable and available. The length of the period contemplated by the term "available" should be disclosed.

3. Significant violations of finance-related **legal or contractual provisions** and actions to address the violations must be disclosed.

4. Separate **principal and interest requirements** to maturity should be disclosed for each of the next 5 years and for 5-year increments thereafter.

5. Disclosures about debt service requirements include interest requirements for **variable-rate debt** calculated using the rate effective at year-end and the terms of rate changes for variable-rate debt.

6. For each of the next 5 years and for 5-year increments thereafter, the reporting government should disclose **minimum lease payments** under capital and noncancelable operating leases.

7. The notes should include a schedule of **changes in short-term debt**; the purpose for which it was issued; and disclosures about beginning and ending balances, increases, and decreases.

8. The notes should include disclosures about **interfund balances and transfers** reported in the fund financial statements. Details should include amounts due or transferred from other funds by individual major fund, nonmajor governmental funds in the aggregate, nonmajor enterprise funds in the aggregate, internal service funds in the aggregate, and fiduciary fund type. Disclosures also should include the purpose for interfund balances and a general description of the main purposes of interfund transfers, balances not expected to be paid within 1 year, and the intended purpose and amount of significant transfers.

9. The notes should include details about **significant receivables and payables** that may have been obscured by aggregation. Significant receivables not expected to be collected within 1 year should be reported.

10. The accounting policy for **encumbrances** is no longer required to be disclosed.

GASBS 39, *Determining Whether Certain Organizations are Component Units*

1. **Component units** (CUs) are legally separate organizations for which the **primary government** (PG) is financially accountable. A CU also may be an entity with a relationship with a PG such that its exclusion from the PG's financial statements would cause them to be misleading or incomplete.

2. A legally separate, tax-exempt organization's financial support of the PG or its other CUs requires treatment of the other organization as a CU if

    a. Almost all of the organization's resources directly benefit the PG, its CUs, or its constituents;

    b. The PG or its CUs can access the majority of those resources; and

    c. These resources are significant to the PG.

3. Other organizations are potential CUs if they are closely related to, or financially integrated with, the PG. Professional judgment is needed to make this determination.

4. Organizations meeting the criteria above should be **discretely presented**.

GASBS 40, *Deposit and Investment Risk Disclosures*

1. This statement amends GASBS 3. For example, **custodial credit risk** disclosures now extend only to

    a. Uninsured deposits by the government that are not supported by collateral or that are supported by collateral held by the pledging financial institution or its agent and

    b. Uninsured investments not registered in the name of the government and held by the counterparty or its agent.

2. Disclosures are made for the primary government and also at lower levels of detail if deposit and investment risks exceed those of the primary government.

3. **Credit quality ratings** of investments in non-U.S. debt securities must be disclosed.

4. **Interest rate risk** disclosures are also required. One of five methods must be chosen for estimating the risk. Terms of investments with fair values highly sensitive to rate changes must be disclosed.

5. Other categories of required disclosures are **concentration of credit risk** (amount and issuer of investments with 5% or more of the total) and **foreign currency risk** (e.g., types of investments and currency denominations).

GASBS 43, *Financial Reporting for Postemployment Benefit Plans Other Than Pension Plans*

1. In general, GASBS 43 follows the same approach as GASBS 25, which addresses reporting by defined benefit pension plans.

2. **Other postemployment benefits (OPEB)** include postemployment healthcare and, if not provided through a pension plan, any other postemployment benefits exclusive of termination offers and benefits. A **plan** is a trust or other fund in which assets are accumulated and from which benefits are paid. GASBS 43 applies if the plan is reported as a trust fund, agency fund, or fiduciary component unit in the fiduciary fund financial statements of an employer or plan sponsor. GASBS 43 also applies when the plan financial statements are separately reported by the plan or its administrators (e.g., a public employee retirement system).

3. If a defined benefit OPEB plan is administered as a trust or the equivalent, two accrual-basis financial statements are presented: the **statement of plan net assets** (fair value and composition of assets, liabilities, and net assets held in trust) and the **statement of changes in plan net assets** (contributions, net investment income, benefits, refunds, and administrative expenses). The **notes** must contain a plan description, a summary of accounting policies, information about contributions and required reserves, current funded status, and actuarial methods and assumptions. Two schedules must be presented: the **schedule of funding progress** (actuarial values of assets and accrued liabilities and their relationship over time) and the **schedule of employer contributions** (annual amounts required and the percentage recognized by the plan). The schedules are required supplementary information (RSI). They must present information for the most recent valuation and the two preceding it.

4. Actuarially-based reported information should be determined in accordance with **parameters** established by GASBS 43 (acceptable methods and assumptions as well as the valuation dates and frequency of valuations). If methods and assumptions used to determine funding requirements meet the parameters, they are required for reporting by the plan and the employer(s). If they do not, the parameters still apply to reported information. When a plan has at least 200 members, the actuarial valuation is performed every two years (three years if the plan has fewer than 200 members). Projected benefits are those under the **current substantive plan**. Moreover, standards of the **Actuarial Standards Board** govern the choice of **actuarial assumptions**, such as the healthcare cost trend rate, member mortality, employee turnover, and retirement dates. An actuarial valuation involves projecting cash outflows for benefits, discounting those benefits, and assigning the present value to future periods based on an **actuarial cost method**. If a plan has fewer than 100 members, an **alternative measurement method** may be used that relies on certain simplified assumptions.

5. A multiemployer defined benefit OPEB plan not administered as a trust or the equivalent is reported in an **agency fund**.

6. A **defined contribution OPEB plan** should follow the reporting principles for fiduciary funds.

GASBS 44, *Economic Condition Reporting: The Statistical Section*
   This statement applies to a statistical section presented with the basic financial statements, rates, and RSI of any state or local government. It incorporates government-wide information.

1. The focus of the information is on the **primary government** (and its blended component units). Nevertheless, information about discretely presented component units may be helpful in evaluating the economic condition of the primary governments.

2. The **objectives** are to provide users with "additional historical perspective, context, and detail." Information is reported in five categories:

    a. **Financial trends** indicate changes in financial position over time. Subcategories are (1) net assets, (2) changes in net assets, (3) governmental fund balances, and (4) changes in those fund balances.

    b. **Revenue capacity** relates to an entity's ability to produce **own-source revenues** (e.g., taxes but not shared revenues). Subcategories are (1) the revenue base (including the **total direct rate** applied), (2) revenue rates, (3) principal revenue payers for a 10-year period, and (4) property tax levies and collections.

    c. **Debt capacity** concerns the entity's debt burden and the ability to issue new debt. Subcategories are (1) outstanding debt and related ratios, (2) general obligation debt and related ratios, (3) direct debt and debt of geographically overlapping governments, (4) debt limitations for a 10-year period, and (5) pledged-revenue coverage of debt.

    d. **Demographic and economic** information pertains to the socioeconomic environment. Subcategories are (1) relevant, current indicators and (2) principal employers over a 10-year period.

    e. **Operating information** furnishes context. Subcategories are (1) numbers of employees (e.g., by function or program), (2) operating indicators (e.g., demand or service levels), and (3) capital assets (volume, usage, and nature). In the separate reports of each **postemployment benefit plan**, the subcategories of operating information are (1) retirees by type of benefit, (2) number of retirees and averages of monthly benefits and final average salary, and (3) participating employers.

3. **Additional information** consistent with the objectives may be reported.

4. **Sources** of information should be identified, and **methods and assumptions** should be explained.

5. **Narrative explanations** should provide analysis of the quantitative data. They address the objectives, the categories of information, unfamiliar concepts, relationships among the data, and unusual trends and data.

GASBS 45, *Accounting and Financial Reporting by Employers for Postemployment Benefits Other Than Pensions*

1. In general, GASBS 45 follows the same approach as GASBS 27, which addresses pension accounting by employers. Furthermore, GASBS 45 is closely related to GASBS 43. The measurement and disclosure requirements of GASBSs 43 and 45 are coordinated.

2. The **accrual basis** is used to measure annual **OPEB cost (AOC)** if the employer is involved in a single-employer or agent multiple-employer defined benefit plan. The AOC equals the **annual required contribution (ARC)** measured using the **parameters** (the requirements for the calculation of actuarially determined information) with an adjustment for any **net OPEB obligation (NOO)** arising when contributions did not equal required amounts. The ARC equals **normal cost** (the part of the actuarial present value of benefits and expenses assigned to the year by the actuarial cost method) plus **amortization of the unfunded actuarial liability** (difference between the actuarial liability and the actuarial value of assets). The maximum amortization period is 30 years.

3. An employer also may use an **alternative measurement method** (simplified assumptions) if it has fewer than 100 plan members. (But if the plan is an agent multiple-employer plan, use of the alternative method must not violate a requirement that the plan obtain an actuarial valuation for plan reporting.)

4. The NOO equals the accumulated difference between AOC and contributions. It includes any transition amount resulting from **optional retroactive application** of GASBS 45. Given a NOO, AOC equals the ARC, one year's interest on the NOO, and an adjustment of the ARC to offset actuarial amortization of prior contribution excesses or deficiencies.

5. **OPEB expense** equal to AOC is recognized in the government-wide statements and in the statements of proprietary funds and fiduciary funds from which contributions were made. **OPEB expenditures** are recognized in the governmental fund statements on the modified accrual basis. Any NOO is reported as a **liability (asset)** in the government-wide statements. An NOO related to contributions from proprietary or fiduciary funds is reported in the statements of those funds as a liability (asset).

6. A **cost-sharing employer** is one who participates in a cost-sharing multiple-employer plan. GASBS 45 is applied by such an employer if the plan is administered as a trust (or the equivalent) and (a) contributions are irrevocable, (b) assets are dedicated to providing benefits, and (c) assets are protected from creditors of the employers or plan administrator. **OPEB expenses or expenditures** are recognized for contractually required contributions on the accrual or modified accrual basis, as appropriate. **OPEB liabilities and assets** for differences between contributions required and made should be recognized, but liabilities and assets related to different plans are not offset. An employer participating in a **defined contribution plan** follows the same basic accounting methods as those of a cost-sharing employer.

GASBS 46, *Net Assets Restricted by Enabling Legislation*

1. **Enabling legislation** permits a government to require payment by external resource providers. It also contains a **legally enforceable** requirement that those resources be used only for the stipulated purpose.

2. Legal enforceability means that the government can be compelled by external parties (e.g., citizens or the courts) to honor the restriction. Whether a restriction meets this criterion is a matter of judgment unless the matter is actually tested in court.

3. **Replacement legislation** results in restriction of resources in accordance with its specified purpose. Judgment is needed to determine whether amounts accumulated under the old law are unrestricted, restricted to the original purpose, or restricted to the new purpose.

4. **Reevaluation** of legal enforceability is necessary if resources are used for an unspecified purpose or if another basis for reconsideration exists. For example, if the restriction is deemed to be no longer legally enforceable, the resources henceforth should be classified as unrestricted. But if the restriction is deemed to be legally enforceable, the balance of restricted net assets is not reduced by the amount of resources used for an unstipulated purpose.

5. The **notes** must disclose the amount of net assets restricted by enabling legislation.

GASBS 47, *Accounting for Termination Benefits*

1. In **accrual basis** statements, an **expense** is debited and a **liability** is credited for **voluntary termination benefits** (e.g., early retirement incentives) when (a) employees have accepted the offer, and (b) an estimate of the cost can be made. Recognition of **involuntary termination benefits** (e.g., severance pay) occurs when (a) the **plan of involuntary termination** has been approved by the appropriate authorities, (b) it has been communicated to the employees, and (c) the cost can be estimated. The plan should meet certain criteria. For example, it should be sufficiently detailed to allow employees to calculate the benefits they will receive. If the plan requires employees to provide **future services**, the liability and expense for post-service benefits are recognized proportionately over the **future service period**. Recognition begins when plan criteria are met. In **modified accrual-basis** statements, **liabilities and expenditures** are recognized when liquidation is normally expected with expendable available financial resources.

2. **Healthcare-related termination benefits** may be offered on an age-related basis in a large program. These benefits are measured at **present value** after consideration of (a) **projected total claims costs** (age-adjusted premiums may serve as an estimate of such costs) and (b) **healthcare cost trends**. If the program is **not large-scale and age-related**, the employer may measure the cost based on projected claims costs (i.e., unadjusted premiums).

3. **Nonhealthcare-related termination benefits** payable in specific amounts at fixed (or determinable) times are measured at the **present value** of expected future payments. (This measure includes an assumption about changes in future cost levels.) If such a specific obligation does not arise under the plan, costs are based on (a) the present value of expected future payments or (b) their undiscounted total at current cost.

4. Termination benefits may alter the employer's obligation under a **defined benefit pension or OPEB plan**. In these cases, GASBS 27 or GASBS 45, respectively, applies.

5. **Required disclosures** include (a) a description of the arrangement, (b) its cost, and (c) significant methods and assumptions.

GASBS 48, *Sales and Pledges of Receivables and Future Revenues and Intra-Entity Transfers of Assets and Future Revenues*

1. GASBS 48 states criteria for determining whether a transfer of specific receivables or future revenues is (a) a **sale** or (b) a **borrowing** secured by collateral. The **proceeds** are accounted for as **revenue** or a **liability** depending on the extent to which the entity retains **control** through **continuing involvement**.

   a. If a transfer of **receivables** is a sale, the difference between their carrying amount and the proceeds is reported in the current **change statements**.

   b. If a transfer of **future revenues** is a sale, the revenue ordinarily is **deferred and amortized**.

2. A government must **not revalue assets** transferred among components of the same **reporting entity**.

   a. GASBS 48 also addresses (1) other issues involving sales within the reporting entity and (2) recognition of **other assets and liabilities**, e.g., residual interests and items subject to recourse provisions.

GASBS 49, *Accounting and Financial Reporting for Pollution Remediation Obligations*

1. This statement does **not** apply to landfill closure and postclosure care obligations within the scope of GASBS 18. For a discussion of municipal solid waste landfill costs, see Subunit 17.4.

2. A state or local government must recognize a **liability** for the costs of remediation if it is aware of the pollution of a site and

   a. An imminent danger exists and the government has little discretion to avoid action;
   b. The government has violated a permit or license;
   c. A regulator has or will hold the government responsible (at least potentially) for cleanup;
   d. The government is or will be sued; or
   e. The government engages, or is legally obligated to engage, in cleanup activities.

3. **Liabilities and expenses** are measured using the **expected cash flows** method.

GASBS 50, *Pension Disclosures*

1. This statement is an amendment of GASBSs 25 and 27. Its goal is to conform the reporting for pensions with that for other postemployment benefits.

2. The notes to the financial statements should disclose the **funded status** of the plan as of the most recent actuarial valuation date.

3. If the **aggregate actuarial cost method** is used to determine the annual required contribution (ARC) of the employer, a schedule of funding progress should be presented as RSI, using the entry age actuarial cost method.

4. The notes to the financial statements should include a reference **linking** the funded status disclosure to the funding progress schedule.

5. If applicable, the notes to the financial statements should disclose legal or contractual **maximum contribution rates**.

6. If an actuarial assumption is different for successive years, the notes to the financial statements should disclose the **initial and ultimate rates**.

GASBS 51, *Accounting and Financial Reporting for Intangible Assets*

1. The goal of this statement is to clarify the guidelines for capitalizing intangible assets.

2. All intangible assets **not specifically excluded** by the scope of this statement **must be capitalized**.

3. **Existing authoritative guidance** related to the accounting and financial reporting for capital assets should be applied to intangible assets, as applicable.

4. An intangible asset should be recognized only if it is **identifiable**. An asset is considered identifiable when it is either:

   a. **Separable,** that is, the asset is capable of being separated or divided from the government and sold, transferred, etc.; or
   b. The asset **arises from contractual** or other legal rights.

5. Outlays associated with the development of **internally generated** intangible assets should not begin to be capitalized until certain stated criteria are met.

   a. Outlays incurred prior to meeting these criteria should be expensed as incurred.
   b. This statement also provides guidance on recognizing **internally generated computer software** as an intangible asset.

GASBS 52, *Land and Other Real Estate Held as Investments by Endowments*

> 1.   Endowments must report these investments at **fair value**. This change from historical cost measurement conforms the accounting with that for similar entities, such as pension plans.

> 2.   Changes in fair value must be reported as **investment income**.

GASBS 53, *Accounting and Financial Reporting for Derivative Instruments* (Testable beginning in April 2009)

> 1.   Most derivatives must be recognized as **assets or liabilities** and measured at **fair value** in **accrual-basis** financial statements.

GASB INTERPRETATIONS

No. 1, *Demand Bonds Issued by State and Local Governmental Entities*, provides that **demand bonds** are to be reported as general long-term liabilities or excluded from current liabilities of proprietary funds if (a) before issuance of financial statements, an arm's-length **take-out (financing) agreement** has been reached to convert bonds put by the bondholders but not resold into another type of long-term debt; (b) the take-out (financing) agreement does not expire for at least 1 year; (c) the agreement is not cancelable and the obligations are not callable; and (d) the lender or investor is financially capable.

> 1.   If all of these conditions are not met, the liability is reported in the fund (often a capital projects fund) that accounts for the bond proceeds. If a take-out agreement expires, a liability for bonds previously reported only in the government-wide statement of net assets is credited in the governmental fund that originally recorded the bond proceeds, and other financing uses is debited. In these situations, redemptions result in recording expenditures in the governmental fund from which debt service is normally paid while reducing the liability by a credit to other financing sources. If average maturities of demand bonds exceed 1 year, they are reported in the government-wide statement of net assets in two components: amounts due within 1 year and in more than 1 year.

No. 2, *Disclosure of Conduit Debt Obligations*, applies to debt issued by a state or local governmental entity expressly to provide capital for a specified third party not within the issuer's reporting entity. The issuer has no obligation beyond resources provided by a related lease or loan. The disclosures include a general description of the arrangement, the aggregate conduit debt outstanding, and a clear indication that the issuer is not liable thereon (beyond related leases or loans).

No. 3, *Financial Reporting for Reverse Repurchase Agreements*, applies when monies from several funds are pooled for investment and the **pool** has **reverse repurchase agreements**. The resulting assets and liabilities are reported separately in the balance sheets of the funds having a risk of loss. Income and costs are reported in the fund operating statements.

> 1.   If income from an agreement related to pool securities associated with one fund becomes an asset of another fund because of a legal or contractual provision, that provision controls the accounting. But, if this situation arises for another reason, income and costs are reported by the fund that recognizes the equity. The transfer to the recipient fund is treated as an interfund transfer.

No. 4, *Accounting and Financial Reporting for Capitalization Contributions to Public Entity Risk Pools*, requires that, given transfer or pooling of risk, these contributions be treated as **deposits** if their return is **probable**. In a governmental fund, fund balance should be reserved. If return is **not probable**, the contributions are reported in the government-wide financial statements or in a proprietary fund as prepaid insurance, with expenses allocated over the coverage period. However, a governmental fund may choose to record the entire amount as an expenditure. Given no transfer or pooling of risk, the contributions are reported as deposits or reductions in claims liabilities.

1. When accounting for **receipts by public entity risk pools**, the pool records a liability if return is probable. If return is not probable, unearned premiums are reported, with premium revenue allocated over not more than 10 years. If risk transfer or pooling does not occur, the contribution is netted with other amounts due to or from a pool participant and an asset or liability is reported.

No. 5, *Property Tax Revenue Recognition in Governmental Funds*, defines when property taxes are deemed to be **available**. The term means "collected within the current period or expected to be collected soon enough thereafter to be used to pay liabilities of the current period."

No. 6, *Recognition and Measurement of Certain Liabilities and Expenditures in Governmental Fund Financial Statements*, applies to entities that use modified accrual accounting. It clarifies the application of standards for determining what parts of certain liabilities should be reported in governmental funds or as general long-term liabilities.

1. Absent a contrary requirement, **governmental fund liabilities and expenditures** should be accrued when incurred for amounts that governments normally timely pay in full from expendable available financial resources, without regard to whether resources are currently available.

2. **Unmatured long-term indebtedness** (other than specific debt of proprietary and trust funds) should be reported as general long-term liabilities. This principle applies not only to formal debt but also to other types of general long-term indebtedness, such as compensated absences, claims and judgments, and other obligations that are not currently due.

3. An **additional governmental fund liability and expenditure** for debt service on general long-term debt may be accrued in excess of the amounts matured if the entity has provided financial resources to a debt service fund for payment of liabilities that will mature early in the following year. **Provided** means that the entity has transferred dedicated resources to that fund.

4. Governmental fund liabilities should be recognized for compensated absences, claims and judgments, special termination benefits, and landfill closure and postclosure care costs if the liabilities are "normally expected to be liquidated with expendable available financial resources." This criterion is met based on whether and to what extent the liabilities **mature** each period.

5. Mere accumulation of financial resources for eventual payment of an unmatured liability is not an outflow of current financial resources. Moreover, no additional governmental fund liability or expenditure is recorded.

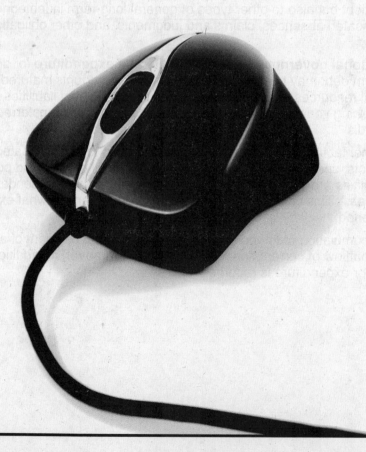

REVIEW CHECKLIST
FINANCIAL

Your objective is to prepare to pass this section of the CPA exam. It is **not** to do a certain amount of work or spend a certain amount of time with this book or other CPA review material/courses. Rather, you **must**

1. Understand the CPA exam thoroughly -- study *CPA Review: A System for Success* and the Introduction in this book.

2. Understand the subject matter in the 20 study units in this book. The list of subunits in each of the 20 study units (presented below and on the following page) should bring to mind core concepts, basic rules, principles, etc.

3. If you have not already done so, prepare a 1- to 2-page summary of each study unit for your final review just before you go to the exam (do not bring notes into the examination room).

Study Unit 1: Concepts and Standards

1.1 Introduction to the Conceptual Framework
1.2 Objectives of Financial Reporting (SFAC 1)
1.3 Qualitative Characteristics of Accounting
     Information (SFAC 2)
1.4 Elements of Financial Statements (SFAC 6)
1.5 Recognition and Measurement Concepts (SFAC 5)
1.6 Cash Flow Information and Present Value
     (SFAC 7)
1.7 Fair Value Measurements (SFAS 157)
1.8 Standards
1.9 Time Value of Money

Study Unit 2: Financial Statements

2.1 Balance Sheet
2.2 Statements of Income, Retained Earnings,
     and Comprehensive Income
2.3 Statement of Cash Flows
2.4 Direct and Indirect Methods of Presenting
     Operating Cash Flows
2.5 Other Financial Statement Presentations

Study Unit 3: Income Statement Items

3.1 Discontinued Operations
3.2 Extraordinary Items
3.3 Accounting Changes and Error Corrections
3.4 Earnings per Share (EPS)
3.5 Long-Term Construction Contracts
3.6 Revenue Recognition after Delivery
3.7 Consignment Accounting

Study Unit 4: Financial Statement Disclosure

4.1 Significant Accounting Policies
4.2 Segment Reporting
4.3 Interim Financial Reporting
4.4 Related Party Disclosures
4.5 Unconditional Purchase Obligations
4.6 Significant Risks and Uncertainties
4.7 Subsequent Events
4.8 Financial Instrument Disclosures

Study Unit 5: Cash and Investments

5.1 Cash
5.2 Fair Value Option (FVO)
5.3 Classification of Investments
5.4 Equity Method
5.5 Investments in Bonds
5.6 Cash Surrender Value

Study Unit 6: Receivables

6.1 Accounts Receivable – Fundamentals
6.2 Accounts Receivable – Discounts and Returns
6.3 Accounts Receivable – Measurement
6.4 Transfers of Receivables and Other Financial Assets
6.5 Notes Receivable
6.6 Notes Receivable – Discounting
6.7 Affiliated Company Receivables
6.8 Balance Sheet Presentation

Study Unit 7: Inventories

7.1 Inventory Fundamentals
7.2 Cost Accounting for Inventory
7.3 Cost Flows – Average Cost, FIFO, and LIFO
7.4 Dollar-Value LIFO
7.5 Lower of Cost or Market (LCM)
7.6 Estimating Inventory

INDEX

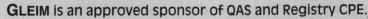

COMPLETE GLEIM CPA SYSTEM

All 4 sections, including Gleim Online, books*, *Test Prep CD-Rom*,
Test Prep for Pocket PC, Audio CDs, plus bonus book bag.

Also available by exam section @ $274.95 (does not include book bag).

*Fifth book: *CPA Review: A System for Success*

☐ $989.95

$_____

COMPLETE GLEIM CMA SYSTEM

Includes: Gleim Online, books*, *Test Prep CD-Rom*,
Test Prep for Pocket PC, Audio CDs, plus bonus book bag.

Also available by exam part @ $213.95 (does not include book bag).

*Fifth book: *CMA Review: A System for Success*

☐ $739.95

$_____

COMPLETE GLEIM CIA SYSTEM

Includes: Gleim Online, books*, *Test Prep CD-Rom*,
Test Prep for Pocket PC, Audio CDs, plus bonus book bag.

Also available by exam part @ $224.95 (does not include book bag).

*Fifth book: *CIA Review: A System for Success*

☐ $824.95

$_____

GLEIM EA REVIEW SYSTEM

Includes: Gleim Online, books, *Test Prep CD-Rom*,
Test Prep for Pocket PC, Audio CDs, plus bonus book bag.

Also available by exam part @ $224.95 (does not include book bag).

☐ $629.95

$_____

"THE GLEIM SERIES" EXAM QUESTIONS AND EXPLANATIONS

Includes: 5 books and *Test Prep CD-Rom*.

Also available by part @ $29.95.

☐ $112.25

$_____

GLEIM ONLINE CPE

Try a FREE 4 hour course at gleim.com/cpe
- Easy-to-Complete
- Informative
- Effective

Contact
GLEIM PUBLICATIONS
for further assistance:

gleim.com
800.874.5346
sales@gleim.com

SUBTOTAL $_____
Complete your
order on the
next page

CPA CMA CIA EA EQE CPE

GLEIM PUBLICATIONS, INC.

P. O. Box 12848   Gainesville, FL 32604

TOLL FREE:	800.874.5346
LOCAL:	352.375.0772
FAX:	352.375.6940
INTERNET:	gleim.com
E-MAIL:	sales@gleim.com

Customer service is available (Eastern Time):

8:00 a.m. - 7:00 p.m., Mon. - Fri.

9:00 a.m. - 2:00 p.m., Saturday

Please have your credit card ready, or save time by ordering online!

SUBTOTAL (from previous page) $_____

Add applicable sales tax for shipments within Florida. _____

Shipping (nonrefundable) 25.00

TOTAL $_____

Fax or write for prices/instructions on shipments outside the 48 contiguous states, or simply order online.

NAME (please print) _____

ADDRESS _____ Apt. _____

(street address required for UPS)

CITY _____ STATE _____ ZIP _____

_____ MC/VISA/DISC _____ Check/M.O.   Daytime Telephone (___) _____

Credit Card No. _____ - _____ - _____ - _____

Exp. _____ / _____   Signature _____

Month / Year

E-mail address _____

---

1. We process and ship orders daily, within one business day over 98.8% of the time. Call by 3:00 pm for same day service.
2. Gleim Publications, Inc. guarantees the immediate refund of all resalable texts, unopened and un-downloaded Test Prep CD-Roms, and unopened audios returned within 30 days. Online courses may be canceled within 30 days if no more than the first study unit or lesson has been accessed. In addition, Online CPE courses may be canceled within 30 days if no more than the Introductory Study Questions have been accessed. This only applies to products that are purchased directly from Gleim Publications, Inc. No refunds will be provided on opened or downloaded Test Prep CD-Rom or audios, partial returns of package sets, or shipping and handling charges. Any freight charges incurred for returned or refused packages will be the customer's responsibility.
3. Please PHOTOCOPY this order form for others.
4. No CODs. Orders from individuals must be prepaid.
5. Shipping and handling charges are nonrefundable.

Prices subject to change without notice.

12/08

For updates and other important information, visit our website.

gleim.com

GLEIM
KNOWLEDGE
TRANSFER
SYSTEMS®

CPA Review: Financial, 2009 Edition, First Printing -- Please complete and mail to us pages 809 and 810 the week following the CPA exam. The information we request is in full compliance with the AICPA's policy on candidate disclosure of exam information.

Please forward your suggestions, corrections, and/or comments concerning this book, as well as topics we need to cover that are currently not explained or not explained thoroughly enough, to **Irvin N. Gleim • c/o Gleim Publications, Inc. • P.O. Box 12848 • University Station • Gainesville, Florida • 32604.** Please include your name and address so we can properly thank you for your interest.

1. _____

2. _____

3. _____

4. _____

5. _____

6. _____

7. _____

8. _____

9. _____

10. _____

CPA Review: Financial, 2009 Edition, First Printing -- Please complete and mail to us pages 809 and 810 the week following the CPA exam. The information we request is in full compliance with the AICPA's policy on candidate disclosure of exam information.

11. _____

12. _____

13. _____

14. _____

15. _____

16. _____

17. _____

18. _____

Remember, for superior service: Mail, email, or fax questions about our materials.
Telephone questions about orders, prices, shipments, or payments.

Name: _____

Address: _____

City/State/Zip: _____

Telephone: Home: _____   Work: _____   Fax: _____

Email: _____